TEXAS A&M UNIVERSITY-TEXARKANA

RIVERSIDE TEXTBOOKS
IN EDUCATION

COMPARATIVE EDUCATION

BY

I. L. KANDEL

*M.A., Manchester; Ph.D., Columbia
Professor of Education and Associate
International Institute, Teachers College
Columbia University*

GREENWOOD PRESS, PUBLISHERS
WESTPORT, CONNECTICUT

Copyright 1933 by Isaac L. Kandel

Reprinted by permission
of the Houghton-Mifflin Company

First Greenwood Reprinting 1970

SBN 8371-3734-9

Printed in the United States of America

**TO
ALAN AND HELEN**

EDITOR'S INTRODUCTION

THE Great War marked the close of an era and the beginning of a new major period in the history of mankind. Many of the aims and purposes and sanctions under which the older generation grew up, in both Europe and America alike, were swept into the discard, and most of those that remained are today experiencing a modification in direction and a change in emphasis which to the older generation is at best disconcerting. In the more important nations of the world the political, social, and economic doctrines which the nineteenth century believed in, and on the basis of which its progress was made, have so given way that today uncertainty exists everywhere as to what are to be the foundations of the life of the State and of the individual in the decades that lie ahead. Youths born since the beginning of the War, in 1914, find themselves today in a world of rapid change which they little understand and to a large degree traveling an uncharted course, while their elders find themselves called upon to readjust their lives, their business and social relations, and their thinking if they are to move forward with the rapidly-changing world in which they find themselves.

In the unrest and uncertainty which has come to the people of all nations, advanced and backward alike, the school has been turned to for help to a degree not previously experienced, and the great changes in educational organization and content which have taken place in all national systems of education since the Peace of Versailles stand as evidence of the important position that education has come to occupy in the modern State. The changes and expansions and new conceptions have been so numerous that the old pre-war descriptions and terminology no longer picture for us what is now being done. The scope of public education has been expanded from a few pre-adolescent and adolescent years to include both infancy and adult life, while the curriculum of the school has been changed from one based largely on skills and drills to one including physical and political well-being and training to adapt youth better to the new needs of an increasingly complex and difficult social, political, economic, and industrial world. In a new way and to a new degree the school has been turned to as the great constructive tool of the modern State. Today nations everywhere conceive of the education of their people as so closely associated with their national, social, economic, industrial, and hygienic progress and the promotion of their national welfare and prosperity that the control and direction of state systems of public instruction have come to be regarded as indispensable state functions. Legislators in democratic nations and dictators alike have accordingly turned to the organization and direction of public education with new interest; the diffusion of political intelligence by means of the school has become a national purpose; the study of economic and social forces has been used as an element in the promotion of policies of social reconstruction, and a new philosophy of education is being evolved that includes the many forces that help shape and direct the individual as a member of the social group. This new emphasis placed on education as an element in national progress is recent and world-wide, though most clearly marked in the leading nations of Europe and in the United States. It is still under way, it is increasing in importance and strength, and its many ramifications make it confusing even to the close student of social change and national progress. Except as the movement is interpreted in terms of some world-wide force it remains largely unrelated and national in character.

The best interpretation of the movement as a whole can be made through a study of the new political, social, and economic forces which have influenced recent changes and development in all leading nations, and for individual nations through a study and interpretation of the national character itself. Differences between national systems of education are far more fundamental than the mere forms of educational organization employed and the types of curricula provided, and can be understood best in terms of the national outlook, which itself is an outgrowth of many forces operating over long periods of time. The individualism and diversity of type found in English education, the centralization and bureaucratic organization of French and Italian education, the sectionalism and the reverence for knowledge and science of the German, the intense nationalism of the Russian, and the long emphasis on democracy and political equality and local liberty of the people of the United States color the organization and administration of education, the curricula, and the methods of instruction in the school of each nation. The national character, and the long series of influences and forces which have made this what it is, have in turn shaped the educational systems of the different nations, and any interpretation of the development of public instruction as a national undertaking must be found in a study of education as an expression of nationalistic forces. The further development of nationalism since the Great War has also contributed to what we find today in the different nations.

So many and so fundamental have been the changes in the educational systems of the leading nations since the Great War that we have for long needed a new description and a new interpretation of what they now provide for the training of their youth. A mere description of the present-day educational system of each nation would be valuable, but far more valuable is such a masterly comparative study of the organization, administration, scope, curricula, and purpose of the principal national school systems as is presented in the present volume, the whole interpreted in the light of national character and national purpose. The book is, to a large degree, a study and interpretation of world progress in educational organization and adaptation in terms of those deep-seated national forces which shape the cultural institutions of mankind, and as such should form an adequate basis for a course, long needed by advanced students in education in our colleges and universities, which will be in effect a philosophy of world educational changes and progress stated in terms of national cultures and national hopes and aspirations. The value of such a study to the student of American educational development will be much greater than is generally supposed. It is the expectation of the publishers and the editor that this volume will meet with a ready welcome from teachers and students of education not alone in the United States, but also from similar workers in all the English-speaking countries of the world.

ELLWOOD P. CUBBERLEY

PREFACE

THE comparison of the educational systems of several countries lends itself to a variety of methods of treatment, depending somewhat on its purpose. One method of approach might be statistical on the analogy of the method of comparing returns of exports and imports, size of armaments, and so on; from this point of view there would be compared the total national expenditures for education, the cost, size and character of school buildings, per capita costs for different items of expenditure in the educational systems, the enrollments, average attendance, and retention of pupils through the different levels of the educational ladder. By another method it might be possible to institute a comparison between education and national welfare and progress as expressed in statistics of illiteracy, the volume of trade and commerce, per capital wealth, or incidence of crime and poverty. These methods are attractive and may some day be useful; at the present stage, as is indicated in the text, it is impossible to institute comparisons of such a character until the raw material, the statistics, becomes more uniform and comparable. Still another method would be to undertake comparative studies of the quality of education in different countries; this, too, may be possible in time, but not before the instruments of measurement have been made more perfect and reliable than they are at present or when aims of education in different countries are more nearly alike, or finally, when tests have been developed which can measure more accurately the results of education rather than of instruction in fundamentals of subject-matter.

In the present volume none of these methods have been followed. The task which has been undertaken is to discuss the meaning of general education, elementary and secondary, in the light of the forces — political, social, and cultural — which determine the character of national systems of education. The problems and purposes of education have in general become somewhat similar in most countries; the solutions are influenced by differences of tradition and culture peculiar to each. The present volume seeks accordingly to serve as a contribution to the philosophy of education in the light both of theory and practice in six of the leading educational laboratories of the world — England, France, Germany, Italy, Russia, and the United States.

To the International Institute of Teachers College, Columbia University, the author is under a deep debt of gratitude both for the opportunities which it has provided to visit four of these countries (the discussion of education in Russia being the only one based on secondary sources) and for its generous provision of books, periodicals, and official publications, which make its library one of the best equipped centers in the world for the study undertaken in this volume.

I. L. KANDEL

NEW YORK
January, 1933

CONTENTS

Introduction xv

I. Education and Nationalism 1

II. Education and National Character 23

III. The State and Education 45
    England 55
    France 59
    Germany 61
    Italy 64
    Russia 69
    United States 76

IV. The Organization of National Systems of Education 83
    England 94
    France 119
    Germany 136
    Italy 155
    Russia 172
    United States 188

V. Administration of Education 207
    England 228
    France 262
    Germany 281
    Italy 297
    Russia 308
    United States 313

CONTENTS

- VI. ELEMENTARY EDUCATION 349
  - England 359
  - France 396
  - Germany 425
  - Italy 455
  - Russia 477
  - United States 486
- VII. PREPARATION OF ELEMENTARY SCHOOL TEACHERS . . 520
  - England 528
  - France 548
  - Germany 565
  - Italy 585
  - Russia 596
  - United States 600
- VIII. SECONDARY EDUCATION 625
  - England 637
  - France 674
  - Germany 707
  - Italy 757
  - Russia 780
  - United States 790
- IX. SECONDARY SCHOOL TEACHERS 827
  - England 831
  - France 835
  - Germany 842
  - Italy 849
  - United States 854
- X. SUMMARY AND CONCLUSIONS 861
- APPENDIX 871
- INDEX 901

INTRODUCTION

It would be difficult to find a period in the history of education which has been marked by such widespread interest and at the same time so much unrest and uncertainty in education as have characterized the last two decades since the outbreak of the Great War. Social unrest, whether political, economic, religious, or cultural, has always been accompanied by discussions of and plans for educational reconstruction, but in the past such reconstruction has been piecemeal. The Renaissance was followed by a reorganization of secondary education; the Reformation was accompanied by proposals for universal elementary education, which was not generally achieved until the nineteenth century under the influences either of the industrial revolution, or of political liberalism, or of the rise of nationalism, or a combination of these; the progressive reform of secondary education was affected by the progress of science and the increased development of international intercourse, both influenced in turn by improved means of communication and the demands of economic competition; finally, vocational education owed its development to the application of science to industry and commerce and the rise of economic nationalism. Progress and reforms were introduced now in one branch of education, now in another; at no time were the needs of a whole system of education from the kindergarten to the university considered from a unitary point of view, determined by the rights and capacities of the individual and the needs of the nation of which he is a member.

The recognition of the significance of education for national welfare was strikingly attested immediately after the outbreak of the War by comparisons which were instituted between their educational systems by the nations which were embroiled. The War, it was felt, was the supreme test of the type of individual produced by each system. To education were attributed, whether rightly or wrongly, the strength and weakness in general and in detail of each nation.[1] The comparisons thus instituted led naturally to a general

[1] See Kandel, I. L., U. S. Office of Education, Bulletins, 1919, No. 9, *Education in Great Britain and Ireland*; No. 21, *Education in Germany*; and No. 43, *Education in France in 1916–18* (Washington, D.C.).

stocktaking of its educational system by each nation. It was not an accident but a natural consequence of these discussions and debates that proposals and plans for educational reform began to be formulated before the close of the War. In Germany the slogan for reform, *Freie Bahn dem Tüchtigen* and the demand for the *Einheitsschule*, in France the movement for the *école unique*, the common school system, and in England the Fisher Act were results attained before the Armistice was signed, and constituted the bases for the educational reconstruction which has taken place since that date.

The post-War period has witnessed a further extension of these movements for reform and reconstruction throughout the whole world. The new social, political and economic conditions and the cultural and intellectual unrest engendered by these gave an added stimulus to the movements for reform in England, Germany, and France; the new political entities which were created by the Treaty of Versailles immediately recognized in education the soundest foundation for their existence, while countries like Russia and Italy, which were transformed by Revolutions, utilized the school as the best means for securing the new national aims. Without entering upon the educational reforms in other countries (Sweden, Turkey, Bulgaria), which are not without significance for the student of education, the realization of the dependence of national welfare upon education is further illustrated by reforms or proposals for reform in countries as far apart as Mexico and India, China and Spain, while the new interest in the education of backward peoples serves as a further illustration of the new era upon which education has entered.

The impending reorganization of education would probably have been achieved in any case, even if the War and its consequences had not produced a new world orientation; the tempo of progress would probably have been slower. Already there are signs that the economic depression through which the world is passing has begun to retard the advances which were expected a few years ago. Much has, however, been achieved already in quickening the interest in education everywhere; the general lines of advance have been thought out; further progress depends upon the world's economic recovery.

For the student of education the development which has taken place in the past two decades, and which still continues, is not without interest. The study of foreign systems of education is not new; since the days when Athens was the school of Greece and "captive Greece took captive her rude conqueror," history is rich in examples of international exchange of ideas, principles, and practices in education. Without discussing the world-wide influence of the great educational philosophers, the interest in the educational systems of foreign countries developed apace from the time when Victor Cousin published his account of education in Prussia, when Horace Mann and Henry Barnard issued their reports, when the English educational commissions sent their investigators, including Matthew Arnold, abroad, and when Sir Michael Sadler at the close of the nineteenth century began the publication of the monumental series of *Special Reports on Educational Subjects*, issued by the English Board of Education. The importance of such reports has been attested more recently by the volume on *Comparative Education*, edited by Professor Peter Sandiford, by the *Educational Yearbooks* of the International Institute of Teachers College, Columbia University, edited by the writer, by the *Yearbook of Education, 1932*, edited by Lord Eustace Percy, and finally by the launching of a quarterly devoted to international education, *Internationale Zeitschrift für Erziehungswissenschaft*, edited by Professor Friedrich Schneider and Professor Paul Monroe. It is impossible here to do more than refer in general terms to the contributions on foreign school systems; the list of monographs and articles is rapidly increasing each year. The need of a bibliography on the subject, comparable to *La Littérature comparée, Essai bibliographique*, by Louis-Paul Betz, which laid the foundations for the study of comparative literature in France, is now becoming urgent.

Despite the volume of literature and the interest in international education, the study of foreign school systems or of comparative education has not yet become established as an important branch in the study of education. The reason is not difficult to find. In the first place, the usual accounts of foreign school systems have been mere descriptions of administration, organization, and practices, which, while interesting in themselves, are frequently not transferable from one country to another. Secondly, such descriptions have been written wholly from the point of view of education alone, without any closely reasoned analysis of what the systems stand for or represent in relation to their national backgrounds, progress, and development. In the third place, the attempt has rarely been made either to allow for differences in national environments or to build up on the basis of comparisons some general trends or principles.[1] Finally, since educational systems inevitably tend to reflect the aims, aspirations, traditions, and characteristics of the nations which they serve, there is a tendency for each nation to regard its own problems as unique, and, therefore, to regard the educational practices of other countries as inapplicable.

That practices, devices, methods, organization, all the detailed aspects which go to make up an educational system cannot be transferred intact from one environment to another, has been amply proved both in the past and in the present.[2] This fact, however, illustrates only the wrong use of comparative education and emphasizes the importance of adaptation as over against assimilation in education. Comparative education has an entirely different function, particularly at the present time when so many of the problems of education are almost universally identical. Among these problems the following may be cited:

> What are the factors which determine the character of an educational system?
> What is the meaning of nationalism?
> What is the relation between education and nationalism?
> What is the relation of the individual to society or the State?
> What is the meaning of freedom in a constituted society?
> Who shall have control of the education of the child?
> What is the place of private education and of private schools?
> How far does the responsibility of society or of the State for the education of its members extend?
> What is the scope of preschool education?
> What is the scope of primary education?
> What is the scope of post-elementary or secondary education?
> What should be the curriculum in each type of school?
> What is the meaning of culture?
> What should be the relation between general and special education?
> How are teachers prepared and what is their status?

[1] From this general statement the works of Sergius Hessen, *Kritische Vergleichung des Schulwesens der anderen Kulturstaaten*, in Nohl, H., and Pallat, L., *Handbuch der Pädagogik* (Langensalza, 1928—), and of Nicholas Hans, *Principles of Educational Policy* (London, 1929) may be excepted.

[2] The transportation of the English system to India, of the American system to the Philippine Islands and Porto Rico, and of foreign systems to China may be cited as a few illustrations.

Should the administration and provision of education be centralized or decentralized?
How can standards be maintained? What should be the place of examinations?
Who shall formulate curricula and courses of study?
What are the essential elements of an educational system?
What is the meaning of equality of educational opportunity?

Since every country is confronted with problems such as these, the study of comparative education assumes a new aspect. Merely to study the educational machinery, the organization and administration of school systems, the curricula and teaching processes, and classroom procedures, would be barren. The chief value of a comparative approach to such problems lies in an analysis of the causes which have produced them, in a comparison of the differences between the various systems and the reasons underlying them, and, finally, in a study of the solutions attempted. In other words, the comparative approach demands first an appreciation of the intangible, impalpable spiritual and cultural forces which underlie an educational system; the factors and forces outside the school matter even more than what goes on inside it. Hence the comparative study of education must be founded on an analysis of the social and political ideals which the school reflects, for the school epitomizes these for transmission and for progress. In order to understand, appreciate, and evaluate the real meaning of the educational system of a nation, it is essential to know something of its history and traditions, of the forces and attitudes governing its social organization, of the political and economic conditions that determine its development. This is all the more true at the present time when educational systems are organized on a national basis, but, as the history of English education proves, the same principle applies to educational systems which are organized on a voluntary basis with little or no governmental control or supervision. It may, indeed, be claimed that systems which are least controlled by an external governmental agency, as in England and the United States, better reflect the variety of forces by which the character of a nation is moulded than do those systems which are subject to rigid centralized control, as in France and pre-War Germany. This fact explains the gap which is so frequently found between theory and practice in education.

For the study of education this approach, if properly conducted, means a comparison of variant philosophies of education based not on theories but on the actual practices which prevail, but in which theories are modified and adapted to suit national characteristics. The study of foreign systems of education means a critical approach and a challenge to one's own philosophy and, therefore, a clearer analysis of the background and basis underlying the educational system of one's own nation. It means, further, the development of a new attitude and a new point of view which may be derived from a knowledge of the reasons for establishing systems of education and of the methods of conducting them. For purposes of illustration some of the problems listed above may be discussed. Thus, one may start with the problem which is probably of the greatest importance at the present time, the relation between education and democracy. What is the significance of education for democracy? A comparison of the use and meaning of the term "democracy" in England, France, and Germany, and of the challenge to it in Russia and Italy cannot fail to throw into bolder relief the American conception of the meaning of democracy and of its implications for education. The different shades of meaning that attach to this ideal have their resultant effects on educational organization and practices, and lead to different interpretations, not only of the concept of equality of opportunity toward which democratic countries are moving, but even of standards of culture and of methods of instruction. The greater part of the world thus constitutes today a species of laboratory in which, so far as education is concerned, varied types of solution are being attempted for the same general range of problems. If it is claimed that education is a science or that scientific methods should be employed in its study, the educator cannot afford, any more than the chemist or physicist, to ignore procedures which are being tried out under conditions somewhat different from those in which he is working.

The significance of this thesis can be further illustrated by discussing some of the other questions which have been cited. One of the permanent questions in the history of education is that of the relation of the individual to the State and to society. How fundamental this problem is may be seen from its effects on such questions as nationalism and patriotism, the content of the curriculum, discipline, and methods of instruction, freedom of thought and indoctrination. The changes in education which are now taking place have their origin in the changes which have taken place since the War. In practice the different attitudes on the relation of the individual to the State and to society are today more effective and potent than the contributions of the psychologists on the nature of the individual or of that theory of education which is based wholly on the principle of individualism. Educational systems are in fact colored far more by prevailing social and political concepts than by psychological theories or educational philosophies which attempt to deal with the individual as an isolated personality. How else, for example, can the different educational procedures in such democracies as France, England, the United States, and the young German Republic be explained, or how can the acceptance of activity methods in Russia and Italy be reconciled with their political dictatorships?

Closely related with this problem are the different types of administration, centralization and decentralization or localism. Here is encountered, not merely the problem of the relation of the individual to society, but the whole complex of traditions and attitudes that govern the relations between parents and children, between families and other social groups, between local and central authorities, and between a nation and its neighbors. Here, too, there must be taken into consideration the status, implications, and effectiveness of a national *Kultur*. This group of problems influencing the character of administration inevitably affects in turn the problems involved in curriculum-making, discipline, and methods. In no small measure the problems considered in this and the preceding paragraphs color the administrative practices dealing with the support of education, the preparation and status of teachers, inspection and supervision, and the formulation of standards. Finally, they affect vitally the conception of progress to the extent that it is determined by governmental or individual and group activity, and depends on public or private effort, on uniformity or variety.

The field of post-elementary education involves a study of the meaning of equality of opportunity and of the implications of the common school idea. Here opportunity is provided of comparing and contrasting the practices of the United States and of Russia of educating all children in the same school and of most other countries in which attempts are being made to establish a variety of schools at the same level organized on a functional basis and adapted to differences in ability and needs. More important, perhaps, than organization and administration, especially in view of the criticisms which are becoming increasingly numerous, is the interpretation in the light of divergent practices of the meaning of culture and liberal education. Closely associated with this general question is another which is of serious concern to most European countries — how to increase educational opportunities without incurring the danger of an educated proletariat, a problem which in turn affects the relations between education and the economic organization of a country.

Another group of questions fundamental to the progress of education is that which centers round the teacher. Not the least significant of these is the place of the teacher in society and in the educational system. What should be the character of teacher preparation and the relation of academic to professional training, and what should be the part of the teacher in promoting educational progress? How much freedom should the teacher enjoy? To what extent should his function be to impart a curriculum and course of study prescribed in detail by the administrative agencies, and to what extent may he be expected to be a scientist as well as a craftsman in education? How much supervision and inspection are desirable and by what standards should effective teaching be measured? What is the place of the textbook in the process of instruction? The implication of these questions for the curriculum and for methods is obvious. In the practices of different countries the answers to these questions are sufficiently varied to furnish the basis for formulating certain principles.

In the last two decades the most extensive activity in education in the United States has been in the field of tests and measurements. The development in this field has been almost as extensive in Germany and significant contributions have been made by a number of English psychologists. A comparison of the results in the three countries, while essentially one for specialists, is worthy of consideration particularly in evaluating the limitations of tests and measurements in the whole program of education, in estimating their effects on defining standards, in suggesting the type of standards that can be defined, in determining problems to be studied, and in perfecting techniques. Closely allied to this field is an examination of the differences in the educational psychologies adopted, consciously or deliberately, as the basis of the educative process. An important cause of differences between various systems of education can be found in the extent to which the doctrine of formal discipline or transfer is accepted.

There are at the present time two outstanding trends which can be distinguished in the study of education. The first is the attempt to make education scientific and objective by the application of statistical methods — all education must have an affirmative value which can be proved and verified statistically. Proceeding from this principle, the further claim is made that a philosophy of education can be formulated only on the basis of objective, statistical measurement. Assuming that the methods of statistical tests and measurements have become sufficiently established to be reliable, all that can be claimed for them is that they can measure results, but they cannot define aims and purposes of education; they may formulate norms, and that only in a limited range of activities, but they cannot set up qualitative standards. The second trend is that philosophy of education which emphasizes the importance of freedom and of individualism in education, most generally without any clear reference to social purposes, or objects of social allegiance, as Professor Dewey terms them. Both trends are inspired by the same point of view — that education has been and still is dominated by tradition, faith, and opinion, that it is formal and meaningless, that the individual is not an active participant in learning those things which have a direct value and significance for him. Both points of view, however, ignore the fact that education is a social process and that today more than ever it is being everywhere organized on national bases. Any sound educational theory must start with this fact and must seek to reconcile the rights of the individual with his position as a member of society and of a State, a problem which is fundamental to the progress of all national systems of education at the present time. To ignore this fact is to incur the risk of discussing education in a vacuum, of setting up an educand analogous to the "economic man" of nineteenth-century economics.

Education, then, must exist for some purposes or ends. The present volume is based on the point of view that educational systems are dominated by national ends, and that it is the duty of educators and teachers to understand the meaning of nationalism and all the forces that contribute to it. Nationalism today is an inescapable fact; because it has been abused and directed to false ends does not absolve the educator from the duty of redirecting it into channels which will ensure the progress of humanity. For nationality properly conceived is for a people what personality is for the individual, the expression of its life and culture.

Comparative education would, accordingly, be meaningless, unless it sought to discover the meaning of nationalism as it furnishes the basis of educational systems. Comparative education does not profess to set up standards by which to measure the quality of various systems of education. The educational statistician may measure results in different countries by the same system of tests, but for the present what can be measured represents on the whole only the rudiments of an education; whether the quality of education in its best sense can ever be measured is at least open to doubt. Each national system of education is characteristic of the nation which has created it and expresses something peculiar to the group which constitutes that nation; to put it in another way, each nation has the educational system that it desires or that it deserves. It is possible, however, by a comparison of problems and practices to disengage certain principles and tendencies, and to build up a philosophy of education, particularly if the prevailing criticisms within a national system are taken into account. The comparative method has in it the possibility of developing a philosophy of education based on practice rather than on the somewhat nebulous basis of metaphysics and ethics. At the same time since educational systems are living things, compounded of traditions, culture, and ideals, their study provides a safeguard against overemphasis of the immediately practical, and of nationalistic control on the one hand and of the freedom of individualism on the other. Beyond this, the study of other systems helps to bring out into relief the meaning and significance, the strength and weakness of our own.

No attempt has been made in the present volume to compare the statistics of education except in the most superficial way. Nomenclature, such as elementary, post-elementary, primary, post-primary, and secondary, while it is not standardized in education, is readily understood from the context. In the case of international statistics uniformity of standards has not yet been achieved. Frequently statistics are not available for the same year; in the absence of an international index number of the cost of living, it is almost futile to attempt to compare figures for the cost of education, for salaries, or per capita expenditures; the length of school year varies in different countries; and, finally, there is an absence of uniformity in organization.[1] In course of time it may be possible to secure some international standards in educational statistics or to evolve methods for reducing the present statistics to common standards.[2]

Comparative education, then, is treated in the present volume as a branch of politics, using the term in the sense in which it was used by the earliest educational theorists — Plato and Aristotle. Education is interpreted not in terms of schoolroom procedures, or in terms of the den, not as something esoteric, but in the only sense in which in modern life it can be conceived — as a part of the activity of humanity, organized into nations, for its own preservation and progress. Starting from this point of view, the meaning of nationalism and the forces which give it character are discussed, since nationalism in turn lends significance to the educational systems which are organized. Beyond this there is another contribution which the comparative study of education may hope to make. This is the development of an internationalism based not on emotion or sentiment, but arising from an appreciative understanding of other nations as well as our own, from the sense that all nations through their systems of education are contributing, each in its own way, to the work and progress of the world, and from a realization of the ambitions and ideals which each nation is endeavoring to hand on through its schools. A study of foreign school systems which neglects the search for the hidden meaning of things found in the schools would merely result in the acquisition of information about another educational system and would be of little value as a contribution to the clarification of thought, to the better development of education as a science, and to the formulation of a comprehensive, all-embracing philosophy of education thoroughly rooted

---

[1] A good example of the fallacy of comparing gross figures is the attempt to contrast the enrollment in the high schools of the United States with the enrollment in secondary schools abroad, ignoring the fact that the high schools enroll all the adolescents of the country, while elsewhere the education of adolescents is provided in a variety of schools — the so-called secondary schools, intermediate schools, and a great variety of vocational, full-time and part-time schools.

[2] An attempt to develop a common international system of educational records and reports has been made by M. Jean-Louis Claparède, Bureau International d'Education, Geneva.

in the culture, ideals, and aspirations which each nation should seek to add to the store of human welfare.[1]

[1] See Demiashkevich, M. J., "Why Comparative Education?" in the *Peabody Journal of Education*, July, 1931, pp. 41 ff., and Schneider, F., "*Internationale Pädagogik, Auslandspädagogik, Vergleichende Erziehungswissenschaft: Geschichte, Wesen, Methoden, Aufgaben und Ergebnisse*," in *Internationale Zeitschrift für Erziehungswissenschaft*, 1931–32, pp. 15 ff., 243 ff., and 392 ff.

CHAPTER I

EDUCATION AND NATIONALISM

EDUCATION AND THE PRESENT CRISIS

THE world is today passing through one of the greatest crises in its history. Shaken to its foundations by the Great War, it has not yet been able to pick up the threads of normal progress. Even before the War a movement of criticism had already set in which began to question all the values in intellectual, social, and economic life which had been inherited from the nineteenth century. The very progress of industrial mechanization on which the nineteenth century had prided itself had accumulated within itself the seeds of unrest and discontent which would in any case have led everywhere to social upheaval. The uncertainty of the situation following the War and a Peace which apparently left nothing settled brought to the focus of attention a whole series of problems which affect every aspect of life, national and international, and for which no satisfactory solutions seem as yet to be available. The political, social, and economic doctrines on which the progress of the nineteenth century appeared to be founded have given way in some countries to complete uncertainty as to the next step, in others to experimentation without any defined sense of direction, and in others, again, to reconstruction on the basis of theories which are accepted with almost religious zeal. The unrest and the uncertainty affect not only those countries which have developed under Western civilization; they have spread to the countries of the Orient, and to no small degree are making themselves felt among peoples who have hitherto been regarded as backward and whose development is now recognized to be bound up with the welfare of more advanced communities.

The history of education can point to numerous examples of changes in the development of educational theories and practices which have been consequent upon changes and crises in political, economic, and social conditions, but never before has education been so sensitive to the problems with which society is confronted. Always intimately bound up with the fabric of life, education has never been looked upon as it is today not only as an important instrument of social control but as one of the most valuable aids for social reconstruction. The world, although it has always paid a tribute to the importance of education, has since the beginning of the century and more particularly since the first days of the War become more acutely conscious of the part that the schools must play in shaping the destinies of the future. The whole field of education has broadened out and expanded in so many directions that the educator of the nineteenth century, concerned with one type of education for the masses, another for the leaders, and still another for the adolescent worker, would scarcely recognize the many ramifications which are being considered today. No longer confined to the cultivation of literacy or of intellectualism or of vocational skills, education is at last beginning to recognize the whole of life — health and physical well-being, political and social training, adaptation to a machine age, emotional and æsthetic development, and preparation for leisure as well as the cultivation of the mind — as the field for its endeavors. And as the problems of life are becoming increasingly complex and as the influences that mould it affect the individual from the cradle to the grave, the scope of education has expanded from what was in the past its major concern — the child and the adolescent — to include in its purview the child of pre-school age at one end and the adult at the other. If, then, education is as broad as life, a philosophy of education cannot be elaborated without taking into account the major forces that play upon the individual as a member of society; and if education is to become not only an instrument of social control but of social reconstruction, it must be more conscious than it has generally been in the past of all those forces which contribute to the development and character of any social organization.

Education and social forces. It is not necessary to go deeply into the history of education to discover the part played by social and political forces in determining the character of an educational system. Athens furnishes perhaps one of the best illustrations in miniature of the interplay of political forces and educational practices; here education was determined by the place of the individual as a citizen, and the full implication of this conception is nowhere better summarized than in Pericles' famous statement in the Funeral Oration:

We alone regard a man who takes no interest in public affairs, not as a harmless, but as a useless character; and if few of us are originators, we are all sound judges of a policy. The great impediment to action is, in our opinion, not discussion, but the want of that knowledge which is gained by discussion preparatory to action. For we have a peculiar power of thinking before we act and of acting, too, whereas other men are courageous from ignorance but hesitate upon reflection.[1]

Because the Greek conception of education was as broad as life itself, simple as it may have been in those days as contrasted with the complexities accumulated in modern civilizations, the philosophical analyses of educational theory by Plato and Aristotle are as fresh and pertinent today as when they were written. While Roman educational theory and practice offered little that went beyond those of the Greeks, the story of the gradual decline of Roman education furnishes an excellent illustration of the thesis that when the schools cease to be invigorated by the vital stream flowing in the social group which they serve they virtually cease to have any real significance. In the mediæval period education derived its purposes and aims from the conception of the individual as a member of the ecclesiastical State, although even at this time other forces, social and economic, strove to assert themselves, and chivalry produced an educational system adapted to its own needs, while the guilds provided a regiment of vocational preparation. The educational theory of the Renaissance, which glorified the individual for his own sake, did not come to its full fruition until it was reënforced and given direction by the Reformation on the one hand and the Counter-Reformation on the other with their doctrines of the domination of the individual by social aims, then the religious character of the State. This conception was inherited by the nineteenth century, but a new note was soon added — the shaping of education to the nationalistic State, which became the strongest factor governing the century.

This permanent truth illustrated in the main streams of the history of education is operative in the present period and has wider ramifications than ever before because of the increasing complexity of the problems with which society is confronted. In the first place, the leading countries of the world had achieved by the close of the nineteenth century systems of elementary education which were almost universal, and, rudimentary as that education was, it undoubtedly succeeded in creating a demand for more. Further expansion of education became inevitable as soon as it was recognized that elementary education alone provided a very inadequate preparation for meeting

[1] Thucydides, I, 70. Jowett's translation.

the problems of modern society. Great as had been the hopes of those who expected social regeneration to result from the mere acquisition of literacy, it was realized at the end of the century that literacy alone does not constitute an education. The rapid development of industry and the emergence of a new industrial revolution created by its increased mechanization have brought in their wake new problems which it is the task of education to solve — the reduction in the hours of labor involve an adequate preparation for the use of leisure; the growing conflicts between capital and labor, short of a complete revolution in the economic bases of life, demand a better education for the representatives of both; and the machine age in turn implies a release of individual effort and energy for other ends than mere living. In other words, while elementary education, which was all that was available to the large masses of individuals in each country, might impart literacy, it failed, because of the immaturity of the pupils exposed to it, to cultivate interests of enduring value and of significance for mature life.

But the industrial and economic environment is only one of the factors which affect education. The significance of education lies in the attempt to conceive it from every aspect of the environment in which the individual lives and moves. The individual is more than a worker; he is a human being with rights, duties, and potentialities of his own; he is a member of a great variety of social groups which satisfy his interests, needs, and aspirations; he is a citizen; and increasingly he is beginning to realize that he must share interests beyond and outside of the national and political group of which he is a member. It is by considerations of such facts that education is being influenced more than at any time in its history. One of the lessons most widely learned during the Great War was that of the worth of the individual; this was due not merely to the realization that in times of crisis every man, woman, and child counts, but to the general recognition that ability is not confined to any social class or group and that any social system must provide for its emergence and particularly by the provision of educational opportunities. But while the War furnished concrete proof of a fact already recognized in theory long before and assumed in practice in the United States, it helped also to confirm another movement which antedated the War. This was the movement, partly the result of education, partly the outcome of class consciousness heightened by the Industrial Revolution, and partly the effect of the slow expansion of liberalism in politics, which was gradually leading everywhere to demands first of all for democratic forms of government and later for democracy as the basis of economic and social as well as of political organization. The nineteenth-century democracy of the ballot-box leading to universal suffrage had been found wanting; in its place there began to be demanded a broader interpretation — democracy as an ideal of life in all its aspects. At the present time the democratic ideal and the recognition of the potential worth of the individual are the two strongest forces which have stimulated the development of education, in theory as yet more than in practice, within the last two decades. And even in those systems which have been set up in opposition to democracy — Fascism critical of it as a form of government and Communism discontented with its economic basis — its educational ideals are none the less exercising some influence. The effects of the democratic ideal and the recognition of individual worth on education will constantly reappear in the discussions of educational developments and tendencies which are the subject of this volume.

SIGNIFICANCE OF NATIONALISM

Behind these two forces, however, there lies another which gives to them and to education their own peculiar interpretation. This force has been the rapid and progressive development of national self-consciousness which marked the nineteenth century as the era of nationalism and which since the Great War has been cultivated with new vigor and intensity as one of the strongest forms of corporate feeling. But while the nineteenth century witnessed the cult of the spirit of nationalism in a sinister direction as the mainspring of prejudice and rivalry between national groups, the dawn of a new era appears to be in sight in which another concept, based on a desire for self-expression and self-determination, may be evolved and directed toward international coöperation and good-will. Already this concept has stirred the minds of men, although it would be futile to claim that those rivalries and antagonisms which culminated in the tragedy of 1914 have even begun to disappear. If the nineteenth century was the era of nationalism, the twentieth promises to become the era of the emergence of self-determining nationalities, a movement which has arisen wherever groups of men feel themselves bound by loyalty to a common ideal, whether in Europe or Asia or Africa or South

America. The redivision of Europe at Versailles was based, however inadequately, on this definition, and to it can be traced some of the burning problems that still confront the world in Palestine, India, China, the Philippines, as well as the demands of minority groups in the newly created as well as among the older nations.

Common racial origin. The concept of nationality does not, however, lend itself readily to such a simple definition as loyalty to a common ideal; there are other factors and explanations that cut across it. There are those who would insist that a nation is or should be a racial unit with common ancestors, common kin, common language, common culture, a common homeland, and certain common characteristics. In this sense, it is claimed that the Zionist movement is both a racial and a national movement; a still more recent movement of a similar type is that for autonomy in Catalonia. On the other hand, the claim for nationality based on community of racial origin, even if true in the groups mentioned, may easily be refuted by reference to any of the nations already in existence; one may begin with the United States and proceed to the history of Italy, or Great Britain, or India, where the mixture of races is obvious to the eye. And yet even in the United States the fiction of a common inheritance is perpetuated in the words of one of the national anthems, "Land where my fathers died."

Language and religion. Language is another factor which has been claimed as the common basis of nationalism and in this sense there may be cited the Americanization movement in the United States, in so far as it seeks to secure community of language and prohibits the maintenance of schools conducted in a foreign tongue, the Germanization of minorities before the War, the Italianization of minorities today, as well as the revival of languages as the basis of new national movements — of Celtic in Ireland, of Hebrew among the Jews, of Catalan in Spain. The claim of language as the cause and basis of national unity is, however, upset by the existence of nations that are bilingual — South Africa, Canada, Switzerland, Belgium — instances that disturb this simple acceptance of language as an explanation of nationalism. At the same time language has in the past played and still plays a very important part in the development of national solidarity, since uniformity of language does make for like-mindedness, a sense of common interest, group consciousness, and a feeling of unlikeness as against the foreigner. But even here the thesis is not irrefutable when it is borne in mind that community of language does not make for like-mindedness between Great Britain and the United States, or between Spain and the South American countries, or between the South American countries themselves. Religion, which for a long time was an important factor in developing nationalism (*cujus regio, ejus religio*), has tended generally to lose its force since religious tolerance began to spread in the nineteenth century.

Common culture. The influences which have been mentioned by no means exhaust the variety of causes that are alleged to furnish the foundations of nationalism. The task of definition is complicated by the connotations that have developed round the words "nation," "nationalism," and "nationality." Nation and nationalism are associated with the existence of a political state; nationality implies a spiritual tie which binds together a group of individuals that feels itself as one, so that a number of nationalities may exist side by side within the same political state. Historically it is possible to trace back the rise of national groups to a number of social instincts: gregariousness and the herd instinct, the instinct for coöperation, and readiness to make sacrifices for the social unit whether through sympathy and love of approval or through fear of disapproval, egoism and self-preservation. The full development of the sense of communion implied by nationality involves the territorial idea, the idea of living together in a definite home-country. Approached from this angle nationalism and nationality may be synthesized in the definition that they represent a spiritual quality which implies a common homeland, corporate life, corporate growth, corporate self-respect and self-consciousness based on community of culture. A nation is then a group of individuals sharing a common culture. To quote Professor Barker:

> Shall we say that a nation is a body of men, inhabiting a definite territory, who normally are drawn from different races, but possess a common stock of thoughts and feelings acquired and transmitted during the course of a common history; who on the whole and in the main, though more in the past than the present, include in that common stock a common religious belief; who generally and as a rule use a common language as the vehicle of their thoughts and feelings; and who, besides common thoughts and feelings, also cherish a common will, and accordingly form, or tend to form, a separate State for the expression and realization of that will? If we so define a nation, we may further define national character as the sum of acquired tendencies which a national society has built on the native basis of its racial blend, its territory,

and the mass and social variety of its population — the house of thought which men have made that their minds may dwell there together.[1]

Nationalism, then, implies a common language, common customs, and a common culture. A nation is a nationality which has acquired self-government — it is nationality plus the State, a nationality possessing its own political institutions governed by its own consent and coextensive with its own national boundaries. To object that this definition does not take into account minority groups which have a sense of like-mindedness is only to say that no definition can be comprehensive. That the definition is almost all-embracing is indicated by the possibility of solving the problem of minorities within the scope of its terms, as is already manifested in Belgium, in Canada, in South Africa, and in the Union of Soviet Republics. For the development of education, the new approach to the whole problem is of the utmost significance. Its progress in the nineteenth century was fostered under the ægis of that conception of nationalism which emphasized the political aspect and power as the end of the national State, which stressed not coöperation but rivalry between nations. Under this conception the individual counted for little as a personality in the development of national power and economic self-interest. Culture as a common basis of nationalism was a state product, a part of the state machinery to promote like-mindedness and loyalty, and hence a definite part of the state system of education, training all to be alike; from this angle culture becomes a force bent and directed to national ends conceived from the political point of view in order to secure discipline, duty, obedience, efficiency, public service. The nation is divided into those who lead and those who are led, those who define the culture which is to become the medium for indoctrinating the masses, and the masses upon whom it is imposed. But national culture, if it is to become the possession of all, and particularly if it is to be dynamic and to grow, is not subject to such narrow definitions as are attempted in a state-controlled régime. In the sense in which the term is used in the recent definitions of nationality, culture implies the spontaneous expression of the individuals of a nation; it arises out of the free interplay between individuals and their environment, and between individuals and groups among themselves. As civilization progresses and increases in complexity, it is becoming

---

[1] Barker, Ernest. *National Character and the Factors in its Formation*, pp. 17 f. New York, Harper & Bros., 1927.

more and more difficult for any state machinery to direct and control it in its manifold ramifications; hence the demand for national self-determination is being followed by a demand for group self-determination, a demand which, although limited for the present to the economic field, may well be extended to others.

Two concepts of nationalism. The world is today confronted with a conflict between these two concepts. On the one hand is the demand for more intense state control whether in the form of a dictatorship of personal power and authority or of a dictatorship of an idea. On the other hand, the difficulties of representative government arising from the variety and complexity of the human affairs that are to be regulated are leading to a demand for an interpretation of democracy in which the individuals or groups of a nation will participate more directly in regulating themselves and their own affairs. Whichever the choice, it is of significance for education.

The philosophy of education aided by the latest researches of psychology may evolve schemes of education, utopian and irrefutable in the abstract, but national systems of education cannot for long remain unresponsive to the demands of the political, social, and economic environment in which they develop. The whole problem of education in the present stage of its development may be approached from one or other of the points of view here presented — of culture as the free and spontaneous expression of individuals or a group of individuals, or of culture as something that is defined by a central agency of the State and devised to secure a common mind and common outlook. Russia and Italy, and to some extent the United States, indicate that a third course is conceivable, a culture which is in part permitted to develop freely and is in part dictated by certain ends, political, economic, or nationalistic.

Psychology of nationalism. The main criteria of nationality are psychological; the growth of nationalism is governed by traditions, historical perspective, and principles and ideas shared in common, leading to pride in group membership, self-consciousness, and the adoption of symbols, holidays, songs, and ceremonials by which these are objectified. The development of nationalism has forced men out of narrow sectionalism into membership in larger social units, and has cultivated loyalty to a state which rises above petty and selfish interests. But it has also raised the problem whether nationalism implies the cult of docility and uniformity in public matters; it has also brought into the foreground the question of the meaning of patriotism and the place of propaganda and indoctrination in the development of men's minds. If patriotism is defined in the spirit of jingoism and imperialism, in terms of pride in the strength, the power, and the superiority of one's nation, the world is in constant danger of a repetition of that catastrophe which overwhelmed it in 1914. If, however, patriotism is defined as loyalty to the moral and spiritual ideals of one's nation, confidence in what it can contribute to the progressive civilization of the world and to the well-being of humanity, acceptance of the right of other nations to embark on a similar mission, and faith that more can be gained for national as well as international progress from coöperation and the pooling of resources than from the pursuit of selfish interests, the world as well as each nation will benefit. If the first view of patriotism is accepted, propaganda and indoctrination in education mean the exploitation of prejudices, bigotry, and human weakness, which colors not only the teaching of patriotism but the whole educative process. If the second definition is adopted, propaganda and indoctrination do not cease to have their place in education, but they imply the cultivation of human intelligence to criticize what is demoralizing and to honor what is choice-worthy. In the one method the emphasis is on dictation, on authority; in the other, the growth of free personality in ability to reach decisions on the basis of knowledge and inquiry is stressed. The danger is as imminent today as it was in the nineteenth century that, because nations have grown up through conflicts, dislike and hostility without, the cult of nationalism and its expression as patriotism may have inherent in it intolerance and hatred of other nations. There are signs, however, that in education at any rate, no matter what the facts may be in politics, it is being recognized that a spirit of nationalism can be cultivated which is ready to play its part in the development of world-mindedness.

NATIONALISM AND EDUCATION

Scope of education. Nationalism is, then, a condition of mind or loyalty to ideals based on a national state. Because it can be conceived only in terms of ideas, intellectual and moral outlook, emotions, and culture in general, education has steadily assumed an increasingly important place in programs of national development. The conceptions underlying national systems of education do not, however, lie immediately on the surface. The forces that actually operate today are more obvious than these. There is at present no corner of the world that is not affected by the educational renaissance, nor is this movement confined to nations which have had established educational systems and traditions, nor to groups which are emerging into nationhood, but the impact has been felt in efforts which are being made for the reorganization of the education of backward peoples. In the main the movements for the reform of national systems of education are inspired by the spread of democracy, but democracy no longer in terms of equality before the ballot-box so much as of equality of opportunity in all aspects of life — political, social and economic — a democracy conceived in terms, not merely of the machinery of government, but of the spirit in which all the relations of the individual to the society of which he is a member are conducted. Alongside of the movement to promote equality of opportunity which developed as a natural trend of the last century towards more liberal and democratic forms of government, there has arisen a widespread recognition of the worth of the individual and the realization of the tremendous amount of intellectual resources latent in all classes and an equally universal recognition of the need of harnessing these resources through education for the improvement of national well-being. It is no accident, no mere result of theoretical considerations that the proposal in education which is most widely discussed today is the attempt to extend further and more diversified education to those classes that have enjoyed it before. Whether it is in terms of a demand for a broad educational highway, or for *carrières ouvertes au talent* or *freie Bahn dem Tüchtigen*, with their corollaries of secondary education for all, the *école unique*, or the *Einheitsschule*, the dominating causes are everywhere the same. If the progress of the movement for the realization of this ideal has been retarded, the reasons are to be found in part in the economic depression from which the world has suffered, and in part in a certain inertia to depart from the traditional practices and ideas in the selection of leaders and in the content of their preparation. Politics and economics are not the only aspects of national life dominated by the vested interests of the *beati possidentes*.

Nationalism and the individual. If the meaning of nationalism is most adequately defined in terms of culture and ideals, it becomes clear that there is scarcely any problem in education that is not in some way or another affected by it. The first problem is the eternal one of the relation of the State to the individual, or, rather, the place of the individual in the State, whether the State exists as an organization to promote the free, moral and spiritual development of the individual, or whether it seeks to preserve and perpetuate itself by moulding all individuals to the same pattern. The answer to this problem determines the whole problem of the administration, support, and maintenance of education, whether they are to be wholly centralized and controlled in the interests of uniformity, or whether some place is to be found for local initiative, local enterprise, and local adaptations to environmental differences. This leads by a natural transition to a consideration of the place of private education in a national system, to what extent is it to be tolerated and encouraged, and to what degree is it to be controlled, supervised, and regimented. Fundamental to these problems is the whole question of the meaning of a national system of education — Is it to be organized in the interests of a class or on the basis of equality of opportunity? Is it to be selective and differentiated, or shall it, in the supposed interests of democracy, offer a single-track institution only? Hitherto elementary education has connoted the education of the masses largely as followers, and secondary education that of the classes, largely the leaders; is the survival of such a dual system of education acceptable and compatible with the demands and meaning of nationalism today? So long as the dual concept of education prevailed, the emphasis in elementary education continued to be placed on the cultivation of literacy and a modicum of information, and in secondary education on culture and liberal disciplines; does the new concept of nationalism have inherent in it another implication — education as life and education for life, which are something more than mere literacy and imply continuity of the process of education from infancy up to and through adult life?

Nationalism and the schools. On the answers to these problems will depend the solution of those problems which are more intimately the concern of the school, of the relations between teacher and pupils. The whole question of the character of the curriculum and of curriculum-making is determined by the national concept and its definition of the relation of the State to the individual. From some points of view the curriculum and course of study may be regarded as a form of propaganda, a type of indoctrination determined by the necessities of the State; in this case the making of the curriculum and the definition of the details of the course of study are controlled wholly by agencies established by the State. If, however, the real meaning of nationalism as a spiritual force is recognized and national culture is considered as the interplay of individual and group interests — intellectual, physical, æsthetic, and moral — freedom and local initiative are encouraged. The inculcation of nationalism and patriotism and the teaching, not only of history, but of geography, literature, art and music, are determined largely by the type of national outlook which prevails.

Ultimately, however, differences between national systems of education consist not so much in the list of subjects that are taught as in the selection of the content of each subject and the use to which it is put. History as a subject of instruction, for example, may in itself be quite neutral and be taught with the aim of developing an appreciation of the sequence of events, to stimulate in the learner a desire to ask, What comes next? On the other hand, it may be and has in the past been employed to develop bigotry and prejudice, patriotism based not on loyalty to a nation's ideals but on hatred of the foreigner. Geography may in a similar way be taught as a science and as a study of the relations of man to his environment, but it may also be abused through an emphasis on national boundaries, on lost provinces, or on the different coloring that sets off one nation from another. Even so apparently innocuous a subject as arithmetic may be bent to patriotic ends.[1] Not only the content but methods of instruction, the place of discipline and freedom, of indoctrination and spontaneity are in national systems of education governed more frequently by aspects of nationalism than by educational theory, however well founded it may be. The place of textbooks, their use and selection, the development and encouragement of corporate life or extra-curricular activities, the preparation and status of teachers, the use and importance of examinations — all of these questions, as will appear subsequently, are more subject to subtle national preconceptions and attitudes than to the theoretical considerations of educational philosophers.

---

[1] See Alexander, T., *The Prussian Elementary Schools* (New York, 1919), for examples of the use of subjects for nationalistic ends, particularly pp. 425–28, 445–51. On the use of history for the inculcation of patriotism of the dangerous kind see Scott, J., *The Menace of Nationalism in Education* (London, 1926); Prudhommeaux, J., *Enquête sur les Livres scolaires d'après Guerre* (Paris, 1923); Pierce, B., *Public Opinion and the Teaching of History in the United States* (New York, 1926); and many others.

Nationalism and internationalism. Finally, it is obvious that any trend towards the development of international understanding or world-mindedness is determined primarily by national emotions and attitudes which, although they may often override the logical demands of the age, are at once the results and the explanations of the character of an educational system. One point is, however, obvious, and that is, that, if the definition of the nation and of nationalism in terms of common spiritual and cultural loyalties is sound, they have nothing to fear from the development of international understanding. Indeed, their proper cult is essential to it, for internationalism properly understood is inconceivable without nationalism, nor does it imply some form of supra-nationalism or cosmopolitanism, but rather the interplay and coöperation between the best spiritual contributions of each national group in the interests of a sane and sound development of world civilization and culture. In the last analysis in the present stage of civilization — with the annihilation of space and time through the improvement of mechanical devices, with the sensitiveness of every part of the world to the slightest changes in the economic and financial sphere, with the interdependence of humanity in the promotion of the sciences and the arts — the self-determination of nations without regard for their neighbors is as unthinkable as the self-realization of the individuals of a nation without regard to their fellow-citizens.

Distinctiveness of national systems of education. It is obvious from the preceding discussion of nationalism and its direct bearing on the character of educational systems, that the educational systems of no two nations can be identical. No country can claim that its educational problems are unique; what is unique are the ways in which each nation approaches these problems, the social situation and the influences that have gone to mould it and to determine the character of the solution which has been reached. In other words each nation today constitutes an experimental laboratory which yields solutions to the same problems in different ways determined by peculiar social traditions and conditions. It is for this reason that the educational systems and practices of one nation cannot be transported to another nation or to other peoples without profound adaptations and modifications; such a course runs the risk of offending local traditions, local genius, the peculiar social, economic, and political conditions of the nation to which the foreign system is transferred.

What are the forces and causes of these differences in national inheritances? Biologically all children have the same start as members of the human race, the same nervous organization, the same instinctive equipment, and the same central tendencies to action qualified by hereditary differences. And yet as they grow up differences of outlook, attitudes, emotions, ideals, become increasingly evident. What are the causes and what are the factors that determine the differences underlying national systems of education despite the fact that in general most nations are confronted by the same problems?

Historical factors. Since modern institutions and culture have been developed out of the interchange between all past experiences and local environments, the most obvious cause of national differences is to be found in a nation's history and traditions. Even those nations which pride themselves on making history rather than on the history of their past cannot escape from the fact that history has left the imprint of all its manifold influences on the minds and culture of their people. In the United States, for example, two important factors have moulded American thought and outlook. The first of these is the dominance of the doctrine of the perfectibility of man, a doctrine imported from France in the middle of the eighteenth century which found its fullest development in the United States in the general acceptance of the ideal of equality of opportunity. The second is to be found in the effects of the frontier and its conquest, which have left a lasting imprint on American character and on American institutions, for this struggle combined with the doctrine of perfectibility has given its particular coloring to the American concept of democracy. Interwoven with these two factors is the strain of Puritanism which some interpreters of American life claim to be still strongly operative. The many-sidedness of English character [1] may be traced to the tradition of individualism, freedom of speech, liberty of conscience, and the doctrine of *laissez faire* which, confronted in the present era by the exigencies of new social and economic conditions, may have to yield, more than it has already done, to some form of social planning and governmental control. The history of English education in the past twenty-five years is full of il-

---

[1] This is fully developed by Sir Michael E. Sadler in his article on "The Philosophy underlying the System of Education in England" in the *Educational Yearbook, 1929*, of the International Institute of Teachers College, Columbia University, pp. 1 ff. (New York, 1930).

lustrations of this conflict between the doctrine of *laissez faire* and governmental prescription, the outcome of which promises to offer a most valuable contribution to the vexed question of the relation of a central authority to local and private organizations.[1] By contrast with the English situation, almost three centuries of centralized administration, organized into a definite pattern over a century ago by Napoleon, have resulted in France in a faith in the wisdom of governmental control and bureaucratic administration against which the recent movement for local self-determination (regionalism) is not likely to make any inroads for many years.

State and Church. Even if the discussion of the influences of history and tradition were limited to education alone, the field becomes almost inexhaustible. Some of the most crucial problems in the reconstruction of the educational systems in England, Germany, France, and Italy may be traced to the age-old partnership between the Church and the school. At the beginning of 1931 this traditional partnership was responsible for an amendment of the bill introduced in the House of Commons to extend the age of compulsory school attendance in England, which would have delayed for some time the operation of the bill had it been accepted by the House of Lords. For three years the most serious educational and political problem in the new German Republic centered round an attempt (the *Reichsschulgesetz*) to restore this partnership into full vigor, a measure which would have resulted in splitting the system of German elementary education into thousands of small parochial schools. One of the chief obstacles to the adoption of the common school system (*école unique*) in France is to be found in the opposition of the Church to the acceptance of a policy which, while it would introduce equality of opportunity, might, it is feared without foundation, be a further step in establishing a state monopoly of education. In Italy the Fascist Government, although not opposed to religious instruction in the schools as an essential part of the tradition of Italian culture, has been compelled by a tradition centuries older than Fascism to place this instruction under clerical supervision.

Class and social distinctions. The most cursory examination of proposals for the reorganization of educational systems conceived with the intention of eliminating the dual tracks of elementary and secondary education and of increasing educational opportunities re-

[1] See Chapters III, IV, and V.

veals that the strongest stumbling-block is to be found, not in the probable increased cost of education, but in the dual origin of elementary and secondary education, in the conception of elementary education as an education for the lower classes and of secondary for the leaders, and in a somewhat narrow conception of the meaning of a liberal education as the proper tradition to be perpetuated in the secondary schools. To the same dual origins and traditions may be attributed the hesitancy in many countries to reorganize the systems of preparing elementary school teachers on the assumption that such preparation should be in the spirit of the traditional elementary schools rather than on a university level. Into the conflict between "progressive" or "new" education and tradition, it is unnecessary to enter in detail. On the one hand, there is a demand for a complete reorganization of curriculum, content, and methods of instruction with an emphasis on the cultivation of freedom, initiative, and independence; on the other, there are stressed drill and discipline, adult needs, the accumulation of examinable information. The traditional faith in literacy as the basis of social salvation and consequently as the aim of the education of the masses, with its emphasis on reading, writing, and arithmetic, stands in the way of the adoption not only of radical but of moderate reforms. No branch of education is more governed by class tradition than secondary; from the social point of view the selective, from the curricular, the classical or linguistic concepts of secondary education still prevail almost universally and block the attempts to democratize educational opportunities and to introduce greater diversification of courses adapted to the needs of adolescents and the changing demands of the new industrial age.

Racial characteristics. In considering the meaning of nationality, reference was made to the claim that one of the bases alleged for its origin is community of race. This claim is carried a stage further with the assumption that differences between nations are due to differences of racial characteristics. Whatever the origin of nations may have been in their early history, community of race plays little part in determining their characteristics; further, no one would affirm today that there are such things as rooted, unchanging racial characteristics. There is, it is true, a tendency to generalize on this subject, and to some it would, indeed, bring comfort and consolation, if there were any truth in the generalization, for Nordic superiority could then be established.[1] There are, however, clear national characteristics which, acquired rather than innate, are marked and have an important influence on outlook and attitudes toward all phases of life, including educational theory and practice. The characteristics themselves are the results of so many changing forces that they do not lend themselves to any clear-cut definition.

Population. Character and outlook may be determined by such factors as the distribution and mobility of a population. A stay-at-home people, particularly if it does not possess adequate means of communication, through roads and railways, press and literature, and the more modern devices of telephone and radio, tends on the whole, because it develops in isolation, to be more cautious and conservative, less curious and more resistant to innovation. The changing status of family life, which has in the past been everywhere a social nursery, and the decline of parental influence exercise important influences on the development of character in general and on the practices of the school. The social attitude to children, whether they are regarded as an investment for old age or as individuals with great potentialities, profoundly affects the retention of children in school, the amount of money devoted to education, the character of the discipline in the home and the school, and, it might be said, the status of the teacher.

Social and economic organization. National character is, again, profoundly affected by the nature and distribution of social organization, whether urban or rural. The large city tends to disintegrate community interests and to dissipate the opportunity of local associations and groups to develop a community of spirit and of interests. The city is the seat of productive originality and offers scope for the development of specialized groups and capacities, and to this extent leaves room for the cultivation of independence of character and for experimentation; the rural organization, on the other hand, varying with the difficulty of aggregation, tends to develop individuality in isolation, to cultivate mastery of the environment without the clash of variety of interests, and to stimulate self-reliance but the self-reliance of the opinionated and conservative. In general the con-

---

[1] My own opinion is that in the United States, where this question of racial characteristics has been most widely discussed, the conflicts of different groups have arisen from a clash of different cultures, different religions, different standards of living, and not least through the attempts at too rapid assimilation of the immigrant with a complete disregard of his background. The economic causes of the conflict need only be mentioned without further discussion.

trast between urban and rural organizations in their influence on character-building and attitudes may be seen in nations which are predominantly industrial and those which are predominantly agricultural. This contrast is well marked if one compares the Germany before 1870 and the Germany since that date, or in present-day France, where a quiet and subtle change is proceeding as the country is gradually moving from an agricultural to an industrial basis, or in England, where there are marked differences in outlook between the industrial North and the rural South. The conflict of interests and differences in temper between rural and urban United States have always exercised a strong influence on national life since the early days of the Republic and in the present crisis are too obvious to need any more comment than to point to the gradually changing attitudes that are proceeding from the gradual industrialization of the Southern States.

Except to those who accept the economic interpretation of history and of national life, the influence of wealth and its distribution on national character and outlook is not on the surface very obvious. It is clear, however, that where wealth serves as a spur to ambition the demand for education as well as for diversification of types of education is likely to be more emphasized than in a country in which there is a more even distribution.[1] At the same time intense competition may lead to the growth of economic levels and types of education presumed to be appropriate to each, while, on the other side, the accumulation of wealth may lead, as in the United States, to the establishment and maintenance of private schools. At the same time the last two results, the provision of differentiated types of schools for different economic levels and the establishment of private schools, may equally be attributed to the existence of social stratification which leads to one type of school for the classes and another for the masses and in general to opposition to public expenditure on education, compensated in part by the provision of opportunities for the poor but able to emerge from their own social level. But these are not the only effects of social stratification; on its extent and distribution depend such contrasts as between conservatism and fixity of tradition, on the one hand, and liberalism, experimentation, and

---

[1] A crude illustration of this thesis may be found in the campaign conducted in the United States about 1918 to encourage young persons to continue their education. See U.S. Office of Education, Bulletin, 1917, No. 22, *The Money Value of Education*.

progress on the other, between inbreeding and continuity and the gradual emergence of vigorous ability and new qualities of character and outlook, between a caste system and a system which provides opportunities for self-realization and ambition, between institutionalism and individuality, between rigidity and plasticity. The significance of these contrasts will emerge in a comparison of national systems of education, but the interplay of these factors is equally marked in a study of the development of educational ideals in the nineteenth century as compared with the present era in individual nations. For the student of comparative education many of the differences between national systems of education can find their only explanation in an examination of the national attitudes and characteristics which are derived from these contrasts.

Political theory. Plato and Aristotle discussed for all time the intimate relations between the character of a people and political theory and forms of government. The development of national systems of education in the nineteenth century only served to give concrete reality to their theoretical discussions. The centralized, autocratic, dictatorial form of government tends to emphasize control through a central agency, to dominate opinion and its formation by what is taught in the schools; the liberal or democratic form of government tends to leave more to local initiative and enterprise, although the fact must be stressed that a republican government is not necessarily liberal or democratic. In the one case there results uniformity and simplicity of organization, a perfected mechanical organization resting on bureaucratic control which maintains universally recognized standards; in the other case, variety, differentiation, and experimentation characterize every phase of social organization resulting in a ragged system with peaks and valleys due to differences in local conditions and local initiative, without uniformity of standards, but with something that is superior — readiness to accept change and reform as conditions demand and to advance to ever-receding goals, an experimental attitude which, if consciously harnessed to principles, is a guarantee of progress. Plato had already noted that there is more scope for variety of human nature in a democracy, but he also warned, and there are concrete examples which prove the truth of his warning, against the danger in a democracy of a dead level of mediocrity. In the centralized system social guidance and direction are determined by a bureaucracy, ready to disregard, because the administrative mind prefers mechanical perfection, local conditions and local interests; in the decentralized system social progress responds more readily to the demands of the public will. Individuality and initiative, whether of persons or of groups, find more opportunity for their realization in a democracy; standardized culture, good form and conventions, conformity are more likely to be characteristic of the autocratic, centralized scheme of organization. And yet, since politics and government constitute only one of the many-colored forces that affect national attitudes, any attempt at generalization is apt to be dangerous.

The list of factors that contribute to the moulding of differences between the character and attitudes of nations is almost inexhaustible, and any further attempt at analysis might lead to mere speculation. This would, for example, be true if it were sought to contrast the divergence of influence exercised by various religions, or to go still further and attempt to explain the acceptance of one denomination rather than another on the basis of race. So far as education is concerned, all that need be insisted upon is that the character of a national system of education may be affected by the relations between the Church and the State; whether national character is differently affected by different forms of creed and worship, it is in the light of recent political events difficult to say. Equally difficult is it at present to anticipate the effects on the future development of nations and of civilization and culture of the adoption of types of social organization which will cut across those already in existence; such, for example, would be the development of occupationalism or grouping by professions and occupations for purposes of self-determination. For education such functional organization of social groups would probably involve a prolongation of general education for all and the consequent postponement of specialization, a reorganization of the systems of vocational preparation, greater emphasis on training in social obligation, and the institution of forms of education which would enrich occupationalism.

Whatever future developments may bring, this fact will always remain true, that a philosophy of education which does not take the major forces that mould and shape national life into account is likely to remain formal and barren. The development of education as a science is possible, but only in a very limited sense. The human element is too complex and human relations are too involved and complicated to be as easily defined and measured for educational purposes as some enthusiasts for a science of education would claim. The facts that must be taken into account by the student of comparative education have been aptly summarized by Robert Bridges in his *Testament of Beauty* (Book IV, lines 918 ff.):

> all men differ each from each, since neither environment
> nor disposition can ever in any two men
> be the same or alike, and therefore (as was said)
> true individuality within the species
> would seem reach'd in mankind.   Again likewise 'tis seen
> how national mentalities are mutually
> incomprehensible and irreconcilable;
> since each group as it rose was determin'd apart
> by conditions of life which none other could share,
> by climate, language, and historic tradition
> estranging evermore; nor are such obstinate bonds
> the weaker for any intrinsic absurdity.[1]

[1] Oxford University Press, 1929.

CHAPTER II

EDUCATION AND NATIONAL CHARACTER

DIFFERENCES between national systems of education are due, as was pointed out in the last chapter, to a series of forces that have gone and still go to mould nations and national character and outlook. Since education represents in the main the conscious effort of society to conserve what it regards as most precious and fundamental to its perpetuation, it is obvious that its nature and organization must be strongly colored by the character and outlook of a nation, shaped and moulded by countless other factors. It must be admitted that there is considerable danger in employing such a generalization as national character. Nothing is more prejudicial to the progress of international understanding than generalizations which would attach labels to different national groups, and such labels are all the more deplorable when they become fixed in uninquiring and immature minds. There is, therefore, no intention here of employing such generalizations as that all Germans are docile, all Frenchmen gay, all Englishmen obstinate and conservative, all Latin peoples passionate and unstable, and all Americans materialistic go-getters. If generalizations are used it is only in the sense that certain groups are likely to act in ways different from other groups according to their history, traditions, environment, ideals, and intellectual outlook; it is not necessary as a consequence to accept the theory that a nation has a soul or mind. Since human beings are what they are, there is room in every group for the development of varieties of character and modes of behavior, and yet when they behave as a group they may collectively manifest the common imprint of those factors which have welded them together. With the progress of mass education, it may well be that certain characteristics may be sublimated in one group and stressed in another.

As one examines national systems of education, the differences are striking. One system is highly centralized and carefully planned in all its parts; another is decentralized, apparently chaotic and unarticulated. One system leaves no room for local initiative and adaptation to local needs; another leaves almost everything in the educational process to local initiative and experimentation except the barest minima to give unity in diversity. One system emphasizes rigid uniformity deliberately; another actually places a premium on variety as the soundest basis of progress. One system stresses the cultivation of the mind and intellectual development, another the formation of character and the will to act. Such differences, which are here stated very broadly, but which will inevitably appear as this work progresses, can find no explanation in educational theories; actually educational theories follow rather than lead — they are the rationalizations of pre-existing conditions. In the light of the attempt of German philosophers to develop a science of education which is autonomous, self-contained, and having its own ends, the point of view here presented must be emphasized. It is no accident or no mere coincidence that the pragmatic philosophy of education is peculiarly American and that American education is founded on the idea of progress, while the French emphasize the progress of ideas and the cult of reason. It is important, therefore, as a means of appreciating and understanding the significance of a national system of education to consider the bearing of a nation's character upon its education.

1. ENGLAND

The English system of education, like the English Constitution and the British Empire, has grown up by a series of accidents, by modifications, adaptations, and expansions, not based upon any theory or on any preconceived planning, but introduced as the occasion or the social needs and changes demanded. Thus the Education Act of 1902 was passed as a happy compromise without any full realization of its implications for the development of a national system of education. Even when the opportunity is offered of establishing a well articulated organization of education in the current proposals to raise the compulsory age of attendance to fifteen and to provide some form of post-elementary education for all boys and girls, the opportunity of adopting a symmetrical design is hardly even considered and new wings in a different style of architecture, as it were, are planned to be added on to a building which is already sufficiently variegated. The explanation is not to be found, as is sometimes alleged, in innate conservatism, or in a desire to perpetuate class distinctions, since the forces aligned against their perpetuation in education are sufficiently strong to oppose such an attempt. The explanation lies rather in the fact that the Englishman dislikes to think or to formulate plans of action, however plausible they may be, before the immediate need for them is apparent on the surface. He prefers to rely on action based on common sense as the need for action arises; his outlook is essentially empirical and relies on his ability to carry out each action with the minimum amount of thought needed for success in meeting a situation. The Englishman, more than any other national, believes that an ounce of practice is worth a pound of theory and that bridges must not be crossed until they are reached, for "You never can tell." Hence Socialism in England is less uncompromising than in other countries and the Russian experiment of social planning makes no appeal there because "it may be very well in theory, but..."

This is by no means a new feature in English character. Burke had already noted it in the *Reflections on the French Revolution*:

By a slow but well sustained progress, the effect of each step is watched; the good or ill success of the first gives light to us in the second; and so, from light to light, we are conducted with safety through the whole series. We see that the parts of the system do not clash. The evils latent in the most promising contrivances are provided for as they arise. One advantage is as little as possible sacrificed to another. We compensate, we reconcile, we balance. We are enabled to unite into a consistent whole the various anomalies and contending principles that are found in the minds and affairs of men. From hence arises, not an excellence in simplicity, but one far superior, an excellence in composition.

This reliance on ability to work institutions, to compromise, to make concessions, to rely on common sense in human affairs rather than on logic, affects not only domestic but also foreign affairs; in neither are rigidly formulated theories and doctrines acceptable. Thus in discussing the problem of a Protocol for a world settlement in 1925 Sir Austin Chamberlain expressed this fundamental feature in English character:

As to the argument that the Protocol is merely the logical conclusion of the Covenant, I profoundly distrust logic when applied to politics and all English history justifies me. Why is it that, as contrasted with other nations, ours has been a peaceful not a violent development? Why is it that great as have been the changes that have taken place in this country, we have had none of those sudden revolutions and reactions that have so frequently affected more logically-minded nations than ourselves? It is because instinct and experience alike teach us that human nature is not logical, that it is unwise to treat political institutions as instruments of logic, and that it is in wisely refraining from pressing conclusions to their logical end that the path of peaceful development and true reform is truly found. (*The Times*, March 25, 1925.)

Because national planning may inevitably lead to governmental dictation and bureaucratic control, the Englishman mistrusts it; he prefers to rely upon the spontaneous activity of individuals or groups. The resistance with which every step in the piecemeal progress of social legislation or national compulsion even in time of war helps to illustrate rather than to refute this statement. The reluctance to rely on government initiative and the suspicion of theories and plans of action have their counterpart in the English attitude to the expert and the specialist; preferring common sense and the conduct of each situation on its own merits the Englishman suspects specialized knowledge because he regards it as narrowing and not sufficiently detached. Hence his preference for the amateur in national and local government and in the management of his social affairs. Hence in educational administration and organization the vast number of voluntary workers and procedure by committees, and in instruction a sceptical attitude to professional training. The expert becomes the bureaucrat and bureaucracy becomes bound up in red tape; when the situation requires it he prefers to proceed straight to his goal with as little external interference as possible. Plasticity and adaptability, intelligence and independence of spirit are to be preferred to formulas and rigid definitions of action; at the same time a system operating on this principle elicits intelligence and independence of spirit.

But if the Englishman is an individualist and regards his home, physically and spiritually, as his castle, his instinct for action flows over into an instinct for coöperation, for team play. Hence he expresses his ideal of life in such terms as "fair play," "playing the game," "it isn't cricket," "good form," for life is a game and must be played according to the rules of the game. The essence of group action is discussion, arbitration, concession, and compromise. This second instinct, as it were, results again in a preference for group self-control and self-determination rather than for state interference. As a consequence social discipline, the rule of law, and law-abidingness are stronger than in societies which are more subject to governmental regimentation. Freedom and liberty for the individual and for social groups to work out their own salvation with a minimum of state interference the Englishman regards as his most priceless possession, and in no field of social endeavor more than in education. As an individual the Englishman believes in the spirit of live and let live; as a member of society he clings to his faith in free coöperation and *esprit de corps*. Although there may today be signs of a movement in the direction of greater state regimentation, even the extreme Left politically has been compelled to learn that it must abide by "the rules of the game" and that the enactment of a social program, however urgently demanded by the exigencies of the time, must not override the fundamental traits of English character.

The following epigram reported to emanate from the Secretariat of the League of Nations, *Un Anglais, c'est un imbecile; deux Anglais, c'est un "match"; trois Anglais, c'est une grande nation*, summarizes the many-colored aspects of English character. It implies the coexistence of all those qualities ascribed to the Englishman by Bishop Creighton — vigor, energy, practical capacity, dogged perseverance, determination not to be beaten, integrity, a love of justice, outspokenness, straightforwardness, and the rest — all qualities which are practical rather than intellectual. At the same time it is difficult, if one refers to the wide range of English literature and particularly English poetry, to deny the existence of qualities which are not covered in this list. English literature in a sense does express these practical aspects of English character with its cult of biography and absorption with character and its behavior, but English poetry, instinct with feeling, with reverence and awe, with mysticism at times, and breathing the love of the beauty of the countryside, displays an aspect of character which rises far above the utilitarian and practical. But when all this has been said, it still remains true that for contributions in the field of pure thought the Englishman has had to rely on the coöperation of his Scottish neighbor.[1] It would, of course, be erroneous to deduce from this analysis that the Englishman is incapable of or has no intellectual interests, but it does mean that he does not place either their cult or the logical discipline which should precede them among the most important of the ideals of life to be attained.

Observing the interplay of national psychologies from the vantage point of the Secretariat of the League of Nations, Señor Madariaga has brilliantly analyzed English character as contrasted with the French:

> As it happens, there is perhaps no clearer contrast there (at Geneva) than that between the two protagonists of the League. England and France seem to have been selected by Providence as the two pure antagonistic elements or

[1] See *Educational Yearbook, 1929*, of the International Institute of Teachers College, Columbia University, pp. 14, 32 f., 108 (New York, 1930).

poles of the international system, forming a couple of opposites comparable to the couple acid-base in chemistry, or to that of the masculine and feminine elements in human life. In Geneva everything gravitates either towards the empirical or towards the theoretical, towards expedients or towards principles, rule of thumb or general law, wait and see or foresight of all contingencies, English ways or French ideas.

In practically every argument between England and France the objective differences due to the inherent conflict of national interests are thus complicated by subjective divergences due no longer to a different perspective but to the different nature of the eye that observes. England brings to Geneva her empirical habits of mind. This means that England nearly always advocates the minimum of pre-established agreements to meet future contingencies. The empirical mind stretches thus as little as possible along the line of time. But it limits itself also in the mental dimension of the present which we call breadth. It shrinks from generalizations. Narrow and shortsighted, the Englishman remains firmly attached to the earth of realities and goes forth like a blind man striking the ground with his stick before he takes a step forward.[1]

The effect of this habit of mind on the development of a national educational system has been to postpone state action as long as possible, and to rely on social or group action — that is, on voluntary enterprise until this should be found to be inadequate. When the State did embark, slowly and tentatively making the initial steps, as it did in 1833 and 1870 in the field of elementary education, in 1888 in technical education, and in 1902 in the general attempt to bring together the various strands that had been woven in the preceding century, it proceeded on the policy of weaving together into one national system public and private schools, schools that are secular and schools that give sectarian religious instruction, "public" schools that are private and private schools that receive state aid, and then devoted itself to setting minimum standards in everything pertaining to the fabric of the school and limiting itself to a minimum definition of what should be taught and how. The result is a system which gives play to the many-sidedness of English life, but which remains to the observer unsystematized, chaotic, vague, yet none the less governed by an accepted principle that social progress comes best not through state action dominating the minds of men but through a sense of responsibility on the part of individuals and groups, through freedom rather than dictation, through individual and group initiative rather than state regulation and prescription. Hence the characteris-

[1] Madariaga, S. de, *I. Americans*, pp. 128 f. (Oxford University Press, 1930).

tic of the English education is variety set in a national framework in which the central authority advises, stimulates, encourages rather than prescribes. Educational laws there are but legislation is introduced after local experimentation and the status of public opinion warrants it. Progress in English education may be slow but progress there is, and the gap between theory and practice is smaller than in countries where education is taken more seriously, because progress proceeds on the basis of experience rather than of scientific principles worked out in the minds of theorists. It is perhaps for these reasons that England is not as rich or as fertile as Germany or the United States in educational theory.

2. FRANCE

If the Englishman is a man of action whose progress is marked by empiricism rather than by theory, the Frenchman is a man of ideas who enjoys to think for the sheer pleasure of thinking and generally without much concern for the outcome of thinking in action. Orderliness, logic, planning, which appear to be absent as the characteristics of English life and organization, are by contrast the outstanding features of the French, a fact brought out in a homely comparison by André Maurois:

London is unintelligible. Paris is geometrical, designed, deliberate. London just happens. In Paris things are done purposely. The Place Vendôme is a place and it has its column right in the middle — designed. Now look at Trafalgar Square! Perfectly absurd! A statue on horseback on one side of the column and on the other side space for such a column — and nothing. Nobody cares. And yet it is beautiful. (Quoted in the *New York Times*, October 29, 1926.)

Señor Madariaga, continuing his comparison of the Englishman and the Frenchman in the passage already quoted, points out that

The Frenchman, on the contrary, comes to Geneva with a mind which nature and training have made an aim in itself. He approaches questions as problems, and while the Englishman is feeling a way out he has already thought out a solution. It is more often than not a perfect solution, applicable on all cases and at all times — so perfect in fact as to stagger the Englishman, who as an empirical man feels as uncomfortable in the presence of perfection as a sailor on land, or a horseman walking. Generalization and foresight are the two qualities of the Frenchman's thought. His method is logic.[1]

[1] Madariaga, *op. cit.*, p. 129. The reader may compare for himself the working of these two methods, the empirical and the logical, in international affairs since 1918.

The chief characteristic of the Frenchman is, then, a tendency to theorize, to emphasize logic and orderliness of mind, clear thinking and planning. *Ce qui n'est pas clair n'est pas Français.* A logically elaborated plan, carefully reasoned out in all its details, is essential for action, even though it disregards human nature, a trait already recognized by Burke:

It is remarkable, that, in a great arrangement of mankind, not one reference whatsoever is to be found to anything moral or anything politic; nothing that relates to the concerns, the actions, the passions, the interests of men. *Hominem non sapiunt.* (*Reflections on the French Revolution.*)

Action, therefore, must obey the laws of reason and must not be misguided by the temporary emotions of the situation under consideration.

The Frenchman is thus an individualist, but his individualism is determined by the rule of reason, while that of the Englishman is governed by the spirit of live and let live; the individualism of the former is rational and intellectual, that of the latter is utilitarian and emotional. Because he is an individualist the Frenchman dislikes to surrender any ideas which he may have reached, whether it is in the use of words, or in literary style, or in political organization at home or in international affairs abroad. Because he lacks the English genius for collective action, he accepts order and the government of law as a social necessity, but French order is official, organized, symmetrical, centralized, and subordinated to bureaucratic control. While the Englishman admires variety and many-sidedness, the Frenchman prefers uniformity and symmetry. That these differences may be explained by differences in geographical location, the insecurity of one country exposed to attack on its landward side and the security of the other protected by the sea on all sides, is immaterial for the present discussion.

If reliance on reason and logic is the basis of French individualism, his attitude to discipline is determined by the same factors. Whereas in England social discipline is the result of willingness to abide by the rules of the game, French discipline is the result of conscious acceptance of control from without to counterbalance the dangers of an excessive emphasis on individualism. Hence French discipline is the result not of conscious social and individual self-control, but is external, imposed from without — through the family, the Church, the

State. Nowhere does the contrast on this point manifest itself more clearly than in the English (one might also add the American) practice of character training through spontaneous activity regulated by the will of the group, and the emphasis in France from the earliest school years upon direct moral instruction and on the reasonable life. The difference between the two points of view stands out markedly again in the uses of the terms "individuality" and "personality."

The individual is such by virtue of the fact that he is different from others. He is a person to the extent that he represents the conscience of truths valid for all and the will to undertake duties common to all. The individual ought to become a person, that is, in a sense he should deindividualize himself, and this is the work of education and of personal effort. (F. Pécaut in the *Educational Yearbook, 1929*, of the International Institute, p. 141.)

The cult of personality stresses the importance of socializing the individual in tune with the highest intellectual ideals and culture of his nation. Since one of the guarantees of national solidarity is the substitution of personality for individuality, education is governed not only by the acceptance of authority in its administration but by control and prescription of what shall be taught. But although prescribed, the curriculum and content of instruction are not ends in themselves, so much as means for the development of ability to think or imparting something with which to think. Hence while the acquisition of French culture and its intellectual traditions furnish one end of education, the educated man is he who can think clearly and lucidly, who has the ability to generalize and to present both movement and order in thought. The selection of the cult of reason, logical precision, and orderliness as the keynote of the French mind is not far-fetched. Where the English and Americans stress social and moral ends and purposes, the French emphasize reason. Compare, for instance, the appeal to the will in the English "be good" as compared with the French appeal to reason in "*sois raisonnable*" or "*sois sage*," in "to be right" as compared with "*avoir raison*," in "to do justice" as compared with "*faire raison*," and in "to get the better of one's vices" with "*avoir raison de ses vices*."[1]

It is in this preëminent characteristic of the Frenchman that there can be found one explanation both of the acceptance of a centralized bureaucratic system of organization and of the worship of an unbroken tradition of culture; it is on this basis that one can appreciate

[1] See Brereton, C., *Studies in Foreign Education*, pp. 214–22 (London, Harrap & Co., 1913).

the insistent demand in the present educational crises that its democratization shall not be at a sacrifice of the traditional *culture générale*, an instrument perfected for the development of reason. For, as Professor Albert Feuillerat has stated:

Our craving for logic, when it becomes excessive, might carry us away and lead us into impossible positions, as indeed it has sometimes done. This is all the more likely because our tendency is toward theories and systems.[1]

There are, of course, other explanations of the devotion to a centralized system of administration, which will be considered later, but in the last analysis it will be found to be true, as has been so pithily stated by a German, F. Sieburg, that the French are more interested in the progress of ideas than in the idea of progress,[2] the one stressing the integrity of the mind, the other the material comforts of the body.

3. GERMANY

The interplay between national character and outlook and social institutions is perhaps more readily subject to analysis in civilizations and cultures in which it has had an opportunity of operating over a long period of time. It does not manifest itself so simply in those nations which have recently undergone the shattering influences of a profound political, social, and economic change. Difficult as it is for the forces of the type under discussion to find free play when this change represents the voluntary expression of the will of a people, the difficulty is considerably intensified in those instances where the change has been effected by force. Hence, while it is possible in a general way to analyze the influences and characteristics of the German temper which are moulding the character of the young Republic, it is almost impossible as yet to see the peculiarly national direction which Communism will take in Russia and Fascism in Italy, both forms of government imposed on the peoples concerned. Even though it is claimed that Communism is universal and recognizes no national distinctions, the peculiar character and outlook of the Russians will undoubtedly give it a Russian flavor, and the Fascism of Italy will, if continued, differ from the type of Fascism which might be developed under traditions of a different type. Since the revolutions in Russia and Italy were established and have at any rate up to

[1] Feuillerat, A., *French Life and Ideals*, translated by V. Barbour, p. 62 (New Haven, Yale University Press, 1925).
[2] In *Who are these French?* (New York, 1932.)

the present been maintained by force, it would be premature to attempt to discover any modifying influences due to the characters of the peoples concerned. Nor is it enough to say that in each case the people have merely substituted one form of dictation to which they have grown accustomed for another, or, in the case of Italy, to claim that Fascism is a direct development out of Italian traditions. If this were true, the authorities in control would not have adopted a new educational program to serve as an instrument of control in the new situation.

The position is somewhat clearer in Germany. Even if it is objected that the Revolution was forced on the country by the results of the War, it must be remembered that despite the common front presented by the country in 1914, there had for a long time been a tradition of liberalism and the rise of industrialism had brought with it the seeds of disaffection. The German people accordingly exercised a free choice in 1918–19 in accepting a republican form of government. Scope was thus provided for the spontaneous interaction of the forces underlying German character except for the limitations imposed by a treaty, which the people affected regard with resentment, and for the disturbing effects of uncertain economic conditions, which Germany shares with the rest of the world.

Out of the imperialistic régime, which was displaced by the Revolution, grew certain popular preconceptions which an analysis of German character labors under the difficulty of having to offset. The outstanding characteristics of German life as described in 1914 were discipline, organization, and the willing acceptance of authority; while this was undoubtedly an accurate description, too little credit was given to the influence, first, of a dominant political philosophy which stressed these qualities as the essential foundations of a state conscious of its destiny, and, secondly, of an educational system which for three generations was deliberately designed to inculcate them. It may even be claimed that these qualities saved Germany in 1918 from a protracted and bloody revolution. History and events since the War would indicate the unsoundness of a generalization that the Germans are by nature submissive; there is evidence that the enforcement of discipline and authority was essential to sublimate a tendency to individualism and liberty. Without going back further than three centuries the world has known three Germanies. The first was a Germany provincial and sectional, cut up into several hundred petty independent States and communities, a Germany which culturally was under the subjection of foreign influences. The second was the Germany of poetry, philosophy, and music, a Germany liberal and humanistic, not only with no strong sense of nationalism, but in the expressions of her intellectual leaders even inclined to cosmopolitanism. It was the period in which there was developed a tradition of liberalism which promised to give an entirely different direction to the development of the country until its growth was checked in Prussia in 1819 and in the rest of Germany in 1848. It is this tradition of liberalism and self-determination, dormant for three generations, which has again been revived and which, complicated by movements in a more radical direction, is one of the elements in Germany's present struggle for existence. Finally, there is the Germany of the imperialistic period, authoritative, dictatorial, with its emphasis on might and power as the ideals to be achieved at home and abroad. But the policy of blood and iron was either not strong enough or was not continued for a period sufficiently long to suppress the main features of German character; it may even be claimed that this policy set up inner antagonisms and opposition the fruits of which were seen in the ready acceptance of the republican form of government.

Far from being uniform in spirit and outlook, the Germans as a people are marked by variety and contrasts like the country which they inhabit. These contrasts may, indeed, be due to the great variety of landscape as well as to the blend and mixture of races out of which the German nation was formed. To a certain extent, too, foreign influences have played their part in making for variety — Slav influence in the north and east, French influence in the west, and Italian influence in the south, just as in the present stage of her development one of the most marked influences is that of American efficiency.

Strong as German nationalism appeared to be in 1914, the late and almost artificial consolidation of the many Germanies into one nation did not last long enough to leave an enduring imprint on the traditional traits. Each State, each section of the country has its own characteristic form of dress, customs, mode of living, and even language and religion.

Even today, anyone understanding the signs may discover under the uniform appearance of the new Germans not only differences of appearance and bearing, dialects and customs, but also of mental point of view and cultural aims; although a common written language, schools, life in cities, and opportunity for travel make for uniformity. One and all are distinguished from each other — the tall, blond, taciturn Frisian, the amiable, vivacious native of the Rhineland, the sober, manly, unimaginative Prussian, the Bavarian who delights in color, flowers, play and song, the humorous and reliable Suabian, the sagacious, restless Saxon, and, above all, that master in the art of living and of supple grace, the Austrian.[1]

To the particularism of the States must be added the independent character of the cities, each of which claims to represent the real Germany and yet has its own peculiar characteristics. By a paradox, Berlin, which has sought to give expression to everything that typifies modern Germany, is in fact the least German of cities, less German, indeed, than such cities as Hamburg, Leipzig, Dresden, Munich. Variety rather than uniformity, particularism rather than universalism are the true German characteristics, which, with the elimination of a dominating authority, the pressure toward loyalty to a single national ideal, and a *Kultur* bureaucratically defined under an exaggerated interpretation of the absolutist State, are today given free play for spontaneous interaction.

Germany is a land in which everything is to be found, every force, every form of mental and physical activity, every kind of organization, all forms of wisdom and folly; much indeed that is peculiar to Germany and not to be met with in other countries. To be German means to wander in a maze of contradictions without being able to win through to any truly national consciousness.[2]

The particularism and sectionalism of the country is further complicated by the peculiarities of the individual character of the German. Contemplative and austere, the German is dialectic and argumentative. Confronted with a situation, he becomes undecided and uncertain as to his course of action because of too great anxiety, not to reach at once a practical solution, but to include in his consideration all of its elements and implications. The German, says Professor Aloys Fischer, wants also the opposite of what he wants; he has a "desire not only for the opposite of what is, but also for the opposite of every one-sided ideal of perfection for that which is." His indeci-

---

[1] Professor Aloys Fischer, in "The Philosophy underlying the National System of Education in Germany," in the *Educational Yearbook, 1929*, of the International Institute of Teachers College, Columbia University, p. 195 (New York, 1930).
[2] Diesel, E., *Germany and the Germans*, p. 283 (London, Macmillan & Co., Ltd., 1931).

sion comes, not from want of knowledge, but from an excessive cultivation of it, which dominates his impulses to action. His inclination to think out and to organize everything, to classify everything, human and material, makes him ponderous, if not pedantic. Not the practical solution of a situation but its effect on his inner personality is too often his primary concern. If to the Englishman life is a game to be played according to rules, to the German it is an educational problem from which some moral lesson is to be derived. This quality of German individualism it is which fills him at one time with pessimism, at another with optimism. It is the same quality which makes him impressionable to external influences; while it makes him intellectually plastic, it inhibits freedom in his expression of thought. This fact is manifested in his language, which, abundant in words and forms, attempts within the confines of the same sentence to include all the intricacies of the process through which his mind passes. The multiplicity of German political parties, the number and variety of clubs and organizations, and the tendency to classify and to label, are all manifestations of the same attitude of mind.

This rational, intellectualistic aspect of German character is counterbalanced by an emotional capacity and strength of feeling which lead him into sentimentality. Hence there comes a tendency to mysticism and irrationalism. This tendency he attempts to synthesize with the rational into a concept of a well-rounded and harmonious life in which the right of the individual to give expression to the laws of his own being is asserted. Outwardly this emotionalism manifests itself in his love of music and appreciation of the beauties of nature, which on the creative side has found its expansion at times in the lyrical quality of his poetry at its best. Combined with his self-assertiveness in the intellectual field, his sentimentality often betrays him into the pursuit and cult of extremes. Like Faust he pushes his search of knowledge to the extreme and equally like Faust he feels

> a youthful, holy, vital bliss
> In every vein and fibre newly glowing.[1]

Wavering and uncertain because he can never be sure of his aims, whether determined on rational or irrational grounds, the German has placed himself under the rule of method, organization, and discipline, at once his strength and his weakness — his strength because

[1] Goethe, *Faust*, Part I, Scene I, p. 19; Bayard Taylor's translation (New York, 1912).

they have given the cohesion which would otherwise be lacking, his weakness because they tend to overemphasize the mechanization of life and destroy its spontaneity. Here a contrast may be found between the easy grace and charm of English or French conventions and the stiffness and formality bordering on the artificial of the German.

There is, however, still another aspect of German character which the world has long known and admired. This is his industry, persistence, and patient perseverance which, harnessed by his reverence for knowledge and science and their application to the material side of life and combined with his acceptance of disciplined order, raised Germany in less than half a century from a congeries of small agricultural States into the first rank among the industrial and commercial powers of the world. As he has always striven for perfection in the realm of knowledge, so in the development of his material civilization he has shown almost unparalleled patience and tenacity of purpose.

The effects of the traits described on his educational system are well known. They have in the past meant thoroughness and efficient adaptation of means to ends, but the system suffered from the imposition of external authority and attempted uniformity which emphasized the cult of the rational and suppressed to a large degree the other aspects of German character. The elimination of this external authority has meant the release of all those tendencies to action which had previously been subordinated in the interests of a single loyalty. Already German literature shows the results in the plethora of educational theories which run the whole gamut from the survival of authoritarian practices to the extremes of the cult of individual freedom. But the exuberance of the first few years will spend itself; already it is clear that Germany has discovered that her task in education lies, not in the substitution of a new kind of uniformity for the old, but in encouraging variety as the basis of a new type of nationalism which puts its trust, not in princes, but in the fullest development of the individual in the light of his own genius, in the true traditions of German life, and in the needs of a new basis of solidarity. This she is finding in the cult of *Deutschtum*, a German culture which will give play to the spontaneous forces in which the nation is so rich, the rational and the irrational, *Natur* and *Kunst*, those two aspects of man's being whose mutual interaction enriches his life. "*Natur*," says Professor Aloys Fischer, "stands for blind force and gifts, for directness of feeling, for natural, unconscious expression, whereas *Kunst* stands for painstaking, conscious limitation, direction, for rational censure and wilful exertion."[1] German life and German education, dominated for over half a century by forces which emphasized *Kunst*, have at last an opportunity of combining them with the forces of *Natur*, of giving expression to the varied aspects of German character.

4. UNITED STATES

The outstanding characteristic of American life is the emphasis on liberty or self-determination. Acquired after a war to win independence, group self-determination, and the rights of man, the ideal of liberty within a democracy was clothed with reality under the influences of an expanding frontier. It was under the frontier conditions that there emerged the more striking features of American character — egalitarianism, resourcefulness, coöperation of social groups, just as the same conditions were the causes of some of the weaknesses of American life as contrasted with European; these are wastefulness of unlimited resources, contempt for the expert and for administration, impatience of restraint, law, and government, and a literal interpretation of the meaning of democracy, later carried over into the intellectual field. The tremendous opportunities afforded by the undeveloped country called for and resulted in a restless, nervous energy, in buoyancy and optimism, and in an emphasis on the immediately practical and on the faith that no idea or ideal is worth anything unless it can be made to work. This aversion to theory was already noted by De Tocqueville, who remarked that "general ideas alarm their minds, which are accustomed to positive calculations and they hold practice in more honor than theory."

The restless energy, the demand for immediate readymade solutions, formulated in a later age as slogans, and the optimism have combined together to develop the conviction that tomorrow must be better than today, that the worship of tradition means stagnation, that every change and every innovation spells progress. The worship of the novel is no new manifestation in the American outlook. It was already apparent in the forties of the last century and was coincident with the rise of the common people, as has been pointed out by Professor C. R. Fish:

[1] *Loc. cit.*, p. 268. Professor Fischer is here referring to Goethe's sonnet, *Natur und Kunst* as an interpretation of German life.

Whereas Washington devoted his attention to bringing his gardens to an exquisite perfection, the men of the thirties and forties sought novelty rather than perfection.[1]

Unwilling to wait for the slow maturing of social or educational institutions, the American tends to pluck up the young shoot by the roots to see how it is growing, to substitute the new even before he is fully assured that the old will not work. This readiness to "scrap" the old for the new is as true in the intellectual field as in industrial and commercial organizations. It is a trait producing a feverishness and instability which at their best may be described as experimentalism, but which prompted by desire for adaptation to the immediately practical rather than guided by a process of serious thinking result too frequently in immature conclusions and insecure foundations. Concretely this improvidence to some extent explains the economic crisis in which the country finds itself after an era of unparalleled prosperity; but it is equally marked in the welter of theories and practices which have arisen with a flourish, had their brief day, and yielded to the new in education in the past thirty years.

If slow adaptation to changing needs is characteristic of the Englishman, and caution and conservatism of the Frenchman, the American is a constant rebel against tradition, and, released from the hold of the past and never really rooted in the present, he presses forward to ends that were never dreamed of, not only in the material field, but — and this is his limitation — in the spiritual and intellectual. While among European nations traditions act, as it were, as a brake on too rapid change, traditions in the United States are ignored or called to mind only to be set aside; while the Europeans tend to cling to an institution because it has become a tradition, the American finds in this reason an argument for its rejection; or, as Sydney Smith said

Others claim honor because of things done by a line of ancestors; an American glories in the achievement of a distant posterity. Others appeal to history; an American appeals to prophecy.[2]

There is, however, another side to the picture. The American may have inherited from the frontier period this spirit of restlessness

---

[1] Fish, C. R., *The Rise of the Common Man*, p. 105 (New York, Macmillan Co., 1927).

[2] It is perhaps not far-fetched to suggest that the great American industrialist's remark that "History is bunk," finds its counterpart in a current movement to substitute "Social Studies" for history in the schools because the lessons of history are not immediately practical and meaningful for living in society today and tomorrow.

which keeps him constantly searching for the new, but it was the conditions of the same period that gave its particular coloring to his conception of democracy. There is rooted in the minds of the American people faith in democracy and pride in its institutions, which have resulted in faith in equality of opportunity and in a genuine desire to give every individual, not merely an equal but often the same chance, ideals which have fundamentally affected both the external and the internal organization of American education. Out of these ideals has grown a widespread belief in individualism, and the measure of the individual is the success with which he has used the equality of opportunity made available for him. This attitude has encouraged and stimulated individual energy, initiative, self-reliance, and enterprise, guided often to no other end than success, since there is imposed on the individual the duty of making the best of himself.

Out of the same frontier conditions which encouraged the growth of individualism and looked with suspicion on governmental interference, there developed the ideal of local coöperation for the common good and the ideal of service and social usefulness. What in other countries has been organized by central governments has in the United States been left to local and group initiative and enterprise under the slogan of "service" for both the individual and society.

Since for the individual there has been held up the ideal of success and for society the ideal of service, and since progress connotes adaptation to immediate practical needs, the American mind tends to direct its attention to the next step, to the future, without any firm anchorage in the past and often without any real consolidation of the present. When this attitude of mind is applied to the world of material things, the essential need in order to secure efficiency is to stress organization and administration, the division and subdivision of each job until responsibility for the performance of each item in the analysis is clearly defined. This practice of job-analysis has been taken over into education, not only in administration where it may be appropriate, but here and there in the content and methods of instruction where nothing can or should be mechanized. In many respects the same type of imaginative qualities, which have been applied to industry and commerce, have been responsible for many of the achievements of American education. In no country has the provision for equality of opportunity in education been carried out so literally as in the United States; at the same time in no country has the influence of business methods and business efficiency been so detrimental to real education. So education must be "advertised" and "sold"; it must have its interchangeable parts known as "units," "points," or "credits"; like industry and commerce, it must constantly survey the field in order to discover and meet the needs of a growing clientèle; and in the same way it must be made subject to itemized measurement to test its efficiency.

By a curious contradiction the United States presents an individualism side by side with uniformity and standardization. Emerson's advice, "Insist on yourself; never imitate," has been forgotten or ignored, for the American of today dislikes to be different from his neighbors. In part large-scale industry and commerce with the nation-wide appeal of their advertisements, partly the mobility of the population, a tendency only increased by the advent of the automobile, partly the fear of the large body of immigrants of appearing unlike their neighbors may be held to be responsible for this uniformity built up on the traditional concept of egalitarianism.[1] One result of this phenomenon is the refusal in education to accept the notion of an *élite*, of selection, and another is the tendency to cater to the average with consequences which tend to make for mediocrity. Because of the expansion of universal education with virtually no limits in the upward direction, De Tocqueville's comment holds true today to a much greater degree than when it was written:

> A middling standard is fixed in America for human knowledge. All approach as near to it as they can; some as they rise, others as they descend. Of course, a multitude of persons are to be found who entertain the same number of ideas on religion, history, science, political economy, legislation, and government. The gifts of intellect proceed directly from God, and man cannot prevent their unequal distribution. But it is at least a consequence of what we have just said, that although the capacities of men are different, as the Creator intended they should be, Americans find the means of putting them to use are equal.[2]

The influence on education of the practical bent of the American mind may be illustrated by another contrast with other nations.

---

[1] A homely but pertinent contrast may be noted in comparing sales arguments in some of the European countries and in the United States. In the former the strongest argument to clinch a sale is that an article is an "exclusive" model, while in the latter it is sold because "everybody is using (or wearing)it." Or the contrast may be illustrated again by the vogue in the one case of customs-made and in the other of ready-made clothing.

[2] De Tocqueville, A., *Democracy in America*, translated by H. Reeve, Vol. I, p. 66 (New York, Century Co., 1898).

The European countries, England, France, and Germany in particular, pride themselves on the quality of education provided for their best minds, and for the best minds the best type of education is considered to lie in a cultural training, or, as the French call it, "disinterested studies." The American emphasis is on the practical and immediate, not on the detached or general but on the direct interests and needs of all the pupils and students. There are, of course, other explanations in educational theory and psychology that account for this approach. Nevertheless, it is significant that in the field of philosophy the only genuinely native contributions to world thought are represented by pragmatism, which is itself the outgrowth of the impact of American life on the American mind. Equally significant is it that until quite recently, when increasing wealth and leisure made it possible, this practical emphasis was not relieved either in the life of the adult or in the work of the school by any adequate attention to the emotional and æsthetic aspects. If progress, even interpreted merely as change, has been the keynote of American life since the establishment of the Republic, it is true today that the country is once more in a stage of transition; if the momentum of that progress has been checked, the retardation is at least providing an opportunity for many to estimate anew the values of life for which the nation has stood in the past and to reconstruct them in the light of present needs.

5. ITALY AND RUSSIA

It is perhaps too early to judge the effect of national character on the new modes of life in Russia and Italy. In both instances it may be claimed that the Communist and Fascist Revolutions, even though directed to developing new social minds in each case, have been made possible by pre-existing conditions. In both instances the backbone of each country was made up of the peasant class. In Italy the peasant is dominated by a strong devotion to traditions and customs; hard-working and thrifty, he is ready to accept a plan of government which protects him against serious economic change and guarantees a certain stability, which was lacking under the liberalism, whose workings he did not understand and which appeared to be leading to anarchy. Fascism ensures the perpetuation of ancient traditions and provides a hierarchical system of administration to which, because of his respect for authority, he can give allegiance. Beyond

EDUCATION AND NATIONAL CHARACTER

this there is a common bond between all Italians in their hero-worship, love of the dramatic, and æsthetic appreciation, all of which are supplied in the personal preëminence of Mussolini, in his sense of the dramatic, and in the cult of a colorful symbolism adopted by Fascism. At once a realist and an idealist, the Italian is ready to accept the situation which is a *fait accompli* and, moreover, is based on an idealistic conception of the State and of Italy's destiny. All these traits of Italian character, it will be noted later, are brought together in a single integrated whole in the most Fascist of all Fascist reforms, that of education.

For the Russian peasant the Revolution, leaving out for the moment the profound economic changes, whose effects on his character may not be discernible for some time, has substituted new controls for the old. For religious orthodoxy there has been substituted economic orthodoxy, in place of the autonomy of the Czar there has been established the autocracy of a Party, and the political and militaristic nationalism has been replaced by a class consciousness which for the present binds the Russian nation together as strongly as the old form. From his struggle with nature the Russian peasant has been enured to the endurance of hardships and privations. Patient and stolid he has become a fatalist, ready to accept what the day brings forth. Events have shown, however, that his newly acquired sense of power may transform these characteristics, and that meekness and humility may not be traits which can be counted on forever. What has been said of the peasant applies to a large majority of the factory laborers, who are peasants but recently transferred to urban and industrial conditions. Since the middle classes have been exterminated, there is no class which stands between this peasant mentality and the control of those in power. With a strong faith in nurture as against nature, the leaders of the Revolution have set before themselves the task of transforming Russian mentality by a conception of the meaning of education which is not paralleled in other countries.

Differences such as those described in the preceding sections justify the statement that the educational system of one nation cannot be transferred to another without considerable readaptation to all that is implied by the new environment. This fact does not, however, mean that each nation or group must live unto itself alone educationally, but it does suggest, first, the improbability of the development of theories and practices in education which are universally applicable, and, secondly, the importance for the student of education of making himself familiar with the cultural background, and all that that implies, of the nation or people among whom he is to work. Theories and principles in the conduct of human affairs can only be adopted as working hypotheses to be checked and modified in the light of all the factors and circumstances which are likely to condition them. Herein lies the basis of social progress; maladjustment and stagnation are the dangers which may threaten any attempt at unmodified transfer of theories through faith in their universal applicability. The history of education is full of examples which illustrate this, and in the present era it is only necessary to refer to the failure of the attempts to transfer the educational practices of a Western nation to backward peoples, to India, or to China. Just as successful instruction implies adaptation to the interests, needs, and capacities of the individual, so a successful national system of education must arise out of and be adapted to the ethos of the nation concerned. Careful diagnosis of all the factors involved and the adaptation of a system on the basis of the results reached are as incumbent on the educator as on the scientist, but, as must be obvious from the discussion of nationalism and of national character, the educator, except when he has an opportunity of starting *de novo*, does not have control of all the factors involved; he should, however, take as many of them as possible into his consideration. For education is a cultural process; like all culture it is the expression of the spirit of a group which must constantly be renewed and reinterpreted in the light of the progress of civilization, that is, the cumulative development of institutions and techniques which make life possible.

CHAPTER III

THE STATE AND EDUCATION [1]

The problem of the control of education. The permanent question in education has always been, "Who shall have control of the education of the child?" The claim for control is disputed by the family, which may insist on its right to educate its children in its own way, generally through the private school; by the Church, which bases its claim on the plea that education is a spiritual process and that religious training is the most important factor in this process; by the State, which argues that, since the State represents the will of its members, it alone should have the right to determine the nature of the means which will guarantee both its own stability and the welfare of its citizens; by educational theorists, who, striving for that freedom which is the result in part of the attainment of independence of their science and in part of the general trend toward occupational self-determination, claim the right to autonomy and the pursuit of their craft in the light of its own inherent character.[2]

The question is not new; it was broached as the fundamental question of education and politics by Plato and Aristotle, who were already familiar with two answers to it — the *laissez faire* practice of the Athenians up to the period of military training, and the state-controlled system of the Spartans. The place assigned to education in Plato's *Republic* gives it its preëminent value as one of the greatest educational treatises of all times. The unity of the State, says Plato, can be assured "if the guardians diligently observe

---

[1] The main part of this chapter appeared in Kandel, I. L., *Essays in Comparative Education*, pp. 9 ff. (New York, 1930).

[2] This claim to autonomy of education as a science (*Eigengesetzlichkeit; innere Logik des Unterrichts und der Erziehung*) is particularly pressed in Germany; although on the English-speaking side nowhere clearly expressed, it underlies the principles of the "new" or "progressive" education. Something of the German idea is suggested in the plea of Principal L. P. Jacks for Dominion Status for Education in his *Education of the Whole Man*, pp. 76 ff. (London, 1931). "The nature of the task on which education is engaged," he argues, "demands before all else that it shall be master in its own house — leaving others to be masters in theirs, under such scheme of coördination as the wit of man can easily devise.... It is only the poorest kind of education, something hardly worthy of the name, that will submit without injury to be the sport of the political vicissitudes and the economic necessities of the moment." The idea of autonomy is also the basis of the proposal for professional self-determination in France.

the one great point, as the saying is, though it should rather be called sufficient than great." This point is "education and rearing. For if by a good education they (the citizens) be made reasonable men, they will readily see through all these questions," which are fundamental to the stability of the State.[1] "If a state has once started well, it exhibits a kind of circular progress. Adherence to a good system of nurture and education creates good natures, and good natures receiving the assistance of a good education, grow still better than they were."[2] In his *Laws*, Plato made the position of Minister of the Education of Youth the greatest of all the great offices of the State which he was planning — a State in which education of both sexes was to be compulsory, since education cannot be allowed to become a secondary or accidental matter and children must be regarded as belonging to the State and not to their parents. From a sense of responsibility and from a consciousness of the importance of his office, the Minister of Education will select his assistants with care for "if young men have been, and are well brought up, then all things go swimmingly" in the State.[3] Aristotle's statement on the subject is as pertinent today as when it was written:

Of all things that I have mentioned, that which contributes most to the permanence of constitutions is the adaptation of education to the form of government [he wrote in the *Politics*; and in the *Ethics* he stated], We laid it down that the end of politics is the highest good, and there is nothing that this science takes so much pains with as producing a certain character in the citizens, that is, making them good and able to do fine actions.

HISTORICAL DEVELOPMENT

Nearly two thousand years elapsed before the question became a practical issue. Voluntaryism was characteristic of Roman education and continued to be the principle on which education was provided even after the Roman Empire had developed the idea of the public school, supported wholly or in part by public funds. During the medieval period the question was unmistakably decided in favor of the Church which took education under its control; from time to time decrees were issued requiring parish priests to provide and

---

[1] Plato, *Republic*, 423 E and 424 A. Davies and Vaughan's translation, p. 122.
[2] See *Laws*, Books VI, 766, and VII, 804 and 813. Jowett's translation.
[3] *Ibid.*

supervise elementary schools, and secondary education was definitely controlled and supervised by the bishops of each diocese regardless of the method of their origin and support. Attempts were made from time to time by individuals (hedge-schoolmasters) to contest this supervision and by city councils to provide their own education, but these protests failed against the established doctrine, which has again been reaffirmed in a recent Encyclical Letter of Pope Pius XI on the *Christian Education of Youth* (1930), wherein it is stated that the right of the Church is "absolutely superior... to any other title in the natural order." This doctrine has been the cause of serious conflicts as the State gradually began to assert the right to determine the character of its educational systems — in the last century in Germany, and more recently in Italy and in Mexico.

The Catholic point of view is, indeed, shared in some countries by other denominations. Thus, in England the Church of England, while accepting state aid for education, insists, with the Catholic and other denominations, on the right to provide its own sectarian schools; in Holland public elementary schools have since 1920 been organized on what is virtually a denominational basis; and in Germany a new *Kulturkampf* was waged from 1925 to 1928 around the proposed *Reichsschulgesetz*, which aimed to conserve denominational interests in elementary education. Nor has the question, despite the laws of 1882 and 1904, been permanently settled in France in favor of a lay system of education controlled by the State. The United States and several South American countries, notably Argentina and Uruguay, have eliminated the religious element entirely from education and have adopted systems of public education wholly under the supervision of the public secular authorities. Yet even in these countries private denominational schools, without public aid and generally under no public supervision whatever, flourish side by side with the public schools and, in the United States, a large proportion of the facilities for higher education has been provided under denominational auspices. At the other extreme Russia has definitely proceeded on the principle that "Religion and Communism are incompatible both theoretically and practically." [1]

---

[1] Bukharin and Preobrazhensky, *The A B C of Communism*, p. 256 (London, 1927). Quoted in Colton, E. T., *The X Y Z of Communism*, p. 250 (New York, 1931).

Between the control of education by ecclesiastical organizations and a secularized system which does not prohibit the establishment of denominational schools, another answer to the problem was found during the period of the Reformation. The adoption at this period of the principle *cujus regio, ejus religio*, resulted, not in the elimination of the control of education by ecclesiastical authorities, but in the development of a partnership between them and the State. This partnership continued, especially in the field of elementary education, in most countries down to the present period, a partnership which is indicated in the subordination of educational and religious affairs to the same Ministry. The State has, however, assumed a larger share of control, which began to increase with the emergence of the political concept of nationalism and the realization that national welfare and security depend upon education.

The theorists of the French Revolution enunciated the principle that the child belongs to the State. Thus, as early as 1763, La Chalotais summed up the position in his *Essai d'Education Nationale* as follows:

> I do not presume to exclude ecclesiastics, but I protest against the exclusion of laymen. I dare claim for the nation an education which depends only on the State, because it belongs essentially to the State; because every State has an inalienable and indefeasible right to instruct its members; because, finally, the children of the State ought to be educated by the members of the State.
>
> It is the State, it is the larger part of the nation that must be kept principally in view in education.[1]

One of the aims of Talleyrand's bill of 1791 to establish a public system of education was

> to teach all children their first and indispensable duties, to instil in them the principles which ought to direct their actions; and to make them happier men and more useful citizens through preserving them from the dangers of ignorance.[2]

Condorcet, while he accepted the principle of a state-controlled system of education, proposed to divorce education from politics by the creation of an autonomous system of education controlled wholly by the teaching profession itself.[3] While the right of the individual

---

[1] Cubberley, E. P., *Readings in the History of Education*, pp. 410–12 (Boston, 1920).

[2] Reisner, E. H., *Nationalism and Education*, p. 13 (New York, Macmillan Co., 1922).

[3] Such a proposal has been recently revived in France, but inspired by syndicalist theory and a desire for professional self-determination.

THE STATE AND EDUCATION 49

to education on the principle of equality of opportunity is mentioned at this period, the chief emphasis in the assertion of the right of the State to establish and control an educational system is placed on the recognition of education as the basis of political stability and security, by making men happier and more useful citizens because enlightened.

It was on this general principle that Napoleon based his decree of 1808 to the effect that "No school, no establishment of instruction whatsoever, may be set up outside the Imperial University and without the authorization of its head." [1] This principle Napoleon had already justified three years earlier when he wrote:

> Of all political questions that [of education] is perhaps the most important. There cannot be a firmly established political state unless there is a teaching body with definitely recognized principles. If the child is not taught from infancy that he ought to be a republican or a monarchist, a Catholic or a free-thinker, the state will not constitute a nation; it will rest on uncertain and shifting foundations; and it will be constantly exposed to disorder and change.[2]

This principle has survived in French education down to the present and a number of additional reasons are advanced to justify it as the foundation of national security and solidarity. It is only within the last fifteen years that education as the right of the individual to equality of opportunity has been reasserted.

The same principle was inherent in the definitive organization of the Prussian system of education before 1800. The *Allgemeine Landrecht*, issued in 1794, provided that

> Schools and universities are state institutions charged with the instruction of youth in useful information and scientific knowledge. Such institutions may be founded only with the knowledge and consent of the State.[3]

The call to patriotism and nationalism which followed the German defeat at Jena in 1806 helped to give further justification to this principle of state control over education. The practical interpretation found its rationalization in the philosophy of Fichte and Hegel, and later in the works of the nationalist historians and propagandists. The State represents the realization of reason and justice in social life; in a word the State alone, as an idealized entity, superior to the

---
[1] Reisner, *op. cit.*, p. 36.   [2] *Ibid.*, p. 35.
[3] Alexander, T., *Prussian Elementary Schools*, p. 24 (New York, Macmillan Co., 1918).

individuals who make it up, has a mission and a destiny to fulfill, and has, therefore, the right to organize that system of education which will realize its *Kultur*. In such a scheme there is no place for individualism, and the State, conscious of its great ends, has the right to make the individual over according to the pattern which it considers best for its own preservation, a pattern determined by those who know and can interpret its mission and destiny to the people concerned. After a brief period of liberalism, finally crushed after the Revolution of 1848, the principle of education as the concern of the political, nationalistic State alone received a more intensive application with the growth of political, military, and economic nationalism in Germany.

The principle of complete state control of education never took a firm hold on English thought. At the time when France was deciding in favor of a state-controlled system of education, the leaders of English thought, including even those who sympathized with French radicalism, were opposed to the provision and organization of education by the State; conservatives were afraid of it because they feared that the enlightenment of the masses would incite them to restlessness and discontent; liberals were suspicious of it because they feared that national education would mean uniformity, indoctrination, and the preservation of the *status quo*. The two aspects of the problem were presented in 1765 by Dr. John Brown in *Thoughts on Civil Liberty, Licentiousness and Faction*, and by Joseph Priestley in *Remarks on a Proposed Code of Education*. Priestley's *Remarks* was a criticism of Brown's main thesis

That, the first and best security of civil liberty consists, in impressing the infant mind with such habits of thought and action, as may correspond with, and promote the appointments of public law.

Public education, as Brown explained in *An Appendix relative to a proposed Code of Education*, should be established for "the preservation of the blessings of society" and to instill principles, religious, moral, and political, "for this great end of public happiness." Priestley agreed with Brown on the importance of education and on the results that would be achieved by such a public system as Brown advocated.

But I should object to the interference of the legislature in this business of education, as prejudicial to the proper design of education, and also to the great ends of civil societies with respect to their present utility; but more especially, as tending to interrupt their progress to a state of greater perfection than they have yet attained to.

State interference in education, in the broadest sense of the word, would put an end to experimentation and therefore to the progressive development of social institutions. Uniformity in education would lead to uniformity of character and outlook; freedom and experimentation would encourage that "variety of original characters" which is the basis of progress, for

It is an universal maxim, that the more liberty is given to every thing which is in a state of growth the more perfect it will become, and when it is grown to its full size, the more amply will it repay its wise parent for the indulgence it gave it in its infant state.

Adam Smith and Malthus, while in general following the same principles as Priestley, advocated a compromise whereby the State might enforce compulsory education and give financial aid for the education of the poor, since, according to Smith, "some attention is necessary in order to prevent the almost entire corruption and degeneracy of the great body of the people"; those who could afford it should be expected to pay for their own education.

Though the state was to derive no advantage from the instruction of the inferior ranks of people, it would still deserve its attention that they should not be altogether uninstructed. The state, however, derives no inconsiderable advantage from their instruction. The more they are instructed, the less liable they are to the delusions of enthusiasm and superstition, which, among ignorant nations, frequently occasion the most dreadful disorders. An instructed and intelligent people, besides, are always more decent and orderly than an ignorant and stupid one.... In free countries, where the safety of government depends very much upon the favourable judgment which the people may form of its conduct, it must surely be of the highest importance that they should not be disposed to judge rashly or capriciously concerning it.[1]

Education was thus to be provided in the interests of national stability for those who could not or would not help themselves; the rest might be expected to provide their own education in the interests of their own advancement. There was thus incorporated into the English tradition the doctrine of *laissez faire*, of non-interference by the State in the progress of social institutions, and Adam Smith's

[1] Smith, Adam, *Wealth of Nations*, Book V, Ch. I, Part III, Art. II, p. 618 (London, 1893).

theory became the basis of the provision of state aid in 1833 to assist voluntary organizations for the education of the poorer classes.

The theory which governed the progress of education in England throughout the nineteenth century and which to a large extent is characteristic of its present administration, when the burden of providing educational facilities is borne mainly by public, state, and local authorities, was enunciated by John Stuart Mill in his essay *On Liberty* (1859). Mill's fundamental thesis is:

> That the whole or any large part of the education of the people should be in State hands, I go as far as anyone in deprecating. All that has been said of the importance of individuality of character, and diversity in opinions and modes of conduct, involves, as of the same unspeakable importance, diversity of education. A general State education is a mere contrivance for moulding people to be exactly like one another: and as the mould in which it casts them is that which pleases the predominant power in the government, whether this be a monarch, a priesthood, an aristocracy, or the majority of the existing generation; in proportion as it is efficient and successful, it establishes a despotism over the mind, leading by natural tendency to one over the body. An education established and controlled by the State should only exist, if it exist at all, as one among many competing experiments, carried on for the purpose of example and stimulus, to keep the others up to a certain standard of excellence.[1]

Herbert Spencer[2] was opposed to state intervention of any kind in education, even to the limited extent accepted by Mill to protect the consumer against his lack of interest and judgment. Spencer's opposition to the state control of education was in general based on the arguments that such education becomes paternalistic and undermines individual and voluntary effort, that the State is no better qualified than the individual to judge what is a right kind of education, and that a state system of education would inevitably result in reducing all to a pattern selected by the State which tends to conserve things as they are. A state system of education would aim to fit individuals to be good citizens. "Hence the proposition is convertible into this — a Government ought to mould children into good citizens, using its own discretion in settling what a good citizen is, and how the child may be moulded into one." It would thus become at once legislator, administrator, teacher, and judge of the

---

[1] Mill, J. S., *On Liberty and Other Essays*, p. 126 (New York, 1926).
[2] See his chapter on National Education in *Social Statics, Abridged and Revised* (New York, 1896). The same ideas can be found in his *Principles of Sociology*.

THE STATE AND EDUCATION

results, with the consequence that there would be no room for experimentation or progress.

That anything like an agreement as to the right way of conducting education is possible in our existing state, few, if any, will pretend. On the choice of subjects to be taught, on the order in which they should be taught, on the manner in which they should be taught, on the moral discipline that should accompany the teaching, on every step that can be taken, from the treatment of our infants up to a college examination, conflicting opinions exist.

Opposed to "the Communist plan of doing everything for everybody," Spencer objected to taxation for education as not within his definition of state duty and as undermining family responsibility. If the provision and control of education were logical, so would be the provision and administration by the State of food, shelter, clothing, and warmth.

CURRENT TENDENCIES

There thus survived into the twentieth century two main principles underlying the relation of the State to education: First, that the State has a right to a virtual monopoly in education, including complete control over all types of education, both public and private; and second, the doctrine of *laissez faire*, with the implication that the State may step in to supply deficiencies. Some changes have, however, taken place in the post-War period. The idea of the unitary political state is gradually receding in favor of a federal or pluralistic idea in which free play is to be given to a freer development and coöperation of group interests, which are too complex and too varied to be subjected to the dictates of a centralized government. The expansion and development of democracies are shifting the emphasis from authority and control to the cultivation of initiative and a sense of responsibility, and are slowly leading to a recognition that the progress of society cannot be left to the uniform action of the State, but is dependent upon color and variety of experiences. In other words, life itself is educative. To the growth of these concepts have contributed not only the increased complexity of life in the modern State, but to a certain extent the new orientation in educational theory itself with its strong emphasis on the individual and on learning through activity, participation, and coöperation in the social environment. It would be rash to claim that this movement, the full fruition of the principles of liberty, is anything more than a tendency. The conflict between the old and new still remains to be fought out even in the most progressive societies, but the tendency is marked even in such authoritarian states as Russia and Italy, both based on occupational groupings, both seeking to inculcate loyalty to an absolutist ideal, and yet both emphasizing in education the same principles as are being propagated in the most advanced school system in which the individual rather than the mass is indicated as the unit.

The implications for the problem under consideration, Who shall have control of the education of the child? are obvious. If the progress of society depends upon the trained initiative of responsible individuals, the burden of providing facilities for their education devolves upon society. The new note of the twentieth century is the recognition of individual worth and of the importance of encouraging its fullest development. Equality of opportunity can only be provided by the concerted efforts of society. Education thus becomes not a police measure of the State established in the interests of its own security and stability, but the right of every individual for the attainment of the fullest development of his abilities, irrespective of his social origin. Thus the Declaration of Geneva, endorsed by the Fifth Assembly of the League of Nations, 1924, bases the rights of the child upon the recognition "that humanity should give the child the best that it has, irrespective of all considerations of race, nationality, and creed." Hence the problem ceases to be one of the control of education and becomes one of the provision of educational facilities for all. If equality of opportunity is accepted as the essential principle of the modern State, then there can be no question but that educational facilities must be provided by the State. If the interests of the State are best served by the fullest development of the individual, and by the promotion of variety of experience rather than by uniformity, then the task of the State is to create the best machinery for their encouragement, and its concern is not that all shall be educated alike in the same institutions, but that all shall have equal opportunities for education accessible to them. Accordingly, the State on these principles does not establish a monopoly to the exclusion of private schools, if there are groups which desire to maintain them, but exercises such supervision as will guarantee adequate standards in all schools.

The problem, however, is not so simple. As was indicated in the first chapter, the State has tended to become synonymous with the nation, and both exist for the promotion of some purposes and ideals. The essential bond of a nation is its cultural heritage, defining cultural in its broadest terms. There at once arises the question as to who shall define this culture. The danger which may follow from the proposal, that the State is primarily concerned with the provision of educational facilities for the fullest development of the individual without exercising a monopoly of such provision, is that it may lead to a system of education based on the cult of individualism without any dominant social purpose. The two extremes of the problem may be illustrated by the educational practices of the United States and of Russia. In the former, although socialization and training for citizenship are professed, there appears to be no clear definition of these terms, with the result that the dominant aim is actually individualistic and training for individual success is uppermost. In the latter, the end of education is definitely propaganda and indoctrination to secure the universal acceptance of Communist ideology. The educational problem is thus to secure a synthesis of the two extremes without incurring on the one hand the danger of excessive individualism devoid of social motives and on the other of such a rigid definition of the social or cultural ideal that it leaves no room for growth and enrichment. In such a synthesis there should be scope for enrichment of the ideal through variety of approach due to differences of environment and the many-sided interests of a complex modern society.

1. ENGLAND

In contrast with those of France and Germany, educational organization and administration in England seem to be devoid of any philosophy or underlying principles. Like the Constitution, English education has grown up in a haphazard fashion without any semblance of design, and today represents at first glance a conglomeration of "public" schools which are private, of private schools which may receive assistance from public funds, of some public schools which are sectarian and others which are undenominational in character. And yet each constitutes a recognized part of the whole national system of education. The long abstention of the State from the provision of education at public expense left the field free for private effort and for the gradual creation of vested interests which could not be set aside when the public system of education was finally established in all its ramifications and the foundation of a national system was laid in 1902 without any clear recognition of its implications for the future. The apparent chaos and existence of public and private education alongside of each other are justified in English political philosophy, which was summarized in the quotation from Mill's essay *On Liberty*.[1]

The English view is that the essence of a national system of education is that the State shall see to it that every citizen is assured of a minimum of education, but the responsibility for providing that minimum is imposed on the parents, who are required to send their children within the compulsory age limits to an efficient school, whether public or private. This minimum was dictated originally by the consideration that mere literacy would result in that feeling of moral responsibility which is essential to social stability and would cultivate that sense of civic and political responsibility which must accompany the progressive extension of the suffrage. Hence the two pleas on which the first tentative steps in the provision of public elementary education were based were "Open a school and close a jail" and "We must now educate our masters." This minimum has gradually been extended for a variety of reasons — the recognition that elementary education in literacy alone is inadequate to secure the social ends desired; as a result of the rise of the working-classes to political power, a rise which was itself due to education, elementary and adult; the recognition that national progress and prosperity are based on as broad an education as possible; and the gradual realization that national welfare demands the provision of equality of educational opportunities which would make possible the fullest development of each individual according to his abilities. It is significant that the program of education implied in this conception of a minimum was incorporated in the manifestoes [2] of the three dominant political parties (Conservative, Liberal, and Labor) in the elections of May, 1929. The exigencies of the present economic situation have seriously retarded the development of this program, but the next step in the provision of the minimum will be an extension of the period of full-time com-

---

[1] *Ante*, p. 52.
[2] These will be found in the *Educational Yearbook, 1928*, of the International Institute of Teachers College, pp. 39 ff. (New York, 1929).

pulsory education up to fifteen and such a reorganization as will ensure in the last four years the elements of a secondary education for all.

Since the responsibility for providing a minimum of education for their children is placed upon the parents, no restrictions are imposed upon the opening of private schools. Legally such schools, in so far as they receive pupils within the limits of compulsory attendance requirements, are subject to inspection by the State, the local authority, or some other recognized agency. In practice the right to inspect private schools has not been exercised and at present the State actually has no accurate knowledge of the number of private schools in existence or of the enrollments therein. A Departmental Committee was appointed in 1930

to survey the present position of the Board of Education and the local education authorities in relation to schools not in receipt of grants from public funds, and to consider what legislative or other changes are desirable for the purpose of securing that the children attending such schools receive an adequate education under suitable conditions.

The appointment of this Committee aroused considerable suspicion and feeling lest the Board, in the words of one of the critics, become "controller, inspector and licenser of schools which it did not aid in any way."

The fundamental theory underlying the relations of the State to education in England is that initiative, growth, and personality can be assured only by allowing reasonable freedom whether education is provided by a public authority or by private effort. It is felt that there is an incompatibility between the enforced uniformity of a bureaucratic system and the varied enterprise possible under a system of administration which is supervisory and advisory. The important national asset to be assured is that experimentation which comes from the free adaptation of education and instruction to local or group needs in order to secure rich variety of character. Personality counts for more than prescription in such a human relationship as is implied by education, and all obstacles to its free action and development must be removed. The proper ideal seems to be, according to Sir Michael Sadler, "variety set in a framework of national organization." The function of the State is to recognize and, when necessary, to aid every kind of efficient and needed school. The well-being of a national system of education, as of individuals, depends on a blend of authority and liberty, of freedom and responsibility, and on an appropriate delimitation of those elements which may be defined and prescribed and those which cannot be organized and made mechanical. Education is a moral affair, and a government, whether national or local, cannot claim a monopoly of moral control; while education should be permeated with a sense of national duty, it does not follow that national duty can be interpreted by the government alone. The national organization should be broad enough to include groups of schools representing different convictions, diverse ways of life, and varied traditions of judgment which result from variety of experience in the complex society of today; the choice of the school should be left to the parents. The chief task of the State is to enforce education under the best possible conditions, and to allow those who will to provide it, taking care only that adequate facilities are supplied within the reach of all at public expense; to this there would be added, on the basis of recent developments, the provision of equality of opportunity to advance beyond the scope of compulsory education.

The State accordingly refrains from prescribing the details of what shall be taught, but through the conditions underlying the distribution of grants for education sets up general standards which are concerned mainly with the *externa* — all those factors that make an efficient educative process possible. Beyond this the responsibility for the comprehensive and progressive development of education is placed upon the local education authorities. In cases of dispute between the central and local authorities which cannot be settled by consultation and conference, recourse is had either to the courts or to Parliament.

State grants are not restricted to schools maintained by public authorities. While private schools of elementary grade may not receive such grants, private secondary schools which are not run for private profit are eligible under certain conditions, such as inspection, general efficiency, and the admission of a percentage of the pupils from public elementary schools free of tuition.

The State does not prescribe curricula and courses of study or methods of instruction, but seeks to exercise its influence by means of Suggestions and Memoranda embodying the best current practices. It refrains from conducting examinations, which are entrusted to a number of recognized agencies. Even in the preparation of teachers the central authority has recently abandoned its former practice of influencing the curricula through its examination syllabus and has delegated the examinations, with some reservations, to regional boards, on whose recommendations the certificates are granted by the Board of Education.

The relation of the State to education in England is thus characterized by stimulus, advice, consultation, and financial rewards to encourage variety and flexibility. The results may be uneven and spotty, but the system of education reflects the essential English characteristics — a horror of theory, fear of mechanical organization, and regard for individual freedom as the fundamental basis for the development of character.

2. FRANCE

France may still be cited as the best example of state centralization or state control in education. The Napoleonic principle survives, but is beginning to be questioned. Additional reasons have been found under the Third Republic to justify this principle. Centralization is justified, not merely on cultural grounds, but as the best protection against aggression both within and without, and as the best guarantee of national solidarity. France cannot forget to remind the world that her frontiers are unprotected and that her soil has several times been violated by foreign armies. But it is not often realized that the Republic still lives in fear of the restoration of a monarchy, a fear which may be groundless, but which still exercises some influence on the French mind. The restoration of the Church to political power is also an eventuality against which centralization in education is regarded as a protective safeguard despite the law against Associations passed in 1904. Fear of the development of a caste system is another factor employed to justify a state control which will hold the balance between classes and provide opportunities for the emergence of talent. On the positive side it is felt that a centralized system with uniform standards and requirements will develop common ideals and common sentiments in the face of the strong appeal of local dialects, customs, and interests. Bureaucratic control of educational administration is, from another point of view, regarded as the soundest guarantee of efficiency. Hence a system of organization in which almost every detail is controlled and prescribed by the Ministry of Public Instruction and carried out by officials directly or indirectly responsible to it. By the time the details of administration have been exhausted by the hierarchy of bureaucrats, so little scope for action is left for the local school committees, which have a place in the scheme of organization, that many refuse to function. The opening and closing of schools, the provision of a large share of the funds, the training and certification of teachers, the approval of textbooks, curricula and courses of study, and the standards of the examinations, which mean so much in the life of the nation — all these, both the *externa* and the *interna*, belong in the last resort to the Minister of Public Instruction. The extent to which the power of any Minister may be employed was well illustrated in 1923-24 when the whole system of secondary studies was changed and rechanged by successive ministerial decrees. This control over public education is extended to private schools which may not be established without the approval of the Ministry, the academy inspector, the departmental officials, the local mayor, and the public prosecutor. It is significant that the pressure to uniformity has resulted in the fact that scarcely any educational experiments of note have come from France.

There is some protest against the system from both lay and professional organizations. There is a demand for regionalism or the adaptation of local administration to local needs in all branches of public concern as well as in education, and for more flexibility and less control from Paris. Up to the present little has been done to meet this demand, except that the latest revision of the elementary course of study leaves to the teachers some room for local adaptation, subject to the approval of the inspectors, and some freedom for local variation has been allowed to normal schools. Should there ever be a movement of larger scope in the direction of decentralization, it is certain that one other dominating element, which serves at present as an argument for centralization, will not be neglected, and that is such an organization of French education as will not deprive France of her preëminent international position as a leader of thought and culture.[1] For the present, however, it does not appear to be likely that French politicians will interrupt their preoccupations with foreign and economic affairs to embark on a program of administra-

---

[1] On regionalism see *l'Université Nouvelle*, two volumes by "Probus" issued by Les Compagnons (Paris, 1919); the organ of Les Compagnons — *l'Université Nouvelle*; Hauser, H. *Le Problème du Régionalisme* (Paris, 1924); and Gooch, R. K., *Regionalism in France* (New York, 1931).

tive decentralization. So far as education is concerned, it is likely to continue for some time longer to be administered and controlled by the State and in the interests of the State. There is every indication, however, that the solution propounded under different conditions by Napoleon and accepted for over a century and a quarter is likely to be rejected when the time comes for the more serious consideration of domestic affairs in France. The regionalist movement, which is not an entirely recent movement, the assertion of the right of every individual to the best education appropriate to his abilities as implied in the movement of the *école unique*, and the claims of teachers' organizations to the right of professional self-determination are the tendencies which point to a national system of education based on greater variation and differentiation and less centralization of effort.[1]

3. GERMANY

The rigid concept of the unitary authoritarian State received a serious blow in Germany in the Revolution of 1918. The constitution of 1919 was based on the democratic concept of the rights of the individual and of groups to self-realization under the protection of the State. Hence a large place is devoted in the Constitution to provisions for the protection of the individual, to education, to freedom of grouping in matters affecting religious outlook, and to occupational groupings. While the uncertain political and economic conditions following the adoption of the Constitution have prevented the realization of all the aspirations of the German people embodied therein, the obvious change which has taken place is expressed in its first Article, "The German Reich is a Republic. The political power emanates from the people." [2] Accordingly the State is not an entity existing metaphysically over and above the individuals who make it up, but an institution representing the will of its members.

The first article in the section of the Constitution devoted to education (Chapter II, Section IV) opens with the statement that "Art, science, and instruction in them are free. The State guarantees their protection and participates in their promotion." [3] At the time when

[1] It is not yet possible to evaluate the influence which will be exercised on this movement by the adaptation to local differences in Alsace and Lorraine. See Hayes, C. J. H., *France, a Nation of Patriots*, Ch. X (New York, 1930).

[2] See McBain, H. L., and Rogers, L., *The New Constitutions of Europe*, p. 176 (New York, Doubleday, Doran and Co., 1923).

[3] *Ibid.*, p. 203.

the draft of the Constitution was being discussed, and since its adoption, an attempt was made to assign a larger place to participation by the Federal Government in education, but, although the Constitution provides for the coöperation of the *Reich*, the States, and the municipalities in the promotion of education, enthusiasm for federal participation waned as soon as it appeared that participation would not be accompanied by financial aid from the federal treasury. With some slight exceptions, adopted in order to ensure some uniformity of standards in the interests of reciprocity, educational affairs are accordingly delegated mainly to the States. One of the serious topics of controversy, the relation of the State to religious instruction, was settled in the Constitution by a liberal provision in which room was found for denominational, interdenominational, and non-sectarian schools, with the right reserved both for teachers and pupils to abstain from giving or receiving religious instruction in the light of their own consciences. In spite of this constitutional provision, however, the question is by no means settled, although a three year conflict on the subject (*Reichsschulgesetz*) has for the time being quieted down.

Education is, then, a matter for each State. In Prussia the functions of the Ministry of Science, Art, and Public Education are broadly conceived and comprise under its supervision the promotion, not only of education and science, but of fine arts as well, including museums, theaters, and moving pictures; some forms of special education and juvenile welfare have been entrusted to other Ministries. The organization of the administrative system has remained unchanged, but something far more important than the organization of the machinery, the spirit underlying administration and the relations between the State and localities and the State and the teachers, has undergone a far-reaching reform. Domination and prescription, the characteristics of an authoritarian State, have been replaced by stimulation, advice, and counsel, which mark a government based on the idea of partnership and coöperation of all parties concerned. This is best illustrated by the introduction of the word *Richtlinien* (suggestions) for the previous *Bestimmung* (decree) and *Verordnung* (ordinance) in such matters as curricula, courses of study, and time-schedules, through which the authoritative State is inclined to exercise its control in the interests of uniformity. This change in the spirit of administration reflects a complete change in the principles underlying the relationship between the State and education. Under the pre-War theory, the State was the repository of *Kultur* and to that end had the right of direction and dictation. The change from a monarchy to a republic has not meant merely a change in the form of government. The Constitution provides that education shall be conducted "in the spirit of German national character and of international conciliation." From this has been adopted the principle that national character and culture cannot be defined *à priori*, that they are rather things which must be slowly built up through education. Another task confronting German education after the collapse of a system of government which was the object of allegiance of all is that of developing a spirit of national solidarity to bind all classes together by an internal rather than an external bond. Hence the task of creating through the school a consciousness of a common culture and therefore of discovering appropriate objects of allegiance.

The new task raises two questions, What constitutes national character? and, Who can define it? Most German States have proceeded on the principle that culture is not one thing alone and that it is not subject to definition by authority. Accordingly the function of the State is to provide those facilities which would lead to the spontaneous development and progress of national culture through the interplay of the individual or of groups and their environment. This explains the substitution of suggestions and outlines which provide scope for adaptation to local conditions, and prescribed courses of study, which make for standardized uniformity. The tendency is thus for the State to allow some freedom and flexibility in the *interna* and to set up standards for the *externa* — buildings, size of classes, length of school term, and the qualifications and salaries of teachers. Another consequence of the changed character of the relations of the State to education is a change in the methods of preparing, particularly, teachers for the elementary schools, from an apprenticeship to a professional basis.

Beyond this the democratic State has another function — the equalization of opportunity for the best development of the individual. Little has been done in Germany to realize the hopes of those who advocated the *Einheitsschule* or the common system, which would have replaced the horizontal system of one school for the classes and one for the masses by the vertical system of schools organized on a functional basis adapted to various abilities. The only installment which has been made so far has been the federal law requiring all children to be educated in the same school (the *Grundschule*) for the first four years of their educational careers. Beyond this the access of bright pupils to secondary education has been facilitated by means of reduction of fees and of an increased number of scholarships, and the creation of a new type of secondary school (*Aufbauschule*) for bright pupils who miss the opportunity of entering the traditionally organized type at the age of ten. The place of private schools has been regulated by the Constitution; the private preparatory school (*Vorschule*), the special privilege of wealthy pupils, has been abolished; private instruction at home is prohibited by law; private schools as a substitute for public schools may be established with the approval of the State, which is granted if they are not inferior to the public schools in equipment, curricula, and qualifications and status of the teachers; private elementary schools may be established only where in any locality there is no public school of the religious belief or the *Weltanschauung* of any group, or for experimental purposes recognized by the authorities. Private schools are subject to inspection by the State; their pupils may be admitted to examinations for certificates granted by the State, and under certain conditions, financial aid may be given by the State to private schools.

4. ITALY

The three countries which have been discussed up to this point — France, Germany, England — and the United States in so far as they represent any common element demonstrate a faith in democratic forms of government and within them various types of relationship of the State to education — France, state control of education in the interests of all; Germany, England, and the United States, state supervision of education with adequate scope in varying degrees in each country for variety, freedom, and experimentation. While it would be dangerous to generalize, certain common tendencies which point to a similarity of aims in the future may be detected: — free and equal opportunities for individual development, regional and group variations, and freedom from centralized dictation and prescription appear to be the central tendencies. In other words, the movement in these countries appears to be away from the concept of the unitary, all-controlling state in the direction of the pluralistic concept implied in local or regional group self-determination. Italy and Russia, however, have embarked on two political experiments which are based directly on criticisms of liberalism and democracy resting on the principle of individualism and which are founded on the theory of the absolute right of the State to define its own ends and purposes and to mould the individual according to the pattern designed by it. The State is not merely a collection of individuals nor is the will of the State merely the sum of the wills of all the individuals who make it up — that is, representative of what is called public opinion. The State has a life and destiny of its own and its citizens are merely instruments for the attainment of those ends which are defined "by those who know." Beyond these common principles which in practice operate somewhat differently, each country has adopted its own solution of the economic problem.

Italy had sought for over a century to develop national unity and to revive an indigenous culture appropriate to the traditions and genius of her people and free from the influences of foreign thought. She had passed in turn under the influences of doctrinaire liberalism, constitutional government, and democracy; during the War she achieved what appeared to be something like national solidarity, and yet at the close of the War the country was again disunited, on the verge of anarchical revolution, and without that leadership which would point a way out of her difficulties; the Fascist Revolution brought about some semblance of peace and order and an ideal of national life, in which would be found a synthesis of the State and the individual, the universal and the particular.

Italian Fascism is the outgrowth of three trends in Italian life and thought. The first is the tradition of the strong state which goes back to the ideal of Dante and Machiavelli. The second is a movement for national union and the national state which struggled for expression in Italian philosophy throughout the nineteenth century. The third is the idealistic concept of the state of Hegel translated into Italian terms to suit Italian traditions. Fascism represents a blend of all three influences. It is more than a political movement; it affects every aspect of state and national life and of the relations of the individual to the State; it is concerned as much with economics as with political organization, and as much with the spiritual as with the material bases of existence. It seeks to awaken the racial and national instincts of the people and to revive a living consciousness of her glorious past, when Rome and Italy were the political, cultural, and spiritual centers of the world. Inspiration for reorganization in the present and preparation for the future are to be found in the living sources of Italy's traditions, for history has inherent in it the unfolding seeds of later progress. The recognition of the common origin of Italian life and culture, which had always survived in the countryside, would assure the unity and solidarity as a nation of which Italians stand so greatly in need. More important, however, than national unity is an ideal to inspire and vitalize it.

Fascism seeks to provide this ideal in a new concept of the national State which is at the same time a challenge to the modern development of democracy. It is in fact a protest against the ideals of democratic government and of individualism which had their roots in the Protestant Reformation and the French Revolution. These ideals, since they placed the individual on a pedestal, imply a mechanical and atomistic concept of the State and of society and are based on the view that the sum of individual interests is the same as the collective interest of the State, and the general will or the ends of the State merely represent the aggregation of individual wills. From this point of view, the State and society exist for the sake of the individuals who compose them and the ends of both are determined by the ends, purposes, and interests of the individuals. Government is merely a mechanical device to hold the balance or "maintain justice" between the conflicting interests of individuals or groups. Representative government and rule by majorities promote the selfish interests of an aggregate of individuals rather than the interests of the State which are directed to the well-being of all. Democratic forms of society are purely materialistic, are dominated by no fixed or stable ideals, and are subject to the whims of changing majorities; the present is isolated from the past, and the spiritual inheritances of the past, which make for the spiritual union of society, are rejected. The State or society exists merely as a means for promoting the happiness of individuals and the essence of social, economic and political life is liberty in an absolute sense, not sacrifice, or discipline, or duty.

Against this ideology Fascism opposes the view that society or the State is something more than the sum of the individuals who compose it, that it is the link between succeeding generations, and that it has ends of its own which may even be in conflict, but are always superior, because more far-seeing and unselfish, to those of the individual. These ends are moral and spiritual and involve language, culture, religion, customs, feelings and volition, economic interests, living conditions, and territory, all dominated by moral values of universal validity which serve to guide progress towards a national ideal. As opposed to the atomistic and mechanistic concept of the State, Fascism sets up an organic and historic concept of a State with a life and purposes of its own over and above those of the individual. The State thus becomes an end; the individuals are at once the means or instruments which may be employed to attain the end and find their happiness as they attain to a complete understanding of the end proposed by the State. Liberty in such a State does not mean self-realization or self-expression of the individual, but rather conquest of oneself in the interests of the State; liberty is not an absolute right, but is contingent upon the purposes of the State, which may concede it to or withdraw it from the individual. The highest ethical value lies not in liberty but in the preëminence of duty; liberty is not a natural right but a concession of the State. Hence sovereignty rests not with the individual members of the nation or their elected representatives, chosen more often than not on the basis of the selfish interests of a party or of the voters, but with the men capable of rising above their immediate private interests and of realizing the aspirations of the State as a unity in relation to its past, present, and future. The leaders are those who are better fitted to govern than others; their authority is derived not from below, from the masses ignorant of anything but their own interests, but from above. Hence government is organized as a hierarchy exercising authority and bearing responsibility. The bases of government are authority, order, and discipline.

The same principles have been applied to the organization of the economic as to the political life of the country; the two aspects have in fact been blended together. The economic life of a democracy is marked by the competitive spirit in which each individual seeks his own interests. Fascism is opposed to orthodox economics based on individualism. On the principle that the collective interests are paramount, no man may do anything that will affect them harmfully. All forms of property and of work are to be administered in the public interest. Hence the Fascist State does not stand by to aid the individual who feels himself aggrieved or injured, but seeks to exercise positive control over the economic situation by organizing society on a corporative basis, a hierarchy of unions under the direction of a special Ministry. In this way the interests of employer, employee, and the State as a whole are conserved and protected, and since political suffrage is dependent upon membership in some form of corporation, the varied group interests of the country find expression through the members sent to the Chamber of Deputies.

Fascism thus seeks to rescue the State from the individual and to emphasize authority, social obligations, and subordination to a hierarchy which constitutes the government because it is conscious of the great ends proposed for the State. The State accordingly is an independent entity which has aims and purposes of its own, which must be authoritative, and which cannot afford to be neutral or indifferent without giving free rein to the unenlightened and blind forces motivated by the selfish interests of its individual members.

Education thus becomes the most important means of enlightening the masses in the ideals of the Fascist State; until it could become universally organized in accordance with these ideals, other means, more forceful and less intellectual, had to be employed. Repression, it was recognized, was the only method by which ignorant opponents could be controlled; the future lay with the younger generation with whom education was to take the place of repression. Since the State is a moral and spiritual affair conscious of moral truths of universal validity, it alone has the right to control education which may be provided by public or other organizations, but always subject to state control which is exercised by a hierarchical administration, in which as little as possible is left to local representative committees. The scope of state action was defined by Giovanni Gentile, who was entrusted with the reform of education in accordance with Fascist ideals:

> We affirm our belief that the State is not a system of hindrances and external juridical controls from which men flee, but an ethical being which, like the conscience of the individual, manifests its personality and achieves its historical growth in human society. Thus it is conscious not of being hedged in by special limits, but of being open, ready, and capable of expanding as a collective and yet individual will. The nation is that will, conscious of itself and of its own historical past, which, as we formulate it in our minds, defines and delineates our nationality, generating an end to be attained, a mission to be realized. For that will, in case of need, our lives are sacrificed, for our

lives are genuine, worthy, and endowed with incontestable value only as they are spent in the accomplishment of that mission.

The State's active and dynamic consciousness is a system of thought, of ideas, of interests to be satisfied and of morality to be realized. Hence the State is, as it ought to be, a teacher; it maintains and develops schools to promote this morality. In the school the State comes to a consciousness of its real being.[1]

The State accordingly comes first, and the function of the educator is to devise such a system of curricula and methods of instruction as will prepare the individual to take his place in it as a self-conscious and active member. Until the stage is reached when the Fascist doctrine has become accepted as a natural and inherent part of Italian life, the task of the hierarchy is to devise methods for the rapid training of its immediate supporters from whom the leaders are to be drawn. The school will serve to educate the large masses; direct training and indoctrination are needed to secure a hierarchical succession. Hence there have been developed what are virtually two parallel systems, one of national education and one deliberately directed to Fascist indoctrination; one consists of the regular organization of schools under the control of the national government, the other of an organization under the direct control of the Fascist Party for the training of its potential members.

5. RUSSIA

Viewed superficially the general principle governing the relations of the State to the individual in Communist Russia bear many points of resemblance to those adopted in Fascist Italy. There is, however, this important difference that the Communist State penetrates more deeply into the life and thought of the individual because the Fascist Revolution failed to discard the traditional bourgeois ideology. Like Fascism, Communism represents fundamentally a criticism of the traditions of democracy and of individualism; it is opposed to that atomistic organization of society which results in individual selfishness and perpetuates the competitive spirit. Democracy and individualism are at once the outcome and the foundation of the bourgeois concept of society rooted in capitalism which encourages the exploitation of the individual for selfish ends. A condition of

---

[1] Circular of November 2, 1922. Quoted and translated in Schneider, H. W., and Clough, S. B., *Making Fascists*, p. 85 (Chicago, University of Chicago Press, 1929).

society based on the rights of the individual perpetuates the notion that the State exists for their protection, with the result that the State represents a struggle for the supremacy of a class, and majority rule is merely the expression of selfish interests grouped together for the time being for their own protection and advancement. A society based on the concept of the freedom of the individual is merely a contrivance to encourage the exploitation of those who cannot help themselves; freedom as well as the cult of individualism are found wherever the State is not sure of its own ends. The State, however, according to both Fascist and Communist ideology, cannot be neutral; it must take a definite position and must confirm that position by force, if necessary, but in the long run preferably by education as the more effective method. The purposes of the State can only be defined by those who know, by those who can gain and perpetuate their control by constantly adding to their numbers new and tested recruits ready and willing to share their principles unequivocally and judged to be fit to rule. Control is thus in the hands of a party, the Fascist in Italy and the Communist in the Union of Soviet Socialist Republics.

All points of resemblance between the two Revolutions end here, for, while Fascism has chosen to develop a national union based on the spiritual ideals derived from Italian tradition, and has retained under certain restrictions the capitalistic organization of society, Communism has undertaken to break ruthlessly with all traditions — political, economic, spiritual, religious, moral, and æsthetic — as the product of bourgeois, and, therefore, capitalistic mentality. Communism is definitely based on the dictatorship of the proletariat, and the State created by Communism is not, as in Italy, merely a perfection of the old machine devised in the interests of a new class but an entirely new machine in which government is vested in the workers. The State cannot be neutral and cannot compromise with the principles for which it stands in order to maintain a balance between various groups — social, religious, or economic.

The dictatorship of the proletariat is incompatible with freedom for the bourgeoisie. This is the very reason why the dictatorship of the proletariat is needed, to deprive the bourgeoisie of freedom; to bind it hand and foot; to make it impossible for it to carry on a struggle against the revolutionary proletariat.

The dictatorship of the proletariat is not only an instrument for the crush-

THE STATE AND EDUCATION

ing of enemies; it is likewise a lever for effecting economic transformation. Private ownership of the means of production must be replaced by social ownership; the bourgeoisie must be deprived of the means of production and exchange, must be "expropriated."

It follows that the conquest of State power is not the conquest of the preexistent organization, but the creation of a new organization, an organization brought into being by the class which has been victorious in the struggle.[1]

The Communist State unlike democracies is not guided by vague, uncertain aims. It made a complete sweep with the past and created a new social order which is founded on government by the proletariat, the manual workers in the cities, to whom were added, but as an afterthought, the peasants who have been gradually drawn into the movement at first by force and then by persuasion. There has thus been set up an aristocracy of labor, directed by the Communist Party consisting of about two million members in a population of about eighty times that number. Membership in the Party can only be acquired by those who in their work and influence have shown unswerving loyalty to the revolutionary cause, who can be recommended by those already in the Party, and who satisfactorily pass through a period of probation. Since no one can be above suspicion, periodical purgings of the Party membership take place, as in the Fascist Party, irrespective of individual standing in its counsels. Through its organization into tens of thousands of groups or "cells" and through its secret service, the Gay-Pay-Oo, the Party is able to keep its finger on the pulse of the country. A rigid discipline is thus enforced in order that the purposes of the Revolution may be attained. Since no one may be neutral, ruthless warfare is waged against individuals who are suspected because of their pre-Revolutionary affiliations or because of their present attitudes of being antagonistic to the Revolution. The class struggle, it is maintained, must be continued until the time when the fundamental principles of the Revolution have been accepted by all without the possibility of question; only when all are of one class, when all are members of the proletariat, will the class struggle disappear. In other words, political neutrality cannot exist and every aspect of life must be "politicized" — that is, imbued with the doctrine for which Communism stands.

Of these doctrines the Communist Party is the guardian until they

[1] Bukharin and Preobrazhensky, *The A B C of Communism*, pp. 80 ff. Quoted in Colton, E. T., *The X Y Z of Communism*, p. 40 (New York, 1931).

have been accepted universally. The development and propagation of these doctrines are in the hands of the Party, with its hierarchical organization reaching down into each cell and culminating in a Central Committee which is elected by the annual congress of the Party and which organizes a Political Bureau responsible for current tasks of organization and administration, and acts as an inner steering committee whose decisions govern the Communist Party and the policies of the Soviet State.

The form of representative government has, however, been retained in the Soviets elected by the proletariat voters, who exercise their suffrage on an occupational rather than a geographical basis. The elections center round individuals, not parties, since for the present there is only one party in the country. The Soviets in turn have a hierarchical organization for the smallest unit which may be a factory or similar center up to the All-Union Congress of Soviets. Although the Soviets, with their organizations paralleling those of the Communist Party, are intended to be the direct representatives of the proletariat, policies and even elections are under the influence of the Party, which manifests itself in the various organs of government — the Central Executive Committee, the Presidium of the Committee, the Council of People's Commissars, and the Council of Labor and Defense with its State Planning Commission — appointed by the All-Union Congress of Soviets which only meets biennially.

There has thus been set up a form of control which is harmonious and closely articulated in all its parts and free from the many contradictions which underlie those forms of government based on the ideals of democracy, freedom, and individualism. This harmony is, however, derived not from the external and superficial forms of organization already described and supplemented by other institutions which fit into the scheme, such as unions, the Red Army and police, the various youth organizations, and the utilization of every conceivable type of influence which may prove to be educative or propagandistic. This harmony comes from devotion to a body of doctrine preached and accepted with the fervor of religious fanaticism and defended with a continuing loyalty found in other countries only in such periodical crises as a war. And yet there is inherent in these doctrines none of the nationalism and patriotism which the Communists regard as bourgeois virtues. The Revolution, indeed, is not nationalistic but definitely international; the ultimate triumph of all the workers of the world would lead to the abolition of national lines and the organization of the world into one large federation of workers' republics.

The Communist order is founded on the collectivist organization of society which involves the abolition of private property in land and the tools of production, and their collective ownership and administration in the interests of all. Only those are to benefit from such an organization who engage in socially useful labor; all others, since they share in the bourgeois tradition of private property and exploitation, stand without the pale, and are not only disfranchised but are deliberately discriminated against in the distribution of the benefits which come from collective ownership — housing, food, and education being among the foremost of these. The advancement of the economic order depends on the rapid industrialization of the country in which labor is glorified as the means of developing common interests; in order to extend the community of interests between manual workers in industry and the peasant on the land, agriculture is to become industrialized on the basis of collective ownership and work. To promote successful industrialization, the development of science must be encouraged, not merely because of its applications, but as an interpretation of life. Through science alone can another body of traditions, which have been employed in the interests of the exploiting classes, be eliminated; superstitions, mysticism, belief in the supernatural, religion ("the opiate of the people") must be abolished by universal training in science which alone can furnish the interpretation of matter, which is the only basis of all existence. The whole explanation of the world of matter and of life, whose chief motives are determined by economic and, therefore, materialistic forces, is to be found in "dialectic materialism."

Accordingly, while the first task of the Communist State is to continue the class struggle until the idea of class is eliminated by the reduction of all society to one class, the most important task is to develop "the new man," the individual brought up from his earliest years in such an environment that it will be impossible for him to entertain any other than the Communist ideology. Education thus becomes in the Union of Soviet Socialist Republics the keystone of its permanence. Other forms of society have paid a tribute to education, but they have professed to keep politics out of education, something which the Communists insist is impossible. All education, all life must be penetrated with politics, and even the schools of capitalistic societies were established and maintained as instruments of the possessing classes. Education unless it is propaganda and directed deliberately to indoctrination is meaningless, and so-called academic freedom is bourgeois humbug. The strength of Communist education lies in its possession of a definite and clear-cut body of doctrine and ideas to impart, closely related to and based on the central principle of its social order — socially useful labor. As contrasted with the vagueness of aims in capitalistic societies, whatever their form of government, with their slogans of loyalty, patriotism, good citizenship, obedience, moral standards, individuality, freedom and initiative, the Communist educators and leaders have a well-defined picture of the kind of citizen who should be the product of the educative process. Obviously he must accept the fundamental principles of the Communist State — collectivism and the abolition of private property, dictatorship of the proletariat under the guidance of the Communist Party, and the abolition of classes through the class struggle. But he must do more than this; he must be a militant revolutionary, not only militant in defense of Communist principles, but active in the interests of social order, and must participate from his earliest years in promoting social welfare by engaging in socially useful labor, the foundation upon which the dictatorship of the proletariat is being built. Because he must be militant and active, he owes it not only to himself but to society to keep himself healthy and sound in body and in mind. Because superstitions and religion bind the individual to meaningless traditions and practices, he must become anti-religious and atheistic on the one hand, and scientific on the other. Finally, he must work for the day when the dictatorship of the proletariat will be established throughout the world. And what is expected of the boy or man is expected equally of the girl or woman whom bourgeois concepts of chivalry have kept in subordination or have exploited. In the words of one of the leading Russian educators, Albert P. Pinkevitch, the aim of education is as follows:

> By way of summary we may state that the aim of nurture and general instruction in Soviet Russia is to aid in the all-round development of a healthy, strong, actively brave, independently thinking and acting man, acquainted with the many sides of contemporary culture, a creature and a

THE STATE AND EDUCATION

warrior in the interests of the proletariat and consequently in the final analysis in the interests of the whole of humanity.[1]

or, more simply:

The aim of training and education in the U.S.S.R. is to bring up fighters for the workers' cause and builders of the socialistic state; men who have an all-round development, are well informed, skilled, physically strong and healthy, filled with collectivistic habits and the joy of living.[2]

The significance of this aim of education in Soviet Russia lies not so much in the clear goal set before the school — examples of efficient adaptation of means to ends in education can be found elsewhere — but in the fact that it penetrates and imbues every aspect of the life of the individual. Nowhere else has the effort been made to put into practice the concept that education is life and life is education. Whether educational practice is for the present successful or not, the theory underlying it is that there can be no break in gauge between the school and society. Education in other societies, certainly until the recent expansion of the movement for adult education began, has been synonymous with the school, while other agencies were regarded as informal; as contrasted with this point of view Communist theory seeks to enlist the whole mechanism of the proletarian State to support its program of education as an "instrument for the creation of a new ideology, of new modes of thought, of a new outlook on the world."[3]

Accordingly, education is regarded as a lifelong process beginning in the nursery and kindergarten with a content and a method governed by the fundamental aim and extending through life with the same basic training in Communist ideology for all, and, as under Fascism, for its guardians special preparation through the organizations rising in the form of a pyramid to the Communist Party at the top. Cultural activities — art, music, dramatics, the moving picture, and all forms of recreation and leisure activities — which elsewhere are regarded as dispensable luxuries which need not be organized or supervised too closely, are all incorporated as parts of the educative process. At the center of all activities is work — manual,

[1] Pinkevitch, A. P., *The New Education in the Soviet Republic*, p. 28 (New York, John Day Co., 1929).
[2] Pinkevitch, A. P., "Development of Public Instruction and Pedagogical Thought in Russia," *Educational Outlook*, May, 1931, Vol. V, p. 195.
[3] Bukharin and Preobrazhensky, *op. cit.*, p. 254. Quoted in Colton, *op. cit.*, p. 210.

social, cultural — any useful labor which contributes both to the training of the individual and to the advancement of the cause. The essence of the Communist theory of education is the penetration of all factors that can be utilized in the creation of Communist mentality by a single, all-comprehending ideal. There is, inherent in the theory, adaptation to a well-defined object of allegiance which is too often lacking in the educational theories of democratic societies with their varied degrees of emphases on character, culture, general or vocational training, intellectual or practical education, the cult of individuality or socialization, citizenship and patriotism. Whatever one's attitude to the Communist Revolution may be, Communist educational theory offers a serious challenge to education in democratic societies to discover in their own systems some social purpose which can exercise a powerful integrating influence analogous to that of the Communist ideology. The problem cannot be dismissed merely by balancing the effects of centralized and decentralized systems. There are centralized systems in democracies, such as Ontario and the Australian Provinces, which seem to have no *raison d'être* in the political or social theories of these States, but appear to be accepted in the interests of efficiency and perpetuated through inertia. On the other hand, Soviet Russia furnishes an example not only of decentralization, guarded by careful selection of teachers and textbooks, but of the encouragement of self-determination of minorities within the limits of Communist ideology.

6. UNITED STATES

The educational system of the United States [1] was fathered by the democratic ideals that began to emerge even before the Revolution, and has been nourished by the industrial development which began early in the nineteenth century and has gained increasing momentum down to the present time. The national ideal, although defined at the infancy of the Republic, did not remain rigid or static, but has been inevitably colored, to some extent enriched, by the gradual expansion of the frontier which filled the greater part of the nineteenth century. The development of American education has been marked

---

[1] The discussion of the relation of the State to education in the United States is based on the author's article on "The Philosophy Underlying the System of Education in the United States" in the *Educational Yearbook, 1929*, of the International Institute of Teachers College, Columbia University, pp. 461 ff. (New York, 1930).

by the interplay between two principles — the recognition that the stability and welfare of the democratic State depend upon universal education and the ideal of equality of opportunity.

The development of national solidarity and of loyalty to the new Republic was obviously one of the first objects of education. Thus Benjamin Rush, in his *Thoughts upon the Mode of Education proper in a Republic*, wished to see a "Supreme Regard to their Country" and "an awareness to the problems of democracy" inculcated in school pupils. The aim of education is to "convert men into republican machines" and by a centralized system "the whole state will be tied together." Equality in education must promote equality in government, says another writer [1] of the period, and is the rock upon which political salvation must be built. As to the provision of education, there was no doubt in the minds of leaders that it must be made at public expense; private schools do not provide for equality of opportunity; they make education the concern of the few. A uniform system of education provided by the State would remove those imperfections and obstructions which come from local differences and inequalities, and would promote harmony and solidarity. The State in the interests of its own perpetuation and progress has a duty to establish a system of education and may for that reason even override the authority of parents; the purpose of such an educational system was regarded to be the promotion of national solidarity and homogeneity of all the people, a purpose already recognized, before the creation of the Republic, by Benjamin Franklin. In his *Proposals relating to the Education of Youth in Pennsylvania* (1749), Franklin had urged the training of teachers. "And this is more necessary now to be provided by the English here, as vast numbers of foreigners are yearly imported among us totally ignorant of our laws, customs, and language." This justification was to become more urgent in the century following.

An enlightened body of citizens was accordingly recognized to be the soundest guarantee of public security. But the theory of the time went beyond this. The importance of education was advocated in the interests of the individual because of a deep conviction in the perfectibility of man. Out of this conviction there emerged the second principle upon which American education is founded: the

---

[1] Coram, R., *Plan for the General Establishment of Schools throughout the United States* (1791).

State must provide a system of education which will guarantee equality of opportunity to each individual. This demand that every boy and girl be given a chance became more insistent at the close of the first quarter of the nineteenth century and the rise of the Jacksonian period of democracy and equalitarianism.

The two demands — enlightenment of the citizens as the basis of national stability and equality of opportunity to enable each individual to make the best of himself — became the foundations upon which American education has been built, the two ideals which have stimulated the establishment of a broad educational highway by the States to whom rather than to the Federal Government the provision of education was delegated. George Washington emphasized enlightenment in his *Farewell Address*:

Promote then, as an object of primary importance, institutions for the general diffusion of knowledge. In proportion as the structure of a government gives force to public opinion, it is essential that public opinion should be enlightened.

Equality of opportunity was stressed by President John Adams:

The whole people must take upon themselves the education of the whole people and must be willing to bear the expense of it. There should not be a district one mile square without a school on it at the expense of the people themselves.

Thomas Jefferson combined both ideals in the two quotations which follow:

If a nation expects to be ignorant and free in a state of civilization it expects what never was and never will be. The functions of every government have propensities to command at will the liberty and property of their constituents. There is no safe deposit for these but with the people themselves; nor can they be safe with them without information.

A system of general information which shall reach every description of our citizens from the richest to the poorest, as it was the earliest, so will it be the latest of all the public concerns in which I shall permit myself to take an interest.

More recently a more complete statement of the American educational ideal was enunciated by Mr. Herbert Hoover before he attained to the Presidency:

The first ideal of our democracy is to maintain a state where each individual shall have an equality of opportunity to take that position in the community to which his intelligence, ability, and ambition entitle him, and that no forces shall continue in the nation which may prevent this free rise. There is a negative quality about this element in our national ideals, for although by this we could keep open the doors of opportunity, it must be supplemented by the second of our great ideals, that is, that we must stimulate and assist each individual in this attainment. The very essence of equality of opportunity requires that we shall give an equal opportunity in education and training to every one of our citizens and thus we arrive at the third of our great national ideals. That is universal and efficient education. If we are to maintain a progressive community and our national ideals we must go even further in education than the routine provision of learning. Education must take upon itself the development of leadership, and leadership calls for character and intelligence as well as learning.

The history of education in the United States begins, accordingly, with the establishment of schools and the means of education because "religion, morality, and knowledge are necessary to good government and the happiness of mankind"; it was developed from the second half of the nineteenth century and more particularly after the decision in the Kalamazoo Case, 1874, which established the principle that the high school is an essential part of the common school system, in the firm conviction that equality of educational opportunity must be guaranteed to every boy and girl irrespective of creed or social status. If the American public has shown a readiness to tax itself to maintain its educational system, it has been in the main to give every boy and girl a chance.

The development of state control of education has been slow in the United States; strong obstacles had to be overcome before the ideal of public education could be realized; opposition to taxation for education had to be removed; the idea of the education of the poor as charity had to be eliminated; a long campaign had to be waged in favor of the non-sectarian public school free and open to all; and the tradition of localism for a long time stood in the way of state control or supervision. Legislation for the promotion of the public school did not, however, imply prohibition of the establishment of private schools, nor did the tendency to use the schools for purposes of political indoctrination manifest itself until late — after the Spanish-American War and more particularly since the Great War. The relation of the State to private education was effectually settled in 1925 in the decision of the United States Supreme Court which declared as unconstitutional the law passed in Oregon to close all private schools and to compel all children to attend the public schools. The principle enunciated in this decision is as follows:

> The fundamental theory of liberty upon which all governments in the Union repose excludes any general power of the State to standardize its children by forcing them to accept instruction from public teachers only. The child is not the mere creature of the State; those who nurture him and direct his destiny have the right coupled with the high duty to recognize and prepare him for additional duties.

The private school is on the whole almost entirely free in most States from any supervision whatever, except that English must be the medium of instruction. But if private schools remain relatively free from public control, this is not true of public schools. The school as a center for indoctrination has always been recognized, but while the character of such indoctrination in other countries, such as pre-War Germany, France, Russia, Italy, and many others, is controlled by the State in its own interests, efforts to define it have been made in the United States by interested groups among the public which bring their influence to bear on state legislatures to foster what they regard as of supreme moment. Nor is indoctrination or propaganda limited to political or nationalistic ideas. The outstanding example is, of course, the Tennessee legislation prohibiting the teaching of the theory of evolution. The phenomenon of legislative prescription of what shall be taught in the schools is not new; so far as the problem of the relation of the State to education is concerned, the significant fact is that public opinion can and does bring its influence to bear on the kind of legislation which it desires even in details of school practice.[1]

Despite this tendency toward state interference in education, which is only a manifestation of the original principle that public stability and progress depend upon education, the control of education in the United States has in the main been local. The demand for federal aid for and participation in education and the movement for greater state control and supervision are prompted rather by the second principle — the provision of equality of educational opportunity with its corollary of improvement of quality by the creation of larger areas of administration. On the whole the State has not

---

[1] See Flanders, J. K., *Legislative Control of the Elementary Curriculum* (New York, 1925); Pierce, B., *Public Opinion and the Teaching of History in the United States* (New York, 1926); and Counts, G. S., *School and Society in Chicago* (New York, 1928).

been looked to for leadership and the powers of the State, with whom the responsibility for education is legally vested, have until recently been but lightly used. Leadership has come from the more progressive communities which under an increasing body of expert administrators have been ready to exercise the autonomy which they enjoy, although legally they may only exercise authority devolved upon them by the State. Another source of leadership has been provided in the nationally recognized centers for the study of education and for the conduct of research.[1] It may, therefore, be said that as compared with most countries the United States does not possess one easily defined formula of national education or a definite social or political pattern according to which its citizens are to be moulded. The State, through its various agencies, readily provides equality of educational opportunity through which each individual may make the best of himself. If a national aim or ideal can be said to dominate the educational systems of other countries, the cult of the individual is the essential characteristic of American education on the general assumption that a sound education will result in good citizenship and in a sense of social obligation. From the point of view of educational theory, this characteristic finds its expression in the movement for the child-centered school, in the proposal that there should be no curriculum fixed in advance, in the practice above the elementary school of adapting education to the actual needs and interests of the individual. At the other extreme are the movements to compensate for the emphasis on individualism by the introduction of social studies, teaching of civics, and the more definite and precise indoctrination demanded by patriotic societies.[2] As compared with such clear-cut and precise aims of education as are found in the systems of pre-War Germany, France, Italy, Russia, and Japan, for instance, the relation of the State to education in the United States continues to be vague and indefinite, as is illustrated in the following statement by Professor Thomas H. Briggs: "The State supports free public schools to perpetuate itself and to promote its own interests. Education is, then, a long-term investment that the State may be a better place in which to live and a better place in which to make

---

[1] See Kandel, I. L., ed., *Twenty-Five Years of American Education*, Ch. I (New York, 1923).
[2] For reflections on the present situation see Bagley, W. C., *Education, Crime, and Social Progress* (New York, 1931).

a living."[1] And yet it is the vagueness and the indefiniteness of purpose which have made education in the United States a great experiment, unstable, flexible, ever seeking to adapt itself to changing needs. There is no sharper contrast between the character of American education and that of countries with more definite aims than is shown by comparing the succession of ideas and changes in curriculum and methods during the past twenty-five years with the fact that the elementary curriculum of Prussia remained unchanged in essentials from 1872 until after 1918, and that of France from 1887 to 1923, while in England the changes have been so gradual that their course is often blurred.

Conclusion. The analysis which has been presented here of the relations of the State to education could be extended to other countries, but in all cases the essential principle would emerge that every State has the type of education that it wills. From the point of view of philosophy of education and of educational psychology, it may, indeed, be possible to conceive of education as autonomous, but the practice of education is in the last analysis dominated by the forces, considered up to the present — nationalism, national character, and the relation of the State to education or the relation between political and social theories underlying the State and education. These forces, it will be found, color the organization of education, its provision and administration, the curricula, courses of study, and methods of instruction. International conferences and congresses on education may be welcomed and may indeed be conducted on a common platform, but education, because it is an instrument of social progress, reflects in the long run the dominant characteristics of the total environment which it seeks to serve[2].

[1] Briggs, T. H., *The Great Investment, Secondary Education in a Democracy*, p. 8 (Cambridge, Mass., Harvard University Press, 1930).
[2] An excellent illustration of this thesis will be found in the *Report of the International Conference on Examinations*, which was organized under the auspices of the Carnegie Corporation and the International Institute of Teachers College, Columbia University, and was attended by representatives from England, Scotland, France, Germany, and Switzerland. (New York, 1931.)

CHAPTER IV

THE ORGANIZATION OF NATIONAL SYSTEMS OF EDUCATION

What is a national system of education? To define a national system of education is not simple, despite the frequent use of the term. The difficulty of finding an adequate definition is not due primarily to the vast range of influences, formal and informal, which enter into the formation of the attitudes and outlook of the members of a nation, but to the absence of a single criterion by which the existence of a national system may be tested. If the problem is approached from the administrative side, a system of education may be called national if it is under the control of a central administrative authority which defines and prescribes virtually every aspect of its organization, curricula, courses of study, methods of instruction, and standards of examination. The French system of education may be taken as one of the best illustrations of this definition, and yet the limitations of this interpretation appear even in the case of France, if the increasing unrest and criticism that spring from a feeling of dissatisfaction with the rigidity of centralized control and a desire to give expression to the many-sided, many-colored aspects of life in a national community are considered. Even in France some forms of education, especially vocational, have not yet been brought entirely under the control of the Ministry of Public Instruction, so that the central authority is not regarded as truly national. In Italy, a Ministry of National Education with supervisory control over every type of education was only created in 1929. If the administrative criterion were applied to England, it might be argued that England does not possess a national system of education because of the extraordinary blend of public and private schools, of council and denominational schools, with little or no control from the central Board of Education. So, too, Germany, the Union of Soviet Socialist Republics, and the United States, each with its own state system and without any or with but limited federal supervision, would equally be ruled out, if subjected to this test.

The existence of a national system of education may be tested by another criterion — the extent to which it is governed in all its parts by a national ideal and common national purposes. A national ideal may be defined for educational ends by a central authority, as in pre-War Prussia, or in France, Italy, and Russia today, even though, as in the latter countries, room is found within the scope of the national ideal for adaptation to local conditions and environments.[1] A national ideal may be equally strong and influential in determining the character of an educational system without being explicitly defined. Germany, for instance, is relying on the emergence of a national ideal from the free interplay of social forces, devotion to republican ideals, and adaptation to local environments subject to the control of commonly recognized standards in order to promote the supreme need of national solidarity. Similarly, England and the United States furnish illustrations of systems of education dominated by common ideals which are elusive and defined with difficulty, despite the absence in each country of an all-embracing central authority. There is a sense, however, in which, even though a national ideal affects every aspect of education, this criterion is inadequate as a complete test of a national system, and that is the existence of varieties of schools intended for different classes in the community and with few opportunities for transfer from one branch of education to another.

Hence, another criterion emerges whereby a system of education may be defined as national if it provides a well-coördinated and carefully articulated gradation of educational opportunities free and open to all and maintained at public expense. If articulation and integration of educational opportunities be employed as a test, then only the Soviet and American systems could be pronounced as truly national. Even in the United States the advocates of federal aid and participation in education claim that the system will not be truly national according to this criterion so long as the present inequality of opportunities in the various states prevails. The movements for the common school (the *Einheitsschule* in Germany,[2] the *école unique* in France, and the reorganization of the school system in England) are evidences of a desire to make systems of education national in the light of this third criterion.

[1] The problem of minority groups is in a somewhat different category and is not discussed here, although a significant contribution to its solution, consonant with the national ideal, is being made in Soviet Russia.

[2] For economic and other reasons the movement in Germany is for the present quiescent.

If the present tendencies are considered — and they are by no means limited to the countries here discussed — a national system of education may be defined as one in which free and equal opportunities are afforded to all according to their abilities and in which education is actuated by certain common purposes. Whether such purposes should be defined by a dominating central authority can be determined only in terms of what is the most desirable concept of nationalism and of an appropriate philosophy of administration,[1] which in turn will determine the existence and status of private schools.

Social distinctions and educational organization. The present tendencies, which appear to justify the definition of a national system of education here given, have, however, emerged into the realm of practical politics since the War. The provision of education in each nation has grown up without plan and without any idea of system. Historically, secondary and higher education for the training of leaders emerged first; the public provision of compulsory elementary education came late and without any thought of articulation with secondary; promoted first in a partnership between Church and State, its control was gradually taken over by the State in the interests of social welfare and national ends.[2] Infant schools and kindergartens came after the establishment of elementary schools, had different origins in theory, and followed practices which are only gradually being integrated with those of the schools which follow them. Vocational education, whether provided through apprenticeship or later with the rapid industrial and commercial expansion in the nineteenth century in special schools, developed apart from both elementary and secondary education. This separation was further manifested in the methods of administration; not only were separate divisions, desirable for functional reasons, created in Ministries of Education, but there existed a certain aloofness between them, while for local administration distinct and independent agencies were created, such as the Provincial School Boards for secondary, and County School Boards for elementary education in Prussia, or academies for secondary, and departments and communes for elementary education in France.[3] The administration of vocational educa-

---

[1] See Chapters I and V.

[2] There is no intention here either of denying the existence or of minimizing the extent of elementary education before it was provided by public authorities.

[3] The same division existed in England until 1902 — school boards for elementary and technical education, committees for technical and secondary education, the one responsible

tion was in fact entrusted to agencies other than those charged with general education.

Historically the different branches of education which constitute a national system have thus developed more or less independently, have been influenced by different social and other forces, and were not the results of organized planning. Systematic planning of educational systems was in fact ignored except in utopias, and in the proposals of Comenius, of the educational theorists of the French Revolution, and of the Chartists in England. Even in the United States, where the ideal of a common democratic system of education was current at the time of the founding of the Republic, it was not until 1874 that the provision of secondary education was pronounced in the Kalamazoo Case as an integral part of the common school system. Accordingly, the educational systems of most countries include infant schools or kindergartens which are not consistently integrated with their elementary schools, intermediate education or middle[1] schools which are not links in a consistent system, secondary education which has until recently had its own preparatory education overlapping with elementary, higher elementary education for pupils of the secondary age level but not conferring the same privileges as secondary education, and a variety of vocational education, part- and full-time, at different levels but also not articulated with other parts of the system. Even the educational systems of the United States, although articulated organically, include schools at different levels which show an absence of close articulation; attempts to close the gaps, which still exist between kindergartens and elementary schools, elementary and high schools, and high schools and colleges, have only begun to be made in the last two decades, and the final form which the American system will assume has nowhere yet been satisfactorily achieved.

Not only are the systems unarticulated and unintegrated, but the various parts have accumulated connotations which reflect their

to the central Education Department and the other in the main to the Science and Art Department.

[1] The term *Mittelschule* as used in Germany is an anomaly, since it is not an intermediate school standing between elementary and secondary schools, but rather the equivalent of central schools in England and higher elementary schools in France; in Austria the term *Mittelschule* refers to secondary schools, a use which would be unequivocal if secondary education had been based on a common primary education, which it was not; in Italy secondary education is known as *Istruzione media*. In Switzerland, again, the *Sekundarschule* is a misnomer, since this type of school is not secondary but intermediate or higher elementary.

origin. Elementary education has everywhere, except in the United States, been considered as the education intended for the masses, which because of their social and economic status were regarded as unfit for secondary education provided for the training of the more favored classes for positions of leadership. Intermediate or higher elementary education was developed to take care of what was regarded as an intermediate social group, able to bear the cost of some education beyond the elementary, but still unable to profit from secondary education. This and other forms of education, chiefly of a vocational character, were provided as substitutes for secondary education. The differences in origin and social purposes between the different branches of education affected their character. Secondary education, which was to prepare the potential leaders, was liberal and cultural in its emphasis; elementary education, intended to train submissive, law-abiding followers, was marked by a pathetic faith in mere literacy, which was to save the lower classes from superstition and immorality, from discontent and crime; "open a school and close a jail" constituted for a long time and in many countries the basis of the appeal for the provision of elementary education. Although elementary education has everywhere been enriched and provided with a curriculum which includes more than the three R's, it has not altogether been able to shake off its traditional connotation; socially it is regarded, except in the United States and Russia, as the education of the lower classes; educationally it is different in quality from secondary education which implies a cultural and liberal training of the mind as contrasted with the mere imparting in the elementary schools of knowledge and information — a contrast which best finds expression in the French *culture générale* of the secondary schools and *l'esprit primaire* of the elementary schools.[1] Thus the social differences which were perpetuated by the educational systems were further intensified by educational differences which divided members of the same nation into educated and uneducated classes.[2] These distinctions have separated the teachers of the various branches of

[1] In Germany the term *Bildung* was never applied to elementary education, while in England the suspicion in the minds of many secondary school teachers that pupils coming to them from the elementary schools were spoiled for secondary education was prevalent for a long time after the provision of public secondary schools.

[2] *Gebildete* and *ungebildete* or *Akademiker* and *Nicht-akademiker* in Germany, a distinction which is found in the more democratic South American countries in the contrast between those who are *universitarios* (including those who have had a secondary education) and those who are not *universitarios*.

education into distinct and independent groups, which are themselves the results of the different attitudes to the type of preparation considered adequate for each branch. This distinction has survived even in the United States, where two years of preparation in normal schools was until recently regarded as sufficient for teachers in elementary schools, while a completed college education was considered essential for high school teachers.

In the descrpitions of national systems which follow, it will be found that most of the distinctions and contrasts, much of the lack of articulation and integration, still survive. For the first time, however, in the history of education, marked discontent with and widespread criticism of this situation have begun to develop, particularly since 1914. It is beginning to be recognized generally that a national system of education must, from the point of view of its organization, be unitary in character, offering equality of opportunity to all according to ability, and differentiated, with a greater variety either of courses in the same school or of schools organized on a functional basis.

The new orientation. The proposals for the reorganization of educational systems are the results of a large number of forces — political, social, economic, educational, and psychological. On the political and social side the spread of democratic forms of government and a new realization of the meaning of democracy have combined to emphasize more than ever before the importance of providing equality of educational opportunities. If democratic forms of government are to succeed, there must be a richer provision of education than in the past; mere literacy, it is recognized, is not adequate, nor can elementary education, however much it may be enriched, furnish a sufficient preparation for participation whether in government or in social and economic life. The demands of modern society are too complex to be met by an elementary education alone. Hence the movements for an extension of compulsory education, part-time or full-time. The same forces, combined with a realization of the worth of every individual and of the great reservoirs of ability and talent which are neglected in educational systems based on class or other distinctions, have led to demands for free access to the highest forms of education according to ability. The pressure of economic competition, national and international, has also contributed to the recognition of the desirability of more adequate preparation for industrial and commercial needs without sacrificing the demands for general education. Educational theory, departing from the somewhat cloistered approach and viewing the problems with which it is confronted in the light of the demands of the whole of life, tends to justify the movement for more education and broader opportunities; the less scholastic it becomes, the wider appear the multiple ramifications of life with which it is called upon to deal. If education is life, then education cannot be restricted to the few years of formal schooling provided hitherto. The contribution from psychology is in the same direction; since the individual is a compound of all the influences of the environment to which he is exposed, then adequate growth — moral, social, physical, æsthetic, and intellectual — cannot be promoted in the few years of compulsory education nor even in secondary education as at present organized. Genetic psychology beginning at one end of the individual's life and studies in adult learning combine to establish the important principle that education is a lifelong process; without necessarily accepting some of the exaggerated emphases of the psycho-analysts, the importance of providing a rich environment which will lay a sound foundation for the growth of the individual cannot be escaped, while at the other end the fact that ability to learn is not confined within narrow age limits stresses the importance of adequate facilities for adult education. From another point of view the psychology of individual differences, which are only beginning to be dimly realized, and then only because of the large numbers of failures in the secondary schools of most countries, is directing attention to the need of far more differentiation of types of education than has been hitherto available. Finally, the place of informal agencies, whether as parts of an established system of education or independent of it — clubs, societies, the whole range of extra-curricular activities, radio, moving pictures, music, and art — is receiving attention which they have never been given before, although their incorporation into the educational systems has nowhere been carried as far as they have in Russia and Italy. The same forces, which are exercising so great an influence toward a reorientation of the problem of organization of education, are affecting as profoundly the whole question of educational methods, are breaking down the walls of the school and are bringing it more closely into relation with the throbbing and multicolored life about it.

The demand for equality of educational opportunities and differentiation of types of education according to individual ability and needs does not, however, obscure the important place which must be assigned to a common general education for all. Differentiation must not be carried to the length of destroying common social or national purposes and of setting up class distinctions through the organized system of schools. The movement for a common national system of education (the *école unique*, the *Einheitsschule*, "secondary education for all") does not imply uniformity of educational provision, although that is the interpretation placed upon it in the American system with its single vertical organization, nor does it exclude differentiation. Essentially the common school idea implies a common foundation for all, elimination of overlapping and special provision for the privileged (as in the former German *Vorschulen* and the French *classes préparatoires*), and a reorganization of schools beyond the common foundation, on the basis not of class distinctions, but of psychological differences and of function. Free education, except for able but poor pupils, is not yet being discussed as a practical policy for the near future, although fees have already begun to be abolished in the secondary schools of France and in a few secondary schools in England. Such a reorganization implies further the adoption of methods for selecting and distributing pupils in the schools best adapted to their abilities, or, in other words, a system of educational and vocational guidance, such as is proposed in France.

The probable plan which will result from the present discussions will consist of some form of pre-school education for pupils from the ages of two to six; primary education for pupils between six and twelve years of age; secondary education for pupils from twelve to eighteen years of age, divided into two stages of four and two or two three-years periods each; and tertiary education in higher institutions of learning and in schools for adults. A reorganization following this plan will involve a change in the present legal provisions for compulsory school attendance and an extension to the age of fifteen so that pupils may take advantage of the lower section of secondary education. In such a plan, primary education would have its logical and natural outlet in some form of secondary education, instead of being left more or less suspended in air like the traditional form of elementary education, while secondary education would include varied types of schools for adolescents in addition to the traditional type of academic school. The functional organization beyond the primary school, if carefully surrounded with safeguards to avoid maladjustment of pupils, would meet the same ends which are sought in the American cosmopolitan high school, which becomes too unwieldy if allowed to grow too big and a sham if the school is so small as not to allow for the employment of more than a limited number of teachers. Two problems are involved. The first is whether the fostering of democratic ideals demands the herding of all in the same school or whether such ideals are not the outcomes of intellectual and emotional attitudes which it is the function of education to develop. The second is the danger that the attempt to provide for a wide range of abilities and needs in the same school may lead to the cult of mediocrity and the sacrifice of the ablest minds for the average. American theory has adopted the provision of the same school with differentiated courses at the secondary level for all; the European tendency is in the direction of an organization of schools on a functional basis.

Private schools. The place of private schools in a national system of education must be determined in the light of the meaning of nationalism. If the emphasis is placed upon rigid conformity and an authoritarian view of government, then private schools will either be prohibited or permitted only under certain sanctions and compelled, either directly by law or indirectly through pressure of state examinations and the privileges dependent on them, to adopt the same standards and practices as the public schools. In either case the assumption is that the State has discovered an ideal and unvarying pattern of nationalism and of culture on which nationalism is based. Such systems fail to give play to the great variety of forces which underlie national life. If, however, private initiative is encouraged and justified because it affords means for variety of practices, for experimentation, for the free expression of aims and ideals of different groups, whether religious or secular, then private schools must be welcomed in the interests of that progress which comes from differentiation. Private schools cannot be exempted from the obligation of meeting the same standards as public schools in respect to the hygienic character of their buildings and equipment, and the qualifications, moral and professional, of their teachers; such requirements imply that private schools should be registered and open to inspection, in the interests, not of standardization, but of the public which uses them. Freedom beyond these requirements imposes on the private schools a certain responsibility, social and educational, for the contribution which they undertake to make to national welfare. Even when the time comes, as it surely must, when the public schools of a national system will enjoy a larger measure of freedom for experimentation than they enjoy at present, and when the traditional lockstep of standardization disappears, private initiative in education will still continue to justify its claim to recognition in the interests of variety and differentiation. The real danger in private education lies not in any departures from standard practices but in its development of class distinctions, in the cult of exclusive and snobbish attitudes in their pupils; such a danger, which even a democratic system like that of the United States shows to be ever present, may be obviated either by requiring a common preparation for all teachers, whether in public or in private schools, or by the maintenance of such standards that good public schools will drive out poor private schools, a reversal, as it were, of Gresham's Law.

Social services and education. The organization of national systems of education involves more than the mere provision of schools. It must include the provision of such services as will enable the pupils to derive the greatest profit from their attendance at school. A pupil who comes to school inadequately fed or clothed is at once at a disadvantage, socially and scholastically; a pupil who is in poor health is not only a menace to his fellow-pupils, but is likely to find his school work burdensome and on the whole to fail to use the opportunities placed at his disposal. Frequent absences from school, it is beginning to be generally recognized, are due to ill-health in the main rather than to delinquency. More attention has, however, been devoted to compelling delinquents or truants to attend school than to the creation of those services which will promote good health. The importance of physical well-being has long been recognized by the inclusion of some form of physical training or the provision of facilities for games and sports as a regular part of an educational program; lessons in health and hygiene, although not so widespread as physical training, have been provided with the same end in view. Beyond these measures, however, both national and educational welfare demand the provision not only of remedial but of preventive measures which will ensure a sound mind in a sound body. This end can only be promoted by a system of medical inspection, and, as experience has proved, of medical treatment and the provision of clinics, and a follow-up system which will link the school to the home and educate parents as well as children. The same responsibility of the school for the health of the child extends to the provision of meals in necessitous cases. The objection, which was at one time more prevalent than at present, that such measures are socialistic or pauperizing, is no more valid here than in the provision of public education. Apart from their contribution to national welfare, such health services, where systematically organized, have made important contributions to the solution of many difficulties attending the educational progress of children; it was no accident, for example, that the existence of many of the instructional problems which have since been taken over by psychologists were first revealed in England by school medical officers. The introduction of medical inspection has led to the provision of special services, not only for defective but also for normal children — open-air schools, open-air activities, holiday camps, special schools for physically defective, and the segregation of the mentally defective.

The change in emphasis from teaching subjects to teaching the child, the outstanding characteristic of current educational theory, has brought with it an increasing interest in the mental growth of the child and with it a more intensive study of the specific difficulties which present themselves in the process of instruction. Already psychological clinics have begun to be established to deal with what are known as problem children. The probability is that out of this small beginning more widespread provision will be made for the school psychologist. It may be expected that a completely organized system of education will include, besides the social services, the services of experts in the scientific aspects and that both services will link the school more closely with the home, a movement with which the development of parents' associations and parental education, which are also in their initial stages, will be associated. A better and more scientific understanding of the child will give reality and concreteness to the demand for better adaptation of education and instruction to the child as an individual. Educational and vocational guidance may in time be so well developed that the traditional test of an education, the examination, will lose some of the importance which has been attached to it. Although it is doubtful whether a science of education will ever be as accurate and infallible as its proponents claim, its further development and refinement are the essential bases for the organization of a system of education in which each pupil will find the school and the instruction best suited to his abilities. Up to the present the possibilities of such an aid to a soundly organized system have been recognized only in France where the creation of a National Bureau of Selection and Distribution of pupils has been advocated as a part of the movement for the *école unique*.[1]

1. ENGLAND

Historical development. The provision of education in England still bears the marks of the historical development of its constituent parts. It thus represents a blend of public and private schools, of denominational and non-sectarian schools, of maintained, aided, and unaided schools, and of overlapping of functions. From the point of view of organization English education is characterized by lack of system, which has resulted from the traditional attitude to the relation of the State to education[2] and to the English reluctance to disturb vested interests which have originated in the activities of well-recognized groups and voluntary agencies. It was not until the passage of the Education Act of 1902 that any attempt was made to reduce the great variety of schools to some system, but much still remained to be done and the task became more complicated with the development of new types of schools which were established to meet new needs. As a result of the *Report on the Education of the Adolescent* (the *Hadow Report* of 1926), another movement for systematization began which has not yet been achieved.

Elementary education began to be developed in the nineteenth century through the efforts of voluntary organizations, of which the most important were the National Society for Promoting the Education of the Poor in the Principles of the Established Church and the British and Foreign School Society. To these, other organizations, local and national, denominational and non-sectarian, were added. It was not until 1833 that Parliament made its first grant for education, which was distributed first through the two leading societies and later through others. The practice of aiding elementary education by means of grants led in 1839 to the creation of a Committee of the Privy Council to supervise their distribution. The further

---

[1] See the annual *Rapport fait au Nom de la Commission des Finances chargée d'examiner le Projet de Loi portant Fixation du Budget Général*, issued since 1924 under the chairmanship of M. Ducos.

[2] See Chapter III.

expansion of elementary education for children whose parents supported themselves by manual labor was stimulated by the Revised Code of 1861, which introduced the vicious "payment by results" system. The recognition of the inadequate supply of schools through voluntary effort and the extension of the suffrage led in 1870 to the enactment of the Elementary Education Act which established a compulsory local rate for education to supply deficiencies not met by voluntary agencies, created school boards, and introduced the principle of compulsory attendance. The Act of 1870 represents the first movement toward a national system of education. Infant schools, which had developed independently of elementary education and were private or public and separate or a constituent part of elementary schools, were now incorporated as a part of elementary education. The Act did not disturb the existing voluntary schools supported by government grants, but set up side by side with them board schools provided by local rates and aided by government grants. Both voluntary and board schools were intended for children of the working classes; those who could afford it sent their children to private schools, not controlled or supervised by any public authority.

Secondary education through the greater part of the nineteenth century was provided by private effort. It was not until 1861 that the Government displayed any interest in secondary education by the appointment of the Clarendon Commission to inquire into the nine "Great Public Schools," followed in 1864 by the Taunton or Schools Inquiry Commission. The second Commission revealed the inadequacy and chaotic nature of the existing provision of secondary education and recommended the creation of local authorities empowered to provide secondary schools out of local rates. Before a third Commission, the Bryce Commission, was appointed in 1894, the situation had already become more complicated in several directions. The elementary schools had begun to expand their curricula and offer secondary school subjects to "ex-Standard" pupils; in some localities "higher grade elementary schools" were established giving a form of lower secondary education. Under the stimulus of grants from the Science and Art Department, created in 1852, organized science schools at the secondary level had begun to be established in 1862 and to increase in numbers.

By the Technical Instruction Act (1889) and the Local Taxation

Act (1890) the county and county borough councils which had been created in 1888 were given power to levy a small tax and to support various forms of technical and secondary education, evening and continuation classes, which had already developed extensively with support from the Science and Art Department, and the training of elementary school teachers. The result of these varied activities was to provide England with facilities for post-elementary education, but still inadequate, unarticulated, and uncoördinated into a system.

The preparation of teachers for elementary schools showed the same variety of development as elementary and secondary education. Training colleges, connected almost invariably with some denominational education association, had begun to be established after 1839. In 1846 a system of preparing elementary teachers through a period of apprenticeship, the pupil-teacher system, was introduced as an improvement of the monitorial plan. A third system of preparing teachers for elementary schools was introduced in 1890 with the establishment of education departments in universities and university colleges. Provision for the preparation of secondary school teachers, although advocated by the Commissions, was practically nonexistent.

Social services for the welfare of school pupils were provided here and there by the benevolent efforts of voluntary organizations, but were in no way organized at public expense as an essential part of the school systems. It was not until the last decade of the century, by laws passed in 1893 and 1899, that school boards were authorized to provide for the elementary education of blind, deaf and dumb, defective, and epileptic children.

The chaos resulting from the existence of overlapping and even competing authorities, local and national, and of the uncoördinated provision of schools led to the creation in 1899 of a national Board of Education and the passage of the Education Act in 1902. The first measure concentrated all the national education authorities in a single board; the second set up local authorities "to consider the educational needs of their areas and take such steps as seem to them desirable, after consultation with the Board of Education, to supply or aid the supply of education other than elementary and *to promote the general coördination of all forms of education.*" This involved the coördination of denominational or voluntary and public elementary schools, of the various types of secondary education, and technical education. Private education and private schools remained unaffected except by the indirect effect of the regulations for compulsory school attendance.

The opportunity for coördination was now made available by law, but time was needed to overcome certain prejudices which had accumulated against a public system of education and the expansion of facilities to other than the well-to-do. Meanwhile, the studies of the educational needs of the various areas revealed the desirability of new types of schools as well as defects in the existing type. At the lower end it was discovered that large numbers of pupils below the age of five were attending schools without adequate provision suited to their ages. There was overlapping between elementary and secondary schools, while a class of pupils was growing up who could profit from continued education but could not undertake a full secondary education. New schools — the central school and a variety of trade and junior and senior technical and commercial schools — were established and still further aggravated the problem of articulation. The Act of 1918 again drew the attention of the local authorities to their responsibility for providing for the progressive development and comprehensive organization of education in their areas "with a view to the establishment of a national system of public education available for all persons capable of profiting thereby."

The school system. Despite the provisions of the Act of 1918, the school system continues to be marked by variety, due not only to the coexistence of private schools but also to the differences in the powers assigned to local authorities according to their size and to the participation of denominational groups in the supply of schools. The smaller authorities (the urban districts and the municipal boroughs), known as Part III authorities, are restricted to the provision of nursery schools and elementary education only, but they may coöperate with the larger, Part II authorities (counties and county boroughs), for the provision of education beyond the elementary stage.[1] The Part II authorities may provide any type of education from the nursery school up to adult education and may assist in the provision of higher education either by grants to universities and university colleges or by the award of scholarships to students attending them.

The system of public schools accordingly begins with the nursery

[1] On the powers of local authorities, see Chapter V.

school for children between the ages of two and five. Although the Education Acts permit the establishment of nursery schools at public expense, the number provided by public authorities in 1930 was only twenty-two, the rest of the total of forty-three being maintained with aid from the Board of Education by voluntary bodies.[1] As a result of a Joint Circular issued in December, 1929, by the Minister of Health and the Board of Education, the growth of the movement was encouraged; the financial emergency, however, prevented the establishment of a large number of new schools which were proposed. The nursery school movement has exercised a great influence on the reorganization of the work provided for children who enter the elementary schools before the age of compulsory attendance. In 1931 there were enrolled in the public elementary schools of England and Wales 159,335 children under the age of five, despite a movement which began some time ago to exclude them. The nursery school idea has, however, furnished a justification for their retention, and in many schools (statistics are not available) the classes for very young children have been organized as nursery classes conducted on the principles underlying the nursery school.

Compulsory attendance begins at the age of five, which may by local by-law be delayed to six, and continues up to the age of fourteen. No pupil may leave school until the end of the term in which he reaches his fourteenth birthday. All exemptions from the compulsory attendance requirement were abolished by the Education Act of 1918. The majority of the children attend public elementary schools. Since 1902 denominational (also known as voluntary or non-provided) schools constitute a part of the provision for public elementary education.

There are thus two types of public elementary schools, the non-provided schools, so called because the buildings are not provided by a public authority but by trustees or managers of some religious denomination, and provided schools. In the former sectarian religious instruction is given as a regular part of the instruction and the managers have a voice in the selection of the teachers; in the provided schools "no religious catechism or religious formulary which is distinctive of any particular denomination is to be taught," according

[1] According to the *Times Educational Supplement*, July 16, 1932, the Parliamentary Secretary to the Board of Education announced that there were fifty-six nursery schools recognized by the Board and fifteen additional schools had been approved to be established.

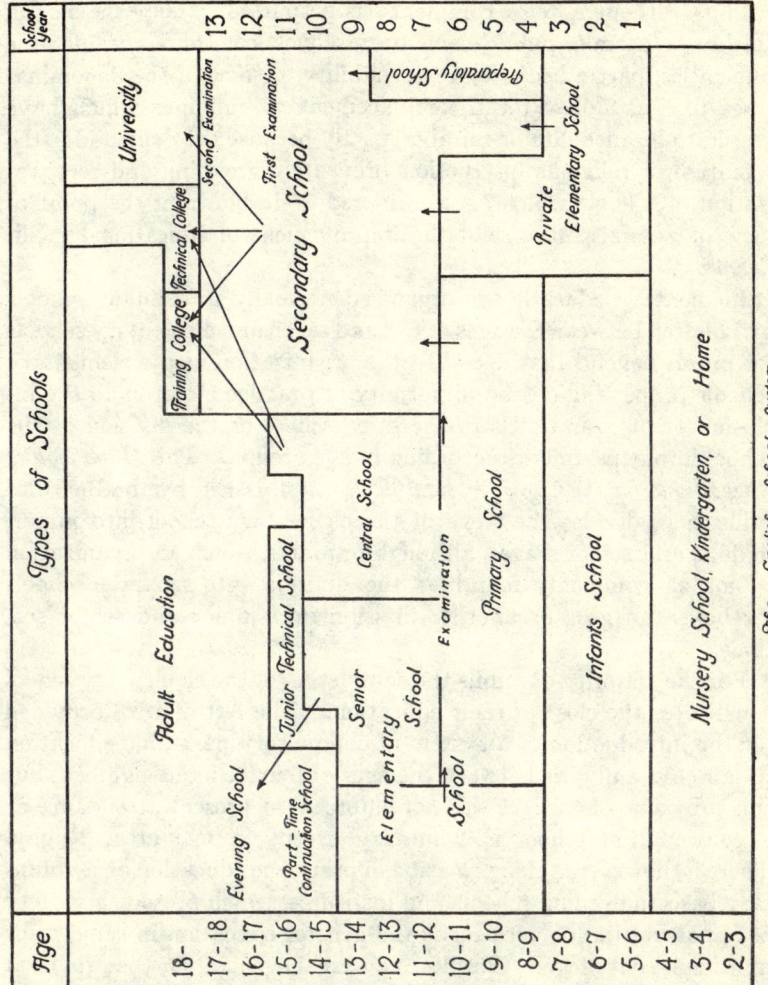

to the famous Cowper-Temple clause of the Act of 1870, but "Bible reading without note or comment" is permitted. The existence of this dual system of public elementary schools has led to considerable difficulties, partly because of the inability of some of the denominations to find money for the replacement of buildings which have ceased to be adequate or suitable, partly because the demand for the retention of religious instruction prevents regrouping and reorganization of schools which are considered desirable from the point of view of administration and the improvement of educational facilities.

Elementary education is organized normally into infant schools for children between the ages of five and seven and elementary schools for pupils beyond that age. In the organization of the elementary schools proper there is no uniformity of practice either as to the inclusion of boys and girls in the same school or the division of the school into departments according to age groups. The *Handbook of Suggestions for the Consideration of Teachers*, issued by the Board of Education, divides the work of the elementary school into junior, middle, and senior stages, although in practice such an organization is not as commonly found as the division into separate schools for boys and girls or another division into junior and senior sections.

For the majority of pupils the completion of the elementary school constitutes the close of their education. The Act of 1918 provided for the introduction of a system of compulsory part-time education for all boys and girls between the ages of fourteen and eighteen, but this provision of the Act was not enforced; at present attendance at a continuation school is voluntary except in one area, Rugby. There is, however, a rich provision of part-time education on a voluntary basis in evening schools and institutes, which provide a variety of opportunities for vocational and general education in some cases up to university level. Besides the formal agencies for the provision of education, England offers a wider variety of adult education than any other country, including provisions by universities, the Workers' Educational Association which coöperates with the universities, the Educational Settlements Association, the Coöperative Union, the Young Men's Christian Association, Working Men's Clubs, the National Adult School Union, the National Council of Labor Unions, Women's Institutes, Rural Community Councils, and a large number of facilities, educational and recreational, organized by local education authorities and voluntary agencies.[1]

For the minority an opportunity is afforded for advancement either to a central or to a secondary school. The practice varies in different parts of the country, but pupils who have completed four or five years of the elementary school and are about eleven years of age (the age range varies from eleven to thirteen) are submitted to a general examination, commonly known as the free place examination; pupils of poor ability may on the advice of the headmasters of their schools be withheld from the examination. As a rule the examination is conducted by boards which include representatives of the administrative officers, and of elementary and secondary school teachers, and consists of written and oral tests. The subjects of these tests include always English and arithmetic and may in addition include history and geography, dictation and spelling, and nature study. An increasing number of authorities are beginning to employ intelligence tests, but these are always supplementary to the written and oral tests. The school records are taken into account in a large number of the examinations. Successful candidates are given an opportunity of entering a central school which is free, or a secondary school without payment of fees. Since admission to such schools requires an undertaking from parents that they will not withdraw their children until the end of four years, and because attendance at such schools involves in some cases additional expenses for books, clothing, travel, and other incidentals, as well as loss of wages, many parents feel unable to allow their children to avail themselves of the opportunity which they have gained. In any case the selection is rigorous, not because of the difficulty of the examinations so much as on account of the lack of accommodation in central and secondary schools at present. Under the provisions of the Education Act of 1918, local authorities may grant maintenance allowances to children and young persons (the English term for boys and girls between the ages of fourteen and eighteen) varying in amount with their ages and the stage of education which they pursue. In addition to maintenance allowances local authorities have established generous systems of scholarship awards which are available in open competition to the ablest pupils at all levels of education after the elementary stage.

[1] For a summary of adult education activities and a bibliography see the *International Handbook of Adult Education* (London, 1929).

The central school is an institution which arose out of a desire to provide for pupils in the elementary schools an opportunity for a form of education which, while lower than the secondary, would be more advanced and more adapted to their needs than the elementary; in other words, it was to be a school in which both general and special training would be given without offering specific vocational courses. Such schools were established about 1910 in London, Manchester, and other cities; the term "central school" was employed to indicate that the school was intended to serve a number of elementary schools in its neighborhood. Central schools offer general, industrial, commercial for boys and girls and domestic arts courses and courses in women's trades for girls and are sufficiently flexible to make possible adjustments to local needs. The length of the courses is four years; in some schools pupils may remain for an additional year. The early success of this type of school stimulated the authors of the Education Act of 1918 to require advanced instruction of a practical character in the senior classes of the elementary schools. Out of this requirement there developed in one direction central classes for practical work used by a number of elementary schools in common and a rapidly increasing number of central schools, admission to which is selective. Abler pupils from central schools may on completing their course continue to a secondary or a technical school.

One of the most striking features in the development of English education has been the increase in the provision of secondary schools. With few exceptions these schools charge fees, but in order to qualify for grants from the Board of Education they are required to admit each year twenty-five per cent of their pupils free of tuition. This provision applies not only to schools which are provided by local authorities at public expense, but also to private schools which are not run for profit and wish to qualify for the Board's grants. In actual practice the percentage of free places prescribed by the Board's regulations were exceeded in 1931 when it had risen to 44.3 per cent for the whole country. Free places are awarded on the basis of the free place examination; fee payers may also be admitted through this examination, but normally there is a separate examination which by many is regarded as of lower standard. The term "secondary school" has not become standardized in respect to the age of beginning secondary work proper or to the length of the course. There are many schools, particularly for girls, which admit pupils to the kindergarten stage and keep them until they are ready to proceed to a university; while many boys' schools admit pupils from private elementary schools at the age of nine or ten. From the point of view of the *Regulations for Secondary Schools* issued by the Board of Education, secondary education extends from about the age of twelve to the age of eighteen, the six year course being divided into two periods of four and two years respectively. The close of the four year period is marked by the First Examination and of the two year period by the Second or Higher Examination conducted by a number of examination boards.[1] Secondary education is devoted to imparting a general liberal education in languages, history and geography, science and mathematics, music and art.

For those pupils who have not been able to proceed to a central or to a secondary school, or who have remained in the elementary school until the end of the course another opportunity for full-time education has been made available in the increased provision of facilities for vocational training. This is offered in junior and senior technical schools, junior and senior commercial schools, domestic science schools, schools for arts and crafts, and art schools. The technical schools offer the greatest variety of courses; some are monotechnic, many are polytechnic. In some important industrial centers advanced work is offered at the university level, but does not lead, except in one instance, to a university degree. The other forms of vocational training — commerce and domestic science — are not as widely developed as the technical. Agricultural education, which, with minor exceptions, is the only branch of education conducted under the supervision of a national agency other than the Board of Education, is under the control of the Ministry of Agriculture which has stimulated the establishment of agricultural schools at different levels, full-time and part-time, by the county authorities. Fees are charged in all types of vocational schools, but as in the case of other branches of education a system of scholarships is available for students of ability.

Beyond the secondary schools pupils may proceed to training colleges for the preparation of elementary school teachers or to universities and university colleges. The training colleges are provided by

[1] See Chapter VIII.

voluntary organizations, chiefly denominational, and by local education authorities with aid from the Board of Education. The universities and university colleges are private institutions and include besides the Universities of Oxford and Cambridge the Universities of London, Manchester, Liverpool, Leeds, Sheffield, Birmingham, Bristol, Reading, and Durham, and the University Colleges at Nottingham, Southampton, Exeter, Hull, and Leicester. These institutions are maintained by income from endowments, fees, and government grants paid through the Universities Grants Committee. Access to the universities has always been open to poor but able students through scholarships obtained in open conditions or provided by endowments for the purpose in a large number of secondary schools. Since 1902 an extensive system of scholarships tenable in universities and colleges have been provided by county and county borough authorities for education, and since 1918 the Board of Education awards two hundred "State" scholarships to boys and girls on the basis of the second or higher certificate examination.

Private education. Side by side with the system of schools provided and maintained by the local authorities with financial aid from the Board of Education, there is an extensive supply of private schools. The number of such schools and of pupils enrolled in them is not available, since the establishment of private schools is not subject to any governmental control. It was not until 1930 that an official committee was appointed to inquire into the extent and efficiency of private education. Under the provisions of the Education Acts the Board of Education and local authorities are legally entitled to inspect private schools which receive pupils within the ages of compulsory attendance, since the law places upon parents the responsibility for the efficient education of their children during this period. It is doubtful whether this indirect grant of the right to inspect private schools has been used, although from time to time parents who educate their children at home have been cited in court to prove that such education is efficient. In all types of private schools other influences are beginning to affect their quality; under the regulations for the superannuation of teachers a limited number of years spent in efficient private schools may be considered as part of the years of service which may be counted for an allowance; similarly, one of the conditions for the registration of teachers in the Royal Society of Teachers (formerly the Teachers' Registration Council) is that applicants must have had a number of years of experience in efficient schools. Both requirements virtually compel private schools to invite inspection by a recognized authority if they wish to secure competent teachers. The new salary scales which offer an attractive career to teachers in public schools exercise the same influence.

Children may accordingly be educated at home by parents, governesses, or tutors, or may be sent to day or boarding schools, depending upon their ages. The supply of private schools ranges from the small kindergarten or primary school to the "public" schools; some are run for the profit of the proprietor; others are administered by boards of governors and may, if they choose, qualify for the grants made by the Board of Education for purposes of secondary education. There is further a great range in quality of education and instruction offered. For young children there are available kindergartens and primary schools for boys or girls or mixed, leading up to entrance to a secondary school, at the age of nine or ten. For boys there have been established a large number of preparatory schools, which admit pupils at the age of eight or nine and prepare them for the entrance examination to one of the "public" schools five years later. The curriculum of the preparatory schools is secondary in character, so that with the public schools they offer a combined secondary course of nine or ten years. These schools are usually small in size, charge fees, and may, at their option be inspected by the Board of Education. The "public" schools for boys, which include a wide range of secondary schools, mostly boarding schools, are those schools which are modeled on the Great Public Schools, such as Eton, Harrow, Winchester, Rugby, Shrewsbury, Charterhouse, and Westminster. The definition of "public" school has, however, been so broadened that there are at present about two hundred schools which are listed in the *Public Schools Yearbook*. Schools of a similar type have begun to be established for girls.

In general private education serves a number of purposes. In the first place, it caters to class distinctions, a certain desire for exclusiveness and vanity which have perpetuated a tradition developed at the time when schools provided at public expense were intended for children of the laboring classes, an association which has carried over to some extent in the attitude toward public secondary schools. Secondly, it is founded on the widespread opinion that "public" schools, because they are boarding schools, offer a type of character education which cannot be equaled in day schools. Finally, private education, it is recognized, has in it the possibility of experimentation, a fact which cannot be denied. Not only the great experiment of Sanderson at Oundle School, and the experiments in the teaching of languages, ancient and modern, by Rouse at the Perse School, but a large number of innovations in the teaching of sciences and history stand to the credit of the "public" schools. In addition there are schools, like Bedales and Abbotsholme and many more recently established schools, which have made and are making important contributions in the field of the new or progressive education. This does not mean that private schools alone can be looked to as centers for novel developments in education, but the freedom from inspection and the *Regulations* of the Board of Education, flexible though they may be, gives them an opportunity not generally enjoyed by public schools. Further, a school which is avowedly experimental tends to secure the support and patronage of groups which are interested in progressive methods in education. The absence of any kind of control or supervision from without, except the voluntary invitation of inspection and submission of pupils to the test of recognized examinations, has led to the establishment of a large number of private schools which an undiscriminating public selects for no other reason than that they are private. Too many schools which would be found to fall below the standard of elementary or secondary schools are allowed to flourish under the general pleas that private education should be recognized as potential centers of experimentation.

The Committee appointed to inquire into schools not in receipt of public funds — that is, private schools — issued its report in May, 1932. The Committee recommended that proprietors of private schools should be required to register their schools with the local education authorities annually, giving certain information. Such schools should be supervised through inspection, either by the Board of Education or the local authority at the option of the proprietors, and must meet certain minimum requirements in fundamental subjects and in regard to the premises. The Committee further recommended that unsatisfactory schools might be given six months' notice in which to improve conditions or to close; cases of non-compliance with such orders should be referred to the courts of summary jurisdiction. Local education authorities should discover the number of private schools in their areas, enforce registration, submit information to the Board of Education, inspect schools unless the Board is invited to do so, and take proceedings against schools failing to register. The Committee estimated that there are in England 10,000 private schools with 400,000 pupils between the ages of five and fourteen and that of these only 1,300 have been inspected by the Board of Education and 1,000 by the local authorities; very few were ever reinspected. It will be noted that the Committee refrains from suggesting standardization or interference with the autonomy of private schools and limits itself to recommending registration and inspection to secure suitable premises and a satisfactory minimum of instruction.

The danger inherent in a system of private education of setting up class distinctions and of failing to develop social attitudes and sympathies has been recognized by a few leaders in "public" schools, but, except for an experimental camp for pupils from "public" schools and from public elementary schools, little has been done to obviate it.

Movement for reorganization of the public system. The complicated character of the existing provision of public education has been generally recognized. It has been realized that from the social point of view the present system is unjust since it does not provide adequate educational opportunities for all, and that from the psychological point of view it is unsound, since it is not adequately adapted to different age levels of the pupils. The problem of reorganization became an issue in the Parliamentary election in May, 1929; the three parties — Conservative, Liberal, Labor — agreed on the importance of its immediate solution. The issue was clearly summarized by Mr. Stanley Baldwin in a message on *A New Step in Education* which he addressed during the election campaign to all engaged in the work of education:

> One of the strongest bonds of union between men is a common education, and England has been the poorer that in her national system of schooling she has not in the past fostered this fellowship of mind. The classification of our schools has been on the lines of social rather than educational distinctions; a youth's school badge has been his social label.[1]

This statement summarized a movement which had already begun during the War for the extension of educational opportunities. The

---

[1] For the message in full and for the programs of the three political parties see the *Educational Yearbook, 1928,* of the International Institute of Teachers College, Columbia University, pp. 39 ff. (New York, 1929).

demand for the provision of secondary education for all and the abolition of what were regarded as substitutes for secondary education, sponsored chiefly but not entirely by the Labor group, stimulated a general inquiry into the education of the adolescent which was entrusted to the Consultative Committee of the Board of Education in 1924. The terms of reference indicated, however, that it was the intention of the Board of Education, which framed them, to leave secondary education undisturbed and to limit the inquiry to the consideration of plans for reorganization outside of the existing provision of secondary education. The terms of reference were as follows:

(1) To consider and report upon the organization, objective, and curriculum of courses of study for children who will remain in full-time attendance at schools, other than secondary schools, up to the age of fifteen, regard being had on the one hand to the requirements of a good general education and the desirability of providing a reasonable variety of curriculum, so far as is practicable, for children of varying tastes and abilities, and on the other to the probable occupations of the pupils in commerce, industry, and agriculture.

(2) Incidentally thereto, to advise as to the arrangements which should be made (*a*) for testing the attainments of the pupils at the end of their course; (*b*) for facilitating in suitable cases the transfer of individual pupils to secondary schools at an age above the normal age of admission.

The Consultative Committee issued its *Report on the Education of the Adolescent* (more frequently referred to as the *Hadow Report*) in 1926. The chief recommendations of the *Report* were (1) that primary education should be regarded as ending at about the age of eleven plus, and that all children should then go forward to some form of post-primary education; (2) that this second stage should as far as possible be organized as a single whole within which there should be variety of types; and (3) that legislation should be passed fixing as from 1932 the age of fifteen years as that to which attendance at school should be obligatory. The general trend of policy contemplating a reorganization of school types at the age of eleven plus had already been outlined in a circular issued by the Board of Education in January, 1925. The reorganization contemplated in the *Report* of the Consultative Committee indicated a break at about the age of eleven, which would mark the close of primary education; at this stage opportunities would be opened to pupils to proceed to secondary schools, which the Committee proposed to call "grammar schools," or to "senior" schools, referred to in the *Report* as "modern schools," both selective and non-selective, or to other types of schools such as the junior technical schools. In a word, the essence of the *Report* was a proposal for a common basis for all children in the publicly provided schools up to the age of eleven, followed by a variety of schools adapted to the different capacities and probable needs of boys and girls at the adolescent stage. The door to educational advancement was to be left open so that pupils could be transferred at all times to schools best adapted to their abilities.

There was thus to be provided for all children some form of postprimary education, which would be given in a variety of four-year courses if compulsory school attendance were extended to the age of fifteen. The proposal for the extension of school age for all up to fifteen was accepted without criticism except by a small group of reactionaries. That such an extension was desirable, not only on educational but on social and economic grounds, was recognized in view of the large number of unemployed young persons. At the close of 1929, the Minister of Education, Sir Charles Trevelyan, in the Labor Government, introduced a bill to extend the compulsory age limit to fifteen by April, 1931. A number of difficulties — such as uncertainty as to the probable requirement of schools and teachers owing to the abnormal fluctuations in the birth-rate since 1918 and the adjustment of the claims of denominational schools — led to the withdrawal of the bill and the substitution of another in 1930. The second bill (the School Attendance Bill) was passed by the House of Commons early in 1931, subject, however, to an amendment that the bill should not go into effect until the enactment of another bill to provide aid to denominational groups for the building of new schools. The rejection of the School Attendance Bill by the House of Lords and the subsequent political and economic crises through which England passed in 1931 have postponed further action.

Despite the postponement of legislative action, however, considerable progress has already been made in the reorganization of the system and in the establishment of senior schools by a number of local education authorities encouraged by a pamphlet issued by the Board of Education in 1928 on *The New Prospect in Education*. The Board stated the problem to be

that of the adaptation of the existing elementary school system so that all the older children, not a selected few, may receive an education suited to their age and special needs, practical in the broadest sense and so organized as to allow for classification and differentiation between pupils of different types of capacity and different aptitudes.

The Board recommended that all children be transferred to a post-primary school at the age of eleven irrespective of their scholastic attainments on the principle that

all the evidence shows that such a child (i.e., who has failed to reach the standard normal to his age) will develop most rapidly if he is placed with other children of his own age in conditions which allow suitable special provision to be made for him.

The bases upon which the new schools are to be built up are variety and differentiation for

if we cannot adjust our curricula so that they meet these varying needs, the compulsory attendance of the child at school becomes a mere constraint, which may well prejudice him for all time against educational influences.

Many authorities included some form of reorganization along the line outlined by the Board in the schemes prepared for the triennial period, 1930–33. Since the Education Act, 1918, empowers local authorities to raise the age of compulsory attendance to fifteen by local by-law, it is not necessary for them to wait for governmental legislation. The reorganization involves coöperation with the denominational groups and an adjustment of the difficulties inherent in the dual system (voluntary and council) of schools, the provision of facilities for travel and of maintenance allowances, and the development of appropriate courses as well as the elaboration of methods of selection and distribution of pupils in schools best suited to their abilities and aptitudes. There will thus be developed a body of experience which, when the time comes, will mean the speedy enactment of the proposed School Attendance Bill. In the meantime the economic crisis of the latter part of 1931 and the retrenchment in public expenditures which it made imperative checked further progress with plans for reorganization.

The recommendations of the *Hadow Report* and the Board's pamphlet on *The New Prospect in Education* both emphasized a break at about the age of eleven and directed attention to the primary school which is to constitute the common foundation for the reorganized school system. In 1928 the Consultative Committee was requested "to inquire and report as to the courses of study suitable for children (other than children in infants' departments) up to the age of eleven in elementary schools, with special reference to children in rural areas." The Committee issued its *Report on the Primary School* in 1931, in which one of the significant features is the adoption of the term "primary school" for education up to the age of eleven, and "secondary" for education from the age of eleven till the end of school life, significant because, unlike the Board in its pamphlet on *The New Prospect*, the Consultative Committee definitely regards all types of post-primary education as secondary in character but differentiated according to the abilities and aptitudes of the pupils. Primary education according to the *Report* falls into two stages, one extending up to the age of seven plus, and the other up to the age of eleven plus; wherever possible the *Report* recommends that the first stage be given separately in infant schools or departments, coöperating closely with the primary schools which in turn should coöperate through periodical conferences with secondary schools of different types. The transition from infant to primary schools should be easy and gradual, a recommendation which means that teachers of lower classes in the latter should be familiar with infant school methods. In rural schools it is desirable that a responsible assistant take charge of the infants. Normally primary schools will be "mixed" or coeducational, with the proviso that the differing needs of boys and girls will be taken care of in such matters as physical education.

When fully developed — and the development will depend more on economic conditions than on the readiness of educators and the public to adopt the plans for reorganization — the English system of education will become more truly national in the sense of providing a carefully articulated organization of schools than ever before in its history. It will continue to consist of both public and private schools but it is not improbable that as a result of the present inquiry into the latter there will be introduced some form of external supervision which will ensure the quality of private education rather than interfere with its organization or internal purposes. The public system will begin with nursery schools, which will be increased in numbers, followed by infant schools leading their pupils at the age of seven into primary schools. The primary schools will keep the pupils up to the age of eleven, when they will be redistributed according to ability and aptitudes into a variety of schools at the secondary level including non-selective and selective schools and secondary schools proper. At the age of fifteen the majority of pupils will complete their full-time education and continue voluntarily in some form of part-time education in continuation and evening schools; the minority will continue in the secondary schools or in some other form of full-time further education, technical or vocational. The system will be crowned by universities, university colleges, technical colleges, and a varied provision of adult education. As contrasted with the American system, the English tendency at the secondary level is in the direction of a functional rather than a unitary organization. From the American point of view such an organization would be criticized as insufficiently democratic and as setting up class education, because of the separation of the pupils into distinct groups at so early an age as eleven. Apart from the question whether democratic institutions are conserved by the educational juxtaposition of pupils in the same schools, the proposed organization imposes on English educators the duty, which is generally recognized in law and in theory, that no pupil shall be debarred from that education by which he is most capable of profiting. This will mean an increase in the provision of maintenance grants [1] and scholarships and ultimately the abolition of fees in secondary schools, which would not involve a serious burden, since nearly half of the pupils now enrolled enjoy free places; a small number of authorities have already abolished fees. There is, however, another task which will be imposed upon the authorities and which is more difficult, and that is to devise methods for discovering abilities and aptitudes on the basis of which the right pupils will be in the right school, a task which even American practice in the cosmopolitan high schools proves not to be as simple as advocates of tests and measurements appear to assume.

Social service and education. No feature in the development of a national system of education has been more striking than the provision in England of those social services which are essential to the successful conduct of education. As is usual in England, much had already been done by voluntary agencies for the amelioration of bad conditions affecting the welfare of school children before it was recognized that such work should be undertaken as a public duty and at public expense. The first step was the Education (Provision of Meals) Act, 1906, which empowered local education authorities to provide meals for necessitous children on the ground that a hungry

[1] An increase in the provision of maintenance grants was proposed in the School Attendance Bill which was passed by the House of Commons in 1931.

child cannot profit from the work of the school. In 1930 about half of the authorities (153 out of 317) provided free meals, including the provision of milk to children reported by their teachers and by welfare workers as necessitous cases. The number of children who avail themselves of this provision each year fluctuates with the conditions of the employment market. A very important contribution of this provision has been the education both of children and parents in the selection of suitable diets; it also had another effect in directing attention to the widespread prevalence of malnutrition, which became one of the tasks of school medical inspection, when it was introduced in the following year, to correct.

School medical officers were first appointed in London in 1890 and in Bradford in 1893, but the importance for educational progress and national welfare of a more general system of school medical inspection was not recognized until after the question was brought to public notice by the reports of the Royal Commission on Physical Training in Scotland (1903), and of an Interdepartmental Committee on Physical Deterioration (1904) and by the Second International Congress on School Hygiene (1907). The two reports agreed in recommending the appointment of school medical officers, the development of physical training, and the feeding of school children. These recommendations were further supplemented and confirmed by the report of the Interdepartmental Committee on Medical Inspection and Feeding of Children in Public Elementary Schools (1905). In 1907 the Education (Administrative Provisions) Act imposed on the local education authorities the duty of providing for the medical inspection of children in elementary schools and gave them power to make arrangements for attending to their health and physical condition. The provision was immediately put into effect and has been rapidly expanded during the twenty-five years that it has been in effect. The system of school medical inspection is under the supervision of the medical department of the Board of Education directed by the Chief Medical Officer who is at the same time Chief Medical Officer of the Ministry of Health, which under the Ministry of Health Act, 1919, delegates that part of its work concerning schools to the Board of Education. The Chief Medical Officer of both Ministries thus serves as a liaison between the service which affects the health of the child and that which is devoted to the promotion of public health in general.

"The original reason for the introduction of a system of medical supervision of school children was that it might fit the children to receive the benefit from the education provided out of public money."[1] Under the present arrangements all children in the public elementary schools must be medically examined at least three times in their school career — at the time of entrance, at the age of eight, and at the age of twelve; some authorities have introduced a fourth examination in the term in which pupils expect to leave school. In addition, children who appear to need attention may be sent by teachers, parents, nurses, and attendance officers for a special examination. By the Education Act, 1918, local authorities were empowered to extend the system of medical inspection to children in nursery schools and in secondary schools; 143 out of the 147 local authorities for higher education provide inspection and 122 treatment. The success of the system has lain not so much in the discovery of the prevalence and distribution of defects and disease among children in school, but in stressing the primary importance of preventive measures through physical training, instruction in health and hygiene, and the education of parents.

The discovery of disease and defects, it was soon revealed, is inadequate without the provision of remedial measures. Ignorance, neglect, and inadequate provision of centers for treatment, readily accessible to parents, frequently rendered the work of the school medical officers nugatory. Voluntary workers, such as the care committees in London and elsewhere, school managers and teachers, gave information of available centers to parents, but often without adequate methods for following up the advice given. The Education Act, 1918, imposed on local authorities the duty of providing medical treatment; parents are expected to pay fees which are very low and which may be waived in necessitous cases. As a result of this measure a large number of clinics have been established. In another direction the work of the school medical service had been rounded out by the employment of school nurses to follow the children into their homes and to see that recommendations of the school medical officers were carried out.

School medical inspection revealed the existence of uncleanliness, malnutrition, skin diseases, defects of vision and hearing, diseases of

[1] *The Health of the School Child, Annual Report of the Chief Medical Officer of the Board of Education for the Year 1930*, p. 83.

the eye, ear, nose, and throat, enlarged tonsils and adenoids, heart disease, tuberculosis, nervous diseases, and deformities. Important contributions have been made to the study of the relation between physical well-being and school progress. The reports of the medical officers may be followed up by the school nurses on the one hand and on the other by the parents either through their own physicians or through the school clinics, of which 1741 have been established to take care of minor ailments — teeth, visual defects, enlarged tonsils and adenoids (operative), ringworm (X-rays), orthopedic cases, and cases needing artificial-light treatment.

A further extension of the work of medical inspection has been due to the growing recognition of differences among school children. Children who are handicapped physically or mentally have long been given special care. It is only recently that attention has been given to the mentally retarded and maladjusted children. To take care particularly of the latter, a small number of child guidance clinics have been established in London, Bath, and Liverpool, while others are being started elsewhere. Under the supervision of psychiatrists and psychologists the clinics are devoting their attention to cases of unexplained backwardness, nervousness, enuresis, misbehavior shown in general lack of control, and other difficulties which it is the province of mental hygienists to consider. The mentally retarded child was the subject of investigation by a recent Committee on Mental Deficiency which in its *Report* (1929) recommended measures to be adopted in the treatment of children of various grades of mental backwardness.

England has thus developed a system of school medical inspection which is probably the most comprehensive and widespread in the world. Taking up the services developed under the provisions of the Maternity and Child Welfare Act, 1918, which empowered local authorities to establish schemes for the welfare of expectant mothers and mothers in childbirth, and for the care of infants up to the age of five not attending school, the system follows the children through up to the age of eighteen so long as they are at school, although the work is as yet not carried out effectively in secondary schools. Since the majority leave school at fourteen, there is a gap between the system of school medical inspection and the National Health Insurance scheme to which wage-earners become eligible only at the age of sixteen. Such a system is cumulative in its effects; the large proportion of the parents of children now in school have themselves experienced some of its benefits and much of the original resistance to what was at one time regarded as state interference has now overcome. The improvement of medical and physical conditions in the school and the relations between the school and the home which the development of medical inspection has promoted has revealed that questions of school attendance are largely concerned with questions of the health of the child and has resulted in close coöperation between the school medical service and the work of attendance officers. There is still another contribution made to child welfare through the system of medical inspection in determining on the basis of physical examinations the fitness of children for employment on school days and for special forms of education as well as in recommending against entry into certain employments after leaving school.

As the system of school medical inspection developed, it directed attention to the importance of improving the organization of physical training and lessons in health and hygiene, and of providing special facilities for various types of physically or mentally defective children. Influenced largely by the study of the health of the child, the central and local authorities have coöperated in the development and use of playgrounds and playing-fields, of after-school recreation centers, of holiday camps, of open-air schools, of special schools for children so seriously handicapped, physically or mentally, that they cannot be adequately cared for in the ordinary schools, and of special classes in these schools for backward and retarded children.[1]

Employment of children. Closely associated with health problems is the employment of children which had been progressively but inadequately regulated until more general measures were imposed by the Education Act, 1918. The Act put an end to the system of half-time employment while still in school of children above the age of twelve, and restricted their employment to two hours on school days and Sundays — one hour before and one hour after school; the hours

---

[1] In 1930 there were employed in the school medical service 1301 school medical and assistant school medical officers, of whom 265 were full-time officers for school medical inspection, 667 were full-time officers of public health, and 369 were part-time officers. In addition 981 specialists (for ophthalmic, aural, anesthetic, X-ray, artificial light, and orthopedic work), and 741 school dentists (439 full-time) were employed. These were assisted by 5485 nurses (2326 district nurses, 1428 full-time school nurses, and 1734 part-time nurses). The total number of children examined was 2,739,297 (1,770,779 routine and 968,518 special cases) or 55.4 per cent of the average attendance. The number of clinics of various kinds provided by local education authorities was 1741.

of employment on Saturdays and holidays are controlled by local by-laws, which may also prohibit the employment of children in certain occupations. Street trading by boys under fifteen and by girls under sixteen and the employment of children under twelve in public entertainments of any kind were forbidden by the Act.

Children and young persons up to the age of seventeen who are habitual truants, or delinquents, or living in homes which are detrimental to their moral welfare, are subject to the provisions of the Children's Act, 1908. In an amendment to this Act introduced in the House of Commons in January, 1932, the age of criminal responsibility is raised to eight. Charges brought against such juveniles must be heard in courts distinct from the ordinary courts; wherever possible one or more women must be associated with the magistrate in trying cases against juveniles. The duty of juvenile courts is to consider the welfare of the children, to remove them from undesirable influences, and to provide proper measures for their training and education on healthy and constructive lines. Since 1908 juvenile courts have been established in London and other large centers. The courts may place youthful offenders under the supervision of probation officers or may commit them for terms up to the age of nineteen to day or residential industrial schools, or to reformatory schools which are similar institutions for adolescents. The amending bill proposes to change the name of industrial and reformatory schools to "approved schools," and permits the commitment of youthful offenders at the age of ten. The administration of the Children's Act is placed under the direction and supervision of the Secretary of State (Home Office) who after inspection may certificate industrial and reformatory schools.

Vocational guidance. The selection of suitable employment for boys and girls leaving school was for a long time conducted informally by teachers, headmasters, school managers, care committees, and other voluntary agencies. In 1910 the Board of Trade issued rules to regulate the relations between labor exchanges established in the previous year and juvenile applicants for employment. The Education (Choice of Employment) Act, passed in the same year, was followed by a memorandum issued by the Board of Trade and the Board of Education to promote coöperation between labor exchanges and local education authorities; where labor exchanges and special advisory committees had not been organized by the Board of Trade, the local education authorities were permitted to set up advisory committees of their own. A Departmental Committee, presided over by Lord Chelmsford and appointed to inquire into certain difficulties which had arisen as a result of the dual control by labor exchanges under the Ministry of Labor (the reorganized Board of Trade) and by advisory committees appointed by local education authorities, recommended that the latter be given the opportunity of assuming sole responsibility for advising young persons between fourteen and eighteen on the choice of employment. Hence, while the central control of the system of finding employment continues to be in the hands of the Ministry of Labor, in the local areas the work may be conducted either by juvenile advisory committees under the Ministry or by juvenile employment committees under the local education authorities aided financially by the Ministry. In practice there is considerable coöperation between the labor and educational agencies. In both cases teachers and headmasters forward detailed records on the physical and mental characteristics of pupils just before they are to leave school; parents are invited to consult and seek advice; employers notify the agencies of vacancies; the agencies, so far as they can, endeavor to find positions suitable to applicants and promising opportunities for continuity and advancement; all seek to coöperate in promoting an interest in continued education. With the rapidly increasing unemployment which affected young persons as well as adults, unemployment benefits were extended to boys and girls between the ages of fifteen and eighteen and are administered by the juvenile employment agencies which were also empowered to establish juvenile unemployment centers. In order to maintain contacts with young persons, for whom employment has been found, a further activity has been developed in connection with such agencies, through schemes for after-care of pupils who have left school up to the age of eighteen. The work is entrusted to after-care or welfare committees which keep in touch with the young persons, their employers, and their homes, give them advice and endeavor to link them up with voluntary organizations which provide recreation facilities and to bring to their attention the opportunities for continued part-time education.

Vocational guidance is in the main empirical in character and owes its success to the experience of those concerned in finding suitable employment for young persons. Technical methods of vocational guidance, utilizing psychological tests, are in their initial stages. Experiments are being conducted in a few selected areas by the Council of Industrial Psychology, which is undertaking a comparison of the results obtained by the empirical methods employed by the existing agencies and by scientific methods used by trained psychologists.

The general tendency of English practice is thus to concentrate the supervision of all activities which concern children and young persons up to the age of eighteen in the hands of educational agencies. This includes not only their formal education, whether full- or part-time, and their health, but also their occupation in suitable careers and their recreation. In this task there coöperate not only the administrative authorities, the schools, the school medical service, the juvenile employment agencies, whether associated with the local education authorities or not, but a large number of voluntary organizations such as the school managers and school care committees and a vast number of clubs and other agencies which seek to promote the physical and other recreative activities of the rising generation. This tendency to recognize the duty of society to supervise the education, interpreted in the broadest sense of the word, of children and young persons and the movement to reorganize the school system from a more unitary point of view represent England's realization that "one of the strongest bonds of union between men is a common education."

2. FRANCE

The present system of education in France is virtually a creation or re-creation of the Third Republic. It is marked by two characteristics — the first is control of education in the hands of the state authority on the principle introduced by Napoleon in 1808; the second is its triple division or the coexistence of elementary, vocational or technical, and secondary systems side by side, each administered by separate sections in the Ministry of Public Instruction, or in the case of some forms of vocational education by other Ministries, without articulation or coördination. Since the War a strong movement has developed in favor of decentralization of educational control and of a unitary system (*école unique*). From the point of view of administrative control and of the definition of aims and purposes, the French system is national; from the point of view of articulation and the provision of opportunities it still continues the division into one type of education for the masses and another for the privileged few, with tenuous links between the two. While the tradition of secondary education goes back to the Napoleonic period,[1] the system of elementary and vocational education was reorganized under the Third Republic. A system of elementary and higher elementary schools had been established under the Guizot Law of 1833, but had practically fallen into desuetude under the reaction following the middle of the century. Free secular elementary education was established under the Third Republic in 1881 and was followed in the next year by a law of compulsory attendance. The lay character of elementary education was progressively assured by the law of 1886, which secularized the teaching body in public schools, and by the law of 1904, which suppressed the teaching congregations and closed all the free schools conducted by them. In 1880 the foundation for vocational education was laid by the creation of trade schools (*écoles manuelles d'apprentissage*), and six years later the higher elementary schools were restored. For young children the *écoles maternelles*, which had existed under various names since 1801, were reorganized by a decree of August 2, 1881. Two years earlier the system of normal schools for elementary school teachers had been revised to meet the new conditions. All the laws and decrees governing the elementary system were brought together in the organic law of 1886 on which the present system rests.

Organization of the system. Public instruction in France is organized on the principles of neutrality in religious matters and laicity. Parents and churches are expected to provide for the religious education of children, and the State coöperates for this purpose to the extent of holding no school sessions on Thursdays. In secondary schools pupils are given religious instruction and participate in religious worship, conducted by ministers of the denominations preferred by the parents; any expense involved is in the case of scholarship holders reimbursed by the State. The situation is, however, different in Alsace-Lorraine, where the French Government has practically been compelled to accept the régime which prevailed under German rule and to refrain from imposing the principles of neutrality and laicity in education. In the restored provinces elementary schools are accordingly organized on a strictly denominational basis — Catholic, Protestant, and Jewish; the normal schools are also

[1] See Chapter III.

Age	Types of Schools	School Year
19–		
18–19	Higher Elementary Normal School — Brevet Supérieur / University and Grandes Ecoles	13
17–18	Normal School / Baccalauréat (Second Part)	12
16–17	Vocational Schools (Lower and Higher) / Baccalauréat (First Part)	11
15–16	Brevet Elémentaire / Higher Primary School / Secondary School (Lycée or College) Public and Private	10
14–15	Classes Complémentaires	9
13–14	Adult Courses or Part-Time Continuation School / Certificat d'Etudes Primaires	8
12–13		7
11–12	Public Elementary School	6
10–11		5
9–10	Preparatory Classes	4
8–9		3
7–8		2
6–7		1
5–6	Classe Enfantine	
4–5	Ecole Maternelle / Private Kindergarten or Home	
3–4		
2–3		

The French School System

denominational (Catholic and Protestant) and candidates are admitted only to institutions of their own faith.

Children between the ages of six and thirteen are required to attend school. Children between the ages of two and six may attend the maternal schools (*écoles maternelles*) wherever they are provided. Every commune must establish one elementary school; where the population is over five hundred a separate school must be provided for girls. A school must be established wherever there are twenty pupils of school age living at a distance of more than three kilometers from a school. The number of schools to be provided and their location are determined by the departmental councils which may order the communal councils to open or close schools or to combine for the establishment and maintenance of a school or may permit villages located in different communes to combine for school purposes. Schools which must be established under the requirements of the law are known as obligatory. Maternal schools or infant classes (*classes enfantines*), usually attached to elementary schools, and higher elementary schools or complementary courses (*cours complémentaires*) generally, and separate schools for girls in communes where the population is less than five hundred may be established by local authorities but with an agreement that they will be maintained for a certain period of years (thirty years if state aid is requested). Such schools are known as obligatory by agreement (*écoles conventionellement obligatoires*). In addition communes may establish schools voluntarily but without any expectation of state or other external aid; such schools (*écoles facultatives*) include separate schools for girls in small communities and maternal schools or infant classes in communes with a population of less than two thousand.

The majority of French children attend the maternal and elementary schools. School attendance even under the compulsory regulations is admittedly poor, particularly in rural areas, where children are employed at very early ages, despite very flexible regulations which permit an adjustment of school hours, terms, and vacations to local needs. By a curious provision pupils who succeed in passing the examination for the certificate of elementary education (*certificat d'études primaires*), which they may take at the age of twelve, are exempted from further attendance at school. A small number of pupils may at the age of ten or eleven be transferred to secondary schools. A somewhat larger number of those who wish to continue their education beyond the primary stage may enter a variety of schools at the age of twelve, provided that they hold the certificate of elementary education; admission to a number of post-primary schools is, however, controlled by competitive entrance examinations. At the age of twelve the educational opportunities branch off in two directions, of which one is administered by the division in the Ministry of Public Instruction for elementary education, and the other, offering industrial, technical, and commercial courses, is under the direction of the Under-Secretary for Fine Arts and Technical Education in the Ministry (some specialized branches of vocational education continue to be administered by a number of other Ministries).

The elementary branch of the educational system includes beyond the elementary schools the complementary courses (*cours complémentaires*), the higher elementary schools (*écoles primaires supérieures*), the normal schools (*écoles normales*), and the higher normal schools (*écoles normales supérieures*). All of these schools run parallel with the secondary schools and universities. The complementary courses are usually attached to the elementary schools and give one or two years of work. The higher elementary schools offer a variety of courses, general and semi-vocational, of from three to five years; the general course serves as a preparation for the entrance examination to the normal schools, which offer a three-year course with here and there a fourth year. The crown of the elementary branch consists of two higher normal schools, at Saint-Cloud for men and at Fontenay-aux-Roses for women, which prepare teachers for higher elementary schools, normal schools, and primary inspectorship in a two-year course. Admission to the normal and higher normal schools is by competitive examination. There is a marked tendency to provide access to the universities and, under certain conditions, to degrees to graduates of these institutions; the higher normal schools are, in fact, sometimes regarded as a part of higher education.

The technical branch, which is under its own special administration, includes the practical schools of commerce and industry (*écoles pratiques de commerce et d'industrie*), which provide a theoretical-practical training; trade or apprenticeship schools (*écoles de métiers*), which are more practical in character; the national vocational schools (*écoles nationales professionnelles*), which offer a four-year training for minor executives, foremen, supervisors, and superintendents in a small number of specialized trades. Advanced vocational training is given in national schools of arts and crafts (*écoles nationales des arts et métiers*) leading up to the central School of Arts and Crafts. Separate schools provide training in commerce and lead up to the Higher School of Commerce in Paris, while a parallel system of lower agricultural schools leads up to the National Agricultural Institute (*Institut National Agronomique*).[1]

Only about one tenth of the pupils who annually leave the elementary school avail themselves of the opportunities for further full-time education. The large majority of the adolescents are thus left uncared for except as they may voluntarily attend the adult courses (*cours d'adultes*), which, despite their name, offer a general continuation of elementary education with some attempts at vocational work. Since 1919 young employees in certain industries are required by the *Loi Astier* to attend part-time schools during working hours up to the age of eighteen; these schools offer vocational training with some general education and are supported in part by the State and by a tax on apprentices paid by employers. Efforts to extend the age of compulsory full-time attendance at school up to fourteen and to introduce a system of compulsory part-time education up to seventeen or eighteen, the importance of which is widely recognized in order to check the exodus from the countryside and to meet the conditions due to the industrialization of France, have been unavailing up to the present.

The secondary branch includes a system of schools which receives pupils at the age of four or five and keeps them until they are prepared to enter on some form of higher education in the universities or special higher institutions (*les Grandes Ecoles*). Until 1925 the lower divisions, whether attached to secondary schools or separate, and including *classes enfantines* and *préparatoires* or *élémentaires*, gave a direct preparation for the secondary schools and had their own programs and specially certificated teachers. In 1925 an important contribution was made toward the realization of the ideal of the common school system (*école unique*) by the abolition of all distinctions between the *classes préparatoires*, which are attended by pupils up to

---

[1] For a detailed account of vocational education in France see the *Educational Yearbook, 1928*, of the International Institute of Teachers College, Columbia University, pp. 277 ff. (New York, 1929).

the age of eleven, and the elementary schools in respect to programs, certification of teachers, and inspection. The only distinction which remains is that the former charge fees.

Secondary education is given in *lycées* or state institutions and in *collèges* or municipal institutions aided by the State; separate schools are maintained for boys and girls, although girls may under certain conditions be admitted to boys' schools.[1] The requirements for admission to the secondary schools are indefinite; pupils coming from the preparatory classes are promoted automatically; others may be admitted to the lowest class on probation; others again may be admitted to the lowest or the next class if they have obtained a scholarship by competitive examinations. Since 1925 the transfer of pupils from higher elementary to the secondary schools has been facilitated. The course of secondary education is seven years in length and culminates in the *baccalauréat* which is the requirement for admission to the universities. Graduates who wish to enter the special higher institutions (*les Grandes Ecoles*) must pass a competitive examination; these institutions include the Higher Normal School, the Polytechnic, schools of mines, schools of roads and bridges, the Central School for Naval Engineering, the Special School of Public Works, the School of Physics and Chemistry, etc.

The secondary schools leading up to higher education are definitely regarded as institutions for the preparation of the *élite* of the nation intellectually. The requirement of fees and other expenditures involved in maintaining adolescents in schools tended to make the basis of selection one of class rather than of ability. It has been frequently charged that many pupils are admitted and retained in the secondary schools solely because their parents can pay the fees, while poor pupils of ability have been deprived of their rightful opportunity, unless they could obtain scholarships in a rigorous competition. To correct this situation two steps have been taken; first, the number of scholarships has been considerably increased, and second, since 1930 fees began to be abolished, starting with the lowest class and advancing, according to the plan, year by year until the whole course has been made free. But the abolition of fees carries with it the maintenance of higher standards; no pupil may remain in a secondary school without the payment of fees unless he obtains a mark of 9 on a scale of 20. The provision of scholarships for poor

[1] See Chapter VIII.

pupils of ability, although expanding each year, provides only for about one eighth of the pupils enrolled.

Private education (*l'enseignement libre*). The system of public education is paralleled by a system of private education. The establishment of private schools is carefully regulated, not in order to ensure the monopoly of the State, but to guarantee the quality of education. It is with the same end in view that parents who educate their children at home must submit them each year after the second year of compulsory education to an examination by special committees in subjects which the children would have studied had they attended a school. A private school is one which receives no financial assistance of any kind from any public authority, local or central; local authorities, however, may give poor pupils attending private schools the same kind of aid which they would receive in public schools, and the scholarships granted by the State to children of soldiers killed or wounded in the War may be held in private schools. Since 1904 all denominational teaching congregations have been deprived of the right to open and maintain schools.

Private schools may be established by individuals or associations, even of secular priests — that is, priests who have not taken the vows of a religious congregation. No private school may be opened without strict inquiry by the local and state authorities and no foreigner may establish a school without permission of the Minister of Public Instruction. The opening and conduct of schools are carefully governed by strict regulations which require that the buildings are adequate hygienically, that the teachers are French and have the same qualifications as teachers in public schools, and that the schools are open at all times to government inspectors who have the right to examine the list of employees, the register of pupils, and the work done as recorded in the pupils' exercise books. Beyond this, private schools are free to organize their time-tables and courses of study and to employ whatever methods of instruction they please, subject only to the restriction that books prohibited by the Higher Council of Public Instruction may not be used for class instruction or distributed as prizes. In 1930 the enrollment in private elementary schools was 853,344 pupils as compared with 3,661,800 pupils in public schools; in private secondary schools the enrollment was 128,161 as compared with 174,097 in public *lycées* and *collèges*.

Since advancement on the educational ladder and access to liberal professions and to appointments in the public services are dependent upon the passing of state examinations, whether qualifying or competitive, the contribution of private education — with a few notable exceptions like the *Ecole des Roches* — to the progress of education through experimentation has been slight. Thus, even though there is a large number of private institutions of higher education, many of which have made distinguished contributions to French life and thought, they cannot confer degrees (*grades*) which entitle the holder to practice a profession and which may be granted only by the State; they may, however, confer titles (*titres*) in the fields in which they provide training. From the point of view of the character of education, the State does in practice exercise a monopoly, even though it is liberal in granting permission to establish private schools and in leaving to parents the liberty to choose the type of school which they desire for their children.

The provision of scholarships. By a system of scholarships the French Government has sought to provide opportunities for education at various levels beyond the elementary schools. The most important of these are available for pupils between the ages of twelve and sixteen. The series of scholarships, arranged in four groups, gives access according to the ages of the candidates to higher elementary schools, secondary schools, and vocational schools. Candidates for entrance to the preparatory classes attached to higher elementary schools or to practical schools of commerce and industry, or to the first class of the secondary schools must be under thirteen in the year of examination; candidates for entrance into the first year of the higher elementary and practical schools or the second class of the secondary schools must be under fourteen; for each of these groups there is a common examination; the examinations for the remaining two series, open to candidates under fifteen and sixteen, become more specialized and are restricted to admission to the second and third years of the higher elementary and practical schools. The standards of the examinations are determined by a Higher Committee on National Scholarships (*Comité Supérieur des Bourses Nationales*), appointed by the Ministry. The examinations are conducted by special departmental committees and the results assessed by regional committees in order to secure uniformity of standards. The award of the scholarships is made by the Minister. Every examination is divided into two parts — written, which is eliminatory, and oral. The value of the scholarships varies; they may provide maintenance for day pupils, for day boarders, and for full boarders. The amount awarded in each case depends upon the family conditions — income, number of children to be educated, and national service. Up to the age of sixteen, scholarship holders may on application to the Minister be transferred from one of the three types of schools for which scholarships are awarded to any other, depending upon their aptitude as indicated by their school records. The majority of the scholarships available are awarded in these four series. Others are provided for pupils in the national vocational schools and all other branches of education. For pupils who complete the courses of the higher elementary schools, scholarships are awarded for foreign travel. The total amount of funds available for scholarships is appropriated in the annual budget of the Government and is determined by financial considerations rather than by educational needs.[1]

Social services and education. France has not established a national system of school medical inspection nor any comprehensive public scheme to supervise the health of children. Children are, however, reached through a variety of organizations coöperating with the *Ministère de l'Hygiène, de l'Assistance Publique, et de la Prévoyance Sociale* (Ministry of Health, Charities, and Social Insurance); among these are the *Conseil Supérieur de l'Hygiène de France, Conseil Supérieur de l'Assistance Publique, Conseil Supérieur de la Natalité, Conseil Supérieur de la Protection de l'Enfance*, and the *Commission Supérieure de la Tuberculose*. There are in addition numerous private organizations, like the *Associations d'Hygiène Sociale, Gouttes de Lait*, and *Consultations de Nourissons*, the last two especially interested in infant welfare. In general, adequate provision is made for the prenatal and postnatal care of mothers and for the welfare of children during the period of lactation. For pre-school children between the ages of two and five, if they attend maternal schools or infant classes, some provision may be made by the local appointment of school doctors to examine the pupils every six months. Beyond this period departments and communes may establish local systems of school medical inspection which coöperate

---

[1] For detailed accounts of the scholarship system, the methods and content of examinations, see *Programme des Conditions d'Attribution des Bourses Nationales, 1re et 2e Séries* and *Programme des Conditions à Remplir pour l'Obtention des Bourses d'Enseignement Primaire* (Vuibert, Paris).

with the public health service and receive aid from national funds. Communal and departmental medical officers are allowed to enter schools only with the approval of the local prefect and are limited to the sanitary inspection of the buildings, to look into matters concerning school hygiene and communicable diseases, and to examine in a general way the health of the children. In 1929 only 30 out of the 89 departments and 1693 out of 27,000 communes had established a school medical service. The department of the Seine, which includes Paris, has a large staff of 180 school medical officers (*médecins inspecteurs des écoles* or *médecins scolaires*). Rarely, however, are children examined more than once in their school career — on entrance into elementary schools. The attitude of the medical profession is an obstacle to the development of an adequate system of diagnosis and treatment. Pupils needing care may be referred to the social hygiene dispensaries where they may be given treatment only if indigent. In boarding schools at all levels, including secondary and normal schools, the appointment of a doctor is the common practice, but except for keeping records of height, weight and chest measurements, his sphere of activity is limited to cases actually needing medical attention. For weakly, anemic, and malnourished children some three hundred open-air schools are maintained by public, private, and philanthropic organizations — some are day schools, others boarding schools, and others are open only in the summer. Parents are expected to make some payment for their children and the State makes a contribution of about fifty per cent of the cost. Since 1922 a Society for Open-Air Schools has been active in promoting interest in their development and in 1930 inaugurated a series of short courses for training teachers for such institutions.

The general welfare of pupils is promoted by voluntary organizations, such as (1) *comités de patronage*, committees of ladies appointed by the academy inspector with the advice of the mayor in each locality to look into the general conditions of maternal schools and to raise funds for the benefit of the pupils; (2) the *caisses des écoles* or benefit funds for the use of schools which must be established in all communes and administered by a board to encourage and facilitate regular school attendance by poor children through rewards and the supply of clothing, shoes, and school books; the funds are raised by subscriptions, gifts, proceeds of entertainments, and grants from local school committees; (3) *comités de patronage* in higher elementary schools and complementary courses, which consist of educational officials, the local mayor, the presidents of local chambers of commerce and agriculture, the school principal, and one or more teachers, two members elected each year, and representatives of the local vocational interests, and a doctor appointed for three-year periods by the rector. The function of these committees is to promote the interests of the schools and the pupils, advise on the adaptation of courses to local needs, to encourage and assist the exchange of pupils at home and abroad, to find employment for the more capable pupils when they complete the course, to appoint some of their members to visit and report on the schools periodically, and to interest themselves in other matters affecting the progress of the institutions to which they are attached. Similar committees are appointed for secondary schools for girls and for vocational schools. Under a system of administration which is so highly centralized and official as it is in France, the organization of voluntary organizations like the *comité de patronage* affords the only means for direct contact between the schools and the public; in no case, however, do the committees have a right to interfere with the purely educational aspects, with the progress of instruction, or with the teachers, unless they are permitted to offer advice.

Special schools. For retarded and abnormal children, special schools were established by a law of April 15, 1909. These schools (*écoles de perfectionnement pour enfants arriérés et anormaux*), which may be separate or annexed to a regular school in the form of special classes, are intended for retarded and abnormal children within the ages of compulsory attendance, and may be day or boarding schools. The buildings are erected by the localities with aid from the State and are maintained by the communes and the departments; the salaries of teachers, who must have a special certificate, are paid by the State. Pupils to be assigned to special schools or classes are selected by committees consisting of the local primary inspector, the principal or teachers of the special schools, and by a doctor after an examination in the presence of their parents. Each school is administered by its own board and has its own *comité de patronage*. The size of classes in special schools is limited to a maximum of twenty, and the curriculum places greater emphasis on manual and practical work than on intellectual.

Employment of children. Children below the age of thirteen may not be employed in industrial occupations unless they have obtained the certificate of elementary education at the age of twelve. The hours of work for young persons in industries has recently been restricted to eight hours a day. Although the selection of occupations is still somewhat haphazard and although teachers and principals play an important part in giving advice, there has been a rapid development of systematic vocational guidance. Indeed, the work initiated by Binet and Simon has been more fully developed in this field than in general education. Vocational guidance bureaus are being established in the larger industrial centers and a Commission for Vocational Guidance has been created in the department for technical education in the Ministry of Public Instruction to investigate and to furnish information on the problem. In 1928 the National Institute for Vocational Guidance (*Institut National d'Orientation Professionnelle*) was organized to conduct research in the subject and to train vocational counselors in the latest scientific methods; the Institute also conducts short intensive courses for teachers, many of whom are encouraged to attend by the award of scholarships.

In the agricultural areas the control of the employment of school children is somewhat loose; children of school age may be exempted from school attendance for three months during the school year to assist their parents; those working for others in any agricultural occupation may be allowed to attend school on a part-time basis; reference has already been made to the flexible organization of school sessions and vacations which renders it possible to adjust school attendance to agricultural needs. Similar conditions prevail on the seaboard; boys between the ages of ten and thirteen may be exempted from school attendance for three months during the school year to work as cabin-boys (*mousses*) on fishing and other vessels. There are traditional and economic conditions which the French authorities up to the present have not succeeded in overcoming.

The common school movement. The present organization of the French system of education has given rise to considerable criticism based not only on the educational but on the social and economic needs of France. Agitation for reform was begun during the War by *Les Compagnons de l' Université Nouvelle*, a group of young educators who formed an organization to promote the complete reorganization of the educational system. The fundamental idea inherent in their proposals was the organization of a system that would promote the interests of the nation as a whole, that would eliminate class distinctions, that would provide equality of opportunity for all, and that would, as a result, utilize all the resources of talent and ability wherever found. The implication was not a common, identical, or uniform education for all above the elementary stage, but the inauguration of a system in which all branches of education would be properly coördinated and in which pupils would find that education that was best suited to their abilities.

The proposals of *Les Compagnons* attracted widespread attention, and since the War have been the chief subject of discussion and debate, not only in professional circles, but in lay newspapers and magazines and in Parliament. In the last few years they have become the center of acrimonious political debate. The opponents of the *école unique* profess to see in it an attempt to establish a uniform, state-controlled system, and an attack on the right of parents to select private (and in the main clerically controlled) schools for their children. This attack is, however, specious, for fundamentally the movement for the *école unique* is intended to promote the greatest efficiency in national education, first, by bringing all education, some of which is still under the charge of various Ministries, under the supervision of a national Ministry of Education; and secondly, to establish a system of coördinated schools at various levels for the recruiting and training of ability, wherever found, not merely along the traditional intellectual lines, but along whatever lines France in her present stage of development may need leaders. The ideas underlying the movement were well summarized by Anatole France, in *La Vie en Fleur*:

> The same education for all, rich and poor. All will attend the primary school. Those among them who show the highest aptitudes will be allowed to have a secondary education, which, without fees, will bring together on the same benches the *élite* of the bourgeois and the *élite* of the proletarian youth. From this *élite* will proceed an *élite* to the higher schools of science and art.

M. Léon Brunschvieg explained the ideas by an analogy:

> It is important that all the children of France should be considered alike as living plants, whose spontaneous growth will be assured by the same methods; only the trunk will be allowed to grow up to a certain height before the

branches are permitted to shoot out without the opposition of any artificial obstacle to the expansion of their being, whose innate powers will raise each up to the level designed for it.[1]

In 1924, M. François Albert, Minister of Public Instruction in M. Herriot's Cabinet, appointed a *Commission de l'Ecole Unique* to inquire into the problem; the *Ligue de l'Enseignement* appointed its own commission; and the problem was discussed in a series of lectures at the *Ecole des Hautes Etudes Sociales*. These are cited as examples, out of many hundreds, of the interest in the subject of the common school. The general trend of the discussions has been in favor of a reorganization of the school system into four levels: (1) a common elementary education (ages six to twelve); (2) a lower secondary level of four years (ages twelve to sixteen); (3) a higher secondary level (ages sixteen to nineteen); and (4) a higher level in universities, technical institutes, and similar centers.

Of these tendencies some have already been realized. Since 1925 a common primary education has been adopted for all children up to between the ages of eleven and twelve. Pupils are not required to attend the same school, but whatever school they attend within this period follows the same curriculum, is taught by teachers with the same qualifications, and is inspected by primary school inspectors. This provision means that the advantages hitherto enjoyed by pupils who attended the *classes élémentaires* or *préparatoires*, associated with the secondary schools, are now abolished. These classes still continue to charge fees, but the work is not directly preparatory to the secondary schools. All pupils who are candidates for admission to the secondary schools accordingly start on an equal footing. Another contribution to the realization of the *école unique* has been the institution of a common scholarship examination for candidates who wish to enter the secondary, the higher primary, or the technical schools; not only may candidates hold these scholarships in any one of these schools, but they may, after an exploratory period, transfer them from one to another. The money set aside in the budgets for scholarships has increased considerably in the last few years. Transfer from the higher elementary schools to the upper section of the secondary school proper has been facilitated.

Circumstances, rather than principles, have, however, hastened the development of a common school at the second level (ages twelve

[1] *Un Ministère de l'Education Nationale*, p. 79 (Paris, 1922).

to sixteen). In an effort to secure retrenchment, it was proposed, in 1925–26, to close the smaller secondary schools — usually *collèges* maintained by municipalities and having small enrollments. In order to save these institutions, higher elementary or technical schools, or in some cases both, were brought together under the same roof as the *collèges*, and teachers were used, where possible, interchangeably in the two or three types of courses. Since pupils in the higher elementary and technical schools are free scholars, parents of pupils in the secondary sections proper, the *collèges*, protested against the exaction of fees. In 1928 the Government decided to abolish fees in the cosmopolitan schools, a decision which affected about one hundred institutions. Parents of pupils in the *collèges* now protested against the payment of fees in the upper sections, the third level of the proposed *école unique*, and these also were abolished in 1929. Since these decisions were obviously unfair to parents who continued to pay fees in secondary schools to which higher elementary or technical schools were not attached, the Government decided to abolish all fees for secondary education, beginning in 1930 with the lowest class, and advancing progressively year by year until their abolition throughout the secondary schools.[1] The abolition of fees has been accompanied by the requirement of a scholarship standard in the secondary schools, so that pupils who fail to reach it are required either to leave or to pay fees.

The development of free education at the second level has raised a number of serious problems. The first is that of selection. It is objected that the standards of admission to the various schools at this level are higher for poor children with ability, who are selected by competitive scholarship examinations, than for the children of the rich who are admitted to the *lycées* and *collèges* by entrance examinations. The commissions already mentioned have advocated the establishment of a Permanent Commission for Selection and Guidance in the Ministry of Education (*Commission Permanente de Sélection et d'Orientation*), which would devise satisfactory methods of assigning pupils to the type of schools that is best suited to the abilities of the pupils. The second problem is that of extending the equality of opportunities. The abolition of tuition fees is only a small contribution to the solution of this problem. Many parents

---

[1] In September, 1932, the Minister of Public Instruction, M. De Monzie, proposed that all fees be abolished throughout the secondary schools in 1933.

are ignorant of the opportunities already available; others withhold their children from secondary education because they need their help, in work or wages, at the earliest possible opportunity; prolonged education would not merely involve loss of wages, but additional expense for books, clothing, and, frequently, board away from home. Children of teachers and wards of the nation (children who lost their fathers in the War) are already provided for in these matters if they can meet the standards. The only solution is to take the next step implied in the democratization and equalization of opportunities, and that is to extend the system of maintenance grants (*bourses d'entretien*) to all deserving pupils.

The *école unique* is, then, according to a summary of M. Ducos, from the point of view of the individual, the right of every human being to acquire the highest and clearest consciousness of the world and of himself of which he is capable; from the point of view of the State it is its duty to provide the individual with the means of attaining this end; it also implies at the same time the duty and right to stimulate and to recruit the *élites*, the duty and the right to prepare them by the most appropriate methods. In other words, France is conscious today of the need of educating, not merely one type of leaders (*élite*) — the intellectual type produced by her traditional secondary education — but a variety of types (*élites*) as demanded by her changing social, industrial, and commercial conditions.

The democratization of education in France implies, then, an extension of educational opportunities according to ability. The more advanced education becomes, the more selective it is to be, but along differentiated lines. On one point all the supporters of the reforms are agreed, that there shall be no surrender of quality of education. The traditional characteristics of French culture are to be preserved and promoted. This France feels that she owes to herself, and to the leadership that she has enjoyed for so long in the world of culture. The intellectual *élites* are to be educated to safeguard the claims of general culture through various methods of approach — classical, modern, scientific and technical humanism; that is, that type of education that arouses a consciousness of the essential problems that confront man as man and as citizen, that stimulates an intellectual interest in all forms of life, that cultivates the habit of going to the facts and from the facts to ideas, that develops an all-round view and a delicate feeling for shades of meanings and a critical judgment that is always ready to seize the manifold aspects and relations of life. On this there is to be no compromise, but the selection and training of the intellectual *élites* are to be paralleled by provisions for the selection and training of *élites* in other walks of life.[1] A complete program of democratic education, according to the Minister of Public Instruction, involves free tuition, selection and distribution or guidance (*gratuité, sélection, et rationalisation*).

3. GERMANY

The organization and provision of schools in Germany have in the main been left to the States which compose the Republic, and although Article 143 of the Constitution of Weimar (1919) provided for the coöperation in this matter of the Federal Government (*Reich*), the States, and municipalities, the action of the Federal Government has been very limited. As long as it was hoped that the Federal Government might coöperate financially in the support of education, its participation was welcomed, but after 1924, when it was announced that this expectation could not be fulfilled, interest in its coöperation waned. The action of the Federal Government was accordingly restricted to implementing the provision of the Constitution that the systems of schools should be based on a common foundation of four years in the *Grundschule* and to the adoption and supervision of common standards in the secondary schools and the universities.[2] Beyond this, the Constitution laid down certain provisions on private schools, the preparation of teachers for elementary schools, the supervision of teachers by professional experts, the relation of the States to religious instruction, continuation schools, and aid to poor children of ability to secure other than elementary education. These provisions have, however, remained normative and have not been embodied in common legislative enactments, either federal or state.

During and after the War there was a widespread movement for

[1] On the *école unique* the best accounts are to be found in the annual *Rapport fait au Nom de la Commission des Finances chargée d'examiner le Projet de Loi portant Fixation du Budget général*, especially the reports issued since 1924 under the chairmanship of M. Ducos. Summaries of these reports are to be found in the *Revue Universitaire*. See also *L'Université Nouvelle; Projet de Statut Organique de l'Enseignement public instituant l'Ecole Unique*, issued by the *Comité d'Etude et d'Action Pour l'Ecole Unique* (Paris, 1927); and *Educational Yearbooks, 1928* and *1930*, of the International Institute of Teachers College, Columbia University (New York, 1929 and 1931).

[2] See Chapter V.

a radical reorganization of the school system on the principle of the *Einheitsschule*,[1] with a common foundation up to the age of twelve, followed by a system of differentiated schools at the secondary level. The idea was not new; it had already been suggested in the *Promemoria* prepared by Süvern in 1817 and was discussed by teachers during the period preceding the Revolution of 1848. The more recent proposals have not been carried out, partly because of the opposition of the forces controlling secondary and higher education who feared that any attempt to postpone the beginning of secondary education to the age of twelve, as was planned in the scheme for a common education would be detrimental to standards, partly because a complete reorganization would have meant a financial burden which the country could not bear. If the movement for the *Einheitsschule* failed to secure a reconstruction of the school system from the point of view of organization and administration, it succeeded in leaving behind it the nucleus of another idea, that whatever the organization of schools might be, they should all be bound together by a common ideal; spiritual and national unity must be promoted by reference to a common aim, the progressive development of *Deutschtum*. Although a large body of the teachers and educators is not deceived by the casuistry of the arguments put forward to shelve the movement for reorganization of schools, which was actually attempted in Thuringia while the Left Wing was in power up to 1924, it cannot be denied that the new interpretation of the *Einheitsschule* has had an important influence in promoting at least a tendency toward unity of aims and ideals in the various types of schools which make up the educational systems of each State, and to give a common character to the schools of the whole nation. It is in this rather than in the administrative sense, then, that Germany may be said to have a national system of education.

The German tradition. To have secured this measure of unity, which expresses itself in a certain common attack on materials and methods of instruction calculated to enrich the common *Deutschtum* and to promote national solidarity, is an achievement which carried German education a stage beyond the practices of the pre-War system. For the German tradition, like the tradition everywhere

[1] The *Einheitsschule* in this form is not to be confused with another movement under the same name which was current in the eighties for the reorganization of secondary schools on a common basis.

else except in the United States, was to provide one type of education for the masses, about ninety per cent of the population, and another for the classes, the potential leaders, making up the rest of the population, the two types of education differing in content, methods, and aims. The purpose of the elementary school (*Volksschule*) was to train God-fearing, law-abiding, self-supporting subjects; the object of the secondary schools was to train the future leaders for administration, the professions, the economic and intellectual life of the country. The connection between the two systems was slight; unless a pupil was transferred to a secondary school at the age of nine (and the majority advanced normally from the preparatory schools or *Vorschulen* rather than from the elementary schools), the chances of securing a secondary education were negligible; only about one pupil in ten thousand entered a secondary school after completing the full eight years of an elementary school. With the gradual development and recognition of the need for providing for the masses something more than elementary schools, the elementary branch of the dual system was gradually extended to provide for a form of intermediate education and part-time continuation schools and to link up with a variety of vocational schools and reached up to the normal schools for the training of elementary school teachers (*Volksschullehrerseminarien*). Side by side with the secondary schools there were developed commercial and technical schools at the secondary level. The distinction between the two systems — the elementary and secondary — which overlapped considerably so far as the ages of the pupils were concerned, lay not only in the social and class differences, but in the privileges and rights conferred by the two. Of these the most important was the one-year military privilege (*Einjährigerschein*), which not only entitled its holder to specially favorable conditions in the scheme of compulsory military service, but opened up certain careers to him; this privilege was reserved only to those who completed six years of secondary education at about the age of fifteen. It was only with difficulty that this privilege was secured for those who completed the intermediate school (*Mittelschule*) at the same age, provided that they had studied two foreign languages and for those who graduated from the normal schools at the age of twenty. A further distinction between the two systems was that access to the universities could only be secured through the secondary branch by pupils who passed the *Reifeprüfung* or *Abi-*

turientenexamen; except, under restricted conditions in Saxony, graduates of the normal schools were not admitted to the universities.

The educational system was dominated by another tradition, the close participation of the churches in education, a tradition perpetuated in the control both of education and religious affairs by the same Ministry; thus the title of the Ministry in Prussia until the post-War change was *Ministerium für geistlichen-und-Unterrichtsangelegenheiten*. This partnership implied the perpetuation of another tradition — the inclusion of religious instruction in the schools as a compulsory subject and the supervision of teachers by the clergy. Elementary schools were organized either on a denominational basis — Evangelical, Catholic, or, in some cases, Jewish — or interdenominational (*Simultanschulen*). The local supervision of the elementary schools was entrusted to the pastor or priest, and in many smaller communities the teachers were, particularly in Prussia, the servants both of the Church and the school and were responsible for the performance of duties in both.

The Constitution and the schools. Without entering at this stage into a discussion of the characteristic features of the schools themselves which pointed to the necessity of internal reform of curricula and methods, the traditions described furnished the background for reconstruction under the Republic. The first attack was made on the *Vorschule* as a class institution, which was regarded as a menace to national and social solidarity and placed the children of those who could pay the fees in a special position of privilege. The *Vorschule*, which was attended by pupils between the ages of six and nine, was abolished by the Constitution, and the *Grundschule* or foundation school was established in its place as the common school for all between the ages of six and ten (Article 146). The second attack was made on the system of teacher-preparation; the normal schools were abolished by Article 143 of the Constitution, which provided that the preparation of elementary school teachers should be organized "according to the principles which apply generally to higher education," a provision which established a much-desired link between the elementary and secondary branches of the system. The third problem, that of the relation of the State to religious instruction, was regulated by Articles 146 and 149 of the Constitution; religious instruction continues to be a part of the regular school curriculum, but the way has been opened for the establishment of secular schools (*weltliche*

Schulen); further, no child may be compelled to participate in religious instruction or in church celebrations without the consent of its parents or guardians, and no teacher may be compelled to give religious instruction against his will. By Article 143 of the Constitution, which provides that the supervision of schools shall be conducted by full-time officials who are professionally trained, the control of the clergy over elementary school teachers was curtailed.

The present system. The Constitution requires that education shall be compulsory and universal for all children between the ages of six and fourteen in full-time attendance and from fourteen to eighteen in part-time continuation schools. In elementary and continuation schools books and school supplies must be provided free of cost. The provision of institutions for pre-school children is not extensive and does not form a part of the general school system. In general, schools for young children are provided by private organizations, but are always under the supervision of the public authorities — in Prussia of the Ministry for Public Welfare which supervises the external arrangements and the Ministry of Education which looks after the pedagogical side and the certification of teachers. In some of the larger cities classes for pre-school children are organized in the elementary schools. Although such schools bear the name of kindergartens, they do not follow Froebelian principles, which never exercised a great influence in Germany. There is at present a conflict between the advocates of the Montessori principles and those who would prefer to see the schools organized on the basis of children's activities.

Compulsory school attendance begins in most of the German States at the age of six and continues up to fourteen. Children may be admitted to school a few months before their sixth birthday if physically and mentally fit for the work. With the abolition of the *Vorschule*, all children are required to attend the *Grundschule* or common foundation school for the first four years of their school life; since the enactment of the Federal *Grundschulgesetz* in 1920, the law has been amended and bright pupils may be transferred to a secondary school after only three years of attendance at the *Grundschule*. This concession was made in response to parents who objected that under the original requirement the combined period of attendance at the *Grundschule* (four years) and at a secondary school (nine years)

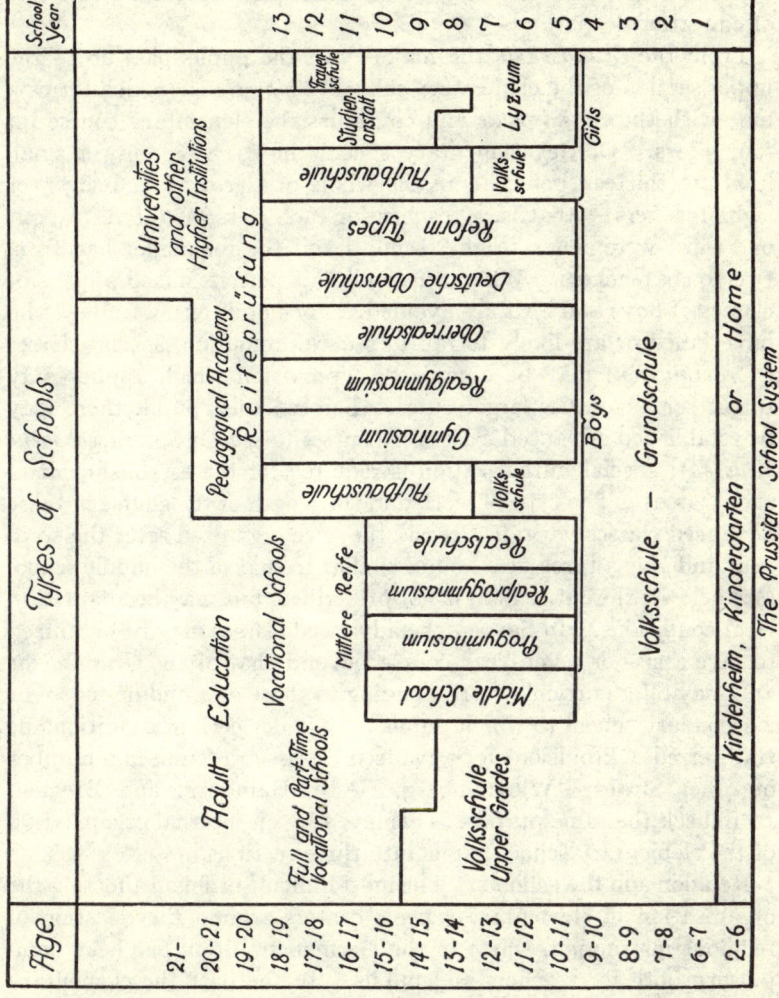

would have increased the total period of attendance by one year beyond the pre-War period, with the consequent increase in the cost of education.

From the *Grundschule* the majority of the pupils pass on to the upper section of the elementary school (*Volksschule*), which forms a unit with the *Grundschule* and continues the elementary course for four years. Of the elementary schools in 1927–28, only a small fraction (thirteen per cent) in the whole of Germany had seven or eight teachers — that is, a teacher for each class; of the rest about one third were single teacher schools and the remainder had from two to six teachers. Wherever conditions permit, mixed schools or classes of boys and girls are avoided. For pupils of low ability who have failed or are likely to fail to secure promotion, special classes (*Förderklassen*) may be organized, a provision which applies only to the schools in the larger cities. For the abler pupils there may be established advanced classes or courses (*Begabtenklassen, gehobene Klassen*); special authorization is required for the establishment of such classes. The type of work and the length of the course in these advanced classes vary; in Prussia they are organized after the sixth year and give a three-year course similar to that of the middle school (see below); the curriculum is not prescribed, but may be adapted to local conditions. In Saxony the advanced classes may be organized to give a six- or seven-year course beyond that of the *Grundschule* and may offer curricula corresponding to those of a middle school or a secondary school to which pupils may under certain conditions be transferred. Provisions for advanced classes are found in a number of other States — Württemberg, Hesse, Hamburg, and Bremen. In Lübeck the same purpose is achieved by an internal organization of the elementary school pupils into three sections.

Religion and the schools. The most difficult problem affecting the organization of elementary schools centers around the question of religious instruction, which in the German tradition has been compulsory both for teachers and pupils. In the past the elementary schools were organized on a denominational (*konfessionelle Schulen*) basis or were interdenominational (*simultan-* or *paritätische Schulen*). There was no uniformity of practice throughout the country; where the denominations form large and distinct groups, some States, such as Prussia and Bavaria, have established separate schools for each with interdenominational schools for minorities, while others (Baden and Hesse) have only interdenominational schools; Württemberg has only denominational schools; most of the other States (Saxony, Thuringia, Hamburg, Anhalt, Bremen) have only one school for all children. The Constitution, as has already been pointed out, provided for freedom of conscience for both teachers and pupils on the declaration of their parents or guardians, but, while suggesting the possibility of the creation of secular schools (Article 146), it retained the existing situation until the enactment of a new federal law (Article 174). Despite three attempts made since 1921 to give reality to the constitutional principle, the Federal Government has been unsuccessful in securing the enactment of a law (*Reichsschulgesetz*). The last bill introduced in the Federal Diet in 1927 proposed the establishment of denominational (*Bekenntnisschulen*), interdenominational (*Gemeinschaftsschulen*, a new name replacing the traditional *Simultanschulen*), and secular (*weltliche*) schools or schools representing the convictions (*Weltanschauung*) of particular groups; the bill aroused such antagonism from all parties as almost to wreck the Government, and was withdrawn. In the meantime the number of parents and teachers who availed themselves of the right to exemption from religious instruction was so large that measures had to be taken to take care of the pupils withdrawn. Although contrary to law, regard for the situation has compelled the Prussian authorities to organize such pupils in special classes (*Sammelklassen*) or to provide community schools (*Gemeinschaftsschulen*) with denominational and secular sections under one principal (*Rektor*), with assistant principals (*Konrektoren*). Teachers for the secular classes or schools may only be appointed at their own request. During the period normally assigned for religious instruction, no other subject of the elementary school studies may be taught, but some form of moral-social instruction (*lebenskundlicher Unterricht*) may be given. The opponents of denominational schools have organized the *Bund der freien Schulgesellschaften Deutschlands*, whose organ is *Die freie weltliche Schule*. The interests of the Catholic Church, which in 1925 concluded a *Concordat* with Bavaria to safeguard the education of Catholics, were protected by an agreement (*Vertrag*) between the Holy See and Prussia concluded in 1929, when negotiations were also begun by Prussia to reach an agreement with the Protestant Churches. There are involved in the whole problem social and political questions which go far beyond the immediate cause of strained relations between political and denominational or secular groups.

Continuation schools. Full-time education for the majority of pupils comes to a close at the end of the term in which they reach their fourteenth birthday. The Federal Constitution (Article 145) requires that all boys and girls receive a part-time education up to the age of eighteen, but, since this provision has not been defined by a federal law, the regulation of part-time school attendance has been left to the States. In Prussia the duty of carrying out the requirement for part-time education has been left to the communities and districts, with the result that young persons are compelled to attend some form of continuation school only where it has been provided by local by-laws. At present from eighty to ninety per cent of the boys and fifty per cent of the girls come under the compulsory requirements and mainly in the industrial centers, while girls are almost entirely neglected in the agricultural areas. The requirements of compulsory attendance may be met by attendance at *Werkschulen*, schools established by the large industrial concerns for their young employees. In a number of other states — Saxony, Württemberg, Thuringia, Hesse, Hamburg, Lippe, and Lübeck — compulsory attendance is obligatory for boys, but is not so general for girls. Generally the period of compulsory attendance is for three years; the number of hours of attendance per week varies from six to nine; in some places it is more, in others, mainly in rural areas, less. The tendency since 1920 has been to organize the work of the continuation schools in close relationship with the occupation in which the pupils are already engaged without neglecting their general education. Hence the majority of the continuation schools are now known as *Berufsschulen* (vocational schools), the general term *Fortbildungsschulen* being reserved for those schools which devote themselves merely to a continuation of the general work of the elementary schools.

Intermediate Schools. For the minority of pupils who do not continue from the *Grundschule* to the upper section of the elementary school and who either obtain free tuition or maintenance grants or whose parents can afford to pay the necessary fees, two choices are open: they may proceed to a middle school (*Mittelschule*) or to a secondary school (*höhere Schule*). The middle schools are institutions which provide a variety of courses intermediate between those of the elementary and of the secondary school, and are under the supervision of that branch in the Ministries of Education concerned with elementary education. Separate schools for boys and girls are the rule except in very small localities. The courses, which last for six years, may be general in character or may be organized with an industrial or commercial bias or, in the case of girls, adapted with a view to their future occupations. In some middle schools a course may be offered which runs parallel with the secondary school emphasizing modern languages and prepares for transfer to the upper sections. In Prussia *Rektoratschulen*, or schools which are formed in small localities and give the first four or five years of one of the secondary school courses, and lower secondary schools for girls (*höhere Mädchenschulen*) are classified as middle schools. *Mittelschulen*, similar to those of Prussia, are found in Thuringia, Mecklenburg-Schwerin, Brunswick, Oldenburg, Anhalt, Lippe, and Württemberg.

Secondary education. The other alternative for pupils who proceed neither to the upper section of the elementary nor to a middle school is some form of secondary education. With a few slight exceptions secondary education is organized separately for boys and girls. For boys a variety of schools are available — the *Gymnasium* or classical school, the *Realgymnasium* or semi-classical school, the *Oberrealschule* or modern-language-science school, and the *Deutsche Oberschule* or German cultural school created since the War. All of these schools offer nine-year courses; there are in addition a number of six-year schools which parallel the first three mentioned — the *Progymnasium*, *Realprogymnasium*, and *Realschule*. By organizing a common foundation, schools offering a combination of the above types have been established — the *Reformgymnasium* and the *Reformrealgymnasium*, both nine-year schools. For girls the cosmopolitan type of secondary school has been established with a common foundation, the *Lyzeum* of six years branching out into courses similar to those provided for boys (*Studienanstalt*), and providing one- or two-year courses for girls who wish to prepare themselves for some form of social service (*Frauenschule*). Graduation from the nine-year courses confers the right of admission to the universities and technical high schools. Besides the *Deutsche Oberschule* another innovation since the War has been the establishment of the *Aufbauschule*, a six-year school intended primarily to be provided in smaller localities and rural areas, but spreading gradually in the larger centers. The *Aufbauschule* furnishes an opportunity for the abler pupils who continue their education in the upper section of the elementary schools and are selected on the basis of their ability for transfer to this secondary school, which in a six-year course following that either of the *Oberrealschule* or of the *Deutsche Oberschule* brings the pupils up to the standard required for admission to the universities. The types of schools mentioned are found throughout the country; Bavaria alone has not established the *Deutsche Oberschule* or the *Aufbauschule*, and although graduates of these schools from other States are admitted to Bavarian universities they are not eligible to the professional examinations of that State. Fees are charged in all secondary schools, but may be reduced or remitted under certain conditions and maintenance grants (*Erziehungsbeihilfen*) may be awarded to the ablest pupils, boys or girls, on the recommendation of the schools which they have attended. The provision of maintenance grants follows the requirement of Article 146 of the Constitution that aid be given by the Federal Government, the States, and municipalities "to enable those in poor circumstances to attend secondary schools and higher institutions of learning." In order to make higher education accessible to young men and women who missed the opportunities for secondary education earlier and who have already entered upon wage-earning occupations, experiments have begun with evening secondary schools (*Abendgymnasien*) which prepare the students for the *Abiturientenprüfung* required for admission to the universities.

Vocational education. Opportunities for specialized training are provided by vocational schools at different levels. There is probably no other country in the world which provides as wide a range and variety of vocational schools as does Germany. For those who cannot devote full time to vocational preparation, there are available the compulsory continuation schools (*Berufsschulen*) which supplement the training that the pupils receive in the occupations which they have already selected. Full-time vocational schools have been established in all phases of the complicated economic life of the country — agriculture, gardening, animal husbandry, forestry, and fishery; every branch of industry for which training can in any way be organized; commerce and transportation, insurance, hotel and restaurant management; arts and crafts; domestic service and household arts; and social welfare work. Courses varying from one to three years are provided for the training of skilled artisans, foremen and supervisors, and executives and managers; admission to the lower courses is based on the completion of an elementary education, to the higher course on the completion of at least six years of a secondary or middle school course. The highest training is given in technical high schools (*Technische Hochschulen*) and commercial higher schools (*Handelshochschulen*) which are of university rank and for admission require the completion of a nine-year secondary course or its equivalent. In the task of providing and organizing vocational education there are associated the public authorities, chambers of commerce, and chambers of industry. With the rapid development of vocational education and with the increase of diversity and specialization of occupations, the importance of systematic guidance (*Berufsberatung*) has been recognized. Bureaus of vocational guidance have been created all over the country, which seek, through promoting the coöperation of the schools, teachers, parents, and employers, to adjust the choice of occupations to the inclinations and aptitudes of the applicants and to the economic situation. The problem, it is realized, is not merely one of finding employment, but of disseminating vocational information and adjusting the human element to the economic organization in the best interests of society as a whole. The progress of vocational guidance has been accompanied by the development of psychological tests of aptitude, so that vocational guidance, where technically conducted, includes a physical examination, a scholastic test, an intelligence test, and several tests of practical abilities. The *Zentralinstitut für Erziehung und Unterricht*, the Federal Ministry of Labor (*Reichsarbeitsverwaltung*) and the Federal Employment Exchange Office (*Reichsamt für Arbeitsvermittlung*) coöperate in promoting the advancement of vocational guidance throughout the country.

Adult education. Higher education is given in twenty-five universities and ten technical high schools. To enable poor students to proceed to the universities, loan funds and a national but unofficial scholarship fund (*Studienstiftung des deutschen Volkes*), raised by voluntary contributions, have been established. There is in addition a large number of other institutions devoted to special purposes, including those for the preparation of elementary school teachers organized in three forms, independently as in Prussia, affiliated with universities as in Saxony and Thuringia, or integral parts of a university as in Hamburg. Since the War there has been a progressive development of adult education under a variety of auspices — political, religious, educational, and other interests. University extension courses, libraries, museums, theaters, concerts, and radio are all directed to the education of adults on the theory, first, that progress depends upon the intelligent participation in all aspects of national life by all the people, and, secondly, that, unless some means are provided for the widespread dissemination of knowledge, its rapid advancement in all fields would result in the division of the population into the educated classes and the uneducated masses equipped with nothing more than literacy. One of the most promising developments in adult education is the spread of the people's university (*Volkshochschule*), which, owing to the failure of the universities to coöperate extensively, has become largely a working-class movement, exposed to political, economic, and religious exploitation. The aim of the *Volkshochschule* is to organize study courses rather than to offer isolated, unconnected series of lectures. Indeed, the method advocated for the conduct of such courses is discussion rather than lecture, and the students are expected to participate by the preparation of written papers. Public authorities are urged to give their support to the movement by placing rooms at the disposal of the people's universities, by organizing committees for their promotion, and by establishing advisory councils to assist in the selection of suitable leaders. As a part of the development of the *Volkshochschule*, residential settlements (*Volkshochschulheime*) have been established, where working men and women can spend two or three weeks as members of a study circle (*Arbeitsgemeinschaft*). The difference between the *Volkshochschule* and the settlements lies in the fact that the former are expected to be non-partisan, while the latter are definitely propagandistic. The Federal Ministry of the Interior and the state Ministries of Education have sections devoted to the promotion of adult education, a task in which they are assisted by the *Akademie der Volksbildner*, the *Reichsverband der deutschen Volkshochschule*, in Jena, and the *Zentralstelle für Volkshochschulstatistik* in Leipzig.

Private education. Following the principle that schools and education are the concern of the State, private education has always been carefully regulated. By Article 147 of the Constitution the principle that private schools which are established as a subtitute for public schools require the approval of state authorities was again emphasized. Approval of the establishment of a private school may only be granted where there is not available a private school of the denomination or conviction of parents or guardians, or if it is in the interests of educational progress — that is, an experimental school (*Versuchsschule*). Private preparatory schools (*Vorschulen*) have been entirely abolished except in a few instances where undue economic hardship would have been entailed on the teachers concerned or where compensation could not be provided; such schools must follow the regulations for the *Grundschule* and may transfer pupils to secondary schools under the same conditions as from the *Grundschule*.

Private schools may be established with the approval of the authorities if they are in every respect — aims, curricula, qualifications and status of teachers — at least of the same standard as public schools and are not established in the interests of a class, social or economic. By a federal agreement, reached in 1927, private schools must furnish a guarantee of financial competence, must enter into approved contracts with their teachers, must make provision for the social insurance of teachers, and must protect the teachers against unjust dismissal. The service of teachers in some private schools may be counted towards a pension, if they transfer to a public school. The opening of private schools for minority groups, especially Polish and Danish, must be approved and the use of the mother-tongue as the vehicle of instruction must be permitted, German being required as one of the subjects of the curriculum. Aid may be given to private elementary schools if maintained by private associations or church organizations and if supported by private contributions, but the grants must not exceed the per capita allowances which would have been paid had the pupils attended public schools. Permission to open private schools must be sought from the local supervisory authority, but can only be granted by the Ministry of Education.

All private schools of whatever grade must be open to supervision by the public authorities, which have the right to inspect the external and internal organization — buildings, qualifications of teachers, textbooks, and other books, and the general moral and social character of the institutions concerned. The right to conduct examinations is granted to private secondary schools, but their control is entirely in the hands of officials employed in the public school system.

The same strict regulations apply to the approval of private tutors, teachers, and schools of music and physical training, and of foreign languages or trades, commerce, and industry. The concern of the State is to protect society and the individual against incompetence and fraud in education as well as to guarantee the moral character of individuals and institutions which offer instruction in any field. Thus teachers who are dismissed from public schools for professional incompetence or on moral grounds cannot expect to obtain permission to engage in private instruction. Foreigners who wish to open schools or to give private instruction or natives who desire to do the same for foreign pupils and students can only obtain permission from the Ministry of Education in each State. As a rule permission to engage in private education is given only to individuals and not to institutions, and is revocable, when necessary in the opinion of the authorities; approval by the authorities does not confer the right to use the fact for advertising purposes.

Social services and education. The serious effects of the War and post-War period on the health of the new generation directed attention to the importance of providing measures for the improvement of their physical welfare. The Constitution (Article 7) empowered the Federal Government to introduce legislation for "the protection of maternity, infancy, childhood, and adolescence," guaranteed the right of children to "education for physical, intellectual, and social efficiency" (Article 120), and authorized state and local authorities to pass measures for the protection of youth "against exploitation as well as against moral, spiritual, or physical neglect." Such a *Reichsgesetz für Jugendwohlfahrt* (Federal Child Welfare Law) was enacted on July 9, 1923, and, combined with the establishment of sickness funds, polyclinics, sanatoria and convalescent homes under the schemes of social insurance, has provided measures for the promotion of the welfare of infants and young children.

The supervision of hygienic and physical conditions of schools and the health of children in general had for many years been entrusted in Prussia to the district public health officers (*Kreisärzte*) under the direction of the Ministry of Public Welfare (*Volkswohlfahrtsministerium*). These officers were required to visit schools of their districts and other educational institutions at least once in five years and to promote an interest on the part of parents, teachers, and the communities in problems of hygiene affecting the welfare of school children. Local educational authorities were authorized to make special arrangements for weak or needy children, for the provision of meals and clothing and the organization of open-air schools, vacation camps, or special schools. Secondary and other schools under the supervision of the Provincial School Boards are inspected only on special request. The health officers are further charged with the control of contagious diseases, the examination of blind, dumb, and backward children before they are assigned to institutions established for their care, and the approval of plans for new or the reconstruction of old buildings.

Since the War there has been an increase in Prussia in the number of school medical officers who are governed by regulations issued in 1927 by the Ministry of Public Welfare. School medical inspection is not compulsory by state laws, but may be established by local authorities. Where it is established, school doctors are expected to examine all pupils either immediately before or after entering elementary schools, before leaving when advice may be given on the choice of occupations, and once in between these two examinations. In Berlin, which employs nearly one hundred full-time school medical officers, pupils are examined every two years. Children who are found defective in physique or backward in intelligence may be required to postpone their entrance to school or else placed on a special list to be reëxamined periodically. The duties of the school medical officers are similar in other respects to those of the public health officers. Treatment may be provided by the school doctors or by others on his recommendation, but is not free; as a general rule it is obtained, if the pupils are children of insured persons, in the polyclinics or dispensaries of the sickness funds. Special provision is made for remedial exercises, orthopedic treatment, convalescent homes, and prophylactic institutions. In the larger centers special schools have been established for children suffering from malnutrition, anemia, myopia, deafness, and speech defects. School nurses (*Schulfürsorgerinnen*) are being appointed in larger numbers to assist the school medical officers and to follow pupils into their homes. Dental clinics and the care of teeth are provided more generally than school medical inspection or treatment; the clinics are established specially for the schools, or are connected with dispensaries or other health centers; the introduction of ambulatory clinics has made it possible for this form of service to reach out into the rural areas.

More widespread than direct medical inspection is the development of the provisions for health instruction and for physical training with more attention to play and games and activities in the open, of which the *Wanderungen* or excursions and hikes are the most important. The establishment of youth hostels (*Jugendherberge*) has made possible for all children holidays in the open at a cost within the reach of most parents, while many secondary schools have organized their own camps which serve as centers for study and recreation.

For backward children who are educable, but who cannot maintain the pace of normal pupils, Germany was long a pioneer in the establishment of auxiliary day schools (*Hilfsschulen*), to which children may be assigned on the advice of teachers and doctors with the consent of their parents. In these schools the curriculum, which is of a more practical nature than in the regular schools, and the time-schedule are adapted to the children's abilities by teachers who have received special training. Blind, deaf, and crippled children must with the consent of their parents be assigned to special residential institutions for their care, education, and vocational training. Special schools and classes are provided for children defective in other ways — vision, hearing, and speech.

Delinquent children or children whose home influences are detrimental to their proper moral upbringing fall under the provisions of the *Reichsgesetz für Jugendwohlfahrt* (Federal Child Welfare Law) of 1923, further defined in Prussia by laws and decrees issued in 1924 and 1926, providing for the creation of Juvenile Boards (*Jugendämter*) which include in their membership experts, teachers, ministers of religion, and others interested in youth welfare. The duties of the Juvenile Boards include the supervision of foster children, care of minors who need assistance, coöperation in the supervision of delinquents under probation, care of war orphans and children of mutilated soldiers, and coöperation with other authorities charged with the supervision of children and young persons — the police and juvenile courts, created in 1923 to deal with juvenile offenders between the ages of fourteen and eighteen (younger children are dealt with by the Juvenile Boards and may be committed to reformatories but not to prisons). The Juvenile Boards also have certain responsibilities for the supervision of the employment of children and youth.

The employment of children is regulated in Germany by the *Reichsgewerbeordnung* (1869), *Reichsgesetz betreffs Kinderarbeit* (1903), and the *Hausarbeitsgesetz* (1911). Children under thirteen years of age may not be employed in trade or commerce; if over thirteen and exempt from school attendance, their work is limited to six hours a day. Children of school age, if engaged in permissible occupations, may not be employed between the hours of 8 P.M. and 8 A.M. nor before school hours, nor for more than three hours a day (four hours when school is not in session). The employment of children in theatrical performances, the film industry, or any form of the liquor trade is carefully restricted, and for the first two occupations permission may be granted only under special conditions. The employment of children under the age of ten by their own parents or under the age of twelve by others is in most occupations forbidden. Work-cards (*Arbeitskarten*) must be obtained by children who are employed by others than their own parents and are subject to police supervision. Teachers are urged to give special attention to children whose work seems to be affected by their employment; on their recommendation the work-cards held by such children may be withdrawn.

Present difficulties. It is impossible under the present political and economic conditions to anticipate the general direction of Germany's educational system. Any approximation to the idea of the *Einheitsschule* as an organization has been postponed indefinitely. The Thuringian experiment, which was planned on the following scheme:

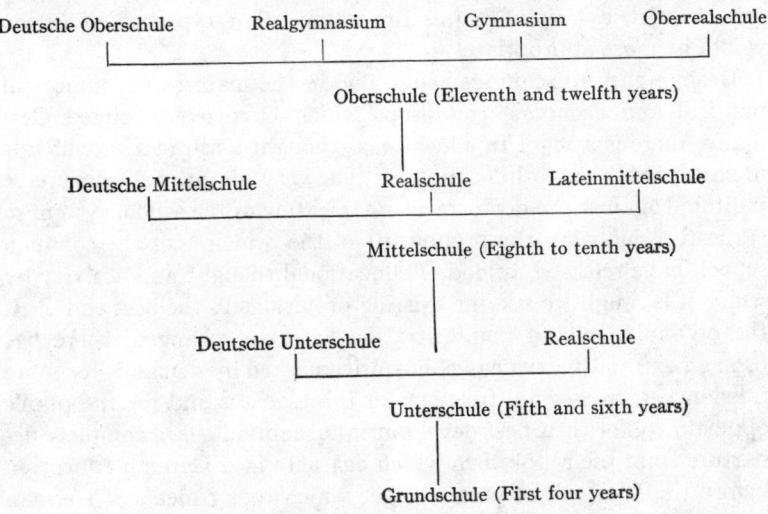

was abandoned with the change in political supremacy from the Left to the Right Wing in 1924. The provisions of the Constitution which were inspired by another interpretation of the principle of the *Einheitsschule* — the establishment of the common *Grundschule* for four years, freedom of conscience in religious matters, but the retention of the sectarian basis of organization in the elementary schools, the free supply of books and school equipment in all but the secondary schools, the abolition of private schools, the award of scholarships and maintenance grants for poor but able pupils, and the preparation of elementary school teachers on the university level — all these provisions have in one way or another been modified, so that little but the skeleton of the principle survives. Amendments have made it possible to enter secondary schools with only three years of attendance at the *Grundschule*; private schools paralleling the elementary have been allowed to continue through inability to provide compensation to their owners or to absorb their teachers in public schools; the religious difficulties have been increased through the *de facto* development of secular schools and classes; the institutions for the preparation of elementary school teachers, though all based on the completion of a secondary education, are not uniformly organized; and the creation of opportunities for poor but able pupils is determined by political rather than national considerations, while the pressure of economic competition is filling the existing secondary schools with a host of pupils for whom other types of education would be more appropriate.

Despite these discouragements, due in the main to the abnormal political and economic conditions which have overwhelmed Germany, there is a vigor in educational thought and practice which is unparalleled in any other country. The very conditions, which have militated against the democratic organization of the school system so earnestly sought by the proponents of the principle of the common school, have released a flood of educational thought and activity by which it is sought to use the existing provisions to the best ends. If the organization and administration have not changed, there has been an extraordinary change in spirit, marked by demands for more freedom — professional freedom for the teachers and for the pupils opportunity for their best development as individuals, a complete departure from the absolutism which characterized German education before the War. The great danger which today menaces German education is that the high ideal, which was set for it in the Constitution (Article 148), that it should be conducted "in the spirit of German national character and of international conciliation" — *Bildung zum Deutschtum* and *Bildung zur Humanität* — may be thwarted by conditions imposed upon the country by forces over which it has no control. A nation driven in on itself, with its future mortgaged for several generations to external powers, and without hope, torn by internal dissension, can hardly be expected to cultivate an educational ideal based on aspirations of friendship and peace within and without.

4. ITALY

Italy was confronted with two outstanding problems in the reconstruction of her educational system which was inevitable after the adoption of the Fascist régime. The first was the provision of an increased supply of elementary education and the liquidation of illiteracy; the second, the reorganization of post-primary, including secondary, education in order to provide an adequately trained personnel for her economic development and to deflect the large numbers of students who were flocking through the traditional secondary schools to the universities and thence to the already overcrowded professions. The principle which was adopted for the organization of the school system was the one employed in the reform of the administrative scheme, that of a hierarchy; to schools were to be assigned specific functions with avenues of promotion only for the ablest pupils and students, the whole scheme being dominated by a system of qualifying and competitive examinations affecting both teachers and pupils. In this way it was hoped that the right school would be found for the right pupil with selective devices which would at the top reduce the competition of an educated proletariat, the cause of much of the political agitation before and after the War. Beyond this there remained the task of inspiring the schools at all levels with powerful motives and ideals of patriotism and national culture. To this task in particular were directed the efforts of Gentile whose philosophy of absolute idealism harmonized with the tenets of Fascist ideology. Of educational legislation Italy had had an abundance, but, despite the dreams of her national philosophers throughout the nineteenth century, there was lacking either the spirit or the ability to make it effective. Fascism brought to the country a new sense of national obligation; Gentile's philosophy set up the claims of the State as paramount. Educationally the problem now resolved itself into one of reconciling the demand for centralization with the desirability of releasing the energies of local groups to make their contributions to national culture.

The educational tradition. The Casati Law, enacted originally in 1859 for the Kingdom of Sardinia and later applied to the Kingdom of Italy had furnished the basis for elementary education until the close of the War. Under this law the provision of elementary education was left to municipalities which were provincial or local capitals and to districts with a population of over ten thousand; elsewhere, or in localities which waived their rights, schools were established by the provincial education committees. Compulsory attendance was required under the Casati Law for only three years. The law was obeyed by the localities according to their means, since they did not receive state aid. The Coppino Act of 1877 extended the period of compulsory attendance to four years, which was further extended in 1904 by the Orlando Law to six years (that is, to the age of twelve) in the larger communities. The same law provided for the establishment of evening and Sunday schools for adult illiterates, introduced state aid, and assigned certain privileges for those who completed the elementary course, such as the rights to vote, to carry arms, to secure employment in public services. In 1906 an effort was made by the Sonnino Law to bring elementary education to the scattered populations in southern Italy and the islands through ambulatory schools and schools with two or three sessions a day. The Daneo-Credaro Law, passed in 1911, attempted to improve the bad conditions which were revealed by examinations, the short duration of the courses, and the poor preparation of teachers.

Repeated legislation on the same subject is always evidence of its ineffectiveness; it was obvious that the laws on elementary education remained pious intentions and that progress was negligible. A survey undertaken by the Ministry of Public Instruction in 1922-23 showed that only 264 communes (local divisions varying from cities to townships) out of the total of 8354 exercised the right to establish schools, and of these the majority were in the industrialized North; the rest left the supply of schools to the provincial authorities. While the supply of classes and teachers was fairly adequate, their distribution was uneven. The percentage of illiteracy rose from 11 per cent in Piedmont to 59 in the central provinces, and 65 and 70 in the southern provinces. The number of pupils enrolled fell from 90 per cent in the North to 41 per cent in the South, and the average attendance from 94 per cent to 32 per cent. Of the pupils in schools only 60 per cent completed the course under the most favorable conditions and 18 per cent under the worst. Classes were either very small or very large; public interest in education was slight and the standards of the teaching profession were low.

The Casati Law of 1859 had also laid the foundations for a system of secondary education which consisted of classical *ginnasi-licei* and technical institutes leading to the universities and normal schools. The dissatisfaction with secondary education and the uncertainty as to its purpose is best indicated by the fact that twenty reforms were initiated by laws and decrees before the recent reform of 1923 was adopted. Secondary school teachers were inadequately prepared, did not enjoy full-time positions in any one school, and were concerned only with their special subjects. The student body was turbulent and undisciplined, examinations were poorly controlled, and discrimination was exercised against private schools. These conditions continued until the eve of the Gentile Reform in 1923 and constituted its background.

The present system. The provision of schools has been regulated by Royal Decrees issued in 1923 and subsequently codified, so far as elementary education is concerned, in the *Testo Unico*, January 22, 1925, and the *Testo Unico*, February 5, 1928. Secondary education is governed by the Royal Decrees, May 6, 1923, No. 1054, and October 14, 1923, No. 2345, and by the Royal Decree of October 6, 1930, No. 1379.

Pre-schools. Provision for the education of young children has been made in Italy for just over a century. The first institution for their physical and educational care was established in 1827 by Ferrante Aporti, one of the leading educational statesmen of the first half of the nineteenth century. His work, begun in Cremona with the organization of the *asilo per l'infanzia*, attracted widespread attention and was speedily imitated. In 1844 Aporti was invited to the University of Turin to establish a school for the training of teachers of young children. From this small beginning the *asilo d'infanzia* spread throughout the country for the education of children between the ages of three and seven. This peculiarly Italian institution, which had much in common with the schools of Pestalozzi, found a com-

Age	Types of Schools					School year
19–	Part-Time Continuation School			Higher Normal School	University and Higher Technical Schools	
18–19				Professional Examination	Matriculation Examination	12
17–18				Leaving Exam.	Liceo Classico	11
16–17			Commercial Surveying and other Technical Courses *Istituto*	Liceo Femminile (Upper Course)	Liceo Scientifico	10
15–16						9
14–15					Entrance Exam.	8
13–14	Corso Integrativo¹	Scuola di Avviamento al Lavoro¹	Entrance Examination	Istituto Magistrale (Lower Course)	Istituto Tecnico (Lower Course)	7
12–13					Ginnasio	6
11–12		Scuola Complementare¹	Trade and Lower Technical Schools			5
10–11			Entrance Examination			4
9–10	Elementary School					3
8–9						
7–8						2
6–7						1
5–6	Scuola Materna Grado Preparatorio					
4–5						
3–4	Nursery Schools					
2–3						

The Italian School System

¹ The *Scuola di Avviamento al Lavoro* is intended to replace the *Corso Integrativo* and the *Scuola Complementare*, which are, however, still found

petitor in the growth, after the first establishment in Venice in 1871, of the Froebelian kindergarten (*giardino d'infanzia*). A third contribution to the education of young children followed after the establishment of the first house of childhood (*casa dei bambini*) in Rome in 1907 by Dr. Maria Montessori. Pre-school children are taken care of in *pre-asile*, *asili materni*, in *nidi* or *crèches*.

Schools for young children are provided by public, private, and charitable or religious organizations. The threefold tradition has been unified since 1923 by the application of the single name *la scuola materna* or *il grado preparatorio* to every school, however provided, intended for young children between the ages of three and six. The term *giardino d'infanzia* is still retained for the school attached to normal schools for purposes of observation and demonstration. The two names which are now given to the infant school, indicate the dual purpose which it serves — it is at once expected to give young children the attention which they would receive in a good home and to induct them gradually into the work of the elementary school.

Elementary education. Compulsory attendance begins at the age of six and continues up to fourteen. The upper limit was largely a gesture to meet the standard laid down in the Washington Convention; the requirements of the law cannot even yet be complied with, partly through lack of schools and partly on account of economic conditions. Further, the regulation of child labor has not yet been brought into agreement with the compulsory attendance law, so that children over the age of twelve may still be employed in industry. Schools must be open during ten months each year from September 1 to June 30 for from 180 to 216 days. Two sessions are held each day except on Thursdays, but where conditions require it schools may be run with one session of five hours every day in the week. Further, school terms and school sessions may be adapted to local circumstances in accordance with occupational demands. The whole elementary school course is divided into four stages: the preparatory stage for children from three to six; the next stage or *corso inferiore* is three years in length and is followed by the *corso superiore*, two years in length; beyond this stage there may be organized supplementary pre-vocational courses (*corsi integrativi di avviamento professionale*). In the larger cities elementary schools have all the four stages; in general, however, not more than the first three or only the lower and upper courses, or even only the lower course, may be found. By the

Royal Decree of October 6, 1930, No. 1379, which created the new *scuola secondaria di avviamento al lavoro,* local authorities are permitted to replace the *corsi integrativi* with the new type of school; if the *corsi integrativi* are retained, their duration may be reduced to one or two years.

Elementary schools are divided into "classified" and "unclassified" schools. The classified are those in provincial capitals and large towns, or schools which provide the lower and upper courses, or schools which have at least forty pupils. Unclassified schools are divided into two types, "aided" or "provisional." The aided schools are schools maintained by private individuals with the approval of the state *provveditore* or regional superintendent of education. Such schools may be opened and receive state aid wherever fifteen pupils can be collected in parishes, around any temporary industrial enterprise, in agricultural districts, at meeting places of shepherds, at a railroad station, or in any place where the population is widely scattered and a permanent or regular school would be too expensive. Financial assistance may be given for a schoolhouse if there are more than five pupils. Provisional schools are those established in localities with less than forty pupils and with an attendance of more than fifteen pupils; aid is granted if more than ten pupils pass the annual promotion examinations. Schools of this type are established by the State on the recommendation of the *provveditore*, and are maintained and supported by societies or corporations recognized by the State; the curriculum only covers that of the lower course, but the function of these schools extends beyond the provision of education to pupils of school age and is directed to the liquidation of illiteracy among adults.

Religion and schools. Religious instruction, from which pupils may be exempted on the request of parents or guardians, constitutes a required subject in all elementary schools. The Casati Law, 1859, included it as a required subject and it was continued as such under the Coppino Law, 1877, although sentiment was beginning to grow against it. In 1904 religious instruction was placed outside of the regular hours of instruction, and in 1908 its provision was left to the option of the communes. Mussolini on coming into power made a solemn promise in 1922 to assign an important place in education to religious instruction. In Gentile's philosophy a new value was given to religion, not as dogma, but as an essential part of the Italian cultural tradition and as an introduction to the study of the relation of man to the supernatural. Hence, it followed as a matter of course that the Royal Decree of October 1, 1923, declared that, as "the foundation and crown of elementary education at all levels, Christian doctrine will be taught according to the form established by the Catholic tradition." It was not, however, the intention of the author of the decree that such instruction should be dogmatic; to Gentile religious instruction at the elementary stage was to take the place of philosophy at the higher. At the same time the ecclesiastical authorities were to be consulted by the *provveditore* in judging the fitness of teachers or others to impart religious instruction. Strained relations between the State and the Church led to conflicts on the subject of religious instruction, the content, and textbooks. In 1929, in the Treaty and Concordat between Italy and the Holy See, it was agreed that religious instruction should be imparted by teachers, priests, and religious approved by the ecclesiastical authorities and certificated by the bishops, whose approval of textbooks was also accepted.

Post-elementary education. Only a small minority of the elementary school pupils continue their formal education beyond the first five years. A small number may enter upon the *corsi integrativi*; for the rest a variety of post-elementary schools, general and vocational, are provided under the direction, since 1929, of the Ministry of National Education. In the organization of the system of post-elementary or secondary education (*scuole medie*), two aims were in the mind of the reformer; first, to organize the schools on a functional basis, each with its own cultural or vocational purpose; and second, to make the system progressively selective by means of examinations. Admission to all post-elementary schools is controlled by an entrance examination. Of those who continue their full-time education the majority enter the *scuola complementare* (supplementary school), corresponding somewhat to the English central school, the German *Mittelschule*, and the French *école primaire supérieure*; it is, in fact, a higher elementary school, which offers a three-year general course, is self-contained, and is not articulated with any other institution beyond it; its leaving certificate confers no privileges, but students may by passing additional examinations enter a kindergarten training school, a normal school, or the lower section of a technical institute. Since 1930 the supplementary school may be replaced by the *scuola secondaria di avviamento al lavoro*. Created by the Royal Decree-

Law of October 6, 1930, this school is intended to provide compulsory post-elementary education to pupils who have completed the upper course of the elementary school or who have reached the age of ten and passed an examination for entrance into a secondary school. The courses are vocational in character to give a preparation for trade, agriculture, and employment in industry or commerce. Two or more types of courses may be given in the same school which must be provided with workshops or a piece of land, for the lease of which the Ministry makes annual appropriations. The schools are supported by the State, provinces, communes, provincial economic councils, and any other interested organization. Pupils who complete the course may be admitted to the fourth year of a technical institute or a normal school or the new technical school established under the law of June 15, 1931, on passing an entrance examination. There are no tuition fees, but fees of 25 lire a year must be paid for practical work and typewriting, and of 125 lire for the *licenza* or leaving certificate.

Three other choices are open: the lower section of a normal school (*istituto magistrale*), or of a technical institute, each with a four-year course, or the classical school (*ginnasio*) with a five-year course. From the normal school pupils may, on passing an entrance examination, continue for three additional years to the girls' secondary school (*liceo femminile*) or to the advanced section of the normal school. The girls' school confers a leaving certificate at the end of the course and after the necessary examinations; successful completion of the normal school is accompanied by the teacher's certificate; graduates of both schools may continue the advanced study of education in the *Istituti Superiori di Magistero* (higher normal schools) of which there are three state-maintained at Rome, Florence, and Messina, and three recognized at Milan, Turin, and Naples. From the lower section of the technical institute students may, on passing an entrance examination, continue for four years in the upper section, where they may elect either a commercial or a surveying course, or they may enter the scientific lyceum (*liceo scientifico*); the graduates of the *ginnasio* may take an entrance examination and continue for three additional years the course of the *liceo classico*. Graduates of the technical institute receive a vocational certificate; those who pass the leaving examination of either the scientific or the classical *liceo* are awarded certificates which admit them either to a university or to a technical high school at the university level. Thus, as will be seen later in discussing the administrative system, the organization of secondary education is based upon the principle of a hierarchy, emergence to the top being governed by qualifying, admission, or competitive examinations. Tuition fees are charged in all the secondary schools here discussed, except the *scuola secondaria di avviamento al lavoro*, and in addition a variety of special fees are fixed for examinations and diplomas or certificates.

By a law of June 15, 1931, No. 889, vocational education was reorganized. Besides the *istituto tecnico*, (1) a new technical school, giving two- or three-year courses in agriculture, trade, industry, or commerce, and based on the *scuola secondaria di avviamento al lavoro*; (2) three-year trade schools for girls; (3) schools to prepare teachers for girls' trade schools; and (4) vocational continuation schools (*corsi per maestranza*), open to all workers and compulsory for adolescents under eighteen, for eight hours a week or two hundred hours a year, were established. These schools admit pupils by examination and award certificates or licenses on the completion of the courses provided. In the technical institutes provision has been made for the addition of nautical and industrial courses in addition to the existing courses in agriculture, surveying, and commerce.

Higher education. The public universities, twenty-one in number, were classified by a Royal Decree of September 30, 1923, No. 2102, into two groups: Group A includes those which are supported entirely by the State (the Universities of Bologna, Cagliari, Genoa, Naples, Padua, Palermo, Pavia, Pisa, Rome, and Turin); Group B includes those universities which receive aid from the State and provincial or communal authorities (the Universities of Parma, Perugia, Catania, Messina, Siena, Sassari, Modena, Macerata, Bari, Florence, and Milan). This classification was undertaken in the hope that weaker institutions would disappear through lack of support. Events have proved, however, that the intense loyalty and local pride in the higher institutions have refused to see them closed. In addition to the public universities there are three private or "free" universities at Ferrara, Camerino, and Urbino.

Private education. Anyone who possesses the qualifications required of teachers in corresponding public schools may open a private school; parents may, if they choose, educate their children at home, if they give evidence of ability to do so; directors of institutions for orphan or abandoned children are required to see that they comply with the regulations for compulsory education. In all cases children educated in private schools must present themselves each year for the examinations conducted at public schools. In the field of secondary education, Gentile and his colleagues proceeded definitely on the principle that the State should not continue the monopoly which it formerly enjoyed by discriminating against private schools through the examinations. The establishment of private schools is, in fact, encouraged in the hope that competition between them and public schools in the common examinations conducted by the State would serve as a spur to the latter.

Social service and education. Perhaps one of the most distinctive features of Italian education is the part played by voluntary organizations in the promotion of the education of infants, children, and adults, and in the provision of a variety of social welfare services. The tendency of the Government since 1924 has been to incorporate these organizations (*Enti morali*) as semi-official agencies delegated to carry on their social-educational activities, particularly in areas which are not readily accessible, where the population is dispersed, or where local government is not well organized. The most important of the educational corporations, all of which were established before the War and at least two in the last century, are *L'Associazione Nazionale per gli Interessi del Mezzogiorno* (southern provinces, Sicily and Sardinia), *Il Comitato Ligure per l'Educazione del Popolo* (Liguria), *Il Consorzio Nazionale di Emigrazione e Lavoro* (southern provinces), *Ente Nazionale di Cultura* (Tuscany, Emilia, and Romagna), *Ente Pugliese di Cultura popolare e di Educazione professionale* (southern provinces), *l'Opera nazionale di Assistenza all'Italia Redenta* (the reconquered provinces), *Le Scuole per i Contadini dell' Agro Romano e delle Paludi Pontine* (provinces around Rome), and *L'Umanitaria* (Milan). All of these corporations had their origin in a desire of their members to create opportunities for education in the backward provinces and especially, among the peasants and mountaineers, although a few concerned themselves with the improvement, general and vocational, of urban workers. They established evening and holiday schools for adult illiterates, provided schools for infants and children, made reading material and school supplies accessible at low cost, organized a great variety of vocational courses, especially in agriculture, farming, viniculture, and domestic arts; some stimulated the development of peasant home industries; others directed their attention to the improvement of sanitary and health conditions and the organization of recreational activities. In 1928 the Government entrusted the management of unclassified schools and schools for adults in Sicily, Calabria, and Sardinia to the National Balilla Institution which in 1930 had 1553 schools with an enrollment of about 55,000 pupils under its charge.

When an attack upon illiteracy was begun after the War, the Minister of Public Instruction, Corbino, created the *Opera contro Analfabetismo* in 1921, later reorganized as the *Comitato contro Analfabetismo* in the Ministry, to coördinate all the activities for the liquidation of illiteracy. In 1924 the Ministry adopted the policy of delegating to the various corporations the task of providing schools for children and adults, and in 1927 entrusted to them the administration of unclassified rural schools under the supervision of the State. Responsibility for the provision of education in those parts of the country, which as a rule do not have the resources to help themselves, is thus divided between the State and semi-public corporations; the State aids through the payment of salaries and the award of prizes, the corporations stimulate and encourage popular interest in education. The programs of the corporations are so elastic that they are able to pass from one stage to another as the foundations are slowly built. Thus evening and holiday courses for illiterates gradually give way to vocational courses or to the development of libraries or the promotion of adult recreative activities — dramatics, sports, moving pictures, or the provision of popular libraries and cheap books. Running through all the activities is a program for the improvement of health and sanitation and for campaigns against malaria, tuberculosis, and other diseases.

Committees of patronage. Every commune is required to have a committee of patronage (*patronato scolastico*); in the larger cities several committees may be established for different sections. Each committee consists of its founders, donors, and ordinary or annual members, and is administered by a committee of five selected by the whole committee in accordance with its own regulations approved by the *provveditore* of the region. Organized originally at the close of the nineteenth century on the model of the French *patronage scolaire*, these committees were given legal status in 1904 and their scope expanded progressively until codified in the *Testo Unico* of 1925. The committees of patronage are expected (1) to encourage and stimulate regular school attendance by the provision of such practical aids as will help poor pupils — school lunches, shoes, clothing, books, and school supplies, and (2) to promote the progress of popular education by the provision of school facilities, the establishment of schools for young children, the supply of libraries, donations of materials to illustrate and enrich instruction, the organization of recreative activities, and of parents' meetings. To promote their work the committees of patronage administer funds raised by subscriptions, state aid, grants from the local authorities, and gifts and bequests. The local authorities are authorized to make annual appropriations to aid poor pupils if adequate funds are not made available by philanthropic organizations. Since 1930 the general supervision of the committees of patronage in each commune is entrusted to the *Comitato Communale dell' Opera Nazionale Balilla*; in provincial capitals their administration is in the hands of a committee of five appointed by the president of the *Opera Nazionale Balilla* supervised by the provincial committee of the Balilla organization.

School coöperatives. In order to promote thrift, coöperation, and a sense of interdependence, funds for mutual aid may be established among the pupils in each school. The idea of the coöperative benefit funds (*mutualità scolastica*) was borrowed from France, and first introduced into Italy at Ancona in 1903. The school coöperatives began to develop rapidly after 1906, and in 1910 they were linked up by law with the National Fund for Social Insurance (*Cassa nazionale per le Assicurazione sociale*). The purpose of the coöperatives is to provide aid for weak and ailing children by sending them to convalescent homes in the mountains or by the sea, to promote physical and recreational activities, and to secure membership for the national insurance scheme. The coöperatives are administered by teachers and parents of the pupils who may be interested in their purposes. Coöperatives may be grouped together to form local and provincial organizations. In 1929 the whole system was placed under the supervision of a national organization, the *Ente Nazionale per la Mutualità Scolastica*. One form of coöperation is prescribed by the elementary school code — every school is required to have a library and all pupils are obliged, unless excused on grounds of poverty, to make a weekly contribution of ten *centesimi* in city and five *centesimi* in rural schools.

Balilla. Crowning all the activities for the promotion of physical and recreational improvement is the work of the *Opera Nazionale*

Balilla (National Balilla Institution). Originating in conflicts between young Fascist sympathizers and youthful Communists in Milan, there was organized first the *Avanguardia Fascista*, whose membership was drawn chiefly from secondary school pupils. In 1922 there was organized the *Gruppo Balilla* for boys between the ages of eight and fourteen. The name Balilla was taken from the nickname of a youthful Genoese hero, Giambattista Perasso, in the war against Austria in 1746. In 1926 the *Opera Nazionale Balilla* was incorporated by law as a voluntary organization maintained by the Fascist Party and private contributions with aid from the Ministry of the Interior. Through the central, provincial, and communal councils Balilla reaches to every corner of Italy. As defined in a decree of January 9, 1927, the aims of the organization are to promote the physical and moral development of the younger generation in accordance with the new ideals of Italian life. The organization is definitely nationalist, patriotic, and Fascist. It aims to promote spiritual and cultural values; to encourage religious education and worship; to disseminate a sentiment for discipline, order, responsibility, altruism, and honor; to train the individual to become a good parent, citizen, and soldier; to provide through gymnastics and sports preparation for more direct military training; and finally, to prepare future Fascists and supporters of the Fascist doctrine. Boys may enlist at the age of eight and remain in the *Gruppi Balilla* until fourteen, when they become members of the *Avanguardia Fascista*; at seventeen their pre-military training begins, and at eighteen at the ceremony of the Fascist levies which takes place throughout Italy on the anniversary of the founding of the *fasci di combattimento* (fighting Fasci), they enter the Voluntary Militia for National Security. In each of the last three years since 1929 more than 90,000 trained *Avanguardisti* have taken a solemn oath of loyalty to the Duce and Fascism and became members of the Fascist Party.

From the start the Balilla organization assumed a military form, with troops, companies, centuries, cohorts, and legions (*squadre, manipoli, centurie, coorti, legioni*); training is provided not only in military but in aviation, naval, cycling, and skiing sections. The officers are drawn from the ranks of elementary and secondary school teachers or from the Fascist Militia. The Balilla is a combination of a variety of boys' organizations found in other countries, such as scouts, church lads' brigades, boys' clubs, pioneers, and cadet corps.

In addition the Institution has undertaken an extensive health program and system of medical treatment under its own staff of doctors and nurses and connected with clinics, dispensaries, convalescent homes, colonies for sun-baths, seaside and mountain colonies, and camps. An accident insurance scheme to provide protection for total and partial disablement was initiated in 1929. In 1927 the Minister of Education advised teachers to urge boys to join Balilla, as one of the strongest instruments for ensuring national greatness.

Arrayed in an attractive uniform (black shirt, blue scarf, military cap, and olive-gray trousers), which may be worn in school, the members of Balilla participate in all national and religious celebrations, have their regular route marches, and have made available for them all types of activities, physical, cultural, and recreational, which the Italian school tradition could never have sponsored. Reaching out to every part of Italy, the *Opera Balilla* has undertaken not only the promotion of the physical regeneration of the young, but the provision of educational and recreational facilities. Vocational education, the encouragement of æsthetic pursuits by the award of national prizes and scholarships, the provision of libraries, moving pictures, and dramatic performances in their own clubhouses (*Case dei Balilla*) — all combine to develop new attitudes of loyalty and devotion. Beyond this the organization arranges educational and patriotic tours of the country, has an extensive scheme of colonies and camps in summer and winter, and each year takes a number of the older members (*Avanguardisti*) on a cruise in the Mediterranean. On the physical side the Balilla has been one of the strongest forces in the development of an interest in sports and gymnastics, in the provision of municipal stadia, in the promotion of local and national contests and competitions, and in the training of instructors of physical education. For the last purpose there was established in 1928 a Fascist Academy, which offers a two-year course of preparation to students who have graduated from secondary schools, and an advanced two year-course open to graduates in medicine was organized in 1929 and intended to lead to a doctor's degree in physical education. A special building has been set aside for the Academy in the Foro Mussolini, the national center for athletic and gymnastic activities in Rome. The two aspects of the work of Balilla are symbolically summarized in its motto, *Libro e Moschetto* (The Book and the Musket). In 1930 the Institution had a membership of 1,974, 822 younger boys and adolescents, distributed in 592 legions under the command of 5588 officers of the Fascist Militia.

Girls have not been neglected in this broad program for national regeneration. Corresponding to the *Gruppi Balilla* are the *Piccole Italiane* (girls from eight to fourteen) and the *Giovani Italiane* (girls from fourteen to eighteen). Here, besides the physical and recreational activities and patriotic education, special activities adapted to the needs of girls are provided.

The importance of these organizations for boys and girls for national advancement was recognized in 1929 when the *Opera Nazionale Balilla*, including the organization for girls, was placed under the Ministry of Public Instruction, the title of which was changed by a Royal Decree-Law of November 14, 1929, to the Ministry of National Education (*Ministero dell' Educazione Nazionale*). Mussolini in referring to this change reaffirmed the principle that

> the State not only has the right but the duty to educate its people, not merely to give them instruction, which after all could be adequately provided by private venture. It is accordingly quite logical that the *Opera Nazionale Balilla* should pass to the Ministry of National Education, particularly since the *Opera Nazionale Balilla* has undertaken the task of physical education in all schools.

Two new under-secretaryships have been created in the Ministry, the one with general supervision over the *Opera Nazionale Balilla* and *Giovani e Piccole Italiane*, the other to have special charge of physical education.

Care of infancy. Boys and girls between the ages of eight and eighteen are thus provided for by the organizations described in the last section. Infants and young children come under the protection of the *Opera Nazionale per la Protezione e l'Assistenza della Maternità e dell' Infanzia*, established by law in 1925 and governed by regulations issued in 1926. The purpose of these measures is to coordinate all activities for the welfare of mothers, infants, and children, whether public or private. The *Opera* seeks to secure protection of these children against disease and neglect, and against exploitation in public performances; it endeavors to stimulate all agencies concerned in the health and welfare of the young, such as those already described. The work of this organization has been supported since 1927 by a tax on unmarried men between twenty-five and sixty-five.

School medical inspection. The care of the health of children, through a system of school medical inspection, is not yet widespread in Italy. The health officers in the communes and provinces are expected to interest themselves in the physical welfare of poor children, to select weak and ailing children to be sent to convalescent homes or open-air schools, and to discover mentally defective children who need care and instruction either in special schools or institutions. School medical officers are found in the larger towns and cities. Genoa, for example, has twelve full-time school medical officers who examine pupils annually and advise but do not give treatment, when necessary; simple treatment may, however, be given by nurses (*vigilatrici*) and in the case of poor children by specialists. Milan has fourteen full-time school medical officers and forty-four nurses; schools are visited by the doctors every week and more frequently by the nurses, who may give minor treatment. Poor children needing treatment are referred to polyclinics or dispensaries. Dental treatment is more frequently and regularly provided than medical in most parts of the country.

Children who are physically weak may be assigned to open-air schools or to colonies, of which a large number have been provided by public and private organizations; some are in the mountains, some on the seacoast; others along the banks of rivers, especially the Po and the Tiber. Mentally defective children are trained in special schools either day (*scuola ausiliaria*) or residential (*asilo-scuola*).

Adult education. Reference has already been made to the large number of semi-public organizations which are engaged in the fight on illiteracy. As illiteracy declines, the same organizations undertake the next step for the improvement of the education of adults through the provision of vocational courses or recreational facilities and libraries. A society for the development of employees' welfare schemes was organized in 1919 through private initiative; the society also undertook the promotion of education and recreational activities among adults. Four years later the society became the active agent of the National Confederation of Fascist Syndicates to carry out the same purposes. In 1925 the society was reorganized by law as the *Opera Nazionale Dopolavoro* (National Organization for Leisure-Time Activities), with power to federate clubs, societies, and other groups for athletic, educational, and artistic activities. In 1929 the organization became both a Fascist and a governmental institution under the direction of the Secretary of the National Fascist Party. The activities of the organization are administered through a national office which functions through provincial and local centers.

The programme of the *Opera Nazionale Dopolavoro* is divided into four great sections: *Instruction* (culture for the people and the teaching of trades): *Artistic education* (dramatic societies, music and chorus singing, kinematography, wireless, folklore); *Physical education* (Italian Excursion Federation and Central Sporting Commission); *Social welfare and hygiene* (dwellings, hygiene, provision for the future, leisure-time occupation for the various classes of workmen).[1]

The educational program includes general and vocational courses conducted usually by elementary and secondary school teachers who receive recognition by the award of special orders of merit which are taken into account in competitions and examinations for promotion; educational films and libraries play an important part in the development of this program. On the artistic side the *Opera Nazionale Dopolavoro* organizes art exhibitions, dramatic performances, and "Cars of Thespis." The athletic program includes not only the promotion of a wide variety of sports and athletics, but tours to all parts of the country organized by the Italian Excursion Federation. On the social and hygienic side the organization has arranged exhibits to illustrate improved housing and furnishing, encourages the development of allotments and kitchen and flower gardens, and conducts campaigns for health education. In 1930 the *Opera Nazionale Dopolavoro* had under its direction about 12,000 clubs, societies, and other organizations with 1,622,140 members. Adult education thus constitutes an important part of the Fascist program and at the same time rounds out the educational system on the general principle that all education is a concern of the State.

Conclusion. The organization of the school system in Italy is thus in its initial stages. It represents an effort to harness the advancement of education to the national and economic reconstruction of the country. The essential spirit of this effort, as in the case of Soviet Russia, is the recognition that educational progress cannot advance without the intellectual and emotional support of the public, that the development of an educational system depends upon the close coöperation of all who are concerned in its promotion. The

[1] Sillani, T. *What is Fascism and Why?*, p. 211 (London, Ernest Benn, Ltd., 1931).

State is not content to rely on its own efforts, but has enlisted all the public agencies — the provinces and communes — as far as possible; but it has gone beyond these and incorporated by its side all organizations of private origin and delegated to them powers as semi-official agencies to coöperate in the common task. For the State and these organizations the ideal is formulated by the Fascist Party, which, as it gradually became identified with the State, has in a very subtle way extended its control over all agencies directed to the promotion of facilities for education. In Italy, as in Russia, it is characteristic of the system which is being developed that there is no break in gauge between education and life, but the definition of both is gradually being moulded in the interests of the Fascist régime.

5. RUSSIA

In discussing the organization of education in the Union of Soviet Socialist Republics, it is difficult to draw a line of demarcation between formal and informal education, so intimately are all agencies and activities of an educative character bound up with, and directed toward securing, unswerving loyalty to the basic principles of the Revolution. It is impossible to indicate the point at which formal schooling stops and informal agencies which affect the attitudes and outlooks, intellectual and emotional, of men begin, since all constitute part of a widespread scheme organized to promote unquestioning devotion to the communist cause, in a social order in which everybody must make a choice and which can tolerate no neutrals. In no other system is the principle that education is life and life is education so completely carried out; whatever affects the minds and hearts of men is utilized and organized for the main end — the interests of Party, whether one is a member or not. Hence not only the schools, as understood everywhere else, but extra-school activities of children and youths, their work and the work of adults, their recreation, their individual and group activities are all brought within the scope of education in its broadest interpretation. Hence the educational system includes not only schools but industrial and agricultural enterprises, the whole of economic life, all political organizations, clubs and centers for youth and adults, the arts, the drama, music, moving pictures, radio, parks and playgrounds, health and sports. All such activities are organized, fostered, and dominated "in strict accord with the main principles of Soviet power."

The Revolution, it is claimed, constitutes a complete break with the past; in overthrowing Czarism the Revolution sought to establish a new social order built on an entirely different ideology. Viewed from one point of view, that of the new economic order, this claim is irrefutable; viewed from another, the thesis may be put forward that the Revolution took as its point of departure the main principles upon which Czarism rested and proceeded to build up a social order on principles diametrically opposed to them. Czarism rested upon the three principles of autocracy, orthodoxy, and nationalism. The Soviet régime is based upon the principle of government by the workers and peasants and the elimination of classes; where Czarism emphasized orthodoxy, the Soviet State is definitely anti-religious; while for nationalism the Communist hopes in time to substitute internationalism. The cynic may claim that, despite the professions of the Revolution, the Czarist principles are still dominant in new forms. The autocracy of the Czar has been replaced by the autocracy of the Communist Party, many-headed, perhaps, but still a minority of less than two millions controlling a population of one hundred and sixty millions. For religious orthodoxy there has been substituted the acceptance of political, social, and economic orthodoxy which brooks no dissenters. Finally, the Soviet attitude on nationalism seems paradoxical in the light of the tolerant recognition of national minorities each with its own language and culture.

In the organization of education, the characteristics of the Czarist system have in the same way served as the starting-point for the new order. Where the pre-Revolutionary school had a religious foundation, the new school is not only lay but actively anti-religious. As contrasted with the old system based on class distinctions, the new school is open to all with a preference for the workers and peasants While the old school was formal and academic and in its upper stages was definitely directed to provide an escape from practical, manual occupations, labor has been made the pivot on which the new school turns. While the old secondary school was devoted to disinterested studies, and especially to the classical languages, the new school cultivates the sciences and practical subjects. The new school as contrasted with the old is coeducational. Finally, where the old régime mistrusted and prohibited student organizations, the new actively promotes them as an important instrument for the education of the younger generation, provided that they are in accord with the accepted principles of the new social order.

The history of Russian education had, indeed, very little to contribute either to the new régime or to any liberal system. Except for occasional spurts of liberalism under Alexander I and Alexander II, which were stopped before they could show any results, education in the nineteenth century was inadequate for the masses and narrowly limited for the classes. It was not until 1905, with the organization of the first Duma, that active efforts began to be made to extend elementary education to the masses and to make post-elementary education accessible to more pupils without distinctions of class. Every Minister of Public Instruction, from 1905 up to the eve of the Revolution, endeavored to secure the enactment of a progressive program of education. Although national legislation failed, the local authorities (*zemstvos*) showed considerable initiative in providing elementary schools to supplement those established by the Holy Synod; as the *zemstvo* schools increased, the Synod schools declined. In 1907 the first bill to create a system of universal education was introduced, but was not passed by the Duma until the following year. The local authorities were to draw up plans for elementary education in their districts, subject to the approval of the state authorities; the local agencies were to build the schools, the State was to make grants for salaries and equipment. A four-year course of elementary education was to be made compulsory for children from eight to twelve years of age, wherever schools were provided. In 1912 a scheme was drafted to make elementary education both compulsory and universal within fifteen years. During this period secondary education was modernized, and made more accessible to the children of workers and peasants; secondary schools were established for girls who were given the same privileges as boys; a system of higher elementary schools was created; and it was even proposed to permit minorities to conduct schools in their own vernacular. The intentions were good, but came too late to stem the revolutionary tide. When the new order was established, it took over a population of which seventy per cent was illiterate.

Present system. Except for the uncertain and tentative gropings for a more liberal system of education which took place for about a decade preceding the Revolution and for a somewhat broader and more profound study of educational theory, the Soviet State began its program of educational reorganization with a clean slate. The ideology of the Revolution would in any case have involved a complete change, for its fundamental principle is that the school cannot be divorced from the political, economic, and cultural régime from which it must take its being and which it must serve. As early as October 29, 1917, the Soviet Government announced that the basis of its educational program must include the liquidation of illiteracy, the provision of free, compulsory, secular education for all, the highest possible education for all who wished to avail themselves of it, the preparation of an adequate body of trained teachers, and unlimited support for the provision of education. Internal conflicts, lack of funds, and the refusal of many teachers to join the Communist ranks prevented any serious attempt to carry out these proposals during the period of militant Communism from 1917 to 1921. Lenin's statement, made in 1920, that "in an illiterate country it is impossible to build a Communist State," soon began to bear fruit. The program was further defined and elaborated by the Eighth Congress of the Communist Party in 1923. The school must be used as an agency for the elimination of all social classes and for building the Communist State. To this end education must be free and compulsory for all without distinction of sex up to the age of seventeen and must begin as early as possible with the widespread establishment of pre-schools. All must be enabled to attend school by the provision of food, clothing, shoes, and school supplies at public expense. The new school must be organized as the unified labor school closely related to industry, social utility, and production, and must be godless or anti-religious, coeducational, and taught in the native tongue of the pupils. The aim of the school must be to indoctrinate all in the ideals of communism. For persons over seventeen, vocational education must be provided and for all toilers opportunities for higher education. All agencies — museums, theaters, etc. — must be utilized for purposes of Communist propaganda. Education must be organized along three main lines — general or social, vocational and technical, and political. Religious instruction had already been entirely eliminated from all public and private educational institutions; it may be given privately to individual pupils and in organized centers only to students above the age of eighteen. The dominating principle that education is the concern of the State alone has affected the place of private education. Private schools have been tolerated to provide either elementary education where a locality is unable to establish its own school or technical or vocational training. In the first case the private elementary school is regarded as a temporary arrangement until adequate funds are available for a public school; in the second case the private technical school is accepted because it may provide courses supplementary to those of the public schools and the subjects taught are regarded as innocuous politically; in both instances strict supervision is exercised by the public authorities.

In practice a dual system was established — the first, consisting mainly but not wholly of the formal agencies, was administered by the central and local educational authorities in each of the constituent republics of the Union; the second, directed to the interests of workers and peasants, or, more broadly, all toilers, was organized and conducted by the Party. The tendency in the last few years has been to draw the two more closely together.

Care of infants. Since the fundamental principle upon which Soviet education rests is that education means "conditioning" the learner in a specific direction, one of the first tasks undertaken was the establishment of *crèches* and nurseries for infants whose mothers are at work or unable to give them adequate care. These institutions, which may be associated with factories or collective farms, are under the supervision of the Commissariat of Public Health. Their purpose is to ensure the healthy development of infants through medical supervision and physical activities; but their function is also educational, and even at this stage educational and socially useful activities according to Soviet principles may be begun. The number of *crèches* and nurseries is inadequate, but they serve as important centers for the dissemination of information on the care of infants and children which are supplemented by the public laws and measures for the protection of maternity, and the provision of consultation centers for mothers and children, and with milk stations. Some evidence of the effectiveness of these organizations for infant and child welfare is already forthcoming in the decline of infantile mortality.

Pre-schools. Social or general education begins in the pre-schools or kindergartens to which children are admitted at the age of three and which are under the People's Commissariat of Education. These schools, day or residential, have adopted a negative attitude to the pedagogy of Froebel and Montessori as artificial and foreign

Age	Education of Children and Youth	Education of Adults
Above 22 Years	Research Institutes and Higher Courses	
17 to 22 Years	Universities and Higher Schools	Communist University
15 to 17 Years	Second Division of Secondary School and Special Courses / Technicums	Workers' Faculties / Adult School of Second Grade / Soviet Party School of Second Grade
12 to 15 Years	First Division of Secondary School / Vocational School / School of Working Apprenticeship / School of Peasant Youth	Soviet Party School of First Grade
8 to 12 Years	Primary School	Adult School of First Grade / School of Political Literacy
3 to 8 Years	Kindergarten and other Pre-School Institutions	School of the Liquidation of Illiteracy
Under 3 Years	Nursery	

General Scheme of the System of Public Education in the R.S.F.S.R.
After Pinkevitch, Albert P. "The New Education in the Soviet Republic, p. 45   New York, 1929

to Soviet ideas and begin, through physical activities, collective work, and the development of a materialistic outlook, which is directed against childish beliefs and folk superstitions, to induct the pupils into the first notions of Marxism and Soviet principles. In addition to the permanent kindergartens, of which there were 5690 with 331,623 pupils in 1930–31, there are summer kindergartens and homes, hearths and playgrounds, which in 1931 reached five million children. Plans were made in 1931 for the general introduction of pre-school education for children between three and six; seven-year children are to be educated in preparatory classes attached to the primary schools.

Elementary education. Primary education is given in the unified labor school which gives a four-year course. Despite the efforts of the Soviet Governments to introduce universal compulsory education, it was not until the Central Committee of the Communist Party, acting on a resolution of the Sixteenth Communist Congress, gave instructions on July 25, 1930, to the Commissariats for Education in the republics that active steps were taken to provide universal education, which is compulsory for boys and girls from eight to twelve. The full program was to be accomplished by 1934. In 1931, the third year under the Five-Year Plan, a decisive advance was reported in all the republics; the Russian Soviet Federation of Socialist Republics reported an enrollment in primary schools of 8,709,937 pupils, an increase of 28.4 per cent over the number in 1929–30 and 105.7 per cent of the plan of the Commissariat of Education; in the autonomous republics the enrollment was 1,506,013 pupils; in the Ukraine 98.2 per cent of the children between eight and ten were registered in primary schools, an increase of 22 per cent over the preceding year. Similar reports were made by all the other republics of the Union, each indicating a more rapid development than had been originally planned. It was expected that by October 1, 1932, illiteracy, at least among the young, would have been entirely eliminated. Pupils who miss the opportunity of attending the regular primary schools or who begin school later are taken care of between the ages of eleven and fifteen in special schools, where in one or two years a foundation is laid either for further education or for self-education.

Secondary education. The primary schools are known as schools of the first grade; these are followed by schools of the second grade.

which may be independent or attached to schools of the first grade and continue the course for three additional years, general in character but with a vocational bias and practical work. Beyond this, some schools provide courses of two additional years, which are either definitely vocational and train the intermediate cadre for factories and offices, or prepare students for admission to the universities and higher institutions.

These schools, which normally overlap with elementary and secondary schools elsewhere, are paralleled by another system of schools. Pupils from primary schools may proceed for three years to schools attached to factories, or trades, or workshops. In the rural areas there has been organized since 1927 seven-year schools for peasant youths, which include the primary schools, or the last three years may be established separately; the purpose of these schools is to coordinate general and vocational education centering around agricultural activities and intended to train farmers and coöperators. In the cities a similar seven-year school has been established, but attached to factories and industrial enterprises to give a general and practical training. In 1930–31 there were 4326 schools for peasant youth with an enrollment of 600,026 pupils, and over 500 factory schools attended by 300,000 pupils.

Technicums. For students who have completed a seven-year course there is available further training in the three- or four-year technicums devoted to specialized training for industrial and agricultural occupations, business management and administration in industry and agriculture, arts and crafts (graphic and plastic arts, theater, music), medical assistants (nurses, midwives, social service), and teaching (pre-school, elementary schools, and extra-school activities). In 1930–31 there were 2998 technicums with an enrollment of 609,064 students.

Higher education. Higher education is provided in universities and special institutions of a specialized character. Their function is to train specialists in the professions, to conduct research, and to disseminate knowledge. Students who have completed the nine-year school are admitted on passing entrance examinations; those who have passed through a workers' faculty are admitted without examination; where the number of students is limited, preference is given to toilers (workers and peasants) or their children. The special higher institutions provide advanced technical training in sciences and mathematics applied to industry and agriculture. In 1928-29 there were 128 higher institutions (including 21 universities) with an enrollment of 167,100 students.

Another type of higher education is that provided for toilers in the workers' faculties (*Rabfaks*), some independent, others, the majority, attached to higher institutions, but with their own corps of teachers. The workers' faculty serves the dual purpose of giving advanced general and vocational training and of preparing for entrance to a higher institution students above the age of eighteen who have already had three years of occupational experience. The courses are three years in length for full-time day students, or four years, if attended in the evenings. In 1928-29 the number of workers' faculties was 164 and the student enrollment was 52,900.

Education and politics. Up to this point there have been described those institutions which are organized to give a general or social education and vocational or professional preparation. It would be fallacious, however, to apply to the Soviet system of education the distinction which exists elsewhere between general and special education; both constitute part of the same process; all are dominated by the polytechnic ideal in a social order where class distinctions are eliminated and all institutions are conducted in the interests of and inspired by labor. Throughout the whole process of education there runs another purpose, that of indoctrinating in the Soviet ideology or politicization. Success in both aims — polytechnization and politicization — has been delayed by the inadequate supply and preparation of teachers. The Soviet authorities have, indeed, been confronted with a formidable task in providing schools and securing an adequate personnel on all fronts. The situation is being attacked and may be met in one direction by the improvement of the material status of elementary school teachers, not only by raising salaries, which have increased from 30 roubles ($15) in 1924 to 90 roubles ($45) a month in 1932, but by extending to them the privileges of workers and peasants in the purchase of necessary supplies. Politicization will proceed more rapidly in formal school instruction through the improved preparation of teachers and their better appreciation of the new pedagogy; this will supplement the extensive, extra-scholastic activities which are directed by the Party rulers.

Polytechnization of schools. The problem of polytechnization has been equally difficult. The new pedagogy, already conceived in outline before the Revolution,[1] stresses the importance of labor as the core of instruction, but as conceived by teachers the criticism has grown that it is as colorless as "activity" instruction in other countries. The factory schools, closely associated with working enterprises, have pointed the way experimentally. The demands of the Five-Year Plan for qualified workers perhaps more than educational or cultural theory have been influential in promoting speedier reconstruction to secure the polytechnization of schools. The Fourteenth All-Russian Congress of Soviets urged in 1929 the necessity of "preparing highly cultured workers capable of understanding new technical improvements and of actively participating in the socialistic organization of public economy." It was felt that the Marxian principle of polytechnic training which would give the child and the adolescent an acquaintance with the scientific bases of all the productive processes, as well as practical skills and ability to use the simplest tools of production, had not been carried out except in factory schools and schools for peasant youth, which were experimental and few in number. This principle, that education must be related to the toil of the workers and peasants in order to develop active participation in collective labor, had been reiterated by Lenin.

The Sixteenth All-Russian Congress of Soviets continued the criticism of the existing school as tending to impart dead knowledge, bookishness, drill and verbalism, and again urged the immediate integration of schools with mills, factories, machine tractor stations, *sovhozes* (state farms), and *kolhozes* (collective farms). Through such an integration the teachers would be in a better position to help in the advancement of the socialistic State and of collectivization. Polytechnic schools, as an integral part of industrial and agricultural enterprises, would eliminate class divisions, the distinctions between city and village, and the gap between manual and brain workers. If teachers are to perform the task of harnessing the schools to the Five-Year Plan successfully, they must be retrained; indeed, it is suggested that the best type of school principal and administrator would be a person who had had experience as a worker, or that successful polytechnization could be secured if the enterprises with which the schools were associated provided the necessary technical leadership and advice.

[1] See especially Pinkevitch, A. P., *The New Education in the Soviet Republic*, Ch. VIII (New York, 1929).

Under the new scheme elementary schools would induct the pupils into practical work and acquaintance with the simplest mechanical tools. Older pupils in the second grade schools would spend part of their time in workshops or on farms, where they would participate in actual processes, or in laboratories for testing and experimenting with materials. Mathematics, physics, chemistry, and natural sciences in general would constitute the backbone of the curriculum. In order to secure guidance for the new direction, centers for research are to be established to investigate the problems of the new education in general, the psychology and pedagogy of the new movement, as well as methods, texts, and other instructional aids. In the promotion of the new program, an active part of the burden would be borne by the Party organization for children and adolescents — the Pioneers and the Komsomol.

Adult education. The educational program of the Soviet régime does not stop with the formal education given in full-time schools. It was recognized from the start that the success of the Communist cause depended upon a literate public and the all-round development of members of a communistic society. The program thus involved two tasks — the liquidation of illiteracy and party indoctrination, both of which are in most cases combined. For the liquidation of illiteracy and semi-illiteracy, centers were established all over the country, in factories, in the Red Army, and in other places where the need was apparent. In this task the organizations for Communist youth have participated extensively. The educational work undertaken in these centers consists, not merely in teaching the three R's and in raising the educational level of the toilers, but also in training in the political ideology of the new social order and to some extent in securing leaders for local groups. For beginners special textbooks have been prepared, based on industrial or agricultural occupations. Beyond this, the aim is to impart facility in reading newspapers and in using books, and in writing and reading letters.

Above the schools for illiterates there have been organized schools for workers and peasants above the age of seventeen, which in three-year courses of some twenty hours a week aim to give the same instruction as in the full-time second grade schools. The courses include practical work related to the students' occupations, studies closely related to life and directed to develop an appreciation of the significance of work, work in laboratories and libraries, and visits to farms, factories, and museums. A further extension of advanced education is provided in evening courses for students above the age of eighteen, who attend two to four hours a week for one or two years. Here the courses are both general and special, political and coöperative, agricultural and industrial. The next stage is provided by workers' evening universities, offering two- or three-year courses at a higher level and with a still stronger emphasis on political training and specialization; political training includes the study of Leninism, the history of the class struggle and economics; the specialized courses include sociology, trade-unionism, coöperation, electrotechnics, chemistry, mechanics, etc.

These semi-formal part-time schools are intimately bound up with a great variety of informal agencies for adult education. Clubs in the industrial centers and village reading rooms in the rural sections combine recreational and political activities, serve as centers for the liquidation of illiteracy and for guidance in self-education. Moving pictures, dramatic performances, concerts, lectures, forums for discussions, the wall newspaper, the living newspaper (dramatization of news), political propaganda and publicity for new movements planned by the Party and governmental authorities, excursions, and study circles are included among the activities of these agencies to raise the educational level of the masses and to train ardent supporters of the Communist ideology. To the same end libraries, stationary and traveling, have been developed on a large scale, not merely to provide books but to give guidance and advice on reading and self-study, which are further promoted by a state system of correspondence courses and instruction by radio at various levels. Finally, a note of symbolism is added by the widespread erection in factories, clubs, reading rooms, and other centers of Red Corners, shrines to Lenin and his works, a substitute for the ever-present ikon of pre-Revolutionary days. Through the great variety of agencies provided for the cultural and material uplift of the masses it is claimed that

On October 1, 1932, the U.S.S.R. will be a literate country throughout. This is entirely secured by the introduction in 1930 of general four-year elementary education and by the imminent final elimination of illiteracy among youths and adults in the school year 1931–32.[1]

[1] Avksentievsky, D., "Education in the U.S.S.R.," *Soviet Culture Bulletin*, No. 6–7, 1931, p. 18. From the statistics given on the same page "in 1931 the U.S.S.R. numbers already over 75 per cent of literate people"; all that was left to be accomplished in 1932 (up to October 1) was to liquidate the illiteracy of the remaining 25 per cent, a remarkable tribute both to the organization and to the methods of instruction!

Informal education. Few countries have so effectively undertaken to utilize their cultural agencies for the general education of the masses. Museums, theaters, concerts, opera, hitherto the preserves of the well-to-do or the intellectuals, have been organized and brought within the reach of the toilers. Particular attention has been given to museums, art collections, and national monuments which are visited by the thousands under the direction of trained instructors. Not only have the pre-Revolutionary collections of art and sculpture been reorganized and placed at the disposal of the workers and peasants, but museums of a new character have been created — educational, historical, anti-religious, industrial, and agricultural — and directed more to political indoctrination than to cultural education. Similarly the theater and moving picture, free to develop independently on the artistic side, are censored and controlled for political ends. The Moscow Park of Culture and Rest, founded in 1929, combines most of the activities mentioned above as a center for mass education. Places are provided for the care of children under the direction of experienced teachers, while for the parents there are available libraries, theaters, moving pictures, museums, and sports grounds. Demonstrations are arranged to illustrate progress in factories, mills, and collective farms. Lectures are given on health and sanitation, on cultural and industrial developments. The "Shock-Workers' Avenue" is devoted to statues of the heroes of the new society — the best shock-workers. Museums of art, exhibitions illustrating conditions before and after the Revolution, dramatic and musical performances and workshops combine cultural and political propaganda. Study circles, recreation halls, and "one-day rest houses" round out what is the largest single center for mass education in its broadest sense. The annual budget for the Park is 6,000,000 roubles ($3,000,000).[1]

Political education. At whatever point the vast educational structure of the Soviet State is touched, it is obvious that it is dominated by the political motive. Education, according to Communist theory, has no meaning except in the social order from which it takes its being; education cannot be autonomous, and there is no such thing as *Eigengesetzlichkeit der Erziehung* claimed by German educational theorists; education accordingly must be synonymous with

---

[1] Bodrov, S., The "Moscow Park of Culture and Rest," *Soviet Culture Bulletin*, September. 1931, pp. 12 f.

indoctrination and propaganda in all its stages and in all its processes, even though instruction must follow the psychological characteristics of the individual. All members of the Communist society must be "conditioned" by education and their environment into an acceptance of the dominant doctrines. Beyond the indoctrination of the masses, however, the training of leaders is essential, and this is a task for the Party and through Party machinery. For this purpose there has been established a hierarchy of organizations from whose ranks are drawn the future Party members and leaders by a process of training, testing, and selection.

The training and selection of the future Party members is arranged in three stages: the Octobrists for children from six to fourteen; the Pioneers from ten to seventeen; the League of Communist Youth, or Komsomols, from fourteen to twenty-three; members may be admitted to the Communist Party at the age of eighteen. There is thus, as a result of the overlapping of ages, an interlocking of all groups, which means that changes in Party programs or problems of immediate urgency at once become the concern of members of all ages. Further, the hierarchical organization deprives the movement of the spontaneity of youth movements in other countries except Italy. It is estimated that about twenty per cent of the population within the age groups represented by the three organizations are enrolled. The performance of socially useful labor and political education constitutes a common bond between the three groups and the activities of each become progressively broader and have more ramifications with the age of the members. On the educational side all are trained to understand the meaning of the life and struggle of the laboring proletariat and the significance of Leninism; all are trained to do missionary work and to help the peasants and workers to the extent of their ability; all are drilled and disciplined in the obligation to be ready at all times to help the Communist cause, and in the realization of their duty to fit themselves for life and the war on capitalism and the bourgeois system by study. As they grow older, the more are the members expected to participate in productive work and to accept assignments wherever the needs of the moment or of the Party may demand. Health and physical fitness are enjoined on all, not only as the ideals of the Communist life, but as the basis of military preparedness. Each older group has its obligations to the next younger group as brothers, guides, and advisers. Admission to the ranks of the Pioneers and Komsomols is through a period of probation, activity, and study; retention in the ranks depends upon active interest, work, and proved loyalty to the new way of life. Constant "purgings" of the organizations, as in the Communist Party, ensure the retention only of those who can be trusted as the new men with new minds. While the Octobrist groups constitute important recruiting centers, it is chiefly the Pioneer and Komsomol organizations which are regarded as the serious schools for Party training. The Pioneers in their schools and the Komsomols in schools and at work are expected to exercise a vigilance and leadership over their fellows of the same age. Where self-government is organized, the Pioneers are expected to exercise control; where new ventures are to be created — as, for example, the creation of factory schools and schools for peasant youth — the direction has frequently been assumed by the Komsomols. These organizations thus help "to unite the more active children into a fermenting element for new experiments and to serve as initiator and leader in the social and political development of the entire school." In the recent movement for the polytechnization of schools, both groups are looked upon as important links between schools and factories or other economic enterprises, just as they have played a leading rôle in the movement for the liquidation of illiteracy and in the spread of the new political doctrines. Through these groups and by means of such activities the Communist Party recruits or rather selects its members, with the result that it has been able with a membership of about two millions to control a population eighty times as large.

Conclusion. Frankly accepting the principle that education is propaganda and that the attempt to separate schools from politics is bourgeois hypocrisy, the Soviet régime has organized an educational structure which is at all points closely related to and an expression of the life which it plans to set up. Starting with the notion that religion is "the opiate of the people," it has not only launched a campaign against religion, but seeks to root out all mysticism and superstition by the cult of a materialistic outlook; moral training based on supernatural or class sanctions is to be replaced by a morality derived from and subservient to the class struggle. The link between school and life is labor, for "before they can engage in politics, science, art, or religion, people must first of all satisfy their need for food, drink, clothing, and shelter." Hence labor in the schools cannot be defined merely in terms of manual activities, but must be real and, as the present move toward polytechnization indicates, that reality must be given concrete expression by connecting the schools with labor enterprises — factories, farms, and workshops. Only in this way can the whole program of the school at any level become permeated with ideas of collectivism and work as the basis of the social order. The school must be not only a vehicle of the principles of Communism in general, but also an instrument through which the proletariat may affect the proletarian and non-proletarian strata of the laboring masses with a view to training up a generation capable of finally establishing Communism.[1] The same association of school and labor will furnish the basis for political indoctrination, since labor organized on collective and communistic principles is an expression of the new social order. To ensure successful politicization the Communist Party has created organizations of its own, not only for the training and selection of its own members, but as leaders in the campaign of political propaganda. Culture, as the expression of the life of the nation, is attained by direct participation in the real activities of life and is enriched by the opportunities afforded to the masses for the enjoyment of music, art, and the drama.

In the theory underlying the Soviet educational experiment there is nothing fundamentally novel; the history of education beginning with Plato and Aristotle presents adequate examples of the doctrine that the educational organization of a state must be determined by its nature. In practice the Russian experiment presents the first example in modern times of a school system intimately bound up with, and deriving its inspiration at every point from, the fundamental principles on which the State is founded. In this respect it offers a challenge to those systems, based on the principles of democracy, which emphasize the cult of individualism, and accepts the thesis that the culture of a nation is not something that can be defined and prescribed once and for all, but grows out of its traditions in a process of adaptation to a changing world. Discarding nineteenth-century liberalism and the principles of freedom which flowed from it and which dominate educational theory today, the Soviet experiment proceeds on the theory that only after rigorous indoctrination can the individual be trusted to be free. It must be admitted that Soviet theory looks upon proletarian dictatorship, which is as autocratic as

[1] Pinkevitch, *op. cit.*, p. 29.

Czarist absolutism ever was, as a temporary measure to be continued until all vestiges of the class struggle have been removed and the victory of the workers and peasants has been assured, not only in the Soviet Union but throughout the world. In the meantime Communist ideology has no place for the notions current in bourgeois societies — individualism, selection, variety, activity methods unrelated to the realities of labor, the dualism between cultural and vocational training, and adaptation of education to a changing civilization. From the point of view of logic there is a perfect case for the Soviet experiment; the fundamental problem is whether human institutions are governed by logic alone.

6. UNITED STATES

The organization of the educational system of the United States is free from many of the implications which are found in other countries, where its different branches and levels have sprung from different origins. As contrasted with other countries, the system is national in the sense that it is built up on the single-ladder plan in which the various levels are articulated with each other and that it is dominated in the main by a common aim. The system is not national, however, from the administrative point of view, since, by the omission of reference to the subject, the Constitution left the provision of education to the States. Within the States education is a state affair, but may be delegated to local authorities. The aims and purposes of education are national, partly because they are based on the universal acceptance of the principle of equality of opportunity, partly because of the mobility of the population which, as it moved from one State to another in the conquest of the frontier, took its educational traditions and practices with it, and to a large degree through the existence of national professional organizations, activities of standardizing agencies especially in secondary and higher education, centers for the study of education which attract students from all parts of the country, research and other foundations whose activities are nation-wide in scope, and the dissemination of a common body of educational literature throughout the whole country. The United States Office of Education, the United States Children's Bureau, and the Federal Board for Vocational Education are national agencies for the collection and distribution of information on the progress of education, but they exercise no direct control over the provision of education or interference in its organization and administration with the exception that the Federal Board for Vocational Education sets up certain standards for the allocation of grants for vocational education administered under state regulations.

The principles underlying the organization and provision of education in the United States were derived from French political philosophy of the eighteenth century defined by the progressive development of the ideals of democracy in the century following the foundation of the Republic. The provision of a democratic system of education built up on the principle of equality of opportunity was inspired by two dominant ideas — faith in the perfectibility of man and a firm conviction that loyalty to republican ideals and democratic equality could be assured by the organization of an educational system provided and maintained at public expense. The general framework of a system based on these principles was already sketched before the close of the eighteenth century.[1] Incorporated as an important part of American political philosophy, these principles were adopted by the leading statesmen of the nineteenth century, and, through them, became an accepted part of the ideals of the American public.[2] Although the Federal Constitution made no reference to education, the state constitutions which were written during the nineteenth century sought to give reality to the principles and ideals already current. Despite the general acceptance of the ideals of a sound system of education free and open to all, it was to take nearly three quarters of a century before they became effective in practice. The gradual movement westward, accompanied by the breakdown of traditions, the development of commerce and industry which was hastened by new inventions and the use of steam and power, the rise of cities and emergence of new social problems through new influxes of immigrants, the demands of organized labor, and the breakdown of class distinctions which became increasingly marked during and following the Jacksonian period — all these forces helped to reënforce the demand of those statesmen and educators who saw in public education the bulwark against ignorance and the foundation of good government. It required many battles on many fronts to secure the widespread establishment of the public school as an institution

[1] See Hansen, A. O., *Liberalism in American Education in the Eighteenth Century* (New York, 1926).
[2] See U.S. Bureau of Education *Bulletin*, 1913, No. 28, *Expressions on Education by American Statesmen and Publicists* (Washington, D.C., 1913).

for all the children of all the people, free, non-sectarian, compulsory, and maintained at public expense. In many places there was encountered opposition to the payment of taxes for education; in others the charity idea of education for the poor prevailed; and in others again sectarian schools had been established and its supporters demanded aid from public funds. The deep-rooted tradition of localism was an obstacle to the introduction of state control and supervision of education. Finally, antagonism to the extension of free education beyond the elementary school was met. Most of the opposition was overcome after the middle of the century and the way was opened for building up a public system of education, including, after the decision in the Kalamazoo Case (1874), the provision of free secondary education. Free state universities had already begun to be established in the first quarter of the century. The public school was now generally accepted, in the words of George S. Boutwell, Secretary of the Massachusetts Board of Education (1853-58), as "a school established by the public — supported chiefly or entirely by the public, controlled by the public, and accessible to the public upon terms of equality, without special charge for tuition." The rapid progress of industry and commerce following the conquest of the frontier (1890) and the great increase in the wealth of the country made possible a wide expansion of the educational system from the pre-school up to the university and the diversification of courses suited to the needs of the whole population. This expansion was, however, very uneven and was most marked in the urban areas; a reorganization of administrative units and of the methods of appropriating and distributing public funds for education helped to increase education facilities in rural areas without, however, reaching all parts of the country equally. Since 1917 there has been a widespread demand for increased aid from the Federal Government for educational purposes in order to equalize opportunities everywhere.

The present system. Although there still exists considerable diversity in the provision of educational opportunities and much variety of practice due to the differences in the size and character (urban or rural) of the administrative areas and in the effectiveness of state control, the general framework of the system of schools is clearer than in any other part of the world. It consists of a ladder or, preferably, a broad highway, of schools starting with the elementary school, entered generally at the age of six, and leading without a break up to the college and university. An investigation made by the United States Office of Education in 1928 showed that of 1000 pupils entering the elementary schools, 974 reached the sixth grade, 855 the seventh, 768 the eighth; 610 proceeded to the high schools, 438 continued to the second year, 321 to the third, 268 to the fourth, and 260 completed the course; 160 went on to colleges and of these 50 graduated.

Pre-school education. The education of very young children has become a subject of interest in the last decade and has produced two movements — one for the education of parents in the care and upbringing of children, not only from infancy up to the entrance to school, but throughout their school years, and the other for the establishment of nursery schools for infants and young children. Parental education has been promoted by federal, state, and local authorities, by private associations, through courses in home economics in high schools and colleges, by educational foundations, and through parent-teachers' associations organized in schools, and local, regional, and national groups. The aim of parental education is to promote an intelligent interest in the development and training of children in the home and at school. The second aspect of the movement, that for the establishment of nursery schools, has made slower progress; 121 nursery schools had been established in 1928 mainly through private effort and in connection with institutions for the advanced study of education and for research into the development of the child.

More widespread than nursery schools are the kindergartens, which enroll 700,000 children, usually between the ages of four and six. The majority of the pupils (about eighty per cent) attend public kindergartens maintained by cities with a population of more than 10,000; the remainder are found in private kindergartens. Most of the public kindergartens are housed in public elementary schools. On educational and psychological grounds there is a tendency to group the kindergartens and the first, and occasionally the second, years of the elementary school into a single unit known as the kindergarten-primary stage, a grouping which is simplified by the fact that elementary schools including the kindergartens are usually under the direction of one principal.

Elementary education. The majority of the children of the country begin their educational career on entrance to the first grade of the elementary school at the age of six. There is, however, no uniformity in the regulation of compulsory attendance throughout the country; although the principle of compulsory education has been accepted in all States, the requirements vary considerably in such matters as age of attendance, minimum length of school term, and scholastic attainments necessary to obtain labor permits.

In 1928 the average length of school terms was 171.5 days, with a range from 138.9 days in Mississippi to 188 days in New Hampshire; each child attended school an average of 140.4 days, with a range from 98.1 days in Mississippi to 171 days in Michigan. The percentage of attendance was 81.8 ranging from 67.1 per cent in Oklahoma to 92.3 per cent in Indiana. The figures for larger cities are in general higher than the averages for the States would indicate; the maximum length of school term in cities is 10 months or 200 days.

Educational opportunities thus vary from State to State in matters of compulsory attendance and length of school term, which in the main affect children who attend elementary schools. There is, however, further inequality, due to the fact that more than half of the elementary schools of the country are in rural areas and are taught by one teacher; about twenty per cent of the children enrolled in the elementary schools of the country are found in these schools. Another six per cent attend schools which have but two teachers responsible for all the grades. In order to correct this situation, there began nearly a quarter of a century ago a movement to improve the opportunities of rural children by transporting them at public expense to consolidated schools; about five per cent of the total number of pupils enrolled in elementary schools attend consolidated schools; in some cases the first four years are spent in a local single-teacher school. Thus about one third of the elementary school population enrolled in public schools are found in schools which are operated under rural conditions, or, to put it in another way, they come from organized localities with a total population of less than 2500. Nearly one fourth of the elementary school teachers of the country are found in rural single-teacher schools; of these the majority are inadequately prepared, and, while many change their positions frequently of their own accord, many more are exposed to insecurity of tenure. These conditions have for many years stimulated an interest in the improvement of rural education, have led to an increase in the number

Age	Types of Schools				School Year
22 –			Graduate School		
21-22	Adult Education		University		16
20-21					15
19-20		Normal Sch. or Teachers College	Undergraduate College		14
18-19					13
17-18			Senior High School		12
16-17	Part-Time Continuation Sch	Four Year High School			11
15-16					10
14-15					9
13-14			Junior High School		8
12-13					7
11-12		Elementary School			6
10-11					5
9-10					4
8-9					3
7-8					2
6-7					1
4-6	Kindergarten		Home		
2-4	Nursery School				

The American School System

of consolidated schools and the provision of transportation, and to some extent have been a contributory cause for the movements for federal aid for education and for a revision of the methods of distributing school funds in order to secure a better distribution of educational opportunities, both in quantity and in quality.

More than two thirds of the children of the country enrolled in elementary schools are found in urban schools in cities with a population of 2500 or more. The length of the elementary school course varies; in the Southern States it is most generally seven years; in other parts of the country it is eight years. In order to provide for the better articulation between elementary and secondary education, there has been a widespread movement which began in 1908 to organize elementary schools on a six-year basis and to create the junior high school immediately upon this foundation.

Secondary education. As contrasted with other countries, secondary education in the United States is free and is a direct continuation of elementary education. Where the schools are seven or eight years in length, the duration of the high school or secondary course is four years; where the six-year elementary school has been adopted, the whole length of the course is six years, usually divided into junior and senior high schools, each with a three-year course. The high school, whatever the length of its course, is an institution which seeks to provide an education for all adolescents who have completed the elementary grades. A direct continuation of the elementary school, the high school does not have any entrance requirements and is selective only to the extent that pupils are compelled by home conditions to enter some wage-earning occupation at the earliest permissible age. On the other hand, with the gradual raising of the age of compulsory education and the introduction of part-time education in many States, a large number of adolescents attend the high school who would under other conditions take up some employment. Confronted with an unselected body of pupils of every degree of ability, the high school has undertaken to perform the functions of every type of school which is provided in other countries in separate schools for adolescents — the secondary schools, intermediate schools, trade and vocational schools, agricultural schools, commercial and domestic science schools. With an enrollment of more than five million boys and girls between twelve and eighteen years of age, the high school is today attended by about half of the adolescent population, while in

California the numbers reach nearly eighty per cent. Except in the largest cities, the high schools are organized on the comprehensive or cosmopolitan plan and offer a variety of courses or subjects which are organized to meet the diverse needs of their pupils. Coeducation is the rule except in a small number of high schools, chiefly in the East.

Continuation schools. Since the high school is so far-reaching in the work which it offers, the unitary system, which is characteristic of the United States, is not very much disturbed by the existence of a great variety of schools. There is available a small number of vocational industrial schools which offer more intensive specialized training than is found in high schools, but in general pupils who do not attend the high schools use the opportunities afforded by part-time schools. Part-time compulsory attendance at continuation schools has been introduced in twenty-seven states, but the regulations include so many exemptions that their general applicability is not extensive; usually continuation schools may be required to be established in areas of a certain size or with a definite number of pupils; or attendance may be obligatory only where schools are available, or exemptions may be granted for personal or family reasons. Thirteen of the States require attendance between the ages of fourteen and sixteen; eight between fourteen and eighteen; two between sixteen and eighteen; two between fourteen and seventeen; two up to eighteen; one up to seventeen; and in one no age limits are specified. The hours of attendance vary from four to eight a week. The work of the continuation schools is generally organized with a vocational bias. Part-time day and evening courses which are not compulsory are also available in such occupations as home economics, commerce, trade and agriculture.

Higher education. Beyond the high school, pupils may continue their educational careers to the colleges and universities, to technical institutes, and to normal school and teachers' colleges. Here certain standards of admission are interposed. In a few Eastern colleges students are admitted by an entrance examination, conducted by each college concerned, or by certificates obtained through examinations conducted by the College Entrance Examination Board in New York, or by certificates granted by high schools, either accredited by one or more colleges and universities or by regional standardizing agencies, of which the North Central Association is the outstanding example.[1] A few institutions of college grade have adopted a system of admission by intelligence tests and school records, combined in some cases with one of the other methods. The requirements for admission to the normal schools and teachers colleges may vary somewhat from this general pattern. In general the tendency is to make the articulation between the high schools and colleges, particularly the state institutions, as close as possible by eliminating any barriers which would be implied by imposing prescribed subject requirements. The rapid increase in the number of pupils in the high schools has had its natural consequence in a great increase in the numbers proceeding to the colleges. Partly to divert this stream, partly to provide as extended opportunities as possible readily accessible to the public in their own locality, junior colleges have been established by adding two further years to the high school or as independent institutions; in a few cases smaller colleges have abolished the last two years of their courses for reasons of economy and have become affiliated with other colleges and universities. This movement is still in its infancy, but is making rapid progress, which points to a possible reorganization of the educational system from the six-three-three plan to a six-four-four plan — that is, six years of elementary school, four years of junior high school, and four years of senior high school. Such a reorganization would mean the completion of the first two years of college work, which is equivalent to the completion of secondary education in most European countries, in the same institution, to be followed either by entrance into some occupation or by continued professional or specialized study in a higher institution. The State and a small number of municipal institutions are free except for certain charges for registration and incidentals; other institutions, of which the large majority are denominational, charge fees. The college in the United States may be an independent institution or part of a university, but in all cases its work is devoted to offering undergraduate courses leading in four years up to the first degree. The function of the university is to provide post-graduate work — that is, work following the attainment of the first degree. As a rule the first two years of the college courses are general in character, and specialization, whether academic, professional, or preprofessional, begins in the third year and may be continued into the university.

[1] See Chapter VIII.

The normal schools and teachers colleges are institutions which offer from two to four years of preparation for candidates who intend to enter the teaching profession, generally but not universally as teachers in elementary schools. With few exceptions these institutions are maintained by public authorities, State, county, or city. High school teachers are in the main prepared in colleges and universities.

Adult education. Adult education was in the past century provided by lyceums, chautauquas, and university extension departments. The great increase of foreigners directed attention to the importance of measures for Americanizing them at least to the extent of providing more training in the use of English and in the elements of American citizenship. More recently the scope and meaning of adult education have been expanded with the realization that formal schooling is inadequate as a preparation for the complex life of modern society. There has not been in this country as elsewhere a spontaneous development of working-class education; the number of organizations deliberately directed to proletarian propaganda is not significant. In addition to extension work conducted by the universities and under the auspices of the Federal Government under the operation of the Smith-Lever Act, a large number of voluntary organizations have been created to promote adult education. Among these are the National Congress of Parents and Teachers, the American Library Association, the National Committee on Home Education, and the American Association for Adult Education. A strong impetus has been given to the development of adult education by the results of Professor E. L. Thorndike's studies of adult learning, which indicated that, contrary to generally accepted opinion, adults are rarely too old to learn, provided that they can be reached along the lines of their own interests.[1]

Private schools. The large majority of children in the United States are educated in public schools, which are free and nonsectarian. Although public opinion is in general opposed to private education because of the fear that it may tend to set up class and other distinctions, there is no legislation anywhere in the country against the establishment of private schools. Virtually the only control which is exercised over them is the right of public authorities to inspect their registers under the regulations for compulsory at-

[1] Thorndike, E. L., *Adult Learning* (New York, 1928).

tendance. Since the War, a few States have forbidden the conduct of instruction in private schools in a foreign language. In no case is aid from public funds given to private schools. The principle upon which the existence of private schools rests was enunciated by the United States Supreme Court on June 1, 1925, when the attempt made by the State of Oregon to forbid the establishment of private schools was declared to be unconstitutional. The statement was as follows:

> The fundamental theory of liberty upon which all governments in this Union repose excludes any general power of the State to standardize its children by forcing them to accept instruction from public teachers only. The child is not the mere creature of the State; those who nurture him and direct his destiny have the right, coupled with the high duty, to recognize and prepare him for additional duties.

Private schools fall into two groups — those established for experimental purposes or in the secondary field to prepare for college, and those created in the interests of some denomination. The large majority of private schools fall into the second group and within this group the majority are Roman Catholic. While the private schools show an increase in numbers and in enrollments, the increase is proportionate only to the growth of the population and is less than in public schools. The total enrollment in private schools of all types, elementary and secondary, represents less than ten per cent of all the pupils enrolled in schools throughout the country. The figures upon which this estimate is based do not include pupils enrolled in private vocational schools, chiefly business colleges, whose number is not ascertainable.

Social welfare service in schools. In *The Children's Charter*, drawn up by President Hoover's White House Conference on Child Health and Protection,[1] there were emphasized the importance of pre-natal and post-natal care of mothers, protection of child health from birth through adolescence, health instruction, measures for the care of physically and mentally handicapped children, the care of the delinquent children, and protection of every child against labor conditions detrimental to his health and welfare. Extensive campaigns have been launched to stimulate the health supervision and care of the pre-school child; courses in motherhood in schools and colleges, the provision of milk stations and feeding centers, the es-

[1] *White House Conference*, 1930, pp. 45 ff. (New York, 1931).

tablishment of children's bureaus, and a variety of publicity activities all play their part in these campaigns in which school authorities, the United States Office of Education and the Children's Bureau, women's clubs, and the National Congress of Parents and Teachers participate. The Maternity and Infancy (Sterling-Towner) Act of 1921 provides for coöperation between the Federal Government and state departments in promoting the health and care of mothers and infants; the work is administered by the Children's Bureau. A recent inquiry, however, reveals that the interest of parents in the health of infants and pre-school children, as evidenced by consultations with physicians, tends to decline after the first year.[1] Health work in schools was begun in Boston in 1894; in 1899 Connecticut passed the first state law providing for medical inspection. Despite these early beginnings, however, the development of adequate systems of school medical inspection has been slow. About half the States of the country require some form of medical inspection of children, but the full implications of such laws have been carried out systematically only in a few of the larger cities. The supervision of the health of children is administered in some localities under the local public health authority, in others under the board of education, in others again under a system of coöperation between the two. Thus in New York the duties of medical inspection of children are in the hands of the Board of Public Health. In Boston, Cleveland, Denver, and Kansas City special divisions acting under the Boards of Education perform these duties. In Milwaukee a School Hygiene division of the Health Department bears the responsibility for school medical inspection, while in Detroit the work is conducted jointly by the Board of Health and the Board of Education. In California the health supervision of pupils and school buildings is entrusted by law to boards of education; in Virginia it is the joint responsibility of the educational and health authorities. There is thus no uniformity of practice throughout the country, and, in the absence of a federal authority directly concerned with the health of the child, no information is available either as to the extent or effectiveness of school medical inspection. The general theory on the subject is in favor of concentrating all matters concerning the health of the

[1] "Health Protection for the Pre-school Child," *White House Conference on Child Health and Protection* (New York, 1931).

child, medical inspection, and health instruction in the hands of the education authorities.

Despite the apparent inadequacy of widespread systems of school medical inspection, few subjects have been so extensively discussed in the last two decades as has the health of the child. Health programs have been given publicity, not only by school authorities, but by a large number of voluntary organizations like the Red Cross, Anti-Tuberculosis organizations, the Federation of Women's Clubs, Chambers of Commerce, and the American Child Health Associations. Such programs are, however, concerned more with health and physical education in the schools than with the general organization of systems of school medical inspection for remedial and preventive measures. Systems which provide for periodical inspection are rare, but, apart from the control of contagious diseases, and immunization against smallpox and diphtheria, teachers and school nurses are entrusted with the task of discovering children who need medical attention in cases of malnutrition and ear, eye, and nose troubles. In an authoritative work the present trend is stated to be as follows:

> The school physician is becoming more and more a medical consultant and less a badly rushed examiner. Cases which require definite medical opinion are referred to him and he will gradually examine fewer supposedly normal children in his school work, except when unusual service is provided. His time will be used in a way which will make the best use of his medical skill and training.[1]

The practice as to treatment varies; where nurses are employed and the cases are simple, they follow the child into the home; in more serious cases the parents are expected to consult their own physician or are referred to a clinic, dispensary, or hospital; in some rural areas traveling clinics have been provided by state health departments or by the Red Cross or other voluntary organization. The dental clinic is the one most commonly found in different parts of the country, but here again the amount and character of the treatment given varies — in some cities the work is limited to examination of the teeth and recommendation of treatment; in others full treatment may be given. On the school side lessons on the proper care of the teeth constitute an important part of the program of health instruction.

[1] Wood, T. D., and Rowell, H. G., *Health Supervision and Medical Inspection of Schools*, p. 218. (Philadelphia, W. B. Saunders Company, 1927.)

In general it may be said that as contrasted with England the tendency in the United States is to place greater emphasis on direct health instruction and on the promotion of coöperation between the school, the home, and the health services in all that concerns the health of the child; medical inspection is considered desirable but

school health service should do nothing for the child that can be done effectively in the family, unless it is something done primarily to educate the child or his parents. Remedial and curative work should be left to the family. While the promotion of health is one of the cardinal objectives of the school program, no service should be performed in such a manner that it takes away the fundamental privilege or responsibility of the home in relation to its children.[1]

The logic of this argument which, if applied to public education, would play havoc with the principle of equality of opportunity, does not affect the treatment of physically and mentally handicapped children. Although there is adequate evidence of the wide prevalence of malnutrition among school children, free meals are rarely provided by public authorities even in necessitous cases; here again greater reliance is placed on direct instruction in health and diet and the careful supervision of lunch-rooms and cafeterias in schools. A few localities have organized special nutrition classes. For the physically handicapped — anemic, sickly, tubercular, hard of hearing, myopic, cripples, epileptics, and cardiac cases — special classes or schools are organized in the larger cities; coöperation between state and local authorities provides for the institutional care of the blind and the deaf and dumb, although in the case of the blind there is a tendency to train them to take their places in the regular schools. New York State provides scholarships to enable blind students to continue their work in high schools and colleges with the aid of a reader. The treatment of backward children depends entirely upon the degree and nature of their backwardness. The application of intelligence tests, the degree of retardation, and more extensively, in recent years, careful diagnosis by psychologists and psychiatrists in psychological clinics, with the coöperation of physicians when necessary, have determined the type of training or education to be given to the mentally deficient. These measures vary from retention in regular classes if segregation is likely to do more harm

---

[1] Report of the Sub-Committee on the Administration of the School Health Program. *White House Conference on Child Health and Protection* p. 11 (New York, Century Co., 1932).

than good, or grouping in ungraded, retarded, or special classes under teachers who are specially selected for the work and who are trained to adapt instruction to the needs of these pupils, to commitment to special institutions.

Employment of children. The employment of children is regulated by state laws. Federal laws which were passed on the subject in 1916 and 1919 were declared unconstitutional, and an attempt to secure the consent of the states to a constitutional amendment in 1924 was ineffective. In the absence of federal regulation, the same variety prevails in the laws, administration, and control of child labor under the state laws as in the case of compulsory school attendance, full-time and part-time. National concern on the subject is promoted by voluntary agencies such as the National Consumers' League, the National Committee on Child Labor, and the American Federation of Labor; the Children's Bureau, which was created in 1912 under the United States Department of Labor, is entrusted with the general task of securing and disseminating information on all matters affecting the welfare of children — infant mortality, juvenile courts, dangerous occupations, accidents and diseases of children, employment, and legislation concerning children. State laws on the employment of children deal with the minimum age at which children may be employed, physical and educational requirements for obtaining employment certificates or work permits, and the hours of labor. The minimum age at which children may begin work varies from fourteen to sixteen, but so many exemptions are provided in the laws that many children are employed before attaining the minimum age prescribed in any state law. Nor is there any general regulation of the kind of work in which children may engage; agriculture and domestic service, employment by parents and home work are in most cases not regulated; dangerous occupations from which children are excluded vary from State to State; finally, the occupations in which they may engage may be described by the laws in such general terms as "any gainful occupations" or may be listed in detail. Street-trading is regulated by laws in about half the States, but three fourths of the States permit children under twelve to engage in it. The hours of labor of children under sixteen range from eight hours a day and forty-four hours a week to ten per day for six days a week. Night work after 6 or 7 P.M. is prohibited in all but thirteen States. A physical examination is required for obtaining an employment certificate in twenty-seven States; the completion of eight grades is prescribed for the same purpose in only one third of the States; while in the rest this requirement varies from the completion of the fourth to the eighth grade or merely the attainment of the fourteenth birthday. The employment certificate is as a rule granted on a specific promise of employment and must be renewed when a change takes place within two years following the prescribed minimum age. Regulations on the employment of children during school terms are rarely found, and employment during vacations is controlled by the requirement of work permits in only a small number of States. The administration of state regulations of child labor is entrusted to state boards of health or state labor departments or industrial commissions which usually delegate the local administration to school officials, but, in the absence frequently of adequate measures of supervision, considerable variations may be found within a State in the interpretations of the laws. In New York State a general employment certificate may be granted by local school officials to applicants between the ages of fourteen and seventeen who have completed eight grades of the elementary school and have a promise of employment; the State Commissioner of Education, coöperating with the Commissioner of Health and the Industrial Commissioner, prescribes the form and content of the employment certificate; the law is enforced by the Industrial Commissioner, school attendance officials, and local school superintendents; employers must report the beginning of a minor's employment within three days.

The problem of child labor is intimately bound up with that of the choice of the right occupation. With pupils in elementary schools little is being done in the way of guidance, but with high schools pupils considerable progress is being made in this direction. The junior high school, for example, has as one of its chief functions the task of discovering the vocational fitness of pupils by the provision of exploratory courses, on the basis of which their programs may be organized. In high schools in general the positions of educational and vocational counselors, whose function it is to discover the aptitudes of the pupils and to advise them on the choice of curricula and occupations. Courses in occupations are offered in a large number of high schools in order to aid the pupils in making intelligent choices. Beyond this, vocational guidance bureaus, public and private, have been established which by means of psychotechnical tests endeavor to discover the interests and aptitudes of applicants, to advise and to place them.

Dependent children. Dependent children are cared for by voluntary non-sectarian agencies, usually children's aid societies of which the New York Children's Aid Society, established in 1853, was the first, by societies under religious auspices, and, in a few cases, by state authorities like the Division of Child Guardianship of the Massachusetts Department of Public Welfare or the Children's Bureau of the Minnesota State Board of Control. The interests of these organizations are promoted by the National Children's Home and Welfare Associations. The general tendency in dealing with dependent children is to provide them with satisfactory homes, first, if the mother is alive, by the grant of a pension which is provided by law in forty-two States; secondly, by placing them in foster homes; and, only in the last resort, by sending them to institutions.

Neglected children, who are distinguished from dependent children by the fact that they live under conditions detrimental to their physical and moral welfare, and delinquent children, come under the purview of juvenile courts, or domestic relations or family courts. Juvenile courts, first established in 1900, are found in all but two States and in all large cities. Their jurisdiction may extend to minors of all ages up to seventeen; in California the age limit is twenty-one. Girls are usually brought before women referees. The aim of the juvenile courts is primarily to recommend measures for the reform of the children brought before it rather than to mete out punishment. Educators, physicians, psychologists, psychiatrists, and social workers in increasing numbers are called in to coöperate with the juvenile courts. The juvenile court is, however, beginning to be looked upon as the last resort. Preventive measures are regarded as more important in the case of maladjusted or problem children. Since the organization in 1909 of the National Committee for Mental Hygiene and the Juvenile Psychopathic Institute in Chicago, and more particularly since 1921 when the Commonwealth Fund began to aid their development, the spread of psychological or child guidance clinics has been rapid. The aim of these clinics is through medical, psychological, and psychiatric diagnoses to discover the causes of maladjustment and to recommend measures for their removal with the help and advice of social workers.

Recreation and welfare. Concern for the welfare of children up to the age of eighteen is promoted by a large number of organizations which are national in scope and either have local and regional branches or coöperate with other organizations for the same purpose. Among these organizations are the Children's Bureau of the United States Department of Labor, state bureaus or departments of child welfare, the National Child Labor Committee, the Child Welfare League of America, the National Child Welfare Association, the American Child Health Association, the Child Study Association of America, the Playground and Recreation Association, and the National Congress of Parents and Teachers.

It might almost be argued on an examination of the provisions that more attention is given to the welfare of handicapped, neglected, dependent, and delinquent children than to the normal. The responsibility for the welfare of normal children is naturally left to the parents, but, with the increasing complexity of modern life and the decline of family control, interest in the importance of providing adequate means for play and recreation is growing. A recent investigation[1] reveals the fact that playground facilities are available for only five and a half millions of the thirty million children of the country, and that such facilities are almost non-existent for rural children. Vacation schools, which were started in New York in 1897, were provided in 447 cities in 1928 and reached less than half a million children; such schools are intended to provide pupils with an opportunity of advancing in their studies or, if retarded, to catch up; usually instruction is provided for three or four hours each day, but with little opportunity for play and recreation after school hours. Summer play schools are being organized under the auspices of the Child Study Association; twenty-four such schools, of which twenty-one were in New York, were provided in 1930. The popularity of summer camps is spreading; although there are 300 camps maintained by municipal authorities, there are no examples of any directly conducted by school authorities. The majority of the summer camps are provided by private organizations, including commercial ventures, boy and girl scout associations, Y.M.C.A. and Y.W.C.A., fraternal orders, and the 4 H clubs under the United States Department of Agriculture. In 1929 it was estimated that about 1,150,000

[1] "Summer Vacation Activities of the School Child," *White House Conference on Child Health and Protection* (New York, 1932).

enjoyed the opportunity of spending from two to eight weeks in summer camps.

In general it may be concluded that reports and discussions of the various groups which participated in the White House Conferences in 1930 and 1931 reveal the fact that parental responsibility alone cannot be relied upon to provide all that is considered essential for the promotion of child welfare — health, play, and recreation, and a sound basis for the growth and cultivation of interests. Whether the recommendations of the many committees at this Conference will lead to larger public provision for child welfare, it is too early to say; one thing is certain, and that is, that anything beyond the provision of educational facilities and all that is involved therein is likely to be criticized as socialistic and as interfering with the proper exercise of parental responsibility. Such criticism will have to be confronted with the fact that, in providing free education for all "from the gutter to the university," the United States set an example of socialistic legislation which has not yet been matched by any other country in the world. Other countries are, however, pointing the way to a realization that a sound system of education cannot stop short of measures which will ensure complete supervision, in coöperation with the home, of the welfare of the child.

CHAPTER V

ADMINISTRATION OF EDUCATION

The scope of educational administration. From the provision of elementary schools for the masses and a relatively small number of secondary schools for a selected group, the organization of education has become one of the largest of the public enterprises undertaken by most countries today. From the point of view of expenditure alone, the cost of education ranks among the first three of the items in national budgets; if local and capital expenditures and the cost of private education were taken into account, there can be no doubt that education would rank as the leading enterprise undertaken by most governments. Thus the percentage of expenditures on the four major items in the national budgets of England, France, and Italy as follows:

	ARMY (per cent)	NAVY (per cent)	AIR FORCE (per cent)	EDUCATION (per cent)
England	4.5	5.8	2.0	6.4
France	12.9	5.7	4.5	6.0
Italy	12.8	5.6	3.3	6.6

Corresponding figures for Germany, the Union of Soviet Republics, and the United States cannot be given, since the cost of education is in the main borne by the several States of these countries, while the cost of defense is borne by the central governments.

The management of such a vast enterprise inevitably implies the establishment of some machinery for its administration. To a great extent the administration of education is not exempt from the principles of efficiency which govern the administration and organization of any other extensive undertaking which involves the coöperative activity of a large personnel for the attainment of some particular end. There is, however, a very real danger of confusing, because of some superficial resemblances, the administration of education with the administrations of an industrial or commercial or other similar organization. The latter is concerned either with the production or the sale of some material product, measurable in quantity and quality; education, however, deals with human beings, and, while it is concerned with standards, cannot be either successful or efficient if it aims at standardization. A system of educational administration which ignores the fact that those concerned in it, whether as educators or educands, are individuals with personalities must result in formalism and stagnation, and even administration in industry and commerce is likely to be in the long run more successful if it does not neglect the human element. It is, accordingly, only to a limited extent that the administration of education overlaps with other types of administration. Hence its problems assume a different character, and that not merely because of the ends for which it exists, but also because of the variety of interests with which it must concern itself — pupils and students, teachers, parents, a multiplicity of other groups, the community and the nation. There is always present, however, the danger that, as a consequence of the vastness of the enterprise, serious mistakes may be committed by concentrating on the machinery of administration rather than on the ends which it should seek to promote; this danger is all the greater because in industry and commerce the ends are more or less clearly recognized, while education is too elusive an affair to be bound by a formula. Even in industry and business that administration which is least obtrusive often turns out to be the most efficient and successful.

Factors determining the character of administration. The character of educational administration is determined in general by two factors — the theory of the State and the theory of education which may be prevalent in a country, although, as will appear later, exceptions to this general statement do exist. As a rule, however, the authoritarian State tends to adopt a highly centralized system of administration, while the federative State, the State which recognizes the rights of local groups and communities to self-determination, is content to exercise a minimum of interference, to enter into a partnership with its constituent areas, and to delegate to them a certain amount of responsibility for the administration of their own affairs. From the educational point of view, a centralized system of administration seeks to secure uniformity and to mould the rising generation according to a preconceived pattern; its methods are those of indoctrination. The decentralized system aims to promote adaptation to the local environment and variety; its methods are empirical and experimental in a broad sense. The first system assumes the responsibility of controlling every aspect of the educative process; the second is satisfied to set up minimum standards and to leave the rest to local initiative.

Systems of administration are colored and affected not only by the political character of the State which they serve; they are governed also by the attitudes to national culture. Where the ideal of a fixed, unchanging national culture prevails, a centralized system of administration is set up to protect it against change; where national culture is conceived as the outgrowth of the free intercourse of men, of the impact of mind upon mind, and of the adaptation of man to his changing environment, decentralized system of administration, which gives free play to these interactions, is likely to result. To state the differences in such simple terms does not mean that certain difficulties and cross-currents are ignored; even in a centralized system freedom may be permitted at certain levels of the educative process (academic freedom, for example, in the German universities before the War, and free activity methods in the schools of Russia and Italy after certain guarantees of loyalty to the existing régime are established), while in a decentralized system certain restrictions on freedom may be found (the avoidance of politics and controversial issues in the English and American schools and control of the teaching of history and of nationalism in the latter).

Finally, the type of administration adopted in any country may be determined by the origin of the national system of education. In the European countries national systems of education were built up and developed by the respective governments on the principle that in this field the right of the State is supreme. Thus the *Allgemeine Landrecht*, issued in Prussia in 1794, incorporated into the code a principle already recognized in Germany that "Schools and universities are state institutions.... Such institutions may be founded only with the knowledge and consent of the State"; in France Napoleon's decree of March 17, 1808, incorporated the same principle, that "No school, no establishment of instruction whatsoever, may be set up outside the Imperial University and without the authorization of its head"; the Italian system of education had its origin in the Casati Law of 1859. It is unnecessary to enter into the reasons for the adoption of this principle; so far as the administration of education is concerned, the result was the establishment of a state monopoly in education and of a central machine for its organization and control. Centralized systems of education have, of course, had other than purely political or nationalistic origins; thus they are characteristic of many parts of the British Dominions (some of the Canadian Provinces, the Australian States, and New Zealand), and many Latin-American countries where the exigencies of scattered communities demanded some kind of central governmental action to make the provision of schools possible, without, however, assuming a monopoly of right. Neither the contribution of centralized control to building up systems of education nor their efficiency up to a certain point can be denied, but the defects of centralization outweigh the advantages, for, while it secures uniformity, it breeds inertia and destroys that spirit of initiative which keeps education alive; while it presents superficially a clean-cut and tidily organized scheme of administration, it prevents the development of that adaptation to local differences which contributes to the progress and advancement of national culture; and although all schools are treated alike, the result is monotony unrelieved by the color which comes from variety.

Decentralized systems of administration have in general developed fortuitously; the theory on which they are based has usually been a rationalization to justify their continuance. In England, although there are numerous examples of state intervention,[1] there has not, until recently, been developed a theory of national education. Schools were provided, privately by individuals or groups, and when the State entered into the field of education, it entered as a partner. The doctrine of *laissez faire* was transferred from economic to political theory, and the principle of local or group initiative was adapted as the basis for the development of a national system of education. As the system began to expand after 1902, it was recognized that the duty of the State is to aid, to advise, to encourage, and to stimulate rather than to control education. The system of education is thus being developed through local effort and initiative rather than through the exercise of the sovereign right of the State. The process of development in the United States has been somewhat similar; schools were established and administered by the local districts with little control from the States, with the result that, when the principle was definitely established that the right to provide and control educa-

---

[1] See De Montmorency, J. E. G., *State Intervention in English Education* (Cambridge, 1902).

tion is vested in governments, the competing principle of local autonomy was retained with the understanding that the local authorities exercised their powers in education by devolution from the State. Hence the outstanding features of both the English and the American system of education are variety and an absence of uniformity. Instead of the simplicity and smoothness of the centralized systems, the English and American present a ragged edge of peaks and dales; the absence of uniformity is more than counterbalanced by the leadership and guidance provided for each country by the progressive authorities, for it is characteristic of the centralized system that the minimum prescription often becomes the maximum, while the decentralized system provides room for experimentation and adaptation to changing needs. There is always the problem, however, in the decentralized system of the backward or the indifferent area; the result in some places of the existence of social groups which provide for their own children through private schools, in others of ignorance and negligence. It is the recognition of this defect that is leading to the realization that, if equality of educational opportunities is to be provided, the size of local areas must be enlarged by consolidation of small districts or by their incorporation in larger areas. Such a movement would not, however, militate against the fundamental principles upon which centralization rests.

The purpose of administration. The problem of the administration of education may be considered from an entirely different point of view from those presented. Fundamentally the purpose of educational administration is to bring pupils and teachers together under such conditions as will most successfully promote the ends of education; or, as an eminent English administrator stated,

To enable the right pupils to receive the right education from the right teachers, at a cost within the means of the State, under conditions which will enable the pupils best to profit by their training.[1]

The question which immediately presents itself is, Who is to determine the character of the "right education"? The question can only be answered by considering those who are concerned in the process and ends of education. Obviously the first group concerned consists of the parents, but as experience shows this obligation is not always recognized by parents; but there are other groups — the

[1] Balfour, Sir Graham, *Educational Administration*, p. 38 (London, The Clarendon Press, Oxford, 1921).

community and the various groups which make it up, and the nation — which, in so far as they are interested in social progress and national well-being, have a paramount concern in providing the necessary machinery of education without, however, overriding the right of parents to provide for their children an education which the other groups concerned can pronounce efficient. There are, however, other factors which determine concepts of "right education" — history and tradition, political and nationalistic ends, cultural purposes, national character, and the survival of class distinctions which demand one type of education for the masses and another for the classes.[1]

It may be objected that the teachers have not been mentioned. There is, it is true, a movement for professional autonomy in education; if this movement means (as it seems to mean in the new or progressive education, in "free" education) that the ends of education can be determined only on the basis of the principle of growth determined wholly by a philosophy and methods based on the physiology and psychology of the pupil, the movement is untenable. Autonomy in education can only mean that the selection of content and the educative process must be organized in the light of a philosophy of education, but such a philosophy cannot escape the influences of the environment (human and material) in which the school exists. The concept "school and society" has a very definite and real implication that the school exists for society. This does not mean the perpetuation of the rigidity and inflexibility which result in systems wholly controlled by society through its central government, but it does throw the responsibility upon the teacher and upon educators of understandingly interpreting the civilization and culture of the society which they serve and of giving them meaning in the school. On the other hand, this point of view also connotes that education is a coöperative affair which cannot successfully be conducted without the interest and support of those groups which make up society, whether local or national.

The same criticism is applicable to systems which are centrally administered, that, even though they may provide room for the creation of local groups, they are more concerned with the production of common patterns through uniformity of control, curricula, courses of study, time-schedules, methods, and standards of exami-

[1] These factors have been considered at greater length in other chapters.

nations; under such conditions the local group is but the lengthened shadow of the central authority. The essential features of administration in such systems are expert bureaucracy and control through regulations, decrees, and laws. It is in such systems of centralization carried to excess that the administrator could, as did a Minister of Public Instruction of France in the middle of the last century, point out with pride that at a particular moment all pupils in all schools of a certain type throughout the country were engaged in reading the same page in the same author.[1] The most serious defect of centralization, however, is that it is too frequently concerned with ends defined without regard to those who are to participate in the educative process. There is no lack of efficiency in such a system, but it is an efficiency which consists of the best adaptation of means to ends that are fixed and defined. Thus the curriculum and course of study for Prussian elementary schools remained virtually unchanged between 1872 and 1921, and those for French elementary schools between 1887 and 1923, despite the fact that social and economic conditions had changed in that time, progress had been made in educational theory and psychology, and the teachers were more than ready to undertake experiments in new directions. A centralized administration means too frequently that progress is too closely controlled by the superior authorities and that changes occur only when it dictates them, while normally social and educational progress is determined rather in an atmosphere which leaves room for free adaptation of institutions to changing demands; progress depends essentially upon an experimental attitude. For this type of progress decentralization is necessary, and even in each area the school should enjoy a certain measure of freedom and self-determination, limited only by such prescriptions as will guarantee equality of opportunity and minimum standards of achievement.

Functions of a central authority. If the last statement is accepted, the ideal system should represent the coöperation of both local and central authorities. In an ideal system the functions of a central authority should include the supervision of the administration of such laws as the State is justified in the interests of society and the

---

[1] Perhaps it was the effect of the same type of centralization which made it possible for the author in 1909 to hear a lesson in one Prussian normal school continued on the following day in another normal school some thirty miles away. Somewhat the same effect is produced in Argentina, where all the secondary schools irrespective of size and location had several years ago exactly the same type of scientific apparatus, entirely irrespective of their needs.

nation to enact. Beyond this, the central authority (1) should aid, advise, stimulate, and reward educational effort; (2) should promote the development of an efficient because articulated system; (3) should, as the result of its command of information and practices, suggest minimum standards to be attained; (4) should exercise leadership and give guidance without, however, encroaching on the freedom of other authorities; (5) should encourage and promote research and investigations; and (6) should make available accurate information and reports.

The constitution of the central authority is determined by the nature of the duties which it undertakes. Since the authority exists to conduct functions delegated to it by the Government in the interests of all, its direction should be entrusted to an official responsible at once to the political party in power and to the representatives of the nation.[1] Despite the recognized importance of education and its cost, this position is in most countries regarded as one of the less important of the cabinet portfolios. Whether the national minister of education should be a person with experience in education is an open question; in those countries where the minister has both the power of legislation (by decrees) and of execution, he may at times be carried away by his own enthusiasm for reform and a desire to leave his mark on the development of education.[2] On the other hand, a minister with a rich experience in education may at critical junctures in the history of education be the best man for the position, as, for example, Jules Ferry in France, H. A. L. Fisher and Lord Eustace Percy in England, Carl Becker in Prussia, and Giovanni Gentile in Italy.

Since the duration in office of a minister of education is determined by political rather than educational conditions, and since education in general should be placed above political considerations, the burden and responsibility for national administration, the drafting of policies, and the supervision of progress fall upon the permanent staff. The character of the work of such a staff is determined by the administrative character of the system; in a centralized system

---

[1] The situation is different in the American States, where the arguments are strongly in favor of an official appointed for a term of years or for an indefinite term.

[2] The best examples of this attitude are to be found in Latin American countries, where each minister feels that it is his duty to mark his period of office by the introduction of some change by decree, however inconsequential this change may be, as, for instance, a modification of the time-tables.

the tendency is to emphasize the supervision of laws, decrees, and regulations, to stress the legal aspects of a system already fixed and defined; in such a system the permanent staff consists of two sets of officials — one group with a legal training to conduct the business of the Ministry and another to act as field agents, both devoted to the task of seeing that official regulations are carried out with accuracy of detail. Where the emphasis is less upon the details of administration and more upon education proper, the permanent staff tends to be made up more of persons who have had experience in the field, and the function of the field agents, the inspectors, is to advise, consult, stimulate, and gather information rather than to control and dictate.

Control of *externa* and *interna*. These differences between centralized and decentralized systems lead to a consideration of those aspects of education in which control may properly be exercised by central and local authorities in the interests of education. The centralized system assumes control virtually over all aspects of education — the enactment of laws, decrees, and regulations, the limits of compulsory attendance, the establishment and closing of schools, the character of the school buildings, the preparation and certification of teachers, the curricula and courses of study and even methods of instruction in all types of schools, standards of achievement, textbooks, the prescription of salary scales, local administration, and the internal management of schools. Bureaucracy omits no detail, so that when the teacher confronts the pupils in a classroom, sometimes decorated and adorned according to regulations, he becomes practically the mouthpiece of the central authority, a skilled craftsman very frequently but hewing to the line. Now the question which at once arises is whether this is education or propaganda; whether such a system does not destroy the character of the school as a human institution and of instruction as the impact of mind upon mind. Because the essence of such a system of administration is mechanization, the results are often mechanical, rigid, and formal, and superficially the pupils acquire a certain body of content which is neither their own nor their teacher's; it is in such systems that mass education is run at its worst. What is mechanized tends to be destroyed; what is over-organized tends to be killed.

Sound administration must be governed by the end to be achieved, and the end in modern education is the creation of such conditions as will best promote the growth and development of the educand and encourage the exercise of professional freedom by the teacher. This means in turn such an analysis of the functions of administration as will reduce to routine what can be so reduced and encourage freedom where it should be encouraged. A system of education obviously must rest on legal enactment which makes its provision possible and which allocates powers and duties. Laws and regulations may well deal, since it is in the interests of the nation as a whole, with the compulsory attendance, length of school year, the character of buildings and playgrounds from the educational and hygienic standpoints, medical inspection and health, the size of classes, the qualifications, salaries, and pensions of teachers, the provision of a coördinated system of schools to ensure equality of opportunity — these are the mechanics of an educational system which seek to set up those conditions under which the process of education can best be conducted. They are the *externa* which make it possible to bring the right pupil to the right school under the right teacher; they ensure that equality of opportunity which democratic systems of education are seeking to provide. The *interna*, those aspects of education for the promotion of which teachers and pupils are brought together, are the curricula, courses of study, methods of instruction, textbooks, and standards. These are aspects of education which cannot be legislated and prescribed from above if genuine progress, adaptation to the pupils and their environment, and professional initiative on the part of the teachers are to be encouraged. If the central authority regards itself as the constituted guardian and interpreter of national culture, if nationalism and the national ideal are to be defined from the same source, if the aim of education is to mould all individuals according to a particular pattern, or if a perverted notion of efficiency accepts uniformity bureaucratically determined and controlled, the *interna* may be prescribed by the central authority and not changed until it chooses to do so. If, however, the principle is accepted that national culture is not something that can be reduced to a formula and that national ideals cannot be centrally defined, and if the promotion of initiative, growth, and personality based on a sense of social duty and obligation is the end of education, then the educative process and everything involved in it cannot be governmentalized. The central authority may, however, on the basis of the information at its disposal furnish guidance through suggestions and reports without interfering with that freedom of experimentation which makes for variety of character.

Such a system of decentralization, in which each school practically becomes a unit of administration, does not imply autonomy of education nor does it involve the risk of anarchy, provided that the foundation of successful education is secured — the sound preparation of teachers. Such a preparation, if genuinely professional, should furnish the teachers with an intelligent appreciation of the meaning of national education, with a philosophy, with understanding through psychology of children, with mastery of subject-matter and its distribution according to levels of the pupils, with some ideas of standards — all of which tend to prevent too radical a departure from certain norms. Beyond this there are the suggestions which may come from both central and local authorities, coöperation with colleagues in the making of curricula and courses of study, textbooks, certain traditional demands from parents, training in service, and the assistance from time to time of supervisors and inspectors. Freedom at best is relative; but the professional background of the teachers, if assured, furnishes a guarantee against the abuse of freedom.

Participation of teachers in administration. A sound system of administration should, therefore, be concerned with the definition of the *externa* and with the promotion of decentralization, freedom and initiative in the *interna*, the former to provide equality of opportunity, the latter to encourage the development of the professional growth of teachers through a consciousness of the responsibility which devolves on them because of the freedom that they enjoy. These ends cannot be promoted by bureaucratic methods, whether they result from the exercise of the sovereign right of the State as in some European countries, or from the application to education of principles of efficiency derived from industrial and commercial organizations as in the United States. So long as teachers are expected merely to carry out regulations issued by the superior authorities, the question of their participation in administration hardly arises; they are merely servants of, rather than partners in, the administrative scheme. If, however, their position as members of a free and responsible profession is recognized, they may well claim the right to participate in the administration of education. The question at once arises what the nature of this participation should be. There are among teachers groups which demand direct representation in the central and local administrative boards of education; in England the establishment of a "real" Board of Education has been advocated, and in the United States it is urged that teachers be appointed as members of local boards. Such a practice would place the teachers in the position of being at the same time employers and employees, with the danger that they would place the interests of their own group first. But if there are serious objections to proposals of this nature, none can be raised against setting up machinery whereby the best professional intelligence of teachers cannot be consulted. In the Russian Soviet Republic proposals for legislation are brought annually before the Union of Teachers; in France and Italy there are higher councils of education made up of appointees and representatives of all branches of the educational profession; in England there is a Consultative Committee whose advice and recommendations are sought by the Board of Education and which is from time to time requested to conduct investigations of crucial issues, while opportunities are provided to secure the opinions of representative teachers' organizations; in the United States no provision is made either for the country as a whole or in the separate States whereby teachers as a group may be consulted, although legislative lobbying by teachers' organizations is not unknown; in the German States a hierarchy of teachers' councils has been established, but nowhere on a state-wide scale. Undoubtedly much is to be gained for the progress of education by capitalizing the professional intelligence of teachers, while failure to provide official channels for its expression may lead to unrest and agitation.

Participation of parents in administration. The situation is somewhat different in the case of another group which has a direct, personal interest in the progress and process of education — parents. They can bring their influence to bear as taxpayers and voters for representatives in local and national government. Even here, however, there are sound arguments for stimulating the interest of parents in education beyond the immediate concern for their own children by setting up organizations to represent their views. In the first place, except in those localities in the United States where boards of education and even officials are elected, the issues in local and national elections are so complicated that the question of education rarely stands out as a prominent issue, and even where boards of education, as in the United States, and education committees, as in Scotland until recently, are elected at special elections, it has been found that the percentage of voters is very small. The best argument for the organization of parent groups is that, in a period in which education is in a stage of transition with an increase in the facilities and consequently the cost and with changes in curriculum and methods, such an organization furnishes the means for educating the parents themselves. Parents' meetings and parents' associations in connection with individual schools have existed in the past, but it is only in recent years that the educative possibilities of such organizations have been recognized and attempts have been made to unite them into local and larger groups with the ultimate development of national associations. This end has been achieved in the United States; in Germany and Holland school and local parents' councils are required to be established by law; elsewhere the development of similar organizations has depended upon the interest of a school principal or a superintendent or director of education.

The tendency to provide such opportunities for eliciting the views of teachers and parents, although only a recent manifestation, combined with the multiplication of educational associations for lay and professional groups, national and international, represents not merely a quickening of interest in education, but ultimately an attack on the rigid centralization which characterized the administration of education in the past. From the political point of view this movement indicates discontent with the assumption of a monopoly of control by the State; from the educational point of view it manifests the realization that education is a human affair and the school a human institution, and that both may become sterile and formal if mechanized and over-organized, as they must inevitably be if they are deprived of freedom to adapt themselves and to grow out of the differences in local environments. Education cannot be successfully conducted if it is regimented, whether by regulations, decrees, and laws, or by standardized efficiency methods however logical and scientific, for education is not a commodity that can be standardized. The fundamental danger of rigid control through a central authority is its tendency to pass beyond those aspects which make education possible to the process itself and to disregard those elements which make for a rich national life and for a culture which is the real expression of the aspirations and ideals of a people. Events proved the soundness of John Stuart Mill's statement (in his essay *On Liberty*) that

A general state education is merely a contrivance for moulding people to be exactly like one another, and as the mould in which it casts them is that which pleases the predominant power in the government... it establishes a despotism over the mind, leading by natural tendency to one over the body.

Educational finance. The aims of educational administration in a modern society may be stated to be, first, the provision of equality of educational opportunity whereby the individual will find accessible to him the best type of education of which he is capable of profiting, and, second, the organization of those facilities which will render possible the transmission, interpretation, and development of national culture and the civilization upon which it is based. The first of these aims has only begun to be recognized universally within the last generation; the second has been the aim which all national systems of education have sought to promote, but have tended to define through a central authority. The position adopted in these and other pages of the present volume is that a national culture cannot be so defined and progress at the same time. The best method for providing that variety of outlook and of interpretation which is essential to the progress of national culture is that which provides for the free play between man and his environment, and this can only be achieved under a decentralized system. The State, however, has the right, in its own interests and in the interests of the individuals who make it up, to prescribe certain minimum requirements and standards which the local groups must meet; beyond this it has the duty of employing its resources to equalize educational opportunities, so that no individual will be deprived of them because of accident of residence. These considerations give rise to two problems: the first is that of the financial support of education; the second, of the size of the local areas for education.

In those countries where the State has virtually assumed a monopoly of education, the machinery of administration has been controlled wholly by the central authorities. Each country was divided up into areas which existed, in some places solely for purposes of educational administration (the academy in France, for instance, or the new regions in Italy), in other places for purposes of general public administration (the *Provinz* and the *Regierung* in Prussia). These in general were and are artificial areas without any real relation to the natural groupings of the population; when these are reached, so little is left for the local communities to perform in the field of educational administration that public interest in schools is almost non-existent. In such systems the major part of the financial burden is usually borne by the central authority, which assumes the cost of teachers' salaries and pensions, and controls the provision of schools by the local community by rigorous prescriptions. The localities may even construct and maintain excellent school buildings, but once the school is established, the right of interference or even of entry by representatives of the community is denied. The progress of education is retained in the hands of the central authority and the opportunity of enlisting public interest and intelligence by the grant of a certain amount of autonomy is lost. The financial arrangements are such that only the conduct of the system as it exists is taken care of, instead of being employed to elicit a sense of responsibility for local progress by providing some reward for it.

At the other end of the scale is the district system, still widespread in the United States, under which each local area enjoys full autonomy devolved upon it by the State, but with no encouragement from the State to accomplish more than the minimum which the community is willing to provide, irrespective often of its financial ability. In the one case the administration and control of education are so far removed from the local areas that they take no interest in it; in the other the local area may be so small or so indifferent that it is unable or fails to provide such educational facilities as will provide equality of opportunity.

Intermediate between these two systems is that in which the provision of education is based on coöperation between the central and the local authorities. Here the central authority prescribes the minimum required from each local area and encourages local initiative and progress by bearing a substantial part of the cost of education. An illustration of this practice is afforded by the English system in which the cost of education is divided equally between the central and local governments.[1] It differs from the American system in defining the size of the area responsible for education, but developments since the size of areas was defined by the Education Act of 1902 show that advancing programs of education, based on a fuller recognition of the principle of equality of opportunity may require the elimination of smaller areas.[2] The provision of schools can no longer be determined solely on the basis of the financial ability of the locality. Hence the movement in the United States for the consolidation of schools; in England Lord Haldane advocated a plan for creating provincial educational areas, a plan which is subject to the same criticism as the French, that any administrative organization which is so large as to diminish local interest in education is likely to defeat its purposes in the interests of a fallacious concept of efficiency. The size of an area of local educational administration should be determined rather from the point of view of its ability to provide a variety of educational opportunities at a time when it is generally recognized that universal elementary education is not enough to meet the present demands of society.

The advocate of a centralized system may urge two objections — first, that progress can be more quickly and more uniformly secured by central regulation, and second, that, since the cost of education, however raised, is ultimately borne by the same taxpayer, it is more efficient and more convenient to provide it from a central source. The answer to these objections is simple. A comparison of centralized and decentralized systems certainly proves that uniformity is more characteristic of the former than of the latter, but it proves equally that there is greater inertia to change under the former. Further, while it is true that the decentralized system is uneven, that there are peaks and dales in the amount of progress achieved at any one time, there is a certain capillarity by which the backward areas are attracted by the example of the more progressive, which in turn continue their advance.[3] What the decentral-

---

[1] The history of the central schools in England seems to indicate that local authorities may themselves bear the cost of types of education which the central authority is not prepared to sanction or recognize.

[2] Some of the Part III areas which were set up for elementary education are, it is recognized, too small today to carry out adequately the responsibility assigned to them in 1918 for the comprehensive and progressive development of education; particularly has this fact been brought out in the present movement for the reorganization of the school system into primary and senior schools.

[3] This can easily be demonstrated both in England and the United States in such matters as the gradual raising of school age, reform of curricula and methods, and provision of new types of schools.

ized system loses in uniformity, it more than gains through that vigor and variety which come from a sense of local responsibility and the freedom to experiment.

The arguments which apply to decentralization on the administrative side apply equally to a discussion of the financial aspects. Without entering into a consideration of the ideal methods of financing education, an equable distribution of the cost of education between central and local authorities provides a method of imposing responsibility for and interest in educational progress; it means, further, that every discussion of the cost of education must inevitably constitute an education of those responsible for meeting it. If an educational budget calls forth interest at a low materialistic level, it at least provides an opportunity for publicity without which the progress of the educational machine must inevitably be retarded. It is not an accident that methods of educational publicity, educational handbooks, education weeks and days, and parents' and other associations have increased at the same time as the cost of education has everywhere begun to mount higher than was thought possible before 1914. Here, if anywhere, is to be found the best argument for arousing public interest in education at as many sources as possible and more especially at those sources at which local and central taxes are levied. It has, indeed, been with this in mind, although other reasons contributed as well, that in many localities in the United States the budget for education and the tax by which the funds are raised have been segregated from the general budget for other purposes of local administration.

A partnership between central and local authorities in bearing the cost of education should in general be determined by the principle of securing, so far as possible, the equalization of educational opportunities. The time is rapidly coming when elementary education alone cannot be regarded as an adequate minimum for the future citizens of a modern society. As was pointed out in Chapter IV, the provision of education is reaching out below and beyond primary education; a well-organized system implies variety of types of schools, which it is in the interest of the collective group, or State, as a whole to bring within the reach of the growing generation. Beyond the provision of this minimum an equable partnership must consider the needs of a locality in terms of its ability to support such schools. Finally, in order to encourage initiative and progress, some reward for local effort might be provided. A system of educational finance must, like a system of administration, promote the ideal of placing the right pupil under the right teacher in the right school, but this minimum must constantly be advanced as social demands change. A successful system of education inevitably means more education, but how the increasing cost of this progress is to be met must be answered not by educators but by statesmen, who today hold in their hands the opportunity of shifting national expenditures from destructive to constructive ends.

Local administration. Much of what has already been said on the relation of the State to education applies with even greater force to local administration. The fundamental principle is the same — its function is to promote equality of educational opportunity and the transmission, interpretation, and enrichment of national culture in the light of the local environment. The centralized system leaves little to the interplay of local forces; frequently the executive officer of a locality is an official of the central department, and, even when provision is made for a local school committee, whether directly or indirectly representing the community, it has no power to determine educational policy. This system prevails in France and Italy, and, while the tradition in Germany, is gradually being modified. The decentralized system implies local autonomy, but local autonomy within certain restrictions set up by and certain rights reserved to the central authority. The advantages of local autonomy have already been discussed; they rest fundamentally on the principles that democracy in government is itself educative, provides for liberty, and elicits responsibility, and that education is a process of adaptation to and growth out of the environment in which the school is located.

Where local communities have been entrusted with autonomy in the administration of education, two types of representative bodies have been created. While both bodies are elected, they differ in so far as they are directly or indirectly elected. The directly elected or *ad hoc* school board, education committee, or board of education prevailed in England from 1870 to 1902 and in Scotland from 1918 to 1929, and is common in the United States. The indirectly elected education committee, which is the present form in England and Scotland, is a committee of the local council whose members are elected for general purposes of local administration; another type, which is appointed by some elected official, usually the mayor, is found in the United States. The practice of having education committees or boards of education specially elected is based on two aims — first, to bring the problems of education directly to the attention of the voters, and, secondly, in the United States in particular, to take education out of "politics" by entrusting its general administration to representatives who are interested in its progress. In practice the method has not succeeded in the United States; it did not in Scotland bring out more than a small proportion of the voters for the special elections, nor has it always resulted in eliminating "politics," as understood in the United States, from education. The arguments in favor of the indirectly elected education committee is that education is not necessarily a greater concern to the public than any other question of local government, and that from the point of view of finance it is of some advantage to coördinate and balance all local expenditures for which the taxpayer is responsible. To meet the criticism that the representatives elected for the conduct of local governments may have neither knowledge of nor interest in education, provision has been made under the English and Scottish laws to "coöpt" members who can supply both and who can assist the education committees in their deliberations.

Whatever the form of the local education committees or boards of education, it is generally recognized that they do not adequately represent all groups which have an interest in or may contribute to the progress of education. The teaching body, for instance, has in some places expressed a desire to participate in the administration of education, and, while the weight of the arguments is against direct participation, everything is to be gained by providing more definite machinery for securing its advice than exists today. In the gradual democratization of the system of administration, Prussia has provided for the development of a hierarchy of teachers' councils (*Lehrerbeiräte*) rising from the local to district councils. Advisory councils have been organized extensively in the field of vocational education, and in England and Scotland for youth welfare, but other sources of opinion and advice have not been as systematically organized in other phases of education. An opportunity offers itself of capitalizing the intelligent support of parents through the associations which are rapidly developing. Indirectly this is the aim of the legal requirement in England that all new schemes in education be duly brought to the notice of the public concerned. These tendencies should not mean any diminution in the responsibility of the organ specifically charged with the administration of education, but it does mean that the purpose for which such administration exists is too delicate a matter to be imposed upon the public without utilizing every opportunity for enlisting its intelligent participation. The function and duty of the local administrative body is to define policies, but in the definition of these policies as wide a range of opinion as possible should be elicited.

The executive official. So long as education was a simple matter and was directed mainly to the spread of literacy with somewhat restricted opportunities beyond this, administration was also relatively simple. Under those conditions the executive official of a school board was little more than a recording secretary or clerk. Today even local education has assumed the proportions of a vast enterprise concerned with a range of activities from the education of the young child to the education of the adult. The great variety of the educational organization means that the layman, who is a member of an education committee or a board of education, cannot hope to be familiar with its problems and needs the guidance of experts. The growth and expansion of education have been accompanied by the gradual emergence of such experts whose duties are not merely executive but advisory as well. The position of the director of education in England, the superintendent of schools in the United States, and the *Stadtschulrat* in Germany, although local autonomy has not advanced as far in this as in the other two countries, has slowly evolved in the past generation in response to the new demands. One of the youngest professions, that of the educational administrator, calls for a variety of abilities and training that is unparalleled in other professions. The educational administrator must in the first place himself be a man with a breadth of culture and education; he must be familiar with the educational problems of a modern society and possess a knowledge not merely of the details of school organization, methods, and curricula, but also of the contributions of medicine and psychology to the progress of the child; he must be something of a financier, a business man, a lawyer, and an architect; he must have the ability in a constantly expanding service to select his staff of experts and to direct their work to a common end; he must be able by word and pen to enlist the interest and support of the public; to carry the teaching body with him and, to influence his committee or board, he must possess the tact of a diplomat and the skill of the politician; in all matters he must be a statesman, able to consolidate whatever progress he has made and to plan for the continuance of that progress to meet new demands; he must combine firmness based on knowledge and conviction with the insight to delegate responsibility in such a way that it will call forth ability in others. With his expert qualifications he must combine outstanding qualities of personality.

The development of the position and the many-sided activities in which the director of education is called upon to engage have in the United States led to the organization of special courses of training; in England greater stress has been placed upon general education, experience, and personality, but there are indications that the possibility of specialized training is being considered.[1] The provision of specialized training has on the whole been extremely salutary in the United States and has succeeded in giving dignity to the position of superintendent of schools and in improving his conditions of service generally. There is, however, a very real danger that the intensity of specialization may result in a stronger emphasis on administration than on education, on efficiency of practice than on educational statesmanship. Efficiency, it cannot be denied, is essential, but, if it becomes a fetish, the main purpose for which it exists is apt to be forgotten, and it may exercise as potent a strangle-hold as bureaucracy; administration under such conditions becomes obtrusive and tends to over-standardization without releasing the initiative of those who are directly associated with education and instruction — the teachers. While in the English system the introduction of specialized preparation would have contributions to make, the American systems still have much to learn from the English balance between freedom and responsibility, between standardization and flexibility, between the *externa* and the *interna*.

The various types of problems of administration will appear in

[1] The University of Leeds has for several years provided courses in educational administration and the provision of such courses is planned in the Institute of Education which is to be established in the University of London. The difference between England and the United States in this matter is indicated by a comparison of the literature to be found under the title of educational administration in the two countries.

the consideration of the administrative systems of the countries discussed in this volume: France and Italy, highly centralized on hierarchical principles; the Soviet Republics and the German States, centralized with the beginnings of decentralization; England, a blend of centralization and decentralization; and the United States, decentralized, but with strong tendencies in the direction of greater state control and increased participation on the part of the Federal Government. There is probably no "pure" system anywhere, for, while the Soviet Republics claim to have local autonomy, the control of the central governments and of the common ideology deprives it of meaning; Italian education is administered by a hierarchy, but curricula and methods, especially in the elementary schools, are based on activity principles, which imply a certain autonomy for the schools; England has developed a coöperative partnership between the central and local authorities, but while the former refrains from exercising any control over the *interna*, some fear is at times expressed that the increasing share of the educational burden may lead to increasing interference with local autonomy; the United States presents a picture of a large number of decentralized autonomous systems, with a tendency in some States toward greater control by the state authority, but each system within itself reproduces some of the characteristics which accompany centralization, or, to put the situation in another way, the system in the United States is the unit, rather than the school, as in England. It is clear, however, that there is a movement toward systems of administration in which there will be an adequate adjustment between the claims of the central and the local governments. In the development of such systems the starting-point must be the two purposes of educational administration already discussed — the equalization of educational opportunities and the promotion of those facilities which will ensure the transmission, interpretation, and advancement of national culture.

1. ENGLAND

History and principles. There are few national systems of education which show less evidence of planning than the English. Viewed from the outside, the provision of education in England appears to consist of a collection of unarticulated and uncoördinated systems, which seem to have no connection with each other. It is made up of "public" schools which are private; of "private" schools which receive aid from public funds; of denominational and non-sectarian schools enjoying equal recognition and almost identical financial support from the national and local treasuries; of a large number of private-venture schools which are independent of any public supervision whatever and whose number is as yet undetermined; of secondary schools which receive pupils from the kindergarten stage on; of schools classed as elementary which provide secondary school subjects; of local authorities which are entirely unrestricted as to the type and range of education that they may supply; and of other authorities which are concerned with elementary education only. When the functions of the central authority are examined, it is found that it does not prescribe curricula and methods or textbooks, and has recently surrendered its control over the preparation of teachers, and when the powers of the local authorities are investigated, there appears to be the same loose relationship to the schools under their control. If the investigation is carried still further, it is discovered that the real unit of English education is the school which enjoys the right and responsibility to exercise freedom, initiative, and independence rarely found in any other country. Further inquiry reveals, however, that since 1902 England has been moving in the direction of creating a national system.

The explanation of this apparent chaos and confusion is to be found in the historical development of English education and in the English philosophy of government. While Prussia began to organize a state system of education before the beginning of the nineteenth century, while the general framework of a system was outlined in France under Napoleon in 1808, and while the ideals of a national system but not of national control were formulated in the United States during the early days of the Republic, England only began tentatively to provide national grants for education in 1833 without contemplating either the implications of such grants or any plan of national education. Six years later, a special committee of the Privy Council was created chiefly "to superintend the application of any sums voted by Parliament for the purpose of promoting public education," and only secondarily "for the consideration of all matters affecting the education of the people." Public schools were not yet established, but the grants were divided between the National Society and the British and Foreign School Society and other organizations maintaining schools. Government inspection was made a condition of all grants. In 1856 the Education Department was created to take charge of the work of the Committee of Council and the position of Vice-President of the Committee was established, responsible to the House of Commons for the distribution of the grants and to answer questions on education. Three years earlier, the Department of Science and Art, which had already existed under other forms and names, was constituted. Secondary education was still left without either state aid or state supervision. In 1861 the payment by results system was introduced by Mr. Robert Lowe to encourage the development of elementary education, and in 1870 the Education Act was passed which authorized the election of school boards and the levy of local rates to provide elementary schools where the supply was inadequate. Compulsory school attendance was not introduced until 1876. Thus, almost by inadvertence and mainly through the distribution of grants the Government was drawn into the consideration of elementary education and the promotion of the study of science and art.

Secondary education was provided wholly through private effort and the State, when it undertook to survey the supply, was legally authorized to do so only in so far as those schools were in enjoyment of endowments. The great surveys of secondary education which took place between 1861 and 1869 revealed the inadequacy of the provision both in quality and quantity, but the recommendations of the two commissions of inquiry (1864 and 1868), that some forms of state and local control be introduced, succeeded only in arousing strong opposition to governmental interference. The result was that the Endowed Schools Act (1869) was passed without setting up local authorities and without introducing inspection and examination of secondary schools as had been proposed, but establishing another body, the Endowed School Commissioners, to frame schemes for the reorganization of endowed schools. In 1874 the powers of the Commissioners were transferred to the Charity Commissioners.

The growing demand for some form of education more advanced than elementary was met by the more ambitious schools boards by the provision of higher grade schools, for which grants were received from the Education Department and in some cases from the Department of Science and Art. In 1889 a new type of education and a new authority were introduced under the Technical Instruction Act which made the County and County Borough Councils (local authorities created in 1888) responsible for technical instruction, including instruction in science and art and "any other forms of instruction (including modern languages and commercial and agricultural subjects)" with the approval of the Science and Art Department. Technical instruction was supported by local rates and government grants ("whiskey money") under the Local Taxation (Customs and Excise) Act of 1890.

The result of such partial and *ad hoc* legislation was to set up competing and overlapping authorities and a supply of schools which were in no way articulated or coördinated. In 1894 the Royal Commission on Secondary Education (with Mr. Bryce as chairman) was appointed to "consider the best methods of establishing a well-organized system of secondary education in England." The recommendations of this Commission for the first time outlined a framework for a national system of education. Although concerned in the main with secondary education, the Commission recommended among other matters the establishment of a central authority and of local authorities on which the local school boards were to be represented, with power to levy rates and to aid secondary schools whether provided by the local authorities or not.

By the close of the century, it was realized that further progress with the development of education was barred by the existence of three central authorities (the Education Department, the Department of Science and Art, and the educational division of the Charity Commissioners), of school boards and technical instruction committees, and of voluntary schools which were beginning to feel the pressure of the increasing cost of elementary education. Among these competing and overlapping authorities the cause of an adequate system of secondary education was lost. In the meantime the provision of higher education had begun to be extended by the development of local universities and university colleges, many of which were constrained to give secondary education because of the inadequate preparation of their students. Before steps could be taken to reorganize the administrative system generally, it was recognized that a single central authority for education must be established. In 1899 the Board of Education was created by Act of Parliament to take over the duties of the Education Department and the Science and Art Department; by Orders in Council issued in 1900, 1901, and

1902, the powers of dealing with educational endowments were transferred from the Charity Commissioners to the Board; the provision of the Act that the supervision of agricultural education be also transferred to the Board has never been carried out.

The immediate reorganization of the system of local administration was precipitated almost by accident. In 1901 the action of Mr. Cockerton, district auditor under the Local Government Board, in disallowing the expenditure of the London School Board for advanced instruction beyond the implications of the Public Elementary School Code, was upheld by the Court of Appeal. This decision meant that school boards were acting illegally in providing higher grade schools, evening schools, and classes for adults, all of which were regarded as institutions of higher education, and therefore outside of the powers of school boards set up to provide elementary education. Temporary measures were adopted to meet the situation, but the Government immediately undertook the reform of the administrative system, which was passed as the Education Act, 1902, and except for some clarification under the Education Act, 1918, established the present authorities for the supply of education.

Throughout the period which has been discussed there is evident a certain hesitancy on the part of the State to embark on a nationwide program of education, a policy which is regarded as one of the paramount rights of the State in all other countries. This hesitancy was due in part to the predominance of the doctrine of *laissez faire* which dominated English political philosophy throughout the nineteenth century, and in part to its corollary, fear of governmental control and interference in the conduct of social affairs. This aspect of English national life has already been discussed in earlier chapters (Chapters II and III). The best expression of the English attitude on the subject is to be found in John Stuart Mill's essay *On Liberty*. Like his predecessors in the same school of thought, Mill accepted the principle that the State may compel parents to educate their children, but parents should be left free to choose whatever school they desired for their children. The State may set up a system of schools, but only as one among a number of competitive experiments conducted for the purpose of demonstrating certain standards of excellence to stimulate the others. In Mill's opinion

A general state education is merely a contrivance for moulding people to be exactly like one another, and as the mould in which it cases them is that which pleases the predominant power in the government... it establishes a despotism over the mind, leading by natural tendency to one over the body.

The control of education by the State would militate against the preservation of individuality of character, diversity of opinions, and of modes of conduct which might result from the provision of diverse types of education. Initiative, growth, personality, can only be assured by allowing reasonable freedom, and rich variety of character can only be assured by free experiment. It is in the interests of the State to see that every citizen is assured of a minimum of education; any interference beyond this would result in an enforced uniformity and bureaucratic control incompatible with variety of enterprise and experimentation. A national system of education can be assured by accepting a national ideal, but a national ideal can neither be defined nor enforced by government without becoming formal and sterile, deprived of all opportunity of adaptation to changing conditions and free expression of individual conscience. An educational system, if it is to be sound, must leave room for the free and spontaneous interplay of ideas.

This attitude has survived to the present, despite the fact that the importance of the public provision of education has been generally accepted in the interests of national progress and equality of opportunity for the individual. Circumstances — international competition and the War — in the first case, and the emergence of the working classes to power and a more fundamental concept of democracy in the second, rather than deliberate change of policy, have been responsible for the movement to develop a national system of education. But the fundamental problem still remains for England how to develop an administrative organization which will at once conserve the principles of freedom and yet bring educational opportunities within the reach of all; in other words, is mass education on a national scale compatible with variety and experimentation? This is the problem which has confronted state and local administrators and educators since the passing of the Education Act in 1902. The right and practical ideal, according to Sir Michael Sadler, is "variety set in a framework of national organization."[1]

---

[1] That the ideal of voluntaryism in education is not altogether dead in England may be seen in Sir Roland K. Wilson's *The Province of the State* (London, 1911). A few years ago Mr. Frank Roscoe, Secretary of the Royal Society of Teachers, suggested that taxes and rates for educational purposes should be prorated among parents, who should be free to

Fear of concentration of power in the hands of a central authority and suspicion of bureaucratic control were responsible for the withdrawal of Mr. Fisher's first bill in 1917 and its introduction in an amended form in the following year. The reasons for the opposition to the first draft, apart from some antagonism to the provision of compulsory continuation schools, were prompted by the fear that the Board of Education would be given compulsory powers without reference to Parliament or the courts. The bill gave power to the Board to alter schemes for the organization of education in their areas prepared and submitted to it by the local authorities. It provided for the creation of provincial associations by a combination of local authorities. The Board was given the right to transfer the powers of smaller to larger authorities and to regulate the amount of expenditures by local authorities for attendance of members at educational meetings and conferences. Finally, the bill gave the Board the right to determine the powers of local authorities under the Education Acts. All these provisions of the 1917 bill were withdrawn from the bill submitted in 1918; had they been passed, the Board of Education would have become at once a legislative, executive, and judicial body, and would have been placed in the same position as ministries of public instruction in the centralized systems in Europe and elsewhere.

The history of English education in the nineteenth century pointed to the development of a national system, but a national system which would refrain from setting up a system of centralized bureaucratic control and uniformity; which would leave to parents the right to choose their own schools, but would provide opportunities through public provision to those who could not afford to bear the burden of the cost of extended education; which would meet the supply and cost of education through the coöperation of state and local authorities, but which would set up a system of partnership between the state and local authorities rather than one in which the latter would be dominated and coerced by the former. It is such a system which has gradually been developed not so much in conformity with any preconceived theory, but in response to situations as they arose. The administrative system has developed step by step without any plan

choose the school which they wish their children to attend. The attitude survives, of course, most strongly in the group interested in safeguarding the complete independence of private schools, which have been the subject of a recent investigation (see p. 106).

and without any fixed goal; it is still in the process of development and any changes which may take place will be accidental rather than anticipated. Administrative procedures in England are not standardized nor the result of theory, unless the vague suspicion of superior control and desire for freedom and variety can be called a theory; it is based wholly on the Englishman's reliance on his ability to work and adapt institutions to meet changing situations as they arise.[1]

CENTRAL ADMINISTRATION

The central authority for education in England and Wales is the Board of Education which was created under the Education Act, 1899, and charged "with the superintendence of matters relating to education in England and Wales." The Board took over the powers and duties of the Education Department and of the Department of Science and Art, and subsequently the functions of the Charity Commissioners relating to education were transferred to it. Under the law the Board consists of the President, the Lord President of the Council, the principal Secretaries of State, the First Lord of the Treasury, and the Chancellor of the Exchequer; in practice the Board has never met. The responsibility for the conduct of the Board rests upon the President who is a member of the Cabinet and is thus a political appointee, and is assisted by a Parliamentary Secretary who is a member of Parliament and represents the President in his absence or if they are not both members of the same House. Except at critical stages in the development of education, the position of the President of the Board of Education has not been and is not yet regarded as one of the more important in the Cabinet. The President, referred to more frequently now as Minister of Education, holds office as long as his Party is in power or until he is transferred to another portfolio; the Right Honorable H. A. L. Fisher was in office for nearly six years and was also one of the few Presidents who had had experience as an educator.

The duties of the President and the Parliamentary Secretary are to represent the Board of Education in Parliament, to discuss educa-

---

[1] It is significant that, while there are several excellent descriptive accounts of the English administrative system, there is only one small pamphlet of sixty-two pages (Balfour, Sir Graham, *Educational Administration*) which discusses principles. The University of Leeds is the only institution which offers courses leading to a diploma in Educational Administration; it is planned to provide training for educational administrators in the Institute of Education, recently created in the University of London.

tional policies, to answer questions on education, and to present and explain the educational budget before Parliament each year. In general he is responsible for the conduct of the Board's officials. Increasingly, as the importance of education has come to be recognized, the President and the Parliamentary Secretary have been brought into closer touch with the public and have in recent years contributed significantly to stimulating the interest of the public in education.

The immediate conduct of administration is entrusted to the permanent staff of the Board, whose chief officer is the Permanent Secretary. In the absence of any more detailed statement of the powers of the Board than the authority to superintend education, the responsibility for the development of policies and principles has devolved upon the permanent staff, subject to consultation with the President. The definition of policies and principles has been guided by circumstances and the gradual expansion of the provision of education. The permanence of the staff ensures continuity of policy without, however, developing rigidity. In relation to the public educational services of the country, it is the function of the Board to see that the local education authorities in the exercise of the powers entrusted to them under the Education Acts provide an adequate supply of schools at different levels, to see that schools are accessible and regularly attended, and in general to promote the efficiency of education. It is at this point that the position of the Board differs from that of national ministries of education in other countries. The Board cannot exercise compulsory powers over the local authorities, unless they fail to fulfill any of their duties under the Education Act, 1921, and then only after a public hearing. It can, however, influence local authorities indirectly in two ways — through consultation and discussion, and by withholding the government grants. The Board does not provide or administer educational institutions except the Royal College of Art, the Victoria and Albert Museum, and the Science Museum; it has no direct relations with teachers, after they have been granted their certificates or have been recognized, until they retire and become eligible for pensions; it does not prescribe curricula, courses of study or textbooks, or conduct examinations; except in so far as they prepare teachers, it has no authority over universities and university colleges, which have been placed since 1919 under the University Grants Committee;

finally, it does not exercise any control over reformatory and industrial schools for delinquent children, which are supervised by the Home Office, or over agricultural education, which is administered by the Board of Agriculture. Its influence and authority are derived from its duty as a grant-distributing agency of the Government. By virtue of this power the Board can call upon local education authorities to submit schemes or programs "for the progressive development and comprehensive organization of education" in their areas within the powers entrusted to them by the Education (Consolidation) Act, 1921, and conduct inquiries to discover whether these powers are exercised; it may require local authorities to submit reports, returns, and information; and it may prescribe the conditions under which grants will be paid. It is the last provision which gives the Board the authority to inspect schools, and to inquire into the local organization of education, the adequacy of the school buildings, the provision of medical inspection, the qualifications of teachers, the suitability of time-tables and curricula, and the keeping of records and returns. Failure to satisfy the Board of the efficiency of local administration on these points may involve either reduction or complete loss of the grant. Opportunities are, however, provided before such action is taken for consultation, discussion, and arbitration.[1]

On the surface it would appear that the control of education by means of the grant gives the Board as much authority as is enjoyed under the compulsory powers exercised by ministries in other countries. Actually this is not the case in practice. On the material side, the *externa* — buildings, qualifications and remunerations of teachers, size of classes, length of school year and of school sessions, and medical inspection and treatment — certain definite and recognizable standards can be set up; on the *interna*, the actual con-

[1] A good illustration of the relations of the Board to a local authority was afforded in Lowestoft a few years ago, when the teachers went on strike on the salary question. The parents of the school children, sympathizing with the teachers, engaged them to open schools and could, therefore, not be proceeded against because the children were being efficiently educated by qualified teachers. The local authority could not be dissolved because the Board does not possess such authority. The only action that the Board could and did take immediately was to reduce the grants because the authority's schools, taught by unqualified teachers, were inefficient. Had the local authority continued to be recalcitrant and refused to come to an agreement with the teachers on the salary question, the Board would have been authorized under Section 150 of the Education Act, 1921, to hold a public inquiry and make an order to compel the authority to fulfill their duty "and any such order may be enforced by mandamus."

tent and conduct of instruction, the Board refrains from prescription. In all cases local circumstances are taken into account and, if disagreement between the central and local authorities develops, ample opportunity is provided for discussion. Nor does the Board have fixed standards of efficiency; the Board is ready to advise, suggest, stimulate, and reward authorities, but the standards of efficiency are flexible and change with the times. The flexibility of education is nowhere better illustrated than in the definitions of the Education Act, 1921, which the Board has to administer: "The expression 'elementary school' means... a school or department of a school at which elementary education is the principal part of the education there given," and, "The expression 'higher education' means education other than elementary education." Until 1926 the Board in its Code for Elementary Schools, issued annually, listed the subjects of elementary education; since that date even this statement has been eliminated, and the only reference to the subject is that the curriculum shall be "suitable," a principle followed also in the Regulations for Secondary Schools.

Accordingly there is a very real distinction between centralization of control in such countries as France and pre-War Prussia and in England. In the former both the *externa* and the *interna* were carefully regulated, while in England the *externa*, all those conditions which are necessary to bring pupils to the schools and to enable them to profit from the instruction, are regulated, but even under the regulations are subject to discussion; while the *interna*, those aspects of the educational process which go on in the schools and classrooms are left undefined and elastic, thus permitting local initiative and local adaptation. The principle adopted by the Board was enunciated, in the original Prefatory Memorandum to the *Suggestions for the Consideration of Teachers and Others Concerned in the Work of Public Elementary Schools*, as follows:

> Neither the present volume nor any subsequent developments or amendments of it are designed to impose any regulations supplementary to those contained in the Code (which has since been changed). The only uniformity of practice that the Board of Education desire to see in the teaching of public elementary schools is that each teacher shall think for himself, and work out for himself, such methods of teaching as may use his powers to the best advantage and be best suited to the particular needs and conditions of the school. Uniformity in details of practice (except in the mere routine of school management) is not desirable even if it were attainable. But freedom implies a corresponding responsibility in its use.

It is obvious, then, that the relations between the Board and the local education authorities and the schools is one of partnership, the Board neither assuming nor exercising authority except in pursuance of the legal requirements and the distribution of grants. It follows from this that, except for certain routine requirements, the Board must enter into individual relationships with each local education authority and, as far as possible, with the schools. This it does through the office staff and through its inspectors.

Until 1922 the Board of Education was divided for administrative purposes into departments corresponding to the main branches in education (elementary, secondary, technological, and training of teachers). In 1922 this organization was abandoned and replaced by a horizontal departmentalization based on a territorial division of the country, so that each official was made responsible for the consideration, from a unified point of view, of all branches of education in the territory assigned to him. In 1907 a separate department for Wales was created in the Board. The general work of the Board is supervised by the Secretariat consisting of the permanent secretary, the deputy secretary, the permanent secretary of the Welsh Department, three principle assistant secretaries responsible respectively for elementary, secondary, and technical education, and five assistant secretaries. The remaining divisions consist of the following branches: establishment (personnel), finance, legal, and medical, and the following divisions: training of teachers, pensions, territorial, and teachers' salaries. There are in addition the architect's office, the Office of Special Inquiries and Reports, and the Welsh Department. The officers of the staff are appointed through the Civil Service Commission and through promotion from the lower to the administrative class. Each official of the territorial divisions is thus responsible for conducting the relations between the Board and the local authorities in his area whether by correspondence or direct conference. Through him direct personal relations are established between the local officials and the Board, and in him the Board finds a source of information on the whole educational situation in the division assigned to him.

The organization of the inspectorial staff is moving somewhat in the same direction. There are three chief inspectors for elementary, secondary, and technical education, of whom one is the senior chief inspector responsible for the whole staff, which consists of divisional inspectors, inspectors and assistant inspectors for elementary, secondary, technical and continuation, art and special schools, and a chief woman inspector responsible in general for the women inspectors. Candidates for the inspectorate are appointed by Order in Council on the advice of the President of the Board acting on the recommendation of a selection committee. The specific qualifications of candidates are not defined. The time has passed when the chief requirement of recruits for the inspectorate was a "detached mind." The expansion of education and the change in the relationship of the Board to local authorities and schools demand

men and women of academic distinction, high general ability, wide outlook and steady sense of balance and perspective, together with those personal qualities which are indispensable for dealing with the great variety of men and women engaged in different capacities in the service of education.[1]

With the progress of education the character of inspection has changed from the inquisitorial and dictatorial type to one which conceives its responsibility to be rather to consult, to advise and encourage teachers and local authorities, to discover and to disseminate ideas that make for progress and improvement, in general to serve, in the words of a former Permanent Secretary, Sir L. Amherst Selby-Bigge, as "agents of cross-fertilization." The inspectors, no longer guided by routine and detailed instructions from headquarters, are becoming more and more the intelligence officers for both the central and the local authorities whose function it is to discover the best that there is in educational practice and organization and to pass it on; they are at once students and teachers, and in the last decade their experience has been utilized in the organization of refresher courses for teachers conducted by the Board. This does not mean that the emphasis is placed upon the study of education or the cult of "pedagese"; if the English inspectorate is successful and commands the respect both of teachers and local officials, it is, first, because of the authority of opinions and views derived from the wide range of their experience, and, second, because their work is based on a knowledge of what can be achieved rather than on theoretical considerations. Advice, guidance, and encouragement for the improvement of educational organization and instruction, and the collection of information which furnishes the

[1] Selby-Bigge, Sir L. Amherst, *The Board of Education*, p. 158 (London, G. P. Putnam's Sons, Ltd., 1927).

basis for reports issued by the Board, are assuming a place of greater importance among the duties of the inspectors than the mere routine of direct inspection of schools. In practice a "full" inspection of secondary schools takes place once in seven years; elementary schools are visited once in three years; but, although routine inspections are decreasing in number and frequency, the inspectors utilize other methods — consultations and conferences with teachers — to keep in touch with the state of education in their areas. The change in the character of inspection is indicated concretely in the reduction in the number of inspectors (376 in 1924 and 338 in 1932), a reduction due to a change of policy as much as to financial reasons. From another point of view the change reflects the progress of local administration and of the professional standards of teachers.

On several matters affecting education the Board shares control with other ministries. In 1919 the Ministry of Health, which was established in that year and which in addition to supervision of public health took over the powers and duties of the Local Government Board, was charged with the control of school medical inspection and treatment, but was empowered to make arrangements with the Board to continue in the exercise of powers and duties in this matter as it had done since its introduction in 1907. The connection between the two ministries is maintained by the Chief Medical Officer of the Ministry of Health who is also the Chief Medical Officer of the Board. In carrying out the duties formerly exercised by the Local Government Board, the Ministry of Health controls the raising of loans for the purchase of school sites, for buildings and equipment, or for other capital expenditures. The education of unemployed adolescents and vocational placement are under the joint control of the Board and the Ministry of Labor.

For the collection of information on education, the Board in addition to relying on the reports of its inspectors maintains an Office of Special Inquiries and Reports whose duty it is to collect and supply information on education at home and abroad and to make reports on special matters referred to it. The Office was established in 1894 and under its first director, Mr. (now Sir) Michael Sadler, issued a series of volumes on education throughout the world which will be of permanent value and models of their kind. After providing in these reports the general foundation of information on educational subjects, the activity of the Office in this field was temporarily suspended, but was again revived as new problems arose and another series of reports (the *Educational Pamphlets*) began to be issued. In addition to its functions as an Office of Special Inquiries and Reports, this branch of the Board has charge of an extensive library on all phases of education, is responsible for arranging the exchange of teachers between England, the Dominions, and other countries, assists the Colonial Office in selecting teachers for the Crown Colonies, serves as the foreign correspondent of the Board, and advises foreign visitors who desire to study education in England.

The fear expressed at the time when the creation of the Board was being considered that it might become a bureaucratic organization was met by the provision of the Board of Education Act, 1899, for the establishment of a Consultative Committee to advise the Board on "any matter referred to the Committee by the Board." The Consultative Committee was established by Order in Council in 1900 and reconstituted in 1920. The Committee consists of twenty-one members of whom not less than two thirds must be qualified to represent the views of universities and other bodies interested in education. Members are appointed by the President of the Board, seven going out of office every second year. The Committee has contributed during the period of its existence a series of significant reports on the most pressing problems of the day, of which the two most recently issued (on the *Education of the Adolescent* and on the *Primary School*) are likely to affect fundamentally the future organization of education in England. Since the Consultative Committee was established originally on the understanding that it would not be permitted to impair the full responsibility of the President of the Board, its reports are advisory only and the Board may or may not act upon them.

In addition to the Consultative Committee, the Board is assisted in framing its policies by the advice of other committees. Among these is the Juvenile Organizations Committee which originated in 1916 as a Central Committee to assist the Home Office in dealing with the problem of juvenile delinquency, and was transferred in 1919 to the Board of Education. The Committee, which consists of forty-four members representing organizations concerned with the social and physical welfare of children and adolescents, sponsors and promotes the formation of similar committees to coöperate with local education authorities. To provide for the development of adult education, to coördinate the work in this field, to create an agency to coöperate with private and public organizations, and to advise the Board, there was established in 1920 the Adult Education Committee, which has prepared and published a number of papers on the subject of adult education. Since the Board does not itself conduct examinations of secondary schools, but has an interest in their conduct and standards, there was organized in 1917 the Secondary Schools Examinations Council to advise the Board, and to coördinate the standards of the bodies which are recognized by the Board for the conduct of examinations in secondary schools. The Council is made up of representatives of universities, of associations of local education authorities, and of the Royal Society of Teachers. In 1929, as a result of the relaxation of the Board's control over the training of teachers, a Central Advisory Committee for the Certification of Teachers was constituted to coördinate the work of the regional joint boards for the training of teachers (see Chapter VII). The Committee consists of twenty-five members representing universities and university colleges, local education authorities, governing bodies and faculties of training colleges, the teaching profession as a whole, and domestic subjects. From time to time the Board appoints Departmental Committees or, with the coöperation of other ministries, Inter-Departmental Committees to investigate and report on special problems of education; reports have been issued by such committees on the *Organization of Secondary Education in England and Wales*, on *Scholarships and Free Places*, on the *Teaching of English in England*, and on the *Training of Teachers for Public Elementary Schools*. Another series of reports (on the place of *Natural Sciences*, on *Modern Languages*, and on the *Classics* in education) was prepared by special committees appointed toward the close of the War by Mr. Lloyd George as Prime Minister.

Reference was made earlier to the fact that the Board does not appoint or pay the salaries of teachers. Since 1929 it has with one reservation surrendered its control over the preparation or examination of teachers to regional joint boards, although it has retained the power to certificate them (see Chapter VII). Teachers in public schools are employees of the local education authorities, who appoint them and pay their salaries. The Board has refrained from setting up scales of salaries. To meet the crisis which developed in this matter after the War and to secure some measure of uniformity of remuneration, a Joint Committee was appointed representing teachers, through the National Union of Teachers, and the local education authorities as their employers

to secure the orderly and progressive solution of the salary problem in public elementary schools, by agreement on a national basis, and in correlation with the solution of the salary problem in secondary schools.

Lord Burnham was appointed chairman of this committee and of two similar committees, consisting of representatives of the teachers' associations in the branches of education concerned, created to deal with salaries in secondary and technical schools. The committees formulated scales of salary, adjusted to different parts of the country — four scales for teachers in elementary schools and two for teachers in secondary and technical schools. The scale appropriate in any area was to be adopted by agreement between the teachers and their local authorities. Once adopted, the Board undertook to pay grants to meet the expenditure, but adjusted in such a way that no authority would gain financially by paying salaries lower than the appropriate scale. The scales were adopted in the first instance for five years, and at the expiration of the period in 1925 were renewed and have continued in effect up to the present.[1] The Board accordingly does not determine the salary scales, but has an interest in them partly because the appropriations to be made each year by Parliament are related to the expenditures of local authorities, and partly because the progress of education is intimately related to the material welfare of the teachers.

Although the Board of Education has for many years certificated teachers for public elementary schools, it does not maintain a register of teachers duly qualified to teach in all types of schools. The need of such a register has been recognized for more than sixty years. Several efforts, beginning with Mr. Forster's Endowed Schools Bill, 1869, were made to establish a system of registration, but without success until 1899, when the Board of Education Act included a

---

[1] Since the present discussion is concerned with the principle underlying the relations of the Board to teachers' salaries, it is not necessary to enter into any details on the reductions in the scales due to the voluntary contributions required during the period of financial difficulties, the contributions under the pension system, or the further difficulties which have resulted in the past two years leading to further deductions. The whole question of scales of salary is to be reopened again in 1933.

provision for the creation of a Teachers' Registration Council. Dissatisfaction with the methods of registration led to the abandonment of the scheme in 1907. In 1912 the Privy Council, acting on the authorization of Parliament, established a Teachers' Registration Council of forty-four members nominated by universities and teachers' associations. The constitution of the Council was amended in 1926 and the membership was increased to fifty, consisting of twelve registered teachers elected by the universities, thirty-six members elected by registered teachers according to the branch of education in which they are engaged, and two additional members appointed by the Council to represent types of teaching not already included. In 1929 the body of registered teachers was authorized by the King to be known as the Royal Society of Teachers, for which the Teachers' Registration Council acts as the executive agent. The duty of the Council is to draw up and maintain a register of teachers qualified for registration under conditions of training and experience set up by the Council. Registration is not compulsory, but in 1931 the number of registered teachers was over 90,000. The establishment of the Teachers' Registration Council illustrates two tendencies — first, the refusal of the Board to control the teachers directly, and, second, a movement for professional self-determination for teachers analogous to that found in the legal, medical, and other professions in England. Since the conditions for registration require professional preparation and experience in an efficient school, the influence of the Council in recent years has been strong, not only in encouraging the former, but also in raising standards in private schools if they desire to secure teachers who look forward to registration. From another point of view, since the Council does not distinguish between teachers engaged in different types of work or between public and private (or independent) schools, it serves as an important agency for the development of a national body of teachers.

The Board of Education as the central authority for national education has thus surrounded itself with a number of organizations which have been and are developed as the need arises and of which the Consultative Committee is the only statutory body. Through these organizations the Board, while it has not divested itself of authority, has surrendered some of those administrative functions which in a centralized system are regarded as essential for purposes of control. Through these agencies the Board of Education has access to the best thought on education represented by both professional and lay groups. The practice of consultation, not only with these agencies, but with teachers' organizations, local education authorities, and others not concerned directly with education, acts as a brake on precipitate and bureaucratic action. There is, however, another check on bureaucratic action, common to education as well as other concerns of public administration: questions may always be raised in Parliament on any matters that concern the governmental machinery. Although members of Parliament are not always intelligent on matters of education, there are some who have been teachers or who are members or officials of teachers' organizations, and all may be prompted by their constituents. The result is that questions concerning education from the minutest details to questions of policy are put at almost every session to the President of the Board of Education and answered either by him or the Parliamentary Secretary.[1] From time to time proposals are made that the Board of Education require the teaching of certain subjects or the use of certain methods of instruction. Invariably the answer given by the President of the Board may be illustrated by the reply given in 1927 by Lord Eustace Percy to a deputation of the Royal Society of St. George which urged that the direct and systematic teaching of patriotism be made a compulsory part of the curricula of schools:

> When it came to the question of a mandate from the Board, it had always been one of the principles of educational administration in this country that as little as possible should be laid down by the Central Department; that the Department, in matters of teaching, curriculum, pedagogics, and so on, should act by advice — by instruction in the sense of suggestion — by the issue of teachers' handbooks rather than by direct regulation.... If governments, whether local or central, begin to prescribe to the teacher a certain method of teaching, or even attempt to influence him in such matters, we run the risk of all those evils that we have seen in various forms, both in the Prussia of the past and in the Russia of to-day.[2]

There has thus been evolved a number of principles governing the relations between the Board and the education of the country.

---

[1] Thus, during April, 1932, questions on the following subjects were asked: the number and distribution of free places in secondary schools; the number of children leaving elementary schools at the school-leaving age; the provision of free meals in schools; the provision and use of moving pictures in schools; the cost of education.

[2] See Kandel, I. L., *Essays in Comparative Education*, pp. 35 ff. (New York, 1930).

There are, of course, criticisms and charges of "tyranny," but on the whole these are less frequent than in the early years of the century when the task of constructing the framework of a national system of education had to be performed. Increasingly the Board is becoming an agency to guide, advise, encourage, and stimulate the progressive development of education through its inspectorate, publications of its own and of its advisory and other committees, and above all through consultation and discussion with representatives of local education authorities and of teachers directly or of their associations. The importance of the last method of coöperation was dealt with at length by Lord Eustace Percy, then President of the Board, when he met a number of representatives of the Association of Education Authorities:

Lord Eustace Percy said it was very good of them to ask him to meet them, and he very much valued the opportunity of meeting the Association in bulk, as he had already met its representatives on a number of occasions. He was sure he had nothing novel to speak about, but he would like to emphasize his really sincere desire to see closer coöperation and consultation between the Board and the local education authorities in all matters of administration and policy. He thought that their representatives who had met him during the last six months would admit that he had done his best to enter into personal relations with them as far as he could. He wished to see that in the future the local authorities were given their proper place as the authorities primarily responsible in each area for education and the progress of education, and it was with this object that he addressed to them the other day a somewhat voluminous document on the subject of the local programme.

He had always felt that it was vain and futile for a gentleman sitting in a room in Whitehall to attempt to lay down the particular advances in education which should be carried out over a given period. That could only be judged by the Local Authorities, and he had asked them in that circular for an expression of their views, a lead from them as to the directions in which they thought extension of educational facilities or reorganisation was primarily needed.

The consultation which the Board of Education could carry on with the educational authorities was in three ways. Direct consultation was always by far the most effective method, but there were 318 such authorities in the country, and the amount of direct personal consultation by any President of the Board was clearly very limited.

Next there was consultation in Parliament, in the House of Commons; that was immensely important, and its importance was too often ignored. Parliament was created historically for the main purpose of enabling the Government to consult with the Local Authorities, and it was in that way that Parliament was originally established, and that was it which had given to our

Parliamentary system its quite peculiar character distinct from the Parliamentary systems of other nations. It remained true today that on matters affecting local authorities, the House of Commons was the most original sphere of joint consultation between the local authorities and the Government.

It was often said that local authorities had not been consulted in a matter which had been very fully debated in the House of Commons. Local authorities should use their representatives in Parliament even more than at present as responsible consultants with the Government.

The third method was represented by their Association there that day. The problems of local government had expanded during the last fifty years in such a way that it was impossible to carry out consultation on anything but the broadest matters of policy in the House of Commons, and on many big questions local authorities must consult with the Board or other Government department through Associations such as their own, which was the most important link and the link most frequently used between them and the President of the Board of Education.[1]

Beyond this, the Board has entered into a partnership with local authorities through the annual distribution of grants, which serves as a method for bringing its authority to bear.

Since the relations between the Board and organizations representing education are informal and not statutory or provided for by law, proposals have been made for the creation of a "real Board" to include representatives of Parliament, local education authorities, and the teaching profession. Such a Board, it is argued, would be more than a mere phantom, would meet at specific times, would secure continuity of policy which, it is charged, is lacking under the present system of changing Presidents, would serve as a real advisory board, and would serve as a check on bureaucratic control. That such a Board would ever be established seems unlikely, not only because the present system already provides channels for consulting a wider variety of opinion than would be conveniently represented in a single Board, but because such a Board could not be directly responsible to Parliament on the financial side, and, if it were granted the exercise of authority, would impair the authority and responsibility which are imposed on the President as on other ministries.

LOCAL ADMINISTRATION

The local administration of education was organized under the Education Act of 1902 and for London under the Act of 1903. Under

[1] *School Government Chronicle*, May 23, 1925, pp. 356 f.

these Acts the existing authorities for education described earlier were abolished and the existing areas for local government (counties, county boroughs, municipal boroughs, and urban districts) were established as the units for educational administration. The elected councils of these areas were constituted the local education authorities, with the powers and duties of providing elementary education, to supply or aid the supply of education other than elementary, and to coördinate all forms of education in their areas. The administrative county is one of the traditional divisions of England; in some cases the larger counties (Yorkshire and Lincolnshire) have been subdivided, and London with its contiguous area has been set up as a county. The county borough is a city with not less than 50,000 population; the municipal borough is a city with a population of over 10,000 at the census of 1901, and the urban district is an organized administrative area, corresponding to the American township, with a population of over 20,000 at the time of the same census. Not only are the areas unequal in size and population, but no steps have been taken in subsequent Acts to reallocate powers and duties, especially of the smaller authorities, to correspond with the increase or decrease of population. The counties and county boroughs were entrusted with the provision of elementary education and, if they so desired, of higher education; the municipal boroughs and urban districts were made responsible for elementary education only, but could levy a small rate for the support of higher education which went to the counties providing it. There are 62 counties, 83 county boroughs, 131 municipal or non-county boroughs, and 40 urban districts, which with the London County Council gives a total of 317 local authorities for education. The Act of 1918 made the local education authorities responsible for the progressive development and comprehensive organization of education in their areas and required them to prepare and submit schemes to the Board of Education showing how such development was to be promoted.

There are thus two types of authorities, one with powers and duties in respect to all branches of education and social services connected with it, and the other only in respect to elementary education. Following the divisions of the Education Act, 1902, which defined these powers and duties, the former are known as "Part II Authorities" and the latter as "Part III Authorities," a nomenclature which has been disturbed by the reorganization of the legal provisions under the Education (Consolidation) Act, 1921. In each area there is elected a council for the conduct of local government; for the expedition of business, every council after it is constituted is divided into committees (finance, gas, electricity, etc.). All matters dealing with education, except the raising of rates or borrowing money, must be referred to an education committee. The method of appointing education committees varies in different localities; sometimes the members are appointed by the mayor, sometimes by ballot, sometimes on the principle of proportional representation of the constituent parties. Since the members of the councils are elected on a general platform, in which education may not appear as an issue, and may have no familiarity with the problems of education, the education committees are required in addition to elect councilors, who must be in a majority, to provide for the inclusion of women and for the appointment (by the council) of persons of experience in education and acquainted with the needs of various kinds of schools in the area. The last are known as coöpted members and may be teachers,[1] principals of private schools, representatives of universities, or any other person generally interested in education. Coöpted members have the same powers, duties, and privileges as the elected members on the committee. The size of committees is not determined by any regulations and varies according to the scheme adopted from five to as many as fifty (thirty-eight councilors and twelve coöpted members) in London.

Although a council is required to exercise its powers and duties as the local education authority through an education committee, the amount of authority which it may delegate to this committee varies. The education committee by law is prohibited from raising rates or borrowing money;[2] beyond this, it may have delegated to it all other powers and duties of the council without any further restriction than the presentation of periodical reports to the council; in such cases the decisions of the committee are final. Elsewhere the delegation may

---

[1] Under the Education Act, 1921, First Schedule, Part III, "Any person shall be disqualified for being a member of an education committee who, by reason of holding an office or place of profit, or having any share or interest in a contract or employment, is disqualified for being a member of the council appointing the education committee, but no such disqualification shall apply to a person by reason only of his holding office in a school or college aided, provided or maintained by the council" (or maintained but not provided by the council).

[2] The Education Committee of the London County Council may approve proposals involving capital or maintenance expenditure not exceeding £500 without reference to the Finance Committee of the Council.

be restricted so as to reserve the right of approval or amendment or rejection of resolutions reached by the committee. The difference in the character of the delegation, while relatively unimportant in itself, affects the work of the administrative office for education. The increase in the amount and variety of the powers and duties of the education committees, whose members serve without pay and are engaged in other occupations, has led to the formation of sub-committees and even sub-committees of sub-committees. The number of these will vary with the amount of work to be considered. The powers and duties of the education committee of the London County Council are divided among seven sub-committees: accommodation and attendance; books and apparatus; elementary education; general purposes; higher education; special services; teaching staff. The chairman, vice-chairman, and deputy chairman of the Council and the chairman and vice-chairman of the education committee are *ex officio* members of every standing sub-committee. The Manchester education committee also has seven sub-committees, as follows: Municipal College of Technology; higher education; elementary education; administrative; sites and school buildings; finance and audit; and general purposes; in addition there are twenty-two special committees of the sub-committees. The Warwickshire education committee is divided into nine committees: finance; elementary education; school attendance and medical inspection; higher education; further education; sites and buildings; joint advisory committee; dismissals; and agricultural education. Smaller areas may have only three committees; all education committees have a general purposes sub-committee, which affords an opportunity for discussing matters at other than public meetings.

Local education authorities for elementary education, and therefore all local authorities, are required by the Act to maintain and keep efficient all public elementary schools within their areas which are necessary and have the control of all expenditure required for that purpose "except such expenditure as is left to managers of non-provided schools." This requirement includes the administration of school attendance, with power to enforce on parents the duty of providing efficient education for their children, the provision of medical inspection and treatment, the organization of practical and advanced instruction, and suitable provision for the education of blind and deaf children and of defective and epileptic children; in non-provided schools the local education authorities are responsible for all secular instruction. Adequate provision must be made to secure that children or young persons shall not be debarred, through inability to pay fees, from receiving the benefits of any form of education by which they are capable of profiting. In addition to the duties imposed upon them, local authorities have power to provide nursery schools, play centers, vacation schools, holiday camps and other arrangements for social and physical training of children, meals for necessitous children, and transportation. After 1918 they became responsible for the administration of the Employment of Children Act, 1903, the Prevention of Cruelty to Children Act, 1904, and the Children Act, 1908, which means that they are authorized to make by-laws to regulate the employment of children and street-trading by children and young persons under sixteen, and to prosecute for cruelty to children.

The local education authorities for higher education — that is, in counties and county boroughs — are required "to consider the educational needs of their areas and to take such steps as seem to them desirable after consultation with the Board of Education, to supply or aid the supply of higher education, and to promote the general coördination of all forms of education." The limit on the amount of rate which might be levied for this purpose, imposed in 1902, was removed in 1918, and authorities were permitted "to spend such sums as they think fit" for that purpose. Non-county or municipal boroughs and urban districts have the same power in respect to higher education, but are restricted in the amount of rate which they may raise for this purpose to a levy of one penny in the pound. Under these provisions an authority may supply any type of school other than elementary, may train teachers, may award scholarships, may make grants to universities, and may make provision for higher education outside their area in cases where they consider it expedient to do so. In practice the power of the non-county boroughs and urban districts is exercised in coöperation with the authority of the county in which they are located, or, in some cases, of the neighboring county borough.

The organization described means in effect, as contrasted with American practices, that the small rural district has no powers for educational purposes. Schools are provided by the county in which they are situated or, if there are non-provided or denominational schools available, these are also under the supervision for secular education of the county authority. In the Part III authorities (municipal boroughs and urban districts), elementary education is provided by the local education authority and higher education by the county authority with their financial coöperation, a system somewhat analogous to the high school districts in Illinois and in California. About twenty-five Part III authorities maintain their own secondary schools. Although the survival of the smaller Part III authorities is justified, as is the district system in the United States, on the ground that it promotes and maintains local interest in education, many difficulties of organization have arisen at a time when the educational program is being expanded. The Education Act, 1921, does in fact provide for coöperation between two types of authorities and for federation of any two educational areas for coöperative purposes under joint bodies of managers. The permission implied in this provision has rarely been used, since Part III authorities are rarely willing to accept transfer to a larger authority. Various methods of coöperation between authorities have, however, been devised. That there is some dissatisfaction with the status of Part III authorities is indicated in the enactment of the Education (Local Authorities) Act, 1931, which prevents the creation of new authorities of this type in the future. On the other hand, the realization of the importance of maintaining direct contacts with the public and of promoting popular interest in education in the larger county authorities has led to the establishment of representative district committees (Kent has 24 such committees, Lancashire 34 for elementary and 100 for higher education, West Riding 112, and Middlesex 13 for higher education).

Voluntary workers. Probably no other educational system in the world has the advantage of such an extensive system of voluntary assistance as does England. The desire to promote popular interest and the fear of bureaucratic control have led to the development of a system of managers for schools or groups of schools, a system which antedated the Education Act, 1902. Every local authority is required to appoint a body of managers for each school or for a group of schools in its area. In the larger areas the authority must appoint four managers and the smaller authority two; in the smaller areas the authority may appoint any number that it decides. This requirement applies to schools provided by the authority (see Chapter VI). In the case of non-provided or denominational schools, the body of managers consists of the foundation managers or trustees and representatives of the education authority in the proportion of four to two. The functions of the managers are mainly advisory and include no financial control except of voluntary funds raised for specific purposes. They may visit schools and have access to the records. They are expected to advise the authority on matters affecting school premises, such as alterations and enlargements, ventilation, lighting, heating, and sanitary conditions, and equipment. They may be consulted on the appointment of teachers, and in non-provided schools have the right to make appointments subject to the approval of the authority so far as qualifications to give secular instruction are concerned. They may investigate complaints against teachers, but can only recommend to the authority the action to be taken. In general they act as patrons of the school and interest themselves in promoting the welfare of the children. The managers serve in the main as a link between the school and the public on the one side and between the school and the committee on the other. Their success depends not so much on the extent of the powers and duties assigned to them as on their personal interest and influence. In secondary schools boards of governors perform functions similar to those of managers.

In a few areas groups of voluntary assistants have been developed to aid in social welfare activities in connection with the schools. These groups are generally known as the care committees, which have been most extensively developed in London. Originally established to discover cases of necessity under the Education (Provision of Meals) Act, 1906, the duties of the care committees have been expanded. They are expected to familiarize themselves with the home conditions of pupils in elementary schools, to advise parents on matters affecting the welfare of their children, to direct them to charitable organizations, and in other ways to provide such information and guidance as will enable the children to profit from their attendance at school. They have established clubs and other means of recreation, organized play centers and vacation schools, and advised on the choice of employment. In general they perform the functions of paid social workers and of visiting teachers in the United States. The care of adolescents who have left school has been taken over by other committees variously known as Juvenile Employment Committees, Juvenile Advisory Committees, and Juvenile Organizations Committees, which advise on the choice of employment, assist applicants to secure employment, and in general promote the educational, social, and recreational interests of adolescents.

Finally, the coöperation of teachers is secured informally through consultation, conference, and appointment of special committees, more formally in some areas by the creation of consultative committees. The character and constitution of these committees vary; in some areas the members are appointed by the chief education officer or the education committee; in others some are appointed in this way, others are elected by the teachers; some areas have consultative committees only for elementary education, others for each branch of education. In Manchester the consultative committee represents all branches of the teaching service and is consulted from time to time by the director of education or seeks the advice of the director. In addition to the consultative committee, Manchester also has an advisory committee of fourteen members, seven teachers and seven members of the education committee; to this committee there may be referred, either by teachers or the education committee, any questions of educational interest. In Warwickshire teachers' consultative committees have been constituted in each of the six districts of the county, consisting of three members appointed by the County Teachers' Association and not more than three by the education committee; each district committee may coöpt three additional members representing secondary, technical, and continuation schools respectively. One representative from each district committee, together with the teacher members of the County Education Committee's Joint Advisory Board, constitute the County Consultative Committee. In general the duties of the committees are to encourage the exchange of ideas on education among the teachers of the districts and county, to confer with government inspectors, to act in a general advisory capacity to teachers, managers, and the education committee, and to nominate representatives to serve as examiners for county minor scholarships in their districts.

Executive officials. It is clear that such a vast organization requires guidance and direction. In the days of the school boards, when the work of the elementary schools was more rigidly controlled by the central authority, or of the technical instruction committees, when the number of schools to be administered was small, the work to be performed could be handled by a clerk or secretary. The situation has changed since 1902; larger areas have been established, and the concept of education, both in its organization and in its aims, has been considerably enlarged. The Education Act, 1921, while it deals extensively with the powers and duties of local education authorities, somewhat characteristically leaves the organization and appointment of an administrative staff to their discretion, as follows:

> A local education authority may appoint necessary officers, including teachers, to hold office during the pleasure of the authority, and may assign to them such salaries or remuneration (if any) as they think fit, and may remove any of these officers.

Accordingly the development of an organizing and administrative staff has grown with the progress of education. Immediately following the reorganization under the Education Act, 1902, many authorities took over either the clerk of the school board or the secretary of the technical instruction committee, who in the larger areas were men of considerable experience and insight, but in many other instances were hardly competent for the broader responsibilities entailed in the new program. There is in each area an administrative officer, variously known as clerk, secretary, or chief education officer, or more frequently director of education. Nowhere are the requirements for this position defined, nor, except for the slight provision mentioned on page 227, has a system of training been developed. As in the case of government inspectors, it is felt that a good education and a strong personality are more desirable than technical preparation or expertness. The duties of a director are so varied that all-round preparation for the position may, indeed, be impossible. Not only is he responsible for the business side of his office — finance, buildings, equipment, and so on — but he must be an educator of many parts if he is to command the confidence of all teachers. Beyond this, he is responsible for preparing the business to be discussed by the education committee and its various sub-committees. Indeed, his function as an educator begins with the members of his committees and particularly with the chairmen.

The director of education is always a university graduate who has had experience in education as teacher, principal, or inspector. With the increase in the size of administrative staffs, it is becoming more usual to appoint to the more important positions men who have acquired experience in an education office. Vacancies are advertised; applications are considered by a sub-committee; a short list is prepared of suitable candidates, from among whom the final selection is made by the whole committee. Appointments are made by and held at the pleasure of the local education authority. The salaries vary with the size of the areas and range from £400 to £2500.

The number of administrative officials differs according to the size of an area and the powers and duties for which it is responsible. In a small Part III authority the administrative duties may be discharged by a director or secretary with one or two assistants and a few clerks. The County of Warwickshire is administered by a director of education, an assistant director, an assistant director for higher education, a chief juvenile employment officer, three organizers of further education, an agricultural organizer, a horticultural adviser, a chief and six assistant school medical officers, three school dentists, and an attendance officer. Manchester, which is a county borough with a population of 755,900, has a director, deputy director, a chief and four principal assistants, a chief inspector with a deputy chief inspector and six inspectors, a school medical officer with twenty assistant school medical officers, eleven school dentists, an organizer of physical education with two assistants, a music adviser with six assistants, an accountant, a surveyor, a superintendent of the by-laws department, a supervisor of juvenile employment, and a superintendent of stores. The organization of the staff of the education committee of the London County Council stands in a class by itself and is, of course, not typical or representative.

The success of an educational system is increasingly determined by the ability of the director or chief education officer. Here, too, as in the case of the central authority, much depends, not upon the director's right to impose his authority, but upon his ability to inspire in those under him, whether as administrators, inspectors, or teachers, the feeling that they are partners in a common enterprise, that the best work can only be done, not through dictation from above, but in an atmosphere of freedom and delegated responsibility. Just as the central authority has gradually assumed the position of guide and adviser, so the administration of a local authority is carried on in the same spirit. Just as the central authority refrains from prescribing curricula, courses of study, and methods of instruction, so the local officials, while issuing suggestions on these matters from time to time, place the responsibility for them upon the principals and teachers in the schools. There have been instances, though very few, in which directors have been charged with interference or with excessive "directing,"[1] but such instances are on the whole rare. As was indicated above, there is a growing tendency to provide channels for consultation and coöperation with those immediately concerned with the conduct of education and instruction.

It is possible to differentiate three types of administration. There is, first, the bureaucratic, which is based on the assumption of the right of the State to control. There is, second, the type of administration which attempts to introduce into education all those methods and principles of organization and direction which have been developed in business and industry, a practice which is desirable up to a certain point, the fabric of education, but which seriously militates against sound education if carried beyond that point, and may result in a control as unjustifiable as any bureaucracy. There is, third, the type of administration which is common in England, that of the amateur, that which regards expertness as limiting and restrictive, as involving the risk of failure to see the other man's point of view. The amateur has no definite plans, no formulas, no schemes which he is not ready to drop if the situation demands their modification or if better ones are offered, nor is he in danger of developing such habits of routine as will obscure the ends for which he is working.

Procedure by schemes. The Act of 1918 made local education authorities responsible for the progressive development and comprehensive organization of education in their areas and introduced the procedure by schemes whereby the authorities were required to survey the educational needs of their areas and draw up schemes for development over a period of ten years. The responsibility for drafting such schemes fell upon the administrative staffs and especially upon the directors of education. The financial stringency which began in 1920 made it impossible either for the Board of Education or local authorities to enter into commitments over a long period of years, and in 1925 the procedure by short-term programs covering three-year periods was adopted. About one hundred schemes had already been drafted by that time and laid down the framework for

[1] See Norwood, C., *The English System of Education* (London, 1928) and *The English Tradition of Education* (London, 1931). It is difficult at times to decide whether charges of excessive use of authority are not due to the traditional conflict between voluntaryism and public control, between the private school tradition and what may sometimes be the exigencies of a developing public system which seems, however, to be making an effort to retain the best of the tradition of independence.

further development. Procedure by schemes or programs produces the same effect as periodical surveys in the United States, with the difference that they are not prepared by experts called in from outside the areas concerned. It involves a canvass of the existing situation and planning for further expansion within the means of the locality and the probable financial aid from the central authority. A program must be submitted for consideration to other authorities which may be affected by them and to parents or other persons or groups interested in education in order to ascertain their views before it is presented to the Board, which may approve it, whereupon it must be put into effect, or, if it does not approve, must arrange for consultation with the authority concerned, and, if requested by the authority, must hold a public inquiry. If agreement cannot be reached, the matter must be referred to Parliament. The responsibility thus rests with the authority, not only to prepare a program, but to be able to justify and defend it. It is significant that no case has yet occurred of such disagreement between the Board and a local authority that Parliamentary action has had to be resorted to. It is such a system that makes the adaptation of education to local conditions possible, and provides scope for flexibility and variety within a national system.

Educational finance. The influence of the Board of Education is exercised through consultation and discussion, the consideration and approval of schemes, and the distribution of the grant. The cost of education is borne almost equally by the central and local authorities. The national funds are raised mainly by income tax, death duties, customs, excise, and various forms of indirect taxation. The budget for education is drawn up annually and presented to Parliament by the President of the Board. From the appropriations approved by Parliament grants are assigned for the maintenance of the Board, for distribution to local and other school authorities, and for pensions to teachers. Grants to universities are made by the Treasury, for agricultural education by the Ministry of Agriculture, for the education of delinquent or neglected children by the Home Office.

The local education authorities derive their revenues for purposes of local administration from rates or local taxes levied upon occupiers of land or buildings, from licenses, fines, penalties, etc., and from income from property, fees, profits from trading, etc., supplemented by grants in aid from the Government. The budgets for educational purposes are drawn up in most areas by the education committee, submitted to the finance committee of the local council, and passed by the council.

The educational grant from the Government to each local authority is calculated for elementary education in accordance with the following formula: thirty-six shillings per unit of average attendance, sixty per cent of the salaries of teachers including employers' contributions for pensions, fifty per cent of the cost of special services (medical inspection and treatment, schools for defective children, feeding of necessitous children, organization of physical training, nursery schools, etc.), twenty per cent (raised to fifty per cent in 1929 for a period of three years) of other approved expenditure. From the sum so derived there is deducted the product of a rate of seven pence in the pound, a measure which is intended to provide favorable treatment for the poorer areas. If the formula does not yield a grant equal to half of the total approved expenditure, the total is raised to that figure. Approved expenditure does not include payments made to other local authorities or schools which receive aid directly from the Board or other central department, teachers' salaries in excess of the agreed national scale, superannuation of officers other than teachers. Any authority wishing to spend beyond the standard set for certain branches of expenditure must justify the proposed excess in advance.

The grants for higher education amount to fifty per cent of the approved expenditure; part of the national fund out of which this grant is paid is obtained from the Treasury in the form of residue grant ("whiskey money"), revenue assigned originally for technical instruction in 1890. In the case of training colleges for teachers, which are conducted by a few authorities, but whose product is employed by others, a sum of £70,000 is withdrawn from all authorities in proportion to their size and paid as an extra allowance to those authorities which maintain such colleges.

Proposals for capital expenditures exceeding £1,000 must be submitted in detail to the Board of Education, which, if it approves, signifies its readiness to support an application for a loan. Such application must be submitted to the Ministry of Health with a formal resolution of the local council. Loans are approved by the Ministry of Health for a definite period of years — sixty years for land, thirty years for permanent buildings, and ten to fifteen years for lighter buildings and equipment. Money may be obtained by loan floated in open market for a period of years or from the sale of short-term mortgage bonds, or may be borrowed by the smaller authorities from the Public Works Loan Board. Loans may be extinguished in equalized annual payments or by annual charges on revenue expenditures covering interest and a portion of the capital.

The financial crisis in August, 1931, had as its immediate consequence a proposal for a serious reduction of the budget of the Board of Education. The grant for teachers' salaries was reduced from 60 per cent to 50 per cent, involving a cut of 15 per cent in teachers' salaries; the grant for loan charges for buildings from 50 per cent to 20 per cent; to balance these reductions the capitation grant was raised from 36s. per unit of attendance to 40s. 6d. The reduction in teachers' salaries was finally left at 10 per cent and the capitation grant was raised to 45s. per unit, and limitations were placed on the number of free places to be awarded annually in secondary schools. The situation is to be reviewed again in 1933, but whether the principles upon which the grants are based will then be changed is uncertain, although they have for some time been subject to criticism.

Conclusion. It is mainly at the time of such crises as that through which England passed in 1931 that the power which the Board of Education may exercise through the grant distribution becomes manifest. Normally the Board is content, so far as financial conditions permit, to allow local educational authorities to make such progress as they can justify and to assume half the cost of the expenditure. The history of the relations between the Board and the local and other education authorities indicates a constant desire to encourage freedom and initiative; in so far as the concerns of education can be regulated, regulations are issued, but without encroaching upon those aspects of its organization that should not be regulated. The *externa* and *interna* seem to be nowhere better separated administratively than under the English system. The principles which have been developed in practice in the relations of the central to the local authorities have guided the relations between the administrative officials and the schools under their care. Conflicts have arisen, particularly when secondary schools, which were formerly independent, came under the control of a local authority, but these have been so rare as to serve rather as the exceptions which throw light on and confirm the inherent principles of administration accepted in England. It is due to these principles that no two schools not only in England but in any one area are alike, and it is due to the prevailing sensitiveness to freedom and the acceptance of responsibility that in the practice of education England is still free from that mechanization and standardization which characterize those systems which are controlled either bureaucratically or in the name of efficiency, both of which may equally result in uniformity. The contrast between the centralized, authoritarian system and the system which seeks to guide and advise, while leaving as much freedom as possible to local autonomy, has nowhere been better drawn than by H. G. Wells in *Mr. Britling Sees It Through*[1] (p. 67):

To organize or discipline or mould characters or press authority is to assume that you have reached finality in your general philosophy. It implies an assured end.... We know we haven't finality and so we are open and apologetic, and receptive, rather than wilful.... You see all organization with its implication of finality is death.... What you organize you kill.... The reality of life is adventure, not performance. What isn't adventure isn't life. What can be ruled about can be machined. But priests and schoolmasters and bureaucrats get hold of life and try to make it *all* rules, *all* etiquette, *all* regulations and correctitude.

2. FRANCE

Centralization. France continues to furnish the outstanding example of centralized administration in education as well as in all functions of government. While in other countries centralization has been justified by political philosophy (Imperialism in Germany, Communism in Russia, and Fascism in Italy), a large number of considerations other than political have helped to perpetuate the control of all governmental functions — political, social, economic, and cultural — in the hands of a central authority. Centralization, first definitely established in the seventeenth century under Louis XIV as an accepted principle, has survived all changes of governmental forms from the Revolution to the present time. While under the Bourbons the principle of the State as the source of all blessings, or *étatisme*, was promulgated, under the Revolution the principle of centralization, involving the abolition of all local and provincial autonomy, was adopted as the best method of protecting the rights of the individual. Napoleon built up a machinery of administration based on the monopolistic concept of the Bourbons and

[1] New York, The Macmillan Company.

on the centralizing tendencies of the Revolution and established a form of government which has persisted down to the present. Three centuries of tradition have thus contributed to make the acceptance of administration one of the fixed characteristics of the French social heritage.[1]

If he were asked to justify the practice of centralization, the Frenchman would probably answer that it has worked in the past, localizes responsibility, and leaves him free to attend to his own affairs. But there are other reasons for its survival and persistence. The Third Republic is founded on the ideal of a France "one and indivisible"; France must offer a united front against all divisive forces; national security must come first (sécurité d'abord), and any encroachments on the authority of the State would be subversive. Centralization guarantees this united front against internal and external aggression. Fear of external aggression has influenced French politics since 1870; internally she is still afraid of monarchist tendencies and of the restoration of clerical influence. While France has little to fear from a movement to restore monarchy, there is widespread a strong feeling that only through a lay, secular system of education, controlled by a central authority, can the country protect itself against a revival of clerical influence.

Through centralization France hopes to present a united front against aggression and at the same time to promote national unity. For, despite the tradition of administrative centralization, the French are a nation of individualists, a paradox perhaps, but a paradox which is due to the emphasis on national security and solidarity, on the one hand, and on the cult of reason as the highest form of intellectual expression by the individual on the other. Centralization is thus justified as an instrument for protection against excessive individualism. The State thus becomes at once the guarantor of liberty, equality, and fraternity, of the rights of the individual in general, and the repository and guardian of national culture. At present it is perhaps in the second position more than in the first that the explanation of centralization of education is to be found. The State is not merely the patron of arts, science, and letters through definitely constituted agencies, such, for example, as the Academy, but sees to it that all Frenchmen receive a share of that French culture which the State defines and prescribes. French

[1] Le Bon, G., *The Crowd*, pp. 100 f. (London, 1903).

culture thus becomes in turn an instrument of control against individualism, a point emphasized recently by M. Bouglé:

> If you now ask me to tell you what we understand by general culture and why we defend it, I would, in answer to the second question, answer that we defend it because we are a nation of individualists and because we wish to be a democratic nation. We are, therefore, compelled to impart a minimum of general culture, even to the humblest citizens, simply because they are citizens.[1]

How the Frenchman would define *culture générale* is not clear, but that he would emphasize above all else the cultivation of the French language as a common bond and as an instrument of thinking is obvious from a study of all educational regulations. The emphasis on a common language explains the official opposition to the introduction of the use of dialects and the study of dialectical literatures in the elementary schools. This point of view was clearly expressed in a Ministerial Circular issued by M. Anatole de Monzie on August 14, 1926, rejecting the petition of a group of Provençal leaders to permit the use of local dialects as vehicles of instruction in elementary schools. The case against localism was summed up by a quotation from de Musset, that "He alone is truly French in heart and soul, from head to foot, who knows, speaks, and reads the French language."[2] Not only the national language, but geography, history, and moral instruction, as phases of French culture, must accordingly be under the control of the State. The concern for the maintenance of the standards of French culture is not determined merely by internal policy; France feels that her influence in the world, especially in Eastern Enrope, Asia Minor, and Latin America, for the past three centuries has been due to her preëminence in the field of letters. To maintain the standards on which her influence depends, control by a central authority, it is argued, is essential. Except for the program of the *école unique*, the discussions on education in professional circles, in the press, and in Parliament, have in the past ten years turned not on political but on cultural issues. In the *crise d'agrégations* a few years ago, when it appeared that the best educated young Frenchmen were turning to industry and commerce rather than to literary and professional pursuits, the effect on

[1] *Conference on Examinations*, held at Eastbourne, England, May, 1931, p. 46 (New York, 1931).

[2] See Hayes, C. J. H., *France, A Nation of Patriots*, where the circular is given in full, p. 313 (New York, 1930).

the outside world was viewed with as much alarm as the effect at home.

The survival of centralization is due to still another factor. Paris has always been the political, administrative, and cultural center of France in a much more real sense than the capitals of any other country, with the exception of the capitals in Latin America, which in general have adopted France as their models. Public opinion in France is moulded largely by what goes on in Paris, and Paris is the lodestar of all ambitious Frenchmen. Centralization in France has been described "as a sword the handle of which is in the capital and the point in the rest of the State." The fiction of Paris as the country's center was for a time even carried so far as to determine the building of railroad communications on a most uneconomical plan. Culturally the dominance of the capital would discourage local initiative and variations, were it not for the fact that there are other forces which, as will be shown later, are beginning to assert the right of localities to self-determination. Administratively and economically the reference of all problems and questions to the center means inevitable delay and a slackening of progress.

Finally, three centuries of experience with centralization have given the Frenchman a feeling of confidence in an expert bureaucracy nationally controlled in the face of frequently changing Ministries. He may laugh at and ridicule red tape, but the concentration of responsibility in the controlled *administration* or officialdom leaves him with a feeling of assurance that all will turn out well; that his liberty and equality are safer in the hands of a central administration than if subjected to the conflict of groups, whether official or not; that much which he regards as more valuable might have to be surrendered if the tempo of life were increased. He would in any event prefer the uniformity of centralized action to the whims and caprices of local government which is at present in the hands of 90 departments and 38,000 communes.

Centralization of administration is, then, the accepted form of government in France. Although it is not without its critics, it is accepted because it has been the tradition of three centuries, because it is regarded as the best guarantee and protection of the rights of the individual, because it makes for national unity and solidarity, because it preserves the basic traditions of French culture, because to the logical mind it is neat and symmetrical in its organization, and because it provides expert service. The general framework of centralization introduced by Napoleon remains intact. It was modified somewhat by the laws of August 10, 1871, and of April 5, 1884, which entrusted certain powers in local government to departments and communes. Local autonomy, however, is restricted in financial matters, decisions of elected councils are subject to central control, and local officials are directly responsible to the central authorities. These restrictions are nowhere more obvious than in the field of education, where the central authority controls the *externa* and tolerates no interference in the *interna*.

THE SYSTEM OF ADMINISTRATION

The Central authority. The control of education in France is thus wholly a concern of the State. Its administration is entrusted to the Ministry of Public Instruction and Fine Arts (*Ministère de l'Instruction Publique et des Beaux Arts*), at the head of which is the Minister selected by the Premier with the approval of the President.[1] The duration of office of a minister is thus dependent upon the life of the Cabinet of which he is a member. In view of the instability of French political parties, cabinets in general have been short-lived, with the result that in the past century about half of the Ministers of Public Instruction have held office for less than six months. Despite the responsibilities involved and the amount of money devoted to education, the position of the Ministry of Public Instruction is not regarded as one of the important portfolios.

The Minister is responsible to Parliament for the conduct of national education, executes the laws, drafts and countersigns decrees which have the power of law when signed by the President, prepares the budget, and is responsible for the supervision of all educational institutions, public and private. He nominates for appointment by the President the important officials in the educational service — directors of divisions in the Ministry, inspectors-general, academy inspectors, and rectors of academies — and has the right to make certain appointments himself — primary inspectors and teachers and professors in all schools and universities. He hears appeals in cases

[1] On the appointment of the Cabinet under M. Herriot on June 3, 1932, M. A. de Monzie was nominated *Ministre de l'Education Nationale*, a title which the advocates of the common school have urged for some time and which seems to have been adopted without any formal discussion or legal procedure other than a decree.

ADMINISTRATION OF EDUCATION

of conflict and has disciplinary authority over all officials whom he appoints. He prescribes, with the advice of the officials of the Ministry and the Higher Council, the curricula, courses of study, and methods of instruction for all schools, the examination requirements and scholarship awards, and all administrative regulations governing the conduct of education.

The powers described may on the surface appear to be matters of routine. Actually the Minister of Public Instruction, like all other ministers in France, is invested with far more authority than is indicated in the preceding paragraph, since he has by virtue of his position legislative as well as executive powers. Legislation in France proceeds by two methods; the first is by legislative enactments (*lois*) by Parliament, the second by decrees (*decrets*) signed by the President and countersigned by the Minister concerned. Educational legislation thus consists of laws and decrees. These are further defined by regulations (*arrêtés*) issued by the Minister, who in addition may communicate opinions through memoranda (*circulaires*). The medium of communication of all ministries is the *Journal Officiel*; the particular organ of the Ministry of Public Instruction is the monthly *Bulletin Administratif du Ministère de l'Instruction Publique*.[1] It is the power of issuing decrees that confers so much authority as well as responsibility upon the French Minister. The Bérard reform of secondary education furnishes an excellent illustration. At the close of 1920, M. Léon Bérard was appointed Minister of Public Instruction, and at the first meeting of the Higher Council of Public Instruction in January, 1921, he presented his proposals for the reform of secondary education, which had been the subject of criticism for several years. Briefly his proposal was to make four years of Latin and two years of Greek compulsory for all boys in secondary schools. The members of the Council were requested to answer a questionnaire on the subject, but the unfavorable replies were ignored. A storm of criticism broke out in educational circles and in the press. M. Bérard, however, proceeded with his plans which he justified in letters to the President and to the Parliamentary Committees on Education, and presented his proposals to the Chamber of Deputies which discussed them at length in 1922 without reaching a vote. In May, 1923, a decree in-

[1] Since the issue of June 15 this has been published under the title *Bulletin Administratif du Ministère de l'Education Nationale*.

troducing the reform was issued, signed by the President, M. Millerand, and countersigned by M. Bérard.[1] The reform was to go into effect in the following October for the entering class in boys' secondary schools. In May, 1924, M. Poincaré's Cabinet, of which M. Bérard was a member, was defeated; M. Herriot became Premier, appointed M. François Albert as Minister of Public Instruction, and a new decree was issued repealing the Bérard reform and abolishing compulsory Latin and Greek.

The authority of the Minister is subject to control by Parliament which frequently discusses general problems of education. The consideration of the annual budget in particular offers opportunities for such discussions on the basis of extensive reports prepared by the special committees on the subject appointed by the Chamber of Deputies and the Senate. The lengthy discussions of the Bérard reform, which resolved themselves into heated debates on the value of the classics and their place in modern culture, have been mentioned;[2] more recently the preliminary general preparation which should be required of candidates for admission to the study of law and medicine and for teachers of the humanistic subjects in secondary schools and the problem of the *école unique* (the common school) have been the subjects of debate. There is probably no other country in which Parliament discusses problems of education as assiduously as in France, but in general it will be found that where the debates are most heated the members are concerned not so much with the questions of educational politics as with the preservation of standards of French culture.

The Minister is assisted in his official duties by a cabinet, consisting usually of aspiring young politicians, the Higher Council of Public Instruction, and the permanent staff of the Ministry. The members of the cabinet attend to correspondence and matters requiring the Minister's personal attention, act as intermediaries between the Minister and Parliament, edit the *Bulletin Administratif*, and recommend candidates for academic distinctions. The Higher Council of Public Instruction (*Conseil Supérieur de l'Instruction Publique*) is a miniature educational parliament which advises the Minister on all problems of education on which it must be consulted by law or

---

[1] The Chamber of Deputies in a debate, after the decree had already been passed by a vote of 306 to 216 supported the reform.

[2] See Kandel, I. L., *The Reform of Secondary Education in France* (New York, 1924).

ADMINISTRATION OF EDUCATION

which are referred to it. The Council, over which the Minister presides, consists of fifty-six members, of whom thirteen are appointed (nine by the President to represent public education and four by the Minister for private education), and the rest elected by their own respective groups (twenty-seven for universities and other institutions of higher education, ten for secondary, and six for elementary education). Each member holds office for four years and may be reappointed or reëlected. The Council meets regularly twice a yeai and may be summoned for special sessions. The Minister must consult the Council on all questions concerning courses of study, methods of instruction, examinations, administrative regulations, discipline, the supervision of private schools, textbooks, and applications from foreigners to open or conduct schools. The Council also acts as a court of appeal on disciplinary matters, as, for example, on appeals brought by teachers against the action of local officials or councils or by individuals who are refused permission by a local body to open a school.

Between the regular sessions of the Council, current affairs are conducted by a permanent section (*section permanente*) which consists of 15 members of the Council, including 9 appointed by the President and 6 selected by the Minister from the elected members. The section prepares all business to be considered by the Council, advises the Minister on the establishment of normal schools, on the interdiction of textbooks and books for libraries and prizes in schools, and on any other questions of courses, administration, or discipline referred to it by the Minister or proposed by a member of the Council.

Administration of vocational education. Until 1920 the Ministry of Public Instruction was responsible only for general education and general vocational schools. The administration of specialized vocational education was in the hands of the Ministry of Commerce and the Ministry of Agriculture, while a few other ministries (War, Navy, and Public Works) had charge of technical training in their own fields. In 1920 the control of vocational education, hitherto under the Ministry of Commerce, was transferred to the Ministry of Public Instruction and placed in charge of an Under-Secretary of State; after a period of indecision and changes in status, the position was confirmed by a decree issued on August 5, 1929. The Under-Secretary for the Minister is responsible for the general administration, organization, and support of vocational education; his powers in this field parallel those of the Minister in the general field. Like the Minister, the Under-Secretary of State for Vocational Education is assisted by a personal cabinet and a Higher Council of Vocational Education which consists of 150 regular members and 56 alternates, *ex officio*, appointed and elected to represent employers and employees, departmental committees for vocational education, and teachers. An executive committee (*commission permanente*) keeps in close touch with the progress of vocational education between the regular sessions of the Council.

Administration of physical education. The widespread interest in physical education which followed the War led to the consideration of schemes for promoting it on a national basis. For a few years the direction of physical education was entrusted to the Ministry of War. Gradually it was transferred to the Ministry of Public Instruction, and placed in 1923 in charge of an academy inspector, and two years later of an inspector-general; in 1929 an Under-Secretary of State for Physical Education was attached to the Ministry of Public Instruction and made responsible for the organization and extension of physical education in all types of schools and universities and for the preparation of teachers. The general line of progress has already been defined by several consultative commissions appointed since 1922 to consider the subject. The Under-Secretary of State for Physical Education is assisted by a personal cabinet, but there is as yet no Higher Council to advise him.

The permanent staff. The Ministry of Public Instruction and Fine Arts is divided into six departments (*direction*) — higher, secondary, elementary, vocational education, fine arts, and accounts, and a smaller division for physical education (*services de l'éducation physique*). Each department is administered by a director and is subdivided into bureaus (three for higher education, five each for the other educational departments, six for fine arts, and three for accounts). To each bureau is assigned the administration of special questions within its field — inspection, courses of study, discipline, scholarships, personnel, buildings, finance and accounts, and so on. The department of fine arts has general charge of public buildings, historical monuments, museums and expositions, architectural works, theaters, and moving pictures.

The immediate links between the Ministry and the educational institutions of the country are the fifty-eight inspectors-general, of whom there are nineteen for secondary education (four for sciences, nine for letters, three for modern languages, one for drawing, and two to supervise the financial administration of schools); for elementary education (including normal and higher elementary schools) there are twenty inspectors-general of whom one is appointed for drawing, four for primary schools, four (women) for maternal schools, and one for administrative matters, while the rest are unassigned; nine inspectors-general, including one woman, superintend the progress of vocational education. The inspectors-general are appointed by the President on the recommendation of the Minister of Public Instruction. Their offices are in Paris, and they are assigned to inspection tours each year by the Minister or are appointed to conduct special investigations from time to time.

The Minister is further assisted in making appointments and promotions by three consultative committees (*comités consultatifs*), one for higher education divided into commissions representing the various faculties and consisting of *ex officio*, appointed and elected members; one for secondary education consisting of inspectors-general of secondary education, the rectors of academies, the director and adjunct-director of the Higher Normal School, the bureau chiefs of the department for secondary education, and the inspectors of the Academy of Paris; one for elementary education including the director of the department for elementary education, the directors of the departments for secondary and higher education, the inspectors-general for elementary education, the rectors of academies, the directors of the Higher Primary Normal Schools, a chief of the first bureau in the department for elementary education, and academy inspectors or professors on special assignments; and one for *Collège Chaptal* and the higher elementary schools in Paris.

The Ministry is directly responsible for the administration of a number of learned societies and academies grouped together as the *Institut de France*, of a number of higher institutions of learning like the *Collège de France*, the *Ecole Nationale des Chartes*, the *Ecole Nationale des Langues Orientales Vivantes*, the *Ecole Pratique des hautes Etudes*, the *Muséum d'Histoire Naturelle*, the *Bureau des Longitudes*, the *Observatoire de Paris-Meudon*, the *Bibliothèque Nationale*, and the *Musée Pédagogique*. Immediately dependent on the Ministry are three special offices — the *Office National des Uni-*

versités et Ecoles Françaises, which promotes intellectual relations and student and teacher exchange between France and foreign countries; the *Office National des Pupilles de la Nation*, which looks after the wards of the nation, orphans of soldiers killed in the War; and the *Office National des Recherches Scientifiques et Industrielles et des Inventions*, a national patent office.

Local administration. There is thus organized at the center a system concerned with the direction of every phase of educational policy and administration. Every need is apparently foreseen and arranged for by law, decree, regulation, circular, or instruction. All that is required is machinery to set the whole system into motion throughout the country. The State reaches either directly through its officials or indirectly by correspondence into every school in every hamlet. Local administration is but an extension of the central authority; certain powers are conferred on local councils, but their execution is subject to the control of the Ministry and its officials.

The academies. For administrative purposes France (including Algiers) is divided into seventeen academies, in each of which there is a university. The responsible official for the conduct and control of education in the academy is the rector, who is both the president of the university and the chief representative of the Ministry of Public Instruction in the academy. The rector is appointed from the ranks of university professors by the President on the nomination of the Minister of Public Instruction. Responsible legally for all branches of education, the rector devotes his attention more directly to higher and secondary education and normal and higher elementary schools. He selects candidates for appointments, advises the Ministry on educational questions, supervises the conduct of examinations, for which he may himself set the subjects of compositions, appoints members of examining commissions, approves the selection of textbooks, and presides over the committee on the award of national scholarships, and is in general responsible for the efficient administration and supervision of public and private education in his academy.

The rector is assisted by an Academic Council which consists of the academy inspectors and of representatives of higher and secondary education, of departmental and communal councils, of private secondary schools. The Council serves as an advisory cabinet on problems of secondary education. The technical advisers of the

ADMINISTRATION OF EDUCATION

rector are the academy and primary inspectors. The academy inspectors, of whom there are ninety-eight for the whole country, and except in the larger areas one for each department, are appointed by the President on the recommendation of the Minister with the advice of the combined consultative committees for elementary and secondary education. The qualifications for appointment are the possession of a doctorate in letters or sciences, or an *agrégation* or the certificate of aptitude for a primary inspectorship together with a *licence d'enseignement*; in addition several years of experience as a teacher, principal, or inspector in some branch of education are required. The first appointment is for a probationary period of two years. The academy inspector has the right to inspect any school in his area and is required to visit secondary schools once a term, is directly responsible for the conduct and progress of elementary and secondary education, is vice-president of the departmental council for education and president of the administrative council of secondary and normal schools in his area and of the departmental textbook commission. He appoints elementary school teachers as probationers, recommends their permanent appointment by the prefect of the department, and exercises disciplinary authority over them; he nominates the examining committees for the teachers' certificate (*certificat d'aptitude pédagogique*) and for the certificate of primary studies (*certificat d'études primaires élémentaires*); he advises on applications to open private schools and has the authority to initiate proceedings against teachers in private elementary schools, if necessary. He is, in a word, the superintendent of education in his department charged with the execution of powers entrusted to him by the Ministry, but without authority to initiate policy. He prepares a report each year on the progress of education, which is first presented to the departmental council for education and transmitted through the general departmental council to the Minister.

In the field of elementary education, which includes maternal schools, elementary schools, higher elementary schools, and normal schools, the academy inspectors are assisted by primary inspectors. To be appointed as primary inspectors, men and women candidates must be twenty-five years of age, must have had at least five years of experience as teachers and must have obtained by examination the *certificat d'aptitude à l'inspection primaire et à la direction des écoles normales*, or a *licence* in letters or sciences. Appointments are made by the Minister, who decides on the number and size of inspection areas. The first appointment is for a probationary period of two years; final appointment is made on the recommendation of the rector of the academy concerned acting on the advice of the permanent committee of the consultative committee for elementary education. No inspector may be appointed to the district in which he was born or trained. Primary inspectors are placed directly under the authority of the academy inspectors, but they are also subject to instructions from the rector, academy inspectors, and the Minister; in other words, they are not responsible to any local council. They inspect public and private elementary schools, distribute pupils in the classes, approve the time-schedule, inspect public school buildings before their opening is sanctioned, advise on the procedure for opening or closing of schools, the establishment of private schools, the organization of adult courses, and of school funds (*caisses d'écoles*). They conduct teachers' conferences, are members of departmental textbook commissions, superintend the administration of the school attendance law, conduct the examination for the certificate of elementary school studies, and are members of the examination committees for the *brevet élémentaire* and *brevet supérieur*. Finally, they advise the academy inspector on the promotion, transfer, and disciplining of teachers. As a rule there is one primary inspector for each *arrondissement* or the administrative area consisting of several communes under the charge of a sub-prefect; in the larger *arrondissement* the inspection of boys' schools may be entrusted to a man and of girls' and maternal schools to a woman. In general each primary inspector is responsible for the supervision of about two hundred teachers.

Departments. What is left after the centralized system of education has completed its control over the educational system is entrusted to local administration. Since 1871 the departments, and since 1884 the communes, have been given a certain amount of autonomy, subject, however, to the control of the central Government. The head of each of the ninety departments into which France is divided is the prefect, who, although appointed by the Minister of the Interior, is responsible according to the variety of his functions to a number of ministries. Thus, among other things he is the head of the elementary school system, confers permanent appointment on teachers, supervises the accounts and expenditures for education by the departments, determines on the location of schools,

ADMINISTRATION OF EDUCATION 275

supervises the award of scholarships to higher elementary schools, and is chairman of the departmental council for education, of which the academy inspector is the vice-chairman. The departmental council consists of the prefect, the academy inspector, four members of the general departmental council, which is elected by the communal councils of the department, four elementary school teachers elected by their colleagues, the principals of the two normal schools usually found in each department, representatives of private schools, and two primary inspectors appointed by the Minister of Public Instruction. The council meets once every three months, and at the call of the prefect; it exists to advise the prefect and not to represent the public, which is not admitted to its sessions. Its functions are advisory: it may recommend reforms and discusses the annual report of the academy inspector; it considers requests from teachers to act as secretaries to the communal mayors or of women to teach in boys' schools; it advises on the number and location of schools and the number of teachers required and supervises school medical inspection. Members may visit schools, but may only concern themselves with the school building, questions of sanitation, and the deportment of the pupils; under no circumstances may they interfere with matters affecting instruction. The council has certain disciplinary powers over teachers and is consulted on the opening of private schools. Beyond this, the council is responsible for certain expenditures for education which will be discussed below.

Communes. The local area next in importance for the administration of education is the commune. There are in France about 38,000 communes varying in size of population from hamlets with less than fifty inhabitants to the dozen larger communes with populations from 100,000 to 400,000 and two with populations of over 1,000,000. The commune in general is similar to the American township and is rarely wholly rural or wholly urban. The chief official of a commune is the mayor, who, although he is nominated by the elected communal council, is responsible to the prefect and to the central Government. For educational purposes the mayor is charged with the supervision of school buildings, proposing new buildings, recommending the opening of private schools, promoting school attendance, and keeping the school census. In relation to the teachers he has no authority. He is assisted by a communal school board (*commission municipal scolaire*), which includes delegates from cantons (mainly judiciary areas) appointed by the academy inspector, and members appointed by the communal council, which is itself elected by the people; the primary inspector is *ex officio* a member of all school boards in his area. The school board meets once every three months or on call by its president, the mayor, or the primary inspector. Its meetings are not public. The school board is responsible for the supervision of attendance, the administration of a voluntary school fund (*caisse d'école*), and encourages attendance by the award of prizes and the grant of aid in needy cases.

The duties of the school boards are relatively so unimportant that there have been cases where communal councils have refused to appoint them or when appointed the boards have refused to meet. Their decisions may be overridden by the departmental councils for education and by the prefects, who have the right to require communes to close schools, to open new ones, to set aside a site and to provide buildings. Should a commune refuse to carry out these requirements, the prefect is authorized, with the advice of the departmental building and health officials, to select the site, plan and erect the building, and charge the cost to the commune concerned. As will be shown later, the communes have certain financial obligations. The most important functions of local boards are thus to provide elementary buildings and promote school attendance; they do not even have the right of entry into schools and with instruction they are not permitted to interfere; parents and inspectors may appeal from the decisions of the local school boards to the departmental councils. The principle which defines the position of the school boards was enunciated more than a generation ago in a Ministerial Circular to their members:

It is not within your province to burden yourselves with the subjects of instruction, with the criticism of methods, books or equipment, since the courses of study are today prescribed in full details by the authorities charged with this duty.

Educational finance. The cost of education is shared by the State, departments, and communes, and is met by the general taxes levied by the three partners in government. The sources of revenue of the State are: (1) income and related taxes; (2) taxes assimilated with direct taxes — that is, levied on luxuries and fees for services; (3) indirect taxes including registration taxes on legal documents, stamp taxes, taxes on business turnover, customs duties, taxes on commodities, and excise taxes; and (4) revenues from state monopolies and taxes on gambling. The departments levy: (1) *centimes additionnels* or centimes added to the direct taxes imposed by the State; (2) taxes on land, buildings, rentals, and license taxes on trades and professions — the amount of these is fixed by law; and in addition (3) extraordinary or deficiency tax whose maximum is fixed each year in the Finance Law. From these sources the departments raise half of their revenues; the rest is derived from the State. The communes levy a greater variety of taxes than the departments, for besides the *centimes additionnels* they retain a share of the indirect taxes of the State (*fonds communs*), impose local taxes on dogs, entertainments, animals for sale or slaughter, and other taxes sanctioned by the Government, and derive revenues from fees, licenses, and tolls and from communal property; the *octroi*, or duty on foods, fuel, and other commodities entering a commune, has virtually disappeared. State grants are made by the State for a variety of purposes.[1]

The expenditures for education vary according as they are ordinary, extraordinary, or adopted by agreement. In the field of elementary education, which includes maternal, elementary, higher elementary, and normal schools, the State assumes as ordinary expenditures the cost of all salaries and of supplements for special positions as principals, the maintenance of students in normal schools, the maintenance of normal schools less the cost of repairs and equipment, and aid to necessitous communes. The departments are responsible for the maintenance and repair of normal school buildings, the provision and maintenance of an office for the academy inspector, additional salary grants to primary inspectors, the cost of the board of normal school students who do not live in the dormitories, the supply of materials for manual work in normal schools, and the publication of a departmental bulletin of elementary education. The communes pay the indemnities for rent to teachers, the wages of assistants in maternal schools, the cost of teachers' lodgings and repairs, light and heat of the schools, and supply school materials and equipment, including materials for manual work.

Under the heading of extraordinary expenditures, the State gives grants-in-aid to departments and communes to pay the interest on loans for buildings; the departments supply the sites and buildings

---

[1] On the French taxation system in general see Haig, R. M., *The Public Finances of Post-War France* (New York, 1929).

for normal schools, and the communes the sites and buildings for elementary schools. In addition to the ordinary and extraordinary charges, there are expenditures which the State, departments, and communes may assume voluntarily, but once they are assumed they must be continued by agreement for a period of years. Thus departments are only required to provide normal schools, one for each sex, and communes must provide elementary schools, and, if the population exceeds five hundred, separate schools must be supplied for boys and girls unless the department council authorizes a mixed school; communes with more than two thousand population must maintain maternal schools or infant classes; at their own option communes may provide maternal schools and infant classes, when not so required by law, and higher elementary schools, but once established such schools must be maintained for a period of years — thirty years, if state aid is requested; once established such optional schools become obligatory by agreement between the communes and the State (*conventionnellement obligatoires*) and receive aid on the same basis as schools required by law. In addition the State may by agreement undertake to give grants-in-aid of manual work in normal schools, school funds (*caisses d'écoles*), instruction in special subjects, apparatus, books for libraries, and educational museums; the departments may grant additions to the salaries of inspectors and teachers, funds for prizes, and subsidies for school funds; the communes may grant additions to teachers' salaries, provide funds for equipment, books, prizes and scholarships, may maintain optional schools or classes, and may subsidize the school funds.

In the field of secondary education, the State assumes the whole cost of salaries of personnel in *lycées* and the maintenance and repair of buildings; the revenue from tuition fees will gradually disappear with their progressive abolition, but the receipts for board or partial board belong to the State. The cost of *collèges* or communal secondary schools is shared by the State and the communes; the salaries, increments, and other additions are paid by the State, while the communes are responsible for the provision of the sites and buildings, their maintenance and upkeep, and for the supply of materials and equipment.

Conclusion. There has thus been set up in France a vast machine for the control of education which leaves nothing to local initiative, from detailed prescriptions of the furniture and equipment in the classroom of a maternal school to the examinations and requirements for entrance to the highest professions. This system has not, however, escaped criticism and protest. It explains, for instance, the emergence of powerful teachers' organizations in which are grouped together members of different religious and political beliefs, militarists and pacifists, conservatives and progressives in education. The criticisms on the educational side were brought to the fore by the activities of *Les Compagnons de l'Université Nouvelle*, the Advocates of the New Educational System, organized formally in 1919, but already in existence before the close of the War. The functions of government, according to *Les Compagnons*, have become so vast that they can no longer be conducted from one center. Centralization of such functions, and particularly of education, tend to subordinate the individual and to suppress initiative and, therefore, progress. The central Government insists on unifying and organizing all activities, on setting up its own values and reducing everything to uniformity, requiring from the individual only devotion and obedience to the existing system. Under a false concept of unity the country is condemned to the control of a bureaucracy and natural groupings are destroyed. Each branch of education is dominated by the same prescribed methods, curricula, and courses of study, the same examinations and competitions. Neither national union nor national culture can be promoted in such ways; the abstract notion of unity should be replaced by a unity of composition.[1]

These criticisms parallel the criticisms of centralization emanating from a group which sponsors the movement known as *régionalisme*, a movement to redistribute France into more homogeneous groupings than the artificial departments created during the Revolution. Originating as a cultural movement for the preservation and promotion of local dialects, languages, customs, and traditions, the regionalist movement has found support from other groups which recognize that France would gain socially, economically, and administratively, as well as culturally, from a system of decentralization. The centralized system had already been subjected to criticism in the middle of the last century, when Pierre Joseph Proudhon urged the minority groups which had common traditions of language and literature to coöperate against the tyranny of state centralization. The term *régionalisme* began to be used about 1892, and as a movement was

[1] See *L'Université Nouvelle*, issued by *Les Compagnons*, two vols. (Paris, 1919).

sponsored by the French Regionalist Federation, which, under the leadership of Charles-Brun and through its monthly, *L'Action Régionaliste*, has gained a large number of adherents. On the political side the regionalist movement urges the creation of administrative areas larger than the departments; on the cultural side it seeks to promote the use of dialects in schools situated in localities where dialects are used (Basque, Provençal, Corsican, Breton, Flemish, and German). The first plan was considered by a Parliamentary Committee, which in October, 1923, reported in favor of regionalism and presented the draft of a bill to divide the country into some thirty regions. The second proposal was embodied in a resolution of the Regionalist Federation at its meeting in February, 1926; the attitude of the Minister of Public Instruction on the subject has already been mentioned (p. 264.)[1]

Although considerable progress is being made by cultural regionalism, the present political situation, with its secular emphasis on solidarity and security, is likely to postpone for many years the adoption of administrative regionalism or decentralization. And yet some progress is being made in education: important changes, influenced by Montessori and kindergarten methods, are being introduced in the maternal schools; the higher elementary schools are within limits free to adapt the courses and their content to local needs, a practice which has recently been sanctioned in the normal schools; similar freedom is tolerated in vocational education, where the chambers of industry and of commerce are given some right to participate in the administration; and in elementary education the latest regulations state that "the time-schedule (as prescribed) should not assume an absolutely imperative character," and that

> the teacher will enjoy greater liberty. We do not guide each one of his steps. We repose confidence in him. He may leave out or take up any question, present or postpone a certain detail, according to the level of his class. On the other hand, the teacher may and even should vary his teaching according to the needs of his pupils and adapt his instruction to the conditions of local life.

These statements are obviously concessions to the times; in practice, however, they are meaningless and must remain meaningless so long as most of the other characteristics of the system remain

---

[1] See Gooch, R. K., *Regionalism in France* (New York, 1931); and Hayes, C. J. H., *France: A Nation of Patriots*, Ch. XI (New York, 1930).

unchanged — inspection, courses of study, textbooks, examinations, preparation and promotion of teachers, and so on. Such professions may indicate a slight change in attitude, but they do not attack the root of the evils which are the subject of criticism. Whether a radical reform of the administrative system is possible in the near future remains to be seen. It is significant that the *Projet de Statut Organique de l'Enseignement Public instituant l'Ecole Unique présenté au Parlement et à l'Opinion Publique*,[1] a plan of reorganization prepared by a committee representing some thirty-five societies, educational and social, did not regard the question of decentralization as of sufficient importance to be considered. Fundamentally it would appear that centralization is a fact accepted by the French people; if decentralization is introduced to any great extent, it will probably take the form already indicated of granting greater freedom to the teachers. A system which is so logically and symmetrically organized as to appear to be the result of deliberate construction is not likely to be surrendered for a system which may more intimately represent the many facets of national life, but may arouse fears for the security of the nation, one and indivisible.

3. GERMANY
THE FEDERAL GOVERNMENT AND EDUCATION

Education and politics. The development of educational administration in the States which constitute the German Republic affords an excellent illustration of the relation between the forms of administration and the progressive democratization. For, with the exception of certain changes in the titles of some of the central authorities, the administrative systems have remained unchanged since the Revolution, but they have been imbued with a new spirit, partly through the allocation of more autonomy to the localities and partly through increased participation by teachers and parents. Within this change, the degree to which administration is imbued with the new spirit varies with the political complexion of the parties in power. Since the establishment of the Republic, the political situation has been so unstable that a normal development in political and social affairs has been almost out of the question. Education has been caught in the maelstrom of parties as much as any other political concern. There are fluctuations from Left to Right, not

[1] *Comité d'Etudes et d'Action "Pour l'Ecole Unique"* (Paris, 1927).

only in the different States, but even in each State. The preparation of elementary school teachers is an excellent illustration of the effect of political outlook in education. Although the Constitution guaranteed the basic principle that such teachers should complete a regular secondary school course and that their training should be in institutions on a university level, the Federal Government refrained from implementing this constitutional provision and left the organization to the States. The result has been an absence of uniformity of principle, due as much to politics as to rationalization on educational grounds. Thus Bavaria and Württemberg delayed the reorganization as long as possible; Prussia was content to meet the minimum implications of the provision and established two-year pedagogical academies outside of the universities; Thuringia, after providing for the preparation of elementary school teachers in the University of Jena, changed her plan with the advent to power of a less radical political party and adopted with Saxony a system in which teachers are prepared partly in the university and partly in a separate pedagogical institute; Hamburg, with strong leanings toward the Left, trains her teachers in the University. Similarly, Thuringia immediately after the Revolution reorganized her educational system along the lines of the common school idea, the *Einheitsschule*, but reverted to the more normal system as soon as the Left party was driven from office. The attitude of Bavaria to innovations in secondary education, the creation of the *Deutsche Oberschule* and the *Aufbauschule*, may be cited as another example of the same influences.

The Federal Government (*Reich*) and education. According to Article 143 of the Weimar Constitution, 1919, the Federal Government (*Reich*), the States, and the municipalities are required to coöperate in the organization of education; Article 10 authorized the Federal Government to define the guiding principles for the educational system, including higher education, which were to furnish the basis for specific legislation by the States. It was intended, when the question was discussed in the Federal Educational Conference (*Reichsschulkonferenz*), 1920, that such common guiding principles should be issued only for those aspects of education in which national uniformity was desirable, such as the preparation of elementary school teachers, the foundation school (*Grundschule*), minimum essentials of each type of school, length of school year, nomenclature, reciprocal recognition of certificates, and statistical reports. In enlarging the participation of the Federal Government in education beyond the sphere previously exercised by the Imperial Government, there was the further intention that it should assume part of the cost of education, particularly for teachers' salaries and for the financial relief of the local communities. The Federal Government in the exercise of the powers entrusted to it by the Constitution did not proceed beyond the drafting of the Common School Law (*Grundschulgesetz*) in 1920. Interest in federal participation disappeared after the Federal Chancellor declared in 1924 that "the conduct of the school and educational systems will, in accordance with the regulations of a forthcoming federal law, be left to the States to be organized independently." Since this statement appeared in a Tax Ordinance, it was understood that financial aid would not be forthcoming from the Federal Government. This fact, combined with the failure of the Federal Government despite ten attempts between 1921 and 1928 to define the relations of the schools to religious instruction (*Reichsvolksschulgesetz*), has had the effect of diminishing interest in federal participation.

The Federal Government does, however, maintain an informal connection with the educational affairs of the country. In 1924 the Imperial Education Committee was replaced by an Education Committee (*Ausschuss für das Unterrichtswesen*) which consists of seven representatives of the State ministries and whose function it is to arrange agreements on fundamental questions of educational organization in which uniformity appears to be desirable, to consider the effect of educational legislation of one State on the others, and to discuss principles for fundamental laws. The Committee is under the Federal Ministry of the Interior, which has a section devoted to culture and schools (*Abteilung III. für Bildung und Schule*), responsible for securing and supplying information on education, social care and welfare of children, and physical education. For educational information it maintains a library and issues the *Archiv für Volksbildung*; on social care and welfare it publishes the *Deutsches Archiv für Jugendwohlfahrt*; and for physical education there is associated with it a Federal Council representing various organizations interested in the development of this branch. On the whole, neither the committee nor the section is likely to exercise any serious influence on the further progress of education in the States, which have learned in the last decade that the future of education in Germany rests in their hands.

The States are, however, limited in their freedom by certain constitutional provisions as follows:

Article 10. The Federal Government may by law prescribe fundamental principles with respect to... (2) Education, including higher education and scientific libraries.

Article 142. Art, science, and instruction in them are free. The State guarantees their protection and participates in their promotion.

Article 143. The education of youth shall be provided for through public institutions. The Federal Government, the states, and the municipalities shall coöperate in their organization.

Training of teachers shall be uniformly regulated for the Federal Government according to principles which apply generally to higher education.

Teachers in public schools shall have the rights and duties of state officials.

Article 144. The entire school system shall be under the supervision of the state; the latter may permit the municipalities to participate therein. Supervision of schools shall be carried on by technically trained officials who are mainly occupied with this duty.

Article 145. Compulsory education shall be universal. This purpose shall be served primarily by the elementary school with at least eight school years, followed by the continuation school up to the completion of the eighteenth year. Instruction and school supplies shall be free in elementary and continuation schools.

Article 146. The public school system shall be organically constructed. The middle and secondary school system shall be developed on the basis of a *Grundschule* common to all. This development shall be governed by the varying requirements of vocations; and the admission of a child to a particular school shall be governed by his ability and aptitude and not by his economic and social position or the religious belief of his parents.

Nevertheless, within the municipalities, upon the request of those persons having the right to education, elementary schools of their own religious belief or of their *Weltanschauung* shall be established, provided that an organized school system in the sense of Paragraph 1 is not thereby interfered with. The wishes of those persons having the right to education shall be considered so far as possible. Detailed regulations shall be prescribed by state legislation on the basis of a federal law.

To enable those in poor circumstances to attend secondary and higher schools, the Federal Government, the states, and the municipalities shall provide public funds, especially educational allowances, for the parents of children who are considered qualified for further education in middle and secondary schools until the completion of such education.

Article 147. Private schools as a substitute for public schools shall require the approval of the state and shall be subject to laws of the states. Such approval shall be granted if the standard of the private schools in their curricula and equipment, as well as in professional training of their teachers, does not fall below that of public schools, and if no discrimination against pupils on account of the economic standing of their parents is fostered. Such approval shall be denied if the economic and legal status of the teachers is not sufficiently safeguarded.

Private elementary schools shall be established only if, for a minority of those persons having a right to education whose wishes must be taken into consideration according to Article 146, Paragraph 2, there is in the municipality no public elementary school of their religious belief or of their *Weltanschauung*, or if the educational administration recognizes in it a special pedagogical interest.

Private preparatory schools are abolished.

The existing laws shall continue in force for private schools which do not serve as substitutes for public schools.

Article 148. In all schools effort shall be made to develop moral education, public-mindedness, and personal and vocational efficiency in the spirit of the German national character and of international conciliation.

Instruction in public schools shall take care not to offend the sensibilities of those of contrary opinions.

Civic education and manual training shall be part of the curricula of the schools. Every pupil shall at the end of his obligatory schooling receive a copy of the Constitution.

The Federal Government, the states, and the municipalities shall foster popular education, including people's universities.

Article 149. Religious instruction shall be part of the regular school curriculum with the exception of non-sectarian (secular) schools. Such instruction shall be given in harmony with the fundamental principles of the religious association concerned without prejudice to the right of supervision by the state.

Teachers shall give religious instruction and conduct church ceremonies only upon declaration of their willingness to do so; participation in religious instruction and in church celebrations and acts shall depend upon a declaration of willingness by those who control the religious education of the child.

Theological faculties in institutions of higher learning shall be maintained.

Article 174. Until the promulgation of a national law provided for in Article 146, Paragraph 2, the existing legal status shall continue. The law shall give special consideration to parts of the Republic in which schools legally exist that are not divided according to religious beliefs.[1]

As already pointed out, the only federal law which has been passed to implement these provisions has been the *Grundschulgesetz*, 1920, followed by Suggestions (*Richtlinien*), issued in 1921 to put the law into effect, and further Suggestions on the Curriculum of the *Grund-*

[1] The translation of the constitutional provisions is from McBain, H. L., and Rogers, L., *The New Constitutions of Europe* (New York, Doubleday, Doran & Company, Inc., 1923); the words "Federal Government" have been substituted for *Reich*.

schule, issued in 1925. No further action has been taken to regulate the preparation of elementary school teachers on a national basis, and the Federal Government has failed to secure the enactment of a *Reichsvolksschulgesetz* to deal with the organization of elementary schools in respect of religious instruction.

THE ADMINISTRATION OF EDUCATION IN PRUSSIA

The administration of education is thus left to the States. Some of the causes of differences between them have been indicated. So far as the organization of schools is concerned, there is a certain uniformity throughout the country, although some of the States (Hamburg and Saxony) are beginning to break the traditional mould in the organization of schools for senior elementary school pupils, a break which may in time lead to a complete reform. Although the details of the administrative systems differ in some respects — as, for example, in the units of administration and the allocation of some branches of education to ministries and authorities other than the educational — the general tendency is everywhere toward a relaxation of the rigid bureaucratic control which prevailed before the War. Prussia is here discussed, not because that State is typical nor because it is the most progressive (it has been outstripped by several other States), but because it still tends to dominate German life.

There is as yet no code governing education in Prussia; the system is regulated by the Constitution, and federal and state laws dealing with particular questions, ministerial decrees and administrative regulations. There are still in force laws and regulations which go as far back as the *Allgemeine Landrecht* (1794) and which were accumulated throughout the nineteenth century. The control of education is distributed among several ministries. General education is regulated and supervised by the Ministry for Science, Art, and Public Education (*Ministerium für Wissenschaft, Kunst, und Volksbildung*), reorganized in 1918; commercial education is administered by the Ministry of Commerce (*Handelsministerium*); agricultural education, with some exceptions under the Ministry for Science, Art, and Public Education, is under the supervision of the Ministry of Agriculture, Forests, and Domains (*Ministerium für Landwirtschaft, Forsten, und Domänen*); and child welfare and school medical inspection has been placed since 1919 under the Ministry of Public

Welfare (*Volkswohlfahrtsministerium*), coöperating with the educational Ministry.[1]

The Ministry for Science, Art, and Public Education is directed by the Minister, who is a member of the Ministry of State, assisted by an Under-Secretary of State (*Staatssekretär*). The Minister, except in certain matters which must be referred to the Ministry of State, is solely responsible for the administration of his department. He prepares educational bills and the budget, represents education in Parliament, issues decrees dealing with the internal management of schools, outlines of courses of study, regulations for examinations and other matters, approves materials of instruction, equipment, and textbooks, appoints the higher administrative officials, and passes on the action of subordinate administrative authorities. Decrees of the Minister, after publication in the official organ of the Ministry, the *Zentralblatt für die gesamte Unterrichtsverwaltung in Preussen*, acquire the force of laws. The Ministry is divided into a number of sections — personnel, general, higher education and research, elementary education, secondary education, art, adult education, physical education, accounts, and religious affairs. The division for higher education supervises universities, technical high schools, academies, research, and state libraries; the division for art is responsible for theaters, public monuments, museums, and advanced art education; the elementary school division superintends elementary education and the preparation of teachers for elementary schools; the division for physical education has under its charge the High School for Physical Education. The work of each division is carried out by a director assisted by councilors (*Regierungsräte, Oberregierungsräte, Ministerialräte*), who have had either a legal or educational preparation. The most important change which has taken place since the Ministry was reorganized has been the introduction of more councilors with training and experience in education, including elementary.

[1] The administration of education is distributed somewhat similarly in Saxony, where the *Ministerium für Volksbildung* is responsible for all education except vocational, which is entrusted to the *Wirtschaftsministerium* (Ministry of State Economy); a few institutions are under the Ministry of Finance and others under the Ministry of the Interior. In Bavaria the *Staatsministerium für Unterricht und Kultus* is solely responsible for educational affairs, as are also the *Kultusministerium* in Württemberg and the *Ministerium des Kultus und Unterrichts* in Baden. In the Free State of Hamburg the *Oberschulbehörde* has charge of all education except vocational, administered by the *Berufsschulbehörde*, and higher under the *Hochschulbehörde*.

There are associated with the Ministry a number of important commissions, bureaus, and institutes. In 1928 a Textbook Commission (*Prüfstelle für Lehrbücher*) was established, whose members, selected according to their subjects, are appointed by the Minister for three-year terms; publishers are required to submit eight copies of every textbook published, to be considered and reported upon by experts to the Commission which recommends to the Minister the action to be taken.

The Ministry maintains a State Bureau of Information on Education (*Staatliche Auskunftsstelle für Schulwesen*), which, established in 1899 to furnish information on textbooks for use in secondary schools, broadened its scope and supplies information on education in Germany and abroad, issues periodical reports on the status of secondary and other education in Prussia, and maintains a list of secondary school teachers.

Established in the same year as the State Bureau of Information, the State Bureau for Instruction in Natural Sciences (*Staatliche Hauptstelle für den naturwissenschaftlichen Unterricht*) furnishes information on textbooks, materials of instruction, and equipment for use in teaching mathematics and sciences, and conducts extension courses for teachers of these subjects. In 1920 a similar center was established in Düsseldorf.

The *Zentralinstitut für Erziehung und Unterricht* was established in 1915 as an inter-ministerial Institute for Education and Instruction, which combines a variety of functions — collection and distribution of information, collections of books and materials of instruction, courses for teachers, conduct of educational tours at home and abroad, research, and publications. The Institute, supported by contributions from the Ministries of Education of the German States, maintains a number of special divisions: office for the examination of and advice on educational films; office on educational information; advisory office on music and gramophone records; and an advisory office on vocational guidance. The monthly organ of the Institute is the *Pädagogische Zentralblatt*; the Institute also publishes an annual (*Jahrbuch*) which in the last few years has appeared under the title *Das Deutsche Schulwesen*.

Provincial School Board. The administrative duties of the Ministry are delegated for secondary education to the Provincial School Boards (*Provinzialschulkollegien*), which were established in 1817 and regulated by a Cabinet Order of 1825. There are at present thirteen such boards which consist of educational experts with some members who have had legal training, appointed by the Minister. Each board is under the chairmanship of the Chief President of the Province, who usually delegates his functions without surrendering authority or responsibility to a vice-president. The Provincial School Boards are responsible chiefly for the supervision of secondary education and the educational institutions for the blind and the deaf. In the field of secondary education the boards supervise the training of teachers, their examination and appointment, advise on problems of secondary schools, and inspect and conduct examination of elementary school teachers. In Berlin-Lichterfelde, which is the center of the Province of Brandenburg, the Provincial School Board has general charge of elementary as well as higher education, and of vocational education delegated to it by the Ministry of Commerce. Each province may issue regulations which have the effect of laws in its own area, if approved by the Minister.

County School Boards. The conduct of elementary education, except in Berlin, is delegated to thirty-four counties (*Regierungen*), which were created at the same time as the provinces, when special sections for religious and educational affairs were established in them. Each section is administered by a school board consisting of administrative, architectural, medical, legal, and educational councilors appointed by the *Regierungspräsident*, who is the chairman of the board, but delegates his functions increasingly to a director with educational training and experience. The school board of a *Regierung* administers and supervises elementary and middle schools, higher schools for girls, kindergartens, private schools and instruction, and schools for music, dancing, cinemas, and drama; it also supervises certain extra-school matters, the administration of school properties and endowments, and religious affairs; and it appoints and supervises elementary school teachers. Like the Provincial School Board the school board of a *Regierung* may issue regulations legally binding only in its area, if published in the official organ, the *Regierungsblatt*.

Inspection. Direct contact between the administrative authorities and the schools are maintained by the *Oberschulräte*, attached to the Provincial School Boards, who inspect secondary schools, and by the *Schulräte*, attached to the *Regierungen*, who inspect elementary schools and have certain duties in respect to private schools and private education. Both grades of officials are appointed by the Minister of Science, Art, and Public Education, the former from the ranks of secondary school teachers and principals, the latter from the elementary school branch on the recommendation of the school boards of the counties. Since the Revolution a long-standing grievance of the elementary school teachers was abolished by the constitutional provision that their inspection should be placed in the hands of professional trained experts. Not only has the clerical part-time inspector been abolished, but teachers' councils (*Lehrerräte* and *Lehrervertretungen*) are requested to recommend suitable candidates; even the title of the official has been changed from *Kreisschulinspektor* or *Ortsschulinspektor* (district or local inspector) to *Schulrat* (school councilor or adviser). The inspectors for elementary education are the direct representatives of the *Regierungen* and are expected to act as leaders and advisers of teachers, to inspect and report upon schools, to approve courses of study, to conduct conferences of teachers, and in general to promote the progress and development of education by improving local conditions. The inspectors are the educational advisers who coöperate with the teachers; according to the recent regulations they must encourage good and promising teachers to use their opportunities for the exercise of freedom and independence, and must deal patiently with poor teachers; they are particularly charged with the oversight of young teachers during their period of probation and of the study groups (*Arbeitsgemeinschaften*) in which they prepare for their second examination. Beyond these duties the *Schulräte* must be invited to attend meetings of local school committees, where they may participate in the discussions, offer advice, object, if necessary, to any resolutions, which must then be submitted for consideration to the next superior authority. They grant permission to teach to private teachers and exercise disciplinary authority within certain limits over both public and private teachers. In general the change in the character and spirit of inspection is one of the outstanding features of the system developed since the Revolution, best illustrated by the gradual disappearance of rigid uniformity which used to mark the Prussian schools and by the fever of experimentation which at times seems to the observer to be a good argument for the retention of some form of control or guidance from without. In some cities the state inspector may serve as city school superintendent (*Stadtschulrat*).

ADMINISTRATION OF EDUCATION

Local authorities. Up to this point the authorities and officials for the administration of education have been direct representatives of the Ministry. Certain aspects of educational administration are allocated to local authorities, but, on the principle that the control of education is an inherent right of the State, such local authorities have no status in the process of education or direct authority over teachers and their work. For administrative purposes local authorities are divided into two groups — city and rural districts. In recognized cities the administration and provision of elementary education is entrusted to school deputation (*Schuldeputationen*) in all matters except finance (the levy of taxes, preparation of the budget, and control of school properties). The school deputation consists of the mayor, one to three members of the local civil service (*Magistrat*), including in some cities the city school superintendent (*Stadtschulrat*), the same number of representatives of the city council (*Stadtverordnetenversammlung*), and of teachers elected by their colleagues, and the senior pastor of the Evangelical Church, the senior priest of the Catholic Church, and the rabbi, if twenty Jewish children are enrolled in the local schools; the school inspector must be invited to attend meetings of the deputation. The duties of the school deputation include general supervision and development of elementary education, location of new school buildings, repair of old buildings, supply of equipment and apparatus, enforcement of school attendance laws, selection of teachers for appointment by the *Regierungen*, the exercise of some disciplinary powers over teachers, preparation of the educational budget for the city council, and the successful operation of laws affecting schools; the school deputation may provide meals for necessitous children, open-air schools, auxiliary classes, holiday homes, and any other activities for the social welfare of the children. Members, who otherwise do not enjoy this right, may be assigned to visit schools, but without any authority to interfere with the instructional process.

To facilitate its work, a deputation may appoint special committees, as for school attendance, general oversight of children, etc. In larger cities committees (*Schulkommissionen*) may be appointed for a single school or for a number of schools to look after its general interests, to promote the relations between school and home, to organize social welfare activities, and to make recommendations to the school deputation for the improvement of the fabric of the school.

Greater Berlin, which received its present organization in 1920, in addition to a central *Deputation für das Schulwesen*, which administers all branches of education, has a number of district school deputations *Bezirksschuldeputationen*) for elementary and middle schools and district school committees (*Bezirksschulausschüsse*) for secondary schools. Elsewhere cities which have provided their own secondary schools have committees for secondary education independent of the school deputation.

The administration of elementary education in rural communities, villages, and landed estates is conducted on the same principle. The local government is responsible for all school finance and property, while the conduct of the schools is in the hands of a local school board (*Schulvorstand*) assisted by a district inspector. The board consists of the president of the community, a teacher, the ranking Protestant pastor and Catholic priest, if children of both denominations attend the schools, and from two to six local citizens elected by the community council and approved by the *Regierung*. The duties of the school board are similar to those of the school deputation; they have general responsibility for the enforcement of school laws and administration of the schools without any authority over the teachers in matters of instruction. Districts may be united for educational purposes, as *Gesamtschulverbände*, which are administered by school boards (*Schulvorstände*) organized in the same way as for single districts.

Teachers' councils. The representation of teachers on school deputations and school boards is not an innovation. Since the Revolution, teachers have, however, acquired a right to greater participation in administration in an advisory and consultative capacity. In 1918 there were organized a number of teachers' councils informally and without any legal sanction. The constitution of such councils (*Bezirkslehrerräte* [1]) as agencies to coöperate with the *Regierungen* was officially recognized by a number of decrees issued in 1919, although their powers have not yet been clearly defined. They are expected to advise the *Regierungen* on general problems of education and especially on matters affecting teachers; they may present petitions, memoranda, and reports and may be represented on committees for the final appointment of teachers. They are consulted on the qualifications of candidates for appointment as in-

[1] Also referred to, but not officially, as *Lehrerkammer*.

spectors. Notices of meetings together with the agenda must be sent to the *Regierungen*, which may select representatives to attend. Teachers' councils have been formed in smaller districts (*Kreislehrerräte*) which exercise functions corresponding to those of the *Bezirkslehrerräte*, but have no official recognition. Similar councils have been organized for administrative purposes in individual schools (see p. 716 f.).[1]

Parents' councils. Since the Revolution, efforts have been made to extend the interest and participation of parents in educational affairs. During the nineteenth century, individual principals and groups of teachers had organized parents' meetings and parents' evenings, but these were informal and enjoyed no official recognition. In a number of States (Hamburg, Saxony, Bavaria, Thuringia, Hesse) the creation of parents' councils is required by laws passed since 1918. In Prussia their existence has been recognized by decrees issued on October 1, 1918, for secondary schools, and on November 5, 1919, for elementary and middle schools. Their purpose is to promote better relations between school and home, and to develop among parents an interest in education at a time when important changes in practice are being made. A parents' council (*Elternbeirat*) must be elected for every school by parents who have children in the school, one member for every fifty children; the term of office is two years; five members constitute the minimum size of a council. The councils are advisory only and have no power or authority to give effect to their resolutions or views. Meetings are held twice a year and may be specially called at the request of the teachers or two thirds of the members. Principals and teachers are required to attend such meetings and to offer advice and suggestions. The councils may arrange meetings for parents. Although restricted in their powers, the parents' councils constitute important agencies for the education of parents themselves as well as for the discussion of problems directly affecting their children.

The regulations make no provision for the organization of a hierarchy of parents' councils culminating in one central council, but a number of national parents' associations, organized mainly on

---

[1] Except in Hamburg, which, though recognized as a state, is a large city, there are no state teachers' councils. The relations between the Ministries and existing teachers' councils are frequently determined by the character of the political party in power. The use of teachers' councils was part of the movement, recognized in the Constitution, for the organization of councils of employers and employees, which has not been effectively carried out.

party lines relating particularly to the problem of religious instruction, have been established. Among these are the *Reichselternverband* (Protestant), *Die Elternvereinigungen des evangelischen Schulkartells* (Protestant), *Katholische Schulorganisation* (Catholic), *Bund der freien Schulgesellschaften* (secular), *Deutscher Eltern- und Volksbund* (interdenominational), *Reichsverband der Elternbeiräte mittlerer Schulen Deutschlands* (non-party), *Freie Arbeitsgemeinschaft von Elternbeiräte an höheren Schulen Deutschlands* (non-party), and *Gesellschaft zur Förderung haüslicher Erziehung*. Each of these organizations publishes its own journal. The development of parents' councils and their national organizations represents an important contrast between the old and the new in Prussian educational administration and a change from the pre-War attitude that the school and its affairs are concerns of the State alone. To this change the constitutional provision (Article 120) made an important contribution in recognizing the existence of a partnership in the education of the young between parents and the State:

Article 120. The education of their children for physical, intellectual, and social efficiency is the highest duty and natural right of parents, whose activities shall be supervised by the political community.

Educational finance. The maintenance of schools is based either on legal regulations or on the general supervisory powers of the localities. The cost of education is met by income from permanent revenues of the education authority (school property and endowments), and annual income (school fees, if any, state aid, and a share of the federal income tax levied locally). Until the system was reformed in 1920, state aid was granted when localities could not support their schools themselves; under the present system the main charges are met first out of state aid, fees and revenues, deficits being made up out of local general taxes (there are no special taxes for education). In 1920 a *Landesschulkasse* was established to serve as a clearing-house for the administration of funds from the state and local authorities, which must make up in the *Landesschulkasse* any deficits not covered otherwise.

The *Landesschulkasse*, which is not a state office nor an official department, but an organization to pool the financial activities of the education authorities, is administered by a treasurer appointed by representatives of the local bodies. It pays: (1) the salaries of teachers and family allowances; (2) pensions and allowances for dependents; (3) grants for the cost of removal; (4) salaries of substitutes; (5) grants in aid of necessitous areas; and (6) grants for rent. These payments are made out of revenues derived by the *Landesschulkasse* from state grants, miscellaneous income, contributions for certain teachers' positions, and deficits made up by contributions from the school authorities.

The cost of education is thus borne by the State and the communities. The payments of the State to the *Landesschulkasse* consist of (1) a sum equal to one fourth of the full compensation of teachers (salaries, rent indemnity, local indemnity, and family allowances); (2) one fourth of the cost of pensions and allowances for dependents; (3) a contribution provided in the state budget for emergency contributions and aid to necessitous areas; and (4) a per capita grant (*Beschulungsgeld*), calculated on the basis of sixty pupils per teacher, the total amount for which must not amount in any one year to more than one half of the estimated cost of salaries, pensions, allowances, and additional grants. The communities contribute amounts calculated on the basis of the number of teachers employed (*Stellenbeiträge*).

According to the law it is intended that the State shall bear three fourths of the cost of salaries — one fourth through its grant and one half through the *Beschulungsgeld*; the communities contribute the balance. Localities must in addition themselves provide the cost for the provision of activities beyond the minimum (advanced classes, classes with less than sixty pupils, salaries of substitutes, etc.).

A similar system has been established for the support of middle schools, the *Landesmittelschulkasse*. The cost of secondary education provided by the State is borne wholly by the State; in the schools provided by the communities the current cost of maintaining the buildings is borne by the local authorities and the cost of salaries by the State.

Capital expenditures (purchase of school sites and buildings) are borne by the localities. Under special circumstances state aid may be given for the construction of buildings. In small localities with less than seven teachers, the State is required by law to contribute one third of the cost of building (*Baudrittel*) after certain charges, amounting to five hundred marks for each teacher and the expenditure for unskilled labor and hauling, have been deducted from the gross cost. To communities with more than seven but less than one hundred teachers the State may give assistance from a fund annually appropriated to the State and distributed to the *Regierungen* for the purpose. In all cases the *Regierungen* and the central authority must be consulted and their approval of the proposal to build and the plans of construction must be obtained.

Conclusion. Prussia — and what is true of Prussia applies in general to the rest of Germany — is thus developing liberal principles of administration. The form and machinery still continue unchanged and a study of these alone does not at first glance reveal these principles. Increased opportunities for consultation with parents and teachers, the introduction into the system of men and women who have themselves had professional training and experience, the change in the character of inspection, and the improved preparation of elementary school teachers are all indicative of the new spirit. But far more important than these is the departure from the old practice of prescribing curricula and courses of study by decrees and regulations (*Erlässe* and *Bestimmungen*) and the substitution for these of suggestions or outlines (*Richtlinien*) on the basis of which each school develops its own course of study in the light of the teachers' professional ability and intelligence and of the environment in which the school is placed. Although such courses are still subject to the approval of the inspectors, this only means that freedom must be tempered by responsibility. The new system at least accomplishes what the old system failed to do — it encourages initiative and independence among the teachers, who are beginning to work out their problems through coöperative study groups (*Arbeitsgemeinschaften*) in each school, if the staff is large enough, or in districts. The mechanical standardization and uniformity which used to prevail are no longer to be found; no two schools are alike, and every form of instruction and curriculum from the conservative to the radical can be found, even in the same system. Germany is gradually discovering that the main purpose of administration is not to secure a standardized uniformity, but to devise a scheme whereby teachers will be released to devote their best efforts to the task of education. The common bond is no longer provided by detailed prescriptions of curricula, courses, and methods prepared by a centralized bureaucracy, but by means of suggestions which will enable each teacher and each school to contribute in their own ways to the development of a progressive national culture (*Deutschtum*). It is not an accident that the new spirit in administration was introduced at the same time that steps were taken to place the preparation of teachers on a genuinely professional level. The full development of the new trend remains for the future; the period since the close of the War and the present has been for Germany too critical and too unstable for the realization of republican ideals. At least this much has been gained — a formula has been discovered which may be the happy mean between rigid centralization of the past and the post-War demands of a group of the teachers for complete professional autonomy.

4. ITALY

Aims of the reform. Two tasks confronted those who undertook to reform the Italian system of education in 1923. The first task was to define the aims and purposes in accordance with the principles of the Fascist Revolution; the second to remove the defects and weaknesses which had grown up in the administrative system since its organization under the Casati Law of 1859. The principles of the Fascist Revolution in so far as they affect education have already been discussed in Chapter III; Fascism implies the absolutist character of the State as a moral entity, as an ethical substance, representing the collective will of the individuals who must subordinate themselves to it through conscious acceptance of the duties imposed upon them rather than by assertion of their own rights. The State, in other words, conscious of its moral destiny, has the right to impose upon its citizens the type of government and the type of education best adapted to its preservation. These principles define the ends of education and the character of the administration by which it is to be achieved. The aims of all educational institutions, whether formal or informal, are to promote the spiritual unity of the members of the State, and hence a national consciousness, both directed to a deepening appreciation and the advancement of *Italianità*, or the mission or destiny of Italy. In a system governed by such principles, there is no room for those popular representative institutions demanded by liberal democracy. The only form of administration compatible with the ideals of the Fascist State is a hierarchical organization, in which the constituent parts derive their rights and powers from the central authority. The watchwords of Fascism in the words of Mussolini are discipline, work, and harmony, and these can only be promoted by a well-organized administrative hierarchy.

The defects and weaknesses of the system which was displaced by the Fascist Revolution had arisen from a bureaucracy which was not inspired by strong ethical motives and from an excess of local autonomy without adequate direction and control by a central authority conscious of its powers. Governmental administration suffered from the multiplication of offices and personnel without a clear definition of duties or of responsibility; local administration was ineffective because of the existence of an excessive number of areas too small and too poor to be entrusted with the provision and maintenance of schools. The Law of June 4, 1911, had attempted to correct these weaknesses by depriving a large number of communes of the right to administer their own schools; only the capitals of provinces and of other large regional areas, and communes which had less than twenty-five per cent illiterates among their inhabitants could retain this right; for the rest, and even for those communes which were entitled to local administration, but waived the right, control and supervision were transferred to new provincial authorities. In the sixty-nine provinces (to which five new provinces were added after the War) the administration of education was in the charge of the provincial superintendents (*provveditori*), assisted by a number of councils. The ineffectiveness of the whole system was indicated by the very slow progress which was made in grappling with the problem of illiteracy, the poor discipline in the teaching profession as a whole, and in the loose organization of secondary education.

The Fascist Government as soon as it entered into power at once attacked the abuses in the central administration. A ruthless onslaught was made upon the excessive number of governmental employees of all grades. By decrees issued on December 21, 1922, and on January 25, 1923, the personnel was reduced by dismissals for the good of the service or by retirement. Adequate qualifications were required of those who remained and of new appointees; the personnel was classified into groups and sub-groups with opportunities for advancement in each and for transfer from lower to higher groups on merit only; functions were defined, and responsibility located; and the whole system was reorganized in the interests of efficiency and in accordance with Fascist principles. This reform affected all branches of central administration as well as education.

Centralization of all functions was adopted as a deliberate principle on the theory that state action could better be promoted by a hierarchical organization of the administrative system than by decentralization and devolution of powers to locally elected bodies. The few, among them Giuseppe Lombardo-Radice, one of Italy's outstanding educators, who favored decentralization in the interests of variety and growth, received no hearing. Local autonomy would, indeed, be incompatible with the ideology of Fascism.

The central authority. By Royal Decree of July 16, 1923, No. 1753, the general control and supervision of educational and cultural affairs were entrusted to a Minister of Public Instruction assisted by an Under-Secretary of State. The title of the Ministry was changed by Royal Decree-Law of September 12, 1929, from Ministry of Public Instruction (*Ministero della Pubblica Istruzione*) to Ministry of National Education (*Ministero dell' Educazione Nazionale*) and another Under-Secretary, responsible for the development of physical and youth education, was added. The new designation of the Ministry was a logical consequence of a movement which had already begun in 1928, when by a decree issued in June the institutions previously under the control of the Ministry of National Economy — that is, technical and vocational schools — had been transferred to the Ministry of Public Instruction. In announcing the change of nomenclature, Mussolini stated that its purpose was "to reaffirm a principle in its most explicit form, that the State not only has the right but also the duty to educate its people, and not merely to instruct them, for which after all private venture would be sufficient." The duties assigned to the Minister of National Education are: (1) the direction and promotion of public national education; (2) the supervision of private schools, public morality, and culture; (3) the custody of the artistic treasures of the nation and the encouragement of fine arts; (4) the decision of questions of discipline and conflicts in the whole system; and (5) the review or annulment of actions of administrative officials which do not conform to the laws and regulations. Both the Minister and the Under-Secretaries are assisted by personal cabinets whose members act as spokesmen on educational affairs in Parliament, prepare matters to be submitted to the Council of Ministers and decrees.

Legislation. Educational legislation may be effected by two methods, by Parliament or by decree-laws (*decreti-leggi*) prepared by the Minister and signed by the King. The Minister has the power to codify existing laws and decrees, provided no new matter is added, in the form of *testi unici*; he may himself issue decrees and regulations (*regolamenti*) which define the application of laws and decrees and acquire the force of law when published in the *Gazzetta Ufficiale*; he may further publish regulations (*ordinanze*) affecting such matters of routine as dates of examinations and competitions, and circulars (*circolari*) or interpretative instructions. The general laws, decrees, and regulations of the State in all branches of government are published in the *Gazzetta Ufficiale*; these are in turn reprinted in the *Bollettino Ufficiale* of the Ministry of National Education, which in addition contains ordinances, circulars, lists of appointments and promotions, courses of study, and all other information which the Ministry desires to disseminate. Much of this information was reprinted with local material in the bulletins issued by regional superintendents; to avoid this duplication these bulletins were suppressed and the *Scuola Fascista*, the organ of the National Association of Fascist Teachers, was enlarged to serve as a semi-official journal of educational information.

Organization of the Ministry. The reorganization of the Ministry was effected by Ministerial Decree of June 28, 1923, and subsequent additions affecting the division of academies and libraries and physical education. The Ministry contains seven departments for (1) elementary education; (2) secondary education; (3) technical education; (4) higher education; (5) antiquities and fine arts; (6) academies and libraries; and (7) physical education. Each of the departments is under a director-general and is in turn subdivided into divisions and sections, to each of which specific functions are assigned. To one department, for example, is assigned general questions of administration and of personnel; another is concerned with the whole field of elementary education — personnel, legislation, disputes, and through various sections with the administration of elementary education, provision and organization of schools, social services, statistics and publications, finance, hygiene, and buildings; a third department has charge of secondary education — personnel, private and accredited schools, types of schools, examinations, and so on. Each department has a small staff of chief, higher, and central inspectors (three higher and six central for elementary and one general, two higher, and six central for secondary education; five inspectors for technical education; and one general and one higher inspector for state educational institutions, accredited and private secondary schools); for the regional inspection of secondary schools the Minister may appoint university professors and principals of secondary schools for three years; in addition, he may at any time appoint inspectors to conduct special investigations. For the administration of educational finance there is a general bureau of accounts which, although attached to the Ministry of National Education, is responsible, as are similar bureaus in other ministries, to the Ministry of Finance.

Higher Council of Public Instruction. With the Ministry are associated a number of consultative and advisory committees. For education the most important of these is the Higher Council of Public Instruction (*Consiglio Superiore della Pubblica Istruzione*) which was reorganized by Royal Decree, November 29, 1928.[1] The Council consists of forty-six members appointed by Royal Decree on the recommendation of the Minister; it is presided over by the Minister, or in his absence by a vice-president appointed from the members by the King. The Council is divided into six sections: higher education, classical, scientific secondary education and teacher training; secondary technical education; elementary education; art education; and physical education. Each section has an executive committee, and the members of all these committees constitute the executive committee of the Council, presided over by the senior chairman of the sections. The members of the Council hold office for four-year overlapping terms. The director-generals of the departments are voting members of the Council and of its sections. The duties of the Council are to advise on all questions referred to it by the Minister, to exercise the right of inspecting universities and other institutions of higher education, and to conduct investigations and to report on the general condition of public education. For the supervision of current affairs and the preparation of agenda for the meetings of the Council a permanent committee (*Giunta del Consiglio Superiore della Pubblica Istruzione*) is appointed consisting of the vice-president and eight members of the Council selected by the Minister. A Higher Council of Antiquities and Fine Arts advises the Minister on the questions in its field. A National Research Council (*Consiglio nazionale delle ricerche*) serves the Minister as the center of informa-

[1] *Bollettino Ufficiale*, 1929, pp. 39 ff.

tion on the development and progress of science and learning at home and abroad. The coördination of education and public health is entrusted to a Consultative Committee for Hygiene and School Welfare (*Commissione consultiva per l'igiene e l'assistenza scolastica e per l'igiene pedagogica*). On problems affecting libraries the Minister consults the Library Committee (*Commissione centrale per le biblioteche*).

Administration of personnel. The administration of all matters affecting state officials is entrusted to a Council of Administration (*Consiglio di Amministrazione*), which consists of the general directors and the director of personnel in the Ministry and is presided over by the Under-Secretary of State for Education; questions of discipline are brought before the First Commission in the case of elementary school teachers (*La I Commissione per i ricorsi dei maestri elementari e i procedimenti disciplinari a loro carico*), and for secondary school teachers before the Second Commission (*La II Commissione per i ricorsi degli insegnanti medi e i procedimenti disciplinari a loro carico*). The members of both commissions are appointed by the Minister for four-year overlapping terms. The First Commission consists of three legal and educational experts, one supervisor of instruction from an autonomous commune, and two elementary school teachers who have had ten years of service. The Second Commission includes, besides three legal and educational experts, a principal and a teacher of the upper section of a secondary school, and a director or recognized teacher of an accredited or private secondary school. Appeals may be brought to the commissions against the actions of the regional disciplinary councils.

Local administration. For purposes of local administration, the provincial system adopted in 1911 was abolished and replaced by a regional system. The country is divided into nineteen regions varying in size, population, and the number of provinces included.[1] The larger cities were given the privilege of administering their own affairs, but less than three per cent of the communes (205 in 1928) have availed themselves of the opportunity. At the head of each regional area is the superintendent of education (*provveditore agli*

---

[1] The nineteen regions and their capitals are as follows: Lombardy (Milan); Piedmont (Turin); Veneto (Venice); Sicily (Palermo); Emilia (Bologna); Campania (Naples); Tuscany (Florence); Puglia (Bari); Calabria (Cosenza); Marche (Zara); Venezia Giulia (Trieste); Venezia Tridentino (Trento); Lazio (Rome); Umbria (Perugia); Sardinia (Cagliari); Liguria (Genoa); Basilicata (Potenza); Molise (Campobasso); Abruzzi (Aquila).

studi), who has charge of elementary and secondary education in general and concerns himself primarily with questions of organization and administration, leaving the immediate supervision of education to the inspectors, supervisors, and principals of his region. The *provveditori agli studi* are appointed by the Minister, who may select the most suitable candidates from officials in the central or regional administration or from principals and teachers in secondary schools, or from any persons of recognized scholarship, experience, and personality, who are not already in the educational service.

The duties of the *provveditore* are to exercise general supervision over all public and private education in his region; approve the selection of textbooks; hear appeals against the decisions of inspectors; order the closing of schools for health reasons; approve standards for competitive examinations for teachers; transfer, dismiss, and retire teachers with the advice of the education committee; exercise disciplinary authority over teachers and impose penalties when necessary; and appoint committees to inquire into cases of negligence of communes in complying with the education law. He has under his direct supervision the personnel of his department. The office of the *provveditore* is maintained by contributions from the provinces under his jurisdiction with some aid from the State.

Each *provveditore* is assisted by an education committee for elementary education (*consiglio scolastico per gli affari della istruzione elementare*), a council on discipline for elementary school teachers (*consiglio di disciplina per i maestri elementari*), and a council for secondary education (*giunta per le scuole medie*). The education committee consists of six members appointed by the Minister, and includes the principal of a secondary school, a public health official, and four other members conversant with the problems of elementary education. The members hold office for four years and may be reappointed after an interval of two years. The duties of this committee are to advise the *provveditore*, who is its chairman, on the administration of funds, to approve school regulations, to recommend the disciplinary measures against teachers, and to discuss any other matters submitted to it. The council on discipline consists of four members under the *provveditore* appointed in the same way and for the same terms as members of the education committee; it includes two members of the education committee, one secondary school teacher and one elementary school teacher or principal according to whether the case under consideration is that of a teacher or a principal. The council hears cases of discipline which involve dismissal, suspension, or interdiction. The council for secondary education includes the *provveditore*, as chairman, and four members — a university professor or other person of distinction in scholarship, two principals and one teacher of the upper section of a secondary school. The council is consulted on questions of accrediting or transforming secondary schools, or opening of private secondary schools; every two years it draws up a list of teachers qualified for promotion to principalships.

Each administrative area is divided into inspectional divisions under a royal inspector (*regio ispettore scolastico*) and supervisory districts under an educational supervisor (*direttore didattico*). Appointments as inspectors or supervisors are obtained by competitive examination open to candidates who have the appropriate qualifications, which are secured by a period of training in a Royal Higher Normal School. The royal inspectors are required to look after the public and private schools in their areas, to authorize the opening of private schools, to provide substitutes in cases of absence of a supervisor, to issue certificates of service to teachers, to grant leaves of absence, to assign classes, to report on their inspection visits, and to decide appeals against the actions of the supervisors. The supervisors visit schools more frequently than the inspectors, assign teachers to classes each year, report on their work, receive requests for leave of absence and substitutes, appoint examination committees for elementary schools, and make recommendations for the reorganization of schools.

Within the regional administrative areas there are a few communes, the capitals of provinces and of certain districts, which may, if they choose, enjoy autonomy in educational affairs, especially elementary education. The control of education in such cases is in the hands of the mayor (*podestà*) and the local communal council. The professional control is entrusted to communal supervisors (*direttori didattici communali*) who must have the same qualifications as the governmental supervisors and must be paid at least the same salaries; sectional supervisors must be appointed in communes with more than two hundred teachers — one for every thirty classes. The regional *provveditore* is expected to exercise a certain general oversight even over communes which enjoy autonomy and may recommend the withdrawal of the privilege of local administration in cases of neglect of duty.

Educational finance. The cost of education is borne by the State, the provinces, and the communes, but under conditions that vary for elementary and secondary education and for autonomous and dependent communes. All communes are required to provide suitable sites and adequate buildings for elementary schools together with heat, light, service, equipment, and school supplies. Under the Casati Law all communes were autonomous and were required to meet all the expenses for education, but received some aid from the State; as salaries and the length of schooling increased, the State assumed a larger percentage of the cost. The grants varied from year to year according to the number of schools maintained and the ability of the communes. In 1911 the various grants were consolidated and the State undertook to pay a fixed sum to the communes each year; in 1920 this principle was reaffirmed, but as salaries were increased, the dependent communes were required to make a fixed contribution of 800 lire a year toward the salary of each teacher. The amount of this contribution is subject to revision every five years by the **Ministry** of Education in coöperation with the Ministry of Finance. The cost of services supplementary to elementary education, such as infant schools, committees of patronage, libraries for schools, the public, and the teachers, and social services, are supported by state grants made on the recommendation of the *provveditori*. The autonomous communes until 1931 bore the cost of maintaining their schools with contributions from the State; by Royal decree of September 14, 1931, the State assumed the burdens borne by the local budgets of such communes for salaries and indemnities to teachers in order to systematize the conditions for all the personnel. This means that such communes must provide a sum annually to pay the salaries of the teachers according to the prevailing scale and for the number of teachers recognized as adequate by the Ministry of Education, and in addition a percentage of the remaining charges according to a prescribed scale. The scale published in 1928 provided for contributions from the State to the 205 autonomous communes then recognized, ranging from 40 per cent in Brescia to 82 per cent in Cefalu, Sicily. The practice is reversed in the case of the dependent communes, in which the State provides for the maintenance of schools with contributions from the communes toward teachers' salaries.

All communes and recognized associations are required to provide buildings, the plans for which must be accepted by the *provveditore* acting on the advice of the engineering and health departments of the region and approved by the Ministries of Education and of Public Works. A teacher's residence must be attached to a school in rural communes where no other living accommodations are available. In order to purchase sites and erect school buildings, communes may borrow money from the National Loan and Deposit Fund or from agricultural credit banks or from savings banks. Interest charges on such loans are met by grants from the Ministry of National Education coöperating with the Ministry of Finance; the payments for amortization must be provided for in the local budgets.

The State, the provinces, and communes coöperate in the provision and maintenance of secondary schools. The State pays the salaries of principals and teachers and of the clerical staff in *licei-ginnasi* and *istituti magistrali*, and in the backward provinces of Basilicate and Sardinia in *istituti tecnici* and *scuole complementari;* it also provides materials for instruction and scientific equipment in all schools except *licei scientifici*. The provinces are required to contribute to the maintenance of *licei scientifici* and *istituti tecnici* and the communes to the maintenance of all other types of secondary schools not already provided for (e.g., *scuole complementari* and *licei femminili*). This means that in their respective fields the provinces and communes must provide the buildings, equipment, heat, light, and all other expenses, and the clerical and mechanical staff, assistants and janitors, where not provided by the State. In the *licei scientifici* and *istituti tecnici* the province supplies the instructional and scientific materials. Under the regulations of the Royal Decrees of March 11, 1923, and June 7, 1923, all communes are required to make certain contributions varying with the size of the locality and the types of schools which they may provide. Institutions which must be established are the *licei-ginnasi* in provincial capitals and the *istituti tecnici* in provincial capitals or some other communes; all *istituti magistrali*; the *scuole complementari* in provincial capitals or other communes with a population exceeding 30,000; optional schools are all other types, like the *licei scientifici* and *licei femminili*. The relative distribution of state and local expenditures for education may be indicated roughly for purposes of comparison; the state expenditure for 1928–29 was 1,394,000,000 lire, while in 1928 the local expenditure was 605,842,000 lire.

Conclusion. The Italian system of educational administration is thus highly centralized on the principle that the State has the right to determine the educational destinies of the country in the light of the political and social principles upon which it rests. In so far as there is decentralization, it exists in the interests of efficiency; administrative efficiency and local administration are but an extension of the powers of the central authority through officials whom it appoints directly either on the basis of competitive examinations open to candidates who are professionally qualified or by selection for the highest positions; e.g., the *provveditori agli studi* from persons of recognized qualifications and experience. The *provveditori* are in turn assisted by councils whose membership is made up of individuals who have professional qualifications. In this scheme no place is provided for popularly elected boards or committees, a situation due only in part to the inefficiency of such bodies in the past and more directly the logical consequence of the Fascist ideology. This principle is carried still further in the care which is taken in selecting teachers, who must in the first place prove their competence through competitive examinations, and in the second place must be acceptable to the Fascist régime. Although teachers in elementary and secondary schools are not required to take the same oath of loyalty to Fascism as are university professors, it is certainly expected that they will not be critical of the established social order.

The rigor of centralization is more apparent on the surface than in practice. For, although everything seems to be carefully regulated from above by the central authority in the interests of administrative efficiency, and although care is taken in securing teachers who are amenable, in practice adequate room is allowed for self-determination in professional matters. The central authority not only encourages the selection of schools to conduct experiments in schools below the secondary level, but the courses of study are issued in the form of suggestions, and adequate scope is left for variety and adaptation to local conditions within the constituted form of the social order. As will be seen, particularly in the chapter on Elementary Education, the work of the pre-elementary and elementary schools is based on activity principles, the essential features of which are adaptation and freedom. There is thus an apparent paradox, which is explicable; politically the schools are not free, educationally they are — a situation which is also found under the Soviet system. The paradox is due to the merging in Fascism of two main ideas — the political and the cultural. From the point of view of political philosophy, Fascism is based on the Hegelian idea of the absolutist state; from the point of view of educational philosophy, as represented by Gentile and Lombardo-Radice, but with different interpretations, individual development is only possible through activity built up on the environment, and national culture is not something which can be defined from a central office, but is itself living and growing. For Gentile the individual should be active, growing, and self-determining, but within the limits set by the collective will or the social order; to Lombardo-Radice the acceptance of any limitations to growth was incompatible with the true meaning of the new educational philosophy. Hence for Gentile the State is omnipotent and the administration of its functions must be centralized and built up on the hierarchical principle; Lombardo-Radice, and with him the largest teachers' association, before it had been transformed into a Fascist Union (*Associazione Fascista della Scuola*), favored decentralization, not merely to ensure administrative authority, but to encourage self-determination and growth of national culture through the interplay of social forces from the bottom up, — that is, from the local units in enjoyment of autonomy. Such an attitude is, however, diametrically opposed to the principles underlying the Fascist State, which was definitely established as a criticism of the democratic forms of government. For the present Fascism can point to the efficiency of its system as illustrated by the increased expenditures, the reduction of illiteracy, the increase of schools and attendance, and the provision of a greater variety of schools and educational opportunities than existed before the Revolution.

5. RUSSIA

For purposes of educational administration, each of the Republics which constitute the Union of Soviet Socialist Republics is autonomous. The Union as such does not maintain a department or authority for education, nor does it exercise any control over education in the constituent Republics. Indirectly, however, since the U.S.S.R. is dominated by the Communist Party, and, since the character of the educational system is dictated by Communist principles, there is throughout the Union a tendency toward uniformity, which is further promoted by conferences between the people's commissars for education in each of the Republics. The Russian Socialist Federated Soviet Republic (R.S.F.S.R.) may be taken as an illustration of the administrative system.

Educational affairs in the R.S.F.S.R. are under the control of the People's Commissar for Education, who is appointed annually by the All-Russian Central Executive Committee and is eligible to reappointment.[1] The People's Commissar is assisted by a board (*Collegium*) consisting of members approved by the Council of People's Commissars and of representatives of the Central Committee of the Union of Workers in Education and Art. The distinctive characteristic of the central authority is derived from the breadth of the concept of education which it is called upon to administer. It controls and supervises, not only education in the technical sense of the word, but scientific organizations, museums, theaters, moving pictures, music and art, and state publications.

The work of the People's Commissariat (or Ministry) for Education (*Narkompros*) is distributed among eleven departments. (1) The Department of Administration and Organization is responsible for the administration and organization of the work of the Commissariat and local authorities, of finances, buildings, etc. (2) The direction of the education of children of pre-school and school age and the social welfare of minors is in the hands of the Department for Social and Polytechnic Education. (3) Vocational education (the training of experts in industry, agriculture, education, art, health, and other fields) is supervised by the Department for Vocational Education. (4) Pre-school education and educational work among adults are controlled by a Department for this purpose. (5) The Board of Education in non-Russian-speaking nationalities is responsible for education among non-Russian-speaking minorities. (6) The State Scientific Council is a research rather than an administrative agency, responsible for the study of educational methods, the preparation of curricula and courses of study for all educational institutions. (7) The Department for Scientific and Art Institutions supervises academies, scientific societies, research institutes, meteorological and biological stations, and other scientific institutions; it is also charged with the safeguarding of historical monuments, works of art and museums, and the conduct of state theaters, cir-

---

[1] A. V. Lunacharsky held the position of People's Commissar for Education from the October Revolution to 1930.

cuses, and musical institutes. (8) The Department for Literature and Publications exercises control over publications, moving pictures, and theatrical repertoires. Associated with, but not actual departments of, the Commissariat are: (9) the State Publishing Agency; (10) the Board of Management for State Moving-Picture Enterprises; (11) the Supply Board which superintends the provision of general educational equipment. The last three departments are commercial concerns in which the Commissariat for Education has controlling interests.

A mere enumeration of the boards of the Commissariat fails to indicate the scope of their activities. Through its boards and departments the Commissariat defines, but does not directly prescribe, the scope of general and social education throughout the country in accordance with the ideology of the new social order; it performs the same function for vocational and professional education, and through an occupational census determines the number of students to be trained in every field of activity which requires such preparation; it has undertaken the responsibility for the liquidation of illiteracy and for developing a program of political education; it stimulates and encourages the development of the fine arts, music, and drama; it plans, controls, and censors publications of every kind, whether newspapers, periodicals, pamphlets, or books; it promotes the establishment of scientific institutions to make them readily accessible in all parts of the country for study, research, and the dissemination of scientific knowledge; and, finally, it collects information of a financial and statistical nature in all matters affecting education.

In the provision and control of education, the People's Commissariat for Education is only one of many agencies. The Cultural and Educational Department of the Central Council of Workers' Unions supervises political education and the organization and provision of clubs and libraries in labor unions. Political education in the Red Army is promoted by the People's Commissar for the Army, while educational activities among railroad and water transport workers is superintended by the People's Commissar for Transport. The coördination of education with industry, particularly scientific and practical research related to the economic life of the country, is supervised by the Supreme Council of National Education. Finally, an extensive educational program is conducted by the Communist Party through the organizations for children and young people

(Octobrists, Pioneers, and Komsomols), the training ground for its future members, and the establishment of Party schools ranging from the education of illiterates to the Communist universities.

The links between the People's Commissar for Education and the country are the inspectors and the Union of Workers in Education, which is consulted on new programs in education and to which the People's Commissar makes an annual report. The inspectors are a late development in the history of Soviet educational administration. At first the Commissariat planned to control education throughout the country by the creation of official representative departments, a measure due in part to a feeling of uncertainty as to the attitude of the teachers to the Revolution, and in part to uncertainty as to the fate of the Revolution. Once firmly established, the central authority proceeded more definitely in the direction of decentralization.

Local administration. For administrative purposes Russia is divided into villages, rural districts, counties, and provinces. In each area soviets are elected; the executive committees of the soviets appoint the local departments of education responsible in the first instance to the executive committee which appoints it and always subject to the scrutiny of the representatives of the Communist Party. The local departments are responsible for the general organization and administration of all education in their areas except higher education, the appointment of teachers, and the preparation of the budget for education. In each school a council is appointed including the teachers and representatives of the lower personnel (clerks and janitors), the school physician, the Communist Party, the workers' unions, and the Komsomols. The school principal, who is a member of the school council, is not bound by the resolutions of the council and may in certain cases act without submitting the question concerned to the council for preliminary discussion.

Educational finance. Under the Czarist régime the major part of the cost of education was borne by the State. Since the Revolution the major part of the cost of education is borne by the local communities. Thus in 1913 the State bore 59.6 per cent of the cost of education and the localities 40.4 per cent; in 1926–27 the burden falling on the localities was 70.7 per cent and on the State 29.3 per cent. In addition to public funds, appropriations for education are made by industrial organizations for vocational education, by the transport system for the training of its workers, by workers' unions and other economic organizations for political education, by the Party and professional organizations for cultural activities among their members, and by social welfare agencies for the care of delinquent children and the liquidation of illiteracy. A certain revenue is derived from fees and the sale of the products of vocational schools.

Conclusion. The Russian educational system represents the harnessing of all social, economic, and political agencies for cooperation in the development through schools and other educational agencies of the new social order. As contrasted with a centralized system like the French or even with the local systems in the United States the progress of education is determined not so much by administrative machinery as by the dominance of clearly defined ends. The new ideals, it is true, have been imposed by force, but, as in Italy, force is giving way to propaganda through educational institutions. The Soviet educational reform is the most Communist of the Communist Revolution, just as education in Italy is the most Fascist of the Fascist Revolution. In both cases education as indoctrination is frankly accepted, and the individual is to be moulded according to the mould into which the Party in power seeks to form him. And yet in both countries the administrative authorities are content to set the stage, to define clearly the purposes and aims of education, to develop an administrative and teaching personnel which, if not actively, at least passively, must accept these purposes. Beyond this, teachers are free, with the resulting paradox in both countries that courses of study are not prescribed in detail, teachers are expected to organize their syllabuses in accordance with the local environment, and the method of education and instruction which is virtually prescribed is the activity method. The individual is free, but the scope and range of his freedom are circumscribed. Whether the hope of the leaders of the Revolution, that education will in time result in the elimination of the rigorous control of propaganda and indoctrination, will be realized remains to be seen. For the present the Soviet system of administration seeks to define for the individual the truth which is to make him free.

6. UNITED STATES

Characteristics of the American system of administration. The administration of education in the United States represents a conflict between two tendencies. The first of these, due to the historical development of government, is the desire of the public in the various units in which it is organized to control its own affairs; the second, the development of the last generation, is the result of a movement to apply the principles of efficient management and of scientific control to the types of education which the public wishes to provide. As already noted by the English educator, Sir Joshua Fitch, in 1901:

> There is no uniformity in the methods or machinery of education in the States. But in its stead there prevails much of the local patriotism, which makes each of the leading communities proud of its own institutions, and keenly solicitous to produce such examples of good work as may prove worthy of imitation in other states and cities. Hence America may be regarded as a laboratory in which educational experiments are being tried out on a great scale, under conditions exceptionally favorable to the encouragement of inventiveness and fresh enthusiasm, and to the discovery of new methods and new truths.

This experimentation is animated by common and deep-rooted faith in education and the desire to provide equality of educational opportunity for all. As contrasted with most European systems, there is an absence in the United States of universal, clearly defined goals, prescribed by a central authority, or even a widespread concept of national culture which might determine the ends in a system locally administered. The Federal Government, with some minor exceptions, exercises no control over education, and, although such control is by law vested in the individual States, it is still true that the educational affairs of the country are administered by some 150,000 local school boards. The movement toward centralization, which is obvious in many States at the present time, and the proposals for greater federal participation through federal aid for education, do not represent a tendency on the part either of the States or of the Federal Government to assert paramount and sovereign rights in education so much as a desire to give reality to the traditional faith in education by creating larger units of administration which will make possible the greater pooling of resources in order to distribute more equably the opportunities for education. There is thus a conflict between the claims of localities, however small, to administer their own affairs in education, as there is on a larger scale suspicion that any extended participation in education by the Federal Government would interfere with state rights. In a word, the conflict at present is between the tradition of local autonomy and a movement toward greater efficiency in education which would result from the creation of larger units of administration. The National Advisory Committee on Education stated the position thus in 1931:

> The American people must face the problem of conflict between our traditional policy of State and local autonomy and this growing trend toward federal centralization. It may well be that apparent immediate educational efficiencies which are the aim of centralized federal management of education, may be completely counterbalanced by other ultimate losses in special and political functioning. It is the conviction of this Committee that harm results when intimacy between schools and their patrons and neighbours is disturbed by remote control of a distant authority. Weakened personal and local responsibility for so important a social function as public education may ultimately sap the foundations of popular interest and of support which historically have been among the major factors in the development of the United States of the most democratic system of education in the world.[1]

The motive underlying the movement for larger administrative units with increased supervisory authority springs from a desire to improve the educational facilities accessible to each individual rather than from a desire on the part of the States to dominate education in their own interests. In so far as there is a tendency toward centralization in some States, a tendency which is likely to spread throughout the country as the conviction becomes more widespread that the smaller units are unable through their own efforts to provide the range and variety of education which should be accessible to every boy and girl, the explanation will not be found in any attempt to look for a national, all-inclusive, dominant aim, political or cultural, for something equivalent to the aims of the French centralized system, or of Communism in Soviet Russia, or of Fascism in Italy. The movement toward centralization is motivated by reasons of administrative efficiency rather than by any

---

[1] National Advisory Committee on Education, *Federal Relations to Education*, Part I, pp. 12 f.

intention of dominating or controlling the conduct of education in the interests of a sovereign State.

The State, as it gradually steps in and seeks to give reality to the right which it enjoys constitutionally and legally, does so by setting up minimum standards of efficiency and improved methods of financial support without seeking to impose uniformity of educational procedures and practices. The theory underlying the administration of education is that progress depends upon free experimentation and variety. Until recently this theory has been put into practice empirically; the tendency in the last two decades has been to promote the progress of education by the application of methods of efficiency, already developed in industry and commerce, and of scientific control, so far as such control is possible in social affairs. Scientific methods, controlled experimentation, principles of efficiency take the place in the United States of the strongly centralized authority found in other countries. The leadership exercised by such an authority elsewhere has been assumed in the United States by institutions for the study of education and by the development of trained professional experts. The place of the former was recognized by Dr. James E. Russell, formerly Dean of Teachers College, Columbia University, as early as 1900, when he wrote that

University departments of education have as their special function the investigation of educational foundations, the interpretation of educational ideals, the invention of educational methods, and the application of educational principles. The science of education... needs to be developed and made over to fit modern conditions.

Leadership in educational progress. The need of such leadership in the absence of controlling governmental authorities became increasingly pressing as the provision of education began to be expanded and the expenditures advanced with the growing wealth of the country. There was uncertainty as to aims, processes, and methods; there were few, if any, external agencies for appraisal either of the quantity or the quality of education; there were no standards of expenditures. All that was available was unbounded faith in education and desire to extend opportunities for it; popular will and consent on which the progress of education depended had themselves to be educated. These needs helped to confirm the status defined by Dean Russell for the newly created departments of education in universities — in administration of trained superintendents, in educational theory of professors of education, in methods of appraisal of experts in the newly created methods of tests and measurements. In administration the superintendent of schools could no longer proceed by mere empiricism and routine; educational progress depended upon his ability to educate his public up to new standards, and in a society in which business efficiency is one of the cardinal virtues he was expected to be no less efficient in the conduct of his office than the director of a large industrial concern spending an equal amount of money. Scientific tests and measurements were utilized increasingly to test the quality of education and to set up standards, which elsewhere are defined by a central authority and appraised by government inspectors. Aims and methods were defined by experts in the light of current practices, experimentation, and the contributions of psychology and sociology. With the advancement and expansion of education, specialization has become narrower and more detailed, with the result that today there are to be found experts in school buildings, in educational finances and school accounting, in curriculum-making, in the various branches and types of education,[1] in extra-curricular activities, and in higher education.

About 1911 the practice began to be adopted of inviting experts in the various fields to investigate local or state systems of education and to make recommendations for reorganization and improvement. For the conduct of such investigations or "surveys," experts were invited from university departments of education, from successful practitioners, and from the educational foundations [2] which began to be established in the early years of the present century. In this way the study of education was kept in close touch with practice in the field, while the reports and recommendations of surveys furnished for the country as a whole that guidance and leadership which in other countries are provided by governmental direction.

[1] Parental education, pre-school education, kindergarten-primary education, elementary education, junior high school, senior high school (with experts in its specialized courses), teacher-preparation, junior college, college and higher education, and adult education.

[2] Among the leading foundations which have contributed to the progress of education, not only through grants and endowments, but through the conduct of surveys and the study of special educational problems, are: (1) the General Education Board, established in 1902; (2) the Carnegie Foundation for the Advancement of Teaching, 1906; (3) the Russell Sage Foundation, 1907; and (4) the Commonwealth Fund, 1918.

From 1913 on there began to be organized local bureaus of reference and research as agencies for continued investigations of educational problems in the place of the occasional survey. The work of such bureaus varies; in some cases their investigations cover the whole field of education, in others only the administrative and statistical aspects, and in others again only tests and measurements of school practices. The work of both city and state bureaus and of university bureaus of research culminated in 1916 in the organization of the National Association of Directors of Educational Research, now the Educational Research Association.

The progress of American education, apart from such control as is exercised by the state authorities and by legislation, is thus determined by experimentation and self-examination, by imitation, and, if the term may be used, by capillary attraction — the more advanced systems setting the pace for the rest. This is due not only to the mobility of the population and of the teaching profession and the nation-wide dissemination of educational literature and school textbooks, but also to the activities of a large number of educational associations, such as the National Education Association, which maintains a Research Division, the Department of Superintendence, the National Society for the Study of Education, the National Society of College Teachers of Education, Section L of the American Association for the Advancement of Science, and a vast number of associations, national and state, of specialists in the field of education. Nor can the influence of graduate study of education in institutions which draw their students from the whole country, particularly for the summer sessions, be neglected as a factor in the development of national aims, ideals, and practices in education.

It is from this point of view that it is possible to speak of an American system of education in the sense that it is dominated by more or less common aims and aspirations. The general framework of education tends to be the same, and the language of education is the same; the differences and variety which are characteristic of the country are due to the absence of central control, whether federal or state, to the differences in the size of the administrative units with consequent differences in the amount of money that they can devote for education, in their ability to provide for efficient administration, and often in the attitude of the population to education. It is perhaps a characteristic of American democracy that in studying its educational system it is necessary to start with all the informal and extra-legal agencies which have grown up as the progress of education demanded rather than to follow the procedure employed in the study of other countries of beginning with the central authorities and tracing the delegation of powers to local units. American education has been built from the local units up and the tendency to centralization in the States has been influenced by the introduction of efficiency methods in the administration of the larger local units and a desire to extend to the smaller units the advantages of educational opportunities which they cannot afford unaided.

The Federal Government and education. The Constitution of the United States makes no reference to education. The Tenth Amendment, which was adopted in 1791 and provided that "powers not delegated to the United States by the Constitution, nor prohibited by it to the States, are reserved to the States respectively, or to the people," left education, as one of the powers not mentioned in the Constitution, to the control of the States. In 1867 a Federal Department of Education was created, but two years later was reduced to the rank of a Bureau in the Department of the Interior, a position which it has retained up to the present; in 1930 the Bureau of Education returned to its original legal designation as the Office of Education. Administered by the United States Commissioner of Education, the Office of Education is primarily an agency for the collection of statistics and for the dissemination of information on education. Except for the supervision of schools for Eskimos and Indians in Alaska, the Office of Education exercises no administrative authority in the field of education. Despite its small annual appropriation ($510,000 for 1932), the Office has helped to focus attention on the progress and development of education through its current publications, its *Biennial Surveys of Education*, its researches and reports of investigations conducted by it at the request of state and local authorities. During the last two years several national investigations — into educational finance, the preparation of teachers, and secondary education — have been conducted under the supervision of the Office. The influence of the Office of Education is in general no greater than the personal prestige and competence of its Commissioner and the members of its staff.

Similar in scope is the Children's Bureau established in 1912 and placed under the Department of Commerce and Labor. The Bureau is charged with the duty of investigating and reporting on all matters concerning the welfare of children — infant mortality, orphan and delinquent children, accidents and diseases of children, employment of, and legislation affecting, children. In 1921 the Bureau was entrusted with the administration of the Sheppard-Towner Maternity Aid Act which provided funds for coöperation with the States in "promoting the welfare and hygiene of maternity and infancy."

To promote coöperation with the States in the provision and extension of vocational education, there was created in 1917 the Federal Board for Vocational Education, which is independent of the Office of Education and administers the annual appropriation made under the Smith-Hughes Act (1917), supplemented by the George-Reed Act (1929) for the promotion of vocational education in institutions below the college level, including training in agriculture, trade, and industry; in 1920 the administration of the Civilian Vocational Rehabilitation Act (Smith-Bankhead Act) was added to the duties of the Board.

The Department of Agriculture, in addition to conducting research and disseminating information on all subjects within the field of administration, supervises the land-grant colleges established under the Morrill Acts (1862 and 1890), the agricultural experiment stations under the Hatch Act (1887), supplemented by the Adams Act (1906) and the Purnell Act (1925), extension work in agriculture and home economics under the Smith-Lever Act (1914), supplemented by the Capper-Ketcham Act (1929). The education of Indians is supervised by the Office of Indian Affairs in the Department of the Interior, while the Insular Bureau in the War Department exercises general supervision over education in the Philippines and Porto Rico. Beyond this the Federal Government maintains institutions for the training of officers for the army and navy, subsidizes the training of reserve officers in colleges and universities through the Reserve Officers' Training Corps, maintains the Library of Congress, the Smithsonian Institution, and a number of similar institutions, and through Congress exercises oversight over education in the District of Columbia.

Federal aid for education. Although education is by implication left to the States, it is obvious from the preceding statement that the Federal Government has in practice developed a somewhat extensive participation in education. Nor is such participation confined to guidance and advice; it has been accompanied almost from the establishment of the Republic by large grants, at first in the form of land, later by direct money grants appropriated for a variety of purposes by Congress. The Ordinance of 1785, which ordered a land survey, provided that lot No. 16 of every township be reserved for the maintenance of schools. The Ordinance of 1787, which enunciated the principle that "schools and the means of education shall be forever encouraged," made no grants, but began in 1802, when Ohio was admitted, the practice of giving each State on admission the sixteenth section of land in each township for the maintenance of schools; after 1850 two, and later four, sections were allotted to new states; to these other lands swamp and saline lands were added; in the case of the States more recently admitted — Oklahoma, Arizona, and New Mexico — the grants were even more liberal.

In 1862, with the passage of the Morrill Act, a new policy was adopted of making grants for specific purposes — in this case for the promotion of education at the college level in agriculture and the mechanic arts. The Hatch Act (1887), to create agricultural experiment stations, introduced a practice which has since been extending of granting annual appropriations to the States for purposes indicated in the various Acts. From 1911 the States were required as a condition for receiving federal grants to make available an amount of money equal to the sum received, and to pass acts of assent to the provisions of the Federal Acts as passed. In each case where federal grants are distributed, the conditions are stipulated in the Act, and the Department, Bureau, or Board charged with their distribution has the authority to approve or reject plans proposed by the States for carrying out the purposes of such aid; the strongest control is exercised through a scrutiny of the accounts. Excluding income from land grants, where they have not been dissipated, the federal appropriations for aid for general and special education in 1930 amounted to $23,778,000, distributed as follows: Office of Education, $351,624; agricultural and mechanical colleges, $2,550,000; agricultural experiment stations, $4,335,000; agricultural extension work, $7,662,936; vocational education, $7,800,000; and vocational rehabilitation, $1,079,120.

Despite the amount of money devoted to education by the Federal Government, it cannot be claimed that there has yet been developed a satisfactory body of principles to govern the relations between the federal and the state authorities. On the one hand there is a marked and widespread fear that too detailed prescriptions by the former of the purposes on which federal grants should be paid would in time mean encroachment on States' rights; on the other hand it is not clear that a scrutiny of accounts is the best method of supervising the efficiency of the education which it is desired to promote. Despite the absence of clear principles on which the relations between the Federal Government and the States might be based, there has since 1917 been a widespread movement to increase the participation of the Federal Government in education, first, by the creation of a Federal Department of Education, and secondly, by an increasing federal aid for education. The arguments for a Federal Department of Education with a Secretary in the Cabinet are that it would raise education in prestige and dignity as one of the major concerns of the Government and that it would give greater authority and influence to the central agency. Increased federal aid is justified on the grounds that education, however it may be administered, is in the end of importance to the nation as a whole, and that wealth is not equally distributed throughout the country, with the result that there are serious inequalities in the provision of every aspect of education both in quantity and quality. Only by pooling the resources of the country as a whole can such inequalities be removed. Those who sponsor the proposals for increased federal participation in education deny, however, that it would be followed by increased control, the dangers of which are nowhere ignored.

The National Advisory Committee on Education, appointed in 1929 by Secretary Ray Lyman Wilbur, of the Department of the Interior, in its report on *Federal Relations to Education* (Washington, D.C., 1931), recommended the establishment of a Department of Education with a Secretary of Education at its head, in which all the functions now exercised in education by various departments and bureaus should be concentrated and coördinated. All future grants to States should be in aid of education in general rather than for specific purposes; such aid should be spent by each State for any or all educational purposes as the State itself may direct. Local autonomy should be maintained and developed. The expenditures of federal aid would be controlled by annual audits or, in the words of the report (p. 38):

> The only restriction placed by federal legislation on such educational grants should be the provision that every State, when it accepts the grant, agrees to make each year to the federal headquarters for education a full report on all questions on which the federal headquarters for education may require information concerning the manner in which the State has used the grant.

By this method it is hoped to avoid the danger of interference by the federal authority in the educational affairs of the States; but there has also been avoided the real issue — how to devise a system of coöperation between the Federal Government and the States which would result in federal aid to the States with some guarantee that such aid is efficiently administered.[1]

STATE ADMINISTRATION OF EDUCATION

Development of state control. The administration of education, as has been pointed out, is a state affair, safeguarded by the constitutions of the several States or by school laws and confirmed by a number of legal decisions,[2] which have proceeded on the principle that "the whole State is interested in the education of children of the State." Since the development of governmental control by the States developed from the small local communities to the larger unit, a tradition of local control was strongly established before the movement for State unification began, at first tentatively before the middle of the nineteenth century, somewhat more rapidly after 1875, and definitely after 1900. The problem confronting the development of state centralization is one of reconciling popular control with administrative efficiency and the vote of the people with a continuously progressive policy. The expanding scope of education and the fuller recognition of the meaning of equality of educational opportunities have brought with them the realization that the American ideal of education cannot be achieved by complete delegation of authority to the smaller communities, which for a variety of reasons are likely to be indifferent to the problems of education and in all cases financially unable to meet the increasing cost of an en-

[1] For the present the issue is unimportant; the present economic and financial situation makes it unlikely that it will become a question of practical politics for some time to come.
[2] See Cubberley, E. P., *Public School Administration*, pp. 18 ff. (Boston, 1929).

larged program. The pace for the country was set by the larger cities — which were the first to provide increased opportunities — to levy more money for education, and to introduce efficient methods of administration into the field of education. Proposals for the improvement of state administration must count with the existence of more than 150,000 local areas — districts, towns, townships, counties, and cities — varying in size of population and wealth, to which the States have delegated their authority in the matter of education. By law and by constitutional provision, however, the States have the right to intervene at any time, to withdraw such delegated authority, to change the size of areas, and to promote the efficiency of education as they see fit. The powers with which the state is entrusted have been clearly summarized by Professor Ellwood P. Cubberley in the following statement:

> It ought to be essentially the business of the State to formulate a constructive policy for the development of the education of the people of the State, and to change this policy from time to time as the changing needs of the State may seem to require. This may involve more than the mere regulation of schools, and may properly include such educational agencies and efforts as libraries, playgrounds, health supervision, and adult education. Instead of being a passive tax-gatherer and law-giver, the State should become an active, energetic agent, working for the moral, intellectual, and social improvement and advancement of its people. The formulation of minimum standards for the various forms of public education, the raising of these standards from time to time, the protection of these standards from being lowered by private agencies, and the stimulation of communities to additional educational activity, is a fundamental right and duty of the State. On the other hand, to find what can safely be left to local initiative and control, and then to pass this down, ought to be as much a function of proper state school administration as is the removal from community control of matters which communities cannot longer handle with a reasonable degree of effectiveness. Unity in essentials and liberty in non-essentials, as high minimum standards for all as is possible, constant stimulation to communities to exceed the minima required, and large liberty to communities in the choice of methods and tools and in the extension of educational advantages and opportunities, ought to be cardinal principles in a State's educational policy and in its relations to its subordinate governmental units.[1]

The state and the curriculum. The character of state administration of education is thus determined by the American tradition of local government, on the one hand, and, on the other, by the recogni-

[1] Cubberley, E. P., *Public School Administration*, pp. 28 f. (Boston, 1929).

tion that the interests of efficiency, progress, and equalization of opportunities demand greater intervention on the part of the state authority. The authority of each State in education is derived from the constitution or from its school laws. Because the tradition of popular control in education has survived, the people through their elected representatives may be said to exercise an important influence on its development. The example of the Tennessee Legislature, which prohibited the teaching of evolution in the schools and universities of the State, is not isolated. Not only do school laws prescribe in many cases what must be taught in the schools, but special laws are passed from time to time, as the whim of the legislators moves them or as particular groups bring pressure to bear upon the legislatures. There may thus be found legislative provisions concerning (1) the teaching of nationalism (flag display and flag exercises, teaching of patriotism and patriotic songs, prohibition of foreign languages as languages of instruction, teaching of the History and Constitution of the United States and the State, and the observance of special days); (2) the teaching of health and prohibition; (3) conservation of life and property; (4) special practical and cultural subjects (agriculture, drawing, music, household arts, industrial arts, bookkeeping, exhibitions of school work, cotton grading, and art); (5) humaneness (humane treatment of animals and birds and their importance, and prohibition of vivisection and animal experimentation); (6) fundamental subjects (arithmetic, English, geography, penmanship, reading, and spelling); (7) religious and ethical subjects (sectarian doctrine, Bible reading, and social and ethical conduct); (8) miscellaneous subjects (elementary science, algebra, metric system, forestry and plant life, use of dictionaries, Darwinism, and reading of survey maps).[1] Temporary enthusiasms, popular demand, pressure by interested groups, and faith in the efficacy of instruction to secure immediate results explain such interference by legislatures and the difficulty which still exists of drawing a line of demarcation between the part which such bodies may well play in representing their electorates and the part which should be left to the judgment of professional experts.

State authorities. The diversity of American practices in the administration of education and the conflict between traditions and progressive tendencies are nowhere better illustrated than in the

[1] See Flanders, J. K., *Legislative Control of the Elementary Curriculum* (New York, 1925).

description of the state authorities for education and their executive officials. The state board of education has emerged from an organization which began to be developed rapidly after its establishment in Massachusetts in 1837. The functions of educational administration, supervision, and definition of policies were for a long time not given special prominence in the organization of state boards of education, which were created originally to look after school funds and lands. By gradual steps the functions of such boards were enlarged and have become in some States as extensive as those of a Ministry of Education in other countries, although there are still many States in which special boards to administer higher education, normal schools and teachers' colleges continue to exist.

There is accordingly no uniformity either in the constitution or the functions of state boards of education. Six of the forty-eight States have no boards; in nine states (Colorado, Florida, Kentucky, Mississippi, Missouri, Nevada, North Carolina, Oregon, and Texas) the state board consists of state officials (generally the governor, the treasurer, the secretary of State, the attorney-general, the auditor, and the superintendent of public instruction); in twenty-four states (Alabama, Arizona, Arkansas, Connecticut, Georgia, Idaho, Indiana, Kansas, Louisiana, Michigan, Montana, New Hampshire, New Mexico, North Dakota, Oklahoma, Pennsylvania, Rhode Island, South Carolina, Tennessee, Utah, Virginia, West Virginia, Washington, and Wyoming) the boards are composed of state officials *ex officio*, school officials, and laymen either appointed or elected; nine state boards (California, Delaware, Iowa, Maryland, Massachusetts, Minnesota, New Jersey, New York, and Vermont) consist of members elected by the legislatures or appointed by the governors. The title most generally used for this body is State Board of Education; other designations are the Board of Regents of the University of the State of New York, the Advisory Board of Education (Massachusetts), the State Council of Education (Pennsylvania), and the State Board of Administration (North Dakota). The boards vary in size from three to thirteen members (most frequently seven), and in their terms of office — two to twelve years (most usually six years). Most frequently the lay members of the boards are appointed by the governor with or without confirmation by the Senate of the State concerned. In a few States the members of the boards receive an annual compensation (ranging from $100 to $3000) and expenses; in others they are paid a *per diem* allowance and expenses with some limitation on the number of meetings for which payment will be made; in others they are reimbursed for expenses; and finally, in a few States in which the members are *ex officio* on the board no payment is made at all.

The powers and duties of State boards vary; in some States they are responsible for the control of school finances; in others there is added general supervision of state institutions; in the progressive systems the boards exercise general supervision and control over all educational affairs — the enforcement of laws, consideration of policies, finance, budget, appointment of executive officials and staff of the department of education — and act in a consultative and advisory capacity to the chief executive. There is in general a tendency to restrict the powers of the boards of legislative and regulative functions, and to the definition of policies, and to leave the exercise of administrative duties to the chief executive official and his staff. The state board, in other words, should represent the best opinion of the people of the State. It is for this reason that the election of members is advocated in place of *ex officio* state officers or appointment, since in the last two methods there is danger of the intrusion of politics; for the same reason those who advocate the election of members also urge special elections, separate from general political elections, and on a non-partisan basis.

The chief state educational official. One obstacle in the way of an appropriate demarcation of functions between the state boards and their chief executive official, generally known as state superintendent of public instruction, but also as superintendent of public schools and commissioner of education, is the fact that this position is still in most States political in character. The state superintendent of public instruction is elected in thirty-three States at the regular political elections; in six States he is appointed by the governors; and in nine States by the state boards of education. Except in the last instances the candidate for the position must usually be a resident of the State in which he seeks election or appointment. The qualifications vary from the requirement that the candidate be a person of educational standing or hold a teacher's life certificate to the requirement that he be a college graduate with professional preparation and several years of experience. Where the executive official is appointed by a state board, the best available candidates in the country may be appointed; generally it is in these States that he is known as commissioner of education. Not only is there a wide variety in methods of selection and qualifications, but the salaries range from $2000 to $12,000 a year (the mode being $5000). The term of office varies from one to six years (most frequently four years). Limitations of residence, qualifications, term of office, and salary as well as the necessity of standing at a political election mean that in general candidates are not well qualified for the larger scope of administration, which is today demanded of the chief executive, but that frequently they would have working under them men and women who are better paid and better qualified. The situation is different in those States in which the best person available is appointed for a term of years with every probability of renewal and at a salary commensurate with the dignity of the office. It is in such States that the new trends toward a proper interpretation of the functions of the State in education and toward efficient administration are being developed and that examples are being set up for the country as a whole. For the more progressive States are those in which political considerations have in the main been set aside and the best persons available are selected to serve as members of the boards of education and as the chief executives; it is here, too, that a proper distribution of functions has become possible — the state board acting in a deliberative, consultative, and advisory capacity, and the chief executive assuming responsibility for the execution of the board's policies and for administration in general.

The powers and duties of the chief executive, the state superintendent of public instruction or the commissioner of education, in the progressive States include general supervision and control over all aspects of education, the enforcement of laws and regulations, the development of public opinion, consultation with educational officials in the local areas, the execution of state policies, supervision of educational finances and expenditures, the classification of schools, certification of teachers, the preparation or supervision of the preparation of curricula, courses of study and lists of textbooks, the collection of statistical returns, reports and publications, the arrangement of conferences, the supervision of special and vocational education, and control of standards of buildings, sanitation, health and child welfare. He is responsible for leadership and guidance in education throughout the State.

State departments of education. The gradual change in the status of the state authority for education and the rapid growth of the functions of the chief executive have led in time to the development of state departments of education; that is, the executive branch as distingushed from the state boards. Here again there is no uniformity of practice; in some States the number of staff officers is as low as five, while in Pennsylvania the number rises to over seventy. In Missouri the staff of the state department of education includes besides the state superintendent a director and assistant director of vocational education and rehabilitation, a chief clerk, inspectors of teacher training institutions, high schools and rural schools, supervisors of agriculture, home economics, industrial rehabilitation, trade and industry, and negro schools, a statistician, and rehabilitation field officers. The state department of education in Maryland consists of the state superintendent, an assistant superintendent, supervisors of physical education, rural schools, elementary education, high schools, music, and colored schools, a director of vocational education, a bureau of educational measurement, a statistician and assistant statistician, a chief clerk, an auditor, and a credential secretary. The New York state department, which is one of the largest in the country, consists of the commissioner of education, a deputy and three assistant commissioners, and the following divisions and bureaus: administration (including publication and statistical bureaus), archives and history, attendance, examination and inspection, professional examinations, special schools, finance, law, library extension, school buildings and grounds, visual instruction, vocational and extension education (including Americanization and rehabilitation divisions), educational measurement, rural education, medical inspection, teacher training and certification, physical education, and state normal schools; the commissioner is also responsible for the supervision of the state museum and state library, the boards of managers of the state normal schools, and the board of trustees of New York State College.

The general tendency is thus in the direction of entrusting the administration of education to trained experts. The examples of this development which have been cited illustrate this direction. The problem of reconciling popular control with efficient administration is being solved by allowing the people to elect a state board or to elect an official who appoints such a board, and by developing a service of experts responsible to the board which represent the people either directly or indirectly. Always in the background is the control of the legislature which has an opportunity to exercise it either through its right to intervene by law in the work of the schools and when discussing the appropriations for education.

LOCAL ADMINISTRATION

Despite the apparent expansion of the authority of the State, the account presented in the last section represents a comparatively recent tendency. It is still true to say of American education that its control is largely local through the exercise of powers delegated by the States. The chief areas of administration are districts, towns and townships, counties, and cities. The evolution, which is still proceeding, has been from smaller to larger units of administration.

District system. The smallest unit, which has persisted from the time when with the gradual movement of the population and inadequate means of communication the New England town was gradually split up, is the district. Although the praises of the small district school have been sung, the district, which spread as an area of educational administration in the Middle-West, North-Central, and Northwestern States, proved to be the greatest stumbling-block to sound educational progress. Administered by elected school trustees, usually three in number, the school districts have proved to be inadequate in every way — buildings, salaries for competent teachers, financial support, equipment, and textbooks. So strong, however, has been the traditions of local control, that despite the fact that the powers of school trustees have been considerably curtailed in the past half-century or more, it is difficult to convince their clientèle of the desirability of large areas to secure better schools. With the development of communication and the provision of transportation, however, the district system is on the way to absorption into larger units.

Towns and townships. In New England the school district was reabsorbed in the town, a natural geographical area including rural and urban settlements, but constituting for educational purposes one unit administered by a single school board. The township found in the North-Central States is analogous to the New England towns, but because it is an area which was artificially constructed and for educational purposes does not include the urban or city centers, it is not as well adapted for school organization as the town.[1]

Counties. Next in size to the township is the county, an organization which varies in size, but is found in the South, the Middle-West and Western States. Whether the county is to play an important part for educational administration depends upon the extent to which the county constitutes an essential part for other governmental purposes. In some States, where the county was the original unit of administration, it constitutes the natural unit for education; elsewhere, if the smaller areas have been traditional, the authority of the State must be invoked to overcome opposition to transfer. In Maryland, Utah, and some of the Southern States educational progress has been determined by the county unit; in others a county organization coexists with local areas which insist on retaining a measure of autonomy. While the county, although in some States it seems too large, generally appears to be the most appropriate area for the administration of education outside of cities, a definite scheme of organization has not yet been developed. In some States the county board of education is elected, and in others it is appointed under certain legal restrictions by the county supervisors; elsewhere a board of education with full authority has not yet been evolved, but its functions are exercised in part by county high school boards as in Nevada, by county textbooks commissions as in Iowa and South Dakota, and by county boards of examiners who examine and certificate teachers. There is, however, found everywhere a county school superintendent, who in most instances is an elected official despite the increasing importance of his position as an administrator and leader in education. The duties of a county superintendent include the general administration and supervision of education, enforcement of laws and regulations, and in general the exercise within his own area of powers delegated to the county by the State for the development and progress of education. He is charged with responsibility particularly in two directions — the improvement of rural schools by careful selection of their teachers and organization of the curriculum or by consolidation and trans-

---

[1] For the English reader the urban district may be compared to the New England town except that the town has more powers and duties in education than the Part III authority. The Mid-West township, without the urban centers, would compare with the rural areas in England, which for educational purposes are subordinated to the counties.

portation, and the provision of adequate facilities for high school education. The aim of those who consider the county as the desirable area for educational administration is to secure the introduction into the rural and semi-rural areas of methods of efficient administration similar to those which have been developed in the cities. Before this can be effected, however, another tradition, that of electing the county superintendent, must be abandoned in favor of appointing a trained individual appointed on the basis of adequate professional qualifications at a salary commensurate with the position and on a reasonable tenure. Such a measure would again mean a blow to the tradition of popular control through direct election.

Cities. It is in the cities, however, that there have been developed the characteristic features of American educational administration. This has been due not merely to the size of the cities — many of them are quite small — nor to the fact that under their charters they enjoy almost complete autonomy in education subject always to the permanent authority of the State, but has been the result in part of the greater wealth of the modern city, the clearer recognition of the problems to be faced, and particularly to the emergence, gradual but assured, of a trained personnel, appointed on the basis of professional qualifications instead of being elected for considerations that are not always educational. It is in the cities that there has been elaborated the principle of retaining popular control and of reconciling it with the interests of educational efficiency and at the same time of rescuing the schools, generally but not universally, from the bane of what is in the United States called "politics," but which elsewhere would be regarded as the use of the schools for the ulterior, selfish interests of a group. The process of cleansing the school systems from the bane of such "politics" has proceeded rapidly in the last two decades, and not the least of the causes which have produced these results has been the improvement in the professional preparation of the teachers and of the administrative officials. There are, of course, instances of backsliding, of attempts to make capital out of the schools, but these become rarer and arouse popular indignation to a degree unknown a generation ago. The schools have been placed above politics, just as nearly a century ago the danger of conflict over religious issues was removed by secularizing all public education.

In a large measure the separation of schools from politics has been effected by invoking the principle that, although a board of education may be a part of a local municipal government, it is responsible ultimately, not to the city council, but to the State from whence its powers and authority are derived. The board of education to which in most cities the responsibility for the administration of schools has been entrusted has evolved out of the school committee which was appointed at public meetings and, so long as education was a simple affair, frequently administered the schools directly. As cities grew in size, either by union of wards or districts or by the extension of boundaries, and as the provision of education was expanded and became more complex, such direct administration became impossible, and there was gradually evolved out of the position of clerk or secretary of the school committee that of the superintendent of schools. There survived out of the traditional status of the school committee, however, the problem of more clearly defining the powers and duties of what came to be called the board of education and of the newly evolved executive official. The solution of this problem was particularly acute because in most cases the boards of education tended to be very large, in some cases exceeding one hundred members, and in others they were elected by wards, whose representatives often placed the interests of the schools in their own areas above those of the whole city. The boards of education, it was recognized, had a dual function in so far as they represented the people of their area and exercised powers delegated to them by the State.

The division of functions between boards of education and their chief executive, which has universally been accepted in theory and in most cities in practice, is that the boards represent the will of the people, define educational policies, and exercise general supervision and control over the proper conduct and development of educational affairs, whose direct administration is left to the superintendent of schools and his staff. On one side the boards are responsible to the public in their areas and on the other to the state authority for carrying out the powers and duties assigned to them either by law or by charter. In general, state laws prescribe the minimum requirements for educational development, leaving a large degree of authority to the localities for their own self-determination and progress within the financial resources available for the purpose.

Up to this point boards of education have been referred to as agencies of administration independent of the municipal governments in their areas. This in fact is the situation in most cities, but such independence is not always complete. The administration of education involves the levy of taxes and the expenditure of funds. In this matter complete independence, which theorists of educational administration desire to see achieved, has been attained only in a few localities. In some cities the boards of education are fiscally independent and have complete charge over the budget for education, the raising of funds, and their expenditure subject only to such limits as may be set by law; elsewhere the boards are fiscally dependent and subject in matters of finance to the control of another municipal authority. The arguments for fiscal independence are that in this way boards of education can bring the cause of education directly to the public, that the funds necessary for carrying out the minimum requirements and for expanding an educational program can best be secured by direct taxation, and that by this method educational finances can be considered without the danger of intruding political or other alien considerations. In Pennsylvania generally and in New York, Minnesota, and Wisconsin, some cities enjoy fiscal independence; on the other hand, in some of the larger cities, such as New York, Rochester, Buffalo, Springfield (Massachusetts), Baltimore, Minneapolis, and St. Paul, the boards of education must submit their fiscal affairs to the approval and control of another authority.

As the administration of education and of its problems have grown in complexity and as the position of expert administrators has been evolved, the large board of education has come to be regarded as unwieldy and its discussions time-consuming. The tendency has accordingly been to reduce the size of boards to five, seven, or nine members; larger boards are found, but are unusual. The majority of the boards of education are elected, in a few cities at special elections which are considered advisable, not only because education is then kept distinct from party politics, but because they provide opportunities of bringing educational issues before the public; where boards are not elected, the members are appointed by the mayor or by the city council, and in a few instances by the court. There are no restrictions as to eligibility for membership of boards of education; virtually the only class which is in practice excluded is that of teachers, on the grounds that as members they might be expected to pass upon questions affecting their own interests and would thus be placed in a position of employer and employee at the same time, and that it is undesirable to have on boards individuals who, because of their professional familiarity with the problems to be discussed, could prevent the direct expression of lay public opinion or who would be tempted to interfere in the activities properly belonging to the superintendent. To the objection that the small size of the boards prevents the representation of minority groups, the answer is usually given that such groups always have access to the public and to the board by other methods than direct representation. The tenure of office of board members is usually four years. In order to secure continuity of policy, the appointments or elections are for overlapping terms.

The functions of boards of education are to determine policies presented by the superintendent; to select and appoint trained expert officials; to issue by-laws, rules and regulations; to select building sites and to determine in general the need of expansion of educational facilities; to pass on the budget; to formulate salary schedules; to approve, on the recommendation of the superintendent, courses of study, textbooks, and appointments, and to exercise general supervision over educational affairs. With the reduction in the size of the boards and the delegation of the administration to the expert superintendent and his staff, there has been a tendency to abolish standing committees, which, it is thought, are time-consuming and handicap the efficiency of administration. Special committees may, however, be appointed for the consideration of special questions, to be dissolved when their reports have been made. The chief function of a board is stated to be the selection of a well-trained and qualified executive responsible to and holding the confidence of the board. The administration of education in the last two decades has been developed on the analogy of big business; the board of education then assumes the position of a board of directors, responsible to the shareholders, in this case the public, and delegating the detailed administration to trained officials.

City school superintendent. It is on this principle that the position of the superintendent of schools and his staff has developed in city systems, a position which has become one of increasing importance as the programs of education have been expanded. With the increased importance of the position and clearer definition of status, opportunities have been developed during the last two decades for specialized training of administrative experts. Until such training was organized, it was usual for the superintendent to acquire his experience on the job. The appointment of superintendents is as a rule not required in all state school laws, nor are his powers and duties defined by them, nor with a few exceptions are the qualifications which he must have prescribed beyond the mere requirement that he must hold a teacher's certificate; the State of Minnesota requires superintendents to be college graduates holding a high school teacher's certificate and to have had about a year of professional study including courses in school administration. Generally superintendents are college or normal school graduates who have taught or have been principals of high schools before their appointment. Although opportunities for training are provided, it has not yet become an absolute requirement.[1]

The nature of the training provided for superintendents of schools (in the field of educational administration) is indicated in the following announcement of a one-year course offered at Teachers College, Columbia University:

The solution of administrative problems, laboratory work for the development of special techniques, and the visitation of school systems will occupy the major portion of the students' time in this course.

This course and the second major course for superintendents of schools present the field of educational administration for superintendents of schools on the basis of an analysis of the work of this professional executive. Problems which have actually occurred in the experience of superintendents of schools will be presented for solution by the students. The problems presented in this course will be those most commonly occurring in the experience of a superintendent of schools, and will vary from those found in a small school system to those which must be met in the larger communities.

Among the fields from which one or more problems will be selected for solution are the following: the relation of the National Government to education, the state's responsibility for education, the organization and functions of state departments of education, state support of education, local units of administration — the county, the township, the district and the special city district — the constitution of state, city and county boards of education and their relation to other governmental bodies — the organization of the administrative and supervisory corps with particular reference to line and staff organization — the organization of school systems; elementary schools, in-

---

[1] Among many other matters which have been the subjects of research, a study has been made of "Personality Traits of School Administrators," by Lide, E. S., in *Educational Research Bulletin*, Ohio State University, Vol. VII, No. 7 (April 3, 1929). Twenty-five judges expressed their opinion that among the most important traits are magnetism, punctuality, promptness, sociability, thoroughness, and industry; resourcefulness, leadership, breadth of interest, broadmindedness and intelligence received the fewest votes!

cluding a consideration of the platoon or duplicate school plan, departmental teaching and special classes; the classification and progress of children, group adjustments; the junior high school; the senior high school, special and comprehensive; continuation schools, vocational schools, adult education — the curricula — the development of courses of study — textbooks and materials of instruction — measuring the results of teaching — supervision — pupil accounting — the continuing census and attendance service — school health administration and physical education — statistical methods applied to the problems of administration — business administration, including the unit and dual control types of organization, fiscal dependence and independence, administrative offices, pay-roll procedure and accounting, supply management, cost finding and cost accounting, preservation and protection of school property and budget making — the training, selection, tenure, salaries, promotions and pensions of teachers, teachers organizations, professional ethics — the selection of school sites, building and equipment including plans and specifications, scoring the plant, building program, financing capital outlays, budgeting equipment, local, state and federal school finance, records and reports — relation of superintendent to the community, parent-teacher associations.

During the Spring Session students in the course will have opportunity, under the supervision of members of the staff, to visit elementary schools, junior high schools, senior high schools, vocational schools, special classes, administrative offices, and research bureaus, in school systems in and near New York City.

The course may be continued for a second year, when the same or similar topics are considered more intensively, and provision is made for participation by the students in the conduct of surveys or other special investigations. The students are expected in addition to follow courses selected from the fields of economics, government, taxation, social economy, statistics, comparative education, educational sociology, history of education, philosophy of education, educational psychology, or any of the other specialized branches of education.

The chief functions of the superintendent are to carry out the policies agreed upon by his board, to administer the system of schools entrusted to him, to supervise their successful operation, and to consider the needs for progressive development. His duties are educative in character; in relation to the board, he must keep the members informed of the progress and needs of the system and formulate policies for their consideration; in relation to the public, he must develop, not only among the patrons of the schools, but among all taxpayers, an intelligent interest in the work of the schools; in relation to his staff and teachers, he is required to coördinate their work and see that they carry out their assigned duties in an atmosphere which allows room for freedom and initiative. He must, in short, be the responsible leader in the educational development of his community, and since in the United States there is much less guidance or direction from the central authority than in any other country, he must be a student of education able to derive advantage from all the non-official sources of information, guidance, and help which have been described earlier.

As contrasted with European school systems, there is an absence in the United States of a division between different branches of education; each city may establish any type of education that is within its financial means from the kindergarten up to higher education, without the distinction between competing authorities, in which elementary education is left in the main to the local authority, secondary education is controlled more directly by the State, and vocational education is placed under the supervision of still another authority. Nor is there that distinction which prevails in England between local authorities according to the size of their population. In 1930 there were 2850 cities and towns with more than 2500 inhabitants; of these 2075 had less than 10,000 inhabitants, 519 between 10,000 and 30,000, 188 between 30,000 and 100,000, and 68 over 100,000. Any community classed as a city may, however, provide whatever schools in the educational ladder it can afford, without that differentiation between Part II and Part III authorities which is maintained in England. Thus the school law of the State of Pennsylvania (1927) provides in Section 401 that

The board of school directors in every school district in the Commonwealth shall establish, equip, furnish, and maintain a sufficient number of elementary public schools, in compliance with the provisions of this act, to educate every person, residing in such district between the ages of six and twenty-one years, who may attend; and may establish, equip, furnish, and maintain the following additional schools and departments for the education and recreation of persons residing in said district, which said additional schools or departments, when established, shall be an integral part of the public school system in such school district, and shall be so administered, namely: high schools, manual training schools, vocational schools, domestic science schools, evening schools, agricultural schools, kindergartens, libraries, museums, reading rooms, gymnasiums, playgrounds, schools for the blind, the deaf, and mentally deficient, truant schools, parental schools, schools for adults, public lectures — together with such other schools or educational departments as they, in their wisdom, may see proper to establish.[1]

[1] *School Law of the State of Pennsylvania*, 1927, p. 38.

The provision of educational facilities and all the necessary equipment depends accordingly upon "the wisdom" of each locality. It is on creating and developing this "wisdom" that the success of the superintendent of schools depends and, since educational development depends not so much upon the prescriptions of a state authority or on what is described in the United States as "overhead direction," each authority, depending upon its financial ability, endeavors to follow the leadership of the more progressive. It is significant in this connection that the theory of administration has been developed, not on the basis of abstract principles, but out of a comparison of what localities of different sizes can accomplish; city is pitted against city, the competitive spirit is aroused, and the reputation of cities depends, as may be seen in advertisements or booms which are indulged in from time to time, not on beauty of location or size, but upon the availability and supply of schools.

Publicity and education. It is accordingly one of the characteristics of American education that one of the important functions of the superintendent in the exercise of educational leadership is to develop and organize public demands and adapt the development of schools to meet them. Since standards and prescriptions are not defined by a central agency, except in such matters as compulsory attendance, length of school year, qualifications of teachers, buildings, and subjects which must be taught, the successful superintendent is he who is able to win his public over to new and progressive methods. If the American public is willing to devote money to education because of its faith in it, that faith must be constantly kept alive and increased by taking the public into partnership in the continuous and progressive reconstruction and shaping of education. If advertising has made big business in the United States, then publicity has made the progressive development and expansion of education possible. A central authority may by regulation dictate a line of policy, but in such cases the minimum requirements may often become the maximum with which a locality rests content; a local system, however, can only be changed, modified, and adapted to meet new ends as the administrator is able to command the confidence of his public and has its intelligent coöperation.

To arouse public intelligence the superintendent has at his disposal the periodical elections of members of the board of education, or the annual presentation of the budget, or occasional campaigns for bond issues for capital expenditures; or he may secure the coöperation of outside experts of national reputation to conduct surveys, comprehensive in scope, or for some special investigation (finance, buildings, curricula, etc.). More important than these means are the methods of constant publicity, of keeping education before the public through the press or by special publications as well as annual reports; not mere statistical records, but documents addressed to and intended for the enlightenment of the public. Publicity has been to education what advertising is to business. Some localities maintain an official specially appointed to take charge of publicity; elsewhere the superintendent himself assumes responsibility for it, and is always expected to use every opportunity of keeping the problem of education before the public and fraternal, business, service, religious, and other associations. In addition, the public is kept in close touch with the schools by the organization of school exhibits, special programs, education weeks, health weeks, music weeks, and "know-your-school" weeks. Finally, one of the most important methods of reaching the public has been the development and organization of parent-teacher associations definitely established to promote a better and more intelligent understanding of the work of the schools and to enlist the coöperation of parents in their development. Such associations are now found in every locality and have been organized into state organizations and a national society. Through lectures, conferences, reading, and discussion groups, parents are informed both on what the schools are doing and on what they might be expected to do to keep abreast of new and progressive movements. Closely associated with the parent-teacher organizations is the recent development of parent education which grew out of the recognition of the importance of the child's early years and of an intelligent start in the home. In the promotion of parent education there coöperate not only the parent-teacher associations, but child clinics, nursery schools, university education departments, special research centers, the Child Study Association of America, the National Congress of Parents and Teachers, and a number of magazines and books directed to the subject.

Administrative staff. An obvious result of the expansion of school systems and the multifarious ramifications of education from infancy to adulthood has been an increase in the responsibilities of the superintendent of schools and with it an increase in the size of the administrative staff to whom he can delegate the supervision of the many duties now involved in the administration of education. A city of the size of Denver, with a population of about a quarter of a million, has the following administrative staff: superintendent of schools, an auditor, an attorney, a secretary of the board of education, a deputy superintendent, two assistant superintendents, directors of curriculum, of elementary education, and measurements, and a staff of supervisors for libraries, industrial arts, home economics, art, health education, attendance, health service, the grades, doctors, dentists, nurses, and a business manager with assistants in charge of buildings, equipment, and supplies. The size of an administrative staff depends, of course, upon the number and types of schools provided and the enrollment of pupils. The Denver organization indicates the scope of administration which is being developed. The amount of authority that a superintendent delegates to the officials under him depends upon his own good sense; in some cities he assumes direct control over all details, while in others his chief function is to coördinate their activities and to encourage the exercise of freedom and responsibility on the part of the staff members whom he regards as specialists. Ultimately he is responsible for their conduct of office, as he is originally for their selection and recommendation to his board of education for appointment. There are a few cities in which the responsibility for administration is divided between the superintendent of schools, who is placed in charge of all educational and instructional matters, and a business manager, who has supervision of buildings, equipment, supplies, and financial matters; occasionally a third executive official, the chief engineer, is placed in charge of all matters relating to buildings. Divided responsibility of this kind is in general regarded as unsound and detrimental to the authority of the superintendent, who, according to the best theory and practice of administration, should "be directly responsible to the board of education for the efficient operation of all school functions of the board of education," including the administration of its business affairs, for the management of which a business manager or assistant superintendent, under the direction of the superintendent, should be appointed.

The superintendent may have, in addition to the staff of experts already described, a bureau of research, to assist him in the study of educational problems. Since the first establishment of such a bureau of research in Baltimore in 1912, about seventy cities have organized such departments for the conduct of investigations and research. The activities of such bureaus vary and may include some or all of the following types of study: classification of pupils, development and application of intelligence and achievement tests, curriculum revision, preparation and preservation of records and reports, study and selection of textbooks, finance and budget, vocational guidance, organization of special classes and psychiatric clinics, publicity, and any other of the great multiplicity of problems which present themselves in a large system of schools.

The participation of teachers in administration is almost negligible. The theory of administration is opposed to the inclusion of teachers on boards of education, while other methods of enlisting their coöperation have not been extensively developed. Teachers' councils have been established to assist the superintendent in an advisory capacity in less than one hundred cities and their influence on educational affairs is slight. That teachers should participate directly in administration is nowhere advocated and would indeed be undesirable, but that advantage of their professional experience is not taken more extensively is significant perhaps of the application of principles of industrial management to education. To some extent the status enjoyed by teachers is due to their poor training in the past, a condition which is being rapidly corrected, and to their uncertainty of tenure; in part it is due to the fact that superintendents have created other opportunities, through conferences and institutes, for meeting teachers. The importance of permanent organizations which should serve as channels of communication and consultation between teachers and superintendents has not been fully recognized,[1] with the result that teachers' organizations tend in some cities to resort to political methods, lobbying, and pressure on board members to bring their views to the front. A new tendency is, however, percep-

[1] The establishment of teachers' councils was extensively discussed from 1919 to 1924. A few had been organized before this period (Dallas, Texas, 1909; Boston, 1910; Chicago, 1913; and Cleveland, Ohio, 1917). In 1924 the number of teachers' councils had reached 86; since that date interest in their existence has waned, because of a suspicion that the sponsors of the movement were "disgruntled and radical teachers, who feel sure that they, and all other teachers, are being ground down by an oppressive system." (E. E. Lewis, *Personnel Problems of the Teaching Staff*, p. 388 f., New York, 1925.) The assumption of the leadership of the movement by the Federation of Teachers' Councils, which amalgamated itself with the American Federation of Labor contributed considerably in arousing this suspicion. See Ortman, E. J., *Teacher Councils, the Organized Means for Securing the Coöperation of all Workers in the School* (Montpelier, Vermont, 1923).

tible in the methods which have been adopted in the last decade for curriculum revision. In the past (and still quite generally), curricula, courses of study, lists of textbooks, and even methods of instruction have been prepared and issued by the administrative staff. With the improvement in the professional preparation of teachers and the realization that the coöperation of teachers should be secured in matters in which they are qualified to pass opinions, they have in a few centers (Denver, Colorado, and Houston, Texas, are outstanding examples) been called upon to coöperate in the making of curricula and courses of study. This practice may or may not represent the inauguration of a new policy to secure increased participation, where such participation is warranted, by the teachers. It is, however, characteristic of American administration to emphasize guidance, organization, dictation, and leadership by the administrator, and the putting into practice of orders and prescriptions by the teachers, since provision for consultation and advice is rarely made even in individual schools, in which the principal is the administrative head and the teachers "his" staff. That there are dangers in such an interpretation of administrative efficiency is obvious. It has meant that school systems derive their character from the ability and competence of their superintendents and that the school as a living institution is often lacking in that personality and uniqueness which are derived from the enjoyment of initiative and freedom on the part of their principals and teachers. The emphasis on administration is even carried so far that there are some who would train prospective superintendents of schools immediately upon graduation from college and without any preliminary experience in the actual work of the classroom.

Educational finance. The cost of education is borne by funds provided by the Federal Government, the states, and the local subdivisions (school districts, towns, townships, counties, and cities). Less than one per cent of the revenue for educational purposes are contributed by the Federal Government, and the contributions from the states amount to less than seventeen per cent. Hence the burden of educational expenditures falls upon the local areas. Changes in the distribution of population, economic shifts, the development of large industrial centers, and the decline of agriculture have all resulted in producing serious inequalities in the ability of localities to maintain schools out of their own resources. That these inequalities are striking is revealed by statistical investigations showing the length of school year, the salaries of teachers, the per capita cost per child, the amount of wealth available for the education of each child, and the provision of educational opportunities beyond a bare minimum. To these facts may be added the differences in the character of school buildings ranging from richly equipped palaces to hovels with barely any equipment at all. As a result of these inequalities, whereby the education available for a child is determined by the residence of his parents, proposals have been made for increased participation of the Federal Government to the extent of increased support of schools, proposals which up to the present have not yet met with success, and for the provision of increased state support sufficient to guarantee a minimum educational program for every child in the country.

State funds are derived from a variety of sources, the most general form being a tax on property. To these are added other sources, such as taxes on income, corporations, inheritance, business and occupations, severance on all or some natural products, tobacco, and other miscellaneous items. Taking the country as a whole there is no uniformity of practice in the type of tax which is levied; there is, however, widespread agreement that a general tax on property is unsound, partly because of inequalities in values and partly because of possible dishonesty in the assessments. From the general funds obtained by any one or several of the methods indicated, funds are appropriated for educational purposes. In addition to funds from taxes, thirty-seven States use the interest from permanent funds for educational purposes, but the amount derived from this source forms a small part, from one to thirteen per cent, of the total funds available. In some States certain taxes are earmarked for educational purposes. In practically all of the States the funds for education are derived from appropriations made by the legislatures. Generally a direct educational tax is preferred to appropriations, since it guarantees a stable revenue and increases automatically with the increase in population, while the periodical, usually biennial, request for appropriations is apt to mean the intrusion of political considerations into education.

The methods of apportioning funds to the local authorities for education vary from simple grants based upon the school census to grants based on elaborate formulas intended to equalize the burden and to guarantee a minimum program of education for each child.

These methods include apportionment: (1) on the basis of the number of children between the ages of six and twenty-one, whether they are in school or not; (2) on the basis of the number of pupils enrolled in the schools; (3) on the basis of average daily attendance; (4) on the basis of aggregate attendance; (5) on the basis of minimum salaries for teachers, either the actual number employed or the number needed for a prescribed number of pupils; and (6) on a combination of two or more of these methods; in one state (New Jersey) the amount of taxes paid by a district is returned to it. In an analysis prepared by Professor F. H. Swift (*Federal and State Policies in Public School Finance in the United States*, p. 247)[1] the chief methods of apportionment used were distributed as follows in 1925–26:

School census: Alabama, Arkansas, Colorado, Connecticut, Georgia, Idaho, Indiana, Iowa, Kansas, Kentucky, Louisiana, Maine, Maryland, Michigan, Mississippi, Montana, Nebraska, New Mexico, North Dakota, Oklahoma, Oregon, South Dakota, Texas, Utah, and Virginia.

Enrollment or attendance for a fixed period: Delaware and Minnesota.

Average daily attendance: Arizona, Florida, Illinois, Rhode Island, and Tennessee.

Weighted aggregate attendance: Washington.

Per teacher: Massachusetts, Missouri, New Hampshire, New York, North Carolina, Ohio, Pennsylvania, South Carolina, Vermont, West Virginia, Wisconsin, and Wyoming.

Per teacher unit: California and Nevada.

In addition, grants apportioned by these methods may be supplemented by grants to districts with low taxable valuations or to encourage the provision of expanded programs, such as high schools, consolidated schools, transportation, libraries, special classes, and instruction in trade, agriculture, and home economics; a few States provide aid for the cost of buildings.

The combination of various methods is based on a desire to assist school districts according to their financial ability and the effort they put forth, a principle which experts on the subject have pronounced unsound. There has in the last decade developed considerable unrest on the whole problem of educational finance. From one point of view the existing methods of state aid have been found ineffective in reducing inequalities; from another it is argued that, since education is a state affair and in the interests of the State, the State should assume a larger share of the burden ranging, according

[1] Boston, Ginn & Co., 1932.

to a number of proposals, from forty to seventy-five per cent. The one remedy to which all investigations of the subject point is that the chief duty of the State is to adopt an equalization policy which will guarantee a minimum program of education for every child, allowing any locality which has the resources to do so to go as far as it pleases beyond this minimum. There still remains the problem of defining such a minimum program, whether it is to be defined by the state authority on abstract principles, or on the basis of cost per pupil, or cost per teacher, or some combination of these. One plan, which has generally commended itself and was adopted first in New York State in 1925, is that devised by Professor Paul R. Mort for measuring the educational need of a community which should serve as the basis for state aid. The measure of school burdens is the "weighted pupil" — that is, "a pupil taught in the type of community and in a school of the size (average daily attendance) within a range in which the cost of providing a uniform program remains practically unaffected by any increase or decrease in average daily attendance." The minimum program of education which the State should undertake to make generally accessible includes the types of schools already available, and the provision of such additional facilities as may be necessary to carry out the program. The cost of the minimum program is determined by the current expense per "weighted pupil" or unit of need (that is, allowance per teacher on the basis of the number of pupils assigned to him) in communities of the State which have an average amount of wealth for each pupil. By its policy of equalizing the amount of money available to provide an education program, the State undertakes in addition to other forms of aid to bring all localities at least up to the level of the average communities already meeting this standard.

The development and extension of such methods of aiding localities must ultimately mean the assumption by the States of an increased share of the cost of education and consequently increased control. In the mean time localities continue to bear the major part of the cost, which is met by local taxation. The authorities for levying local taxes are generally municipal agencies other than the boards of education; the taxes may be collected by the district or by the county auditor and treasurer and returned to the district, or, in cities, by the local tax collector and placed at the disposal of the board of education if fiscally independent and preparing its own budget.

The most common source of local revenue is a tax on property. Revenues may be derived from other than local taxes and state aid in the form of gifts and bequests, interest on funds or bank deposits, and tuition for the education of non-residents, but these are inconsiderable in amount. Capital expenditures — as, for example, for the construction of buildings — are met by bond issues.

Conclusion. The administration and organization of education in the United States have developed in response to changing needs based on the traditional faith in education and the principle that educational opportunities should be provided for all. In this respect the nearest analogy is the recent evolution in England, with the difference that the significance of education at public expense is a development of the twentieth century. The two countries again have in common a strong faith in local autonomy which is only gradually giving place to increasing participation and supervision by a central authority in the interests of all. As contrasted with some centralized systems, there is an absence in the United States of a conscious political philosophy which would justify control by the State; if the authority of the State is increasing, it is due to a desire to remove inequalities in the amount of funds available for education and to equalize opportunities. As this authority increases, there must be developed some principles upon which a due allocation of powers and duties between the State and localities may be based, or upon which will be defined the scope of state control and prescription and the degree to which initiative and responsibility can be left to the localities. In time this may mean an increase in the size of local areas and the disappearance of the struggling district system. What may be accomplished in areas which are adequate in size and in command of adequate resources is already indicated in the development and progress of city systems, in which a body of administrative principles and practices has been evolved, again not on the basis of any philosophy or theory, but in response to changing conditions. Nor has this progress been dictated by central authorities; it has in itself been the result of educating the public, whose coöperation has been made easier because of the aggregation of wealth in the cities. In the absence of strong central authorities, educational advancement has been stimulated by the spirit of emulation and competition. Indeed, it may be affirmed that the whole body of knowledge, known as educational administration, has been built up by a comparative study of what the market will bear; what one system can accomplish, it has been argued, another of the same size and resources can achieve. Standards have been built up not on the basis of theory but of practical achievement.

With the enlargement and expansion of the scope of education and its supply, there has developed the position of the superintendent of schools who has applied to the vast enterprise principles of administrative efficiency borrowed from big business. If the administration of American education is open to criticism, it is not because these principles are unsound or inapplicable, but because an adequate distinction has not been made between those aspects of administration which can be mechanized and reduced to standards and routine and those which concern those human relations which are properly called education. There is a very real weakness in carrying the analogy between the administration of education and the administration of big business too far; in the one the whole machinery must be so organized that waste motion is eliminated and the result is a standardized, marketable product; in the other the mechanical organization is important only to the extent that it removes difficulties and leaves the well-trained teacher free but responsible in carrying out the task for which the school is created. To standardize costs, accounting, buildings, equipment, reports and records is one thing and necessary for efficiency; to attempt in the interests of efficiency to standardize curricula, courses of study, textbooks, and even methods of instruction by administrative procedures and to measure the results by standardized tests, which should serve as guides rather than ends, is another, and tends to defeat the purposes for which education exists — the liberation of the individual, the teacher as much as the pupil. Between bureaucratic control and methods of efficiency as applied to the educative and instructional process there is on the whole not much to choose. It is doubtful whether much is gained by applying industrial terminology to educational administration, if the school becomes a plant and the teacher the operator of the machine. And yet the situation can be understood in the light of the history of American education and the inadequacy of teacher preparation until recently. In the provision of the fabric of education and the provision of variety of opportunities, the administration of education in the American cities has a record of which it may well be proud. But it is still true that further progress must look to increased decentralization based upon the professional competence of the teachers, for the best type of administration is that which is least obtrusive and in which the aim of efficiency is to release those forces which will make for the best education, for efficiency cannot be its own end, and, if it exists at all, it must exist in the interests of the children to be educated and of the society for which they are to be educated. If American administration has accomplished much in analyzing the units to be educated, as compared with most other countries much still remains for it to do in defining the aims and objectives from the point of view of a social and national purpose.

CHAPTER VI

ELEMENTARY EDUCATION

The tradition of elementary education. The history of elementary education, more than any other branch of education, is an epitome of the social and political history of each nation. In it are reflected the place of the Church and of religion, the gradual supersession of the influence of the Church by the State, the changes in social organization and the status of social classes, the gradual emergence of nationalism and of nationalist indoctrination, the rise of the working classes and an appreciation of the importance of economic life and organization, and the gradual development of an appreciation of the worth of the individual as a human being, and therefore of the meaning of democracy. From another point of view, the development of the elementary school represents all the changes which have taken place, not only in social values, but in the attitude to knowledge and literacy, in the kind of knowledge that is of most worth, in the meaning of intelligence and the methods of its development, in the relation of mental and physical activities, in the learning process, and, in general, in the concept of what makes a whole individual.

Elementary education in the nineteenth century was everywhere, except in the United States, regarded as an instrument for training the children of the masses, the lower classes, to be content with the position in which it had pleased the Lord to place them. Through instruction in the elements of literacy, the three R's combined with religious instruction, it was expected that society would find a protection against immorality, superstition, and crime. As the spirit of nationalism developed, another aim, training in loyalty and patriotism, was added. The purposes of the elementary school were determined by a deep-rooted faith in knowledge as power and knowledge as virtue; literacy was regarded as the best panacea for all social ills. Hence the wide acceptance of Guizot's slogan, "Open a school and close a jail." Through the acquisition of knowledge, the individual was to acquire, not merely the skills and techniques which would adjust him to his environment, but a training in character. As formulated by Herbart, the theory of education was that knowledge provides the basis of ideas and ideas make the man. The type and amount of knowledge considered desirable to secure these ends were selected by the adult generation without any attempt to take into account the stages of immaturity or maturity of the educand, the pupil to be educated, a principle which has survived to the present in the French statement that the pupil in the elementary school should learn those things of which no individual should be ignorant. To the objection that a program or curriculum based on this principle was too difficult, the answer was that the very difficulties themselves were valuable, since they called for effort, hard work, and perseverance, which are moral virtues and so provide a training for character, and, in addition, they train the mind. Whether from the moral or the psychological point of view, the fundamental basis upon which education rested was discipline.

Gradually the curriculum of the elementary school was expanded under the influence of Auguste Comte and the positivists, of Herbart, and of Herbert Spencer; to this expansion the emergence of the working classes, the rapid growth of industry in factories, the development of adult education, the rise of the press and the supply of cheaper books, and the increase in the means and methods of communication also contributed. But the emphasis continued to be upon knowledge, and the expansion of the elementary school curriculum meant additions and accretions to the information which was to be imparted. The increasing difficulties of this situation were met by the development of methods which would simplify and facilitate the acquisition or the learning process. The good pupil was the one whose mind was well filled with the knowledge, facts, and information supplied by the teacher or obtained from books, as tested by annual examinations. The result of such an education, which was to provide a store of knowledge as a preparation for life, was an emphasis on intellectualism, bookishness, memorization, repetition, and discipline. In the development of a perfect technique for successfully carrying out the principles of such an education, the German system attracted widespread attention.

The defects of this education were that it ignored the nature and needs of the individual, accepted a static concept of the culture to be transmitted to the new generation, and was unrelated to the changing demands of society. Under such a system the successful teacher was he who faithfully carried out the prescriptions of a detailed course of study and produced good results which could be measured by examinations. In such a system there was no room for the teacher who sought to develop the individual as an all-round personality. The distinction between the two methods was to be found in every country in the distinction between elementary and secondary education: the function of the former was to impart a certain amount of information; the function of the latter to train students and scholars in methods of acquiring information. The work of the former was completed, except where it was continued in part-time education more directly related to vocational purposes, when the pupils were released from compulsory school attendance; the work of the latter was looked upon as a foundation for further study and the cultivation of new interests. The distinction between the two was not merely one of class, but of quality, a distinction expressed in Germany by the different connotation of the words *Akademiker* and *Nicht-Akademiker*; or in the connotation of the French *esprit primaire*, the elementary school mind, as distinguished from the mind trained by secondary or higher education.

Social status of the elementary school. The opening of the twentieth century witnessed the beginning of a changing attitude to elementary education. The United States had already given an example of an educational system in which the elementary school constituted the lower part of a continuous system, although in general character it did not differ from the elementary school elsewhere. The changes in Europe are moving in the direction of the American system — the recognition of the elementary school as the school which provides a common educational foundation for all, to be followed at the next stage by differentiated types of secondary education. This movement, which is in its infancy, is accompanied by a movement to change the terminology and to avoid the connotations which have grown up around the term "elementary" education. The first stage is to be called "primary," to be followed by "secondary" education. Russia and Italy have adopted the ladder system, an organization in which the primary school is the common foundation for all; Germany requires all pupils during the first four years of compulsory education to attend the common foundation schools (*Grundschule*); France, since 1925, requires the same curriculum and course of study to be followed in all primary schools, whether public or private; in England the movement to reorganize the whole system on the foundation of a primary school is well on its way in the principle stated by Mr. Stanley Baldwin that

> One of the strongest bonds of union between men is a common education. England has been the poorer that in her national system of schooling she has not in the past fostered this fellowship of the mind. The classification of our schools has been on the lines of social rather than educational distinctions.... The great new fabric is already taking shape; the outworn "elementary" structure is at last being superseded.[1]

The elementary school and the progress of educational theory. As democratic institutions develop, the elementary school as an institution for the education of the masses is changing to an institution for the common education of all. But the development of a richer and more comprehensive appreciation of the significance of democracy implies more than a change in the social status of the elementary school as an organization; because it connotes a change in the attitude to the individual as an independent, responsible personality and recognizes his worth as a human being, it implies also a change in the character of the internal organization and work of the elementary school. This change, which has accompanied the broader conception of democracy, has been supported by changes in educational theory and in the sciences upon which it is based. The metaphysical, structural psychology, on which the faculty psychology of the nineteenth century was based, has yielded to physiological and genetic psychology, directed to the scientific study of the individual as a whole. A new educational philosophy has undermined the importance attached to knowledge *quâ* knowledge and stressed the principle that its worth and value can only be measured by its reality, meaningfulness, and use to the learner. On the side of the learning process, the result of a combination of the new psychology and the new philosophy has been to direct attention to the importance of active participation by the learner in place of the passive memorization and learning which had characterized the traditional school. The individual, in other words, learns through his own experience — through sensory, perceptual, motor, and emotional activities; he must be a free and active participant in his own education, and the function of the school is to provide an environment which will introduce the learner to a variety of many-sided experiences, growing out of and

---

[1] In his "Message on a New Step in Education"; see *Educational Yearbook, 1928*, of the International Institute, Teachers College, Columbia University, p. 39 (New York, 1929).

related to his interests, needs, and capacities. Not knowledge for its own sake, but knowledge related to life, methods of thinking and criticism, the acquisition of the tools and technique of acquiring experience, interpreting it, and using it as an instrument of control should be the aim of education. The definition of the content of school work in terms of experience means the inclusion of activities which in the traditional scheme, if they were given any consideration at all, were regarded as subordinate to intellectual training — music, fine arts, drama, physical and manual activities.

The individual and society. As an immediate reaction against traditional practices and methods, the new psychology and philosophy were seized upon by extremists as a justification for abolishing all controls in the school — external discipline, curriculum fixed in advance, extrinsic standards and tests. The advocates of freedom, guided by respect for the child's individuality, were willing to follow the child whithersoever he might lead. Experiments, conducted on the principle that the only true freedom is that which originates in the true self of the individual, free from the control of material or quasi-material forces and laws, have been valuable because they illustrated the pitfalls of the extremist position and drew attention to the fact that the individual represents only one datum in the educative process.

The individual is born with certain tendencies, abilities, and potentialities; the function of education is to provide the environment and the experiences by which the individual will grow into a responsible member of society, responsible not merely for his own self-realization, but also for the realization of the best in the society to which he belongs. The school is not merely a vacuum for the spontaneous self-expression of the individual; it is itself a social organization which mediates between the individual and society and provides opportunities for sharing in activities which society regards as valuable. It may be objected that the traditional school performed this function, but the objection is not valid, because the activities of the traditional school were selected without any consideration for the individual's interests or capacities and he was adjusted to them through discipline and authority. The only activities which can be of value in developing the individual as a socially responsible personality are those which represent the major aspects of culture of the society in which he lives, but they must be meaningful and of significance to the learner according to the stage of his development; only in this sense can he become an active agent in acquiring mastery of his environment. This means further that the teacher must be, not a dictator of lessons to be learned, but a guide and organizer of the activities in which the pupil is to engage and through which he realizes himself.

Even when the claims of activities which are meaningful to the individual and of value to society as representing a part of its culture are accepted, there are those who fear that a definite program in the mind of the teacher — or a curriculum fixed in advance — would militate against the self-expression and creative originality of the pupil. The advocates of self-expression and creative originality are content with anything which they regard as the direct result of the pupil's own experience, forgetting that such immature experience needs guidance, that expression requires training in rules and techniques, and that for the immature their reaction to any experience is creative. The emphasis of this group is always on the process rather than on the acquisition or the result. For this position, as in the radical interpretations of freedom, the reason is to be found in a swing of the pendulum away from the traditional practices of formalism, mechanical learning without comprehension, dictation, and indoctrination. The compromise will be found in a proper adjustment between activities or curriculum closely related to the developing interests of the pupils and expanding in range and richness with their own development and active methods of instruction and learning to merge into the accepted values of society, or, to put it in another way, in a reconciliation between freedom and responsibility. The so-called child-centered school is meaningless unless it implies that the child is but the starting-point of a process which is guided by the teacher.

Early education. The forces which have led to a change in the function and organization of the elementary school, because they have directed attention to a consideration of the child, have equally stressed the importance of the early years. The development of the individual is determined, not only by his nature, but also by his nurture or environment. Compulsory education generally begins at about the age of six; some countries have provided schools for children before this age, but the infant schools of the nineteenth century, whether in England, France, or Italy, were regarded as preparatory to the elementary schools and introduced formal subjects in a rudimentary form; the kindergarten, which pointed in another direction and laid stress on games and activities, whether Froebelian or neo-Froebelian, were mainly private institutions for children of the well-to-do, and the Montessori method of auto-education came still later. Influenced by the kindergarten and Montessori methods, by the new psychology, and by the recognition of the importance of health and good physical habits, the infant schools were gradually transformed and more attention was given to play, games, and activities of children in a healthy environment. Still more recently, as a result partly of the contribution of psychoanalysis and its insistence on the dangers of early miseducation, and partly of a movement from considerations of social welfare to provide for the children of the working classes an environment comparable with that enjoyed by children of the well-to-do, the nursery schools have been established and are exerting an influence on the character of the educative care given to very young children. Similar attention is being given to the stage which precedes nursery and infant schools; care is being given in institutions (*crèches*, *Krippen*, children's homes, day nurseries) to children as soon as they can be left by their parents. All these movements represent a realization that education is a lifelong process, and all the influences, physical and spiritual, that affect the individual determine the character of his development.

Curriculum and courses of study. As long as the function of the elementary school was restricted to imparting a fixed amount of knowledge, the three R's to which enrichment subjects were later added, and as long as it was believed that the same content would serve all educative purposes — training of character, development of skills and techniques, and mental training — the problem of who should prepare the curriculum and courses of study was relatively unimportant. Because teachers were inadequately trained, or because they were trained merely to carry into practice what was prescribed, or because the State definitely intended to use the schools for purposes of nationalistic indoctrination, curriculum and courses of study have in the main been prepared and prescribed by a central authority. Even in the United States, where central control was negligible, they were prepared in each area by the administrative officers, and in England, where the central authority was in the main an agency for the inspection of schools and for distributing grants, the work of the elementary schools was dominated by the annual examinations conducted by the inspector.

The movement for greater freedom for the child has been accompanied by its correlative, greater freedom for the teacher. If the child and his interests are to be the starting-point, and if education is the process of understanding and mastering one's environment, then the work of the school must be related to both, and a curriculum or course of study uniform for a large area becomes an anomaly. Hence the tendency is at present to abandon the prescribed curriculum and course of study, and to issue suggestions which serve as a basis for adapting the work of the school to the locality in which it is situated. Hence, also, a movement for the better preparation of teachers on a higher standard. France and the United States alone have retained prescribed courses of study, but in the former country permission is given to the teachers to make adaptations to local needs, and in the latter there is a tendency to enlist the participation of teachers in the preparation of courses of study to be adopted, however, in all the schools of a system. In England, the German states, the Soviet Republics, and Italy, the practice of issuing suggestions instead of prescribed regulations has been adopted.

Freedom to adapt the curriculum and course of study to the needs and interests of pupils and to the local environment furnishes only the starting-point from which the work of the school is to reach out until the pupils are introduced to the larger environment of the society, the nation, and the world in which they live. Such culture is obviously colored by the history and traditions of the country in which it has been developed. With the development of the nationalistic spirit in the nineteenth century, it was further colored by an attempt to utilize it for nationalistic indoctrination out of narrow loyalties. The development of patriotism is important and cannot be denied a place in education, but unless it involves at the same time a series of loyalties to the home and the social institutions of which the pupil is a member, and with them a sense of service and a realization that culture and civilization have been a collective achievement in which one's own nation has borne a share along with others, such training will result in a nationalistic spirit which looks upon other nations with suspicion and hatred. The narrow type of patriotic education has not disappeared, but much has been achieved already in so far as it is possible today to talk in the schools of international understanding and of a common humanity based on common knowledge and devoted to common ends.

Methods of instruction. Education, accordingly, must have a definite end or purpose: to base it solely on the growth of the individual and his interests is to court anarchy; to impose on the individual content whose significance he does not understand but which he learns, in the superficial sense of memorizing, is to court failure. The tendency today is to bring the two together — the individual with his interests and capacities, and the culture which he is to make his own. The method which mediates between the two is the activity of the learner motivated by recognition of meanings. The school is accordingly being changed from a passive, learning school (*Lernschule*), which cultivated verbalism and the use of books, into an active school (*Arbeitsschule*; *école active*) in which the pupil is an active participant in the learning process, no longer limited to the acquisition of knowledge and information from books or from the teacher, but engaging in a variety of activities which train him in the use of hand and eye, give him opportunities for the exercise of his mind and body, and do not neglect the development of his emotions through æsthetic experiences.

Such are the general tendencies in the progress of elementary education. The conflict between the old school and the new school has not yet been settled; but as the following sections will show, the new tendencies are dominant in every country, with the exception of France, with her strong convictions that the function of the school is to transmit those things of which no individual should be ignorant and with a proud faith in her own cultural traditions, all the other countries which are discussed in the following sections illustrate the new tendencies. There are differences, to be sure, which result from national traditions, national characteristics, and national values, and from the conceptions of the State and society in relation to the individual [1] — Russia uses her school system as an instrument of indoctrination in socialistic principles; in Italy education is dominated by Fascist ideals; Germany and England, but England less consciously than Germany, stress the importance of the cultural heritage; the United States, because there has not yet been developed

[1] See Chapter III.

any deep or profound conviction or faith in a national culture. emphasizes the individual more and is restlessly searching for the best means and methods appropriate for the promotion of his growth and development.

The present a stage of transition. Elementary education is thus in a stage of transition full of uncertainties and groping for new expression. The preparation for teachers in this process of reconstruction has not yet been adequately adapted to the new situation, except perhaps in Germany and in a few English training colleges. This much has been achieved, that the nineteenth-century tradition is no longer accepted as adequate to present conditions. Science has accumulated a vast store of knowledge about the nature of the individual, even though complete agreement has not yet been (and perhaps never will be) reached on the subject. Much thought is being given to the nature of the content of the elementary school curriculum and to the process of instruction. The standardized methods and formulas of the nineteenth century have given way to countless experiments which will bear fruit in the future. How much of these results, and whether the genuinely valuable aspects of an education can be submitted to objective measurement, is another question which only the future will answer. Upon this, however, the tendencies which will be described in the following sections are agreed, that the purpose of elementary education is to lay the foundations for, or to initiate the development of, an independent individual, as a member of society, trained to think and feel, and conscious of his responsibilities, with a mastery through appreciative understanding over himself and his environment. The individual with his original nature is the starting-point, society and all that it means with its culture and civilization, and the world of nature and of man, furnish the environment from which the educative experiences, or curriculum content, are derived. That the school can go beyond this and be used as an instrument for the reorganization and reconstruction of society not even a Russian educator, like Pinkevitch, accepts, ready though he is to believe in the theory that education can change human nature.

We are not supporters of the thesis that an existing society can be changed through the school. To make the school the embryo of a future socialistic order is impossible for the simple reason that the school cannot be independent of its environment. Moreover, the school should be most intimately related to the contemporary life; it should study, observe, and participate in an organized way in that life. The school will of course reflect the existing situation; and the children because of their imitativeness and suggestibility, are naturally influenced by their surroundings.[1]

To adopt the French phrase, "the school is the school," an institution created by society to perpetuate itself; but the school must be responsive to contemporary life if it is to save itself from the danger of becoming artificial and meaningless, formal and mechanical. The weakness of elementary education in the nineteenth century lay in the fact that it was directed solely to transmission of the acquired heritage and the perpetuation of existing social and political orders. Today the world finds itself in a stage of change and transition, still uncertain of the future, confronted with economic, national and international problems which it has never before in its history been called upon to solve, and standing at the beginning of an era in which every aspect of life is being affected by the advances of science whose progress is apparently unlimited. In the light of these conditions, education assumes a new function; the school becomes an instrument of reconstruction, not in the sense that it creates a new social order, but that it so equips the individual that he understands the world around him, has some appreciation of the civilization and culture which have made it what it is today, and with an interest, because of a sense of social responsibility, in contributing to its progress. This is the function of education in general, in which the elementary school is only one stage, but an important stage because its task is today to lay the foundations of a process which should continue through life. The elementary school can only interpret the life of the society which it serves, express the highest aspirations and ideals which society sets before itself; as an institution for creating a new social order, it would be meaningless, even if it were tolerated.

1. ENGLAND

History. Elementary education in England does not lend itself to easy classification by any convenient pedagogical formula. It cannot be described as conservative or progressive, but has in it the elements of both. It has none and yet has all of the characteristic features of other systems. It is not, like the French system, in-

[1] Pinkevitch, A. P., *The New Education in the Soviet Republic*, pp. 153 f. (New York, 1929).

spired by a deep-rooted passion for national culture, although its curriculum is founded on a belief in the value of the best that has been said and thought. Unlike the German system, it does not bear the stamp of any dominant philosophy or theory of education, but is ready to tolerate any experiment in curriculum or method which a teacher can justify. It is not dominated, like Russian or Italian education, by any particular political or economic or social ideology, and yet is able to cultivate loyalty to ideals of government and democracy. Finally, while it is not governed, like the American, by efficiency as an aim and encourages variety and freedom, with all its vagueness it is administratively efficient. While England, like France, can point to a distinguished list of educational statesmen — Bentham, John Stuart Mill, Lord Brougham, Sir James Kay-Shuttleworth, Lord Shaftesbury, W. E. Forster, Sir Michael Sadler, and H. A. L. Fisher — with a few outstanding exceptions (J. J. Findlay and Sir Percy Nunn) she has on the whole not made any important contribution to the philosophy of education; the progress of education has not been influenced by great theories, although some influence has been exercised, but as a rule indirectly, by Pestalozzi, Froebel, Herbart, Kerschensteiner, and John Dewey. Since the abolition of the "payment-by-results" system in the nineties, elementary, like secondary education, has relied upon the personality of the teacher more than on nationally accepted theories or governmental rules and regulations.

The English system of elementary education had its origin in the philanthropic and religious movements at the beginning of the nineteenth century and was provided until 1870 by voluntary organizations. To some of these the State began in 1833 to give financial assistance, which soon led to the establishment of a national Education Department (1839) and the introduction of a system of inspection on the principle of "no grants without inspection." It was not until 1870 that public authorities, school boards, were permitted by the Education Act of that year to establish elementary schools out of local rates, where the supply was inadequate. There was thus created a dual system of elementary schools, some established and maintained by voluntary organizations, mainly denominational, others provided by publicly elected school boards, which were not permitted to give denominational religious instruction. Although the schools under the dual system were intended for children

ELEMENTARY EDUCATION

of the lower orders, the well-to-do providing for the education of their children at home or in private schools, fees were charged in all schools, with exemption for the poor, until they were abolished in 1891. Compulsory attendance at school was not introduced until 1876, the Act of 1870 having empowered local authorities to pass by-laws requiring children to attend school between the ages of five and twelve; the Act of 1876 made education compulsory up to the age of ten and based the employment of children from ten to fourteen on the attainment of certain scholastic standards; in 1900 local authorities were permitted to pass by-laws requiring full-time attendance up to the age of fourteen; in 1914 there were still 70,000 children of school age who were engaged in half-time employment.

The aim of the elementary schools was to impart the essentials of an education, the three R's mainly and religious instruction. The work of the schools was regulated first by inspection, and, after the publication by Mr. Robert Lowe, vice-president of the Committee of Council on Education, of the Revised Code in 1862, by annual examinations of all the pupils conducted by the government inspectors. The government grants were based on the results of the examinations. For thirty years, until the practice was abolished in 1895, and for some years following the abolition, the chief features of elementary education were moulded by the payment-by-results system with its emphasis on drill and discipline, repetition and memorization. While the effects were in the main harmful to the progress of education, the system did not fail at the same time to stress the importance of the ideals of accuracy and thoroughness. Nor was the curriculum of the schools restricted altogether within the limits of a few subjects; some subjects were obligatory in all schools, others were optional for pupils above the first class (Standard I), and others, known as "specifics," were optional for pupils in the last three years of the course (Standards IV to VI);[1] a Seventh Standard and even a so-called ex-Seventh standard were added after 1882.

The larger industrial centers, in which elementary education was administered by enlightened school boards, were unwilling, in the absence of an adequate supply of secondary education, to restrict

---

[1] The obligatory subjects were the three R's and needlework (for girls); the optional subjects were English, geography, history, and elementary science; the specifics included algebra, geometry, languages (English literature, elements of Latin, French, or German), domestic economy and cooking.

the opportunities of abler boys and girls, and not only added the extra standards, but also organized higher grade or higher elementary schools which gave a form of lower secondary education. The refusal of a government auditor to sanction expenditure by the London school board on subjects which were not strictly elementary (the Cockerton Case), combined with the universal recognition, following the *Report* of the Bryce Commission, of the need of a system of public secondary education, precipitated a situation which made a revision of the education law inevitable. The elementary school of the nineteenth century had outlived its usefulness. The voluntary organizations were no longer able to secure adequate funds to maintain their schools, and more and better education in a genuinely national system was demanded. The Board of Education was created in 1899 by a combination of a number of national departments concerned with various aspects of education, and in 1902 the administrative organization was changed and the provision of secondary education out of public funds, local and state, was made possible.[1] A new spirit had already been injected into elementary education before this by the abolition of the payment-by-results system and the substitution of inspection for examinations.

PRESENT SYSTEM

Provision of schools. By the Act of 1902 the dual system of elementary schools was continued, but placed under one authority — the county, county borough, municipal borough, or urban district councils. In areas which are unorganized for educational purposes — that is, rural areas — elementary education is under the control of the county authority. Each of the authorities mentioned is responsible for the maintenance of both the denominational and the strictly public schools. The difference between the denominational, voluntary, or, more usually, "non-provided" schools and the "provided" schools is that the buildings of the former are the property of a body of trustees and rented to the education authority at a charge sufficient to cover the cost of reasonable "wear and tear"; the trustees retain certain rights in the appointment of the teachers with respect to their ability to give religious instruction of their denomination. The "provided" schools are built and maintained wholly by the education authority. Both types of schools now constitute parts of the public system of elementary education.

[1] On administration of education in England see Chapter V.

Religious instruction. Religious instruction is given in all schools, but in the provided schools it is controlled by the Cowper-Temple Clause (Clause 28 of the Education Act, 1870), which requires that "no religious catechism or formulary which is distinctive of any particular denomination shall be taught in the school." This has meant in practice the inclusion of the reading of the Bible without comment, and the teaching of the Apostles' Creed, the Lord's Prayer, and the Ten Commandments. A number of local education authorities — the West Riding of Yorkshire, Cambridgeshire, Lancashire, Leicestershire, Oxfordshire, Hampshire, Middlesex, and others — have issued syllabuses for religious instruction which have been prepared by the coöperation of teachers, the clergy of the Anglican Church, and ministers of the Free Churches, and adopted not only in their own but in other areas. All children are expected to receive religious instruction, usually given by the class teacher, unless their parents claim exemption under the conscience clause of the Education Act. The first period of the day, usually half an hour, from 9 A.M. to 9.30 A.M., is set aside for religious instruction, a period which is often curtailed by taking of attendance and marking of registers.

In non-provided schools the religious instruction is definitely denominational and is given by the teachers, who may be selected for appointment because of their religious affiliation. New non-provided schools may be established, but if a local education authority refuses it recognition, which means the assumption of a certain share in the cost of maintenance, the final decision rests with the Board of Education. Religious instruction is not supervised by the Board's inspectors; in non-provided schools it may be inspected by the managers or trustees of the school or as they may arrange, usually by a minister of the denomination concerned.

The increasing cost of education, the inability of most of the denominations to replaced their school buildings, which in many cases are old and outworn, the development of interdenominational syllabuses, and the recent movement to reorganize the system of schools, have focussed attention on the defects of the dual system and the need of some reform. The *Church Assembly Report of the Commission on Religious Education*,[1] known as the Archbishops' Commission, recommends that local education authorities be empowered by Parliament

[1] London, 1929.

to make such arrangements as they may think fit for religious instruction for all children of their area, in accordance with the religion of their parents, notwithstanding the prohibition of the Cowper-Temple clause.

The Commission also recommended state building grants for the purpose of adapting the buildings of non-provided schools to the needs of the proposed senior schools.[1]

The first recommendation would mean the organization of elementary schools as interdenominational schools (the German *Simultanschulen*); the second would relieve the denominational organizations of one of the chief causes of their present difficulties — inability to find money for new buildings. No action has yet been taken to give effect to these recommendations, but two authorities, Bradford and West Riding, have entered into a Covenant "for twenty-one years or more" to take over non-provided schools on condition that the religious instruction follow the regular syllabuses of the authorities and that the denominations concerned provide for denominational religious instruction at their own expense on two days a week at such times and places as they may elect.

The time has passed when the reform of elementary education and the religious question were synonymous, as they were in 1902 and 1906. All the denominations, except the Roman Catholic, because of financial pressure and the education authorities in the interests of economy and a common public system, are ready to compromise on the subject of religious instruction and the dual system. On March 31, 1931, the various types of public elementary schools in England and Wales were distributed as follows:

	Schools	Average Enrollment	Average Attendance
Council	9,698	3,696,360	3,289,736
Church of England	9,598 *	1,403,765 *	1,253,321 *
Wesleyan	113	20,866	18,592
Roman Catholic	1,188	376,782	331,753
Jewish	13	5,291	4,597
Other voluntary schools	257	35,708	32,077
Total	20,867	5,538,772	4,930,076

* It will be gathered from a comparison of the number of schools with the enrollment that the majority of the Church of England schools are small schools in rural districts.

[1] The School Attendance Bill, which proposed to extend full-time compulsory education to fifteen, was passed in the House of Commons, 1931, with an amendment which provided that the bill, if enacted, was not to become effective until provision was made to assist voluntary organizations with grants for buildings; the bill was rejected in the House of Lords.

Private schools. Beside the public elementary schools, there is a large number of private schools, which are required to be efficient, but which at present are not subject to inspection except under the indirect requirement of the law that children of compulsory school age must be efficiently educated. Statistics of the number of private schools and the children attending them are not available, but it is estimated that about 350,000 boys and girls between six and fourteen receive private education either at home or in schools.[1]

Compulsory attendance. The Education Act, 1921, places upon parents the obligation of causing their children of not less than five nor more than fourteen years of age to attend school, unless under efficient instruction in some other manner, for reasons of health, or because a public elementary school is not available within two miles of the residence of a child under eleven, or three miles if over that age, and suitable means of conveyance are not provided by the local education authority beyond these limits. The law thus requires compulsory education, and may be met by attendance at any school, public or private, or by instruction at home, provided that the education is efficient. Since 1918 no child may leave school except at the end of the term in which the fourteenth year is reached. Local authorities were also empowered by the Act passed in that year to pass by-laws extending compulsory attendance to fifteen or even sixteen with the approval of the Board of Education; the number of authorities which have availed themselves of this power is negligible.

Compulsory attendance regulations are administered by the local education authorities through their school attendance committees and school attendance officers. The latter are responsible for the preparation of the school census and investigations of absences. With the improvement of education and the introduction since 1907 of a system of school medical inspection, the large majority of absences are no longer due to truancy and neglect, but to illness. It has even been suggested that the functions of school attendance officers should be taken over by school nurses. In any case, the position of the school attendance officers has become more like that of the welfare workers. Cases of repeated absence without cause are brought first before the school attendance committees or their sub-

---

[1] Percy, Lord E., *The Year Book of Education, 1932*, p. 127 (London, 1931). See also pp. 104 ff. above.

committees, and only in the last resort to the magistrates' — usually juvenile — courts. Habitual truants may be committed to special schools — reformatory and day industrial schools.

The percentage of average attendance for the whole of England and Wales in 1930–31 was 89 per cent. This high percentage is attained not only through the efficiency of the administration of attendance and the growing popularity of the schools, but by the fact that a part of the government grant is calculated on the basis of attendance, the interest of the teachers who have emphasized the importance of regularity and punctuality, and competitions between schools, classes, and pupils. It is not improbable that a higher percentage of attendance might be attained were it not for the rigorous regulations of the school medical service.

The organization of schools. The elementary school is rapidly becoming the common school of the whole population, a position which it had secured, not through pressure of official regulations, but because of its progressive improvement in buildings, teachers, and curriculum. There is, however, a complete absence of uniformity in the organization of the schools. Because of its separate origin in the nineteenth century, the infant school, intended for children between the ages of five and seven, has everywhere continued to be organized as a separate department with its own principal and staff, and even in small schools it is usual to have a separate teacher for the infants. Under the pressure of economic conditions, many working mothers are compelled to send children to school before the age of five, but no child is admitted under the age of three. For these children there have been organized, although for reasons of accommodation the upper limit is sometimes exceeded, babies' classes, which are gradually being transformed, under the influence of the nursery school movement, into nursery classes.

Beyond the infant school all uniformity of organization ceases even in the organization of schools under the same authority. In some schools boys and girls from seven to fourteen may be in separate departments; in others they may be in junior mixed departments from seven to eleven and continue the last three years in senior mixed departments; elsewhere they may be in junior mixed departments and then separated for the last three years into departments for senior boys or senior girls. The *Handbook of Suggestions for the Consideration of Teachers and Others Concerned in the Work of Public*

Elementary Schools, issued by the Board of Education,[1] is based upon four stages of school life: (1) the "nursery" stage for children under the age of compulsory attendance (three to five); (2) the "infants'" stage from the age of five to about eight; (3) the "junior" stage up to the age of eleven plus; and (4) the "senior" stage including the last three years of schooling. At the close of the "junior" stage, the better pupils are usually selected by examination for transfer to a central or a secondary school.

The movement for the provision of some form of post-primary or secondary education for all pupils is based in general on the organization adopted by the Board. The *Report on the Education of the Adolescent* (1926), followed by the Board's pamphlet, *The New Prospect in Education* (1928), recommended a definite break at or about the age of eleven; education up to that age was to be given in the primary school, including the infants' and junior departments; beyond that age and up to the age of fifteen, which was proposed as the upper limit of compulsory attendance, pupils were to attend a variety of schools according to their ability and bent — the modern school, selective and non-selective, or the secondary school. The failure to enact the School Attendance Bill, which would have given effect to these recommendations, left the local authorities with the reorganization of the school system in their own way. Many have already begun to organize senior schools as separate units for pupils between eleven and fourteen: the difficulties are not so great in the larger areas, but in the rural areas they are intensified by the existence of the dual system and the refusal of trustees to send their older pupils to the senior schools without some guarantee as to their religious instruction and to face a reduction in the size of their own schools.

The Consultative Committee, in its *Report on the Primary School*,[2] repeats the recommendation made in its *Report on the Education of the Adolescent*, that pupils should be transferred to some form of secondary school at the age of eleven plus. It proceeded to recommend that the education of children up to eleven be given in two stages, one extending to the age of seven plus and the other from seven plus to eleven plus. The recommendations of the Consultative Committee will undoubtedly constitute the basis on which the elementary school system of the future will be organized throughout the

---

[1] The latest edition was issued in 1927. [2] London, 1931.

country, as it has already begun to be reorganized in a few areas. The present organization is indicated in the following figures which give the number of departments for 1931:

there were 426 departments for senior boys, 421 for senior girls, 505 senior mixed, 2797 for boys, 2928 for girls, 12,815 mixed 348 for junior boys, 416 for junior girls, 3285 junior mixed, and 6422 for infants — a total of 30,363.

Articulation. One of the difficulties involved in the present organization of schools by departments is to secure an unbroken articulation between them. In the absence of specific requirements prescribed by a central authority, each department is autonomous and articulation depends upon voluntary consultation and coöperation between the head teachers concerned. The problem of articulation is particularly difficult at a time when theories and practices, especially in the education of young children, are changing; the work of infants' departments are tending to become freer and the transition between this and the next stage is at times too abrupt. The *Report on the Primary School*, while recommending the retention of the infants' department as a separate unit, emphasizes the importance of articulation with the junior school, which constitutes the next stage.

Size of class. There are no rigorous or standardized regulations on the size of classes. For some time the Board of Education has encouraged the adoption of forty-five children in a class as the maximum. Owing to the economic situation and the fluctuations in enrollments since the War, this maximum has frequently been exceeded. *The Primary School Report* recommends that "A class in a primary school should not contain more than forty pupils, and, where there are a considerable proportion of retarded children, it should be much smaller." [1]

Of a total of 152,062 classes in 1931, 14,219 had less than 20 pupils, 30,527 classes had between 20 and 30 pupils, 47,590 between 30 and 40 pupils, 51,155 between 40 and 50 pupils, 8504 between 50 and 60 pupils, and 67 over 60 pupils.

Nursery schools. The necessity, which became urgent during the War, of providing for the care of infants and young children whose mothers were absent from home and at work during the day, helped to focus attention on their needs. The actual situation, combined with the emphasis of the school medical service on the importance of

[1] *The Primary School*, pp. xxviii and 107 (London, 1931).

a sound foundation of good health and with the rapidly developing study of the growth of children, helped to arouse public interest in a type of school, the nursery school, which had been first established by Rachel and Margaret McMillan in one of the slum districts of London in 1908. The Education Act, 1918, permitted local education authorities to establish and maintain *crèches* or day nurseries in which infants might be received from one month old and kept until they are three years old or more, and nursery schools for children between the age of two and five years, out of local rates, half the cost being borne by grants from the Board of Education. The value of the nursery school, which aims to provide for young children living under social conditions detrimental to their health and good training an environment similar to that enjoyed by children in good homes, has been universally recognized. The financial conditions of the last decade have, however, prevented any extensive establishment of such schools. There were in 1931 about 150 day nurseries, and 44 public and 11 private nursery schools;[1] a number of local education authorities have already presented plans for new nursery schools. The general principles of the nursery school have been adopted in the reorganization, in infants' schools, of babies' classes for children between the ages of three to five, into nursery classes. From the point of view of the health of the pre-school child, nursery classes and nursery schools continue the work begun in maternity and child welfare centers which have been established under the Maternity and Child Welfare Act of 1919; beyond this stage the care of the child's health is supervised under the system of school medical inspection, established in 1907.

Administration of elementary schools. The responsibility for the administration of elementary schools or departments of such schools rests upon the head teacher, head master, or head mistress. There are no uniform regulations governing the appointments to this position; each authority has its own system. Generally the position is filled by promotion from the ranks of teachers within a system, sometimes by inviting applications through advertisements; some authorities have an eligible list of candidates prepared on the recommendations of the local inspectors. The tendency at present is to appoint only certificated teachers who have had a number of years of successful experience; in very small schools, owing to unsatisfactory condi-

[1] See also note on page 98.

tions of salary and living, uncertificated teachers are still appointed to headships.

Head teachers are expected to devote a number of periods a week to class instruction, but their chief functions are to guide and supervise their staff; to promote the unity of school work by frequent consultations, discussions, and conferences; to prepare the curriculum, time-schedule, and course of study with the advice and assistance of their teachers; to conduct periodical examinations, and to assume a large share of the responsibility for the classification and promotion of pupils. They are expected to supervise the work of their teachers and in particular to give as much assistance as possible to young teachers; and, finally, they are responsible for the general routine work of administration, the keeping of records, and the preparation of reports.

Aim of elementary education. The aim of elementary education varies somewhat in the different stages. The purpose of the nursery schools and classes is to provide an environment which will promote the health and happiness of the children and at the same time cultivate their early interests through play and games, movement and exercise, form and color, song and story. This aim is continued into the infants' classes, where the activities expand in range and become the basis of what are later organized as subjects.

The aim of elementary education has been defined as follows in the Annual *Code* issued by the Board of Education from 1904 to 1926:

> The purpose of the public elementary school is to form and strengthen the character and to develop the intelligence of the children entrusted to it, and to make the best use of the school years available in assisting both girls and boys, according to their different needs, to fit themselves, practically as well as intellectually, for the work of life.[1]

To this statement may be added the more recent definitions of the aim of the primary school:

> Its primary aim must be to aid children, while they are children, to be healthy, and, so far as is possible, happy children, vigorous in body and lively in mind, in order that later, as with widening experience they grow towards maturity, the knowledge which life demands may more easily be mastered and the necessary accomplishments more readily acquired.[2]

---

[1] See *Handbook of Suggestions for the Consideration of Teachers and Others Concerned in the Work of Public Elementary Schools*, p. 8 (London, 1927).
[2] *The Primary School*, p. xvi.

ELEMENTARY EDUCATION

Referring to the curriculum of the primary school, the Consultative Committee in its *Report* declared:

Its aim should be to develop in a child the fundamental human powers and to awaken him to the fundamental interests of civilized life so far as those powers and interests lie within the compass of childhood, to encourage him to attain gradually to that control and orderly management of his energies, impulses and emotions, which is the essence of moral and intellectual discipline, to help him to discover the idea of duty and to ensue it, and to open out his imagination and his sympathies in such a way that he may be prepared to understand and to follow in later years the highest examples of excellence in life and conduct.[1]

As in all English definitions of education, character-formation comes first; it implies the development of certain habits of conduct and behavior, intellectual, emotional, and moral, and the cultivation of certain ideals. Beyond and contributory to this common aim, the elementary school has the task of development of health and vigor of body, of cultivating intellectual habits, of arousing alertness and a taste for further study and work, and of laying the foundations and giving the tools for self-education. As compared with the aim of the elementary school in the nineteenth century, with its emphasis on thorough mastery of a few subjects, the aim today is to impart the elements of liberal education, or, in the words of Sir Michael Sadler, to give "new things to love and admire." [2] Through individual as through coöperative activities the pupils are to be trained to discipline themselves and to become sensitive to the meaning of duty for themselves and to society. All those qualities which are implied by freedom and independence must be developed, but they must be tempered by an appreciation of the similar rights of others.

In the elaboration of these aims a distinct change is noted. The English school has always emphasized character-formation, but the methods in the past have been in the main extra-curricular; increasingly the contribution which may be made by a suitable organization of the curriculum and content of instruction has begun to be recognized. This represents a movement toward the recognition of the education of the whole man; whatever contributes to the education of the individual cannot be divided into separate and distinct departments which are unrelated to each other. A similar change has taken place in the concept of discipline; discipline, it is recognized,

[1] *The Primary School*, p. 93.
[2] *Our Public Elementary Schools*, p. 8 (London, 1926).

cannot be discarded, but the external discipline of tradition, suppression of the individual by authority, must be replaced by free self-discipline accepted because it is necessary to the existence of any social organization. Corporal punishment has not been abolished, but it is administered with less frequency and reserved for serious offenses.

Curriculum and courses of study. The work of the nursery school is determined by its aim — provision for the healthy and active growth of young children, and to some extent by the nature of its buildings and equipment. Some nursery schools, following a principle insisted upon by Margaret McMillan, consist of gardens and buildings attached, and most of the work is carried on in the open air; others, including also nursery classes, have buildings with gardens or playgrounds attached, and the major part of the activities are carried on indoors. The nursery schools take care of children for the whole day, from 8 A.M. to 5 P.M.; the nursery classes for the shorter school day. In both provision is made for feeding the children; the parents,

PROGRAM OF NURSERY CLASSES

A.M.
9:00– 9:50 Arrival and registration. Hymn. Prayer. Visit offices. Put on handky bags. Handky drill. Breathing exercises.
9:50–10:00 Rhythmic exercises or games.
10:00–10:15 Chats and picture talks.
10:15–10:50 Preparation for lunch. Wash hands. Set table. Have lunch. Tidy up.
10:50–11:05 Free play.
11:05–11:35 Short rest. Sense Training on Monday, Wednesday, and Friday; singing on Tuesday and Thursday.
11:35–11:50 Nursery rhymes and drawing on Monday and Friday; aloplast on Tuesday; paper tearing or folding or cutting on Wednesday; finger plays or beads on Thursday.
11:50–12:00 Learning to put on coats, etc. Grace and dismissal.

P.M.
1:30– 2:30 Arrival and registration. Inspection of class. Handky drill. Visit offices and prepare for rest. Quiet occupations for those who do not sleep.
2:30– 2:40 Wake up and put on shoes or clogs.
2:40– 2:55 Free play.
2:55– 3:30 Story, followed by dramatization on Monday; free drawing on Tuesday; Brick building on Wednesday; toys on Thursday; rocking horse and singing rhymes on Friday.
3:30– 3:45 Dressing. Prayer. Dismissal.

as far as possible, contribute what they can. So far as one can speak of a curriculum at the nursery stage, it is directed to the cultivation of good habits through bathing and washing, dressing and undressing, coöperative activities in the preparation for meals and other activities. Much of the time is devoted to play and games, training of the senses through color, size, and number; formal subjects, as such, have no place, but a foundation is laid for them through the care and observation of animals and plants, singing, group games, story-telling, art work, and the development of good habits of speech. In some cases the work of nursery schools and classes has been influenced by the spirit, but not by the details, of the Montessori method. Although attention is given to the individual child, the nursery schools have not been established as centers for psychological research, as have many similar institutions in the United States. Because of the age of the children, the nursery schools and classes have attracted the interest of parents and in that way have become centers that influence the home environment to which the children return from school.

In infant and elementary schools neither the Board of Education nor the local education authorities prescribe either the list of subjects to be taught — the courses of study, or the time-schedules. The legal definition of elementary education is that it is "that education which constitutes the whole or the principal part of the work of an elementary school." The Board of Education until 1926 issued an Annual *Code* in which the subjects of an elementary school curriculum were indicated without any requirement that all subjects should be taught in all schools, but the practice has been discontinued. The only guidance furnished by the Board is the *Handbook of Suggestions for the Consideration of Teachers and Others Concerned in the Work of Public Elementary Schools*, first issued in 1905 and revised periodically until 1927. The *Handbook* is prepared by the inspectors of the Board on the basis of their observations in the field and with the coöperation of teachers. The *Handbook* is thus a compilation which is eminently practical and a guide which represents what can actually be achieved. The *Suggestions* are not governed by any particular theory or philosophy, but illustrate the variety of practices which result from the freedom enjoyed by the teachers. The only subject in which the Board, influenced by the medical inspection branch, requires its syllabus to be followed is physical training, but even in this case a local authority may use its own syllabus provided that it can secure the approval of the inspectors.

The Board definitely refrains from prescribing the curriculum or its details because, according to the *Suggestions*:

> It is not possible to lay down any rule as to the exact number of the subjects which should be taken in an individual school. The choice, indeed, cannot be in practice absolutely free. It is in part determined by public opinion as expressing the needs of the community in which the scholars live. [Language, reading and writing, arithmetic and measurement, hygiene, physical and moral training cannot be omitted.] But in selecting other subjects the decision is not always so easy.... The curriculum must vary to some extent with the qualifications of the teaching staff.... Variations in the curriculum will often correspond to the special needs and circumstances of the scholars.[1]

This does not mean that the English elementary school is curriculum-centered or that the interests of the children are ignored.

> He [the teacher] certainly must become, if he is not one already, a close and sympathetic student of the nature of his pupils. He must be able to range himself mentally alongside them and ready to modify his teaching to meet their needs. Briefly, his task is to make the most of the mental qualities which already exist in them and are seeking opportunities for exercise, their motives, interests, and instincts; their sense of wonder and romance; their natural curiosity, constructiveness, combativeness, and so forth. His starting point must be no rigid syllabus or subject, but the children as they really are; he must work always with the grain of their minds, try never to cut across it.[1]

But if the children are the starting-point, the ends are determined by the purposes for which the school exists and the civilization and culture which they are to share. Freedom must be combined with its correlative, responsibility.

An almost unlimited degree of freedom for children is sometimes advocated nowadays. It has been proposed that they should choose their own subjects, make their own rules and time-tables, work or not as they feel inclined. Nothing of this kind is suggested here, except perhaps in the case of individual pupils who are nearing the end of their school life. There is a due mean between a system which counteracts the natural aspirations of the children and one which in the name of freedom refuses them the aid and guidance they require. Children cannot be treated from the outset as if they were possessed of mature judgment, experience, and self-knowledge. But they can be treated as natural beings, and the teacher should see to it that the purpose of the work they are required to do does not remain a mystery, either to them

---

[1] *Handbook of Suggestions*, pp. 38 f.   [1] *Handbook of Suggestions*, p. 13.

or to himself. Its ultimate purpose may not be fully within their comprehension, or may be too remote to appeal to them directly. The teacher should then endeavor to invest it with an immediate purpose which should, if possible, take the intrinsic form of putting it to some practical use, rather than an extrinsic form, such as the gaining of marks.[1]

The success of education at any stage depends upon the personality of the teachers, free and responsible, understanding children, but also appreciating the purpose of education, guided not by plans and methods prescribed by others and exacted by rigorous supervision, but by their own insight and experience. In view of the tendency in the United States toward curriculum-making by experts, the periodic vogue of methods, the control through administrative devices, supervision, standardized tests, and so on, students of education cannot too often be reminded of the importance of the teacher in the educational process. On this point it is pertinent to quote two statements from the *Report on the Primary School*:

The National Association of Inspectors of Schools and Educational Organizers argue that the greatest single factor in education was, or should be, the personality of the teacher, since schools were neither made nor marred by curricula (p. 76).
Different methods will be used not only in different subjects, but also in teaching the same subject in different circumstances of school organization, numbers, situation, and equipment, and different teachers will face similar problems in different ways. In a vital sense, method is the teacher's style, the outward expression of his educational faith and experience. If his instruction is to be a living influence upon his pupils, his methods must in the end be an individual expression of his modes of thought, feeling, and outlook, and not merely the application of general rules, however sound (p. 151).

Freedom for the teacher who understands his pupils is the first essential. The curriculum will represent an "introduction to the major interests of society as derived from man's civilization and culture, or certain elements of experience, because they are part of the common life of mankind."

Here is the touchstone, Sir Percy Nunn has declared, by which the claims of a subject for a place in the time-table can be infallibly tested. Does it represent one of the great movements of the human spirit, one of the major forms into which the creative impulses of man have been shaped and disciplined? If it does, then its admission cannot be contested. If it does not, it must be set aside; it may usefully be included in some special courses of

[1] *Handbook of Suggestions*, p. 16.

technical education, but it is not qualified to be an element in the education of the people.[1]

In no part of English education has a greater transformation taken place than in the infants' schools. From classrooms equipped with galleries in which large classes were huddled together under a disciplinary régime as strict as in the upper schools and a curriculum which in the main was formal and preparatory, the infants' schools

TIME-SCHEDULE OF AN INFANTS' SCHOOL

	Class 1 (min.)	Class 2 (min.)	Class 3 (min.)
Registration and religious instruction — A.M.	150	150	150
Registration, grace and personal hygiene — P.M.	75	75	75
Prayer, songs and dismissal	25	25	25
Free play — A.M. and P.M.	150	150	150
Free movement between periods (3)	75	75	75
Number	125	125	125
English { Reading and doing	190	200	200
Composition, grammar, and dictation	150	100	75
Script writing, poetry, and words of songs	65	75	95
Nature. Conversation. Stories. Picture. Chats. History and geography	140	115	165
Physical exercises { Games and dancing, exercises	150	150	150
Personal hygiene			
Music and band	60	50	50
Handwork { Knitting and needlework, Drawing, Expression work, Plasticine, Toymaking, Individual occupations	220	235	190
Total number of minutes	1,575	1,575	1,575

have become centers of free movement and activities proper to the interests of the children in attendance. No longer is the emphasis placed upon the acquisition of the three R's and adjustment to the demands of the next Standard, but upon a variety of activities and experiences out of which the need for the rudiments of the so-called subjects emerge. Play and games, speech-training with clear articulation and freedom in expression, story-telling and conversation, painting, drawing, music, dancing, nature study, and manual activities provide a range of experiences on which are based the introduction to reading, writing, and arithmetic with an emphasis on concreteness and reality and within the scope of the pupils' comprehension. The common-sense principle is followed that a normal child, as a re-

[1] *Report of the British Association*, 1923, p. 267. See also a similar statement by Sir Percy Nunn in *Report on Examinations*, pp. 54 f. (New York, 1931).

sult of the environment in which he has been brought up, even before he enters school has an interest in the so-called formal subjects, despite modern theories to the contrary. The change in the character of the infants' school has been effected in part by the greater freedom introduced into the school atmosphere in general in the last generation, in part by the progressive methods of the kindergarten and by Montessori methods, and to some extent by the nursery school. In turn, the methods of the infants' schools are affecting the work of the early years of the elementary school and the transition from the one to the other is not as abrupt as it once was.

The normal subjects of an elementary school are religious instruction, English language and literature, writing, arithmetic, drawing and modeling, nature study, geography, history, singing and music, hygiene and physical training, manual work, and domestic subjects (needlework, cooking, laundry work, and household management). Moral instruction is rarely taught as a separate subject. The *Education Act*, 1918, contained a provision, now incorporated in the *Education Act*, 1921, Section 20, requiring local authorities to include practical instruction suitable to the ages, abilities, and requirements of the children, and to provide courses in advanced instruction for the

TIME-SCHEDULE OF A JUNIOR MIXED ELEMENTARY SCHOOL

SUBJECTS	IIA	II	IIIA	III	IVA, VA	IV, V
Religious instruction	175	175	175	175	175	175
Arithmetic	230	230	230	230	230	230
Physical training *	75	75	75	75	75	75
Geography	110	110	110	110	110	110
English †	195	195	195	195	230	230
Recreation	100	100	100	100	100	100
Drawing	150	150	150	150	150	150
Needlework ‡	120	120	120	120	120	120
History	70	70	60	60	60	60
Handwork	60	60	60	60	60	60
Poetry	70	70	60	60	60	60
Music	70	70	60	60	60	60
Dancing and rhythmic exercise	50	50	50	50	50	50
Optional	70	70	110	100	110	110
Observational lessons	80	80	80	80	80	80
Reading	145	145	140	135	100	100
Total	1,650	1,650	1,650	1,650	1,650	1,650

* Boys attend baths for swimming on Friday afternoons.
† English includes grammar, composition, and exercises auxiliary to composition.
‡ Handwork is correlated with arithmetic, drawing, nature study, geography, history.

older pupils. The curriculum, courses of study, and time-schedules are prepared in each school, sometimes by the head teacher, most usually by the head teacher and his staff. Wherever possible a teacher who has specialized in some subject of the curriculum prepares the syllabus in that subject for the whole school. The responsibility, however, rests upon the head teacher; the courses of study or syllabuses and the time-schedules must be approved by the government inspectors, who do not withhold approval if the head teacher can justify his position. In the preparation of courses of study, head teachers and teachers are guided by tradition, by their professional knowledge, by the *Suggestions* and *Memoranda* of the Board of Education, by special reports, such as that on *The Teaching of English*, and in some areas by suggestions issued by the local education authority. Another source of influence is to be found in the increasing number of short summer courses on the subjects of the curriculum, organized either by the Board of Education and given by its inspectors or other specialists, or by education authorities, such as those of Kent and West Riding of Yorkshire, and courses and conferences for teachers provided during the school year by some education authorities. Such a system permits adaptation to the local environment, encourages freedom, and elicits responsibility. It is characteristic of the system that the courses of study are rarely printed, sometimes typewritten, usually written by hand, evidence at least that they are not intended to be permanent and are subject to modification as the occasion requires.

The Consultative Committee in its *Report on the Primary School* recommends that in the early years the curriculum be integrated on the basis of the common experience underlying all subjects (the German *Gesamtunterricht*) and correlated with the natural movement of children's minds. Such integrated instruction, whether in the form of projects or through close correlation of subjects, must, as the child grows older, give place to subjects "which have their own self-sufficient motives," and in which regular and systematic work is desirable. Similarly, while room should be provided for individual study, this must be alternated with group instruction. On the question of methods, the English attitude is pragmatic — those methods are best which produce the best results. The statement on the subject in the *Report on the Primary School* is as follows:

Since the immediate aim of teaching is that the pupil shall become an active learner, any method which is claimed, on reasonable grounds, to conduce to that end is worthy of unbiased study.

The well-tried methods of corporate teaching have an indispensable place in the school economy, and should not be discarded wholesale in obedience to insufficiently tested theories.

Nevertheless, there are occasions and purposes for which they are clearly not so suitable as methods which, while not depriving pupils of the stimulus, inspiration, and guidance of the teacher, yet leave him reasonable scope to ensue his own special interests, to learn in his own way, and to acquire the priceless habit of independent purposeful work.

While these considerations are of general validity, they apply specially to small rural schools, where, from the nature of the use, class-organization and class-teaching must have a particularly limited value.

Finally, while we deprecate experiments ill-considered or carried out under conditions clearly unfavourable to success, we hope that, as teachers come to grips with the special problems of the primary school, ways and means will be found of giving effect to what is sound in the suggestions of those who criticise the present predominance of the class-method. In particular, we hope that where individual methods are employed with unmistakable success in an infant school, the teachers in the lower classes of the primary school will consider carefully the propriety of so adjusting their own methods that there is no serious break in continuity as the child passes from the one to the other.[1]

Curriculum organization and standards. The general character of the infants' school curriculum has already been indicated. The fact that compulsory education begins one year earlier in England than in any other country, and the acceptance of the principle that young children do manifest an interest in what are usually called formal subjects, render it possible to set up a standard whereby pupils at the age of eight or nine may, in addition to the variety of other activities in which they engage, be expected to be able to read an easy book, tell or write a simple narrative, and have a command of the first notions of arithmetic and measurement. From this stage on, the work becomes more systematic with less emphasis on mere freedom and pleasure than on exactness. The standard to be attained by pupils at about the age of eleven is that

The scholars should be able to express themselves with fair ease and correctness on matters which fall within their experience or which they have read about in books. They should have learned accurately all the simple processes in arithmetic and made at least the first steps in mensuration. In handwork and drawing, they should now be showing more technical skill and be aiming at more difficult subjects and a closer finish. The outlines of his-

---

[1] *The Primary School*, p. 152 f.

tory and geography will be forming in their minds, though no attempt should have been made to teach them details, or generalizations, which they cannot properly assimilate.[1]

The weakest part of the work of the English elementary school has in the past been that of the senior stage (pupils from eleven to fourteen). This has been due to a number of causes; under the selective system the best pupils were generally transferred to an intermediate or secondary school at about the age of eleven; much time was wasted on repetition of work already done; the smaller number of pupils made an adequate system of classification difficult; in the last year, until the Education Act, 1918, required pupils to remain in school until the end of the term in which they reached their fourteenth birthday, the classes were constantly reduced as pupils dropped out. The Education Act, 1918, attempted to attack the difficulties by imposing upon local authorities the duty of providing advanced instruction and a variety of practical work for pupils in the senior stage. The *Suggestions* recommended in the advanced instruction laid more emphasis on self-education through extensive reading, local, social, and European history, practical work in science and geography, and in mathematics the introduction of algebraical symbols and graphical methods. For practical work, the opportunities for a variety of manual activities for boys and for housecraft or domestic science were increased, in the larger schools by the provision of workshops and model apartments, for pupils in the smaller schools by the organization of central workshops or domestic science centers used in common by pupils from a number of schools.

It is possible here to give only the main features of the English course of study as defined in the Board's *Handbook of Suggestions*. The subject which is regarded as the most important, because it is a means of expression and understanding and underlies the work in all other subjects, is English. Every teacher should, in fact, be a teacher of English. The aim of the school should be to encourage good and correct English and its simple, direct, and unaffected written and oral expression. While aiming to correct bad English, the use of dialects should not be altogether discouraged, because they "have a history and associations which entitle them to respect." English should be regarded as a unified subject which offers opportunities for a variety of exercises through speech, reading, and writing. Beginning with

[1] *Handbook of Suggestions*, pp. 55 f.

conversation which should develop naturally out of concrete situations (the home, play, pictures, stories, and dramatization), the pupil is introduced to reading and oral and written expression. The subjects for composition and spelling lists should be within the range of the pupils' ability and experience. The purpose of reading, prose and poetry, should be to cultivate pleasure and appreciation; after the preliminary foundations through the use of readers, pupils should as early as possible be introduced to the masterpieces of literature appropriate to their stage of development. The range of reading suggested for the senior stage includes Scott, Dickens, Shakespeare, Kingsley, *Robinson Crusoe, Masterman Ready, Tom Brown's Schooldays*, and books of travel, adventure, and biography. Attention is given both to reading aloud and to silent reading, and special emphasis is placed upon good speech, accurate voice-production, and careful articulation.[1] Freedom and breadth have taken the place of the narrow, formal drill in fundamentals; practice is regarded as necessary in spelling, some grammar is essential, and rules and techniques are desirable in writing compositions, but the practical needs have replaced the formal and deductive methods.

Although the teaching of arithmetic has undergone considerable change, the subject is still regarded as one of the most important in the elementary curriculum and absorbs about one fifth of the weekly time allotment. Meaningless drill has been replaced by ability to apply number to everyday life, and the practical and useful are kept constantly in mind. Simple geometry and mensuration through handwork and drawing are associated with arithmetic. Graphic methods and algebraical symbols are taught to older pupils where circumstances are favorable.

In the teaching of history and geography, there is an absence of any attempt to use these subjects for purposes of nationalistic indoctrination. The purpose of history instruction is to develop a sense of continuity and of cause and effect. The teaching of history varies with the capacity and interests of the teacher.

It is of more value to give the pupil some idea of the right spirit in which he may approach the study of history in later life than to burden his memory with details which can have little or no significance for him. If the subject is made so attractive that the pupil is constantly asking himself "What comes next?" and if when his schooldays are over he continues to read and study history, the teacher has achieved his purpose.[2]

[1] See Meader, Emma Grant, *Teaching Speech in the Elementary School* (New York, 1928).
[2] *Handbook of Suggestions*, p. 120.

In the lower classes an appeal should be made to the imagination through simple and attractive narratives, legend, and the story of the British and foreign heroes, and, if taught at all, as a subject, history at this stage should be limited to the older period of British history which is the least complex and the most picturesque. The older pupils should acquire a connected view of the main outlines of British history and of the changes which have led to the social and industrial life of the present. Controversial aspects of economic and political development should be omitted, since "There is scope enough for all children's powers in those aspects of history which are not of this character, and the discussion of topics on which they are unable to exercise their judgment is useless." [1] In addition to its value as a cultural subject, history may also be made an instrument of moral training in lessons of heroism, unselfishness, loyalty to an ideal, and "how the patriot has helped his country." Finally, the history of Great Britain and of the British Commonwealth of Nations should be taught as a part of world history leading to a discussion of international coöperation, the League of Nations, and the ideals for which it stands.[2]

Geography, which may be closely associated but not necessarily integrated with history, is a subject which provides opportunities for observation of and reasoning upon scientific facts within the child's experience. Through it the teacher should awaken an interest in the environment, lives and habits of people, illustrate the interdependence of the world, and develop a knowledge of the principles of geography and power to apply them. As a subject, geography is a link between the humanistic and scientific subjects and is accordingly a study of man and his world.

Elementary science developed out of the nineteenth-century object lessons. Starting with the observation of common things, the subject aims to deepen the pupils' interest in the world around them and in the simple phenomena of nature, to train them in habits of scientific observation and thinking with an avoidance at this stage of technical terms. The selection of the topics to be treated depends upon the interest of the teacher and his ability to use the opportunities provided by the environment of the school. Like geography, elementary science can be correlated with other subjects.

[1] *Handbook of Suggestions*, p. 132.
[2] *Handbook of Suggestions* contains an *Appendix on the League of Nations*.

The school journey has long been advocated as a valuable aid to instruction. First promoted by the School Journeys Association, the school journey has been adopted widely and in many areas special facilities are provided for reducing the cost of travel. In history, geography, science, and art, the school journey provides endless opportunities, not only for making the work of the classroom concrete and real, but in developing an appreciation and knowledge of the local resources and in their historical and geographical significance as well as through museums and art collections. More than this, it can cultivate an appreciation of the pleasures of open-air life and the opportunities available for educational and recreational activities. The recent establishment of Youth Hostels is a valuable contribution to this aspect of school life.

Finally, an important part of the work of any English school is the attention given to physical training for the promotion of health and for the development of character. All schools are required to have a playground, which is in most cases unsatisfactory; in addition, the regulations of the Board of Education permit teachers to take their pupils to open spaces and playing-fields, often set aside in municipal parks, or made available by the National Playing-Fields Association. Physical training, which includes also formal classwork in hygiene, is on the formal side dominated by the Swedish system and on the informal side provides for a great variety of games, dances, and sports; for swimming, pupils are taken to public swimming baths. The emphasis in physical training is on honest, cheerful, and strenuous play and the cultivation, not of perfection of skill, but of an appreciation of the rules and spirit of the games.[1] In many areas special organizers, half the cost of whose salaries is borne by the Board's grants, have been appointed to coördinate physical training, to offer courses for teachers, to supervise and in general to promote the progressive development of this branch of the work of the elementary school.

Textbooks. The Board of Education does not publish a list of textbooks for the use of schools, nor are they in the elementary schools used as extensively as in the United States, partly because of the cost, partly because the "recitation" method has never been

---

[1] See *The Syllabus of Physical Training for Schools* (1919), *Syllabus of Physical Training for Schools: Supplement for Older Girls* (1927), *Reference Book of Gymnastic Training for Boys* (1927), and *Handbook of Suggestions on Health Education* (1928), all issued by the Board of Education.

widespread, and partly because there is gradually developing a tendency to use a wider range of books and sources than are provided by the textbook. Suggestive lists are drawn up by a number of local education authorities (e.g., London, Kent, West Riding of Yorkshire), and central stores are available where teachers may examine books; the selection is made, however, by the head teachers and their staffs for each school. Free textbooks are provided to the pupils, but remain the property of the schools and in most cases are kept in the schools. For a long time schools have coöperated with public libraries in securing books for general reading; more recently many schools have begun to create their own libraries; here and there teachers organize class libraries consisting of books lent for a period by the pupils themselves. The limitation on expenditures imposed by economic conditions rather than by administrative regulations restricts any extended purchase of textbooks and libraries. In any case, however, as is true in the making of courses of study, head teachers and their staffs enjoy freedom of choice, with such guidance as may be afforded, in the selection of the books used in their schools.[1]

Control of elementary education. Throughout the discussion of English elementary education, the outstanding characteristic has been freedom. The work of the elementary school is not controlled by prescribed time-schedules, curriculum, or courses of study. Each school is a unit and the responsibility for its progress rests upon the head teacher and his staff. There is thus an absence of standardization and of uniformity; reliance is placed upon the insight and personality of the teachers and opportunities for reasoned experimentation are provided. Public elementary education is marked by variety of practice ranging from the traditional and formal to a radical free school.[2]

There are, however, certain controls which, though indirect, are none the less effective. There is as everywhere an undefined public demand, which, whether sound or not, expects the schools to achieve certain results. From professional preparation, even though all teachers have not had it, certain norms are derived which guide the work of the school. The *Suggestions* and other publications of the Board, lectures, courses, and conferences organized by the Board,

[1] See *Report of the Consultative Committee on Books in Elementary Schools* (London, 1928).
[2] At Kearsely, near Bury, Lancashire.

local authorities, or professional associations set up a definite standard of aims and ideals. The system of inspection by inspectors of the Board and of some local authorities, although not as rigorous as supervision in the United States, tend to spread common standards, which are suggestive, if not prescriptive. External examinations for pupils in elementary schools are discouraged. There has, however, developed out of the necessity of a system which does not provide free secondary education for all the practice of holding an examination for pupils at about the age of eleven on the basis of which the selection of the abler boys and girls to be transferred to secondary or central schools is made. In some areas all pupils at this age are required to take the examination; in others, only those who are recommended by their teachers are presented; in all cases, the examination tends to be indicative of the standard of attainment expected by pupils at the age of eleven; leaving out of account the danger of cramming, the examination becomes normative. On the whole, however, the pressure of this examination is not felt, and, as will be seen later, the examination is administered and organized in such a way that direct cramming or preparation is discouraged.

Movement for reorganization of the education system. The arrangements suggested for the improvement of the work in the senior stage of elementary education neglected the pupils over eleven who were retarded and remained in the lower Standards, likely to leave without any preparation for the life before them. This situation, combined with the movement to provide for all pupils above the age of eleven the advantage of some form of secondary education, has led to proposals for a reorganization of the whole system of education into four well-defined stages: the pre-school or nursery school for children up to the age of five; the infants' stage, up to seven; the primary stage, up to eleven; and the secondary stage, divided into two stages — one up to fourteen or fifteen, the other up to eighteen. The first three stages will offer a common foundation for all; the last stages will provide a variety of schools and courses.

The transition would have been facilitated if the School Attendance Bill, which passed the House of Commons, but was rejected by the House of Lords in 1931, had been enacted. The bill sought to give effect to the recommendations of the Consultative Committee on the Education of the Adolescent, which urged a break at eleven plus, the extension of compulsory education to fifteen, and the provision in the last four years of some form of secondary education. The pamphlet of the Board of Education on the *New Prospect in Education*,[1] issued in 1928, encouraged local education authorities to proceed with the reorganization, to establish senior schools, and to transfer to these all pupils at age of eleven, irrespective of scholastic attainments. Since the senior school constitutes a new stage above the primary, and since it is not classified as a part of the provision of secondary education, it is more convenient to consider it, together with other types of schools already in existence, as a part of the system of intermediate education. This classification is perhaps not altogether happy, but it distinguishes the schools within it from primary and from secondary schools and places them in a category side by side with the French *écoles primaires supérieures* and the German *Mittelschulen*. The movement for reorganization, it will be noted, is similar to that which has been taking place in the United States in the development of what is known as the six-three-three plan (six years of primary education, followed by three years of junior high school and three years of senior high school), with the important distinction, however, that the junior high school is definitely intermediate between the primary school and the senior high school, while intermediate education, except for the minority, is not articulated with a continuing higher stage in the European system.

INTERMEDIATE EDUCATION

The gradual expansion of elementary education after 1870 and the absence of an adequate supply of secondary schools led to the creation of higher grade and higher elementary schools which gave a lower form of secondary education to pupils who remain in school until fourteen or fifteen. The need of such types of schools did not disappear with the provision of secondary education at public expense after the enactment of the Education Act, 1902. The regulations governing the higher elementary schools were in general considered unsatisfactory for the needs of boys and girls who could remain in school up to the age of fifteen, since the curriculum had to be "of a specially and predominantly scientific type." In 1910 the London County Council after a period of investigation decided to establish a series of schools to be called "central schools," giving a four-year course to boys and girls selected from the elementary schools at about the age of eleven plus. The same plan was adopted by a number of

[1] *Education Pamphlet*, No. 60 (London, 1928).

other authorities (Manchester, Bradford). The Education Act, 1918, through its requirement of advanced instruction and practical work in the senior stage of the elementary schools, encouraged the development of a number of other experiments. The Consultative Committee, while conducting its investigations into the education of the adolescent, found that the following types of organizations were in existence: the selective central school, the slightly selective central school, non-selective central schools, higher tops and senior standard departments, and a combination of some of these. The Consultative Committee recommended a reorganization, to which reference has already been made, — the transfer of all pupils to some form of junior secondary school (modern school), either selective or non-selective, at the age of eleven plus; although not included in its terms of reference, the arrangements for the transfer of able pupils to the existing secondary schools (grammar school) were included in the scheme. The further recommendation of the Committee that the compulsory age for school attendance be extended to fifteen has not yet been given legal effect.

Pending legislation, the present situation is as follows: Local education authorities are proceeding with the reorganization of the school system on a voluntary basis. The break or the age of differentiation is eleven; at this age pupils are examined, and the best are selected for free places in secondary schools; the next on the list are selected for admission to central schools; the rest continue in the senior departments of elementary schools or are assigned to senior schools. The central school normally offers a four-year course, the senior school a three-year course.

The senior school. The senior school may be a separate institution or the senior division of an elementary school with its own organization. Since the pupils are older, they may be expected to walk a longer distance to school or provision may be made for their transportation, particularly in rural areas. Pupils are in general transferred to the senior school on an age basis, irrespective of scholastic attainments, on the principle that a retarded child will develop most rapidly if he is placed with other children of his own age in conditions which allow suitable provision to be made for him. He needs the stimulus of a new environment, possibly even more than does the child of normal attainments, and his presence in a class of younger children is as harmful to them as to himself.[1]

[1] *The New Prospect in Education*, p. 11.

Separate schools are recommended for boys and girls, whenever the numbers are adequate.

The curriculum of the senior schools has not been prescribed nor have suggestions been issued beyond those already contained in the Board's *Handbook of Suggestions* and the Consultative Committee's *Report on the Education of the Adolescent*. In general the senior schools continue the work of the primary school to a more advanced stage and add a variety of practical work adapted to the circumstances of each locality; thus, in the rural senior schools, while the basic subjects remain the same as in urban areas, opportunities are provided, without an undue emphasis on the rural bias, to relate the work to the rural environment in all subjects and particularly in handwork for boys and domestic science for girls. From another point of view, the curriculum of the senior schools overlaps with that of the lower stages of the secondary schools. The curriculum, recommended for the senior schools in the West Riding of Yorkshire by the

Time-Schedule of a Senior School

Subject	Class III (St. V) (minutes)	Class II (St. VI) (minutes)	Class I (St. VII) (minutes)
Religious instruction	150	150	150
Arithmetic	225	180	180
Domestic arithmetic	..	30	..
Algebra	..	65	65
Practical mathematics	30	45	45
Reading	95	95	75 + Bible literature 35
Composition and silent reading	125	90	90
English *	140	110 + 65 (girls)	110
Poetry	100	70	65
History and civics	100	100	95
Art (boys)	150	150	140
Art (girls)	45	65	65
Physical exercise or swimming	60	60	60
Games (girls) †	..	45	30
Practical science (boys)	30	140	140
Biology (girls)	110	75	..
Domestic science (girls)	65	..	65
Geography	..	95	100
Needlework (girls)	145	150	150
Singing (girls)	150	60	60
Singing (boys)	30	..	..
Manual instruction (boys)	60	140	140
Domestic arts (girls)	..	..	140
Optional	30	..	..
General knowledge	30	..	..

* Girls have two English periods (private study, etc.), when boys are at manual instruction.
† Games: Girls play netball, hockey, and rounders.
  Boys play cricket and football under supervision out of school hours.

Consultative Committee on the Curriculum of the Senior School, includes, in the four-year course which is planned, English language and literature, a foreign language, geography and history, mathematics, elementary science (including gardening), art (drawing and craft), music, physical training, housecraft, and hygiene. In the larger schools parallel sections are organized in which pupils are classified according to ability, and in which the courses of study are adapted to their capacities. The foreign language selected for the senior schools is French. Mathematics may include arithmetic and practical measurements, history of mathematics, metric system, geometry, algebra, graphs, and trigonometry. Under elementary science are included general elementary science, followed by physics, biology, rural science, and hygiene. One important advantage which the senior schools may possess over the traditional organization will be better equipment, more apparatus, libraries, and special rooms.[1]

The curriculum of the senior schools is being planned on the recommendation of the *Report on the Education of the Adolescent* (p. 84) that

A humane or liberal education is not one given through books alone, but one which brings children into contact with the larger interests of mankind; and the aim of the schools... should be to provide an education by means of a curriculum containing large opportunities for practical work and related to living interests. In the earlier years the curriculum in these schools should have much in common with that provided in the schools at present known as "secondary"; it should include a foreign language, subject to permission to omit it in special cases, and it should be given a practical bias only in the last two years.

The senior schools are non-selective; they are intended for pupils who fail, in the examination for pupils at the age of eleven, to secure free admission to a selective senior or central school or to a secondary school. Such an examination is now conducted by most authorities, — in some it is compulsory for all pupils, in others it is voluntary and taken with the advice of the teachers. The examination is administered by a committee which may include members of the education committee, administrative officers, and representatives of teachers in elementary and secondary schools. The examination may be in one or two stages; where the latter practice is followed, the first stage is eliminatory, and the papers are marked usually by the head teachers of each school, following detailed instructions; the second stage is

[1] *Report of the Consultative Committee on the Curriculum of the Senior School* (Wakefield 1931).

conducted and marked by external examiners. The subjects of the examination always include arithmetic and English (dictation and spelling), sometimes history, geography, and nature study. In some areas the written examination is followed by an oral test for all candidates, or for those who reached a certain level in the written test, or for border-line cases; occasionally the oral test is administered by the secondary school to which the successful candidates will be admitted. School records are generally taken into account, and in a minority of the areas intelligence tests are used, but always supplementary to other examinations.[1] On the results of the examination, candidates are offered free admission to secondary or to central schools in order of merit to the number of free places available.[2]

Central schools. The origin of the central schools has already been given. They are schools intended for boys and girls who can remain in school for four years beyond the age of eleven, and have proved their ability in a selective examination, but are not considered sufficiently able to profit from a secondary education. The distinction between those who do and those who do not proceed to a secondary school is somewhat arbitrary; the general assumption is that the secondary school is intended for the academically minded and the central school for the practical minded. The difference in the curricula of the two types of school is also based on this distinction.

The central school offers a course of four years (occasionally five). It differs from the elementary school in that classes are smaller, the equipment somewhat superior, and the teachers selected and paid a bonus in addition to the elementary teachers' scale of salaries; as compared with the secondary schools, the classes are somewhat larger, the teachers are not always university graduates, although they are trained, the salaries are lower, and the work becomes more practical in the last two years. One very important consideration in the establishment of the central schools is that they are cheaper. A few years ago it was estimated that the cost per place in an elementary school was £26, in a central school £38, and in a secondary school £66, while the average cost per pupil was £11 10s. in an ele-

---

[1] In its *Report on the Primary School*, p. 127, the Consultative Committee expressed the opinion that "carefully devised group intelligence tests may be a useful factor in selection, but it would be inadvisable to rely on such tests alone." See also the Consultative Committee's *Report on Psychological Tests of Educable Capacity* (London, 1929).

[2] See Board of Education, *Education Pamphlet*, No. 63, *Memorandum on Examinations for Scholarships and Free Places in Secondary Schools* (London, 1928).

mentary school, £18 in a central school, and £34 in a secondary school.

The aims of the central schools, as announced at the opening of such a school at Morley in 1928, are as follows:

1. To widen the outlook of the pupils so that they may become intelligent citizens.
2. To give them the basis of a sound literary and scientific training so that they may learn to reason correctly and draw legitimate conclusions.
3. To train them to use their hands so that, if need be, they can afterwards follow skilled occupations, and make intelligent and profitable use of their leisure time.
4. To develop the æsthetic taste through the medium of art (drawing, painting, and music).
5. To teach them the elements of a foreign language (French) to open their minds to the difficulty of nations speaking different languages understanding one another, and to assist somewhat in the "rapprochement" of the nations of the world, which is so much to be desired.
6. To give them physical training and games to develop their bodies, to train them in swift judgment, accurate movement and coöperation, and to inculcate the ideals of fairness and good-will together with self-reliance, restraint and courage.[1]

The London central schools, which have served as a model for others, have provided for all pupils in the first two years, including English, mathematics (algebra and geometry), science, history, geography, art, music, handwork, and domestic science and needlework; French is included especially for pupils who plan to continue in the commercial course of the last two years. The work of the second half of the course becomes more definitely practical; without being definitely vocational, the courses are given a bias — commercial, industrial, or domestic. In the course with a commercial bias, bookkeeping, economics, commercial correspondence, shorthand, and typewriting, are added; in the industrial course more time is given to manual work of various kinds; in the domestic course for girls domestic science, household management, and the needlecrafts are given special attention. In some central schools the general course is continued in the last two years.

A comparison of the time allotted to the different subjects of the curriculum in secondary and central schools shows how very slight is the distinction between the two types. (See page 393.)

[1] *School Government Chronicle,* Jan. 28, 1928, p. 60.

TIME-SCHEDULE OF A MIXED SELECTIVE CENTRAL SCHOOL IN A RURAL AREA

SUBJECTS	IV A (min.)	IV B (min.)	III A (min.)	III B (min.)	II A (min.)	II B (min.)	I A (min.)	I B (min.)
English	210	210	210	210	245	245	245	245
History	105	105	70	70	70	70	70	70
Geography	105	70	105	70	105	105	105	105
French	175	..	175	..	175	175	175	175
Mathematics	175	245	210 } * 175 }	245	210	245 } † 210 }	210	210
Needlework (girls)	70	140	70	140	70	70	70	70
Mechanical drawing (boys)	..	70	..	140	70	70	70	70
Mechanical drawing (girls)	..	..	..	..	..	..	35	35
Surveying	..	70	..	..	..	..	..	..
Science (boys)	70	210	140 } * 70 }	210	140	140	140	140
Science (girls)	..	140	..	140	140	140	105	105
Art (boys)	70	70	70	70	70	70	70	70
Art (girls)	70	140	70	140	70	70	70	70
Handicraft	140	210	140	210	140	140	140	140
Housecraft	140	210	140	210	140	140	140	140
Commercial	175	..	175	..	..	..	..	..
Music	35	35	70	70	70	70	70	70
Physical training	35	35	35	35	35	35	35	35
Games	70	70	70	70	70	70	70	70
Gardening	..	..	140*	..	..	140†	..	..
Private study	70	..	70	..	..	..	..	..

* These are boys who will not be completing a full Form III course and who may be taking up Farm Service. Instead of French and part of the commercial course they take gardening and extra periods in mathematics, devoted to rural problems; they study bookkeeping and have extra science.

† These are boys who are judged unable to profit by a study of French; they, therefore, take up school gardening and extra mathematics.

Because the first four years of the secondary course culminates in an examination whose certificate carries some weight in securing employment, a number of central schools in London and elsewhere have tended to prepare their pupils for this examination and have not only sacrificed the interests of many pupils for the sake of the few, but have departed from the original purpose of the central schools to provide a differentiated type of education. It is now proposed, since certificates play an important part in the vocational career of the adolescent, to establish a distinct system of examination for central schools. An experiment along these lines has been tried in Manchester.

The chief source of the difficulty has, of course, not been attacked, nor can the problem be solved until it is recognized in England (as well as in France and Germany where the problem is similar) that all education beyond the break at about eleven should be classified as secondary, but that within this category there is room for differen-

ELEMENTARY EDUCATION

SUBJECT TIME-ANALYSIS IN MINUTES FOR ONE WEEK OF A FOUR-YEAR COURSE IN A SECONDARY SCHOOL FOR BOYS, A SECONDARY SCHOOL FOR GIRLS, A CENTRAL SCHOOL FOR BOYS, AND A CENTRAL SCHOOL FOR GIRLS [1]

BOYS

Subject	First Year		Second Year		Third Year			Fourth Year		
	S.	C.	S.	C.	S.	C.		S.	C.	
						Tech.	Com.		Tech.	Com.
English	225	385	180	345	180	335	340	180	285	335
History	135	120	90	90	90	90	100	135	90	100
Geography	135	120	90	90	90	100	110	90	100	100
Mathematics	270	385	270	320	270	420	330	315	315	315
Science	90	140	135	160	270	220	...	270	220	...
Languages	270	105	450	130	450	...	195	450	...	205
Commercial subjects	...	...	...	...	...	...	320	...	...	350
Handicraft	135	...	90	120	...	150	...	...	240	...
Drawing	90	90	90	120	90	120	...	...	195	...
Music	90	60	45	65	...	...	...	...	...	...
Scripture	45	60	45	60	45	60	60	45	60	60
Physical training	90	60	90	60	90	60	60	90	60	50
Recreation, preparation, prayers, school opening	75	125	75	90	75	95	135	75	85	135
Total in minutes per week	1,650	1,650	1,650	1,650	1,650	1,650	1,650	1,650	1,650	1,650

GIRLS

Subject	First Year		Second Year		Third Year			Fourth Year		
	S.	C.	S.	C.	S.	C.		S.	C.	
						Gen'l.	Com.		Gen'l.	Com.
English	320	345	160	300	160	375	345	120	285	285
History	80	80	80	80	80	120	90	80	90	90
Geography	80	90	80	80	40	120	90	80	140	140
Mathematics	160	285	200	280	200	310	330	240	350	260
Science	80	80	80	135	160	90	80	200 or 120	140	...
Languages	200	185	160 or 320	180	160 or 320	210	180	320 or 160	190	190
Commercial subjects	...	...	...	...	...	...	250	...	...	400
Handicraft (domestic)	80	220	240 or 80	230	240 or 80	80	...	... or 240	110	...
Drawing	80	80	80	80	80	60	...	80	60	...
Music	40	65	40	65	40	65	65	40	65	65
Scripture	80	60	80	60	40	60	60	40	60	60
Physical training	160	60	160	60	160	60	60	160	60	60
Recreation, preparation, prayers, school opening	290	100	290	100	290	100	100	290	100	100
Total in minutes per week	1,650	1,650	1,650	1,650	1,650	1,650	1,650	1,650	1,650	1,650

[1] From a *Report on Education in Other Lands*, by James McRae, M.A., Chief Inspector of Primary Schools, p. 27. Published by the Education Department, Victoria.

tiated types of schools for pupils of different abilities and capacities. Such a system would demand alertness on the part of the authorities and of teachers to see that pupils are adequately classified and that opportunities for transfer from one type of school to another are always open. England has already reached the realization that educational organization cannot be based, without encountering considerable difficulties, on social considerations. The opportunity for a reorganization on educational grounds and the abilities of pupils will be provided when all children will be assured of an education for four years beyond the age of eleven. The problem was well stated by the Director of Education for Kent, Mr. E. Salter Davies, before the Consultative Committee on the Education of the Adolescent:

> It can be laid down as a postulate that the organization of the education of children in the bulk up to fifteen or sixteen years of age cannot be carried out effectively so long as the practice prevails of thinking in terms of more or less parallel educational systems instead of concentrating on the problem of the education of adolescents as a whole.[1]

The United States, in solving the problem, has adopted the common school for all, providing differentiated courses within each school.[2] England and other European countries, have an opportunity of creating a democratic system of education in which schools will be organized on a functional basis, and in which the right pupil will find his way into the right school with the right curriculum adapted to his needs and capacities.

Conclusion. Elementary education in England has made remarkable progress since the beginning of the century, a progress in which the guiding hand of the Board of Education may be seen, but which has in no small manner been due to intelligent and sympathetic direction of administrators who have been called forth by the opportunity and by principals and teachers who have wisely used the freedom which is granted to them. That there are backward districts, no one would deny. Those, however, who would judge the progress of education by the amount of money spent or by the material fabric of the schools (buildings, equipment, and supplies) will fail to catch the

---

[1] *Report on the Education of the Adolescent*, p. 73.

[2] One of the serious criticisms of the American system is that in the zeal to provide identical opportunities for all, the interests of the able students have been sacrificed. See Thorndike, E. L., "The Distribution of Education," *School Review*, May, 1932, pp. 335 ff. See also Chapter VIII in the present volume.

spirit underlying the educative process.[1] The absence of standardization of uniformity in methods and courses of study, and of a dominating philosophy of education is apt to mislead the superficial observer. Particularly is this likely to be true in the case of the observer armed with a list of detailed objectives, based on a mechanistic psychology and on the principles derived from the canons of industrial efficiency, and convinced that certain results can only be obtained by specific methods adapted to their attainment. Nowhere is this better illustrated than in the teaching of reading and the fundamentals of language; an examination of the *Suggestions* on this point would reveal methods which have long been discarded by the scientific students of education, and yet the results of the two systems would be discouraging to the advocates of a "science" of education. There would here be found some arguments for the theory that those methods are best which work best.[2]

Not only has progress been made in methods of instruction, but the courses of study have undergone a process of revision and reconstruction; the formal and disciplinary elements have been discarded and greater emphasis is being placed upon those elements which have meaning and significance to the pupil. Here again the reform has not been carried out under the ægis of any philosophy or theory, but largely by trial and error [3] guided by a more sympathetic understanding of the child. The change which has taken place in the internal organization of the elementary school reflects also the change in the public attitude toward it. The elementary school has gradually become the common school for all. With this concept as the starting-point, the whole system is beginning to be reorganized on the principle that national welfare and progress depend upon sound education and the provision of equality of educational opportunity to each according to his ability. This is the stage which has been reached; the reorganization is not complete, and, as usual in all matters of social progress in England, the problem of reorganization is being solved by trial and error. When the desirable form has been

[1] Considerable progress has, of course, been made in replacing antiquated with modern buildings.

[2] There is undoubtedly need of objective comparisons of different methods of instruction in English and American schools. Such a comparison of results in fundamental subjects has been made recently by the Scottish Research Council, which tends to corroborate the statement made above.

[3] Dr. P. Ballard has wittily called this the Bessemer Process in Education. See *The Changing School*, Chapter XV (London, 1926).

achieved, legislative action will follow to consolidate the gains which have been made and to provide for the advance to the next stage. If convincing proof is desired of the achievements of the English elementary school, it will not be found in results of examinations or by objective tests and measurements, but in a concrete visual comparison such as is afforded by the photographs of children in elementary schools in the same districts of London thirty years ago and today.[1] More remarkable perhaps than the progress itself is the fact that the major portion of it has taken place in the period of economic strain following the War. Whatever the results may be on the intellectual side, there has been an improvement in manners and in physique; there may be, although it has not been proved, less accuracy and thoroughness, but they are balanced by greater alertness and adaptability. In other respects England, like all other countries, is confronted by problems which always accrue in a period of social transition, unrest, and uncertainty, when society is released from its old moorings and values and has not yet found new objects of allegiance.

2. FRANCE

General character of French education. In an era of educational reform, when virtually all her neighbors are reorganizing their educational systems and practices, France stands out for her staunch loyalty to theories elaborated in a period of intellectual revolt and put into practice when the Third Republic was established. France has produced a long list of distinguished educational statesmen — Jules Ferry, Paul Bert, Octave Gréard, Félix Pécaut, Ferdinand Buisson, and Louis Liard — who laid the foundations of her educational system; through Gabriel Compayré she contributed to the study of the history of education, and through Alfred Binet and Dr. T. Simon she gave to the world an instrument of educational research which has been more fully elaborated and applied in other educational systems than her own; the French concept of culture has exercised a dominating influence over a large part of Europe, Asia Minor, and South America. In the field of educational theory, however, it would be difficult to discover any French educator whose work is known outside

---

[1] See the *Annual Report of the London County Council* on the Elementary Schools of London, 1925, Appendix 1 (London, 1925), and *The London Education Service*, pp. 52 ff. (London, 1927).

of his country.[1] The French system of education is peculiarly national and rooted in the soil of French ideals, French philosophy, and French culture.

The explanation of this situation is not to be found in the rigid centralization of educational administration; centralization is to be explained rather by the French emphasis on logical organization, by profound faith in and reverence for French culture, which must become the heritage of all her citizens, and by the desire to preserve French national solidarity through imparting the common heritage in the schools. There is another important factor which can be cited as an explanation of the character of French education in general and elementary education in particular; France has not developed a child psychology which in other countries has been so effective in changing the character of the elementary school. The child is still regarded as a miniature adult, and instruction still emphasizes the cult of reason and logic rather than activity and behavior at the child's level. By development and growth of the child, French pedagogy still understands increased mastery of subject-matter through the development of reason, and subject-matter is built up, not on the interests of the child, but as an introduction to French culture. The place of reason in French life has been excellently illustrated by Cloudesley Brereton in his discussion of "Moral Instruction in France." Referring to the varied uses of the word *raison* in the French language he writes:

> They intrude, in fact, into the moral domain and even into the sphere of action.... Note for instance the moral *nuances* in the uses of *avoir raison* (to be in the right), *donner raison à quelqu'un* (own that some one is in the right), *dire avec raison* (rightly, justly, equitably), *entendre raison* (to comply with something just), *comme de raison* (as is just), *pour valoir ce que de raison* (in equity), *entrer en raison avec quelq'un* (to remonstrate, reason together, — as to *rights* and *wrongs*), *lui demander raison de quelque chose* (ask him to justify himself), *rendre raison de quelque chose* (to justify), *point de raison* (justification).
>
> Note again the *nuance* of action implied in the phrases *avoir raison de ses vices* (to get the better of his vices), *demander raison au tyran* (challenge, attack), *faire raison* (render justice), *conter ses raisons* (business). But the full strength of the word raison is best seen or felt in such phrases as *raison suffisante* (sovereign reason), *raison d'être* or *raison d'état*.[2]

---

[1] Auguste Comte's philosophy of positivism and its educational interpretation would, of course, have to be excepted. Emile Durkheim is known outside of France as a sociologist by many students who do not know that he was professor of education at the Sorbonne.

[2] Brereton, Cloudesley, *Studies in Foreign Education*, p. 219 (London, Harrap, 1913).

Where the English language emphasizes conduct or behavior, the French stress reason.

The character of elementary education is thus derived from the emphasis on French culture and on the development of reason. The work of the school must provide for the progress of the pupil in both directions. Through a curriculum based on French culture, he will be introduced to the great spirit of humanism and a body of knowledge and information common to all French citizens; through the cult of reason he will develop the highest and most important human quality. To culture he will be introduced gradually as he passes through the various stages of his psychological development; at first the emphasis will be on the concrete and training of the senses; the next stage will give him the foundation of knowledge and information; at the third stage the emphasis will be more on the abstract and on training in deductive reasoning. The course of the child's education is mapped out in advance and the map is gradually filled in as he grows more mature; hence the curriculum is organized on the concentric method, and expands by reviews and repetition through the three stages of the pupil's development. Facts first, then ideas, but facts and ideas derived from the body of knowledge which society has come to regard as the proper heritage of its members. The principles of method are based, not on the activity of the child based on his interests as they react to his environment, but on the theory that the child must learn first before he can express himself or create. Activities, problems, projects, which are in the foreground of the new educational philosophy, have not replaced the French emphasis on receptivity, assimilation, and then creation. The pupil must understand, in the best sense of the word, all that is taught him, but what is taught him is determined by the kind of individual that society desires to reproduce as man and as citizen, for "the civilization which education must transmit is something different from the nature of the individual and cannot be attained by following nature," that is, the interests and urges of the child. The intellectual sympathy with the child which "is carried to extremes, even to the point of wishing to derive the methods of education solely from a consideration of children's characteristics," makes little appeal to the majority of French educators. He agrees with the new philosophy of education that the aim of education is the development of the personality of the child, but he starts, not with the premise of the autonomy of the child, but with the conviction that the family, society, and the State are the trustees of the child's right to an education, and differs from the progressives in his interpretation of personality.

French philosophers, as is well known, distinguish between individuality and personality. The individual is such by virtue of the fact that he is different from others. He is a person to the extent that he represents the conscience of truths valid for all and the will to undertake duties common to all. The individual ought to become a person, that is, in a sense he should de-individualize himself, and this is the work of education and of personal effort.[1]

From the point of view of the new education this attitude to the curriculum to be imparted in the school would be described as "extrinsic," as "fixed in advance," as "impositions." The same attitude governs the views on discipline. Beginning in the family, the French notion of discipline is based on authority, at first of persons, then of moral law. The school as a miniature society must be governed by a body of rules, a code which is gradually converted into a moral law, whose atmosphere dominates the spirit of the school. On the theory of self-discipline, the French educator is skeptical.

Experiments along these lines [says M. Pécaut] have been made here and there, but too infrequently to justify any generalized conclusions; in fact, where they succeed, it is difficult to discern what is the result of pupil effort and what is due to the authority, concealed but ever present, of the teacher.[2]

Elementary education, then, represents the will of the State, of the adult members of society, their culture and their traditions, and their aspirations. Because the French State has determined, since the establishment of the Third Republic, for reasons which have their origin in history and not because of antagonism to religion, to separate Church and State, the French school is a lay, secular school. The State, desiring to maintain impartiality in matters of religion, decided to establish its school on principles acceptable to all. But in remaining lay and neutral in religion, the State has not surrendered its right and responsibility to impart instruction in moral ideas acceptable to all and a common spiritual bond to all. The State has not, however, refused to recognize the right of parents to provide for

---

[1] *Educational Yearbook, 1929*, p. 141. This and the other quotations in the above paragraphs are taken from Félix Pécaut's article in this volume on "The Philosophy Underlying the National System of Education in France."

[2] *Educational Yearbook, 1929*, p. 171.

the religious instruction of their children in their own way. For this purpose all schools are closed on Thursday, and parents may follow the dictates of their own consciences in arranging or refusing to arrange for the religious instruction of their children through the spiritual teachers of the denominations to which they belong. Such religious instruction may not be given in a building used as a public or private school, nor by a public school teacher, nor during regular school hours; the only exception which is permitted is that pupils may be excused during school hours to attend religious exercises during the week preceding their first communion.

The ideal of the lay schools, it must be remembered, is not an innovation of the Third Republic. It was inherent in the educational thought of the Revolution; and the ideal of the lay teacher as the priest of intelligence and the leader of progress was expressed by Victor Hugo, *A propos d' Horace* (*Les Contemplations*, 1831):

> Chaque village aura, dans un temple rustique
> Dans la lumière, au lieu du magister antique,
> Trop noir pour que jamais le jour y pénétrât,
> L'instituteur lucide et grave, magistrat
> Du progrès, médecin de l'ignorance et prêtre
> De l'idée: et dans l'ombre on verra disparaître
> L'éternel écolier et l'éternel pédant.

THE ELEMENTARY SCHOOL SYSTEM

The elementary school system in France includes all those schools and institutions which belong to the branch of elementary as distinguished from higher education. There are accordingly included not only the elementary school proper (*l'école primaire*), but the maternal or infant school which precedes it (*l'école maternelle et la classe enfantine*), and the higher elementary school (*l'école primaire supérieure*), and the institutions for the preparation of teachers for these schools (*l'école normale primaire et l'école normale primaire supérieure*).[1]

L'école maternelle. The maternal or infant school is an institution for children below the age of compulsory attendance, which grew out of the *salle d'asile*, a charitable institution, based on the ideas of Oberlin and Père Girard, and established by regulations issued in 1837 "to provide maternal care and the early stage of edu-

---

[1] These are discussed in Chapter VII.

cation suitable to the ages of the pupils." The law of June 16, 1881, recognized the *salle d'asile* as a part of the system of free public education. Under the present title of *école maternelle et la classe enfantine*, this institution was incorporated into the system in the Law of October 30, 1886, the charter of elementary education; the organization and work of the school were defined by a decree and *arrêté* (regulation) issued on January 18, 1887, which have continued to constitute the basis of the maternal school up to the present. The provision of a maternal school is not, like that of an elementary school, compulsory, but it may be established at the option of the municipalities, but, once established, it must be maintained for a period of ten years by agreement between the commune and the State and state aid is given for its support. This regulation applies only to municipalities with a population of 2000, of whom 1200 are concentrated in a town or village; municipalities of smaller size may also establish such schools, but wholly at their own expense.

The maternal school is "an institution for the stage in education in which children of both sexes, between the ages of two and six, receive in common the care required for their physical, moral, and intellectual development." In municipalities with less than 2000 population, a *classe enfantine* may be annexed to the elementary school, under the charge of the principal, and performs the same function as the maternal school, which is an independent institution under its own principal (*directrice*). The construction and equipment of the maternal school are defined in detail by the regulations issued in 1927: waiting-rooms must be provided for parents, rooms must be set aside for classroom activities, rest and recreation; a court and playground must be available; the school must be equipped with a kitchen, a medicine cupboard, cloakrooms, washbowls, sanitary arrangements, and cots; the school furniture must consist of movable chairs and tables; for instructional and recreational activities each school must have a supply of toys, sand-trays, wagons, and carts, jumping-ropes, hoops, pails, balls, beads, paper for cutting, weaving, and folding, raffia, wool and cotton, scissors, and clay, cubes, bricks, rings, sticks, pictures, slates and crayons, and a tuning-fork. The regulations express a pious wish, on the whole, since the movement to reform the *école maternelle*, which began nearly thirty years ago, has not yet met with success, due in part to the scholastic tradition of the past and the demand of parents that their children be taught as early as possible to read, write, and cipher, in part to the inadequate differentiation in the preparation of the teachers, and in part to the fact that many of the schools are inspected by elementary school inspectors rather than by experts, a weakness which has been greatly reduced in recent years.

Children are admitted to the *école maternelle* at the age of two and remain until the age of six. No child may be admitted without a medical certificate; absences are carefully checked to prevent the spread of disease; and a medical officer is expected to visit once a month. The teachers must hold a *brevet supérieur* (see Chapter VII), with special qualifications in the theory of education in the maternal school, puericulture, hygiene, and the sciences applied to these subjects. Principals must have the same qualifications and five years of experience in a maternal school. In addition, there is appointed an unqualified assistant (*femme de service*) to look after the cleanliness and physical needs of the children. Increasingly the inspection of maternal schools is being entrusted to inspectresses with special qualifications; candidates for appointment must be twenty-five years of age and hold the *brevet supérieur* and the *certificat d'aptitude pédagogique* or some recognized equivalents, must have had five years of teaching experience in an elementary or secondary school, and must pass a special examination. The examination consists in the written part of two essays, one on some subject in the theory of education in the maternal school, and the other on the hygiene of the maternal school. The oral examination includes the discussion of some problems on the education and hygiene of the maternal school and questions on the law and administration of such school. In addition, a report of an inspection of a maternal school must be presented.

The size of a maternal school is limited to 150 pupils; where the number exceeds 50, an assistant principal is appointed. The size of each class is limited to 25, pupils being divided into two groups according to age and intelligence — usually those below and those above the age of five being grouped together. The curriculum consists of (1) physical exercises: breathing exercises, games, and movements accompanied by songs; (2) sensory exercises, manual work, and drawing; (3) exercises in observing things and familiar objects; (4) exercises for the development of moral habits; (5) exercises in language and recitation; and (6) introductory exercises in reading, writing, and arithmetic for the older pupils. In a circular issued by the Ministry of Public Instruction on November 10, 1931, the following distribution of time is suggested:

Recreation and personal care...................	5 periods
Rhythmic exercises............................	2
Sense-training and observation................	2
Modeling and drawing.........................	2
Manual work..................................	2
Singing and music.............................	2
Recitation and story-telling...................	2
Arithmetic....................................	2
Language, speech, and oral exercises...........	10
Total.............................	29

During the last few years a tendency in a new direction has been noticeable, with less concern for formal school work and instruction and more emphasis on play and free activities. This may be the result of the spread of the Montessori theory; it may be a return to the original method suggested by earlier regulations which stated that the best method is that which gives the name to the school — "the closest imitation of the educational procedure of an intelligent and devoted mother — a method essentially natural, personal, and always open to new suggestions, always ready to expand and to reform." Freedom, health and happiness, the promotion of spontaneous and joyful activity, training in observation and thinking, and physical and moral development are the characteristics of the new tendency. Despite this, much still remains to be done to bring the French maternal school up to the level of the pre-schools elsewhere, and not the least important of the innovations, assuming that brighter buildings could be secured, would be the abandonment of the depressing, if useful and economical, black smock.

Elementary education. Public elementary education has its origin in the *Loi Guizot* of 1833, which required every commune to establish an elementary school, but failed to impose compulsory attendance. The reactionary *Loi Falloux* (1850) practically placed the control of education in the hands of the ecclesiastical authorities and lowered the qualifications which the *Loi Guizot* had required of teachers; the slow progress of elementary education was indicated in 1865 by the fact that 26 per cent of the men and 44 per cent of the women were unable to sign the marriage certificates. Victor Duruy, recognizing the importance of education at a time when universal suffrage had been granted, proposed to make elementary education free and compulsory; the *Loi Duruy*, which was passed in 1867, failed to secure those two essentials of public education, but did succeed in requiring communes to tax themselves for the maintenance of schools, curtailed the influence of the Church, regulated the qualifications of teachers, introduced the school funds (*caisses d'écoles*) to aid poor pupils, and added geography and history to the curriculum.

The defeat of France by the German schoolmaster in 1870 at once drove home to the leading statesmen the recognition that the problem of elementary education must be one of the first tasks to be considered in the reconstruction which followed the establishment of the Third Republic. Jules Simon announced that he would introduce a bill to make school attendance compulsory, but the National Assembly showed no interest in it. Ten years later the program of the reformers began to be realized: elementary education was made free by the law of June 16, 1881; by the law of March 28, 1882, school attendance was made compulsory for all children between the ages of six and thirteen and the lay secular course of study was introduced; finally, the whole system was codified by the Organic Law of October 30, 1886, defined by the decree and *arrêté* of January 18, 1887.

Compulsory attendance. Elementary education is compulsory for all children between the ages of six and thirteen; they may attend public or private schools or be educated at home; in the last case pupils must be submitted, after the third school year, to an annual examination conducted by a committee consisting of an elementary school inspector or his deputy, a cantonal delegate, and another person holding a recognized certificate. In localities where a maternal school or infant class is not available children may be admitted at the age of five.

A school census is drawn up each year by the mayor, assisted by the school committee, and a notice is sent to parents who have children of school age. All children must be registered in a school fifteen days before the beginning of the scholastic year, or a statement must be submitted by their parents of the provision made for their education otherwise. Parents and guardians are responsible for the school attendance of their children or wards; in cases of inexcusable absence, the school committee (*commission scolaire*) may post the names of parents or guardians on the public notice-board of the town hall for a period of fifteen days or a month. For further repetitions, a penalty of a fine from eleven to fifteen francs, or imprisonment for five days or more, may be imposed.

The administration of compulsory attendance is perhaps the weakest feature of French education. School committees may exempt pupils above the age of eleven, if living and working for their parents or guardians, from attendance for three months in a year, provided the approval of the elementary school inspector is obtained for exemptions of more than fifteen days; with the approval of the departmental council, a school committee may exempt pupils for one or two periods a day to engage in farm work for employers other than their parents. Pupils who pass the examination, which they may take at the age of twelve, and obtain the *certificat d'études primaires*, are exempted from further attendance at school. Repeated efforts have been made to require attendance for the full period during which schools are in session, but the poor success of such efforts prevent further attempts to extend compulsory education up to fourteen. France did not sign the Geneva Convention of 1921. Teachers and inspectors are urged to use their influence to improve regularity of attendance. One result of the poor administration of compulsory attendance, which is explained by the lack of an adequate supply of labor in the agricultural areas, the unwillingness of school committees to use the authority with which they are endowed, and to some extent the failure, until recently, to adapt the school curriculum to rural conditions, has been a perceptible increase of illiteracy. France had succeeded before the War in reducing the percentage of illiteracy to 3 per cent; in 1924, of 235,325 conscripts called to the colors, 13,838, or 6.2 per cent, were unable to read or write.[1] The figure continued to increase and in 1928 had reached nearly 9 per cent.[2]

[1] Quoted by Albert Thomas in an address on *La Prolongation de la Scolarité et ses Répercussions sociales*. See *L'Hygiène par l'Exemple*, January-February, 1928, pp. 11 ff.

[2] According to a report quoted in the *Living Age* (January 12, 1924, p. 50), from *L'Intransigeant*, out of 700 recruits at one army station, two out of every ten could be classed as educated in the ordinary sense of the term; of the remaining eight, five on the average could read and write a little, two could spell with great difficulty, and the eighth was quite illiterate. In justification, it may be stated that these recruits had passed through the period of compulsory school age during the War.

The elementary school. The elementary education of all French children is today the same, whether given in public elementary school, or in private schools, at home, or in the preparatory classes of secondary schools. The majority of children, however, attend public elementary schools, which must be provided in every commune. Separate schools are maintained for boys and girls in communes with more than five hundred inhabitants, unless special permission is obtained to establish a mixed school. The teachers (*instituteurs* and *institutrices*) must have recognized qualifications (the *brevet élémentaire*) granted on an examination in the work of a higher elementary school, the *brevet supérieur*, obtained by examination at the end of the normal school course, and the *certificat d'aptitude pédagogique*, conferred as the result of an examination after at least two years of service.[1] Boys must be taught by men, girls and mixed classes of boys and girls by women; in exceptional cases women, provided that they are related to the principal, may teach in boys' schools.

All elementary education is under the supervision of inspectors — general, specially assigned to this field, academy inspectors, and elementary school inspectors.[2] A large number of the public elementary schools are single-teacher schools. In schools with two or more classes, a principal (*directeur* or *directrice*) is appointed; for this position no special examinations or qualifications are required except that candidates must be at least twenty-one years of age. Principals who do not have charge of a definite class, as they do in small schools, are required to give four hours of instruction each week in one of the essential subjects of the curriculum; from this duty they can only be exempted in schools with an enrollment of three hundred pupils. On the principal devolves the responsibility for the sound organization of instruction, of helping and supervising the teachers, especially the young teachers in his school, of providing for satisfactory articulation between the different classes, and of maintaining with his teachers constant relations between the school and the home, the locality, civic life, and educational institutions. Although not required by law or regulations, the practice of organizing a teachers' council (*conseil des maîtres*) has grown up since 1908, which through conferences and meetings maintains the unity of work in the school, promotes the interest of the teachers and their

[1] See further, Chapter VII.   [2] See further, Chapter V.

professional growth. Meeting at the beginning and end of each school year, and at least once a term, the council drafts regulations for the internal organization of the school, assigns pupils and teachers to their classes, and determines on promotions from the maternal school or infant class outside of the regular period. Disciplinary measures and rewards to pupils are meted out by the council. It is, however, the opportunity for discussing educational problems — the time-schedule, adaptation of the course of study, consideration of methods of instruction, provision and maintenance of the school library — which gives such councils their importance. Administrative action recommended by the teachers' councils are subject to the approval of the local elementary school inspector.

The aim of elementary education. The aim of elementary education which determines the character of the curriculum was summarized in a statement by Octave Gréard, who organized the system of elementary education in Paris and later, as vice-rector of the University of Paris and chairman of many commissions, exercised a strong influence on the development of education in France. This statement, which was formulated by Gréard in 1887, and is still accepted as valid in the *Instruction* issued in 1923, is as follows:

> The object of elementary education is not to burden the different subjects that are treated with everything that can be learned, but to learn well in each of the branches that of which we cannot be permitted to be ignorant.

The aim of elementary education is accordingly to preserve and transmit the treasures of acquired truth, to enlighten the consciences, to strengthen the judgments, and in general to develop the pupils physically, morally, and intellectually. Elementary education should be both utilitarian and educational, for

> We have no intention of abandoning either one of the two aims which have been assigned to elementary education. We do not overlook the fact that most of our pupils, from the time they leave us, will have to work for a living; and we desire to supply them with a fund of practical knowledge which tomorrow will serve them in their vocation. But we do not forget, furthermore, that we should be forming in them the man and the citizen that they are to become tomorrow. Concern with urgent realities will not cause us to neglect the cult of the ideal.[1]

---

[1] From the *Instruction, 20 Juin, 1923, relative au Nouveau Plan d'Etudes des Ecoles Elémentaires.* See Kandel, I. L., *French Elementary Schools, Official Courses of Study,* p. 54 (New York, 1926).

The elementary school pupil is expected to leave school with a fund of practical knowledge and some appreciation of the meaning of civilization. French philosophy of education, as interpreted by the Ministry of Public Instruction, thus emphasizes social control and adult needs rather than the direct and immediate needs and interests of the pupils.

Curriculum and course of study. It follows from this aim and from the character of the French administrative system that the curriculum and course of study of the elementary schools are prescribed and defined by law, and by decrees and regulations issued by the Ministry of Public Instruction. In the preparation of the courses of study the inspectors and the Higher Council of Public Instruction coöperate, but responsibility and authority for its enforcement are vested in the Ministry. The basic foundation of the curriculum and the course of study was laid by the Decree of January 18, 1887, and the regulation of the same date. It is significant of the French conviction on the subject that no extensive revision was made until a new course of study was issued on February 23, 1923, followed by *Instruction* published on June 20 of that year. The revision was undertaken, as is explained in the *Instruction*, not because the historical curriculum and course of study were unsound, but because they had not been put into practice in the spirit which had been intended.

"What demand does the reform meet? Has the system drafted by the authors of our school laws revealed itself as defective?" are questions asked in the new *Instruction*. The answer is:

By no means. Each time that one reads over the statement in the *Instructions* of 1887, one is filled with admiration. It is thus not without apprehension that we have decided to apply to this structure the modifications that time has rendered necessary. We have taken care, of course, not to affect the outstanding features, and however important certain innovations may appear, the general tone remains the same. In reforming the institution, we intend to remain faithful to the principles of the founders.

But experience has proved that, in order to obtain a better application of these principles, there was need of a definite statement on the proper use of the time allowed, of simplifying and graduating the programs, of vitalizing the methods, and coördinating the subjects. To define, to simplify, to graduate, to vitalize, and to coördinate, such has been our aim.[1]

---

[1] Kandel, *op. cit.*, p. 45.

Teachers had failed to understand the regulations, had not followed the organization of the course of studies strictly, had tended to crowd it into a shorter period than was intended through fear lest pupils might leave school without completing it, and had overburdened the pupils. The new *Instruction* aimed to clarify the organization, to simplify the program, and, as a result of the simplification, to leave greater freedom to the teacher in retaining or adding or even omitting certain topics, and in adapting the work to the needs of his pupil and the conditions of local life.

The course of study is organized, not by years or classes, but by courses: for children from the age of six to seven (*cours préparatoire*), one year; for children between the ages of seven and nine (*cours élémentaire*), two years; for children between the ages of nine and eleven (*cours moyen*), two years; for children between the ages of eleven to thirteen (*cours supérieur*), two years. In each course beyond the preparatory the second year was in the old course of study largely a repetition and review of the first; while something of the concentric method of organization is retained, it has lost its rigidity in the new *Instruction*, for

With pupils ranging from six to thirteen years of age, it would be dangerous to give up all repetition and review. There are lessons to which it is necessary to return in the various courses, so that the pupil may complete, according as he is more capable of understanding and reasoning, the notions previously taught. But if it is desired that the child should study with pleasure and profit, the monotony of repetition and distaste for what as already been studied should be avoided.... Give, then, to your pupil the impression that he is progressing; that he is discovering a new realm. Instead of the concentric, take in preference the progressive method.[1]

The prescribed subjects of instruction in the elementary school curriculum are as follows: moral and civic instruction, reading and writing, French, arithmetic and the metric system, history and geography (especially of France), object lessons and elementary science, drawing, singing, manual work for boys (applied chiefly to agriculture), and needlework for girls, physical and military training. The language of instruction must be French except in Alsace-Lorraine where bilingualism has been sanctioned since 1926. The time-distribution of the subjects are as follows:

[1] Kandel, *op. cit.*, p. 51.

OFFICIAL TIME-SCHEDULE

	PREP. SEC. Hrs.	ELEM. COURSE		MIDDLE COURSE		HIGHER COURSE		TOTAL	
		B. Hrs.	G. Hrs.	B. Hrs.	G. Hrs.	B. Hrs.	G. Hrs.	Boys Hrs.	Girls Hrs.
Moral and civic instruction.........	1¼	1¼	1¼	1¼	1¼	1½	1½	5¼	5¼
Reading.............	10	7	6½	3	3	2½	2½	22½	22
Writing.............	5	2½	2½	1½	1½	¾	¾	9¾	9¾
French.............	2½	5	5	7½	7	7½	7	22½	21½
History and geography............		2½	2½	3	3	3	3	8½	8½
Arithmetic and geometry..........	2½	3½	3½	4½	4½	5	5	15½	15½
Physical and natural science..........	1¼	1½	1½	2½	2	2½	2½	7¾	7¼
Drawing............	1	1	1	1	1	1	1	4	4
Manual work.......	1½	1	1½	1	2	1½	2	5	7
Music (inc. singing).	1¼	1	1	1	1	1	1	4¼	4¼
Physical training....	1¾	2	2	2	2	2	2	7¾	7¾
Recreation..........	2	1¾	1¾	1¾	1¾	1¾	1¾	7¼	7¼
Total hours....	30	30	30	30	30	30	30	120	120

Within this distribution each school may make up its own time-schedule subject to the approval of the elementary school inspector.

It is clear from the discussion on the preceding pages that the work of the French elementary school continues to be based on the dualism between subject-matter and pupil, which the new education seeks to eliminate. The French theory is that there is a body of facts, information, knowledge, of which no person can be permitted to be ignorant:

We do not ask that each child be left to do just as he likes, according to his fancy; the school is no more a playroom than it is a prison; the school is the school — a gathering of children who work whole-heartedly for their common education, under the guidance of the teacher.

The function of the teacher is to act as an intermediary between the subject-matter to be learned and the pupil by appealing to his interest and inspiring him with enthusiasm for his work. The pupil should be guided to take pleasure in his work, "conscious of working towards the realization of a beautiful ideal."

The only method that is suitable to teaching elementary grades is that which provides for an interchange between the teacher and the pupils; which maintains between them, so to speak, a continuous exchange of ideas, varied, flexible, and cleverly graded.

The methods of instruction follow in the main three steps — exposition by the teacher, discussion through questions and answers, and summaries in the form of an idea, a formula, a *cliché*, a short statement to be entered into the pupils' exercise books and memorized. These steps are illustrated with particular clarity in the textbooks on moral instruction; the teacher makes a general statement, develops it by questions and answers, and leads up to a summary sentence which synthesizes the point reached and which is then entered into the exercise books as the resolutions to be adopted by the pupils; this is followed by reading of selections to illustrate the discussion, and then by an exercise to be done by the pupils. The resolutions reached in a lesson on good health intended for pupils between the ages of nine and thirteen were as follows:

(1) Good health is incomparable wealth for all.
(2) Good health is not real and complete unless it applies both to the body and to all those faculties that are called the soul.
(3) He who only takes care of his body is like the workman who stops with the care of the body.
(4) Good health of the soul regulates that of the body.
(5) Only those are well who have a sound body and a sound soul.[1]

Nothing could better illustrate the French emphasis on the abstract idea than a lesson of this kind.

The regulations set up a standard curriculum, but do not exclude freedom or variety which comes from the teacher's cultural background and skill in instruction. There appears to be an increasing tendency to permit adaptation to local conditions, a tendency which is due to the influence of foreign practice, the advocacy of new methods by *Les Compagnons*, and the realization that the failure of the rural schools is the result of failure to adapt the programs to the rural environment. Recent circulars have encouraged the normal schools to devote some attention to the preparation of teachers for single-teacher schools, and elementary schools to stress the local environment and to give attention to the occupations of young children. What is demanded of all schools is that what is done should be done thoroughly. Knowledge and information continue to be emphasized, but so are attention, activity, observation, and judgment, as the desirable ends of education. The *In-*

---

[1] From Garcin, F., *Le Livre Auxiliaire du Maître pour la Morale Active aux Cours Moyen et Supérieur* (Paris, 1924).

struction urges "more air, more ease, more freedom, more joy, and finally, more work." None the less, it would be a mistake to confuse these recommendations with those of the new education. France offers in her educational system an example of a country which has definite convictions as to what shall be taught; starting with a prescribed, standard curriculum, she recognizes the value of good expository teaching which, while it seeks to impart a definite round of subjects to be learned, does not fail to pay due regard to the child.

Of the subjects of the curriculum those which are considered as the most important besides the fundamentals are moral instruction and French. The training of character should take precedence over that of intelligence and overlaps both physical and intellectual training. The three forms of training really constitute one whole, for through intellectual training judgment is developed and the cultivation of the judgment is the best way of training the will, to which physical education also contributes. The process of moral instruction follows the three stages of the child's development — from the concrete through a mixture of concrete and abstract to ideas; hence it emphasizes habit-formation and opportunities for moral judgment in school conduct and culminates in a body of moral ideas. With moral instruction is combined civic training in the duties of the individual as man and as citizen, and the study of government despite the emphasis in the *Instruction* on the practical aspects of moral training. The course of study (the upper course with pupils from eleven to thirteen discusses conscience and character, self-education, and the various aspects of solidarity) and the textbooks on moral instruction bring out clearly the influence of Descartes in French education and the emphasis on reason and the reasoned life.

The teaching of the French language derives its importance, not only because it is looked upon as an instrument for maintaining and disseminating a beautiful language and a beautiful literature, but because it is a valuable means for strengthening national unity. To overcome the *patois* of the village and the dialect of the province, particular attention is paid to recitation and elocution, to grammar and vocabulary exercises, until in the last stage the command of language and ideas is tested by exercises in composition and the pupil is introduced to simple canons of taste and appreciation through reading of French literature.

Through history and geography, the pupil is introduced to a knowledge of France and her relations in the past and in the present with the rest of the world. Both subjects have another function to perform than that of conveying information; both can be employed to develop and cultivate patriotic feeling; the rights of science and the rights of truth are not opposed. Hence "French patriotism has nothing to fear from truth.... The place of France in the world is sufficiently great and her rôle sufficiently noble to justify a sincere kind of instruction, scrupulously truthful." And yet the French elementary school teachers through their largest professional organizations threatened in 1926 to refuse to use the current history textbooks unless all expressions of hatred were removed, and in addition, undertook the preparation of a textbook, which, in the opinion of the organization, would be more accurately representative of the truth.[1]

Some idea of the organization of the curriculum on the concentric method and of the emphasis on repetition and review may be obtained from the following analysis of the monthly and weekly course of study in geography and history contained in a handbook which was prepared for teachers by two normal school principals and which elaborates in detail the course of study prescribed by the Ministry:[2]

GEOGRAPHY
Elementary Course

First Year	*Second Year*
Local	Review (2 months)
Plans	Asia, Africa, Europe (1 month)
Terminology	France (6 months)
Asia	Review (1 month)
Australia	
Africa	
America	
Europe	
Great countries	
Review (1 month)	

---

[1] Prudhommeaux, J., *Pour la Paix par l'Ecole* (Nîmes, 1928); German translation, *Der Kampf um das Geschichtsbuch in Frankreich* (Leipzig, 1929).

[2] Gay, P. H. and Mortreux, O., *Programmes Officiels des Ecoles Primaires Elémentaires, 1923, Texte officielle, Repartition Mensuelle et Hebdomadaire, Emploi du Temps — Documents Annexes* (Paris, 1924). A translation of this work will be found in Kandel, I. L., *op. cit.*, pp. 121 ff.

France
  Physical
  Industrial
Review (1 month)

Middle Course

Review (3 months)
France (7 months)
France — Colonial Possessions

France (8 months)
  Industrial
  Colonial Possessions
Europe
Asia
Africa
America
Review (1 month)
France

Upper Course

Europe
  Relief, physical
  British Isles
  All countries
Asia
France and her Colonies (5 months)
Germany

HISTORY

Elementary Course

First Year

France to 1453
Review (1 month)

Second Year

Review (3 months)
France to 1610
  Inventions and discoveries
  Art, Renaissance, Religion
  Review (1 month)

Middle Course

Review (1 month)
France to 1815

Review (2 months)
France 1815–1918
Review

Upper Course

Review to 1919
Review of the Review (1 month)

Ancient History
  Egypt, Greece, Jews, Romans, Christianity, Germans
Review of France (7 months)
Relations to England and Prussia
Review (1 month)

It is unnecessary to discuss the other subjects of the curriculum in detail. They may be characterized, like the rest of the course of study, as somewhat formal, factual, and informational, but leaning somewhat to the practical implications. Increased attention is being given to local and regional studies, and excursions are being introduced to secure and supplement the materials of instruction.

Such excursions (*excursions* or *promenades*), if made during regular class hours, must receive the authorization of the local inspector; if made on Thursdays or Sundays, such approval is not required, the State assuming responsibility for accidents which are not the result of serious negligence on the part of the teachers.

There is thus a tendency toward the new or progressive in education, but only within the limits of the prescribed curriculum. Educational experimentation of a radical character is not encouraged, except in extra-curricular activities, such as self-government and organization of pupils' coöperatives. In the literature of progressive education there is to be noted only one instance of a free experiment in the field of elementary education, that conducted by M. R. Cousinet, a government inspector, who was given an opportunity in his district to try out courses of study and methods of instruction, following the models of the new education developed outside of France.[1]

Administrative controls. Although the regulations speak of freedom for the teachers, the administrative controls have not been changed. The method of teacher preparation is still of the apprenticeship type and teachers grow up in the elementary branch of the educational system. In their school work they are supervised by inspectors whose approval is needed for every act not already prescribed and whose duty it is to see that prescribed regulations are carried out. In their instruction they are limited by the regulations which define the curriculum, course of study, and methods of instruction, and in addition, have available a number of manuals which work out the government regulations in detail and weekly professional journals which devote a part of each number to lesson plans and answers to examination questions.[2] Every pupil is required to have an exercise book in which the first task in each subject is written at the beginning of each month (*cahier de devoirs mensuels*); at the teacher's option another exercise book may be provided in which a pupil enters the work of each day (*cahier de roulement*); both serve as records for inspectors and parents of the work done by the teacher, the progress of the pupils, and the care with which corrections and revisions are made; the *cahiers de*

---

[1] In the field of secondary education there are more, e.g., *l'Ecole des Roches, Collège de Normandie*, and *l'Ecole de l'Ile de France*.
[2] See, for example, *L'Ecole et la Vie, L'Ecole Libératrice, Manuel Général de l'Instruction*.

devoirs mensuels are retained by the school and not given to the pupils until they leave. Another important link with tradition in education is the close interest of parents in the work of their children, which, based on a strong faith in the tradition, manifests itself in a demand for the same kind of work as they did in their own school days. Two other methods of control are textbooks and examinations.

Textbooks. The selection of textbooks to be used in elementary schools passes through the hands of a number of committees. Each year fully appointed teachers in each canton meet under the chairmanship of a primary inspector and prepare a report recommending the addition and elimination of textbooks. This report is submitted to the academy inspector, who in turn transmits it to a departmental committee, over which he presides, consisting of the normal school faculties, of the teacher members of the departmental council, and cantonal delegates selected by this council. The list drawn up by the committee is submitted for approval to the rector of the academy and adopted, if he approves. In case of disapproval it is referred to the Minister of Public Instruction, who has the final decision with the advice of the permanent section of the Higher Council of Public Instruction. No book, pamphlet, or manuscript may be introduced into a school except with the sanction of the academy inspector. Books for prize distribution may be selected by the teachers themselves or by the municipal authorities with the sanction of the primary inspector. The Higher Council may, however, prohibit certain books even here.

Under Article 7 of the Decree of January 29, 1890, the books that pupils are required to have are definitely prescribed. Thus, in the lower course a pupil must have a reader; in the middle course a reader, an elementary grammar with exercises, an elementary arithmetic, a small atlas, and a history of France; and in the upper course a reader, a grammar with exercises, an arithmetic, a history of France or a history covering the prescribed course, an atlas, and a textbook on morals and civics. A pupil refusing to use one of the books included in the list of the department may be excluded from school.

Examinations. Pupils are promoted each year on the basis of their records and the recommendations of their teachers to the principal or the *conseil des maîtres*. At the end of the course the State conducts an examination for the certificate of primary studies (*certificat d'études primaires*), which serves to test both pupils and schools. Pupils may present themselves if they are twelve years of age in the year of the examination. The examination is conducted by a commission consisting of a primary inspector, a representative of a normal school, higher elementary school or of an elementary school with a *cours complémentaire*, and two teachers not engaged in a school of the canton in which the examination is held. Each examination is held in the capital of a canton. Provision is made to include women on the commission for examining girls.

The examination is oral and written. The latter, the topics for which are selected by an academy inspector, includes an essay in a simple subject (50 minutes); dictation and questions on the sense and language (40 minutes); two reasoning problems in practical arithmetic and the metric system (50 minutes); an essay or questions on history and geography or everyday science applied to agriculture, industry, commerce, fishery (according to the locality), infant care, hygiene (40 minutes), and a simple drawing exercise and handwork (50 minutes). The oral examination, lasting from twenty to twenty-five minutes and open to the public, includes a test in reading and questions on the sense and language of the text, recitation of a poem selected from a list presented by the candidate, a song, a test in mental arithmetic, and a very simple physical exercise. The questions for the written examination are prepared by the academy inspector from the syllabus issued by the Ministry; the oral questions are based on the same syllabus, which covers in the main the work of the middle course with some selections from that of the upper course.

A definite system of marking is prescribed on a scale of 10, as follows; 1–2, bad; 3–4, middling; 5, passable; 6, sufficiently good; 7–8, good; 9–10, very good. The examining commission reports the results to the academy inspector who grants the certificate to successful candidates and transmits his report to the rector of the academy through whom it reaches the Ministry. Thus, in the last analysis, it is the Ministry that is the controlling authority in all matters affecting the school. The authorities have endeavored in the last year to discourage preparation and cramming for the examination and to develop types of tests which would call for observation and reflection, but without much success in either direction. The authorities do not appear as yet to have achieved their ideal.

The examination which crowns the work of the schools should not, because of poor selection of tests, result in setting a premium on bookish and abstract methods. In banishing them from the *certificat d'études primaires*, the Higher Council has tried again to affirm its confidence in those intuitive and active methods which should more and more be given a place of honor in the elementary school.[1]

The examination has been subjected to criticism and has been fraught with certain dangers which the new *Instruction* and regulations seek to avoid. On the whole, however, its retention is strongly desired by parents, since it serves to establish standards and helps to link the public to the schools in a country in which certificates and diplomas play perhaps too great a part. The statistics do not indicate the number of pupils eligible to take the examination, but in 1931, of 98,583 boys who presented themselves, 82,490 passed the written examination and 82,372 the oral; of 90,116 girls, 75,878 passed the written examination and 75,805 the oral; about 84 per cent of those who took the examination obtained the certificate.

INTERMEDIATE EDUCATION

Higher elementary schools. The large majority of pupils leave school either on obtaining the certificate of elementary school studies or on reaching the age of thirteen, the upper limit of the period of compulsory school attendance. For those who do not proceed to a secondary school or to a vocational school, there is available the higher elementary school (*école primaire supérieure*), established in 1833 by the *Loi Guizot*. The higher elementary schools offer a three-year course open to boys and girls who have reached the age of twelve and may be established only at the request of the communes. Their establishment cannot, like that of elementary schools, be made compulsory; once they are established, however, they must be maintained for a period of years, usually thirty, if state aid is granted. The aim of the higher elementary schools is to train the intermediate grade of officials in the administrative and economic occupations of the country. Since their establishment is usually determined upon by the local authorities, these schools enjoy a

[1] *Journal Officiel*, January 13, 1928.

certain latitude in providing the type of course best adapted to the locality. The faculty consists of a principal, professors, assistant professors, teachers, and foremen. A distinction is made between the teachers who have the special qualifications for teaching in higher elementary schools (*professeurs de lettres, de sciences, ou de langues vivantes*), and those who have elementary school or other certificates. Principals and professors must hold the *certificat d'aptitude au professorat des écoles normales et des écoles primaires supérieures*, obtained by examination usually following special preparation, or a *licence* (university degree). Assistant professors are teachers who do not hold these qualifications, but have had three years of teaching experience in a post-elementary, secondary, or vocational school. Principals are required to teach for ten periods a week except in schools with more than 150 pupils; professors teach twenty periods a week and are responsible for five periods of supervision of pupils.

To be admitted to a higher elementary school, candidates must be twelve years of age, hold the *certificat d'études primaires*, and have spent at least one year in the upper course of an elementary school, or they may be admitted by examination or if they have obtained a national scholarship. Pupils over eleven years of age may be admitted to the preparatory class, if there is one, in which the work of the upper course is covered.

Every higher elementary school must have a room for drawing, a library, a laboratory, museum, gymnasium, playground, and workshops equipped to give the instruction appropriate to each curriculum offered (for example, machinery for the industrial section, a demonstration field for the agricultural, and equipment for practical household work for the household arts section). A committee of patronage is appointed for each school, consisting of the rector, academy inspector, elementary school inspector, principal of the school, the mayor, the presidents of the Chamber of Commerce and the Chamber of Agriculture, and others elected by their colleagues or appointed to represent the teachers, local interests, and medicine. The chief function of the committee is to look after the general welfare of the school, maintain close relations with the local public, promote foreign travel and study and the exchange of pupils, appoint members to visit the school at least twice a year, and advise through a standing sub-committee on the organization of curricula.

Each school may determine the number of curricula which it will offer, making the selection from the general, industrial, agricultural, or household arts sections. A section preparing for the entrance examination to normal schools may also be established. The curriculum of the first year is common to all sections, and the general subjects are common to all the courses. The subjects of the curricula and the courses of study are prescribed by the Ministry of Public Instruction (*arrêté*, August 18, 1920), but principals, with the advice of their teachers' councils, are free to adapt them to local needs and to select the necessary textbooks subject to the approval of the rectors; in matters of administration, the action of the principals and the teachers' councils must be approved by the academy inspectors.

The subjects of the curricula, prescribed in the official regulations, are: moral instruction; civics, elementary political economy, and everyday law; French language and literature; modern foreign languages (English, German, Italian, or Spanish); national history and introduction to general history; geography; practical arithmetic, rapid calculation; algebra and geometry; elementary physical and natural sciences; practical principles of hygiene; writing, stenography and typewriting; artistic and geometrical design and modeling; singing; physical education, and for boys, military training; and the special courses — theory and practice of industry, commerce, and agriculture, including mechanics, technology, industrial chemistry, industrial electricity, theory of agricultural chemistry, merchandise, transportation and customs, bookkeeping, accounting, etc. To these are added practical work for boys in the workshop, laboratory, agriculture and horticulture, and for girls in household economy, care of infants, household management, care of linen, dressmaking, cookery, and care of the home, garden, farm, etc.

The time-schedules suggested in the regulations are as shown in tables on pages 421 and 422.

The organization of the courses of study follows in general the lines laid down for the elementary schools rather than the methods of the secondary schools. The distinction between the higher elementary school and the secondary school is that the work of the former must be more practical and that of the latter more academic; the one emphasizes acquisition of knowledge and information, the other more formal intellectual training. It is this distinction which

ELEMENTARY EDUCATION

Higher Elementary Schools
COURSES FOR BOYS

	Common Course	General Course		Agricultural Course		Industrial Course		Commercial Course	
	First year	Second year	Third year	Second year	Third year	Second year	Third year	Second year	Third year
Moral instruction, civics, everyday law, economics.	1	1	1	1	1	1	1	1	1
French............	4	4	4	3	3	3	3	4	4
Modern languages	3	4	4	..	..	..	..	4	4
History..........	1	1	1	1	1	1	1	1	1
Geography.......	1	1	1	1	1	1	1	1	1
Mathematics.....	3	3	3	3	3	3	3	3	3
Mechanics.......	..	..	..	1	1	1	2	..	..
Physics and chemistry...........	2	2	2	3	3	3	3	2	3
Natural sciences and hygiene ...	1	1	1	1	1	1	1	1	1
Technology......	..	..	..	1	1	1	1	1	1
Agriculture......	..	..	..	2	2	..	..	..	..
Artistic design and modeling......	2	2	2	..	..	2	2	..	..
Geometrical design............	1	1	1	1	1	3	3	..	..
Writing..........	1*	..	..	..	..	..	..	..	..
Stenography and typewriting....	3*	..	..	..	..	..	..	3	3
Bookkeeping.....	..	..	..	1	..	..	..	3	3
Singing (1 hour optional).......	2	2	2	2*	2*	2*	2*	2	2
Gymnastics......	2	2	2	2*	2*	2*	2*	2	2
Shopwork, laboratory, agriculture, horticulture..........	4	4	4	9	9	12	12	1	1
Total.......	31	28	28	32	31	36	37	29	30
Compulsory	26	27	27	29	28	33	34	30	30
Optional ..	5	1	1	3	3	3	3	1	1

* Optional.

created difficulties when higher elementary and secondary schools were brought together into one institution, and which represents the chief line of demarcation between *l'enseignement primaire* and *l'enseignement secondaire*, an artificial distinction, but one which has been perpetuated by social and historical causes. Like the central school in England and the *Mittelschule* in Prussia, the *école primaire supérieure* is secondary in character and more nearly equivalent to the American high school than the secondary school proper in

COURSES FOR GIRLS

	COMMON COURSE	GENERAL COURSE		COMMERCIAL COURSE		DOMESTIC ARTS COURSE	
	First year	Second year	Third year	Second year	Third year	Second year	Third year
Moral instruction, civics, everyday law, economics..	1	1	1	1	1	1	1
French........................	4	4	4	4	4	3	3
Modern languages............	3	4	4	4	4	..	..
History......................	1	1	1	1	1	1	1
Geography...................	1	1	1	1	2	1	1
Mathematics..................	3	3	3	3	3	2	2
Physics and chemistry........	2	2	2	2	2	2	2
Natural sciences and hygiene..	1	1	1	1	1	1	1
Technology...................	..	..	..	1	1	..	..
Artistic design and modeling..	2	2	2	..	..	2	2
Geometrical design...........	1	1	1	1	1	1	1
Writing......................	1*	..	..	1	1	..	..
Stenography and typewriting..	3*	..	..	4	4	..	..
Bookkeeping..................	..	..	..	2	2	..	..
Domestic economy............	..	1	1	..	..	1	1
Singing (1 hour optional)....	2	2	2	2	2	2	2
Gymnastics...................	2	2	2	2	2	2	2
Lingerie, clothing, fashions, cookery, household management, garden, farm, infant care..................	6	6	6	..	..	12	12
Total....................	33	31	31	30	31	31	31
Compulsory..............	28	30	30	30	30	30	30
Optional.................	5	1	1	..	1	1	1

* Optional.

those countries. The advocates of the *école unique* hope to secure the recognition of the higher elementary school as one of several differentiated institutions in education at the secondary level. Opportunities are now provided whereby pupils may transfer from the higher elementary to the secondary school and national scholarships may be held interchangeably in one or the other.

The three-year course of the higher elementary school culminates in an examination for the *brevet d'enseignement primaire supérieur*. Candidates must be at least fifteen years of age, must present their *livret de scolarité*, or record book of their scholastic progress (attendance, marks, and conduct). The general examination committee, appointed by the rector, consists of an academy inspector or a deputy, and five members selected from elementary school inspectors and teachers in secondary, normal, and higher elementary schools. The questions for the written examination are prepared by a committee of academy inspectors under the chairmanship of the rector. The examination is conducted in each school by a special committee. The written examination is based on the general subjects for all and on the special subjects of each section; the oral examination covers the subjects not included in the written examination; the practical test is based on the characteristic vocational work of each section. The candidates are marked on a scale from zero to 20, and must obtain an average mark in each of the three tests to pass; a mark of less than 5 in French composition is eliminatory. The *brevet d'enseignement supérieur* as a certificate is valuable for securing certain appointments; it is required for admission to certain schools such as the schools of arts and crafts (*écoles des arts et métiers*) and for the competition for scholarships for foreign travel. Although the higher elementary schools were intended to train pupils for intermediate positions in administrative and economic occupations, a large proportion of the graduates enter the civil service or continue their studies and become teachers.

Cours complémentaires. In localities which cannot afford to establish a higher elementary school there may be organized in an existing elementary school a *cours complémentaire* (full-time continuation course), giving a curriculum of one or two years to pupils who are admitted under the same conditions as to the higher elementary schools. Under the direction of the principal of the elementary school, the work of the *cours complémentaire* must be divided between two special teachers, one for letters and one for sciences. The curriculum, so far as differences of time permit, is similar to that of the higher elementary schools. The time distribution and subjects of instruction, which may be varied, are as follows:

	1ST YEAR	2D YEAR
Moral Instruction (first year), Civics (second year)	1	1
French	6	6
History	1½	1½
Geography	1½	1½
Mathematics	6	3
Physical and natural sciences	3	6
Drawing	3	3
Manual work	3½	3½
Writing	½	½
Singing	2	2
Physical education	2	2
Total	30	30

Conclusion. French elementary and higher elementary education bear the stamp of the national respect for intelligence, judgment, ideas, and their relationship. Both start with the conviction that there is a certain body of knowledge which must become the possession of every citizen and that the task of the school is to see that the pupils acquire it. The emphasis is in the main on instruction rather than on education. "The school is the school," created by society to produce citizens with a common background of information and ideas, loyal to the ideals and traditions of the nation, and accepting hard work and effort as a duty. In so far as new educational ideas — and those mainly from abroad — exercise any influence, an attempt is being made to adapt them to the existing system rather than to reconstruct it radically. The pattern remains the same; the methods by which this pattern is achieved are beginning to be modified; the traditional attitude to the child, the traditional psychology, continues unchanged.

The system is not without its critics, but it is significant that the most serious discussion in the last few years has centered round the problem of overburdening (*surmenage*) the pupils in all types of schools without any other proposals than for the reduction in the number of hours of work in school and at home, and this despite the fact that the regulations for the elementary schools, issued in 1923, aimed definitely at reducing the overloaded programs. Nor has the other problem which has been so widely discussed since 1918, that of the *école unique*, attacked the fundamental basis so much as the organization of the system. The advocacy of new methods, of activity and vitality of the curriculum, by *Les Compagnons* has on the whole been relegated to the background.

And yet there is a certain unrest. If the authorities are not interested in radical reforms, a number of other organizations representing parents and reform groups (such as *Le Redressement Français*) are directing their attention to the problems of educational reconstruction. Excessive bureaucratic control and uniformity are being criticized; opportunities for experimental schools and increased autonomy in existing schools are advocated; a reduction in the number and importance of examinations is proposed; the textbooks with their burden of facts are criticized. In general, the demand is made that the claims of the present *Instruction* for "more air, more ease, more freedom, more joy," be clothed with greater reality in the schools, with less emphasis on intellectual and more on moral and social training through active participation of the pupils in the conduct of their affairs as well as in the process of instruction. Finally, there is the long-standing criticism of those who are concerned with secondary and higher education that the elementary schools do not teach their pupils how to think or how to study (*apprendre à apprendre*), but fill them with a mass of inert facts and ideas which results in what they call the "primary school mentality" (*l'esprit primaire*).

3. GERMANY

Education and the Revolution. The Revolution in Germany did more than substitute one form of government for another; it deprived the country of those objects of allegiance, to the cult of which the schools had been devoted. For elementary education a new aim had to be formulated to replace the traditional training of "God-fearing, loyal, and self-supporting subjects." The Federal Constitution redefined the aim in broad, general terms; Article 148 provided that

In all schools effort shall be made to develop moral education, public-mindedness, and personal and vocational efficiency in the spirit of the German national character and of international conciliation... Civic training and activity instruction shall be part of the curricula of the schools.

Religious instruction was retained as part of the regular school curriculum, but the rights of conscience, both of teachers and of pupils, were protected, and the establishment of secular schools or schools representing the spiritual outlook (*Weltanschauung*) of parents was permitted. A federal law to regulate the status of religious instruction was provided in the Constitution, but, as was pointed out in an earlier chapter,[1] the Federal Government, despite several attempts, has not succeeded in securing the enactment of a law (*Reichschulgesetz*) to regulate the organization of schools from this point of view. Finally, the Constitution provided for the abolition of the old methods of preparing teachers for elementary schools and by requiring the completion of a full secondary school course before such preparation, substituted for an apprenticeship type of training a system organized on the university level.[2]

[1] See Chapter IV.   [2] See Chapter VIII.

In a country as intellectually restless as Germany, it would have been surprising if any delay in reforming education should have had to wait for the formulation of new theories and philosophies of education. Although the principles upon which the schools were founded and the practices within the schools were rigidly regulated by central authorities, there was no similar check on freedom of thought and of expression, providing that the existing political régime was not attacked. There was, accordingly, no lack of educational theories, psychologies of education, and new methods of instruction and curriculum-making, once the opportunity for considering them as practical issues was afforded. Teachers' organizations through their study circles, psychologists in their experimental laboratories, philosophers, and a small band of practitioners who had undertaken educational experiments in private schools had built up a body of literature which was at once critical of existing practices and pointed the way in new directions, to which the Youth Movement (*Jugendbewegung*) had sought to give expression.

The teachers' organizations maintained active study circles which not only provided opportunities for teachers in practice to extend the limited education which they had received in the normal schools, but which served as centers for the elaboration of materials of instruction in their own localities (*Heimatkunde*, especially history, geography, and nature study). In the latter connection, teachers had already begun to take their classes on excursions of discovery and exploration which tempered the bookishness of classroom instruction by contacts with the concrete (*Schulwanderungen*). Shortly before the War, the Prussian authorities had sanctioned a few experiments in environmental studies (*Heimatkunde*) in the elementary schools.[1] In Leipzig the teachers' association had organized an important laboratory for experimental psychology, inspired by the new tendencies in this field inaugurated by Wilhelm Wundt, Ernst Meumann, and Wilhelm Stern, who broke away from the traditional metaphysical and abstract discussions of psychology. Criticism of experimental, mechanistic, and voluntaristic psychology led in time to the development of new schools of psychology, with which the names of *Gestalt* and *Struktur* are associated, based on the objection that experimental psychology cannot explain all mental functions and emphasizing larger units or wholes rather than discrete nervous processes.

[1] Alexander, T., *Prussian Elementary Schools*, Chapter XVII (New York, 1918).

On the practical side, a number of private schools had been established as centers for educational experimentation. Free from all restrictions except the official requirement that their teachers must be as well qualified as teachers in public schools, and the pressure of parents that their children be enabled to pass the official examinations, these schools were in fact protests against many of the characteristic features of the public schools. To free education from the pressure of modern industrialization, they were established in the country and found there opportunities for healthy living, abundant physical activities, and a return to nature. In place of the competitive spirit, they sought to develop a sense of social responsibility and broad human sympathy. To offset the rigid intellectualism developed in the public schools, they emphasized the free play of emotional life through the cultivation of the fine arts, music, and manual skills and the provision of opportunities for self-expression and for self-government. In contrast to the public schools, some of these experimental schools were coeducational. Influenced largely by Cecil Reddie's experiment at Abbotsholme, England, Hermann Lietz developed in his *Landerziehungsheime* (country home schools) at *Ilsenburg* (1898), *Haubinda* (1901), and *Bieberstein* (1904) which soon became models for many other schools organized on the same principles. Other centers of reform influence were the *Hauslehrerschule* established at Berlin-Lichterfelde (1906) by Berthold Otto, the *Freie Schulgemeinde Wickersdorf* (1906) of Gustave Wyneken, and the *Odenwaldschule* of Paul Geheeb.

Those progressive schools represented a general spirit of unrest which pervaded the country from the close of the nineteenth century and which was most widely represented by the Youth Movement, described by Friedrich Wilhelm Foerster, himself a radical critic of the official educational philosophy, as "a moral rejuvenescence of the German people, the return of the German soul to its best traditions." The Youth Movement was more than a rebellion of youth against the restrictions and conventions imposed on them by the adult generation and by the school authorities. It was inspired by clear and definite constructive ideas; it emphasized a return to nature and simplicity, free from the incubus of the conventions and artificialities of industrialized urban life; it laid stress upon freedom for youth to determine its own life in accordance with its own ideals rather than the standards imposed by others; it preached the gospel of social responsibility and brotherhood; and it sought to spread an appreciation of the real foundation of German culture — its music, art, drama, folkways, and folk customs — instead of the conventional culture of the schoolroom.

From various angles educational theory concentrated its attack upon the same weaknesses and defects as did the leaders of the progressive schools and of the Youth Movement. The schools were too mechanical and formal; they placed a premium on the mastery of knowledge and information without giving any training in its acquisition; the work was bookish, artificial, and unrelated to the life and interests of the pupils; false standards had been set up which resulted in pressure from the home or the pupils and from the authorities on the teacher; freedom and self-expression were unknown and the process of instruction had developed into a sterile method of questions by the teacher and answers by the pupils, who were themselves never allowed to question; æsthetic and creative activities were ignored, although formal training in drawing and singing were included in the curriculum. In a word, the elementary schools were dominated by the spirit of intellectualism derived from secondary and higher education, but limited, prescribed, and defined by the official regulations. Such a system afforded no opportunities for the development of free personalities, but moulded all according to a standard pattern, which, when supplemented by vocational and military training, perpetuated the existing caste system.

Educational theorists were agreed in their criticisms of the existing system; and in their emphasis on the cult of personality they differed only in the solutions which they were prepared to offer. While all were ready to take the individual, his interests and needs, as the starting-point, some wished to leave the process of education wholly to the development of these interests and needs, others set up specific ends which they derived either from the claims of the State and of society or from a theory of cultural values. Common to all, but differing somewhat in the interpretation of its meaning, was the advocacy of activity (*Arbeit*) on the part of the learner in the educative process rather than of the mere passive absorption of knowledge. Once the pressure of official control was removed, as it has been in the new German education, the school became the battle-ground of the educational theories which were associated with the names of Friedrich Paulsen, long an opponent of bureaucratic control in education, Wilhelm Dilthey, Eduard Spranger, Theodor Litt, Georg Kerschensteiner, Hugo Gaudig, and Paul Oestreich, each of whom stressed the importance of the educand as an individual personality to be developed, but differed in the ends to be attained. The radicals, under the leadership of Paul Oestreich, emphasized freedom above all else, *vom Kinde aus*; Gaudig and Kerschensteiner were the leading advocates of the activity principle (*Arbeitsprinzip*), but differed in their interpretations of it; Spranger and Litt stress the importance of a theory of cultural values and of cultural unity which educands are to make their own.

The influence of Spranger and Litt has dominated in the main the development of a theory of secondary education, but has not been without its effect on elementary education. Because of their more immediate applicability in school practice, the influence of Gaudig and Kerschensteiner, who had already put their theories into practice — the first in girls' secondary school in Leipzig, the second as superintendent of schools in Munich — has been greater than that of the philosophers. Gaudig, starting with the potentialities of the child, advocated an emphasis on free spiritual development, or self-activity under the guidance of the teachers and of the schools as cooperative communities (*Arbeitsgemeinschaften*), but he limited the activities in the main to the methods of acquiring information rather than to the organization of new materials of instruction; the school is to be an *Arbeitsschule* rather than a *Lernschule*, but the techniques of learning rather than the content are to be changed. Kerschensteiner, perhaps because his work brought him more directly into contact with elementary and post-elementary school pupils, showed greater breadth in his interpretation of the activity principle, through which each individual was to be trained to become a responsible, co-operating citizen for ennobling society and the State. Recognizing the importance of vocations in developing the worth of the individual as a person and a citizen, he emphasized the place of manual work, of drawing, of civic instruction, and gradually extended the application of the activity methods in these subjects to others. But in contrast to the encyclopedic character of the official courses of study, Kerschensteiner advocated less content, but more thoroughness, less bookishness and greater reality, less knowledge and more experiencing. Starting with manual activities, he gradually extended the principle of activity to intellectual (*geistige Arbeit*) and physical (*körperliche Arbeit*) sides of the school curriculum. From the concentration on civic training as the end of education, Kerschensteiner gradually accepted Spranger's philosophy, that a fully developed personality implies mastery and appreciation of cultural possessions — language, literature, fine arts and music, techniques and skills, science and religion, social customs and law — which serve two ends in providing the content for the development of personality, but only if the individual is an active agent in making them his own. Many-sided character, developed emotionally as well as intellectually, can be cultivated only by a process through which the individual enters into the possession of values which are social. His early emphasis on civic instruction Kerschensteiner reconciled with his later point of view by defining the State, not as a preëxisting entity, but as a cultural institution which exists for the free development of human personality.

The task which confronted the reformers of German education was defined, first, by the change in the form of government from a monarchy, which demanded the training of loyal subjects, to a republic which, by implication at least, rests upon the independent judgment of citizens. Secondly, the traditional division of the people into classes, each with its own form of education, had to be replaced by a system which for a period of years would train the future citizens in the same schools and which throughout their educational careers would seek to cultivate the same objects of loyalty as a basis of national solidarity. Third, there had to be substituted for bureaucratic control a certain measure of freedom to the localities and to the teachers. Finally, education in all its branches had to be imbued with the spirit of the new orientation, the emphasis on the individual as a growing personality as contrasted with the traditional aim of indoctrination and moulding of standardized patterns. Except for an extreme group which saw in the Revolution an opportunity for anarchy or an absolute concept of freedom, there was general agreement that the aim of elementary education must be to develop responsible, independent citizens, but citizens loyal to republican ideals and striving to appreciate and enrich the cultural foundations upon which the new Republic rests. For the State is more than a political instrument; it is a form of social organization which exists for the promotion of moral and cultural ends. Education must accordingly be conducted, in the words of the Constitution, "in the spirit of national character and of international reconciliation."

The data of the educational process are thus the individual and his environment. The process of education is the gradual acquisition by the pupil of mastery over and understanding of this environment in accordance with his developing potentialities. The content of the curriculum is not derived solely from books, but from experience in an enlarging environment. Education must be rooted in the soil of the people (*Bodenständigkeit*); and as the pupils grow, the process is one of expansion from their immediate environment (*Heimat*) to an understanding and appreciation of the meaning of life (*Leben*). The materials of instruction or curriculum must be derived from those aspects of life with which the pupils at each stage of development are familiar (*Heimatkunde*, knowledge of the environment), and which furnish the real and concrete relations between school and life outside. The function of the teacher is to create opportunities for the gradual expansion of the pupil's horizon, in part through vicarious experiences — that is, through books, in part through excursions. Through language and literature there is developed an appreciation of the best expressions of the ideals of the nation; through history a knowledge of the processes by which civilization and its institutions have developed; through geography an understanding of the relations of man to nature and of the interrelations of different parts of the world; through a study of nature an idea of elementary science and of the service of science to man. For the pupils the process must not be merely the acquisition of factual information, but a creative discovery. Beyond this, the school must develop the emotional side of the pupils' lives through the arts, music, manual, and physical activities. As the pupils grow older, they begin to realize that their own national culture has been and is influenced by the culture of other peoples and nations; *Heimatkunde*, knowledge and understanding of the national environment, is the common point of reference for elementary as for secondary schools, with the difference that the latter can take its pupils further afield in discussing foreign influences which have helped to mould German culture and civilization.

The process of education must be the active participation of the pupils, which will result in their intellectual, moral, and emotional development and growth. As contrasted with the traditional emphasis on precept and example, the method of activity (*Arbeitsprinzip*) implies on the part of the pupils ability to recognize and formulate problems to select the means and methods of their solution through independent planning, and to verify and criticize the results. Recognition of a problem, observation, and collection of data furnish the opportunities for a variety of forms of expression — oral, written, graphic, dramatic, musical, and manual. The necessity for observation, comparison, application, and verification in order to carry a task through to its desired end is in itself the basis of moral training, since it calls for perseverance, self-control, and truth. But the school is not a collection of isolated individuals bound to each other by common subjection to the authority of the teachers; it is a social organization, a section of life, a coöperative working community (*Arbeitsgemeinschaft*), which seeks through the promotion of group planning and group activities to develop the ideals of self-sacrifice, coöperation, and a sense of social duty and responsibility. The individual is free, but he learns that his freedom is restricted by the values created by his environment and by the right of his fellows to equal freedom.

The reform movement aims to cultivate the totality, the whole being of the individual. Experience is one and undivided; its logical separation into discrete compartments called subjects has no place in the minds of young children and even for older children; it is only tradition that has determined that the time of the school shall be distributed into a variety of periods assigned to disconnected activities to be studied. From this approach there was derived the demand for integrated programs of instruction (*Gesamtunterricht*), which implies the abolition of time-tables and the splitting of the total activity of the pupils into separate subjects. It emphasizes the unity of experience in young children, the enrichment of that experience through the environment, and the gradual emergence of the need for techniques and the three R's. The traditional school, because it was artificially organized round subjects, set up a distinction between school and home, and school and the background which the child of the age of six has already accumulated. Through integrated instruction the home and background of the child are incorporated into the school as experience to be further developed. The principle of *Gesamtunterricht* has in general been adopted as the basis of instruction for the first two years of school life; drill in the fundamentals still continues to be regarded as an important educational foundation by all but the most radical theorists, but the fundamentals must be drawn out of the matrix of the child's experience rather than be imposed upon him. In other directions integrated instruction, an expansion and reinterpretation of the earlier concept of correlation, is followed; the excursions in particular lend themselves to such treatment, or it may be found in combinations of various forms of expression round one subject.

These in general are the trends of the new German theories of education — respect for personality (*vom Kinde aus*), the derivation of materials of instruction from the expanding environment (*Heimatkunde*), training of a common loyalty to German ideals and culture (*Bildung zum Deutschtum*), excursions as a method of enrichment (*Wandern*), integrated instruction (*Gesamtunterricht*), and activity methods (*Arbeitsunterricht*). It would be a fallacy, however, to conclude that all these features will be found in all German schools, but what is true is that all forms of education from the absolutely free to the conservative can be discovered, even in the schools of one city. Human nature being what it is, this is to be expected. The majority of teachers in the German schools were trained under the old methods; some with long years of experience were satisfied with the old system; others, who were applying the prescribed methods and courses of study under protest and against their convictions, readily broke away in new directions as soon as opportunities for liberalism were created. For some the Revolution meant the abolition of all supervisory authorities and self-determination, which manifested itself in the movement for the abolition of the position of principals or their election by the teachers; in some cases the same principle inspired pupils to demand participation in the administration of schools and even a voice in the selection of their teachers. In Hamburg a number of schools (*Gemeinschaftsschulen*) were organized on Tolstoyan principles, and teachers, pupils, parents, and any other persons who felt that they had anything to contribute were allowed a voice not only in the administration, but in the determination of what should be taught as well as when and how. Pupils participated as their disposition moved them. Anarchy, however, soon gave place to organization and coöperation.

More important than such radical ventures into the new was the change in the spirit of the authorities, who recognized the importance of freedom in the new political régime. Not only did they sanction the establishment of experimental schools (*Versuchsschulen*) in the public school system, but they realized that the day of uniformity and standardization had passed. The system of inspection was reformed, and in place of uniform, prescribed curricula and courses of study, the authorities issued Suggestions (*Richtlinien*), leaving to the teachers the responsibility for making their own courses of study with the help of the Suggestions and in the light of local needs; the duty of inspectors became one, not of control, but of sympathetic discussion and guidance. This change in administrative practices gave the teachers their opportunity; some could reconcile the Suggestions with established practices; others could now, alone, or in coöperation with other teachers in their district, or through their associations, adapt them to the canons of the new theories. For standardized uniformity there were now substituted freedom and variety; for bureaucratic control, general standards and outlines and the professional responsibility of the teachers. The first four or five years of the new régime were years of feverish experimentation; gradually better understanding of the practical situation, and to some extent the effect of the economic crises which have meant increased size of classes and reduction in the funds available for school supplies and equipment, have produced more normal conditions. Variety of educational efforts still remains the characteristic of the new systems and the theories and principles which have been described continue to inspire teachers and schools, but there is less of the exaggerated interpretations of freedom which marked the earlier experiments.

THE SYSTEM OF ELEMENTARY EDUCATION

Provision of Schools. Pre-school education has not been fully developed. For children below the age of three there are available *crèches* (*Krippen*) and children's homes (*Kinderheime*). Children above the age of three may be sent to *Kleinkinderschulen* or *Kindergärten*, the majority of which are private and may only be opened with the approval of the authorities. In addition, young children as well as children of school age out of school hours may be looked after in *Kinderhorte*, which provide a variety of play and manual activities. The supervision of these institutions is, in Prussia, in the hands of the Ministry of Social Welfare (*Volkswohlfahrtsministerium*) in so far as the welfare side and organization of their work is concerned; instructional work is supervised by the Ministry of Education. All teachers and leaders in these institutions must be trained and hold state certificates.

Elementary education in Germany is provided in *Volksschulen*, which since the Revolution are divided into two sections, the foundation school (*Grundschule*) of four years and the upper section, also of four years. The *Grundschule* is the common four-year school which all children, irrespective of class distinction, are required to attend, unless they are enrolled in private schools or are educated at home under exceptional conditions. The *Grundschule* represents a compromise; a common six-year school was advocated by the sponsors of the *Einheitsschule*. The private schools are those which were in existence before the Revolution or are recognized as experimental schools. The preparatory school (*Vorschule*) for secondary education has been abolished, and private schools which are substitutes for public schools are tolerated, despite a constitutional provision (Article 147) for their abolition, only because neither the Federal nor the State Governments are in a position to compensate their owners, if they are closed. Pupils may be educated at home only if their physical condition, certified by a doctor, is such that they ought not to attend a public school.

The *Grundschule* is thus the foundation school in which the majority of German children receive the first four years of their education. By amendments to the constitutional provision, which were passed as a result of protests from parents,[1] gifted children may complete the course of the *Grundschule* in three years.

From the *Grundschule* the majority of the pupils pass on to the upper section of the *Volksschule* for four additional years,[2] the rest continuing their education in middle or secondary schools. In practice the *Grundschule* and the upper section constitute an unbroken unit under one administration. Only thirteen per cent of the elementary schools in Germany are fully organized with a separate class for each year; one third of the schools are single-teacher schools. The desire to provide better educational opportunities for children who remain in the elementary schools has led to the establishment in most States of advanced classes (*gehobene Klassen*), which enables pupils to remain in school for one or two additional years beyond the eighth; fees may be charged in these classes, which in some schools are organized into distinct units, and foreign language and mathematics may be added to the curriculum. For pupils who are retarded, there is a

[1] The requirement of four years' attendance in the *Grundschule*, followed by nine years in a secondary school, would have extended the period of education by one year beyond the traditional twelve.
[2] In Bavaria three years.

grouping of special classes (*Förderklassen*); pupils who are retarded in the last year before they leave school may be given special instruction in the fundamentals in concluding classes (*Abschlussklassen*); pupils who appear likely to fail to secure their promotions may be given additional instruction (*Nachhilfe-unterricht*). For backward but educable pupils there have been organized special schools (*Hilfsschulen*), which were first organized in Mannheim; to such schools pupils may be assigned, after spending one or two years in a regular school, on the recommendation of their teachers and after a medical examination; the curriculum of the *Hilfsschulen* is devoted mainly to training of hand and eye through a variety of manual activities.

Education and religion. Religious instruction is given in all schools; the Constitution, however, provides that pupils may be exempted from it at the request of their parents and teachers may only give it, if they choose to do so. The relation of the religious question to schools and the organization of the schools on denominational or undenominational lines were discussed in Chapter IV. In Prussia the majority of the schools are denominational (*konfessionelle Schulen*) — that is, Protestant, Catholic, or Jewish; a few are interdenominational (*Simultanschulen* or *paritätische Schulen*) in which the pupils receive religious instruction from teachers or ministers of their own denomination. Since the industrial areas are in the main opposed to religious instruction, difficulties arose in some schools because of the large number of requests for exemptions, and the practice developed of organizing such pupils in collective classes (*Sammelklassen*) and of establishing special secular schools (*Sammelschulen*), to which were assigned, but at their own request, only teachers who refused to give religious instruction.[1]

Compulsory attendance. The Constitution (Article 145) required compulsory education to be universal with full-time attendance at school for at least eight years, followed by part-time attendance up to eighteen. This is not an innovation in Germany, but the proposed

[1] In 1929 there were in Prussia 23,147 Protestant schools, 8741 Catholic, 9 of various Protestant sects, 96 Jewish, 1173 interdenominational, and 249 secular. In the Protestant schools 96.6 per cent of the pupils were Protestant, in the Catholic schools 99.1 per cent were Catholic, and in the interdenominational schools 58.4 per cent were Protestant and 39.2 per cent were Catholic; in the secular schools 25.5 per cent were Protestant, 0.3 per cent Catholic, and 69 per cent belonged to various denominations. Of the teachers, 396 Protestants and 118 Catholics refused to give religious instruction, while 458 had no affiliations with any denomination — a very small percentage of the total of over 111,000 teachers; of the pupils 30,520 Protestants and 5446 Catholics were withdrawn from religious instruction and 77,315 had no religious affiliations, about 3 per cent of the total enrollment.

abolition of private schools has introduced school compulsion (*Schulpflicht*) in place of compulsory education (*Unterrichtspflicht*); the old laws compelled parents and guardians to have their children and wards educated, but left the choice of school to their discretion; under the constitutional provision and state laws, which require attendance at a *Grundschule*, the choice of school has been withdrawn.

Compulsory education in Prussia has been regulated anew by a decree of December 15, 1927, which became effective on January 4, 1928. All children who are physically and mentally mature must enter school at the beginning of the school year nearest to the sixth birthday and remain in attendance until the end of the year in which they reach their fourteenth birthday. Exceptions are allowed at both ends; children who are weak or mentally immature may postpone entrance by a year, and pupils who have already been assured of employment may, if they are fourteen years of age, leave before the end of the school year. Pupils who receive private instruction must be examined periodically to discover whether they cannot attend a public school. The census of pupils eligible for school attendance is prepared in each locality by the police and sent to the school authorities at the beginning of each school year; the pupils are then assigned to the school which they must attend. The responsibility for regular attendance falls upon parents or guardians, who are liable, in cases of unjustifiable absences of pupils, to a fine ranging from 1 to 25 Mark; employers who knowingly employ pupils of school age during school hours are liable to a fine up to 150 Mark. Absences are reported by the teachers through the regular channels to the police. Pupils who move from one school district to another or from one town to another must provide themselves with a certificate of dismissal and must enroll in another school within six weeks. Blind children must attend an institution from the age of six to fourteen; deaf-mutes from seven to fifteen.

Text and schoolbooks. All pupils must be provided with textbooks and school supplies required for instruction at the cost of their parents; aid may be given to poor pupils unable to purchase them, or a loan library may be provided for their use. No textbook may be introduced into any school without permission of the county and central authorities. Pupils must have primers, readers, song-books, books for religious instruction (approved by the Ministry and the denominational authorities), slates and pencils (in lower classes), and exercise books for the different subjects. The single textbooks never played a very important part in class instruction in Germany; they were used as reference books after the lesson had been given by the teacher. With the introduction of activity methods the textbook as such is assuming a position of even lesser importance, while libraries and source materials become more appropriate than outlines and summaries.

Organization and administration of schools. Separate elementary schools are provided in Prussia for boys and girls in all schools with more than three classes, and women teachers are not allowed to have classes in which there are boys. The large majority of schools in Prussia in 1927 had less than three classes; of 33,405 elementary schools in 1927, 14,076 were single-teacher schools, 6492 schools had two teachers, 4529 three teachers, 1808 four teachers, 959 five teachers, 851 six teachers, and 4790 had seven or eight teachers.

The size of classes is determined indirectly by the method of state appropriation of funds, which employs the basis of one teacher for sixty pupils; localities which desire to have smaller classes must bear the additional cost out of their own funds. Directly, a decree of May 24, 1922, set the maximum number of pupils in a class at eighty; a later decree of October 4, 1926, provided for an average class size of forty-five pupils; when the number exceeds fifty, an additional teacher must be employed. The economic conditions in Germany have prevented the effective realization of the movement for lower classes.

The schools are administered by principals (*Schulleiter*); in schools with at least three teachers and less than six, the principal is known as the head teacher (*Hauptlehrer*); in schools with six or more teachers he has the title of *Rektor*. The special examination for this position was abolished in 1920 and the selection is made on the basis of general qualifications, experience, and ability. The *Hauptlehrer* receive a remuneration in addition to their regular salaries as teachers of 500 Mark a year; the *Rektoren*, an addition of 1200 Mark. In schools with six teachers or more, one of the teachers may be designated as associate principal (*Konrektor*); a second associate is appointed in schools with fourteen teachers or more; the additional remuneration of a *Konrektor* is 500 Mark. The principals and assistant principals are not the superiors of the teachers, but are officials charged with certain administrative duties in addition to teaching (the *Rektoren* must teach at least twelve periods a week; the *Kon-*

rektoren have full charge of a class). The principal is responsible for the administration of his school to the authorities, keeps the records of the school, conducts its official correspondence, and is the intermediary between the school and the parents or the public; beyond this, he has other duties which may be assigned to him by his council of teachers. The *Konrektor* is the deputy of the *Rektor* and is assigned special duties such as the care of the school library, social welfare work among the pupils, the administration of the school bank, special instruction, the organization of parents' councils and meetings, and any other tasks designated by the teachers' council.

The principal is not the superior of the teachers, but a peer among peers. The demands of the teachers for participation in the administration of schools were finally met by a decree issued on September 20, 1919, which provided for the creation of teachers' councils in each school (*Lehrerkonferenz*). All teachers holding permanent appointments and other teachers with at least six months of service are eligible to membership in the councils. The functions of the councils are to look after the general welfare of their schools, to confer on and discuss methods of instruction, assignment of classes, promotions of pupils, use of school funds, the provision of school materials and supplies, and coöperation to secure unity of work. The principal is the chairman of the council; on its advice, he may visit older teachers in their classrooms, criticize, and discuss their work with them; under the regulations, he is expected to supervise young teachers, those who have not yet received their permanent appointments. The administration of schools has thus been placed on a collegiate basis with the principal serving as the executive officer of his council, a practice which is feasible in a system in which there are few schools with more than twenty classes.

Curriculum. The curriculm and course of study in elementary schools are governed by state regulations, with the exception that general suggestions for the organization and work of the *Grundschule* were issued by the Federal Government. With legislation and suggestions for the *Grundschule* in 1920 and 1921, federal influence on elementary education came to a close; even these were supplemented by state suggestions. Federal legislation defined the scope of the *Grundschule* and required the closing of preparatory schools (*Gesetz betreffend die Grundschule und Aufhebung der Vorschulen*, April 28, 1920, amended by a law of April 18, 1925, making three years attendance at the *Grundschule* permissive); on July 18, 1921, a decree was issued giving suggestions on the aims and organization of the *Grundschule* (*Richtlinien für die Zielbesetzung und die innere Gestaltung der Grundschule*), which served as a basis for the curriculum suggestions prepared by each State.

The significant changes which have taken place since the Revolution in the preparation of curricula and courses of study have been, first, that they are no longer issued by the central authorities as decrees or laws which are immutable, but as suggestions (*Richtlinien*) on the basis of which each school or locality prepares its own course of study; secondly, that to an increased extent teachers participate in their preparation through coöperative activity in each school, or through district committees, or through teachers' associations; from time to time experienced teachers may be invited to coöperate with inspectors or the central authorities. Thus, the Prussian decree of March 16, 1928 (*Richtlinien zur Aufstellung von Lehrplänen für die Grundschule*), specifically requires that

> In the construction of the courses of study for individual schools opportunity for coöperation in the widest sense must be granted to the teaching staff.[1]

Aim of the Grundschule. The aim of the *Grundschule* as defined in the federal decree of July 18, 1921, is as follows:

> The first four years of school have their own goal and unified sphere of activity. Their goal is the gradual unfolding of the child's abilities out of the instinct for play and movement toward a normal desire for work which manifests itself inside the school community.[2]

This statement is further elaborated as follows in the Prussian decree of March 3, 1921:

> The *Grundschule*, as the common school for all children in the first four years of school, has the task of giving to the children who attend it a basic training on which not only the *Volksschule* in its last four years can be built, but also the middle and secondary schools with their more extended instruction. Therefore, it must awaken and train all the spiritual and physical forces of the children and equip them with those knowledges and skills which, as groundwork for every type of further instruction, are absolutely essential.[3]

---

[1] Kandel, I. L., and Alexander, T., *The Reorganization of Education in Prussia*, p. 193 (New York, 1927).
[2] *Ibid.*, p. 191.   [3] *Ibid.*, p. 193.

In detail the suggestions recommend the development of the abilities of the children through play and movement, leading gradually over to instructional activities which will introduce them to an understanding of their physical and cultural environment. Through practical activities they should receive a training of hand and eye and the foundation for the cultivation of various modes of expression; training in the mother-tongue should be cultivated through practical activity accompanied by drawing, modeling, cutting out, and observation; physical training should be developed through games, excursions, gymnastics, and sports. The materials of instruction should be related to and derived from the home and local environment of the children, and the choice of subjects and activities should be determined by the pupils' background, according to districts and localities, sex, ability, and interests. In other words, the basis of curriculum-making in the *Grundschule* should be *Heimatkunde* (the home, yard, garden, schoolhouse, street and market, the countryside, life and work at home and in school, and in the shop, factory, and on the farm). Such a background provides the materials for story-telling, dramatization of fairy and other tales, singing and recitation of folk and children's rhymes and poems, modeling, drawing, and other manual activities. The study of the environment extended by excursions supplies the content for geography, history, nature study, local myths and traditions. The environment must be treated as a whole and out of the integrated instruction (*Gesamtunterricht*) in the first year there should be derived the subjects which constitute the work of the last three years. The *Grundschule* must not be a *Lernschule*, in which the pupils acquire information from the teachers, but an activity school (*Arbeitsschule*) which stimulates them to learn through self-experienced activity and through coöperation with their teachers and their fellow-pupils. Throughout the course the emphasis is to be placed on various forms of expression and activities. Unity and integration are to be observed by the provision, suggested in a decree of March 23, 1923, that pupils be taught by the same teachers for two year periods.

The time-schedule which follows is intended for a fully graded school; schools which do not have four separate classes for each of the four years are expected to conform to the time-distribution suggested. The work of the first year should be organized as an integrated whole

(*Gesamtunterricht*); permission may be obtained to continue the integrated program for one or more years beyond the first.

TIME-SCHEDULE OF THE GRUNDSCHULE

Subject	Year 1*	Year 2	Year 3	Year 4
Religion		4	4	4
Environmental study (*Heimatkunde*)		⎫	⎫	⎫
German		⎬ 9	⎬ 10	⎬ 11 (10)†
Writing		⎭ 2	⎭ 2	⎭ 2
Arithmetic		4	4	4
Drawing			2 (1)	2 (1)
Singing		1	2 (1)	2
Physical training		2	2	3 (2)
Sewing			(2)	(2)
Total	18	22	26	28

* The work of the first year is organized as an integrated whole (*Gesamtunterricht*).
† The figures in parentheses are for girls only.

Aim of the last four years of the Volksschule. The aim of the upper section of the *Volksschule* is determined not only by the general principles governing education — the interests of the pupils, close articulation with the environment (*Heimat*), and activity methods — but also by the special consideration that for most pupils this course will be the end of full-time education, and that they will enter immediately on practical careers and continue their education chiefly in vocational schools; a few will be found eligible for transfer to a secondary school (*Aufbauschule*) at the age of thirteen. In general, however, at this stage, too, the educational needs of the pupils and the objective of the constant and symmetrical development of their whole being, especially with reference to their emotions and will, must be the deciding factor.[1] Self-activity, intellectual as well as physical, must continue to be the basis of instruction.

The coöperation of the pupil must not consist chiefly in the absorption of knowledge, but the objectives of instruction are to be worked out under the guidance of the teacher through observation, experiment, investigation, independent reading, and verification.[2]

A wide range of concrete activities provides opportunities for a variety of forms of instruction and study — the preparation of sketches, drawings, and instructional materials — especially for

---

[1] Kandel, I. L., and Alexander, T., *op. cit.*, p. 203. [2] *Ibid.*, p. 204.

geometry, geography, and nature study — the organization of collections, experiments in natural science, the care of animals, school gardening, and, for girls, sewing and home economics. School excursions (*Wandertage*), which serve primarily for physical education and must be arranged for one day each month and for shorter periods as occasion demands, bring the pupils into contact with a wide variety of experiences and materials of instruction — observation of plant and animal life, of earth and weather conditions, problems of business and labor, agricultural and industrial activities, and monuments and records of historical significance. In the promotion of reality in education and understanding of community and social life, every possible agency provided by the locality must be utilized, whether in city or in country. Direct experience must be supplemented by the use of books, schools and public libraries, and museums. The real contrast between the old and the new school lies in the fact that the walls of the schoolroom have been removed and the materials of instruction, instead of being provided through the cold, factual form of books or the teacher's exposition, are derived from living contact with the environment. The school excursions as such are not an innovation in German education; it is their application in the new education which has acquired a new significance. With the establishment of a nation-wide network of youth hostels (*Jugendherbergen*) pupils can be accommodated at a very low cost in any part of Germany, an opportunity which is extensively used by whole classes accompanied by their teachers during the vacations.

The curriculum includes religion (or moral instruction for pupils exempted from religious instruction), German, history, and civics, geography, natural science, arithmetic, geometry, drawing, music, physical training, and sewing for girls, with manual training for boys and home economics for girls where these can be provided. The Suggestions (*Richtlinien zur Aufstellung von Lehrplänen für die oberen Jahrgänge der Volksschule*, Decree of October 15, 1922), issued by the Ministry are intended to suggest standards to be attained in each class rather than to prescribe details to be carried out. The responsibility for working out courses of study in accordance with the local environment devolves upon the teachers.

The guiding principles (of the Suggestions) determine and limit in general the materials that are to be treated. The choice and distribution in particular are matters for the courses of study to be drafted for the individual school, in the organization of which the principle of basing the instruction upon life in the community must be respected. The amount of materials to be chosen varies with the school. In all schools, however, care must be taken that the materials prescribed in the curriculum are not superficially treated, but may be thoroughly worked through from an intellectual point of view. Schools of few classes, in order to be able to secure a richer selection of materials, may organize their work on the basis of alternating year courses.[1]

The time-schedule suggested is as follows:

TIME-SCHEDULE OF UPPER SECTION OF THE VOLKSSCHULE

Subject	Boys' School				Girls' School			
	5	6	7	8	5	6	7	8
Religion	4	4	4	4	4	4	4	4
German	8	7	6–7	6–7	7–8	7	6–7	6–7
History and civics	2	2	2	3	2	2	2	3
Geography	2	2	2	2	2	2	2	2
Natural science	2	3–4	4	3	2	2–3	3	3
Arithmetic ⎱ Geometry ⎰	4–5	5–6	5–6	5–6	3–4	4	4	3
Drawing	2	2	2	2	2	2	2	2
Singing	2	2	2	2	2	2	2	2
Physical training	2–3	3	3	3	2	3	3	3
Manual training	2	2	2	2	..	..	..	..
Sewing	..	..	..	..	2	2–3	2–3	2–3
Total	28–30	30–32	30–32	30–32	28–30	30–32	30–32	30–32

The Suggestions no longer define the course of study in detail or by years; they are, as they are intended to be, guides or principles for the teachers. Religious instruction varies with each denomination; since the schools are in the main denominational, beyond the common aim of religious and moral training stress is laid upon instruction in dogmatic tenets of each denomination. The aim in teaching of German is to cultivate mastery in the oral and written use of the mother-tongue, to develop an appreciation of the native language and literature, and to stimulate further reading with pleasure; as compared with the traditional practice, although it is not neglected, less emphasis is placed on the formal side of language study (grammar and spelling), while in the study of literature more attention is paid to variety and breadth in the selection of readers and books than on repetition and memorization which tend to kill pleasure in reading. Instruction in history has been completely re-

[1] Kandel, I. L., and Alexander, T., *op. cit.*, pp. 205 f.

vised, and, in place of the former emphasis on inculcation of loyalty to the Hohenzollerns (whose portraits have been removed from all schools and classrooms) and on the study of war [1] there has been substituted the study of the development of the German people and the German State as illustrated in their political, social, economic, and cultural progress. 'The highest law of history instruction must be to come as near as possible to historical truth.' Love of the people and of the fatherland and a sense of civic and social responsibility must be aroused. Civic instruction is to be given through history first and must culminate in a study of the Federal and Prussian Constitutions.[2] Party politics must be avoided in the schools, and pupils in all schools must receive instruction in the nature, duties, and aims of the League of Nations (Decree, May 28, 1927).

For geography the local environment is the starting-point; its aim is to develop familiarity with the home district and Germany and to give a general knowledge of foreign countries. With the assistance of the Meteorological Institute in Berlin, schools are encouraged to study meteorological charts and to establish observation stations. Germany's need of colonies is to be stressed; illustrative material for this purpose is provided by the Colonial Institute in Berlin; in the same way, through the *Verein für das Deutschtum im Ausland*, also in Berlin, the cultural bonds between Germans at home and abroad are cultivated. Through natural science the pupils are introduced in an elementary fashion to botany, zoölogy, physiology, physics, chemistry, geology, and agriculture; an important part of the instruction in this subject is assigned to physiology, hygiene, health, temperance, and care of infants. The number sense, the place of mathematics in life, the meaning of quantitative form and measurement are taught through arithmetic and geometry. Drawing aims to cultivate the use of form and color as a means of expression, and through music joy in song, feeling for tone qualities, and training in singing as a leisure and cultural activity through membership in choral societies are cultivated. Manual training for boys is closely correlated with other subjects of the curriculum, as is also the study of home economics by girls.

[1] The use of textbooks which glorify war and false interpretation of the World War and its causes are forbidden.

[2] A common decree was issued by the Ministers of Education on July 19, 1922, containing suggestions for the coöperation of schools and universities for the protection of the Republic. See Kandel, I. L., and Alexander, T., *op. cit.*, pp. 213 ff.

Physical education has been given special attention since the War, partly to provide a substitute for compulsory military training, which has been abolished, and partly to repair the ravages of the War and post-War period on the health of the nation. Care is paid in the selection of principals and inspectors to discover their interest in and understanding of the importance of physical education, to which the attention of teachers and parents is directed. Pupils may be exempted from physical instruction only on a doctor's certificate which must be periodically renewed. The time assigned to the instruction may be supplemented by folk and other games, marches, skating, and sledding in winter, and swimming in summer wherever possible; for these activities one afternoon a week (*Spielnachmittag*) must be set aside. Information on the literature of the various aspects of physical education is supplied by the *Museum für Leibesübungen* and through the *Deutsches Archiv für Leibesübungen* in Berlin.

There are no examinations in the Prussian elementary schools at the end of each year or of the whole course. Promotions are made on the recommendations of the class teachers with the approval of the teachers' council.

INTERMEDIATE EDUCATION

In Germany, as in most European countries, the need arose of some type of schools which, while not strictly vocational, would provide an education somewhat more advanced and longer than the elementary school course. Generally the demand for such schools was made by parents who were unable to pay the high fees or to undertake the cost of a full secondary education for their children, but who desired on payment of smaller fees school conditions somewhat better than prevailed in the elementary schools. The intermediate school is in fact a hybrid — higher in standard than the elementary, but lower than the secondary and catering to the demands of the less well-to-do middle classes.

In Prussia intermediate education, which is not strictly intermediate between any two distinct types of schools, either elementary or higher, but overlaps both, is provided in the *Mittlere Schulen* or *Mittelschulen*, which sprang up in the nineteenth century as *höhere Bürgerschulen*, advanced elementary schools charging fees, or as *Rektoratschulen* or *Lateinschulen*, lower secondary schools, charging fees and established in smaller localities which were unable to maintain a recognized secondary school. The first of these two types was not officially recognized and organized until 1894, and was assigned a more definite position in 1910. Both types were incorporated in the system of intermediate education (*Mittelschulwesen*) and given new regulations by a decree issued on June 1, 1925. The middle school is intended, first, to give a general and prevocational preparation to those pupils who intend to enter the intermediate ranks of employment in trade and commerce, agriculture and forestry, and the administrative services, and, in the case of girls, a preparation for the home; and, secondly, to provide in smaller localities a course parallel to that of the first six years of a secondary school and qualifying pupils for entrance to the last three years of a full secondary school.

Middle schools, although recognized and regulated by the state authorities, are provided and maintained either by local authorities or by private societies; under certain conditions poor localities may receive state aid in addition to grants for the salaries of the teachers. Public middle schools may be administered by the same authority which has charge of elementary education, or may have special boards of governors; they are supervised by elementary school inspectors. The chief characteristics of the middle schools are as follows: they are better equipped than the elementary schools; the classes in general are smaller; tuition fees (from 60 Mark to 240 Mark a year in public schools and 72 Mark to 600 Mark a year in private schools) are charged; the pupils come from better homes; the course is six years in length above the *Grundschule*; the teachers must have special certificates as middle school teachers[1] or as specialists in such subjects as music, drawing, physical training, sewing, gardening, manual training, and home economics; women are allowed to teach boys and mixed classes may be taught by men or women, although, wherever possible, separate schools or departments must be established for boys and girls. The maximum size of classes is fifty in the lower and forty-five in the upper sections.

Pupils who have completed the *Grundschule*, normally in four years, under special conditions in three, may be admitted to a middle school on passing an entrance examination or, if the middle school is in close relations with the elementary school, on the recommendations of the teachers. The entrance examination, which covers the

[1] See Chapter VII.

work of the *Grundschule*, is conducted by a committee of teachers representing the school which the candidates have attended and the school which they wish to enter; where a number of schools are concerned, a central representative committee may be established. The general records of the candidates must be taken into account and the examination may be supplemented by psychological tests, provided the examiners are competent to use them. If the number of successful candidates exceeds the number that can be accommodated, the selection is made by the teachers of the school which they wish to enter. Scholarships may be provided for needy but able pupils.

Aim of the middle school. The aim of the middle school is defined indirectly in the regulations of June 1, 1925:

> The development in the fields of manual activity, industrial art, commerce and industry, agricultural and forestry demands increased preparation of boys and girls for these vocational branches. In connection therewith there is need also of a suitable type of preparation for many sorts of intermediate positions in the administrative service of the State or municipalities, as well as in the larger industrial and commercial enterprises.[1]

Since the elementary school is limited in its scope and the secondary school is definitely directed to academic training, the middle school can provide both for general education and for the vocational needs described.

Curricula. The regulations suggest a variety of curricula for middle schools, but beyond requiring the teaching of one foreign language and indicating the minimum and maximum number of hours in the language, mathematics, and natural science subjects and in drawing, each school is permitted to adapt its program to the special needs in order to give special attention to those subjects which are especially important for later vocations. Bookkeeping must be included under arithmetic for all pupils and as a separate subject in special courses; shorthand and typewriting are elective subjects; home economics for girls and manual training for boys are elective subjects, but may, at the option of local authorities, be made compulsory. The curriculum of the first three years must as far as possible be common for all courses; differentiation begins in the fourth year. Localities which cannot provide a variety of curricula are expected to provide the general course only, although exceptions may be permitted for urgent reasons. In middle schools which are defi-

---

[1] Kandel, I. L., and Alexander, T., *op. cit.*, p. 232.

ELEMENTARY EDUCATION 449

nitely designed to prepare for continuation in the secondary schools, the program includes a second foreign language and follows that of the non-classical schools — the *Oberrealschule, Deutsche Oberschule, Aufbauschule, Reformrealgymnasium*, and, for girls, the *Studienanstalt*.[1]

The following curricula are suggested: general for boys and girls, commerce and trade and industry for boys, and commerce and trade and domestic economy and social welfare for girls, and secondary school preparatory. Courses in agriculture, navigation, and mining may be organized where local conditions are appropriate. For girls a seventh year may be added to the domestic economy and social welfare course (*Hausfrauenklasse*). The subjects and time-schedules of the courses for boys and girls are shown in the tables on pages 450 and 451.[2]

To the course in domestic economy and social welfare for girls there may be added an additional year (*Hausfrauenklasse*) which includes the following subjects: religion and knowledge of life, 2 hours; German and sociology, 3; theory of education and kindergarten principles, 3; hygiene, including care of children and sick, 1; civics and economics, 2; domestic economy (household accounts, nutrition, and domestic science), 3; music, 1; kindergarten work and care of infants, 5; physical training, 1; sewing, 4; drawing and handwork, 2; cooking, housework, and gardening, 7; total 34 hours.

The subjects and time-schedule for middle schools which also prepare for secondary schools, Plan V in the regulations, are shown in the table on page 452.

The methods of instruction and the organization of the courses of study are governed by the principles which have been described earlier. Emphasis is placed on activity instruction and on close articulation of all subjects with the local environment, with present problems, and with concrete situations. Subjects which are closely related culturally should, as far as possible, be united, as, for example, German, history, geography, and foreign languages; mathematics and science; manual work and drawing with other subjects. Since the subjects are taught by specialist teachers, the importance of coöperation and frequent conferences becomes even more necessary than in the elementary schools. As compared with the work of the

[1] See Chapter VIII.
[2] In the following tables the curricula described in the regulations as Plans I and II for boys and Plans III and IV for girls have been combined.

TIME-SCHEDULES FOR BOYS' MIDDLE SCHOOLS*

Subjects	Common						General			Commerce and Trade			Industry		
	VI	V	IV	III	II	I	III	II	I	III	II	I	III	II	I
Religion	2	2	2	2	2	2	2	2	2	2	2	2	2	2	2
German	6	5	5	5	5	5	5–6	5–6	5–6	5–6	5–6	5–6	5–6	5–6	5–6
History			2	2	2	2	2	2	2	2–3	2	2–3	2	2	2–3
Geography	2	2	2	2	2	2	2	2	2	2	2	2	2	2	2
First foreign language	6	4–5	4–5	3–5	3–5	3–5	3–5	3–5	3–5	5–6	5–6	5–6	3–4	3–4	3–4
Second foreign language			(3–5)	(3–5)	(3–5)	(3–5)	(3–5)	(3–5)	(3–5)	(3–5)	(3–5)	(3–5)	(2–3)	(2–3)	(2–3)
Arithmetic (bookkeeping), geometry	4	4–5	4–5	5–6	5–6	5–6	5–6	5–6	5–6	5–6	5–6	5–6	6–7	6–7	6–7
Natural sciences	2	2–3	2–3	3–4	3–4	3–4	2–3	2–3	2–3	2–3	2–3	2–3	4–5	4–5	4–5
Drawing	2	2	2	2	2	2	2	2	2	2	2	2	3–4	3–4	3–4
Manual training	(2)	(2)	(2)	(2)	(2)	(2)							(3)	(3)	(3)
Gardening				(1–2)	(1–2)	(1–2)							(1–2)	(1–2)	(1–2)
Music	2	2	2	1	1	1	1	1	1	1	1	1	1	1	1
Physical training †	3	3	3	3	3	3	3	3	3	3	3	3	3	3	3
Shorthand and typewriting				(1)	(1)		(1)	(1)	(2)						
Maximum number of hours of required subjects	29	30	30	32	32	32	32	32	32	32	32	32	32	32	32

* The number of hours in the subjects grouped with a brace, ⌢, may be distributed in other ways. The hours in elective subjects are designated by parentheses.
† In addition to the hours provided for this subject, one day a month is set aside for excursions (*Wandertage*), and games afternoons (*Spielnachmittage*) must be arranged.

TIME-SCHEDULES FOR GIRLS' MIDDLE SCHOOLS *

Subjects	Common VI	Common V	Common IV	General III	General II	General I	Commerce and Trade III	Commerce and Trade II	Commerce and Trade I	Domestic Economy and Social Welfare III	Domestic Economy and Social Welfare II	Domestic Economy and Social Welfare I
Religion	2	2	2	2	2	2	2	2	2	2	2	2
German	}6	5	5	5	5	5	5–6	5–6	5–6	5	5	4–5
History		}2	}2	}2	}2	}2	}2	}2	}2	}2	}2	}2
Geography	2	}2	}2	}2	}2	}2	}2	}2	}2	}2	}2	}1
First foreign language	6	4–5	4–5	}3–5	}3–5	}3–5	}5–6	}5–6	}5–6	}3–5	}3–5	}3
Second foreign language	..	..	(3–5)	(3–5)	(3–5)	(3–5)	(3–5)	(3–5)	(3–5)	(3–5)	(3–5)	(3)
Arithmetic (bookkeeping), geometry	3	3–4	3–4	4–5	4–5	4–5	4–5	4–5	4–5	4–5	4–5	2–3
Natural sciences	2	2	2–3	2–3	2–3	2–3	2–3	2–3	2–3	2–3	2–3	2
Drawing	2	2	2	2	2	2	2	2	2	2	2	1
Manual training	2	..	..	(1)	(1)	(1)	..	..	..	(1)	(1)	..
Gardening	..	..	..	(1–2)	(1–2)	(1–2)	..	..	..	(1–2)	(1–2)	..
Sewing	2	..	2	2	2	2	..	..	..	2	2	4
Domestic economy	..	..	..	..	(3–4)	(3–4)	..	..	..	..	(3–4)	4
Hygiene (nursing and care of children)	..	..	..	..	..	..	..	..	..	..	..	4
Music	2	3	2	2	2	2	2	2	2	2	2	2
Physical training	3	3	3	3	3	3	3	3	3	3	3	1
Shorthand and typewriting	..	..	..	(1)	(1)	..	(1)	(1)	(2)	(1)	(1)	..
Maximum number of hours of required subjects	30	30	31	31	31	31	32	32	32	31	31	32

* See note to time-schedule for boys.

Time-Schedule for Middle Schools Preparatory to Secondary Schools

Subject	VI–IV (as in Plan I, Common Course)	Number of Hour in Class			Total
		III	II	I	
1. Religion *	6	2	2	2	12
2. German	16	3–5	3–5	3–5	25–31
3. History	4	2–3	2–3	2–3	10–13
4. Geography	6	2	2	2	12
5. First foreign language	14–16	(3–5)	(3–5)	(3–5)	23–31
6. Second foreign language	3–5	(3–5)	(3–5)	(3–5)	12–20
7. Mathematics	12–14	4–6	4–6	4–6	24–32
8. Natural science	6–8	3–4	3–4	4–5	16–21
9. Drawing	6	2	2	2	12
10. Music	6	1	1	1	9
11. Physical training †	9	3	3	3	18
12. Sewing for girls	6	2	2	2	12
Maximum number of hours of required work	89	34	36	36	195

* See *Erlass vom 10, Januar 1017–U III D 2089 1*.
† To the three hours for physical training are added in all classes the play afternoons and the monthly excursion day which are required.

secondary schools, that of the middle schools is less academic, less directed to preparation for further study in higher institutions. The teachers with the exception of a small minority are men and women who, after a few years of experience in elementary schools, have taken the special examination for middle school teachers; of the rest, some are specialists in drawing, music, manual and physical training; a minority have had university training and are qualified to teach in secondary schools. The difference in standards between intermediate and secondary education is further illustrated by the fact that only those who have followed the special preparatory course in the middle school are permitted to continue in a secondary school.

Pupils are promoted at the end of each year on their records and the recommendations of their teachers. In response to repeated demands from teachers, who wished to have the status of middle schools defined in relation to other institutions attended by pupils of the same age, the Ministry issued a decree on March 22, 1927, establishing a leaving certificate (*Zeugnis der mittleren Reife*), to which pupils who have successfully completed the course of a middle school, recognized advanced classes (*gehobene Klassen*) attached to an elementary school, and six years of a secondary school course, are eligible. The possession of this intermediate certificate is not equivalent to the *Obersekunda-Reife*, obtained after six years in a secondary school and entitling its holder to continue the work of the last three years, nor does it confer any special privileges (*Berechtigungen*) except the right of admission to certain higher vocational schools (e.g., for commerce and agriculture).

In 1928 there were in Prussia 1143 middle schools (591 public, 379 private, and 173 *Rektoratschulen*) attended by 175,783 pupils and taught by 9938 teachers.

The *Mittelschule* is an obvious illustration of the need of differentiated types of schools and of education as pupils develop beyond the elementary stage. It equally illustrates the survival in Germany of class distinctions in education. More serious than these features is the fact that it represents the continuance of refusal to face the facts and reorganize the whole system of education in such a way that the various stages will be clearly marked and distinguished, but that in each stage above the primary there will be such variety and differentiation as will adequately meet the differences in capacity and the interests of the pupils. The *Mittelschule* is in many respects, excluding the continued organization of the curricula, very similar in standards and aims to the American high school, despite the difference in the ages of the pupils in the two types of schools. In many ways its work overlaps that of the secondary schools, but in order to maintain a strict distinction between them, a somewhat farfetched distinction is made between the practical emphasis in the one and the academic in the other, a distinction which will hardly hold if activity methods are employed in all schools. The existence of the *Mittelschule*, of the *Aufbauschule*, and the various types of reform secondary schools, illustrates the needless over-organization which exists in Germany and the wisdom of those who have advocated a common foundation followed by differentiation or the idea of the *Einheitsschule*.

Conclusion. The reform of education in Germany since the Revolution closely parallels the reform which followed the defeat at Jena in 1806. Then, as now, the nation had been defeated and realized that national reorganization could only be achieved through educational reconstruction. In the early nineteenth-century reform, however, attention was devoted mainly to secondary education; in the reconstruction since 1918 the whole of the educational system has been affected, but the most thoroughgoing reform has been in the field of elementary education and the preparation of teachers for elementary schools. The principle of educational reform, accepted then as now, is that national unity and national solidarity can be attained only through loyalty to a common culture shared in by independent, responsible individuals; the difference between the past and the present is that the former stressed the content of instruction, the latter, aided by the progress of educational theory, the method. In both periods the reforms were animated by a spirit of liberalism, but while in the first this spirit was gradually destroyed by the pusillanimity of the reigning monarchs, in the second the reaction is being caused more by the economic conditions which affect the rest of the world as well as Germany and by the failure of these powers whose destiny is bound up with the fate of Germany to strengthen the forces which are genuinely loyal to the development of democratic institutions in the spirit of the Weimar Constitution. The trend to narrow nationalism and the movement toward the Right wing in politics are the results, not of the will of the German people, but of world politics whose development the international mind has failed to inspire.

As a result of the new philosophy of education and as a protest against the pre-War system, German educators have begun to realize the meaning of freedom — in administration, in teaching, and in learning. Freedom, however, implies in education guidance by teachers who have themselves been trained to be free; the first radical reform which was undertaken was accordingly that in the preparation of teachers. The number of teachers who have had the advantage of the new preparation has been small up to the present, but liberalization of administrative practices, the organization of teachers' councils, the change in the spirit of methods of inspection as well as the system of preparation have given the teachers a feeling for the dignity of their work which can only be appreciated by members of a profession rather than servants of a machine-like organization. Added to this have been the contributions of theorists, the results of experimentation, and the guiding suggestions of the authorities, all of which have created a ferment disturbing to the calm indifference of a system whose operation is prescribed in every detail. Freedom and variety are today the characteristics of German elementary education; the exuberant license which prompted the more radical experiments, more striking as protests than as contributions to education, have given place to a reasoned reconciliation of freedom and responsibility. The claims of the child, the educand, as a developing human being are recognized, but they are not cultivated to the neglect of a common national end, the appreciation and understanding and advancement of German culture. Political, militaristic, and nationalistic indoctrination have been replaced by the development of the free, independent citizen, responsible for and inspired by the rich cultural forces of the nation of which he is a member.

These are the ideals which German education is striving to achieve and would achieve in a period of normal development. It must again be pointed out, however, that, unlike the Soviet Revolution, the German Revolution was not a complete break with Germany's cultural past and that the old and the new continue side by side; except by compulsion all teachers cannot be made over to one pattern. But, although schools can be found in Germany today which still bear upon them the marks of the old tradition, a new day has dawned in German education, and the responsible leaders will in the new era be the teachers; and, if the forces of reaction do not secure control, the German schoolmaster, trained to understand the child on the one hand and to interpret his environment on the other, will again win the victory, but this time for German democracy.

4. ITALY

History. The reform of elementary education in Italy, which took place in 1923, was inspired by discontent with its past development, by a new philosophy, and by Fascism. From its foundation by the Casati Law of 1859, Italian education had not suffered from neglect by the legislators, but educational laws, not motivated by any definite principles, were piecemeal and in general remained good intentions. The Casati Law required the establishment of elementary schools, one for boys and one for girls, in every commune so far as local resources permitted the carrying out of the law. The Coppino Law of July 15, 1877, following the unification of Italy, sought through education to train Italians, and made attendance compulsory from the age of six at least for the lower course — that is, up to the age of nine or ten. Compulsory attendance was extended to twelve and state aid was introduced by the Orlando Law of July 8, 1904, which also required adult illiterates to attend school in the evenings on pain of forfeiting certain rights and privileges — the franchise, public employment, and permits to hunt and carry arms. The Sonnino Law, July 15, 1906, provided for the establishment of state schools in districts with scattered population. Finally, the Daneo-Credaro Law, June 4, 1911, recognizing the ineffectiveness of local autonomy in education, set up provincial organizations to establish schools at the cost of the State in poor or indifferent communities; the effect of state aid was to lead to the surrender of local autonomy, with the result that an investigation conducted in 1923 revealed that only 264 localities out of 8354 had retained the right to provide elementary education; the majority of the autonomous communes were in the North. The percentage of illiteracy ranged from 11 per cent in Piedmont to 70 per cent in Calabria. The proportion of pupils enrolled in the elementary schools varied from 90 per cent in the Northern provinces, mainly industrial, to 59 per cent in Sicily and 41 per cent in Calabria, while of those enrolled, 94 per cent attended schools regularly in the most progressive province, Venetia, and only 47 per cent in Sicily and 32 per cent in Calabria. The number of pupils who succeeded in passing the annual examinations and securing their promotion, and the uneven distribution in the size of classes, ranging in some places from one pupil to more than sixty in others, revealed the failure of the laws to secure any real progress.[1] Inefficient administration, inadequate preparation, and poor professional discipline were other causes which, besides an inert public opinion, militated against an adequate execution of even the low minimum prescribed by the laws.

On the educational side elementary education was dominated by the philosophy of positivism, which emphasized knowledge for its own sake, placed science on a pedestal, was rationalistic and tended to set up standards and ideals which did not correspond in any way with the customs, prejudices, and ideals of the people. Combined with an emphasis on secularism, positivism had the effect of making the schools unreal, divorced from life, and external. Influenced in part by German educational theory and methods and in part by French rationalism and the analytical trend, the curriculum of the Italian elementary schools had become encyclopedic in content and atomistic in methods. The teacher, under the direction of detailed

---

[1] See Ministero della Pubblica Istruzione. Direzione generale per l'Istruzione Elementare. *Relazione sul Numero, la Distribuzione ed il Funzionamento delle Scuole Elementare* (Rome, 1923).

prescriptions and relying on a professional preparation which emphasized methods, rules, techniques, and devices, was set apart as a lay priest ministering knowledge and the sciences to the neglect of life around him and the real spirit and interests of the child.

Against the positivistic trend in nineteenth century philosophy a new philosophy of idealism was opposed by Benedetto Croce and Giovanni Gentile, who with the establishment in 1903 of *La Critica*, a philosophical journal, gradually built a school to which the younger Italians flocked. The interpreter of this philosophy for educational purposes was Gentile, who began with an attack on the unreality of the work of all schools, elementary and secondary, and on the prevailing dualism between mind and reality. Between these Gentile would recognize no distinction; reality does not exist by nature, but is the creation of the mind, of the spirit by the pure act of thought. The only true reality is the human spirit; education is philosophy in action and cannot be built up on the basis of biological analysis or of a psychology which separates the mind from reality and the world. Such a separation means the development of rules, techniques, devices, and methods, which are posited on theories of how the mind works, and instruction becomes the process of filling the mind with knowledge, facts, and information. This process is all the more unsound in a system which prides itself on being secular, neutral, agnostic, skeptical, and materialistic. Education under these conditions becomes a pseudo-science, abstract and divorced from reality, and in turn emphasizes, not the growth of man as man, the development of personality, experience as a formative factor, but informational and instrumental teaching, the tools rather than the spirit and culture. The traditional school set up three entities — the teacher, the content, and the pupil — and the intermediaries between the first and third consist of methods, which mechanize the process of education, makes it pedantic and schematic.

What is then needed to bring about an educational reform? Not a revision of the curriculum or new courses of study with the addition of new subjects, but a fundamental change of outlook and acceptance of the philosophy of active idealism. True education is possible only through personal experience, not by imbibing doses of knowledge and information ladled out by the teacher. Hence the center of the educative process is the child, not the teacher nor the content nor methods of instruction. Hence, also, the emphasis on the personality of the child as a human being with a spirit whose free growth must be encouraged and must be respected. What the child brings with him to school and his environment — his family, his religion, the folklore in which he has grown up, the dialect which he speaks, his nationality, and history of which he is a part — cannot be ignored. Education means, accordingly, the free development of the spirit and is a spiritual activity, which is one and cannot be divided and atomized into a multiplicity of aims, purposes, and objectives; it is one, as that reality which is the creation of the mind is one. Breadth of mind does not come from rationalization or intellectual liberalism as ends in themselves, but from enlightenment which grows from breadth of experience and self-cultivation. The function of the teacher is not to transmit his wisdom to the child, a process which would still leave it as an external, unrelated thing, but to provide opportunities for enriched experiences flowing from and based upon the curiosity, interests, and emotional life of the child, his inner world, his recreational life, and his joy in the beautiful.

The mind is one, and its method is the act of creating reality; but three categories can be recognized in this creative activity of the mind which brings about unity between the Ego and the non-Ego, between the subjective and the objective. These categories are art, religion, and philosophy, which must be the points at which education becomes philosophy in action. By art Gentile does not mean instruction in art, but the way in which the mind of the artist operates in expressing his concept of the world; art is pure subjectivity, the expression of the self, and the formation of personality. Artistic or æsthetic teaching, accordingly, is not limited to one field, but it is the formation of personality through expression and activity in any field — penmanship, composition, and play as much as drawing and music. Religion is consciousness of the object and the idea of God, or the omnipotence and omnipresence of spirit as manifested in the world of man with which the individual spirit must enter into harmony. Man is a man to the extent that he becomes a man — that is to the extent that his spirit becomes a part of the human spirit and his will becomes will at the same time as it is the will of all. But by religion Gentile does not mean the teaching of a religious creed, but religion as the essence of the growth of the mind itself, applicable to the conquest of the sciences as of religion in the narrower sense. The reconciliation between art, the subjective, and religion, the objective, is

ELEMENTARY EDUCATION

brought about by philosophy which creates the unity between the two. Hence a theory of education for all teachers is this "clear, precise, and sincere concept of reality, which opens our eyes in philosophy and making us fully conscious of our nature, realizes it in full by establishing in us that mind which is the only legitimate and effective teacher."

The essential principles of the reform from the point of view of this philosophy are freedom and activity — freedom for the schools, the teachers, and the pupils to follow the principles of their own development, and activity of teachers and pupils. The authority of the teacher depends upon his ability to promote the progressive human and spiritual development of the pupils and upon his own ability to grow and cultivate himself. Freedom, however, implies a responsibility to coöperate in the development of culture, "which is the progressive conquest of freedom," in the interests of the nation as a whole, for

National cultures have never been more conscious than now of the higher needs of the mind, needs that are not only æsthetic and abstractly intellectual, but also ethical and religious. For a school without an ethical and religious content is an absurdity. The school is not the form and means of the elevation of the mind; but it is precisely that elevation itself; it is the formation of men and consciences. There is no conscience that has a form indifferent to its own content and to its own faith. Every faith is sacred; but it must be a faith. The Italian school which the State, the supreme conscience of the Italian people, must maintain with serious determination and a firm understanding of its own duty, must be a human school for its universal faith; but also it must always be an Italian school for its national faith.[1]

In this process of building a national culture, the school must remain free as a developing, growing institution changing the content of its work as the spirit changes. Such work cannot be defined by officially prescribed courses of study and regulations, which Gentile had already insisted in 1920, three years before his reform, must be abandoned.

Away with pre-established programmes, then, of every description! Spiritual activity works only in the plenitude of freedom.... What we need to do is to wait, observe, and have faith. For God will reveal himself to us, and

[1] Quoted in *Educational Yearbook, 1929*, of the International Institute, Teachers College, Columbia University, pp. 388 f. Gentile's most important discussion of educational theory is his *Sommario di Pedagogia come Scienza filosofica*, in two volumes (Bari, 1924). His *La Reforma dell' Educazione* (Bari, 1920) was translated by Bigongiari, D., *The Reform of Education* (New York, 1922).

God is the very Spirit of ours which at every moment prescribes its law to itself and thus determines its own content.[1]

In the development of his reform, Gentile as Minister of Education was assisted by Giuseppe Lombardo-Radice, who was Director of Elementary Education in his Ministry. Lombardo-Radice brought to the task the inspired enthusiasm of long years of experience with children and the training of teachers. A modern Pestalozzi, he had built up his philosophy of education by observation and practice. With Gentile he was opposed to the materialistic, positivist tradition in Italian education. The process of education should develop by intuition, not through presenting a mass of objects to be studied by the pupil, but as a manifestation of his life and the evolution of ideas which he derives from his own experience. This process can be promoted by encouraging free and frank expression whether in the use of dialect and the mother-tongue, or in composition, singing, and art, or in play and recreational activities. The child must be respected as an investigator, an explorer, a student of nature and the great documents of the human spirit in religion, science, history, and literature rather than as a learner of formal manuals and textbooks. Only in this way can the child develop his personality as an independent, self-respecting individual and not a tool of others; only in this way can his spirit grow into a realization of itself as at one with the spirit of humanity.[2] Education is growth through self-conscious activity, for the free man is the creator of his own personality through play and work.

In Ernesto Codignola, Director of the Royal Higher Normal School in Florence, Gentile found another active collaborator, whose influence has been exercised not only through his opportunities for training the higher officials in the educational service, but in his interpretations of the history of education and philosophy, addresses to teachers, and the publications of educational and cultural journals. His influence has been especially strong in the emphasis which he has always placed on the reform of the preparation of teachers and in his attack on the exaggerated value attached to so-called professional subjects — theory and method, which in his opinion, as in that of

[1] Gentile, G., *The Reform of Education*, translated by D. Bigongiari, Chapter X (New York, Hartcourt, Brace & Co., 1922).

[2] Lombardo-Radice's most important works are his *Nuovi Saggi di Propaganda pedagogica*, (Turin, 1922); *Educazione e Diseducazione* (Turin, 1923); and *Vita nuova della Scuola del Popolo* (Rome, 1925).

Gentile, should be replaced by broad cultural training and philosophy.[1]

Because Gentile's philosophy of idealism emphasized the absolute, the omnipotence of the spirit, and the significance of historical truth, it was accepted as the philosophy of Fascism, and Gentile was selected to undertake "the most Fascist of all reforms," the reform of education. There was nothing contradictory between his emphasis on the supremacy of the spirit and the Fascist emphasis on the supremacy of the State and of the nation, nor between his plea for individual growth and the organization of a hierarchical administration, for an individual's will and spirit realizes itself in the will and spirit of others. But while Gentile and his associates realized the essential importance of nationalism and of national culture as the environment for the growth of personality, their aims were remote from attempting to cultivate political nationalism. And yet the place which they assigned to the study of popular heroes as manifestations of the human and national spirit furnished a ready opportunity for those who wished to use the schools for political ends; hero-worship could conveniently be turned to advantage in favor of a dictator, and the affirmation of the ideal values of Italy could easily be made to start with Vittorio Veneto. Hence it is significant that after Gentile, on completing his reform, retired from the Ministry (Lombardo-Radice had already retired because of his opposition to the tendency to mix education and politics), the schools have become increasingly Fascist. The direction of physical education was placed under the control of the *Opera Balilla*, a Fascist organization, incorporated under the National Ministry of Education in 1929. In 1928, in a discussion with the Minister of Public Instruction, Mussolini declared that his policy called for a new code of elementary education to educate the younger generation in the new atmosphere created by Fascism and to arouse in it a clear consciousness of (*a*) what the Italian people has been and hopes to become in history; (*b*) her contribution through discoveries and inventions to the knowledge, art, and civilization of the world; (*c*) the beauty and wealth of the Italian soil; and (*d*) the contributions made by Italians scattered over the world to the productive activity of diverse nations. The aim must be

---

[1] Codignola's writings include *La Reforma della Coltura magistrale* (Catania, 1917); *La Pedagogia rivoluzionaria* (2d ed., Florence, 1925); and *Il Problema dell' Educazione nazionale in Italia* (Florence, 1925).

the "Fascistization of all schools not only in their courses of study but in their personnel." In an earlier address Mussolini had made the following statement:

> The Government demands that the school shall derive its inspiration from Fascism; it demands that school shall not be, I do not say, hostile but not even aloof from Fascism, or agnostic in the face of Fascism; it demands that every school in every grade and in all its instruction train Italian youth to understand Fascism, to ennoble itself through Fascism, and in the historical atmosphere created by the Fascist Revolution. (*Discorso all'Augusteo.*)

Although teachers are not required to take an oath of allegiance to Fascism as are university professors, they do take an oath of allegiance to the Government. Early weeding out of anti-Fascist teachers and the presence in all schools of teachers who are members of the Fascist Party have had the same effect as direct compulsion. In the classrooms the portraits of the King and the Duce and the Crucifix on the walls, the presence of black-shirt teachers, who are members of the Party, and pupils in the uniform of the *Balilla*, and the Fascist salute [1] are ever-present reminders of the Fascist ideal of "work, discipline, and harmony." The control of textbooks and the publication of a series by the Government contribute to the same ends — the political direction of the schools. One of the strongest factors, however, has been the incorporation of the *Opera Balilla* in the Ministry of National Education, its control of physical education, and the influence which it exercises through its members, boys and girls, who are in the schools.

THE ORGANIZATION OF ELEMENTARY EDUCATION

The system of schools. The system of elementary education, which is free, includes the preparatory stage (*grado preparatorio*) given in pre-schools (*asili d'infanzia, asili infantili, giardini d'infanzia, scuole materne*) [2] for pupils from the age of three to six, the lower stage (*grado inferiore*) of three grades, and the higher stage (*grado*

---

[1] The Fascist salute, a revival of the ancient Roman salute with outstretched arm (*Saluto Romano Fascista*, is justified as a sane Fascist and hygienic practice, "destined to exercise the most beneficent influence on the formation of the character of the young." The Fascist salute was required in the schools in an official circular of January 2, 1926 (*Bollettino Officiale*, January 5, 1926).

[2] The last name, *scuole materne*, is the title used for the pre-school in the Code for Elementary Education (*Testo unico delle Leggi e Norme giuridiche sulla Istruzione elementare, e sulle sue Opere d'Integrazione*, 1928). The official name has not succeeded in ousting the traditional use of *Asili d'infanzia* or *asili infantili*.

ELEMENTARY EDUCATION

superiore). Until 1930 these stages were supplemented by a pre-vocational course of two or three years, known as the *corso integrativo di avviamento professionale*. The Royal Decree-Law of October 6, No. 1379, transferred this course to the lower secondary level as a *Scuola secundaria di avviamento al lavoro*,[1] thus abolishing the distinction, which is still found in France (*école primaire supérieure*), in Germany (*Mittelschule*), and in England (senior schools, central schools), between intermediate or higher elementary and secondary education.

Compulsory attendance. Compulsory attendance begins at the age of six and continues up to the age of fourteen. The length of the school year is ten months; pupils who for economic reasons cannot attend school for the school year must have the same number of lesson periods as are required for the whole year. Schools are open every day in the week except on Thursday and Sunday. Pupils must attend the type of elementary school provided in their locality — that is, graded, ungraded, or aided school [2] — and must remain in such school until the completion of their fourteenth year unless there are available in the neighborhood other courses and institutions of an educational and cultural nature. Responsibility for the school attendance of children of school age is placed upon parents, guardians, and employers, and, in the case of orphan children, on the directors of institutions or private individuals to whose care they are assigned. Parents and guardians who undertake to provide for the education of their children or wards in their own way must prove their technical and financial ability to do so. Private schools may be opened and maintained by persons who have the same qualifications as teachers in public schools. Pupils who are educated privately at home or in schools must be submitted to the regular examinations conducted for public school pupils. Blind and deaf-mute children, who are not abnormal in other ways, are also compelled to attend school, deaf-mutes up to the age of sixteen; for such pupils special schools, public or private, having, if they wish, infant sections, are recognized as schools to which state aid may be given and in which the principals and staff must have special preparation; the same requirements of examinations are set up for these defective as for normal children.

[1] See Chapter VIII.
[2] The variety of types of elementary schools is given in Chapter IV.

A list of children who reach the age of compulsory attendance is prepared each year by the mayor (*podestà*) of each locality and submitted to the government inspector. The names of such pupils who are not in attendance at the annual opening of the schools is posted on official notice-boards and, if a satisfactory explanation of their absence is not given by those responsible for their attendance, proceedings may be begun against them. The penalty which may be imposed rises from a fine of two lire, increasing for repeated non-observance of the law to fifty lire; these amounts are doubled in case of employers who knowingly employ children of school age. A similar procedure is followed against parents and others for unjustifiable absences of the children for whose education they are responsible.

There has been a notable increase in the number of children enrolled in the schools since 1926–27, as is shown in the following table: [1]

YEAR	CLASS-ROOMS	TEACHERS	CHILDREN OF SCHOOL AGE			PUPILS ENROLLED		
			Boys	Girls	Total	Boys	Girls	Total
1926–27	89,399	92,535	2,345,932	2,140,986	4,486,918	1,847,107	1,646,608	3,593,715
1927–28	90,210	93,912	2,445,954	2,244,537	4,690,491	1,964,026	1,738,104	3,702,130
1928–29	91,307	94,497	2,384,530	2,189,832	4,574,362	2,050,357	1,829,122	3,979,479
1929–30	90,633	94,148	2,482,400	2,266,462	4,748,862	2,194,893	1,958,891	4,153,784

The figures for private elementary schools are as follows: [2]

YEAR	SCHOOLS	PRINCIPALS		TEACHERS			PUPILS ENROLLED		
		M.	W.	M.	W.	Total	Boys	Girls	Total
1926–27	2466	378	1202	802	5337	7719	51,029	89,812	140,841
1927–28	2551	405	1242	839	5737	8223	52,024	91,192	143,216
1928–29	2616	432	1293	884	5811	8420	55,094	94,493	149,587
1929–30	2563	370	1333	724	5649	8076	56,782	103,712	160,494

Pre-school education. All pre-schools for children between the ages of three and six are recognized legally as the preparatory stage of elementary education. Attendance is not compulsory nor is the establishment of such institutions compulsory. The *asilo d'infanzia* is an old established institution in Italy; the first *asilo* was opened in Cremona in 1827 by Ferrante Aporti (1781–1858), a priest, philanthropist, and educator, whose activities, inspired by Pestalozzi and Père Girard, on behalf of young children and whose educational writings set a stamp on the pre-school which survived even after the

---

[1] Based on the *Compendio Statistico*, p. 55, of the *Istituto Centrale di Statistica* (Rome, 1931).
[2] *Ibid.*, p. 56.

introduction into Italy of the Froebelian methods. Another influence on the development of the *asilo* was that of the sisters Rosa and Carolina Agazzi, who, in 1894, reorganized an old *asilo* at Mompiano in Brescia and were supported in their work and theories by Professor Pietro Pasquali. Their contribution lay in the utilization of a rural environment for the enrichment of the lives of young children. Here they developed their own equipment, devised special methods for teaching singing, emphasized instruction in the mother-tongue and training of the senses, and through play and natural activities promoted the mental, moral, and physical advancement of the pupils; a sense of responsibility was cultivated in the older pupils, who were required to take care of the younger. The Agazzi system, which attracted attention at the Educational Congress held at Turin in 1898, was adopted by the city of Trieste in 1910. In 1915 it was pronounced as a model for pre-schools by the Minister of Public Instruction, and after the War was adopted for the *asili* established by the *Opera Nazionale di Assistenza per l'Italia redenta* (National Association to Assist Liberated Italy). A third direction from an Italian educator has been given to pre-school education by Madame Maria Montessori, who in 1907 established the first *Casa dei bambini* and there developed her theory of auto-education and the use of didactic materials. It is difficult to gauge the influence of Montessori in her own country; by those educators who have been influenced by the new philosophy of education her system is criticized as narrow, rigid, formal, and mechanical on the one hand, and as lacking in social purposes and vitality on the other.[1]

The provision of pre-schools for children between three and six has increased rapidly. This increase has been due both to the interest of the Government and the activity of the *Opera Nazionale per l'Assistenza e la Protezione della Maternità e dell'Infanzia* (National Association for the Assistance and Protection of Maternity and Infancy) which has sponsored child care, nursery schools and *crèches*, as well as the pre-schools of the type of the *asilo*. From 4587 *asili* in 1915 the number rose to 5902 with over 400,000 children in 1922, to 7076 in 1926–27 with an enrollment of 607,891 children, and to 9546 with

---

[1] It is significant that in two encyclopedias of education, the *Dizionario delle Scienze Pedagogiche* (2 vols., Milan, 1929) and the *Enciclopedia delle Enciclopedie*, vol. *Pedagogia* (Rome, n.d., but containing references to legislation as recent as 1930), there is no article on Montessori, although the latter discusses her work under the heading of *Le Case dei bambini* in the article on *Educazione Prescolastico*).

749,876 children in 1929–30. In the last year, 1043 provided free meals to all children in attendance, 2431 free only to the poor, and 912 made a charge for them. Distributed according to methods employed, 422 used those of Montessori, 1283 those of Aporti, 1458 those of Froebel, and in 6383 the methods were mixed. The schools in 1929–30 were in charge of 5903 directresses, 10,851 teachers and 4061 assistants.

Teachers in the preparatory stage must have special qualifications and hold a certificate of capacity to teach in this stage. They may be trained in six government schools of methods (*scuole di metodo per l'educazione materna*) which offer three-year courses, or in summer and other special courses, or in other institutions which provide the necessary preparation. Since 1926 the Ministry has been authorized to sanction and aid recognized associations in conducting experiments to differentiate the methods of instruction in the preparatory and elementary stages and to train teachers.

As defined by the regulations, "the preparatory stage is recreational in character and aims to train the first manifestations of intellect and character to the pupils." Besides simple prayers the curriculum includes singing of simple nursery and patriotic songs and music, free gymnastic and rhythmic games and exercises, simple exercises in manipulation, plastic and manual work, gardening and care of domestic animals, elementary general information and correction of popular prejudices and superstitions, and reading, recitation, and dramatization. The time-schedule, divided into thirty-five brief periods per week is as follows:

Subjects:
Religion...	1
Singing, free drawing, calligraphy, recitation.................	4
Elementary information and recreative intellectual occupations	6
Gardening, manual activities, domestic activities, physical activities and games, meals and hygienic care.............	24
	35

The absence of formalism, the opportunities for experimentation, and the interest of the committees of patronage (*patronati scolastici*) have placed the *scuole materne* among the most attractive institutions in Italian education. It is in these schools that Lombardo-Radice's insistence on the cultivation of the spirit of childhood, joy in life, and joy in play is best illustrated. At present, however, only about one fourth of the children between the ages are provided for in pre-schools.

Elementary schools. Elementary education until 1930 included the lower stage of three years (*corso inferiore*), the upper stage of two years (*corso superiore*), and the prevocational stage (*corso integrativo*) of two or three years. In 1930 the last stage, as already stated, was transformed with the *scuola complementare* into the *scuola di avviamento al lavoro* and transferred to the secondary level. The first two stages are given in the graded schools (*scuole classificate*); the *scuole non classificate*, or ungraded schools, are found mainly in rural areas and offer, as a rule, only the lower stage. The maximum size of a class according to the regulations is sixty; if this number is exceeded for a period of two years, an additional teacher must be appointed or the class divided and taught in alternate sessions.

The work of elementary schools is governed by the Royal Decree of October 1, 1923, No. 2185, incorporated in the *Testo Unico* (1928), the regulations on the time-schedule, courses of study, methods of instruction for elementary schools (*Ordinamento*, November 11, 1923), and the regulations on the courses of study in the mixed elementary rural schools (*Ordinamento*, January 21, 1924). The curricula are defined in general terms in the Code; that of the lower stage includes the following subjects:

1. Prayers and fundamental ideas of Christianity, — short and clear sentences and stories of immediate bearing taken from the Scriptures and especially from the Gospels; stories from sacred history; illustrations of the Pater Noster.
2. Reading and writing.
3. Elementary arithmetic and the metric system.
4. Oral exercises in translation from dialect; easy exercises in written composition; recitation of national hymns and poetry.
5. General information with special provision for direct experiences in agricultural and industrial work; knowledge of works of art, records, and monuments.
6. Elementary geography.
7. In schools which do not have a higher stage, the history of the Risorgimento up to the present.

The curriculum of the upper stage continues to develop the work begun in the lower and includes:

1. Readings on Catholic morals and dogma based on the Ten Command-

ments and the parables in the Gospel; principles of religious life and worship; Sacraments and rites according to the Catholic creed and practices.

2. Reading of books useful as guides in the problems of home and society.

3. History and geography, particularly of Italy; elementary notions and reading about the structure — geographical, administrative, agricultural, industrial, commercial, banking, and employment conditions — of those countries to which the immigration of the locality is directed.

4. Elementary study and reading of the political organization, administration of justice, the duties and rights as man and citizen; elements of economics.

5. Elementary arithmetic and geometry.

6. Elementary science; formation of collections of specimens obtained on school journeys; hygiene.

7. Applied design.

8. Physical education.

The prevocational course (*corso integrativo*), which is retained pending the reorganization introduced in 1930, continues the general studies, and adds applied design, plastic work, elements of mechanical work, elementary knowledge of electrical appliances for the home, theory and practice of agriculture, fundamentals of some manual trade, elements and practice of seafaring, cooking, and domestic arts, repairs, bookkeeping, and any other course approved by the *provveditore* (superintendent).

The courses of study and time-schedules issued on November 11, 1923, were published, not as prescribed requirements, but as suggestions (*indicativo*), leaving to the teachers the task of drawing up the courses for their own schools and classes.

The courses of study are intended to be suggestive only. They suggest to the teacher the result which the State expects from his work in each school year, leaving him free to use appropriate methods to attain it. For a number of reasons these are always diverse and variable according to the real situation in which the teacher finds himself in a given school environment, and according to the personal culture of the teacher and the special stamp which he will have succeeded in the course of a watchful experience in giving to his own spirit as an educator.

This freedom imposed upon the teachers the responsibility "of constantly renewing their own culture, not with the aid of petty manuals in which are collected the crumbs of knowledge, but at the living fountains of the true culture of the people." And so too with reference to the methods of instruction:

Each teacher must discover the methods of instruction, as a living norm, in himself aided by the study of those authors who have meditated on education, or have given accounts of their spiritual experiences, or have developed suggestive activities through the children, in whom the norms, though not expressed, are at all times implicit. Above all, the teacher will perfect his own instructional activity, living with warm enthusiasm the life of his people, listening insatiably to the voices of the Great, already studied in the years of professional preparation, and looking for new guides for his thinking in good books not previously read. In this way he will succeed in realizing his progress and will bring into the school the vibrant echo of his study.

The three important features which the reform has sought to emphasize are religious instruction, æsthetic training, and self-expression and self-activity of the pupils. According to the Code, "instruction in the Christian doctrine according to the form handed down in Catholic tradition is the foundation and crown of elementary education in all its stages." Gentile's emphasis on religious instruction as the search of the spirit for the eternal, the beginnings in the elementary stage of philosophy, has been explained earlier. Neither he nor his associates intended to emphasize dogmatic teaching: this was brought about later as a result of the Concordat with the Vatican in 1929 (see Chapter IV). Teachers are not required to give religious instruction unless they can do so with a clear conscience. In any case, those who do give it must be approved by the ecclesiastical authorities, whose approval is also required for the textbooks which are used.

Æsthetic education is not limited to art instruction, but must inspire every lesson. From the point of view of the philosophy of Gentile and of Lombardo-Radice, it means the slow groping for perfection through self-expression. It dominates in particular the work in language and literature, in singing and music, in play, and, of course, in art. Perhaps the most characteristic feature in all Italian elementary schools today is the illustrated diary which pupils above the first class are required to keep, and the illustrated monthly and annual composition. The suggestions for diaries of pupils in the third year (ages 8-9) include the following topics: Descriptions of all events in the life of the school with free comments, such as notes of lessons, excuses for absence, praise and reproval received, difficulties overcome, records of stories told by the teacher, descriptions of games, interesting facts about the school, notable events and celebrations. In the higher classes this content is supplemented with accounts of books read. The diaries must be illustrated. One form of diary which is widespread is the *Calendario alla Montesca*, or daily illustrated records of observations of nature (weather, plants, flowers, farming, etc.) which was first elaborated in the schools of *La Montesca* and *Rovigliano* in Città di Castello (Umbria), established for the children of farmers on the estates of Alice and Leopold Franchetti in 1901. The *Calendario*, because it is more systematic, provides for a closer relation to life than the diary which is left to the spontaneity of the pupils and which too frequently becomes formal and inept through repetition and uncritical in selection. The *Calendario*, without encroaching on the free expression of the pupils, has the advantage of defining the scope of their observation and activity.

Instruction in singing progresses from simple nursery and folk and patriotic songs to the study of music, intonation, proper use of the voice and expression, and choral singing. Art work is closely associated with all other subjects with a strong emphasis on free expression in line and color; in the last three classes the study of artistic masterpieces is introduced. The same principle is followed in the teaching of language and literature; while grammar and the study of words are not neglected, the free expression of the pupils is encouraged in oral and written practice; in the selection of reading, teachers are urged to introduce the pupils to the "voices of the Great," to the masterpieces of literature, "for the greatest authors are always the most simple" and bring the reader into harmony with the spirit of humanity; but this does not mean that the literary expression of the people, their folklore and dialect, should be ignored. As was pointed out in Chapter IV, every school is required to have a library maintained by the contributions of the pupils, the communes, and other associations. History and geography are limited in the main to the study of Italy and the region in which the school is located; in the fifth year the course in history includes the study of the great heroes of Italian history — painters, sculptors, architects, scientific discoverers, the Italian army and navy, the World War, the development of public services in Italy, the condition of labor, and the national resources as compared with other countries.

Two other courses leave room for a variety of activities and the introduction of the elementary sciences — there are *nozioni varie* (general information) and *occupazioni intellettuali recreativi* (recreational intellectual activities). The former give a large place to hygiene and relations to parents, to the school, to fellow-pupils, and much of the information included under the term "social studies" in American schools. In the fifth class the *nozioni varie* are divided into *scienze fisiche e naturali e nozioni organichi di igiene* (physical and natural sciences and organic notions of hygiene) and *nozioni di diritto e di economica* (elements of government and economics). The first of these courses is intensely concrete and practical, including in hygiene simple descriptions of the anatomy and physiology of the human body and lessons on health, with visits to laundries, bakeries, factories, hospitals, hygiene laboratory, and athletic clubs. The course in physical and natural sciences is more concerned with giving the pupils some notion of their place in modern society — the mineral resources of the country, hydro-electric power, climate and thermal stations, application of chemistry to industry, and botany and agricultural development.

Recreative intellectual activities aim to train the pupils in the art of play and healthy leisure occupations — indoor games, charades, riddles, story-telling, folklore and traditions in dialect. Every subject of the curriculum — geography, history, arithmetic, manual activities — is drawn upon and their recreational uses are indicated. The development of school journeys and of regional studies contribute to the same end and help to keep the work of the schools in close touch with realities.

Educational experiments. Not only are freedom of adaptation and activity of the pupils emphasized in all the regulations, but schools may obtain special permission to undertake experiments. By the Royal Decree-Law of February, 1926, No. 206, the Minister of Education may authorize associations, which are in his judgment competent for the task, to organize semi-annual or annual courses to experiment with different methods in elementary education. Such courses may be granted state subsidies. Teachers who wish to take such courses must already hold the official certificates of capacity to teach and must also have had a number of years of experience. Those who receive the diplomas granted at the end of such courses may receive appointments in experimental schools. Many such schools have been officially recognized and conduct their experiments under the supervision of inspectors. Educational experimentation is not new in Italy; that of the Sisters Agazzi has already been mentioned, while Montessori's work is known all over the world. The schools of *La Montesca* and *Rovigliano* in Città di Castello, established in 1901 by Alice and Leopold Franchetti for the children of agricultural laborers, developed an interesting program especially adapted to children living in a rural environment. *La Scuola Rinnovata* or *La Rinnova* (known also as *Ghisolfa*, from the district in Milan where the school is located) was established by Madame Giuseppina Pizzigoni in 1911, as a public experimental school built upon the activities and experiences of the pupils, emphasizing work in the open, manual occupations, play and games; the school carries the pupils from the preparatory stage up to the close of the compulsory attendance period and in the last years provides prevocational training in well-equipped shops. Madame Pizzigoni succeeded in developing a real school colony with spacious buildings, extensive playgrounds, and a swimming-pool; besides providing a hygienic environment and supplying meals to the pupils, Madame Pizzigoni added an adequate system of medical inspection. The various cultural associations (see Chapter IV) and other private organizations have been responsible for experimentation in rural schools. Open-air schools, the earliest of which was the Trotter School in Milan, have been increased in numbers not only for physically defective children but for all.[1]

The spirit of experimentation and innovation is undoubtedly in the air in the Italian elementary schools, inspired not only by the new tendencies in educational theory, which in a sense Italy shares with other countries, but also by a realization of the new task imposed upon the school by the Fascist Revolution. Educational experimentation requires, however, teachers who are better prepared than those whose task is prescribed by government regulations. Despite the emphasis on the new spirit in education, on freedom for the pupils, the discipline still remains formal and mechanical; except in the preparatory stage, there is not that freedom of movement which is expected in the new schools. There is in fact a real conflict between the new theory and the Fascist emphasis on discipline. The teacher brought up under one tradition changes to the new with some difficulty, with the result that even the "free" diary and composition become stilted, formal, and mechanical.

Textbooks. The Italian teacher's freedom is still restricted in two directions. He has no voice in selecting textbooks and state examina-

[1] For other experimental schools see Ferrière, A., *L'Aube de l'Ecole sereine en Italie* (Paris, 1927).

tions have been retained. No textbook may be used which has not been approved by the Ministry of Education and included in its official list. All publishers and authors are required to submit five copies of each book for examination by special commissioners; the fee for such examination is 120 lire. The critical reports on books which are approved are published; unfavorable reports are transmitted on request to the publishers and authors concerned. The influence of this system was particularly noticeable in the new and revised editions of the history textbooks which were published about 1928; all contained additional chapters written in almost identical form on the part played by Italy in the World War, her victories, the Fascist Revolution, and the work of *Il Duce*. In other words, textbook-writing is governed by the suggested course of study issued by the Ministry. In 1927 the Government undertook to publish its own series of elementary school textbooks, on the plea that in this way the cost of books could be kept down at a time of economic stringency. At the opening of the twenty-eighth session of Parliament the King pronounced the *libro del Stato* as the "indispensable instrument for the revival of culture and national education." The pupils purchase their own textbooks, poor pupils receiving assistance from the *cassa scolastica* and the *patronato scolastico* (see Chapter IV). The fact that uniformity of textbooks militates against the development of freedom of instruction does not seem to have been raised. Copies of approved textbooks must be deposited in the office of the *provveditore*.

Examinations. During the five years of the elementary course (*corso inferiore* and *corso superiore*) pupils are promoted to the second, third, and fifth class on the basis of their records (*scrutinio*), and tests conducted by the teachers in the last week of the school year; promotion to the fourth — that is, from the lower to the upper stage — is based on an examination conducted by a committee consisting of the supervisor (*direttore didattico*) or a delegate appointed by him, the class teacher, and another teacher specially selected for the purpose. Pupils who on their records or in the examinations are deficient in more than two subjects may take another examination at the beginning of the following school year and be promoted if they pass. Pupils who are educated at home or in private schools are required to submit to examinations, also conducted by special committees, for the certificates of elementary education, which consist of (1) certificate of promotion or admission to the different classes; (2) certificate of the lower grade on completing the third year; and (3) certificate of elementary studies (*certificato di compimento*) at the end of the fifth year. Where the *corsi integrativi* (sixth to eighth year) are provided, pupils are promoted to the sixth year by examination, and on the successful completion of the course, receive a certificate indicating that they have completed the period of compulsory attendance required by the law; this certificate (*certificato di adempimento dell'obbligo scolastico*) serves as a labor permit (*di speciale ideonità al lavoro*). Pupils who reach the age of fourteen without having completed the whole course may receive on request a certificate indicating the stage that they have reached. Every pupil, whether in public or private schools, is required to provide himself annually with a record book (*pagella scolastica*) in which are recorded his attendance, promotions, and success in examinations. In 1929–30 a total of 3,633,115 pupils (1,915,329 boys and 1,717,786 girls) were examined, of whom 2,678, 740 pupils (1,382,140 boys and 1,296,600 girls), or 74 per cent, were promoted. In the *scrutinio* and in the examinations, pupils are given one of four marks: unsatisfactory, satisfactory, good, praiseworthy (*insufficiente, sufficiente, buono, lodevole*), and are passed on the last three marks only.

Time-schedule. The time-distribution of subjects in the elementary school suggested in the regulations is as follows:

	I	II	III	IV	V	Prevocational
Religion	1½	1½	2	2	2	2
Singing, free drawing, calligraphy, recitation	2½	2½	4	5	5	3
Reading, writing, and language	7	6	5	5	4	3
Spelling	...	2	2	...	...	...
Arithmetic, geometrical design, bookkeeping	4	4	4	3	3	2
General information, and recreational activities	4	4	4	1	1	1
Gardening, manual work, household arts, physical training and play, meals, and hygiene care	6	5	4	4	4	...
Physical and natural sciences, hygiene	...	...	...	2	2	3
History and geography	...	...	...	3	3	2
Elementary government and economics	...	...	...	...	1	1
Vocational work	...	...	...	...	...	8
Total	25	25	25	25	25	25

Physical education. It will be noticed that physical training and play are not given a separate place in the time-schedule. The promotion of physical education, which is strongly stressed by the Fascist authorities, was at first placed under the supervision of a special association (*Ente Nazionale di Educazione Fisica*); by a decree issued in 1927 its organization and administration were placed under the care of the *Opera Nazionale Balilla*, which in turn became an official branch of the Ministry of National Education in 1929. Under the regulations issued by the *Opera Balilla* four periods of half an hour each were assigned to physical exercises in the third, fourth, and fifth years, and two periods a week of an hour each in the sixth, seventh, and eighth years and in secondary schools. The organization and supervision of physical training were placed in the hands of the provincial and communal committees acting through a director and office of physical education and sports, which draw up courses and train elementary school teachers for this branch of the school work. In addition, special teachers of physical education and sports are trained in a three-year course in the *Scuola Superiore Fascista* in Rome. In addition to direct physical training, the directors are required to see that facilities for sports and athletics are made accessible in every locality, that school excursions and exercises in the open are arranged, and that pupils are entered for athletic and gymnastic competitions and exhibitions.

Opera Balilla. It is through the far-reaching work of the *Opera Nazionale Balilla* perhaps more than through direct instruction in the classroom that the synthesis between education and nationalism as defined by the Fascist authorities is accomplished. For besides being the recruiting and training organization for the Fascist Party, the *Opera Balilla* through its members and through the great variety of its activities,[1] in and out of school, exercises a determining influence on the patriotic and national development of youth. Open to boys from the age of eight to the age of eighteen, the *Opera Balilla* recruits the majority of its members from pupils in the elementary schools. Thus in 1930 there were 981,947 boys between the ages of eight and fourteen in the junior branch technically known as *Balilla* and 371,529 youths between fourteen and eighteen in the senior branch, *Avanguardisti*. The section for girls had in the junior branch, *Piccole Italiane*, girls from six to twelve, had 670,183

---

[1] These were described in Chapter IV.

members and 98,000 girls in the senior branch (*Giovani Italiane*). From the point of view of national education, the *Opera Balilla*, with its symbolism, its uniform, its military organization and discipline, its provision of the many-sided opportunities for outdoor life, and its emphasis on religious devotion, moral character, and duty, is a powerful instrument for national unity, which, in many respects, transcends the influence of the schools. On the surface, the organized and disciplined activities of the *Opera Balilla* seem to be diametrically opposed to the philosophy with which Gentile sought to inspire Italian education. Actually, the contradiction is only superficial and the difference is one of methods. What Gentile and his collaborators hoped to secure by free activity and expression — the reconciliation of the spirit of the individual with the spirit of the absolute, for practical purposes the State, and of his will with the will of others, defined in Italy by the Fascist Party — the *Opera Balilla* as the active agent of the Party secures by direct action, training, indoctrination, and discipline. Gentile directed his attention to the process, *Opera Balilla* to the result, and with both man becomes free in so far as he recognizes the authority of the State.

Conclusion. The significance of the Italian reform in education lies in the congruence of the two directions upon which it is based — the philosophical and the political or national — which give education a unity which it never enjoyed before 1923. Despite the control of a strong political ideal, the Italian system illustrates how much scope can still be left for free experimentation and differentiation. One may disagree with the critical attitude of contemporary Italian leaders on what are regarded as the essentials of professional preparation — time will indicate the modifications which must be introduced — but the reform has already shown what a body of teachers, inspired by a potent ideal, can accomplish. As contrasted with those countries in which scientific experimentation in education is regarded as holding the key to progress, Italian education stands out because of its emphasis on the educand as a whole personality or a spirit in process of development and growth rather than as a bundle of nervous connections to be trained; against the analytical method which claims to experiment without a clear concept of a goal defined by the environment in which it serves, Italian education is a constant protest. By a curious paradox, the process of education is defined in terms which are almost similar by the idealists in Italy and the pragmatists in the United States; they part company, however, when the pragmatist refuses to define the ends of individual growth and the idealist finds them in the Fascist State.

5. RUSSIA

Theory of Soviet education. The educational reform of the Soviet Revolution represents a blend of revolutionary educational theories which had already been current in Russia for at least half a century earlier, of the new educational philosophy of freedom and activity, and of the control of education in the interests of the new social order. Many of the ideas which have been put into practice or incorporated into theory since the Revolution had been enunciated by the leading Russian educational theorists of the nineteenth century: V. V. Belinsky and N. I. Pirogov, with their emphasis on educating the individual as a man; K. D. Ushinsky, who insisted on the importance of national culture as the basis of instruction, suggested the outlines of the "complex" method, and laid the foundations of a science of education; Leo N. Tolstoy, who preached the doctrine of absolute freedom in education; and S. N. Kuvenko and P. A. Kropotkin, who placed labor in the center of the educative process. In 1905, S. T. Shatsky inaugurated an experimental school in Moscow based on his observations in the United States, and six years later, having moved the school to the country, he reorganized it on the basis of domestic and agricultural activities, close relationship to economic life, and self-activity and responsibility. The control of education by the State and by the Orthodox Church prevented any extensive application of the new education in the schools. Something else, however, was lacking — a social order in which the new education would have real meaning.

This meaning was provided by the Revolution and the principles upon which it was based. Its permanent success depended upon a close articulation between the schools, the new order, and the Communist ideology. In the first place, all education must be politicized; in the words of Lenin, "Our task in the school world is to overthrow the bourgeoisie, and we declare openly that the school, apart from life, apart from politics, is a lie and hypocrisy." For educational purposes this principle was elaborated by the educational leaders of the Revolution, Lunacharsky, Pokrovski, Pinkevitch, Shatsky, and Krupskaya, and in a measure by others, such as

Blonsky and Kalashnikov, who were not so clearly identified with Communism. Education can only have meaning, is the central contention of this group, in so far as it is identified with the social environment in which it functions and to which it contributes. The dominant interests of the Revolution are those of the workers, soldiers, and peasants. The function of the school is to prepare the future builders of socialist society and champions of the ideals of the proletariat, and this function can only be carried out successfully to the extent that the educative process is directly oriented toward labor, nature, and society, which provide the content of instruction. Only through looking at these three elements as a complex can the unity of education be preserved, a principle which is synthesized in Marx's definition of education:

> By education we mean three things: first, mental education; second, physical training as given in schools by means of gymnastics and military training; and third, technical education which introduces the prospective worker to the general principles of all the processes of production and at the same time gives to children practical information regarding the use of various working tools.[1]

Only through labor, nature, and society can the school give reality to education and direct it to the ultimate aim, the acceptance of the ideology of the new order, which rests upon productive activity and collectivism of the proletariat. Hence the school is definitely an instrument of indoctrination, a vehicle for inculcating the principles of Communism. To the extent that this principle is accepted can freedom in working out the aim of education be tolerated and the development of the individual through his own activities and participation be permitted. The aim of education is thus defined, not in terms of an abstract philosophy, but in accordance with the paramount claims of the social order.

> The major aim of general instruction [says Pinkevitch] is the development of an outlook upon the world. This involves the introduction of the individual to an understanding and evaluation of the entire cultural heritage of the present time. Our socialistic understanding and Marxian evaluation will of course differ fundamentally from those of the bourgeoisie. We must educate warriors for socialism who clearly understand the problems of their class and are able to evaluate independently all of the most important expressions of the contemporary culture. This does not mean that we make no allowances

[1] Quoted in Pinkevitch, A. P., *The New Education in the Soviet Republic*, p. 193 (New York, John Day Co., 1929).

for the needs of individual development. We dream of a man fully equipped with all the knowledge of the present day and to whom all that is truly beautiful is near; we dream of an active, strong man, struggling through the revolutionary classes of contemporary society for a realization of ideals which throughout the world will bring peace and happiness to all mankind. Such a conception of the aim of general instruction in no way contradicts the aim of professional instruction.... A man must have an allround education and at the same time know well some particular specialty.[1]

The ideal Communist citizen, which it is the task of education to mould, is thus described by Professor Thomas Woody:

The new citizen believes in, and can justify by Marxian dialectic, the *dictatorship* of the Communist Party, or as is generally said, the dictatorship of the Proletariat. He is *militant* in his defense and advocacy of it. He must be an *activist*. Though it seems a paradox at first glance, he is to be class-conscious; yet he is to become, at the same time, a *classless* mind. He believes in *universal labor*, holds the laborer in high regard, and the exploiter in greatest contempt. His mind must be secular (dominated by science) and atheistic, *political, collectivistic, and non-nationalistic*, and positively *international*. He must be healthy in the physical sense, a sound mind in a sound body. It is to be a sexless mind, i.e., recognizing no preferences based on sex. He who possesses these is the new man.[2]

Here are enunciated clear, definite, and unmistakable aims and ideals to be attained, by comparison with which the aims of education as usually stated, "development of character," "training of personality," "training of citizens," "imparting of culture," and even the innumerable objectives which are set up by American education without relation to a dominant aim, pale into insignificance as vague and intangible. Soviet education sets up a definite pattern according to which the individual is to be moulded, and because the school is constantly kept in close touch with its environment and is constantly under the supervision of the official and unofficial control of the constituted authorities and of members of the Party. From this pattern are derived all the ends — cultural, spiritual, intellectual, moral, and physical — of education, and in turn unity of purpose is derived from it. Religious training has, of course, been banned with religion and the schools are dominated by another form of orthodoxy — the politico-economic. Moral and ethical training based on religious and absolutist concepts has been

[1] Pinkevitch, *op. cit.*, p. 28.
[2] Woody, Thomas, *New Minds: New Men?* p. 42 (New York, Macmillan Co., 1932).

discarded as bourgeois practice, and its place has been taken by "proletarian class norms in the way in which we see them in the concrete historic environment of today" (Pinkevitch). The whole of education is dominated by dialectic materialism, the concept that the history of mankind can only be explained in terms of its economic development and changes in the methods of production and exchange. An existing society cannot be changed through the school, but the school must reflect society as it is and be intimately related to contemporary life, which in the new social order derives its significance only in the light of the collective activity and production of the proletariat.

From the point of view of a science of education, to which Russian educators have made extensive contributions through the centers for scientific research in Moscow and Leningrad, corroboration is furnished in the emphasis which is placed upon nurture or environment as a potent educative force. Education thus becomes the process of "conditioning" the pupil. And this the Soviet school has undertaken to achieve by surrounding him with an environment, material and intellectual, to which he can respond only in one way. The strength of Soviet education lies in the absence of a break in gauge, in a consistency of methods and ends, which was only partially achieved in the Jesuit and in the pre-War Prussian systems.

ORGANIZATION OF ELEMENTARY EDUCATION

Pre-schools. Since education is regarded as one of the strongest influences in the development and perpetuation of the new social order, it should begin at as early a stage as possible. Infancy and childhood are the most important periods in the life of the individual. Unable to carry out one of the fundamental ideas of Communism, the training and education of children from their earliest infancy in state institutions, the new order has sought to achieve the same end as nearly as possible by establishing institutions — *crèches*, children's homes, nurseries — in which infants can be left during the day. Such institutions serve two ends — the early physical and social training of children and the emancipation of women of the working classes to take their place side by side with men. Here the infants are provided with a healthy environment, are fed, are surrounded with didactic materials, acquire their first social training through their playmates, and begin to engage in socially useful labor in so far as they can help

ELEMENTARY EDUCATION

to keep the school clean, to look after themselves, and develop certain habits of responsibility.

In the kindergartens, which follow the infant stage, the children begin to participate actively in building up their own lives through socially useful labor and the establishment of close associations between the school and contemporary life. At this stage, the formal educational influences begin through labor, nature, and society. The pupils engage in activities which are imitative of the work of adults, are trained in collectivistic habits, and develop their powers through creative pursuits. Fairy tales have been banned as relics of bourgeois class conflict and folk stories as survivals of superstitions, and their place has been taken by an extensive children's literature closer to the realities and the materialism of the day. Even toys have been transformed into miniature reproductions of tools and instruments used by adults. The curriculum includes nature study, talks, and stories which give the pupils concrete understanding of the life about them, reading, writing, arithmetic, play, music, and art.

Before the close of the pre-school period, at about the age of eight, children become eligible for membership in *Oktiabrata* (Octobrists), the organization which represents the first stage in the training of future members of the Communist Party and which links the young child with the organizations for his older brothers and sisters, the Pioneers and the Komsomols (League of Communist Youth). But membership in the Octobrists means more than this; it means, so far as the intelligence of the children permits, the recognition of consecration to a cause and active work in the school and out of it in its interests. The task set before the Octobrists by Lenin was as follows: "First, and most important, constantly help the workers and peasants in their struggle; second, study; third, and last, make strong your own organization." [1]

Elementary education. Compulsory education, where schools are available, begins at the age of eight and continues up to the age of twelve. Elementary education is given the first four years of the unified labor school of seven or nine years, which, it is hoped, will in time be attended by all children between the ages of eight and seventeen.[2] The unified labor school is free, secular, and coeducational, and it is required by law to be open 190 days in the country areas and 205 days

---

[1] Woody, Thomas, *op. cit.*, p. 114.
[2] The statistics of pre-schools and elementary schools have been given in Chapter IV.

in the cities for from four- to six-hour periods a day; in 1928 the average number of days on which schools were open in twelve countries was 155.5 days in the rural districts and 180 days in the cities.

From what has preceded, the aim of the elementary school is clear; it is to give instruction in knowledge and habits and education in the broadest meaning of the term — sense training, development of native abilities, intelligence and will, the cultivation of an outlook on the world definitely based on class consciousness. Knowledge and information are, however, not the main ends but incidental outcomes from the study of labor, nature, and society directed to the social revolution. At the center of all activities stands socially useful labor, both in and out of school, which gives the Soviet school its polytechnical nature, thus defined by Krupskaya:

> This does not mean a school in which one studies several trades, but rather a school where children learn to understand the essence of the laboring processes, the substance of labor activity of the people, and the conditions of success in work. It is a school where children learn to know the extent of their powers.[1]

The program of the labor school was indicated in 1918, worked out by the State Scientific Council in the Commissariat of Education, and issued in 1923. The method of organization of the course of study is that known as the complex (*Gesamtunterricht* in Germany, integrated instruction in the United States), but differing from the German and American practices in being directly related to those major phases of human life — nature, labor, and society. In other words, instead of organizing the curriculum in the traditional fashion, by subjects, the course of study is developed round central themes related to the phases indicated. The general outline of the curriculum is indicated in the following scheme:[2]

GRADE	NATURE	LABOR	SOCIETY
1	Seasons.	Immediately surrounding labor life of both village and city family.	Family and school.
2	Air, water, soil. Nature and care of cultivated plants and animals which surround man.	Labor life of village or city block in which child lives.	Social institutions of village and city.

[1] Quoted in Pinkevitch, *op. cit.*, p. 200.   [2] As given in Pinkevitch, *op. cit.*, p. 305.

ELEMENTARY EDUCATION

Grade	Nature	Labor	Society
3	Elementary observations (information) in physics and chemistry, nature of local region; life of human body.	Economics of local region.	Provincial social institutions. Picture of past of one's own country.
4	Geography of Russia and other countries. Life of human body.	State economy of Russian Republic and other countries.	Organization of State in Russia and other countries. Pictures of past of humanity.

The curriculum is centered around the three major themes, which, when divided into a large number of themes and topics, become the course of study, as illustrated in the following analysis:[1]

Country School — Town School

First Year

Country School:
1. The first steps in school.
2. Family work in autumn.
3. The protection of health. Participation in the celebration of the Anniversary of the October Revolution.
4. Preparation for the winter and winter work. Participation in the celebration of Lenin's Day.
5. Life and labor in the winter.
6. The approach of spring and preparation for spring work. Participation in the May Day celebration.
7. Spring work. Participation of the children in spring work.
8. Participation in the examination. Exhibition of the school.

Town School:
1. The first steps in school.
2. The protection of health.
3. Life and labor of a family in the autumn.
4. Preparation for the winter, and life and labor in the winter.
5. The coming of spring, and spring work.

Second Year

Country School:
1. Children's life and labor in the summer, and the beginning of autumn work in the school.

Town School:
1. Children's life and labor in the summer.

---

[1] *Educational Yearbook, 1927*, of the International Institute, Teachers College, Columbia University, pp. 324 ff. (New York, 1928).

Country School	Town School
2. Autumn work in the village. Participation in the celebration of the October Revolution.	2. The town in the autumn.
3. The protection of health in the family and in the village.	3. The protection of health in the family and in the town.
4. Village life and labor in the winter.	4. Life and labor in towns.
5. The beginning of spring work and preparation for spring work. Participation in the May Day festivity.	5. Spring, and spring work.
6. Spring work in villages. Account of work done during the school years and plans for the summer.	

Third Year

1. *The village:* Harvest and agricultural produce; the village and environs; local trades, village life, and village organizations.	1. *The town:* The town and its environs. The labor of the town; commerce and cultural life of the town.
2. *Town and village:* Factories and works, city life. The cultural life in town and village.	2. *The village:* Cultivation of fields, manure, seasons of fruit, sowing.
3. *Spring in the village and the work of the peasant:* Tilling land; rivers and lakes in the spring; the meadows; beehives. Participation of the school in the May Day festivity. Account of the work done during the year.	3. *The work of the group during spring and summer:* Work on the piece of land belonging to the school. Rivers and lakes; the woods in the spring; the meadows.

Fourth Year

1. The Union of Soviet Republics. The earth as a sphere. Climate. The place of nature and labor in rural economy in our country. Rural economy in different localities of U.S.S.R. Accounts of agriculture in other countries. The northern borders of U.S.S.R. The southern borders of U.S.S.R. The industries of U.S.S.R. The origin of U.S.S.R. The government of U.S.S.R. The Communist Party. The relation between important foreign states (Germany, England, France, and the United States).
2. The care of the Soviet Government for improvement in the standard of life of the workers of U.S.S.R.
3. Topics from other work done during the four years.

In the earlier suggestions for carrying out the work of the unified school on the basis of the complex, it was intended that the so-called fundamental subjects — reading, writing, and arithmetic — be taught incidentally. As it was proved in practice that this could not be done or that these subjects were taught surreptitiously, the time-schedules were modified and special lessons in them were introduced. The "complex" scheme does, however, provide for social education through labor and the study of contemporary life, for music and rhythmic activities, for art, and for physical training. The study of nature leads over gradually to the study of science as furnishing the materialistic explanation of life and the instrument of social and industrial progress.

The most effective influences of the school are exercised, not so much through actual instruction, which is important in itself and follows the methods of the new education, but through the provision of opportunities for self-organization and self-government, school excursions to factories, museums, public institutions, and the intimate relationship with the junior organizations of the Communist Party — the Pioneers and the Komsomols. Commissions of the pupils are organized for sanitary, economic, cultural, and record purposes in each class and for each school and culminate in student councils responsible for the general interests of the school as a whole. Clubs and circles may be established for a variety of purposes. The most active spirits in the schools from the point of view of the Communist order are the Pioneers, members of the Children's Organization of Young Pioneers, who are admitted into the organization at the age of ten and continue until they are sixteen. Before admission to membership they must serve a period of probation and prove their sincerity and understanding of Pioneer ideals. In relation to the school of which he is a member, the Pioneer is a recognized leader. Distinguished by his badge, tie, and salute, the law of his group calls upon him to assume such leadership and be an example to his comrades:

> He will not avoid those who stand apart but go to them, try to draw them into his work and acquaint them with the organization. In school the Pioneer must actively share in school life, support discipline, and draw others into club activities, circles and games; arrange meetings and explain the tasks and purposes of Pioneers — and especially the commands of our leader and teacher, Comrade Lenin.[1]

As leader, he must stand out as an example in his studies, in his

[1] Quoted in Woody, Thomas, *op. cit.*, p. 110.

physical life, and in helpfulness to others; as a future Party member he must be an activist. Constantly under the eyes of his comrades and under the direction and leadership of a member of the next higher organization in the hierarchy, the Komsomols, the Pioneer is an active instrument of socio-political education in his school and a constant reminder that the school must be a part of contemporary life, an institution which is an extension of the new social order of government in the interests of the proletariat.

It is this social status of the school in the Soviet Republic which gives it life and meaning. In theory, at any rate, it seeks to carry out the principle that education is life and not a preparation for life in a more real sense than in other countries where this principle has been adopted. In practice the school may lag behind the theory, but only because the teachers until recently have either been lukewarm in their allegiance to the new education or inadequately prepared for the new task assigned to them. This much may, however, be said, that the Soviet ideology and Soviet educational theory constitute an unbroken circle; that it does not shrink from the acceptance of education as indoctrination,[1] even while it accepts the principle of freedom and respect for individual development; that it recognizes and utilizes every formative influence which will mould the future citizen into a loyal member of the social order. That school practices may be open to criticism may be true, but the magnificence of the whole concept upon which education is based and which takes one back to Plato's *Republic* can only be criticized when democracies have set before themselves the concept of social education which will be the moral equivalent of the Soviet Republic.[2]

6. UNITED STATES

History. The elementary school in the United States is today what it has always been intended to be — the common school of all

---

[1] If M. Ilin's *New Russia's Primer*, translated by Counts, G. S., and Lodge, N. (New York, 1931), is a good sample of the modern Russian textbook, Russian educators have discovered a more effective and more powerful technique for indoctrination than the Prussian pre-War elementary school teachers employed. See Alexander, T., *Prussian Elementary Schools* (New York, 1918).

[2] According to a leading article in *Pravda*, August 29, 1932 (translated by Mrs. N. P. Lodge), the Central Committee of the Communist Party is critical of the work of the schools, both elementary and secondary, which have failed to give a thorough training in subject-matter and to train the pupils intellectually and morally. The Committee recommends more attention to subjects as such, to systematic teaching, to the use of textbooks, and to greater flexibility of methods, and places upon principals and teachers greater responsibility for the maintenance of discipline among pupils.

the people, with the exception of the very small number whose children attend private schools. The idea of a public elementary school had been incorporated in American traditions as early as 1642 when in Massachusetts parents and masters were required to teach children to read, a provision which was changed in 1647, by the "Old Deluder Satan" Law, into a requirement that every town of fifty householders must appoint a teacher to give instruction in reading and writing. After many vicissitudes and amendments increasing the penalty for failure to establish schools, the law was virtually a dead letter when the Republic was established. From this time on the political motive for providing schools was substituted for the religious; the schools were to promote solidarity, freedom, and good citizenship.

Although seven States provided in their constitutions for the creation of systems of public education, nearly a generation elapsed before public elementary schools began to be established in considerable numbers. Public consciousness was aroused as in England by the development of Sunday schools, the organization of philanthropic associations for the establishment of schools, the rise of Lancasterian schools, and the creation of societies to conduct propaganda in favor of public education. No small part was played in arousing public opinion by workingmen's associations and by public-spirited citizens — DeWitt Clinton, Lyman Beecher, Calvin E. Stowe, James G. Carter, Horace Mann, Henry Barnard, and many others. The characteristics of the public school were that it must be free, common to all without class distinctions, non-sectarian, supported by public taxation, and supervised by the public authorities.

The task which confronted the leaders was not always simple. Opposition had to be overcome to the idea of the non-sectarian schools, to the abolition of tuition, to the levy of taxes for education, and to the introduction of state control over education. The rise of the common people during and following the Jacksonian era, the development of urban centers consequent on the expansion of industrial enterprises, and the gradual increase in the number of immigrants were factors, which, besides the active propaganda of educational and civic leaders, gradually broke down the opposition. By the middle of the century in some States, and after the Civil War in others, the principle of the public elementary school was generally accepted.

During the first stage in the evolution of the public elementary school there were no definite principles governing either the length of the course or its content. Starting with the three R's, the curriculum was gradually expanded; as the pupils increased in number and age, the elementary school was divided into primary, intermediate and grammar schools or into primary and grammar schools. To the earlier subjects there were added geography, grammar, composition, history, and music. Following the division of schools into stages, the grades themselves were slowly divided into classes until by the middle of the century there emerged the public elementary school with seven (generally in the South), eight (the normal type), and nine (in New England) classes or grades. This development was, however, possible only in the larger centers of population; the survival of the district system and the large rural population have militated against the universal adoption of graded schools until the present day, although efforts were made to grade the work of the ungraded schools into eight divisions.

The progress of elementary education was determined in the second half of the nineteenth century by the expansion of industry, the gradual conquest of the frontier, the rapidly increasing number of immigrants, and improvement in the means of communication. On the educational side changes in the curriculum were influenced by the development of normal schools, the introduction of Pestalozzian methods, and the spread of Herbartian and Froebelian philosophy. The curriculum continued to expand by the accretion of new subjects — drawing, manual work for boys and domestic arts for girls. In general, however, there had not yet been formulated a distinctively American philosophy of education adapted to the distinctively American idea of the public elementary school.

It was not until the last decade of the nineteenth century that a characteristically American attack on education began to be made. To this there contributed the establishment of chairs of education in universities and the development of departments or schools of education, the organization of educational associations like the National Education Association and the National Herbart Society, the beginnings of the child-study movement, and the work of such leaders as Francis Parker and John Dewey. The rise of national consciousness following the Spanish-American War and the rapid increase in national wealth combined with criticisms, which were leveled against every aspect of education from within the professional groups, led to a period of unrest and transition which has not yet closed. From the point of view of organization, it was felt that the break at the close of eight years of elementary education was unsatisfactory in so far as it postponed the beginning of secondary education to the age of fourteen; this led to a movement for a six-year elementary school, to be followed by three years in the junior and three years in the senior high school. At the other end, the kindergarten, which was rapidly being established as a part of the public school system, was not integrally articulated with the early grades of the primary school. The curriculum and methods of the elementary school were also subjected to the criticism that they were formal and perpetuated antiquated processes, utterly unadapted to the life and needs of the child. It was out of this setting that there emerged the problems which still surround the development of the elementary school.

THE PRESENT SYSTEM

Provision of schools. It was pointed out above in Chapter V that the control of education is vested in each State and that the Federal Government, with certain reservations, does not exercise any regulative authority over education. Each State delegates to the local areas — districts, towns, townships, and cities — the power to provide educational facilities under its supervision and with its financial aid, the extent of which varies considerably in different parts of the country. The provision of elementary schools is mandatory in every State by legislative enactment, but the extent and duration of elementary education varies from State to State and in different parts of the same State; the elementary school may give a six years' course articulated with the junior high school; more generally the course is eight years in length; in the South the length of the course is still seven years; in parts of New England nine years. It may or not be preceded by the kindergarten. There are still about 160,000 schools, in which the pupils are ungraded and are taught by a single teacher; this situation, which means a denial of equality of opportunity, has been remedied by the establishment of consolidated schools to which the pupils are transported daily. Between the ungraded and the graded schools — six classes or more with their own teachers — there are schools with two or more teachers. There thus exists a great variety in the opportunities even within the field of elementary education: magnificent buildings in one area may be matched by hovels in others; in one area the public school system may provide opportunities from the kindergarten up to entrance to college or even beyond, while another has only an ungraded, one-room school taught by a teacher with slight qualifications; the average number of days of school attendance in 1928 ranged from 98.1 days to 171 days in the year, and the percentage of average attendance from 67.1 per cent to 92.3 per cent; the average cost for current expenditures per pupil in average daily attendance varied from $34.35 to $144.56, while the amount per pupil for capital outlays ranged from $2.77 to more than $30 for the country as a whole, and in city systems from $25.57 per pupil for all current expenses to $216.77. There is thus an absence of uniformity in standards, quantity, and quality in the American elementary schools and in the further absence of a central controlling agency. All that can be attempted in a study of elementary education is to present a general picture of the present status and of the tendencies in the future.

Compulsory attendance. Compulsory attendance laws are now found in all States, but there is no uniformity of practice either in the ages of the pupils or the duration of the period of attendance. The first compulsory attendance law, requiring attendance at school for twelve weeks a year between the ages of eight and fourteen, was passed in Massachusetts in 1852. The example of Massachusetts had been followed by twenty-five States by 1889, but according to a report of the United States Commissioner of Education, the laws were inoperative except in Connecticut and Massachusetts. Some provision for compulsory attendance had been made by all but six Southern States by 1914; in 1920 the enactment of a compulsory attendance law by Mississippi made attendance compulsory throughout the country. The adoption of the principle of compulsory attendance does not signify uniformity of standards, as may be seen from the following summary showing the age requirements:

6–18 Ohio; 6–16 New Mexico; 7–14 Louisiana, North Carolina; 7–15 Arkansas and Virginia; 7–16 Connecticut, District of Columbia, Florida, Illinois, Indiana, Iowa, Kansas, Kentucky, Massachusetts, Michigan, Mississippi, Missouri, Nebraska, New Jersey, Rhode Island, Tennessee, West Virginia, Wisconsin, Wyoming; 7–17 Delaware, Maine, Maryland, North Dakota; 7–18 Nevada; 8–14 Georgia, South Carolina, Texas; 8–16 Alabama,

Arizona, California, Colorado, Minnesota, Montana, New Hampshire, Pennsylvania, Vermont, Washington; 8–17 South Dakota; 8–18 Idaho, Oklahoma, Utah; 9–15 Oregon.

The variations in length of attendance required is as follows:

No minimum laid down, Alabama; 3 months, Oklahoma; 4 months, Florida, Mississippi; 5 months, Utah; 6 months, Arkansas, Colorado, Georgia, Indiana, North Carolina, Texas; 7 months, Idaho, Illinois, Kentucky, Louisiana, Michigan, Minnesota, New Mexico, North Dakota, South Carolina, Virginia; 7½ months, Maine; 8 months, Arizona, California, Delaware, Iowa, Kansas, Massachusetts, Missouri, Nevada, Ohio, Oregon, Pennsylvania, South Dakota, Tennessee, Washington, West Virginia, Wisconsin, Wyoming; 8½ months, Vermont; 9 months, District of Columbia, Maryland, Montana, Nebraska, New Hampshire, New Jersey, New York, Rhode Island; 9½ months, Connecticut.

These variations are still further aggravated by the inadequate methods of enforcing compulsory attendance laws. Except in cities and in the larger units of administration, such as counties, enforcement is unsatisfactory. In the larger areas special departments of school attendance have been established charged with the duties of drawing up and keeping the school census up to date and of encouraging and enforcing attendance. The work of the attendance departments in some larger cities is supplemented by visiting teachers, whose function it is to investigate, not only cases of irregular attendance, but their causes, and on the basis of such investigation to make appropriate recommendations to the classroom teachers or to the parents to ensure the proper scholastic or physical adjustment of the pupils concerned. Beyond this, difficult cases of irregular attendance are met by the establishment of special classes and special schools; habitual truants may be committed to parental schools, which are either day or residential and in which the work and discipline are adapted to meet the peculiar needs of the pupils so committed.

Poor attendance is particularly characteristic of the rural schools and may be the result of climatic conditions, distance, inadequate means of transportation, illness, or, in many cases, an unsuitable curriculum or poor teaching. Much depends in such schools upon the influence of the teacher, perhaps more upon the adaptation of the curriculum to the rural environment.

Religious education. The American public elementary school was established as a non-sectarian, secular institution in which sectarian instruction is not permitted. The establishment of denominational or "parochial" schools is nowhere prohibited; the attempt made in Oregon to require all children up to the age of sixteen to attend public schools was declared unconstitutional in 1924. Denominational elementary schools are not given aid from public funds anywhere in the country, nor are they supervised or inspected, although inspection by state authorities is provided for in twenty States. In Nebraska, South Carolina, and South Dakota denominational schools must be approved by the public school authorities; in a number of other States standards are set up in the curriculum and quality of instruction, but are rarely enforced. Perhaps the only general requirement is that denominational schools must report the attendance and enrollment of pupils. The large majority of such schools are Roman Catholic; in 1928 there were 7764 Roman Catholic parochial schools with an enrollment of 2,201,942 pupils.

Although sectarian schools, sectarian instruction, and sectarian control of public schools are prohibited, religious instruction is not forbidden directly and in Virginia is actually permitted by law. Where found, however, religious instruction in elementary schools consists merely in the reading of the Bible without comment. Beyond this, religious instruction does not form a part of the regular curriculum and does not appear on the time-schedules. There has, however, recently begun a movement to permit pupils to attend religious instruction provided by denominational or interdenominational groups during school time.

Pre-schools and kindergartens. The large majority of American children are found in the public elementary schools. A smaller number, between the ages of four and six, attend kindergartens where they are available, and a still smaller number are sent to pre-schools which have recently been introduced into the United States and are still mainly private in character. Although the pre-school or nursery school was established under the influence of similar schools in Europe, the motives are somewhat different. They have been promoted in the interests of psychological and educational research rather than for the philanthropic desire to provide for the children of the poor opportunities similar to those enjoyed by the children of the well-to-do. A number of organizations interested in the study and physical welfare of children and in the promotion of better care of children in the home have contributed to their development; among these are the Child Study Association, the National Committee for Mental Hygiene, the American Child Health Association, and the National Congress of Parents and Teachers. Their promotion has been based on the principle that the first six years of the child's life are the most important for physical development, mental growth, the acquisition of language and other habits, and emotional adjustments, and that many of the ills of later life may be attributed to faulty training in childhood. Hence the nursery schools must be centers not only for research, but also for the training of parents.

The nursery school is accordingly to be distinguished from day nurseries, of which there are about 600 provided by philanthropic, religious, and welfare associations, run for profit, or attached to social settlements, industries, and public schools (Los Angeles is the only city maintaining the last type). The interests of the day nurseries are promoted by the National Federation of Day Nurseries. The nursery schools have been established by coöperative groups of parents (Chicago, Boston, Smith College), or in connection with clinics (Yale Psycho-Clinic Guidance Nursery), or attached to departments of education (Teachers College, Columbia University; Iowa State College of Agriculture; University of Iowa; University of California in Los Angeles; and a number of teachers colleges), or by private endeavor for research purposes (Bureau of Educational Experiments, New York, and Merrill-Palmer School of Home-Making, Detroit). Two nursery schools are provided in the public school system in Los Angeles (Normandie Nursery School) and Chicago (Franklin Public School Nursery). In 1928 there were 121 nursery schools in the country.

The aim of the nursery school is to discover the best conditions for meeting the needs of growth. The work of the nursery schools is by no means standardized, but in general they admit children from the age of about sixteen months and keep them up to the age of four years. The character of the buildings varies and there is an absence of that standardization which in England is due to the influence of Margaret and Rachel McMillan. The common aim of the nursery schools is to promote simple healthful living, cleanliness, planned diet, and a variety of activities, through play, music, story, and rhythm. Many schools keep careful records, not only of the health but the conduct and experiences of the children. The schools receive the children at about 8.30 in the morning and keep them for half or a full day, up to 5.30 in the afternoon. There is still great variation in the work of the nursery schools in the types of buildings, length of session, size of groups under one teacher, fees, and work. Some schools have a flexible program; in others there is a fixed timetable. The present status of nursery schools was clearly summarized in the following statement:

> There has been no crystallization of the programs of education for young children in nursery schools. Questions which are still controversial include the size, kind, and quality of play materials and of physical apparatus; the amount of independent personal care and care for property to be expected of children at two, three, and four year age levels; the size of group which a nursery school can handle, and the desirability of conducting organized group work; the amount of indoor and outdoor play; adequate provision of food for mid-morning, noon and afternoon lunch; the values of conducting nursery schools a full day or a half day; types of records to be kept each day, each week, and at other times during the school year; the details of physical examination considered essential and methods of preventing contagion; adequate methods of giving mental and social tests. Even this list of controversial questions does not complete the problems continually arising in nursery schools.[1]

The kindergarten was introduced into the United States by German immigrants; the first school of this type was established in 1855 in Watertown, Wisconsin, by Mrs. Carl Schurz, who had studied with Froebel. In 1860 Miss Elizabeth Peabody established a kindergarten in Boston and encouraged the opening of a private training school for kindergartners by Madame Matilde Kriege and her daughter in 1868. Four years later Miss Marie Boelte opened a training school in New York; a student of this school, Miss Susan Blow, was invited by William T. Harris to establish the first public kindergarten in St. Louis. From that time public and private kindergartens continued to be established, but are still found most generally only in the larger cities. In 1928 the enrollment of children between the ages of four and six was 700,000.

Originally conducted wholly on the principles laid down by Froebel, the modern kindergarten has today discarded almost all of them. The chief emphasis is placed upon the development of good habits, training in social behavior, formation of character, and sound physi-

[1] U.S. Office of Education, Bulletin, 1930, No. 16. *Biennial Survey of Education, 1926-1928*, pp. 286 f.

cal progress. The program of the kindergarten consists in the main of a variety of activities which may serve partly as a means for socializing the child and aiding the child to adapt himself to his environment, and partly to provide an accumulation of experiences which will furnish an enriched environment and may later serve as a foundation for beginning formal subjects — language, reading, writing, and numbering. The aim of the kindergarten has been defined as the provision of "a happy, colorful, and joyous environment, where children may really live together." The activities developed to attain this aim are play, dramatization, constructive and creative work (music, art, handwork), and games.

The kindergarten in its origin was an addition to the elementary school, attached to but not a part of it. Different in origin and governed by different aims and principles, the two departments were generally not articulated satisfactorily, with the result that the transition from the kindergarten to the first grade was too abrupt. There has accordingly developed a movement to correct this defect by extending to the first, and in some cases, even to the second grade, the organization of the school work on the basis of activities and by introducing formal subjects very gradually. The whole period so organized from a unitary point of view has come to be known as the kindergarten-primary stage and in many school systems has administratively been placed under one supervisor.

THE ELEMENTARY SCHOOL

Organization. The elementary school is the school attended by the majority of children of school age. Normally children are admitted at the age of six, even in those States where the compulsory attendance laws specify a later age of entrance. The duration of the elementary school period is in most systems eight years, except in the Southern States, where it is seven years, in some New England States, where it is nine, and in those areas where the junior high school, admitting pupils after six years of elementary education, have been established. Schools which have several teachers are administered by a principal, appointed by the local board of education on the recommendation of its superintendent from candidates who generally must hold a special certificate for the position or have qualifications higher than those required of classroom teachers.

The responsibility of the principal extends to the general administration of his school and the supervision of the teachers under him. One of the most general criticisms of the work of elementary school principals is that so much of their time is devoted to routine details, keeping of records, and other clerical duties that little is left for educational leadership and supervision of classroom instruction. Since the administration of education tends to be centralized in local systems, leadership and direction come too frequently from the superintendent and his staff, and schools bear the impress of these leaders rather than of the principals and teachers. Principals are rarely expected to construct a curriculum or course of study for their schools, since these are made out by the central offices and passed on. A certain amount of initiative is, however, left to each school for the preparation of the time-schedule, the assignment of classes to teachers, and adaptation of the course of study to the peculiar needs of a school. In schools with more than two hundred pupils, the principal is generally relieved from teaching. As the administrative and supervisory official, he has the right to supervise his teachers and to use whatever methods he may consider desirable.

Promotion and classification of pupils. Schools vary in size from the small rural school with less than ten pupils to the large city school with more than one thousand pupils. The question of the optimum size of school has not been considered. The size of classes varies from thirty to forty; on this question a number of investigations have been conducted, but have not yielded conclusive results — some studies point to a class of thirty or less, others seem to indicate that the size of class is immaterial so far as results are concerned. The promotion and classification of pupils constitute one of the important functions of the principal in a graded school, but even here he may be limited by a plan determined by the administrative staff of the system in which the school is located.

With few exceptions the usual practice is to divide the work of each year into two sections (A and B), and to promote pupils every six months; hence the nomenclature of classes generally found goes from the lowest class, 1B, 1A, 2B, 2A up to 8A. In larger schools parallel classes are provided which render classification and promotion more flexible, an end which is attained in other systems (e.g., St. Louis) by quarterly promotions. Pupils are classified on the basis of ability, which is tested either by examinations or by tests. Recently this method of homogeneous grouping has been challenged on the ground that it is artificial and does not provide for the intermingling of different types of ability found outside the school, and that labeling of classes as fast or slow, or advanced or backward, is unjust to the pupils.[1]

Various plans have been adopted to create systems of classification and promotion which will be most appropriate to individual ability. Detroit divides each grade into X, Y, and Z classes for the bright, normal, and slow pupils respectively; for the slow group, the curriculum is limited to the minimum essentials; the curriculum of the normal group is modestly enriched; and for the bright group, it is greatly enriched. Where parallel classes have been adopted, as in Cambridge, Massachusetts, Portland, Oregon, and Norfolk, Virginia, the pupils are divided into fast and slow groups, the latter taking eight years and the former six years to complete the course; the work of each group is so synchronized that pupils may be transferred from one to the other as occasion arises. In Batavia slow pupils are given special assistance by an extra teacher to enable them to keep up with the others of their class, a plan similar to that of Pueblo, where slow pupils are sent to a special teacher. Other variations which seek to adapt the work to the ability of each pupil are special or extra promotions, which are not regarded with favor, vacation schools in which retarded pupils may catch up with their classes or accelerated pupils may gain time, and special or ungraded rooms in which the special difficulties of backward pupils are investigated and corrected. The recognition of individual differences has led to the construction of diagnostic tests and of practice materials whereby defects may be discovered and corrected.

The most radical departure from normal practices has been introduced in Winnetka, Illinois, where Superintendent Carleton Washburne has adopted a modified form of the Dalton Plan of individual instruction. Recognizing individual differences and variation in abilities, Washburne has divided the curriculum into the common essentials and group and creative activities. The former consist of the fundamental processes which require practice, speed, and accuracy. For these subjects there have been developed carefully graded tasks at which each pupil works at his own pace; definite goals are set and the pupil tests himself from time to time before proceeding to the next stage; he may, when necessary, seek the help

[1] See Burr, M. Y., *A Study of Homogeneous Grouping*, etc. (New York, 1931).

of his teacher. The group and creative activities include literature, history, geography, music, art, play and assemblies, and manual work, which are studied by the class as a whole. Another form of the experiment which enables pupils to progress at their own rate is the Dalton Plan, which differs from the Winnetka Plan in that it is not limited to certain subjects, in the monthly assignment system, and in other details. Although developed by an American educator, Miss Helen Parkhurst, the Dalton Plan, except in modified form and with limitations, has not had a wide following in the United States.

While it does not bear directly on the question of classification and promotion, the "platoon" school is an experiment in the reorganization of school activities. Originating primarily as a device to provide adequate accommodation for a rapidly increasing population (in Gary, Indiana), the idea of the "platoon" school has been elevated to the status of an educational principle. Since the home provides decreasing opportunities for worthy educational activities, it is the duty of the school to add to its existing program those activities which were formerly provided in the home. Further, in view of the large cost of modern school buildings, there is economic waste in leaving any part of them unused not only after the school day, but also during the regular sessions. Accordingly, the platoon plan aims to make the maximum use of the school. Each school under this system, which has been adopted with more or less modifications by nearly 120 cities, divides the pupils into two or three, but generally two groups or platoons; while one group is receiving class instruction or study, the other is engaged in work (music, drawing, nature study in the laboratory, or library), or play (physical training or assemblies in the auditorium). The characteristic of the platoon school on the curricular side is accordingly its division into "work-study-play." The platoon school, it is claimed, can provide better equipment, specialized teachers, special rooms, and an enriched curriculum, and the pupils can be kept busy at a variety of activities during the whole school day. Since they are taught by specialist teachers, the community of each group is retained by providing "home rooms" under a teacher charged with its supervision.

The aim of elementary education. The aim of the American elementary school has been determined by a number of factors. The first of these is the heterogeneous character of the population, occupying a vast area and made up of individuals and groups drawn from all parts of Europe and differing in language, customs, and standard of values. The second is the democratic form of government which implies an absence of distinction and demands an education which will prepare for the responsibilities of a common citizenship. The third factor is the contribution of psychology to better knowledge of the child and of the methods of his growth through the learning process. The fourth is derived from the philosophical consideration of the relation of the individual to society and the State with a strong emphasis on his right to free growth and development. The fifth is the characteristically American emphasis on adaptation to changing needs, a tendency to look to the immediate present and future, and a refusal to be bound by traditions. All of these factors have led to the development of a pragmatic point of view which sets up values in terms of direct utility either to the individual or to society. The traditional aim of imparting a certain amount or kinds of knowledge, knowledge as power, or knowledge for its own sake, is no longer accepted as a defensible aim of education. The strongest influence in the development of a new aim of education in the United States has been the philosophy of John Dewey, with its insistence that "the school should be life and not a preparation for life" and that "the school cannot be a preparation for social life except as it reproduces conditions of social life."

The integrating and socializing aim of elementary education has been defined by Professor T. H. Briggs as follows:

In such an organization of education as exists or will exist, in the United States, the most important purposes of the elementary school are conceived to be, first, to furnish the common training necessary for all children "regardless of sex, social status, or future vocation"; and, second, by means of this common training, to integrate the future citizens of our democracy.[1]

In discussing the aims of education in other countries, it was possible to cite the statements found in the official publications of the respective ministries. The absence of such a central authority in the United States renders it impossible to cite aims which are generally accepted; of theoretical statements there is no end; the nearest analogy to an official definition of aims is to be found in the statements issued from time to time by committees appointed by the Department of Superintendence to investigate the reorganization of the curriculum. In general, American education is seeking to dis-

[1] Briggs, T. H., *The Junior High School*, p. 20 f. (Boston, Houghton Mifflin Co., 1920).

tinguish between (1) the *aims* which determine the whole process of education or of instruction in a single subject, (2) *objectives* which should determine the organization of the curriculum for the attainment of various ends, and (3) *outcomes*, or the expected results of instruction. Thus there may be one large comprehensive aim governing elementary education and within elementary education there may be included arithmetic; in the organization of this subject there are innumerable objectives within the four fundamental processes; the outcomes of instruction are skills and techniques in and knowledge of numbers and their relations. This method of attack, it is claimed, has the advantage of specificity and of clear adaptation of ends to means. It is derived from the method of job analysis in industry where every process has its own operation and all the processes yield a clearly defined result. It is based scientifically upon the stimulus-response theory (the S-R bonds) of mechanistic psychology, which emphasizes specificity of learning. In this process it is sometimes forgotten that in education the whole is greater than a combination of its parts.

In the studies of curriculum organization, which have been conducted since 1924 by the Department of Superintendence and which are summaries of current practices, this is the method which has been pursued. The *Fifth Yearbook* of the Department begins with an analysis of the common aim of American education:

> What are America's educational ideals? Education for life and service in a democracy cannot rest upon capricious or indefinite theories. It must have for its basis a sound and reliable philosophy. Fortunately, the founders of the Republic planned a nation in accordance with definite purposes, to achieve which they framed the Constitution.
>
> Officially they promulgated these six purposes in the preamble: (1) a more perfect union, (2) justice, (3) domestic tranquillity, (4) the common defence, (5) general welfare, (6) preservation of the blessings of liberty. They held the conviction that these should be secured by education. Since that time the States have provided for schools at public expense, taxing all for the general welfare. In tax-supported schools these American ideals are permanent. Upon their realization depends the perpetuity of our government which is composed of citizens. The progress of the Republic is conditioned by the development of its citizenry. To keep the citizenry at a rising level, schools have been established at public expense.[1]

On the basis of this statement the following common aim was formulated:

[1] Department of Superintendence, *Fifth Yearbook*, p. 9 (Washington, D.C., 1927).

The common or ultimate purpose of American education is the development of the kind of citizenship that will guarantee both the preservation and the promotion of public welfare. To carry out this common aim, the four following general objectives have been set up:

1. To promote the development of an understanding and an adequate evaluation of the self.
2. To promote the development of an understanding and an appreciation of the world of nature.
3. To promote the development of an understanding and an appreciation of organized society.
4. To promote the development of an appreciation of the force of law and of love that is operating universally.

Another statement of "the main objectives which should guide education in a democracy" was published in 1918 in a *Report* of the Commission on the Reorganization of Secondary Education, appointed by the National Education Association. Although issued under the title of *Cardinal Principles of Secondary Education*, the following objectives have been accepted as applying equally to elementary education: (1) health; (2) command of fundamental processes; (3) worthy home membership; (4) vocation; (5) citizenship; (6) worthy use of leisure; and (7) ethical character.

These statements of aims apply to all education; the specific objectives of elementary education were defined in these terms:

(1) Advance the child, although by no means perfect him in his ability to read, write, and speak correctly the English language, and to know and to use intelligently the elementary processes of arithmetic.

(2) Advance the child in his ability to know and to observe the laws of physical and mental health and well-being and to appreciate the meaning of life and of nature.

(3) Advance the child in his ability to know and to appreciate the geography and history of his own community, state, and nation, and of the world at large; to sense his share in the social, civic, and industrial order of such a democracy as ours, and to meet the full obligations which such knowledge and appreciation should engender, to the end that justice, sympathy and loyalty may characterize his personal and community life.

(4) Advance the child in his ability to share intelligently and appreciatively in the fine and musical arts as they are related to the three great universal needs of food, clothing, and shelter.[1]

Social efficiency and good citizenship are, then, the chief ends of

---

[1] This and the other quotations will be found in the Department of Superintendence, *Seventh Yearbook*, Chapter IV, pp. 79 ff. (Washington, D.C., 1929).

education. Starting from this point, the objectives may be derived. These may be analyzed simply as by Superintendent H. B. Wilson on the occasion of the revision of the course of study of the Berkeley Public Schools into vital or physical efficiency, vocational efficiency (right use of leisure), civic efficiency, and moral and religious efficiency, with outcomes in knowledge, habits, and skills, and attitudes in each. The job-analysis method has, however, gone much farther; Professor Franklin K. Bobbitt, in his *Curriculum-Making in Los Angeles*,

listed over one thousand definite, particularized objectives in human abilities, habits, attitudes, appreciations, skills, powers, and judgment, personal characteristics, etc. These were all classified under the following ten divisions:

(1) Social intercommunication, mainly language.
(2) Physical efficiency, the development and maintenance of one's physical powers.
(3) Unspecialized practical labors, such as repairing simple mechanical devices used in the home, driving a motor car, etc.
(4) Occupational objectives, the labor of one's calling.
(5) Efficient citizenship, the activities of the efficient citizen.
(6) Social efficiency, activities involved in one's general social relationships and behavior.
(7) Leisure occupations — recreations and amusements.
(8) General mental efficiency — its development and maintenance.
(9) Religious attitudes and activities.
(10) Parental responsibilities — activities, the upbringing of children and the maintenance of home life.[1]

Into the more theoretical discussions of the aims of education, it is impossible to enter here, not only because of their variety, but also because for the present they do not represent the actual situation in America except in some experimental, public and private, schools. In general they concentrate more on the free development of the individual, his needs, interests, and capacities, and on creative activity rather than on the social aim, which is expected somehow to be the ultimate outcome. The contrast between the old and the new theories of education is well pointed out in the following exposition of the *Opposite Poles in Educational Theory*:

[1] Department of Superintendence, *Second Yearbook*, p. 87 f. (Washington, D.C., 1929).

OPPOSITE POLES IN EDUCATIONAL THEORY[1]

Theory of Repression	*Theory of Expression*
1. Education is preparation for adult life, it ends when maturity is reached. It is primarily a reshaping, reformatory process for the child, who is looked upon as a bundle of original sin.	1. Education is life; it continues throughout life. It is an unfolding process. Spontaneous self-expression is the means employed; and unrepressed child nature is its own best guide.
2. The aim of the curriculum is to prepare for future opportunities and responsibilities. The curriculum necessarily involves much that is distasteful and foreign to the child's immediate interests.	2. The aim of the curriculum is to stimulate and encourage children to grow by providing for them, through a rich and suggestive environment, activities in which they joyously engage.
3. The method of teaching is formal drill on set assignments logically arranged. Rigid discipline moulds the child into adult conformity.	3. The method of teaching is following the inner urge of the child which results in spontaneous activity. Freedom and self-expression best develop latent talent.
4. Training results from acquiring, through memorization, the facts that make up the social heritage of the race.	4. Training results from meaningful activity growing out of the child's needs and interests.
5. Learning is a cold storage process by which the child stores up facts and skills for future use.	5. Learning is the acquisition of facts and skills essential to the fulfillment of the child's immediate interests.
6. Through education the child is inculcated with accepted doctrines and imbued with the sanctity of established institutions and vested rights.	6. Through education the child is imbued with a spirit of irreverence for blind tradition and a critical attitude toward things as they are.
7. School equipment is simple — a room, a teacher of the drill — master type, a rod, and a book.	7. School equipment is varied and attempts to duplicate life situations. The teacher is a sympathetic observer of childhood.
8. Child activity in itself has no justification. Childhood is merely a period of intensive preparation for successful participation in adult life.	8. Childhood is its own justification. It should be a period of carefree self-expression untrammeled by the demands of adulthood with its unfulfilled anticipations.
9. Too much education is feared. Education beyond one's station is to	9. The more education the better. Through education every child can

[1] National Education Association, *Research Bulletin*, Vol. III, Nos. 4 and 5, Sept.–Nov., 1925, p. 118.

be deplored. Early entrance into industry and the early assumption of adult responsibilities should be encouraged.

be brought to a higher level or station in life. The period of youth and school attendance should be extended.

Curriculum and courses of study. The outstanding preoccupation in American education during the past ten years has been the study of curriculum problems, which arose out of a feeling of discontent with the traditional program of the elementary (and secondary schools). This program is criticized as a purposeless and unorganized accretion of subjects which emphasize the acquisition of more or less useless facts, information, and knowledge, stress discipline and intellectual training, and neglect the development of the total personality of the individual in relation to his present environment. In the task of curriculum revision have participated not only the official agencies for the administration of education, state and local, but national organizations like the Department of Superintendence of the National Education Association, the National Society for the Study of Education, individual leaders in the field of education (both general and "curriculum experts"), and research divisions of university departments of education.

The movement for the revision of the curriculum and courses of study has resulted from a number of different factors. So far as the content and aims of the curriculum are concerned, each State in the country and in most States each local district has been a law unto itself, and this variety has manifested itself also in great diversity in the amount of time devoted to the different subjects. These differences are shown in the accompanying table in which the amount of time given to the elementary subjects in the schools of Seattle is compared with the average amount of time given in forty-nine cities of over 100,000 population.

In spite of this diversity, which from one point of view is desirable, it is felt that there are certain national ideals that need to be cultivated. So much time has been devoted to methods that the realization of purposes and the improvement of subjects have been disregarded. On the other hand, the making of curricula and courses of study has been too much dominated by convention and traditions to the neglect of the demands of everyday life. The curricula have grown by the accretion of subjects and subject-matter without any careful synthesis or interpretation. Courses

Comparison of the Time Allotments in Number of Minutes per Week by Grades in the Seattle Schools with the Average Allotments in Forty-Nine Large Cities *

Subjects Taught		I	II	III	IV	V	VI	VII	VIII	Total
Language	49 Cities	130	141	167	176	187	194	207	215	1417
	Seattle	0	50	75	110	200	225	225	225	1110
Reading	49 Cities	421	404	332	245	182	141	142	136	2003
	Seattle	600	525	425	310	135	135	225	212	2567
Spelling	49 Cities	39	82	87	85	82	78	72	73	598
	Seattle	0	75	100	100	60	60	60	60	515
Penmanship	49 Cities	67	72	77	78	77	75	63	58	567
	Seattle	50	75	75	75	60	60	60	60	515
Arithmetic	49 Cities	64	143	193	206	211	211	212	211	1451
	Seattle	0	150	250	240	225	255	250	200	1570
History	49 Cities	17	19	30	54	84	97	148	167	616
	Seattle	100	30	50	75	135	135	250	125	900
Civics	49 Cities	9	12	11	12	14	15	23	27	123
	Seattle	0	30	25	25	35	30	0	75	220
Geography	49 Cities	11	14	59	137	156	162	137	84	760
	Seattle	0	0	50	100	180	180	0	112	622
Science	49 Cities	22	23	23	23	21	21	22	26	181
	Seattle	38	20	25	25	25	40	40	40	253
Hygiene	49 Cities	16	16	16	22	27	27	25	22	173
	Seattle	37	20	25	25	25	25	35	35	227
Physical Training	49 Cities	90	67	89	90	90	89	98	104	737
	Seattle	0	0	50	50	50	50	50	50	300
Supervised Play	49 Cities	22	19	18	14	16	16	16	15	136
	Seattle	150	150	100	50	50	50	50	50	650
Recess	49 Cities	105	106	106	96	91	90	84	74	752
	Seattle	100	100	100	100	100	100	100	100	800
Industrial Arts	49 Cities	22	22	25	30	50	65	90	106	410
	Seattle	25	50	63	60	60	0	0	0	258
Drawing	49 Cities	87	88	87	86	82	75	77	79	661
	Seattle	75	50	63	75	75	75	75	75	563
Music	49 Cities	71	74	74	77	76	74	70	75	591
	Seattle	75	75	75	80	80	80	80	80	625
Miscellaneous	49 Cities	97	93	99	97	99	98	88	87	758
	Seattle	0	0	0	50	50	50	50	50	250

* Department of Superintendence, *Second Yearbook*, p. 140 (Washington, D.C., 1929).

of study have been imitated and copied, while the influence of textbooks has been detrimental to freedom and local adaptation.

There is today "a great need for a scientific determination and general acceptance by both educators and laymen of the aims and objectives of modern elementary education. If education is to be placed on a thoroughly scientific basis, outcomes must be considered in the determination of processes. Selection of objectives is the first step toward putting education on a firm foundation."[1] Accordingly, the questions that are being asked in the present survey of the curriculum are as follows:

Is the present course of study in harmony with present social and individual needs? Is it in harmony with advancing educational practice based upon the rapidly developing science of education?... How shall a program of revision be organized which will result in the best possible course of study? How should provision be made for continuous modification and improvement of this course? How may the teaching corps be stimulated actively to participate in the revision and intelligently to coöperate in its interpretation in the classroom? How may the community be brought into sympathetic understanding of the whole program?[2]

Underlying the movement is a new attitude which has developed in the twentieth century, opposed to the narrow conception that the function of the school is to provide training in a few simple tools. Modern life has become so complex, the number and diversity of pupils in schools so great, that the curriculum calls for a new orientation; not merely pruning of dead material and the addition of new topics, but a complete, thoroughgoing revision is necessary if the school is to contribute to successful life in society.

Determination of content. The general trend of aim in curriculum-making having been discovered, the next problem is to devise methods for determining the content. Professor Bobbitt thus summarized the steps in curriculum construction:

(1) Determination of objectives; (2) Formulation of guiding principles; (3) Selection of pupil experiences; (4) Selection of needed materials; (5) Placing experiences in proper sequence as determined by maturity; (6) Experimentation to test placing of experiences; (7) Welding the experiences found suitable for any particular year or term in a thoroughly correlated instruction; (8) Constant revision in the light of experiences and experimentation.[3]

---

[1] Department of Superintendence, *Second Yearbook*, p. 94 (Washington, D.C., 1929).
[2] *Ibid., Fourth Yearbook*, p. 28.   [3] *Ibid., Second Yearbook*, p. 102.

Somewhat similar were the suggestions of Professor W. W. Charters:

(1) Determine the ideals and activities which constitute the major objectives. (2) Analyze these and continue the analysis until working units are obtained. (3) Arrange them in order of importance. (4) Raise to positions of high rank in these lists those ideals and activities which are of great value for children even though low in value for adults. (5) Determine the number of most important ideals and activities which can be mastered in the time allotted to school, after eliminating those which can be learned outside of school. (6) Arrange the material in proper constructional order, according to the psychological nature of children and the texture of the materials.[1]

Professor Otis W. Caldwell, formerly Director of the Lincoln School of Teachers College, Columbia University, emphasized the importance of considering the needs of the pupils for whom a curriculum is being made.

I wish to state certain principles which it seems should be clearly defined for use in any reorganization of the school subjects of a study.

1. *Pupils' attitude toward school subjects.* Children learn best, retain longest, and find learning most stimulating and most usefully available, when the subject matter and methods of school work are engaging and genuine, not repulsive and artificial.... Subject-matter should be so selected and used that more should be gained than has been in the past from its inherent significance to pupils.

2. *Pupils must succeed in school subjects if they are to be educated.* Subjects should be so selected and used, and pupils and subjects should be so graded that more pupils will succeed, in order that later achievement may also be had.

3. *The rate and quality of learning are improved by an increase in the number of senses used.* There is too large an omission of fundamental experiences which involve touch, taste, sight... the experiences of the daily life for which we say we are preparing our pupils.... We have fallen into a conventional education of words.

4. *The subjects should be organized and used so that pupils may teach one another.* Education has never made adequate use of the fact that children learn much from one another, and our present subject organization does not favor such mutual teaching.... The topics and content of studies should be such that pupils can come into mutual and coöperative mastery of them.

5. *The school's organization is a legitimate and necessary part of the subjects of instruction.* School is training for social effectiveness, the school institution must itself be socially effective. To be so the educational processes must be coöperative, and the activities and procedures which enter into the school's organization must be used as true subject-matter material.... This means that school curricula and methods and building organizations must be

[1] Department of Superintendence, *Second Yearbook*, p. 102.

participated in by pupils, and that the school's own organization is a part of the school's curricular possession, not a personal possession of the administrative officers.... Ideas will never be carried out unless they are embodied in the machinery.[1]

The making of courses of study. The universal practice in the United States has been until recently that the curriculum and courses of study have been prepared in great detail by the superintendent of education himself, or with the aid of his administrative staff, and handed on to the teachers. The methods of preparation have varied — in some cases the curriculum and courses of study have been mere imitations of others recognized as standard; in others they have been based on and followed the textbooks which were prescribed. To some extent, the subjects and the curriculum have been prescribed in legislative enactments; among these are flag exercises, fire prevention, temperance, health, physiology, history from certain national points of view, and so on.[2] The past ten years have witnessed the beginnings of a movement to enlist the participation of teachers in the preparation of the curriculum and courses of study. Starting in Denver, the movement has extended to other large cities, among these Detroit, Cincinnati, Dayton, St. Louis, and Houston. In Denver the curriculum revision was the result of the coöperative activity of teachers, principals, supervisors, and university and other agencies which were engaged in curriculum investigations; experts were invited for consultation, criticism, and advice. Teachers and principals were organized into separate committees for each subject and special arrangements were made to enable members of such committees to attend meetings during school time. Following the publication of the courses of study, a department of curriculum revision was established to maintain a continuous revision.

The Denver experiment and the continued unrest in curricular matters not only stimulated other cities to undertake similar revisions, but led to the creation of departments of curriculum research as a part of the administrative organization in a number of cities or attached to schools of education in universities; it led at the same time to the emergence of the "curriculum specialists" available for consultation and advice. Among the studies under-

[1] Department of Superintendence, *Second Yearbook*, pp. 103 f.
[2] See Flanders, J., *Legislative Control of the Elementary Curriculum* (New York, 1925).

taken in this connection are the following, given in an account of the work of the Bureau of Curriculum Research of Teachers College, Columbia University:

(1) Analyzing the outstanding courses so as to determine: (a) general trends and tendencies, (b) the overlapping of content and experience materials, (c) the best projects in various subjects as well as those which disregard subject-matter lines entirely, (d) the best drill devices in the various phases of different subjects.

(2) Studying, by various methods, classroom teaching in outstanding school systems and experimental schools, in order: (a) to compare the work as outlined in the courses of study with actual practice, and (b) to note wherein the work in the classroom differs from ideal and theoretical schemes.

(3) Analyzing textbooks.

(4) Making curriculum materials more usable by setting up tentative suggestions for adaptation to various communities. Some of the factors which should be considered in this study are size of the community, preparation of teachers, individual differences of pupils, types of administrative organization and the like.[1]

Not only is this a period of transition, but there is inevitably a gap between theory and practice. Hence, while theory stresses that education is life and not a preparation for life, that the curriculum should consist of experiences and activities which represent real "life situations" or actual problems as they arise in the social environment of the school, in actual practice published courses of study range from detailed prescriptions of facts, information, and skills to be imparted to suggestive outlines of activities meaningful and significant to the pupils at their particular stage of development.

Not only are courses of study, in the preparation of which teachers have had no part, prescribed, but supervisors are employed to guide the teachers in carrying out these prescriptions, and, while external examinations have generally been abandoned, standardized tests or achievement tests tend to lead to the same result, which is further promoted by the use of prescribed textbooks. Knowledge, facts, and information at one end of the scale contrast with the revision of courses of study based on analyses of contemporary American life and its needs on the one hand, and the study of pupil capacities, interests, needs, rates of learning, and other individual characteristics on the other; the methods of arriving at this revision are meas-

[1] Stratemeyer, F., and Bruner, H. E., *Rating Elementary School Courses of Study*, pp. 170 f. (New York, Teachers College, Columbia University, 1926).

Average Amounts of Time in Minutes per Week and Percentages of Time in Each Grade Allotted to the Subjects by Forty-Four Cities in 1926*

Subject	Grade 1		Grade 2		Grade 3		Grade 4		Grade 5		Grade 6		Total Grades 1–6	
	Min.	%	Min.	%	Min.	%	Min.	%	Min.	%	Min.	%	Min.	%
Three R's:														
Reading	388	28.8	348	24.3	293	19.1	212	13.4	168	10.4	149	9.2	1558	17.1
Phonics	68	5.0	51	3.6	24	1.6	5	0.3	1	0.1	1	0.1	150	1.6
Literature	22	1.6	22	1.5	35	2.3	25	1.6	26	1.6	27	1.7	157	1.7
Arithmetic	80	5.9	146	10.2	196	12.8	211	13.3	215	13.3	215	13.3	1063	11.6
Language and grammar	86	6.4	104	7.2	136	8.8	158	10.0	169	10.5	173	10.7	826	9.1
Penmanship	74	5.5	80	5.6	84	5.5	85	5.4	82	5.1	79	4.9	484	5.3
Spelling	31	2.3	82	5.7	94	6.1	96	6.1	93	5.8	89	5.5	485	5.3
Total three R's	749	55.5	833	58.1	862	56.2	792	50.1	754	46.8	733	45.4	4723	51.7
Content Subjects:														
Geography	4	0.3	7	0.5	58	3.8	133	8.4	160	9.9	164	10.2	526	5.8
History	8	0.6	11	0.8	26	1.7	57	3.6	94	5.8	113	7.0	309	3.4
Social science	2	0.1	3	0.2	3	0.2	5	0.3	6	0.4	6	0.4	25	0.3
Citizenship and civics	11	0.8	12	0.8	14	0.9	16	1.0	19	1.2	21	1.3	93	1.0
Nature study and elementary science	21	1.6	23	1.6	21	1.4	19	1.2	17	1.0	16	1.0	117	1.3
Total content	46	3.4	56	3.9	122	8.0	230	14.5	296	18.3	320	19.9	1070	11.8
Special Subjects:														
Art and drawing	71	5.3	73	5.1	74	4.8	73	4.6	72	4.5	70	4.3	433	4.7
Music	74	5.5	76	5.3	77	5.0	80	5.0	79	4.9	77	4.8	463	5.1
Household and manual arts	2	0.1	2	0.1	3	0.2	6	0.4	18	1.1	30	1.8	61	0.7
Hand work	30	2.2	22	1.5	13	0.8	9	0.6	6	0.4	5	0.3	85	0.9
Projects and achievements	8	0.6	6	0.4	6	0.4	5	0.3	4	0.2	2	0.1	31	0.3
Health education	30	2.2	31	2.2	37	2.4	44	2.8	51	3.2	52	3.2	245	2.7
Physical training	79	5.9	79	5.5	81	5.3	81	5.1	80	5.0	80	5.0	480	5.3
Recess	111	8.2	112	7.8	109	7.1	103	6.5	97	6.0	92	5.7	624	6.8
Opening exercises	51	3.8	53	3.7	52	3.4	49	3.1	48	3.0	47	2.9	300	3.3
Supervised study	18	1.3	24	1.7	31	2.0	44	2.8	49	3.0	52	3.2	218	2.4
Unassigned and free time	49	3.6	43	3.0	42	2.7	39	2.5	37	2.3	33	2.0	243	2.7
Miscellaneous	29	2.1	25	1.7	26	1.7	26	1.6	22	1.4	22	1.4	150	1.6
Total special	552	40.9	546	38.0	551	35.8	559	35.4	563	35.0	562	34.7	3333	36.5
Total all subjects	1347	99.8	1435	100.0	1535	100.0	1581	100.0	1613	100.0	1615	100.0	9126	100.0

* From Mann, C. H., *How Schools Use Their Time*, p. 23 (New York, 1928).

Average Amounts of Time in Minutes per Week and Percentages of Time in Each Grade Recommended for the Elementary Subjects by Fifteen States in 1926*

Subject	Grade 1		Grade 2		Grade 3		Grade 4		Grade 5		Grade 6		Total Grades 1–6	
	Min.	%	Min.	%	Min.	%	Min.	%	Min.	%	Min.	%	Min.	%
Three R's:														
Reading	382	28.2	367	26.1	317	20.1	259	16.1	194	11.8	179	10.8	1698	18.4
Phonics	18	1.3	15	1.1	13	.8	8	.5	7	.4	7	.4	68	.7
Literature	4	.3	4	.3	5	.3	5	.3	10	.6	10	.6	38	.4
Arithmetic	67	4.9	105	7.5	179	11.4	186	11.6	198	12.0	198	12.0	933	10.1
Language and grammar	126	9.3	127	9.0	149	9.5	158	9.8	166	10.1	174	10.5	900	9.7
Penmanship	62	4.6	75	5.3	79	5.0	84	5.2	83	5.1	82	5.0	465	5.0
Spelling	27	2.0	65	4.6	87	5.5	88	5.5	81	4.9	80	4.8	428	4.6
Total three R's	686	50.6	758	53.9	829	52.6	788	49.0	739	44.9	730	44.1	4530	48.9
Content subjects:														
Geography	14	1.0	14	1.0	59	3.8	115	7.1	164	10.0	166	10.1	532	5.8
History	24	1.8	24	1.7	45	2.9	80	5.0	140	8.5	132	8.0	445	4.8
Citizenship and civics	12	.9	12	.9	14	.9	14	.9	15	.9	25	1.5	92	1.0
Nature study and elementary science	39	2.9	43	3.1	35	2.2	30	1.9	30	1.8	30	1.8	207	2.2
Total content	89	6.6	93	6.7	153	9.8	239	14.9	349	21.2	353	21.4	1276	13.8
Special subjects:														
Art and drawing	113	8.3	107	7.6	115	7.3	104	6.5	81	4.9	85	5.2	605	6.6
Music	76	5.6	82	5.8	80	5.1	80	5.0	80	4.9	79	4.8	477	5.2
Household and manual arts	35	2.6	36	2.6	35	2.2	36	2.2	53	3.2	54	3.3	249	2.7
Health education	36	2.7	36	2.6	44	2.8	53	3.3	50	3.0	54	3.3	273	3.0
Physical training	77	5.7	73	5.2	69	4.4	68	4.2	63	3.8	57	3.5	407	4.4
Recess	121	8.9	120	8.5	124	7.9	120	7.5	119	7.2	117	7.1	721	7.8
Opening exercises	48	3.5	48	3.4	48	3.0	48	3.0	46	2.8	46	2.8	284	3.1
Unassigned and free time	35	2.6	29	2.1	53	3.4	59	3.7	56	3.4	59	3.6	291	3.2
Miscellaneous	39	2.9	23	1.6	24	1.5	12	.7	12	.7	15	.9	125	1.3
Total special	580	42.8	554	39.4	592	37.6	580	36.1	560	33.9	566	34.5	3432	37.3
Total all subjects	1355	100.0	1405	100.0	1574	100.0	1607	100.0	1648	100.0	1649	100.0	9238	100.0

* From Mann, C. H., *How Schools Use Their Time*, p. 38 (New York, 1928).

urements, statistical records, analyses, and controlled experimentation.

The great variety of education practices throughout the country has already been illustrated above (see Table, page 505). It may be further amplified by the accompanying tables (pages 510, 511) which give at the same time the lists of subjects found in the elementary schools of the country; although the tables present the figures for 1926, there has probably not been any substantial change in the general situation.

There are thus no established norms either as to the subjects taught or the time allotted to them. There is still less uniformity in the courses of study despite the nation-wide discussion of the problem by a large number of agencies. Some courses prescribe the details which are to be taught in each subject; others are textbooks and guides on educational theory and methods. The Wisconsin Course of Study, for example, in the section on geography discusses the aims, gives general suggestions in methods and organization, a general statement of content by grades, a summary of the standards of accomplishment to be reached, and a list of books on content and method to be used by the teachers. This procedure is followed in all subjects. The Denver Course of Study in arithmetic may be cited as another example of a course which is at once a textbook in subject-matter, general and special methods, standards, and reference material. Opening with a General Introduction, it discusses general aims, how the course of study meets general aims, relation between content and method in achieving the end, value of knowing the course as a whole, development of character traits, and a concluding summary. This is followed by Suggestions Relative to Instruction (development, methods of presentation, drill, motivation through interest, application — the thought side of arithmetic), the Elimination of Difficulties in Reasoning, Individualization — Suggestions for Diagnosis of Difficulties and Remedial Instruction, General Suggestions, Tests and Results of Scientific Investigation: Relative Value of Subject-Matter. Each of these sections is illustrated by practical examples. The remainder of the volume (376 pages) is devoted to the distribution of the course in the grades, with further statements of aims, suggestions, standards of attainment, and examples for each of the six grades. The same procedure is followed in volumes on the other subjects of the curriculum. More usually the courses of study,

ELEMENTARY EDUCATION

after a few general suggestions, give itemized lists of the topics to be treated in each class. Another form of course of study, which is gradually disappearing, is that which directly follows a selected textbook both in organization and content.

Textbooks. Despite progressive movements in curriculum, it is still true that the textbook method of instruction (the "recitation" method) and of subject-matter organization is the dominant practice throughout the country. In its origin the textbook was introduced into American schools to compensate for the poor preparation of teachers and in time it has become difficult to dislodge. Free textbooks were introduced in Philadelphia in 1818 and in Massachusetts in 1844. In 1927 twenty States required by law the free distribution of textbooks to pupils, twenty-three States had permissive laws, and five had no regulations on the subject. The practice of providing free textbooks is almost universal and particularly to pupils in elementary schools. In twenty-five States uniform textbooks are adopted in all parts except the independent cities, six States permit county adoption, and seventeen allow local adoption. Textbooks are selected in eleven of the States which have uniform adoption by the state board of education; in other States special textbook commissions are appointed; in the localities the selection is made by the boards of education; rarely do teachers participate in the selection. Not only is there uniformity of textbooks in many States, but the period of adoption is over a long term of years, three for four years, twenty-one for five years, nine for six years, two for eight years, and one for ten years.[1]

The extensive market and the competition for adoption have resulted in the production of textbooks which are superior in many respects to the European in form, make-up, binding, print, and illustrations. Textbooks are prepared by teachers at all levels of the system and leading experts in subject-matter and in theory have participated either individually or in coöperation. Selection committees, advised by their officials, are guided generally by certain standards for measuring both the material and scientific character of books submitted to them. The aim in the preparation of textbooks is to base them upon the latest contributions from the side of theory, methods and curriculum principles and in certain fundamental subjects of tests and measurements. So far as textbooks are

[1] See Tidwell, C. J., *State Control of Textbooks* (New York, 1928).

concerned, they are in general beyond criticism; difficulties arise, however, when the single textbook rather than the teacher's mastery of the subject of instruction becomes the sole reliance both of teacher and pupils. This is what is meant by the "recitation" method, which, despite all theoretical discussions of progressive methods, prevails very widely — the teacher assigns a certain number of pages in a textbook to be "studied," and on the following day the pupils must be ready to answer questions on them; hence much depends on the quality of the textbook and the extent of instruction and guidance that the pupil may derive from it. Changes in methods of instruction are proceeding rapidly; the single textbook is gradually being replaced, not only by the use of several or by supplementary books, but also by the development of library methods. The extensive use of the textbook has been a corollary of poor preparation of teachers, and, as professional preparation improves and a proper balance between the attainment of mastery of content and methods is secured, the textbook method, but probably not the textbook, will be relegated into the background for purposes of consultation and reference as in most European countries.

Methods of instruction. The textbook or recitation method still continues to be the characteristic method of instruction in American elementary schools. It has been subjected to severe criticism as emphasizing only the acquisition of knowledge, of dead cold facts, and of information unrelated to the life and needs of the learner. After the five formal steps of Herbart had been discarded, efforts were made to supersede or to supplement the recitation method by training pupils in how to think and how to study, a training which was accompanied by library work. But this method still seemed to imply the study or reorganization of what was regarded as the cut-and-dried material of one or several textbooks. Training in how to study was a step in the direction of a wider range of activities than were possible under the recitation methods, but the activities were still scholastic and did not arise out of life situations which should determine the purposes of the pupils' activities. Accordingly, there developed out of the ever-widening influence of pragmatic philosophy in education, combined with the laws of learning, based on the mechanistic psychology, a new general method, the "project method." "A project is any unit of purposeful experience, any instance of purposeful activity, where dominating purpose, as an inner urge,

(1) fixes the aim (or end) of the action, (2) guides the process, (3) furnishes its drive, its inner motivation for its vigorous prosecution." Psychologically this means that learning is based on three laws: (1) law of readiness; (2) law of exercise (use and disuse); and (3) law of effect or the satisfactory attainment of the purpose. The project method has on the whole been more discussed than practiced except in a few experimental schools and with younger children.[1]

The project method, if not carried out according to its definition, combined with the criticism of subject-matter prescribed merely as content to be learned, has led to a new approach to both curriculum and methods. The curriculum, according to the advocates of the new philosophy, should consist of activities and experiences arising out of the lives of the pupils and methods should vary according to the ends to be attained. This means, in turn, a complete change from the traditional subject organization of the curriculum to integrated subject-matter. The child does not distinguish between subjects *quâ* subjects; his experience at any one time is whole and integrated; so, too, his school activities and subjects, as they have been known, should be introduced as the need for them emerges. This is, of course, the American analogy for the German *Gesamtunterricht*, but appears to have been arrived at independently. At present, it is found in public schools more frequently in such integrations as "social studies," a blend of history, civics, geography, and hygiene, or "general science," a course based on study of the science of everyday life and drawing upon hygiene, biology, botany, chemistry, and physics. In its more general form the integrated curriculum is found in the kindergarten and early primary grades and more often in experimental schools.

Into a discussion of the development of special methods of teaching the different subjects of the elementary school curriculum, it is impossible to enter here. On the whole, much of the time in the courses of professional preparation has been devoted to the study of special methods with inadequate attention to the mastery of the subjects themselves. This emphasis has tended to restrict professional growth and to militate against freedom and flexibility in the classroom. The movements for the revision of the curriculum and for the de-

---

[1] The laws of learning have been subjected to criticism as an inadequate explanation of learning except at the lower levels by Professor B. H. Bode in his *Conflicting Psychologies of Learning* (New York, 1929).

velopment of training of teachers through professional subject-matter are helping to reduce the emphasis hitherto placed on special methods.

Control of the teaching process. Only in a limited sense, however, can it be said that education in the United States is characterized by freedom and flexibility. There is variety in so far as each State is responsible for its own system of education and each local unit — whether town, township, county, or city — enjoys a certain independence. But within each local unit every school tends to be dominated by the same principles and functions. The character of a school is determined not by its principal and staff, but by the policy of the superintendent in charge of the whole system of which it is a part. Through the prescribed courses of study and sometimes prescribed methods, through teacher-rating schemes (in some areas), through teachers' institutes, held at the beginning of each school year to discuss the work of the year, through supervision, and through tests and other forms of standardization, the freedom of the teacher tends to be limited. On the other hand, there are distinct evidences of a change. The participation of teachers in the preparation of courses of study, which has already been mentioned, is an advance in the right direction. Scientific tests and measurements are no longer accepted as having the infallibility of the yardstick and are regarded as valuable mainly for diagnostic purposes. Teachers' institutes are changing in character and are becoming more practical with opportunities for discussion by the teachers. The mobility of teachers and the pursuit of further study in summer sessions or during a longer term are helping to create professional attitudes which will in the end result in greater professional freedom and flexibility. Finally, the nature of supervision, which at one time was directed to securing uniformity of practices, has changed; the function of the supervisor is to help the teacher and through the teacher to improve instruction; the supervisor no longer exercises the authority of a policeman, but rather that of a special expert, ready to guide, assist, and advise. Despite these advances, American elementary education suffers from the impermanence of the profession, which means a constant change of personnel. From this point of view, it is not feminization of the teaching profession which is the weakness of American schools, but the fact that neither men nor women enter the profession as a permanent career, women leaving for marriage

ELEMENTARY EDUCATION 517

and men for more remunerative careers either within the profession of education itself or elsewhere.

Private schools. The establishment of private schools is virtually unrestricted; public authorities may in some States have the right of entry, but in general the only limitations are that enrollment and attendance must be reported. According to the figures for 1927-28 there were enrolled in private schools of all kinds 2,134,999 pupils (1,002,336 boys and 1,132,663 girls), the majority attending parochial schools of the Roman Catholic Church. The only influential private schools are those which are definitely established for experimental purposes. Of these some are entirely private, others are attached to university schools of education. It would be difficult to gauge the influence of private experimental schools; in the development of new curricula, courses of study, and methods, they have played a part which public schools, with their emphasis until recently on mass education and uniformity, were not able to undertake. The contributions of such private schools range all the way from the absolute concept of freedom to more moderate experimentation with such materials as are used in the public schools. In general, they have adopted the following principles enunciated by the Progressive Education Association:

The following is a statement of the goals toward which the new education is tending. It is safe to say that no school has attained them all, nor are they put forth as the specific aims of any one group or organization. Rather they are a general summing up of such characteristics as find expression in some part throughout all forward-looking education.

The child's physical well-being. One of the most important considerations of the school is the health of the pupils. Space in which to move about, light and air, clean, well-ventilated buildings, attention to proper nutrition, access to the out-of-doors and greater use of it, are all necessary. There should be frequent use of adequate playgrounds. The school should observe closely the physical condition of each pupil, and, in coöperation with the home, make abundant health available to every child.

Opportunity for full development. Opportunity for initiative and self-expression should be provided in an environment rich in interesting material, the free use of which will release the creative energies of the child.

Social Development and Discipline. Group consciousness is developed in children through participation in the school as a community. Discipline should be a matter of self-mastery rather than external compulsion, and character development the result of social experience, and of the recognition of spiritual forces and resources underlying all nature, life, and conduct. A coeducational student body, and a faculty of both men and women, constitute a normal life situation for character and development.

Beauty of environment. The school should furnish an environment that is simple, natural, and beautiful.

Interest the motive of all work. Interest should be satisfied and developed primarily through (1) direct and indirect contact with the world and its activities, (2) use and application of knowledge thus gained, (3) correlation between different subjects, (4) the consciousness of achievement.

The curriculum. The curriculum should be based on the nature and needs of childhood and youth, with the idea of acquiring knowledge as far as possible through the scientific method of first-hand observation, investigation, experiment, and independent search for material. Through these activities the world of books and abstract ideas is entered. The school should increasingly widen the circle of the child's world, leading him not only to appreciation of national ideals, but also to a realization of the interdependence of peoples and international good-will.

The teacher as a guide. The teacher should guide the pupil in observing, experimenting and forming judgments that he may learn how to use various sources of information including life activities as well as books, and how to reason about the information thus acquired, and how to express logically and effectively the conclusion reached. The teacher should be given latitude to express his own initiative and originality.

Scientific study of pupil development. The school should study and endeavor to meet the individual needs and capacities of each child. School records should not be confined to the marks given by teachers to show the advancement of pupils in their study of subjects, but should also include both objective and subjective reports on those physical, mental, emotional, and social characteristics which concern both school and adult life, and which can be affected by the school and the home. Such records should be used as a guide for the treatment of each pupil and should also serve to focus the attention of the teacher on the all important work of child development.

Coöperation between school and home. Since the child's life at school and at home is an integral whole, the school cannot accomplish its purpose without the active support and intelligent coöperation of the parents. Reciprocally the school should aid the home in problems concerned with the child.

The School a contributor to educational progress. The school should be an educational laboratory, where new methods are encouraged, and where the best of the past is leavened by the discoveries of the present, and the result freely added to the sum of educational knowledge.[1]

Conclusion. In view of the wide extent and variety of the country, it may be rash to present any general conclusion on elementary education in the United States. Variety marks the compulsory attendance

---

[1] It is not yet clear how the progressives plan to reconcile these principles with the more recent movement sponsored by the Progressive Education Association for "social reconstruction through education."

laws and their enforcement, the length of the school year, the character of the buildings, the quality of the teachers and of teaching, the nature and scope of the curriculum and the courses of study, and the expenditure. If approached from this point of view, the country is far from providing equality of opportunity. Certain general tendencies do, however, stand out. The elementary school is the common school of all the children, and not only the common foundation, but the lower stage of a system which reaches from the kindergarten to the university. In the absence of a central educational authority for the whole country and of strong central authorities in all States, the burden of educational progress is borne by local systems, which are free to experiment, by institutions for the study of education, and by the societies for the scientific study of education. To some extent, the mobility of teachers and educators tends to the spread of certain norms for the whole country, and in the same way the use of the same textbooks over a large area has the same effect. But more characteristic than these facts are the vigor and imagination which are applied to the advance of educational progress. From this point of view the American school systems constitute a veritable laboratory. The very qualities, however, which are the strength of American education, as contrasted with education in other countries, are at once its weakness. There is on the whole too strong a tendency to develop education as an autonomous science, or, in other words, to found education on scientific theory to the neglect of the social environment in which it functions. The reason for this is to be found, not in a lack of vision (there is perhaps too much of this), but in the absence of any strong, dominating, cultural tradition. Hence the cult of the individual and of individual success; hence the reference in all curriculum discussions to the needs and abilities of the child and in more radical circles to the activities and experience of the child as the only guides worth considering. American education — and what is said of elementary applies equally to other branches of education — unlike education in other countries, does not grow out of, and does not merge into, a consciously recognized culture. Because it lacks this solid foundation, there is a tendency to experiment in every direction with a naïve faith that the canons of science can be applied to human affairs.

CHAPTER VII

PREPARATION OF ELEMENTARY SCHOOL TEACHERS

History. The preparation of elementary school teachers began simultaneously with the rise of public systems of elementary education. Its history thus begins in the nineteenth century, although the necessity of providing some preparation had been frequently recognized earlier. Richard Mulcaster, John Lily, John Brinsley, and Charles Hoole in England and Ratke and Comenius were among the first leaders of educational thought who advocated the training of teachers. To Duke Ernst the Pious belongs the honor of recognizing its importance as the basis of a sound system of education, and although he was himself unable, owing to a depleted treasury, to organize institutions for the preparation of teachers, he left an injunction for their development in his will, drawn up in 1654. It was not until 1694 that his grandson, Frederick II of Gotha, established a number of *seminaria scolastica*. The experiment was short-lived and was soon overshadowed by the efforts of leaders in the pietist movement for the extension of education, with which the names of August Hermann Francke, J. C. Schienmeyer, and J. J. Hecker were associated. It was, however, the Pestalozzian movement which exercised a permanent influence on the development of institutions for the preparation of elementary school teachers in Germany at a time when, following the disaster at Jena in 1806, the importance of education as an essential instrument of national reconstruction was recognized. Through the efforts of disciples who were inspired by Pestalozzi, among whom were Plamann, Zeller, Henning, Denzel, Dinter, Harnisch, and Diesterweg, the idea of preparing teachers in special institutions (*Lehrerseminare*) became firmly established in Germany by 1825.

In France the first institution for the training of elementary school teachers was established by the Convention in 1794 and opened in the following year in Paris as the *école normale* which became the prototype of similar institutions in other parts of the world and gave its name to the characteristic institution later established in the United States. The first beginnings of a system of teacher training in England were associated with the monitorial system developed by Andrew Bell and the National Society for the Education of the Poor in the Principles of the Established Church (1811) and by Joseph Lancaster and the British and Foreign School Society (1814). It was not until some twenty years later that an active movement began for the establishment of normal schools or training colleges. In 1835 John Arthur Roebuck unsuccessfully introduced a bill in Parliament for the creation of normal schools on the model of the French. One of the first proposals of the Committee of Council on Education, set up in 1839, was to establish a national normal school with a model school attached; owing to the opposition of the two societies mentioned, the funds already voted by Parliament and later increased were used to assist these and other denominational societies to erect training colleges. Side by side with this development there was introduced in 1846 the pupil-teacher system of training; the two systems have continued up to the present time. In the United States the preparation of teachers for elementary schools was first undertaken by the academies, the earliest of which was established in Philadelphia as a result of proposals made by Benjamin Franklin in 1749. The contribution of the academies, although widespread and adopted by the Legislature in New York State, was not regarded as satisfactory. A campaign for the establishment of special institutions began to be promoted actively about 1825 by W. E. Russell, Thomas Gallaudet, Samuel R. Hall, who opened the first private normal school at Concord, Vermont, in 1823, and James G. Carter who later came to be known as the "Father of Normal Schools." Carter's efforts were crowned by the first legislative enactment in favor of normal schools in Massachusetts in 1838 and by the opening of the first public normal school in the United States at Lexington, Massachusetts, in the following year. The legislation and the normal school set the pattern for the country and displaced the preparation of teachers in academies. By the middle of the nineteenth century both the principle and the practice of preparing teachers were definitely established in the four countries considered here and began to exercise a profound influence in other parts of the world.

Changing status. The subsequent development of systems for preparing teachers has been determined largely by the changing character of public elementary education in each country and by the progress of educational theory. So long as the emphasis in elementary education was mainly upon literacy and the teaching of the three R's, an adequate training in these subjects and in simple methods of instruction were regarded as sufficient and the test of an education consisted in evidence of mastery of these subjects. The social status of elementary education as the education of the masses helped to confirm this point of view, so well illustrated in the reactionary legislation passed in 1854 in Prussia through fear that too much education had inclined the elementary school teachers toward liberalism in politics. The development of compulsory and universal elementary education and the gradual social changes toward the end of the nineteenth century led to demands, not only for more education, but on the part of teachers for a type of preparation which was not limited merely to training in ability to give instruction in the rudiments. The movements for enriching the curriculum of the elementary schools and the rise of strong professional organizations combined to lead to an agitation for the preparation of teachers on a higher level than was provided. Secondary education as a minimum preliminary education and the organization of teacher-training institutions on a university level began to be demanded. Progress was slow; in some cases political, in others economic reasons were obstacles to reconstruction. The gradual recognition at the beginning of the twentieth century of the enlarged scope of the elementary school as an institution to give not merely instruction but an education in the broadest sense, the development of educational theory and psychology, which carried the conviction that the teacher's task consists of more than merely imparting information, the gradual movement toward the acceptance of the elementary school as the common school for all and not for the masses alone, and the realization of the meaning of education as an instrument of social and national welfare — all these factors have helped to support the movement for better systems of preparing teachers for elementary schools.

This movement, however, represents inherently something more than a mere increase in the number of years of preparation or the organization of teacher-training institutions on a university level. It involves a change from an apprenticeship to a professional basis of preparation. So long as the function of elementary education was looked upon as the imparting of a knowledge of the three R's and perhaps history and geography, the acquisition of subject-matter and rules for imparting it — tricks of the trade — was regarded as an adequate preparation. The increasing complexity of the task of education, the recognition of each pupil as an individual, and the increasing recognition that an educational institution cannot be run as an institution in which the teacher's sole function is to carry out orders from above, whether in the form of prescribed curricula, courses of study, and methods of instruction, or of standardized examinations, all pointed in the same direction, that the teacher's preparation must be on a professional basis and that the teacher must be trained to teach through mastery not of rules but of principles. In other words, if the task of education, as Sir John Adams has described it, is to teach John x, then the teacher must know, not only x, but John, and his probable reaction to x. But he must know more than x, the subject; he must understand its significance in the environment in which he teaches, its educative value, and its relation to all other subjects, its pertinence for John's development, as well as the methods by which John's interest can be aroused to master it. The same holds true if, as in the "new" or "progressive" education, the teacher seeks to start with John's interests and to organize his environment for their growth.

There is, too, a further change which is taking place. So long as the school was conceived in its original sense as a place of leisure, an institution, sheltered and divorced from the main currents of life, in which certain subjects were to be imparted, an emphasis on subject-matter and methods still constituted an adequate preparation. The school cannot, however, be divorced from "politics," and literacy or mental training alone do not give an adequate preparation for the complex demands of modern life. Without necessarily accepting the theory of Soviet educators, that the school must be an institution for indoctrination in the ideology on which the State is founded, educational theory in general accepts the principle that the school must inevitably be colored by the environment in which the school functions. The teacher must accordingly be not only a master of the subjects which he professes, but he must understand the relation of the school to social and national welfare as expressed not only on its cultural side but in its everyday manifestations — social, political, and economic.

The expansion of the scope and significance of the teacher's position implies as a natural corollary an extension of the period of preparation. Throughout the nineteenth century the vision of the intending elementary school teacher was restricted to his future occupation; selected at an early age from an elementary school, he was prepared either in an elementary school or in an institution administered by the authorities responsible for elementary education. As a consequence he was never able to shake off what the French call *l'esprit primaire*, a tendency to worship primary facts and information rather than ideas; narrow intellectual contacts inevitably resulted in narrow points of view. The tendency today is to postpone the early choice of teaching as a vocation by providing a complete general education in a secondary school followed by preparation in an institution on the university level.

The problems of teacher preparation. The prolongation of the period of preparation does not, however, simplify the problems involved. While it is true that the introduction of a preliminary general education gives the teacher-candidate a broader background than is possible when the training institution is a direct continuation of the elementary school, the professional preparation of the teacher must include the methods of teaching the subjects which make up, as it were, the tools of his trade. Further, the time is passed when the claim that he who knows can teach can be justified; this means that preparation must include not only what to teach but how to teach. In the United States the emphasis tended for a long time to be on methods, on how to teach, as the most important part of professional preparation; in England both aspects were included, but subject-matter was taught by one group and methods by another group of instructors, the student often being expected to integrate and synthesize the two sides himself. The practice of the German *Lehrerseminare* was to synthesize the two, the teacher of arithmetic, for example, being responsible for the content of the subject, the study of its place in education, and the methods of teaching it as well as demonstration and supervision of practice in it. In other words, the teaching of each subject was professionalized; the German practice, however, was open to the criticism of devoting too much time to an extended review of the subjects of the elementary school without providing adequate opportunities of introducing the students to the standards of a higher education.

The problem of organizing adequate systems for preparing teachers is still further complicated by the recognition of the necessity of providing differentiated training for different stages of elementary education and for different environmental conditions. Provision must now be made for the preparation of teachers for nursery schools, for infant schools and kindergartens, for primary grades, and for intermediate schools, which for the time being still hover between elementary and secondary schools. A larger problem is the adaptation of teacher-preparation to the needs of urban and rural areas, a problem which has been directly attacked only in the United States and indirectly in England by the retention of a lower level of training for prospective rural school teachers.

In the reforms which are taking place in the preparation of teachers an attempt is being made to prolong the general, all-round education of the students, to give them a deeper and broader insight into the content and significance of the subjects which they are to teach, and at the same time to associate special methods simultaneously with the study of each subject. The tendency is thus to professionalize subject-matter. Beyond this, the preparation of the teacher involves the study of the so-called professional subjects — the history and theory of education, educational psychology, and general theory of method; these traditional subjects are gradually being increased by the addition of tests and measurements, sociology, and special aspects of psychology. Finally, the practical aspect, induction into teaching, constitutes the third important phase of the problem. This problem is beset by difficulties more of an administrative than of a theoretical character due to the inadequacy of practice institutions directly under the control of the training institutions. These difficulties, combined with the increased responsibilities which have fallen on the teacher, have led to the recognition that the few years devoted to professional preparation could not be relied upon to produce a finished teacher and that a period of probation is necessary before a young teacher can be given a permanent appointment.

The rapidity with which educational reforms are taking place and the growing recognition that the school must be adapted to social progress have in turn directed attention to the fact that the training of the teacher cannot be restricted to the years of preparation, but must be continued throughout his career. For this purpose some countries have relied upon staffs of inspectors or supervisors to keep teachers up to the mark; elsewhere active professional organizations have helped to keep teachers in touch with educational progress; generally the tendency is to organize more formal methods for training teachers in service by means of conferences, study groups, and summer courses. A teacher who does not grow tends to stagnate and to become mechanical. Again the change in the character of education is demonstrated: when education was largely instruction in a somewhat fixed round of subjects, the initial training with occasional further study was adequate for the situation; the new place of the school in society, the necessity of overhauling subjects and curricula periodically, the participation of the teachers in the making of courses of study, the constant expansion and progress of educational theory which in turn are the results of experimentation, have so broadened the professional equipment of the teacher that two or three years of initial preparation are no longer sufficient to keep the teacher abreast of the times.

The changing character of the school, involving as it does an extension of the period of preparation, has begun to exercise another influence which is economic and social in character. Although the idea was gradually discarded in the nineteenth century that anybody was competent enough to teach in an elementary school, the low esteem in which the education of the masses was held attached to the teachers in the schools intended for them. Salaries were also commensurate with the esteem of the schools and with the length of preparation required for teaching in them. The development of a professional consciousness which led to the creation of teachers' associations, the changes which have taken place more recently in the status of elementary education, and the gradual prolongation of the period of preparation have resulted in a slow but definite improvement in the status of elementary school teachers and in increased remuneration. In other words, the profession of teaching is not exempt from the general principles which govern supply and demand in other occupations. In addition to improvements in the remuneration of teachers which open up a genuine career, there have been provided protection against disability and retiring allowances. There are still difficulties to be overcome on the economic side; in some countries there is the problem of equal pay for men and women, or of the adjustment of salary scales to family responsibilities or to variations in the cost of living. The extension of the period of preparation which may in time, and in some places has, become almost as long for elementary as for secondary school teachers, may bring in its train a demand for single salary scales with which some American authorities are now experimenting. Tenure, on the whole, has not been a serious problem in European countries or in England, except occasionally in voluntary or non-provided schools, but in the United States there is still room for improvement. For the present, however, the important point is that there has been an appreciable improvement in the status of elementary school teachers such as could hardly have been anticipated at the beginning of the century. Progress will depend to some extent on the general acceptance of the elementary school as the common school for all and on the increased recognition of the significance of the school for social and national welfare. Improvement of status will have the further salutary effect of directing the attention and interest of teachers away from preoccupation with their economic condition toward closer study of the more fundamental and important problems of education.

The tendencies described above will be found exemplified more or less in the accounts of the systems for the preparation of teachers presented in the following pages. At one end is the Italian reform of 1923, which, providing for the preparation of teachers in schools at the secondary level, is based on the assumption that the successful teacher is he who is thoroughly imbued with the cultural and spiritual aspirations of his country and for whom preoccupation with methods and educational theory, rather than a broad philosophical understanding of life, is a hindrance rather than a help. France has still retained the nineteenth-century attitude to teachers as servants of the State trained to carry out prescribed regulations. England is in a stage of transition and reform which represent a tendency to place the preparation of teachers on a university level with an emphasis on genuine professionalization; at the same time the traditional pupil-teacher system is retained for the training of rural school teachers. The United States represents every type of teacher-training from training in high schools to preparation in teachers' colleges and schools of education in universities. Germany again sets the standard, as she did at another level in the nineteenth century, by organizing the preparation of teachers on a university level either in independent institutions, in institutions affiliated with universities, or in universities. Soviet Russia stands outside of the general stream in training teachers for elementary schools in institutions at the secondary level and in the intimate association of this training with the polytechnization of all schools.

1. ENGLAND

History. The preparation of elementary school teachers was strongly influenced until recently by its dual origin in the pupil-teacher system and in training colleges. The former was introduced in 1846 by a Minute of the Committee of Council on Education for which Sir James Kay-Shuttleworth, who had seen the system at work in Holland, was responsible. It was definitely an apprenticeship system in which boys and girls were indentured at the age of thirteen to the headmaster of an elementary school for five years; the pupil-teachers taught during the day and after school hours continued their general education under the direction of their headmasters. At the close of the period they were submitted to the examination for the Queen's Scholarships, a competitive test by which the best candidates were selected to continue their preparation in training colleges.

The apprenticeship practice began to decline gradually after the Act of 1870 established a system of public elementary schools and the need of a broader academic preparation began to be recognized. The age of pupil-teachers was raised to sixteen in urban centers and to fifteen in rural areas; center classes were established in 1874 and were gradually organized toward the close of the century into pupil-teacher centers; academic preparation was emphasized and for one year the pupil-teachers were required to obtain practical teaching experience. Those who passed the Queen's Scholarship Examinations proceeded to training colleges; those who failed became uncertificated teachers, but might later obtain certificates by examination without training, a practice introduced in 1847.

Training colleges began to be established first by the two leading educational societies, the British and Foreign School Society and the National Society, with the help of grants for buildings allotted to them in 1839 by the Committee of Council on Education; other denominational societies — Wesleyan, Congregational, and Roman Catholic — began to open their own colleges. The Borough Road School, in which monitors had been trained since 1805, was reorganized in 1842 and became a training college, but had already been preceded by one institution opened in 1836 by the Home and Colonial School Society to train female teachers and another established in

1840 by James Kay (later Sir James Kay-Shuttleworth) to train teachers for pauper schools. With the help of building and per capita grants from the Government, the number of training colleges increased rapidly in the next twenty years. They were assured by the pupil-teacher system of a supply of adequately prepared teachers.

The dual system — pupil teacherships and training colleges — continued to provide the large majority of elementary school teachers. From 1846 to 1861 salaries were paid directly by the Government and teachers virtually enjoyed the status of civil servants. In the absence of publicly maintained secondary schools, the system was the only one practicable under the circumstances; its chief weakness was that it was wholly unrelated to any other branch of education — the students came from elementary schools, were pupil-teachers in elementary schools, were trained by teachers whose sole experience had been in elementary schools, and returned to elementary schools. The only opportunity open to the more ambitious teachers was to prepare for the external degrees of the University of London. Despite the limitations of the practice, which became still more restricted when the vicious system of payment by results was introduced in 1861, the elementary school teachers performed a notable service in the progress of education. The desirability of introducing another spirit in elementary education began to be recognized and in 1888 the Cross Commission recommended the establishment of day training departments in universities and university colleges which had by that time begun to flourish in increased numbers. Two years later the recommendation was embodied in the Code, and a third method of preparing teachers was thus adopted at the university level.

The Education Act of 1902 created new possibilities and opportunities. In the first place, the Act permitted the larger local education authorities (counties and county boroughs) to provide secondary schools out of local rates with the help of government grants. Secondly, the same authorities were allowed to establish their own training colleges, for the building of which the Government began to give grants in 1906. The establishment of secondary schools created a new route by which intending teachers could obtain their preliminary training. Pupil-teacher centers were retained, especially in the rural areas, but gradually the majority of intending teachers, who were given free tuition and maintenance allowances, began to pass through the secondary schools. The difference between the two methods was that a candidate who entered a pupil-teacher center remained up to the age of sixteen and then became a pupil-teacher up to the age of eighteen, when on passing an examination he might become an uncertificated teacher or enter a training college. The candidate who entered a secondary school pursued a general course also up to the age of sixteen, and then, if recommended by his headmaster and on signing a declaration to become a teacher, received a bursary or grant to continue his education for another year; at the end of this period he might, if he had passed an examination qualifying him for entrance to a training college, continue his studies there or become a student-teacher. The student-teacher year was divided between observation and practice in an elementary school and further study in a secondary school; at the end of the year the student teacher, if he had passed the necessary examination, might enter a training college or training department of a university or become an uncertificated teacher. The training colleges gave a two-year course, the university training departments originally a three-year course and after 1911 a four-year course, the first three in preparation for an academic degree, the fourth devoted to professional training.

This system continued until it began to be subjected to criticism which led to the appointment of a Departmental Committee in 1923

to review the arrangements for the training of teachers for public elementary schools, and to consider what changes, if any, in the organization or finance of the existing system are desirable in order that a supply of well qualified teachers adjustable to the demands of the shools may be secured, regard being had to (*a*) the economy of public funds; (*b*) the attractions offered to young persons by the teaching profession as compared with other professions and occupations; (*c*) the facilities afforded by secondary schools and universities for acquiring academic qualifications.

The Committee in its *Report*, published in 1925, in considering the problem of recruiting teachers, expressed itself as opposed to the practice of aiding intending teachers before the age of sixteen, and was of the opinion that the most effective method of securing a qualified supply of teachers is through satisfactory salaries, tenure, and pensions, improved conditions of school life, and freedom from undue administrative control. It recommended the ultimate elimination of supplementary and uncertificated teachers and the discontinuance of the acting teachers' certificate, whereby an untrained teacher could obtain a certificate by examination. It deprecated the system of student and pupil teacherships, but admitted that the latter might have to be retained in rural areas, where secondary schools were not accessible. The Committee rejected as not practicable the suggestion that all teachers should be trained in universities, but recommended a closer connection between training colleges and universities.

The Committee thus attacked some of the defects of the system of preparing teachers which had been accumulated in the course of its development. Among these were the premature recruiting of candidates for the teaching profession, the retention of the student-teacher year, the segregation of candidates in separate centers, and the isolation of the training colleges. The improvement of salary scales and the provision of a sound superannuation scheme had already made the teaching profession sufficiently attractive to dispense with artificial aids to secure a supply of candidates. The student-teacher year had been taken over from the pupil-teacher system on the assumption that a period of practical experience in elementary schools was desirable as a basis for testing the suitability of candidates and for the subsequent professional study. In practice some school principals devoted attention to the student-teachers assigned to them; in general the student-teachers without guidance picked up habits which they had later to unlearn. The training colleges had developed in isolation in the nineteenth century and in the twentieth had been left suspended without constituting an integral part of the system of higher education; academically and professionally they enjoyed little independence, since they were controlled by the prescription of courses and examinations in the *Regulations* of the Board of Education.

The Board of Education at once proceeded to take steps to put the recommendations of the Committee into effect. In 1925 a Circular (1372) was issued by the Board announcing the intention of discontinuing its practice of conducting the final examinations in training colleges; this was followed in 1926 by an invitation to universities and training colleges to consider plans for coöperation between them. The *Regulations for the Training of Teachers*, issued in 1926, omitted any reference to the student-teacher year and Circular 1383 (1926), while confirming the Departmental Committee's recommendation against its retention, permitted such local authorities as wished to do so, to continue the practice. The detailed syllabus and examination requirements were replaced by a general statement that

> The course of education and professional training in a training college must be in accordance with a suitable curriculum and must include systematic study of the principles and practice of teaching. Satisfactory arrangements must be made for the examination of students at the end of their course. In the case of training colleges other than those for domestic subjects, adequate provision must be made in approved schools for practice in teaching under proper supervision, and students who have not had practical experience as teachers in an approved capacity must spend at least twelve weeks of their course in such practice.

In thus releasing the institutions for the preparation of teachers from its control, the Board of Education looked to the adoption of the practice which prevails in the preparation for other professions in England. The preparation of lawyers and doctors, for example, is controlled entirely by the organizations which represent these professions — the Incorporated Law Society and the Inns of Court and the General Medical Council; only those who have obtained certificates granted by such bodies are permitted to engage in the practice of the professions concerned. Accordingly, the control of the preparation of teachers would, under the continued supervision of the Board, because of its general interest and the grant of financial aid, be transferred to those organizations directly concerned with the preparation and employment of teachers — the universities, training colleges, local education authorities, and teachers' associations.

To carry out the recommendations made on this point by the Departmental Committee and the Board of Education, a Committee on Universities and Training Colleges was appointed and issued its recommendations in 1928. The Committee suggested the division of the country into twelve regional groups to promote contacts between the universities and training colleges. In each of these groups a joint board was to be set up, consisting of representatives of the universities, training colleges, and local education authorities, and charged with the duty of defining standards, curricula, courses of study, and examination requirements. To coördinate the work of the regional boards it was recommended that a Central Advisory Committee for the Certification of Teachers be created, consisting in turn of representatives of the institutions concerned, to consider standards, curricula, and the scope and range of examinations.

THE PRESENT SYSTEM

Preliminary education. The main lines of the present system can now be described. The recommendations of the Departmental Committee and of the Board of Education have already begun to bear fruit and a full-time secondary education up to the age of eligibility for entrance to a training college or university training department has been adopted as the requirement for preliminary training. In 1930 the number of pupil-teachers in centers had fallen to about one quarter of the number in 1927; of the total number (1160) 761 were rural pupil-teachers. The number of student-teachers was about one third of the number in 1927. The class of teachers known as "supplementary" still survives; the only qualification required for appointment as supplementary teachers is that candidates shall be suitable women over eighteen years of age and in good health; there are no requirements of academic attainments or of training. They may be employed, if the Board's inspectors certify them as having teaching ability, but always upon a temporary basis, in the infants' or lower classes in rural schools. They are never, as is sometimes the case in the United States with teachers with scarcely better qualifications, in sole charge of a school. The normal practice will henceforth be that boys and girls will enter a secondary school between the ages of eleven and twelve and will there pursue a general academic course without being ear-marked for teaching or any other occupation. At the age of sixteen they may become candidates for bursarships offered by a number of local education authorities to suitable students who intend to become teachers in public schools. The bursarships carry free tuition and maintenance allowances for one or two years.

Whether candidates for the teaching profession obtain scholarships or bursarships, they are expected to pass the First Secondary School Examination [1] and to have reached the age of eighteen, if they wish to be admitted to a training college, or, if they intend to apply for admission to a university training department, they must be seventeen years of age and must have passed either a matriculation examination or the First Examination with sufficient credits to be exempted from the matriculation requirement. Owing to the limited accommodation, admission to training colleges and university training departments is selective; the age and examination requirements

[1] See Chapter VIII.

are the minima; beyond these candidates must submit a certificate of good health and testimonials as to character and promise, and in most cases are interviewed. Admission to a course of preparation is thus in a sense competitive; the best students find their way into the university training departments, the next best into training colleges; those who fail to secure admission still have the opportunity of becoming uncertificated teachers, or they may enter some training institution as non-recognized students, in which case they assume the total cost of preparation themselves. The new system guarantees an adequate academic and general education such as is required in general for admission to preparation for other professions. The able student may even continue this general education and pass the Second School or Advanced Examination, which overlaps to some extent with the first year of work required for an academic degree. A candidate who enters a training institution as a recognized student must sign a declaration of intention to complete the course and to follow thereafter the profession of teacher in a public school, with the understanding that preparation for the teaching career is the sole purpose of his taking advantage of the public funds provided for the preparation of teachers.

Training colleges. Unlike institutions devoted to the same purpose in other countries, the training college is not a state institution; it is supported by the State, but since 1928, when the new system was introduced, it is no longer state-controlled. It may be provided — that is, established and maintained by a public education authority — or non-provided or established and maintained by a voluntary, usually a denominational, society. In 1930–31 there were 74 two-year training colleges provided as follows: (*a*) by a university, 1; (*b*) by a local education authority, 22; (*c*) by other bodies, 51 (Church of England, 29; Roman Catholic, 8; Wesleyan, 2; and undenominational, 12). The colleges are residential or day or both day and residential institutions.

The Board of Education bears a share of the cost of building training colleges, in the case of local education authorities up to half of the cost. The contributions for maintenance, salaries, and scholarships are paid to local authorities up to half of the cost of the approved expenditures; to non-provided institutions the annual grants are paid on a per capita basis as follows: for tuition, £28 for men and £26 for women students; for maintenance, £43 for men and

PREPARATION OF ELEMENTARY TEACHERS

£34 for women; for non-resident students, £26 for men and £20 for women (these sums may be paid through the colleges direct to students in cases of need).[1] In the provided colleges there are as a rule no tuition fees; in the non-provided colleges students pay the difference between the actual cost and the income derived from grants and other sources. Needy students in provided institutions may receive monetary assistance. Since only a small number of the local education authorities maintain training colleges, whose graduates may accept employment anywhere in the country, the Board of Education raises a fund of £70,000 annually by deducting from the grants made to those authorities which do not maintain colleges and distributing it to those which do.

The staffs or faculties of the training colleges include in increasing numbers men and women who have had a university preparation and hold an honors degree (that is, they have specialized intensively in some one or two subjects) and some experience in teaching, although not necessarily or always in elementary schools, a defect frequently criticized by those who detect a certain divorce between the work of the training colleges and the needs of elementary schools. The old distinction between subject-matter and methods, which used to be marked by the presence on the staffs of masters or mistresses of method, has disappeared. Each lecturer is responsible both for courses in the subjects in which he is a specialist, and in methods of teaching them, as well as for the organization of periods for observation and demonstration in the schools. Professional subjects — principles and theory, history and psychology of education — are taught by lecturers in education who are in general responsible for the arrangements for the practical teaching of the students. The salaries of lecturers in training colleges are slightly higher than those provided by the Burnham Committee for secondary school teachers.

Courses in training colleges. Until 1929 the Board of Education prescribed the curricula and courses of study in training colleges. Since that time the system recommended by the Departmental Committee, the Board of Education, and the Committee on Universities and Training Colleges has been adopted, and twelve regional groups, including universities and training colleges, have been created to set up standards of courses and examinations. Each group

[1] These grants were reduced by Amendments to the *Regulations* issued in 1931 and 1932.

is administered by a representative body variously known as a delegacy, joint board, or board of administration. Thus the Board of Administration for Yorkshire Training Colleges includes representatives of the governing bodies and principals of training colleges, of the two universities (Leeds and Sheffield), and the University college (Hull), and of local education authorities in Yorkshire. The Board is assisted by three agencies: (1) an advisory council representing all types of schools, universities, training colleges, and local education authorities to discuss and make recommendations on suggestions for the development of the training of teachers; (2) boards of studies to consider courses of study and the selection of examiners; and (3) boards of examiners to approve questions drafted for examinations, and to consider the reports of the examiners, both internal and external. Each regional group is permitted to charge fees for examinations, part of which is paid by the candidates and part (£1.10.0 per candidate) is contributed by the Board. In order to secure a certain uniformity of standard and to provide a medium for the discussion of common problems, a Central Advisory Committee has been created of twenty-five members, as follows: eight representing universities, four local education authorities, four training colleges, four training college staffs, four the teaching profession, and one domestic subjects.

Since the whole system of joint boards is recent and is regarded as experimental, there has been a tendency in the framing of courses of study and requirements for examinations to cling to the traditions established by the Board of Education during its period of control in these matters. In general the aim of the training colleges is to approach their problem from a single point of view, that of giving professional preparation, and, while the teaching of subjects is on a standard in advance of that of the secondary school, it is expected that they will be taught with a view to their use in schools; beyond this opportunity is to be provided to students to select one subject and to pursue it to an advanced standard. The courses are divided into three groups — professional, general or academic, and practical.

The Board of Administration for the Yorkshire Training Colleges prescribed the following Regulations for the final examination in 1931:

>Professional subjects
>1. Principles and practice of teaching
>2. Hygiene
>3. Physical training (theory and practice)

General subjects [1]
Group A
1. English
2. History
3. Geography
4. Mathematics
5. General elementary science (ordinary standard only)
6. French (advanced standard only)
7. Physics (advanced standard only)
8. Chemistry (advanced standard only)
9. Biology (advanced standard only)

Group B
1. Music (theory and practice)
2. Drawing
3. Needlework and handwork (for women)
4. Handwork (for men; advanced standard only)
5. Gardening (advanced standard only)

All students are examined in the professional subjects; [2] in the general courses they may offer four subjects at ordinary standard, or two subjects at ordinary and one at advanced standard, or one subject at ordinary and two at advanced standard. English must in all cases be one of the subjects taken, and whatever selection is made, subjects must be chosen from both Groups A and B. The examination does not as a rule include papers in general elementary science, drawing (ordinary standard), needlework, handwork for women, the practice of teaching, or the practice of physical training, which are tested chiefly by inspection, supplemented by written papers, if desirable; in practical music, gardening, and advanced science, the written papers are in all cases supplemented by inspection. The grouping of subjects and the standard taken are in general determined by the type of work in which the student intends to engage — ordinary work in the elementary school, work with children over eleven, and work with infants. There is accordingly an opportunity for differentiation which until recently has been somewhat empirical. The proposed reorganization of the system into infants, junior and senior schools will provide a better opportunity for specialized preparation than in the past. Specialization for work in rural schools is not provided except that where possible observation and practice in such schools are arranged.

[1] Both ordinary and advanced standards unless otherwise indicated.
[2] Some boards include voice training, reading and recitation, drawing and handwork among these subjects.

Under the *Regulations* of the Board, all students who have not already had some experience are expected to devote twelve weeks to teaching practice during their period of preparation. The provisions for practice teaching vary; few training colleges have their own schools, but all arrange for the use of public schools, some of which may be specially designated as demonstration schools, others for observation and practice only. But even where schools are selected as demonstration schools, the staffs of the training colleges do not have complete control of their management and courses. In general, observation and demonstration are looked after by the subject-matter lecturers, and the continued practice by the lectures in education. It cannot be said that the situation is satisfactory; with the elimination of the student-teacher year, the situation may, indeed, become worse, for unreliable as the results of the student-teacher year were, it did bring the intending teacher into close contact with elementary schools. A remedy for the situation was found several years ago by the introduction of a year of probation; originally introduced as a measure of economy to save a year's salary increment, a few authorities have realized the opportunity provided by this year if the probationers were placed under careful and sympathetic guidance; as a general rule, however, the success of the probationary year as an induction to the practical problems of teaching depends upon the ability and interest of the head teacher under whom the probationer secures her first appointment.

Candidates who pass the final examination conducted by one of the regional boards are granted a certificate, provided that they satisfy the inspectors of the Board of Education as to their ability in practical teaching. The Board has retained this connection with the certification of teachers because of its interest in the quality of teachers throughout the country; where desired by an examining body, the Board's inspectors will also test candidates in practical subjects. Candidates who obtain the certificates of the regional boards and satisfy the inspectors in practical teaching are recognized as certificated teachers after a year of probation. There has thus been developed a system of teacher preparation governed by standards which the profession will determine for itself with the advice of the Board of Education. The result which has been attained is best expressed in the words of former Prime Minister Stanley Baldwin:

The new entrant to the profession is no longer regarded as a government trainee for a government job, segregated in a special institution, meeting none but his own type. The crown of his work no longer takes the form of a government licence to teach. By converting the certificate into a diploma granted by a joint body representing both the university and the training colleges, the Board are enabling students to train alongside men and women destined for other careers. The teacher is thus being drawn out of a backwater into the main stream of the liberal professions, and sees life from more than one angle.[1]

University training departments. Since the requirements for admission to university training departments connected with universities and university colleges are higher than for entrance to a training college, the more able students obtain their preparation by this route which was introduced in 1890. In 1930–31 there were twenty-two training departments in universities and university colleges. It became obvious, soon after the introduction of this system and the rapid increase in the supply of secondary schools after the Education Act of 1902 was passed, that students who obtained degrees preferred to look for appointment in secondary schools. For some time the period of preparation was three years, during which the student devoted his time to the courses required for the academic degree and to professional courses required for the teacher's certificate, a heavy burden which was lifted in 1911 by the introduction of a fourth year. The time was now divided, three years being devoted to the attainment of a degree (pass or honors) and the last year to professional training. Since this practice virtually removed any distinction between preparation for teaching at the secondary and elementary level, the Board of Education, in its *Regulations* of 1926, accepted the situation and dispensed with administrative distinctions between elementary and secondary training colleges and between university training departments and other training colleges.

University training departments receive grants from the Board of Education as follows: £35 for each recognized student in the fourth year of the course, a grant to cover the cost of fees for the degree course and an additional £5 per student for general supervision, and a grant paid to each recognized student (£26 for men and £20 for

---

[1] From Mr. Baldwin's Message, A New Step in Education. *Educational Yearbook, 1928*, pp. 39 ff. The reader is reminded that the Message was issued during the political campaign of May, 1929, as an account of the achievements of the Conservative Party. There was, however, no change of policy in respect to the preparation of teachers in the Labor régime which followed.

women living at home; £43 for men and £34 for women residing in hostels).[1]

The students in university training departments devote the first three years to academic courses leading to a degree either on the pass or ordinary level, which is characterized by extensive study of a number of subjects, or on the honors level, which implies specialization in one or more subjects closely allied (e.g., classics, Latin and a modern language, modern languages, history, mathematics and physics, physics, chemistry, etc.). On the professional side little difference is made in the work of the students, except that those who have a clear intention of teaching in the elementary schools must take courses in practical subjects. Teaching practice provided for according to the *Regulations* of the Board is arranged in both elementary and secondary schools. The course terminates with an examination conducted by the university, or in the case of university colleges by a degree-granting university which provides for the examination of external students; while there are variations in the character of this examination, it generally includes the professional subjects and methods of teaching special subjects. Successful candidates are awarded a diploma in education which entitles the holder to the elementary teachers' certificate, if the holder has had practical experience in an elementary school; candidates who fail to reach the requirements for the diploma may be recommended for a certificate.

As the reorganization of the system of education proceeds, it seems probable that candidates who complete a four-year course will be employed in secondary, central, or senior schools, and graduates of training colleges in infants or junior schools. Such an arrangement may result in a more general recognition of the need of more carefully organized differentiation of courses along functional lines. The four-year system, besides providing a supply of teachers with a thorough academic training and professional preparation, has also furnished the group from which head teachers of elementary schools have been drawn, since a degree has become a general requirement for this position.

Other institutions for the preparation of teachers. In addition to the two-year training colleges, which may offer a third-year course for specialized training, and the university training departments, there are a number of institutions for the preparation of special

[1] These sums were reduced in 1931.

teachers. Six colleges prepare teachers of infants and young children to take the examinations of the National Froebel Union, whose certificates are recognized by the Board. Teachers of handicrafts may be trained in the third-year course of a training college or in two technical institutions, Loughborough College and Shoreditch Technical Institute, which have organized two-year courses for the purpose. Teachers of domestic subjects may receive their training in special colleges which offer two- or three-year courses. Art teachers are prepared either in schools of art or in the third-year course of training colleges. Preparation of teachers of physical training is provided in the training colleges either in the regular two-year course or in the third-year course.[1]

Rural school teachers receive their preparation either in secondary schools or in pupil-teacher centers. The former may become uncertificated teachers in rural schools after passing a First School Examination. Following a *Report of the Departmental Committee on the Training of Rural Teachers*, issued in 1929, it was decided to retain the pupil-teacher centers and to provide for them a course of study terminating in a special examination the conduct of which was placed in the hands of the Oxford Examination Delegacy and the Cambridge Examinations Syndicate. This examination differs from the First School Examination only in the fact that a foreign language is optional. The papers in English, history, geography, a foreign language, drawing, and needlework are identical with those set in the First School Examinations; those in elementary mathematics, natural science, music, gardening, hygiene with housecraft, and handicraft are based on special courses of study. Except for English, including an oral examination, and natural science, candidates are given permission to select from these subjects which are arranged in groups. Practical subjects are tested by inspection. The minimum age at which candidates take the examination is seventeen. Those who pass the examination may continue their further preparation in a training college.

The Departmental Committee reported that "the special needs of

---

[1] In 1930–31 the total number of students in training was 19,484 (6,757 men and 12,727 women), distributed as follows: university training departments, 6,462 (3,393 men and 3,069 women); post-graduate training colleges, 70 (7 men and 63 women); two-year training colleges 11,941 (3,354 men and 8,587 women); training colleges for domestic subjects, 988 women; 23 graduate students (3 men and 20 women) were in training in secondary schools under a scheme somewhat like the Prussian.

rural schools receive insufficient direct attention," and recommended that, in view of the reorganization of the school system into junior and senior schools, more important places be assigned to biological science, rural economics, professional subjects, and practical acquaintance with rural school work, and that the content of courses in general should refer more directly to rural school teaching.

Certification of teachers. The Board of Education recognizes for purposes of the grant three types of elementary school teachers: (1) The supplementary teachers whose only qualifications are age, physical fitness, and approval by the inspectors. The number of teachers of this type decreases every year; thus in 1931 there were 7270 supplementary teachers in regular employment as contrasted with 7497 in the previous year. It must again be made clear that such teachers are usually assigned to teach infants and younger children and never have charge of a school, as may happen with teachers with no better qualifications in the United States. (2) The uncertificated teachers whose qualifications at least guarantee a preparation equivalent to the requirements for admission to a training college. With the gradual disappearance of the pupil-teacher system and the student-teacher year, the new generation of uncertificated teachers will enter upon their work without any professional preparation. The abolition in 1929 of the acting teacher's certificate, granted on examination by the Board of Education to experienced but untrained teachers, the lower scales of salary paid to them, the refusal of the more progressive authorities to appoint them, and the absence of opportunities of promotion to principalships are already having their effect upon the number of uncertificated teachers. In 1931 there were regularly employed 30,632 uncertificated teachers, over seven hundred less than in 1930 (31,385). The larger authorities (London County and county boroughs) employed only about 18 per cent of the total number of uncertificated teachers. Their status will be further affected by the reorganization of the school system and the probability is that they will be limited to work in infants and junior schools. The opportunity is always open to those who wish, and can afford to do so, to enter a training college. (3) The third group consists of certificated teachers, who for the present include those who obtained their certificates by training and examination or by examination without training. The avenue to the second type of certificate (acting teachers' certificate) has now been closed. The improved scales of salaries and the adoption of a sound superannuation system, combined with the refusal of many authorities to employ any but certificated teachers, have increased their number; in 1931 there were in regular employment 126,245 certificated teachers as contrasted with 124,597 in 1930. Slightly more than fifty per cent of these teachers were in the service of the larger authorities.

The total number of teachers employed in public elementary schools in 1931 was 168,934, a number which included, in addition to the three types mentioned, teachers of special subjects and handicrafts who were not certificated. Of the total 43,775 teachers were men and 125,159 were women. The general principle which is followed is that senior boys — that is, boys above the age of eleven — shall be taught by men.

Status of teachers. The progressive improvement of the preparation of teachers has been accompanied by a marked improvement in their status. As contrasted with the practice which is common in other European countries, English teachers are not civil servants — that is, employees of the central Government, but of the local education authorities, or, in the case of non-provided schools, of the managers. Like all public employees, teachers hold their positions during the pleasure of the employing authority. Wherever positions are abolished owing to legally recognized reorganizations, teachers are entitled to compensation for loss of office. Local education authorities and managers of non-provided schools with the consent of such authorities may dismiss teachers on educational grounds or for misconduct; managers of non-provided schools have the further power to dismiss teachers on grounds connected with the giving of religious instruction. Teachers who are dismissed may of course resort to the courts. Their interests are protected by the powerful professional organization, the National Union of Teachers (N.U.T.), which places at their disposal, whenever necessary, the resources of its legal department. Dismissals of teachers are on the whole rare; this does not mean that all teachers are perfectly competent, but that it is extremely difficult to define in a court of law the meaning of teaching competence. Generally, measures are taken in cases of incompetence to give a teacher an opportunity in a different environment — in another class or another school under a different headmaster. Nowhere, however, is the teacher so much at the mercy of the administrative officials or the local education authority as he is in the United States. The English system furnishes one of the best illustrations of indefinite tenure or "tenure during pleasure," which, on the one hand, because of tradition is free from the uncertainties which are found where there is no system of tenure, and, on the other hand, free from the abuses which are often found where teachers have secured the right to permanent tenure.

Salaries. Since teachers are not employees of the central authority, the Board of Education does not prescribe the scales of salary to be paid. The general principle is that salaries should be determined by those concerned in them, the teachers and their employers, the local education authorities; the interest of the Board of Education is involved because the central Government makes annual grants for educational purposes, including salaries. An improvement in the remuneration of teachers had long been overdue and, although increases were paid here and there to meet the higher cost of living following the War, they were uncertain and wholly dependent upon the good-will of the local authorities. To correct this situation and to give reality to the new status of education which it had been the purpose of the Education Act of 1918 to promote, a number of Standing Joint Committees was set up in 1919 under the chairmanship of Lord Burnham to consider the drafting of scales of salary for elementary, secondary, and technical school teachers. The Committee on Salaries for elementary school teachers consisted of representatives of teachers through the National Union of Teachers and representatives of local education authorities through the County Councils Association, Municipal Corporations, and the Association of Education Committees. A provisional minimum scale was issued in 1920; a year later four scales of salary were drawn up, adjusted somewhat roughly to the cost of living in different parts of the country and subject to revision in 1925. The allocation of scales to the various areas was made by the Committee and accepted by all but 19 of the 318 local authorities; in these areas agreement was reached through the intervention of the Board. It must be noted that under the Education Act, 1918, the Board contributed grants on account of salaries equivalent to sixty per cent of the expenditure. Before the scales had been generally introduced, they were subjected in 1922 to a deduction of five per cent as a contribution toward pensions; in 1923 the teachers voluntarily submitted to another abatement of five per cent in view of the economic crisis at that time.

When the date for revision approached in 1925, there was evidence that the local authorities and the central Government were anxious to effect economies. Disagreement between the teachers and employing authorities on the amount of deduction to be adopted led to the reappointment of the Salary Committee, again with Lord Burnham as arbitrator. The result of the arbitration was the publication of new scales of salary which represented a compromise between the standards proposed by the teachers and those of the authorities. Under the new scheme a probationary year of service was introduced so that the first increment of salaries was not added until after two years of service. The amount of increment was reduced and the period between the minimum and maximum salaries was increased. The salaries of women were adjusted to approximately four fifths of those of men with similar qualifications. The Board of Education undertook to intervene by means of its grants in cases where the efficiency of the educational service was prejudiced or endangered by the unreasonable action of a local authority, an undertaking which was later incorporated in the Elementary School Code in the statement that "there shall be no saving to local rates by not paying the allotted scale if, in the opinion of the Board, the efficiency of the provision of elementary education is endangered." To permit flexibility in the award of special financial recognition for special work, the Board also expressed itself as ready to recognize such special arrangements for grant purposes.

The Burnham award was adopted for six years from March 31, 1925. When that period expired the existing arrangements were continued for another year, but a few months later the financial crisis developed, there was a change of government, and the demand for retrenchment, especially in public services, became urgent. An Economy Committee under the chairmanship of Sir George May had prior to this crisis recommended a cut of fifteen per cent in teachers' salaries, which was subsequently reduced to ten per cent. This reduction will continue until the end of the financial year when the whole question of salaries will again be reconsidered by the Burnham Committees. The local authorities and the Government desire to see a reduction in the scales corresponding to the reduction in the cost of living; the leading teachers' organization, the National Union of Teachers, claims that the salary scales were originally adopted in order to make teaching a profession which would attract ability, irrespective of any consideration of the cost of living; the women teachers have been opposed to the existing scales because of sex differentiation, while a section of the men teachers feel that the difference in the salaries of the two sexes is not great enough; a compromise between the two groups was a proposal to make additions to the normal scales in accordance with family obligations; head teachers or principals are discontented with the present method of calculating their salaries on the basis of the size of schools; and, finally, the reorganization of the school system into junior and senior schools and other schools on the secondary level may require more differentiation in the scales of salary than existed under the old system. The advance made since 1913 is indicated by a comparison of the average salary in that year (£119 for men and £74 for women, and £104 for all teachers) with the average salary in 1930 (£334 for men, £254 for women if certificated; £324 for all men, £217 for all women, and £245 for all teachers).

Pensions. The status of teachers was further improved by a radical revision of the pension system in 1922 and again in 1925. Elementary school teachers had, since 1898, enjoyed the benefits of a deferred annuity system which was inadequate in amount and which proved to be actuarially unsound. A Departmental Committee appointed in 1922 recommended the adoption of a contributory system to which teachers, employers, and the State would contribute. A superannuation scheme on this basis was established in 1922 and revised in 1925 (Teachers' Superannuation Act). The present system includes all elementary school teachers, administrative officers and inspectors, and teachers in grant-aided schools and institutions below those of university rank. The teachers and others eligible under the Act contribute five per cent of their salaries annually and the local education authorities an equal amount, which is reduced by grants from the Board of Education for this purpose to less than two and a half per cent of the cost of salaries. Teachers who have had thirty years of service may retire at the age of sixty, or, if the period of qualifying service [1] is less than thirty years, at

---

[1] Various types of service may be calculated for this purpose — recognized service before April 1, 1926, contributory service subsequent to that date, and approved external service in other than grant-earning schools, Universities, Scotland, the civil service. or such as may be approved by the Treasury.

the age of sixty-five, which is the age of compulsory retirement for all teachers. The superannuation allowance is one-eightieth of the average salary for the last five years of pensionable service for each year of service with a maximum of half of the average salary plus a lump sum gratuity, paid at the time of retirement, of one thirtieth of average salary for each year of service with the same maximum. Disability allowances are paid after ten years of service, or, if disability occurs earlier, a short service gratuity of one twelfth of annual salary for each year of pensionable service is granted. To teachers who leave the profession or who fail to qualify for the benefits of the scheme or if the benefits are less than the accumulated contributions, the contributions, compounded at three per cent interest, are returned.

This scheme, while a considerable improvement on the deferred annuity system, has been subjected to a number of criticisms. The allowances are not calculated on the basis of accumulated contributions, but on length of service and average salary in the last five years of service at a time when salaries are subject to fluctuations. The cost of the system has only been vaguely estimated and the contributions are not funded but used to pay current annual obligations, most of which are on account of accrued liabilities, or allowances due to teachers who performed the major part of their service before the system was adopted. In other words, the future solvency of the plan depends on the pledge of the Government, which may at any time be overridden by national interests of greater importance. The progress of the system is to be watched and an actuarial survey is due in 1933; the probability is that it will then be too early to discover any trends of importance.

Conclusion. Despite the uncertainties of the pension scheme and the probable adjustment of salaries in the present year, there can be no doubt that there has been a considerable advance in the economic, professional, and social status of elementary school teachers since 1918. Increased or improved preparation, better remuneration and protection against disability and old age, greater freedom from administrative control and more sympathetic administration have completely changed the character of the elementary school teacher's career. To these may be added a rich and vigorous associational activity, which, as it becomes relieved of the burden of fighting for economic welfare, is directing increased attention to professional problems important to the schools and the public. This situation is reflected in the gradual but marked increase in "refresher" and other courses for general and professional improvement, conducted by universities, local authorities, professional groups, and the Board of Education. While training in service of this and other types is not as extensive as in the United States, it may also be said that it is not as much loaded in favor of professional courses as it is in this country. Finally, the absence of regimentation from above, whether by a bureaucracy or in the interests of "efficiency," leaves more to the teacher's freedom and initiative, but increases his sense of responsibility. The change in the status of English elementary school teachers can be illustrated in no better way than by referring to the high standard held before them, a standard which would have been inconceivable thirty years ago, by one who was during his whole career associated with them as teacher and inspector: "Every teacher should have his own theory of teaching and his own philosophy of education; but they can be built only upon long experience and mature reflection." [1]

2. FRANCE

History. The preparation of elementary school teachers in France is still based on the general lines on which the system was organized soon after the establishment of the Third Republic by Jules Ferry and Ferdinand Buisson. The idea of establishing normal schools for the preparation of teachers had already been adopted by the Convention acting on a report prepared by Lakanal in 1794 and was continued under Napoleon, but with little result until a normal school opened in Strasbourg in 1811 provided a model which was soon copied elsewhere. The regulations issued on December 14, 1832, under Guizot's influence required each department to establish a normal school offering a two-year course under state control. In 1842 the first normal school for girls was created, and three years later a regulation was issued requiring teachers in normal schools to have experience in elementary schools. The programs of the normal schools were somewhat liberal in scope and for that reason aroused the suspicion that they tended to train teachers with a broader

---

[1] Ward, H. (formerly Chief Inspector for the Training of Teachers in the Board of Education), "The Training of Teachers," in Wilson, J. Dover, *The Schools of England*, p. 224 (London, 1928).

preparation than was regarded as necessary for teaching in elementary schools and thus to make them discontented with their work. This suspicion, which was also current in Germany at the same time, led in France to the reactionary *Loi Falloux*, which reduced the programs of the normal schools to the range of the elementary schools, but extended the period of preparation to three years. A more liberal spirit was introduced by Duruy in 1866; a year later, Duruy placed the preparation of girls on the same footing as that of boys.

The reorganization of the normal school system was effected by legislation introduced by Ferry and Buisson. In 1879 each department was required to maintain two normal schools, one for men and one for women; in 1880 a special examination was introduced for normal school professors of letters and science and was further defined in 1887; in the same year an institution (*école normale supérieure primaire*) to prepare candidates for these examinations was established at Fontenay-aux-Roses for women, followed two years later by the creation of a similar institution for men at Saint-Cloud; in 1882 an examination for candidates for directorships of normal schools was introduced. In 1881 the normal school curriculum was liberalized by the inclusion of algebra, modern languages, and manual work. Except for a modification of the regulations in 1905, the character of the normal schools remained unchanged until 1920, when a new curriculum and courses of study were published.

THE PRESENT SYSTEM

Provision of normal schools. The preparation of elementary school teachers is entirely under the control of the State, which prepares the curriculum and courses of study, supervises the normal schools, selects the candidates, appoints the teachers, provides for the maintenance of the students, and bears the cost of teachers' salaries. Under the regulations each department is required to provide two normal schools, one for men and one for women, and to supply and maintain the buildings. Actually there are only eighty-eight normal schools for each sex in France, and three for men and four for girls in Algeria and Tunis; in other words, two of the departments do not provide normal schools. Some of the institutions are very small, in some cases with less than thirty students, but local pride prevents the smaller departments from availing themselves of the legal provision to combine with their neighbors for the purpose of maintaining larger schools. All the normal schools are boarding institutions (*internats*), but provision is made for partial boarders and for day students.

Administration of normal schools. The normal schools are governed in general by state regulations, and are under the immediate supervision of the rector and inspectors of the academy in which they are situated. Each school has an administrative board consisting of an academy inspector, four members appointed by the rector, and two members delegated by the *conseil générale* of the department. The function of the board is to discuss problems of management, to prepare the budget, to visit the school with which it is associated once a month, and to submit an annual report through the prefect of the department to the rector on the material condition of the institution. Responsibility for the internal administration of a normal school is vested in the director, who is assisted by a bursar (*économe*), and the faculty which meets in conference once a month.

The normal school faculty. The faculty of a normal school consists of the director, the bursar, professors of letters and science, teachers of special subjects such as foreign languages, drawing, singing, music, gymnastics, and manual work, and the principal of the practice school. Each member of the faculty must possess the special qualifications prescribed for his position. For appointment as a professor of letters or science, candidates must hold the *certificat d'aptitude au professorat dans les écoles normales et des écoles primaires supérieures*. This certificate is awarded by the State under the following conditions: Candidates must pass two examinations separated by an interval of at least one year. For the first examination they must be at least nineteen years of age, be in good health, and hold the *brevet supérieur*,[1] the *baccalauréat*,[2] or the *diplôme de fin d'études secondaires*.[2] For the second examination they must be at least twenty-one years of age, be in good health, and must have had at least two years of practical experience. The first examination is a qualifying examination, but is also required for admission to the higher primary normal school up to the number of vacancies at Fontenay-aux-Roses and Saint-Cloud, which are represented on the examining juries by their directors and professors.

[1] See Chapter VI.   [2] See Chapter VIII.

The second examination is competitive, only that number of candidates being selected which is necessary to fill available vacancies. Both examinations are based on syllabi issued each year by the Ministry of Public Instruction.[1] The written test of the first part of the examination, from which holders of a *licence* in letters or sciences may under certain conditions be exempted, includes for the professorship in letters an essay on a question or text in French literature (five hours); an essay on a question or text in philosophy (four hours); an essay on a question in modern and contemporary history (four hours); and an essay on a question in geography (four hours). The oral examination includes an *explication* of a text in a foreign language (Latin or modern) after three quarters of an hour's preparation; questions in modern and contemporary history, and geography. For professors in science the written examination includes tests in arithmetic and algebra (three hours), geometry (three and a half hours), physics (four hours), chemistry (two hours), and natural science (five hours); the oral test covers the same subjects with practical work, setting up experiments and reports on them in the sciences.

The second examination is organized in a similar way, but opportunity is provided for specialization; the professorship in letters may be in French language and literature, or history and geography, or in a modern foreign language (English, German, Italian, Spanish, and Arabic); that in science in the mathematical and physical, in the physical, chemical and natural, or in the applied sciences. In addition to the written and oral test there is a supplementary test in illustrative design and in handwork (wood or metal for men, dressmaking, knitting or embroidery for women).

The certificate of aptitude for a professorship (or a *licence* in letters or science) is the minimum requirement of candidates for the *certificat d'aptitude à l'inspection primaire et à la direction des écoles normales*. They must be twenty-five years of age and must have had five years of practical teaching experience. Teachers who have had at least ten years of experience are exempt from the requirement of the certificate of aptitude for a professorship. The examination for the certificate of aptitude for a directorship (which is also valid for an elementary school inspectorship) is both written and oral. The

---

[1] Under the following title: *Programmes des Examens du Certificat d'Aptitude au Professorat des Ecoles Normales et des Ecoles Primaires Supérieures.*

written part, taken in the capital of an academy, consists of two essays (five hours being allowed for the preparation of each), one on education or educational psychology, and one on ethics or sociology based on the normal school course of study. Candidates who are successful in this part are summoned to Paris for the oral examination, which includes (1) the *explication* of a passage selected by lot from a list of authors issued every three years by the Ministry after one hour of preparation; (2) the discussion of an educational problem, after two hours of preparation; (3) the discussion of a problem of educational administration, after one hour of preparation; (4) report of a visit of inspection to a maternal, elementary, higher elementary, or normal school.

The principalship of a practice school connected with a normal school may be held by a professor who has had at least three years of experience in an elementary school or teachers who have their permanent certificate and have had at least ten years of experience in some institution of public education; an assistant in such a practice school must have had at least five years of experience.

Other members of the normal school staffs, including the bursar, must hold the certificates prescribed for their special fields of instruction or administration. In normal schools with more than seventy pupils, the number of professors is fixed at five; if the enrollment is between thirty-six and seventy, at four; if the number is less than thirty-six, at three. Each professor is expected to give twenty hours of instruction a week and to devote five hours a week to the supervision of study; directors are required to give six hours a week of instruction (always in ethics and education) in schools with more than thirty-six pupils and in addition ten hours of instruction in science or twelve in letters in smaller schools.

The scale of salaries of professors, men and women, is as follows:

Class	Seine and Seine-et-Oise	Other Departments
First	37,000 francs	30,000 francs
Second	34,000	27,000
Third	31,000	24,000
Fourth	28,000	21,000
Fifth	25,000	18,000
Sixth	22,000	15,000

Directors receive salaries on the same scale with residence and the addition of the following supplements:

PREPARATION OF ELEMENTARY TEACHERS

GRADE	SEINE AND SEINE-ET-OISE	OTHER DEPARTMENTS
1	7,000 francs	6,000 francs
2	6,000	5,000
3	5,000	4,000
4	4,000	3,000

Professors who also hold the position of bursar are entitled to residence and salary additions of 1000, 1500, or 2000 francs, according to grade. Those who are also principals of the practice school attached to the normal school receive the same additions to salary.

Admission of students. Admission to normal schools is competitive. Each year the council of each department reports through the prefect and the rector to the Minister of Public Instruction the number of teachers which it is likely to need; on the basis of this report the number of students to be admitted to the normal schools is determined. Candidates for admission must be French, between the ages of fifteen and nineteen, in good health and of good character; they are required to sign an undertaking that they will serve for ten years in a public school or refund to the State the cost of their maintenance in the normal schools, including the cost of board, laundry, books, and the value of scholarships for clothing, if they have held these. The selection of a normal school is a delicate matter, since every graduate must teach for a period of years in the department in which he has been trained unless he obtains permission to seek an appointment elsewhere.

The preliminary requirements for candidacy are followed by an examination, that for the *brevet élémentaire* being used. This examination is based on the course of the general section of the higher elementary schools,[1] in which most intending teachers receive their preparation. The examination is written and oral. The written tests, which are taken at local centers, include an essay in morals or literature (two and a half hours), a paper on history and geography (one and a half hours), a test in mathematics (arithmetic, algebra, and geometry, one and a half hours), and a paper on physical or natural sciences (one and a half hours); the first two papers are also marked for writing and spelling. The best candidates are permitted to proceed to a normal school for the oral test, which includes questions in mathematics, morals and civics, history and geography,

---

[1] See Chapter VI.

physical and natural sciences, drawing, singing, gymnastics, and, for girls, needlework. The candidates who rank highest on the list are awarded scholarships of admission to the normal schools up to the limit prescribed by the Minister; those who obtain marks above the average but are not eligible for admission are awarded the *brevet élémentaire*. The scholarships cover the cost of full or partial board and in some instances maintenance grants. The severity of the competition is indicated by the following table which gives the number of applicants and the number admitted:

	Men		Women	
	Applicants	Admitted	Applicants	Admitted
1927	4,700	1,787	6,659	1,911
1928	5,375	1,864	6,590	1,986
1929	6,101	1,967	7,198	2,104
1930	7,048	2,125	8,011	2,182
1931	6,327[1]	2,163	7,321[1]	2,176

Curriculum and courses of study. The latest regulations on the curriculum and courses of study in normal schools were issued on August 18, 1920. The new regulations aimed to give a more definite character to the normal schools as institutions for professional preparation. It was felt that preceding the revision the normal schools suffered from a confusion of aims; on the one hand, they were too much like continuations of the higher elementary schools, and on the other they attempted to give the elements of a higher education. Under the regulations of 1905 the first two years had been devoted to general academic studies culminating in the examination for the *brevet supérieur* and the last year solely to professional studies. The regulations of 1920 seek to permeate all the work of the three years with the professional aim, while placing the general studies on a higher level; graduation from the higher elementary school is to furnish the starting-point leading up to the standard of the *classe de philosophie* in a secondary school or the work of the first year of a liberal arts faculty. The examination for the *brevet supérieur* has been postponed to the end of the course. The normal school is thus primarily a professional institution and not a university or a center for educational research. Its work is differentiated from that of the higher elementary school, in the first

---

[1] The reduction in the number of applicants for admission in 1931 is explained partly by the abolition of fees in secondary schools and partly by the fact that the fall in the birth-rate during the War is beginning to show itself at this stage.

PREPARATION OF ELEMENTARY TEACHERS

place, by an avoidance of emphasis on the mere acquisition of information, and, secondly, by introducing the students to methods of research and the use of source materials. To this end the schools are encouraged to utilize activity methods and in the sciences to study the materials offered by the environment.

The curriculum includes the following subjects:

General and professional ethics
Elements of educational psychology and sociology; principles of science
Theory of education
French language and literature
One modern foreign language
History
Geography
Arithmetic and algebra
Surveying and levelling (for men)
Physical and natural sciences and their chief applications; hygiene, and, for women, domestic economy and care of infants
Agriculture (for men), and horticulture
Drawing
Singing and music
Gymnastics
Manual work

The number of periods devoted to these subjects per week is given in the accompanying table.

Subjects	First Year		Second Year		Third Year		Total	
	M	W	M	W	M	W	M	W
Educational psychology and sociology. Education. Ethics. Philosophy of science...............	2	2	2	2	2	2	6	6
French language and literature....	4	4	4	4	4	4	12	12
History and geography............	3	3	3	3	2½	2½	8½	8½
Modern foreign language..........	2	2	2	2	2	2	6	6
Mathematics.....................	3	3	3	3	2	1	8	7
Physical and natural sciences. Hygiene. Laboratory. Domestic economy (for women)...........	4	4	4	4	4	5	12	13
Theory of agriculture.............	..	..	1	..	1	..	2	..
Drawing and modelling............	2	2	2	2	2	2	6	6
Geometrical drawing..............	1	1	1	1	1	1	3	3
Singing and music................	2	2	2	2	2	2	6	6
Gymnastics......................	2	2	2	2	2	2	6	6
Manual work and agriculture......	4	4	4	4	4	4	12	12
Total......................	29	29	30	29	28½	27½	87½	85½

An examination of the course of study (*Plan d'Etudes et Pro-*

grammes des Ecoles Normales), which for the first time leaves a certain latitude to the professors in the selection of topics and books for discussion and encourages adaptation to local differences, does not warrant the conclusion that the desire to permeate the work of the normal schools with the professional point of view has been carried out. General and professional studies are still kept distinct, and, although the professors are required to participate in the induction of the cadet-teachers (*élèves-maîtres* or *élèves-maîtresses*) into the practice of teaching, there is no indication in the courses of study that the subjects of general instruction are treated from the point of view of their use in elementary schools. Indeed, there appears to be a distinct separation between the two, since in the second year one hour a week is devoted, under the caption of *Pédagogie*, to the study of special methods in the elementary school subjects. The standards attained in general academic subjects have been raised, not only on the principle that every teacher must be an educated person, but to make possible the access of normal school graduates to the universities, which has been effected under certain conditions since the regulations appeared in 1920. Educational psychology still follows in the main the metaphysical approach, although opportunity is provided for general observation and measurement of school children and for the study of Binet-Simon tests. Educational theory includes the study of principles, general methods, and classroom management in the first year, special methods in the second, and the administration and organization of education in the third. The course in educational sociology includes the discussion of the economic organization of society, the place of the family in society and its relation to the school and the child, civics, religion, art, and science studied from the sociological point of view. The study of general principles of science is a study in logic, methods of the various sciences, science of life, and science and reason. As in all French educational institutions the course in ethics (*morale*) is intended to take the place of religious instruction and deals in general with moral ideas and ideals, supplemented in another course by a study of professional ethics and the relations of the teacher to the pupils, their parents, the profession, and the authorities.

The preparation of the teachers on the professional side is extended by observation and practice. Each normal school has available for this purpose either a school directly associated with it (*école an-*

nexe) or some other school in the locality designated for the purpose (*école d'application*). Normal schools for women must have access to a maternal and infant school either as a part of their own practice schools or assigned to them in the locality. The qualifications of the director of the *école annexe* have already been described; teachers in these schools must themselves be normal school graduates with at least five years of teaching experience. Directors and teachers in the *écoles d'application* are only required to be graduates of normal schools. The contact of students with the practice schools is continued throughout the three years of the course. All are required to spend at least fifty half-days a year in the schools; the first year is devoted to observation and reports; the second to observation and occasional teaching in the presence of the director, professors, or classroom teachers; in the last year opportunities are provided for more continued independent teaching in a number of subjects. The professors of general subjects as well as the normal school director participate in supervising the students' practice. In the last year of the course a weekly educational conference is held at which a demonstration lesson followed by discussion may be given, or a problem of method or discipline is discussed, or pupils' written work or school textbooks are criticized, or, finally, an extract from educational literature is critically analyzed (*expliquée*).[1] The members of the normal school faculty and the directors of the practice schools are present at these conferences.

The practical training of the cadet-teachers is not restricted to the schools associated with the normal schools. In order to extend the variety of their experiences they may be assigned for several weeks to selected teachers at a distance from the normal schools, or they may be required to participate in extra-school activities (*œuvres complémentaires*) or to organize lectures or courses for adults. In general the tendency is to give the students as many opportunities as possible to become familiar with the possibilities of the profession of which they hope to become members.

Examinations. Students are examined at the end of each year

[1] The terms *expliquer* and *explication de textes* have a definite connotation in French educational literature. Originally developed by the Jesuits and carried over very generally in classical instruction for nearly three centuries, it has in France been applied to a variety of subjects. The method involves the detailed, critical analysis of any written text with a thorough and minute discussion and implication of almost every word. In the United States the method has been introduced by M. de Sauzé in the teaching of modern languages in Cleveland, and by Professor A. Cru in Teachers College, Columbia University.

and may be required to repeat the work of the year or be dismissed. Each examination counts as a part of the examination for the *brevet supérieur*, which is also open to candidates not prepared in a normal school but who hold the *brevet élémentaire*, or the *brevet* of a higher elementary school, or have passed the first part of the *baccalauréat* or hold the *diplôme de fin d'études secondaires*, and who are at least seventeen years of age. The examinations, which are both written and oral, are based each year, in the case of normal school students, on the work of the year; other candidates may take all the tests at one time or in two separate sessions. The majority of those who take the examination are, of course, normal school students, as is indicated in the following figures for 1926:

	NUMBER TAKING EXAMINATION	NUMBER PASSING	PER CENT PASSING
Normal school candidates:			
Men	1,953	1,696	86.3
Women	2,016	1,861	92.3
Other candidates:			
Men	183	87	47.5
Women	1,111	689	62.0

School life. The normal schools, like other French schools, have not as yet developed an active corporate life. Not only is the program of studies heavy, but the life and work of each day are carefully regulated. Slowly the schools are being affected by the general interest in athletics, but they do not yet constitute a recognized part of the school activities. The day of the normal school student is regulated as follows:

	5.45 A.M.	Rise (dress and put room in order)
6.15 to	7.15	Study
7.15 to	7.30	Breakfast
7.30 to	7.55	Clean room
8.00 to	12.00	Classes (except on Thursdays)
12.00 to	12.30 P.M.	Lunch
12.30 to	1.30	Recreation
1.30 to	4.30	Classes; 1 hour of study (except on Thursdays and Saturday afternoons)
4.30 to	5.00	Recreation and lunch
5.00 to	7.30	Study
7.30 to	8.00	Dinner
8.00 to	8.30	Recreation
8.30 to	9.30	Study
	9.30	Retire

On Thursdays there are no classes, but two hours are devoted in normal schools for men to military instruction and three hours are left entirely free; on Sundays students are entirely free after 10 A.M.

Ten hours a day are thus normally devoted to classwork and study. Men students may leave the normal school premises only on Sundays and holidays; women are only permitted to go out at the request of their parents. Students are permitted to receive correspondence from persons listed by their parents. Such details may on the whole be unimportant and may have a different significance under different social régimes; they do, however, serve to indicate that, while the new regulations seek to raise the intellectual level in the normal schools, the control and discipline of the pupils still follow the traditions of the nineteenth century. What the effect is on the professional initiative of the teachers it is impossible to estimate, since the same type of administrative discipline dominates the practices of the schools to which the normal school graduate proceeds. M. Lapie, who was in large measure responsible for the revision of the regulations for normal schools, advocated the introduction of self-government in these institutions in order to cultivate initiative and responsibility on the part of the students; his recommendations have not, however, been put into practice.[1]

Certification. The lowest qualification which is accepted for appointment as teachers is the *brevet élémentaire* already described (Chapter VI), which at least guarantees three years of academic preparation beyond the regular elementary school; the minimum age for appointment is eighteen. It confers no claim to permanent appointment or assignment on the salary scale. The *brevet supérieur*, granted on the completion of the normal school course and the examination based on it, entitled the holder to appointment as an *instituteur* or *institutrice stagiaire* — that is, an elementary school teacher on temporary appointment made by an academy inspector. The temporary certificate may be converted, after at least two years of experience and passing the examination, for the *certificat d'aptitude pédagogique*, provided the candidates are twenty years of age. The examination is professional in character, and consists in teaching a class for three hours (the instruction must include singing and gymnastics) and questions on educational administration, school management, and practical problems in education; the exercise books of

[1] See Lapie, P., *Pédagogie française* (Paris, 1926).

the candidate's class are examined. The certificate is not awarded to men until they have completed their period of military service. On obtaining the certificate the teachers become *titulaires* and are eligible to permanent appointment and advancement on the salary scale. The appointment as *titulaire* is made by the prefect of a department acting for the Minister of Public Instruction and on the advice of an academy inspector.

From this point on advancement depends upon the ability and ambition of the teacher. He may become the principal of a school; if he passes the necessary examinations he may advance to a position in a higher elementary or normal school on obtaining the *certificat d'aptitude au professorat des écoles normales et des écoles primaires supérieures*, which constitutes a stage to appointment as director of a normal school, or inspector of elementary schools on obtaining the *certificat d'aptitude à l'inspection primaire et à la direction des écoles normales*. The last two positions are the highest in the elementary branch of the educational system. A small number on passing the required examinations may transfer to the secondary branch; in general this procedure is unusual and promotion is sought within the elementary branch proper.

Training in service. The continued training of teachers after their preliminary preparation is entrusted to academy and primary inspectors who organize conferences periodically for the teachers of one or more cantons. The conferences, which teachers must attend, are devoted wholly to the discussion of the theory and practice of education. Beyond this, the dependence of promotions on examinations serves as a stimulus to continued study. Courses are available in universities and in normal schools, where they may be given by university professors. Scholarships are available for attendance at universities or for foreign travel in the case of teachers who plan to qualify as teachers of foreign languages. Each year the ablest teachers may compete for admission to the two higher primary normal schools at Saint-Cloud (for men) and Fontenay-aux-Roses (for women). These institutions prepare professors for higher elementary and normal schools as specialists in the two main branches of letters (French, foreign languages, history and geography) or sciences (physical and mathematical, chemical and natural, or applied) in a two-year course; a third year may be spent in preparation for the examination for normal school directorships or primary inspectorships. A few students from these institutions may take the examination for the *certificat d'aptitude à l'enseignement secondaire* and thence proceed through the *licence d'enseignement* to the *agrégation* and so enter service in the secondary schools. The members of the faculties of Saint-Cloud and Fontenay-aux-Roses are recruited from local secondary schools or from the Sorbonne. The students who succeed in obtaining admission receive free tuition and board.

Status of teachers. Since they are members of the civil service, the French teachers already enjoy a satisfactory status; in the smaller communes they may often be the best educated persons next to the priest; in the larger centers social gradations based on educational qualifications are still marked. Once appointed to office as *titulaires*, the teachers enjoy permanent tenure which can only be disturbed on account of serious misconduct or professional incompetence. They may be reprimanded, censured, suspended, or dismissed, but in all cases their interests are protected and no teacher may be dismissed without a hearing nor by any one superior official. The recommendation of dismissal may come from an academy inspector, but it is not carried out until the departmental council and the prefect have considered the case. All documents in the case are available to the teacher, who has the right to be represented by the professional organization of which he is a member and to appeal to the Minister and the Higher Council of Public Instruction.

On the material side the teachers enjoy salary scales fixed by the State for the country as a whole and allowances for disability and superannuation. Owing to the fluctuations in the cost of living and in the stability of the franc, salary scales have been revised several times since 1918. The present scale of salaries is as follows:

Stagiaires	10,500 francs
Sixth class	11,500
Fifth class	13,000
Fourth class	14,500
Third class	16,000
Second class	17,500
First class	19,000

The salary scales are basic for the whole country and are the same for men and women; in order to equalize them, the teachers are granted a number of supplements (*indemnités*) varying with the size of the locality in which they serve; in other words, they are adjusted to the cost of living in different parts of the country and to personal needs. Teachers are entitled to a residence or an allowance for rent which is paid by the communes according to their size and on a scale fixed by the prefect of the department; they range from 100 to 900 francs a year on the following scale:

Cities with less than 1,000 population........	100 to 200 francs
Cities between 1,000 and 3,000..........	150 to 250
Cities between 3,001 and 9,000..........	180 to 400
Cities between 9,001 and 12,000..........	230 to 450
Cities between 12,001 and 18,000..........	260 to 500
Cities between 18,001 and 36,000..........	300 to 600
Cities between 36,001 and 60,000..........	340 to 650
Cities between 60,001 and 100,000..........	380 to 700
Cities over 100,000......................	450 to 900

A slight addition may be made to these sums in those cases, which are not infrequent, where both husband and wife are engaged in educational or other state service. Another allowance is paid varying with the locality in which the school is situated; this allowance ranges from 291.20 francs to 1747.20 francs, and is graded on the following scale:

Paris...............................	1,747.20 francs
Suburbs of Paris.........................	1,528.80
Cities of over 150,000 population...........	1,310.40
Cities between 100,001 and 150,000.........	1,092.00
Cities between 70,001 and 100,000.........	873.60
Cities between 40,001 and 70,000.........	728.00
Cities between 20,001 and 40,000.........	582.40
Cities between 10,001 and 20,000.........	436.80
Cities between 5,001 and 10,000.........	291.20

A further addition consists of family allowances depending upon the number of children in a teacher's family; the allowances are paid for each dependent child up to the age of sixteen, or, if the child is being educated, up to the age of twenty-one; the allowances increase progressively from 660 francs for the first child, 960 francs for the second, 1560 francs for the third, and 1920 francs for each child beyond the third.

Teachers who are transferred from one school to another are given a grant to defray the expenses of moving. In cases of ill-health, leave of absence on full pay is given up to three months; in the case of married women, leave of absence on full pay is granted for childbirth, one month before and one month after the confinement. Beyond this, teachers are given reductions on the railways for five trips a year, receive free tuition for their children who are day pupils in secondary schools, and for themselves if they study in a university for the *licence*, and may be given financial aid in serious cases of need. Additional allowances are paid to principals of schools, as follows:

Schools with 2 classes	800 francs
Schools with 3 to 4 classes	1,600
Schools with 5 to 9 classes	2,800
Schools with 10 or more classes	3,500

Protection against disability and old age is provided by a contributory system to which the teachers contribute six per cent of their salaries a year. They may retire at the age of fifty-five after twenty-five years of service on an allowance equal to one fiftieth of the average salary during the last three years of service multiplied by the number of years of completed service; these amounts may be increased if retirement is postponed; additions are also paid on the basis of the number of children raised up to the age of sixteen. Married women may retire after fifteen years of service, but do not become eligible to an allowance until they reach the age prescribed for it. A disability allowance is granted after fifteen years of service on the basis of one fiftieth of average salary for each year of service; if disability occurs after less than fifteen years of service, a life annuity based on the capitalized contributions is paid. The system makes provision for widows and orphans of deceased teachers.

Conclusion. Despite the apparently satisfactory conditions of service, there is considerable unrest among the elementary school teachers of France. The unrest on the whole is not primarily concerned with the material conditions of the teachers, but is due to discontent with their professional status and the class organization of the educational system as a whole. Professional organizations are recognized by law, but professional syndicalism, although prohibited, actually flourishes, and at present the *Syndicat des Instituteurs* is perhaps one of the strongest associations of the elementary school teachers, who may also be members of the *Fédération Générale de l'Enseignement*. The common bond of discontent brings together in the same groups teachers from different branches of education, and of different political, religious, and economic views. In general the associations would like to see a complete reorganization of the educational system on the basis of the common school, equal educational opportunities, and differentiation of post-primary education. So far as the normal school is concerned, their criticism is that it is still isolated, often located in small centers without adequate opportunities for intellectual growth and development. The preparation of teachers begins too early, and, although the latest regulations have attempted to raise the standard of general cultural education, the graduate of the normal school does not enjoy the same privileges as the *bachelier* of a secondary school. The situation is being remedied to some extent by the acceptance of the *brevet supérieur* for admission to some science faculties; the faculties of letters do not, however, recognize anything below the certificate for professors in normal and higher elementary schools. Postponement of the beginning of professional training, a sound general education in a secondary school, and preparation on a university level are among the proposals which are made. The universities, as at present constituted, are not equipped to prepare teachers, although here and there courses are offered in education and in educational and experimental psychology. Further, it is objected, although the admission of normal school graduates to the universities reduces the force of this objection, that they are not prepared for study at a university level, that they have too much of the *esprit primaire*, the primary mind which accepts all information and facts as of equal value without interest or ability to inquire into sources. The second objection the regulations of 1920 have attempted to meet.

The whole problem of teacher-preparation is closely associated with the character of the administrative system. Preparation on a higher level implies professional freedom and responsibility. The intense centralization of the French system assumes all responsibility by prescribing curricula and courses of study, methods to a large extent, and examinations, and restricts the freedom to a minimum even in the latest regulations of 1923, which permit some local adaptation. It is not, therefore, an accident that the same groups which are interested in the reorganization of the educational system and improvement in the preparation of teachers also advocate decentralization of the administrative system. Perhaps the best criticism of the professional preparation of teachers can be found in the educational journals [1] for elementary school teachers. Each of these contains in its weekly issue a section devoted to lesson plans based upon questions set in the examinations for the *certificat d'études primaires* or upon the prescribed courses of study; this, as nothing else could be, is evidence at least of the control exercised by the government regulations, if not entirely of the failure of the preparation given in the normal schools to provide the basis for professional freedom and growth.

3. GERMANY

History. In the preparation of teachers for elementary schools, Germany again bids fair to assume the leadership in the twentieth century as she did in the nineteenth. The political situation has changed and with it the status of the elementary schools, for although the organization of the school system as a whole has not been radically modified in the post-War period, the ideals governing the elementary schools have undergone a complete revision. In the nineteenth century, particularly in the second half of the century, the aim of elementary education had been the training of loyal, law-abiding subjects; the aim today is the development of free, intelligent, and active citizens. The change of aims has led to a profound change in the character of teacher-preparation. Under the old régime Germany had succeeded in developing a system for the preparation of teachers which was probably the most efficient that the world has seen with the exception of that of the Jesuits, if efficiency is defined as the best adaptation of means to secure clearly formulated ends. There was no break in gauge between the character of teacher-preparation and the work of the elementary schools. The responsibility of the elementary schools was to train submissive and unquestioning obedience to authority, and the duty of the teachers was to carry out the regulations prescribed by their official superiors in the same spirit. Curriculum, courses of study, and methods of instruction were prescribed by the Ministry of Education in each State, and the purpose of preparation was to train and discipline the teachers to carry these out without question. The teachers, in other words, were expected to be mouthpieces of the state governments, skilled craftsmen rather than independent practitioners of a profession guided by the demands of different environments for

[1] For example: *L'Ecole et la Vie, Manuel d'Enseignement, L'Ecole Libératrice*

variety and adaptation. The regulations prescribed a certain amount of knowledge and information to be imparted to the pupils; the teachers were trained to impart this with the skill best adapted to secure the ends desired.

These were not, however, the principles upon which the system of teacher-preparation was established in the early part of the nineteenth century, when its great founders, Harnisch and Diesterweg, were influenced by the Pestalozzian movement. The aim at this time was to give teachers a general, intellectual training not limited to the subjects which they were to teach in the elementary schools. The future teachers must receive a liberal preparation and must be trained to think rather than be mere followers of routine and mechanical practices. Since the Prussian educational authorities did not define and prescribe the work of the normal schools, Harnisch at Weissenfels and Diesterweg at Mörs and later in Berlin were able, under the impulse of the liberal movement, to develop a system of preparation which went far to arouse a strong professional feeling among teachers not only in Prussia but throughout Germany. It was under the impulse of this professional consciousness that the teachers' associations were formed which were strong enough to formulate in 1848 the ideal bases for the further development of their profession. These demands were as follows: (1) Abolition of clerical control of schools. (2) The abolition of the isolated preparatory institutions and the preparation of candidates for entrance to normal schools in higher elementary schools. (3) A higher and more liberal curriculum in the normal schools. (4) The removal of the normal schools to university towns and their organization into professional institutions. (5) The recognition of teachers as civil servants and exemption from lower church duties. (6) Inspection of schools by professionally trained experts. (7) The representation of teachers on local school committees.

Only two of these demands, the fifth and seventh, were secured, it is interesting to note, before the Revolution of 1918. Indeed, the year 1848 marks the beginning of a reaction in the preparation and status of teachers. Placing the responsibility for the disorders of that year on the normal schools and the teachers that they had prepared, the Prussian Government in 1854 issued regulations which restricted the work of the normal schools to imparting those subjects which were taught in the elementary schools, controlled the reading of the students, limited the scope of the professional studies, and tightened more securely the political and clerical control over the teachers. The regulations of 1854 were modified in a more liberal direction in 1872, partly through the influence of Saxony, which in 1865 made access to the University of Leipzig possible for the best graduates of the normal schools, and partly through the active propaganda conducted in and out of Parliament by Diesterweg almost up to his death in 1866. Teachers were given the status of civil servants and the curriculum of the normal schools was expanded, particularly on the scientific side and by the introduction of French as an optional subject. Except for a slight modification in the curriculum in 1901, the general spirit of teacher-preparation remained unchanged until the recent reform.

The chief characteristics of teacher-preparation until this reform was introduced were as follows. Candidates were selected at the age of fourteen on completing the elementary school and began their preliminary training, in Prussia, in *Präparandenanstalten*, where the elementary school course was continued for three years under teachers who were themselves elementary school teachers. At the end of the preparatory course candidates were admitted to the normal schools (*Lehrerseminare*), maintained by the State and organized on a denominational basis. Here the three-year course was devoted, except for the study of physics and chemistry and French, to an intensive review of the subjects of the elementary schools, professional subjects, and observation and participation in the work of the practice schools. The strength of the system lay in no sense in breadth of preparation, but in undeviating disciplining in the work which lay before the students. Every lesson had to be given in such a way that it could be reproduced in the elementary schools; every lesson was intensely practical, and, since the same instructor, himself trained in a normal school and with several years of teaching in elementary schools, was responsible for subject-matter, demonstration lessons, and supervision of the cadets in practice teaching, the whole of the work was closely integrated or professionalized, but at the level of the elementary schools. Discipline was strict; corporate activities were discouraged; the whole régime was almost military in character. Successful completion of the normal school course entitled the young teacher to probationary appointment which became permanent on passing a second examination and the completion, in the case of men, of the required military service. The only concession which was made to the recognition that normal schools were not merely exalted elementary schools was the grant to the graduates at about the age of twenty of the one-year military service privilege, obtained by secondary school pupils at about the age of fifteen.

Despite this somewhat limited but efficient preparation, which turned out skilled craftsmen, there was an intense professional activity among the teachers directed wholly by their own organizations. Discontent with a system, which isolated the normal schools from all other institutions at a higher level and refused to admit into the lives and minds of the future teachers the breath of anything but the elementary spirit, had its political effects; teachers, although they could not be members, because since 1872 they had been given the status of civil servants, sympathized in large numbers with the programs of the Social Democratic Party. On the educational side there were widespread discussions of plans for reorganization of the system, demands for the preparation of teachers on a higher level, and proposals for the improvement of curricula and methods. It was no accident that after the War the first Prussian Minister of Education, Karl Haenisch, was a former elementary school teacher, and that a large number of elementary school teachers won places in the state and federal Parliaments.

The Revolution of 1918 made possible the realization of the demands of the elementary school teaching profession for preparation on a higher level, a preparation which would substitute for the traditional apprenticeship type of training a new system based on principles governing the preparation for other professions. The recognition that a new responsibility and a new status were to be assigned to the elementary schools, that a change in the political character of the State inevitably implied a change in the character of education, was widespread. But the demands of the teachers had social and economic implications as well; improved training on a professional rather than a craftsmanship basis would, it was expected, mean an improvement in their status which had been depressed, it was felt, because of the character of their preparation.

The fundamental principle upon which the reform was to be based was defined in the Federal Constitution of 1919. According to Article 143, 2, "The preparation of all teachers shall be uniformly regulated for the *Reich* according to principles which apply generally to higher education." This provision spelt the abolition of the traditional preparatory and normal schools, the preliminary education of future teachers in schools leading up to the universities, and their professional preparation at the university level. A discussion of the problem at the *Reichsschulkonferenz* (the Federal Educational Conference), which was held in 1920 and offered to representatives of all branches of education and others concerned in its provision and maintenance an opportunity of considering the basic principles of reform, resulted in the acceptance of a number of theses bearing on the preparation of teachers. Since all teachers are members of the same profession, they should have a common preliminary preparation followed by a period of study, varied according to the needs of the various types of schools, in a university. Elementary school teachers should be required to follow a three-year course in pedagogical institutes as constituent parts of universities in which the members of the different faculties would give instruction. Separate teachers colleges, whether in the universities or not, were rejected. The courses for teachers should include both professional and academic studies with opportunities for intensive study of one subject elected by the student according to his own interests.

For some time it was expected that the Federal Government would issue regulations and suggestions to serve as a common basis for the organization of institutions for preparing teachers. This expectation was bound up with the hope that the Federal Government would also participate in the new system with financial aid. After it was announced in the Third Federal Tax Ordinance, issued in 1924, that the Government had neither the resources nor the intention of aiding any part of the educational systems, it was understood that the States were free to proceed alone with the organization of education without waiting for a lead from the Federal Government.[1] Steps were immediately taken, if not already begun, to abolish preparatory and normal schools; in Prussia the last of these were closed in 1926; in most of the other States, except Bavaria, in 1928. Owing to the great excess in the supply of teachers, quick action was not needed to reorganize the system of preparation.

[1] On the relation of the Federal Government to education see Chapter V.

THE PRESENT SYSTEM

The Constitution had set up only the common basis of providing for the preliminary education of all intending teachers in institutions leading to the universities — that is, in secondary schools; beyond this, each State by the inaction of the Federal Government was left free to devise its own system of preparing teachers. The problem of selecting the type of secondary school course best adapted to the future needs of elementary school teachers was not difficult; it was decided that such a course should be modern in character — that is to say, the *Gymnasium* and *Realgymnasium* were practically ruled out; for the modern courses a choice remained between the *Oberrealschule* and the *Deutsche Oberschule*.[1] Since the latter emphasized German cultural subjects, it was generally regarded as preferable to the *Oberrealschule*. There was, however, another problem to be solved; in the past a large number of teachers had been recruited from the rural districts and small towns which in general were not provided with secondary schools or else only with those of the classical type. The abolition of the normal school which was generally located in these areas left a number of buildings available for other purposes. These were converted into a new type of secondary school, the *Aufbauschule*, open to boys and girls entering from elementary schools at the age of thirteen. The *Aufbauschule* offers a six-year course, following the curriculum of either the *Oberrealschule* or the *Deutsche Oberschule*, and leading up to the *Abiturientenprüfung*, which carries with it the privilege of university entrance. The regulations do not discourage preliminary education in any of the secondary schools, but ordinarily the *Deutsche Oberschule* type, whether in the nine-year school or in the *Aufbauschule*, is preferred.

More serious and difficult was the question of the type of institution to be created for professional preparation. The Constitution provided that it must be at the university level, but did not specify that it must be a part of, or affiliated with, the universities. The teachers in general desired the preparation to be given in the existing universities. Against this course it was argued that the universities are primarily institutions for academic study and research; that they are not equipped to provide professional preparation, only one part

---

[1] On the secondary schools, see Chapter VIII.

of which — philosophy and education — could be offered; that new arrangements would have to be introduced to provide training in practice and in the skill subjects required in the elementary schools; and that, in Prussia at any rate, secondary school teachers are not prepared professionally in the universities. In these arguments there was, of course, a great deal of truth, but political considerations entered. The universities would have been overwhelmed with a great increase of students for whom special provision would have to be made; the temptation would always be present to devote a little more time to university studies and transfer to the secondary school branch; and, finally, preparation in the universities might make the teachers dissatisfied with the prospect of entering upon the humble but important work of the rural school. The solutions reached in the different States followed somewhat the political lines. Thus Prussia and Bavaria with leanings toward the Right favored the two-year independent *Pädagogische Akademie* (teachers college); Saxony, taking a middle position, compromised by splitting the preparation between the universities and pedagogical institutes; Socialist Hamburg incorporated the preparation in the local university. The story of the development of the system in Thuringia to some extent illustrates the shift from one point of view to another as influenced by the political changes in that State. Thuringia from 1918 until 1924 had been overwhelmingly Socialist; during that period it was proposed to prepare teachers at the University of Jena. In 1924 political control was transferred from the Left toward the Right and the immediate consequence was a modification of the plan in favor of that adopted by Saxony — academic preparation in the University and professional in a pedagogical institute. The smaller States follow one or other of the three systems indicated, or delegate the preparation of their teachers to other States.

Prussia decided to adopt the two-year teachers colleges; the general principles on which they were to be established were defined in a Memorandum on the Preparation of Elementary School Teachers (*Neugestaltung der Volksschullehrerbildung*) issued on July 20, 1925. The aim of these colleges was not to be merely the training of classroom teachers, but educators and teachers of the people, living in contact with them and with the realities of life, able to develop their cultural needs and to cultivate the intellectual, moral, and æsthetic values ever present in their environment. The teacher must be equipped with knowledge of his subjects, but he must during his period of preparation acquire ability, not necessarily in academic research, but insight into the cultural possibilities of the environment in which he may be placed. Through professional studies he must acquire a professional ideal which will inspire every aspect of his work and give him a realization of the significance of education for the development of local and national culture and for the promotion of social welfare. In the work of the teachers colleges the emphasis must be on the development of personality rather than of skilled craftsmanship.

It was planned to establish ultimately thirty-five teachers colleges (*Pädagogische Akademien*). Three were opened at Easter 1926, two Protestant institutions at Kiel and Elbing, and one Catholic at Bonn, the first two for men and women, the last at first for men alone. In 1927 an interdenominational college was opened at Frankfurt-am-Main; in 1929 four more were added at Breslau, Erfurt, Hannover, and Dortmund (all Protestant and coeducational), and in the following year further additions were made at Frankfurt-a-d-Oder, Stettin, Halle, Altona, Cassel (Protestant) and Beuthen (Catholic). By 1931 fifteen colleges had been established. It is to be observed that the colleges were organized, with the exception of that at Frankfurt-am-Main, as sectarian institutions and that they were practically all coeducational.[1] The original intention of admitting three hundred students to each college was not carried out owing to the oversupply of teachers already available.

Students who seek admission to the colleges must present a biography, a certificate of graduation from a secondary school, and a certificate of health. Successful applicants must pass a further test in music (singing and the playing of the violin, piano, or organ) women candidates must demonstrate their ability in sewing. The students do not pay tuition fees, but provide for their own maintenance, state assistance being granted in necessitous cases. Dormitories are not provided in the colleges, but day homes or unions and reading-rooms are made available for the students who live in lodgings. It is estimated that the annual cost of living for each student is 1000 Mark. An important innovation is the encouragement of

---

[1] The oversupply of teachers and the serious financial crisis which imposed severe measure of economy on the Government compelled it in November, 1931, to decide on the closing of five teachers colleges at Easter, 1932, and to distribute their students among the remaining colleges, which were not to admit any new students at that time.

student self-government, particularly in the care and organization of the homes or unions which are placed at their disposal. The social relations between students and faculty are more intimate and genial than they used to be in the traditional normal schools.

The faculty. The teachers colleges are under the general supervision of the Ministry of Education, one member of which is delegated to coöperate with the faculties. All appointments are made by the Minister of Education. The faculties consist of a director, professors, docents, and instructors. Responsibility for administration is vested in the director with the coöperation of his colleagues. Some difficulty was experienced in the initial stages of the new venture in securing the type of personnel best adapted to the work. Fundamentally the character of teacher preparation is determined by the needs of the elementary school and of public education. On the one hand, the future teacher must be given a thorough mastery of subject-matter directed to use in the elementary school; on the other, he must receive the necessary preparation in professional studies, methods, practice, and the skill subjects (music, art, handwork); the teachers colleges, however, are on the university level. The problem was how to find professors and instructors who had had a university training and experience in elementary schools. During the period of transition a solution could not be found immediately and a compromise had inevitably to be accepted; the faculties were made up of members, some of whom had had elementary school experience without academic training, while others were university trained, but had had no experience in elementary schools. It is hoped that in time it will be possible to establish requirements for appointment which will combine both types of preparation. To emphasize the recognition of teachers colleges as institutions of university rank, the members of the faculties, with the exception of the teachers of the skill subjects, have been given the title of "Professor." The salary scales in the teachers colleges were as follows according to the regulations of 1927: Director and about one fourth of the professors, 9000 Mark, rising to 14,000 Mark (in exceptional cases to 15,000 Mark); one half of the professors, 7500 Mark, rising to 11,600 Mark (13,600 Mark in exceptional cases); and the remaining fourth of the professors, 5700 Mark, rising to 9000 Mark (11,600 Mark in exceptional cases); to the salaries are added indemnities for rent.

Curriculum and courses of study. The Ministry of Education, recognizing the experimental character of the teachers colleges, refrained from issuing uniform curricula and courses of study, but in 1927 issued suggestions on the basis of which the faculty of each college was expected to formulate its own course of study. The curriculum is distributed into four main divisions: (1) professional subjects; (2) materials and methods of instruction in elementary school subjects; (3) training in skill subjects, combined with observation and practice teaching; and (4) elective studies. The distribution of subjects by hours is indicated in the following table:[1]

	Hours	
Education		
Theory	4	
History	8	
School hygiene	2	
School management — economy	2	
Materials — methods of elementary school subjects	17 (18)	
Sociology	3	
Practice teaching	19	55 (56)
Allied Sciences:		
Philosophy	4	
Psychology	9	
Religion	2	
Geography (local)	1	
Ethnology (local)	1	
Animal and plant biology (local)	1	
Physiology and Anatomy	1	
Political and social economy	2	21
Fine and Practical Art Training:		
Music	20 (16)	
Speech	1	
Manual training or sewing	3 (6)	
Physical training	12	
Drawing	2	38 (37)
		114 Sem. hrs.

The organization of the curriculum may be illustrated by the organization of the curriculum at the Bonn Teachers College.

[1] Alexander, T. *The Training of Elementary Teachers in Germany*, p. 73 (New York, 1929).

PROGRAM AT BONN TEACHERS' COLLEGE

	First Semester Hours	Second Semester Hours	Third Semester Hours	Fourth Semester Hours
I. Academic Lectures and Practica	Introduction to Philosophy 2 Physiology and Anatomy.. 1 General Psychology...... 2 Practicum in General Psychology............ 1 Systematic Pedagogy..... 2 Practicum in General Theory of Teaching and Education............... 3 Introduction to Study of Elements of Religion.... 1 Local Geography......... 2 Local Plant and Animal Biology................ 1 Local Ethnology......... 1 Introduction to Political and Social Economy.... 2	Introduction to Philosophy 2 Differential Psychology... 2 Psychological Laboratory. 1 History of Education..... 2 Practicum in the History of Education............ 2 Speech................. 1 Content and Method of Elementary School Subjects: Religion................ 1 German................ 2 History of Civics........ 1 Arithmetic & Geometry.. 2 Nature Study........... 1 Music.................. 1	Structural Psychology.... 2 Psychological Laboratory. 1 History of Education..... 2 Practicum and History of Education............ 2 Materials and Methods of the Elementary School: Religion............... 2 German and Activity Instruction............. 2 Geography.............. 1 Drawing................ 1 Physical Training........ 1	School Hygiene.......... 2 School Management...... 1 Practicum and School Management........... 1 Practical Social Pedagogy.. 2 Practicum in Social Pedagogy................. 1
II. Practical and Fine Arts	Blackboard Drawing..... 1 Music.................. 5 Physical Training........ 3	Drawing................ 1 Music.................. 5 Physical Training........ 3 Manual Training........ 1	Music.................. 5 Physical Training........ 3	Music.................. 5 Physical Training........ 3 Manual Training........ 1
III. Introduction to the Practice of Teaching	First introduction into the practice of teaching to the study of the educational process............... 3	Observation, teaching and discussion............. 2	Observation, teaching and discussion............. 8	Observation, teaching and discussion............. 8
Required hours	29	30	30	24
IV. Electives				

In addition, students are required to attend a number of lectures and practica offered in a variety of fields: education; religion; German; history and civics; geography, local and folk study; mathematics; natural science; music, drawing; manual training; and physical training.

The program of each student requires about thirty hours of required studies each week; beyond this, he is expected to attend the special lectures which he may elect. The two years of the course hardly suffice to carry out the aims set before the teachers colleges. The chief difficulty is that of reconciling the claims of study of academic subjects at the higher level and the needs of the teachers in their future work. Although the students enter the colleges with a rich background of liberal education obtained in the secondary schools, it must be reorganized for purposes of the elementary schools. Great stress is placed, however, not so much upon lecturing about the various subjects of the elementary school curriculum, but upon training the cadet-teachers in independent development of the materials of instruction by studying and analyzing the opportunities provided in different environments; in other words, just as *Bodenständigkeit* and *Heimatkunde*, leading to *Lebenskunde*, constitute the basis of the elementary school work, so it becomes the aim of the colleges to impart a profound understanding of the meaning of these terms for the development of a curriculum. Class instruction and lectures are supplemented by special study rooms, laboratories, and excursions for shorter or longer periods, which create opportunities for the development of free activity groups (*freie Arbeitsgemeinschaften*) of students who have a common interest. While these methods aim at cultivating initiative and independence on the part of the student and to open his intellectual vision to a world that is not bound up in books, it is not the intention of the teachers colleges to train research workers; the aim is rather to enable the students to see how knowledge and information have been developed rather than to extend their limit by new discoveries. Essentially the difference between the methods of the old and new type of teacher-preparation lies in the attempt to develop activity and curiosity rather than to fill the minds of the students.

The function of a teachers college is not, however, wholly academic and intellectual, but ultimately practical. Here the colleges are confronted by another difficulty created by the decision of the

Ministry to abandon the practice school attached to the training institutions. Administrative and financial difficulties were too great to provide a separate school directly under the control of each college. Accordingly, it is expected that public elementary schools in the locality of a college will be employed for purposes of observation, participation, and practice by the students. Such schools, while provided and administered by the local authorities, are placed under the supervision of the director or some professor of the local teachers college, thus giving them a certain latitude in determining the character of the schools and in the selection of some of the teachers. Students are inducted into the practical aspects of teaching through observation which begins in the first semester and is continued throughout the course in such a way that opportunity is provided for them to become familiar with the content, method, and practice in nearly all the subjects of the elementary school curriculum. Practice teaching begins in the third semester; generally, students in small groups of four or five are assigned to a class for several subjects, each one being expected to be ready to give the lesson, if called upon, while the others observe; at the end of four weeks the groups are rotated and sent to other classes. Lesson plans are prepared and supervised by the subject-matter specialists of the college and the conduct of the lesson is discussed with the group by them and the teacher in charge of the practice class. Generally, each student is expected to have some practice in teaching religion, German, and arithmetic. The chief criticism of the arrangements made for practice teaching is that the teaching is not consecutive, but broken up into a number of isolated lessons. To obviate this criticism, students are encouraged to become assistants in rural and other schools during the college vacations, when they might obtain complete charge of a class under the supervision of the regular teachers.

In order to extend the range of their observation and a knowledge of the scope of the school organization, students are expected to visit, not only a number of elementary schools, but schools for defectives, schools in eleemosynary institutions, garden schools, open-air schools, experimental schools, kindergartens, nursery schools, recreation centers, and other educational agencies. The same purpose underlies the more extended tours, not only to educational institutions, but to museums, social welfare institutions, conferences, and so on.

First teachers' examination (*Erste Lehrerprüfung*). The two-year course in the teachers colleges culminates in a final examination which is also the first teachers' examination, regulated by a decree issued on April 10, 1928. Candidates must submit a biography, a maturity certificate from a secondary school, and a certificate of regular attendance at a teachers college and participation in elective courses and practice. Attached to the application for examination are the reports of the professors and instructors on the candidate's record. Candidates may be refused admission to the examination if for any reason the records of the application are unsatisfactory. The examination committee, which consists of the teachers college faculty and an educational official of the county (*Regierung*) in which the college is situated, is presided over by a chairman appointed by the Ministry; a representative of the Protestant or Catholic denomination, as the case may be, is also invited to attend the examination.

The written part of the examination consists of an essay on a problem in education or in an allied field selected by the candidates from lists drawn up by the instructors of the field chosen; eight weeks are allowed for the preparation of the essay, which is marked by a member of the examining committee appointed by the chairman. All the essays must be available to all the examiners at least three days before the oral examination. The subjects of the oral examination fall into two main groups: (1) Professional — theory of education, history of education, psychology, philosophy, school management, school hygiene, and educational sociology. All candidates are examined in theory of education and psychology, and any two of the other subjects. (2) Subject-matter and methods — (*a*) religion, German, and arithmetic or geometry; (*b*) history, civics, geography, and nature study; (*c*) music, drawing, manual work (or sewing); (*d*) physical training. All candidates are examined in the subjects under (*a*) and one subject in the other groups at their choice. The examination in religion may be dispensed with by candidates who refuse to take it on conscientious grounds. In the subject-matter and methods examination, candidates must show familiarity with the *Suggestions for the Curricula of Elementary Schools* and a knowledge of the most important methods of instruction in five subjects as well as ability to determine the educative value of curriculum materials and to discuss them in relation to the ages and maturity of pupils at various levels and to the needs of a locality or the nation as a whole. The test, in other words, is not so much verbal mastery of content, but professional judgment and standards of application.

The results of an examination are determined by a candidate's performance — not only in the subjects in which he is examined and in the essay, but also on his record in other subjects as reported by his instructors. Success or failure is decided by vote of the whole committee; the grades are "excellent," "good," "satisfactory," "failed." Those who pass the examination receive a certificate which entitles them to appointment as probationary teachers.

Second teachers' examination. Permanent appointment is dependent upon the successful passing of the second teachers' examination (*Zweite Lehrerprüfung*), the regulations for which were issued on June 25, 1928, to become effective on April 1, 1929. The requirements for permanent appointment in existence before the new regulations were issued were continued until March 21, 1930; under these requirements teachers could obtain permanent appointment by successful participation in a study course (*Arbeitsgemeinschaft*) for two years. The new regulations require teachers to present themselves for the second examination after from two to four years of active employment. Each applicant must submit the certificate of the first teachers' examination and a full account of his professional career and further study; to the application is added a report from the inspector (*Schulrat*) of his district. The county school board decides on the admission of a candidate to the examination, which is conducted by a committee consisting of a county educational official (*Regierungsrat*) or inspector as chairman, the inspector of the candidate's school, a member of the teachers college faculty appointed by the Minister of Education, and an elementary school teacher or principal selected from a list prepared with the advice of the district teachers' council (*Bezirkslehrerrat*); the principal of the candidate's school may be present at the examination. If the examination includes religious instruction, the examiner must be of the same denomination as the candidate; if the candidate is a woman, the examining committee must include a woman.

The examination, which takes place in the candidate's school, is wholly professional and practical. The committee observes the instruction of the teacher in his own class in at least two subjects which must be selected from religion, German, arithmetic or geometry, history, civics, geography, and natural science. The instruction observed is followed by a discussion in which the teacher is expected to show a scientific grasp of principles of teaching and education and the administrative regulations for schools. The results of the examination are marked "excellent," "good," "satisfactory," or "failed." Teachers who fail twice in the examination or who do not present themselves for the examination within five years after passing the first teachers' examination are dismissed from the service.

Training in service. The period of probation required before appointment is made permanent serves as a stimulus to further study. But beyond this, German elementary school teachers have always been active in continuing their education, both academic and professional, largely through their own organizations. Study groups (*Arbeitsgemeinschaften*) have increased in number as a result of the greater professional freedom which has been given to teachers, particularly in the development of curricula and courses of study and in the advancement and encouragement of experimental schools. The teachers colleges have also assumed a certain responsibility for the further training of teachers who return to their own institutions for conferences and lecture courses. Similar provision is made by local authorities and by the *Zentralinstitut für Erziehung und Unterricht*[1] in Berlin which has become an active agency in this work; it arranges exhibits, demonstrations, conferences and courses, and conducts study tours in Germany and abroad. Finally, the increased participation of teachers in the administration of their own schools and of education in general through their school, district, and regional councils has been an effective measure in developing both their status and their professional consciousness.

Status of teachers. Teachers are civil servants even though they may not be appointed directly by the State. Their position as civil servants does not, however, diminish in any way their rights and duties as citizens. They may belong to any organizations, political or otherwise, that they please, may participate actively in party politics, and may hold political office. A large number of them are today found as members of local councils and as representatives in the state and federal Parliaments. Their status from this point view is likely to continue to improve as more teachers enter the service after a period of preparation in the teachers colleges.

[1] See Chapter V.

Salaries. As public employees teachers receive salaries which are determined by a federal salary law for the whole country, even though the salaries are not paid by the Federal Government. The amount of basal salary paid depends upon the salary group or category to which they are assigned; there are altogether twelve groups for all public employees. The remuneration of elementary school teachers includes the basal salary, rent indemnity, and allowance for children, and provisions for disability and retirement. The basal salary rises in Prussia from 2800 Mark to 5000 Mark in twenty years from the date of permanent appointment, with four increments of 250 Mark each and six of 200 Mark each. Head teachers and principals receive an additional annual grant ranging from 200 Mark to 1400 Mark, varying with the size of school and number of teachers employed. The rent indemnity, where a house is not provided, varies with the teacher's position and salary and the location of the school, and ranges from 258 Mark to 1152 Mark. The allowance for children is 20 Mark a month for the first two, 25 Mark a month for the next two, and 30 Mark a month for each child beyond the fourth; the allowances are paid for children up to the age of sixteen and may be continued up to twenty-one if the child is engaged in study.

The retiring and disability allowances have been included as part of the remuneration, for, since the system is not contributory, the allowances are technically provided for by deferred payments; that is to say, salaries are reduced by the amount which must be reserved to meet the obligations created by these allowances ultimately. Teachers become eligible to disability allowances after ten years of service and may retire voluntarily at sixty-five. The allowance after ten years of service consists of thirty-five per cent of salary, rising by two per cent annually for each year of service up to twenty-five and thereafter by one per cent of salary up to forty years of service, with a maximum of eighty per cent of final salary. For pension purposes only basal salary and rent indemnity are taken into account. Widows of teachers receive allowances of sixty per cent of the pension which the teacher received if retired or to which he would have been entitled. Children of deceased teachers receive one fifth of the widow's allowance, if she is alive, or one third, if not.

Preparation of teachers in other States. A number of German States have adopted systems of preparing teachers similar to that of Prussia — that is, in teachers colleges or training institutions; among these are Baden, Mecklenburg-Schwerin, Oldenburg, Waldeck, and Bavaria. Other States have not reorganized their systems or have teachers trained in a neighboring State or have adopted a three-year course in affiliation with or as part of the universities. Those which have adopted the affiliated plan are Saxony, Thuringia, Hesse (two-year course), and Brunswick; Anhalt and Lippe use the facilities provided by Thuringia in Jena. Hamburg prepares teachers wholly in the university of that city.

In Saxony the preparation of teachers, following a regulation passed on April 3, 1923, was organized on a three-year basis in part at the University of Leipzig and the Technical University (*Technische Hochschule*) in Dresden and pedagogical institutes (*Pädagogische Institute*) in the two cities. In general, the responsibility of the universities is to provide the courses in general and academic subjects, and of the pedagogical institutes to give the training in the theory and practice of education. Thus, every student in Dresden is expected to take the following courses at the *Technische Hochschule*: history and principles of education, psychology of childhood and adolescence, anthropology and hygiene, German language and literature, government, and one elective subject; eighty of the total of one hundred and eighty semester hours of the three-year course are devoted to these subjects. The arrangement of subjects is somewhat similar at the University of Leipzig, but the amount of time devoted to them is less. The pedagogical institutes in both cases assume the responsibility for the professional preparation in special and general methods, introduction to practical instruction, and training in the skill subjects (art, music, and physical training). As compared with the two-year course in Prussian teachers colleges, the system adopted in Saxony has the obvious advantage of an additional year which furnishes opportunities for the more intensive study of the materials and methods of instruction in the elementary schools, especially in the practica. Observation, demonstration, experiments, research, and some practice teaching take place in the schools belonging to the institutes. Each of the members of the faculty of the institutes is responsible for instruction in the practice schools. In Dresden observation is continued during the first three semesters; actual participation in teaching is provided for usually in local public schools, when the institutes are closed for the summer vacation.

The examination at the close of the course in Saxony includes the preparation of two essays, one on a problem of practical education; two months are allowed for their preparation. The oral examination includes questions on the following major subjects: education, school management, school organization and law, and special methods on two elementary school subjects, philosophy, history of education, and psychology; the minor subjects are anthropology and hygiene and one elective subject. Saxony does not require a second examination for final appointment.

Elementary school teachers in Hamburg receive their preparation wholly in the School of Education of the University under a law issued on December 20, 1926. The length of the course is three years and it includes the following main divisions of study: education, philosophy, and psychology; elective academic or skill subject, art, remedial education, and observation and practice. Observation, participation, and practice are provided for in the demonstration school of the School of Education. Upon the observation and demonstrations in this school are based the study of methods of instruction in the subjects of the elementary school curriculum. More intensive practice teaching is arranged for in the public schools of the city under the supervision of its teachers; it is continued for six weeks between the third and fourth semesters and is followed by a second period between the fifth and sixth semesters of four weeks' participation in social welfare work and educational activities for children and adolescents. The first examination at the end of the course for eligibility to appointment as a probationary teacher includes: (1) the preparation of two essays, one in education and one in an elective subject; (2) written examinations on education, philosophy, and psychology, and one other subject selected from the elementary school curriculum or any other academic subject; (3) an oral examination on the same subjects as in the written test; and (4) a practical examination at the choice of the examiners in teaching, physical training, fine arts, or natural science. Permanent appointment is based on a second examination taken after at least three years of school experience; this examination is practical in character and is similar to the second examination in Prussia, with the additional requirement that candidates must demonstrate their ability in the teaching of physical training, drawing, music, manual training (for men), and sewing and household arts (for women). Opportunities for further study are provided in a special institute for the training of teachers in service.

Conclusion. Three forces have been influential in determining the present reform in the preparation of teachers in Germany. Discontent with their status, economic and political, under the Imperial régime contributed very largely to the demand for a type of professional preparation which would improve it in both aspects. Undoubtedly the narrow, even though effective, character of the training given in the old normal schools justified this discontent. The Revolution and the realization that its success and the development of a new national spirit which would give real expression to the best in German culture led to the recognition that the schools must be given a new orientation the responsibility for whose success would devolve upon the teachers. Inevitably the traditional form of training was inadequate for the assumption of such a responsibility. From another point of view the development of education as an independent science or field of knowledge, with its own content and methods, inspired the plea for autonomy in education (*Eigengesetzlichkeit der Erziehung*), a movement for professional freedom and self-determination, which could only be realized by a new system of professional preparation more nearly akin to the spirit underlying the preparation for other liberal professions. Those who feared that the increased demands, both in the length and cost of the preparation which has been adopted, would diminish the number of suitable candidates failed to take into account the inspiration of the youth movement (*Jugendbewegung*) and the missionary spirit which influenced German youth immediately after the War.[1] Actually far more candidates present themselves for admission to the teachers colleges of various types than can be accepted. To some extent, but not wholly, this may be attributed to the intense economic struggle which confronts youth everywhere, but more particularly in Central Europe.

Whatever the causes, Germany has taken the lead in adopting for the preparation of teachers for elementary schools the highest standards to be found anywhere in the world. The nature of these standards may bring about a change in the social group from which

[1] For the change which has taken place and the intensely narrow spirit of nationalism which is now sweeping Germany the intransigent attitude of some foreign powers, which have produced the present situation, rather than the domestic situation itself, must bear the responsibility.

teachers have in the past been recruited — the rural and artisan classes; but opportunities are already being provided to retain these by means of scholarships and other financial aid. The problem is whether teachers, trained in the new system, will be willing to serve, even during the probationary period, in the small rural school. The German answer has always been that physicians and the clergy have always been ready to settle in rural areas; the advanced training will probably not prove a deterrent, but rather a stimulus to the young teacher to contribute to the rebuilding of his country. The serious crisis through which Germany is now passing and which has already compelled the authorities to close a number of teachers colleges postpones for many years the opportunity of estimating the results of the reform, which is of supreme interest for all interested in education. The experiment means more than an improvement in the professional preparation of elementary school teachers; it means, with the gradual approximation of the time spent on preparation to that of secondary school teachers, the ultimate development of a single teaching profession, prepared according to the various functions which it is called upon to perform.

4. ITALY

History. The reform of education following the Fascist Revolution inevitably affected the status and the preparation of elementary school teachers. A reorganization in this field had long been overdue, for it had been the subject of a special investigation in 1918. The preparation of teachers for elementary schools had been provided for under the Casati Law of 1859 in separate normal schools for boys at the age of sixteen and girls at the age of fifteen. The training was mainly a continuation of the work of the elementary school with an emphasis on practice teaching in the second and third years of the three-year course. In 1896 the course of study was modified by the Gianturco Law which required the organization of practice and infant schools in connection with the normal schools and introduced a final examination for a teacher's certificate, which was a condition of eligibility for the competitions for appointment to vacancies. In 1911 a two-year course of training for elementary school teachers was instituted in *ginnasi* with four-year courses. In 1912 the *Unione Magistrale Nazionale* (National Teachers Union) at its Congress in Bologna recommended a complete reorganization of the system and the establishment of institutions with a seven-year course, five to be devoted to general education and two to professional preparation. Beyond this, the Union advocated the creation of facilities for further training of teachers in service. In the following year the Ministry of Public Instruction appointed a committee to consider a number of problems in the preparation of teachers: how to meet the demands of general and professional training; the length of the course as a whole and the distribution of time between the two parts; and curricula and courses of study. The recommendations of the committee were identical with those of the Union. A reform along these lines was proposed in a bill introduced by Minister Credaro in 1914: the whole course was to be seven years in length following elementary education; the first five years were to be devoted to general culture and the last two to a review of general education with special reference to the elementary schools, and to the study of education and social ethics with practice teaching; in the last year the study of agriculture, hygiene, and physical training were to be included. Nothing came of this plan, which was again modified in 1918 in a proposal to organize a seven-year course, separate for men and women, the first six years to be devoted to general education and the last year to professional preparation.

During the same period there had been established two higher normal schools, in Rome and Florence, to provide opportunities for women teachers who wished to prepare for positions as principals of schools; similar opportunities had also been created in schools of education for men in the universities and in special courses elsewhere for advanced study (*corsi di perfezionamento*). The characteristics of both stages of training were the same; the institutions were virtually isolated from the main currents of education and devoted closely to preparation for the elementary schools; in both the greatest difficulty was the problem of adjusting the claims of general culture studies and of professional preparation.

The problem, on the whole, was not difficult when considered from this point of view or in the light of the character of elementary education. Italy had long been under the influence of positivist philosophy and in education this meant an emphasis on the acquisition of an organized body of knowledge. In practice this emphasis resulted in memorization, formalism, and bookishness. On the professional side the task was to prepare teachers with a thorough command of methods and techniques. The same consequence followed also from the introduction of the Herbartian principles.

THE PRESENT SYSTEM

The new orientation. The Gentile reform, which emphasized humanism and the awakening of the spirit, the cult of personality through activity and sympathetic insight on the part of the teacher into the meaning of the Italian tradition and of humanism, on the one hand, and into the inner urge of the pupils for spiritual expression and activity, on the other, was not compatible with a methodology which stressed mechanisms and artificial devices as something extrinsic both to subject-matter and to the personality of the pupils. In other words, the Gentile reform was in essence opposed to the traditional practices in preparing teachers. The leading exponent of the new approach was Professor Ernesto Codignola, Director of the *R. Istituto Superiore di Magistero* in Florence, who had for many years been a critic of the normal schools and the principles upon which their work was based. Education, according to Codignola, is a spiritual process and anything which stands between the teacher and the pupil disturbs this process. Methods tend to dominate and to mechanize the spirit and to reduce instruction to mere routine. Hence the best preparation of the teacher lies, not in the study of principles of education and of methods of teaching, but in the thorough penetration of the humanistic spirit. On the professional side the best preparation of the teacher is provided by the study of philosophy, of which education is a part, and whose function it is to illustrate the nature of the spirit and the process of its development. Methods are only meaningful, not as external devices, but as the expression of a spiritual form, constantly active and constantly changing as conditions, pupils, or environment change. Not mastery of methods nor even an encyclopedic command of knowledge alone makes the good teacher, but an active mind, a firm will, an exquisite feeling for art, and consciousness of the harmonious and universal in man. Applied to the problem of preparing teachers, this means a different approach; the problem is not what knowledge or methods are necessary for the teacher, but what is best adapted to giving him that consciousness of his own and the pupils' humanity. Not didactic formulas, but how to reach the inner souls of the pupils and how to respect the human spirit in them, is the lesson that the future teacher must learn. This lesson can, in Codignola's opinion, be acquired only by thorough study of the humanities and of philosophy which seeks to interpret them in the light of universals.[1]

The reorganization of the preparation of elementary school teachers followed the principles advocated by Codignola. All existing institutions — the normal schools and courses in *ginnasi*, the *corsi di perfezionamento*, and the schools of education in universities — were abolished, and were replaced by new institutions (*istituti magistrali*) as a part of the secondary school systems. Institutions of this type may only be established by government decree. Pupils, boys and girls, are admitted on completing five years of the elementary school at the minimum age of ten and on passing an entrance examination. The length of the course in the *istituti magistrali* is seven years, divided into two periods of four and three years each. Transfer from the lower to the upper section of the course is based on an entrance examination.

The curriculum of the *istituti magistrali* is wholly academic. The subjects and the weekly time-distribution are given in the accompanying tables.

TIME-SCHEDULE
Istituto Magistrale

SUBJECTS	LOWER COURSE			
	I YEAR (hours)	II YEAR (hours)	III YEAR (hours)	IV YEAR (hours)
Italian language	8	4	4	4
Latin language	..	6	6	6
History and geography	4	2	2	2
Mathematics	3	2	2	3
Foreign language	..	4	4	4
Drawing	3	2	2	2
Music and singing	2	2	2	2
Musical instrument *	(2)	(2)	(2)	(2)
Total	20	22	22	23

* Optional.

The *istituto magistrale* does not differ in content or methods of instruction or in organization and administration from other schools at the secondary level.[2] The only connection between this institution and the obvious purpose for which it is created is to be found in the discussion of educational theory in the philosophy course. Every

[1] See *La Riforma della cultura magistrale* (1917); *Il Problema dell' Educazione nazionale in Italia* (1925). [2] See Chapter VIII.

PREPARATION OF ELEMENTARY TEACHERS

TIME-SCHEDULE

Istituto Magistrale

SUBJECTS	UPPER COURSE		
	I YEAR (hours)	II YEAR (hours)	III YEAR (hours)
Italian language and literature	4	5	4
Latin language and literature	5	4	4
Philosophy and education	4	5	6
History	3	4	4
Mathematics and physics	3	4	4
Natural science, geography and hygiene	3	2	3
Drawing	2	1	1
Music and singing	2	1	1
Musical instrument *	(2)	(2)	(2)
Total	26	26	27

* Optional.

institute is required to have associated with it a kindergarten, or *casa dei bambini*, primarily for purposes of observation and not for practice teaching.

At the end of the whole course candidates must pass an examination in all the subjects of the upper section. The oral examination in philosophy and education which are characteristic of the normal institute covers the following program:

Knowledge and evaluation of children's literature.

Selections from the history of schools and of educational theory.

The æsthetic problem and teaching of art. The candidate must show a knowledge of at least one of the following works: Plato, *Republic*, X; Aristotle, *Poetics* (extracts); Vico, *Scienza nuova* (extracts referring to the problem of art); Kant, *Critique of Judgment* and *Æsthetic Judgment*; Croce, *Breviario di Estetica*.

The problem of religion and the teaching of religion. The candidate must show a knowledge of at least one of the following works: Plato, *Euthyphro*; Aristotle, *Metaphysics*, XII; Cicero, *De Natura Deorum* (Part I or II); Saint Paul's *Epistles*; Vico, *Scienza nuova* (Providence); Mazzini, *Idee religiose* (extracts); Gioberti, *Riforma Cattolica* (extracts); Royce, *The Problem of Christianity*.

The problem of consciousness and the teaching of science, based on a knowledge of at least one of the following works: Aristotle, *Organon*; Descartes, *Méditations* (extracts); Locke, *On the Understanding* (extracts); Leibniz, *Nouveaux Essais*; Kant, *Critique of Pure Reason* (extracts) and *Prolegomena*; Galluppi, *Saggio* (extracts); Rosmini, *Esposizione del suo Sistema*; Spaventa, *Logica e Metaphysica* (Part I).

The moral problem and moral instruction, based on a knowledge of at least one of the following works: Aristotle, *Nichomachean Ethics* (extracts); New

Testament; Spinoza, *Ethics* (Part III); Kant, *Critique of Practical Reason* and *Metaphysics of Morals*; Rosmini, *Principi di Scienza morale* and *Storia dei Sistemi*.

Discussion of an educational classic selected from the following: Comenius, *Great Didactic; Ratio Studiorum*; Locke, *Thoughts on Education*; Basedow, *Appeal to the Friends of Humanity*; Vico, *De Nostri Temporis Studiorum Ratione* (extracts); Rousseau, *Emile*; Kant, *On Pedagogy*; Cuoco, *Pagine scelte*; Pestalozzi (selected writings); Froebel, *Education of Man* and selected writings; Fichte, *The Vocation of Man* and *Addresses to the German Nation*; Schelling, *Lectures on the Method of Academic Studies*; Necker de Saussure, *L'Education Progressive*; Richter, *Levana*; Rosmini, *Del Principio supremo*.

Discussion of a modern or contemporary educational work: Capponi, Lambruschini, Gioberti, Mazzini, De Sanctis, Gabelli, Ardigo, James, E. Caird, Arnold, Laberthonnière, Boutroux, etc.

According to the regulations the aim of the oral examination is not so much to test the knowledge acquired by the candidates as their ability to discuss questions and problems from the philosophical point of view. When it is recalled that pupils begin the study of philosophy and education at the age of fourteen or fifteen, that they are examined at the age of seventeen or eighteen, and that the duration of the oral examination is but thirty minutes, some doubt may be expressed of the virtue of such a course. The pupils acquire a certain glibness in discussing theories and principles, wide in range, but, although the use of textbooks and compendia is forbidden, the feeling cannot be resisted that the glibness is the result of instruction by the teacher rather than "inner penetration of the spirit" of the sources read.

Appointment. Candidates who pass the final examination in the *istituti magistrali* are given the *abilitazione all' insegnamento elementare* or *abilitazione magistrale*, a certificate of aptitude as elementary teachers, which is the minimum qualification required, not for appointment, but for the competition for appointment, in an elementary school. Vacancies are advertised each year by the *provveditore agli studi* or regional superintendent of public education or by the councils of autonomous communities. Candidates must submit with their applications the certificate, a statement of physical fitness, proof of citizenship, and testimonials of character; if men, they must be over eighteen years of age, and, if women, over seventeen years of age. They are then submitted to a public competitive examination (*concorso pubblico*) conducted by commissions appointed either by the superintendent or the autonomous community which may delegate the conduct of the examination to the superintendent. The examination consists of a written essay on an educational problem and an oral test based largely on the programs of the *istituto magistrale*. On the basis of the results the candidates are arranged in order of merit and the best are assigned to the available vacancies in boys', girls', or mixed schools; the highest on the list have, of course, a certain preference in the choice of a position.

After obtaining their first appointments, teachers must serve a probationary period of three years as *maestri straordinari*, corresponding to the French *instituteurs stagiaires*; at the end of this period they are appointed on the favorable report of the inspectors as *maestri ordinari*, the French *instituteurs titulaires*. No teacher may transfer from one school to another unless he has spent two years in the same post; exceptions are made only for reasons of health or for family considerations.

The line of advancement of elementary school teachers is within the field of elementary education itself. The *maestro elementare* may become a *direttore didattico* or supervisor and then an *ispettore scolastico*. Promotion is secured by further study in the *Istituti Superiori di Magistero*, three maintained by the State in Rome, Florence, and Messina, and three private in Milan, Turin, and Naples. The Royal Higher Teachers Colleges offer two-year courses preparing for positions as *direttori didattici*, and four-year courses preparing teachers of literature in secondary schools, of philosophy and education in normal institutes, and inspectors. Admission is secured by competitive examination which is the same for all courses. The examination is written and oral; the written test includes an essay in philosophy and education, or history or Italian literature and a translation from Latin; the oral test is on philosophy and education, Italian and Latin language and literature, and history and geography. The annual fees are 350 lire for tuition and 140 lire for the examinations in the four-year course; additional fees are charged for the entrance examination, matriculation, contribution to the school fund, the examination for the diploma, and the diploma (445 lire for the four-year course and 210 lire for the two-year course). The Government each year selects by competition forty teachers who are assigned to the two-year course and retain their salaries and positions during their period of study; one fourth of these teachers are selected from the new provinces. In addition, fees are remitted wholly or partially to candidates who rank highest in the competitive examination and can prove the need of financial assistance. Finally, the Minister of Public Instruction awards a number of scholarships annually to students recommended by the administrative council of each institute.

The curriculum for the two-year course leading to the *diploma di direzione didattica* includes the following subjects: Italian and Latin language and literature, education, German language and literature (two-year courses in each), and history, geography, philosophy, elements of public law and educational legislation, school hygiene, and foreign literature (one-year course in each). The diploma awarded by examination at the end of the course is a certificate of eligibility for the competitive examination by which the *direttori didattici* are selected each year up to the number of available vacancies. The minimum age for appointment is thirty; candidates must have had at least three years of teaching experience. The function of the *direttori didattici* is in the main supervisory; they assign teachers to their classes, issue time-schedules and programs of work, arrange for examinations, and in general supervise instruction and progress in the schools, reporting each year to the inspectors of their districts; in the larger areas they may be assisted by sub-directors.

The four-year course for teachers of philosophy and education and for inspectors includes in the first two years the following subjects: Italian and Latin language and literature, philosophy, education, and German language and literature (two-year courses in each) and English language and literature, history, geography, elements of public law and educational legislation, and school hygiene (one-year course in each). The subjects of the last two years are Latin language and literature (two-year course) and philosophy and education (one-year course in each) and at least two other courses selected from the subjects of the first two years and pursued for one year. The final examination leads to the award of the *diploma di pedagogia e filosofia* or the *abilitazione all'ispettorato scolastico*, both of which are only certificates of eligibility for the competitive examinations for appointment. Candidates for inspectorships must be *direttori didattici* with two years of experience or teachers with fifteen years of experience; appointments are divided equally between the two groups; one fifth of the inspectorships are reserved for women.

Status of teachers. Before appointment teachers, like all public officials, must take the following oath:

I swear loyalty to the King and his successors, to observe the Constitution and other laws of the State faithfully, to fulfil all the duties of my office diligently and with zeal for the public good and the interests of the Administration, scrupulously guarding the secret of office and conducting myself, in public and private, in accordance with the dignity of my position. I swear that I do not nor will belong to associations or parties whose activity cannot be reconciled with the duties of my office. I swear to carry out all my duties to the sole end of the inseparable good of the King and my country.

As recently as 1928 teachers were not required to be declared Fascists, but a strong hint had already been given by Mussolini in one of his addresses (*Discorso all'Augosteo*) to the effect that teachers were expected to support the Fascist régime (see p. 462). After a number of dismissals for political reasons, the question whether teachers were or were not Fascists ceased to be of importance. Many of the teachers are members of the Party and many are officers of the *Balilla* organization.

After appointment as *ordinari*, teachers enjoy permanent tenure, but are subject to dismissal for incompetence or misconduct, with the right of appeal to the disciplinary council of the regional superintendent (*provveditore agli studi*) and beyond it to the Higher Council of Public Instruction. The organization is thus hierarchical with responsibility fixed by law at each stage. The importance of this organization, which is the result of the Gentile reform, can only be understood in the light of the conditions which prevailed in the profession in the period preceding it. Insubordination, lack of discipline, frequent and readily condoned absences, and professional incompetence, as indicated by the examination of pupils and in the competitions for advancement, had produced a state of chaos; efforts at improvement led to strikes among the teachers. The situation was immediately improved by the removal of the incompetent and superannuated, by a reform in the system of preparation, by the introduction of a hierarchical system, and above all by an amelioration of the salary conditions, which were probably more responsible for the unrest and discontent than any other cause.

Under the Gentile reform the salaries of elementary school teachers were almost immediately doubled; from a minimum of 3000 lire a year and a maximum of 5600 lire they were raised to a minimum of

5600 lire and a maximum of 9500 lire. Since 1923 salaries have been further increased to a minimum of 5900 lire, rising in twenty-eight years to a maximum of 10,000 lire, with a supplement for active service ranging from 1300 to 1800 lire a year and an addition of 800 lire a year for service in schools with double sessions. No provision is made for teachers' homes or for rent or other indemnities as in France. Local communes, particularly in rural areas, may provide homes, but teachers are not entitled to such a benefit as of right.

A pension fund (*monte-pensioni*) for elementary school teachers was established in 1878; after periodical revisions the regulations governing the system were codified by Royal Decree of March 23, 1931 (*Regio Decreto*, 23 Marzo, 1931, No. 707). The system has been placed under the supervision of the Administrative Council of the Loan and Trust Fund and the State Insurance Associations. The cost of administration of the pension fund is provided for annually by appropriations granted on the recommendation of the Minister of Finance. The fund is made up of contributions paid by the teachers in elementary schools and their employers (the State, communes, or other recognized educational corporations) and gifts and bequests. The decree regulates the nature of the investments and provides for quinquennial valuations. Teachers are required to pay into the fund eight per cent of their salaries annually, which is duplicated by their employers. Disability and retirement allowances are paid out of the fund accumulated at compound interest. Teachers may be retired on account of ill-health with an allowance after ten years of service or on reaching the age of sixty after the same period of service; a retiring allowance may be obtained on reaching the age of sixty after twenty years of service or after forty years of service without any age requirement. Disability allowances consist of three fourths of the allowance to which a teacher would be entitled if eligible for retirement; the retiring allowances consist of the annuities purchasable with the accumulated contributions standing to a teacher's account, but limited to a maximum equal to the average of the salary received in the last three years of service and raised to certain prescribed minima based on the length of service. Provision is made under the same scheme for the protection of widows and orphans of teachers who die in service or after retirement. A somewhat different system exists for the retirement of administrative officials (inspectors and supervisors), who may be retired at the age of sixty after twenty years of service or after forty years of service without any conditions as to age. The retiring allowance in such cases consists of one fortieth of the first 4000 lire of the average salary received in the last three years of service and an addition of one sixtieth of the balance of the average salary over 4000 lire for each year of service, with a maximum allowance of four fifths of the average salary.

Conclusion. The new Italian system of preparing teachers for the elementary school, determined as it is by the idealistic philosophy underlying the whole reform of education, is frankly a challenge to the traditional and current practice. Sound in insisting on a broad cultural and general background for every teacher, the complete negation of the value of professional training raises many doubts of the ultimate success of the system. That there is much truth in the view that overemphasis on methodology tends to lead to sterility and mechanization cannot be denied, but it is questionable whether the difficulty can be solved by talking about education and avoiding the practical induction of the young teacher into its conduct. The result in practice will be that Italian teachers will secure their initiation into practice at the expense of the pupils entrusted to them during their three years of probation with such guidance as they may receive from *direttori didattici* and *ispettori scolastici* — a reactionary step which has in it the inherent danger that the teacher may become more mechanical and formal than without any professional preparation. This is particularly serious at a time when the essence of the elementary school reform is to impose greater responsibility upon the teacher in framing courses of study adapted to the local environment and in conducting instruction on activity principles. In other words, in seeking to make the teacher free, as the new system of preparation does, it fails on the practical side to give him that professional training which alone can make him free.

The reform has, however, achieved one notable accomplishment — a change in the status of elementary school teachers and of elementary education by incorporating both as essential parts of the great national Revolution. Incorporation of the normal institutes into the secondary school system, improved salaries, opportunities for advancement, better discipline, and more freedom have already exercised their influence. Beyond this, a new sphere of activity has been opened for elementary school teachers in the service of educating adolescents and adults outside of regular school hours and in participating in the national movement as officers in the *Balilla* organization. The new spirit is perhaps more marked in smaller and remote corners of Italy where the rural school teachers seem to be inspired with missionary zeal; in the cities the opportunity provided for experimentation produces the same result. In both cases, however, it is doubtful whether the new spirit can yet be attributed to the new system of teacher-preparation; the new spirit was in fact already present under the influence of the cultural awakening which had begun in Italy many years before the Revolution.

5. RUSSIA

The preparation of teachers in the Soviet Union is dominated by two main objectives. The first is to secure teachers who are loyal to the existing political ideology; the second is to reorganize the character of the preparation in such a way as to promote the close relationship between education and the economic goals which are to be attained. In the pre-Revolutionary system elementary school teachers had been trained in normal schools of the traditional type and in girls' *gymnasia*. Through the organization in 1905 of the All-Russian Teachers' Union, in which membership was open to teachers in all grades of schools and universities, a strong professional spirit had begun to be developed, even though there was no great improvement in the material conditions of teachers in elementary schools. The part which education was to play in the social reconstruction of the Revolution was immediately recognized, and it was with this in mind that Lenin declared that "We must raise our teacher to a height such as he had not attained and never will be able to attain in a bourgeois society." Despite this declaration the conditions of the teaching profession, socially and materially, continued to be unimproved until the past year.

The preparation of teachers was not reorganized until 1924, when, instead of being assigned to separate institutions, it was provided in the technicums or in the last two years of the nine-year secondary schools. In these institutions are prepared teachers for pre-schools, first grade schools, and for lower schools for political enlightenment. The character of the preparation is thus determined by the predominantly vocational bias of the institutions in which it is given. Admission to the pedagogical technicum is based on the completion of the seven-year school, which usually takes place at about the age of fifteen. The length of the course is four years. Each pedagogical technicum has an industrial or agricultural bias, determined by the predominant local conditions. As contrasted with the academic and professional emphases found elsewhere and with the movement for autonomy in education, the preparation of teachers in the Soviet Union is subordinated to the aims of the unified labor school and of participation in socially useful labor. There is, in other words, no break in gauge between the preparation of the teacher and the aims of education, which are determined by the needs of the workers. This synthesis is emphasized all the more because the teacher is expected to be a leader in the cultural work of his locality. Labor thus becomes the center in the scheme of teacher-training as it is in education. Accordingly, the future teacher is expected to acquire a certain amount of skill whether in a trade or in agriculture, for it is from variety of practical experience that his influence will be determined. Beyond this, the studies must include the scientific studies which are fundamental to an understanding of the nature of the child and of the educative process (anatomy, physiology, biology, pedology, and psychology), and the social sciences, with an emphasis on Marxian philosophy and dialectic materialism.

The first two years of the four-year course in the pedagogical technicum are devoted to general and professional studies, visits to all types of educational institutions, and a study of the educational systems in the Soviet Republics. The last two years are more intensively professional in character and are devoted to the study of social science, methods, and practice, with participation in the work of the locality (industrial or agricultural), and to training in conducting campaigns against illiteracy, work with homeless children, children's clubs and libraries, and participation in youth movements. At a recent meeting of the Central Committee of the Communist Party (reported in *Izvestia*, September, 1931) it was resolved that all teachers be required to learn the fundamentals of production in factories, soviet farms, machine tractor stations, and collective farms, and the methods of the work of polytechnization. Increasingly the statement is repeated that the teacher is not only the chief agent in the educative process, but the organizer and leader of his community.

The curriculum and time-distribution for the various subjects of the four-year course in a pedagogical technicum with an agricultural bias in the Russian Republic are shown in the accompanying table. (See opposite page.)

The courses in the pedagogical sections of the nine-year secondary schools, which are given in the eighth and ninth years, are similar in general to those in the first two years of the pedagogical technicum, the major part of the time being devoted to professional studies and practice.

Status of teachers. The All-Russian Teachers' Union was dissolved early in the history of the Revolution and reorganized, but without restoring the confidence of the authorities in the teachers. That many of the older teachers (and the majority had inevitably been trained under the old régime) did not sympathize actively with the Revolution is certain. About 1924 the Union was reorganized as the Educational Workers' Union, including all workers in public education, students, school medical officers, clerks and janitors, and was made a constituent part of the General Workers' Union. In 1925 the Educational Workers' Union declared its loyalty to the Communist Party and decided to throw in its lot with the workers in the construction of the new life and the new order. That suspicion is not altogether allayed was indicated at the conference of the Central Committee of the Communist Party (referred to above) which urged all members to take an interest in the schools and to supervise the teachers, especially those of the social and political disciplines; the Central Committee of Komsomols was at the same time encouraged to select candidates for the teaching profession from trustworthy Pioneers.

Materially the conditions of teachers continued without improvement until 1931, when it was decided by the Council of People's Commissars in Russia to raise the existing salaries by twenty-five to thirty per cent and to extend to teachers the privilege of purchasing provisions and merchandise at the same rates as workers. Salaries, the same for men and women, are established in five zones and vary with the cost of living, and the grade of school. In 1927–28 elementary teachers in rural areas received about 46 roubles and in cities 54 roubles a month; in 1932 salaries were raised to 90 roubles a month, a

CURRICULUM AND TIME-DISTRIBUTION IN THE PEDAGOGICAL TECHNICUM

Subjects	Number of Hours per Week		Subjects	Number of Hours per Week	
	I year	II year		III year	IV year
Mathematics	4	4	Theory of evolution	3	..
Physics	3	3	History of the class struggle	3	..
Chemistry	6	6	Economic policy	2	..
Natural science			Constitution	1	..
Agriculture	2	2	Historical materialism	..	3
Vernacular	5	5	Environmental study	1	..
Foreign language	2	2	Foreign language	2	2
History of the class struggle	2	2	Pedology	4	..
Economic geography	3	..	Problems of the organization of instruction by complexes	1	2
Political economy	..	2	Methods of the vernacular	2	2
Activity instruction *	3	3	Methods in arithmetic	2	2
Drawing	2	2	Methods in nature study	2	2
Music and singing	2	2	Methods in social sciences	1	2
Physical education	2	2	Methods in activity instruction *	2	1
Introduction to pedology	2	3	Methods in drawing	2	1
Educational system of the R.S.F.S.R.	2	2	Methods in singing	2	1
			Methods in physical education	1	1
			Pedagogical practice	6	13
			Pedological practice	..	2
			Political enlightenment		2
Total	40	40	Total	37†	36†

* It is not clear, from the use of the term *Arbeitsunterricht* employed in the report from which this table is taken (see note following), whether it refers to manual instruction or the activity principle.
† The totals given in the last two columns are 41 and 40 respectively in the publication of the People's Commissariat for Education in the R.S.F.S.R., *Die Volksbildung in der Russischen Sozialistischen Föderativen Sowjetrepublik*, p. 34 (Moscow, 1926).

rouble being worth about 50 cents. Teachers in the first grade schools are required to teach twenty-four hours a week; in the second grade schools eighteen hours a week, with additional compensation for additional work. Lodgings are provided for teachers in villages; unemployment benefits and medical care are provided for all; married women may retain their positions and two months' leave of absence are granted for childbirth. Teachers, like workers, enjoy special concessions for the education of their children, may retire on a non-contributory pension after twenty-five years of service, and are entitled, like workers, to the privilege of purchasing supplies and of using clubs and rest-houses.

The Educational Workers' Union, to which all engaged in public education must belong, is supported by contributions from the members of two per cent of salary, and has a membership of 800,000. All education bills and plans for curricula and courses of study, which are drawn up by the Education Department (*Narkompros*), are presented to the Union for suggestions and final approval; its advice is sought in the appointment of principals, and the People's Commissar for Education makes an annual report at the Conference of the Union. The extent of this participation implies, as does the character of the preparation given, that the teacher is expected above all to be a partisan, and not a member of a free profession, which in Soviet ideology would for education be a contradiction in terms. Up to the present the teacher in the Soviet Republics is still far from having attained, from the point of view of professional preparation or of status, the exalted position which Lenin assigned to him.

6. UNITED STATES

History. The great variety of practices and standards which prevail in the educational systems of the United States is nowhere so well illustrated as in the preparation of teachers. Here are reflected the wide divergences which prevail in the economic conditions, the popular attitude to education, the weakness of local control, and the status of teachers. All levels of teacher-preparation are found from high school training classes, county normal schools, and state normal schools to teachers colleges and education departments in colleges and universities. While the educational system was gradually developed during the nineteenth and rapidly expanded during the twentieth century on the principle of equality of opportunity and adaptation to changing social demands, the institutions for the training of teachers, which began to be provided in the third decade of the nineteenth century, continued to maintain an existence almost isolated from the influences which governed the growth of the rest of the system. This was due in the main to two causes: first, the control and administration of education were to a large degree decentralized, and, second, the normal schools, until an adequate supply of secondary education was available, had to perform a dual function in providing both the preliminary academic education and the professional training. To these a third cause, closely associated with the first, might be adduced in the reluctance of the state authorities to enforce basic standards for the certification of teachers, with the result that in some localities teachers were appointed on the basis of simple examinations conducted by the local school committee or on the basis of a variety of certificates granted by several overlapping authorities and valid for terms of different duration from one year to life. Only within the last two decades has there been a concentrated effort to secure some order out of the confused and complicated situation, and to define certain minimum requirements for the preparation of teachers; but, although progress has been made in this direction, the reorganization of the systems of certification has barely been initiated.

The desirability of giving teachers some preparation for the work which they were to undertake began to be advocated in the second decade of the last century, when the establishment of teacher-training institutions began to be urged by James L. Kingsley, William Russell, Samuel R. Hall, Thomas Gallaudet, and James G. Carter. The movement gained momentum in the thirties as a consequence of reports on the Prussian system of teacher-training which were disseminated widely by Charles Brooks, Calvin E. Stowe, and Alexander D. Bache, and particularly by the translation of Cousin's *Report on Public Instruction in Prussia*. To James G. Carter, who was assisted in his efforts by Horace Mann, is due the credit for the establishment of the first state normal school in the country at Lexington, Massachusetts, in 1839. This institution served as a model for other States and in time superseded the practice adopted in New York State in 1827 of training teachers in academies or secondary schools which received special grants for this purpose. Connecticut through the efforts of Henry Barnard established the first state normal school at New Britain in 1850; Michigan followed in 1853 with the opening of the state normal school at Ypsilanti; and even New York State was influenced by the practice of creating independent institutions for the training of teachers in the establishment of the New York State Normal School at Albany in 1843, while retaining for some time the academy system. From these early beginnings the normal school system spread throughout the country. Unfortunately, certification requirements were not made dependent on training, so that the majority of teachers, until within the last twenty years, although certificated, were untrained professionally.

While the normal schools helped to keep alive and to foster the idea of professional preparation for teachers, they were confronted with serious difficulties. The length of the course was unstandardized and even where it was defined many students failed to complete it; the entrance requirements were low, often not more than an elementary education, with the result that the course of training had to include both academic and professional preparation; frequently the academic work consisted of little more than a review of the subjects of the "common school" branches, while the so-called professional courses — principles of education, methods, and practice — consumed a major part of the time. Two traditions were built up during this formative period, which continued almost up to 1910; one was the restriction of academic studies to the subjects of the elementary school; the second was an overemphasis on the professional subjects or techniques.

With the gradual expansion in the supply of high schools after 1905, it became increasingly possible to raise the entrance requirements to normal schools and to demand graduation from high school for admission, a practice which had already been introduced in the New York State Normal College at Albany in 1890 and in Massachusetts in 1894. Beginning in 1908, a definite movement was launched to set up as the minimum period of preparation a two-year course in a normal school following graduation from high school. This standard was urged again in 1920 as the result of an extensive inquiry into the *Professional Preparation of Teachers for American Public Schools* conducted by the Carnegie Foundation for the Advancement of Teachers. Scarcely had this standard begun to be adopted, when, as a result of the improved economic status of teachers, the prosperity of the country, and the expanding program of the elementary school, a new movement was initiated to extend the period of preparation to four years and to convert the normal schools into teachers colleges.

This, the latest movement in the organization and advancement of teacher-preparation, was not new. As long ago as 1879 a paper had been read before the Normal Department of the National Education Association on *Professional Degrees for Teachers*, which were already being granted in several States. The nomenclature of these degrees it is not necessary to discuss here; it was not until after 1900 that some institutions began to expand their courses to four years and to award not only the degree of Bachelor, but that of Master, of Arts. A number of institutions had already adopted the title of college; the Michigan State Normal School at Ypsilanti became the Michigan State Normal College in 1897; Illinois had gone even further when it established its training institution in 1857 as the Illinois State Normal University. The introduction of degrees did not, however, mean the discontinuance of shorter courses in the same institutions. The real significance of the movement was that the teacher-training institutions were entering into competition with the liberal arts colleges and were undertaking the preparation of teachers for high schools as well as for elementary schools. By 1930 a number of States had raised the period of preparation for elementary school certificates awarded on the basis of training from two to three years; a smaller number, including California and New York, required four years of preparation. The direction of the movement for raising normal schools to the status of teachers colleges was defined by the American Association of Teachers Colleges, which was organized in 1917.

The result of all these tendencies is a bewildering variety of practices ranging from high school training to preparation requiring four years of study at the collegiate level. Cutting across the array of practices between these extremes are the certification requirements which have in many States not been adjusted to the systems of training. The situation can, of course, be explained in part by the existence of a large number of small single-teacher schools in which teachers receive low salaries and are under annual contracts of employment only, and in part by the fact that the centralization of educational control in the hands of the state authorities is in its initial stages in many States. There is thus a range of schools from the small single-teacher rural school, with a term of about one hundred and twenty days, to the urban school, elaborately equipped, providing a varied curriculum, employing specialized teachers, and having a term of about two hundred days. The various types and degrees of preparation of teachers are thus determined by economic and social status, by the grade of work, and by the public interest in education.

THE PRESENT SYSTEM

Since there is such a variation in the practices of preparing teachers in the United States, ranging from the high school to the universities, it is impossible to do more than present a general picture.

The outstanding tendency at present, due to the increase in teachers' salaries during the past decade, is the gradual elimination of the lowest types of preparation. The preparation in high schools consists of a few simple courses in education in addition to academic subjects; in the county training classes the major part of the work of the year following, as a rule, graduation from high school is devoted to the study of professional subjects. Teachers prepared in this way secure employment in rural schools of which they are in sole charge, responsible for the work of all the grades.

Since 1920 there has been a marked tendency to set up as the minimum desirable requirement two years of preparation following graduation from the high school. This preparation is given in state, county, and city normal schools, in private normal schools, and in teachers colleges. In 1930 the number of these institutions was as follows: state normal schools, 66; city normal schools, 26; county normal schools, 47; private normal schools, 58; teachers colleges, 134; and private teachers colleges, 6. The current trend is in the direction of a decrease of normal schools of different types and their conversion into teachers colleges, which offer a variety of courses ranging from one to four years. The majority of the teacher-training institutions, except where indicated in their description, are maintained by the state authorities, which meet the greater part of the annual cost of operation by appropriations. Until recently most of the normal schools and teachers colleges were administered by their own governing bodies, a practice still found in twelve States;

the objection to this practice is that it encourages excessive rivalry and competition for appropriations. The defects of this situation have been overcome in many States by placing the institutions concerned directly under the state department of education, as in Alabama, California, Connecticut, Louisiana, Maryland, Massachusetts, New Hampshire, Oklahoma, Tennessee, Vermont, and Virginia; in other States special boards have been created to supervise the preparation of teachers, as in Colorado, Indiana, Maine, Michigan, Minnesota, Nebraska, Texas, and Wisconsin; in thirteen States one board has been established for all state institutions of higher education, including universities, liberal arts colleges, teachers colleges, and normal schools. While these systems of coördinating the preparation of teachers in each State represent a great advance, there is still left the difficulty of adjusting the relations between the teachers colleges and normal schools and the state institutions for higher education, particularly as these are also concerned with the preparation of teachers.

Standardization. Although there have for a long time existed organizations for the consideration of problems affecting institutions for the preparation of teachers, it has only been within the last few years that a concerted effort has been made to define minimum standards for their organization. This task was undertaken and has been promoted by the American Association of Teachers Colleges, which performs the same function as the associations for standardizing secondary schools and colleges. The Association defines as a teachers college a state, municipal, or incorporated private institution which admits students who have completed a high school course, offers at least one four-year unified curriculum devoted to the preparation of teachers, and has the legal right to confer degrees; a normal school is a similar institution offering curricula of two or more years in length, but not leading to a degree. The members of the faculty of such institutions must hold the master's degree or its equivalent. The standards further define the desirable maximum of the number of teaching periods per week, and require the maintenance of a practice school, the provision of adequate library facilities, the appropriate organization of curricula, and the prescription of organized requirements for the award of degrees.

The standards prescribed by the Association represent the direction in which it is desired to move. During the present period of transition many teachers colleges still offer one-, two-, and three-year courses in addition to the four-year course, while many normal schools offer three- as well as two-year courses. This confusion is attributable, however, not merely to the transition stage, but to the fact that certification laws have not yet adjusted their requirements to the new trends, and many institutions undertake to prepare teachers for high schools as well as for elementary. While there is a tendency to define the function of teachers colleges and normal schools, the criticism is still current that they are undertaking more than lies within their province and are thereby in danger of missing the primary objective for which they exist. A few teachers colleges, besides providing courses which lead to the bachelor's degree, are beginning to offer graduate work and to award higher degrees.

The creation of teachers colleges offering four year courses, the increase in salaries, and an oversupply of teachers have rendered it possible to raise the minimum requirement for the certification of elementary school teachers to two years of preparation, as is done in Colorado, Connecticut, Idaho, Indiana, Louisiana, New Jersey, Oregon, Pennsylvania, Utah, and Vermont; three States have raised the requirement to three years — Arizona, Massachusetts, New York, and Washington (to become effective in 1933); California and the District of Columbia (to become effective in 1934) and a few cities, such as New York, require four years of preparation.

Admission requirements. The minimum requirement for admission to normal schools and teachers colleges is graduation from high school. The oversupply of teachers has had the effect of introducing selective methods of admission. These include the requirement that candidates for admission must have had a high record of scholarship in their high schools, or the use of intelligence or standard achievement tests. One State admits candidates by examinations. Others require a personal interview. A health and physical examination, and recommendations and statements of character from high school principals, are required generally. Only nine States demand a declaration of intention to teach. Experiments have been undertaken to devise personality and diagnostic tests of fitness for the teaching profession, but up to the present without any great degree of success. In general, from the scholastic point of view it is claimed that the students entering normal schools and teachers colleges are slightly inferior to those who proceed to liberal arts colleges. From the social point of view the few investigations which have been made indicate that intending teachers are drawn from the homes of skilled and unskilled labor in industrial areas and from farm homes in agricultural areas. Tuition fees are not charged in public institutions for the preparation of teachers; generally matriculation and incidental fees must be paid. The students are themselves responsible for the payment of the cost of board and lodging; they may receive aid for this purpose from loan funds or defray their expenses by "working their way through" the period of preparation.

Curricula. Serious consideration has been given to the problem of curricula in the institutions for the preparation of teachers. While it has always been a subject of discussion, attention was directed to the problem as a result of the publication by the Carnegie Foundation for the Advancement of Teaching of its *Curricula Designed for the Professional Preparation of Teachers*, in 1927, and of its report on the *Professional Preparation of Teachers for American Public schools*, in 1920. The problem is more complicated than in most other countries, not only because most institutions have until recently enjoyed a great deal of independence from any state control, but also because of the practice, which is common, of providing preparation in the same institution for different branches of the educational service. Hence, while the European institutions tend on the whole to provide one type of preparation for elementary school teachers, leaving to special institutions the preparation of teachers of young children, the American normal schools and teachers colleges attempt to prepare teachers for the kindergarten, the kindergarten-primary grades, the primary, intermediate, and upper grades, rural school, junior high school, and senior high school.

The problem became somewhat more complicated with the introduction of three- and four-year courses, for which no precedents existed except in the liberal arts college. The tendency in the four-year courses was to prolong general, liberal education for the first two years and to concentrate on professional preparation in the last two years, a practice which brought the teachers colleges into direct competition with the junior colleges, which have spread rapidly in the last decade. The normal school courses of two years had themselves not developed a sound policy. The development of high schools had by 1920 made it unnecessary for them to stress general or academic preparation; the practice of concentrating on reviews of elementary school subjects had already begun to disappear. Fundamentally the crucial problem, it began to be recognized, particularly after the publication of the reports of the Carnegie Foundation, was not one of choosing between a liberal or general education and professional preparation for the future teacher, or of superimposing professional or liberal courses, but of devising curricula in which the professional needs of the teacher would serve as the integrating nucleus. The preparation of teachers in the United States has suffered, and perhaps still suffers, from an overemphasis on professional subjects divorced from content. Since, however, the teacher's tools are subjects to be used for the attainment of particular ends, it was realized that appropriate professional preparation consists in the professionalization of subject-matter, a principle of which Professor W. C. Bagley has been the outstanding advocate. On the one hand, it is not enough for the teacher to be a master of the subjects which he professes, and on the other to study methods divorced from content is inadequate. The teacher must see the subjects in the light of their place in the development of culture and civilization and from the point of view of the growing child. Professionalization serves to integrate mastery of subject-matter with methods and with practice and gives a functional unity to the preparation of the teacher. It does not, as is sometimes objected, mean a restriction of the academic subjects to the standards needed in the elementary schools, but demands, indeed, a breadth of knowledge and perspective which are not present when academic subjects are taught in separate compartments devoid of any application. The principle of professionalization of subject-matter does more than orient the organization of subjects; it incorporates more directly than ever the utilization of the practice or training school as an essential adjunct in the preparation of teachers for purposes of observation, participation, demonstration, and practice teaching. The simplicity of this principle, which, *mutatis mutandis*, applies equally to preparation for other professions, does not reduce the administrative difficulties involved in the provision of practice schools adequate in size to meet the new place assigned to it. Properly organized, the practice school serves as a point of concentration for the work of normal schools and teachers colleges and provides the best opportunity of eliminating the traditional dualism between academic and professional subjects by directing attention to the main objective of these institutions — the education of the child. This objective may be sometimes forgotten in faculties composed of specialists in academic subjects with little preparation in education and specialists in professional subjects who are apt to overestimate the importance of the technical studies.

This dualism, which has been traditional not only in the United States but also in other countries, is being gradually attacked, although some recent studies, such as that of W. W. Charters and D. Waples in the *Commonwealth Teacher-Training Study* (Chicago, 1929), influenced by the job analysis technique employed in industry, indicate that the solution has not yet been reached. Such studies seek to analyze the duties and traits of teachers, to draft an itemized and detailed list of the activities of teachers, and to rate these in order of importance as a basis for making curricula for teacher-training institutions. Such studies would result in perpetuating the apprenticeship principle of preparing teachers rather than in promoting the professional character of the work.

As at present organized, the curricula of teacher-training institutions include three main divisions, the extent to which they are coordinated depending upon whether the whole task is looked upon from a unitary point of view. These divisions are: (1) academic and cultural subjects (generally English, history, and social sciences, economics, science, and physical training); (2) professional subjects (generally principles of education or teaching, special methods, educational psychology, history of education, and educational methods); and (3) observation, participation, and independent practice. As a rule room is left in most curricula for the election of some subjects by the students. Within this general framework provision is made for functional specialization for various branches of educational service — kindergarten, kindergarten-primary, primary, intermediate or upper grades, and junior or senior high school.

Curricula and courses of study are either prescribed by state authorities or prepared in each institution. In both cases their preparation is entrusted to numerous committees assisted by experts in the preparation of teachers. The principles which serve to guide such committees vary. In some cases they are based on the method of job-analysis — the needs of the area to be supplied, the duties of the teacher, and the traits of teaching success; in others they are more directly adapted to the prevailing curricula and courses of study in schools for which teachers are being prepared; in others again, but less frequently, the whole framework of the curricular organization is inspired by a definite philosophy of education which starts with the needs of the growing child. In the first type there is inherent the danger of emphasizing the "tricks of the trade"; in the second, it is objected that curricula may be adapted too much to the *status quo*; in the third, the aim is to permeate the whole of the curriculum with a philosophy which is to guide the future work of the teacher and give him a certain degree of flexibility and independence. While it is obvious that the third type is the ideal and emphasizes the professional rather than the craftsmanship ideal of teaching, it encounters the difficulty that under the prevailing practices of administration and organization the teacher in the United States is still too much controlled from above — by prescribed curricula and courses of study, supervision, tests of various kinds, and textbooks, all of which involve the danger of creating a gap between the system of preparing teachers and school conditions as they exist.

Whatever the principle upon which the curricula are based, they include academic and professional subjects. The selection of the academic subjects is determined partly by the type of teaching in which the intending teacher plans to specialize and partly by the need of extending his general cultural education. The professional subjects tend to be more closely adapted to the work of the teacher. History of education, which at one time held a commanding position, is gradually being subordinated to other subjects and the emphasis placed more upon recent developments with greater stress on the growth of practice than on theory or philosophy. Philosophy of education is generally postponed to the last year of a four-year course or to the period of post-graduate study. Educational sociology, whose scope is as yet not clearly defined, is as a rule not a required subject. The emphasis is placed upon educational psychology (the growth of the child, individual differences, laws of learning, psychology of various subjects), principles of teaching or general methods, special methods, and classroom management. Generally, a foundation for these studies is laid in a course which is usually called "introduction to teaching" or "introduction to education." In all the subjects more stress is placed upon the practical than the theoretical aspects of education, but on the whole the nature of the content as well as the selection of subjects is determined by the availability of textbooks. Closely linked up with both academic and professional studies are observation and practice in the training or practice schools.

The majority of teacher-training institutions have their own practice schools; others use the local public schools. The practice schools are organized under a director of training and have their own staffs of critic teachers, who serve as demonstrators and advisers of the young teachers in practice. Critic teachers are teachers who have been selected or in many cases have had special training for their positions, which are somewhat better paid than those in the ordinary public schools. The practice schools serve as centers for observation, participation or occasional teaching practice and assistance to the critic teacher, and independent practice. To an increasing extent members of the normal school and teachers college faculties are closely associated both with the work of the practice school and the supervision of the students in their own subjects. The chief difficulty which is always encountered is the problem of securing schools of adequate size for the large number of students usually enrolled. As a consequence a large number of students leave the teacher-training institutions without any practice at all. The amount of practice teaching also varies considerably in different institutions. In 1929–30 the median number of hours of practice was 190 in state normal schools, 270 in city normal schools, 26 in county normal schools, 225 in private normal schools, and 150 in teachers colleges. One result of these variations is the practice of placing young and inexperienced teachers under special supervision during a probationary period; in some cases the supervision is conducted by supervisors in the school system to which the teacher is appointed, in others by members of the faculty in which he was appointed. A few institutions have adopted the practice of conducting special conferences for recent graduates who return for a week to discuss the problems and difficulties which they have encountered during their first year of teaching; their places during the conference are taken by senior students in the institutions where the conference is held.

In the following pages are presented a few samples of curricula in two-, three-, and four-year teacher-training institutions.

Two-Year Curriculum for Primary Teachers, State Teachers College, Fredericksburg, Virginia [1]

First Year

Fall Quarter	Winter Quarter	Spring Quarter *
General art	Art in the elementary grades	Reading and language
Educational psychology	Educational psychology	English fundamentals
English fundamentals	English fundamentals	Gymnasium
Music	Music	History of the United States
Gymnasium	Gymnasium	
Geography of the United States	History of the United States	
One of the following:		
History of education	History of education	History of education
Children's literature	Children's literature	Children's literature
Arithmetic	Arithmetic	Arithmetic

Second Year

Art appreciation	Children's literature	Nature Study
Educational sociology	Oral reading	Citizenship
Tests and measurements	Music appreciation	Geography of Eurasia or Geography of Southern Lands
Supervised teaching	Gymnasium	
Principles of teaching		

* In addition to the subjects listed students may elect courses in Art appreciation, Public school music, or Music appreciation.

In the second year students may elect courses in music or other subjects by permission. The students are divided into three groups, each of which is assigned to teaching practice for one of the three quarters. The only course taken during the period of supervised teaching is that in principles of teaching.

Three-Year Curricula for Kindergarten-Primary, Intermediate and Grammar Grade Teachers State Normal School, Cortland, New York [2]

Semester I	Semester II	Semester III
Introduction to teaching and observation	Educational psychology	Kindergarten theory
Library methods	Literature	Methods of teaching history
Science	Health education	Literature
History of civilization	Oral expression	Methods of teaching geography
Geography	Arithmetic	
	Music	

[1] This institution offers in addition to the curriculum here given, curricula for the grades (two years), elementary teachers, principals, and supervisors, high school teachers, principals and supervisors, commercial education, physical education, music, and home economics (all four-year courses).

[2] The institution also offers three-year courses in physical education, nutrition, and open air classes.

PREPARATION OF ELEMENTARY TEACHERS

SEMESTER I	SEMESTER II	SEMESTER III
Written expression	Educational biology	Methods of teaching reading
Art		Health education
Penmanship		Art
		Special kindergarten-primary methods

SEMESTER IV	SEMESTER V	SEMESTER VI
Principles of education	Specialized psychology	History of education
Educational methods	Sociology	Economics
Methods of teaching arithmetic	Music	Electives
Children's literature	Technique of teaching	Practice teaching
Practice teaching	Art	Methods of teaching penmanship
Music	Practice teaching	
Elective	Modern European history	

The institution has a practice or training school with seven hundred pupils; students are required to spend more than one hundred hours in observation and ten weeks in actual teaching with charge of a class for stated periods each day. The curricula for each of the three groups — kindergarten-primary, intermediate, and grammar grade teachers — are selected from the above list of subjects according to its needs.

FOUR-YEAR COURSE, STATE TEACHERS COLLEGE, GREELEY, COLORADO

The curricula are built upon four principles: (1) the inclusion of a common group of general, cultural, and background courses; (2) the inclusion of a common group of professional courses; (3) the inclusion of a group of courses in each curriculum to give adequate instruction and preparation for a specific teaching job; (4) leaving ample room for individual choices by students so that their education may be suited to their own likes and preferences while preparing them for a definite place in the teaching profession.

The Core Required Subjects

FIRST YEAR	SECOND YEAR	THIRD YEAR	FOURTH YEAR
Fall			
Introduction to the social world	Student teaching		Student teaching
Introduction to education	Psychology of learning		
Hygiene	Physical education		
Introduction to science			
Physical education			

First Year	Second Year	Third Year	Fourth Year
Winter			
Art appreciation	Contributions of the ancient and medieval world to modern civilization	General sociology	
Outline of literature			
Outline of music			
Introduction to science			
Physical education	Physical education		
Spring			
Outline of literature	Expansion of European civilization in modern times		Philosophy of education
Pre-teaching observation			
Introduction to educational psychology	Physical education		
Physical education			

Requirements for Majors

Kindergarten-Primary Major	Rural Major
First Year	First Year

Winter

Language arts in primary grades

Winter

Agriculture for teachers

Spring

Pre-teaching observation
Social arts in primary grades
Teaching of history and civics

Spring

Pre-teaching observation
Language arts in intermediate grades
Teaching of history and civics

Second Year	Second Year

Fall

Student teaching

Fall

Student teaching

Winter

Music, rudiments and method
Fine art methods
Kindergarten-primary methods
Child development

Winter

Rural school management
Principles of education
Electives

Spring

Biological elementary science
Principles of education
Rural school problems
Home geography

Spring

Biological elementary science
Methods and materials in geography for intermediate grades
Methods and materials in arithmetic
Fine art methods in intermediate grades
Electives

PREPARATION OF ELEMENTARY TEACHERS

Third Year

Fall
Instruction in spelling and reading
Making the school curriculum
Electives

Winter
Instruction in content subjects
History of education in the United States
Industrial arts methods
Elective

Spring
Instruction in handwriting, composition, and arithmetic
Teachers' classroom tests
Elective

Fourth Year

Fall
Creative education
Electives

Winter
Genetics and eugenics
Electives

Spring
Personality and social behavior
Electives

Third Year

Fall
Instruction in spelling and reading
Recent developments in rural life
Social and industrial history of the United States

Winter
Methods and materials in geography for intermediate grades
Electives

Spring
Instruction in handwriting, composition, and arithmetic
Teachers' classroom tests
Expansion of European civilization in modern times

Fourth Year

Fall
Making the school curriculum
Electives

Winter
Instruction in content subjects
Electives

Spring
Personality and social behavior
Electives

Courses are similarly organized for teachers who plan to teach in intermediate, upper grades, and junior high schools, and as specialist teachers in high schools; the last group is expected to take courses organized into majors and minors. The State Teachers College grants both undergraduate and graduate degrees.

Student life. Very few normal schools or teachers colleges have their own dormitories; students live in boarding-houses, clubs, fraternity or sorority houses, which are under the general supervision of the authorities. Student life is organized very much like that in liberal arts colleges. While sports and physical activities are everywhere encouraged, the preponderance of women prevents that emphasis on athleticism so common in the colleges. The social life of the students is promoted by the clubs, sororities, and fraternities, and a variety of societies organized for cultural or recreational purposes. The responsibility for government and the control of student affairs is entrusted to student representative councils or to the whole student body.

Certification of teachers. The chief obstacle in the way of the progressive development of teacher-preparation lies in the vagueness and diversity of the practices of granting teachers' certificates. Traditionally certificates were awarded by local authorities on the basis of examinations often with little or no specific requirement as to preparation, whether academic or professional. The present tendency is in the direction of more rigid control by the state authorities, the simplification of practices, the elimination of examinations, and the award of certificates on the basis of diplomas earned in recognized institutions. Although the movement is in this direction, the goal is still far from being reached; there still exist low-grade, emergency, temporary, provisional, and life certificates awarded on the basis of examinations and renewable, except in the last type, periodically. The following examples of certificates may be cited:

In California the state board of education issues a life diploma in all schools of the State upon recommendation of a county board of education, which in turn is authorized upon presentation of credentials issued by the state board to grant a great variety of certificates, valid for two or five years and renewable for the same terms, for school administration, general, special, or departmental supervision, kindergarten-primary or general elementary schools, junior high school or general secondary, special subjects, educational research and guidance, vocational arts and trade and industrial occupations, and health and development certificates.

In Kansas the State Teachers College issues life diplomas valid in any school, life certificates valid in elementary, junior, and two-year high schools, and special subject life certificates, as well as three-year certificates. The state board of education grants in addition life certificates on college graduation, three-year certificates renewable for life, permanent certificates, three-year certificates renewable for three-year periods on the basis of further study or examination, and special certificates for special subjects or departments. Still another type of certificates, the first grade certificate valid for three years and the second grade certificate valid for two years, are granted by county boards of examiners.

In Massachusetts certificates may be issued by the state or by local committees. There are, however, two marked tendencies: the first is to centralize the power of certification in the hands of the state authority, and, second, to abolish certification by examination in favor of the acceptance of credentials based on a specified period of study in recognized institutions. Both tendencies will make the improved organization of teacher-preparation possible.

Appointment of teachers. The minimum requirements for appointment have been indicated in the discussion of the methods of preparation and certification; as may be expected, they show a wide range of variation from less than high school graduation for teachers in rural schools to four years of preparation in the more progressive cities. In 1930-31 in cities with populations of 2500 and over, 74.7 per cent of the teachers were required to have two years of preparation, 16.1 per cent three years, and 6.1 four years beyond the high school. In addition to preparation, many cities require candidates for appointment to have some experience; 18 per cent require one year, 22.4 per cent two years, and 1.1 per cent more than two years. The majority of the cities will not appoint married women teachers, but the practice varies when a single woman teacher already in service marries — in three fifths of the cities they are required to resign at once or at the end of the school year, and in the remainder they may continue to teach. Leave of absence without pay is provided for maternity in a number of cities. Despite serious objections to the practice, more than half of the cities prefer to appoint local residents, a practice which is still more common in rural areas. The selection of candidates for appointment is a function of the superintendents of education, who in most cases interview candidates personally and in addition use other methods, such as application blanks, recommendations, written and physical examinations, and observation of instruction. The sources from which suitable candidates are available are: (1) commercial agencies; (2) appointment bureaus in normal schools, colleges, and universities; and (3) appointment bureaus maintained by state departments of education or state teachers associations. Appointments are held from the boards of education.

Tenure. The most common practice throughout the country is the appointment of teachers on annual contracts which may be renewed or discontinued, often without notice. While this practice of "hire and fire" is most usual in rural areas, the annual contract is still the most commonly found even in cities, of which 60.1 per cent elect teachers annually or enter into contracts for one year only; 27.5 per cent grant permanent appointments after a probationary period, usually of three years; 12.1 per cent appoint teachers to indefinite tenure subject to termination at the end of any year. Teachers are protected by state-wide tenure laws in Indiana, Maryland, Montana, New Jersey, and New York, and in California in districts with eight teachers or more; the larger cities have their own tenure laws. The argument for annual appointments is that incompetent teachers can be more easily dismissed; the argument for permanent tenure is that it is the only method by which teachers can be protected against wrongful dismissal for political or other reasons not always connected with teaching ability; the obstacle to the introduction of indefinite tenure, which is generally recognized as the soundest practice, is the difficulty of defining teaching ability and competence in such a way that the courts would accept reasons for dismissal on such grounds. Efforts to establish merit or efficiency scales have up to the present proved to be unsatisfactory.

Salaries. Teachers' salaries have followed a decidedly upward trend in the past ten years. The median salaries paid to teachers in city kindergartens and elementary schools in 1930-31 are shown in the accompanying table on page 619.[1]

The median salaries paid to elementary school principals in the United States were as follows in 1931:

Cities	Teaching Principals	Supervising Principals
Over 100,000	$2,436	$3,519
Between 30,000 and 100,000	2,011	2,646
Between 10,000 and 30,000	1,572	1,925
Between 5,000 and 10,000	1,583	2,239
Between 2,500 and 5,000	1,409	2,175

Salary scales have been adopted in more than three fourths of the cities with populations over 2500, but are more frequently found in the larger than in the smaller cities. The scales are based on the

[1] Based on the Research Bulletin of the National Education Association, Vol. IX, No. 3. May, 1931, *Salaries in City School Systems, 1930-31* (Washington, D.C., 1931).

number of years of service, amount of professional training, ratings on efficiency scales, position held, and sex. The periods within which the maxima on the scales adopted range from five to fifteen years, although longer scales are found. About three fourths of the school systems require continued professional or other study in

MEDIAN SALARIES PAID TEACHERS IN CITIES OF THE UNITED STATES

STATES	OVER 100,000 POPULATION		30,000 TO 100,000 POPULATION		10,000 TO 30,000 POPULATION	5,000 TO 10,000 POPULATION	2,500 TO 5,000 POPULATION
	K.	E.S.	K.	E.S.	E.S.	K. and E.S.	E.S.
United States	$2,077	$2,118	$1,609	$1,609	$1,428	$1,303	$1,162
Alabama	...	1,610	...	1,171	953	890	791
Arizona	...	...	1,450	1,795	...	1,452	1,508
Arkansas	...	...	...	1,332	983	824	779
California	1,962	2,287	1,900	1,954	1,732	1,591	1,583
Colorado	2,220	2,227	1,750	1,638	1,530	1,298	1,284
Connecticut	1,725	1,856	1,818	1,840	1,840	1,376	1,253
Delaware	1,600	2,010	...	...	...	...	1,038
District of Columbia	2,226	2,219	...	...	...	...	...
Florida	1,250	1,208	...	below 1,000	882	872	754
Georgia	1,719	1,754	1,050	1,310	914	891	858
Idaho	...	...	...	...	1,514	1,279	1,173
Illinois	2,511	2,516	1,461	1,554	1,310	1,275	1,103
Indiana	1,680	1,882	1,388	1,539	1,386	1,156	1,165
Iowa	1,895	1,859	1,459	1,505	1,283	1,132	1,100
Kansas	1,550	1,746	1,583	1,721	1,291	1,194	1,026
Kentucky	1,536	1,508	1,268	1,400	1,037	923	912
Louisiana	1,340	1,709	...	1,079	...	...	1,017
Maine	...	...	1,522	1,538	1,234	977	894
Maryland	...	1,660	...	1,199	1,152	...	1,228
Massachusetts	1,876	1,953	1,561	1,651	1,525	1,348	1,265
Michigan	1,919	2,003	1,584	1,699	1,453	1,350	1,301
Minnesota	1,745	1,797	...	...	1,496	1,177	1,165
Mississippi	...	...	1,043	1,033	1,201	1,061	1,003
Missouri	2,209	2,120	...	1,186	1,180	1,032	868
Montana	...	...	...	1,807	1,650	1,388	...
Nebraska	2,090	2,110	1,640	1,602	1,333	1,177	1,113
New Hampshire	...	...	1,532	1,546	1,230	1,100	1,011
Nevada	...	...	...	...	1,538	...	...
New Jersey	2,440	2,230	1,981	2,180	1,801	1,578	1,502
New Mexico	...	...	...	...	1,433	1,288	1,282
New York	2,601	2,652	1,901	1,910	1,742	1,735	1,637
North Carolina	...	...	...	1,343	1,098	1,080	1,139
North Dakota	...	...	...	...	1,446	1,246	1,143
Ohio	2,050	2,037	1,650	1,603	1,310	1,233	1,120
Oklahoma	1,517	1,903	...	1,253	1,109	958	948
Oregon	1,725	2,213	...	...	1,238	1,252	1,217
Pennsylvania	1,886	2,073	1,613	1,719	1,450	1,420	1,142
Rhode Island	1,850	1,794	1,615	1,615	1,437	1,308	1,239
South Carolina	...	...	...	1,253	1,249	1,008	950
South Dakota	...	...	1,530	1,523	1,301	...	1,226
Tennessee	1,170	1,503	...	...	1,013	831	815
Texas	1,267	1,029	1,383	1,241	1,041	960	936
Utah	1,775	1,557	...	1,342	838	1,156	1,067
Vermont	...	...	...	...	1,300	1,232	900
Virginia	1,500	1,507	...	1,358	1,174	984	833
Washington	2,000	1,933	...	1,541	1,411	1,273	1,265
West Virginia	...	...	1,279	1,493	1,158	...	1,122
Wisconsin	2,265	2,390	1,521	1,681	1,362	1,268	1,216
Wyoming	...	...	...	...	1,707	1,480	1,540

summer schools or extension courses as requirements for salary increases. Although efficiency ratings are regarded as desirable bases for the award of salary increases, rating scales have not yet been devised which give complete satisfaction or command the confidence of teachers; the mistrust of such devices is indicated by the fact that less than eleven per cent of the cities employ them. In theory an adequate array of arguments may be produced in favor of a single salary scale for all teachers, irrespective of the type of school in which they teach; in practice its adoption is beset by many administrative difficulties and particularly by the problem of supply and demand for certain positions. At present the single salary scale has been adopted by an insignificant number of school systems. The question of sex differentiation in salary scales is relatively unimportant in elementary schools, since the percentage of men teachers is so very small; in the junior high schools 42 per cent and in the senior high schools 54.8 per cent of the cities pay higher salaries to men than to women. Supermaximum salaries are paid in 44.1 per cent of the cities to teachers who have exceptional qualifications as indicated by successful classroom instruction and continued professional study.[1] The two tables on page 621 indicate the methods of organizing salary schedules.

Pensions. The improvement of salaries for teachers has been accompanied by the development during the past few years of sound retirement systems. Teachers' retirement systems have been in existence since the close of the last century, but it was not until the Carnegie Foundation for the Advancement of Teaching began to study the problem of the principles underlying sound systems that a revision of them began to be made. The older systems either were based on inadequate contributions or else were of the free or non-contributory type. The sound systems which have been established recently are based on contributions of teachers and employers accumulated at compound interest and provide protection against old age and disability. To protect the funds measures are taken to meet the accrued liabilities — that is, the payment of allowances to teachers already in service when the systems are launched. The return of contributions, optional forms of allowances, periodical

---

[1] On teachers' salaries see Elsbree, W. S., *Teachers' Salaries* (New York, 1931), and Research Bulletin of the National Education Association, *Salaries in City School Systems*, 1930–31, Vol. IX, No. 3, May, 1931.

PREPARATION OF ELEMENTARY TEACHERS

actuarial evaluations, the keeping of individual accounts and establishment of a reserve basis, and optional and compulsory limits for retirement are some of the features of the sounder systems.

There are at the present time state retirement systems in the District of Columbia and twenty-two States (Arizona, California, Connecticut, Illinois, Indiana, Maine, Maryland, Massachusetts, Michigan, Minnesota, Montana, Nevada, New Jersey, New York, North Dakota, Ohio, Pennsylvania, Rhode Island, Vermont, Virginia, Washington, Wisconsin). In addition, a large number of cities, both within these States and in others, have their own systems. Normally, membership in retirement funds is optional with teachers already in service, but compulsory for new entrants into the service. Of the state systems, nineteen require both the em-

ELEMENTARY SCHOOL TEACHERS' SALARY SCHEDULES
1. SPRINGFIELD, MASSACHUSETTS

SCHEDULES	YEARS OF TRAINING	MINIMUM	YEARLY INCREMENTS	MAXIMUM
I	Successful completion of a two-year course in normal school or equivalent.	$1200	8 × $100	$2000
II	Successful completion of a three-year course in normal school or equivalent	1300	9 × $100	2200
III	Successful completion of four years of college work with a standard bachelor's degree or equivalent.	1400	9 × $100	2300

2. BRONXVILLE, NEW YORK

TRAINING	YEARS OF EXPERIENCE						
	0	1	2	3	4	5	6
Two years' normal	$1500	$1800	$2034	$2209	$2341	$2441	$2516
Three years' normal or third college year	1563	1926	2223	2398	2530	2630	2705
A.B., B.S., Ph.B.	1563	1926	2244	2587	2719	2819	2894
A.M.	1563	1926	2244	2587	2908	3008	3083

TRAINING	YEARS OF EXPERIENCE					
	7	8	9	10	11	12
Two years' normal	$2576	$2626	$2676	$2726	$2756	$2786
Three years' normal or third college year	2765	2815	2865	2915	2945	2975
A.B., B.S., Ph.B.	2954	3004	3054	3104	3134	3164
A.M.	3143	3193	3243	3293	3323	3353

ployer and the teacher to pay contributions. Practice varies as to the contributions of teachers; some systems require a flat annual payment, others a percentage of salary. Provision is made in most systems for the return of contributions in whole or in part in cases of death or on leaving the service prior to retirement. The conditions of retirement are governed by length of service, which varies in range from ten to forty years — thirty years being the most usual — and age, usually sixty as the minimum requirement and seventy as the compulsory limit. The amount of the retiring allowance is either a flat rate or in the sounder systems an annuity purchased by the contributions accumulated at compound interest; disability allowances are determined in the same way.[1]

Improvement of teachers in service. The in-service training of teachers is probably more widespread in the United States than in other countries. Arising at a time when the initial preparation was inadequate, the practice has been retained and extended, not only to meet the rapid advance of the science of education, but as a method for the continuous improvement of teachers. The methods of in-service training are many and varied. Reference has already been made to the follow-up systems used by normal schools and teachers colleges to keep in touch and assist their graduates in the first year or two of their experience. This is supplemented in all systems by supervisors, general and special, who not only visit teachers in their classrooms, but conduct conferences on special problems. Teachers' institutes and conferences are organized very generally, in some localities by the educational authorities, in others by the teachers' associations. Rating scales of efficiency, of which the use of achievement tests constitutes a part, are employed by nearly half of the city school systems as a method of improving teachers; it will be noticed that rating scales are more frequently used for this purpose than for promotion on salary schedules. Generally such scales are the results of the coöperative action of the administrators, supervisors, and teachers. Although used fairly extensively, there is still no widespread confidence in such scales. By far the most general system employed for the improvement of teachers in service is attendance at summer sessions, which are now conducted by col-

[1] On the subject of pensions see the reports and bulletins of the Carnegie Foundation, and the Research Bulletins of the National Education Association, especially *Current Issues in Teacher Retirement*, Vol. VIII, No. 5, November, 1930, which contains a bibliography.

leges and universities, normal schools and teachers colleges; it is estimated that about one teacher in four spends the summer vacation in attendance on courses in summer schools. About five per cent of the cities either grant bonuses for such attendance or take it into consideration for salary increases. Another practice which is also distinctively American is the granting of extended leave of absence for professional improvement either by formal study or by travel. In 1930–31, 616 cities reported that they granted leave of absence for professional improvement, 290 for travel, and 352 for rest. In practically all but 10 per cent of the cities such leave of absence is granted without salary; 31 cities, mostly the largest, grant leave of absence with half salary, and a few with full salary less the pay of a substitute.

Status of teachers. Considerable contribution to the improvement of the professional status of teachers has been made by their professional organizations, especially the National Education Association and the state associations, which conduct conferences, publish journals, and maintain bureaus of research and information. The full growth and development of these organizations have been recent, so that it is difficult to estimate their contribution to educational politics. The local organizations in the larger cities have in the main been concerned with the promotion of the interests of their own members, sometimes in opposition to the policies of the authorities. The larger associations have limited themselves too narrowly to education and instruction, and, as contrasted with the activities of similar associations in England, France, and Germany, their work has been mainly that of assembling, disseminating, and interpreting information on current tendencies rather than of leadership. Whether due to the fact that the overwhelming majority of teachers are women, or whatever the cause, the teachers of the country, despite their numbers, have not taken concerted steps to promote and protect their professional, as contrasted with their material, interests. The result is that the principle upon which education in the United States is based, that it is a public concern, is still interpreted to mean that the public has the right to interfere in matters which are properly not its concern — teacher tenure, curriculum prescription, acceptance or rejection of textbooks for reasons which are not educational. Undoubtedly much of this situation can be attributed to the fact that teaching in general has only recently begun to evolve out of what has been described as a procession into a real profession. The rising standards of preliminary preparation, improved salaries and retirement systems, and better conditions of tenure are tending to produce more stable conditions and longer professional service. One defect still remains: the fact that the rewards of the profession do not lie in its separate branches, with the result that teachers not only tend to move from one place to another, but also from one branch to another — from elementary schools to junior or senior high schools or to the administrative branches or to higher institutions. While from one point of view mobility of teachers from place to place or from one branch of education to another is salutary, it tends to develop a restlessness from which in the long run the smooth progress of education, particularly in the smaller areas, is likely to suffer.

CHAPTER VIII

SECONDARY EDUCATION

The problem of secondary education has become perhaps the most important and the most difficult of all the problems which today confront the educator and the statesman. Whatever the conflicts which are involved in any discussion of elementary education may be, there is at least more likelihood of agreement about its content and its methods than in the case of secondary education, partly because its universal distribution has in the main been accepted and partly because the interests of the clientèle concerned have not become as diversified as is the case with pupils of secondary school age. Elementary education has on the whole been more progressive, more responsive to changing demands, than has secondary, and educational theorists have devoted more thought to this branch than to secondary.

Secondary education, it may be said, is today the victim of its own traditions, which, however fine and noble they may have been, have set up certain barriers to clear thinking on the subject and have increased the difficulties created by a new age and by new demands. In the Greek and Roman periods secondary education was definitely regarded as a preparation for active participation in the duties of the citizen, and it was only in the Imperial period that education gradually began to be divorced from the realities of life. The medieval period, inheriting the grammar school established in the Roman era, adapted it to its own needs and employed secondary education as a preparation for the scholar-clerk to serve the State and the Church, and, when the universities appeared, as a preparation for more advanced studies. The same purposes survived into the Renaissance and Reformation periods, but with an enriched content which before long also became formal. Despite the gradual secularization of public offices and of the professions, the same type of secondary education which had served as a preparation for service in the Church was retained. This retention was justified on two grounds, first, that the content of the curriculum taught in the Latin grammar school constituted the best training for the mind, and, second, that it furnished the only sound foundation for a liberal education. Efforts were made from the sixteenth century on to introduce modern subjects — foreign languages, the vernacular, history and geography, and sciences — into the secondary curriculum, but for a long time with little success so far as the official schools and even the universities were concerned. Through all these periods, however, secondary education was still open and accessible to the poor boy of ability, either through free education and scholarships or the sacrifices of his family.

A change gradually began to make itself felt in the eighteenth century as the social and economic situation began to change. The curriculum of the secondary school had become narrow and formal; new subjects, more closely pertinent to the actual needs of life, were demanded; new types of schools slowly began to emerge, giving a more direct preparation for vocational careers. As a result the secondary school became an institution for those who could afford to devote the time needed for the lengthy course or for poor pupils whose ability secured assistance for them to proceed as far as the university. In either case secondary education gradually began to become the education of a class. This situation was strengthened by the universities, which insisted on preparation in a certain limited round of subjects as a condition of admission, and by government regulations at the beginning of the nineteenth century, which, as in France and Germany, conferred certain privileges on students who completed a secondary school course which also happened to be the particular course sanctioned and approved by the universities. This was the classical course of the *Gymnasium* in Germany, of the *lycée* in France, of the "public" school in England. Justified by tradition in all countries and prescribed by government regulation in France and Germany, the classical secondary school established a monopoly of secondary education which it became the task of the nineteenth century to break down.

The gradual emergence of the middle classes, the rapid development of commerce and industry, and the still more remarkable development and expansion of the sciences led to demands for types of secondary schools to meet the new social and economic needs. New schools were established and even received official recognition, but it was not until the opening of the twentieth century that they succeeded in securing the same privileges as the classical secondary school. In attaining these privileges the new types of schools offering modern curricula were gradually moulded into the same shape and form as the classical school. In other words, while the addition of new schools or new courses in existing schools made possible a better adaptation to an increasing clientèle, the association of privileges with secondary education exercised a pressure to conformity with reference to standards, methods of instruction, examinations, and the concept of liberal education. The reforms in secondary education which took place at the beginning of the present century thus represent accretions of new subjects — the vernacular, modern foreign languages, modern history, more mathematics, and sciences — rather than a fundamental reconsideration of the purposes of secondary education. Liberal education was still defined too narrowly in terms of the best that had been said and thought in the past, and secondary education in general as a preparation for university education which imparted at the same time, but in degrees varying with the subjects studied, a sound mental training. The privileges conferred on pupils completing secondary education in whole or in part made it desirable both for social and for economic reasons and attracted a clientèle which with some limited exceptions could pay for it. The expansion and enrichment of elementary education led to a demand for some form of further education, which was met by the provision of intermediate or higher primary schools. But, although these schools might overlap with a part of secondary education, they did not entitle their pupils to any privileges. The secondary school was essentially the school which, because of its class limitations and curriculum, was regarded as the institution for the selection and training of the *élite*, of those who were to become the leaders in public affairs and in the professions.

The United States early began to break away from the European type of secondary education and to provide equality of opportunity on the principle that every boy and girl must be given a chance. Although a certain specified course continued for a long time to be required for admission to the colleges, the principle of equality of opportunity played an important part in bringing about greater elasticity and flexibility than was found in Europe in the provision of subjects in the secondary schools. But while secondary education in Europe remained narrow because of adherence to a restricted and traditional concept of liberal education, in the United States it developed on no other principle than that the individual was to be given a chance, which meant in practice the provision of a round of subjects adapted to his needs and capacities. While this principle, combined with growing flexibility in the requirements for admission to college, made possible the remarkable expansion and provision of free secondary education at public expense, this development has not been guided by any recognized philosophy of purpose. A haphazard aggregation of subjects, which are put together on the mechanical principle that all subjects taught for the same length of time have the same value, and which are adapted to the interests and abilities of the individual pupils, seems to furnish the basic foundation of a secondary education. While the defects underlying secondary education in the United States center round the adequacy for educational purposes of many of the more than three hundred courses now found in the high schools, the difficulty of organization which is now confronting the rest of the world has been solved by the establishment of the high school as the natural continuation for all pupils of the elementary school. Secondary education has ceased to be the school for the direct selection of an *élite* and has become an institution open to all according to their needs and abilities.

One fact is clear, that there is in the field of secondary education universal unrest to which a number of factors have contributed. The first of these is the full realization of the meaning of democracy, which is itself the result of the development of democratic institutions and of education, and which is today called upon to meet the challenge from Communism on the one side and Fascism on the other. The liberalism of the nineteenth century, based on the conviction that political and social salvation would come from the grant of universal suffrage, has been found wanting. The demand today is for something more than political democracy and for more equality of opportunity — social, economic, and educational. This implies an obligation on society to provide equality of opportunity for the fullest development of the individual, and on the individual an obligation to contribute of his best to the welfare of society. This demand for the permeation of all social institutions with the spirit of democracy is accompanied by a recognition of the worth of the individual, a realization of the tremendous wastage of human resources and of individual ability caused by a social and educational system which failed to provide equality of opportunity and set up such barriers that only the ablest and strongest could surmount either if they came from homes which could support them or had such native ability that they could win aid through scholarships. To a great extent a demand for more education is the result in the leading countries of nearly a century of universal elementary education, although the tradition of secondary education as the education of a class has made the so-called lower classes suspicious of it even when opportunities to it are opened by means of free tuition and scholarships, as in England and France.

To these forces must be added the realization of the importance of education for the promotion of national well-being in all its aspects. This realization is everywhere becoming stronger because of the increased complexities of modern life which demand on every hand better trained and enriched intelligence on the part of the individual in all his social, political, and economic relations. The increased mechanization of industry is in turn creating problems which education will be called upon to solve. Hitherto the adolescent who did not proceed to a secondary school either entered upon an occupation in and through which he received his training or some school which prepared him for an occupation. The present economic crisis, which has brought unemployment in its train, as well as the mechanization of industry, has revealed that in general the opportunities for the employment of adolescents will be increasingly reduced. Confronted with this problem and the demand for equality of educational opportunity, society will probably be required before long to extend its tutelage over the adolescent and extend compulsory education throughout the period of adolescence. Secondary education for all is a movement which has already begun; in the United States it is represented by the remarkable increase in the enrollment of adolescents in high schools; in Germany it took the form of a proposal for the *Einheitsschule*, in France for the *école unique*, and in England for the extension of compulsory education for all up to the age of fifteen, the last four years of the period to be devoted to a type of junior secondary education.

The problem, however, is not merely one of the organization of facilities for secondary education, but involves a reconsideration of the meaning and purpose of secondary education. The assumption upon which secondary education was based in the past, an assumption which still survives in many places, was that a limited number of subjects, preferably literary, could serve the various functions of giving a mental training, preparing for higher education, and imparting a liberal education or general culture. The increasing enrollment in the secondary schools of most countries, due in some to the privileges which they conferred, in others to their more generous provision and accessibility combined with higher standards of living which enable parents to dispense with the earnings of their children, have revealed that the traditional curriculum and purposes of secondary education must be more varied and differentiated to meet the differences in ability and interests of the pupils. Criticisms are already being heard in Europe, as they were a generation ago in the United States, that it is unjust to submit all pupils to examinations which are based on requirements regarded as appropriate for admission to a university and to courses leading to professional careers. So long as secondary education was selective, society was able to absorb both the product of secondary schools and of the universities. The rise of the middle classes and the progressive improvement in the standards of living have led to an increase, not only in the enrollments in the secondary schools, but also in the numbers seeking to enter the professions, with the result that there has developed everywhere the danger of producing an intellectual proletariat, the inevitable danger which accompanies an education for status. Approached from this point of view the problem of secondary education becomes one not merely of selection but of distribution — that is, such an expansion of its aims that an adequate adjustment can be made to individual differences without affecting the main purpose of imparting a liberal education to all. The reform of secondary education in Italy in 1923 was undertaken in part with the end in view of diverting students from the type of secondary education which leads to the universities and the professions;[1] in France the proposal has been made that a National Bureau of Selection and Distribution be created as part of the general reform looking to the *école unique*; in England the *Report of the Consultative Committee on the Education of the Adolescent* accepted the principle of a variety of post-primary schools performing various functions adapted to the needs and abilities of the pupils; in the United States training for leadership as an aim of the high school is no

---

[1] A similar purpose but with different methods underlies the recent reform adopted in Chile with a view to adjusting the supply of students to the demands in the various professions. See *Educational Yearbook, 1930*, of the International Institute of Teachers College, Columbia University, pp. 125 ff. (New York, 1931).

longer discussed. In Germany the situation has been aggravated by the economic situation, with the result that the secondary schools are crowded with pupils, many of whom are sent at a sacrifice on the part of their parents in order to secure the privileged diplomas which will give them a better start in the competition for appointments, since even the trades have begun to demand the certificate granted at the end of six years of secondary education. This overcrowding and the failure to introduce adequately differentiated courses have given rise to the criticism that scholastic standards are being lowered — a criticism which reflects rather on the organization of the courses than on the quality of the pupils. One of the principles upon which the future reform of secondary education must be based is the statement of the English headmaster, Edward Thring, that "There is no stupid boy."

While the influences discussed up to this point have begun to affect discussions in secondary education, in practice a definite issue has not yet been reached. In the first place, the economic crisis which has affected the whole world has inevitably delayed educational reconstruction which would involve larger expenditures for salaries, equipment, and buildings, as well as the prospect of abolishing fees and providing maintenance grants in many cases. Secondly, those who have been brought up in the traditional concept of a liberal education as well as university authorities, who feel that the traditional preparation is the best foundation for advanced academic and professional studies, object to a reconstruction which may involve a complete revision of the traditional features of the secondary school and with it a lowering of standards of scholarship. There is as much hesitation today before the proposal to extend the opportunities of secondary education as there was in many countries a century ago when it was proposed to establish universal, compulsory elementary education.

That there are serious difficulties involved cannot be denied, but it would be folly to believe that they cannot be surmounted. Of these the financial difficulty is not insoluble, for, as the mechanization of industry develops further, the choice before nations will be the provision of educational opportunities or the payment of unemployment doles to adolescents. The real difficulty lies in the adoption of adequately differentiated courses adapted to the great variety of individual differences, when all adolescents continue their education beyond the primary school, while at the same time retaining the elements of a liberal education. At present the admission and retention of pupils in secondary schools is based on examinations; how reliable such examinations are as tests of capacity and achievement is still uncertain; all that can be said at the present is that the examinations are conducted in subjects which are required for admission to the universities and are imposed on all irrespective of their future careers. Virtually the same examinations are employed for purposes of selection regardless both of the capacities and future needs of the pupils. Should secondary education for all be adopted and with it the principle of broad differentiation of schools or courses, methods of selection and guidance will have to be adopted other than the traditional type of examination devised for academic purposes. Involved in this problem is the whole question of the meaning of general intelligence and how it may be trained; whether, indeed, the imparting of a culture based on a few subjects is of universal efficacy for intellectual training; and, finally, whether there is not rather a general factor of intelligence which may be trained through any subject.

A radical reform involving secondary education for all and an adequate system of guidance, selection, and distribution into a variety of differentiated courses would mean the deathblow to secondary education for status, which is so characteristic of the European systems, which results in overpressure on pupils to meet the standards, which diverts a portion of the population into the overcrowded professions, and which results in the creation of an intellectual proletariat. It would mean an organization in which each pupil would follow the course best suited to his abilities and aptitudes; it would also involve such constant oversight of the pupil as would make it possible at all stages to transfer him to the appropriate course demanded by his development.

The problems of administration and organization are not insurmountable. When these have been settled, the problem of the purpose and content of secondary education still remains to be solved. Shall these be general or special, cultural or vocational? The question can only be answered by positing others, What is the place of the individual in society? Is he first a worker or a citizen in its broadest sense? So far as work is concerned, two facts must be taken into account, both based on the increased mechanization of industry and the economic changes which are pending. Increased mechanization will probably mean a reduction in the need for protracted vocational preparation; whether that preparation is to be given in schools —

which can never be adequately equipped for the purpose — or whether it is to be given in the factories and offices under such conditions as will avoid exploitation, need not be discussed here. Another result of this trend will be a reduction in the hours of labor and an increase in available leisure. The question whether secondary education should be general or special may be discussed from another point of view. The traditional justification of a secondary education limited to a narrow round of subjects has in general been that they afforded a training of the mind, even if they were in themselves of little direct and immediate value for life. This broad statement of the value of general training has been challenged by some psychologists who professed to prove experimentally that formal discipline or the amount of transfer of training is negligible and the value of any subject is specific and direct. This point of view, which is essentially that adopted in the United States and which means that one subject is as good as another, implies the negation of any theory of educational values; on such a theory "pushpin is as good as poetry," as Bentham remarked. Between the two extremes, the acceptance of the theory of formal discipline and its virtual negation, there may be accepted a modified theory of general intelligence, a theory that intelligence or the mind does not consist merely of a collection of innumerable specific bonds, but that over and above these there is a general factor of intelligence. Wherever the scientific truth may lie, there is a consensus of opinion among employers that they would prefer an employee who is well educated to one who is specially trained for his work.

If, then, the main function of secondary education is to train the citizen first, leaving his vocational preparation to other schools and agencies, the problem is, What shall be the content of this general training? In other words, what is the meaning of a liberal education, the education of the free man, free as a citizen and free to use his leisure? Definitions of liberal education crowd the pages of histories of education and of literature; in the hands of the schoolman, however, they have been reduced to a limited number of subjects, some of which are even today regarded as of preëminent value. No particular virtue, however, lies in subjects as such; whatever value they possess depends upon the skill of the teacher to make them living and pertinent to the vibrating life about the pupil, even though certain propedeutic elements are inevitable. Liberal education can, indeed, not be defined in terms of subjects; its real test is the change produced in the pupil, and such change cannot be measured in terms of individual values, but of values essential to the maintenance and progress of society. The function of a liberal education is to provide the means for the unfolding and development of personality in its fourfold aspects — physical, social and moral, æsthetic, and intellectual. Never since the days of the Greeks have these four aspects been given equal attention. Attention has in general been devoted primarily to intellectual training in the hope that somehow or other moral and emotional aspects would be cultivated indirectly. The real measure of a successful liberal education is the extent to which it cultivates judgment and discrimination, good taste and sensitiveness to beauty, moderation and tolerance, ideals and convictions, open-mindedness and curiosity, reverence and awe, the power of intellectual and æsthetic enjoyment, abiding interests, and a sense of social obligation. The end is not command of subject-matter or the amassing of knowledge for its own sake, but the cultivation of a balanced personality; the subjects that may contribute to this end can only be selected in so far as they have at one and the same time some significance for the sympathetic understanding of the world in which we live and are suitable for the development of the particular abilities of each individual concerned. Such an approach to the secondary school curricula would involve a reëxamination of the subjects which are now found and a redirection of the content; it would also mean the inclusion of new subjects, such as music and the art, in positions of greater importance than they have hitherto enjoyed. The same criterion would also serve as a basis of greater differentiation in the secondary education of girls than is provided at present in most countries. Ultimately the success of an education depends upon a body of skilled teachers united by a common aim to which they seek to contribute through their own special subjects.

An examination of the practice of secondary education in the countries which will be considered in the following pages will reveal different methods and aims; each system in its own way has something to contribute to the theory of secondary education. Radical reforms in the traditional concept of secondary education have not yet been embodied into practice except in the United States and Soviet Russia. None the less, no country can be said to be free from the unrest which has been described and which will furnish the basis of a reorganization which seems inevitable in the not distant future. Whatever the outcome of the unrest in each country, the ultimate solution will be colored by those ideals toward which each system is already directed.

English secondary education is characterized by an emphasis on those qualities which are regarded as the most important in the relations of the individual to his fellow-citizens. If intellectual training is not regarded as the paramount end of education, although for the best minds it is as rich and broad as will be found in any other country, every boy and girl is expected to learn the meaning of "fair play" and "playing the game" in life; and yet even the intellectual training offered has improved considerably in the last quarter of a century. Where the emphasis lies is well illustrated in the following tribute paid to the secondary schools by a former director of education:

> The Secondary Schools are doing a great work. Every year they turn out nearly 100,000 boys and girls with minds comparatively trained, with a fairly solid mass of necessary knowledge, with self-respect and a sense of responsibility, with a love of fairplay and an incipient civic sense which they have learned on the playing field.[1]

The French secondary schools are devoted to the development of *culture générale* and the training of reason. The system is deliberately designed to select an *élite* by means of a rigorous training in *études désintéressés*, general culture divorced from any utilitarian motives and introducing the pupils to a full heritage of the humanities as they have developed through and out of the literature of the classics. Although the classical tradition was modified by the reforms of 1901 and 1925, the essence of the reforms has been an attempt to find the modern equivalent of classical humanism. Whether through the classical humanities or through the modern humanities, French secondary education seeks to develop the spiritual and intellectual sides of the individual, not by amassing knowledge but through a critical approach to it. The justification for this practice is to be found in a faith that a mind well trained furnishes that alertness and adaptability which will enable the individual to turn later to any career. But no Frenchman will deny that the system is for the few, that it is intellectually aristocratic.

Secondary education in Germany has not yet found itself. It is generally recognized that the emphasis on *allgemeine Bildung*, general

---

[1] King, Bolton, *Schools of Today*, p. 91 (New York, E. P. Dutton and Co., 1929).

all-round cultural training, which was the aim of secondary education before the War, is unsound, because it was defined primarily in terms of subjects and an encyclopedism which exercised a great pressure on the pupils. The new aim seeks to place the emphasis on the cult of personality, but a personality effective in the tasks that confront the new Germany. Humanism (*Bildung zur Humanität*) is still the aim and still furnishes the means, but the emphasis is shifted from the amassing of knowledge and information to an understanding and appreciation of *Deutschtum*. The intellectualistic emphasis is retained, but it is recognized that intellectual training does not cultivate the total personality. The change in content is to be accompanied by a change in methods of instruction which provide greater and richer opportunities for individual activity. The reform in theory has, however, not been as difficult as the problem of retraining the teachers who are confronted, not only with new aims but with a clientèle drawn in increasing numbers from a new stratum of society.

The reform of secondary education in Italy was directed toward the attainment of two purposes. The first was to extend the opportunities for some form of post-elementary education to all, but through the establishment of a variety of schools — general, prevocational, and vocational. The second purpose was to organize the system of secondary education in such a way that there would be progressive selection of the ablest students by means of examinations, and by means of this selection to deflect the excessive numbers seeking admission through the universities to the overcrowded professions and public services. Running through the whole reform is the aim to transform the bookish character of the curriculum and instruction and to vitalize them through the inspiration of Italian culture. In Russia secondary education is a constituent part of the unified labor school. In the reform no room could be found for the traditional culture, which is regarded as a bourgeois inheritance. The secondary, like the lower section of the unified labor school is devoted to training students for the everyday life activities of Communist society.

In the United States secondary education is still, as it has been for the past quarter of a century, in a process of reconstruction. As contrasted with the European system, there is an absence of clearly defined aims, due in no small measure to the fact that the high school has ceased to be the school for the few and seeks to meet the needs of all pupils who in other countries are distributed among a great variety of schools. So far as there is any recognizable principle, it does not lie either in a rooted faith in a cultural tradition or in a profound esteem of scholarship so much as in a desire to adapt curricula and courses to the needs and capacities of the individual. At best American secondary education is frankly experimental; it seeks to adapt itself to the needs of American life and to discover those elements of culture which are justifiable in a highly industrialized society. It refuses to accept anything merely because it is traditional and attempts by experiments and tested results to discover what is most appropriate both for the individual and for society. If at best it may be said that it is seeking to reinterpret culture in terms of life to be lived under the peculiar social and economic conditions of American life, in practice it represents a blend of the old and the new, and, from the point of view of the curriculum, an accretion of subjects added more or less haphazard in response to individual needs rather than an attempt at its reconstruction in the light of a reformulated concept of culture. The difficulties of American secondary education as contrasted with European are due to the discarding of the traditional faith in general training or formal discipline and a desire to meet the differentiated needs and capacities of the individual without any clear guidance of social or cultural purposes. These difficulties are only intensified by the rapid increase of the enrollment and the absence of an adequate supply of suitably trained teachers.

I. ENGLAND [1]

RECENT HISTORICAL DEVELOPMENT

State intervention. The Clarendon Commission. Secondary education in England is provided through a variety of schools, some wholly provided and maintained at public expense, some private but receiving aid from the local and state authorities under certain conditions, some entirely private and unsupervised unless they choose to invite inspection by a recognized authority. Although secondary education has had a long history, its provision at public expense is of comparatively recent origin. It was, indeed, not until the second half of the nineteenth century that the State began to manifest any real interest in the supply of secondary education. The first move-

---

[1] For a detailed account of the history of English education see Kandel, I. L., *History of Secondary Education* (Boston, Houghton Mifflin Company, 1930).

ment in the direction of state intervention was the appointment in 1861 of the Clarendon Commission to inquire "into the nature of the endowments, funds, and revenues belonging to or received by" the nine great "public" schools (Eton, Winchester, Westminster, Charterhouse, Harrow, Rugby, Shrewsbury, St. Paul's, and Merchant Taylors'), and "into the administration and management of the said colleges, schools, and foundations, and into the system of studies respectively pursued therein, as well as into the methods, subjects, and extent of the instruction given to the students." The *Report* of this Commission, which was issued in 1864 and resulted in the enactment in 1868 of the Public Schools Act for the administrative reorganization of the first seven of the schools mentioned, only served to direct attention to the need of a wider investigation into the state of secondary education in the country.

The Schools Inquiry Commission. In 1864 the Taunton or Schools Inquiry Commission was appointed to inquire into the condition and needs of secondary schools not included under the terms of reference of the Clarendon Commission. The *Report* of the Schools Inquiry Commission, issued in 1868, revealed that the supply of secondary education was inadequate, particularly in areas where it was most needed; that there was an absence of a clear conception both of the purposes of secondary education and of the needs of the pupils; that no recognizable standards were apparent; that owing to poor methods of instruction and untrained teachers the results were unsatisfactory even in the classical subjects, which constituted the backbone of the curriculum. Matthew Arnold, impressed with the secondary school systems which, as one of the assistant commissioners, he had studied in France, Germany, Switzerland, and Italy, urged upon the country the importance of organizing its secondary schools. The Commission in its *Report* recommended the establishment of a central authority for the following purposes: (1) to consider schemes for the reorganization of educational endowments to be submitted to Parliament for final approval; (2) to appoint inspectors of endowed schools; (3) to audit accounts of such schools; and (4) to decide whether certain charities reported as useless, mischievous, or for obsolete purposes should be converted to educational uses. The Commission further recommended the division of the country into a number of administrative areas under authorities charged with the coördination of secondary education and the preparation of schemes for submission to the central authority. To improve the standards of education, the creation of an examination council was recommended to examine pupils, to certificate after examination candidates for the teaching profession, and to promote the improvement of schools by the publication of annual reports. Various grades of schools were to be established adapted to the needs of pupils coming from different social classes. When the Endowed Schools Acts of 1869 and 1874 were passed, it was recognized that the more important recommendations of the Commission had been ignored and that England had missed the opportunity of creating a system of secondary education on a national basis.

Professional organization. Although the reports of the two Commissions did not lead to effective action by the State, the revelation of the defects of secondary education and the suggestion of state control exercised a powerful influence on the headmasters of the leading "public" and endowed schools. Mainly through the influence of Edward Thring of Uppingham, the Headmasters' Conference was organized in 1869. Urged by the Conference, Oxford and Cambridge in 1873 established a Joint Board to inspect and examine schools and to grant certificates to successful pupils. The improvement of schools which resulted from the coöperation of members in the Conference, and other professional organizations whose formation was stimulated in large measure by the creation of the Conference, from the establishment of the Joint Board, and particularly from the efforts of a distinguished line of headmasters, did not affect the fundamental problem of providing an adequate supply of secondary schools adapted to the growing needs of the country and differentiated according to the abilities and needs of the pupils.

Changing social conditions. While the Government failed to follow the recommendations of its Commissions, the social and economic conditions of the country were developing so rapidly that some form of education beyond the elementary became increasingly urgent. The well-being of the country was promoted by mildly socialistic legislation affecting health, housing, and labor conditions; the working-classes began to develop a political self-consciousness; free public libraries and art galleries, maintained out of local rates, were established; the rapid expansion of Germany began to challenge England's preëminence in the industrial and commercial fields; the development of elementary education, the creation of new universities and university colleges, and the organization of university extension and of other forms of adult education — all these forces helped to focus attention on the inadequate provision of secondary education. If the Government refrained from meeting the demand, other methods were adopted. Under the stimulus of grants from the Science and Art Department, the elementary schools began to provide advanced classes for pupils who could remain in school beyond the compulsory age limit; organized science schools, giving day and evening instruction, were established; and technical instruction, very broadly interpreted, began to be provided, under the Technical Instruction Act of 1889 and the Local Taxation (Customs and Excise) Act of 1890, by the local authorities created by the Local Government Act of 1888. But the provision of these facilities only served to increase the confusion and chaos of the unorganized and unarticulated system.

The Bryce Commission. In 1894 the Bryce Commission, which for the first time included three women among its sixteen members, was appointed to consider "the best methods of establishing a well-organized system of education in England" taking into account the facilities already available. The Commission recommended in its *Report* the creation of (1) a central authority for education as a government department under a Minister responsible to Parliament; (2) a representative Educational Council to act in an advisory capacity; and (3) local educational authorities to make adequate provision for secondary education. The recommendations of the Commission also included the inspection of schools, the professional preparation and registration of teachers, and some general principles governing the curricula of secondary schools.

PROGRESS TOWARD A NATIONAL SYSTEM

The Education Act of 1902. The recommendations of the Bryce Commission met with a better fate than those of its predecessors. In 1899 the Board of Education was established and in 1902 the Education Act was passed, placing upon the counties and county boroughs the responsibility of providing an adequate supply of secondary education having regard to facilities already available in their areas. The Act at once corrected a situation which had been precipitated in 1899 by the refusal of Mr. Cockerton, a government auditor, to sanction expenditures of the London School Board on education other than elementary, and on the instruction of persons who were not children except as provided under the Technical Instruction Act. The responsibility was now placed by the Act upon the local authorities "to supply or aid the supply of education, other than elementary, and to promote the general coördination of all forms of education," a responsibility which was defined in more detail in the Education Act of 1921:

With a view to the establishment of a national system of public education available for all persons capable of profiting thereby, it shall be the duty of the council of every county and county borough so far as their powers extend to contribute thereto by providing for the progressive development and comprehensive organization of education in respect of their area.

The problems confronting both the Board of Education and the local authorities were many. A central authority was inevitably looked upon with suspicion and fear of control and domination. As a result of the developments of the last quarter of the nineteenth century, the meaning and purpose of secondary education had become somewhat confused. There were no standards as to ages and retention of pupils and none as to the content of a secondary education; in one group of secondary schools the emphasis was on the study of the classics, in the other, governed by the regulations of the Science and Art Department, it was on the sciences. The confusion was only increased by the existence of a variety of standards prescribed by a vast number of examination boards. The persistence of social class distinctions presented a serious obstacle to sound organization. Finally, there was the fear that an extension of secondary education to classes of society which had never enjoyed it before would involve a lowering of standards. Guidance was found through numerous surveys which were instituted by local education authorities, in the investigations conducted by the inspectors of the Board, and in the *Regulations for Secondary Schools* which the Board began to issue in 1903.

Organization and types of secondary schools. The problem which confronted the country after the passing of the Education Act of 1902 was how to draw together the existing types of secondary schools to which the new public type was now to be added into the semblance of a national system. The existing supply was characterized by variety in origin, in financial support, in standards, and in the ages of their pupils. It must, however, be remembered that the term "secondary education" has in England, as it has in practically all countries except the United States, a definite connotation. Accordingly there are not included in this discussion types of schools, such as central schools, trade schools, junior technical schools, and others which, although intended for pupils of the lower age range in the secondary schools, do not fall within the definition of secondary education as generally accepted. While the American high school is the school for all adolescents, the English secondary school offers only that general type of curriculum known in the United States as academic. From the point of view of supply, the following types of secondary schools may be distinguished:

1. *"Public" schools.* The first group consists of the "public" schools, a term which is now used to include those schools which meet the conditions for eligibility of their headmasters to membership in the Headmasters' Conference. These conditions are that the scheme of the school is satisfactory, that the governing body and the headmaster are independent, that the enrollment is adequate, that a certain number of the pupils passed each year to the Universities of Oxford and Cambridge, and that a good proportion pass the school certificate examination. The group includes, besides the great "public" schools, about one hundred and fifty others which, whether of old or of recent foundation, have assimilated the traditions of the older "public" schools.[1] The majority are boarding schools, the pupils living in "houses" or dormitories; the fees range from £150 to £300 a year, but scholarships are available; and most of the pupils are admitted at about the age of thirteen, on the basis of a common entrance examination for which they are prepared in preparatory schools. While there are many boarding schools for girls, some of which, like St. Leonard's and Roedean, are modeled on the "public" schools for boys, they have not on the whole assumed the place in English life and education enjoyed by the corresponding schools for boys.

The preparatory schools in turn constitute a part of the system of "public" schools, are fee-paying private day or boarding schools, admit pupils at about the age of nine, and, as far as possible, reproduce the characteristics of the schools to which they serve as the gateway. The exact number of these schools is unknown, but about

[1] A list of these schools will be found in the *Schoolmasters' Yearbook* and a description of each in the *Public Schools Yearbook.*

550 of them are represented in the Association of Preparatory Schools, founded in 1892. Considered from the point of view of the ages of the pupils attending them, the preparatory schools parallel the elementary schools; considered from the point of view of their purpose, the preparatory schools lay the foundations in subjects properly regarded as of secondary level. Accordingly, the curriculum includes the elementary subjects, Latin, French, mathematics, and Greek, which has recently become optional. The establishment of a common entrance examination has helped to standardize the preparatory schools, which, besides equipping for this examination, also have the task of preparing their better pupils for entrance scholarships to the "public" schools, which are awarded on a competitive basis.

In the curriculum of the "public" schools the study of the classics long constituted the backbone of the instruction for most pupils. Since the beginning of the present century, however, partly as a result of the general revision of the content of secondary education throughout the country, partly through the influence of the school certificate examinations and changing social conditions under which the upper classes have gradually turned toward trade and commerce, adequate provision is made today for differentiation of courses in modern languages, science and mathematics, English and history, and other subjects. The masters are drawn in the main from the two older universities, to which the majority of the pupils who continue their education later proceed. Since the War, and to a large degree because of the qualities displayed by the product of the "public" schools, the number of applicants for admission has increased tremendously, and new institutions have been established on the same lines. It is not, however, social exclusiveness nor the intellectual training which have given these schools the hold that they have on the public imagination, despite the attacks made on them during and since the War, so much as the qualities cultivated by the corporate life, the games and athletics that are associated with what is called the "public school spirit." That the "public" schools deliberately set themselves the task of maintaining the *status quo* or that they aim at direct indoctrination in politics, economics, and social affairs is apt to be an exaggeration of those critics who profess to look upon such schools as nurseries of class-consciousness. The probability is that these schools are as innocent of deliberate and direct indoctrination as the American high schools or colleges. That the "public" schools do set a definite stamp on their product cannot be denied, but the impress of that stamp is made rather through the nature of the environment in which the pupils spend their adolescent years, and the too great detachment and remoteness of the curriculum from the realities of life. The "public" school, because it is a boarding school, is a miniature community, membership in which depends upon acceptance of the standards of what is called "good form." The weakness of these standards is that they place a premium on certain modes of behavior and correctness of manners ("the method of wearing a waistcoat," as Sir James Barrie said once in discussing the "public" school spirit), attitudes which are not entirely absent from certain institutions in the United States. On the intellectual side a change has been taking place for some time. The practice of dismissing pupils who fail to secure promotion after spending two years in the same class is an effective instrument at one end of the scale. More important than this is the leavening influence of external examinations, of inspection which many "public" schools after considerable hesitation have invited from the Board, and of the competition from the new secondary schools which have a more numerous clientèle to draw upon and are beginning from the scholastic standpoint to compete on equal terms with the "public" schools at least in the modern subjects. Nor can the social and economic crisis through which England is passing fail to exercise a powerful pressure to secure an adequate educational preparation for life. That those actively concerned in the work of the "public" schools are not ignorant of their problems may be seen from the participation of headmasters and assistant masters in the discussion of educational problems; they may not be radical in their points of view (English educational theory is rarely inclined to be radical), but they have contributed their share to the reform of instruction and content in special subjects. Fundamentally, however, it is the pattern of the English gentleman which the "public" schools endeavor to cultivate which gives them their character and in turn affects the ideals of education throughout the country. Thoughtful leaders in the "public" school system have always been aware of the dangers involved in the separation of classes, and have attempted through participation of their pupils in settlement work, in the Boy Scout movement, and in mixed camps of "public" school and elementary school pupils to cultivate sympathetic understanding. Such activities, it may be charged, may produce a certain condescending attitude on the part of the upper to the lower classes instead of a genuine understanding of the social problems involved. However that may be, if the "public" schools fail to give a direct training in social affairs, the explanation is to be found in two causes: The first is the deliberate exclusion of controversial subjects from the school program, and the second is a traditional faith in general education, which affect both "public" and other types of schools.

2. *Day grammar and high schools*. The second group of schools consists of a large number of day schools — grammar schools or high schools for boys or girls — many of which are as old as the older "public" schools. Because of their character as local schools, this group has been more responsive to public demands and social changes, with the result that the modernization of the curriculum began somewhat earlier than in the "public" schools. From the scholastic point of view these schools are organized in much the same way as the "public" schools and compete with them on equal terms, and while their affiliations have traditionally been with the older universities, many have established close relations with the newer or provincial universities. Pupils may be admitted before the age of twelve from private or from elementary schools and may remain up to the age of eighteen, although the majority leave after taking the first school certificate examination at about the age of sixteen. This group of schools is supported by income from endowments, from fees which range from about £10 to £30 a year, and from grants from the local and central authorities paid under certain conditions, the chief of which is that they admit a proportion of the pupils coming from elementary schools free of tuition. So far as conditions permit, the ideals and practices of the corporate life of "public" schools are here also reproduced.

3. *Council secondary schools*. The third group consists of council schools, public schools in the real sense of the term, provided and maintained by the local authorities empowered to do so under the provisions of the Education Act of 1902. These schools may be for boys or for girls or may be mixed. Of the four types of authorities for education, only the counties and county boroughs are permitted to establish secondary schools, although the municipal boroughs may levy a small rate which they contribute toward the cost of

secondary education in the counties in which they are located. This organization means that pupils living in rural or urban districts or in municipal boroughs attend secondary schools provided by the counties.

Many of the council schools are new foundations; some have been private schools which, because they were in danger of losing their clientèle to the new schools, found it more advantageous to be transferred to a public authority; others were previously higher elementary or organized science or technical schools. Each school is administered under a scheme approved by the Board of Education which requires the organization of a governing body, including representatives of the local education authority. The headmaster, selected by the governing body, and appointed by the local education authority is responsible for the internal administration of his school to his governing body and for the external or business matters to the local education authority. Under the *Regulations* of the Board of Education, the headmaster must have a right to a voice in the appointment and dismissal of teachers, to submit proposals to and to be consulted by his board of governors. One of the difficulties which has arisen in the development of the council secondary schools is that of the due distribution of the rights and duties of the headmasters and governing bodies on the one hand, and the local education authorities and their directors of education on the other. The Headmasters' Conference, indeed, refuses to admit to its membership a school which is otherwise eligible, if the independence of the headmaster is not safeguarded. The administrative principle which is universally recognized may be stated in two forms, either that "Schools are living things; they are not machine-made, mass-produced shops for the sale of instruction," [1] or that "No school can flourish where the head is not ruler in his land and a school controlled by outsiders is bound to lose status." [2]

The council schools charge fees generally lower than in the other types of schools, are more closely articulated with the elementary schools from which a large proportion of the pupils are drawn between the ages of eleven and twelve, and retain the majority of the pupils enrolled for a four-year course. Because of their origin as higher elementary, organized science, or technical schools, in many

---

[1] Quoted in Legge, J., *The Rising Tide*, p. 88 (London, 1929).
[2] King, Bolton, *Schools of Today*, p. 93 (New York, E. P. Dutton and Co, 1929).

cases there was a tendency at first to emphasize the scientific branches; a more balanced curriculum has, however, been developed under the influence of the Board of Education and the requirements of the school certificate examination, although instruction in the ancient classics does not enjoy the same position as in the other two groups of schools. The majority of the pupils who continue their education beyond the secondary stage to some extent, because the preliminary preparation of future elementary school teachers is given in these schools, proceed to the newer universities, from which, too, a larger percentage of the teachers are drawn. The development of the council schools, considering the comparatively short period of their existence and the fact that they have had to build up their own traditions, has been remarkable. At present their best pupils have begun to compete favorably for the open scholarships at the universities with the pupils from the older schools, a healthy situation for the maintenance and advancement of standards in all types of schools. In the same way a gradual advance has been made in the development of corporate life, and athletic activities.

4. *Private schools.* The last group consists of private schools of all degrees of quality. Their number is at present unknown, for the provision of the Education Act of 1918, which provided for their registration with the Board of Education for statistical purposes mainly, was not put into effect. In December, 1930, a committee was appointed to look into the number, status, and general character of all private schools. Their interests are represented by the Independent Schools Association, which claims on their behalf that parents have the right to choose the school to which they will send their children and that such schools are in general desirable as centers for variation and experimentation. Private schools are not subject to any public control except technically in respect of pupils within the range of the compulsory attendance laws. They may, however, on application be inspected by the Board of Education or by a local education authority, or by any other inspecting agency, such as a university; many of them submit their pupils to recognized external examinations; and finally, their standards may be indirectly affected under the conditions which have been set up for the registration of teachers, and for eligibility to the national superannuation system for teachers, service for a number of years in an efficient school being required in both cases. No school which is run for private profit

is eligible for a grant under the *Regulations* of the Board of Education.

REGULATIONS OF THE BOARD OF EDUCATION

Development of a national system of secondary education. Despite the variety of the types of schools, a recognized national system of secondary education has been developed in the main by three forces — the requirements of the universities for entrance and for competitive scholarships, the requirements of the examining bodies concerned in the examination of secondary schools, and the *Regulations* of the Board of Education. The definition of the scope and meaning of secondary education, the duration of an adequate period of education, the prolongation of this period, and a definition of the content of a secondary education have all been given national recognition through the *Regulations*. The Board from the start undertook to discourage the practice, which was not uncommon, of sending boys and girls to secondary schools for one or two years "to be finished" or "to acquire a polish." The *Regulations* require that an adequate number of the pupils be retained for a period of four years, with the result that many schools and local education authorities generally demand an undertaking from parents to keep their children in school for this period. Because of their influence on the character of its corporate life and on scholastic standards, the Board also takes into consideration the number of pupils who remain in a school beyond the age of sixteen.

Since the Education Act of 1902 was directed to the development of a coördinated system of schools, the Board devoted its attention from the first to securing a proper articulation between elementary and secondary education, which was all the more necessary as there was no unanimity in practice as to the age for beginning secondary education. Accordingly, the *Regulations* require that for purposes of recognition "the school must be a school for pupils who intend to remain for at least four years and up to at least the age of sixteen. It must provide a course of general education of a kind and amount suited to an age range at least from twelve to seventeen." The grants of the Board are based on the number of pupils in a school beyond the age of twelve, although reduced grants are paid in respect of pupils between the ages of ten and twelve.

Beyond this effort on the part of the Board of Education to define secondary education in terms of its duration, one of the chief tasks for which it was made responsible was to stimulate the provision of secondary education. This it was able to do through the usual English practice of entering into a partnership with the local education authorities and with individual schools which satisfactorily met the conditions prescribed for securing a grant. The first difficulty to be overcome was to allay the suspicion that participation by a state authority in the provision of education would in the end mean bureaucratic control and imposition from above. This was done by drawing a line of demarcation between administration and education, or control and advice. So far as the material side of education is concerned, the Board undertook to define the standards which schools applying for a grant must meet in the matter of *externa*; on the side of the *interna* the Board has refrained from controlling curricula, courses of study, time-schedules, and internal administration, with the reservation that these must be subject to the approval of its inspectors, which means in the last analysis that responsibility is imposed on the headmaster and his staff to think through and defend their policies.

The Board of Education inspects not only schools which apply for a grant, but also those schools which for one reason or another do not desire a grant, but wish to have the opinion of external assessors whose experience with the whole field of secondary education gives them satisfactory standards of comparison. The Board accordingly issues a list of efficient schools recognized for grant and of schools recognized as efficient but not as eligible for the grant. The fear of bureaucratic control, which was manifested when the Board was established with powers to inspect schools, has gradually disappeared and many of the great "public" and independent schools have invited and welcomed its inspection and are found today in the list of efficient but not grant-earning schools.

A school applying for a grant — and any school is eligible for it provided that it is not run for private profit — is subjected to a full inspection by the Board's inspectors, which is repeated at stated periods, and must present a scheme for approval by the Board. The conditions upon which the grant is awarded is that the buildings and equipment must be satisfactory; that the school is open for thirty-six weeks in the year; that the staff is suitable and sufficient in number and with adequate qualifications; that salaries must not be based on the amount of annual grant received; that the size of classes must be limited to thirty pupils; that a satisfactory percentage of the pupils are retained for four years; and that free places are provided for pupils coming from elementary schools up to twenty-five per cent of the enrollment, on the principle that state-supported schools must be accessible to all and not be "class" institutions.

The last provision, introduced in 1907, aroused serious misgivings and threw a considerable amount of light on the prevalence of social class distinctions in England. The private schools depending upon the support of fee-paying pupils feared that the introduction of a new social element would seriously affect their clientèle. Some of these schools were transferred to local education authorities and became council schools; others were permitted to admit a lower percentage, but not less than ten per cent, of the pupils from elementary schools. Generally it was felt, particularly by teachers in the schools, that the elementary school product, because of the character of elementary education and the lack of cultural advantages in their homes, would be unfitted for secondary education. Time has proved that this fear was groundless; not only do free-placers remain in school longer than fee-payers, but a larger proportion of them succeed in the certificate examinations, and proceed to the universities. That the policy of the Board has been more than justified is indicated in the increase of the percentage for free places almost up to fifty per cent and in some fifteen systems in the abolition of fees.

The progress made under this system will in all probability be checked by new regulations issued by the Board in September, 1932, to become effective on April 1, 1933. According to *Circular 1421*, which accompanied the draft *Regulations for Secondary Schools for 1933*, the Board undertook

to take account of two criticisms which have recently been made with increasing force, viz., that (*a*) the system of admitting pupils free to secondary schools without regard to the capacity of parents to pay is needlessly wasteful of public funds, and runs counter to the principle now generally accepted, that where educational awards are made by public or quasi-public bodies the amount of any assistance given should vary according to the circumstances of the successful candidates, (*b*) the fees charged often bear but a small proportion to the cost of the education provided, and are frequently not adequate having regard to what parents can afford to pay.

Accordingly, under the new *Regulations* all schools must charge fees but must maintain facilities for poor parents to obtain for their children the benefits of secondary education. The average per capita cost for secondary education is about £35; the *Regulations* now propose that fees shall constitute a larger proportion of this sum than they have done hitherto, and, while not desiring to lay down any uniform standard, the Board recommends a minimum fee of £9.9.0; fee payers will continue to be admitted on a qualifying examination. All schools in receipt of grants will be required to offer each year special places (a term which is now substituted for "free places") subject to the prescribed minumum and maximum limits, that is to say, 25 per cent and 50 per cent of the total number of admissions in the previous school year. The special places will be awarded on the basis of competitive examinations under the same arrangements as for free places, but exemption from fees will be granted only to the children of parents whose income is £3 or £4 a week, but, in considering proposals put forward for approval, the Board will have regard to the particular circumstances of an educational area and the rate of fee to be charged.

The terms of *Circular 1421* and the *Regulations* have been approved by Parliament and will become effective on April 1, 1933, despite the opposition of leaders in education, professional associations, and many local authorities. That the change is reactionary is obvious; that it has been inspired by a desire to reduce the burden on taxation is specious in the light of official statements that the total savings expected will amount only to £400,000 a year; that it is contrary to public welfare and progress can be proved by the subsequent achievements of students who gained their first opportunity for higher education under the free place system. The argument that "where educational awards are made by public or quasi-public bodies the amount of any assistance given should vary according to the circumstances of the successful candidates" would, of course, apply equally to elementary education and the special services connected therewith. Finally, the adoption of a "means" test for special places will seriously affect those classes whose income is just above the proposed limits and from which the larger proportion of free-placers have been drawn. Whatever the reasons which have prompted this reactionary step, it is interesting to note that almost at the same time that the *Circular* and the *Regulations* were issued the French Minister of Education announced that he would speed up the policy adopted in 1929 and abolish all tuition fees for secondary education in 1933.

PROGRESS OF SECONDARY EDUCATION

The progress of secondary education since 1902 has been rapid. In 1903-04, the first year for which figures for grant-earning schools are available, there were 407 schools; in 1931 (March 31), this number had increased to 1367 in England and Wales (1218 in England alone). These schools were distributed, from the point of view of their provision, as follows: 720 were council schools, 87 Roman Catholic schools, 458 foundation and other schools, and 102 Welsh Intermediate Schools. Of the total 500 were schools for boys, 485 for girls, and 382 were mixed. The enrollment has increased from 31,716 in 1902 to 411,309 (217,110 boys and 194,199 girls) in 1931. The number of schools recognized as efficient but not on the grant list was 362 in England and Wales (343 in England), with 64,622 pupils (32,193 boys and 32,429 girls). There were in addition 228 preparatory schools with 16,647 pupils, which were recognized as efficient. It must be remembered that these figures do not include a large number of secondary schools which are not grant-earning and do not apply for inspection by the Board, nor, as contrasted with the high school enrollment in the United States, do they include schools giving technical or other forms of vocational education. On the other hand, the enrollment in the grant-aided schools include pupils below high school age in the United States; the number of pupils below the age of twelve was 45,883 (16,939 boys and 28,944 girls).

More significant than the increase in the total enrollment has been the success of the movement to make secondary education accessible to pupils coming from the elementary schools. The proportion of such pupils in grant-aided schools was 76.1 per cent in 1931. The total number of free-place pupils in the same year was 194,095 or 44.3 per cent of the pupils. The percentage of free places ranges from under 25 per cent up to 75 per cent and over, but any reduction below the standard requirement of 25 per cent can only be permitted by the Board after considering the special circumstances of the school concerned. Free secondary education has been adopted in some fifteen areas (74 schools in all), but the extension of this practice, although proposed from time to time in Parliament, and considered as a logical development in the *Report of the Departmental Committee on Scholarships and Free Places* (London, 1920), has not yet come within the range of practical politics. At present the income from fees in grant-earning schools represents about forty per cent of the total cost, the remainder being met out of local and state funds and to a slight extent out of income from endowments.

The number of pupils between the ages of eleven and sixteen in grant-earning schools was 302,987 or nearly 74 per cent of the total enrollment. The average length of school life after the age of eleven was 4 years 8 months for boys and 4 years 9 months for girls, while the average leaving age for boys was 16 years 7 months and 16 years 7 months for girls. As a measure of the success of secondary education, it is to be noted that the average length of school life has increased by over two years since 1908–09 and the average leaving age has increased by a little over one year. To this may be added the increase in the number of advanced courses, which rose from 483 in 1929–30 to 494 in 1930–31. In 1908–09 the number of pupils proceeding to a university was 1056 (695 boys and 361 girls) as compared with 4132 (2701 boys and 1431 girls) in 1930–31. Perhaps more striking than these figures as indicating the increased opportunities for pupils coming from elementary schools is the fact that a larger percentage continue in the secondary schools than do the fee-paying pupils and that of the number proceeding to a university 64.4 per cent were ex-elementary school pupils.

ORGANIZATION

Organization of secondary schools. As contrasted with the secondary schools of other countries, there is an almost complete absence of uniformity in the organization of the English schools. Except that each school, if of sufficient size, has adopted a uniform division into six forms, additional forms ("Shell," "Remove," "Transitus") have been intercalated in the interests of flexibility. The same reason has led to the adoption of several classes within each form, to which pupils are assigned according to ability. The result is that the system of promotion is elastic. In schools which provide advanced work or advanced courses (see p. 664), the common practice is that pupils spend two years in the Sixth, or highest, Form. The Board of Education prescribes a normal limit of 30 as the size of classes in grant-earning schools; this limit was, however, exceeded in 1930 in 4494 classes, in 155 of which there were more than 35 pupils.

If generalizations about the administrative organization are impossible, still less possible is it to generalize about the organization of studies. In the older and larger schools modern and classical sides are found from the start; in others there may be a common foundation branching out later into these two sides; in others again provision is made for pupils who have had several years on the language sides to enter other sides which place an emphasis on science or mathematics or both, and on history. The organization is still further increased in complexity by the regrouping of pupils into sets for some special subjects such as mathematics or a second foreign language. In all cases, however, pupils are assigned to a form master who is responsible in the lower forms usually for the teaching of a foreign language and English subjects (English, history, and geography) and who exercises a general supervision over the pupils in his forms. For pupils in day schools the form-room is their home. In boarding schools the pupils are divided into houses and are responsible to their housemaster, a practice which has been adopted in a few day schools partly to provide for such personal supervision and guidance, and partly to promote the corporate life of the school through the organization of the pupils into groups. However vague and indistinct the methods of organization may be, they are of considerable importance in conserving the individual characteristics and independence of each school. The only fixed points which are common to all schools are the standard and requirements of the First School or School Certificate Examination, to which pupils are expected to be submitted after a four-year course, and the Second or Higher Certificate Examination taken two years later (see p. 666).

Admission of pupils. Pupils are normally admitted on the basis of an examination. The "public" schools rely on the results of the common entrance examination. The subjects in which papers are set in this examination are Latin translation, grammar and composition; history; geography; arithmetic, algebra, geometry; French; Scripture and English; Greek translation and grammar (optional); Eton requires Latin verse. In other schools, particularly council schools, the entrance examination is based on the fundamental subjects and English, supplemented usually by an oral examination. The free-place pupils are selected in each area on the basis of a common examination taken usually between the ages of eleven and twelve (see p. 101). This practice of a dual system of examinations

SECONDARY EDUCATION

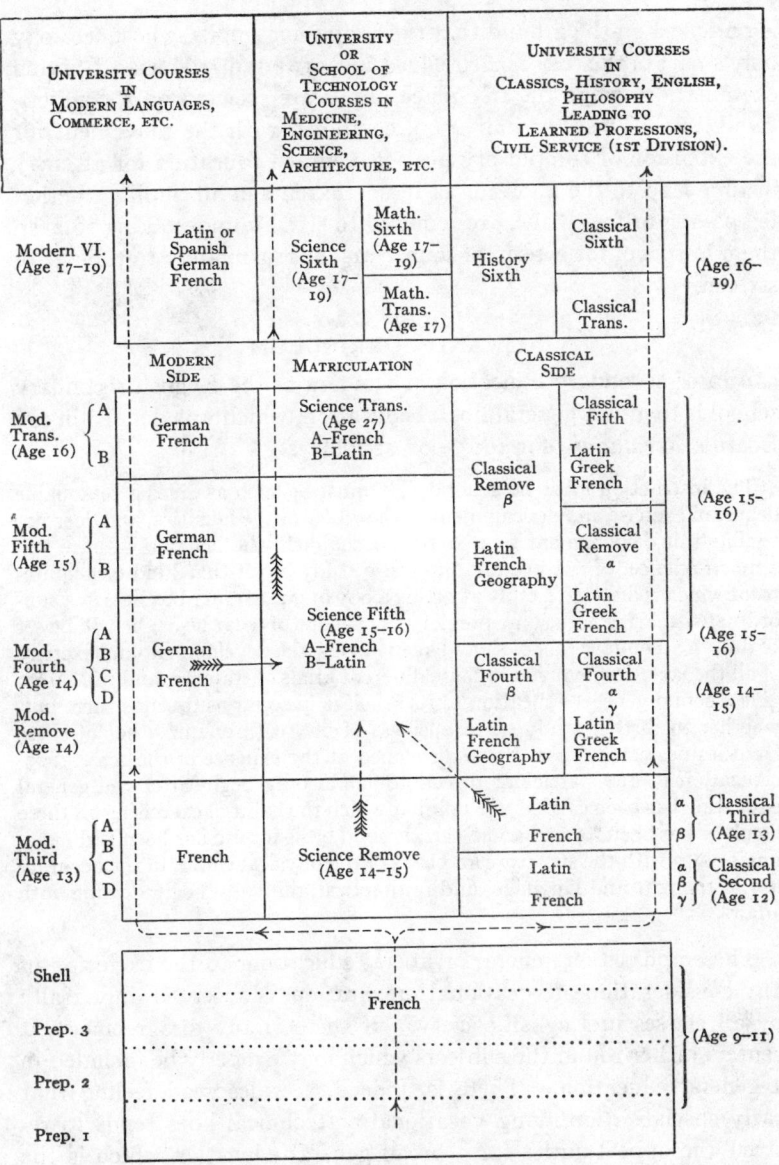

The above Diagram shows the various stages of a boy's progress from the Lower Forms to the Upper in the several departments into which the Manchester Grammar School is divided.

is criticized on the ground that the fee-paying pupils, whose fees pay only a part of the cost of their education, are admitted on a qualifying examination, while the free-place pupils are selected on a competitive basis. This discrimination, combined with the movement for the extension of compulsory post-elementary education for all, may in time lead to the abolition of fees. Parents of all pupils, whether fee-paying or free-place, are required to sign an undertaking to keep them in school for a term of four years, approximately to the age of sixteen.

AIM AND CURRICULUM

Aim of secondary education. The aim of the English secondary school is to give a general liberal education, which was defined in the Board's *Regulations* for 1905–06 [1] as follows:

> The instruction must be general; i.e., must be such as gives a reasonable degree of exercise and development of the whole of the faculties, and does not confine this development to a particular channel, whether that of pure and applied science, of literary and linguistic study, or of that kind of acquirement which is directed simply at fitting a boy or girl to enter business in a subordinate capacity with some previous knowledge of what he or she will be set to do. A secondary school should keep in view the development and exercise of all the faculties involved in these different kinds of training, and will fail to give a sound general education to its scholars in so far as it sends them out, whether to further study or to business of life, with one or other of these faculties neglected, or with one developed at the expense of the rest. Specialization in any particular direction should only begin after the general education has been carried to a point at which the habit of exercising all these faculties has been formed and a certain solid basis for life has been laid in acquaintance with the structure and laws of the physical world, in the accurate use of thought and language, and in practical ability to begin dealing with affairs.

The emphasis on general or liberal education, to the exclusion of any consideration of vocational preparation, is accepted universally by all classes in English society. If there is any disagreement, it centers rather round the subjects which may properly be included in a general education. There is, indeed, a widespread feeling that early specialization along vocational or technical lines tends to restrict the opportunities for a broad general education which is the foundation of the well-being of man as an individual and as a citi-

---

[1] Board of Education, *Regulations for Secondary Schools, 1905–06*, p. vii (London, 1905).

zen.¹ A general education, indeed, is regarded as the best basis upon which later specialization can be built, so that vocational training should be supplementary to, rather than a part of, secondary education. Whatever any future reorganization of post-primary education may bring, it is widely agreed that a common feature of all schools should be the harmonious development of all the powers — mental, moral, and physical; an increasing number of educators are beginning to urge the importance of æsthetic development. Literature, science, mathematics, art, and practical work should all enable the pupils to understand and interpret the life about him and serve at once as a universal bond of sympathy and as a preparation for the enjoyment of the increased amount of leisure which is following the reduction in the number of working hours. In quite a different sense from that in which it was employed when the provision of elementary education was discussed, secondary education is to give to the new classes in society to which it is being extended that education which had been enjoyed by their masters. Two other reasons may be added for this insistence on general education as the basis of secondary. The first is that there still survives in England, despite the brilliant contribution of some of her psychologists, a strong faith in the virtue of general training, with the consequent suspicion of the narrow training of the specialist. The second is a rooted conviction that a liberal education can best be acquired through a sympathetic study and appreciation of all that has been involved in the evolution of the human spirit. The present, it is felt, is too much with us and too near to afford an adequate perspective. For this reason and because of a desire to keep politics out of the school, the discussion of controversial subjects is eschewed in the classroom.

The scholastic standards in the secondary schools are being raised appreciably as a result of the Board's inspections and publications, the examination system, which, however subject to criticism, does set up definite standards of achievement, the improvement of teaching methods, and the intense economic competition. The average English parent, however, is by no means as interested in this aspect of

¹ The Committee on Education and Industry (England and Wales) endorsed this point of view in its *Report* (Second Part, pp. 32 f.), and, while advocating the introduction of special courses at about the age of fourteen, stated that "it appears essential for educational reasons that it (the special course) should be of quite a general character... rather than through the detailed study of subjects specially related to a particular industry. The proper place for specialized instruction of that kind is, under any system of education, the Technical and not the Secondary School." (London, 1928.)

TIME-SCHEDULE, FIRST FOUR YEARS, MANCHESTER GRAMMAR SCHOOL [1]

CLASSES	CLASSICAL SIDE				MODERN SIDE				SCIENCE SIDE	
	First Year	Second Year	Third Year	Fourth Year	First Year	Second Year	Third Year	Fourth Year	Third Year	Fourth Year
Average Age..........	12	13	14	15	12	13	14	15	14	15
Subject:										
English and history..	5	5	5	5	6	6	5	5	6	6
Geography.........	2	2	..	..	2	2	2	..	..	..
Science.............	1a	3b	2c	..	1a	3b	5d	6d	10e	10e
Art................	2	2	1	2	3	2	..	1	1	1
Latin...............	6	6	5	5	..	..	..	..	..	..
Greek (or geography).	..	..	5	6	..	..	..	..	..	..
Latin or French.....	..	..	..	..	..	..	..	..	5	5
French.............	4	4	4	4	7	6	5	5	..	..
German............	..	..	..	..	..	..	5	5	..	..
Manual............	2	..	..	..	2	2	..	..	..	..
Gymnasium........	1	1	1	1	2	2	1	1	1	1

a = Natural science
b = Physics
c = Chemistry
d = Physics cum chemistry
e = Physics and chemistry as two subjects for matriculation

SIXTH FORM CURRICULUM, MANCHESTER GRAMMAR SCHOOL

	PRINCIPAL SUBJECTS	SUBSIDIARY SUBJECTS	OTHER SUBJECTS NOT FOR H.S.C.
Classical VI	Greek, Latin, ancient history	English, Greek Testament	German or French
Mathematical VI	Pure mathematics, applied mathematics, physics, higher mathematics	Latin	English, German, or Latin
History VI	History, French or Latin, English	Economics	German, Latin, or Greek, French
Science VI	Chemistry, physics, pure and applied mathematics, biology, botany, zoölogy. Of these, boys take chemistry and any two other subjects	Latin or German or French	English
Modern VI	French, German, history	....	English, Latin

[1] From *The Journal of Education* (London), March, 1931, pp. 157 f.

TIME-SCHEDULE, YARDLEY SECONDARY SCHOOL[1]

CLASSES	First year	Second year	Third Year	Fourth year A, B, and C	Fourth year D	Fifth year
Age range at beginning	10.8 to 12.8	11.8 to 13.8	12.8 to 14.8	14.3 to 15.8	13.8 to 15.8	14.8 to 16.0
Girls and boys together						
Scripture	1	1	1	2	2	2
English	5	4	4	4	4	4
History	2	2	2	2	2	2
Geography	2	2	2	2	2	2
Latin		5	4	4		4
French	5	3	4	4	4	4
Mathematics *	7	4 *	5	6	6	6
Nature Study	2					
Art	2	1 (hour)	2 (boys) 1 (girls)	2	2	2
Music	2	1			1	
Boys only						
Woodwork	2	2	2		3	
Physics and chemistry		5	5	5	5	5
Physical Exercises	2	2	1	1	1	1
Girls only						
Needlework and handicraft	2	2	2	2	2	2
Domestic science		2	2		2	
Physics and chemistry		3				
Botany			4	3	3	3
Physical exercises	2	2	1	1	2	1
Total periods	32	32	32	32	32	32

* 3¾ hours.

education as is the French or German. His chief interest is that the school shall develop the character of his children, turn them out imbued with the qualities of an English gentleman or gentlewoman. Hence, while every secondary school realizes the importance to itself and to the country of providing the best facilities for the intellectual training of the best minds, its aim is to do the best possible for the moral or character development of all the pupils. There may be no unanimity on what constitutes a sound modern education, but all are agreed that of equal importance are the development of character, the awakening of a feeling of duty, the cultivation of a sense of responsibility, and training in self-reliance. If the two aims —

[1] From *The Journal of Education* (London). May 1, 1931, p. 296.

the instructional and educative — are rarely synthesized into a consistent philosophy, as is being attempted in German theory at any rate, and if the spirit of the classroom may be quite distinct from the spirit which pervades the playing fields or the corporate activities of the school, this is merely another illustration of the English educator's abhorrence of theory or philosophy of education.

The curriculum. In spite of the insistence on general education, however, its implications for the curriculum had not begun to be formulated until 1917. Before that date the curriculum had tended to grow up piecemeal, some schools throwing the emphasis on the languages, mainly the classical, then on the sciences. As the result of a letter on "The Neglect of Science" which appeared in *The Times* of February 2, 1916, a number of organizations interested in secondary school subjects (the Classical, English, Geographical, Historical, and Modern Languages Associations) appointed representatives to meet with a committee representing the sciences. The conference between the representatives passed the following resolutions in January, 1917:

1. The first object in education is the training of human beings in mind and character, as citizens of a free country, and any technical preparation of boys and girls for a particular profession, occupation, or work must be consistent with this principle.

2. In all schools in which education is normally continued up to or beyond the age of sixteen, and in other schools so far as circumstances permit, the curriculum up to about the age of sixteen should be general and not specialized; and in this curriculum there should be integrally represented English (language and literature), languages and literatures other than English, history, geography, mathematics, natural sciences, art, and manual training.

3. In the opinion of this conference, both natural science and literary subjects should be taught to all students below the age of sixteen.

4. In the case of students who stay at school beyond the age of sixteen, specialization should be gradual and not complete.

5. In many schools of the older type more time is needed for instruction in natural science; and this time can often be obtained by economy in the time allotted to classics, without detriment to the interests of classical education.

6. In many other schools more time is needed for instruction in languages, history, and geography; and it is essential, in the interests of sound education, that time be provided.

7. While it is probably impossible to provide instruction in both Latin and Greek in all secondary schools, provision should be made in every area for teaching in these subjects, so that every boy and girl who is qualified to profit from them, shall have the opportunity of receiving adequate instruction in them.

SECONDARY EDUCATION

TIME-SCHEDULE, HYMERS COLLEGE, HULL [1]

Modern	Classical
6 German	6 Greek
or 4 Latin and 2 Mechanics	or 6 German
or 4 Art and 2 Mechanics	
or 4 Workshops and 2 Mechanics	
or 2 Art, 2 Workshops, and 2 Mechanics	

The time allocations — with alternatives marked * — up to the Sixths are as follows:

SUBJECTS	L3	U3	IVa b	IV cl	Shell	LV m	LV cl	UV m	UV cl
Scripture	1	1	1	1	1	1	1	1	1
English	4	3	4	4	4	4	4	5*	5*
History	2	2	2	2	2	4*	4*	4*	4*
Geography	2	2	2	2	2	4*	4*	4*	4*
Latin	5	6	4*	6	4*	4*	6	4*	8
Mechanics	..	..	2*	..	2*	2*	..	2*	..
French	5	5	5	5	5	6	6	5	5
Greek/German	..	..	6*	6*	6*	6*	6*	6*	6*
Mathematics	6	7	7	7	6	7	7	7	7
Chemistry	2	2	3	..	4	4	2	4	..
Physics	2	2	3	2	4	4	..	4	..
Art	2	2	2*	..	2*	2*	..	2*	..
Music	2	1	..	..	..	..	..	..	..
Workshop	2	2	2*	..	2*	2*	..	2*	..
Commercial	..	..	2	..	2	..	..	..	..
Physical exercise	1	1	1	1	..	..	..	..	..

The average ages of the senior forms on entry are as follows:

L3a,	11.8	IVcl.,	13.11
U3a,	12.7	LVcl.,	15.1
IVa,	13.10	UVcl.,	15.11
LVm,	15.1	UVI,	17.1
UVm,	16.3	I3c,	12.1
LVI,	16.1	U3c,	13.4
I3b,	12.0	IVb,	14.5
U3b,	13.2		

In the advanced courses subjects are taken as follows:

SUBJECTS	MAIN	SUBSIDIARY	NOT FOR EXAMINATION
Classics	Greek, Latin, Ancient History	Scripture, English	Music
Modern Studies	English, French, History	Latin or German	Music, Art, Scripture
Mathematics	Mathematics, Physics	Chemistry, English	Music, Scripture, German
Science	Chemistry, Physics	Mathematics, English	Music, Scripture, German

[1] From *The Journal of Education* (London), July 1, 1931, p. 478.

Interest in the aims of secondary education and in its curriculum was fostered by the activities of the special subject organizations mentioned and by the publications of special reports on the position of natural science, classics, modern languages, and English in a national system of education.[1] These have been supplemented from time to time by the memoranda, suggestions, and *Educational Pamphlets* of the Board of Education, by the development of vacation courses for teachers of special subjects, and by special reports of professional associations of headmasters and headmistresses, and assistant masters and mistresses.

The *Regulations* of the Board of Education require that the secondary school curriculum must provide instruction in the English language and literature, at least one language other than English, geography, history, mathematics, science, and drawing. Provision must also be made for organized games, physical exercises, manual instruction and singing. Where two foreign languages are included, one of them must be Latin except by special permission of the Board, which may also approve the omission of foreign languages altogether, provided "that the instruction in English provides special and adequate linguistic and literary training, and that the teaching staff are qualified to give such instruction."

In girls' schools provision must be made for the inclusion of practical instruction in domestic subjects, such as needlework, cookery, laundry work, housekeeping, and household hygiene; a combination of these subjects may in the case of older girls be substituted partially or wholly for science and for mathematics other than arithmetic.

In a *Report* of the Consultative Committee on *Differentiation of the Curriculum for Boys and Girls respectively in Secondary Schools* (London, 1923), it was recommended that greater freedom should be introduced in the curriculum for both boys and girls, and especially that a more prominent and established place be assigned

---

[1] *Report of the Committee appointed to inquire into the Position of Natural Science in the Educational System of Great Britain* (London, 1918); *Report of the Committee appointed by the Prime Minister to inquire into the Position of Modern Languages in the Educational System of Great Britain* (London, 1918): *Report of the Prime Minister's Committee on the Position of Classics in the Educational System of the United Kingdom* (London, 1921); *The Report of the Departmental Committee appointed to inquire into the Position of English in the Educational System of England* (*The Teaching of English in England*), (London, 1921).

For an analysis of the first two *Reports* see Kandel, I. L., *Education in Great Britain and Ireland*, U.S. Bureau of Education, *Bulletin* (1919) No. 9, pp. 34 ff.; and of the third, Kandel, I. L., *The Classics in England, France, and Germany*, Part III of the *Report of the Classical Investigation* (Princeton, 1925).

to æsthetic training through music, art, and other æsthetic subjects. After recommending measures for assimilating girls' and boys' schools in such subjects as mathematics, physics, English language and literature, manual instruction, domestic subjects, and organized games, the *Report* urged that care should be taken for the protection of girls against physical fatigue and overstrain. Further research into the physical and psychological differences between boys and girls was recommended.

The Board of Education does not itself prescribe courses of study, but exercises an indirect influence through its inspectors, who must approve the curriculum, courses of study, and time-schedule in efficient schools, and through its publication of memoranda and suggestions on various subjects. Each school enjoys freedom, subject to the approval of the inspectors, in organizing its curriculum, courses of study, and time-schedule. The principle upon which the *Regulations* of the Board on this question are based is to "allow and encourage much elasticity in curricula, subject only to the fundamental principle that the school course make effective provision for the development of bodily and mental faculties on broad and human lines in the pupils who are to be the citizens of the future." There is accordingly adequate room for flexibility and elasticity for each school to define the content of a general education, with one important reservation — the requirements of external examinations, but even examination bodies have shown themselves ready to recognize alternative courses (see p. 668).

For the majority of the pupils from the ages of twelve to sixteen a general course, observing a proper balance between the humanities and sciences, is organized, covering a period of four years and culminating in the First or School Certificate Examination conducted by an external examining body. In its Circular 1294, the Board suggested the following time-distribution of subjects in the secondary school curriculum:

Subject	Periods (45 minutes)	Subject	Periods (45 minutes)
English	2–4	Mathematics	6
Languages (2)	9	Drawing	2
Science	6	Music	1
History	2	Manual work,	2
Geography	3	Physical exercises	2
Scripture	1		
Total periods			35–37

Advanced courses. In an effort to encourage the prolongation of school life, and to provide for specialization by pupils intending to pass on to the universities and other places of higher education and research, the Board, in its *Regulations* for 1917–18, proceeded to carry out its plan, already outlined in 1913, to promote by a special grant the organization and development of advanced courses for pupils remaining in school for two years after passing the First Examination. Provision was made first for three such courses:

(A) Science and mathematics.
(B) Classics, viz., the civilization of the ancient world as embodied in the languages, literature, and history of Greece and Rome.
(C) Modern studies, viz., the languages, literature, and history of the countries of Western Europe in modern and medieval times.

Adequate provision for continuing general subjects was required. As a result of protests against the restriction of advanced courses to three groups, the Board of Education permitted the introduction of other groups. To the three courses mentioned above there have now been added the following:

(D) The Civilization (1) of Greece and Rome, and (2) of England or another country of Western Europe in modern times, as embodied in their language, literature, and history.
(E) Geography combined with two other subjects approved by the Board, of which at least one must be history or a science.
(F) Such other combinations of subjects as may be approved by the Board.

The development of advanced courses, which are tested by the Second or Higher Certificate Examination, has introduced a new problem, since they tend to overlap to some extent with the first year of the courses for the general degree in many of the universities, or, in American terms, with the junior college. They have, however, had the effect of raising the general standards in many schools and have encouraged an increasing number of pupils to proceed to the universities. In 1930–31 the number of advanced courses in England was 494 given in 341 schools and distributed as follows: 230 in science and mathematics, 182 in modern subjects, 37 in classics, 7 in classics with modern studies, 5 in geography, and 33 in other combinations of subjects. These figures do not include the provision for advanced work in many schools which have not applied for formal approval by the Board. State scholarships, awarded annually up to a maximum of 200, and tenable normally for three years in an English or Welsh university, are granted on the basis of the examinations for the Second or Higher Certificate.

EXAMINATIONS

Perhaps the most characteristic influence on secondary education has been that of examinations. The absence of a central authority in the nineteenth century and the recognition of the need of some external appraisal of the work of the secondary schools led to the creation of external examining agencies such as the College of Preceptors in 1853 and the Oxford and Cambridge Joint Board in 1873. The Science and Art Department began, through the award of grants on the basis of examination, to encourage the study of science, art, and other subjects in 1872. From that time on the number of examining bodies, representing universities and a great variety of professions, increased without check, with the result that the great variety of standards and requirements caused a constant upheaval in the schools and imposed a tremendous pressure on the pupils who were subjected to them in many cases at the end of each year of their school life.

In 1911 the Consultative Committee of the Board of Education considered the question, and on the basis of its *Report*,[1] the Board of Education in 1914 prepared a scheme to limit the number of examining bodies and to restrict the number of examinations to which pupils were to be subjected to two, the first to be general and taken at about the age of sixteen on the completion of a four-year course, and the second, more specialized, to be taken two years later. The Board put its scheme into operation in 1917. A Secondary Schools Examination Council was set up to act in an advisory capacity, with a membership including representatives of the examining boards of universities, the Teachers' Registration Council, local authorities, and others. The chief function of the Council is to recommend examining bodies for approval, to supervise the maintenance of standards, and to secure the recognition by universities and professional bodies of certificates obtained in the examinations. The Council requires that the coöperation of teachers be secured by the examining bodies.

The Board of Education may under the *Regulations* require schools to submit whole forms for examination by an approved examining

[1] *Report on Examinations in Secondary Schools* (1911).

body, and pays a grant for each pupil who takes an examination. Eight examining bodies have been recognized: the Joint Matriculation Board of the Northern Universities, the Universities of London, Bristol, and Durham, the Central Welsh Board, the Oxford and Cambridge Schools Examination Board, the Oxford Delegacy for Local Examinations, and the Cambridge Local Examinations Syndicate.

As an example of the requirements of the First or School Certificate, Examination, the following arrangement of subjects prescribed by the Oxford and Cambridge Schools Examination Board may be cited:

Group I. (1) Scripture knowledge. (2) English. (3) History. (4) Geography.
Group II. (1) Latin. (2) Greek. (3) French. (4) German. (5) Spanish (6) Italian. (7) Arabic.
Group III. (1) Elementary mathematics. (2) Additional mathematics. (3) Physics. (4) Chemistry. (5) Physics and chemistry. (6) General science. (7) Botany. (8) Biology.
Group IV. (1) Music. (2) Drawing. (3) Geometrical and mechanical drawing.[1]

One, but not more than one, of the three subjects in Group IV may be included in the five subjects counting for a certificate. In order to obtain a certificate, candidates must (1) pass in the first three groups separately by reaching a satisfactory standard in at least one subject in each group; (2) reach a satisfactory standard in five subjects including the three under (1) — not more than one of the subjects may be in Group IV; (3) pass with credit in at least one of the five subjects and satisfy the examiners in the examination as a whole.

In 1931 Group IV was modified on the recommendation of the Council that two of the following subjects should be allowed to count toward the minimum number of subjects required for the award of a certificate: art, music, handicraft, domestic science (including needlework), commercial subjects, geometrical and engineering drawing, and any other subject which may be approved by the Council in special circumstances.

The subjects for the Second or Higher Certificate Examination are

[1] In the requirements of other Boards, there may be included, besides these subjects, art, handicraft, bookkeeping, cookery, laundry work, needlework, housewifery, and domestic science.

based, as a rule, on the advanced courses. In the Oxford and Cambridge Schools Examination Board requirements, the subjects are arranged in the following groups: (1) classical studies; (2) modern studies; (3) mathematics; (4) natural science. In each group a number of subsidiary subjects must be taken.

The number of candidates who took the first examination in 1931 was 66,909, of whom 46,301, or 69.2 per cent, obtained certificates; not all pupils, however, who have spent four years in a secondary school, take the examination. Of 11,016 pupils who took the second examination, 7408, or 67.2 per cent, obtained certificates. The subjects taken in the two examinations, which are as follows, indicate the character of the secondary school curriculum:

First Examination

Subject	Number of Entries	Subject	Number of Entries
English	68,024	Additional mathematics	3,408
French	64,746	Biology	3,075
Mathematics	62,585	Welsh	2,788
History	58,217	Domestic subjects	2,693
Geography	44,698	Greek	2,474
Latin	27,956	Electricity and magnetism	2,497
Chemistry	27,112	General science	2,134
Art	26,850	Mechanics	1,986
Physics	17,998	Commercial subjects	1,751
Religious knowledge	14,835	Handicraft	1,100
Botany	15,073	Spanish	978
German	5,257	Domestic science or hygiene	918
Chemistry with physics	3,825	Music	860
Heat, light and sound	3,447	Economics	732

Second Examination

Subject	Number of Entries	Subject	Number of Entries
Mathematics	4,749	Zoölogy	346
French	4,215	Biology	182
English	4,011	Welsh	120
History	3,524	Economics	157
Physics	3,372	Physics with chemistry	121
Chemistry	3,248	Spanish	97
Latin	2,509	Art	45
Geography	1,005	English with history	41
Greek	989	History with French	18
Ancient history	960	Music	18
Botany	690	Geology	11
German	434	Italian	4

Criticism of examinations. The organization of the examinations has undoubtedly exercised an important influence in defining the scope of the work of the secondary school, and the first school certificate has come to be generally required of applicants for employment in business offices, banks, railways, insurance companies, and similar organizations. The system has, however, begun to be the subject of serious criticisms, not so widely as yet on technical grounds — that is, their reliability and whether they really measure ability — but rather for the reason that they militate against a desirable expansion of the curriculum for those pupils who might profit more from a study of practical subjects. From another point of view the privileges attached to the certificate have proved an obstacle to the independent development of the central schools, which, intended originally for the less academically minded pupils, have tended in many cases to prepare for the certificate examinations (see p. 392). Although some changes have taken place in the list of subjects required for the examination, they have been but slight and have not paid due attention to the remarkable increase since 1917 in the enrollments and consequently to the differences among the pupils. A further difficulty has resulted from the confusion of the certificate requirements with the requirements for entrance to the universities. A curriculum based on the supposed needs for university study is recognized to be inappropriate for all pupils. There is accordingly a demand that the requirements for the school certificate be dissociated from those for university matriculation examinations and that greater encouragement be given to the fine and practical arts. It has been proposed that the foreign language cease to be obligatory in the examinations, that alternative syllabuses be accepted, and that more value should be attached to practical subjects such as art, music, wood and metal work, machine drawing and elementary engineering, domestic science, and practical rural science, subjects which the Secondary Schools Examinations Council has recently recommended.[1]

Alternative courses. At least one county education authority, the West Riding of Yorkshire, has followed the logic of the situation and has introduced alternative courses in some of its secondary

---

[1] See *The School Certificate Examination, being the Report of the Panel of Investigators appointed by the Secondary Schools Examinations Council*, etc. (London, 1932); and Valentine, C. W., *Reliability of Examinations* (London, 1932).

schools for pupils not of the school certificate type. The alternative courses follow the following lines:

(1) Mechanics, machine drawing, and engineering workshop.

(2) (*a*) Handicraft (including wood-turning, sheet-metal work, pattern-making, industrial art applied to engineering or textiles, industrial history, and commercial geography); (*b*) engineering (including that pertaining to heat engines, machine drawing and design, and machine shop practice); or (*c*) textiles (including study of materials, fabrics, cotton, flax, hemp, jute, ramie, silks, artificial fibers, and waste materials, principles of weaving, etc.).

(3) Courses in the management and cultivation of land or (for girls) in country or home occupations.

(4) (*a*) Special courses for girls with academic subjects and art or music or domestic subjects, or crafts, or extra physical training work; (*b*) a business course, including academic subjects and shorthand, bookkeeping, and typewriting. It has been found that a fair proportion of the pupils taking such courses can be presented for one form or other of the school certificate examination even under present regulations; that the work in the alternative and academic courses is common in a number of subjects; and that only a slight amendment of the regulations for the examination is necessary to meet the needs of this group of pupils.[1]

The recent inquiries into the relation between education and industry have emphasized the need, not so much of specialization as of the increase of alternative courses in which attention will be given to the economic aspects of contemporary society. Thus, the Committee on Education for Salesmanship expressed in its *Final Report* [2] the opinion that "some definite study of the organization of commerce and industry would be of value to every future citizen, and should be provided for in every secondary school." So far as the older pupils are concerned, the problem "is how to give these pupils some preparation for a business life, while widening their interests and avoiding undue specialisation."

It is obvious, then, that secondary education in England, after a period of quiet construction, is entering on a new stage of development. As Sir Michael Sadler stated, in a recent discussion of exami-

[1] See County Council of the West Riding of Yorkshire, Education Department, *Alternative Courses in Secondary Schools* (1927).

[2] *Final Report of the Committee on Education for Salesmanship*, pp. 48 ff. (London, 1931.)

nations: "We want one certificate, but different avenues leading up to it. Those avenues should be boldly incongruous, because the two types of mind for which they are designed are dissimilar. But the different avenues should converge on one certificate, and boys as well as girls should be allowed to follow them." [1]

SECONDARY EDUCATION FOR ALL

That there has been progress in the development of secondary education in England is obvious both from the statistical data presented above and from the tendencies toward more marked differentiation of courses. The success of the ex-elementary school pupils has only served to draw attention to the tremendous waste of ability that existed hitherto and still exists, and, combined with other social forces for national reconstruction, has led to a widespread demand for such a reorganization of the system as would provide for an increase of educational opportunities for all and at the same time eliminate the difficulties which arise from the existence of two parallel systems — elementary and secondary. The Education Act of 1918 had already provided that no pupils "should be debarred from receiving the benefits of any form of education by which they are capable of profiting, through inability to pay fees." The Departmental Committee on Scholarships and Free Places reported in 1920 that, in the opinion of experts, seventy-five per cent of the pupils in the elementary schools were intellectually capable of profiting by full-time instruction up to or beyond sixteen.

In 1924 the Consultative Committee of the Board of Education under the chairmanship of Sir Henry Hadow, was requested to consider and report upon the organization, objective, and curriculum of courses of study most suited for pupils who will remain in full-time attendance at schools other than secondary schools up to the age of fifteen. The Committee was requested to consider the requirements of a general education and the desirability of varying courses according to the abilities and probable occupation of the pupils. The Committee in its *Report* [2] recommended that more pupils should pass on to the secondary schools and that provision for some form of post-primary education consisting of a variety of types of schools

---

[1] Sadler, Sir Michael E., "Examinations," in *The New Era*, January, 1929. See also *Report of the International Conference on Examinations* (New York, 1931).
[2] *The Education of the Adolescent* (London, 1926).

and courses should be provided for all pupils from eleven to fifteen.

The exclusion of the secondary schools from the terms of reference prevented the Committee from including them in its recommendations, but the general result would in the end have been the same. All pupils would have a primary education up to the age of eleven and thereafter would be assigned to some one of the various types of post-primary schools according to their abilities and probable future occupations, except that only those proceeding to the secondary schools would be entitled to the privileges attached to the school certificates. The Board of Education in its pamphlet on *The New Prospect in Education* (1928) indicated its general acceptance of the Committee's recommendations, and in the Parliamentary elections of May, 1929, the three political parties — Conservative, Liberal, and Labor — committed themselves to an extension of the age of compulsory school attendance and a reorganization of the school system.[1]

A bill to this effect was introduced in the House of Commons by Sir Charles Trevelyan, Minister of Education in the Labor Government, and was passed in January, 1931, with an amendment safeguarding the interests of denominational schools. In February, 1931, however, the bill was defeated in the House of Lords, and in the disturbed economic situation through which England is passing, action must be postponed until better times return. The interval is, however, being used by the local education authorities for tentative and experimental forms of reorganization. All the tendencies seem to point to a system providing a variety of schools beyond the primary, but all governed by the same ideal and seeking to attain it in different ways. By offering differentiated types of schools, functionally organized instead of herding all pupils into the same school, it is hoped that the danger which confronts a democratic system of education, that of leveling down to a dull mediocrity, will be averted. Such a system no doubt has much to commend it; the interests of democracy can be safeguarded through other methods than the comprehensive secondary school, provided always that doors are left open for the transfer of individual pupils from one type of school to another so that each one finds himself in the school best adapted to his needs and abilities.

[1] See *Educational Yearbook, 1928*, of the International Institute of Teachers College, Columbia University, pp. 39 ff. (New York, 1929).

SCHOOL LIFE

Reference was made in the discussion of the aims of secondary education to the paramount importance attached to character-formation. It is this aim which is the most marked feature of English education, but equally marked is the absence of any formula or definition or theory of character or character-formation. From the point of view of organization, the provision for character-formation, unlike the extra-curricular activities in the high schools and colleges of the United States, is unobtrusive, for the Englishman believes with Wells "that what you organize, you kill." Moral instruction as such, or special courses in civics and citizenship, are but rarely found, and yet the ideals that are sought by such instruction are inculcated. In the day schools and especially in the grant-earning schools religious instruction has a place in the curriculum, but in general religious influences are left to be taken care of by the home and the churches; in the boarding schools great importance is attached to the school chapel and the religious influence which can be exercised by masters with a sympathetic understanding of boys.

So far as direct relations between teachers and pupils in the classroom are concerned, opportunities for training in conduct are seized as they arise. Corporal punishment still survives, but is no longer administered either with the severity or the frequency of former days. The greatest effectiveness in the formation of character is attained outside the classroom. Originating in the boarding schools, which had to provide opportunities for some outlet for youthful energies, the fundamental principle which is universally accepted is that the best method for the formation of character consists in the development of a community spirit, a feeling of corporate life, an *esprit de corps*, of which the required school cap and badge and the school colors are the external symbols. This means that the school stands for something more than instruction, that it has customs, standards, and traditions that must be lived up to. The school is a living organism, a society in miniature which imposes standards of living and of conduct reflecting the standards of the society around it. In this community the teachers play their part, but unobtrusively and in the background. They are ready to advice, to coöperate, and to give encouragement and stimulus, but leadership and direction are left to the pupils. Such a system gives a teacher with a hobby or some pet enthusiasm opportunities which are rarely found in the schools of Europe. The control lies, not in the authority of the teachers, nor in the rigor of discipline, but in a personal sense of duty, of *noblesse oblige*, acquired by years of apprenticeship followed by opportunities for leadership, on the principle that those who wish to govern must first learn to obey.

The standards of conduct are in replica those standards that make for the smooth running of any society. Honesty, uprightness, unselfishness, coöperation, give and take, fair play, playing the game — these are some of the ideals that the English school seeks to cultivate. The organization of corporate life, with the absence of organized cliques like fraternities and sororities, provides opportunities for the emergence of leaders and for the exercise of initiative; it develops ability to see the other man's point of view; it trains in tenacity of purpose that is often unreasoning, but a tenacity based on the feeling that even the most uncongenial task once undertaken must be carried to a finish, whether for the group, the school, or the community. But the system has its dangers whether from the subtle tyranny of which the adolescent is at times capable, or from the narrowness and exclusiveness of small communities, such as are the boarding schools, shut off from contacts with other worlds than their own.

Such are the ideals that are held to constitute the ends of character-training. The means are those that any healthy-minded group of adolescent boys and girls would adopt. Athletics, games, sports loom large in the schools as they do in national life, but they have been saved from that exploitation which has menaced their proper educational influence in American high schools and colleges. To give all pupils an opportunity of participating in physical activities, although participation in most of the boarding schools is compulsory, the greatest variety of athletics and games in addition to formal gymnastics and drill are encouraged — football (Rugby and soccer), cricket, tennis, fives, hockey, lacrosse, swimming, cross-country running, and track. In recent years rambling, hiking, and camping have become increasingly common and popular. Athletics, however, do not constitute the only outlet; any form of adolescent activity which is of social value or which emerges from the interests of various groups has its devotees — debating societies, literary and scientific societies, stamp-collectors' clubs, natural history clubs, wireless clubs, photographic clubs, chess clubs, music clubs, dramatic societies, glee clubs, school orchestras, scout and girl guide organizations, the school magazine, and many others. Running through all these activities is the system of self-government, the prefect or monitor system, in which, except in the gravest cases, discipline is to a large extent entrusted to the older pupils, a practice which not only trains in qualities of leadership, but also inculcates a rule, often forgotten, that the duty of obedience is of equal importance with ability to lead.

2. FRANCE [1]

HISTORICAL DEVELOPMENT

Creation of *lycées* and *collèges*. Of the leading countries of the world there is probably none which has clung so tenaciously to its ideal of secondary education as has France. Formulated in the seventeenth century the ideal of *culture générale* has persisted to the present day despite modifications which may have been introduced from time to time, and has been rigorously preserved under the highly centralized system of administration. The modern form of secondary education was inaugurated in 1802 with the establishment of the *lycées* which abolished the system created under the Revolution. Under the Act of 1806 a national system of administration was created and two years later was placed under the charge of the Imperial University, which administered the *lycées* directly, supervised the communal secondary schools or *collèges*, and inspected all private schools. In 1808 the *Ecole Normale Supérieure* was created by law and opened in 1810 to prepare teachers for the secondary schools. The subjects of instruction in the *lycées*, as prescribed in 1809 and extended to the *collèges* in 1812, included "those studies that are needed to prepare students to enter the faculties" — Latin, Greek, French, history, mythology, geography, mathematics in the first five years, and logic, metaphysics, ethics, optics, and astronomy, or mathematics, natural history, physics and chemistry, in the last year. A seventh year, devoted mainly to philosophy, was added in 1814. For some twenty years secondary education was dominated by a reactionary spirit, an emphasis on classics, and mistrust of modern studies and sciences.

Demand for modernization. Despite a profound belief in the educative value of the classics, which had produced so many leaders

[1] For a more detailed history of French secondary education see Kandel, I. L., *History of Secondary Education* (Boston, Houghton Mifflin Company, 1930).

in French life, had given the nation a fund of common ideas, and had cultivated good taste and appreciation of the beautiful, there was spreading the opinion that the secondary schools were too remote from the real world. In the interests of French commerce, agriculture, and industry, and because of the rapid expansion of the sciences, it was felt that the curriculum must be modernized. Schools were authorized in 1829 to establish courses for special groups "in sciences and their application to industry, modern languages, and the theory of commerce." Guizot sought a solution by establishing higher elementary schools in 1833, but popular sentiment looked askance at this type as a substitute for the fully privileged secondary school.

Bifurcation. In 1852 secondary education was reformed by the establishment of a common course of three years, followed by a bifurcation into two courses, one literary and the other scientific, and both with a core of common subjects. One course led up to the *baccalauréat ès lettres* and the Faculties of Letters and Law, the other to the *baccalauréat ès sciences* and the Faculties of Science and Medicine, and the special schools (*les grandes écoles*), or to industrial and commercial pursuits. Eleven years later, in 1863, the system of bifurcation was suppressed by Victor Duruy for a variety of reasons — pressure on the pupils, selection of the scientific course to escape Latin, lack of teachers of modern foreign languages. Duruy attempted to meet the need by creating a special course (*l'enseignement spécial*) giving a three- or four-year continuation of elementary education to prepare foremen, managers, and minor officials. The new course was unpopular from the start; it was felt that it was intended for pupils incapable of pursuing the regular course of the *lycée*, and it failed to carry with it the prestige of the *lycée*.

Unrest in secondary education. The unrest in secondary education began to increase after the Franco-Prussian War. Reforms of various degress of importance were introduced, but the system was not thoroughly overhauled to satisfy all demands until the close of the century. The problem of secondary education was still discussed in terms of subjects best adapted to give a liberal education, which usually meant a comparison of the value of classical and modern subjects. A serious attack had been launched against the classics in 1885 by R. Frary in his *le question du Latin*, in which he demanded a complete reform of secondary education to give France her rightful place in the world competition. Educated opinion — and this included the views, not only of educators in schools and universities, but of the leaders in French social and political life — was opposed to an attack on the existing régime. The determining factors in organizing a curriculum were, it was felt, the educational and disciplinary values of the subjects rather than demands of utility. The true aims of education should be the cultivation of a taste for study, training in methods of work, and the development of ability to understand, assimilate, and even to create. The chief means of education lies in letters, which develop neatness, precision, and logic; which elevate and ennoble by intercourse with great minds and the examples of perfect masterpieces; and which transmit the heritage of ideas and traditions embodying the experience of the best endowed races. Specialization at an early age must be avoided. There was a further reason for the faith in the classics, and that was, in the words of M. Gréard, that "classical culture is the basis of our literature, of our arts, of our history, and of all our traditions. It has been the leaven of the genius of France. It is the school of thought, and of the thought that liberates."

Reform of 1902. In 1898 a Parliamentary Commission on Education was appointed under the presidency of M. Alexandre Ribot. The Commission, after an extensive inquiry recommended that the classical tradition be maintained and strengthened, but that the modern course, which had been introduced in 1890, should be extended and given equal recognition so far as the privileges of secondary education were concerned. In 1902 the system was reformed and classical and modern courses, leading to a single *baccalauréat*, were established side by side. The new system provided for a course of seven years, divided into two cycles of four and three years respectively. The first cycle allowed a choice of two sections, one with Latin and the other emphasizing French, sciences, and drawing. Greek could be taken up in the third year. The first cycle was to be complete in itself, and to lead to a *certificat d'études secondaires* on the recommendations of the faculty and the record of the pupils. In the first two years of the second cycle a choice of four courses was available, as follows: (1) Latin and Greek; (2) Latin with more advanced study of modern languages; (3) Latin with more advanced study of sciences; and (4) modern languages and sciences. At the close of each course students could present themselves for the first part of the examination of the *baccalauréat*. In the last year, the seventh, a choice between specialization in philosophy or in mathematics was offered, followed at the close by the second part of the *baccalauréat*.

The choice thus lay between Latin and modern languages and sciences; the common subjects were history and geography and mathematics and sciences; but the last two groups of subjects were allotted more time in the modern course. The secondary school thus attempted, though with varied content, to retain the French loyalty to the classical spirit and to incorporate, side by side with it, the scientific spirit.

The reform was a compromise and satisfied no one. Criticism of the whole educational system was intensified during the War. Not only was there discontent with the reform, but new demands were added, particularly for better articulation between elementary and secondary education and for an increase of opportunities for secondary and higher education. It was widely agreed that secondary education should be open to ability irrespective of class and that it should be general in character rather than specialized, but in any event its purpose would be to impart a liberal education and to select an *élite* for positions of leadership. A group of educational reformers, *Les Compagnons de l'Université Nouvelle*, aroused nation-wide interest by its demand for a thoroughgoing reform of the whole system of French education with provision for a number of differentiated secondary courses following a common elementary education and adapted to the various needs and capacities of the pupils.

The Bérard reform.[1] The reform undertaken by M. Léon Bérard, who became Minister of Public Instruction in 1921, was destined to disappoint most of the demands. He proposed to abolish the system of 1902 and to replace it with a new system which would require four years of compulsory Latin and two years of compulsory Greek, followed by two optional courses, classical or modern, for the next two years, and culminating with a year of specialization in philosophy or mathematics. The arguments for compulsory classics were based on the spiritual affinity between French and classical culture and the disciplinary value of a classical training. The claims of democracy could be met, not by subject-matter, but by making all secondary education sufficiently accessible to all pupils of ability, irrespective

---

[1] For a detailed account see Kandel, I. L., *The Reform of Secondary Education in France* (New York, 1924).

of their social origin. The new system, which had been the subject of serious and protracted discussion in Parliament, but without a vote until after the decree was published, and which became a major political and educational issue, was promulgated by a Ministerial Decree of May 3, 1923. Almost before it could go into effect there was a change of Ministry, and M. Bérard's successor, M. François Albert, by a decree issued in August, 1924, repealed the compulsory requirement of Latin and Greek and restored the modern language option. By a series of decrees and regulations the present system of secondary education was organized in 1925.

THE PRESENT SYSTEM

Provision and supply. Secondary education is provided in two types of schools, *lycées* and *collèges*, organized separately for boys and girls. Under special conditions to be noted later, girls may be admitted to boys' schools and young boys to the lower sections of girls' schools. The *lycées* are provided and maintained wholly by the State. The *collèges* are institutions established by municipalities with the approval of the Ministry of Public Instruction which takes into consideration the ability of the locality to support such a school and the need for it. Since 1925 every municipality which has a *collège* or desires to establish one must enter into a contract with the State and furnish a guarantee that it will maintain the school for ten years. The cost of a *collège* is now divided between the State and the municipality; the State undertakes the payment of salaries to the regular instructional staff and supervisors of boarding pupils (*maîtres d'internat*), and the municipality is responsible for the provision and maintenance of adequate buildings and equipment. Fees for tuition are collected by the municipality and transferred to the State, which returns from ten to fifteen per cent to the municipality as a contribution toward maintenance charges. Revenues derived from fees for boarding pupils are retained by the municipality. How these arrangements will be affected by the progressive abolition of fees has not yet been determined; the burden will in all probability be assumed by the State.

Beyond these administrative differences there is another distinction between the *lycées* and *collèges*. As a general rule teachers in the *lycées* must be *agrégés*; teachers in *collèges* must hold the lower qualification of the *licence*; in general other members of the staff of the *collèges* possess lower qualifications than their colleagues in similar positions in the *lycées*. Otherwise, the curriculum, courses of study and standards are identical in the two schools.

Organization. Both *lycées* and *collèges* may receive day pupils, semi-boarders and full boarders. Tuition fees were charged in all schools until 1930, when they were abolished for the first class with the understanding that they were to be abolished for all pupils year by year until free secondary education was provided.[1] For poor pupils of ability a scholarship system, which has always existed, has been considerably extended in the last ten years. In 1913 the amount spent on scholarships by the Government was 3,000,000 francs; in 1930-31 the amount was raised to 51,616,666 francs and for 1931-32 an appropriation of 57,645,666 francs was to be devoted to scholarships in secondary, higher elementary, and technical schools. It is a serious reflection, however, on the attitude of certain grades of society that they will not avail themselves of the opportunities provided for secondary education by the abolition of fees and the provision of scholarships. Many parents of the artisan or peasant class fear, not only that the incidental costs of a protracted education may prove burdensome, but that such an education will remove the children from the class to which they belong.

Most secondary schools have preparatory sections in which tuition is charged and which parallel the elementary school system. The work of these sections was definitely directed to prepare for admission to the secondary divisions, included subjects in their curriculum which would be regarded as secondary, and was taught by teachers with special qualifications. Since 1924, however, all distinctions between the *classes préparatories* and the primary school up to the end of the *cours moyens* were abolished; teachers in the preparatory sections are required to have the same qualifications and are inspected under the same system as teachers in the elementary schools. In 1925 provision was made for the admission to these sections of pupils from the elementary schools free of tuition, regard being had in the selection to their ability and promise to continue in the secondary school and the available accommodations. These measures were adopted as installments of the proposal to establish a common school system (*école unique*) and to equalize for children

---

[1] In September, 1932, M. de Monzie, the Minister of National Education, expressed his intention of securing the abolition of tuition fees for secondary education in 1933.

of all classes opportunities for secondary education. The progressive abolition of fees was begun in 1930 with the same end in view, but it is not intended, for the present, to make secondary education free for all in the sense in which this phrase is employed in the United States. Secondary education, indeed, continues to be selective, and the abolition of fees has been accompanied by provisions for the maintenance of scholarship standards as a condition of what is regarded as a privilege; *sélection* and *gratuité* must, the French say, go together. For pupils of ability there are scholarships and maintenance grants which have been discussed above (p. 127).

The regulations for admission to the secondary divisions — that is, the *lycées* and *collèges* — are somewhat indefinite. Pupils who complete the work of the preparatory sections are promoted automatically to the lowest class of the secondary school (*sixième*); pupils who obtain scholarships may be admitted to the second class (*cinquième*); pupils who hold the *certificat d'études primaires* (see p. 416 f.) may be admitted to either of these classes; other pupils may be admitted on probation to the lowest class and retained on a decision of all the teachers of this class.

Separate schools are provided for boys and girls, but boys may be admitted to the preparatory sections of girls' schools under certain conditions — proximity of the school to the home or the presence of an older sister in the school. Until 1930 girls were only admitted to boys' schools if there was no separate school available for them in their locality, but are never admitted to schools with a larger enrollment than two hundred pupils and never to a number in excess of fifty, a figure which is scaled down in proportion to the number of boys in the school concerned. Where an adequate number of girls was available, but was not large enough for the establishment of a *collège*, a municipality might create *cours secondaires*; this somewhat unorganized form of secondary education often furnishes the nucleus for the later establishment of a *collège*. If no other facilities were available, girls might be admitted to the sixth year (*première*) or the seventh year (*classe de philosophie* or *classe de mathématiques*) to prepare for admission to the special higher institutions (*les grandes écoles*). In 1930, according to a circular issued by the Ministry (February 4), permission was given to admit girls to any secondary school up to a maximum of fifty without regard to the number of boys enrolled; when the number of girls exceeds fifty, a separate school must be established for them.

Not only are there separate schools for boys and girls, but the courses are to some extent distinct. After the War in particular the number of girls who desire to prepare for the *baccalauréat* and to proceed to the universities began to increase. Until 1924 the girls' schools provided a single common course of five years leading to the *diplôme de fin d'études secondaires*, with special arrangements for those who wished to prepare for the *baccalauréat*. In 1924 the system was changed; the general course, culminating in the *diplôme*, was extended to six years, and a seven-year course, similar to that for boys, leading to the *baccalauréat*, was organized.

Except for the six-year course for girls, which leads to the *diplôme*, and which may be extended since 1931 to a seventh year in preparation for the *diplôme complémentaire d'études secondaires* with specialization in philosophy or science, the length of the courses in *lycées* and *collèges* is seven years, the classes being numbered from *sixième* to *première*, and culminating in a *classe de philosophie* and a *classe de mathématiques*. Promotions from one class to another are made at the end of each year by the principal on the basis of the combined reports of all the teachers by whom the pupil has been taught. Pupils are marked on a scale from zero to 20; a mark of 10 exempts a pupil from further examination; a pupil who receives a mark below 10 must take an examination after the summer vacation, on the basis of which he is promoted or required to repeat the year. The first part of the *baccalauréat* is taken at the end of *première*, the second after the *classe de philosophie* or the *classe de mathématiques*. In a number of schools provision is made for students who have obtained the *baccalauréat* to continue in special classes (*classes de mathématiques spéciales*, *classes de rhétoriques supérieures*) to prepare in an additional year of study for the competitive examinations admitting to the special higher institutions (*les grandes écoles*).

There are no definite prescriptions for the size of classes, but it is expected that the regular classes will have an enrollment of from thirty to thirty-five pupils. The maximum may be raised to forty in the four highest classes; for classes in science and history the regulations suggested an organization for from forty to fifty pupils. With the rapid increase in the number of pupils enrolled in secondary schools in the last few years, combined with economies in the provision of additional teachers, the average size of classes for the country has also increased considerably.

The school staff. The staff of a secondary school consists of the principal (known as the *proviseur* in the *lycées*, *principal* in the *collèges*, and *directrice* in girls' schools); of *censeurs*, responsible for the supervision of discipline; of *économats* or bursars, responsible for financial administration; of *professeurs*, variously graded according to qualifications and years of service and subject-matter fields — that is, general academic subjects or special subjects such as drawing, music, gymnastics; *répétiteurs* in boys' and *répétitrices* in girls' schools, assistants responsible for the general disciplinary and instructional supervision of day pupils, who may after a period of service be appointed as *professeurs adjoints*; and *maîtres* and *maîtresses d'internat*, assistants responsible for the supervision of boarders.

Internal administration. Each *lycée* and each *collège* has an administrative board (*conseil d'administration*) with a membership in the case of a *lycée* consisting of the rector of the academy, an academy inspector, the prefect or under-prefect, the mayor, the principal, the bursar, elected representatives of the staff, and representatives of parents of pupils in the school and of the alumni. On the administrative board of a *collège* there are additional members representing the local public health office and chambers of commerce, agriculture, and trade and industry. Each board is required to meet four times a year. The duties of the administrative board include consideration of the finances of the school, the appropriateness of the courses to local needs, and the appointment of a member to visit the school in the company of an academy inspector and the principal and to report once a quarter on the external conditions of the school.

There are associated with many of the secondary schools alumni associations (*associations d'anciens élèves*) and *comités de patronage*, whose function is to promote the welfare of the pupils by the establishment of scholarships and prizes and advising pupils at the time when they leave school.

For instructional purposes there are two councils. The first, the *conseil de classe*, consists of the teachers of each class who meet four times a year for the purpose of coördinating the work of the class represented and to avoid overpressure of the pupils. The second, the *conseil d'enseignement*, consists of the teachers grouped by subjects or by allied subjects, meeting at the beginning and end of each year to coördinate and articulate the work of the school as a whole, to secure a certain degree of harmony in methods, and to provide measures for the avoidance of repetition and overlapping.

Purpose of secondary education. The purpose of French secondary education, which underlies all reforms, remains essentially unchanged and continues in the best French tradition. Secondary education is definitely provided and organized to secure an *élite*, and, whatever modifications may be introduced with the fuller development of the movement for the *école unique*, they will still be based on the principle that the function of education as it advances upward is selective. The types of abilities to be selected may be amplified, but the fundamental purpose will still remain the same; or, in other words, the future will see the organization of a system of selection on the basis of more differentiated courses. Accepting the logic of individual differences, French educators and statesmen interested in education do not recognize that there is any incompatibility between selection and democratic ideals; any other solution, they fear, would involve the serious danger of colorless mediocrity and lowering of intellectual standards. At the same time the extension of educational opportunities, supported by the abolition of fees and the award of scholarships and maintenance grants is generally accepted as the basis of a solution of the problem of education in a democracy; careers must be open to talent irrespective of wealth and social class. This principle has always been recognized and the careers of the late President of the Republic (M. Doumer) and the former Premier (M. Laval) are modern examples of it, but the door to advancement has not been opened as widely as it might have been. The economic changes through which France is slowly passing — from an agricultural to an industrial society — and the social changes which may result therefrom are important factors which are today leading to a broader conception of the scope of secondary education.

Few countries, however, approach the problem of the character of secondary education with such clarity of aims and objectives as does France. The starting-point rests on the firm conviction that the predominance of French culture which France has now enjoyed for nearly three centuries, and which she has contributed to a large part of the world, must be preserved. The purpose of secondary education is, accordingly, to transmit general culture, *culture générale*; the attainment of the purpose is to be secured by a *culture d'esprit*, an elusive term to which the English translation, intellectual training, can by means do justice. It does not imply merely verbal mastery of French or other cultures, ancient or modern, or of sciences and mathematics. It means the utilization of these subjects and the methods of their acquisition for the attainment of those qualities which are the marks of the educated man. These are a sense of balance, moderation, orderliness, liberty, humanism, reason, and enlightenment (*lumière*). Through *études désintéressés*, general studies, French secondary education aims to cultivate judgment, taste, appreciation, and an ability to think clearly and logically, for *ce qui n'est pas clair n'est pas Français*. The success of such an education is measured, not in terms of ability to reproduce knowledge and information, but in power to use abstract ideas, to see the general in the particular. More concretely expressed, the measure of a sound liberal education is ability to speak well and to write well (*bien dire et bien écrire*), not because of an exaggerated emphasis on elegance of language and style, but because such ability is the outward indication of clear thinking. Hence the emphasis that the French more than any others place upon command of their own language; the study of foreign cultures, whether ancient or modern, as of other subjects, is directed to a better appreciation of the mother-tongue. This explains the recent movement for the coördination of various subjects in each year and the reminder to the teachers "that they are not specialists, each one giving instruction independently of his colleagues, but that they are collaborators participating in a common task and pursuing one end coöperatively."[1] But intellectual training is not the only end sought by an education which emphasizes clarity of thought and reasoning. Underlying this aim is also a moral purpose on the principle of Pascal, *Travaillons donc à bien penser, c'est le principe de la morale*.

According to the *Instructions* on the secondary school course:

> It is not the function of secondary education to prepare pupils who have a definite profession in mind nor even to point them toward one or other of the great intellectual routes in which the activities of man deploy themselves. It does something more and better; its task is, without preparing for anything specific, to make the pupils apt for everything. It forges in them, with the care and diligence of the artist, conscious of the growing difficulty of his task, the powerful and delicate tool for their future conquests, that is, a vigorous and fine intellect, ready for all the beautiful adventures of the mind.... At an uncertain age in which tastes, interests, and aptitudes begin

[1] *Arrêtes* of September 23, 1930, and April 30, 1931.

to manifest themselves without any surety whether they are still artificial and temporary or real and permanent, the rôle of the teacher is precisely to prevent the pupil from throwing himself wholly on the side of his youthful whims.

Curriculum and courses of study. The present organization of the *lycées* and *collèges* for boys, and to some extent of the courses in the *lycées* and *collèges* for girls, preparing for the *baccalauréat* is based on the regulations of 1925. The essential features of the plan then introduced are as follows: All pupils are required for the first six years to follow the same courses in the general subjects. In the first four years there is an option between Latin (Section A) and modern foreign languages (Section B); Greek has been made optional for pupils taking Latin and is begun in the third year, when pupils in Section B add a second modern foreign language. In the fifth (*classe de seconde*) and sixth (*classe de première*) years the options are classics (Section A), Latin and modern foreign languages (Section A^1), and modern foreign languages (Section B). In order to provide a balanced course for all and to correct the defects of the reform of 1902, the other subjects — French, language and literature, history, geography, mathematics, and sciences — are the same. The aim in general is to prevent early specialization, and to give a liberal education on both the literary and scientific sides. The coördination of the courses in each year and throughout the six years is one of the tasks assigned to the class councils (*conseils de classe*) and the councils on instruction of the school as a whole (*conseils d'enseignement*).[1] Only in the last year, after the first part of the examination for the *baccalauréat* has been passed, is opportunity provided for specialization — in the *classe de philosophie* and the *classe de mathématiques*. The work of the secondary schools is crowned by passing, at the end of the seventh year, the second part of the examination for the *baccalauréat* which entitles to admission to the universities. The *baccalauréat* is a step toward the competitive examinations (*concours*) for admission to the great special institutions at the university level (*les grandes écoles*); students usually remain in those *lycées*, where they are provided for an additional year of preparation for the *concours* either in the *classe de mathématiques spéciales* or *classe de rhétoriques supérieures*.

[1] A somewhat similar plan is recommended for the making of courses of study in Prussian secondary schools — a marked contrast to the American practice of making out programs of unrelated subjects for each pupil.

Time-Schedule (April, 1931), French Secondary Schools (Boys)

Classe de	Sixième			Cinquième			Quatrième				Troisième				Seconde				Première			
	Common	A	B	Common	A	B	Common	A	A[1]	B	Common	A	A[1]	B	Common	A	A[1]	B	Common	A	A[1]	B
French	4	..	3	4	..	3	3	..	2	4	4	..	1	2½	3	..	..	1	3½	..	..	1
Latin	..	6	..	..	6	..	..	5	6	..	..	4	6	..	..	3½	5	..	..	4	5	..
Greek	..	..	..	..	..	..	..	3	..	..	..	3	..	..	..	4	..	..	..	3½	..	..
History	1½	..	..	1½	..	..	..	..	..	..	2	..	..	..	2	..	..	..	..	..	..	..
Geography	1	..	..	1	..	..	3½	..	..	..	1	..	..	½	1	..	..	..	3½	..	..	..
Modern languages	3	..	3	3	..	3	3	..	..	4	3	..	..	4	1½	..	2	6	1½	..	2	6
Mathematics	2	..	..	2	..	..	3	..	..	..	3	..	..	..	4	..	..	..	3½	..	..	..
Natural sciences	1½	..	..	1½	..	..	1	..	..	..	1	..	..	..	..	..	..	..	..	..	..	..
Physics and chemistry	..	..	..	..	..	..	..	..	..	..	..	..	..	..	3	..	..	..	4	..	..	..
Drawing	2	..	..	2	..	..	1½	..	..	..	1	..	..	..	..	..	..	..	..	..	..	..
Art	..	..	..	..	..	..	..	..	..	..	½	..	..	..	..	..	½	½	..	..	½	½
	15	6	6	15	6	6	15	8	8	8	15½	7	7	7	14½	7½	7½	7½	16	7½	7½	7½
Total, each section	21			21			23				22½				22½				23½			

Classe de	Philosophie	Mathématiques
Philosophy	8½	3
History	2½	2
Geography	1	1
Literary studies	2	..
Modern languages	2	2
Mathematics	1½	9
Physics and chemistry	4	5½
Natural sciences	2	2½
	24	25

Note: Included in the above time-schedule are the time allotments for practical work in sciences and history and geography, and for supervised study. Drawing is an optional subject in the last three years. Provision must be made outside of this schedule for physical training, and may be made for excursions and conferences arising out of the classwork.

The revision of the time-schedule, the emphasis on coördination of subjects, and certain restrictions on the amount of homework to be done have been dictated by a desire to reduce the pressure (*surmenage*) on the pupils. Although the movement against *surmenage* in all types of schools began with the parents, there are many who seem to test the success of a school by the amount of work done by the pupils at home. In addition to the measures taken in the regulations which have introduced supervised study periods and recommend the prohibition of homework for both boarders and day pupils after the evening meal, the *Instructions* of 1931 stress the part that methods of instruction may play in reducing the pressure on the pupils. One aspect of secondary education, which France shared with Germany, appears to have been overlooked, the social and economic pressure to secure the privileges (*sanctions*) which accompany the successful completion of the secondary school course. This pressure is in turn affected by the character of the examinations.

The courses of study (*Programmes de l'Enseignement Secondaire des Garçons*) are prepared and issued by the Ministry with the coöperation and advice of the Higher Council of Public Instruction and are expected to be known by administrators, teachers, parents, and pupils. There is to be noted in the latest courses of study a tendency to stress the idea that they are intended to be suggestive only and to leave a greater latitude to the teachers themselves in the actual choice of the work to be done within each class, provided that care is taken to secure coördination throughout the whole school. Two general principles are expected to be observed by all teachers; every lesson, whether in the literary or in the scientific branches, must always be a lesson in the correct use of French, and the paramount aim in every lesson in literature must be to develop lasting interests, taste and judgment, and a lofty appreciation of the meaning of life.

The latest revision of the courses of study, based on the criticisms and recommendations of the Commission on Pressure (*surmenage*) in the Schools, reiterates in every subject the importance of avoiding an emphasis on detailed facts and information and on erudition; attention is to be directed to the attainment of the ultimate objectives of general culture — a well-trained rather than an overstocked mind, cultivation of taste, awakening of sympathetic and intelligent appreciation, stimulation of curiosity and intellectual interests. Teachers are warned that what is prescribed in the courses of study for each class is intended as a maximum, which is too often made the minimum, with accompanying pressure on the pupils. Too many teachers, because of their own special preparation or in anticipation of the examinations for the *baccalauréat*, tend to lay too much stress on the acquisition by the pupils of minute details of scholarship, and to overload the pupils by insisting on the memorization of information which is often irrelevant and useless.

The aims of the courses in languages and literature are to give the pupils on one side a thorough command of language as a vehicle of thought and ideas, and on the other to acquaint them with the great masterpieces of the world. The first aim, however, is not to be secured by abstract and theoretical studies of grammar, syntax, and style, but a knowledge of these should grow out of their applications in actual use. Thus, scientific philology and comparative grammar have no place at the secondary level. All instruction in this field is to be directed to the main end, the acquisition of general culture rather than minute scholarship. At the same time the study of foreign languages must be directed, not only to the cultivation of literary taste and critical judgment, but must serve to introduce the pupils to an acquaintance with the modes of life and thought, the civilization and culture of the people whose language is being studied, with the additional acquisition in the case of modern foreign languages of a spoken mastery of the language. The last aim can be fostered by the exchange of pupils, vacation camps, and international correspondence. The choice of the first language is left to each school which should be guided by the needs of the majority of the pupils or of the local situation, and may be made from English, German, Italian, Spanish, Portuguese, Russian, and Arabic. Finally, since direct moral instruction is no longer included in the curriculum until the course in philosophy is reached in the seventh year, the study of languages and literature can contribute to the formation of character through intercourse with great minds and great masterpieces, through the cultivation of humanism in its broadest sense.

In history and geography the same emphasis is placed in the courses of study and the *Instructions* accompanying them on avoidance of excessive detail. Both subjects must be made living and picturesque, appealing to imagination as much as to intelligence. The pupils should be expected through history and geography to acquire an appreciation of the distinctive features and general characteristics of a period, a civilization, or of a country. In history they should obtain a thorough conception of the succession of a chain of events, just as in geography they should appreciate the interrelation of geological, physical, economic, and political factors. In both subjects instruction can be made living and concrete by the use of visual aids, the study of sources, and by excursions. The course of study in history introduces the pupils to the history of the world from the days of prehistoric man down to the present, while stressing in the later classes the history of France and of the world since the middle of the nineteenth century. In geography is included a study of the whole world culminating in a special study of France and the main features of the physical, anthropological, and economic aspects of the subject.

The courses in mathematics and sciences have been revised in the same spirit as the literary subjects; excessive attention to details is to be avoided. Mathematics is carried in the first six years up to algebra (progressions and logarithms) and solid geometry; the study of advanced algebra, analytical geometry, trigonometry, statics, and astronomy is left to the special class in mathematics. The sciences include zoölogy, botany, geology, physiology and hygiene in the first four years, and physics and chemistry in the last three; natural sciences are again included in the last year. The aim of science instruction is to give the pupils a clear idea of the experimental method and of the meaning of scientific theory, both of which are to be acquired, not through the mechanical acquisition of information, but through actual observation and experimentation, criticism, and verification of a law. The time devoted to the sciences is to be divided equally between classwork with demonstrations and laboratory work.

Art as a separate subject was introduced in the course of study issued in 1926. It is a required subject for all pupils in the fourth year and for pupils in sections A^1 and B in the fifth and sixth years. The aim is neither to train specialists nor critics, which would indeed be impossible in the half-hour a week assigned to the subject, nor to give a systematic course in art history, but to develop appreciation and taste through the study of the great masterpieces of painting and sculpture since the Renaissance period. This course in æsthetic appreciation includes not only painting and sculpture but architecture, furniture design, and contemporary decorative art. The method of instruction is analogous to that used for the cultivation of literary appreciation, the *explication de textes*, an emphasis on the whole rather than an excursion into technical details. Indeed, the most effective instruction in art will go hand in hand with history and literature; the pupil should be trained to enter into the sentiments and thoughts of the artist, to learn the silent language of form and color.

The whole course of secondary education is crowned by the study of philosophy in the last year, a feature which the French themselves regard as one of the most important characteristics of their secondary school system. The course aims to give an elementary introduction to psychology, logic, ethics, metaphysics. The teacher in charge of the course may in addition select for intensive study some special phase — such as history of philosophy, experimental or abnormal psychology, æsthetics, formal logic, sociology, and the science of language — or one or more outstanding philosophical works. The purpose of the course is to enrich pupils' intellectual grasp and to lead them to formulate a synthesis of what they have studied. Breadth of view, enlightenment, and independence of judgment are the objectives to be attained. Here perhaps more than in any other subject is the emphasis placed on freedom for growing personalities, and the whole course is to be regarded as an apprenticeship in intellectual freedom. The chief danger to be avoided in the study of philosophy at this stage is abstract thinking, which is to be the goal gradually reached by utilizing the previous studies and concrete examples within the range of the pupils' experience. As far as possible the course should be an exercise in group thinking of the whole class in collaboration with the teacher.

Methods of instruction. An analysis of the courses of study would leave the impression that the emphasis is placed upon the accumulation of a great amount of facts and information. Such an impression is confirmed in many cases by observation of classroom procedure. Too many teachers are in the habit of dictating notes and of lecturing even in the lowest classes. In the hands of the better teachers, however, instruction becomes an art, and, despite an apparent prescription of details in the courses of study, the true scholar is free to roam at will in his own field and not only to inspire the pupils with a reverence for knowledge and for scholarship, but to train in methods of independent study and mastery. None the less the *Instructions* repeatedly warn teachers against too much emphasis on detail, a quantitative rather than a qualitative emphasis.

Every school task should above all be an invitation to reflection, to research, and an appeal to intellectual initiative, however modest that may be; it must not encourage the habit of mechanical work, limited to an assignment. Everything that amounts merely to copying or rewriting of notes, to purely detailed and automatic busy work should be abandoned. (*Instructions*, 1931.)

Nothing is more characteristic of French instruction than the method of *explication de textes*, which, developed first in the teaching of the classical languages, has been adapted to the needs of the French and modern foreign languages. The primary aim of this method is to teach pupils how to read critically and with intelligence, to train their ability to enter intellectually and emotionally into the real spirit of any passage which they may read, and to cultivate a sympathetic understanding of an author's meaning. But literary appreciation of this type is not attained without trained effort; there is involved in it more than attentive reading. The method of *explication de textes* requires detailed attention to everything that contributes meaning: language and style, the contemporary setting and background of a passage, familiarity with its place in the history of literature and of thought, ability to compare and contrast with similar and different types of literature, and finally, the submission of the result of such analysis to criticism, which becomes more refined and discriminating as the pupil grows in training and maturity. The *explication de textes* is to literature what observation, experimentation, and verification are to the sciences and mathematics; it is a training in research, not necessarily to discover something new, but to enable the pupil to put himself in the place of the author whom he may be reading. The method does something more than cultivate intelligent reading; it aims to develop intellectual curiosity and activity; it stimulates the pupil to pursue clarity of thought and ideas, to solve his own difficulties, to be ready to ask and to answer questions arising out of any text; and finally, to read a passage aloud with intelligence and the proper emotional expression. While the method is directed to an end beyond itself, it furnishes at the same time a technique which is of inestimable value to the student. It represents an effort to avoid learning about literature and to initiate the pupil in methods of proceeding direct to the literature itself.

In such a method the textbook and manual have little place. Indeed, the textbook plays an unimportant part in classroom procedure. At the worst teachers replace the textbook by lectures and dictation of notes; at the best the *cahiers* or notebooks which pupils are required to keep for each subject are the substitutes of the textbook. In the *cahiers* the pupils note down, either with the teachers' aid or in the course of their own reading, the essentials of the subjects for which they will be held responsible. In this task they are assisted by the teachers in the periods set aside for supervised study (*travaux dirigés*). Textbooks and manuals are used as works of reference. Despite the efforts of the authorities and the teachers to inculcate methods of study, the pressure of examinations, particularly for the *baccalauréat*, does lead to cramming (*bachotage*) and the use of compendia offering short cuts to learning.

The *baccalauréat*. The final test of the successful completion of secondary education is the examination for the *baccalauréat*, which is at once a leaving certificate and a certificate of admission to any of the faculties of the university. The examination for the *baccalauréat* is taken in two parts; the first part at the end of the sixth is based on the work of the *classe de première*, and the second at the end of the seventh year is based on the work of either the *classe de philosophie* or the *classe de mathématiques*. A fee of fifty francs is charged for each part. The majority of the candidates present themselves for the examination in each series conducted in July; others, including those who fail at the July session, have another opportunity in October. The examinations are conducted at university centers and other towns designated by the Minister of Public Instruction before examining boards composed of professors and instructors in universities and teachers in secondary schools, selected under certain conditions either by the deans of faculties of letters and of sciences or by the rector of the academy. The conduct of the examination, which is both written and oral, is governed by special regulations as to method of marking written work, apportionment of time between different subjects, and the length of each oral test.

The questions and problems for the written examinations may be prepared by the Ministry or by the deans of the faculty of letters or the faculty of sciences in their respective fields. There has been a tendency to increase the number of written tests as offering better evidence of knowledge and intellectual ability, and to give the candidates a choice of three questions on each paper.[1] Candidates who fail in the written tests are excluded from the oral. Each test is weighted and candidates are graded on a scale from zero to 20, 10 being the passing mark. The school record (*livret scolaire*) of the pupil is taken into account in assigning the final mark. The final records are "pass" (10/20 of the marks), "satisfactory" (12/20), "good" (14/20), and "very good" (16/20). Written examinations are given in the following subjects which vary with the section pursued by the candidates:

First Part

Section A: French essay, translation from Greek and Latin, and problems in mathematics and physics.

Section A¹: French essay, translation from Latin, a test in a modern foreign language, and problems in mathematics and physics.

Section B: French essay, tests in two modern foreign languages, and problems in mathematics and physics.

The oral examination includes the following tests:

Section A: Explication de textes in French, Latin, Greek, and a modern foreign language, and questions on history, geography, mathematics, and physical sciences.

Section A¹: Explication de textes in French, Latin, and a modern foreign language, and questions on history, geography, mathematics, and physical sciences.

Section B: Explication de textes in French and modern foreign languages, and questions on history, geography, mathematics, and physical sciences.

The examinations in the second part cover the following subjects:

Second Part

Philosophy: Written examination: A philosophical thesis and problems in physical and natural sciences.

Oral examination: Questions in philosophy, literary studies, history, geography, mathematics and cosmography, physical and natural sciences, and on a modern foreign language.

Mathematics: Written examination: Problems in mathematics and physical sciences, and a philosophical thesis.

Oral examination: Questions on mathematics, physical and natural sciences, philosophy, history, geography, and a modern foreign language.

[1] At the July session (1931) of the Higher Council of Public Instruction, the Minister, M. Mario Roustan, introduced a proposal to reduce the number of written and oral tests; whether candidates would be examined in languages or in mathematics and science would be determined by lot.

In order to ensure uniformity of standards, all reports bearing on the examinations must be submitted to a committee of members selected from the *Comités consultatifs de l'Enseignement Supérieur et Secondaire*, which assesses the results, from time to time compares them with the results attained in previous years, and submits a report to the Minister of Public Instruction.

The examinations for the *baccalauréat* have been the subject of constant review almost since their establishment. Based on the courses of study according to the regulations, they tend to exert pressure on teachers and pupils to master all their details, which is not the intention. The examiners are drawn in the majority from the universities and are accordingly inclined to view each subject from the point of view of their own field of specialization. It is gradually beginning to be recognized that the technique of examining is an art not possessed by every scholar. There is in addition a little uncertainty whether the present type of examination can be a real test of the attainment of the chief objective of secondary education, *culture générale*, or can serve as a method of measuring ability and aptitudes.

Viewed from the standpoint of students and parents, the *baccalauréat* is a serious hurdle to be overcome, not because it is a test of scholarship or of intellectual training or of *culture générale*, but because its possession is an essential prerequisite, not only for admission to the universities and the competitive examinations for admission to the special institutions, but to many intermediate careers. The *baccalauréat* has in a sense an educational, social, and economic value. Hence it becomes an important preoccupation both of students and of parents. The good student will work hard in preparation for the examination because he realizes how much there is to learn, the poor pupil because he realizes his own limitations. Accordingly, however much the teachers may attempt to avoid cramming, there is a suspicion that many pupils rely more on the handy compilations of questions set in previous examinations and on convenient manuals prepared in the various subjects on the basis of what the market will demand. Cramming (*bachotage*) is perhaps inevitable in any system of examinations which follows traditional lines (although it is doubtful whether any successful substitute has yet been discovered), but its existence does not detract from the standard or quality of the education given in the French secondary schools. Slowly French educators are beginning to see the implication both of cramming and of the examination results and are beginning to realize that some measures must be taken to guide and distribute pupils after the primary stage into types of courses best suited to their abilities; for the best minds the present secondary course may still be found to be the best.

There is in some quarters a feeling of unrest concerning the standards of the *baccalauréat* in recent years. There are those who profess to see a lowering in these standards and who claim that students with no further preparation than the *baccalauréat* are not ready to undertake university studies in the faculties of letters and sciences. M. Lapie, rector of the University of Paris, suggested shortly before his death (January 24, 1927) the establishment in all faculties of courses preparatory to advanced education at the university level. Similar courses already exist in the *classes de mathématiques spéciales* and *de rhétoriques supérieures*, which follow the *baccalauréat* and prepare for the special higher institutions. M. Lapie argued that

Between secondary education whose aim is to impart general culture, both literary and scientific, and higher education, where each student limits himself to his special field, there should be established an intermediate course also specialized, in which some would devote themselves wholly to sciences while others would study literature exclusively, but sufficiently general so that the lawyers should not be ignorant of history and historians of philosophy. And who knows but that the introduction of the preliminary year would not make it possible to settle to the general satisfaction the irritating question of the *baccalauréat*? Would there be any disadvantage in leaving the award of this title to committees composed wholly of members of the secondary school teaching body?

This suggestion has met with considerable opposition through fear lest the prestige of the *baccalauréat*, granted on internal examinations, would be lowered. Not much consideration has been given to the question whether the lowering of standards, if it is real, may not be due to the increased enrollments and to the absence of adequately differentiated courses. The whole problem is intimately bound up with the proposed reorganization of the educational system on the plan of the *école unique*.

The *baccalauréat* examination is a qualifying examination and serves as a general standard; beyond this, there is another examination which is competitive in character and exercises to a certain extent the same influence as the open competitive scholarships in

England. This examination is the *concours général*, a national competitive examination open only to boys and girls selected from the pupils in the last two years of the course. The subjects of the examination are based on the courses of study of the *classes de première, philosophie*, and *mathématiques*. The candidates, selected by the teachers of these classes or of subject-matter divisions, must be below eighteen years of age in the year of the competition for the lower *concours* (*classe de première*) and below nineteen for the higher (final year); each school may submit from two to six candidates, the number varying with the enrollment in each class, in each subject. The subjects of the examination and the duration of each test are as follows:

Classe de Première: French essay, 6 hours; Latin translation, 4; Latin prose, 4; Greek translation, 4; history and geography, 6; mathematics, 5.
Classe de Philosophie: Philosophical thesis, 6 hours; history and geography, 6.
Classe de Mathématiques: Mathematics, 6 hours; physics, 6; history and geography, 6.

An examination common for all candidates is given in drawing.

The papers in each subject are set by the Ministry and examined by special committees appointed by the Minister. The list of candidates is drawn up in order of merit; prizes are awarded to the first three on the list and an honorable mention up to a maximum of ten. The prize winners (*lauréats*) are expected to attend at the prize distribution which takes place annually at the Sorbonne and is regarded as the crowning feature in secondary education. Success in the *concours général* carries some distinction, but no privileges; the announcement of the results of the *concours* and the ceremony of the prize distribution tend to focus national interest on secondary education, second only to the more personal and immediate interest in the results of the *baccalauréat* examination.

The following table gives the results of the *baccalauréat* examinations in July, 1929:

Part I

Section	A	A^1	B
Number of candidates			
applying	3,325	6,387	4,580
examined	3,299	6,302	4,507
Failed in written test	1,736	3,682	2,674
Failed after oral test	341	437	446
Passed	1,222	2,183	1,387
Percentage passed	37	34.6	30.7
Range in academies	20 to 58	27.1 to 42.5	24.1 to 38.5

Section	A	A¹	B
Marks			
Very good	1	6	
Good	53	73	45
Fair	297	584	342
Satisfactory	871	1,540	1,000
Total examined		14,108	
Total passed		5,792	
Percentage passed		40.05	

Part II

Section	Philosophy	Mathematics
Number of candidates		
applying	13,929	6,009
examined	13,816	5,915
Failed in written test	5,466	2,109
Failed after oral test	1,697	687
Passed	6,653	3,119
Percentage passed	48.1	52.7
Range in academies	36.7 to 71.9	29.6 to 29.3
Marks		
Very good	18	8
Good	221	163
Fair	1,559	835
Satisfactory	4,855	2,113
Total examined	19,731	
Total passed	7,575	
Percentage passed	38.4	

In 1929 there were still a number of students who had followed the old division of courses. The results in the *baccalauréat* examinations taken by these were as follows:

Section	Latin-Greek	Latin-Modern Languages	Latin-Science	Science-Modern Languages
Number of candidates				
applying	1,722	7,466	2,050	3,381
examined	1,706	7,405	2,032	3,320
Failed in written test	660	3,723	825	1,501
Failed after oral test	263	735	211	300
Passed	783	2,947	996	1,519
Percentage passed	45.8	39.7	49	45.7
Range in academies	34.4 to 59.5	29.4 to 50.1	39.2 to 64	33.1 to 59.5

Section	Latin–Greek	Latin–Modern Languages	Latin–Science	Science–Modern Languages
Marks				
Very good.........	2	4		1
Good.............	14	68	19	47
Fair..............	122	590	170	293
Satisfactory.......	645	2,285	807	1,178
Total examined............		14,463		
Total passed..............		5,245		
Percentage passed.........		36.1		

Secondary education of girls. The provision of public secondary education for girls in France is of comparatively recent origin. The foundation of the present system was laid in the law of M. Camille Sée, passed in 1880. The schools established at this time made no provision for the preparation of girls for the *baccalauréat*, which began to be demanded by an increasing number of girls after 1900. The attitude toward and the restrictions placed upon the admission of girls to boys' schools have been discussed above (p. 680). It was not until March 25, 1924, that a decree was passed for the reorganization of the system, the details of which were defined by the *arrêté* of July 10, 1925. Two courses were created in the *lycées*, *collèges*, and *cours secondaires* (or *collèges* in process of organization) for girls; the first was an extension of the general course from five years to six with the inclusion of the following subjects: French, modern languages, mathematics, science, history, geography, and drawing. To these subjects pupils working for the diploma of secondary education (*diplôme de fin d'études secondaires*) were required to add household management, handwork, music, ancient and foreign literatures in translation, psychology, and ethics. Girls who wish to continue their studies for an additional year may specialize in philosophy or science and after another examination obtain the *diplôme complémentaire d'études secondaire*. The standards and requirements of the second course leading to the examinations for the *baccalauréat* are the same as in the schools for boys, with some slight modifications to provide for instruction in household subjects. Wherever possible the pupils in the two sections follow a common course, the differentiation increasing progressively in the last three years of the second course. By the *arrêté* of July 10, 1925, the courses of study issued for boys' secondary schools were made applicable to secondary schools for girls with such modifications of the time-schedule as may be demanded by their special needs.

The total enrollment of girls in public secondary schools in 1930 was 59,339 (37,198 in *lycées*, 17,446 in *collèges*, and 4,695 in *cours secondaires*) as compared with a total of 138,301 in boys' secondary schools (83,764 in *lycées* and 44,537 in *collèges*). Included in these figures are pupils enrolled in preparatory classes, if these are excluded, there were enrolled in secondary education proper 174,097 in public schools and 128,161 in private schools.

School life. The atmosphere of the French secondary school, whether for boys or for girls, is colored by the fundamental objects for which they exist. The English and American emphasis on character-formation through the organization of the corporate life of the school is not stressed; character-formation as an end of education is not ignored, but the approach to it is almost wholly through the reasoned life. As was pointed out earlier, the humanistic subjects in particular are to be used as instruments for its development. There is also another aspect: secondary education, crowned by the *baccalauréat*, is competitive in so far as it is regarded as the avenue which leads to preferred positions in professional and administrative careers. Accordingly, the pupils are subjected, not only to the pressure of the schools themselves, but also to family, social, and economic pressure which tend to reënforce the intellectualistic atmosphere of the schools. Where the English or the American parent shows perhaps a greater interest in the athletic or personal achievement of his children, with a somewhat lukewarm interest in their intellectual progress, the French parent's attention is directed to intellectual achievement. This emphasis has been criticized for nearly four decades and attention began to be directed to the other aspect by M. Démolins in his book *A quoi tient la Supériorité des Anglo-Saxons*,[1] which appeared in 1897. A few experimental schools, such as the *Ecole des Roches* and the *Ecole de Normandie*, have attempted to establish a new type of school, a blend of the French and English tradition. These experiments, however, and others based on similar principles, have on the whole not caught the imagination of the French public. The regulations in fact prohibit the formation of associations among the pupils with officials, insignia, and a body of

---

[1] The English translation was published under the title *Anglo-Saxon Superiority; To What It Is Due* (New York, n.d.).

rules; these do not apply to the creation of athletic associations. Here and there a few public schools have attempted to encourage athletic activities. The character of the school buildings themselves, with little more provision for exercise than a small court, does not provide the space necessary for extensive movement. The time-schedules provide periods for recreation between classes. Municipalities and sports clubs are urged to place open spaces at the disposal of the schools without expense. The regulations require that pupils, particularly boarders and semi-boarders, be taken on walks (*promenades*) twice a week on Thursdays and Sundays, but even on these occasions opportunities for instruction are not to be neglected, such as nature study, visits to old châteaux, important ruins, battlefields, and so on; from time to time a whole day may be devoted to an excursion.

The Government, however, has for the past two decades sought to encourage the development of athletics and sports throughout the educational system. In the regulations, at any rate, their importance for the development of personality, ideals of self-government, physical agility, and endurance have for long been recognized. It is only within the last three years that actual steps have been taken to promote their expansion by the provision of government grants. Secondary schools are urged to encourage the organization of sports clubs and athletic associations to be affiliated with the national *Union des Sociétés françaises de sports athlétiques*. Considerable inertia on the part of the pupils and a great amount of fear and suspicion on the part of parents will have to be overcome before such a program becomes effective. According to the regulations pupils may only participate in games and athletics with the written authorization of their parents, who must also in a signed statement undertake not to hold the school officials responsible for accidents. The *Union* has made arrangements to secure at low rates insurance policies against accidents incurred on the playing-field. In the meantime the Government, inspired by the examples of Germany and Italy, is rapidly developing its propaganda in favor of wider interest in physical activities throughout the country and is encouraging municipalities to set aside playing-fields and to build stadia. This movement may in time exercise an influence on the secondary schools which is lacking at present.

The new unrest in secondary education. France is again passing through one of those educational crises which marked the development of secondary education during the nineteenth century. There is general unanimity that the traditions of French culture must be preserved and continued at all costs. For the time being the secular conflict between the advocates of the classical and of the modern humanities has been settled; science and mathematics have been accepted by both as a necessary part of a well-balanced liberal education. The unrest of the present is different in kind from that noted in the nineties (see p. 675). It is no longer a question of what subjects are of most worth, but of the type of education to be provided in the post-primary period, the secondary stage, for the increasing body of pupils to whom educational opportunities are to be opened. During and since the War, however, the French themselves have become somewhat disturbed about the validity of this as the only conception of secondary education. The unrest has been brought about by a large number of factors: the large percentage of elimination and mortality in secondary education; the fact that secondary education is still largely the privilege, not only of a minority, but of a minority drawn from the well-to-do classes; that the work of the schools is hampered by the presence of pupils who are retained because their parents can afford to keep them in school; and that the country as a whole is not drawing on the talent and ability of all classes. Finally, France is passing through an economic change from an agricultural to an industrialized society, a change which is opening new opportunities for ability which is not trained, and which is bringing with it a realization that leaders must be prepared not only for intellectual but for a great variety of other careers. This unrest has found expression in the movement for the *école unique*, which is the center of proposals to reorganize the French system of education and to adopt a broader conception of the scope of secondary education.

The principle of the *école unique*, a common school system, was enunciated during the War by *Les Compagnons de l'Université Nouvelle*, a group of young educators who formed an organization to promote the complete reorganization of the French educational system. The fundamental idea inherent in their proposals was the organization of a system that would promote the interests of the nation as a whole; that would eliminate class distinctions; that would provide equality of opportunity for all; and that would, as a result, utilize all the resources of talent and ability wherever found. The implication was not a common, identical, or uniform education for all above the elementary stage, but the inauguration of a system in which all branches of education would be properly coördinated and in which pupils would find that education that was best suited to their abilities.

Widespread interest in a common school. The proposals of *Les Compagnons* attracted widespread attention, and since the War have been the chief subject of discussion and debate, not only in professional circles, but in lay newspapers and magazines and in Parliament. In the last few years they have become the center of acrimonious political debate. The opponents of the *école unique* profess to see in it an attempt to establish a uniform, state-controlled system, and an attack on the right of parents to select private (and in the main clerically controlled) schools for their children. This attack is, however, specious, for fundamentally the movement for the *école unique* is intended to promote the greatest efficiency in national education, first, by bringing all education, some of which is still under the charge of various ministries, under the supervision of a national Ministry of Education; and secondly, to establish a system of coordinated schools at various levels for the recruiting and training of ability, wherever found, not merely along the traditional intellectual lines, but along whatever lines France in her present stage of development may need leaders. The ideas underlying the movement were well summarized by Anatole France, in *La Vie en Fleur*:

> The same education for all, rich and poor. All will attend the primary school. Those among them who show the highest aptitudes will be allowed to have a secondary education, which, without fees, will bring together on the same benches the *élite* of the bourgeois and the *élite* of the proletarian youth. From this *élite* will proceed an *élite* to the higher schools of science and art.

M. Léon Brunschvieg explained the ideas by an analogy:

> It is important that all the children of France should be considered alike as living plants, whose spontaneous growth will be assured by the same methods; only the trunk will be allowed to grow up to a certain height before the branches are permitted to shoot out without the opposition of any artificial obstacle to the expansion of their being, whose innate powers will raise each up to the level designed for it.[1]

In 1924 M. François Albert, Minister of Public Instruction in

---

[1] *Un Ministère de l'Education Nationale*, p. 79 (Paris, 1922).

M. Herriot's Cabinet, appointed a *Commission de l'Ecole Unique* to inquire into the problem; the *Ligue de l'Enseignement* appointed its own Commission; and the problem was discussed in a series of lectures at the *Ecole des Hautes Etudes Sociales*. These are cited as examples, out of many hundreds, of the interest in the subject of the common school. The general trend of the discussion has been in favor of a reorganization of the school system into four levels: (1) a common elementary education (ages six to twelve); (2) a lower secondary level of four years (ages twelve to sixteen); (3) a higher secondary level (ages sixteen to nineteen); and (4) a higher level in universities, technical institutes, and similar centers.

Changes since 1925. Of these tendencies some have already been realized. Since 1925 a common primary education has been adopted for all children up to between the ages of eleven and twelve. Pupils are not required to attend the same school, but whatever school they attend within this period follows the same curriculum, is taught by teachers with the same qualifications, and is inspected by primary school inspectors. This provision means that the advantages hitherto enjoyed by pupils who attended the *classes élémentaires* or *préparatoires*, associated with the secondary schools, are now abolished. These classes still continue to charge fees, but the work is not directly preparatory to the secondary schools. All pupils who are candidates for admission to the secondary schools accordingly start on an equal footing. Another contribution to the realization of the *école unique* has been the institution of a common scholarship examination for candidates who wish to enter the secondary, the higher primary, or the technical schools; not only may candidates hold these scholarships in either one of these schools, but they may, after an exploratory period, transfer them from one to another. The money set aside in the budgets for scholarships has been increased considerably in the last few years. Transfer from the higher elementary schools to the upper section of the secondary school proper has been facilitated.

Circumstances, rather than principles, have, however, hastened the development of a common school at the second level (ages twelve to sixteen). In an effort to secure retrenchment it was proposed, in 1925–26, to close the smaller secondary schools — usually *collèges* maintained by municipalities and having small enrollments. In order to save these institutions, higher elementary or technical schools, or in some cases both, were brought together under the same roof as the *collèges*, and teachers were used, where possible, interchangeably in the two or three types of courses.

The existence of this situation was recognized in the publication of a decree (October 1, 1926), in which provision was made for instruction in subjects common to the first four years of the secondary school and to the preparatory and the three years of the higher elementary school in institutions where the two courses were being given. The common subjects are: French language and literature, a modern foreign language, arithmetic and algebra, natural sciences, drawing, and physical exercises. Both courses are under the direction of one principal and teachers may be used interchangeably in each. The time-schedule for such institutions is as follows:

TIME-SCHEDULE IN SECONDARY AND HIGHER ELEMENTARY SCHOOLS COMBINED

Class	Sixième Preparatory			Cinquième First Year			Quatrième Second Year				Troisième Third Year			
	Common	A	B	Common	A	B	Common	A	A¹	B	Common	A	A¹	B
French language and literature...	4	..	3	4	..	3	4	..	..	3	4	..	..	3
Latin............	..	6	..	..	6	..	..	5	7	..	..	4	6	..
Greek...........	..	..	..	..	..	..	..	3	..	..	..	3	..	..
Modern foreign language.........	4	..	1	4	..	1	3	..	..	4	3	..	..	4
Geography......	1	..	}3	1	..	}3	1	..	..	}3	1	..	..	}2½
History.........	..	2		..	2		..	3*	3*		..	2½†	2½†	
Arithmetic and algebra.........	2	..	..	2	..	..	1	1	1	1	1	1	1	1
Geometry.......	..	..	..	..	..	..	..	1	1	1	..	1	1	1
Natural sciences .	1	..	1	1	..	1	1	..	..	..	1	..	..	..
Drawing........	2	..	..	2	..	..	1½	..	..	..	1½	..	..	..
Physical exercises	2	..	..	2	..	..	2	..	..	..	2	..	..	..
Art.............	..	..	..	..	..	..	..	..	..	..	..	½	½	½
Total........	16	8	8	16	8	8	13½	13	12	12	13½	12	11	12
Total per class....		24	24		24	24	26½	25½		25½		25½	24½	25½

* An additional hour may be added but is optional.
† An additional half hour may be added but is optional.

Since pupils in the higher elementary and technical schools are free scholars, parents of pupils in the secondary sections proper, the *collèges*, protested against the exaction of fees. In 1928 the Government decided to abolish fees in the cosmopolitan schools, a decision which affected about one hundred institutions. Parents of pupils in the *collèges* now protested against the payment of fees in the upper sections, the third level of the proposed *école unique*, and these also were abolished in 1929. Since these decisions were obviously unfair to parents who continued to pay fees in secondary schools to which higher elementary or secondary schools were not attached, the Government adopted the decision to abolish all fees for secondary education, beginning in 1930 with the lowest class, and advancing progressively year by year until their abolition throughout the secondary schools. By a vote taken on January 1, 1931, Parliament committed the country to the acceptance of the principle of free secondary education. It is estimated that the cost to the Government of the assumption of the burden of the fees will amount ultimately only to about fifty-eight million francs or one sixth of the total cost for secondary education. The abolition of fees, which is already operative in the two lowest classes, has been marked by a rapid increase in the number of entrants, which at the beginning of the year 1931-32 amounted to about 22,000. Measures have, however, been taken to prevent too rapid an increase in the enrollments by the requirement of a scholarship standard which pupils must reach if they wish to be allowed to remain in a school.

The problems of selection and equality. The development of free education at the second level has raised a number of serious problems. The first is that of selection. It is objected that the standards of admission to the various schools at this level are higher for poor children with ability, who are selected by competitive scholarship examinations, than for the children of the rich who are admitted to the *lycées* and *collèges* by entrance examinations. The Commissions already mentioned have advocated the establishment of a Permanent Commission for Selection and Guidance in the Ministry of Education (*Commission Permanente de Sélection et d'Orientation*), which would devise satisfactory methods for assigning pupils to the type of schools that is best suited to the abilities of the pupils. The second problem is that of extending the equality of opportunities. The abolition of tuition fees is only a small contribution to the solution of this problem. Many parents are ignorant of the opportunities already available; others withhold their children from secondary education because they need their help, in work or wages, at the earliest possible opportunity; prolonged education would not merely involve loss of wages, but additional expense for books, clothing, and, frequently, board away from home. Children of teachers and wards of the nation (children who lost their fathers in the War) are already provided for in these matters, if they can meet the standards. The only solution is to take the next step implied in the democratization and equalization of opportunities, and that is to extend the system of maintenance grants (*bourses d'entretien*) to all deserving pupils.

The *école unique* is, then, according to a summary of M. Ducos, from the point of view of the individual the right of every human being to acquire the highest and clearest consciousness of the world and of himself of which he is capable; from the point of view of the State it is its duty to provide the individual with the means of attaining this end; it also implies at the same time the duty and right to stimulate and to recruit the *élites*, the duty and the right to prepare them by the most appropriate methods. In other words, France is conscious today of the need of educating not merely one type of leaders (*élite*) — the intellectual type produced by her traditional secondary education — but a variety of types (*élites*) as demanded by her changing social, industrial, and commercial conditions.

Democratization and the old traditions. The democratization of education in France implies, then, an extension of educational opportunities according to ability. The more advanced education becomes, the more selective it is to be, but along differentiated lines. On one point all the supporters of the reforms are agreed, that there shall be no surrender of the quality of education. The traditional characteristics of French culture are to be preserved and promoted. This France feels that she owes to herself and to the leadership that she has enjoyed for so long in the world of culture. The intellectual *élite* is to be educated to safeguard the claims of general culture; that is, that type of education that arouses a consciousness of the essential problems that confront man as man and as citizen, that stimulates an intellectual interest for all forms of life, that cultivates the habit of going to the facts and from the facts to ideas, that develops an all-round view and a delicate feeling for shades of meanings and a critical judgment that is always ready to seize the manifold aspects and relations of life. On this there is to be no compromise, but the selection and training of the intellectual *élite* is to be paralleled by provisions for the selection and training of *élites* in other walks of life.[1] In the words of M. de Monzie the problem of post-elementary education involves free tuition (*gratuité*), selection (*sélection*) and distribution (*rationalisation*).

In his address to the Higher Council of Public Instruction in

[1] For references on the *école unique* see p. 136.

January, 1927, M. Herriot, then Minister of Public Instruction, stated:

> Our task, in fact, is constantly to create an *élite*. I, for my part, feel that keenly. At a time when other forces, less noble, seek to establish themselves, the educational system has the glorious privilege of maintaining the prestige of the spirit, the sovereignty and independence of the idea. It has the duty of courageously teaching democracies that no greater danger menaces them than misunderstanding of the rôle of the *élite*, or, in other words, the danger of leveling downward. Our system by examinations and by competitions maintains the most justifiable method of recruiting.... Is it not in the educational system that the republican ideal must be realized first, and thence spread through the whole State?

3. GERMANY

HISTORICAL DEVELOPMENT [1]

Reorganization after 1806. The meaning and problems of secondary education were nowhere so widely and intensively discussed as in Germany during the nineteenth century. When Prussia [2] in 1806 emerged from the disaster inflicted upon her by Napoleon at Jena, she at once began to direct her attention to the reconstruction of her educational system as one of the essential bases for her recovery. A Bureau of Education was created in 1808 in the Ministry of the Interior, and in 1817 was made a part of the newly created Ministry of Religion, Education, and Public Health. Wilhelm von Humboldt (1763–1835), a scholar, philosopher, and statesman, was called to take charge of the Bureau in 1808, and in the two years of his incumbency he was able to give to education the direction that it needed.

Germany's need at this time was an education which would liberate the potentialities of the individual in the interests of a self-governing community of fellow-citizens, patriotic, liberal, and emancipated from the control of foreign culture. In the field of secondary education this ideal had already been urged as the end of a reorganization proposed under the term Neohumanism. The neohumanistic movement sought to shift the emphasis in the sec-

---

[1] For a more detailed account of the history of secondary education in Germany see Kandel, I. L., *History of Secondary Education* (Boston, Houghton Mifflin Company, 1930).

[2] Although the following pages deal with the development of secondary education in Prussia, they represent in the main the general characteristics of secondary education in the whole of Germany. This is due, not merely to the reciprocal recognition of leaving certificates for entrance to the universities of each State, but since 1875 to the existence of an Imperial Educational Commission whose function was to supervise and approve standards.

ondary schools from Roman life to Greek life and antiquities, and to utilize this content, not for purposes of imitation but for spiritual assimilation, for the cultivation of taste, judgment, and understanding, for the discovery of the principles of creative activity, and for the search for "the good, the true, and the beautiful." Wilhelm von Humboldt was an ardent enthusiast for classical culture conceived in this way and defined the aim of secondary education to be the promotion of all-round culture (*Allgemeine Bildung*). It was around this concept of general culture that the conflict in secondary education revolved for another century as the claims of new subjects and the demands of a changing civilization began to make themselves felt. As developed by von Humboldt and his associates, the purpose of secondary education was defined as the harmonious development of all the powers, with all-round formal cultivation of intelligence, mastery of languages, considerable attainment in mathematics, and some familiarity with sciences and history; Hebrew, French, and other modern languages were optional. Real penetration into the spirit of classical culture, and assimilation of its ideal masterpieces in form and content, were to inspire a new creative age, which, through the activity and self-culture of the individual, was to furnish the solid foundations of a new nationalism, the expression of the living spirit and genius of the German people, now emancipated from the domination of foreign ideals.

The institution which alone could give a course of instruction for the attainment of this program, the *Gymnasium*, was placed in a privileged position and permitted to conduct a leaving examination (*Abiturientenprüfung*) which after 1834 became the sole method of access to the universities. The successful completion of six years of the course conferred the one-year military service privilege (*Einjähriger-freiwilliger Dienst*), and eligibility to some junior positions in the civil service. Schools that were not officially recognized as *Gymnasien* adapted themselves to the new conditions and became *Realschulen*, *Bürgerschulen*, or *Progymnasien*.

Reaction. Following the political reaction which took place in 1819, secondary like other branches of education was subject to bureaucratic control and supervision and the ideal of general culture was directed to serve the ends of the State. Under Johannes Schulze, who had charge of secondary education from 1818 until 1858, secondary education was more and more brought under the detailed regulations of the State. Teachers and pupils were rigorously controlled, both in and out of school; uniformity and standardization were introduced; and the breadth and liberalism of the neohumanistic spirit were gradually eliminated with a renewed emphasis on Latin, which, under the first definite prescription of the course of study in 1837, was assigned 86 hours out of a total of 280 hours in the nine-year course. Greek, Latin, and mathematics absorbed more than half the time (161 hours); the remainder was divided between French, religion, philosophy, history and geography, nature study, drawing, writing, and singing. If Schulze overemphasized scholarship at the expense of liberal education, he made a lasting contribution to education by improving the preparation of teachers, not only for the *Gymnasium*, but for other types of secondary schools, and by raising their dignity and social status.

The *Gymnasium*, however, became the center of attack from a number of directions. There were those who were disturbed by the overpressure on the pupils and the neglect of their physical well-being; some attacked Schulze's interpretation of *Allgemeine Bildung* as encyclopedic and would have preferred to reduce the number of subjects as instruments for the training of all-round ability; finally, the monopoly of the *Gymnasium* was opposed by those who desired to see more attention given to modern languages and sciences, or, rather, who insisted upon differentiated types of secondary education receiving equal recognition and leading to the same privileges. The Revolution of 1848, however, led to a reaction in education as well as in politics, and under Ludwig Wiese, who directed secondary education from 1852 to 1875, a return was made to the ideals of the Reformation period, with an emphasis on Latin and religious instruction. The regulations of 1856 subordinated still further German, French, and science.

Demands for modernization. In the mean time secondary schools other than the *Gymnasium* began to increase in numbers, largely in response to growing demands for modern subjects and sciences. In 1832 the authorities organized a leaving examination from the higher *Bürgerschulen* and the *Realschulen*, and granted to successful pupils the privileges of the one-year military service and admission to lower civil service appointments, but withheld state aid from them. It was not until 1859 that the authorities accepted a compromise solution and organized the modern schools into two types — the nine-year *Realschule erster Ordnung* giving religion, German, Latin, French, English, history and geography, mathematics and science crowned by a leaving examination, and the six-year *Realschule* without Latin. The privilege of admission to the universities continued to be withheld from graduates of the *Realgymnasium*, as the first of these schools came to be known later, until 1870, when they were admitted only to study mathematics, sciences, or modern languages. The increasing pressure of modern demands following the Franco-Prussian War led to the extension of some of the six-year *Realschulen* to nine-year schools (*Oberrealschulen*), which were officially recognized in 1878 to the extent of admitting their graduates to technical high schools.

Reform of 1892. The conflict between the partisans of the three types of secondary schools now became more embittered. The question was not merely one of educational values and the recognition of the equivalence of certain subjects for cultural and disciplinary ends, but a social and economic one. It was feared that the extension of privileges to graduates of the two modern courses would mean intense competition with the graduates of the traditional classical course. Numerous organizations were formed to represent the claims of each form of culture, and countless proposals for reform were put forward. The conflict was brought to a focus by Kaiser Wilhelm II, who called a conference in December, 1890, to investigate the courses of study, to eliminate useless information, to reduce the heavy burden on the pupils, and to seek measures for educating "national young Germans, and not young Greeks and Romans." To some extent the summoning of the conference was inspired by the fear of the spread of socialism through the increase of an unemployed intellectual proletariat (*Hungerkandidaten*).

Following the conference, but departing from some of its recommendations, new regulations were issued in 1892, recognizing the following types of schools: (1) the *Realschule*, the *Progymnasium*, and the *Realprogymnasium*, giving six-year courses; and (2) the *Gymnasium*, the *Realgymnasium*, and the *Oberrealschule*, giving nine-year courses. Schools with a common basis, following either the Altona plan, begun in 1878, or the Frankfort plan, begun in 1890, were also sanctioned. In the detailed courses of study more time was given to German, history, and religious instruction as the common basis of all schools.

Reform of 1901. The reform of 1892, while it defined the character of each school and gave them a common basis in the core subjects, failed to settle the heart of the conflict, the recognition of the equivalence of each group of schools so far as privileges were concerned. Following another conference in 1900, all nine-year schools were declared to be of the same value for general culture, which meant that their graduates would be admitted to the universities. Certain restrictions depending upon the requirements of some of the faculties (law, medicine, and theology) continued to be imposed upon graduates of the *Realgymnasium* and the *Oberrealschule*. In 1901 revised courses of study were issued, directed to linking the old and new cultures and to the promotion of the ends of German national life. The aim of each school was to contribute to the whole national culture through its own particular approach (classical, semi-classical, and modern-language-scientific). Unity was to be assured as far as possible through common elements and common subjects (German, history, and religion), but mainly through uniformity of aims.

Continued unrest. The reform of 1901 was regarded as a compromise and did not quell the criticisms which were directed, not only against the continued emphasis on the classics, but developed from other angles. There were those who demanded a modern education to prepare for modern life in an industrial age; there were others who urged a strong emphasis on German life and culture even to the exclusion of foreign languages; others again pressed for the establishment of a common school system and closer articulation with the elementary school. The outbreak of the World War only served to intensify the criticisms and the agitation for more radical reforms on the basis of German national culture and needs. Another movement, which looked beyond the internal organization of secondary education and the question of educational values with a limited range of subjects, centered around proposals for the complete reorganization of the whole system of education and the adoption of the principles of a common school system (*Einheitsschule*). This was a movement for the extension of educational opportunities on the basis of a common education for all up to the age of twelve and the organization of a variety of secondary school courses differentiated according to the needs and abilities of the pupils. A slight concession to the advocates of this reform was made during the War by the admission to secondary schools of gifted pupils from the elementary schools, selected by intelligence tests.

The German Republic, established in 1918, thus inherited a large number of problems in the field of secondary education. It was confronted with the problem of securing better articulation between elementary and secondary schools and of extending opportunities for secondary education. It had to reconsider the aims and purposes of secondary education, for, despite the professions of the regulations in 1892 and 1901, *Allgemeine Bildung* or general culture was not attained, partly because of the examinations and partly because each teacher, an intense specialist in his own field, virtually insisted on specialization by his pupils and failed to relate his own subject to the major cultural aim; the result was encyclopedism and mastery of information and knowledge with failure to produce the real ends of culture — judgment, discrimination, taste, and appreciation. To encyclopedism and scholarship the cult of personality had been sacrificed. Although Germany had made during the nineteenth century a greater contribution than any other country to the preparation of teachers, it was felt that they were too much dominated by the system and not sufficiently free to depart from tradition and routine. The whole problem of the secondary education of girls, which had grown up independently of that for boys, had to be considered, whether through coeducation or by the provision of separate schools which would provide opportunities paralleling those provided in boys' schools. Finally, there was a small group which felt that the domination of secondary education by privileges (*Berechtigungen*) perverted the real ends of education to an education for status, social and economic.

PROVISION AND ADMINISTRATION OF SECONDARY EDUCATION

Secondary education in Prussia is provided in public and private schools, but both types are equally under state supervision and no school may be established without the approval of the state authorities.[1] Public schools may be established either by the State or by local authorities (*Gemeinden*). In order to secure permission to establish a secondary school, a local authority must prove (1) the need of the type of school which it is proposed to establish, and (2)

[1] On the status of private schools see p. 148 ff.

its ability to maintain such a school without state aid at any time. The proposed site, building, and equipment must be approved, and the local authority must undertake to follow the regulations of the State in matters of the curriculum, course of study, and qualifications and appointment of teachers. The same procedure must be followed if it is proposed to change an existing school of one type into a school of another type, or amalgamate schools of different types, or to close a school entirely.

General administration and supervision. The supervision of secondary education is entrusted by the Ministry to the provincial school boards.[1] The professional members of the board (*Oberschulräte, Oberstudienräte, Studienräte*) are responsible for the inspection of secondary schools. The chief function of the inspectors is to make themselves thoroughly familiar with the work and personnel of each secondary school in their districts. They are expected to visit each school at least once a year and to prepare a short report on its characteristics and progress every four years. Stress is placed, however, not on the reports, but on the personal relations between the inspectors and the staffs of the schools under their jurisdiction. They are thus responsible for the approval of time-schedules and the distribution of the subjects, which are to be so organized that an appropriate balance is maintained between them in the light of the special aim of a particular school and of its general educative function as an institution for the development of character. The inspectors are required to discuss the work of the schools visited with the whole staff and with individual teachers, to make recommendations for improvement in the light of their broader experience, and to see that the recommendations are made effective, not by virtue of his authority, but as the result of personal conference and discussion. Provincial school boards may from time to time appoint senior teachers (*Oberstudienräte*) as special subject advisers (*Fachberater*), who may be assigned to visit schools and to assist at teachers' conferences.

Until the publication of the Administrative Ordinance in 1918,[2] each secondary school had its own board of governors (*Kuratorium*). Since 1918 each locality may create its own committee (*Schulaus-*

---

[1] See p. 288 f.
[2] *Verwaltungsordnung für städtische höhere Lehranstalten, Erlass vom 1 Oktober 1918.* (*Weidmannsche Taschenausgabe.*)

schuss), or, if the area is large enough, several committees for the general supervision and administration of secondary education. The school committee of a city consists of (1) the mayor or a deputy appointed by him as chairman; (2) three administrative officers; (3) three members of the city council; (4) two or three citizens (including women); (5) two to four teachers, including principals.

The duties of a school committee are to exercise supervision over the buildings and equipment; to prepare the annual budget; to coordinate local and state regulations; to determine the grant of free places and reduction in school fees; to act upon requests from teachers for leave of absence of short duration or to undertake employment beyond their regular duties or to reside outside of the area in which they are employed. The chairman of the committee, or some professional member appointed by him, may visit schools and classrooms, but without any right to interfere with instruction, may accompany state officials on the occasion of an inspection, and may be present at and participate in examinations. The committee may suggest to the appropriate city authority [1] the names of candidates to be selected for appointment as teachers or principals; these suggestions need not be followed. In any case the definitive appointment is made by the provincial school board with the approval of the Ministry, and the local authorities are restricted in the selection of candidates to the eligible list prepared by the Ministry.

The school committees thus perform a dual function. From the point of view of the provision of the fabric of secondary education, buildings, equipment, and part of the teachers' remuneration, they represent their locality; from the point of view of the smooth administration of the internal affairs of the schools, they represent the State. Irrespective, however, of whether they receive or do not receive state aid, they have no right to interfere with the purely educational and instructional side of the schools, which are entirely under the supervision of the state authority and the school principal assisted by his staff. The principle upon which this division of duties is justified is that the schools, whether provided by a locality or by the state, perform a state function — the education of all the citizens for the whole State. For the same reason all teachers in public schools are state officials (*Staatsbeamten*).

Internal administration. Responsibility for the internal adminis-

[1] Whether this authority is the elected or the official council has not yet been established.

tration of a secondary school is entrusted to the principal (generally called *Direktor*, or officially, *Studiendirektor*, or, in large schools with more than fifteen classes and in double schools, *Oberstudiendirektor*). The principal, who is appointed by the Minister, is the immediate superior of his staff; a movement, which was pronounced after the War, to designate him as merely a senior colleague, did not succeed. The principal in state schools is directly responsible to the provincial school board of his district, in city schools to the provincial school board and the local school committee, to which he is required to furnish information and advice when called upon. In relation to his school the principal is responsible for the general maintenance of the building and equipment and for the supervision of the progress of education in its broadest sense. Particular stress has been placed during the last two decades on the establishment of friendly relations with parents of the pupils, and since 1918 on coöperation with the parents' council which must be organized in each school.[1] On the instructional side the principal has charge of the admission of pupils, the assignment of classes and subjects to the teachers on his staff, for the preparation of the time-schedules and courses of study, and for the general progress and conduct of the pupils both in and out of school. In double schools and in schools with a large number of boarders, the principal must himself give eight hours of instruction a week; in other schools, twelve hours a week. In the performance of these functions he is expected to visit classrooms, to participate in the instruction, to discuss problems of instruction with each teacher personally, to familiarize himself with the work of each teacher so far as concerns the assignment and correction of written work and the selection of textbooks. If a school is a center for the preparation of teachers, the principal with teachers who are specially selected for the task must supervise the general training of the candidates (*Studienreferendare*). Finally, he must prepare an annual report (*Jahresbericht*) on the progress of the school and approve the inclusion of any other matter, usually a scholarly article, which may be submitted.

The principal is assisted by *Oberstudienräte*, positions which were created in 1920 and to which regular teachers are promoted for special ability. Promotions to this position are made by the provincial school board; in city schools nominations for promotion are

[1] See p. 293 f.

made by the school committee after consultation with the teachers of the school concerned. The *Oberstudienrat*, while continuing his duties as teacher, is expected to relieve the principal of some of the burden of his administrative duties so that he may devote more attention to his supervisory functions. Among the duties which may be assigned to the *Oberstudienrat* are the following: supervision of instruction in his own special field; the administration of one school in the case of double schools; the conduct of conferences of teachers in the lower classes; and the regulation of the relations with the parents of pupils in these classes; participation in the preparation of teachers; and other tasks such as the preparation of statistics and time-schedules.

The staff of each school consists of *Oberstudienräte, Studienräte*, and teachers of such special subjects as music, art, gymnastics, and manual work (*Oberschullehrer*). The principal appoints teachers who are to be responsible for each class (*Klassenleiter* or *Ordinarius*). In the assignment of the class teachers, care is taken that the older teachers are not assigned to the upper classes or the younger teachers to the lower. Each class teacher moves up with his class for several years. The class teacher is responsible for the general supervision of his pupils both in and out of class, supervises their progress, keeps in touch with other teachers who give instruction to his pupils, promotes, as far as possible, coöperation between school and home, and must inform himself on the whole scheme of studies laid out for his class during the year. The number of teaching hours per week are defined by the regulations, and are as follows: twenty-five hours a week up to the age of forty-five, twenty-three hours a week up to the age of fifty-five, and twenty hours a week thereafter for *Oberstudienräte* and *Studienräte*; teachers of music, art, singing, gymnastics, and manual work are required to teach twenty-five hours a week irrespective of age, unless, in the case of teachers of music and art, they have been promoted to the position of *Studienräte*.

Teachers' conferences. For the purpose of promoting the common aim of a school and securing coöperation among the teachers, opportunities for discussion and interchange of views are provided in the organization of conferences of three types: the *Gesamtkonferenz*, the *Klassenkonferenz*, and the *Fachkonferenz*. The *Gesamtkonferenz*, or conference of the whole staff of a school under the chairmanship of the principal, meets once a month or more frequently at the request of one fourth of the teachers, and may discuss such matters as the following: proposals for changing the type of school, reorganization of classes, or modifications of the course of study; requests for funds for equipment; revision of the school regulations on discipline; school celebrations, lectures, excursions, and games afternoons; requests for remission or reduction of fees; regulations for homework and written class exercises; dismissal of pupils; approval of pupils' societies; problems of pupil welfare and vocational guidance; and recommendation of candidates for promotion as *Oberschulräte*. The *Gesamtkonferenz* may appoint a permanent committee of from three to five teachers to act in an advisory capacity to the principal.

The *Klassenkonferenz*, which consists of all the teachers of one class, meets whenever necessary to discuss: the amount and distribution of homework and written class exercises in accordance with the regulations of the *Gesamtkonferenz*; the preparation of pupil reports; the promotion of pupils; and the imposition of serious punishments in so far as they are not required to be submitted to the *Gesamtkonferenz*. The *Fachkonferenz*, or conference of special-subject teachers, meets when necessary to discuss methods of instruction, without, however, interfering in any way with the independence of each teacher; the preparation of new or modifications of existing courses of study; proposals for the introduction of new textbooks and purchase of instructional aids; and suggestions for reading lists for each year.

REFORM OF SECONDARY EDUCATION

Problems of reform. In the reform of secondary education following the War, the German States were confronted with a number of problems. The first was the insistent demand for a complete reorganization of the whole system of education in such a way as to provide equality of opportunity for all according to ability. The radical advocates of such a reorganization proposed the establishment of a common school for all up to the age of twelve and of a variety of secondary schools built upon this foundation. This and similar proposals were rejected for a number of reasons, the chief being the fear that a secondary education leading up to the universities could not be given adequately in less than the traditional nine years.

There were, however, other problems which the reform had to solve besides that of a complete reorganization of the system. The traditional secondary schools had been definitely regarded as institutions for the training of leaders, as class institutions, and were distinct from the schools for the masses in methods and content of instruction. Not only was there a clearly marked gap between secondary and elementary education, but despite the efforts made since 1891 each type of secondary school tended to retain and cultivate its own particular identity without any regard for the development of a common basis between different types. The result was the crystallization of specific forms of secondary schools which rendered increasingly difficult transfer from one to the other, while in each school the emphasis tended to be placed on its own special objectives — whether classical, Latin-modern, or mathematical-scientific, with a consequent loss of a national aim. With the crystallization of forms and the difficulty of transfer, it became increasingly difficult to provide for adequate differentiation for individual pupils, with the consequence that the pressure on pupils for whom a particular course was not adapted became increasingly burdensome. Finally, the schools were dedicated to the cult of intellectualism and of scholarship, often to the neglect of the development of other and equally desirable qualities of personality. It was obvious to all that any reforms which might be undertaken must provide for a common national aim in all the schools, must encourage the fullest development of personality, and must be based upon the principles of elasticity and flexibility.

Preliminary preparation. The system of education has been modified to some extent. The Constitution of 1919 provided that all children should receive a common education for the first four years in a common school, and that the school preparatory to the secondary school should be abolished. Following the constitutional provision, the Federal Government in 1920 passed a law establishing the *Grundschule* or foundation school (see p. 140 f.), giving a common primary education to all irrespective of class distinctions. The purpose of the foundation school, as of the abolition of the preparatory school (*Vorschule*), is to give German children, at least for the first four years of their education, a common fund of ideas on the basis of national solidarity. The establishment of the *Grundschule* had the effect of postponing the beginning of secondary education from nine to ten years of age and thus of extending the total length of education to thirteen instead of twelve years. Since such an extension involved an additional year's expense on parents sending their children to the secondary schools for the whole course, serious protests were made against the requirement of four years of attendance in the *Grundschule*. As a result, permission has been granted to allow bright pupils to complete the course of this school in three instead of in four years.

Admission to secondary schools. On completing the work of the *Grundschule* normally in four years, or in the case of bright pupils in three years, pupils may apply for admission to a secondary school. The admission of pupils is administered by the school principal, who must be guided by the ages of the pupils (pupils over twelve years of age may not be admitted to the lowest class), the number of vacancies in his school, the size of each class which may be concerned, and by the ability of the pupils. There does not exist any uniformity in the methods of admission. In some localities, where definite working arrangements have been established between the lower and the higher school, pupils may be admitted on the recommendations of the teachers in the *Grundschule*; in others, each secondary school conducts its own entrance examination; in still others, there may be a common entrance examination for several schools. Where entrance examinations are employed, two restrictions are imposed; first, the standard must be that of the *Grundschule*, and the subjects must include only general knowledge (*Heimatkunde*), German, arithmetic, and drawing; and second, the examination must be conducted by mixed committees representing teachers in the *Grundschule* and the secondary school. The pupils' school records must always be taken into consideration, and other methods of examination (e.g., tests) may be employed, but only to supplement the traditional methods. Pupils who pass the examination, but who cannot be admitted to the school of their choice, may be referred to other schools; pupils who fail may not repeat the entrance examination for a year.

Fees and free places. The entrance examination thus serves as one method of selection. Another is the cost of secondary education. Free secondary education has not yet become a question of practical politics; the charging of tuition fees is in fact accepted as a definite principle. In Prussia the fees are so adjusted that they supply one third of the cost of each pupil; in 1930 a fee of 250 Mark a year was established on the assumption that the cost of education of each pupil is 750 Mark per pupil. The tuition fee in Prussia is the highest in Germany, with the exception of Hamburg and Bremen.[1] Although secondary education is on principle based on tuition fees, certain adjustments are made; the fees may be reduced where several children in the same family attend secondary schools — the full fee is charged for the first child, seventy-five per cent for the second, fifty per cent for the third, and waived for the rest, but the intellectual ability of the child and the financial ability of the parent applying must justify such a reduction. To assist poor pupils of ability, one fourth of the income from fees may be employed for the remission of fees and the award of maintenance grants; in such awards the principal of a school acts on the advice of his teachers' conference. It is estimated that about thirty per cent of the pupils in the secondary schools of Germany, the distribution varying largely in different parts of the country, enjoy free tuition, while another small percentage is admitted on reduced fees.

Types of schools. The Prussian reform of secondary education, which was begun in 1924, proceeded on the principle that the historical continuity of secondary education must be preserved, since the types of schools which had emerged during its development in the past century gave expression to certain national demands. The Federal Educational Conference (*Reichsschulkonferenz*, 1920) had recommended secondary schools with German cultural subjects as the core, with more attention to current practical demands for civic and social training, and with less emphasis on foreign languages not adapted to the requirements of modern life. The Prussian reform attempted to synthesize these demands with the retention of the traditional types of schools, to which new ones were added. In other words, instead of moving in the direction of a common secondary school with differentiated courses, it was decided to retain the existing types, to create at least one new type, to concentrate on a common core in each, and to permit each type to develop its own particular objective. In the secondary education of girls, which is organized separately, the principle of the common school with differentiated courses, adopted in the reform of 1908, has been

---

[1] The general range of tuition fees is from 90 Mark in Bavaria to 360 Mark in Bremen. These figures apply to state schools. In city schools they may, with the approval of the state authorities, be higher or lower. In some States the fees are flexible and are adjusted to parental income (Thuringia and Brunswick) or even wealth (Oldenburg).

continued. Coeducation has been rejected, and only in exceptional cases may girls be admitted to boys' schools — but only if a suitable girls' school is not available, if the applicants are particularly gifted and in good health, and if the application has the approval of the parents' council in the school, of the teachers, and of the Ministry. In 1929 the enrollment of girls in 427 out of a total of 1122 boys' schools was 10,089, about 3 per cent of the total enrollment; nearly one third (3385) of the girls were in *Reformrealgymnasien*, 1269 in *Oberrealschulen*, 1388 in *Realschulen*, and 2009 in *Aufbauschulen*.

Rising on the foundation of the *Grundschule*, the three pre-War types of secondary schools have been retained — the *Gymnasium*, the *Realgymnasium*, and the *Oberrealschule*. These three types, with two additional types adopted in 1922, the *Deutsche Oberschule* and the *Aufbauschule*, are known as complete institutions (*Vollanstalten*). The *Deutsche Oberschule*, like the three traditional types, is a nine-year school created since the War in response to the demand for a school in which the emphasis would be placed on German subjects and on German culture. It was intended by the proponents of this type that foreign languages should be excluded. The universities stated that they would refuse to admit graduates of this school as matriculated students; a proposed compromise to include one foreign language was also rejected. The new school was accordingly organized with two foreign languages, to which, however, less time is devoted, and greater attention is given to German language and literature and history and geography than in the other types.

The *Aufbauschule*, which is also a new type, was intended to provide opportunities for secondary education to pupils living in smaller towns and rural areas. The abolition of the old normal schools opportunely left buildings available for this purpose. The new school type is intended for gifted pupils who have completed the seventh year of the elementary school and are specially recommended; they are thus normally about the age of thirteen when they enter the six-year course of the *Aufbauschule*. Like the other complete institutions, the *Aufbauschule* prepares its pupils for the secondary school leaving examination (*Abiturientenprüfung*) in six years through a program of studies similar either to that of the *Oberrealschule* or to that of the *Deutsche Oberschule*. The *Aufbauschule* has been recognized provisionally by the universities, and has already made such progress in popular esteem that it is being established in the larger cities as well.

In addition to the complete nine-year schools, there are six-year schools which in general run parallel to the first six years of the complete schools. These incomplete institutions (*Nichtvollanstalten*) are the *Progymnasium*, the *Realprogymnasium*, and the *Realschule*, paralleling the *Gymnasium*, *Realgymnasium*, and *Oberrealschule* respectively.

Each of these schools has its own peculiar objectives, particularly in Prussia. Thus the *Gymnasium* is devoted to the study of the classical languages, Latin and Greek, the *Realgymnasium* to Latin and a modern foreign language, the *Oberrealschule* to mathematics and science, and the *Deutsche Oberrealschule* to German cultural subjects. Since this type of organization tends to be somewhat inflexible to the extent that pupils on entering any one of them have no choice of courses, efforts have been made to introduce more elasticity. Thus, in localities where the only available school is the classical *Gymnasium*, pupils may substitute a modern foreign language in place of Greek, particularly those pupils who plan to leave school after the sixth year. This solution is not regarded as adequate, since the possibility of transfer to other types of schools is still limited. Two other variations, which have long been in existence, have been encouraged. These are the *Reformgymnasium*, which for the first three years offers the same course as the *Reformrealgymnasium* and *Oberrealschule*, beginning with a modern foreign language and postponing Latin to the fourth year; and the *Reformrealgymnasium* of which there are two alternative forms; (*a*) one type in which Latin is not begun until the fourth year; and (*b*) another type in which the beginning of Latin is postponed to the sixth year. The *Reformgymnasium* is not popular in Prussia; the *Reformrealgymnasium* is important because it postpones the choice of specialization along the lines of the *Realgymnasium*, the *Oberrealschule*, or the *Deutsche Oberrealschule* as long as possible. In the light of the obvious need for flexibility (*Bewegungsfreiheit*), the reform in Saxony is moving in the direction of more comprehensive schools either following the type of the *Reformschulen* or providing *Reformzüge* (possibilities of bifurcation) in the last years of the school. As will be pointed out later, other measures besides organizational have been adopted to provide a greater amount of flexibility and elasticity and not merely from the point of view of the needs of intellectual differences, but perhaps even more with the intention of furnishing facilities for the fullest development of personality.

There are not included in this discussion of the types of secondary schools other institutions at the same level in which the emphasis is primarily vocational (commercial or technical). From the German point of view, these do not constitute a part of the secondary school system (*höhere Schulen*). There is in process of development for selected pupils who have completed seven years of the elementary schools a new type of school directed to the study of modern social, economic, and political problems and leading on graduation to the higher commercial schools (*Handelshochschulen*). Owing to the failure to secure recognition for the *Deutsche Oberschule* as originally planned, there are some who hope that this new type of school, the *Wirtschaftsoberschule* will take its place as an institution which will prepare its pupils more directly for modern life.

Organization. The nine-year secondary schools are organized into nine classes named as follows from the lowest class to the top: Sexta (VI), Quinta (V), Quarta (IV), Untertertia (UIII), Obertertia (OIII), Untersekunda (UII), Obersekunda (OII), Unterprima (UI), and Oberprima (OI). The *Aufbauschule* begins with Untertertia; the classes in the six-year schools bear the same nomenclature from Sexta up to Untersekunda. The school year is 240 days in length (including Sundays). Classes are conducted every day except Sunday, and as a general rule in the mornings in order to obviate unnecessary travel to and from school, or, in the case of poorer pupils, the cost of a midday meal. Each period is forty-five minutes in length. One afternoon a week is usually set aside for games and athletics, and one day a month may be devoted to an excursion for study or other purposes.

The size of classes is still fixed by a decree of 1867 which set up a maximum of 50 pupils for the first three classes, 40 for the next three, and 30 in the last three. These figures may be exceeded, but not up to more than 10 per cent above the maximum for each class. The average size of classes in all types of schools in 1927–28 was 27.8, decreasing from an average of 33.4 in the lowest class to 19.1 in the highest. The amount of homework which may be set for each class is regulated as follows: VI, 1 hour; V, 1½ hours; IV to UIII, 2 hours; OIII to OII, 2½ hours; OI, 3 hours as a maximum. The burden

	Gymnasium	Real-gymnasium	Oberrealschule	Deutsche Oberschule	Reformgymnasium	Reformrealgymnasium (1)	Reformrealgymnasium (2)	Aufbauschule
OI								
UI								
OII								Second Modern Language
UII		Second Modern Language	Second Modern Language	Second Modern Language	Second Modern Language / Greek	Second Modern Language / Latin	Latin	
OIII	Greek				Latin / Latin	Second Modern Language		First Modern Language
UIII		First Modern Language	First Modern Language	First Modern Language	First Modern Language		Second Modern Language	
IV	Modern Language						First Modern Language	Volksschule
V		Latin				First Modern Language		7 years
VI	Latin							

Grundschule (4 years; 3 years in special cases)

TYPES OF BOYS' SCHOOLS AND ENROLLMENT, 1912-1927

TYPE	1912		1917		1922		1927	
	Schools	Pupils	Schools	Pupils	Schools	Pupils	Schools	Pupils
Gymnasium and Progymnasium............	352 }	112,991	348 }	100,169	317	90,044	300	83,763
Reformgymnasium and Reformprogymnasium ..	20		23		22	6,305	17	5,638
Realgymnasium and Realprogymnasium.......	125 }	63,923	129 }	74,903	152	39,816	182	39,604
Reformrealgymnasium and Reformrealprogymnasium................	87		116		124	40,585	177	75,225
Oberrealschule and Realschule............	279	76,973	302	80,766	311	97,421	330	93,001
Oberrealschule in Aufbauform............	....	....	....	....	....	....	12	1,673
Deutsche Oberschule................	....	....	....	....	....	....	9	1,261
Deutsche Oberschule in Aufbauform...........	....	....	....	....	2	70	60	7,781
Total............	863	253,887	918	255,838	928	274,301	1,087	307,946

is further reduced by a requirement that the work to be done at home must arise out of work done in class and be ultimately associated with it.

Pupils are promoted at the end of each year on the recommendation of the conference of class teachers which is reached on the basis of the pupils' total records for the year. Pupils cannot be promoted on condition that they take an examination subsequently in subjects in which they have been weak. Pupils who fail to qualify for promotion after two years in the same class must be withdrawn from the school; parents must, however, be given notice in cases where promotion is doubtful at least three months before the close of the school year. Double promotions are permitted, but only with the consent of the pupil's parents. In general pupils are graded in each subject and on their total record as follows: Very good; good; satisfactory; deficient; unsatisfactory. A grade of satisfactory is required for promotion; a poorer grade, provided that it has not been obtained in a major subject of the course, may be compensated by the teacher's report on the personality of a pupil and on some special achievement in another field. In 1927–28 the percentage of promotions from class to class was as follows:

VI... 84.3 per cent	UIII... 82.6 per cent	OII... 82.1 per cent
V.... 85.4	OIII... 80.5	UI.... 84.8
IV... 86.9	UII.... 84.4	OI.... 92.1

Pupils in nine-year institutions, if recommended for promotion from the sixth to the seventh year of the course, receive a certificate, the *Zeugnis der Obersekundareife*, which entitles them to certain privileges of further study or for entrance to certain appointments; pupils in six-year institutions are given the same certification after an examination conducted by a committee consisting of the principal and staff of the school and a representative of the State.

AIMS OF SECONDARY EDUCATION

The reformulation of the aims of secondary education was due in part to the recognized defects of the secondary schools before the War, in part to the recognition of new forces whose influence could no longer be ignored, and in part to changes in educational theory, itself affected by the first two causes. The pre-War system was definitely regarded as selective, not only intellectually but also socially; not only was there an absence of articulation with the elementary schools, but a separate system of preparatory schools (*Vorschule*) gave the necessary preparation for admission to the secondary schools. There was an absence of articulation between the elementary and secondary schools, and the secondary schools themselves were in no sense coördinated either by a common objective or in such a way as to provide ready opportunities for transfer from one to the other.

More serious than defects of organization, which meant the reduction of educational opportunities to a select class, was the intense specialization to which the aim of *Allgemeine Bildung* had been reduced. Each type of school proceeded in its own way in emphasizing its own peculiar characteristics without regard to integration of subjects around a single unitary aim, whether national or individual. The result was an absence of educational articulation with elementary education, on the one hand, and between the various types of secondary schools on the other. The emphasis, it was charged, was too much on specialization and scholarship to the detriment of that development of personality which should be the end of education. While the system produced students with well-filled minds, the results, so far as training in initiative and independence are concerned, were inadequate. More freedom, greater flexibility, a more direct emphasis on social and national aims were recognized as the objectives which must be striven for in the reforms.

The demands of some of the advocates of reform for such a reorganization of the whole system as would provide for a prolongation of the common education of all and an increase in the opportunities for education shattered on the obstacles opposed by the *beati possidentes*, the social and intellectual vested interests of those associated with the traditional secondary schools and the universities. The movement for the *Einheitsschule*, which had as its basis a common elementary education for all up to twelve, failed, and in its place a common four-year school, the *Grundschule*, was adopted. Opportunities have been increased, but only to a slight extent, by provisions for the reduction of fees, scholarships, and maintenance grants. Secondary education has remained selective, and with the award of privileges (*Berechtigungen*), which are granted after the completion of six or more years of the course, continues to have a magnetic attraction for pupils who in their own interests should attend another type of school. The intensification of economic competition and the difficulty of securing employment have tended to crowd into the secondary schools large numbers of pupils who look upon the acquisition of the *Berechtigungen* as an economic investment. At the same time employers are seizing the opportunity of an unfavorable employment situation to insist on the completion of at least six years of secondary education as a qualification for appointment even in such trades as shoemaking, tailoring, and waiting in railway restaurant cars. The pressure toward the secondary schools is illustrated by the steady increase of enrollments since 1912. In that year Prussia, with a population of about 40,000,000, had 863 secondary schools for boys with an enrollment of 253,887 pupils; in 1917 there were 918 schools with an enrollment of 255,838 pupils; in 1922 there were 928 schools with an enrollment of 274,301 pupils; and in 1927, when the population was more than two million less, there were 1087 schools with an enrollment of 307,946 pupils. A part — but up to 1927 only a small part — of this increase may be attributed to the requirement that prospective elementary school teachers must have their preparatory general education in secondary schools.[1] There are those who already profess to see a lowering of intellectual standards, without, however, recognizing that the fault lies with a system which combines education with privileges and which does not as yet provide an adequate range of differentiated courses.

The change to a democratic form of society has, however, had the effect of emphasizing the importance of common elements in the education of citizens in order to promote national solidarity and mutual understanding. The common elements have, indeed, furnished the basis for articulation between secondary and other types of schools and a point of concentration for the courses in each type of secondary school.

The new spirit in education. Liberal education in the new organization is still defined in terms of foreign languages together with the vernacular history and geography, science and mathematics. The choice of the foreign languages — classical, Latin and modern, or modern — gives to each type of school its own peculiar character,

---

[1] The increase has been even greater in the enrollment of girls. In 1912 there were 384 schools with 99,517 pupils; in 1917, 437 schools with 119,359 pupils; in 1922, 509 schools with 119,509 pupils; and in 1927, 550 schools with 131,330 pupils. For the whole of Germany the number of pupils increased from 662,105 (427,644 boys and 234,461 girls) in 1911 to 822,609 (551,322 boys and 271,287 girls) in 1926-27.

but the tendency — more marked in Saxony, for instance, than in Prussia — is to postpone differentiation as long as possible. Except that the subjects are regarded as the prerequisites for academic and professional study in the universities, there has been no compromise with vocational or technical training. The study of these subjects is considered to be the essential for a broad general education, but, if there has been practically no change in the concept of culture, there has been an important change in the organization of the subjects for national and individual ends. One of the most serious problems confronting the German people in their post-War reorganization has been to devise means for the promotion of education that would develop a new sense of social solidarity and loyalty to the republican form of government, to take the place of the bonds of loyalty that had been forged by the monarchy and devotion to the political ends that it had set up. The obvious solution, the adoption of the *Einheitsschule*, was rejected as an organization; indeed, attempts have been made to define this as a spiritual need for common education rather than an institutional necessity. Since the organization has remained virtually unchanged, efforts to promote national cultural solidarity have been made in other directions.

The first of these was the adoption of the pedagogical principle of *Heimatkunde*, or knowledge of the environment, as a common basis for curriculum-making in the elementary and, so far as it can be carried out, in the secondary schools. The important difference between the two educational levels lies in the fact that the interpretation of the environment in the secondary schools would be enriched and broadened by reference to a greater range of factors, national and foreign, that have gone into the making of German culture. The second direction has been the adoption of a more clearly defined national purpose, which with a somewhat different motif had been urged by the Kaiser since the Conference of 1890. The new end to be promoted is *Deutschtum*, German nationalism, German culture — everything that has made and continues to give meaning to German civilization. This does not mean that German secondary education is becoming nationalistic, but it does mean that national values must be taken as terms of reference in building up the content of the school programs.

Change in administrative methods. To this end the change in the spirit of German educational administration has contributed. Rigid prescription of curricula and courses of study has been replaced by the publication by the Ministries of Education of suggestions (*Richtlinien*) to be filled out by the faculties of each school in the light of local conditions. According to this theory the specialist teachers of the various subjects must justify every part of the content that they recommend on the basis of its potential contribution to a better understanding and appreciation of German culture. In a sense this theory recalls the spirit underlying the neohumanistic movement. This tendency has affected not only the organization of the ancient languages, in which chief stress is being placed on the study of foreign cultures and institutions and their relations to German culture and institutions, rather than on the acquisition of a mastery of the spoken language. Following this theory the programs have been divided into core and concentration subjects. The core subjects are those that transmit German culture and are the constants in all types of schools; they are religion, German, history and civics, and geography. To these subjects the others are expected to contribute enrichment as well as to cultivate special and individual interests. The significance of the reform lies in the attempt to meet the criticisms of the old system that it cultivated specialists, and failed to secure any coördination between the various subjects of each program. The old aim of *Allgemeine Bildung*, in which equal attainments were expected in all subjects, now gives way to *Bildung zum Deutschtum*. The differentials in each program are intended to be treated as different methods of approach to an appreciation of national life.

The Youth Movement, and its significance. One of the most serious criticisms of the old system was its strong emphasis on the accumulation of knowledge and information, rather than on the development of power, judgment, taste, and discrimination. It was charged that the schools were successful in imparting information, but failed to cultivate in the pupils ability to meet new situations. Personality and individuality were sacrificed for the accumulation of knowledge; the chief cult of the schools was intellectualism. These criticisms were not new. They were inherent in the revolt of youth that began in 1898, when Karl Fischer, a student in one of the secondary schools in Berlin, organized the first group of *Wandervögel* and laid the foundations for the Youth Movement (*Jugend-*

bewegung), which was to sweep the country and cultivate a new spirit and new attitudes. The movement was a protest against the severe intellectualism of the schools, and represented a yearning for opportunities for emotional expression. Having its roots in eighteenth-century romanticism, the movement preached the gospel of a return to nature and the simple life, free from the restrictions of the conventions and restrictions set up by modern urban life, the control of parents, and the authoritarian discipline of the school. Traveling in small groups, the adherents of the movement wandered over the country under self-elected leaders, living as a family, and cultivating a spirit of independence, strength of body, and a sense of social discipline and coöperation.

For the young rebels the movement stood for the rediscovery of life and of their native land, the inner meaning of both of which they attempted to penetrate; folk-songs and folk-dances to the accompaniment of the guitar (*Zupfgeige*) were revived; love of the country, love of the people, and love of the national traditions became the gospel of the Wanderbirds. The movement spread widely throughout the secondary schools of Germany, and soon was taken up by the girls. The cult of independence, the questioning of authority, and the growing self-reliance of the youth filled the authorities and parents with a feeling of alarm and suspicion. Attempts were made, but unsuccessfully, to bore from within by the introduction of teachers into the groups. The outbreak of the War put a temporary check on the movement, but the ideals for which it stood had had sufficient time to become stamped into the minds and hearts of young Germany, and after the Revolution fitted in admirably with the aims and aspirations of the new Republic. The philosophy of *Deutschtum* and the educational theories, stressing the development of independent personality, found a ready soil on which to build. Although the *Jugendbewegung* has lost some of its idealism and momentum because of its growth and consequent over-organization, and because of the injection of political and sectarian conflicts, its contribution to the reform of the spirit of secondary education has in theory at any rate been marked.[1]

The new aim in education. The *Jugendbewegung* combined with the recognized need for national solidarity to emphasize the culti-

[1] Alexander, T., and Parker, B., *The New Education in Germany*, pp. 3 ff. (New York. 1929).

vation of *Deutschtum* as the concentration point in secondary as in elementary education. Another aspect was contributed by this movement and by educational theory. The old system had been criticized for its emphasis on intellectualism at the expense of the development of judgment, taste, and appreciation; from another point of view the methods of instruction were open to criticism for the stress on memorization, drill, and cramming, and the discipline for its severity. Knowledge, it is recognized, is the essential basis of culture, but not its end; knowledge and information alone deal with externals; their proper fruit is culture, which is eternal and personal, and affecting emotion and will as well as the intellect. Culture implies activity, purpose, creation, and a properly balanced and harmonious personality. Hence education must have as its aim, not the acquisition of knowledge, but the development of all the powers of the individual — the body, the will, and the emotions. The test of an education is not ability to reproduce information, but interest and ability to engage in its discovery, or, in other words, ability to handle new situations.

The new aim of education accordingly demanded new methods of instruction. Here, too, a common bond for elementary and secondary education has been found in the activity principle (*Arbeitsprinzip*). The Prussian *Richtlinien* (suggestions) state definitely that instruction should be fundamentally activity instruction. The activity school (*Arbeitsschule*) aims to cultivate in the individual the highest self-activity, to develop creative powers, and to promote joy in work. All learning should be an activity, a creating, a forming. The teacher must not merely impart information, but must discover content that develops powers, independence, judgment, imagination, and will. The pupil must coöperate in the learning process by appreciation of aims and purposes of the task in which he is engaged, and the spirit of classroom procedure must be one of coöperation and mutual interchange of ideas. The aim of the teacher should be to lead the pupil gradually to independence and initiative in work. To this end the time-schedules provide, in the upper sections of the secondary schools, for the organization of small activity groups (*freie Arbeitsgemeinschaften*) in which the pupils, under sympathetic guidance, may continue intensively to pursue their study either in some of the subjects of the curriculum, or to take up new subjects.

CURRICULA AND COURSES OF STUDY

The principles governing the revision of the curricula and courses of study of the secondary schools were enunciated in *Die Neuordnung des preussischen höheren Schulwesens* prepared by Ministerialrat Hans Richert in 1924. The four main types of secondary schools (*Gymnasium, Realgymnasium, Oberrealschule,* and *Deutsche Oberschule*) are equivalent in value and all are equally responsible for carrying out the aims of secondary education. The primary task of secondary education is in the spirit of the *Einheitsschule* to promote the integration of that specifically national content of subjects which may contribute to the advancement of German intellectual life. *Allgemeine Bildung* must be interpreted, not in terms of specialization in a series of unrelated and uncoördinated subjects, but as the unitary comprehension of all culture. Accordingly, while the cultivation of *Allgemeine Bildung* is the common task of all schools, they are organized on the principle of division of labor, so that each pursues the same goal, but with different methods of approach. In all schools there must be a common core of subjects (*Kernfächer*) — religion, German, history, and geography — but in each school there are the special subjects (*Kursfächer*) which give it its peculiar character or color. The special subjects, however, in turn must be organized in such a way that they help to contribute to a better understanding of the core subjects and in this way to enrich national culture (*Deutschtum*), to the attainment of which all schools must strive. The core subjects not only serve as centers of concentration in each school type and as a common basis for all types, but promote unity and common understanding among schools at all levels. Beyond this, the secondary schools have the further responsibility of providing an adequate preparation to the pupils who will later proceed to the universities, without in any sense undertaking themselves to provide specialized training.

National culture is not the only end to be promoted by secondary education; care must be taken that the personality of the pupil is not neglected either in the selection of materials or in the methods of instruction. The cult of intellectualism and encyclopedic mastery of content, which characterized the old secondary education, must give place to broad cultural training and the development of personality. The lessons of the Youth Movement must not be ignored, and all the potentialities of the individual — mind and body, will and emotions, the rational and the irrational — must be given opportunities for development. Hence more room must be found for handwork, music and fine arts, and civic training, and, through greater flexibility in the organization of the time-schedule, opportunity must be provided for the pupils to pursue their special interests, when they are sufficiently mature to make a choice. The school must be organized as a community for coöperation among teachers and between teachers and pupils.

The responsibility for the preparation of the course of study for each school on the basis of the Suggestions (*Richtlinien*) issued by the Ministry is vested in the principal and his staff working in coöperation in activity groups (*Arbeitsgemeinschaften*). In order to secure unity in a course of study, the coöperation is essential of class teachers, special subject teachers, teachers of skill subjects (*technische Fächer*, such as art, music, manual work, physical training), and of the faculty as a whole. Each group is responsible for the contribution which its work or subjects of instruction may make to the general unity of the program. This object can be further advanced by discussions, conferences, exchange of opinion, visiting of class instruction, and coöperative experimentation.

Special objectives. The special objectives and purposes of each type of school are defined in the Suggestions in detail. The function of the *Gymnasium* is to impart a humanistic training through an emphasis on the cultural values of the classics and their relations to and influence on modern German culture. The *Realgymnasium* has the special task of cultivating an appreciation of the influences exercised upon the development of German culture by Roman civilization and Christianity and by mathematical-scientific thinking. In the *Oberrealschule* the predominant position is held by mathematics and natural sciences which provide intellectual, philosophical, humanitarian, and historical training; the educational objective of this school will be carried out by constant integration between these subjects, modern languages, and the core subjects. The function of the latest addition to the traditional types of secondary schools, the *Deutsche Oberschule*, is to place German culture in the center of the course and from that point of view to study the influences exercised upon its development by its relations with other modern cultures. The *Aufbauschule* may be organized on the model of the *Oberrealschule* or the *Deutsche Oberschule*. Besides the special objectives each school shares the responsibility of the whole of secondary education for the general intellectual and disciplinary training of the pupils.

Not only are the objectives of each school type defined, but the special place of each subject in the curriculum is outlined. Thus the teaching of the mother-tongue must develop a mastery of the language and a thorough appreciation of the cultural values of the language, of its literature and art, and of the people who speak it; the pupils must learn not only to speak, read, and write German, but to feel, live, and think in German. These ends are to be achieved by constant emphasis on good speech in every class, on speech-training, reading aloud and recitation, oral and written exercises on a variety of topics and in various forms, the study of grammar, which will give an insight into the genius of the structure of the language, and extensive reading of literature. Art appreciation, folklore, civic education are natural outcomes of a broad approach to the study of German which will also use the opportunities afforded to it of treating many questions which arise as problems in philosophy.

History has to serve a number of ends. It must not only cultivate a knowledge of the development of the pupil's community, State, and nation, but must lead them to understand the present in the light of the past and develop in them a feeling of political responsibility. Political, economic, and cultural history must be interwoven into a complete picture, and the study of the history of Germany must be connected gradually with the study of world history, and the interdependence of great nations with one another. This subject again offers opportunities for the training in art appreciation, civic education, and certain philosophical concepts. Geography, like history and German, has the task of cultivating love of the native soil, the home and the fatherland, and to train for citizenship. But geography has a dual character; it may be humanistic or scientific and the school should pay attention to both aspects. Starting with local community studies, geography must enable the pupils to read maps with understanding and to use their eyes when observing their environment as well as to appreciate the influence of environment on human development and the physical factors which affect the environment.

The study of foreign languages, whether ancient or modern, must introduce the pupils to the characteristics of the cultural and intellectual life of the people whose language is studied. Whatever the language and literature, their study should contribute to a better appreciation and understanding of the pupil's own language and literature and of the genius of his own people. The influences of the foreign language and literature on the development of German and the interplay between German and other cultures must be emphasized as an essential part of the study. The subjects in this field must also contribute their share to art appreciation, civic education, and philosophy. In the modern foreign languages the pupil should be expected to acquire sufficient ability to use them to express himself orally and in writing on simple subjects or ideas with which he is familiar.

Mathematics and natural sciences also have their special objectives. Accuracy and skill, the correct conception of quantitative values, appreciation of mathematics as an ordered science, training in logical procedure and proof, and knowledge of the philosophical values of mathematical processes and their importance for intellectual history are the ends of instruction in mathematics. The function of the natural sciences is to give an insight into the laws of all natural phenomena and into the significance for life of all natural processes; through physics the pupils are to acquire a comprehensive view of nature and the fundamental theories essential to a physical conception of the world; while chemistry will familiarize them with the most important chemical phenomena in so far as they are important for an understanding of the animate and inanimate world, for housekeeping, or for economic life.

Music, drawing, and art are subjects which serve for the training of personality. In addition to the objectives inherent in the subjects themselves, they have the opportunity of developing feeling and imagination and of stimulating a desire for creative expression. Few subjects are as well suited to give the pupils an appreciation of the importance of the arts for social well-being and for group cooperation.

The Suggestions define the scope of the content in each subject for each year in order to secure uniformity of standards, but within the Suggestions adequate opportunity is provided to the teachers to adapt the work of each class along the lines of their own and the pupils' interests. But the success of a course of study, it is emphasized in the Suggestions in general and in the outlines of each subject, depends on giving adequate attention to concentration in order to secure unified instructional activity. In place of the former emphasis on specialization in subject-matter, the whole work of each school must be directed to the harmonious development of personality, to national, civic, and art education, and to an appreciation of the meaning of each subject in the cultural whole or philosophical penetration. Such an integrated approach, combined with the reduction in the number of hours of classwork, has the further advantage of reducing the burden on the pupils. To the same end the hours for homework have been reduced; homework must grow directly out of class instruction and its preparation must be discussed in advance.

Finally, the success of the reform depends on the employment of methods of instruction which utilize the personal interests and coöperation of the pupils. The emphasis must be, not on transmission of knowledge and memoriter learning, but on the active participation of the pupils through which independence of judgment, will, and imagination may be developed. The teacher is no longer to be a taskmaster, but must stimulate the activity of each pupil and of the class as a group. Hence instruction must be fundamentally activity instruction (*Arbeitsunterricht*). The acquisition of knowledge and the acquisition of ability to do independent work and of a purposeful technique of work must go hand in hand and be developed progressively. On the basis of such training the pupils in the advanced classes will reach a stage of maturity which will enable them to participate successfully in the free activity groups (*freie Arbeitsgemeinschaften*) to which six hours a week may be assigned in the upper sections of each school. The purpose of the free activity groups, which are voluntary, is to provide opportunities for the intensive cultivation of the pupils' own interests in special phases in so far as they arise out of the subjects in the curriculum which they pursue; no provision is made for the study in those groups of subjects not already in the curriculum. In the last years of the course the free activity groups furnish occasions for special research work and the preparation of theses which may be presented by candidates for the leaving examination (*Abiturientenexamen* or *Reifeprüfung*). In order to encourage variety, teachers are advised to redistribute the hours for these groups among different subjects every half-year.

The Ministry places particular stress on the establishment of activity groups for the study of philosophical works related so far as possible to the various subjects of the curriculum. The aim of such philosophical study is not the acquisition of a system of philosophy or philosophical solutions of the latest social problems, but the development of insight into philosophical method, into the intellectual processes of the thinker and their methods of attack.[1]

In the accompanying tables will be found the time-schedules in the main types of schools and a summary table giving the time-distribution for subjects, based on regulations issued on Sept. 14, 1931. It will be noted that special arrangements are made according as the first modern foreign language is French or English. In Prussia the choice between these two languages is left to the local school acting frequently on the request of parents. The general tendency in most States is to begin with English as the first modern language. In addition to the periods prescribed in the schedules a total of 3 periods

1. GYMNASIUM

Subjects	VI	V	IV	U III	O III	U II	O II	U I	O I	Total
Religion	2	2	2	2	2	2	2	2	2	18
German	4	4	3	3	3	3	3	3	3	29
Latin	6	6	6	5	5	5	5	5	5	48
Greek	..	..	..	6	6	6	6	5	5	34
Modern language	..	..	3	2	2	2	2	2	2	15
History (civics)	..	..	2	2	2	2	3	3	3	17
Geography	2	2	2	1	1	1	1	1	1	12
Mathematics	4	4	4	3	3	3	3	4	3	31
Natural sciences	2	2	2	2	2	2	2	2	2	18
Drawing	2	2	2	1*	1*	1*	1*	1*	1*	12
Music	2	2	..	..	..	..	..	..	..	4
Total	24	24	26	27	27	27	28	28	27	238

* Two hours every two weeks.

[1] In the *Jahresberichte der höheren Lehranstalten in Preussen, 1927–28*, pp. 142 ff., there are listed activity groups in 1135 schools with a membership of 17,290 pupils. There will also be found in this volume the nature of the groups and their studies.

SECONDARY EDUCATION

2. REALGYMNASIUM

SUBJECTS	VI	V	IV	U III	O III	U II	O II	U I	O I	TOTAL
Religion	2	2	2	2	2	2	2	2	2	18
German	4	4	3	3	3	3	3	3	3	29
Latin	6	6	6	4	4	3	3	3	3	38
1st modern language	..	..	3	4	4	4	4(3)	4(3)	4(3)	27(24)*
2nd modern language	..	..	..	4	4	3	3(4)	3(4)	3(4)	20(23)*
History (civics)	..	..	2	2	2	3	3	3	3	18
Geography	2	2	2	1	1	1	1	1	1	12
Mathematics	4	4	4	4	4	4	4	4	4	36
Natural sciences	2	2	2	2	2	3	3	3	4	23
Drawing	2	2	2	2	1†	1†	1†	1†	1†	13
Music	2	2	..	..	..	..	..	..	..	4
Total	24	24	26	28	27	27	27	27	28	238

* The figures in brackets apply when English is the first modern language.
† Two hours every two weeks.

3. REFORMREALGYMNASIUM

SUBJECTS	VI	V	IV	U III	O III	U II	O II	U I	O I	TOTAL
Religion	2	2	2	2	2	2	2	2	2	18
German	5	5	5	3	3	3	3	3	3	33
Latin	..	..	..	..	..	4	4	4	4	16
1st modern language	6	6	6	5	5	3	4(3)	4(3)	4(3)	43(40)
2nd modern language	..	..	..	5	5	3	3(4)	3(4)	3(4)	22(25)*
History (civics)	..	..	2	2	3	3	3	3	3	19
Geography	2	2	2	2	1	1	1	1	1	13
Mathematics	4	4	4	4	4	4	4	4	4	36
Natural sciences	2	2	2	2	2	3	3	3	3	22
Drawing	2	2	2	1†	1†	1†	1†	1†	1†	12
Music	2	2	..	..	..	..	..	..	..	4
Total	25	25	25	26	26	27	28	28	28	238

* The figures in brackets apply when English is the first modern language.
† Two hours every two weeks.

4. Oberrealschule

Subjects	VI	V	IV	U III	O III	U II	O II	U I	O I	Total
Religion	2	2	2	2	2	2	2	2	2	18
German	5	5	5	3	3	3	4	4	3	35
1st modern language	6	6	6	5	5	3	3	3	3	40
2nd modern language	..	..	..	5	5	3	3	3	3	22
History (civics)	..	..	2	2	3)	3	3	3	3	19
Geography	2	2	2	2	1)	1	1	1	1	13
Mathematics	4	4	4	4	4	5	5	5	5	40
Natural sciences	2	2	2	2	2	6	5	6	6	33
Drawing	2	2	2	1	1	2	2	1*	1*	14
Music	2	2	..	..	..	..	..	..	..	4
Total	25	25	25	26	26	28	28	28	27	238

*Two hours every two weeks.

5. Deutsche Oberschule

Subjects	VI	V	IV	U III	O III	U II	O II	U I	O I	Total
Religion	2	2	2	2	2	2	2	2	2	18
German	5	5	5	4	4	4	4	4	4	39
1st modern language	6	6	6	5	5	4	4(3)	4(3)	4(3)	44(41)*
2nd modern language	..	..	..	..	..	4	3(4)	3(4)	3(4)	13(16)*
History (civics)	..	..	2	3	3	3	4	4	4	23
Geography	2	2	2	2	2	2	2	2	2	18
Mathematics	4	4	4	4	4	4	4	4	4	36
Natural Sciences	2	2	2	4	4	3	3	4	4	28
Drawing	2	2	2	2	2	2	1†	1†	1†	15
Music	2	2	..	..	..	..	..	..	..	4
Total	25	25	25	26	26	28	27	28	28	238

* The figures in brackets apply when Latin or French is the second modern language.
† Two hours every two weeks.

6. AUFBAUSCHULE

TYPE	DEUTSCHE OBERSCHULE						
SUBJECTS	U III	O III	U II	O II	U I	O I	TOTAL
Religion	2	2	2	2	2	2	12
German	5	5	5	4	4	4	27
1st modern language	7	6	4	4(3)	4(3)	4(3)	29(26)*
2nd modern language	..	..	4	3(4)	3(4)	3(4)	13(16)*
History (civics)	3	3	3	4	4	4	21
Geography	2	2	2	2	2	2	12
Mathematics	5	4	4	4	4	4	25
Natural sciences	4	4	4	4	4	4	24
Drawing	2	2	1‡	2	2	2	11
Total	30	28	29	29	29	29	174

TYPE	OBERREALSCHULE						
SUBJECTS	U III	O III	U II	O II	U I	O I	TOTAL
Religion	2	2	2	2	2	2	12
German	4	4	4	4	4	4	24
1st modern language	6	6	4	4	4(3)	4(3)	28(26)†
2nd modern language	..	..	4	4	3(4)	3(4)	14(16)†
History (civics)	3	3	3	3	3	3	18
Geography	2	2	1	1	1	1	8
Mathematics	6	5	5	5	5	5	31
Natural sciences	4	4	4	6	6	6	30
Drawing	2	2	2	1‡	1‡	1‡	9
Total	29	28	29	30	29	29	174

* The figures in brackets apply when Latin or French is the second foreign language.
† The figures in brackets apply when French is the second modern language.
‡ Two hours every two weeks.

7. TOTAL TIME DISTRIBUTION BY SUBJECTS IN EACH TYPE OF SCHOOL

SUBJECTS	GYM.	RGYM.	REFORM RGYM.	OR.	D.O.	AUFBAUSCHULE	
						OR.	D.O.
Religion	18	18	18	18	18	12	12
German	29	29	33	35	39	24	27
Latin	48	38	16	..	..	..	..
Greek	34	..	..	..	..	..	..
1st modern language	15	27(24)	43(40)	40	44(41)	28(26)	29(26)
2nd modern language	..	20(23)	22(25)	22	13(16)	14(16)	13(16)
History (civics)	17	18	19	19	23	18	21
Geography	12	12	13	13	18	8	12
Mathematics	31	36	36	40	36	31	25
Natural sciences	18	23	22	33	28	30	24
Drawing	12	13	12	14	15	9	11
Music	4	4	4	4	4	..	..
Total	238	238	238	238	238	174	174

a week are assigned for music in all classes above the second, 19 periods a week for physical exercises, and 3 periods a week in the three last years for free activity groups, thus bringing the total for the time-schedules in nine-year schools, up to 263 periods. In the *Aufbauschule* a total of 6 periods are assigned for music, 13 periods for physical exercises, and 3 periods for free activity groups, bringing the total up to 196 periods.

Textbooks. The choice of textbooks is governed by regulations of the Ministry which maintains a state bureau for their examination and approval (*Staatliche Prüfstelle für die Lehrbücher der höheren Schulen*). Publishers are required to submit eight copies of each book intended for use in secondary schools; these are examined and reported upon by standing committees of specialists appointed for three years. Lists of approved books are published each month in the *Zentralblatt* and in the periodical reports of the *Staatliche Auskunftsstelle für Schulwesen*, a central clearing-house for information on all aspects of secondary education. The books to be used in each school are selected from the approved lists by the conference of special-subject teachers in each school and submitted for further approval to the provincial school board. The regulations do not apply to the selection of anthologies, literary texts, and other source materials. Frequent changes of textbooks are discouraged. In order to assist poor students there have been established since 1923 lending libraries (*Hilfsbüchereien*) which are provided and maintained by the authorities responsible for each school with the assistance of publishers.

Teachers of natural sciences may receive advice on equipment from the State Bureau for Instruction in the Natural Sciences (*Staatliche Hauptstelle für den naturwissenschaftlichen Unterricht*) in Berlin. The *Zentralinstitut für Erziehung und Unterricht* furnishes advice on the choice of educational films and gramophone records.

Leaving examination. The new spirit underlying secondary education is nowhere better illustrated than in the leaving or maturity examination (*Abiturientenexamen* or *Reifeprüfung*). From the national point of view this examination is of the greatest importance; since it has been the subject of arrangements for reciprocal recognition between the various States,[1] the examination virtually defines the standards of the nine-year secondary schools throughout Germany. Thus schools leading to the examination must provide courses of nine years; every course must include as obligatory subjects: religious instruction, German, history, geography, mathematics, and natural sciences; in the *Gymnasium* there must be taught Latin, Greek, French, or English; and in the *Realgymnasium* and *Oberrealschule*, French, English, and drawing, with Latin additional in the *Realgymnasium*. The educational authorities, so far as possible, agree on common standards in the courses of study and must see that in each type of school adequate attention is given to the major subjects, although flexibility may be encouraged. Teachers must have the appropriate qualifications to teach their subjects. Certain common principles for the conduct of the examinations were set up. Separate arrangements, to which Bavaria did not subscribe, were made subsequently for the recognition of the *Reifeprüfung* of the *Aufbauschule* (1922) and the *Deutsche Oberschule* (1925). The reciprocal recognition of certificates means that their

---

[1] *Vereinbarung der Länder über die gegenseitige Anerkennung der Reifezeugnisse der höheren Schulen,* December 19, 1922.

holders are entitled to the privileges which attach to them in all the States which have subscribed to the agreement.

The examining commissions in each school consist of a representative of the Ministry of Education as chairman, the school principal, and the teachers of the last year (*Prima*) appointed by the provincial school board; in the case of city schools a member of the Secondary School Committee (*Schulausschuss*) may also be present and sign the leaving certificate, if awarded. Each member is expected to visit the classes, and to acquaint himself with the work of the pupils to be examined. Candidates for the examination must submit a full account of their education, and a statement of the special subjects on which they wish to be examined in the oral test. The admission of candidates to the examination is determined by a conference of teachers of the graduating class; their reports must deal with the character, general ability, ability to do independent work, and anything that may be necessary to give an all-round picture of the candidates — their powers of observation, clearness of intellect, judgment, inventiveness, imagination, expression as well as special abilities and activities both in and out of school, participation in activity groups, gymnastics, athletics, and school life in general. The reports are also expected to refer to the home conditions, economic status, and health of the candidates. Consideration is also given to theses which candidates may prepare in their last year on subjects selected by themselves, and usually based on the work of the free-activity groups; the theses are examined by specialists both in and outside the school, and may be accepted in place of written examinations on the subject discussed, or some allied subject. Finally permission to take the examination is thus based on the all-round quality of a candidate.

The examination consists of two parts, written and oral, and a test in physical education. In the written test all candidates must take German and mathematics; the other subjects vary with the type of course. Thus, in the *Gymnasium* the test is in Latin and Greek; in the *Realgymnasium* and *Reformrealgymnasium* in French and English, or Latin in place of one of these; in the *Oberrealschule* in modern languages and science (physics or chemistry or biology according to choice); in the *Deutsche Oberschule* in one foreign language and history or geography. The purpose of the written examination is not to discover mastery of detailed information, but intellectual maturity and ability to pursue university studies; it is not a test on what has actually been done, but something analogous in order to test independence of treatment. Candidates may use the same aids that they would in their regular work. The grades are determined by the whole examining group, which then decides on the oral subjects in which a candidate is to be examined.

The oral examination covers all the work of *Prima*, and the subject in which a candidate feels himself especially strong. The commission as a rule selects the subjects on the basis of the written examination, on the general principle that it is better to examine in subjects in which candidates have already done well and may be expected to show ability. Broad problems are set in order to give candidates scope to indicate their comprehension, judgment, general grasp, and ability to express themselves; adequate time is allowed for preparation. If a pupil shows inability to handle the problem, the specialist on the topic of the examination may decide whether another is to be given or whether to develop one with the pupil. Every effort is to be made to avoid arbitrariness and caprice, and in estimating the final result of the two parts of the examination all aspects of a particular case must be taken into account rather than a mere arithmetical computation of marks. Candidates whose work is unsatisfactory in German or in the special subjects of the school type concerned may only be passed with the approval of three fourths of the examiners. Candidates who fail may only repeat the examination after the lapse of a year.

The results of the examinations for the *Reifezeugnis* in 1927–28 are shown in the accompanying table; it must be remembered as an explanation of the high percentage of successes that as a rule pupils and the parents of pupils who are likely to fail in the examination are warned in advance and that those who survive to the end of the course are progressively selected:

School	Number of Candidates	Withdrawn	Examined	Passed	Failed	Per cent Passed
Gymnasium	6,093	100	5,993	5,609	384	93.4
Reformgymnasium	251	5	246	234	12	95.1
Realgymnasium	2,954	46	2,908	2,710	198	93.1
Reformrealgymnasium	2,622	28	2,594	2,426	168	93.5
Oberrealschule	4,151	53	4,098	3,819	279	93.1
Oberrealschule in Aufbauschule	41	1	40	35	5	87.5
Deutsche Oberschule in Aufbauschule	406	2	404	389	15	96.2
Total	16,518	235	16,283	15,222	1,061	93.6

By ages the successful candidates were distributed as follows: 849 were 17 years of age; 4274 were 18; 5110 were 19; 2906 were 20; and 1603 were 21 or over.

Of the total number of successful candidates, 11,925, or 78.3 per cent, were planning to continue their studies in the universities or other institutions for higher education.

SCHOOL LIFE

Self-government. The reform spirit is manifested in still another direction in the rise of student activities. Since 1918 efforts have been made with the approval of the Ministry to encourage the development of pupil self-government (*Schülerselbstverwaltung*). Following a decree issued in 1920, each class is expected to elect a spokesman (in the first two classes he is appointed by the teacher). The spokesmen representing the last four years (or in six-year schools the last three) constitute a "pupils' committee" (*Schülerausschuss*) which elects a teacher as adviser to serve as the connecting link between the committee and the staff. Each class meets as a group (*Klassengemeinde*) to discuss problems affecting the interests of the class. Periodically all the classes meet together as a community group (*Schulgemeinde*) either under the chairmanship of the president of the school committee or of a teacher. The purposes of these various organizations are not clearly described; their establishment is encouraged to give the pupils experience in group action of the kind which they will find on leaving school. Activities and discussions of a political nature are prohibited. The intention of the authorities was good, but there is apparently no widespread enthusiasm for self-government, an ideal which cannot be attained by decrees. The whole tradition of German education in the past has been in the opposite direction, that of acceptance of authority, and it will take some time for the new tendency to establish itself.

School societies. More successful than the attempts to promote self-government has been the development of societies and clubs (*Schülervereine*) devoted to a great variety of activities — religious and missionary; literary and scientific; choirs, orchestras, and bands; radio; photography; and dramatics — the more academic types predominating. Societies of a political nature are prohibited, particularly if they tend to be critical of the republican form of government. The formation of a school society and its statutes require the approval of the teachers' conference, which may suspend or abolish a society which contravenes the statutes as approved. School magazines have been established sporadically (in 1928 only twenty-one were reported) and do not appear to meet with much more success than many of the other forms of non-scholastic self-activity.

Games and athletics. Largely as a result of the distressing physical conditions that followed the War and the abolition of compulsory military service, which has always been regarded a school of physical training, and partly as a consequence of the cult of open-air life which was a feature of the *Jugendbewegung*, increased attention is now devoted to gymnastics and athletics throughout Germany. There are still many educators who prefer the traditional type of formal physical training, as modified by recent theory and practice. On the other hand, games, sports, and athletics are more popular with the public and the youth of the country. The most popular forms of athletic activities in the schools are swimming, rowing, *Schlagball* (a form of baseball), football, and track. So great have been the efforts of federal, state, and municipal governments to promote sports and athletics that there are many who fear that an excessive amount of time and interest are devoted to them. While considerable progress has been made in introducing sports and athletics in many schools, it is difficult, particularly among the older pupils, to break down the old academic traditions which have prevailed in schools and universities. The German secondary school pupil of sixteen or over, like his French coeval, tends to be more serious in purpose and intellectual interest than the English or American pupil of the same age. To what extent this is due to the general status of the student in continental Europe generally, and to what extent economic pressure and the urge to obtain the privileges associated with education, cannot be determined. Non-scholastic activities in general are looked upon by older pupils, teachers, and a large part of the public as childish things. One check on their development has been the timidity of parents, which has been somewhat allayed by the introduction of schemes for accident insurance (*Unfallversicherung*) at a low cost. Despite these facts the generalization is true that educators recognize the value of self-government, of school societies, and of games and athletics for character-building, and that an appreciable change of attitude toward these activities has taken place since the close of the War.

Excursions. The activities which have been discussed up to this point are after all importations and do not constitute a part of the German educational tradition. More genuinely characteristic is the educational and recreational use of school excursions (*Wanderungen*), which have been more extensively developed since the War. Although their purpose in the past was primarily recreational, excursions are being increasingly employed for educational and instructional ends. As an extension of classroom instruction and of textbooks, excursions constitute a valuable supplement, since they furnish innumerable opportunities for concrete experiences which give life to school instruction. They may be organized for a day, or a week, or for a longer period; if they are not arranged purely for physical recreation, they must be carefully planned and discussed in advance. Excursions have been facilitated by the organization of a network of youth hostels (*Jugendherberge*) established throughout the country by public and private effort. In addition, many schools have established their own "camps" (*Schulheime, Schülerheime, Schullandheime*), often built by the pupils themselves. Excursions thus provide infinite opportunities, not only for recreational activities, but for supplementary study in most subjects of the curriculum, — history, geography, nature study, art, industries, dialects and folklore. To a considerable degree they have been found valuable in the contributions which they may make to a deeper appreciation of Germany and of *Deutschtum*. Excursions are not, however, restricted to Germany; groups are taken from time to time to Finland, the Scandinavian countries, Italy, France, and England; occasionally whole classes are incorporated for several weeks into a class of the same status in a foreign school, live in the homes of their foreign classmates, and gain something which is far more valuable and lasting for them than mere instruction and exercise in the foreign language — an appreciation of the common humanity of which all are members, a real basis for international understanding and coöperation.

GENERAL SUMMARY

It would be a mistake to conclude that the spirit of reform which permeates educational theory and the official regulations has affected all schools. The political, social, and economic crisis through which Germany has been passing since the War has been too deep-rooted for an educational reform, which seeks to give a new orientation to German secondary education, to establish itself completely. The pressure of economic competition has brought into the secondary schools large numbers of pupils for whom a secondary education of another type than those now provided would be more suitable. The same charge is made as in England, when secondary education began to be opened to a new stratum of society, that pupils coming from uncultured home could not profit from secondary education; such a charge may be proved by time to be groundless, as it has been in England. It is as yet too early to base any generalization on the results of the *Aufbauschule*, whose graduates are about this time ready to complete their university studies. If the experiment with the six-year secondary school should in time justify itself by success, then the advocates of a common primary education up to the age of twelve approximately, to be followed by a variety of secondary courses, will have a powerful argument tor the *Einheitsschule*. So far as the teachers are concerned, they have under the present conditions a legitimate grievance in the fact that the increased enrollment has meant in many cases overcrowded classes.

The success of any educational reform depends on the teachers. Up to the present two facts must be remembered: first, that a relatively small number of new teachers has been added to the schools; and second, that the system of preparing teachers has remained unchanged. As it is organized in Prussia, it still has apprenticeship character, since candidates for the secondary school teaching profession receive the major part of their preparation in the type of schools to which they will be called. This means that there is always inherent the danger that the practices of the older teachers will be transmitted to the younger. Reforms of the scope contemplated in the regulations demand freedom and a critical attitude which can best be acquired through a professional training which is not restricted wholly to prevailing practices.

Another obstacle in the way of reform lies in the fact that the destinies of secondary education are controlled by the demands of the universities and this despite the fact that the secondary schools virtually conduct their own examinations. The universities resist all attempts to vary the types of secondary school too far from the traditional norm, as evidenced by the history of the *Deutsche Oberschule*. Flexibility and elasticity are no doubt the fundamental principles upon which the curricular and organizational reform has been effected, but their range is still restricted within the academic subjects in which foreign languages constitute the central pivot. If secondary education is to be made accessible to larger numbers, then more variety and differentiation than have yet been contemplated must be provided. But as the history of German secondary education during the nineteenth century illustrates, every attempt to recognize a new type of secondary school is regarded as an attack on the sacred citadel of privileges (*Berechtigungen*). From this *impasse* there can be no way out until secondary education is provided for all according to their needs, a vision contemplated by the advocates of the genuine *Einheitsschule* as the central principle of a complete reorganization. For the present German educators do not yet seem to see the logic of present trends, with two consequences. The first is the social danger, which is already present, of an increasing educated proletariat, well prepared but unable to find the employment traditionally regarded as appropriate to their training, and unwilling because of their social status to turn to other occupations. The second is an inevitable tendency to lowering of standards. Thus the faculty of philosophy of the University of Berlin issued a memorandum (*Denkschrift*) in 1928, in which it professed to see a decline in the quality of secondary school graduates. The decline was attributed to the relaxation of the methods and discipline of pre-War days, an implication that the cult of free activity methods has been accompanied by a relaxation in exact standards of scholarship and mastery of content. Although the period between the introduction of the reforms and the date of the report was too short to warrant this conclusion, it was recommended that a preparatory college year be established to bring students up to the standards required for university study (*Wissenschaftliche Arbeit*), a suggestion made at about the same time in Saxony. Recommendations of this type, made also in France (see p. 695), appear to be superficial and to point rather to the need of more penetrating consideration of the trends and meaning of secondary education in a democracy in this industrial age.

SECONDARY EDUCATION OF GIRLS

Secondary education of girls, from the point of view of its provision, organization, and standards, has come within the interest of the States in Germany only during the last quarter of a century. Before 1908, in Prussia, the *höhere Mädchenschulen*, which were provided either by private organizations or by local authorities, were not classified as secondary schools. Not only secondary but higher education was practically closed to girls and women; it was not until 1895 that women were admitted to the universities as auditors and then only with the consent of the instructors concerned. With the reorganization of secondary education in 1908, the possibility was now opened for girls to prepare for the *Abiturientenprüfung* without the unnecessary obstacles which had existed previously; as a consequence their admission to the universities as regularly matriculated students was sanctioned, but still with certain reservations. The active participation of women in public affairs and in social welfare work brought the movement for the emancipation of women within the range of practical politics. Article 22 of the Federal Constitution of 1919 gave women the right to vote, and Article 128 provided that "all citizens without distinction must so far as the laws are concerned and in accordance with their abilities and attainments be admitted to public offices." Secondary education for girls was reorganized in 1923 on the basis of this constitutional guarantee, but without any intention of increasing considerably the numbers proceeding to the universities. Coeducation, which was extensively discussed by the Federal Educational Conference (*Reichsschulkonferenz*), has not been accepted, although gifted girls may be admitted to boys' schools in localities where separate educational provisions do not exist (see p. 721).

Present system. The general framework of the reorganization in Prussia was the reform of 1908. The principles upon which the reorganization rests are that the first task of secondary schools for girls is to improve the training of the German girl as women, housewives, and educators, and that the second is to provide for girls a training which will enable them according to their abilities to take their place in the wide range of practical occupations and to collaborate actively in the political and social life of their communities. Another task of the reorganization was to incorporate the secondary education of girls within the whole system of education, based on the *Grundschule* at the bottom and leading to the universities and other forms of post-secondary education most suited to the needs of women.

All girls must attend the four-year *Grundschule* before entering a secondary school. The conditions of admission and the relaxation of the regulation require four years of attendance at the *Grundschule*

OI	Frauen-schule one or two years	Oberlyzeum	Oberlyzeum of Oberreal-schule type	Deutsche Oberschule	Realgymnasiale Studienanstalt	Gymnasiale Studienanstalt
UI						
OII						Aufbauschule
UII			Lyzeum Second Modern Foreign Language	Second Modern Foreign Language	Second Modern Foreign Language	Greek
OIII					Latin	Latin
UIII						
IV				First Modern Foreign Language		
V						Elementary School (7 years)
VI						
	Grundschule (4 years; occasionally 3 years)					

TIME-SCHEDULE: GIRLS' SECONDARY SCHOOL

Type	Lyzeum							Oberlyzeum					Oberrealschule					Realgymnasium						Gymnasium					
Subjects	VI	V	IV	UIII	OIII	UII	Total	OII	UI	OI	Total		UIII	OIII	OII	UI	OI	Total	UIII	OIII	OII	UII	UI	OI	Total	UIII	OIII	OII	UI	OI	Total
Religion........	2	2	2	2	2	2	12	2	2	2	18		2	2	2	2	2	18	2	2	2	2	2	2	18	2	2	2	2	2	18
German........	5	5	4	4	4	4	26	4	4	4	38		3	3	3	4	3	32	3	3	3	3	3	3	33
Latin..........	..	..	..	..	..	..	..	..	..	..	..		6	5	5	4	4	27	..	..	4	4	4	4	..	7	6	6{7	6{7	6{7	37
Greek.........	..	..	..	..	..	..	..	..	..	..	..		..	..	..	..	..	..	..	..	..	..	..	..	..	..	..	6{7	6{7	6{7	28
1st modern language.....	5	5	4	3	3	4	26	4	4	4	38		4	4	3	3	3	35	3	3	3	3	3	3	35	2	2	2	2	2	27
2nd modern language.....	..	..	..	4	4	4	12	3	3	3	23		4	..	3	3	3	21	..	..	..	..	..	..	16	..	..	..	..	..	..
History (civics)..	..	..	2	2	2	3	9	3	3{1	3{1	18		2	2	3	4	4	18	2	2	2	2	3	3	18	2	2	2	2	3	15
Geography.....	2	2	2	2	2	1	11	2	1	1	15		1	1	1	1	1	14	1	1	1	1	1	1	12	1	1	1	1	1	12
Mathematics...	4	4	4	4	4	4	24	4	4	4	36		5	4	5	5	4	39	4	4	4	4	4	4	36	4{	4{	3	3	3	32
Natural sciences	2	2	2	3	3	2	14	3	3	3	23		4	2	4	5	5	28	2	2	2	2	3	3	21	2{	2{	2	2	2	18
Drawing........	2	2	2	2	2	2	12	2	1*{	1*	16		1*	1*	1*	1*	1*	15	1*	1*	1*	1*	1*	1*	12	2	1*	..	..	..	9
Music..........	2	2	1	..	..	..	5	..	..	..	5		..	..	..	..	..	5	..	..	..	..	..	..	5	..	..	..	..	..	5
Needlework....	2	2	1*	1*	1*	..	7	..	..	..	7		..	..	..	..	..	7	..	..	..	..	..	..	..	..	..	..	..	..	5
Total........	26	26	25	27	27	27	158	27	26	26	237		25	24	25	27	27	237	25	24	27	28	28	28	237	25	24	28	28	29	239

N.B. The six years of the *Lyzeum* serve as the common foundation for the *Oberlyzeum* and the *Oberrealschule* type of the *Studienanstalt:* the first three years of the *Lyzeum* serve as the common foundation for the *Realgymnasium* and *Gymnasium* types. In addition to the schedules above there are added 2 periods for music and 13 for physical exercises in the *Lyzeum*, bringing the total up to 173; in the upper divisions there are added 4 periods (3 periods in the *Gymnasium*) for music, 19 for physical exercises, and 3 periods for free activity groups, bringing the totals up to 263 (264 in the *Gymnasium*) periods.

*Two hours every two weeks.

are the same as those for boys. The system of secondary education for girls differs radically in organization from that for boys, since there is only one school with a common foundation and differentiated courses in the last years, some of which lead up to the *Reifeprüfung* and entrance to the universities, while others provide for the special needs and interests of women — preparation for the home, care of children, teaching, and women's occupations. There is thus eliminated the serious difficulty, which confronts the parents of boys, of selecting from a number of different school types, and the choice of a specialized course is postponed by several years. In other words, the organization of secondary education for girls follows the reform types which are being increasingly provided for boys, and the principle of flexibility (*Bewegungsfreiheit*) is a reality from the start. Besides the reorganized type of secondary school there still survive a large number of public and private *höhere Mädchenschulen*, which, while giving courses similar to that of the lower part of the reorganized school, cannot obtain recognition. Here and there schools organized as are those for boys are found more in States outside of Prussia.

The fundamental course which constitutes the foundation of the girls' secondary school is given in the *Lyzeum*; the subjects of the six-year course of the *Lyzeum*, organized with but slight modifications on the same basis as the first six years of the *Oberrealschule* for boys, are religion, German, two modern foreign languages, history, geography, mathematics, natural science, drawing, and music, with additional hours for sewing and physical training. This course may be continued for three additional years in the *Oberlyzeum*, of which two forms are found — the first, a continuation of the *Lyzeum* which does not prepare for the *Reifeprüfung*; the second, organized in the last three years like the *Oberrealschule*, with more attention to mathematics and sciences, and concluding with the *Reifeprüfung*. At the end of the first three years of the *Lyzeum* that is, in UIII — pupils may enter the *Studienanstalt*, which, besides the *Oberlyzeum* of the *Oberrealschule* type, provides six-year courses corresponding to the *Deutsche Oberschule*, the *Realgymnasium*, and the *Gymnasium*. In addition, there also exists *Aufbauschulen* for girls who may enter from an elementary school at the age of thirteen and continue on a six-year course leading to the *Reifeprüfung*. The organization of a girls' secondary school is illustrated in the diagram on p. 752.

The time-schedules and the time-distribution of the various types, except the *Aufbauschule*, are given on page 753.

SECONDARY EDUCATION

The regulations, the courses of study, and methods of instruction need no further discussion, since, according to the Suggestions (*Richtlinien*), "the instructional objective and courses of study of the corresponding schools for boys apply to the various types of courses for girls." Special attention, however, is to be given in the selection of the content, especially in the core subjects (religion, German, history, and geography), to the place of women in the progress of civilization, to their legal position in the family, in society, and in the State. In general the special characteristics and life purposes of girls receive special consideration so that they may realize the contribution which they can make to the progress of civilization through work in the family, in some vocation, or in some other activity in the interests of general welfare. The reform spirit, which was discussed in connection with secondary education for boys, dominates the work of the girls' secondary schools.

Frauenschule. For those girls who wish to continue their education beyond the *Lyzeum* course, but without taking one of the advanced academic courses, there have been developed special one- and two-year courses in what is known as the *Frauenschule*. The purpose of these courses is to give the student an insight into the problems and techniques of household management, an appreciation of the problems of child care, education, and welfare, and a continuance of their general education for the development of their moral personality and an understanding of the place of the individual in his community. The courses of the *Frauenschule* are intended for the training of women in the home and in occupations — education, social welfare, and women's industries. The courses are not clearly defined, but the following subjects have been suggested for the guidance of the *Frauenschulen*:

One-Year Course	Hours Per year	Per week
a. Household arts; nutrition; household accounts and bookkeeping; cooking; housework; gardening (if possible); and needlework....................	400	10
b. Hygiene with practical work in the care of infants and young children; simple exercises in home nursing.	240	6
Theory of education, especially of young children, with practical work............................	240	6
c. Religion...	40	1
German...	80	2
History, civics and economics...................	120	3
Maximum..	1120	28

In the two-year courses the curriculum may follow one of two forms. In the first form the course of the second year may continue and extend the work of the first year. In the second form the work of the first year is the same as in the one year course, while that of the second is organized as follows:

	Second Year Course	Hours	
		Per year	Per week
a.	Household economy in relation to economics	40	1
	Cooking (special types as for invalids or infants), housework and gardening	300	7½
	Care of clothing and the home	80	2
b.	Hygiene, social hygiene	80	2
	History and organization of social welfare	80	2
	Introduction to practical work in care of infants and children, care of school children, visit to social welfare agencies	360	9
c.	Continuation and extension of general subjects, plus gymnastics and physical activities; an additional subject	as needed	6½
	Maximum	1200	30

A few schools, by the addition of a third year, have since 1927 organized the *Frauenoberschule*. The subjects of the course are the same as those listed above, but the students who complete the three-year course have the advantage of being admitted to institutions for the preparation of teachers of trades, technical and art subjects, and household management.

Statistics. The growth of secondary education for girls is illustrated statistically in the following table:

Type of School	1912		1917		1922		1927	
	Schools	Pupils	Schools	Pupils	Schools	Pupils	Schools	Pupils
Lyzeum	242	89,302	272	107,473	301	108,784	305	101,834
Oberlyzeum	77	5,742	80	5,751	80	2,854	74	6,937
Studienanstalt: Oberrealschule type	3	248	5	411	21	1,007	14	6,287
Realgymnasium	27	3,011	32	4,182	47	4,511	52	8,005
Gymnasium	2	246	2	379	3	498	6	789
Deutsche Oberschule	...	...	...	...	9	661	13	3,302
Deutsche Oberschule in Aufbauschule	...	...	...	...	...	...	12	1,427
Frauenschule	33	768	46	1,163	48	1,194	74	2,749
Total	384	99,517	437	119,359	509	119,509	550	131,330

The percentage of girls passing the *Reifeprüfung* in 1927–28 was 97 per cent; the number of candidates was 3088; of these 22 withdrew before the examination; of the 3066 taking the examination 2975 passed. The majority of the girls, 2077, came from the *Oberlyzeum* (*Oberrealschule* type); 900 came from the *Studienanstalt* (*Gymnasium* and *Realgymnasium* type); and 111 came from the *Deutsche Oberschule*.

4. ITALY
HISTORICAL BACKGROUND

The present system of secondary education in Italy, which was established by the Gentile reform of 1923, is the direct result of sixty years of conflict and unrest on the subject. The foundations of the modern organization of secondary education were laid by the Casati Law of 1859, which sought to depart from the traditional classical monopoly by the addition of more modern and practical forms of secondary education. Side by side with a reorganized classical school, there were created technical institutes and normal schools, designed to deflect students away from the universities and into practical careers. Only one avenue to higher studies was opened to pupils from schools other than the classical *ginnasio-liceo* by the introduction in the technical institutes of a section for physics and mathematics leading its graduates up to the faculties of mathematical, physical, and natural sciences.

The number of classical secondary schools was indirectly limited by the provision that the communities provide the *ginnasi*, giving the first five years of the course, and the State a restricted number of *licei*, giving the last three years of the course. The absence of such restriction and the shorter duration of the technical course, three years in the *scuola tecnica* and three years in the *istituto tecnico*, led to a rapid increase in the number of schools and of pupils. As a consequence the aims and curricula of the technical schools became a mixture of general culture and of practical studies without genuine success on either side. The existence of the physico-mathematical section in the *istituto tecnico* opened access to the universities to students whose general cultural foundation was inadequate. The Casati system was attacked from another side because it had failed to make provision in any school for modern studies. In 1898–99 six *licei moderni* were established by way of experiment, in which German and French were added to the existing curriculum of the classical schools by a slight revision of the time-table. Although the experiment failed, at this time modern sections were set up in the classical schools after 1904.

The Casati Law was further subjected to criticism because of its failure to provide a common foundation for all secondary schools. For this common foundation some advocated Latin as an essential element; others rejected it. Equally uncertain was the question as to the subjects which should constitute the common elements of a cultural education in the secondary schools. The uncertainty and unrest through which secondary education passed in the forty years following the enactment of the Casati Law can only be indicated by reference to the many bills and laws introduced as Minister succeeded Minister. The most significant dates are as follows: Matteucci (1863), Amari (1864), Natoli (1864), Bertini (1865), Berti (1866), Coppino (1867, 1877, 1879, 1881, 1887), De Sanctis (1878), Baccelli (1881), Martini (1886), Boselli (1890), Villari (1891), De Cristoforis (1897), Baccelli (1890), Gallo (1901), Nasi (1903), Bianchi (1905). The situation was still further aggravated by conflicts between competing authorities; some technical courses were under the direction of the Ministry of Education, others under such ministries as those of agriculture, industry, and commerce.

An attempt to settle the unrest in Italian secondary education, which only paralleled the contemporary unrest in England, France, Germany, and the United States, was made in 1905 by the appointment of a Royal Commission, over which Paolo Boselli presided (*Commissione Reale per l'Ordinamento degli Studi Secundari in Italia*). The report (*Relazione*) of the Commission, published in 1909, recommended a functional organization of secondary education to provide a utilitarian preparation for those proceeding to practical careers and a general education for the *élite* intending to proceed to the universities and the liberal professions. Both types of schools were to be based on a common foundation of three years for pupils admitted from the lower elementary schools at the age of ten; this common school was to offer a modern curriculum without Latin. On the common foundation were to be built a higher elementary or continuation school, a technical school, and three *licei* — classical, modern, and scientific. The technical schools were to be assigned to appropriate ministries (agriculture, commerce, or industry) in order to prevent any incursion into the cultural fields proper to the *licei*. Little resulted from the recommendations of the Commission except the organization of modern *licei* offering two modern foreign languages in place of Latin and Greek.

Uncertainty as to aims and curricula did not constitute the sole difficulties which attended secondary education. The secondary school teaching profession was badly organized and poorly remunerated. Each teacher, limited narrowly to his own special subject, had to eke out his salary by going from school to school in order to fill out a weekly program; such a system resulted in many cases in the acceptance of obligations in different schools which made adequate instruction and familiarity with pupils impossible, militated against good discipline, and left no time for study. Disciplinary difficulties were increased by the great increase in enrollments, due in large measure to the deliberate discrimination against private schools and the inadequate provision of schools, as well as by the assumption by the secondary school pupils of some of the prerogatives of university students. Agitation, violence, and strikes were common occurrences almost up to the eve of the Gentile reform. Finally, the system of examinations played havoc with any attempt to maintain standards. Pupils were examined by their own teachers without any external check, and even then only those pupils who had failed to obtain an average mark of 6 on a scale of 10 were examined. Pupils in private schools had to resort to public schools for their examinations and were examined on the whole of the school program, a discrimination which placed the public schools at a considerable advantage. Taking advantage of this situation, all kinds of pressure were brought to bear on the examiners both by the pupils, their organizations, and others interested in them.

The problems which confronted the reformer were not merely educational: they were at once social, economic, and political. Overcrowding in the secondary schools led to overcrowding in the universities and in the liberal professions and to an overproduction of "men of letters, doctors, and rhetoricians." An excess-educated proletariat meant in Italy, as it had done earlier in Germany, so many centers of discontent which found its outlet through agitation in the press and in politics. Overcrowding in the professions meant neglect of economic channels which would be of greater advantage to the individual and to the country as a whole. It was remarked during and after the War that the lower, so-called illiterate masses, the peasants and artisans, had displayed a higher spirit of loyalty and patriotism than the educated classes. Whether this was true or not, it was recognized that the task for the reformer was to establish a secondary school system which would provide opportunities for the able in all classes of society, which would be organized to suit a variety of individual and public needs, which would open the way to higher education only for those capable of profiting thereby, and which would instill in the future leaders of the country a new spirit of idealism and interest in the welfare of the country as a whole.

THE PRESENT SYSTEM

Basis of reform. A fundamental reform of secondary education was long overdue. The attack on the system was begun by the idealist group which rallied around Croce and Gentile. The system had been built up on a concept of equality of opportunities which the group regarded as baseless and which filled the schools with pupils who had neither the ability nor the earnestness to profit by secondary education. The schools had become diploma mills which sent to the universities more candidates for entrance into the professions than the country could absorb, with the consequence that unemployed lawyers, journalists, teachers, and others became the sources of disturbance and agitation. The discrimination against private schools through the system of examinations deprived the public schools of the healthy stimulation which comes from competition. The State could not surrender its duty of providing schools, but such schools must serve as models for the country as a whole, and, instead of being entrenched behind a monopoly such as they enjoyed by controlling the examinations, the standards of secondary education must be raised by the introduction of external examinations to set up standards for all schools, whether public or private. Finally, a genuine profession of secondary school teachers, definitely assigned to a single school and devoted to the real task of education in its broad sense rather than to giving instruction alone, was essential to a successful system of secondary education.

Educational politics following the War supported proposals for reform along these lines. The Popular Party, under the leadership of Sturzo, definitely pronounced itself in favor of a complete reorganization of the educational system on the principle of freedom in all its stages, but under the control of state examinations. That the Party was influenced by religious and political motives is immaterial; the important point is that it supported the program of reform planned by the idealists. The Congress of Fascists which met at Naples in October, 1922, also drew up proposals for the reorganization of the system of education in the interests of a stronger nationalist consciousness and the demands of contemporary needs. It parted company from the other reform groups in refusing to support the principle of state examinations, which would play into the hands of private, especially denominational, schools. The Fascists were, however, in close sympathy with the idealists in their fight against what they regarded as the misinterpretation of the spirit of democracy, in their affirmation of the principle of authority, and in their demand for the development through the school of a strong national ideal. Education in the opinion of both groups must be progressively selective and must direct the rising generation into the types of activities best suited to their abilities; the individualism of the past must be checked by the educative supervision of the pupils in the schools. The one point of disagreement between the Fascists and idealists was their respective positions on the question of state examinations. It was obvious that this disagreement had disappeared when Mussolini appointed Gentile to become Minister of Public Instruction in 1922 and to undertake the reform of Italian education; it was apparent that the difficulties which had confronted Croce in 1921, when he proposed the introduction of state examinations, had been removed.

The Gentile reform. Gentile proceeded on the principle that in the reorganization of secondary education there must be provided opportunities, but opportunities based on the abilities of the pupils rather than on a demagogic concept of equality; that it must accordingly be functional and selective; that each type of school, whether it has a terminal function or is preparatory to another institution, must be dominated by rigorous standards; and that private schools must be placed on a footing of equality with public schools. The system was accordingly reorganized by Royal Decree of May 6, 1923 (No. 1054). Secondary education was founded upon the primary school and was to be provided by a variety of schools to which specific functions were assigned.

The new system includes:

(1) The full-time continuation school (*scuola complementare*) of three years. On completing this course, pupils could either proceed to an institution for the preparation of kindergarten teachers, or enter into minor public or private employment.

(2) The normal school for the preparation of elementary school teachers (*istituto magistrale*) with a seven-year course, divided into two sections of four and three years respectively. Graduation from this school entitles students to become teachers in elementary schools or to enter a higher normal school (*istituto superiore di magistero*).

(3) The technical institute with an eight-year course, divided into two four-year periods. On the completion of the common foundation, pupils may elect either a course in commerce and accounting (*commercio e ragioneria*) or a course in surveying (*agrimensura*) or enter a scientific *liceo* (*liceo scientifico*).

(4) The secondary school for girls (*liceo femminile*), offering a course of three years for girls who have completed the lower section of a normal school or four years of a *ginnasio* or of a technical institute.

(5) The scientific *liceo* (*liceo scientifico*), offering a four-year course to pupils who have completed the lower section of a technical institute or four years of a *ginnasio*. Graduates may enter the faculties of science or medicine in universities or schools of engineering, architecture, and pharmacy.

(6) The classical secondary school (*liceo-ginnasio*), consisting of the *ginnasio* with a five-year course and the *liceo* with a three-year course. Graduates may enter the universities.

(7) In 1930 there was created by the Royal Decree-Law (October 6, 1930, No. 1379) a new type of vocational secondary school, the *scuola secondaria di avviamento al lavoro* (secondary vocational preparatory school), which is intended to take the place of the *corso integrativo* or elementary senior schools and the *scuola complementare*. The establishment of the new type of school is left to the option of the localities. The Government made an appropriation of 7,000,000 lire toward the creation of these schools and local authorities or private corporations were expected to make annual contributions for their support.

These schools are divided into two grades. Those of the first grade include the continuation school, the lower courses of the technical institute and the normal school, and the *ginnasio*; those of the second grade comprise the classical and scientific *licei*, the girls' school, and the higher courses of the technical institute and the normal school.

Each institution is self-contained; promotion from a lower to a higher section in the same school and transfer from one school to another are controlled by entrance examinations. The completion of the continuation school does not entitle pupils to transfer to any of the secondary schools proper. Finally, the graduation certificates from each of the complete secondary schools do not entitle the holders to the same privileges.

Provision and organization of secondary education. The provision of secondary education is thus carefully controlled by the State, and no schools, except the continuation school, may be opened without the consent of the state authority, which in the case of some types — *licei scientifici* and *licei femminili* — may proceed by decree; in the case of others, by law. All secondary education is under the general supervision of the Minister of Public Instruction through the Division for Secondary Education in the Ministry and is inspected either by the permanent inspectors of the Ministry or by experts appointed for a special inspection or inquiry. The number of normal schools is fixed by law. In the provision and maintenance of public secondary schools, the State, provinces, and municipalities are concerned. The provincial authorities are required to provide and maintain the buildings and equipment of technical institutes and scientific *licei* and to pay the salaries of the non-instructional personnel. The municipalities provide and maintain the buildings for other types of schools, while the equipment is provided by the State. The salaries of the non-instructional staff are paid by the municipalities in continuation schools and girls' schools, by the State in the normal and classical schools. A definite scale of contributions is fixed for the municipalities according to their size. The equipment which is provided by each authority includes teachers' and pupils' libraries, maps, works of art, and laboratories for physics, chemistry, and natural sciences.

The general supervision of secondary education in each administrative area is entrusted to the superintendent with whom is associated a board of secondary education (*giunta per l'istruzione media*), which consists, besides the superintendent as chairman, of a university professor or some other person of distinction in letters or science, two secondary school principals, a full instructor of a secondary school of the second grade, appointed by Royal Decree.

Each school is administered by its principal (*preside*), assisted by the faculty acting as a committee (*collegio dei professori*), which deliberates on all matters affecting instruction and discipline, the purchase of equipment and books for the school library, the selection of textbooks from the list approved by the Ministry, and the final coördination and decision on the reports prepared by the teachers on their pupils. A smaller council (*consiglio di presidenza*), consisting of the principal, vice-principal, and a teacher elected by his colleagues, deliberates on questions requiring immediate action. Problems affecting the pupils of each class are discussed by the instructors assigned to it acting as a class council (*consiglio di classe*). The principal may appoint special committees of teachers of special subjects when any problems concerning them arise. Finally, each school is expected to create and administer a school fund (*cassa scolastica*), to assist poor but deserving pupils, to provide additional or elective studies, to promote school celebrations and tours, to purchase equipment and projectoscopes, to assist in participation in competitions and conventions, and to promote the general welfare of the school and its pupils. Such funds, which are administered by a council consisting of the principal and two or more teachers, amounted in 1929 to 10,000,000 lire.

To obviate the difficulties which beset secondary education from the intense specialization of the teachers, who were thereby virtually compelled to support themselves by teaching the same subjects in a variety of schools, the reform clearly defined the scope of each position and the classes in which a teacher could give instruction. This measure was effected by the combination of allied subjects, such as Italian, Latin, history, and geography; or Latin and Italian literature; or a foreign language; or philosophy, history, and political economy; or mathematics and physics; or natural science, chemistry, and geography. By this reform and by the restriction placed on the creation of parallel classes, it was possible to raise teaching to the dignity of a full-time profession.

In addition to public schools, facilities for secondary education are provided by accredited schools (*scuole parreggiati*), private schools, and national boarding schools (*convitti nazionali*). Recognized organizations (*enti morali*) may establish any type of secondary school except the normal. Teachers in such schools must have the same qualifications as teachers in public schools, are subject to the same regulations, and, if transferred to a public school, may count their period of service in the accredited school toward a pension. Private schools may be opened with the approval of the local superintendent (*provveditore*) by any citizen above thirty years of age who holds the same qualifications as teachers in public schools. The qualifications of teachers, the curricula and courses of study, and buildings of private schools must comply with the requirements for all secondary schools; provision must be made for an approved course of physical education; and the schools must always be open to inspection by the superintendent or other person appointed by the Ministry of Public Instruction. National boarding schools are institutions recognized by the state authority, which bears the cost of the salaries of the personnel while the cost of maintenance is met out of fees and income from endowments. Pupils are admitted between the ages of six and twelve, receive their elementary education in the institution which they attend, and their secondary education in local public or accredited schools as a general rule.

In order to avoid the evils of overcrowding in secondary schools by the addition of parallel classes, the number of parallel courses which may be added in each school is strictly defined by the decree governing secondary education. The size of classes is limited to thirty-five. The board of secondary education, which meets regularly once a month or on special occasions determined by the superintendent or Ministry or on the petition of two of its members, deliberates on all problems which affect the successful administration of secondary education.

Admission and fees. Since secondary education is definitely organized on the principle of selection, entrance to each grade is controlled by admission examinations (*esami di ammissione*). To be admitted to the first grades of the secondary school, pupils must have reached the age of ten and pass an examination, which is common to all types except the continuation school. The examinations, written and oral, are conducted by committees consisting of teachers of the type of school to which the candidate seeks admission and an elementary school teacher. Admission from the first grade of a school to the second of the same or of another type is guarded by an examination before a committee composed in the same way. The examination for entrance to the first grade of schools covers the following subjects: Italian, arithmetic and elementary geometry, drawing, and a general oral test to discover general capacity. This is followed for candidates for admission to all schools except the continuation school by an additional written examination on a subject of the oral examination or some general subject lasting three hours and designed to discover their fitness for admission to the particular type of school to which they seek admission. Those who fail in the additional test may be recommended for admission to the continuation school.

Secondary education is not free; in addition to tuition fees there are fees for the various examinations, as indicated in the following table in lire:

Type of School	Entrance Examination	Matriculation	Tuition Fee	Transfer Examination	Final Examination	Diploma
Classical or scientific lyceum.	150	60	300	100	300	...
Gymnasium..................	...	60	160 *	50	...	...
Technical institute						
Lower course...............	...	60	160	50	...	...
Higher course..............	150	60	300	100	250	100
Normal school						
Lower course...............	...	30	100	30	...	...
Higher course..............	50	30	150	30	150	50
Lyceum for girls.............	100	50	200	50	50	20
Continuation school.........	...	25	100	25	50	20
Scuola secondaria di avviamento al lavoro.............	...	25	...	50	...	125

* The tuition fee for the fourth and fifth years is 200 lire per year.

Provision is made for the remission of fees to needy but deserving pupils, the orphans of soldiers killed in the War, children of Italian residents abroad or in Dalmatia, and of non-Italian residents in the new provinces. Exemption from fees is dependent on ability; they may be remitted entirely to pupils who obtain 8 marks on a scale of 10, or to the extent of a half to pupils who obtain 7 marks on a scale of 10.

Curricula and courses of study. The regulations define in general the functions assigned to each type of secondary school. The work

SECONDARY EDUCATION

of each school is governed, however, not by prescribed courses of study, but the official time-schedules, which define the amount of time to be devoted to each subject, and by the prescribed requirements for the various examinations, which in effect define the curriculum of each school. At the close of each school year the faculty committee (*collegio dei professori*) determines for the succeeding year the course of study for each class and for each subject, so that at the end of the course the pupils will be prepared to take their examinations. The textbooks to be used are selected at the same time.

Aims and curricula. The aim of the continuation school,[1] which in general corresponds to the English central school, the French *école primaire supérieure*, and the German *Mittelschule*, rather than to the accepted secondary school, is to continue the elementary school curriculum to a more advanced stage. The subjects of the three-year course are distributed as follows:

TIME-SCHEDULE OF THE CONTINUATION SCHOOL

SUBJECTS	I YEAR	II YEAR	III YEAR
Italian	4	4	3
History and geography	4	4	3
Modern foreign language	4	4	4
Mathematics	4	3	3
Natural sciences	..	2	2
Bookkeeping	..	3	3
Drawing	4	3	3
Caligraphy	2	..	..
Stenography	..	1	2
Total	22	24	23

The aim of the classical secondary school (*liceo-ginnasio*) is to prepare for the university and other institutions of higher learning. The first grade (*ginnasio*) gives a five-year course; the second (*liceo*), a three-year course. To be admitted to the fourth year of the course where Greek is begun and to the *liceo*, pupils must pass an admission examination. The subjects of the eight years are distributed as follows:

[1] The *scuola complementare* (continuation school) is included in this chapter because in the Italian system it is classified as a part of the secondary rather than of the elementary school system.

Time-Schedule of the Liceo-Ginnasio

Subjects	I Year	II Year	III Year	IV Year	V Year	I Year	II Year	III Year
Italian	7	7	7	5	5	4	4	3
Latin	8	7	7	6	6	4	4	3
Greek	..	..	..	4	4	4	4	3
Modern foreign language	..	3	4	4	4	..	..	..
History and geography	5	5	4	3	3	..	..	..
History	..	..	..	..	..	3	3	3
Geography	..	..	..	..	..	..	..	3
Philosophy and political economy	..	..	..	..	..	3	3	3
Mathematics	1	2	2	2	2	4	2	2
Physics	..	..	..	..	..	..	2	3
Natural sciences and chemistry	..	..	..	..	..	3	3	1
History of art	..	..	..	..	..	1	1	2
Total	21	24	24	24	24	26	26	26

The scientific *liceo* is designed to give pupils a scientific preparation for university study of science or medicine, or specialization in engineering, architecture, and pharmacy. Pupils are admitted by examination from the gymnasium or the lower course of the technical institute. The subjects of the four-year courses are as follows:

Time-Schedule of the Liceo-Scientifico

Subjects	I Year	II Year	III Year	IV Year
Italian	4	4	3	3
Latin	5	4	4	3
Modern foreign language	4	4	3	3
History	2	2	3	3
Geography	..	..	..	3
Philosophy and political economy	..	2	3	3
Mathematics	5	3	3	3
Physics	..	2	3	3
Natural science and chemistry	2	3	2	..
Drawing	3	2	2	2
Total	25	26	26	26

The secondary school for girls (*liceo femminile*) is a new institution established under the Gentile reform for the advanced general education of girls who do not intend to continue their education beyond the secondary course. Pupils are admitted by examination after four years in the *ginnasio*, normal school, and the technical institute. The type is deliberately designed to divert the number of girls from vocational and professional careers. Under the Royal Decree of

1923, it was planned to establish twenty such schools throughout the country; five years later, only a few schools were in existence with every prospect of disappearing. The curriculum and time-distribution are as follows:

TIME-SCHEDULE OF THE LICEO-FEMMINILE

SUBJECTS	I YEAR	II YEAR	III YEAR
Italian and Latin	6	6	6
History and geography	3	3	3
Philosophy, law, and political economy	3	3	3
History of art *	(2)	(2)	(2)
French *	(4)	(4)	(4)
German or English	4	4	4
Drawing	3	3	3
Music, singing, and dancing	2	2	2
Instrumental music *	(2)	(2)	(2)
Domestic arts and economy	3	3	3
Total	24	24	24
	(32)	(32)	(32)

* Elective.

The technical institute (*istituto tecnico*) performs two functions: it is an institution which prepares at once for the two vocations of commerce and surveying and for entrance by way of the *liceo scientifico* to the universities. The lower course consists of a common foundation; the upper course offers two courses — commerce and accounting and land surveying. The subjects of the eight-year course are distributed as shown in the table on page 770.

The *scuola secondaria di avviamento al lavoro* was established to provide a general lower secondary school preparation for agriculture, trades, industry, and commerce. The type of course established in each community is determined by local needs, but two or more types may be provided in the same school. The length of the courses is three years. All schools, whether state (*Regie*) or private (*libere*), are under the supervision of the authorities for secondary education. Pupils are admitted on completing an elementary school or by examination at the age of ten. Successful completion of the course entitles the holders of the *licenza* to enter the fourth year of the technical institute or normal school after a further examination in Italian, Latin, and mathematics.

The curricula and time-schedules are shown in tables on pages 771, 772.

TIME-SCHEDULE OF THE ISTITUTO TECNICO

Subjects	Lower Course				Upper Course							
					Commerce and Accounting				Surveying			
	I	II	III	IV	I	II	III	IV	I	II	III	IV
Italian	7	6	6	5	5	5	..	..	5	5	..	..
Latin	7	7	6	6	..	..	..	..	..	..	..	..
History and geography	4	4	2	2	..	..	..	..	..	..	..	..
History	..	..	..	..	..	..	..	..	..	..	..	..
Mathematics	2	2	..	..	5	5	..	..	5	5	..	..
Mathematics and physics	..	..	4	4	6	5	5	4	6	5	3	3
First modern foreign language	..	4	4	4	2	2	..	..	..	..	..	..
Second modern foreign language	..	..	..	..	..	6	5	..	..	..	..	..
Drawing	4	2	2	2	..	..	..	4	4	..	..	2
Stenography	..	..	1	2	..	..	..	..	..	..	..	2
Natural sciences and geography	..	..	..	..	3	3	2	2	3	3	2	..
Surveying	..	..	..	..	..	..	..	..	..	..	4	4
Rural bookkeeping	..	..	..	..	..	..	..	..	..	..	..	2
Political economy	..	..	..	..	2	2	2	4	..	..	..	4
Chemistry	..	..	..	..	..	..	..	..	3	3	3	3
Rural technology	..	..	..	..	..	..	..	..	..	..	..	2
Construction and design	..	..	..	..	..	..	..	..	..	2	7	6
Topography and drawing	..	..	..	..	..	..	..	..	..	..	8	8
Rural legislation	..	..	..	..	..	..	..	8	..	..	2	..
Bookkeeping and accountancy	..	..	..	..	..	..	8	5	..	..	..	..
Law	..	..	..	..	..	..	7	4	..	..	..	..
Finance and statistics	..	..	..	..	2	..	..	..	..	..	..	..
Caligraphy	..	..	..	..	..	..	3	..	..	..	..	..
Industrial chemistry	..	..	..	..	..	..	..	..	..	..	..	..
Total	24	25	25	25	23	26	27	27	23	23	26	27

Time-Schedule of the Scuola Secondaria di Avviamento al Lavoro

Subjects	Agriculture I	Agriculture II	Agriculture III	Vocational Courses Industry I	Industry II	Industry III (a)	III (b)	III (c)	III (d)	Commercial I	Commercial II	Commercial III	Women I	Women II	Women III
Vocational drawing	..	..	2	2	4	4	6	3	4	..	..	..	..	2	4
Applied science	..	..	2	..	..	3	2	2	3	..	..	..	..	..	..
Agriculture and agricultural industry	..	3	3	..	..	..	..	..	..	..	..	..	..	..	..
Zoötechnics	..	..	1	..	..	..	..	..	..	..	..	..	..	..	..
Farm accounts	..	..	2	..	..	..	..	..	..	..	..	..	..	..	..
Technology	..	..	..	..	..	4	2	3	..	..	..	..	..	..	..
Construction	..	..	..	..	..	..	3	..	..	..	..	..	..	..	..
Weaving	..	..	..	..	..	..	..	5	..	..	..	..	3	3	..
Mineral and allied industry	..	..	..	..	..	..	..	..	4	..	..	..	..	..	..
Accounting in mineral industry	..	..	..	..	..	..	..	..	2	..	..	..	..	..	..
Domestic economy	..	..	..	..	..	..	..	..	..	..	..	..	3	3	2
Household accounts	..	..	..	..	..	..	..	..	..	..	..	..	..	..	2
Accounting and bookkeeping	..	..	..	..	..	..	..	..	..	..	2	4	..	..	..
Merchandise	..	..	..	..	..	..	..	..	..	..	2	2	..	..	..
Stenography	..	..	..	..	..	..	..	..	..	..	2	2	..	..	..
Typewriting	..	..	..	..	..	..	..	..	..	..	2	2	..	..	..
Foreign conversation and correspondence	..	..	..	..	..	..	..	..	..	..	..	4	..	..	..
Commercial practice	..	..	..	..	..	..	..	..	..	..	2	4	..	..	..
Practical work	12	11	10	10	10	10	8	8	8	..	..	..	9	9	10
Common subjects	25	14	20	12	14	21	21	21	21	25	8	16	12	14	21
		23	17	25	23	17	17	17	17		23	17	25	23	17
Total	37	37	37	37	37	38	38	38	38	25	31	33	37	37	38

(a) Mechanics and carpenters; (b) masons; (c) weavers; (d) miners.

Time-Schedule of the Scuola Secondaria di Avviamento al Lavoro

Subjects	Common to All		
	I	II	III
Italian	4	4	3
History, geography and Fascist culture	3	3	4
Foreign language	3	3	3
Mathematics	4	3	2
Physical and natural sciences	2	2	..
Hygiene	..	1	1
Drawing	4	2	..
Writing	1	1	..
Physical training	2	2	2
Religion	1	1	1
Choral singing	1	1	1
Total	25	23	17

The function of the normal school (*istituto magistrale*) is to prepare teachers for elementary schools in a seven-year course, divided into two grades of four and three years respectively. The curriculum is definitely organized on the principle that the essential requirement for successful teaching is command of academic subject-matter and philosophical penetration rather than an emphasis on practice teaching and techniques. To each normal school there must be annexed a kindergarten (*giardino d'infanzia*) or a nursery school (*casa dei bambini*). The subjects of the curriculum and their distribution are as follows:

Time-Schedule of the Istituto Magistrale

Subjects	Lower Course				Upper Course		
	I Year	II Year	III Year	IV Year	I Year	II Year	III Year
Italian	8	4	4	4	5	4	4
Latin	..	6	6	6	5	4	4
History	..	..	..	..	3	3	4
Geography	4	2	2	2	..	..	3
Modern foreign language	..	4	4	4	..	..	..
Philosophy and pedagogy	..	..	..	..	4	5	6
Mathematics	3	2	2	2	..	..	..
Mathematics and physics	..	..	..	..	3	4	4
Natural sciences and hygiene	..	..	..	..	2	4	..
Drawing	3	2	2	2	2	1	1
Music and choral singing	2	2	2	2	2	1	1
Instrumental music *	(2)	(2)	(2)	(2)	(2)	(2)	(2)
Total	20 (22)	22 (24)	22 (24)	23 (25)	26 (28)	26 (28)	27 (29)

* Elective.

The spirit of the reform. Some of the reasons which led up to the Gentile reform have already been mentioned and the aims of each type of secondary school have been discussed. The reform was dominated, however, by a far deeper purpose, social and cultural, than the mere mechanical or administrative rearrangement of schools. From the social and economic point of view the reorganization is intended to distribute the coming generation on the basis of interests and abilities in such a way as will best promote the welfare of the country. But while the new system is selective and distributive, secondary education of all types (excluding the continuation school) is dominated by a common cultural aim. Secondary education before the reform was mechanical, encyclopedic, and informational in character, offering to pupils the semblance rather than the reality of culture. What was emphasized was not intellectual or cultural training, but the amassing of items of knowledge and disconnected detailed information obtained at second hand from manuals about literature rather than literature itself and from compendia of the sciences rather than direct observation and experimentation. The supreme test was ability to reproduce the inert, undigested body of knowledge at the time of the examinations, through which the coveted diploma would be obtained.

The reform proposed by the idealists, among whom Gentile was the leading but not the only exponent, is based on the principle that education means growth of personality, spiritual maturing, the development of the individual as a human being. Accordingly, it placed the emphasis, not on memorization and cramming, but on arousing curiosity, on cultivating and training understanding, and on developing appreciation and enjoyment of the cultural heritage of man as man and of the individual as an Italian. The primary task of secondary education is to introduce all pupils to the humanities, to liberal studies, to give them a general rather than a special education first. The cultural foundation, so far as possible common for all pupils and based on Latin language and literature as the source of Italian, must precede the special training for a career. In 1930 religious instruction was added (by the Giuliano Law, June 5, 1930, No. 824) to the curricula of all secondary schools to the extent of one hour a week in each class; in the *istituto magistrale* two hours a week are given in the upper course. Teachers of the subject are selected each year by the principal of the school with the approval of the ecclesiastical authority of the diocese. The syllabus of religious instruction was issued by Royal Decree, July 10, 1930, No. 1015. A sound education must result in the formation of ideals and a new outlook on life. These ends can only be obtained by an education which is real and active and which places the pupil in a position to commune directly with great contributions of man to the culture of the nation and of the world. Hence, in place of manuals the pupil must read literature and philosophy as they came from their authors; in languages he must acquire facility in their use rather than a knowledge of grammar and canons of style; in the sciences he must learn how to experiment. Finally, his progress is to be tested, not by an examination which may measure his mastery of facts and details, but which seeks to discover his spiritual maturity and mastery of himself.

Examinations. If examinations continue to play as important a rôle in Italian education as they have always done, they have been greatly reformed in character and organization. The internal examinations, conducted by the teachers, which at once lowered the standards in the public schools and penalized the private schools, have been replaced by state examinations common to all schools, public and private, and thereby encouraging competition. In character the change has been in the direction indicated in the preceding paragraph — the examinations seek to test the spiritual maturity of the pupil, his fitness neither to continue his education or to enter on a career for which his school has prepared him. The examinations enjoy a position of importance from another point of view, since they virtually define the scope of the curricula and courses of study in the secondary schools. In order to avoid confusion of aims and purposes between the different types of schools, a characteristic examination has been established for each grade and each type. Examinations are not interchangeable with each other.

The following examinations have been instituted: admission (*ammissione*); capacity or aptitude (*ideonità*); promotion (*promozione*); license (*licenza*); qualifying (*abilitazione*); and maturity (*maturità*). The first three are entrance, the last three leaving examinations. All examinations are held in July. Candidates who obtain less than a mark of 6 on a scale of 10 or who do not complete either the written or oral test may be permitted to repeat the examination in October of the same year. All examinations are written and oral; failure in the written examination is eliminatory. The admission examination has already been discussed with reference to first entrance into a secondary school. Entrance from the lower grade to the upper grade of the same or another school or from the third to the fourth year of the *ginnasio* is guarded by an admission examination conducted, as has been pointed out, by teachers of the school which the pupil plans to enter and a teacher from the type of school from which he comes. The examination of capacity or aptitude must be passed by pupils who, coming from an unaccredited or private school, seek admission to a public school. Promotion examinations are required only in the case of pupils who have obtained a mark of less than 6 on a scale of 10 in conduct and progress during the preceding year. The reports of teachers are considered every two months and again at the end of each year by the whole staff (*collegio dei professori*). The license is the leaving examination at the end of the continuation, the vocational preparatory, and girls' schools; the examination is conducted by the teachers of the school concerned.

The qualifying and maturity examinations are more formal in character. The qualifying examination is the leaving examination from technical institutes and normal schools and seeks to establish the ability of candidates for the pursuit of the career for which they have been prepared. The examinations are conducted in the provincial capitals for candidates from the technical institutes and in the administrative centers for educational supervision for candidates from normal schools. The examining commissions are appointed each year by the Minister of Public Instruction on the recommendation of superintendents of education. The maturity examination for candidates from the classical and scientific *licei* is a test of their ability to pursue higher education and is held at prescribed centers only. The examining commissions, appointed by the Minister, consist of not more than one third of university professors or lecturers, at least two thirds of teachers of second grade schools, and a teacher from a private school or a person not connected with the work of education. Members of examining commissions are not permitted to vote on candidates whom they have taught publicly or privately.

Since the examinations determine the character of the curriculum and the courses of study of the secondary schools, the standards which they set up seriously influence the aims. Of the many examinations it is only possible to give the suggestions for the *maturità* from the *liceo classico*. The chief stress is placed upon the language requirements; these are the only subjects in which there are written examinations, lasting six hours in Italian, ten hours in Latin, and five hours in Greek, and oral examinations of thirty minutes in each subject. All other subjects are examined orally as follows: history, twenty minutes; political economy, ten minutes; philosophy, twenty-five minutes; mathematics, fifteen minutes; physics (mechanics, heat, acoustics, electricity and magnetism, cosmography and meteorology), fifteen minutes; history of art, fifteen minutes; chemistry (organic and inorganic), natural science (biology), geography and geology, fifteen minutes.

The purpose of this examination is to test the spiritual maturity of the candidates. In literature the examination "must not be a test of memory but of culture and taste. Can the candidate read our great authors alone? Has he the ability to enjoy them? Has he an adequate background of history and æsthetics for a proper appreciation of their place?" The emphasis throughout is on the direct study of the classics, whether ancient or modern, and their setting in the history of culture. The test in history, which covers the ancient, medieval, and the modern periods, must aim to discover the candidates' sense of interrelationships and continuity. In political economy they must be expected to give evidence of an understanding, not so much of abstract theory as of the influences of economic forces in history. The examination in philosophy is directed to discover ability to analyze problems philosophically with an understanding of the fundamental problems of consciousness and ethics and the chief manifestations of the mind (intellectualism, empiricism, criticism, and idealism), and a knowledge of the particular contributions of the great philosophers. Mathematics serves as a test of the mastery of theory and formulas and as a test of ability to discuss a problem logically and systematically. The examinations in sciences must avoid any stress on mere facts which can be memorized and endeavor to test the candidates' understanding of fundamental concepts and their relations. Finally, the examination in the history of art serves to discover knowledge of the great periods in the development of art in all its branches, and of the development of æsthetics and taste, as well as ability to interpret masterpieces in relation to their epoch.

Whether these lofty aspirations can be tested by examinations is extremely doubtful. The idealism which inspired the Gentile reform is nowhere more manifest than in the statements of the aims of the examinations. Their intent is clear — to eliminate the traditional emphasis on memorization and to substitute therefor active participation by the pupils in their own growth and development. The mere distribution of emphasis in the time-schedules and in the examinations must be detrimental to any serious attempt to achieve balance between the different branches of culture. In the lower grades of all types of schools no provision is made for the teaching of the sciences, while in the upper grades too much content is crowded into too few periods. Girls who begin their education in the lower grades and proceed to the *liceo femminile* are entirely deprived of any opportunities for the study of science. The amount of ground to be covered must inevitably affect adversely the attempt to emphasize reality and experimentation. The reform was launched without much attention to the adequate preparation of the teachers. The insistence of Gentile and his group that education is wholly a matter of the spiritual influence of a well-trained mind on the immature was interpreted in theory and practice as meaning that thorough command of subject-matter makes a good teacher and that training in professional technique and methods interferes with, rather than promotes, freedom in instruction. Certainly five years after the reform was launched it was not easy to distinguish the new methods or the new spirit from the old. Dictation and lecturing still predominated and in language work the atomistic method of dissection of a masterpiece had not disappeared. The reform was well-intentioned and in many respects followed the lines of progressive reform everywhere, but the examination requirements continued to lay the emphasis on the *multa non multum* which has always been the bane of secondary education. The aims may be unimpeachable, but confronted with a formidable program, such as is prescribed for the examination in each subject, few pupils and teachers could resist the temptation of mastering the content rather than utilizing the content as a means to secure the ends proposed — ends which can only be tested by the most refined skill if they can be tested at all.

School life. The character of secondary education during the nineteenth century and up to the period of reform militated against the development of a tradition of corporate life in the schools. The large numbers, in most cases the gloomy buildings, the absence of open spaces, the emphasis on diplomas, and the itinerant character of the teaching profession were all factors which prevented the organization of activities of the right kind among the pupils. Nor is there any indication, either in the proposals for reform put forward by the idealist group or in the reform itself, that the importance of extra-curricular activities was recognized. The regulations governing the aims and curricula of secondary education make no reference to pupil self-government, or even to physical education except by an indirect requirement that time must be provided for it in the arrangement of the time-schedules. The introduction of physical education was the work not of the idealists but of the Fascists.

By a Royal Decree of March 15, 1923, there was created an independent and autonomous body for the promotion and supervision of physical education — the *Ente Nazionale per l'Educazione fisica*. This body was administered by a council of seven members, only one of whom represented the Ministry of Public Instruction. A sum of 2,000,000 lire was provided for 1923–24 to enable the *Ente Nazionale* to organize physical education for secondary schools. Every locality in which there was a secondary school was required to establish committees which through an expert as director supervised physical education in its area. The *Ente Nazionale* was authorized to make use of the facilities provided by gymnastic societies and sports clubs; municipalities were required by the Royal Decree of May 6, 1923, the fundamental decree governing the reform of secondary education, to provide for the maintenance, lighting, and heating of gymnasiums and stadia belonging to the *Ente Nazionale*. In other ways local authorities have been urged to provide stadia and personnel for the promotion of physical education.

The regulations require every public and accredited secondary school to leave two afternoon sessions or a morning and one afternoon session free to enable the pupils to proceed to the gymnasiums and stadia in which they are registered, for their physical education and sports, and a whole period of eight days for an excursion or competitions. No pupil may receive his annual promotion or qualify for a certificate or diploma unless he meets the standards prescribed for this work; exemptions are only granted for reasons of health or physical disability. Private schools must make their own arrangements for physical education, but their pupils must present themselves for examinations each year at recognized centers.

As a result of the criticism of the dualism introduced into education by the separation of physical from general education and of excessive interference by the *Ente Nazionale*, this body was suppressed and its work was transferred on January 1, 1928, to the *Opera Nazionale Balilla*, which is discussed in another connection; in 1929 the *Opera Nazionale Balilla* was itself transferred to the Ministry of National Education (see p. 169).

In addition to these provisions for physical education, provision is made in each school for educational tours, but only as a reward for the better pupils. Under the direction of their teachers, groups have been taken on tours to places of interest in Belgium, France, Germany, and Hungary, and are taken more regularly through Italy. A hostel has been established in one of the secondary schools in Rome which accommodates about a hundred pupils, who may be brought from different parts of the country. Valuable as such tours are for the general advancement of the pupils, they are supplementary to the work of the classroom. They do not take the place nor fulfill the purposes of the organization for corporate life or extracurricular activities.

The conduct and discipline of pupils both in and out of school are governed by a Royal Decree of April 30, 1924. The penalties there provided include private or public admonition, suspension from school for longer or shorter periods, deprivation of the right to promotion without examination, expulsion from the school attended, or exclusion from all public schools. Of the more serious types of punishments the board of secondary education and the Ministry of National Education must be informed; the severest penalties, expulsion or exclusion, are published in the *Bollettino Ufficiale* of the Ministry.

The official attitude to school life thus represents a survival of the traditional control of the pupils, an application of that idealism which dominates educational theory, and the use of the school for Fascist purposes through control of the régime of physical education. It almost appears as though the emphasis on spiritual freedom and growth which underlies the aims of secondary education is balanced and checked on the personal side by the disciplinary measures of the Royal Decree and the political and national ends of the *Opera Nazionale Balilla*, which controls physical education.

5. RUSSIA

In no branch of education has the Soviet régime so completely broken with tradition as in what is usually termed secondary education. Since secondary education dominantly connotes the education of a select group and, since the programs are determined largely in terms of culture which is historically conceived, neither could be accepted in an educational system which seeks to form new minds and to train for new forms of life as defined by Communist ideology. The traditional secondary school has, on the whole, it is objected, remained closed to contemporary life and has deliberately aimed to train its pupils away from work and labor. In this sense it has been an instrument for perpetuating class distinctions and enlarging the gap between the so-called educated classes and the proletariat of workers. Upon these traditions Soviet secondary education has deliberately turned its back. In the first place, the secondary school is the continuation and a part of the unified labor school; in the second, it is not concerned with imparting an education for its own sake, such as liberal education is conceived to be — the French insistence on *études désintéressés* as the constituent part of a liberal education has no meaning for the Russian educator. Secondary education, like all other education, must be dominated by the social, political, and economic ideals of the new social order. Hence it cannot be divorced from labor or from Communist ideology, nor can it be separated from the needs and demands of the community which it serves.

Secondary education constitutes the second grade of the unified labor school and is provided in courses of three or five years' duration, which may be established as independent units or may form the upper sections of a seven- or nine-year school. Since the second grade school is part of the unified labor school, pupils pass into it automatically without any entrance examinations. The seven-year courses have been made compulsory in 1932. Three main types of seven-year schools are found — schools for peasant youth in the agricultural areas, factory or mill schools in industrial regions, and general schools in urban centers. With increased emphasis on polytechnization even the general schools are beginning to be organized on a vocational basis. The last two years of the nine-year school provide for differentiated courses or biases — pedagogical for the preparation of teachers for lower schools, coöperative for agricultural workers or coöperators, and Soviet administration for workers in financial and tax divisions, insurance, or administration. During the past years a great variety of other courses with a vocational bias has been introduced in the last stage of the nine years. Normally pupils in the second grade schools are from twelve to fifteen years of age in the lower stage and from sixteen to seventeen in the upper stage.

The aim of the second grade school is not to prepare for the next stage, but to give a general training for workers in one of the field of socially useful labor without attempting specialized vocational training, and to lay the foundations for continued study. The work of the school thus has three main emphases: (1) to impart a definite body of knowledge or general studies; (2) to give a definite training in socio-political education, including a study of the contemporary struggle of the working classes and the structure of the Soviet State, with an emphasis on the place of labor in society; and (3) introduction to practical work. Other aspects of education — physical training and the arts — are not neglected, and great stress is placed, as it is in all educational institutions, on self-organization and self-government of the pupils.

The subjects of the first three years of a second grade school in an urban center and the time assigned to them are shown on page 782.

The curriculum of the last two years is divided between general subjects and the special subjects of the specialized courses — pedagogical, coöperative, and Soviet Administration, as indicated in the accompanying table (page 783).

The "complex" method of curriculum organization is continued from the first to the second grade, but with a somewhat different emphasis, so, that while the subjects are taught synthetically, their individuality is not destroyed by the integration, as it tends to be in the American general courses. The synthesis or integration is made around large general themes which provide opportunities for the combination of a number of separate disciplines. The ac-

Subjects	V*	VI*	VII*	Total for the Whole Course *†
Social science	4	4	4	408
Russian language and literature	5	5	4	476
Mathematics	4	4	5	442
Natural history	3	4	4	372
Chemistry ‡	1	2	2	170
Physics	4	4	4	408
Geography	2	2	2	204
Foreign languages	3	3	3	306
Labor	3	3	3	306
Plastic art	2	2	2	204
Singing, music, and rhythmics **	2	1½	1½	170
Physical culture	2	1½	1½	170
Total	35	36	36	3638

* Fifth, sixth, and seventh years of the unified labor school.
† The school year is thirty-six weeks in length; two weeks are assigned to organizing and closing.
‡ In the fifth year of study, natural history and chemistry are taught by the one instructor.
** Three hours are devoted in the second and third years to singing, music, rhythmics, and physical culture; this time may be distributed among the other subjects, depending on the conditions of the school, the possibility of organizing separate studies in rhythmics, facilities for physical work, etc.

companying courses of study (pp. 784–86), drawn up by the State Scientific Council, illustrate the complex or synthesis provided in the second grade school around (*a*) nature, its resources and powers; (*b*) man's exploitation of these resources and powers; and (*c*) social life.[1]

Beyond this integration the work of the school is further directed to the dominant emphasis — socially useful activities. Concrete application is constantly provided by associating the studies of the school with observation, study, and practical participation in the economic and community life of the locality in which the school is situated and by more extended excursions to different parts of the Union. In the last two years, indeed, through fear that the schools were not being sufficiently polytechnicized, the educational authorities and the Communist Party have urged, first, that the factory, the farm, or other economic activity be made the laboratory of each school in the district, and, second, that an increasing number of teachers be drawn from men and women who had experience as workers.

In 1928–29 there were 5707 seven-year schools with 2,071,400 pupils; 946 nine-year schools with 635,100 pupils; and 897 independent second grade schools with enrollments of 328,700 pupils; there were in addition 700 schools for peasant youth.

[1] From Pinkevitch, A. S., *The New Education in the Soviet Republic*, pp. 306–08 (New York, 1929).

Subjects	General Course VIII	General Course IX	General Course Total	Special Course	General Course VIII	General Course IX	Special Course VIII	Special Course IX	Total VIII	Total IX	Total for Whole Course
Social science	5	4	306	Pedagogical course							
Russian language and literature	4	4	272	(a) School division	29	26	9	12	38	38	2,584
Mathematics	4	4	272	(b) Pre-school division	29	26	8	12	37	38	2,550
Natural history	3	3	204	(c) Political enlightenment division	29	26	9	12	38	38	2,584
Chemistry	2	2	136	Coöperative course							
Physics	3	3	204	(a) Agricultural-economic coöperative division	29	25	9	13	38	38	2,584
Foreign languages	2	2	136	(b) Consumer's coöperative division	29	25	9	13	38	38	2,584
Plastic art	2	1	102	Soviet administration course							
Singing and music	2	1	102	(a) Financial-taxation division	29	25	7	13	36	38	2,516
Physical culture	2	1*	102	(b) Insurance division	29	25	7	13	36	38	2,516
Total	29	25	1,836	(c) Administrative division	29	25	7	11	36	36	2,448

* Two hours in the pedagogical course, giving a total of 26 periods per week.

II. The Plan of the Program of the First Division of the Secondary School

(Children 12 to 15 years of age)

First Year

Nature: Its Resources and Powers	Man's Exploitation of These Resources and Powers	Social Life
1. Physics and chemistry in so far as they are needed for clear understanding of climate, life of soil, life of plants.	1. Varieties and forms of industry of agricultural economy. Characteristics of agricultural region of Soviet Union. Exploitation and fertilization of soil. Rotational system. Care of plants in field. Tools of labor and village economy. Cultivated agricultural plants. Cattle breeding, poultry raising, and other forms of animal breeding. Small and large scale agriculture.	Peasants and landowners. Rise of serfdom. Struggle of peasants against landowners. Czar and nobility. Autocratic régime. Dictatorship of nobility. Crimean War. Liberation of serfs. Peasants' lack of rights. Redeemed payments. Peasants' limitation of landownership. Peasants' economy. Landowners' economy. Statistics of village economy before war. Peasants' dreams about land. Union of Workers and Peasants. Conquest of power. Land laws.
2. Soil: its composition and characteristics. Kinds of soil in different regions of Russia.	2. Agriculture in Western Europe and America. Results of application of science to agriculture. Renewed land.	Struggle of peasants in West. Jacquerie. Peasants' wars. Great French Revolution.
3. Observations of weather. Meteorology. Climate of various regions of Soviet Union.		
4. Biology. Life of plants, dependence of plants upon environing conditions. Distribution of plant life throughout Soviet Union. Animal world; relation between structure and mode of life. Animals useful and harmful to agricultural economy.		

Students who complete the seven-year school may continue either in the last two years of the nine-year school or enter a technicum; those who finish the nine-year course may enter a university or other higher educational institution, preference being given to students

II. The Plan of the Program of the First Division of the Secondary School

(Children 12 to 15 years of age)

Second Year

Nature: Its Resources and Powers	Man's Exploitation of These Resources and Powers	Social Life
1. Physics and chemistry in so far as they are necessary for an understanding of (1) life of animals and man and (2) application of these sciences to industry (machine construction, locomotives, electricity).	1. Mining of ores, minerals, and fuel.	Workers and capitalists. Hired labor and capital. Private ownership at expense of production. Condition of working class. Union of noblemen and capitalists. Limited monarchy. Republic. Dictatorship of bourgeoisie. Democratic republic.
2. Ores, rocks, metals, mineral fuel. Deposits in Soviet Union.	2. Chemical and mechanical industry. Trade. Manufacture. Factories. Organization of labor in trade, mill, and factory. Development of various branches of industry in Soviet Union and in other countries. Regional industries of Soviet Union.	Capitalism. Competition. Chaos in production. Struggle of labor and capital. Chartists. Year of 1848. Communistic Manifesto — expression of impulses of working class. International union of workers. First International. Attempt of workers to take power into their hands. Paris Commune. Second International. Strikes. Organization of labor. Assimilation into political parties.
3. Technical plants and animals.	3. Technology of products of village economy.	
4. Man as member of animal kingdom. Anatomy and physiology of man.	4. Anthropogeography: man and human society; dependence upon natural environment.	Capitalism in Russia. Remnants of serfdom. Autocracy. Struggles of 1905 and 1917.
5. Hygiene of physical and mental work. Sound and unsound body.	5. Man as a working power. Organization of his labor. Protection of labor and health of workers.	

of proletarian or peasant origin. The courses in the technicums are normally four years in length; each course has a definite vocational bias which after the first two years becomes more progressively specialized. The general subjects of the first two years are similar to those of the last stage of the nine-year school; to these are added the special subjects and practical work either in the school or in the factory. The vocational courses are offered in industry,

II. The Plan of the Program of the First Division of the Secondary School

(Children 12 to 15 years of age)

Third Year

Nature: Its Resources and Powers	Man's Exploitation of These Resources and Powers	Social Life
1. Structure of universe (as revealed by astronomical observations and appropriate divisions of physics and chemistry).	1. Chaos in social organization of labor under capitalism. Unproductive dissipation of productive forces.	Development of capitalism. Trusts. World markets. Colonies. Imperial war of 1914. Unprecedented disintegration produced in Russia by war. Defeats at front. Revolution of 1917. Fall of autocracy. Provisional government. Continuation of war. October revolution. Soviet régime. Foundations of soviet constitution. Its differentiation from parliamentary republics. Dictatorship of proletariat.
2. Structure of matter.	2. Organized economy of country under communism. Rôle of accounting. Rational organization of production.	
3. Derivation and history of land.	3. Soviet régime as transition from capitalism to communism.	
4. Mutation and heredity among organisms.		
5. Artificial and natural selection and origin of species; study of grades of animals and plants, selection and breeding of new species.		Its aim. Five years of dictatorship of proletariat. Third International and future world revolution.
6. Evolution of plant and animal kingdoms. Origin of man.		

agriculture, arts-crafts, and fine arts (music, drama, and art), medicine (samaritani, nurses, dental workers, care of maternity and infancy), and pedagogy. In 1928–29 the 1053 technicums were attended by 207,600 students.

The education of the adolescent or secondary education in the Soviet Union, allowing for some variations in the different Republics, is thus dominated by the vocational aim, partly because all education must be in the interests of the workers, partly because it has definitely been harnessed to the Five-Year Plan. By this aim all the subjects of instruction are governed — the sciences are predominantly applied and practical, the humanities are inspired by the socio-political aims; foreign languages are selected for their utility and preference is given, not to French, which in the old régime was the language of all educated Russians, but to German and English, of which there appears to be greater need at the present time; liberal studies, as they have been generally understood have been discarded; the past, in so far as its study is included, is utilized as an object study in the evils of capitalism and the bourgeois ideology; the new school looks wholly to the present and the future — the building of a new social order as defined by the Communist Party. A Resolution of the Central Committee of the Communist Party, adopted on August 25, 1932, indicates that the experiments both in content and method are not satisfactory; the schools are criticized for overloading and superficiality, lack of coördination, oversimplification of difficult subjects, inadequate historical background for social sciences, and lack of thoroughness in general; on the side of methods there has been too much emphasis on one method and too much relegation of the teacher into the background.

School and society. This task is, however, not completed by formal instruction and training in the classroom; a large place is assigned to training through self-organization and self-government. The Russian educator, however, denies that the purpose of self-organization and self-government is the same as in the bourgeois countries where they are found. Their aim is not as in the bourgeois schools to provide opportunities for the development of individual initiative, independence, and responsibility, and an outlet for adolescent interests not directly included in classroom instruction. Their organization in such schools is artificial and meaningless because they do not reflect the realities found in the life of the community outside the school. Self-government in schools must be used as an educational instrument in the same sense as is the curriculum; it must be vitalized by the same purposes as the larger society of which the school is a part, and the activities for whose sake it is established must be socially useful and not mere mimicry or play. Hence self-organization and self-government must exist for the sake of training the pupil throughout his school life in group participation in the realities of life. The pupils must enjoy complete independence, but must rely on advice and guidance from the teachers and other adults only because their experience is richer and broader, but not because of the exercise of authority or dictation on their part. The school organizations, created and managed by the pupils, must grow from below up and must serve as a link between the school and labor on the farms and in factories, the Red Army, and the life of the proletariat. Only if this aim is kept in view can self-organization and self-government succeed in developing those collective traits which are essential if new forms of social life are to be created. As in the case of the curriculum, courses of study, and methods of instruction, so the freedom enjoyed by pupils and students is beginning to cause some concern. The Resolution of the Central Committee of the Communist Party of August 25, 1932, to which reference was made above, urges the Commissariats of Education to "entrust unquestioned leadership in the work of the school to the teaching personnel," and to impose on principals and teachers the responsibility for the maintenance of discipline.

Although leadership is supposed to come from within the pupil group itself, and the teacher or other adults are counselors and guides, in actual practice self-organization and self-government are dominated in the main by the Pioneers and Komsomols, the junior branches of the Communist Party. Leadership by these groups is urged by the Party itself and by the educational authorities. The People's Commissariat of Education in 1927 thus described the main purposes of self-organization:

> An essential feature of Communistic training is the inculcation of *collectivism*. It is a problem of primary importance for the socialistic school to develop in children the habit of living, learning and working collectively. This work is accomplished best by the development of the activities of children's organizations. The most salutary basis for this is the organization of socially useful work of the school, the connection of the school with Pioneer organizations, arrangement of their activities, the organization of club work at school, the performance of different tasks of the school economy, the improvement of school comforts, the establishment of bonds between different schools, and between schools and other social institutions, and the development of mutual aid within the schools.[1]

Through self-organization and self-government it is expected, according to Pinkevitch,[2] to develop habits of behavior and social instincts, to give practical meaning to socialistic ideology, to culti-

---

[1] Lvov and Sirotkin, *Self-Organization of School Children*, pp. 24–25; translated in Woody, T., *New Minds: New Men?* p. 173 (New York, 1932).

[2] Pinkevitch, A., *The New Education in the Soviet Republic*, p. 213 (New York, 1929).

vate loyalty to the school and friendly relations between teachers and pupils, to stimulate the creative powers, initiative and independence, and to organize the school on a labor basis. The forms of organization and government in which pupils engage vary and room is always provided for the creation of new machinery as needs arise. School pupils are linked to the school administration by electing representatives to the local school committees. For the conduct of their own affairs general school councils are elected which through their executive committees organize and supervise clubs, groups, and circles for sanitary purposes (the promotion of hygiene, cleanliness, physical activities, and sports), for economic life (the launching of campaigns, agricultural life, repair of school buildings, general supervision of the material well-being), for instruction (encouragement of attendance, and criticisms and suggestions for improvement of instruction), and for enlightenment (the promotion of the arts — music, drama, and organization of celebrations). Art, science, political, social, and economic questions, literature, sport, dramatics, music, school journals, wall-newspapers, conduct of libraries, anti-religious or atheistic propaganda — for all these activities self-organization provides scope through circles and clubs which reach out beyond their own schools to the parents, the locality, and beyond.

The whole organization of the education of the adolescent, like all education in the Soviet Union, is marked by unity of purpose which colors every activity involved — curriculum and pupil life, work in the classroom and activities outside of it. The school is not, as it were, a social excrescence, to provide for the sheltered growth of its members until they are old enough to join the main currents of life; the school in a real sense is life.

The system is sound if the major premises are sound. The school is continuous with life and there is no break in gauge between the two, but the increasing polytechnization of education and the tightening of the link between the school and vocations raises the serious question whether a liberal education can be provided on such terms, whether there is not here a confusion between education and training, whether the school routine is not really a greater mimicry of adult life in Soviet than in bourgeois societies. It is significant that the American educator has found something alluring in Russian education. The reason is clear — both have allowed their schools to be dominated by the machine; but the Russian system at least has the merit of professing to seek the control of the machine in the interest of human beings. Time alone will prove whether the new secondary education has much to contribute that cannot already be found in prevocational and vocational schools elsewhere, for the so-called socially useful labor is definitely becoming specialized trade instruction. The contribution to general theory, however, cannot be ignored — that education at any stage must find its meaning and significance in the civilization and culture of the country which it seeks to serve. Undoubtedly Russian criticism of bourgeois secondary education as divorced from life is sound, but the Russian experiment, while harnessing the school to life, has discarded most of the elements of a liberal education which cannot be bounded by life as it is in the immediate present and which cannot serve one master alone.

6. UNITED STATES

HISTORICAL BACKGROUND [1]

The academy period. The tradition of secondary education which is current today in the United States began to be formulated with the establishment of the Republic. The Latin Grammar School which had been transplanted to the colonies from Europe had already begun to be the subject of criticism early in the eighteenth century with the rise of a movement for types of post-elementary education which would be immediately useful and would better meet the demands of a changing society. Although the Latin Grammar School preparing for college continued throughout the eighteenth century to be the typical secondary school, its dominance began to be challenged by the rise of academies, at first private and later public, which either omitted the study of the classics entirely or relegated them to a position subordinate to that of modern subjects. The burden of the new movement is best illustrated in Benjamin Franklin's *Proposal Relating to the Education of Youth in Pennsylvania* (1749) and the establishment of his academy in 1751, which, although it failed to carry out his design, was sympathetic of the demands of his day.

[1] For a fuller account of the history of secondary education in the United States see Kandel, I. L., *History of Secondary Education* (Boston, 1930).

The Republic was created on the foundation of a strong belief in the perfectibility of man, in his capacity for progress, and in his right to an opportunity to realize himself. With the faith in liberty and democracy was combined a clear recognition of the importance of education. The theory of education as enunciated before the close of the eighteenth century demanded flexibility of institutions, education for constructive citizenship, a national or public system of education as opposed to private schools, and due attention to the study and promotion of the sciences and other subjects essential for the advancement of social welfare and progress. "It is certainly laudable," stated one educator of the period, "to pay due regard to those sciences that tend to enlarge the sphere of worldly interest, and without which the various and complicated business of human life cannot be transacted."

The academy, because it was still flexible and not subject to the control of college entrance requirements, as was the Latin Grammar School, was peculiarly adapted to the growing demands of a society in its formative stages. Because it could serve more ends than one, it was the institution that was fostered almost everywhere, and became the secondary school most generally founded in the first half of the nineteenth century by public and private efforts. The academy was not only well adapted to the needs of the time, but it met the liberal demands of those who were giving thought to education. As early as 1797, Massachusetts adopted a policy of aiding both public and private academies, which were to be regarded "as a part of an organized system of public and universal education, as opening the way, for all people, to a higher order of instruction than the common schools can supply."

The same institution, known as the academy or seminary, spread rapidly in all the States and reached its highest development in the country as a whole by 1850. There were at that time 6085 academies with an enrollment of 263,096 pupils, taught by 12,260 teachers, and in receipt of an annual estimated income of $5,831,179. A variation of the broad curriculum of the academy was introduced with the establishment of manual labor institutions which flourished between 1820 and 1840. The general theory underlying the advocacy of manual labor institutions was that they provided an education that is natural, interesting, healthy, and character-forming; that they cultivated habits of industry, independence, and originality; that they diminished the cost of education, increased the country's wealth, and eliminated class distinctions.

Despite the real contributions made by the academy to the provision of facilities for secondary education on a more generous scale than was found during its period of development in any of the European countries, a provision which was accompanied by a broader conception of the purposes of secondary education, it was destined to fill a temporary need only. It was never regarded as fulfilling the democratic ideal of a public system of education, free from the lowest to the highest stage, and was looked upon with some suspicion as a select, exclusive, and aristocratic school, catering chiefly to those who could pay fees and providing only for the more able children of the poor. Public opinion was definitely in favor of a movement for the establishment of a system of free public schools, supported by public taxation, equally open to all, and responding to the genius of the country's democratic institutions.

Rise of the public high school. Liberal theorists and politicians of the early Republic were unanimous in urging the establishment of public systems of education, extending from the lowest to the highest grades. The principle of the provision and control of public education by public authorities was not only widely accepted, but constituted the basis of a number of legislative proposals. State governments, however, were not sufficiently strong or well established before the middle of the nineteenth century either to enforce or to support a system of public high schools. The movement was thus left largely to the initiative of local authorities.

The new era in American secondary education, as contrasted with the academy movement, was inaugurated in Boston in 1821 by the opening of what was at first known as the English Classical School and later as the English High School to distinguish it from the Boston Latin School. The aim of this school was to furnish young men "with the means of completing a good English education and of fitting themselves for all departments of commercial life." The term "high school" had already begun to be used by a few schools which were organized, like the Edinburgh High School, on the monitorial system, but the probability is that its general employment to signify a school giving an education beyond that of the elementary school spread from its use in the new Boston school.

From Boston the high school idea spread to cities in neighboring

States until the movement became fairly general throughout the country, except in the South. In Massachusetts the development of high schools was advanced by the enactment of the law of 1859 which required towns to maintain schools other than the elementary according to their size. More common than a compulsory law of this type was the act passed in New York in 1853, which permitted the legal voters of a district or of two or more adjoining districts to create a board of education with the right to establish or take over an existing academy. A series of laws of the same type gave legal sanction to the general principle underlying a public school system which had always been in the minds of the founders of the Republic. The enactment of laws did not, however, allay the opposition which still continued to exist in some places against the payment of taxes for the advanced education of other people's children, or the suspicion that secondary education would lead to the undemocratic stratification of society.

The matter was brought to an issue in the famous Kalamazoo Case (1874), in which among a number of other contentions it was argued that the common schools mentioned in the Constitution of the State of Michigan did not include high schools, which were part of higher education and should be supported out of funds other than those intended for common schools. The case was carried to the Supreme Court, which refused to accept these contentions and virtually upheld the general public concept of a public high school. This had already been defined in 1850 by Henry Barnard as follows:

By a public or common high school is intended a public or common school for the later and more advanced scholars of the community in which the same is located, in a course of instruction adapted to their age, and intellectual and moral wants, and, to some extent, to their future pursuits in life.

From the administrative point of view, another definition of the public high school was put forward later by George S. Boutwell, Secretary of the Massachusetts Board of Education, in discussing the question, "How can the advantages of a high school education be best secured?"

And, first, the high school must be a public school. A *public* school I understand to be a school established by the public — supported chiefly or entirely by the public, controlled by the public, and accessible to the public upon terms of equality, without special charge for tuition.

After the Kalamazoo decision and following the gradual recovery of the country from the effects of the Civil War, the development of high schools was rapid. It was promoted by the gradual evolution of the state systems of education, the rapidly increasing wealth of the country which followed the change from an agricultural to an industrial order, and the growth in the number of cities and other organized communities. The stages in the provision of high schools were as follows: (1) Legislation permitting cities, towns, incorporated villages, and districts to tax themselves for the maintenance of high schools. (2) The grant of permission to small units to organize high school districts and to tax themselves for their maintenance. (3) The recognition of county units for high school purposes. (4) The grant of special assistance from state or other sources toward the support of high schools.

There was thus settled in the United States more than half a century ago the problem of the common school with which many European and other countries are struggling at present. Not only was the ideal of the broad educational highway from the kindergarten or the first grade of the elementary school accepted, but it was also determined that the same school shall serve the needs of all pupils, boys and girls, coming from the elementary school and remaining until ready to enter college. The elementary school period was to extend over eight years, that of the high school over four. The acceptance of the broad educational highway as the essential guarantee of equality of opportunity brought with it other problems than those of the provision of schools: it meant that there must be organized such a variety of courses as would meet the varied interests and abilities of a growing clientèle of pupils.

The differentiated needs of pupils had been the basis of the establishment first of the academy to provide opportunities which were not found in the Latin Grammar School which was essentially college preparatory. The earliest tendency in the establishment of high schools in New England was to create an English High School to supplement the Classical High School, but as early as 1831 Lowell combined both courses in the same school, and the Worcester High School, opened in 1845, was not only a Classical and English High School, but was also coeducational. The decision was early reached, even in what is often regarded as traditional New England, that the function of the high school was to enable students "to obtain such an education as will fit for any business or station in life." Out of this principle there developed an increasing multiplicity of subjects which in some schools were combined into courses for individual pupils and in others into prescribed courses. In the period from 1896 to 1900, thirty-six different courses emerged, including commercial and manual training courses. In some of the larger centers separate high schools were established giving special courses.

Such an expansion of the curriculum led to unrest which culminated in 1890 in a movement to define, not only the scope of the high school, but also its relation to the college. Two methods had been established to regulate the relation between the high school and college. In 1871 the University of Michigan adopted the practice of accrediting high schools on the report of a Commission of Examiners who visited each school annually; the graduate of an accredited school could be admitted to the university on the recommendation of the school principal or superintendent. The practice was adopted generally in the States of the Middle West and West and helped to standardize the high schools within each State. The problem was not so simple in the Eastern States, where there existed a great diversity of college entrance examinations. A solution was found by the creation of standardizing associations which had their first tentative beginnings at a conference of New England Colleges in 1879 at Trinity College, Hartford. Out of these conferences there arose the New England Association of Colleges and Preparatory Schools formed in 1885. This was followed by the establishment of the Association of Colleges and Preparatory Schools of the Middle States and Maryland in 1892. In 1899 the College Entrance Examination Board was formed to conduct a common entrance examination, the result of which would be generally accepted throughout the country. In the North Central States the need of an organization to promote relations between the secondary schools and colleges of various States was met by the formation of the North Central Association in 1894. Similar associations were established to serve other parts of the country — the Association of Colleges and Preparatory Schools of the Southern States

(1895), and the Northwest Association of Secondary and Higher Schools (1918).

The influence of these associations was local or regional; there was still needed some definition of the scope of secondary education and their relation to colleges which would receive nation-wide recognition. In 1892 the National Education Association appointed a Committee of Ten on Secondary School Studies. The Committee, reporting in 1893, recommended that secondary subjects should be begun earlier; that no distinction should be made between pupils planning to proceed to college and others; that teachers should be better trained; and that flexible and comprehensive courses be organized out of the following major groups of subject proper for secondary schools — languages, mathematics, general history, natural history, physics, and chemistry. The Committee further set up a principle for the equivalence of studies in the sense that all subjects studied for the same length of time under competent teachers are equal to each other. The principle of the equivalence of studies on a time-allotment basis was accepted as the basis of the relations between high schools and colleges by the Committee on College Entrance Requirements which was appointed in 1895 and reported in 1899. Defining the whole high school course in terms of units, the Committee, in order to avoid giving encouragement to unlimited election of subjects, recommended the assignment of a specific number of units to constants (foreign languages, English, mathematics, science, and history).

The time-allotment basis adopted by the two committees meant the acceptance of a quantitative measure as the basis of standardizing the work of the secondary schools, which had already been adopted by the New York State Board of Regents in 1891. The recommendations of the Committee on College Entrance Requirements began to be generally adopted throughout the country after 1906, when the Carnegie Foundation for the Advancement of Teaching employed this ready measure as one method for evaluating college standards. The Foundation's definition of the unit was almost universally accepted, both in colleges and high schools: "a unit is a course of five periods a week throughout an academic year." Besides the quantitative basis for the organization of secondary education, two other principles were enunciated by the Committee on College Entrance Requirements which laid the foundation for the further expansion of secondary education in the United States. The first was:

> Throughout the course of secondary education surely there must be no Procrustean bed which every pupil by some process of dwarfing or stretching must be made to fit, but natural endowments, as soon as discovered, should have full scope, within certain limitations.

The second principle was thus stated:

> The secondary schools are the schools of the people, and the people have demanded and in still more effectual ways will demand, that their courses be practical, beneficial, disciplinary.

THE PRESENT SYSTEM

Differences between European and American concepts of secondary education. The twentieth century opened with the concept of the high school as an institution to meet the needs of the pupils attending it — that is, of adolescent boys and girls — and of the public supporting it. The high school was thus to offer subjects as they were demanded, on the principle that all subjects taught for the same length of time were equal in value. This principle at once furnished an entirely different setting for the further development of secondary education in the United States from that which prevailed in the European countries, where the only result of the period of unrest during the last decade of the nineteenth century had been the grudging recognition of the equivalence of modern with classical languages and of the acceptance of the sciences as proper subjects of a liberal education. Except in England, no provision was made for the expansion of the provision of opportunities for secondary education, which still retained its traditional character of an education for a selected minority. In the case of the American high school, on the other hand, the acceptance of the time-allotment measure opened the door for the admission of a great variety of subjects and aims which in European systems are provided for not in the same but in a variety of institutions differentiated on a functional basis; the American high school is thus, with few exceptions, *par excellence*, the post-elementary school of all its adolescent population. There is the further difference that the high school does not overlap with, but is superimposed upon, the elementary school, and is its natural sequence. There still remained the two problems: first, of considering from as broad a point of view as possible the needs both of the pupils and of the society for which they were to be trained as the basis for the expansion of the curriculum and of courses, and, second, of articulating, more satisfactorily than was the case at the beginning of the century, the elementary and the high school.

Liberal education or the individual. European secondary education is directed to imparting an education which is regarded as liberal or cultural and at the same time as disciplinary in character. The concept of liberal education is approached from the historical or "classical" point of view, as that education which introduces the pupil to the best that has been said and thought in the past. The categories are in a sense absolute and unchanging, and the applications to modern life are expected to be met by the pupil to the extent that his mind is trained. The United States, however, had not built up a strong tradition of liberal education during the nineteenth century and had in fact developed a spirit of realism which was actually opposed to the acceptance of traditions of any kind. This attitude is expressed in the late Professor Inglis's statement in his *Principles of Secondary Education* (1918), that "the terms 'culture' and 'liberal' are purposely avoided here because of their ambiguity in modern educational literature," and that "the indefiniteness and ambiguity of the term 'liberal' renders it profitless to consider the problem in such terms." The American high school thus freed itself at the beginning of the twentieth century of the preconceptions which might lurk in the control of secondary education by the tradition of liberal education, or *culture générale*, or *Allgemeine Bildung*. Starting with a clear sheet, although it is doubtful whether the implications of their respective *Reports* ever occurred to the members of the Committee of Ten or of the Committee on College Entrance Requirements, educators sought, in the reorganization of the high school in the twentieth century, to give reality to the one solid tradition inherited from the nineteenth century — to give a chance to every boy and girl. From this point of view, the individual, rather than any absolute concept of the aim of secondary education, became not only the means but the end of high school reform.

Formal discipline. Another important development helped to undermine the traditional faith in the disciplinary and cultural values of certain subjects usually included in a secondary education. One of the earliest contributions from the recently created laboratories of experimental psychology had been, not merely the complete overthrow of the faculty psychology, but the denial of the validity of the doctrine of formal discipline or transfer of training except under somewhat limited conditions. In other words, an attack was made on the assumption of disciplinary values which had already been claimed by Isocrates and Quintilian, and which had justified the limited secondary school curriculum, more especially from the time of Locke. Disciplinary values, according to this theory, are specific and not general; transfer of training occurs only when there are present, in two or more subjects of instruction, identical elements of content and form. That there is some transfer is not denied, but the real question to be answered was the extent to which it occurs and the method by which it is secured. The problem was thus summarized by Thorndike:

No one can doubt that all of the ordinary forms of home or school training have some influence on mental traits in addition to the specific changes which they make in the particular function the improvement of which is their direct object. On the other hand, no careful observer would assert that the influence upon the other mental traits is comparable in amount to that upon the direct object of training.... The real question is not, "Does improvement of one function alter others?" but, "To what extent, and how, does it?" [1]

The general results of continued experiments showed that the extent of transfer was slight, although more recent studies indicate that the whole problem will probably be reopened.[2] At the time, however, the attack on the disciplinary values fitted in admirably with the temper of the country, which was ready to enter upon an expanded program of secondary education for all and to organize a high school which would meet the diversified demands, not only of those who were planning to enter college, but for all adolescents. The result of the studies of formal discipline and transfer, combined with the quantitative basis of the high school curriculum in terms of units, furnished the "scientific" justification for the introduction of any subject which any group of individuals in any school might

[1] Thorndike, E. L., *The Psychology of Learning*, p. 358 (New York, 1914). See also Thorndike, E. L., *Educational Psychology* (New York, 1910); Heck, W. H., *Mental Discipline and Educational Values* (New York, 1909); and Inglis, A. J., *Principles of Secondary Education*, pp. 394 ff. (Boston, 1918).
[2] Orata, P. T., *Theory of Identical Elements* (Columbus, O., 1928).

demand. That it also undermined any theory of educational values was not noticed for some time.

The public and its schools. Education in European countries, and more particularly secondary education, has in the past been much further removed from the control of the public than in the United States. While there is at present going on in the United States a pronounced movement in the direction of larger areas of control and supervision, the administration of education at the beginning of the century was still provided and administered by the local areas, in which the participation of the public can be not only closer but more exacting. When the time was ripe for the more generous expansion of the opportunities for education beyond the elementary school, the public had to be convinced of the value of the additional expenditure. One consequence, at least, of this interest was that the program of secondary education had to be brought down to the level which the public could understand in terms, not of faith in the value of culture or a liberal education, but of direct and immediate results. The rapidly increasing wealth of the country, which made it possible to dispense with the wages of adolescents or rather to keep them in school beyond the elementary stage, did not relieve administrators of the responsibility of proving that the additional cost of education would yield tangible returns.

Efficiency and education. The same result followed from the application to education of methods employed for testing efficiency in the field of industry. The question which the administrator set himself to answer was whether the pupils already enrolled in the high schools were deriving a reasonable profit from the education provided. Studies of eliminations (or mortality), retention throughout the whole course (at that time four years), and of after-careers immediately following on elimination or graduation from school pointed clearly to the fact that the courses provided were adapted to the needs and aptitudes of only a minority of the pupils enrolled in the high schools.[1] Refusing to accept the European principle

---

[1] See in particular Inglis, A. J., *Principles of Secondary Education*, Ch. IV (Boston, 1918), and Koos, L. V., *The American Secondary School*, Ch. III (New York, 1927). So far as is known to the author, this method of investigating whether the secondary school courses are adapted to the needs and aptitudes of the pupils has been employed outside of the United States only by the Director of Education of the West Riding of Yorkshire (see County Council of the West Riding of Yorkshire, Education Department, *Alternative Courses in*

of *caveat alumnus*, the American administrator proceeded to reorganize the courses of the high schools in such a way that every pupil would find something suited to his needs and abilities.

The new psychology and philosophy of education. In 1907 appeared G. Stanley Hall's monumental work on *Adolescence* (preceded in 1906 by *Youth*), which focussed attention and which threw a flood of light on the period of adolescence as a period of physical and mental growth and of new and changing interests. The appearance of Hall's work stimulated a series of special investigations into the physiological and psychological meaning of adolescence. Not the least important contribution made by Hall was his analysis of the social changes and interests produced by the growing urban environment resulting from the rapid industrial developments, as contrasted with life in a predominantly agricultural environment. The studies of adolescence exercised a profound influence on organization and administration, subject-matter, methods, and discipline in secondary education.[1]

From the point of view of educational philosophy, the strongest influence in redirecting the aims of American education has been that of John Dewey. His general thesis that education is life and not preparation for life, that the function of the school is to foster the growth of the pupils along the lines of their interests rather than to impart subjects that may be of value to them later, and that the aim of education is social, created a revolution in American thought and gave philosophical interpretation to trends that had already manifested themselves. Accordingly, the principles upon which secondary education has been built emphasize the present needs and the growth of the pupils, instead of some future needs; to include subjects in the curriculum because of some assumed deferred values is to court failure; and everything that is taught must have immediate value commensurate with the time devoted to it. On the side both of method and content this theory has been sup-

---

Secondary Schools, 1927). It has also been suggested in Sir Michael Sadler's discussion of "Examinations" in the *New Era*, January, 1929. If only some sixty per cent of the candidates pass the first examination in English secondary schools (a certain percentage leave without attempting it), then the argument would be that the schools concerned are not meeting the standards set up for them, or, alternatively, that the examinations are unsound, or, again, that the instruction may be inadequate. From the American point of view, French secondary education, in which less than fifty per cent of the candidates succeed in passing the *baccalauréat*, must assume the responsibility for those who fail.

[1] Inglis, *op. cit.*, Chs. I to III; Koos, *op. cit.*, Ch. II.

plemented by the psychologist's enunciation of the laws of learning in terms of readiness, effect, and practice.[1]

Education and national wealth. The expansion of facilities for secondary education was made possible, not only because of the traditional faith in education and the equalization of opportunities, but by the remarkable increase of the country's wealth, which rose from $89,000,000,000 in 1900, to $321,000,000,000 in 1922 — an increase unparalleled in the history of the world. Even if due allowance is made for the fluctuation in the value of the dollar, this rise represents an increase of about one hundred per cent. The annual income of the American people showed an equal growth from $27,000,000,000 in 1909, to $91,000,000,000 in 1929. Although only a small fraction of this wealth was devoted to education, it nevertheless made possible a remarkable development in the provision of high schools, the number of these rising from 6005 schools and an enrollment of 519,251 pupils (216,207 boys and 303,044 girls) in 1900, to 22,237 schools and an enrollment of 5,212,179 pupils (2,522,816 boys and 2,689,363 girls) in 1930. To these figures should be added 1978 private secondary schools with an enrollment of 110,797 pupils (55,734 boys and 55,063 girls) in 1900, and 2760 schools with an enrollment of 309,052 pupils (146,517 boys and 162,535 girls) in 1930. The increased enrollment of pupils has been due, not merely to the increase in wealth and the desire of parents and the public to give every boy and girl a chance, but also to the increased complexity of the new industrial age. The rapid development of the utilization of machinery and labor-saving devices has made it possible for industry to dispense with the labor of young persons, so that few boys or girls can obtain employment, under the age of sixteen, that is in any way promising for their future.

Provision and organization of high schools. Except that the American high school is a part of the common school system and is the natural sequence to the elementary school, there is no legal definition of it, as there is of secondary education in other countries. Since it has become the school of all adolescents, it is equally difficult to distinguish the high school by types, although a general distinction between the rural and city high school may be made. In the larger centers there may be found special high schools — technical and commercial — but such a distinction is unpopular

[1] Inglis, *op. cit.*, Ch. I; Koos, *op. cit.*, Ch. II.

and the tendency is overwhelmingly in favor of the so-called "cosmopolitan" or "comprehensive" high school, which undertakes to meet the varied needs of a large clientèle.

The traditional high school, which is still the form most frequently found, is an institution providing four years of education beyond the elementary school. Because of the rapid transition from the elementary to the four-year high school and the difficulties of adjustment imposed on the pupils, and because of the recognition that the psychological changes associated with the beginning of adolescence involve changes of interests and methods before the normal age of entrance into the four-year high school, a redivision of the educational ladder at about the age of twelve began to be urged at the close of the nineteenth century. From another point of view it was realized that there were advantages in beginning certain subjects at an earlier age than was possible in the four-year high school.

The junior high school. In 1888 President Eliot had suggested the desirability of a reorganization of the high school, and in 1893 the Committee of Ten, and in 1899 the Committee on College Entrance Requirements, had also recommended a redivision of elementary and secondary education into two six-year periods, instead of the prevailing division into eight and four years. As a result of these recommendations, which continued to be urged by the Committee of Five of the National Education Association in 1907, 1908, and 1909, a number of cities soon began to reorganize their educational systems, but introduced a further division in the secondary school resulting in the 6-3-3 plan — six years of elementary education, and three years in the junior and three years in the senior high school. Junior high schools were established in Columbus (Ohio) in 1908, Berkeley (California) and Concord (New Hampshire) in 1910, and Los Angeles in 1911. Variations of this plan have been adopted, but in general the 6-3-3 became the more usual form. The movement for reorganization was slow, but by 1930 there were 1842 separately organized junior high schools and 3287 schools with a junior-senior organization. This development has meant the increased retention of boys and girls in school up to the age of fifteen, or one year beyond the usual age for completing the elementary school.[1]

[1] On the junior high school see Briggs, T. H., *Junior High School* (Boston, 1920); Koos, L. V., *Junior High School* (New York, 1927); and Smith, W. A., *Junior High School* (New York, 1925).

The provision of high schools is in general left to the discretion of local administrative areas; only in Vermont and Massachusetts is it mandatory. The development of the provision began with the granting of permission through state laws to cities, towns, and districts to tax themselves for the maintenance and support of high schools. The next stage was the granting of permission to smaller units to combine for the provision of high schools. This was followed by a movement for the extension of administrative areas and the organization of the county as the unit for educational purposes. Finally, the development of adequate opportunities for education beyond the elementary school has been stimulated by the award of special aid by the State. From the point of view of maintenance and support, there is thus to be found a variety of different types of high schools, according as they are provided by a city, a township, a consolidated district (a combination of districts created for high school purposes), a union township, a county, and other combinations of small or large and small administrative units. The equalization of opportunities for high school education has taken the form of free transportation to the nearest available school, the payment of the cost of tuition by a non-high school district to the high school attended by its pupils, the establishment of free dormitories where free lodging is provided, the pupil paying for board at a modest rate.[1] The result is an expansion of facilities for post-elementary education which is unparalleled in any other part of the world. The distribution of these facilities is illustrated by the large number of small schools. Thus, of 22,237 public high schools in 1930 more than one fourth (26.7 per cent) had less than 50 pupils each and yet they enrolled only 3.4 per cent of the pupils in high schools (5,212,179 pupils); 54 per cent of the schools had less than 100 pupils each and enrolled a little over 12 per cent of the pupils. By contrast with the large number of small high schools, almost 5 per cent of the schools had more than 1000 pupils each and enrolled nearly 39 per cent of all the pupils, while more than half of the pupils were in schools with an enrollment of more than 500 pupils each (11.3 per cent of the schools). The average number of pupils enrolled in all the high schools in 1930 was 234. It was estimated in the same year that 47.2 per cent of all the boys and girls

---

[1] See Johnston, C. H., *The Modern High School*, Ch. III (New York, 1916); and Butterworth, J. E., *Problems in State High School Finance* (Yonkers-on-Hudson, 1918).

in the country between the ages of fifteen and eighteen inclusive were enrolled in the high schools. The extension of opportunities, for post-elementary education has applied, although to a far more limited degree, to colored pupils, whose enrollment in high schools, separate in the Southern States, has increased from 8395 in 1900 to 118,897 in 1930. With the negligible exception of about 100 schools, the high schools of the country are coeducational. The reorganization of the high school into a six-year institution, divided into two three-year periods, is proceeding rapidly. In 1930 there were 1842 junior high schools, 3287 junior-senior high schools, and 648 senior high schools, a total of 5777 reorganized high schools out of the total of 22,237 schools. There were thus 16,460 regular high schools of which 13,876 offered the four-year courses, and the remainder three years of work.

The opportunities for secondary education are provided at public expense and of all the pupils receiving this type of education 94.4 per cent attend public schools. As compared with the enrollment of 5,212,179 pupils in public high schools, there were only 309,052 pupils in private high schools and academies, the majority of which (78.5 per cent) are denominational in character.

Standardization. The greatest variety prevails in the methods of providing and maintaining high schools, in size, in length of the course, in length of the school year, in the preparation, certification and remuneration of teachers, and in standards of achievement. The one common element throughout the country is the desire to provide equality of opportunity for all. The common European practice of standardization by means of examinations under the control and supervision of ministries of education, or conducted by recognized boards as in England, is unknown except in New York State, where examinations are conducted by the Board of Regents. The examination system of the College Entrance Examination Board affects but an infinitesimal number of the pupils enrolled in high schools (22,724 in 1929), while entrance examinations have in general been retained mainly in the Eastern colleges.

The place of standardization by examination of the product is taken by measures to standardize the high schools by insistence on external requirements. This is effected by various agencies — by the state authority, by the state university, by regional associations. The State exercises its influence by setting up the conditions under which special aid is granted and by means of inspection, the purpose of which is to see that the conditions of the grants are met. The state universities set up standards for the high schools in respect of the admission of their graduates to the colleges. In some States the state authorities and the state universities coöperate in the employment of the same inspectors; high schools which are found to be satisfactory are placed upon the accredited list of the State or the university concerned or on both. In some States the universities accredit or certify high schools on the basis of the achievements of their graduates. These methods of standardization affect only the high schools within a single State. In order to provide wider areas for standardization, there have been organized regional associations (see p. 795) which exercise a strong influence over the high schools of a number of States. The chief among these are the Association of Colleges and Secondary Schools of the Middle States and Maryland, the North Central Association, the Association of Colleges and Secondary Schools, the New England Association of Colleges and Secondary Schools, and the Northwest Association of Secondary and Higher Schools. There are thus available at least three lists of accredited high schools — those of state departments, those of state universities, and those of interstate or regional associations. Not all high schools are found on all the three lists.

The standards which are usually set up for accrediting high schools deal with the buildings and equipment, the length of term, the course of study, the number of qualifications of teachers, library and laboratory facilities, the teaching load or the number of hours of teaching assigned to each teacher, and the definition of a unit of work. Despite certain variations affecting chiefly the requirements for admission to different colleges, there is developing a tendency toward some uniformity. Thus the National Conference Committee on Standards of Colleges and Secondary Schools, representing a number of national and regional associations, has set up the following standard of measurement for high schools:

A unit represents a year's study in any subject in a secondary school, constituting approximately a quarter of a full year's work.

This statement is designed to afford a standard of measurement for the work done in secondary schools. It takes —

(1) The four-year high school course as a basis and assumes that —

(2) The length of the school year is from thirty-six to forty weeks; that —
(3) A period is from forty to sixty minutes in length; and that —
(4) The study is pursued four or five periods a week;
but under ordinary circumstances a satisfactory year's work in any subject cannot be accomplished in less than 120 sixty-minute hours, or their equivalent. Schools organized on any other than a four-year basis can, nevertheless, estimate their work in terms of this unit.

A four-year secondary school curriculum should be regarded as representing not more than sixteen units of work.[1]

This statement represents the only uniform standard which is common to the various standardizing agencies.

On other points there is considerable variety, the standards of the state agencies being as a rule lower than those of the regional associations. Thus, while the former may in some cases recognize high schools with only two teachers, the North Central Association will accredit only schools with a minimum of five teachers, four of whom must be full-time teachers of academic subjects. On the preparation of teachers there is general unanimity that high school teachers should be college graduates and should have taken a number of courses in education. Although California has been able to go beyond it and to require a year of graduate work for the certification of teachers of academic subjects, this standard is far from being reached. More serious than this defect are the uncertainty and vagueness of the certification requirements in most states and even of the definition of teachers' qualifications prepared by the regional associations. The vagueness of standards is indicated in the following table:

METHODS AND STANDARDS IN CERTIFICATING HIGH SCHOOL TEACHERS AND NUMBER OF STATES USING EACH [2]

METHOD AND STANDARD	NUMBER OF STATES USING
College graduation	45
Equivalent of college course	5
Partial college course	15
Normal school graduation (two years' course)	27
Partial normal course	9
Examination only	16

[1] See U.S. Office of Education Bulletin, 1930, No. 24, *Accredited Secondary Schools in the United States* (Washington, D.C., 1930).
[2] Lowery, M. L., *Certification of High School Teachers* (Philadelphia, 1924).

Although these figures are for 1923, the probability is that the situation has not changed much. It is only recently that the North Central Association, whose standards are generally recognized to be higher than those of any other standardizing agency, has changed a former vague requirement that "teachers shall so far as possible teach only those subjects which they have taught in college" to the requirement that they "must teach in the fields of their major and minor specialization in college preparation." The majority of the States prescribe no academic requirements other than college graduation as a condition for certification. In other words, a teacher may receive a high school teaching certificate which enables him to teach any subject which may be assigned to him. Even where major or minor subjects are required, the vagueness is not removed, since the graduation requirements of colleges vary so much. Few States insist that teachers must be specially qualified in certain subjects or combinations of subjects in order to obtain a teaching certificate. The result is that, while the majority of high school teachers are college graduates, a large number may be found teaching subjects which they themselves never studied in college. These conditions do not apply in the larger urban systems which have their own regulations for certification.

Beyond this, certain standards of general efficiency are set up and are measured by inspection. While the standards are in themselves adequate, inspection is too often infrequent and cursory, except when conducted for the first time to determine the eligibility of a high school to a place on an accredited list. The standards of the North Central Association are as follows:

The efficiency of instruction, the acquired habits of thought and study, the general intellectual and moral tone of a school and the coöperative attitude of the community are paramount factors, and therefore only schools that rank well in these particulars, as evidenced by rigid, thorough-going, sympathetic inspection, shall be considered eligible for the list.

The requirements concerning the program of studies except as they bear on college entrance are nowhere clearly defined. Generally there is recommended, in addition to academic subjects, the introduction of vocational subjects such as agriculture, manual training, household economics, and of commercial subjects into schools where local conditions render such introduction possible. The requirements for admission to colleges of liberal arts in state universities show little uniformity except in English, mathematics, and foreign languages. The number of units of electives which are accepted ranges from three to ten.

Aims of secondary education. The vagueness which is manifest in the standards set up by the various agencies concerned with the subject is parallelled not so much by a vagueness of aims and purposes as by multiplicity. As contrasted with the French aim of *culture générale*, the German aim of *Bildung zum Deutschtum*, and the English aim of character-formation, the high school in the United States suffers from a plethora of objectives without any single aim to give color and character to each. The danger is always present that in aiming at a large number of targets, none of them will be hit. This is due perhaps to two causes. The first is that, as contrasted with the European countries, there is an absence of a dominating tradition of intellectual culture, or, if it may be expressed more broadly, a dominating object of allegiance. The second is the fact that the American high school is still in a stage of transition with a development which has been too rapid to be held within the bounds of a single aim.

The various trends and influences which were responsible for this transition from the last decade of the nineteenth century on were brought to a focus in 1913, when the National Education Association appointed a Commission on the Reorganization of Secondary Education, for the following purposes:

1. To formulate statements of valid aims, efficient methods, and kinds of materials whereby each subject may best serve the needs of high school pupils.
2. To enable the inexperienced teacher to secure at the outset a correct point of view.
3. To place the needs of the high school before all agencies that are training teachers for positions in high schools.
4. To secure college entrance recognition for courses that meet the needs of high school pupils.

The Commission consisted of the following committees — English, social studies, natural sciences, modern languages, ancient languages, household arts, manual arts, music, business, agriculture, a committee on articulation of high school and college, and a reviewing committee. Each of these committees later published their *Reports*, which were issued by the United States Bureau of

Education. Subjects on which these committees did not report were dealt with by independent organizations: the National Committee on Mathematical Requirements of the Mathematical Association issued a *Report on the Reorganization of Mathematics in Secondary Education* in 1923; the Advisory Committee of the American Classical League published its *Classical Investigation* in 1925; the *Reports on Modern Language Teaching* prepared by the American and Canadian Committees on Modern Languages were issued in 1929 and 1930.

The Commission on the Reorganization of Secondary Education issued a general report, in 1918, on *Cardinal Principles of Secondary Education*,[1] in which the basic principles were laid down that secondary education should be determined: (1) by the needs of the society to be served; (2) by the character of the individuals to be educated; and (3) by the knowledge of educational theory and practice available. The Commission drew attention to the growing complexity of community life, and the relations of the individual to state, national, and international affairs; it stressed the development of specialization in industry; and it noted the importance of training for leisure. It summarized the problems of secondary education in two statements:

1. The purpose of democracy is so to organize society that each member may develop his personality primarily through activities designed for the well-being of his fellow-members and of society as a whole.
2. Education in a democracy, both within and without the school, should develop in each individual the knowledge, interests, ideals, habits, and powers whereby he will find his place and use that place to shape both himself and society toward ever nobler ends.

To promote these ends, the curricula of the high schools should be so organized as to meet the following objectives: (1) health; (2) command of fundamental processes; (3) worthy home-membership; (4) vocation; (5) civic education; (6) worthy use of leisure; and (7) ethical character. These objectives gained immediate and wide acceptance and, although they were intended to serve as points for the interrelation of subject-matter and to promote education as a unitary and continuous process, no marked effect followed in the making of courses of study.

Because this statement of objectives appeared too comprehensive

---

[1] U.S. Bureau of Education, Bulletin, 1918, No. 35 (Washington, D.C.).

for a full consideration of the obligations of secondary education, Professor Koos essayed a comprehensive portrait of aims and functions of secondary education, based on published statements of leaders in education. He found the aims and functions of secondary education stated in the following order:

Civic social responsibility, occupational efficiency, recreational and æsthetic participation, individual differences, general or liberal training, physical efficiency, democratic secondary education, college preparation, exploration and guidance, religious training, recognizing adolescence, meeting life's needs, domestic responsibility, intellectual efficiency, training in fundamental processes, training for leadership, selection for higher education, mental discipline, training the senses, and community service.

These statements Koos further formulates into four aims: (1) civic-social-moral responsibility; (2) recreational and æsthetic participation and appreciation; (3) occupational efficiency (including preparation for higher institutions); and (4) physical efficiency. The functions he listed as follows: (1) achieving a democratic secondary education; (2) recognizing individual differences; (3) providing for exploration and guidance; (4) recognizing the adolescent nature of pupils; (5) imparting knowledge and skills in the fundamental processes; and (6) fostering transfer of training (with guarded acceptance).

It will be noticed how far such a statement has advanced beyond the European concept of the aims and functions of secondary education. Fundamentally it represents the recognition that a democratic system of education must be conceived in as broad terms as possible. It avoids any attempt to consider the meaning of liberal education or culture, and rests on a vague optimism that the cause of culture may be advanced if the material needs of the individual and of society are assured. The statement is, however, more definite and objective than that of the Commission on the Reorganization of Secondary Education. At least it is clear that the American high school is intended to cater to the needs of all, and not to select the few who can profit from and appreciate the meaning of a liberal education defined in traditional terms. That the high school is successful in reaching an increasing percentage of the adolescents of the country is shown by the fact that nearly fifty per cent of the boys and girls of the ages of fifteen, sixteen, seventeen, and eighteen were enrolled in public high schools in 1930. That the high school is still selective in character is not due to its aims, but to social conditions which have not yet been attacked,[1] for despite the fact that tuition is free certain groups at the lower end of the economic scale cannot afford to dispense with the wages of their children. Up to the present the provision of maintenance grants for poor but able pupils has not been suggested, although here and there scholarships are provided by private effort.

The aims of the junior high school have been summarized as follows by Professor Thomas H. Briggs:

> First, to continue, in so far as it may seem wise and possible, and in a gradually diminishing degree, common, integrating education; second, to ascertain and reasonably to satisfy pupils' important immediate and assured future needs; third, to explore, by means of material in itself worth while, the interests, aptitudes, and capacities of pupils; fourth, to reveal to them, by material otherwise justifiable, the possibilities in the major fields of learning; and, fifth, to start each pupil on the career which, as a result of the exploratory courses, he, his parents, and the school are convinced is most likely to be of profit to him and to the State.[2]

In general the American attitude which has determined the provision of equality of educational opportunities is indicated in two other statements of Professor Briggs:

> A successful and progressive democracy is possible only if the people make provision for the education of youth not only in the accepted rules of conduct but also in such ways that they may contribute to their improvement. This means all youth, each one made maximally competent according to his natural gifts.[3]

> Education is, then, provided by the State in its own interests, for education is a long-term investment that the State may be a better place in which to live and a better place in which to earn a living.[4]

The curricula of the high schools. The curricula of the high schools reflect the aims and influences which have in the past twenty years combined to affect the American concept of secondary education. As soon as the concept of formal disciplinary training of the mind was discarded, it became essential to discover new psychological bases for the selection of subject-matter; for indirect and remote values there has been substituted an emphasis on the direct and

---

[1] See Counts, G. S., *The Selective Character of American Secondary Education* (Chicago, 1922).

[2] Briggs, T. H., *The Junior High School*, p. 26 (Boston, Houghton Mifflin Co., 1920).

[3] Briggs, T. H., *The Great Investment. Secondary Education in a Democracy*, p. 142 (Cambridge, Massachusetts, 1930).

[4] *Ibid.*, p. 8.

intrinsic outcomes of the subject-matter studied by the pupils and on its immediate effects on habits and conduct. The recognition of individual differences, intensified by the rapid increase in the number proceeding to the high schools, led to an expansion of subjects to meet the varied interests and capacities of the pupils, a result to which the realization that all pupils would not proceed to college also contributed. Another factor which led to a further expansion of the curricula was the recognition of the importance of practical subjects serving the ends both of liberal and vocational education. Finally, the establishment of the junior high school, which means in effect the beginning of secondary education two years earlier than had been traditional in the United States, imposed on the schools such an expansion and reorganization of subjects as would help to carry out the exploratory and guidance functions of this type of school. The change in the relations between the high school and college, introduced by the wide spread of systems of accrediting and certification, has left the high school freer to adopt flexible and elastic programs of study, although it has not yet eliminated entirely certain criticisms of college entrance requirements. In general, the organization of high school curricula is governed by the three following principles formulated by the Commission on the Reorganization of Secondary Education in its *Report on the Cardinal Principles of Secondary Education*:

> The purpose of democracy is so to organize society that each member may develop his personality primarily through activities designed for the well-being of his fellow members and of society as a whole.... Consequently, education in a democracy, both within and without the school, should develop in each individual the knowledge, interests, ideals, habits, and powers whereby he will find his place and use that place to shape both himself and society toward ever nobler ends.

> The doctrine that each individual has a right to the opportunity to develop the best that is in him is reinforced by the belief in the potential, and perchance unique, worth of the individual. The task of education, as of life, is therefore to call forth that potential worth. While seeking to evoke the distinctive excellence of individuals and groups of individuals, the secondary school must be equally zealous to develop those common ideas, common ideals, and common modes of thought, feeling, and action, whereby America through a rich, unified, common life, may render her truest service to a world seeking for democracy among men and nations.

The result of these forces has been a rapid expansion in the list of subjects offered by the high schools. The programs offer as wide a variety of studies as is justified by the capacities and needs of the pupils and the ability of the community to provide them. The curricula are so organized as to ensure a proper balance in accordance with the aims and objectives of secondary education and to enable the pupil to secure the maximum benefit from his stay in school. Hence, as much flexibility as possible is provided, even in smaller and inadequately staffed schools, so that the necessary adjustments can be made by the pupil with a minimum loss of time. As far as possible, differentiation is secured along the lines of significant differences in the careers which pupils are preparing to enter. For the foreigner it is impossible to understand the high school unless he realizes that it is the school for all adolescents and that it performs the functions which, outside of the United States, with very few exceptions, are performed by the secondary school, the higher elementary, middle, or central school, and a variety of trade and vocational schools. It is this fact which explains the current statement that the high schools of the country offer more than three hundred courses.[1] The high school with a specific aim, such as commercial, agricultural, or vocational, is the exception. Of one hundred and fifty-two school systems in 1928, one hundred and thirty-two had the comprehensive form of organization, three the separate plan, and seventeen both.[2]

The function of the junior high school, which includes the seventh, eighth, and ninth grades for pupils from about the age of twelve on, whether organized separately or as a part of the six-year high school, is to provide opportunities for the pupil and the school to discover those subjects best adapted to his interests and abilities; the three years are regarded as an exploratory or "testing-out" period. While the subjects common to a high school education have served to form the nucleus of the curricula, important changes have been made in their organization by bringing several branches of one large field of study together and reorganizing the content on a new basis. This has resulted in such courses as "general mathematics," "general science," "general English," and here and there "general language" courses. The general tendency is to organize a core curriculum with elective subjects; certain subjects such as

[1] The United States Office of Education, Bulletin, 1929, No. 35, pp. 7 ff., announced two hundred and fifty courses in 1926–28.

[2] Department of Superintendence, *Sixth Yearbook, The Development of the High School Curriculum*, 1928, p. 61.

SECONDARY EDUCATION

English, mathematics, social studies, and science must be taken by all pupils, while other subjects are elected on the basis of interest, capacity, or expected needs. The subjects which are generally found in junior high schools are given in the following table:[1]

Mathematics
  Algebra
  Arithmetic
  General mathematics
  Geometry

English
  Grammar
  Language and composition
  Penmanship
  Reading
  Spelling

Science
  Biology
  Botany
  Physiology
  Zoölogy
  Physiography
  General science
  Science

Social Studies
  American history
  Ancient history
  English history
  General history
  Medieval history
  Modern history
  Civics
  Geography

Foreign languages
  Latin
  French
  German
  Spanish

Commercial subjects
  Bookkeeping
  Commercial arithmetic
  Commercial geography
  Stenography
  Typewriting

Fine and practical arts
  Drawing
  Music
  Agriculture
  Cooking
  Sewing
  General shop
  Industrial arts
  Mechanical drawing
  Printing
  Sheet metal work
  Woodworking

Physical education and health
  Athletics
  Calisthenics
  Hygiene
  Nursing
  Physical education
  Sanitation
  Sex hygiene

In the regular four-year high schools and in the senior high schools which continue the junior high schools for three additional years, the same principles of curriculum-making are employed, but with

[1] Quoted from Monroe, W. S., and Herriott, M. E., *Reconstruction of the Secondary-School Curriculum: Its Meaning and Trends.* University of Illinois Bulletin, 1928, No. 41, pp. 82 f.

increasing differentiation. The earlier practice of complete free election of subjects has disappeared, and all pupils are expected to take a certain number of constants or common subjects. The constants are generally English and social studies, although the requirements for college entrance include the addition of such subjects as foreign languages, sciences, and mathematics.

The methods of constructing curricula vary. In some schools pupils may select from a large number of curricula, in which all subjects are prescribed; in others the curricula are made up of constants and variables — that is, of subjects which all pupils are required to take — and subjects which are elected according to the pupil's needs and capacities, usually with the advice of teachers and principals, or of some member of the faculty to whom the position of counselor and adviser is specifically assigned. In no case, however, must the advice offered on the selection of curricula compulsorily be followed; even where advice is based on tests specifically designed to discover the intelligence and capacities of the pupils, it is found that other factors enter which weigh more with both pupils and parents in reaching a final decision.

As an example of the first type of organization, the curricula offered in the Los Angeles High Schools may be cited. They are: agriculture, art, drafting, engineering preparatory, home economics, literary, music, scientific, social science, accounting, salesmanship, automobile industry, building industry, electrical industry, mechanic arts, printing, and elective.[1] In Detroit the high schools offer thirty-one different curricula, as follows:[2]

Architectural drawing	Dietetics	Merchandising
Art	Electricity	Metallurgy
Automotive construction	Engineering (general)	Music (general)
Aviation	Engineering (preparatory)	Music (vocational)
Building construction	Hospital work	Nursing (preparatory)
Cafeteria management	Hotel work	Occupational therapy
Chemistry (industrial)	Home economics	Pottery
College preparatory	Jewelry design	Printing
Commerce	Laundry work	Science
Commercial art	Mechanic arts	Shop (technical)
Costume design		

[1] Counts, G. S., *The Senior High School Curriculum* (Chicago, 1926).
[2] Department of Superintendence, *Sixth Yearbook, The Development of the High School Curriculum*, 1928, p. 68.

The variety of courses, while not so great in small high schools with an enrollment of one hundred pupils or less, still illustrates the same attempt to meet the needs of all types of interests and capacities. The following table gives the titles of courses found in two hundred such small high schools and their frequency:

College preparatory	186	Scientific	3
Normal school preparatory	92	English	2
Commercial	65	Academic	1
Agricultural	53	Classical	1
Vocational, industrial, and manual training	44	Engineering	1
		Latin-scientific	1
Home economics, domestic art	11	Life of the average individual	1
General	8		

The difficulties involved in the attempt to carry out logically the principle of adapting curricula and courses to the assumed interests and needs of the pupils become obvious when it is remembered that of the 22,237 high schools reported in 1929–30, 12,007, or 54 per cent, were small schools with an enrollment of less than one hundred pupils and employing six teachers or less; in 1927–28, 5512, or 30.4 per cent, of the schools had less than three teachers. With such small staffs of teachers the attempt is made to offer from twenty-two to thirty-seven subjects, a situation which, when combined with the indefinite requirements for the certification of high school teachers, results in many teachers being required to teach subjects in which they have had no preparation, in many teachers being assigned subjects which have no conceivable relation to each other, and in many teachers being unduly overburdened. The following table illustrates the results at once of the attempt to provide as large a number of subjects to meet the needs of the pupils and of the inadequacy of certification requirements, since a single teacher is expected to teach each combination cited:[1]

Combinations	Number of Different Subjects Taught
Civics, English, general science, history, Latin, mathematics, science	7
Economics, English, general science, history, mathematics, penmanship, psychology	7
Agriculture, general science, manual training, mathematics, physical education, science	6

[1] Department of Superintendence, *Sixth Yearbook*, p. 101 (Washington, D.C., 1928).

Combinations	Number of Different Subjects Taught
Agriculture, bookkeeping, general science, geography, manual training, physical education..................	6
Bookkeeping, club, economics, English, history, Latin...	6
Chapel, civics, club, general science, history, Latin.....	6
Civics, domestic science, English, general science, history, Latin......................................	6
English, general science, history, mathematics, physiology, Spanish.....................................	6
French, general science, mathematics, music, physical education, science.................................	6
Agriculture, commercial law, English, general science, physical education...............................	5
Agriculture, economics, English, history, physical education..	5
Agriculture, English, history, Latin, psychology.........	5
Agriculture, general science, glee club, history, manual training....................................	5
Agriculture, history, manual training, science, Spanish..	5
Athletics, history, Latin, mathematics, science..........	5
Bookkeeping, civics, English, French, history...........	5
Bookkeeping, Italian, music, physical education, Spanish	5
Civics, general science, history, Latin, physical education	5
Domestic science, English, mathematics, science, Spanish	5
Geography, Latin, manual training, mathematics, science	5

These conditions are still further aggravated by the instability of the teachers themselves, who change positions with the frequency offered by opportunity. "Teachers in small high schools are notoriously young — not infrequently a third are not old enough to vote; inexperienced — sixteen to twenty per cent are beginners and almost half have not taught more than three years; transitory — about forty per cent change positions annually; unprepared — approximately fifty per cent are not college graduates."[1] While conditions are considerably better in the larger city systems, a number of factors which are detrimental to a successful education are common to all high schools. In the first place, the form master of the English schools or the class teacher of the European schools, responsible for a reasonable combination of allied subjects and for the general supervision of the pupil, is not found in American

[1] Bachman, F. P., *Training and Certification of High School Teachers*, p. 66 (Nashville, 1930).

schools. An attempt to correct this deficiency has been made by the organization in the larger schools of "home rooms" under the charge of a teacher responsible for the personal, educational, and social guidance of the pupils assigned to her, but it is doubtful whether the assembly of pupils in the home room, for perhaps thirty minutes a day at most, can ever be as effective as the constant supervision and guidance under a competent teacher for several hours a day. At best the home room can only serve the same ends which are sought in some English day schools by the organization of "houses" — that is, the promotion of activities known as extra-curricular.

Another factor common to all high schools is the discontinuity of the curricular organization which results from the quantitative measure. Except English — and this is not universal — no pupil is required to carry a subject continuously throughout his high school course, whether it is four or six years in length. Measured quantitatively a complete four-year course consists of fifteen units of study (a unit representing a year's study in any subject for four or five periods a week). An average program may include: English, four units; social studies, two units; mathematics, one unit; science, one unit — eight units in all, leaving seven units to be selected from a variety of subjects. Hence it is the unit rather than the richness and potentiality of a subject which is the measure, and frequently continuity may be sacrificed to administrative considerations arising out of the time-schedule. With such an organization conducted by teachers, each responsible for his own subject, it becomes almost impossible to develop programs of study which are closely interrelated and integrated. The assumption that the needs of the pupils will provide the necessary integration is nothing more than an assumption. The desirability of some form of integration is recognized in the grouping of branches of the same subject under one caption, such as "general mathematics," "general science," "social studies," "general language course," but this fails to provide that larger integration which might come from a broad cultural aim, such as is found in France in *culture générale* or in Germany in *Bildung zum Deutschtum*, or even that personal integration which is found in England in the assignment of certain groups of subjects to a form master. The organization of curricula into units, besides resulting in isolation and discreteness of subjects, has the further disadvantage of failing to provide for the continuous pursuit of subjects for a period of years with the opportunity of enrichment and grasp which comes with maturity. The quantitative measure may be a useful method of organization from the point of view of bookkeeping, but it has no place in an educational scheme. Combined with the emphasis on individual needs and interests, the unit system is responsible for a certain shirking of the problem of educational values, so that a unit of stenography is as valuable as a unit of English, and a unit of penmanship and business writing has the same value as a unit of history or of a foreign language. The justification of the principles upon which the quantitative measure and the expansion of the courses offered by the high school are based is that only in this way can the needs, interests, and capacities of the pupils be met; a narrowly prescribed curriculum of the type found in European schools offers a Procrustean bed. The combination of a system of guidance and flexible adaptation of curricula should guarantee a large measure of success on the part of the pupils. And yet there is adequate evidence that this is not achieved. "The second count of the indictment," says Professor Briggs in discussing the American high schools, "would be that there has been no respectable achievement, even in the subjects offered in the secondary school curricula. Evidence on this count is abundant in scientific documents, especially in those that present results of standardized objectives" — in such subjects as mathematics, Latin, modern foreign languages, history and English.[1] The poor results which are found by examinations, objective tests, and the work of freshmen in college, instead of serving as a basis for a correction of defects, are used as an excuse to criticize the subjects concerned or to substitute new subjects "more meaningful" to the pupils. Since the unit system gives the pupil an opportunity of maneuvering his way around from subject to subject, he is exposed to many and becomes master of none. It is doubtful whether satisfactory results can ever be expected from two years devoted to Latin or French, the average amount of time devoted to these subjects. The emphasis on immediate returns for time spent on a subject has led to a neglect of the cumulative value of study and education and

[1] See Briggs, T. H., *The Great Investment in Secondary Education in a Democracy*, pp. 124 ff. (Boston, 1930). See also in this connection the reports of the Carnegie Foundation on the *Study of the Relations of Secondary and Higher Education in Pennsylvania* (New York, 1931).

the stress on the quantitative measure has tended to an underestimate of the place and function of a well-trained teacher. And yet the American high school pupil enjoys many advantages over the European. He is freed from the pressure, social and economic, which comes from the system of privileges; he is given more advice and guidance; in his studies he is not left to his own devices, but is given definite training and supervision both in and out of school; and in most schools he has library facilities which are unsurpassed elsewhere.

The unit, however, is for the country as a whole the only standard which is at present available. The standardizing and accrediting agencies devote their attentions in the main to what may be called the external fabric of the school. Except in New York State the practice of external examinations is unknown. Hence each teacher is responsible for the standards of attainment in his class. In view of the absence of standards in the preparation and certification of teachers, it is obvious that uniformity of qualitative standards cannot be expected and is in fact not found. Whatever may be said in criticism of external examinations, they would appear to be better than no standards at all until all teachers have had such preparation and until certification standards are such that teachers can be trusted to conduct their own examinations without the pressure which inevitably attends even the best-organized system of external examinations.

Since the aims of the American high school and the European secondary schools differ so markedly, it may be hazardous to attempt to institute comparisons. If, however, the work in academic subjects be compared, a basis of comparison is available. The American pupil who graduates from a four-year academic course will have attained approximately the standard expected for the First Schools Examination in England which pupils generally take at about the age of sixteen. Committees on equivalents, appointed some time ago by the American Council on Education, recommended that the graduates of French and German secondary schools should be admitted to the junior year of an American college, and the same would probably apply to English pupils who have obtained the certificate of the Second Examination. Of course, it may be objected that the European pupils are selected in a variety of ways and that the American high school seeks to cater to the average.

Provision for bright pupils. It has been widely recognized in recent years that the provisions for the bright and capable pupils in the American high school have been inadequate and that the first two years of college work are secondary in character. A variety of practices have been adopted to meet the needs of the bright pupils. The most general practice is the homogeneous grouping of pupils which makes more rapid progress possible for the abler pupils. Other methods are the granting of permission to carry an extra subject, additional assignments and library work, double promotion, or the assignment of credits weighted according to achievement. The result of these methods, however, is generally that the bright pupils graduate at too early an age to enter college or a satisfactory wage-earning career.[1]

The junior college. For a variety of reasons — the great increase in the enrollments in colleges and universities in recent years, the desire to extend still further local opportunities for education, the reduction of the cost to parents by keeping pupils at home — the movement for the establishment of junior colleges has grown rapidly. The movement began from one end in 1896, when President William Rainey Harper segregated the first two years of the college work offered by the University of Chicago into an independent unit under the title of the "junior college," and from another in the establishment in 1902 of the Junior College at Joliet, Illinois, in connection with the high school. In 1932 there were 469 junior colleges (181 public and 288 private). The junior college has been defined by the American Association of Junior Colleges as follows:

> The junior college, as at present constituted, comprises several different forms of organization: first, a two-year institution embracing two years of college work in advance of what is ordinarily termed the twelfth grade of an accredited secondary school; secondly, the institution embracing two years of standard collegiate work integrated with one or more contiguous years of fully accredited high school work administered as a single unit. The aims of the curriculum in either case are to meet the needs of the student for maximum growth and development, to further his social maturity, and to enable him to make his greatest contribution as a member of society.

While the functions of the junior college may be preparatory in

---

[1] That the American system of education does not cater adequately to the needs of the bright pupils is the thesis of Professor E. L. Thorndike. See his article on "The Distribution of Education," *School Review*, Vol. XL, May, 1932, pp. 335 ff.

the sense of equipping students to continue their further general or professional studies in a university or professional school, or terminal in the sense of completing a definite course of study, general or vocational, the new institution, particularly if linked with the high school, has the opportunity of enabling bright pupils to reach the same standards of attainment which are now reached by graduates of European secondary schools and at the same age. The development of the junior college has already led to a proposal to reorganize the school system — which today may be on the 8-4 plan (eight years of elementary followed by four years of high school) or the 6-3-3 plan (six years of elementary followed by three years of junior and three years of senior high school) — into a 6-4-4 plan (six years of elementary, four years of junior and four years of senior secondary school). In such a system the bright pupil, following the academic course, will be placed on a level of equality with the European, provided that the system is sufficiently elastic to enable him to proceed at the pace best suited to his abilities.[1]

School life. The expansion of the high school and the recognition of the responsibility of the school to its varied clientèle have led to a remarkable development of extra-curricular activities. These have arisen in part out of the variety of interests which inevitably develop when any large group of individuals are assembled daily. In part they have developed as activities supplementary to the work in certain subjects. Some activities have been sponsored and fostered by such agencies as the Junior Red Cross, Boy Scouts, Girl Scouts, and Camp Fire Girls. Student activities provide opportunities for the development of interests which are not otherwise provided for in the classroom activities and to elicit qualities of personality which academic studies may not give a chance to emerge. The extra-curricular activities offer opportunities for the development of pupil government, self-direction, and leadership, and a diverse number of ways, although athletics appear to be the most prominent, of securing public interest in the schools. The activities which come under the general caption of extra-curricular are in general of three types.

1. Pupil participation in government, including home room, class organizations, student councils, and all the organizations of whatever name, that participate in the government of the life of the school.

[1] On the junior college in general, see Eells, W. C., *The Junior College* (Boston, 1931).

2. All activities that can wholly, or in a large part, grow out of the curriculum work of the school, such as the majority of school clubs.

3. Supplementary school agencies such as the Junior Red Cross, Boy Scouts, Girl Scouts, and Camp Fire Girls.[1]

From the point of view of their organization, student activities are in many schools classified as follows:

Vocational — Engineering club, premedical club, law club, journalism club, school bank, student associations.

Artistic — Symphony orchestra, glee club, military band, art club, bugle corps, fife and drum corps.

Cultural — Dramatic club, classical club, Latin club, German club, Italian club, radio club, school paper.

Athletics — Fencing club, golf club, life saving club, C.M.T.C. club, rifle club, tennis club, play work.[2]

This list is by no means exhaustive, but serves to indicate the general character of student activities in addition to the organizations for self-government. As far as possible they arise out of the spontaneous initiative of the pupils and are organized with the sympathetic interest and support of teachers, many of whom are specifically trained in the theory and conduct of extra-curricular activities. Some of the activities may originate outside of the curriculum and then be incorporated in it; among these are journalism, dramatics, chorus, and orchestra. Others may grow up to supplement the curriculum; among these are Latin and other language clubs. In so far as these activities supplement the work of the classroom, there is a tendency to reward the participants in them by grant of scholastic credit. Extra-curricular activities have in general contributed considerably to the promotion of ideals of good citizenship and of social consciousness, to training in responsibility and leadership, and to the development in the comprehensive high school, in which pupils are organized by subjects, of an *esprit de corps* and a sense of corporate membership which might otherwise be lacking.[3]

It is in the organization and conduct of these activities that the American adolescent shows the practical sense and ability which

---

[1] Department of Superintendence, *Sixth Yearbook, The Development of the High School Curriculum*, 1928, p. 232.

[2] *Ibid.*, p. 239.

[3] See Fretwell, E. K., *Extra-Curricular Activities in Secondary Schools*, which contains an extensive bibliography (Boston, 1931).

characterizes the adult. Academically and scholastically he may be inferior to the European adolescent of the same age; practically he is far superior. It would be futile, however, to attempt to attribute this superiority to his education; it is due entirely to the difference in the social atmosphere in which he lives, an atmosphere which is more favorable to the practical than to the academic or scholastic pursuits and in which the rewards can more easily be achieved. American education, from the elementary school to the universities, is built up on the principle *primum vivere, deinde philosophari;* it is based on the principle of doing, of activity, and of conduct, and in this atmosphere extra-curricular activities find ample means on which to thrive.

The unique character of the American high school. The public high school of the United States is, however, a unique institution. In its present form it is of recent origin and it is still in a stage of transition. In the history of education it is the first experiment in the attempt to provide a suitable education for all the children of all the people at public expense in a single institution; that is, the American high school is essaying the task distributed in other countries among a great variety of schools, only one of which grants the privilege of further advancement to higher education. Few secondary schools elsewhere have won the appreciation and support of the public as have the American high schools. Their social function may be estimated by comparison with the small number of private schools — 2760 with an enrollment of 309,052 pupils, compared with 22,237 public high schools attended by 5,212,179 pupils in 1930. Of the 2760 private schools more than three fourths are denominational, while of the 647 non-sectarian schools some have been established for experimental purposes; others are found mainly in the larger centers of population.

The public high school has thus begun to solve the problem of providing secondary education for all, a problem which is only just becoming a practical issue in other countries. This it has been able to do by breaking with tradition, but its qualitative standards still remain to be developed out of the vast experiment that is proceeding both with subject-matter and methods. This task may perhaps be beset with as many difficulties as now confront those countries that are planning to organize a democratic system of education for adolescents, but fear to surrender that quality of education for the best minds that has been inherited from tradition. The American high school will at least serve the world as an educational laboratory in action, as it has served the United States by distributing a fair average of intellectual training throughout the population, even though it has been for the time being at a sacrifice of the best minds. It represents, as do all American institutions when contrasted with European, the spirit of adventure and innovation which refuses to be bound by tradition and is always ready to break new paths.

It is this spirit which combines at once the elements of strength and weakness of American education, and of the high school in particular — a readiness to face the situation as it exists combined with an impatience to see quick results. The contribution of the United States to the solution of the problem of organizing a democratic system of education is obvious. The tasks of perfecting the machine, of imbuing the schools with a high sense of social purpose in a new age, of maintaining standards of hard work and the will to work and to think hard, of making adaptations that are genuinely educative and not superficially responsive to needs, and at the same time of preserving standards of mental vigor — these still remain to be solved in the future with a teaching personnel commensurate in ability and qualifications with the grandeur of the experiment.

CHAPTER IX
SECONDARY SCHOOL TEACHERS

THE preparation of secondary school teachers has nowhere been given the same amount of attention as that of teachers for elementary schools. The reasons are to be found partly in the historical development of secondary education, partly in a widespread attitude to the problems of instruction at the secondary level. Secondary schools, even when organized autonomously as in France and Germany, have been associated with the universities for which they prepared and have been regarded as a selective institution. From the universities the secondary schools derived the emphasis on the acquisition of subject-matter as the all-important end to be stressed; in other words, the function of the secondary school was to prepare scholars. The best qualification of the teacher, accordingly, was all-round mastery of subject-matter. Since the school was selective, the pupils could be relied upon to look after themselves under the scholarly guidance of the teacher. Since the completion of a secondary school course entitled a successful pupil to certain privileges and conferred on him a definite status, the pressure of academic, social, and economic competition could be counted upon to act as a spur even to the less well-endowed. Hence, from the point of view of teaching, mastery of subject-matter came to be regarded as a completely adequate preparation; from the point of view of the pupil, the burden for progress rested upon him. When the aim of secondary education was conceived more broadly than the mere acquisition of a body of knowledge and character-formation came to be regarded of as much importance as scholarship, as it was in England, the emphasis began to be placed on the personality of the teacher. As Thomas Arnold expressed it, the desirable qualifications of a teacher were activity of mind, interest in his work, and common sense combined with sympathy with and understanding of boys — a Christian spirit and gentlemanly character. Scholarship could be acquired by university study, but personality, the other essential for successful teaching, could not be trained.

Another cause which retarded the development of adequate systems for preparing secondary school teachers was the fact that for a long time they were members or prospective members of the clerical profession or of teaching congregations. The qualifications considered desirable by Arnold for a long time prevented the rise of a lay teaching profession in England, and, even while the number of lay teachers constantly increased in the nineteenth century, the clerical headmaster continued until the beginning of the present century. Tentative efforts were made in the eighteenth century in Germany, by such men as Johann Matthias Gesner, Johann August Ernesti, Christian Gottlieb Heyne, and Friedrich August Wolf, to establish a profession of secondary school teaching independent of the ministry, and toward the end of the century special examinations for secondary school teachers were instituted in Prussia. It was not until the nineteenth century that steps began to be taken to require definite professional preparation, but it seems more than probable that this movement was stimulated more by political ends than a desire to improve the quality of instruction. The establishment in 1808 of the *Ecole Normale Supérieure* in France constituted a part of Napoleon's general legislative enactments to ensure the national character of education in France, while the introduction of a year of probationary training (*Probejahr*) in Prussia in 1826 was prompted by the political reaction which began in 1819, and sought to exercise a rigid political control over secondary and higher education; in other words, political rather than professional reasons determined the introduction of schemes which looked to the selection of trustworthy teachers. Despite its origin, however, the success of the German system of preparing secondary school teachers, which became increasingly professionalized, exercised a strong influence both in England and the United States. Although no tangible results were achieved for some time, proposals at first for the examination and certification of secondary school teachers began to be made by the Schools Inquiry Commission (1868) and subsequent commissions in England, while in the United States the movement for their preparation was associated with the creation of chairs of education at the universities in the last decade of the nineteenth century.

So long as the pupils attending secondary schools constituted a very small minority of the school population and were selected either on the basis of their ability or of wealth which implied a certain cultural background, it might be argued that professional preparation as distinguished from academic preparation was adequate. The rapid increase of opportunities for secondary education and the recognition that such opportunities must not only be made the right of every child, but must be closely articulated with the preliminary education in the elementary schools, place the problem of teacher preparation in a new light. If secondary education is to be the continuation of primary education, then the gap between the untrained teacher in the one branch and the trained teacher in the other must be closed. Further, with the progress of education as a subject of study, it is being increasingly realized that education is broader than instruction in academic subject-matter; that instruction does not consist merely in the transmission of knowledge and information; and that fundamentally the purpose of education at any stage is to train the whole individual. This means a study of educational values, selection from the broad fields known as subject-matter, understanding of the pupil, and the proper adaptation of subject-matter to him, or what is called instruction. The traditional concept of the teacher's position still survives in an exaggerated form in many South American countries, where the teacher visits a school to give and hear lessons and departs at the end of the period to repeat the performance in another school or to attend to the duties of such other occupation as he may pursue. Or it may manifest itself in the teacher giving a series of dictations or lectures or assigning lessons in textbooks on one day and requiring the pupils to "recite" on the next. Some teachers, on the other hand, may be gifted teachers without special preparation, but the supply of such is inadequate, or they may acquire a certain skill in the course of time, but at a sacrifice of several generations of pupils.

It is unnecessary, however, to enlarge on the importance of teacher-preparation, since it is now generally recognized. The problem, however, is to determine the right type of preparation. That a broad cultural foundation and a solid mastery of subject-matter are essentials, no one will deny, but there are many in all countries who would be content with this as the only qualification; the recent tendency in Italy in the preparation both of elementary and of secondary school teachers is based on this ideal plus an emphasis on "spiritual" penetration. The essential point, however, is that at some stage in his preparation the future teacher shall have studied the subjects which he plans to teach from the point of view of the learners whom he will instruct. In France, England, and the United States the attempt is made, with certain exceptions, to superimpose courses in the theory, psychology and history of education, and methods of instruction on top of the academic preparation, but without any integral relation to it. What is forgotten is that the academic subjects are the tools which the teacher has to use, and that somewhere in his preparation the future teacher should acquire a professional attitude, as it were, to the subjects which he plans to teach. Only in rare instances, in the *Ecole Normale Supérieure* in Paris and the London Day Training College, is this interpenetration between subject-matter and its use attempted, less successfully in the former institution because this work is too strictly limited to prescribed courses of study and because the facilities for observation and direct practice are too restricted.[1] The German system, again, although far in advance of those in other countries, is still based on the traditional dualism — academic preparation in the universities and professional preparation in selected secondary schools. Under such a system the German teacher certainly acquires a richer professional preparation than his colleagues elsewhere, but it is open to the criticism that his professional insight is too narrowly cultivated under conditions as they actually exist and tends to a perpetuation of practices which the older teachers have in turn acquired from their predecessors. Excellent as the German system is, it does not make for that freedom, initiative, and growth which should be the ends of a thorough professional preparation, such, for example, as has been instituted for his colleagues who intend to teach in the elementary schools.

Since the universities, and in the United States the colleges, in general retain the traditional attitude that he who knows can teach, and since there are undoubtedly numerous difficulties of an administrative character in providing separate professionalized courses, the future may see a solution, already proposed in Germany, by the establishment of independent institutions for the preparation of secondary school teachers, analogous to the *Ecole*

---

[1] The same criticism would apply to the preparation of secondary school teachers in Ontario, where the dualism between subject-matter and method has been overcome, but the subject-matter is studied strictly in terms of the prescribed courses and textbooks used.

Normale Supérieure.[1] Such a solution would overcome many of the difficulties which surround the problem of providing adequate facilities for observation and practice teaching. Such a solution has been adopted in several state universities in the United States, where schools of education have been established with their own subject-matter specialists for the preparation of secondary school teachers as well as for the advanced study of education. Should the time ever come when the traditional cleavage between various branches of teaching, below the level of the universities, is overcome and a unitary profession of teaching is established on a functional or specialist basis, a single teachers college,[2] analogous to a school of medicine or school of law, might solve many of the difficulties which have been discussed. The increase in the requirements for training for elementary school positions in Germany, England,[3] and the United States is reducing gradually the difference in the length of preparation demanded from elementary and secondary school teachers. While such a solution is not impossible, the economic difficulties and the problem of the adjustment of salary scales are for the present virtually insuperable. And yet the professional preparation of teachers, whether for elementary or for secondary schools, is confronted with the same task — the education of the whole individual rather than mere imparting of subject-matter.

1. ENGLAND

The professional preparation of teachers for secondary schools, although advocated since 1868, when the Schools Inquiry Commission made its report, has been retarded by the characteristic English emphasis on experience, personality, and scholarship.

[1] There are already other examples of this type, but more professionalized; e.g., the remarkable *Escuela de Lenguas Vivas* for training teachers of modern foreign languages in Buenos Aires and the *Istituto Pedagógico* in Santiago, Chile, each with its own practice school.

[2] There is no intention here of recommending as models of such an institution the recently organized teachers colleges of the United States. While it is true that they attempt to prepare teachers for all types of schools and at different levels, their organization and standards, both academic and professional, are too confused as yet to meet the need which is here discussed.

[3] As an example of the *reductio ad absurdum* of the distinction between elementary and secondary school teachers, the English practice might be mentioned of appointing to secondary school positions candidates who had a four-year preparation to teach in elementary schools and of granting elementary school certificates under certain conditions to candidates who prepared for the teacher's diploma, intended as a qualification for teaching in secondary schools!

As recently as 1913, only 180 out of 5246 men teaching in secondary schools reported by the Board of Education, and 1161 out of 5158 women, had been trained specifically to teach in secondary schools. Actually many more had been trained to teach in elementary schools and had received appointments in secondary schools to meet the demand for teachers. The Board of Education, beyond requiring that secondary schools in order to be recognized for purposes of the grant must have a staff of teachers adequate in number and qualifications, has never defined these qualifications or insisted that they be trained. The Board does, however, under its *Regulations* sanction a method of preparing teachers somewhat analogous to that found in Germany. University graduates may under this system be appointed for one year as probationary teachers, receiving a small salary in a recognized grant-earning secondary school. During this period they receive guidance on the practical side and study the theory of education in preparation for an examination for the teacher's diploma conducted by one of the universities. The number of prospective teachers trained in this way is negligible.

Teacher's diploma. The more common system which is followed is in a post-graduate course in the education department of a university, to which any university graduate and students who, although originally admitted to a university with the intention of preparing for elementary schools, have taken a degree in honors and are permitted to transfer to a course of secondary training. The course, which lasts one year, includes normally, on the theoretical side, principles of education, methods of teaching and in some cases special methods, educational psychology, educational hygiene, and history of education; on the practical side, students are assigned to local secondary schools and supervised by the members of the faculty of the education department or of the school to which they are assigned. The *Regulations* of the Board require that at least sixty days be spent in contact with classwork. Students are generally expected to participate in the activities of the school to which they are assigned. At the end of the year an examination is conducted in the professional subjects and one or more lessons are given before the examiners. Papers and essays written during the year and written records of work done during the period of school practice are taken into consideration for the award of the teacher's diploma. In some universities the candidates may hold full-time positions and prepare privately for the examination in theory and practice.

The system on the whole is not satisfactory, and chiefly for two reasons. The first is that, with few notable exceptions, the provision for specialized training in the subjects which the candidates are expected to teach is inadequate. In other words, the professional preparation is superimposed on the academic preparation and the student is expected to make the synthesis between the two in his own way. The second reason lies in the difficulty of providing adequate facilities for guided and supervised practice teaching. The staffs of the schools to which candidates are assigned may or may not be sympathetic with the principle of training, and there is no guarantee that they will give the young teacher the help which he may need.

The adoption of a scale of salaries in 1921 and 1925, opening a satisfactory professional career for secondary school teachers and offering an additional increment to trained graduates, has been effective in increasing the number of trained teachers. To some extent the proposals of the Royal Society of Teachers, formerly the Teachers' Registration Council, to require professional training as a condition of registration has promoted the same ends, even though the Council has not been able to insist upon it and continues to accept three years of successful teaching experience in lieu of training.

Academic preparation. If the progress of professional preparation of secondary school teachers has been slow, the increase in the number of university graduates teaching in secondary schools has been marked. The number of teachers who are not university graduates can in general be explained by the fact that they are teachers in junior classes or teachers of special subjects (art, music, handicraft, domestic subjects, and physical training) who have had their preparation in specialized institutions which do not grant degrees. According to the Board of Education's Statistics for 1930-31 for secondary schools on the grant list of the total number of principals, 1315, only 47 were non-graduates; of the 20,379 teachers 14,918, or 73 per cent, were graduates; of the men 83.5 per cent and of the women 65.5 per cent were graduates. Of the total number of teachers, 12,163, or 56 per cent, were trained; of the graduate teachers 9030, or 55.7 per cent, and of the non-graduate teachers 3131, or 56.8 per cent, were trained.

Under the English system of higher education, university graduates may have taken a degree in honors or a pass or ordinary degree. An honors course involves specialization in one or two fields of study (classics, English, history, modern languages, mathematics, or science); such specialization, however, generally implies also the study of allied fields which may be prescribed. The pass or ordinary course involves a distribution of study over a more extensive list of subjects definitely arranged by groups which avoids that dispersal of interest which characterizes a college course in the United States. From the point of view of standards, the pass degree may be compared with the American baccalaureate degree; unlike the American degree, however, which does not disclose the grades obtained by its possessor, the English graduate is definitely classified (normally there are three classes). The standards for the pass degree vary in the different universities; in general there is a widespread opinion that the pass degree of the older universities is obtained too easily. The specialization required for an honors degree, for which the graduates are also classified, is comparable to that for the M.A., if not the Ph.D., degree in an American university.

In so far as a distinction is made between the two types of degrees, most schools strive to secure a teacher with an honors degree for the upper forms or for special subjects. The additional increment on the salary scale paid to teachers who hold a good honors degree has tended to increase the number of candidates who prepare for this degree. On the other hand, the degree alone is not regarded as an adequate guarantee of good teaching. The emphasis in the selection of teachers is placed more on personality and promise of participation in and wholesome influence on the pupils, whether in class instruction or in their corporate activities. While it would be difficult to find regulations defining their duties, either as to the number of hours of instruction or participation in athletic or other activities, it is generally understood that an interest in the general welfare of the pupils is a part of the professional obligations of the teachers. It is this aspect of the secondary school work which has a particular appeal for the young teacher, as it is the aspect to which England attaches peculiar importance.

Status. While the status of secondary school teachers in England is not so high as in France or Germany (in normal times), there has been a tremendous improvement in their position during the last twenty-five years. This has been due in no small measure to the improvement in the status of secondary education in general, but more perhaps to the development of professional organizations, some of which have performed valuable services in safeguarding their interests, while others, devoted to some special branches of the secondary school curriculum, have promoted the growth of professional groups directed to the improvement of secondary education. Finally, the adoption of a salary scale and the introduction of a pension system have improved the attractiveness of secondary school teaching as a professional career.[1] Certainly much has been done to reduce the disparity in status between English and foreign teachers which was revealed in the report (1910) of the Assistant Masters' Association on *Conditions of Service of Teachers in English and Foreign Secondary Schools.*

2. FRANCE

The preparation of teachers in French secondary schools is largely governed by the requirements for examinations, which are either qualifying (*examens*) or competitive (*concours*). The minimum qualification for eligibility to teach in *collèges* is the *licence d'enseignement;* the competitive examinations are those for the *agrégation*, by which teachers are selected for the *lycées*, and for the *certificats d'aptitude* in letters and science for women, and up to the present only in modern foreign languages for men.

Licence d'enseignement. Until 1920 the minimum requirement for teaching in a secondary school was either the *licence ès lettres* or the *licence ès sciences*, university degrees obtained after two years of residence and granted without any specific reference to the needs of the secondary school. In 1920 there was introduced the *licence d'enseignement* in letters, organized with direct reference to the curricula and instruction to be given in the secondary schools; a similar *licence* was established in 1928 for teachers of the sciences. The difference between the regular *licence* and the *licence d'enseignement* is that, while the choice of the certificates required for the *licence* in letters or science is left to the candidates, the certificates

---

[1] The salary scale for secondary school teachers adopted in 1925 is as follows: For non-graduates, £186, rising by eighteen increments to £384 for men, and £174, rising by sixteen increments to £306 for women; for graduates, £234, rising by eighteen increments to £480 for men, and £216, rising by twelve increments to £384 for women. The scale is somewhat higher in London. Salaries are subject to a five per cent deduction annually under the superannuation scheme and, since October. 1031. to a further deduction of ten per cent as an economy measure.

for the *licence d'enseignement* are prescribed. Candidates for the *licence* must spend four semesters in a university; two of the semesters may be spent in a foreign university. The examinations for each certificate are taken at the end of each of the four semesters and a diploma is granted after all the certificates have been obtained. Following the common practice in French examinations, the examinations for the certificates are written and oral. Failure in the written part eliminates candidates from the oral test.

The certificates required for the *licence ès lettres d'enseignement*, varying with the subjects which the prospective teacher intends to teach, are as follows:

Licence for teaching Philosophy: A. Certificate of general history of philosophy. B. Certificate of psychology. C. Certificate of logic and general philosophy. D. Certificate of ethics and sociology.

Licence for teaching Letters (French and classical humanities): A. Certificate of Greek studies. B. Certificate of Latin studies. C. Certificate of French literature. D. Certificate of grammar and philology.

Licence for teaching History and Geography: A. Certificate of ancient history. B. Certificate of medieval history. C. Certificate of modern and contemporary history. D. Certificate of geography.

Licence for teaching Modern Foreign Languages: A. Certificate of classical literary studies. B. Certificate of foreign literature (English, German, Italian, Spanish, Russian, Arabic). C. Certificate of philology in the foreign language selected. D. Certificate of practical studies in the foreign language selected.[1]

The requirements for the *licence ès sciences d'enseignement* are divided into three groups, one of which may be selected by the candidate: I. Differential and integral calculus, mechanics, general physics. II. General physics, general chemistry, and one of the mathematical sciences listed under I or one of the natural sciences listed in the next group. III. Zoölogy or general physiology, botany or geology, and one of the physical sciences listed under II.

No provision is made in the requirements for either *licence* for the study of professional subjects. The courses offered in the universities are based on the programs prescribed for the examinations. In

---

[1] There is at present a strong movement in the French Chamber and elsewhere to require a knowledge of the ancient classics of all candidates for the *licence* in any of the four fields mentioned.

so far as the candidates receive any preparation for teaching, it consists in the careful organization of subject-matter, in the giving of lessons or reading of papers before the class under the criticism of the professor or of fellow-students, and in practical courses such as the writing of *thèmes, versions* and essays in French or in a foreign language for the *licence ès lettres* and in laboratory work for the *licence ès sciences*.

Certificats d'aptitude à l'enseignement secondaire. The certificates of aptitude are awarded on a competitive basis. The number to be granted is determined each year by the Minister of Public Instruction in accordance with the number of teaching positions to be filled in the subjects for which the certificates are provided. At present there is organized for men only the certificate of aptitude to teach modern foreign languages (*certificat d'aptitude à l'enseignement des langues vivantes dans les lycées et collèges*); for women there are certificates in both letters and sciences which entitle them to teach in secondary schools for girls. Candidates for these certificates must hold the *baccalauréat* or an equivalent foreign degree; or the certificate of aptitude for the preparatory classes in secondary schools; or the certificate of aptitude for teaching special subjects; or the certificate of aptitude for teaching in normal schools. In addition, women may hold the *brevet supérieur* entitling them to teach in an elementary school or the secondary diploma for girls (*diplôme de fin d'études secondaires*). These requirements provide an opportunity for teachers, who have not come through the normal route by way of the secondary school and university, to obtain appointments in secondary schools and to proceed further to the *agrégation*.

For the certificate in modern foreign languages, candidates are required to pass the following examinations (the works to be studied in each language are announced each year by the Ministry): French composition, from which *licenciés* and holders of the certificate of aptitude for teaching in normal schools are exempt (four hours); a *thème* or translation from French into a foreign language (three hours); a *version* or translation from a foreign language into French (three hours); and an essay or composition in the foreign language which the candidate intends to teach (four hours). Candidates who fail in the written examination are not admitted to the oral test, which includes a *thème* and *version*, a *lecture expliquée* in the foreign language, and a discussion of the grammar of a foreign text. Each of the tests lasts at least one hour. Emphasis is placed on the candidate's pronunciation. The examination does not include any tests in professional subjects, but it differs from those for the *licence* in the fact that special attention is paid, especially in the oral examination, to the candidate's ability to present his subject to a class and his familiarity with problems of instruction. In other words, while the examinations for the *licence* stress the candidate's mastery of subject-matter, the examination for the *certificat d'aptitude* stresses his ability to use the subject-matter for purposes of instruction. The examination requirements make no mention of professional study, but many of the candidates have already had some teaching experience and have prepared themselves privately with such help as they may find in special courses in universities.

Agrégation. The highest qualification is the *agrégation*, a competitive examination designed to select teachers for the *lycées*. The number selected each year by this examination is limited to the number of teachers to be appointed in each subject. There are few examinations which are as rigorous as those for the *agrégation*. Since the establishment in 1923 of secondary courses for girls leading up to the *baccalauréat*, it has been felt that the standards for the selection of women teachers must be placed on the same level as those for men. In 1927 it was decided by the Higher Council of Public Instruction to admit women as candidates for the same *agrégations* as men, but the lower requirements were allowed to continue for some time longer. It is proposed gradually to require women to take the same *agrégations* as men in all subjects. This has already been done in letters, philosophy, modern languages, and natural sciences. Candidates may prepare for the examinations either in universities or in the *Ecole Normale Supérieure* for men and the *Ecole Normale Supérieure de l'enseignement secondaire des jeunes filles* at Sèvres for women, although women who pass the competitive examination for entrance to the Higher Normal School for men may be admitted as day students. Admission to the higher normal schools is competitive; wherever facilities are provided, candidates remain in their secondary schools after obtaining the *baccalauréat* in order to prepare for the entrance examination. Although designed for the preparation of secondary school teachers, the Higher Normal School for men has on the whole placed its emphasis on training brilliant scholars rather than teachers, as may be illustrated by the large number of graduates who have obtained distinction in universities and the world of letters in France.

The course to the *agrégation* is carefully guarded by a series of required examinations which must be passed before candidates are admitted to the final test. Thus, candidates must hold the *licence* and the *diplôme d'études supérieures* in the fields in which they present themselves for the *agrégation*. Like the *licence*, the *diplôme* is obtained by passing examinations conducted by the universities, and may be obtained in letters in the following fields: philosophy, classical languages, modern foreign languages, and history and geography; in sciences the diploma may be obtained in mathematics, physical sciences, and natural sciences. The preparation of a thesis is required in each of these fields; in modern languages it must be prepared in the language in which the candidate offers himself for examination. Emphasis is placed in all examinations on a thorough command of French. The diploma is usually obtained one year after the *licence*.

The examinations for the *agrégation* are given in eight groups: philosophy, letters, grammar, history and geography, modern foreign languages (English, German, Spanish, Italian, or Arabic), mathematics, physics and chemistry, and natural sciences. The scope of the examination in each group, authors and problems to be studied, are prescribed annually. Every examination is written and oral, and includes in the oral part the presentation of a lesson on a topic selected from the secondary school course of study; from four to six hours are allowed for the preparation of a lesson under supervision; books and other materials required for its preparation are placed at the disposal of the candidate. The requirements for the *agrégation* may be illustrated from two fields. In the *agrégation des lettres*, the written examination includes translation from and into Latin and Greek (four hours for each of the four tests), and a French composition on one of the prescribed authors (seven hours). The oral test includes the *explication* of Greek, Latin, and French (ancient and modern) texts; for the preparation of each of these half an hour is allowed; and the presentation of a lesson for the preparation of which six hours are allowed. In the *agrégation des sciences naturelles*, the written examination includes three essays — one on a subject assigned a year in advance and dealing with problems in physiology, comparative anatomy, paleontology, etc., and two on subjects taken from the course of study for secondary schools; seven hours are allowed for each essay. The oral examination includes: (a) the selection, arrangement, or preparation of materials to illustrate a lesson selected by the examiners; (b) the preparation and selection of specimens suitable for instructional purposes; (c) a lesson on a subject taken from the lower section of the *lycée;* and (d) a lesson on a subject taken from the upper section. Four hours are allowed for the preparation of the lesson.

To ensure that candidates for the *agrégation* have, in addition to intense specialization in their subjects, acquired some familiarity with the problems of education and the conduct of a class, a *stage pédagogique* was introduced in 1924. Under the more recent regulation of March 5, 1929, the *stage pédagogique* requires: (1) preparation in theory of education to the extent of at least twenty lectures on the history and organization of secondary education in France and abroad and on the teaching of the subjects which a candidate intends to teach; (2) a practical period in a public secondary school. During the practical period, a candidate for three consecutive weeks may follow the work of several teachers of his subjects in one class and observe the progress of his subjects from class to class. In addition, every candidate must participate for two weeks in the management of a class, prepare lessons, correct written work, and engage in other educational procedures. The professors who give the lectures on educational theory and the teachers to whom candidates may be assigned for their practical work are selected each year by the Minister of Public Instruction on the recommendation of the rectors of the academies. Reports, which constitute the basis of a certificate required from each candidate for the *agrégation,* are presented to the rectors by the deans of the faculties and the professors assigned to the task. Candidates who have already had teaching experience are exempted from the *stage pédagogique.*

The creation of the *licence d'enseignement,* the proposal to extend the *certificat d'aptitude à l'enseignement secondaire* to other subjects besides modern languages, and the introduction of the *stage pédagogique* illustrate a change in the French attitude to teacher training. The preëminent position enjoyed by the Higher Normal School and its brilliant record for over a century tended to the adoption of the view that "a good general education, free and disinterested, while it was admirably suited to future savants and writers, was also the most appropriate way in the world for the preparation of teachers."[1] Undoubtedly the standards of the examinations prescribed succeeded admirably in securing teachers who knew what they had to teach and something beyond that, but the result of placing scholars in the secondary school classes, especially the lower classes was too obvious to pass unobserved. Recent regulations have repeatedly warned teachers against excessive dictation, while the more recent public agitation against overburdening (*surmenage*) of pupils and the large number of failures in the *baccalauréat* examinations point to an emphasis on subject-matter rather than the pupil. The *stage pédagogique* follows in its organization and requirements suggestions formulated as long ago as 1902 by M. Ch. Langlois, but does not provide as long a period of practical training as he then suggested. The significance of its introduction lies, not in its organization, which is still somewhat informal, but in the recognition that professional preparation is essential. Up to the present the requirements for appointment, whether in *lycées* or *collèges*, have furnished a guarantee that every teacher is a master of the subjects which he professes; the recent reforms seek to supplement this with a further guarantee that he can teach these subjects at the various levels of the secondary school.

Status. The French secondary school teacher enjoys the status, socially and economically, of all others who have had the same grade of education and hold the same rank in public employment, for they are scholars who are at once members of a liberal profession and of the civil service. Salaries on the whole have not kept up with the fluctuations in the cost of living since the War, despite the efforts which have been made by the authorities to adjust salaries periodically.[2] The problem with which the Government is confronted is

[1] Langlois, Ch., *La Préparation professionelle à l'Enseignement secondaire*, p. 43 (Paris, 1902).

[2] The salaries of principals and professors who hold the *agrégation* are, according to the scale adopted in 1926, as follows: In the *lycées* of Paris, 18,000 to 26,000 francs; in the departmental *lycées*, 15,000 to 21,000 francs; in the girls' schools, 15,300 to 22,300 francs in Paris, and 14,000 to 20,000 francs in the departments. Principals and professors in *collèges* for boys receive from 11,000 to 16,500 francs a year. Heads of departments, *censeurs*, receive the same or slightly higher salaries; professors and teachers of special subjects receive lower salaries. The personnel is divided into six classes, and promotion from one class to another is based on selection or seniority. In addition to the basic salaries, all teachers receive indemnities for rent and family allowances for each dependent child.

rendered all the more serious because of the economic changes which are taking place in France and which make employment in the developing industrial and commercial life of France more attractive, because of the remuneration, than employment in public services, despite the dignity which attaches to it. From time to time France has been confronted with a *crise d'agrégation*, not in secondary education alone, but in other branches of the higher civil service, where similar competitive standards are maintained. The crisis is at times so serious, indeed, that an adequate supply of competent teachers is not available in some subjects. Such crises may be temporary, but through them all and in the midst of agitation for the *école unique*, France and French educators seek to maintain the high standards of the secondary school teaching profession and through it of the school for the recruiting of the *élite*.

3. GERMANY

Although the systems of preparing teachers for secondary schools may vary in some details in the States of the German Republic, the standards are uniform. In all States attendance at a university and professional preparation under state supervision and certification by the State are the prerequisites for appointment throughout the country. In Prussia, examinations for secondary school teachers were introduced in the eighteenth century and a period of probationary service was acquired in 1826. In 1890 an additional year of professional preparation was required with the establishment of seminars. Both the *Seminarjahr* and the *Probejahr* were spent in selected secondary schools. The present system was organized under the examination regulations of July 28, 1917, which combined the two years into a single unit known as the *Vorbereitungsjahre*.

Preliminary requirements. Before being admitted to the period of professional preparation, candidates must have spent at least eight semesters in university study and have passed the state examination (*Staatsexamen pro facultate docendi*). Of the eight semesters, six must be spent in a German university. During their period of university study, candidates for the state examination must have attended courses in education and philosophy and in the subjects which they intend to teach, and must have been members of seminars and practica in these subjects; in the sciences they must have done work in laboratories. Since 1925 they must also have had two semesters of practical training in gymnastics and athletics and two semesters of lectures on physical education, a requirement, which, like the development of physical training in the secondary schools, is an attempt to provide a substitute for the physical training hitherto given during the period of compulsory military service. Those who wish to teach religion, German, modern languages, or history must at some time have had Latin or Greek or English as may be necessary; prospective teachers of modern languages may during the period of university study have attended a foreign university for not more than two semesters; teachers of mathematics, chemistry, and physics may have attended a technical high school of university rank. Applicants for admission to the state examination must present a full statement of their life, the subjects studied, copies of theses which they may have written, a certificate of health, and testimonials from professors whose seminars they attended. If the university course was not well organized, or for reasons of character, applicants may be refused admission to the examination.

Academic examination. The state examination is conducted by academic examination commissions (*Wissenschaftliche Prüfungsämter*) which are found in every university and which consist of university professors and secondary school teachers appointed by the Minister. The subjects of the examination are: (*a*) Compulsory for all: philosophy, ethics, theory of adolescence, logic, and epistemology. (*b*) A choice of three from the following subjects either as majors (*Hauptfächer*) or two majors and one minor (*Nebenfach*): religion, German, Latin, Greek, Hebrew (as a minor), French, English, history, geography, mathematics, physics, chemistry, botany, and zoölogy. (*c*) A wide range of supplementary subjects (*Zusatzfächer*): introduction to philosophy, political science, education, applied mathematics, mineralogy, geology, classical archeology, history of medieval and modern art, comparative philology, Polish, Danish, Swedish, Dutch, Russian, Spanish, Italian, Turkish, Chinese, general history of religion, drawing, physical training, singing, and handwork. The number of supplementary subjects which a candidate may offer is not restricted, but only one may be substituted as a minor.

Each candidate is required to prepare two essays — the first on a problem selected from one of his major subjects and a second on a problem from another major subject or from philosophy. Five months are allowed for the preparation of the theses — three months for the first and two months for the second. Major essays in classical philology must be written in Latin, and in modern languages in the appropriate language; the second essay must be in German. Candidates may submit a published work in lieu of one of the essays. In addition to the essays, the examining commissions may require candidates to take written examinations, each of three hours' duration, in the subjects which they offer. If the work of a candidate in the essays or in the written examinations is unsatisfactory, he may be refused permission to proceed to the oral examination. In both the written and the oral examinations, candidates must give such evidence of familiarity with the literature of their subjects as to indicate their ability for further study and to give life to their instruction in general. The standards expected of the candidates may be judged from the following examples:

English

In order to obtain a certificate in the teaching of English as a major subject, candidates must show ability to comprehend and to translate into German a not too difficult Latin text and late and medieval Latin in so far as he has given attention to it; in this connection he must have a command of the requisite grammatical foundation.

The requirements include:

(a) If the subject is offered as a minor: Knowledge of elementary phonetics, correct and thoroughly grounded expression. Familiarity with grammar and syntax, command of a rich vocabulary and idioms and practice in the spoken use of the language. Ability to translate correctly into German the authors read in secondary schools and to write in the foreign language without serious errors in language and style. Survey of the development of English literature since Shakespeare; several works of the most outstanding poets and prose writers, including the modern period, must be read with understanding. Practice in expressive reading of English poetry.

(b) If the subject is offered as a major: Thorough knowledge of phonetics; correct and thoroughly grounded expression. Thorough accuracy in grammar; ability to explain the grammar scientifically. Knowledge of the historical development of the language from the period of Old English down. Familiarity with the vocabulary and with peculiarities of expression as well as adequate mastery in the written and oral use of the language. Knowledge of the general development of English literature through extensive reading; intensive study of some of the outstanding authors from the earliest period to the present day. Comprehension of the laws of English prosody of the ancient and modern times. Familiarity with the history, philosophy, political institutions and geography of England. Familiarity with the relations between English and German literature.

The examination will be conducted in English so far as this is necessary to discover the ability of the candidates in the spoken use of the language.

Physics

The requirements for the teaching certificate in physics are:

(a) If the subject is offered as a minor: Knowledge of the more important phenomena and laws in the whole range of this science and their applications, as well as ability to derive these laws experimentally. Evidence of successful participation in practical work, and familiarity with the most important apparatus and methods of measurement.

It is essential that the candidate be trained in the principles of chemistry and be informed in the simpler chemical studies.

(b) If the subject is offered as a major: Intensive knowledge of experimental physics and its applications, especially in technology; survey of the historical development of physical science. General survey of the whole field of theoretical physics; detailed familiarity with theoretical mechanics and intensive knowledge of at least one of the other branches. Evidence must be given of scientific work in the laboratory and adequate knowledge of mathematics.

Candidates who do not satisfy the examiners in two major subjects, a minor or supplementary subject, and philosophy are failed, but may repeat the whole examination once more.[1] Success in the examination entitles a candidate to admission to the two-year period of professional preparation, during which he has the title of *Studienreferendar*. The state examination is a test of general culture and mastery of academic subject-matter; only indirectly, in philosophy and in education if offered as a supplementary subject, does the examination have any reference to purely professional preparation.

Practical preparation. The professional preparation and practical training are given in the two preparatory years (*Vorbereitungsjahre*), which are generally spent in two schools, selected for the purpose and under the supervision of the provincial school boards; the first year may be spent in a six-year school; the second in a nine-year school. Not more than eight students are assigned to a school, where they are placed under the direction of the principal and selected teachers, although all members of the staff are expected

---

[1] Candidates may receive a mark of "excellent," "good," "satisfactory," and "unsatisfactory."

to coöperate. Two hours a week throughout the two years are devoted to conferences for the study of professional subjects. The first year is devoted to history of education, the organization of German and especially Prussian education, methods of instruction in the special subjects in which each candidate has certificates, and the marking of pupils' written work; psychology and ethics, methods of teaching the common subjects (German, religion and history) and their place in the curriculum, and the general duties of the teacher are discussed in the second year. In both years, courses are organized in school hygiene, with participation in physical training and welfare activities, principles of discipline, discussions of important educational works, and observation and practice teaching. Unsatisfactory candidates may be dropped during or at the end of the first year; the others continue their preparation in another school. *Studienreferendare* may receive financial aid during their period of training or may be assigned a limited number of teaching periods for which they are paid.

Professional examination. At the end of the second year, candidates who have been given satisfactory reports by the principals and teachers under whom they have been trained and by a secondary school inspector are admitted to the professional examination (*Pädagogische Prüfung*). The reports refer to the character, professional promise, health, research and teaching ability of the candidates. The professional examination is conducted in each province by an examination committee (*Prüfungsausschuss*), appointed by the provincial examination board (*Pädagogische Prüfungsamt*) from among its own members (two members of the provincial school board and a number of secondary school principals and teachers, including women if women candidates present themselves for the examination). The examination is given in three parts. The written examination consists of an essay on some problem of educational theory or methods, based on practical experience. The oral examination takes the form of a discussion by all the candidates of a subject which is selected by the chairman of the examination committee and which is intended to test the ability of the candidates to handle educational and class problems. The third part consists of a lesson of about thirty minutes' duration conducted before the committee on one of two topics assigned at two days' notice, and based on the work done in the last semester of preparation. In the final decision, all factors are taken into consideration — the written and oral examinations, the lesson, and reports on the candidates during their period of preparation. If a candidate fails, the examining committee may decide whether he is to be rejected or permitted to continue his preparation for a half or a full year longer and repeat the examination.

Appointment. Successful candidates, who are now given the title of *Studienassessoren*, are registered by the provincial school boards with a record of their subjects; as, for example, religion; German, history and geography; Latin and Greek; French and English; mathematics and physics; chemistry, natural science and geography; additional subjects. Whatever the combination of subjects, they are in all cases closely related for purposes of instruction. A *Studienassessor* may receive remunerative employment, but final appointment as a *Studienrat* is not guaranteed unless his name is placed on a list of eligible candidates, *Anwärterliste*, prepared by the Ministry of Education in coöperation with the provincial school boards. Candidates who are placed on the eligible list may receive appointments on salaries beginning with ninety-five per cent of the initial salary of a *Studienrat* and rising to one hundred per cent in four years. Registration on the *Anwärterliste* is virtually a guarantee of definitive appointment at the end of five years. The economic uncertainty of the last decade and other factors have not always been favorable to the fulfillment of this guarantee. This means that few who intend to become teachers in secondary schools can hope to obtain final appointment much before they are thirty-two years of age.

The system of selecting teachers in Germany offers a certain guarantee of mastery of the subjects which they intend to teach, but the system of professional preparation is too much of the apprenticeship type, in which the older teachers are more likely to transmit their own methods, aims, and ideals than to encourage progress and reforms which are today in direct contradiction to the traditions under which they were themselves educated and trained. The situation is somewhat aggravated at the present time because political views tend to color attitudes to innovations in education. Hence, while new methods, dominated less by older practices, by requirements of the examinations, and by standards demanded by the universities are being advocated, older methods and practices still survive. It is for these reasons that proposals have been made for a reorganization of the system of preparing teachers. Whether this task should be entrusted to the universities is a question which is open to discussion. The university courses in subject-matter, it is objected, are adequate from the point of view of the research student and specialist, but are too intensive for the future teacher, and neglect entirely their use in the classroom. The universities, on the other hand, insist that their function is to train scholars and not teachers; the courses in education are also given from the same standpoint and are regarded as too general and not sufficiently practical in character. For these reasons it is proposed, but the discussions have not yet proceeded further, to establish separate teachers colleges for the preparation of secondary schools. If the proposals are carried out, the tension which now exists between the universities and those interested in the preparation of teachers would be relieved and the preparation could be placed on a genuinely professional basis in place of the apprenticeship or craftsmanship training which now takes place in the schools. Such a reform, it is recognized, is all the more urgent in view of the progress made in the reform of the preparation of teachers for the elementary schools.

Status. The status of the German secondary school teachers, while it has not lost any of its distinction, has suffered as has that of all middle classes in Germany from the uncertain economic conditions. None the less, for those who can survive the severe competition for admission to the profession a career is offered which is secure, and for which graduated increases in salary, with consideration for family circumstances, allowances for rent, protection allowance for disability and pensions, are provided. So far as changes in status are taking place, they are due to changes in the character of secondary education which demand teachers who are educators in the broadest sense of the term rather than scholars. Scholarship as an essential qualification of the teacher is still emphasized, as is indicated in the requirements for the academic state examination; but scholarship alone, it is recognized, is an inadequate guarantee for the many-sided demands on the teacher in the new secondary education which is being developed. Possibly the change is reflected in the abolition of the old practice of conferring the title of "Professor" on secondary school teachers who have distinguished themselves in the field of scholarship.[1]

4. ITALY

The Gentile reform. The first task which confronted Gentile in the reform of secondary education was to reorganize the whole system of selecting and appointing teachers. Unsystematized and unorganized, the status of the teachers, so specialized that each had to combine a number of periods of instruction in different secondary schools to support himself, was regarded as one of the chief weaknesses of secondary education. Gentile attacked the problem ruthlessly in the interests of the general reform of education. Preceding the general reform introduced by the Royal Decree of May 6, 1923, superfluous positions in the administration of secondary education were abolished, and principals and teachers who had reached the age of sixty and had had forty years of service, or who were judged incompetent, were retired on pensions; principals who were not competent for their administrative positions were reassigned to teaching posts; all teachers were investigated and reclassified. Finally, at the close of 1923 the qualifications for appointment to secondary schools were revised in a general decree which set up new requirements for admission to any of the liberal professions. University degrees and diplomas were no longer regarded as qualifications for the practice of a profession; every aspirant was now required to pass a state examination, for which appropriate degrees and diplomas were essential as prerequisites.

The reform carefully defined the number of teaching positions in each school and the various grades of teachers. The list of teachers required is revised every two years, and no school is permitted without authority to change the number assigned to it. The first classification is into three groups — permanent teachers (*professori di ruolo*), *supplenti* assistants, and *incaricati*, who teach subjects which are not formally organized in definite groups; the two last classes of teachers are appointed annually. The permanent teachers are further divided into three groups: (*a*) those

---

[1] According to the salary schedule of December, 1927, the salaries of *Studienräte* begin at 4400 Mark a year and rise to a maximum of 9600 Mark a year. The scale is, however, divided into four classes with subdivisions in some of them; advancement from one division to another or from one class to another depends upon seniority and promotion. Salaries are supplemented by rent indemnities, family allowances, and local allowances.

who teach in the classical, scientific, and girls' *licei*, in the *ginnasio*, and in the upper sections of the technical and normal schools; (*b*) those who teach literary subjects in the lower courses of the *ginnasio*, technical, and normal schools, continuation schools, and drawing in all schools; (*c*) teachers of music and singing in normal schools, and teachers in kindergartens attached to normal schools.

Selection and examinations. All permanent teachers are selected by examination. For those who wish to teach in government or accredited schools the examination is competitive — that is, only those are selected who are needed each year to fill vacancies. All others who pass the examination receive a diploma of eligibility (*abilitazione*) which entitles them to teach in private schools. An important contribution of the reform has been the abolition of the specialist, who was master of only one subject, and the introduction of a grouping of subjects for which special examinations are prescribed. This reform was intended to emphasize the educative and integrative function of the teacher in place of the traditional emphasis on mere instruction. The reform has, however, introduced another form of specialization — different standards and different groupings for different school types and different sections of the same school, and a distinction between the general examination required for schools in small towns and the special examination for appointment to schools in such cities as Bologna, Florence, Genoa, Milan, Naples, Padua, Palermo, Pisa, Rome, Turin, Trieste, and Venice.

The examinations are conducted by committees of three (two university professors and one principal or teacher), appointed biennially by the Higher Council of Public Instruction, which selects the topics and defines the standards of the examinations. Candidates must be between the ages of eighteen and forty (forty-five for ex-soldiers), and must be Italian citizens of good health and character. The minimum academic prerequisites for admission to candidacy vary with the subjects and schools in which they are to be taught, from a diploma to the *laurea* (the Italian equivalent of the Ph.D.) of a university; other qualifications are accepted or prescribed for special subjects, such as commerce, accounting, finance, political economy, etc. The examinations are open to men and women with certain exceptions (women may not teach classics in *licei*, Italian and history in technical schools, Italian and Latin or philosophy and history in classical and scientific *licei*, and Latin and history in normal schools; men may not become kindergarten teachers). In natural sciences, chemistry, accounting, and agriculture, the examinations are oral; in all other subjects written and oral. Candidates who obtain a mark of less than 7 on a scale of 10 in the written examination are excluded from the oral test. In the general examination, the minimum mark is 7, and in the special, 8; the minimum mark for the diploma of eligibility is 6.

Examinations are given in twenty groups, as follows:

Italian, history and geography (continuation schools).
Italian, Latin, history and geography (lower courses of *ginnasi*, technical and normal schools).
Italian, Latin, Greek, history and geography (upper courses of *ginnasi*).
Classics (classical *licei*).
Italian and history (upper courses of technical and normal schools).
Italian, Latin, and history (classical, scientific and girls' *licei*, and normal schools).
Philosophy and history (classical, scientific and girls' *licei* and courses in philosophy and education in normal schools).
Foreign languages (lower courses in all schools and continuation schools).
Foreign languages (upper courses in all schools).
Science subjects (continuation schools, separate *ginnasi*, and lower courses of technical schools).
Mathematics and physics (classical and scientific *licei*, technical and normal schools).
Natural sciences and chemistry (classical and scientific *licei*, technical and normal schools).
Chemistry (surveying section in technical schools).
Drawing (all schools except classical *licei*).
Bookkeeping and accounting (technical schools).
Law and political economy (technical schools).
Agriculture (technical schools).
Construction and topography (technical schools).
Music and singing (normal schools).
Kindergarten work (normal schools).

The groupings are somewhat similar for the examinations for the diploma for eligibility, with the exception that the schools for which they qualify are not so specifically defined. Separate examinations are prescribed for teachers of the history of art, stenography, and calligraphy.

Teachers who are selected on a competitive basis must accept appointments offered to them in government and accredited schools as probationers (*professori straordinari*) for a period of three years, during which they may be dismissed if, in the opinion of the principal of the school to which they are assigned, their work is unsatisfactory. At the end of the probationary period they become permanent teachers (*professori ordinari di ruolo*). Permanent teachers are placed on a regular scale with annual increments; special increments of salary may be paid to teachers for special merit; those who obtain two such increments are inscribed in a roll of honor (*ruolo d'onore*). Teachers must retire from service with a pension at the age of seventy, or earlier if pronounced incompetent. They are subjected to a rigid code of discipline which provides a series of penalties ranging from warning to dismissal. Supervision is exercised by the principals, the superintendents, the boards of secondary education, and the Higher Council of Public Instruction, which acts as the last court of appeal.

Opportunities for preparing teachers for secondary schools exist, but the institutions in which they were provided were established originally to offer facilities for higher education for women. The two institutions (*R. Istituti Superiori di Magistero*), established in 1882 in Rome and Florence, added to this function that of preparing elementary school teachers (women) for advancement to positions as school principals, teachers in normal schools, and inspectors of elementary schools. In 1924 a third institution was added at Messina, and in 1925 private institutions in Naples, Milan, and Turin were recognized and men were admitted. These higher teachers colleges prepare teachers of Italian and Latin in lower courses of secondary schools, of history and geography in any secondary schools, teachers of education and philosophy in normal schools, inspectors, and elementary school principals. Students are admitted by competitive examination; the course extends over four years. The courses in the *R. Istituto Superiore di Magistero* at Florence for teachers for secondary schools are shown on page 853.

There is general agreement that the reforms introduced by Gentile and his successors in the Ministry were essential if the reform of secondary education was to be successful. The reforms are criticized for two reasons — first, for introducing a new type of specialization which is detrimental to the mobility of teachers, who may be transferred from one type of course or school to another only by taking a new examination; and, second, for the absence of

SECONDARY SCHOOL TEACHERS

Course for Diploma in Letters
First two years

Italian language and literature
Latin language and literature
German language and literature
History
Geography
Philosophy and history of philosophy (one or two years)
Education (one or two years)
English language and literature (one or two years)

Second two years

Italian language and literature (one year)
Latin language and literature
History (one year)
Geography (one year)

At least two other one-year courses selected from Italian, history, geography, philosophy and history of philosophy, education, a foreign language and literature. Of the two courses in education and philosophy in the first biennium one may be taken for one and the other for two years. English may be taken in the first or second biennium.

Course for Diploma in Education and Philosophy and for Inspectors
First two years

Italian language and literature
Latin language and literature
Philosophy and history of philosophy
Education
German language and literature
English language and literature (one year)
History (one year)
Geography (one year)
Public law and educational legislation (one year)
School hygiene (one year)

Second two years

Italian language and literature (two years)
Philosophy and history of philosophy (one year)
Education (one year)

At least two other courses as in column 1. The courses in English, public law and educational legislation and school hygiene may be taken in the first or second biennium.

any provision for testing either the knowledge of professional subjects or competence as teachers. Education, as a subject, is only required for teachers of philosophy in normal schools. As in the preparation of elementary school teachers (see p. 587), so in the selection of secondary school teachers there is considerable suspicion of professional training; the courses in the *R. Istituti Superiori di Magistero* make no provision for training in practice. Complete reliance is placed on the personality of the teachers, their mastery of subject-matter, and their ability to attain the idealistic aims of the Gentile reform because they see the spiritual significance of their subjects in the cultural development of man as man. Observation of actual practice unfortunately leaves the impression that dictation and lecturing still constitute the most usual methods of instruction, even though textbooks covering the matter are in the hands of the pupils, and that the chief activity of the pupils consists of answers to questions on content. Possibly the time since the introduction of the reform has been too short to have penetrated through the school system and the universities. The conclusion cannot be resisted that a system dominated at every strategic point by external examinations, however desirable to obviate the chaos and absence of standards which prevailed in the past, must inevitably lead, after the first enthusiasm for reform has disappeared, to a system in which examinations will dominate and the broad cultural and educative ideal will be subordinated. This is all the more likely to be true in a system in which the future social and economic career of pupils and students is determined by success in examinations.

5. UNITED STATES

To present a picture of the conditions governing the appointment of high school teachers in the United States is not as simple a matter as it is in discussing the secondary school teachers in Europe. The only general statement which can be made is that there is no uniformity of standards. This is due to a large number of causes which affect all aspects of American educators. There is, in the first place, in the case of secondary education, an absence of universally accepted aims. Second, the provision of secondary education is in the hands of a great variety of public authorities, state and local, with varying standards of education and of certification of teachers. Third, the divergences in the sizes of the high schools and the attempt to provide for the needs of all adolescents introduce complications which are not found in European secondary education. Fourth, teaching has not yet become either a profession or a life career. Fifth, the standardizing agencies (see p. 795) have not yet adopted uniform standards of teacher qualifications. Finally, the high schools have increased in number and in enrollments so rapidly that it has been impossible to provide an adequate teaching personnel.[1]

[1] Professor C. H. Judd, in his *Unique Character of American Secondary Education*, goes so far as to doubt whether, in the effort to provide secondary education for all adolescents, it

If the situation in the country as a whole is examined, it is found that high school teachers change their positions frequently, that a large number are immature, and that in many places they do not enjoy security of tenure. In 1927–28 in the high schools accredited by the North Central Association, whose standards are probably the highest in the country, 8453, or 22 per cent, of the teachers were teaching in the reporting high school for the first time. In the same year, of the total number of high schools in the country, 18,116, more than 56 per cent, or 10,248, were small high schools with an enrollment of less than 100 pupils and with six teachers or less; 5512, or 30.43 per cent, had three teachers or less; 75 per cent of all the high schools had enrollments of 200 pupils or less. According to Professor F. P. Bachman,[1] 16 to 20 per cent of the teachers in the small high schools are beginners; 40 per cent change their positions each year; 50 per cent are not college graduates; and about one third are not old enough to vote.

Since every high school, irrespective of size, attempts to meet the needs of all its pupils, the result is that a large number of teachers undertake to teach subjects which they may never have studied themselves, or that many are overloaded with a combination of isolated subjects. In five Southern States, according to figures for 1923–24 and 1928–29, there were high schools in which one teacher offered from 22 to 27 subjects, two teachers from 24 to 36 subjects, four teachers from 24 to 37 subjects, and six more teachers from 28 to 39 subjects.[2] This situation results in overloading them with as many as 30 to 35 periods of instruction with little time for preparation and other duties. A further consequence is the curious combination of subjects in which even the most skillful teachers could not find any points of integration. The following combinations may be cited: agriculture, English, history, Latin and psychology; athletics, his-

will ever be possible to secure an adequate number of well-qualified teachers. The fundamental question, however, is whether a country can for long continue to offer the semblance of a good education without attempting to correct the situation by frankly facing the economic problem involved. Some time it must be realized that the palatial buildings which are being erected for secondary education must have teachers of a quality commensurate with the promise which the buildings offer.

[1] Bachman, F. P., *Training and Certification of High School Teachers*, p. 66 (Nashville, Tennessee, 1930).

[2] Bachman, *op. cit.*, p. 47. That these conditions are not confined to the Southern States is indicated in Hutsen, P. W., *The Scholarship of Teachers in Secondary Schools*, p. 12 ff., which gives the facts for California, Minnesota, Pennsylvania, and Washington (New York, 1927).

tory, Latin, mathematics, and science; bookkeeping, civics, English, French, and history; civics, general science, history, Latin, and physical education.[1] These conditions do not, in general, apply to the high schools of the larger cities, where better functional assignments for teachers are possible.

Whether the conditions described are the results of the methods of certificating high school teachers or whether the methods reflect the conditions, it is impossible to say. The practices of certification vary from certification by examination up to the requirement of college graduation; between these limits certificates may be granted to candidates who have not completed the course of a normal school, and to those who have not completed a college course. A study of the laws and regulations governing teachers' certificates[2] shows that twenty-seven States have no other requirements than college graduation, sixteen States prescribe the major and minor subjects which must have been taken for college graduation, and five States prescribe the specific requirements in terms of the subjects which the candidates plan to teach. In addition, the laws and regulations require from five to twenty-four unit hours of professional subjects (such as educational psychology, principles of secondary education, theory of teaching, special methods, and observation and practice of teaching). California alone requires the completion of a college course and one year of post-graduate professional training. Since few States grant certificates on the basis of specific requirements, and since college graduation offers no guarantee of strict specialization, candidates are too frequently certificated as high school teachers without specific statement of the subjects which they are qualified to teach. In other words, the most general practice is "blanket" certification rather than subject certification.

Even if it is assumed that college graduation, which is required for the highest certificates, has a standardized meaning, and that a candidate has specialized strictly in a few subjects, it does not follow that these subjects have been taught from the point of view of their need in high schools; candidates may, indeed, have specialized in subjects which have not yet found their way into the high school curriculum. Nor does the requirement of a number of pro-

[1] See Department of Superintendence, *Sixth Yearbook, Development of the High School Curriculum*, pp. 94 f. (Washington, 1928), and p. 816 above.

[2] United States Bureau of Education, Bulletin, 1927, No. 19, *State Laws and Regulations Governing Teachers' Certificates* (Washington, D.C., 1928).

fessional courses furnish any guarantee of genuine professional training, since such courses are given apart from the academic subjects without any attempt at professional integration. Of the four leading accrediting agencies (North Central Association, Southern Association, Association of Middle States and Maryland, and the Northwest Association), three have in general based their requirements for the preparation of teachers on the highest requirements for high school teachers' certificates — college graduation and fifteen hours of professional subjects; the Southern Association requires that three fourths of the teachers in a high school must be college graduates and that all teachers must have had professional training. Only one of the Associations, the North Central, has required since 1929 that teachers must teach in the fields of their major and minor specialization during their college courses.

The state universities, as contrasted with the state certification laws and the standards of the accrediting agencies, have begun to make a contribution to a better and more specific preparation of teachers for high schools. Eleven of the universities required that candidates who wish to be recommended for a teacher's certificate specialize in two academic majors or teaching fields; twenty-seven States limit candidates to the study of subjects commonly taught in high schools; twenty-two prescribe more or less the subjects or courses of study; and four prescribe combinations of subjects as they appear in high school courses. It must be remembered, however, that, while this activity on the part of state universities for the improvement of high school teachers is in the right direction, they supply considerably less than half of the numbers of teachers required; that a large number of the remaining candidates come from colleges of liberal arts and teachers colleges; that the certification laws provide a variety of standards and loopholes for escape from specific subject requirements, and that on the whole they do not control the destinies or the ambitions of the high schools which desire to be all things to all pupils, regardless of the availability of teachers. Further, despite the extensive popularity of professional subjects in education, the situation found in European countries also prevails in the United States, widespread mistrust, if not contempt, among subject-matter specialists for theory of education and methods of instruction. Hence, in many institutions it has not been possible

[1] See Bachman, *op. cit.*, pp. 21 ff.

to establish that *rapprochement* and coöperation which are desirable between the academic-subject professors and the professors of education, with the inevitable sacrifice of proper integration of academic and professional subjects. In a few of the leading institutions, the difficulty has been settled by the establishment of schools of education which include on their faculty, besides professors of educational subjects, professors who are specialists in the teaching of academic subjects. Where this solution has been adopted, the schools of education generally, but not universally, advise future teachers on the selection of appropriate courses.

It is obvious, then, that the chief obstacles to the development of a sound profession of teaching are to be found in the state laws and regulations for teachers' certificates and the attempt of small high schools to offer courses for which they do not have an adequate supply of teachers. Too frequently teachers are first appointed to high schools and later assigned the subjects which they are expected to teach, regardless of their qualifications and attainments in these subjects. If one may generalize, it may be said that the chief weakness of high school teachers as compared with European teachers is an absence of profound mastery of subject-matter. Whether this can be compensated by a broader preparation in theory of education and methods is open to serious doubt. According to the *Report of the Classical Investigation* (1925), approximately two thirds of the teachers of Latin in cities of more than 100,000 population had studied the subject for eight years or more; 90.5 per cent for seven years or more; but in high schools of small communities with 2500 or fewer inhabitants, only 18 per cent had studied Latin for eight years or more, and only 28 per cent for seven years or more. The situation was worse among teachers of modern languages; the *Modern Language Investigation* reported in 1929 that teachers of German had had on the average 6.1 years of preparation, of French 4.9 years, and of Spanish 3.9 years.[1] The facts are probably the same in all subjects.

No improvement can be expected in the present position until the blanket general certificate entitling the holder to teach in a high school is abolished and replaced by special subject certificates [2]

[1] It must be noted that in all cases the period of preparation includes the study of the subject in high school and college.

[2] It may even be insisted that such a system of certification is equally desirable for teachers in junior high schools.

or certificates requiring a reasonable combination of allied subjects. Adequate provision needs to be made for the study of subject-matter and its use for instructional purposes. As in the case of elementary school teachers, the preparation of high school teachers should be definitely professional. Finally, the appointment of teachers who are not prepared to teach the subjects assigned to them should be prohibited. Such requirements for certificates may be followed by salutary results for the high schools themselves and a reduction of curricula and courses to those that can be honestly offered by teachers who are adequately prepared. Results of this kind may work a hardship on the small high school, but would at least be better than the superficiality at present tolerated under the guise of offering educational opportunities.

Status. The facts already presented throw a considerable amount of light on the status of high school teachers in the country. Since the professional requirements are not standardized, since teaching is not regarded as a life career (only forty per cent of the high school teachers in 1927–28 were men), and since teachers are in the main nomadic, their status reflects these conditions. Nor is there the traditional respect for learning and education which helps to compensate the European teachers for any discontent he may have with his economic situation. In an industrial society, success is measured in material terms; judged by this measure again, the status of teachers reflects to a great degree the public attitude to a career which is overwhelmingly feminine. The median salaries of high school teachers in 1928–29 were as follows: $2680 in cities of over 100,000 population; $2120 in cities from 30,000 to 100,000; $1869 in cities from 10,000 to 30,000; $1729 in cities from 5000 to 10,000; and $1584 in cities from 2500 to 5000. A good beginning salary in the largest cities is $1531 and the maximum about $4200.[1] The average annual salary of junior high school teachers in cities of 10,000 population or more was $2,039, and of high school teachers $2467. The averages since 1930 are probably lower than these figures.

It is obvious that, as compared with the European secondary school teacher, the status of the American high school teacher is not so high if considered from the points of view of public esteem, standards of preparation, tenure and stability, and remuneration.

---

[1] Bachman, *op. cit.*, p. 3; National Education Association, Research Bulletin, Vol. VII, No. 3, pp. 114 and 121.

The faith of every American citizen in education has been manifested by the creation of opportunities for education and in the erection of magnificent buildings, but it is no exaggeration, in the light of the facts presented, to conclude that the essential element in promoting successful attainment of the ends of education, well-trained teachers, content with their work as life careers, has on the whole been ignored. The problem will only be solved when the country awakens to the realization that education is more than schooling, and that, if quality is desired, those responsible for its conduct must receive a remuneration which will warrant adequate preparation and ensure their adoption of teaching as a permanent career.

CHAPTER X
SUMMARY AND CONCLUSIONS

DESPITE the fact, which must be conceded, that the tempo of educational reconstruction and progress has been retarded by the serious economic and financial conditions which confront the world, the period since the War will stand out in the history of education as marking the beginning of a new era. Not only has the concept of scope of a national system of education been expanded in terms of its provision, but the theories underlying its process are changing. The nineteenth century witnessed the spread of the ideal of universal and compulsory elementary education; with the new era there has been inaugurated the recognition that elementary education, as defined in the nineteenth century in terms of literacy, is inadequate for the increasing complexity of life in the twentieth and that national welfare depends upon the provision of educational opportunities which will carry the individual as far as his abilities permit. The recognition of this fact is not confined to democracies like those of England, France, Germany, and the United States, but underlies the educational reorganization in the dictatorships of Italy and Russia. The implications of the new program do not extend merely to the provision of schools and other educational institutions adapted to every stage of life from infancy to adulthood, but include the adequate organization of measures to promote the health of the individual, not only in the interests of national progress, but as a result of a better understanding of the implications, physical and psychological, of the traditional ideal of a sound mind in a sound body.

The new educational program accordingly contemplates the provision of care for infants, *crèches* and nursery schools, kindergartens or maternal schools, primary schools, post-primary or secondary schools differentiated and varied according to the needs and abilities of the pupils, vocational schools, colleges and universities, and adult education, ranging from schools for the liquidation of adult illiteracy to the organization of opportunities for advanced studies. For the present, it must be admitted, adequate methods for the selection and distribution of pupils and students into the schools best suited to their abilities have not been devised. The American practice of admitting all adolescents to the same school, the high school, is open to serious criticisms, which do not, however, affect the right of every individual to the best education from which he is capable of profiting.[1] The English *Report on the Education of the Adolescent* and the organization of a variety of schools at the secondary level in Italy indicate the scope of the problem, without, however, providing suitable solutions of the problem of selection. One result of the failure to discover a solution in the European countries is the excessive pressure of adolescents to the academic secondary schools under conditions which lead to the production of an educated proletariate. The French proposal for the establishment of a National Bureau of Selection and Distribution suggests the need but fails to recommend the methods.[2]

How long it will take any country to achieve completely the program which has already been inaugurated, it would be impossible to predict. Such achievement will depend more upon the development of an enlightened point of view in the nations concerned than upon their financial ability to support it. Strong prejudices, the outgrowth of centuries of tradition based on class distinctions will be overcome. It must be remembered, however, that a century ago, and in some countries less than a century ago, the same objections were raised against the introduction of compulsory elementary education as are brought against proposals for the extension of education for adolescents. During the century that has elapsed, all conditions which affect the development of education have changed. The concept of democracy as political equality before the ballot box has given place to the concept of democracy in terms of equality of opportunity, political, social, and economic. Universal elementary education is leading to demands for more education. Class distinctions are yielding, slowly but surely, to the assertion of the right of the individual to advance as far as his abilities will permit; and the best method for promoting such advancement is through edu-

---

[1] See Thorndike, E. L., "The Distribution of Education," in *School Review*, May, 1932, pp. 335 ff.

[2] It is not unlikely that the investigations into examinations which are now being conducted in England, Scotland, France, and Germany, following the International Conference on Examinations held at Eastbourne in 1931, may result in recommendations on the point in question.

cation. Finally, education has come to be recognized as the most solid foundation for national welfare and progress.

In the last analysis the progress of education depends upon public enlightenment and willingness to support it. This means, not merely the education of the public through parents' organizations and other methods of propaganda, but measures for increased participation of the public in the administration of education. Much of the opposition on the part of the public to the increasing cost of education is due to failure to understand the purposes and aims of education. Large though the cost of education has become already and is bound to be in the future, the public everywhere fails to realize how little it is in comparison with other forms of national expenditures — the army and navy — or with the expenditures on luxuries and entertainments. The day is passing when education and its provision can be merely the concern of governments, administrative agencies, and the teaching profession. All of these must inevitably provide the leadership and guidance, but they must have behind them a public enlightened on the meaning of educational progress. Centralized systems of education may achieve standards of excellence which are sometimes not attained in systems administered locally, but they neither create nor are they susceptible to changing public demands. Education is a living thing and cannot, without seeming to be artificial, be created according to one pattern applicable over an extensive area. The least centralized systems often reflect the variety of forces and influences which give character to a nation. The principle of a proper balance between central and local control which is the strength of the English system is gradually being adopted in other countries — Germany, Russia, and the United States so far as administration is concerned, and Italy in the freedom assigned to the teaching profession in curriculum organization. Not only political and social but educational theory justify this principle. The proper reconciliation of localism and nationalism is not an insuperable task — minimum standards may be prescribed in order to secure equality of opportunity, systems of inspection may be established not to enforce but to suggest norms, or financial aid may be granted under certain conditions. In the last analysis, however, educational progress is dependent upon enlightened public opinion and sound leadership.

Such leadership has in the past been provided both in centralized and decentralized systems by the administration. The teachers have, on the whole, been relegated to the background and their function restricted to the work of the classroom. The new importance attached to education is nowhere better manifested than in the new tendency to place the preparation of elementary school teachers in Germany, England, and the United States on a university level and the provision in these countries of opportunities for advanced study. This tendency means more than an improvement in the quality of teaching; it represents, in contrast with the training provided in the nineteenth century, the beginnings of a movement to place teaching and education on a professional basis, and to give to teachers a greater opportunity of contributing in the light of their professional experience to the progress and advancement of education.

This tendency cannot, however, be employed as an argument for the self-determination of the teaching profession or for the autonomy of education. From the point of view of public interest the danger of such professional determination has been amply proved by the professions of law and of medicine. Education is a public affair and is governed today by the demands, explicit or implicit, of groups organized into national units. The development of public systems of education accompanied the development of nations in the nineteenth century,[1] and their continued development is sponsored in terms of national interests. But while systems of education must inevitably be organized in national units, there appears to be emerging a new concept of nationalism. The nineteenth-century concept of nationalism has by no means disappeared and the high hopes of a new era of world peace and brotherhood which were entertained after the close of the War have proved illusory; there is, indeed, no lack of evidence of the introduction into schools of the worst forms of nationalism of the last century. Progress may, however, be illustrated by the new tendency to discuss nationalism from the cultural rather than from the militaristic and competitive point of view. Cultural nationalism alone, a nationalism which is the natural expression of the life of a people, can serve as the basis of a national system of education which is natural and not dominated by ends extrinsic to sound education. Patriotism and civic loyalty can only have real and abiding signifi-

[1] See Reisner, E. H., *Nationalism and Education since 1789* (New York, 1922).

cance if they are built up on a recognition of the part played by one's nation in the service of humanity and of international coöperation as the basis of human progress.

Without entering upon speculations as to other possible forms of integration and organization which may be established in the future, in considering educational systems today the fact is that they are organized on national bases and that they are colored by the principles upon which nationalism rests. Despite the differences between educational systems which are due to the differences of national background there are certain points of resemblance in the general approach to the problems, and certain common tendencies toward a new philosophy of education. Throughout the history of education the fundamental aim has always been the transmission of the cultural inheritance which has been regarded as necessary for the preservation of society. From the point of view of methods this aim implied the moulding of the individual to a preconceived pattern, and the development of docility and conformity. Such methods were particularly well adapted to secure the ends of the nationalism and social organization of the nineteenth century with one system of schools for the masses or followers and another for the upper classes or leaders. The emphasis was on indoctrination, the acquisition of knowledge, whether of significance to the individual and society or not, formal learning, discipline imposed by punishments, reverence for tradition, and the acceptance of authority. The result was a gap between school and society, which became wider with the rapidly developing social and cultural changes resulting from the industrial revolution, the progress of science, the development of more rapid means of communication, and the rise of political consciousness among the masses.

All these changes have in the new era produced a revolution in the status of the individual and have brought with it a new recognition of his worth not only in those nations which have become more conscious of the meaning of democratic forms of government, but also in nations like Russia and Italy in which dictatorships have been established to protect the rights of all individuals against the machinations of Parties, even though all Parties are subordinated in the one case to the Communist and in the other to the Fascist. Not only have political and social traditions undergone a revolution, but the rapid advancement of the sciences and of inventions based upon them have tended to produce a certain instability of intellectual outlook which is more or less intolerant of the control of traditions of any kind. Educational theory and psychology have in turn contributed to the same situation with their emphasis on the individual as the starting-point in the educative process and on individual differences in abilities, capacities, and needs. Education, it is argued, has a larger function than the uncritical and unquestioned transmission of the cultural experience of the past; not only must education be a preparation for life, but every stage in its development must be full of meaning and significance to the learner; not only must education equip the individual with the knowledge and skills necessary to understand the society in which he lives, but it must develop in him a critical attitude which will enable him with freedom and discrimination to modify and adapt the social conditions around him to his own needs. The aim of education from this point of view is not to adjust the individual to society as it is, nor to inculcate acquiescence, docility and conformity, but to give him such a training as will enable him to refuse to accept tradition uncritically, to control the conditions under which he lives, and to be intellectually ready for change and progress. This philosophy, which stresses individualism and the freedom of the individual, and which in its extreme form refuses to accept any content fixed in advance and not determined directly by the interests of the learner, is today dominant in the new or progressive schools and in public systems in the *Versuchsschulen* and *Gemeinschaftsschulen* of Germany.

This school of thought ignores two important facts — first, that formal education is not the only means by which the individual is moulded, and second, that "the school is the school," to quote a statement from the French Instructions for Primary Schools, an institution deliberately created to attain certain social or national ends. Nations, in other words, have the type of schools which they desire and define in a sense the "experiences" which individuals are expected to acquire. This does not mean the acceptance of a policy of indoctrination. The task for the educator is to interpret the culture for which a nation stands and to devise the best methods, based on the contributions of psychology, whereby the individual acquires that culture. The day has passed when the sole emphasis in education and instruction can be placed merely on the acquisition of knowledge and information of any kind. Not knowledge alone, but conduct and character based on knowledge are the essentials of citizenship. Education is not cramming or pouring in of knowledge and information, but it is, so far as one institution can do it, the development of the pupil's total personality, his mind and body, emotion and will. It means that the abilities and potentialities of the pupil must be taken into account and the provision of opportunities and experiences for his fullest development with a thoroughly reasoned realization of his responsibility as a member of society. The selection of these experiences must be made from the individual's expanding environment, which constitutes the culture of the society to which he belongs. As was pointed out in earlier chapters, social or national culture is not something fixed but grows and progresses. A national authority may define minimum standards in the interests of equality of opportunity, but the prescription of what shall be taught in schools implies fixity and predetermined patterns of culture rather than recognition of its progressive character as the spontaneous interaction between individuals and their environments.

On the practical side the implication of this philosophy is seen in all the countries discussed in this volume, except France, in the emphasis on activity instruction (*Arbeitsunterricht, méthode active*) which involves two aspects, the utilization of the immediate environment (*Heimatkunde*) of the pupil and his active participation in the process of instruction. But the immediate environment (*Heimat*) is only the starting-point from which experience radiates out until it takes in national culture and at the higher levels those cultures which have influenced its development. The school is an institution which mediates and selects those experiences which society or a nation regards as desirable for its preservation and progress; but the individual is no longer a passive learner, absorbing information and knowledge through fear of disciplinary measures, but an active agent with the right on the basis of his progressive experiences to question, criticize, judge, and evaluate.

Although the new philosophy of education is generally accepted, there are gradations in the extent to which it is adopted in practice. Older countries (England and France) with long established traditions of culture are less ready to sacrifice what is regarded as the essential basis of their national foundations; other countries (Germany) seek to adapt the new forms of social organization to the progressive development of selected traditions as a basis of national solidarity: others again (Italy and Russia) seek to combine activity methods with political indoctrination, thus permitting freedom within certain rigidly defined limits; finally, the United States building upon a tradition that tradition must not be binding, emphasizes change and progress. Generally, however, there is widespread recognition that too strong an emphasis on traditions may lead to the development of prejudices and opposition to needed changes. On the other hand the danger underlying the emphasis on change and progress for their own sakes is the absence of social and national foundations by which their value may be measured.

The tendencies in methods, techniques, and curriculum-making thus point to the acceptance of the same philosophy of education; the solutions in different countries vary, since ultimately these are governed by differences in national backgrounds, environments, and culture, which even the rapid development of means of communication affect but slightly. The value of comparative education lies, not merely in the study of how nations live and think, but in developing an understanding of the forces and factors which lend to each nation its particular characteristics, and an appreciation of the meaning of education for national welfare. It emphasizes the principle that education is a living thing which derives its significance and meaning from all the forces underlying national cultures. Because the study of foreign school systems remains unintelligible without a study of the foundations of national existence, it furnishes an opportunity for comparing the variant concepts of nationalism, for discovering the common elements which make for international understanding, and for understanding intelligently those forces which in the past have militated against and which, if made the bases of education, may again endanger the onward progress of humanity. Such an approach, far from being a menace to the proper inculcation of patriotism, helps to promote a richer appreciation of the strength of each nation and to develop a patriotism based on a realization of the positive contributions which nations can make to human progress rather than on an emphasis on those aspects which stress national differences and lead to suspicion and hatred. These common elements comparative education seeks to discover but in discovering the common elements and the common problems of education, which confront national systems today, there is also discovered the fact that the solutions vary because nations differ each from each, not because of innate conflict of interests, but because each, as the result of different traditions, seeks to express and through education to transmit and develop a culture characteristic of itself; as within each national system, so what matters most for the development and progress of humanity as a whole is color and variety of life; education is a living thing and spontaneous only if it is inspired by the cultural foundations of the people whom it seeks to serve, for

> Truth is as Beauty unconfined:
> Various as Nature is man's Mind:
> Each race and tribe is as a flower
> Set in God's garden with its dower
> Of special instinct; and man's grace
> Compact of all must all embrace.
> China and Ind, Hellas or France,
> Each hath its own inheritance;
> And each to Truth's rich market brings
> Its bright divine imaginings,
> In rival tribute to surprise
> The world with native merchandise.[1]

[1] Bridges, R. S., "England to India," in *October and Other Poems* (The Clarendon Press, Oxford, 1920).

APPENDIX
BIBLIOGRAPHICAL NOTE

THE references which follow present a selection of current works dealing with various aspects of education. The intelligent study of the educational system of any country involves a knowledge of the history of education and of the political, social and cultural backgrounds of the country studied. For the history of education E. P. Cubberley's *History of Education* (Boston, 1920), E. H. Reisner's *Nationalism and Education since 1789* (New York, 1922), and *Comparative Education* edited by P. Sandiford (London, 1928) which deals with the educational systems of six countries before the post-War reorganization, are recommended. For the general backgrounds a number of references will be found in the list given in the following pages, especially the references for the first three chapters. Current information on the development of the countries discussed in this volume will be found in the *Statesman's Yearbook* (London), the *Europa Yearbook* (London), the *Annuaire Général* (Paris), *Annuaire Statistique* (Paris), the *Handbuch des öffentlichen Lebens* (Leipzig), *Statistisches Jahrbuch für das deutsche Reich* (Berlin), the *Almanacco Italiano* (Florence), the *Soviet Union Year-book* (London), the *American Yearbook*, and the *World Almanac* (New York).

Official reports on education are published in England by the Board of Education under the title *Education in* (the year) (London) and by the local education authorities; in Italy the Ministry of National Education issues an *Annuario;* in Germany a semi-official report is issued annually by the *Zentralinstitut für Erziehung und Unterricht* under the title of *Das Deutsche Schulwesen* (Berlin); in the United States, besides the annual and biennial reports of state and local authorities, the United States Office of Education issues a *Biennial Survey of Education* (Washington, D.C.). In France the place of a report of the Ministry of Public Instruction is taken by the annual reports on the budget for education prepared for members of the Chamber of Deputies and the Senate by their respective committees on education; these reports are unfortunately not available to the public, but summaries may be found in such journals as the *Revue Universitaire*.

Some of the central authorities for education publish official journals — the *Bulletin Administratif du Ministère de l'Education Nationale* (fortnightly); the *Zentralblatt für die Gesamte Unterrichts-Verwaltung in Preussen* (fortnightly) of the Prussian Ministry of Science, Art, and Public Education; the *Bollettino Ufficiale del Ministero dell' Educazione Nazionale* (weekly); and the *Komunisticheskoe Prosveshchenie (Communistic Education)* (monthly) issued by the People's Commissariat of Education of the R.S.F.S.R. The English Board of Education, in addition to the publication of regulations, circulars, and memoranda, publishes a series of Educational Pamphlets and from time to time reports of special committees (Consultative and Departmental).

The United States Office of Education issues Bulletins, Pamphlets, and Leaflets, and a monthly journal, *School Life*.

For purposes of general orientation cyclopedias of education will prove valuable. Monroe's *Cyclopedia of Education* (New York, 1911-19), although out of date for current information, still constitutes a useful starting point for the reader; the only other work of a similar kind in English is Foster Watson's *Encyclopedia and Dictionary of Education* (London, 1921-22). The French *Dictionnaire de Pédagogie*, edited by F. Buisson, was published in 1911. Germany, Italy, and Russia have, however, added a number of up-to-date encyclopedias to educational literature. The German works include: the *Pädagogisches Lexikon*, edited by H. Schwarz, four vols. (Leipzig, 1928); *Lexikon der Pädagogik der Gegenwart*, two vols. (Freiburg im Breisgau, 1932); *Handwörterbuch des preussischen Volksschulrechts* by W. Vorbrodt and K. Hermann (Leipzig, 1930); and the *Handbuch der Erziehungswissenschaft*, edited by F. X. Eggersdorfer, M. Ettlinger, G. Raederscheidt, and J. Schröteler (Munich, 1930). The Italian works are the *Dizionario delle Scienze Pedagogiche*, edited by M. Giovanni, two vols. (Milan, 1929), and the *Enciclopedie delle Enciclopedie*, vol. *Pedagogia*, published by A. F. Formiggini (Rome, n.d.). The Russian encyclopedia is the *Pedagogicheskaia Enciclopedia*, edited by A. G. Kalashnikov assisted by M. S. Epstein (Moscow, 1929-30).

The last few years in which there has developed a widening interest in comparative education have witnessed the publication of a number of international yearbooks: the *Educational Yearbook* of the International Institute of Teachers College, Columbia University, first issued in 1925 under the editorship of I. L. Kandel (New York); the *Internationale Jahresberichte für Erziehungswissenschaft* (Breslau), edited by Professor Rudolf Lehmann, of which only two volumes were issued in 1923 and 1928 and which has been discontinued on account of the death of the editor; the *Year Book of Education, 1932*, edited by Lord Eustace Percy (London). A valuable guide to the progress of education is furnished by the *Anuario de Bibliografía pedagógica*, which is edited by Professor Rufino Blanco y Sanchez (Madrid) and includes works in English, Spanish, German, French, and Italian. Finally, there must be added to this list the *Internationale Zeitschrift für Erziehungswissenschaft* (Cologne), a quarterly edited by Professors Friedrich Schneider of Bonn and Paul Monroe of New York; the articles are written in German, French or English with summaries in the other two languages. To list the annuals, general and special, issued in each country would be beyond the scope of this volume; such a list may be found in an article by J. Claparède, *Les Annuaires pédagogiques nationaux et internationaux*, in the *Internationale Zeitschrift für Erziehungswissenschaft*, No. 1, 1931, pp. 130 ff.

Guides to current educational bibliography will be found in the magazines listed below; for Germany in *Deutsche Nationalbibliographie* (Leipzig, fortnightly), and in the *Literarisches Zentralblatt* (Leipzig, fortnightly); and for the United States in the *Educational Index* published since 1929 by the H. W. Wilson Company, and in C. Alexander, *Educational Research*, a pamphlet issued annually by Teachers College, Columbia University, New York.

APPENDIX

The number of educational journals and magazines is so vast that it is possible to present only a selected list of those which are of general interest to the foreign student:

England: *The Times Educational Supplement* (weekly); *Schoolmaster* (weekly); *School Government Chronicle* (monthly); *Educational Outlook* (monthly); *Journal of Education* (monthly); *The New Era* (monthly); *Forum of Education* (quarterly).

France: *L'Ecole et la Vie* (weekly); *L'Ecole Libératrice* (weekly); *L'Information Universitaire* (weekly); *Enseignement Public* (monthly); *Revue Universitaire* (monthly); *Pour l'Ere Nouvelle* (Geneva, monthly).

Germany: *Die Erziehung* (monthly); *Die deutsche Schule* (monthly); *Die Arbeitsschule* (monthly); *Neue Bahnen* (monthly); *Die neue Erziehung* (monthly); *Pädagogische Warte* (monthly); *Pädagogisches Zentralblatt* (monthly); *Allgemeine deutsche Lehrerzeitung* (weekly); *Das werdende Zeitalter* (monthly); *Leipziger Lehrerzeitung* (weekly); *Deutsches Philologenblatt* (weekly).

Italy: *L'Educazione Nazionale* (monthly); *La Rivista Pedagogica* (monthly); *La Cultura Popolare* (monthly); *L'Educazione Fascista* (monthly); *La Nuova Scuola Italiana* (weekly).

Russia: *Na Putiakh k Novoy Shkole* (*On the Road to the New School*) (monthly).

United States: *School and Society* (weekly); *Educational Administration and Supervision* (monthly); *Elementary School Journal* (monthly); *Educational Method* (monthly); *Journal of Higher Education* (monthly); *Progressive Education* (monthly); *Journal of the National Education Association* (monthly); *The Nation's Schools* (monthly); *School Review* (monthly); *Teachers College Record* (monthly).

Chapter I

Nationalism and Education

1. Trace the development of the concept of nationalism.
2. Discuss the essential bases of nationalism.
3. Distinguish between political nationalism and cultural nationalism, and the influence of each on education.
4. Trace the interaction between the development of the concept of nationalism and the development of national systems of education.
5. How is a national culture formed? Can it be defined? Can it be prescribed?
6. Does the school create or interpret national culture?
7. How are curricula, courses of study and methods of instruction affected by nationalism?
8. To what extent can there be freedom in education in a national system of education?
9. What is the place of private schools or of minority groups in a national system of education?
10. Is the development of nationalism compatible with the promotion of internationalism?

References

Allport, F. H., *Social Psychology.* (Boston, 1924.)
Bowman, I., *New World.* (Yonkers, N.Y., 1926.)
Counts, G. S., *The American Road to Culture.* (New York, 1930.)
Fleure, J. H., *Peoples of Europe.* (Oxford, 1922.)
Gaus, J. M., *Great Britain: a Study in Civic Loyalty.* (Chicago, 1929.)
Gooch, G. P., *Nationality.* (London, 1920.)
Harper, S. N., *Civic Training in Soviet Russia.* (Chicago, 1929.)
—— *Making Bolshevists.* (Chicago, 1931.)
Hayes, C. J. H., *Essays on Nationalism.* (New York, 1926.)
—— *France, a Nation of Patriots.* (New York, 1930.)
—— *The Historical Evolution of Modern Nationalism.* (New York, 1931.)
Herbert, S., *Nationality and its Problems.* (London, 1920.)
Jäckh, E., *The New Germany.* (Oxford, 1927.)
Joseph, B., *Nationality, Its Nature and Problems.* (New Haven, 1929.)
Josey, C. C., *Race and National Solidarity.* (New York, 1923.)
Kosok, P., *Germany.* (Chicago, 1932.)
Merriam, C. E., *The Making of Citizens.* (Chicago, 1931.)
Monroe, P., Education and Nationalism, in *Essays in Comparative Education.* (New York, 1927.)
Moon, P. T., *Syllabus on International Relations.* (New York, 1925.)
Partridge, G. E., *The Psychology of Nations.* (New York, 1919.)
Pierce, B. L., *Civic Attitudes in American School Textbooks.* (New York, 1930.)
—— *Public Opinion and the Teaching of History.* (New York, 1926.)
Pillsbury, W. B., *Psychology of Nationality and Internationalism.* (New York, 1919.)
Prudhommeaux, J., *Der Kampf um das Geschichtsbuch in Frankreich.* (Leipzig, 1929.) Tr. from *Pour la Paix par l'Ecole* (Nîmes, 1928.).
—— *Les Livres Scolaires d'après Guerre.* (Paris, 1923.)
Reisner, E. H., *Nationalism and Education since 1789.* (New York, 1922.)
Rose, J. H., *Nationality in Modern History.* (New York, 1916.)
Schneider, H. W., *Making the Fascist State.* (New York, 1928.)
—— and Clough, S. B., *Making Fascists.* (Chicago, 1929.)
Scott, J. F., *The Menace of Nationalism.* (London, 1926.)
—— *Patriots in the Making.* (New York, 1916.)
Stratton, G. M., *Social Psychology of International Conduct.* (New York, 1929.)
Woody, T., *New Minds; New Men?* (New York, 1932.)
Zimmern, A. E., *Nationality and Government.* (London, 1918.)

Chapter II

Education and National Characteristics

1. What is meant by national traits or characteristics?
2. How are differences in national attitudes to be explained?

APPENDIX 875

3. How do differences in national characteristics affect education?
4. What are the factors which produce differences in philosophies underlying education?
5. Can there be conflicts between theories of education and national character?
6. Can national character be changed or modified? What part can the school play in this change?

REFERENCES

Adams, J. T., *Our Business Civilization*. (New York, 1929.)
Barnes, J. S., *Fascism*. (London, 1931.)
Barker, E., *National Character and the Factors in its Formation*. (London, 1927.)
Boutmy, E., *Psychologie Politique du Peuple Américain*. (Paris, 1920.)
Curtius, E. R., *Civilization of France*. (New York, 1930.)
Dibelius, W., *England*. (New York, 1930.)
Diesel, E., *Germany and the Germans*. (London, 1931.)
Eckardt, H. von, *Russia*. (New York, 1932.)
Feuillerat, A., *French Life and Ideals*. (New Haven, 1925.)
Gaus, J. M., *Great Britain, a Study in Civic Loyalty*. (Chicago, 1929.)
Inge, W. R., *England*. (New York, 1926.)
Kandel, I. L., The American Spirit in Education in *Essays in Comparative Education*. (New York, 1930.)
—— edr., *Educational Yearbook, 1929*, of the International Institute, Teachers College, Columbia University. Bibliography. (New York, 1930.)
Keyserling, Count H., *Europe*. (New York, 1928.)
Madariaga, S. de, *Americans*. (London, 1930.)
—— *Englishmen, Frenchmen, Spaniards*. (Oxford, 1928.)
Merriam, C. E., *The Making of Citizens*. (Chicago, 1931.)
Nevinson, H., *The Natives of England*. (New York, 1931.)
Parrington, V. L., *Main Currents in American Thought*, three vols. (New York, 1927.)
Shuster, G., *The Germans*. (New York, 1932.)
Sieburg, F., *Who are these French?* (New York, 1932.)
Siegfried, A., *America Comes of Age*. (New York, 1927.)
—— *France, a Study in Nationality*. (New Haven, 1930.)

CHAPTER III

THE STATE AND EDUCATION

1. Trace the development of state control in education.
2. Compare the Hegelian philosophy of the State with the principles underlying democratic forms of government.
3. What are the arguments for state or national control of education?
4. Does a state or national system of education imply a monopoly of control or supervision?

5. Discuss the Papal Encyclical on Christian Education of Youth (1929) and its bearing on the relation of the State to education.
6. What should be the rights in matters of education of (1) parents; (2) minority groups (national, linguistic, religious, political)? How can such rights be reconciled with the rights of the State?
7. Compare the place of private schools in the six countries discussed in the present volume.
8. What is the effect of different types of state control on the progress of education?
9. What are the causes leading to different types of state relation to education?
10. Discuss the statement that the relation of the State to education is determined by the political character of the State.
11. Discuss the statement that the school cannot be divorced from politics.
12. Can the school contribute to social and political change?
13. Is there any conflict between the character of state control and the progress of national culture?
14. In what sense is a free profession of teachers possible in a state system of education?
15. Does a state system of education necessarily imply indoctrination, political or cultural?

REFERENCES

Barthélemy, J., *The Government of France.* (London, 1924.)
Beard, C., *American Government and Politics.* (New York, 1931.)
Blättner, F., *Das Elternrecht und die Schule.* (Leipzig, 1927.)
Briggs, T. H., *The Great Investment.* (Cambridge, Mass., 1930.)
Bryce, Viscount J. B., *The American Commonwealth.* (New York, 1930.)
—— *Modern Democracies.* (New York, 1924.)
Buisson, F., and Farrington, F. E., *French Educational Ideals Today.* (Yonkers, N.Y., 1919.)
Clarke, F., *Essays in the Politics of Education.* (Oxford, 1923.)
Counts, G. S., *The Soviet Challenge to America.* (New York, 1931.)
Cubberley, E. P., *Public Education in the United States.* (Boston, 1919.)
—— *State School Administration.* (Boston, 1927.)
Deutscher Lehrerverein, Schulpolitisches Jahrbuch. (Berlin.)
Dewey, J., *German Philosophy and Politics.* (New York, 1915.)
Durkheim, E., *Education et Sociologie.* (Paris, 1927.)
Emerson, R., *State and Sovereignty in Modern Germany.* (New Haven, 1928.)
Findlay, J. J., *Foundations of Education*, Vol. I. (London, 1925.)
Gaus, J. M., *Great Britain, a Study in Civic Loyalty.* (Chicago, 1929.)
Giuliano, B., *La Politica scolastica del Governo Nazionale.* (Milan, 1924.)
Gooch, R. K., *Regionalism in France.* (New York, 1931.)
Graham, M. W., *New Constitutions of Europe.* (New York, 1927.)
Griffith, E. S., *The Modern Development of City Government in the United Kingdom and the United States.* (Oxford, 1929.)

APPENDIX

Hans, N., *Principles of Educational Policy*. (London, 1929.)
Harper, S. N., *Civic Training in Russia*. (Chicago, 1929.)
—— *Making Bolshevists*. (Chicago, 1931.)
Harris, G. M., *Local Government in Many Lands*. (London, 1926.)
Hayes, C. J. H., *France, a Nation of Patriots*. (New York, 1930.)
Headlam, M. A., *New Democratic Constitutions of Europe*. (Oxford, 1929.)
Hesse, S., *Kritische Vergleichung des Schulwesens der anderen Kulturstaaten* in Nohl, H., and Pallat, L., *Handbuch der Pädagogik*. (Langensalza, 1928.)
Kandel, I. L., edr., *Educational Yearbook, 1929, and 1932*. (New York, 1930 and 1933.)
—— and Alexander, T., *Reorganization of Education in Prussia*. (New York, 1927.)
Landé, W., *Aktenstücke zum Reichsvolkschulgesetz*. (Leipzig, 1928.)
—— *Die Schule in der Reichsverfassung*. (Berlin, 1929.)
Laski, H., *Authority in the Modern State*. (New Haven, 1919.)
—— *Grammar of Politics*. (New Haven, 1925.)
Lehmann, R., *Staat, Kirche und Schule im Auslande*. (Darmstadt, 1927.)
Lowell, A. L., *The Government of England*. (New York, 1912.)
Maciver, R., *The Modern State*. (London, 1926.)
Mallory, W. H., edr., *Political Handbook of the World*. (New York, 1932.)
McBain, H. L., and Rogers, L., *New Constitutions of Europe*. (New York, 1923.)
Merriam, C. E., *The Making of Citizens*. (Chicago, 1931.)
Ogg, F. A., *English Government and Politics*. (New York, 1929.)
—— *The Governments of Europe*. (New York, 1929.)
Poincaré, H., *How France is Governed*. (New York, 1919.)
Quigley, H., and Clark, R., *Republican Germany*. (New York, 1928.)
Reisner, E. H., *Nationalism and Education since 1789*. (New York, 1922.)
Robson, W. A., *The Development of Local Government*. (London, 1931.)
Scherer, A., *Staat und Kirche in ihrer Verhältnis zur Schule*. (Berlin, 1926.)
Schneider, H. W., *Making the Fascist State*. (New York, 1928.)
—— and Clough, S. B., *Making Fascists*. (Chicago, 1929.)
Strunz, J., edr., *Politik und Pädagogik im Auslande*. (Leipzig, 1931.)
Suzzallo, H., *Our Faith in Education*. (Philadelphia, 1921.)
Woody, T., *New Minds; New Men?* (New York, 1932.)

Chapter IV
The Organization of Educational Systems

1. What are the factors and causes which determine the nature and amount of education provided in a national system of education?
2. What is meant by equality of educational opportunity?
3. Does equality of educational opportunity imply the same schools for all?
4. What are the implications of the common school movement?
5. Does equality of educational opportunity imply the exclusion of the factor of selection?

6. What should be the scope and extent of a national system of education?
7. Does the responsibility of a national system of education extend beyond instruction?
8. Discuss the provisions for the medical inspection of children of school age.
9. Has an educational system any responsibility for the health of pupils?
10. Compare the provisions in different countries for preschool education.
11. What is the responsibility of a national system of education for vocational education?
12. How have changing social, political, and economic conditions affected the provision of agencies for education?
13. Should the control of delinquent children be placed under the educational or the police and judicial authorities?
14. What are the arguments for the inclusion of social welfare activities for children of school age in an educational system?
15. Discuss the reasons for the expansion of the provisions for the education of adults.

REFERENCES
Organization

General
 Bureau International d'Education, *L'Organisation de l'Instruction Publique dans 53 Pays.* (Geneva, 1932.)
 Kandel, I. L., edr., *Educational Yearbook, 1924–.* (New York, 1925–.)

England
 Education Week *Handbooks* issued by many local authorities, e.g., Cornwall, Ilkeston, Bingley, Bradford, Leeds, Manchester, Oldham, Sheffield, etc.
 London County Council, *The London Education Service.* (London, 1927.)
 —— *The Special Services of Education in London.* (London, 1929.)
 Norwood, C., *The English Educational System.* (London, 1928.)
 Percy, Lord Eustace, edr., *The Year Book of Education, 1932.* (London, 1931.)

France
 Guide Général pour la Jeunesse. (Paris, n.d.)
 Richard, C., *L'Enseignement en France.* (Paris, 1925.)

Germany
 Kandel, I. L., and Alexander, T., *Reorganization of Education in Prussia.* (New York, 1927.)
 Löffler, E., *Das öffentliche Bildungswesen in Deutschland.* (Berlin, 1931.)
 Zentralinstitut für Erziehung und Unterricht, *Das Deutsche Schulwesen.* (Berlin, annual.)

Italy
Almanacco Scolastico Nazionale, Anno 1929. (Florence, 1929.)
Goy, H., *La Politique scolaire de la nouvelle Italie*. (Paris, 1926.)
Marraro, H. R., *Nationalism in Italian Education*. (New York, 1927.)

Russia
Hans, N., and Hessen, S., *Educational Policy in Soviet Russia*. (London, 1930.)
Counts, G. S., *The Soviet Challenge to America*. (New York, 1931.)
Pinkevitch, A., *The New Education in Soviet Russia*. (New York, 1929.)
Wilson, L. L. W., *The New Schools of New Russia*. (New York, 1928.)

United States
Hylla, E., *Die Schule der Demokratie*. (Berlin, 1928.)
Cubberley, E. P., *Public Education in the United States*. (Boston, 1919.)
United States Office of Education, *Education in the United States of America*. (Washington, D.C., 1927.)

Social Welfare
Almanacco Scolastico Nazionale, Anno 1929. (Florence, 1929.)
American Child Health Association, *A World Panorama of Health Education*. (New York, 1929.)
Blome, P., *Jugendwohlfahrtseinrichtungen und ihre gesetzlichen Grundlagen* (Halle, 1931.)
Board of Education, *The Health of the Child*. (London, annual.)
Hall, W. C., *Children's Courts*. (London, 1926.)
Hess, W., *Jugendwohlfahrtsrecht*. (Munich, 1926.)
Hirtsiefer, H., *Jugendpflege in Preussen*. (Berlin, 1930.)
International Handbook of Child Care and Protection. (London, 1928.)
King, O. B., *The Employment and Welfare of Juveniles*. (London, 1925.)
Mesurier, L. L., *Boys in Trouble*. (London, 1931.)
Ministry of Labour, England, *Report on the Work of Local Committees for Juvenile Employment*. (London, 1932.)
Newsholme, Sir A., *International Studies on the Relation between the Private and Official Practice of Medicine with special Reference to the Prevention of Disease*. (Baltimore, 1931.)
Nohl, H., *Jugendwohlfahrt*. (Leipzig, 1927.)
Opera Nazionale Balilla, The Opera Nazionale Balilla. (Rome, n.d.)
Percy, Lord Eustace, edr., *The Year Book of Education, 1932*. (London, 1931.)
Stern, E., *Jugendwohlfahrt und Schule*. (Dortmund, 1926.)
Weyl, R., *Das Deutsche Jugendrecht*. (Leipzig, 1927.)
White House Conference on Child Health and Protection. The *Reports* of all the sections published by the Century Company, New York, 1930–32.
Woody, T., *New Minds: New Men?* (New York, 1932.)
Zentralinstitut für Erziehung und Unterricht, *Das Deutsche Schulwesen*. (Berlin, annual.)

Adult Education

International Handbook of Adult Education. (London, 1929.)
World Adult Education Association, *Bulletins.* (London.)

CHAPTER V
ADMINISTRATION OF EDUCATION

1. What are the forces which determine the character of the administration of education in any country?
2. Discuss the advantages and disadvantages of centralized control of education; of local control.
3. From the point of view of a national system of education how can the powers of central and local authorities for education be appropriately distributed?
4. Discuss the distinction between *externa* and *interna* and its implications for the administration of education.
5. What should be the functions of educational administration?
6. How do differences in types of educational administration affect educational progress?
7. What should be the responsibility of an educational authority, central or local, (1) for promoting equality of opportunity; (2) for curricula and courses of study; (3) for the preparation and certification of teachers; (4) for the supervision and inspection of teachers; (5) for educational standards?
8. To what extent should (1) the public, (2) the teachers participate in the administration of education?
9. Discuss the place of parents' meetings and associations in relation to education.
10. Why is bureaucratic control less desirable in education than in any other form of public administration?
11. What should be the bases for the financial support of education? What are the most satisfactory methods for the apportionment of funds for education?

REFERENCES
England

Balfour, Sir G., *Educational Administration.* (Oxford, 1921.)
—— *Educational Systems of Great Britain and Ireland.* (Oxford, 1903.)
Barker, W. R., *The Superannuation of Teachers in England and Wales.* (London, 1926.)
Board of Education, *Education in 1931. Report of the Board of Education and Statistics of Public Education in England and Wales.* (London, 1932.)
—— Report of the Departmental Committee. *Private Schools.* (London, 1932.)

APPENDIX 881

Corlett, J., *A Survey of the Financial Aspects of Elementary Education.* (London, 1929.)
Education Authorities Directory. (London, annual.)
Education Week *Handbooks* issued by many local authorities, e.g., Cornwall, Ilkeston, Bingley, Bradford, Leeds, Manchester, Oldham, Sheffield, etc.
Griffith, E. S., *The Modern Development of City Government in the United Kingdom and the United States.* (Oxford, 1927.)
Ikin, A. E., *The Organization and Administration of the Education Department.* (London, 1926.)
——, and Sparke, H. C., *A Compendium of Precedents, Judgments, Decisions, Opinions, Examples and Notes on the Education Act 1921.* (London, 1931.)
Jennings, H., *The Private Citizen in Public Social Work.* (London, 1930.)
Kandel, I. L., edr., *Educational Yearbook* of the International Institute, Teachers College, Columbia University, *1924–.* (New York, 1925–.)
London County Council, *The Londoner's Education; its History and Development.* (London, 1924.)
—— *The London Education Service.* (London, 1927.)
—— *The Special Services of Education in London.* (London, 1929.)
Moulton, H. F., *The Powers and Duties of Education Authorities.* (London, 1919.)
National Association of Head Teachers, *Education in Lancashire.* (London, 1932.)
Norwood, C., *The English Educational System.* (London, 1928.)
——, *The English Tradition of Education.* (London, 1929.)
Owen, Sir H., and Lithiby, Sir J., *The Education Act, 1921.* (London, 1923.)
Percy, Lord Eustace, edr., *The Year Book of Education, 1932.* (London, 1931.)
Robson, W. D., *The Development of Local Government.* (London, 1931.)
Samuels, H., *Education Committees, their Powers and Duties.* (London, 1928.)
Selby-Bigge, Sir L. A., *The Board of Education.* (London, 1927.)
Simon, E. D., *A City Council from Within.* (London, 1926.)

France
Dion, L., *Recueil Complet de la Législation de l'Enseignement Secondaire.* (Paris, 1929.)
Forsant, O., *Vade-Mecum de l'Enseignement Primaire.* (Paris, 1921.)
Kandel, I. L., edr., *Educational Yearbook* of the International Institute, Teachers College, Columbia University, *1924–.* (New York, 1925–.)
—— edr., *French Elementary Schools. Official Courses of Study.* (New York, 1926.)
Richard, C., *L'Enseignement en France.* (Paris, 1925.)
Soleil, J., *Le Livre des Instituteurs.* (Paris, 1929.)

Germany

Kandel, I. L., edr., *Educational Yearbook* of the International Institute, Teachers College, Columbia University, *1924–*. (New York, 1925–.)

———, and Alexander, T., *The Reorganization of Education in Prussia.* (New York, 1927.)

Kühn, W., *Schulrecht in Preussen.* (Leipzig, 1926.)

Landé, W., *Die Schule in der Reichsverfassung.* (Berlin, 1929.)

Löffler, E., *Das öffentliche Bildungswesen in Deutschland.* (Düsseldorf, 1931.)

Nohl, H., and Pallat, L., *Handbuch der Pädagogik,* Vol. IV. (Langensalza, 1924.)

Nydahl, J., *Das Berliner Schulwesen.* (Berlin, 1928.)

Pottag, A., *Die Bestimmungen über die Volks- und Mittelschulen und über die Ausbildung und die Prüfungen der Lehrer und Lehrerinnen in Preussen.* (Berlin, n.d.)

Rohrscheidt, K. von, *Gesetz betreffend die Unterhaltung der öffentlichen Schulen.* (Berlin, 1931.)

Sachse, A., *Grundzüge des preussischen Volksschulrechts.* (Berlin, 1926.)

Vorbrodt, W., and Hermann, K., *Handwörterbuch des gesamten Schulrechts und der Schul- und Unterrichtsverwaltung in Preussen.* (Leipzig, 1930.)

Weidmannsche Taschenausgaben von Verfügungen der Preussischen Unterrichtsverwaltung. (Berlin.)
Heft 1. *Elternbeirat und Elternbeiratswahlen.*
Heft 31. *Die Verwaltungsordnung für städtische höhere Lehranstalten.*
Heft 34. *Die Landesschulkasse.*
Heft 47. *Etats-, Kassen- und Rechnungswesen.*
Heft 72. *Schuldeputation und Schulvorstand.*

Zentralinstitut für Erziehung und Unterricht, *Das deutsche Schulwesen.* (Berlin, annual.)

Italy

Almanacco Scolastico Nazionale, Anno *1929,* pp. 39 ff. (Florence, 1929.) On pp. 73 ff. will be found a list of the laws, rules and regulations concerning the administration of education in Italy since 1929. Subsequent legislation may be followed in the *Bollettino Ufficiale* of the Ministry of National Education.

Goy, H., *La Politique scolaire de la nouvelle Italie.* (Paris, 1926.)

Kandel, I. L., edr., *Educational Yearbook, 1924,* of the International Institute, pp. 329 ff. (New York, 1925.)

Marraro, H. R., *Nationalism in Italian Education.* (New York, 1927.)

Testo unico delle Leggi e Norme Giuridiche sulla Istruzione elementare, post-elementare e sulla sue Opere d'Integrazione. (Rome, 1928.)

Russia

Counts, G. S., *The Soviet Challenge to America.* (New York, 1931.)

Goode, W. T., *Schools, Teachers and Scholars in Soviet Russia.* (London, 1929.)

Hans, N., and Hessen, S., *Educational Policy in Soviet Russia*. (London, 1930.)
Public Education in the Russian Socialistic Federation of Soviet Republics. (Moscow, 1928.)
Wilson, L. L. W., *The New Schools of New Russia*. (New York, 1928.)

United States
  Alexander, Carter, and Theisen, W. W., *Publicity Campaigns for better School Support*. (Yonkers, N.Y., 1921.)
  Cook, W. A., *Federal and State School Administration*. (New York, 1926.)
  Counts, G. S., *The Social Composition of Boards of Education*. (Chicago 1927.)
  Cubberley, E. P., *Public Education in the United States*. (Boston, 1919.)
  —— *Public School Administration*. (Boston, 1929.)
  —— *State and County Educational Reorganization: The Revised Constitution and School Code of the State of Osceola*. (Boston, 1914.)
  —— *State and County School Administration, Source Book*. (Boston, 1915.)
  —— *State School Administration*. (Boston, 1929.)
  Department of Superintendence of the National Education Association, *Seventh Yearbook*. (Washington, 1929.)
  Engelhardt, F., *Public School Organization and Administration*. (New York, 1931.)
  Engelhardt, N. L., and Alexander, Carter, *School Finance and Business Administration*. (New York, 1927.)
  Engelhardt, N. L., and Engelhardt, F., *Planning School Building Programs*. (New York, 1930.)
  —— *Public School Business Administration*. (New York, 1927.)
  Graves, F. P., *The Administration of American Education*. (New York, 1932.)
  Kandel, I. L., edr., *Twenty-five Years of American Education*, Chs. VII and VIII. (New York, 1924.)
  Li, C. H., *Popular Control of Education in the United States*. (Shanghai, 1928.)
  Lindsay, E. E., *Problems in School Administration*. (New York, 1928.)
  McGaughy, J. R., *Fiscal Administration of City School Systems*. (New York, 1928.)
  Miller, C. R., and C. F., *Publicity and Public Schools*. (New York, 1924.)
  Moehlman, A. B., *Public School Relations*. (Chicago, 1927.)
  Monroe, W. S., *Ten Years of Educational Research, 1918–1927*. (Urbana, Ill., 1928.)
  National Advisory Committee on Education, *Federal Relations to Education*, Parts I and II. (Washington, 1931.)
  Reeder, W. G., *The Business Administration of a School System*. (New York, 1929.)
  —— *The Fundamentals of Public School Administration*. (New York, 1930.)

Sears, J. B., *The School Survey*. (Boston, 1925.)
Strayer, G. D., and Engelhardt, N. L., *Problems in Educational Administration*. (New York, 1925.)
Strayer, G. D., and Haig, R. M., *The Financing of Education in the State of New York*. (New York, 1923.)
Swift, F. H., *Federal and State Policies in Public School Finance in the United States*. (New York, 1931.)

Chapter VI

Elementary Education

1. Discuss the nature and scope of the preschool.
2. Compare the place of nursery schools in Europe and the United States.
3. Compare the nursery school, the kindergarten, the *école maternelle*, and the infant school.
4. Compare the provisions for and the administration of compulsory school attendance.
5. Trace the development of elementary education and the survival of an elementary school tradition.
6. What is the influence of the elementary school tradition on present practices?
7. What is the implication of the change of the term "elementary" to the term "primary" education?
8. Compare the aims of elementary education in the countries considered.
9. What are the factors which determine the character of the elementary school curriculum?
10. Who should make the course of study?
11. Should the elementary school course of study be based on national objectives? local environment? needs and interests of the pupils?
12. Compare the prescribed courses of study in one country with courses of study based on "Suggestions" or "Outlines."
13. Can there be any education without indoctrination?
14. What is meant by activity instruction?
15. What is the connotation of German *Heimatkunde* in English, American, and Italian schools?
16. Discuss the significant changes in methods of instruction which have been introduced in elementary schools in the last two decades. What has produced these changes?
17. What should be the place of examinations in elementary schools?
18. Compare the standards of attainment expected in the elementary schools of the countries considered.
19. Discuss the types and character of inspection and supervision in the countries considered.
20. Discuss the contribution of "progressive" or "new" education to elementary education.
21. Discuss the place of textbooks, their selection and use, in elementary schools.

22. Compare the time allotted to the subjects of the elementary school curriculum in the countries considered.
23. Discuss the relations of elementary to post-elementary education.

REFERENCES

General

Kandel, I. L., edr., *Educational Yearbook, 1924*, pp. 481 ff.; *1925*, pp. 467 ff. (New York, 1925 and 1926.)

New Education Fellowship, *Towards a New Education*. (New York, 1930.)

Reisner, E. H., *Nationalism and Education since 1789*. (New York, 1922.)

England

Adamson, J. W., *English Education, 1789–1902*. (Cambridge, 1930.)

Ashby, A. W., and Byles, P. G., *Rural Education*. (Oxford, 1923.)

Ashby, M. K., *The Country School. Its Practice and Problems*. (Oxford, 1929.)

Ballard, P. B., *The Changing School*. (London, 1926.)

Birchenough, C., *History of Elementary Education in England and Wales*. (London, 1925.)

Blyton, E., *Modern Teaching in the Infant School*. (London, 1932.)

Board of Education, *Handbook of Suggestions for the Consideration of Teachers and Others Concerned in the Work of Public Elementary Schools*. (London, 1927.)

—— *Handbook of Suggestions on Health Education*. (London, 1928.)

—— *The New Prospect in Education*. (London, 1928.)

—— Consultative Committee, *Report on the Education of the Adolescent*. (London, 1926.)

—— *Report on the Primary School*. (London, 1931.)

Cholmely, R. F., and others, *The Case for Nursery Schools*. (London, 1929.)

Findlay, J. J., *Foundations of Education*, two vols. (London, 1925 and 1927.)

Hey, Spurley, *The Central School*. (Manchester, 1924.)

Ikin, A. E., and Sparke, H. C., *A Compendium of Precedents, Judgments, Decisions, Opinions, Examples and Notes on the Education Act 1921*. (London, 1931.)

Kimmins, C. W., and Rennie, B., *Triumph of the Dalton Plan*. (London, 1932.)

Lay, E. J. S., edr., *Macmillan's Teaching in Practice*, six vols. (London, 1931.)

Lochhead, J., *The Education of Young Children in England*. (New York, 1932.)

Lynch, A. P., *Rise and Progress of the Dalton Plan*. (London, 1926.)

McMillan, M., *The Nursery School*. (London, 1930.)

Nunn, Sir T. P., *Education, its Data and first Principles*. (London, 1930.)

APPENDIX

Owen, G., *Nursery School Education*. (London, 1920.)
Percy, Lord Eustace, edr., *The Year Book of Education, 1932*. (London, 1931.)
Sadler, Sir M. E., *Our Public Elementary Schools*. (London, 1926.)
Sleight, W. G., *The Organization and Curricula of Schools*. (London, 1920.)
Smith, F., *History of English Elementary Education*. (London, 1931.)
Smith, H. B., edr., *Education at Work*. (Manchester, 1927.)
West Riding of Yorkshire, Education Department, *Report of the Consultative Committee on the Curriculum of the Senior School*. (Wakefield, 1931.)
Wilson, J. D., edr., *The Schools of England*. (London, 1930.)
Wise, M., *English Village Schools*. (London, 1931.)

France

Brereton, C., *Studies in Foreign Education*. (London, 1913.)
Buisson, F., and Farrington, F. E., *French Educational Ideals*. (New York, 1919.)
Farrington, F. E., *Public Primary School System of France*. (New York, 1906.)
Forsant, O., *Vade-Mecum de l'Enseignement Primaire*. (Paris, 1921.)
Hayes, C. J. H., *France, a Nation of Patriots*. (New York, 1930.)
Kandel, I. L., edr., *Educational Yearbook, 1929*, pp. 461 ff. (New York, 1930.)
—— edr., *French Elementary Schools. Official Courses of Study*. (New York, 1926.)
Lantenois, A., *Ce que l'Instituteur doit savoir*. (Paris, 1930.)
Lapie, P., *Pédagogie Française*. (Paris, 1926.)
Schwartz, L., *Nouveau Code de l'Instruction Primaire*. (Paris, 1930.)
Soleil, J., *Le Livre des Instituteurs*. (Paris, 1929.)

Germany

Alexander, T., *Training of Elementary Teachers in Germany*. (New York, 1929.)
—— and Parker, B., *The New Education in the German Republic*. (New York, 1929.)
Gaudig, H., edr., *Freie geistige Schularbeit*. (Breslau, 1925.)
Hilker, F., *Deutsche Schulversuche*. (Berlin, 1924.)
Kandel, I. L., and Alexander, T., *Reorganization of Education in Prussia*. (New York, 1927.)
Karsen, F., *Deutsche Versuchsschulen der Gegenwart und ihre Probleme*. (Leipzig, 1923.)
—— *Die neuen Schulen in Deutschland*. (Langensalza, 1924.)
Kerschensteiner, G., *Begriff der Arbeitsschule*. (Leipzig, 1925.)
Kühn, W., *Schulrecht in Preussen*. (Leipzig, 1926.)
Oestreich, P., edr., *Die Produktionsschule*. (Berlin, 1924.)
Pottag, A., *Die Bestimmungen über die Volks- und Mittelschulen und über*

APPENDIX 887

die Ausbildung und die Prüfungen der Lehrer und Lehrerinnen in Preussen. (Berlin, n.d.)
Pretzel, C. L. U., Hylla, E., and Nadolle, L., *Neuzeitliche Volkschularbeit, Winke zur Durchführung der preussischen Lehrplanrichtlinien.* (Langensalza, 1924.)
Sachse, A., *Grundzüge des preussischen Volksschulrechts.* (Berlin, 1926.)
Scheibner, O., *Zwanzig Jahre Arbeitsschule in Idee und Gestaltung.* (Leipzig, 1928.)
Weidmannsche Taschenausgaben von Verfügungen der Preussischen Unterrichtsverwaltung. (Berlin.)
Heft 18. *Die Grundschule.*
Heft 26. *Die Mittelschule.*
Heft 40, a and b. *Die Bestimmungen über Einführung von Lehrbüchern.*
Heft 43. *Sammelklassen und Sammelschulen.*
Heft 53. *Privatschule und Privatunterricht.*
Heft 57. *Die Schulpflicht.*
Heft 59. *Religionsunterricht.*
Zentralinstitut für Erziehung und Unterricht, *Das Deutsche Schulwesen.* (Berlin, annual.)

Italy
Almanacco Scolastico Nazionale, Anno 1929. (Florence, 1929.) On pp. 191 ff. will be found a list of all the laws, rules and regulations governing elementary education from 1906 to 1928. All laws, rules and regulations subsequent to 1928 can be found in the *Bollettino Ufficiale* of the Ministry of National Education.
Codignola, E., *Il Problema dell'Educazione Nazionale in Italia.* (Florence, 1925.)
Ferrière, A., *L'Aube de l'Ecole Sereine en Italie.* (Paris, 1927.)
Gentile, G., *La Riforma dell'Educazione*, tr. by D. Bigongiari, *The Reform of Education.* (New York, 1922.)
Goy, H., *La Politique scolaire de la Nouvelle Italie.* (Paris, 1926.)
—— *Nouveau Code de l'Enseignement Primaire Italien.* (Paris, 1926.)
Lombardo-Radice, G., *Educazione e Diseducazione.* (Florence, 1923.)
—— *Acconto ai Maestri.* (Turin, 1925.)
—— *La Riforma della Scuole Elementare*, two vols. (Palermo, 1925 and 1926.)
Marraro, H. R., *Nationalism in Italian Education.* (New York, 1927.)
Testo unico delle Leggi e Norme Giuridiche sulla Istruzione elementare, postelementare e sulla sue Opere d'Integrazione. (Rome, 1928.)

Russia
Counts, G. S., *The Soviet Challenge to America.* (New York, 1931.)
Dewey, J., *Impressions of Soviet Russia and the Revolutionary World.* (New York, 1928.)
Hans, N., and Hessen, S., *Educational Policy in Soviet Russia.* (London, 1930.)

Harper, S. N., *Civic Training in Soviet Russia.* (Chicago, 1929.)
—— *Making Bolshevists.* (Chicago, 1931.)
Kandel, I. L., edr., *Educational Yearbook, 1927*, pp. 315 ff. (New York, 1928.)
Pinkevitch, A. P., *The New Education in the Soviet Republic.* (New York, 1929.)
Public Education in the Russian Socialistic Federation of Soviet Republics. (Moscow, 1928.)
Wilson, L. L. W., *The New Schools of New Russia.* (New York, 1928.)
Woody, T., *New Minds: New Men?* (New York, 1932.)

United States
Bagley, W. C., and Keith, J., *An Introduction to Teaching.* (New York, 1924.)
Bain, E. W., *An Analytical Study of Teaching in Nursery School, Kindergarten, and First Grade.* (New York, 1929.)
Blatz, W. E., and Bott, H., *Parents and the Preschool Child.* (New York, 1929.)
Bobbitt, F., *How to Make a Curriculum.* (Boston, 1924.)
Bode, B. H., *Modern Educational Theories.* (New York, 1927.)
Bonser, F. G., *The Elementary School Curriculum.* (New York, 1923.)
Briggs, T. H., *Curriculum Problems.* (New York, 1926.)
Brim, O., *Rural Education.* (New York, 1923.)
Burton, W. H., edr., *The Supervision of Elementary Subjects.* (New York, 1929.)
Butterworth, J. E., *Rural School Administration.* (New York, 1926.)
Charters, W. W., *Curriculum Problems.* (New York, 1923.)
Cobb, S., *The New Leaven.* (New York, 1928.)
Cubberley, E. P., *Public Education in the United States.* (Boston, 1919.)
Davis, S. E., *Teaching the Elementary Curricula.* (New York, 1931.)
Dewey, J., *Democracy and Education.* (New York, 1922.)
Department of Superintendence of the National Education Association, Second Yearbook, 1924, *The Elementary School Curriculum;* Third Yearbook, 1925, *Research in Constructing the Elementary School Curriculum;* Fourth Yearbook, 1926, *The Nation at Work on the Public School Curriculum,* Seventh Yearbook, 1929, *The Articulation of the Units of American Education.* (Washington, D.C.)
Forest, I., *Preschool Education.* (New York, 1927.)
Foster, J. L., and Mattson, M. L., *Nursery School Procedure.* (New York, 1929.)
Hillegas, M. B., *The Elements of Classroom Supervision.* (New York, 1931.)
Hopkins, L. T., *Curriculum Principles and Practices.* (New York, 1929.)
Johnson, H. M., *Children in the Nursery School.* (New York, 1928.)
Kilpatrick, W. H., *Education for a Changing Civilization.* (New York, 1931.)
—— *Foundations of Method.* (New York, 1925.)

Knight, E. W., *Education in the United States*. (New York, 1929.)
Lincoln Elementary School Staff, Teachers College, Columbia University, *Curriculum Making in an Elementary School*. (Boston, 1927.)
Mearns, H., *Creative Youth*. (New York, 1925.)
Moore, A. E., *The Primary School; the Improvement of its Organization and Instruction*. (Boston, 1925.)
National Society for the Study of Education, Twenty-sixth Yearbook, 1927, I — *Curriculum-making*, II — *The Foundation of Curriculum-making*; Twenty-eighth Yearbook, 1930, *Preschool and Parental Education*; Thirtieth Yearbook, 1931, I — *Status of Rural Education*, II — *The Textbook in American Education*. (Bloomington, Ill.)
Reavis, W. C., Pierce, B., and Stullken, E. H., *The Elementary School, its Organization and Administration*. (Chicago, 1931.)
Reeder, E. H., *Simplifying Teaching*. (Chicago, 1929.)
Reisner, E. H., *The Evolution of the Common School*. (New York, 1930.
Rugg, H., and Shumaker, A., *The Child-Centered School*. (Yonkers, N.Y., 1928.)
Spain, C. H., *The Platoon School*. (New York, 1924.)
United States Office of Education, 1932, Bibliography No. 5, *Good References on Nursery Education*. (Washington, D.C., 1932.)
—— Bulletin, 1932, No. 9, *Nursery Schools. Their Rise and Development in the United States*. (Washington, D.C., 1932.)

Chapter VII

Preparation of Elementary School Teachers

1. Discuss the tradition underlying the preparation of elementary school teachers and its effects upon standards.
2. How is the emphasis upon methods as over against subject-matter to be explained?
3. What are the arguments for raising standards in the preparation of elementary school teachers? What is the relation of such standards to the status of elementary schools?
4. What should be the minimum preliminary preparation of elementary school teachers?
5. Should elementary school teachers be prepared in universities or in independent professional institutions?
6. Compare the systems of preparing elementary school teachers in the countries discussed.
7. What is meant by professionalized subject-matter?
8. How should the time for subject-matter and methods be distributed?
9. Discuss the place and nature of the practice school in the preparation of teachers.
10. Should a probationary period be required for the certification of teachers?
11. Compare the status of elementary school teachers in the countries discussed.

12. Is the character of the preparation of elementary teachers affected by the aims of elementary education?
13. Distinguish between systems of teacher preparation based on the principles of teaching as an art and teaching as a profession.
14. Compare the provisions made for the training of teachers in service.

REFERENCES

General
    Kandel, I. L., edr., *Educational Yearbook, 1927*, pp. 455 ff. (New York, 1928.)
    McNeil, M., *A Comparative Study of Entrance to Teacher-Training Institutions.* (New York, 1930.)

England
    Barker, W. R., *The Superannuation of Teachers in England and Wales.* (London, 1926.)
    Board of Education, *Regulations for the Training of Teachers.* (London, 1926.)
    —— *Report of the Committee on Universities and Training Colleges.* (London, 1928.)
    Jones, L. G. E., *Training of Teachers in England and Wales.* (Oxford, 1923.)
    Percy, Lord Eustace, edr., *The Year Book of Education, 1932*, pp. 271 ff. and 453 ff. (London, 1931.)
    Report of the Departmental Committee on the Training of Teachers for Public Elementary Schools. (London, 1925.)
    Report of the Standing Committee on Standard Scales for Teachers in Public Elementary Schools, Third. (London, 1927.)
    Sandiford, P., *The Training of Teachers in England and Wales.* (New York, 1910.)
    Teachers Registration Council Order, 1926.
    Teachers Superannuation Acts, 1925 and 1928; *Rules,* 1926; *Amending Rules,* 1930.

France
    Farrington, F. E., *The Public Primary School System of France.* (New York, 1906.)
    Jones, L. G. E., *The Training of Teachers in England and Wales.* (Oxford, 1923.)
    Lantenois, A., *Ce que l'Instituteur doit Savoir.* (Paris, 1930.)
    Organisation et Programmes des Ecoles primaires supérieures et des Ecoles normales avec Instructions préliminaires. (Paris, 1920.)
    Richard, C., *L'Enseignement en France.* (Paris, 1925.)
    Soleil, J., *Le Livre des Instituteurs.* (Paris, 1929.)

Germany
    Alexander, T., *Training of Elementary Teachers in Germany.* (New York, 1929.)

Becker, C. H., *Die Pädagogische Akademie im Aufbau unseres nationalen Bildungswesens*. (Leipzig, 1925.)
—— *Secondary Education and Teacher Training in Germany*. (New York, 1931.)
Gesetz über die Ausbildung der Volksschullehrer vom 20 Dezember, 1926. Hamburgisches Gesetz- und Verordnungsblatt, No. 142, pp. 789 f.
Kandel, I. L., and Alexander, T., *Reorganization of Education in Prussia*. (New York, 1927.)
Kerschensteiner, G., *Die Seele des Erziehers und das Problem der Lehrerbildung*. (Leipzig, 1921.)
Kühn, W., *Schulrecht in Preussen*. (Leipzig, 1926.)
Litt, T., *Berufsstudium und Allgemeinbildung auf der Universität*. (Leipzig, 1920.)
Neuordnung der Volksschullehrerbildung in Preussen. Denkschrift des Preussischen Ministeriums für Wissenschaft, Kunst, und Volksbildung. Zentralblatt für das gesamte Unterrichtswesen, 1925, pp. 245 ff.
Neuregelung der Lehrerbildung in Sachsen, Beschlüsse des Sächsischen Landestages von 23 März, 1923. Deutsche Schule, vol. 28, pp. 209 ff.
Oestreich, P., and Tacke, O., *Der neue Lehrer. Die notwendige Lehrerbildung*. (Osterwieck, 1926.)
Petersen, P., *Der Bildungsweg des neuen Erziehers*. (Jena, 1925.)
Pottag, A., *Die Bestimmungen über die Volks- und Mittelschule und über die Ausbildung und die Prüfugen der Lehrer und Lehrerinnen in Preussen*. (Berlin, n.d.)
Reichsschulkonferenz, Die, 1920. (Leipzig, 1921.)
Rein, W., *Zur gegenwärtigen Lage der Lehrerbildung*. (Langensalza, 1924.)
Sachse, A., *Grundzüge des preussischen Volksschulrechts*. (Berlin, 1926.)
Schwartz, H., *Aufgabe und Einrichtung der Pädagogischen Akademien*. (Berlin, 1926.)
—— *Die Lehrerbildungsfrage und ihre Lösung*. (Leipzig, 1926.)
Seyfert, R., and Richter, J., *Gesetzliche Grundlagen und Studienordnung der akademischen Lehrerbildung im Freistaat Sachsen*. (Leipzig, 1925.)
Spranger, E., *Gedanken über Lehrerbildung*. (Leipzig, 1920.)
Tews, J., *Ein einheitliche Lehrerstand, die Voraussetzung und Grundlage der Volkseinheitsschule. Pädagogisches Magazin*, No. 3. (Osterwieck, 1920.)
Weidmannsche Taschenausgaben von Verfügungen der Preussischen Unterrichtsverwaltung. (Berlin.)
Heft 32. *Ruhegehalt und Hinterbliebenenversorgung der Volksschullehrer*.
Heft 54 and 55. *Der Volksschullehrer*.
Heft 56. *Gehaltsverhältnisse der Volksschullehrer*.
Heft 60. *Der Mittelschullehrer*.
Heft 64. *Der Junglehrer*.
Heft 65. *Dienstanweisung für die Direktoren (Direktorinnen) und Lehrer (Lehrerinnen)*.
Heft 67. *Die strafrechtliche Stellung des Lehrers*.
Heft 70. *Die Pädagogische Akademien*.

Italy
  Almanacco Scolastico Nazionale, Anno 1929. (Florence, 1929.) An account of the legal and economic status of elementary school teachers is given on pp. 103 ff. On pp. 191 ff. will be found a list of all laws, rules, and regulations governing elementary education and the status of teachers; on pp. 323 ff. are given the laws, rules, and regulations for secondary education, including institutions for the preparation of elementary school teachers.
  Codignola, E., *La Riforma della Cultura magistrale.* (Catania, 1917.)
  Gentile, G., *La Nuova Scuola Media*, pp. 197 ff. (Florence, 1925.)
  Goy, H., *La Politique Scolaire de la Nouvelle Italie.* (Paris, 1926.)
  Lombardo-Radice, G., *La Riforma della Scuole Elementare*, two vols. (Palermo, 1925 and 1926.)
  Marraro, H., *Nationalism in Italian Education.* (New York, 1927.)
  Testo Unico delle Leggi e Norme Giuridiche sulla Istruzione elementare, post-elementare e sulla sue Opere d'Integrazione. (Rome, 1928.)

Russia
  Goode, W. T., *Schools, Teachers and Scholars in Soviet Russia.* (London, 1929.)
  Hans, N., and Hessen, S., *Educational Policy in Soviet Russia.* (London, 1930.)
  Pinkevitch, A. P., *The New Education in the Soviet Republic.* (New York, 1929.)
  Public Education in the Russian Socialistic Federation of Soviet Republics. (Moscow, 1928.)
  Wilson, L. L. W., *The New Schools of New Russia.* (New York, 1928.)
  Woody, T., *New Minds: New Men?* (New York, 1932.)

United States
  Agnew, W. D., *The Administration of Professional Schools for Teachers.* (Baltimore, 1925.)
  American Association of Teachers Colleges, *Yearbooks.*
  Armentrout, W. D., *The Conduct of Student Teaching in State Teachers Colleges.* (Greeley, Colo., 1927.)
  Carnegie Foundation for the Advancement of Teaching, Bulletin No. 14. *The Professional Preparation of Teachers for American Public Schools.* (New York, 1920.)
  Charters, W. W., and Waples, D., *The Commonwealth Teacher-Training Study.* (Chicago, 1929.)
  Hill, C. M., *A Decade of Progress in Teacher Training.* (New York, 1927.)
  Mead, A. R., *Supervised Student Teaching.* (Richmond, 1930.)
  Pangburn, J. M., *The Evolution of the American Teachers College.* (New York, 1932.)
  Randolph, L. D., *The Professional Treatment of Subject-Matter.* (Baltimore, 1924.)

APPENDIX

United States Office of Education, *Biennial Survey of Education, 1928–1930.* (Washington, D.C., 1932.)

Chapter VIII
Secondary Education

1. Discuss the tradition of secondary education in each of the six countries described.
2. Consider the social and other changes which are producing a reorientation on the subject of secondary education.
3. What has been the effect of examinations and privileges on the character of secondary education?
4. What is meant by the statement that secondary education is for status?
5. Contrast the American high school with the secondary school in Europe. What provisions are made for the non-academic pupils in European schools?
6. Consider the relations between elementary and secondary education.
7. Should secondary education be selective or open to all? What are the implications for secondary education of equality of opportunity?
8. What is the relation between secondary education and future vocations? between secondary education and leisure?
9. To what extent should secondary education be adapted to individual differences?
10. How is the survival in Europe of the disciplinary concept of secondary education to be explained? What has been the effect in the United States of discarding this concept?
11. Compare the scope and standards set in the subjects taught in secondary schools.
12. Discuss the status of examinations for secondary schools.
13. Compare the quality of secondary education.
14. Discuss the changes in the definitions of liberal education.
15. Compare the aims of secondary education.
16. Discuss the place of extra-curricular activities or corporate life in the school.
17. Consider the influence of the universities on secondary education.
18. To what extent is or should the secondary education of girls be differentiated from that for boys?
19. Discuss the implications of the common school movement.

References

General

Carnegie Foundation for the Advancement of Teaching, Bulletin No. 20. *The Quality of the Educational Process in the United States and Europe.* (New York, 1927.)

Conference on Examinations. (New York, 1931.)

Kandel, I. L., *Essays in Comparative Education*, pp. 172 ff. (New York, 1930.)

—— *History of Secondary Education.* (Boston, 1930.)
—— edr., *Educational Yearbook, 1926*, pp. 459 ff., and *1930*. (New York, 1927 and 1931.)

England
Adamson, J. W., *English Education, 1789–1902.* (London, 1930.)
Archer, R. L., *Secondary Education in the Nineteenth Century.* (Cambridge, 1921.)
Board of Education, *Education Pamphlets*, many of which deal with aspects of secondary education.
—— *The New Prospect in Education.* (London, 1928.)
—— Annual Reports of the Board of Education, now issued under the title *Education in 1931*, etc. See especially *Report for 1923–24*. (London.)
—— *Regulations for Secondary Schools.* (London, annual.)
—— *List of Secondary Schools and Preparatory Schools in England recognized by the Board of Education, List 60.* (London, annual.)
—— Consultative Committee, *The Education of the Adolescent.* (London, 1926.)
—— Departmental Committee, *Report on Scholarships and Free Places.* (London, 1926.)
Carnegie Foundation for the Advancement of Teaching, Bulletin No. 18, *Games and Sports in British Schools and Universities.* (New York, 1927.)
Darwin, B., *The English Public School.* (London, 1929.)
Durlston, K., *The Preparatory School System.* (London, 1926.)
Ellis, G. S. M., *The Poor Student and the University.* (London, 1925.)
Girls' School Yearbook. (London, annual.)
Howard, B. A., *The Mixed School: A Study of Coeducation.* (London, 1928.)
King, B., *Schools of Today.* (London, 1929.)
King, P., *Preparatory School Ideas.* (London, 1926.)
Legge, J. G., *The Rising Tide.* (London, 1929.)
Lindsay, K., *Social Progress and Educational Waste.* (London, 1926.)
Norwood, C., *The English Educational System.* (London, 1928.)
—— *The English Tradition of Education.* (London, 1929.)
Pekin, L. B., *Public Schools, their Failure and their Reform.* (London, 1932.)
Percy, Lord Eustace, edr., *The Year Book of Education, 1932*, pp. 174 ff. (London, 1931.)
Public Schools Year Book. (London, annual.)
Sadler, Sir M. E., *The Outlook in Secondary Education.* (New York, 1930.)
Schoolmasters' Yearbook. (London, annual.)
Tawney, R. H., *Secondary Education for All.* (London, 1922.)
Waugh, A., *Public School Life.* (London, 1922.)

APPENDIX

France

Dion, L., *Recueil Complet de la Législation de l'Enseignement Secondaire.* (Paris, 1929.)

Farrington, F. E., *French Secondary Schools.* (New York, 1910.)

Kandel, I. L., *The Reform of Secondary Education in France.* (New York, 1924.)

Laue F., *Das französische Schulwesen.* (Leipzig, 1926).

Official Publications:

Horaires et Programmes de l'Enseignement Secondaire de Garçons. (Vuibert, Paris.)

Instructions complémentaires du 27 Août 1927 relatives à l'Application du Nouveau Plan d'Etudes Secondaires. (Vuibert, Paris.)

Instructions du 2 Septembre 1925 relatives à l'Application des Programmes de l'Enseignement Secondaire dans les Lycées et Collèges, complétées par les Instructions du 30 Avril 1931. (Vuibert, Paris.)

Plan d'Etudes de l'Enseignement Secondaire des Jeunes Filles. (Vuibert, Paris.)

Programmes du Baccalauréat de l'Enseignement Secondaire. (Vuibert, Paris.)

Richard, C., *L'Enseignement en France.* (Paris, 1925.)

Germany

Alexander, T., and Parker, B., *The New Education in the German Republic.* (New York, 1929.)

Becker, C. H., *Secondary Education and Teacher Training in Germany.* (New York, 1931.)

Kandel, I. L., and Alexander, T., *Reorganization of Education in Prussia.* (New York, 1927.)

Kellerman, F., *The Effect of the World War on European Education.* (Cambridge, Mass., 1928.)

Kühn, W., *Schulrecht in Preussen.* (Leipzig, 1926.)

McMurry, R., Mueller, M., and Alexander, T., *Modern Foreign Languages in France and Germany: The Training of Teachers and Methods of Instruction.* (New York, 1930.)

Reichsschulkonferenz, Die, 1920. (Leipzig, 1921.)

Richert, C., *Neuordnung der höheren Schulen in Preussen.* (Berlin, 1924.)

Riesenbürger, W., *Die rechtlichen Grundlagen des mittleren und höheren Schulwesens in Preussen.* (Langensalza, 1927.)

Russell, J. E., *German Higher Schools.* (New York, 1913.)

Staatliche Auskunftstelle für Schulwesen, Jahresberichte der höheren Lehranstalten in Preussen, 1927–28. (Berlin, 1930.)

Weidmannsche Taschenausgaben von Verfügungen der Preussischen Unterrichtsverwaltung. (Berlin.)

Heft 6. *Richtlinien für einen Lehrplan der Deutschen Oberschule und der Aufbauschule.*

Heft 16. *Die Frauenschule mit angegliederten Lehrgänge.*

Heft 19 and 20. *Richtlinien für die Lehrpläne der höheren Schulen Preussens.*
Heft 22. *Die Aufbauschule in Preussen.*
Heft 23. *Schülerheime.*
Heft 25. *Studium ohne Reifezeugnis in Preussen.*
Heft 31. *Die Verwaltungsordnung für städtische höhere Lehranstalten.*
Heft 33. *Schüler und Schülerin der höheren Schule.*
Heft 41. *Versetzungs- und Prüfungsbestimmungen für die öffentlichen höheren Lehranstalten.*
Heft 46. *Schulgeld.*
Heft 62. *Der Studiendirektor als Verwaltungsbeamter.*

Zentralinstitut für Erziehung und Unterricht, *Das Deutsche Schulwesen.* (Berlin, annual.)

Zur Neuordnung des höheren Schulwesens in Sachsen. Denkschrift des Ministeriums für Volksbildung.

Italy

Almanacco Scolastico Nazionale, Anno 1929. (Florence, 1929.) On pp. 323 ff. will be found a list of all the laws, rules, and regulations governing secondary education from 1859 to 1928. All laws, rules, and regulations subsequent to 1928 can be found in the *Bollettino Ufficiale* of the Ministry of National Education.

Annali della Istruzione Media.

Codignola, E., *Il Problema dell'Educazione Nazionale in Italia.* (Florence, 1930.)

Gentile, G., *La Nuova Scuola Media.* (Florence, 1925.)

Goy, H., *La Politique scolaire de la Nouvelle Italie.* (Paris, 1926.)

Marraro, H. R., *Nationalism in Italian Education.* (New York, 1927.)

Ministero della Pubblica Istruzione, *Raccolta di Norme Legislative e Regolamentari sull'Ordinamento dell'Istruzione media.* (Rome, 1927.)

Severi, L., and Sangiorgio, G., *Manuale di Legislazione sull' Istruzione Media.* (Rome n.d., but probably 1926.)

Russia

Counts, G. S., *The Soviet Challenge to America.* (New York, 1931.)
Hans, N., and Hessen, S., *Educational Policy in Soviet Russia.* (London, 1930.)
Harper, S. N., *Civic Training in Soviet Russia.* (Chicago, 1929.)
—— *Making Bolshevists.* (Chicago, 1931.)
Ognyov, N., *Diary of a Communist Schoolboy.* (New York, 1928.)
Pinkevitch, A. P., *The New Education in the Soviet Republic.* (New York, 1929.)
Public Education in the Russian Socialistic Federation of Soviet Republics. (Moscow, 1928.)
Soviet Culture Review. (Moscow, monthly).
Soviet Union Year-book. (London, annual.)
Wilson, L. L. W., *The New Schools of New Russia.* (New York, 1928.)
Woody, T., *New Minds: New Men?* (New York, 1932.)

APPENDIX

United States
    Briggs, T. H., *Curriculum Problems.* (New York, 1926.)
    —— *The Great Investment.* (Cambridge, Mass., 1930.)
    —— *The Junior High School.* (Boston, 1920.)
    Brown, E. E., *Making of Our Middle Schools.* (New York, 1926.)
    Counts, G. S., *Secondary Education and Industrialism.* (Cambridge, Mass., 1929.)
    —— *Senior High School Curriculum.* (Chicago, 1926.)
    Cox, P. W. L., *Curriculum Adjustment in the Secondary School.* (Philadelphia, 1925.)
    —— and Long, F. E., *Principles of Secondary Education.* (Boston, 1932.)
    Eells, W. C., *The Junior College.* (Boston, 1931.)
    Fretwell, E. K., *Extra-Curricular Activities in the Secondary School.* (Boston, 1931.)
    Inglis, A. J., *Principles of Secondary Education.* (Boston, 1918.)
    Koos, L. V., *Private and Public Secondary Education: a Comparative Study.* (Chicago, 1931.)
    —— *The American Secondary School.* (New York, 1927.)
    —— *The Junior College.* (New York, 1925.)
    —— *The Junior High School.* (New York, 1920.)
    —— and Kefauver, G. N., *Guidance in Secondary Schools.* (New York, 1932.)
    Morrison, H. C., *Practice of Teaching in the Secondary School.* (Chicago, 1931.)
    Snedden, D., *American Secondary Schools in 1960.* (New York, 1931.)
    Stuart, M. H., *The Comprehensive High School.* (New York, 1926.)
    Uhl, W. L., *Secondary School Curricula.* (Yonkers, N.Y., 1927.)

Chapter IX
Preparation of Secondary School Teachers

1. Compare the history of the preparation of elementary and secondary school teachers.
2. Why is the preparation of secondary school teachers regarded as less important than that of elementary school teachers?
3. Discuss the statement that the preparation of secondary school teachers has emphasized subject-matter while that of elementary school teachers has stressed methods.
4. Compare the systems of preparing teachers for secondary schools, noting the peculiar emphasis in each.
5. Should secondary school teachers be prepared in universities or in independent professional institutions?
6. Compare the methods of certificating secondary school teachers.

References
England
    Kandel, I. L., *History of Secondary Education*, pp. 384 ff. (Boston, 1930.)
    —— edr., *Educational Yearbook, 1927*, pp. 486 ff. (New York, 1928.)

Percy, Lord Eustace, edr., *The Year Book of Education, 1932*, pp. 279 ff., 454 f. (London, 1931.)

France
Demiashkevich, M. J., the French and German Academic Examinations and Degrees. *School and Society*, vol. 34, pp. 515 ff. (New York, weekly.)
Kandel, I. L., *History of Secondary Education*, pp. 226 ff. (Boston, 1928.)
—— edr., *Educational Yearbook, 1927*, pp. 517 ff. (New York, 1928.)
McMurry, R., Mueller, M., and Alexander, T., *Modern Foreign Languages in France and Germany: The Training of Teachers and Methods of Instruction.* (New York, 1930.)
Richard, C., *L'Enseignement en France.* (Paris, 1925.)
United States Office of Education, Pamphlet No. 29, *Official Certificates, Diplomas and Degrees Granted in France.* (Washington, 1932.)

Germany
Brown, J. F., *Training of Teachers for Secondary Schools in Germany and the United States.* (New York, 1911.)
Kandel, I. L., *History of Secondary Education*, pp. 276 ff. (Boston, 1930.)
—— edr., *Educational Yearbook, 1927*, pp. 562 ff. (New York, 1928.)
Learned, W. S., *Der Oberlehrer.* (Cambridge, Mass., 1914.)
Weidmannsche Taschenaugsgaben von Verfügungen der Preussischen Unterrichtsverwaltung. (Berlin.)
Heft 2. *Die wissenschaftliche Staatsprüfung der Philologen.*
Heft 3. *Der Studienreferendar.*
Heft 7. *Der Studienassessor.*
Heft 27–30. *Der Studienrat.*
Heft 62. *Der Studiendirektor als Verwaltungsbeamter.*

Italy
Goy, H., *La Politique Scolaire de la nouvelle Italie*, pp. 253 ff. (Paris, 1926.)
Marraro, H. R., *Nationalism in Italian Education*, pp. 56 ff. (New York, 1927.)
Ministero dell'Educazione Nazionale, Regio decreto 27 Novembre, 1924, No. 2367 — Regolamento sullo Stato dei Presidi, dei Professore e del Personale assistente, di Segreteria e Subalterno dei Regi Istituti Medi di Istruzione. Bollettino Ufficiale, April 14, 1925, pp. 2031 ff.
—— *Programmi per i concorsi a Cattedre di Regi Ins!ituti Medi d'Istruzione e per l'Abilitazione all'Esercizio professionale dell'Insegnamento Medio.* (Rome, 1930.)

Russia
Goode, W. T., *Schools, Teachers and Scholars in Soviet Russia.* (London, 1929.)
Hans, N., and Hessen, S., *Educational Policy in Soviet Russia.* (London, 1930.)

Public Education in the Russian Socialistic Federation of Soviet Republics. (Moscow, 1928.)
Wilson, L. L. W., *The New Schools of New Russia.* (New York, 1928.)
Woody, T., *New Minds: New Men?* (New York, 1932.)

United States
  Bachman, F. P., *Training and Certification of High School Teachers.* (Nashville, Tenn., 1930.)
  Fitzpatrick, E. A., and Hutson, P. W., *The Scholarship of Teachers in Secondary Schools.* (New York, 1927.)
  Purin, C. M., *The Training of Teachers of Modern Foreign Languages.* (New York, 1929.)
  United States Office of Education, Bulletin, 1927, No. 19, *State Laws and Regulations Governing Teachers' Certificates.* (Washington, D. C., 1927.)

INDEX

Abbotsholme, 106, 427
Abendgymnasium, 146
Abilitazione all'insegnamento elementare, 590
Abilitazione all'ispettorato, 592
Abilitazione examination, 774
Abilitazione magistrale, 590
Abiturientenexamen, see Abiturientenprüfung
Abiturientenprüfung, 138 f., 146, 708, 721, 743 ff., 751
Abnormal children, 130
Abschlussklassen, 436
Abteilung III für Bildung und Schule, 283
Academic Councils, 272 f.
Academies, American, 790 f.; French, 221, 272 f.
Academy inspectors, 272 f.
Accident insurance, German schools, 747
Accredited schools, Italy, 764 f.
Accrediting, system of, 195, 795
Action Régionaliste, l', 280
Activity groups, 732, 734, 737
Activity instruction, 867
Activity principle, 428 ff., 441 f., 732
Adams Act, 319
Adams, John, 78
Adams, Sir John, 523
Administration of education, 207 ff.; central authority and, 213 ff.; educational finance and, 220 ff.; executive officials, 226 ff.; *externa* and *interna* in, 215 ff.; factors affecting, 208 ff.; in England, 228 ff.; in France, 262 ff.; in Germany, 281 ff.; in Italy, 297 ff.; in Russia, 308 ff.; in the United States, 313 ff.; local authorities and, 224 ff.; parent participation in, 218 ff.; purpose of, 211 ff.; scope of, 207 f.; teacher participation in, 217 ff.; types of, 258
Administration, purposes of, 211; training in, 227, 335 f.
Administrators, 226 ff.; training of, 227
Admission, secondary schools, 654 f.; Germany, 719; Italy, 765 f.; teacher training institutions, United States, 606 f.; to pedagogical academies, 572
Adolescent, education of the, 107 ff., 367, 387, 670
Adult education, 147 f., 182 f.; in England, 100 f.; in France, 124; in Italy, 170 f.; in the United States, 197
Adult Education Committee, 243
Advanced courses, 664
Æsthetic education, 468 f.

Agazzi, Rosa and Carolina, 465, 471
Age requirements for school attendance, 490 f.
Agrégation, 273, 838 ff.
Agrégés, 678
Agricultural education, 103
Agriculture, Board of, 237
Aims, educational, 865 ff.; elementary, 370 ff., 407 ff., 440 ff., 468, 477 f., 498 ff.; intermediate, 387, 390 f., 419 f., 447; secondary, 656 ff., 683 ff., 726 ff., 767 ff., 781, 795, 809 ff.
Akademie der Volksbildner, 148
Akademiker, 351
Alabama, 325, 344, 605, 619
Alaska, 318
Albert, M. François, 133, 268, 678, 702
Alexander I, 174
Alexander II, 174
Allgemeine Bildung, 635 f., 708 f., 712, 727, 730, 733, 798
Allgemeine Landrecht, 49, 209, 286
All-Russia Teachers' Union, 596 ff.
Alsace-Lorraine, 120
Alternative courses, 668 f.
Amari, 758
American Association for Adult Education, 197
American Association for the Advancement of Science, 317
American Association of Teachers Colleges, 605 f.
American Child Health Association, 200, 205, 493
American Classical League, Advisory Committee of, 810
American Federation of Labor, 202
American Library Association, 197
Anhalt, 143, 145, 582
Anti-tuberculosis organizations, 201
Anwärterliste, 847
Aporti, Ferrante, 157, 464 ff.
Appointment, teachers', permanent, 579; temporary, 578 f.
Apportionment of funds, 343
Arbeitsgemeinschaften, 148, 290, 296, 429, 432
Arbeitskarten, 153
Arbeitsprinzip, 428 ff., 732
Arbeitsschule, 357, 429, 441
Arbeitsunterricht, 433, 737, 867
Archbishops' Commission, 363
Archiv für Volksbildung, 283
Argentina and religious instruction, 47

INDEX

Aristotle, 46
Arithmetic, teaching of, 381; in Germany, 445
Arizona, 325, 344, 606, 619, 621
Arkansas, 325, 344, 619
Arnold, Matthew, 638
Arnold, Thomas, 827
Arrêtés, 267
Articulation of schools, 368
Asili materni, 159
Asili d'infanzia, 462, 464 ff.
Asilo per l'infanzia, 157 f.
Asilo-scuola, 170
Association of Colleges and Preparatory Schools of the Middle States and Maryland, 795, 806, 857
Association of Colleges and Preparatory Schools of the Southern States, 795 f., 806
Association of Preparatory Schools, 643
Associations, private, and education, 164 f.
Associations, teachers', 543 f., 546, 563 f.
Associazione Fascista della Scuola, 308
Associazione Nazionale per gli Interessi del Mezzogiorno, 164
Athletics and games in secondary schools, 673; in France, 700; in Germany, 747
Attendance, average, 366; length of, 491
Attendance, compulsory, *see* Compulsory attendance
Aufbauschule, 64, 145 f., 282, 721 ff.
Ausschuss für Unterrichtswesen, 283
Australian states, centralization in, 76, 210
Autonomy of education, 45, 184, 584
Auxiliary schools, 152
Avanguardia Fascista, 167
Avanguardisti, 167, 475

Baccalauréat, 125, 550, 558, 676, 692 ff.; *ès lettres*, 675; *ès sciences*, 675
Baccelli, 758
Bache, Alexander D., 601
Bachman, F. P., 855
Bachotage, 694
Backward children, 201, 436
Baden, 142, 287, 582
Bagley, W. C., 608
Baldwin, Mr. Stanley, 107, 352
Balilla, see *Opera Nazionale Balilla*
Baltimore, 333, 341
Bari, University of, 163
Barker, Ernest, 7
Barnard, Henry, 487, 602, 793
Barrie, Sir James, 644
Bath, 115
Baudrittel, 295
Bavaria, 142 f., 282, 287, 293, 582
Becker, Carl, 214
Bedales, 106
Beecher, Lyman, 487

Begabtenklassen, 142
Bekenntnisschulen, 143
Belinksy, V. V., 477
Bell, Andrew, 521
Bentham, 360
Bérard, M. Léon, 267, 677
Bérard reform, 267 f., 677
Berechtigungen, 453, 712, 726 ff., 750
Berkeley, Cal., 803
Berlin, 151, 292
Bert, Paul, 396
Berti, 758
Bertini, 758
Berufsberatung, 147
Berufsschulen, 144, 146 f.
Beschulungsgeld, 295
Bestimmungen, 296
Bewegungsfreiheit, 722, 754
Bezirkslehrerräte, 292
Bezirksschuldeputationen, 292
Bianchi, 758
Bible reading, United States, 492
Bibliography, 871 ff.
Bibliothèque Nationale, 271
Bieberstein, 427
Bifurcation, 675
Bildung zum Deutschtum, 155, 433
Bildung zur Humanität, 155, 636
Binet, Alfred, 131, 396
Birmingham, University of, 104
Blind children, 152, 201
Blonsky, 478
Blow, Susan, 494
Board of Education Act, 231 f.
Board of education, city, 331 f.; state, 325 f.
Board of Education, England, 96, 235 ff., 362, 640
Board of Trade, England, and juvenile employment, 117
Boards of education, 224
Bobbitt, Franklin K., 502, 506
Bodenständigkeit, 431
Boelte, Marie, 494
Bollettino Ufficiale, 300
Bologna, University of, 163
Borough Road School, 528
Boselli, Paolo, 758
Boston, 493; English High School, 792; school medical inspection in, 199
Bouglé, M., 264
Bourses d'entretien, 135, 706
Boutwell, George S., 190, 793
Boy Scouts, 823
Bradford, 113, 364, 387
Bremen, 142 f.
Brereton, Cloudesley, 397
Brevet d'enseignement primaire supérieur, 422
Brevet élémentaire, 274, 406, 553 f., 558 f.

INDEX

Brevet supérieur, 274, 402, 406, 550, 554, 558 f.
Bridges, Robert, quoted, 22, 869
Briggs, T. H., 81 f., 479, 812, 820
Brinsley, John, 520
Bristol, University of, 104, 666
British and Foreign School Society, 94, 521, 528
Bronxville, N.Y., 621
Brooks, Charles, 601
Brougham, Lord, 360
Brown, John, 50 f.
Brunschvieg, M. Léon, 132 f., 702
Brunswick, 145, 582
Bryce Commission, 95, 362, 640
Bryce, Mr., 231
Buffalo, 333
Buisson, Ferdinand, 396, 548 f.
Bulletin Administratif, 267 f.
Bund der freien Schulgesellschaften Deutschlands, 143
Bureau des Longitudes, 271
Bureau of Curriculum Research, Teachers College, Columbia University, 509
Bureau of Education, United States, 318
Bureau of Educational Experiments, New York, 493
Bureaucracy, 215; English attitude toward, 26
Bureaus of reference and research, 317, 340 f.
Bürgerschulen, 446 f., 708
Burke, 25, 30
Burnham Committees, 544 ff.
Burnham, Lord, 244, 544

Cagliari, University of, 163
Cahiers, 692; *de devoirs mensuels*, 415 f.; *de roulement*, 415
Caisses d'école, 129, 274, 276, 278, 404
Calabria, educational conditions in, 456
Caldwell, Otis W., 507
Calendario alla Montesca, 469
California, 325, 344, 603, 605 f., 616, 618 f., 621, 807, 856; high school enrollment in, 195; juvenile courts in, 204; school medical inspection in, 199; University of, 493
Cambridge Local Examinations Sydicate, 541, 666
Cambridge, Mass., 497
Cambridge, University of, 104
Cambridgeshire, 363
Camp Fire Girls, 823
Camps, summer, 205
Canada, centralization in, 210
Capper-Ketcham Act, 319
Care committees, 114, 254 f.
Carnegie Foundation for the Advancement of Teaching, 316, 602, 607 f., 619 ff., 796
Carter, James G., 487, 521, 601

Casa dei Balilla, 168
Casa dei bambini, 159, 465
Casati Law, 156 f., 160, 209, 297, 305, 455, 585, 757 f.
Cassa nazionale per le Assicurazione sociale, 166
Cassa scolastica, 473, 764
Catania, University of, 163
Censeurs, 682
Centimes additionels, 277
Central Advisory Committee for the Certification of Teachers, 243
Central Advisory Committee on the preparation of teachers, 532, 536
Central authority, 266 ff., 299; functions of a, 213 f.
Central Council of Workers' Unions, 316
Central schools, 101 f., 386 f., 390 ff.
Central Welsh Board, 666
Centralization, 59 ff., 208 ff., 262 ff., 299, 307, 863 f.; and decentralization, 228
Certificat d'aptitude à l'enseignement secondaire, 561, 837 f.
Certificat d'aptitude à l'inspection primaire et à la direction des écoles normales, 273, 551, 560
Certificat d'aptitude au professorat des écoles normales et des écoles primaires supérieures, 419, 550, 560
Certificat d'aptitude pédagogique, 273, 402, 406, 559
Certificat d'études primaires, 122, 405, 417 ff.
Certificat d'études primaires élémentaires, 273
Certificat d'études secondaires, 676
Certificate, leaving, 452 f.
Certification for college entrance, 195
Certification of high school teachers, 856 f.
Certification of teachers, England, 542 f.; France, 559 f.; United States, 616 f.
Certificato di adempimento dell'obbligo scolastico, 474
Certificato di compimento, 474
Certificato di speciale ideonità al lavoro, 474
Chamberlain, Sir Austen, 25
Chambers of Commerce, 200
Character-formation, 643 f., 672 ff.; English aim of, 371
Character, national, and education, 23 ff.
Charity Commissioners, 230 ff.
Charles-Brun, 280
Charterhouse, 105, 638
Charters, W. W., 507, 609
Chartists, 86
Chelmsford, Lord, 118
Chicago, 493
Child Guardianship, Division of, Massachusetts Department of Public Welfare, 204
Child labor, 202 f.

INDEX

Child Study Association of America, 205, 339, 493
Child Welfare League of America, 205
Child-centered school, 354, 374
Children, employment of, *see* Employment of children
Children's Act, 1908, 117, 252
Children's Bureau, Minnesota State Board of Control, 204
Children's Charter, 198
Children's homes, 355
Children's Organization of Young Pioneers, 485
Christian Education of Youth, Encyclical on, 47
Church and education, 45 ff.; elementary, 349
Church and state in education, 16
Churches, representation of, on local bodies, 291
Cincinnati, 508
Circolari, 300
Cities, administration in American, 331 ff.
Civic instruction, Germany, 445
Civil Service Commission, 239
Civilian Vocational Rehabilitation Act, 319
Clarendon Commission, 95, 637 f.
Class distinctions and education, 16 f., 349
Classe de mathématiques, 680 f., 685; *spéciales*, 695
Classe de philosophie, 680 f., 685
Classe de rhétoriques supérieures, 681, 685, 695
Classes élémentaires, 124, 133, 703
Classes enfantines, 122, 124, 400
Classes préparatoires, 90, 124, 133, 679, 703
Classes, size of, 368, 438, 467, 650, 681, 723
Classical education, 626, 674 f.
Classical Investigation, Report of the, 858
Classification of pupils, 496 ff.
Classified schools in Italy, 160, 165
Clinics, child guidance, 115, 204; dental, 151; school, 115
Clinton, De Witt, 487
Clubs, women's, 199
Cockerton Case, 232, 362, 640
Code for Elementary Schools, 238
Codignola, Ernesto, 460 f., 587 f.
Coeducation, 721, 795; Germany, 751
Collège de France, 271
College Entrance Examination Board, 195, 795, 805 f.
College of Preceptors, 665
Collèges, 125, 134, 694 ff.
Colleges, American, 195 f.
Collegio dei professori, 764, 767, 775
Colonial Institute, Berlin, 445
Colorado, 325, 344, 605 f., 619
Columbia, District of, education in, 319
Columbus, O., 803
Comenius, 86, 520

Comitato Communale dell'Opera Nazionale Balilla, 166
Comitato contro Analfabetismo, 165
Comitato Ligure per l'Educazione del Popolo, 164
Comité Supérieur des Bourses Nationales, 127
Comités consultatifs, 271
Commercial high schools, 723
Commissars, 309
Commission de l'Ecole Unique, 133, 703
Commission municipal scolaire, 275 f.
Commission on the Reorganization of Secondary Education, 501, 809 ff., 813
Commission Permanent de Sélection et d'Orientation, 134
Commission scolaire, 405
Commission Supérieur de la Tuberculose, 128
Commissione consultiva per l'igiene e l'assistenza scolastica e per l'igiene pedagogica, 302
Commissions on secondary education, 230 f.
Committee of Five, 803
Committee of Ten on Secondary School Studies, 796, 798, 803
Committee on College Entrance Requirements, 796, 798, 803
Committees, education, 224
Committees, school, 714
Common school, American, meaning of, 794; idea, 351
Common school movement, 131 ff.; France, 700 ff.
Commonwealth Fund, 204, 316
Commonwealth Teacher-Training Study, 609
Communes, French, 275 f.
Communism and education, 172 f., 175 f., 180, 182 ff., 187, 308 ff.; and Fascism, 312; and secondary education, 780 ff.; concept of, 69 ff.; educational aims of, 478; influence of, in Russia, 32 f.
Communist Party, Resolution of Central Committee, 788
Compagnons de l'Université Nouvelle, les, 131 f., 279, 411, 424, 677, 701
Compayré, Gabriel, 396
"Complex" method, 482, 781
Compulsory attendance, 230, 354, 361, 365, 436 f., 490 f.; England, 98; France, 122 f., 404 f.; Germany, 140; Italy, 159, 455 f., 463 f.; Russia, 178; United States, 192
Comte, Auguste, 350, 397
Concentric method, 413 f.
Concerts, 184
Concord, N.H., 803
Concordat, 143
Concorso pubblico, 590
Concours général, 696
Condorcet, 48
Congregations, religious, and education, 126

INDEX 905

Connecticut, 325, 344, 601 f., 605 f., 619, 621
Conseil d'administration, 682
Conseil d'enseignement, 682, 685
Conseil de classe, 682, 685
Conseil des maîtres, 406 f., 416
Conseil Supérieur de l'Assistance Publique, 128
Conseil Supérieur de l'Hygiène de France, 128
Conseil Supérieur de la Natalité, 128
Conseil Supérieur de l'Instruction Publique, 268
Conseil Supérieur de la Protection de l'Enfance, 128
Consiglio di Amministrazione, 302
Consiglio di classe, 764
Consiglio di disciplina per i maestri elementari, 303
Consiglio di presidenza, 764
Consiglio Nazionale delle Ricerche, 301
Consiglio scolastico per gli affari della istruzione elementare, 303
Consiglio Superiore della Pubblica Istruzione, 301
Consolidation, school, 192, 222
Consorzio Nazionale di Emigrazione e Lavoro, 164
Constitution, Federal, and education, Germany, 718
Constitution, German, 148, 150; and education, 136, 281 ff.; and preparation of teachers, 568 f.; and schools, 139 f., 144.
Constitution, United States, and education, 188 f., 318
Consultative Committee, England, 218, 242; and examinations, 665
Consultative Committee for Hygiene and School Welfare, 302
Consultative committees, French, 271; teachers and, 255
Continuation schools, 144; in United States, 195
Convitti nazionali, 765
Coöperatives, school, 166
Coöperative Union, 100
Coöption, 225
Coppino, 758
Coppino Act, 156, 160
Coppino Law, 455
Corbino, Minister, 165
Core subjects, 733
Corporal punishment, 372
Corporate life, 672 ff.
Corsi di perfezionamento, 586, 588
Corsi integrativi di avviamento profesionale, 159 ff.
Corsi per maestranza, 163
Corso inferiore, 159, 467
Corso integrativo, 463, 468
Corso superiore, 159, 467

Council of Industrial Psychology, 119
Council secondary schools, 645 ff.
Councils, parents', 293 f.; teachers', 218, 225, 290, 292 f., 349
Counties, 249, 330 f.
County borough councils, 231
County boroughs, 249
County councils, 231
County School Boards, Prussian, 289
County superintendent, 330 f.
Cours complémentaires, 123, 417, 423
Cours d'adultes, 124
Cours élémentaire, 409
Cours moyen, 409
Cours préparatoire, 409
Cours secondaires, 698
Cours supérieur, 409
Courses of study, making of, United States, 508
Courses of study, *see* Curriculum
Cousin, Victor, 601
Cousinet, R., 415
Cowper-Temple Clause, 100, 363
Crèches, 159, 176, 355, 369, 434, 465, 480
Credaro, Minister, 586
Crippled children, 152
Crise d'agrégation, 264
Critic teachers, 611
Critica, La, 457
Croce, Benedetto, 457, 760
Cross Commission, 521
Cru, Professor A., 557
Cubberley, Ellwood P., 323
Culture d'esprit, 683 f.
Culture, French, concept of, 396 ff.
Culture, national, and administration, 209
Culture générale, 264, 635, 675, 683, 798
Culture in the United States, 798
Curricula Designed for the Professional Preparation of Teachers, 607
Curriculum, *école maternelle*, 401 ff.
Curriculum, elementary school, 349, 355 ff.; England, 372 ff.; France, 408 ff.; Germany, 439 ff.; Italy 467 ff.; Russia, 482 ff.; United States, 504 ff.
Curriculum, intermediate school, England, 388 ff.; France, 420 ff.; Germany, 448 ff.
Curriculum, secondary school, England, 656 ff.; France, 685 ff.; Germany, 733 ff.; Italy, 766 ff.; Russia, 781 ff.; United States, 812 ff.
Curriculum, teacher training institutions, England, 535 ff.; France, 554 ff.; Germany, 574 ff.; Italy, 588 ff.; Russia, 597 ff.; United States, 607, ff.
Curriculum, state and, 323 f.
Curriculum-making, teachers and, 342

Dalton Plan, 497 f.

INDEX

Daneo-Credaro Law, 156, 456
Dante, 65
Das Deutsche Schulwesen, 288
Davies, E. Salter, 394
Day nurseries, 369, 493
Dayton, 508
De Cristoforis, 758
De Sanctis, 758
Deaf and dumb children, 152, 201
Decentralization, 863 f.; and centralization, 228; of administration, 208 ff.
Decreti-leggi, 299 f.
Decrets, 267
Defective children, 151, 170
Degrees in France, 127
Delaware, 325, 344, 619
Delinquency, juvenile, 242 f.
Democracy and education, 3 f., 189 f., 705 f.; concept of, 862
Démolins, M., 699
Denominational organization in Alsace-Lorraine, 120 ff.
Denominational schools, 98 f., 362, 492
Dental clinics, 151, 200
Denver, 340, 342, 508, 512; school medical inspection in, 199
Denzel, 520
Department of Superintendence, 317, 505
Departmental Committees, 243
Departmental Council for Education, 275
Departments, French, 274 f.
Departments of education, state, 328
Dependent children, 204
Detroit, 497, 508; high school curricula in, 816; school medical inspection in, 199
Deutsche Oberschule, 145 f., 282, 721 ff.
Deutscher Eltern- und Volksbund, 294
Deutsches Archiv für Jugendwohlfahrt, 283
Deutsches Archiv für Leibesübungen, 446
Deutschtum, 36, 137, 297, 636, 729 ff.
Dewey, John, 360, 488, 499, 801
Dialect, teaching of, 264, 280; use of, 412
Die freie weltliche Schule, 143
Diesel, E., 35
Diesterweg, 520, 566
Differentiation, 89 f.
Differentiation of the Curriculum for Boys and Girls respectively in Secondary Schools, 662
Dilthey, Wilhelm, 429
Dinter, 520
Diploma di direzione didattica, 592
Diploma di pedagogia e filosofia, 592
Diplôme complémentaire d'études secondaires, 681, 698
Diplôme de fin d'études secondaires, 550, 558, 681, 698
Directeur, 406
Directors of education, 226 ff., 255 ff.
Directrices, 406, 682

Direktor, 715
Direttore didattico, 304, 591 f.
Discipline, English concept of, 371 f.; formal, 798 ff.; French concept of, 399; Italian secondary schools, 779; Russia, 788
Dispensaries, social hygiene, 129
District of Columbia, 606, 619
District system, 329
Dopolavoro, 170
Doumer, M., 683
Drawing, teaching of, Germany, 445
Dresden, Technical High School, 582
Ducos, M., 135, 706
Duma, 174
Durham, University of, 104, 666
Durkheim, Emile, 397
Duruy, Loi, 404
Duruy, Victor, 675

Ecole active, 357
Ecole annexe, 556 f.
Ecole conventionellement obligatoire, 122
Ecole d'application, 557
Ecole de métiers, 123
Ecole de Normandie, 699
Ecole de perfectionnement pour enfants arriérés et anormaux, 130
Ecole des Hautes Etudes Sociales, 133
Ecole des Roches, 126, 699
Ecole facultative, 122
Ecole manuelle d'apprentissage, 120
Ecole maternelle, 120 f., 400 ff.; curriculum of, 401 ff.; teachers in, 402
Ecole nationale des arts et métiers, 124
Ecole Nationale des Chartes, 271
Ecole Nationale des Langues Orientales Vivantes, 271
Ecole nationale professionelle, 123
Ecole normale, 123, 520
Ecole normale primaire, 400
Ecole normale primaire supérieure, 400, 549
Ecole normale supérieure, 123, 674, 828, 830, 838 f.; Sèvres, 838 f.
Ecole pratique de commerce et d'industrie, 123
Ecole Pratique des hautes Etudes, 271
Ecole primaire, 400
Ecole primaire supérieure, 123, 386, 400, 418 ff.
Ecole unique, 61, 84, 90, 119, 124 f., 131 ff., 268, 422, 424, 629 f., 679, 683, 695, 700 ff.
Economats, 682
Edinburgh High School, 792
Education Act, 1870, 230, 360, 363
Education Act, 1902, 95 f., 232, 248 ff., 386, 640, 645, 648
Education Act, 1918, 96, 98, 101 f., 109, 114, 116, 232, 234, 249, 369, 377, 380, 387, 647, 670
Education Act, 1922, 529

INDEX 907

Education (Administrative Provisions) Act, 1907, 113
Education (Choice of Employment) Act, 1910, 117
Education (Consolidation) Act, 1921, 237 f., 250, 256, 365, 377, 641
Education (Local Authorities) Act, 1931, 253
Education (Provision of Meals) Act, 1906, 112, 254
Education, aims of, 865 ff.
Education and democracy, 706
Education and efficiency, 800 f.
Education and national character, 23; in England, 24 ff.; in France, 29 ff.; in Germany, 32 ff.; in Italy, 32 f., 42 ff.; in Russia, 32 f., 42 ff.; in United States, 38 ff.
Education and nationalism, 864 f.
Education and politics, 172 f., 175, f., 180, 182 ff., 187, 281 f., 570, 780 ff.
Education and propaganda, 184 f.
Education and religion, 139
Education and Salesmanship, Committee on, 669
Education and social distinctions, 85 ff.
Education and social services, 92 f.
Education, boards of, 224
Education committees, 224
Education, control of, 45
Education Department, England, 230 f., 360
Education, informal, 184
Education of the Adolescent, Report on the, 94, 108 ff., 367, 670
Education, theory of, and education, 208 ff.
Education Workers' Union, 600
Educational finance, 305 f., 311, 342 ff.
Educational Research Association, 317
Educational theory, criticism of, 457, 460 f.
Efficiency and education, 502, 800 f.
Egalitarianism, 41
Eigengesetzlichkeit der Erziehung, 584
Einheitsschule, 63, 84, 90, 136, 153 ff., 282, 435, 629, 711, 727, 729
Einjähriger-freiwilliger Dienst, 138, 708
Einjährigerschein, 138, 708
Elections, school, 225
Elementary Education Act, 1870, 95
Elementary education, England, 98 ff., 359 ff.; France, 119 ff., 396 ff.; Germany, 138, 140 ff., 359 ff., 425 ff.; Italy, 156 f., 159 ff., 455 ff.; Russia, 174, 177, 477 ff.; United States, 191 ff., 486 ff.
Elementary education, 349 ff.; aims of, 361; tradition of, 349 ff.
Elementary school curriculum, England, 372 ff.
Elementary schools, administration of, 369 f.; organization of, 366; stages in French, 409
Eliminations, study of, 800

Eliot, President, 803
Elite, 135, 632, 683, 706; and secondary education, 627; training of, 125
·*Elternbeirat*, 293
Elternvereinigungen des evangelischen Schulkartells, Die, 294
Emerson, 41
Employment certificates, 203
Employment Exchange Office, Federal, 147
Employment of Children Act, 1903, 252
Employment of children, 116 f., 131, 152 f., 202 ff.
Endowed Schools Act, 1869, 230, 639
Endowed Schools Act, 1874, 639
England, administration in, 228 ff.; central authority, 235 ff.; executive officials, 255 ff.; finance, 259 ff.; local authorities, 248 ff.; principles of, 246 ff., 261 f.; teachers' consultative committees, 255; voluntary workers, 253 ff.
England, educational system of, 83, 94 ff.
England, elementary education in, 351, 354 f., 359 ff.; administration, 369 f.; aims, 370 ff.; central schools, 390 ff.; compulsory attendance, 365 f.; curriculum, 372 ff.; history, 359 ff.; nursery schools, 368 f.; present system, 362 ff.; religious instruction, 363 f.; senior school, 386 ff.; textbooks, 383 f.
England, national character and education in, 24 ff.
England, organization of education in, 94 ff.
England, preparation of elementary school teachers, 528 ff.; certification, 542 f.; history, 528 ff.; preliminary education, 533 f.; present system, 533 ff.; training colleges, 528 ff., 534 ff.; university training departments, 530, 539 f.
England, preparation of secondary school teachers, 831 ff.
England, reorganization of educational system in, 385 ff.
England, secondary education in, 635, 637 ff.; admission, 654; advanced courses, 664 f.; aim and curriculum, 656 ff.; examinations, 665 ff.; history, 637 ff.; national system, 639 ff.; organization, 641 ff.; 653 ff.; progress, 652 f.; *Regulations* for, 648 ff.; school life, 672 ff.
England, state and education in, 55 ff.
English High School, Boston, 793 f.
English, teaching of, 380 f.
English, Teaching of, Report on the, 378
Enrollments, American high schools, 802; school, Italy, 456; secondary schools, Germany, 728
Enseignement libre, 126 f.
Enseignement spécial, l', 675
Ente Nazionale di Cultura, 164

INDEX

Ente Nazionale di Educazione Fisica, 475
Ente Nazionale per l'Educazione fisica, 778
Ente Nazionale per la Mutualità, 166
Ente Pugliese di Cultura popolare e di Educazione professionale, 164
Enti morali, 164, 765
Environment and education, 431, 441 f.
Equality in education, 705
Equality of opportunity, 89 f.
Erlässe, 296
Ernesti, Johann August, 828
Ernst the Pious, Duke, 520
Erziehungsbeihilfen, 146
Esami di ammissione, 765, 774
Escuela de Lenguas Vivas, 831
Eskimos, education of, 318
Esprit, primaire, 351, 425, 524, 564
Eton, 105, 638
Etudes désintéressés, 635, 684
Examinations, 631 f.; at eleven plus, 389 f.; college entrance, 195; English secondary school, 665 f.; French elementary school, 416 f.; French secondary school, 692 ff.; German elementary school, 446; German secondary school, 743 ff.; Italian elementary school, 473 f.; Italian secondary school, 774 ff.; state, and private education, 126 f.; teachers', 577 ff.
Excursions, 151; school, 426, 433, 443, 748
Executive officials, 226 ff., 255 ff.
Exeter University College, 104
Expenditures, capital, 260; governmental, 207
Experimental schools, Germany, 433 f.
Experiments, educational, 517 f.; French, 415; Italian, 471 f.
Explication, 551 f., 557; *de textes*, 690 f.
Externa, 227 f., 237 f., 261, 649; and *interna*, 58, 60, 63, 215 f.
Extra-curricular activities, 672 ff., 699 f., 746 ff., 778 f., 787 ff., 823 ff.

Fachkonferenz, 716 f.
Factory schools, 181
Faculty, pedagogical academies, 573
Falloux, Loi, 403, 549
Family, allowances for, 562; and education, 45
Fascism and communism, 312
Fascism and education, 155 ff., 297 ff., 461 f.
Fascism, concept of, 66 ff.; influence of, in Italy, 32 f.
Fascist Academy, 168
Fascists, Congress of, and education, 761
Federal aid, 319 f.; movement for, in the United States, 190, 194
Federal Board for Vocational Education, 188 f., 319
Federal Child Welfare Law, German, 150

Federal Constitution, German, and education, 425
Federal Department of Education, 318
Federal Educational Conference, 282 ff., 751
Federal Government, German, and education, 136, 282 f.; United States, and education, 313 ff., 318 ff., 342 f.
Federal grants, 320
Fédération Générale de l'Enseignement, 563
Federation of Women's Clubs, 200
Fees, American colleges and universities, 196; French secondary schools, 134, 704 f.; German secondary schools, 719 f.; Italian secondary schools, 765 f.
Ferry, Jules, 214, 396, 548 f.
Feuillerat, Albert, 32
Fichte, 49
Films, educational, 743
Finance, educational, 220, 259 ff., 305 f., 311, 342 ff.; French, 276 ff.; Prussia, 294 f.
Findlay, J. J., 360
First examination, 103
First School Examination, 654
Fiscal independence, 332 f.
Fischer, Aloys, 34 f.
Fischer, Karl, 730
Fish, C. R., 38 f.
Fisher, H. A. L., 234 f., 244, 360
Fitch, Sir Joshua, 313
Five Year Plan and education, 178, 181
Florence, 586, 591; University of, 163
Florida, 325, 344, 619
Foerster, Friedrich Wilhelm, 427
Fonds communs, 277
Fontenay-aux-Roses, 123, 549 f., 560
Förderklassen, 142, 436
Formal discipline, 798 ff.
Forster, W. E., 244, 360
Fortbildungsschulen, 144
Foundation school, 283 f.
France, administration in, 228, 262 ff.; central authority, 266 f.; centralization, 262 ff.; educational finance, 276 ff.; inspectors, 270 ff.; local authorities, 272 ff.
France, Anatole, 132, 702
France, educational system of, 83, 119 ff.
France, elementary education in, 351, 354, 396 ff.; aim, 407 f.; character of, 396 f.; compulsory attendance, 404 f.; curriculum, 408 ff.; *école maternelle*, 400 ff.; elementary schools, 403 ff.; examinations, 416 f.; history, 403 f.; intermediate education, 418 ff.; methods, 411 ff.; system, 400 ff.; textbooks, 416
France, governmental expenditures in, 207
France, national character and education in, 29 ff.
France, organization of education in, 119 ff.
France, preparation of elementary school

INDEX

teachers, 548 ff.; administration, 550; admission, 552 f.; certification, 559 f.; curriculum, 554 ff.; examinations, 557 f.; faculty, 550 ff.; present system, 549 ff.; school life, 558 f.
France, preparation of secondary school teachers, 835 ff.
France, secondary education, 635, 674 ff.; administration, 682 f.; aim, 683 ff.; *baccalauréat*, 692 ff.; curriculum, 685 ff.; faculty, 682; girls, 698 f.; history, 674 f.; methods of instruction, 690 f.; organization, 679 f.; provision of schools, 678 f.; school life, 699 f.
France, state and education in, 59 ff.
Franchetti, Alice and Leopold, 470, 472
Francke, August Hermann, 520
Franklin, Benjamin, 77, 790
Franklin Public School Nursery, Chicago, 493
Frary, R., 675
Frauenoberschule, 755 f.
Frauenschule, 145, 755 f.
Frederick II of Gotha, 520
Free places, 102; England, 650; France, 680; Germany, 719 f.
Freedom in education, 374 f.
Freedom, meaning of, 459
Freedom, local, 356
Freie Arbeitsgemeinschaft von Elternbeiräte an höheren Schulen Deutschlands, 294
Freie Arbeitsgemeinschaften, 732, 734, 737
Freie Schulgemeinde Wickersdorf, 427
French, teaching of, in France, 412
Froebel, 140, 159, 176, 355, 360, 488, 494
Froebelianism, 465 f.

Gallaudet, Thomas, 521, 601
Gallo, 758
Games and athletics, German secondary schools, 747
Gary, Ind., 498
Gaudig, Hugo, 429
Gazzetta Ufficiale, 300
Geheeb, Paul, 427
Gemeinschaftsschulen, 143, 433, 866
General Education Board, 316
General science, 814, 819
Geneva Convention, 405
Geneva, Declaration of, 54
Genoa, University of, 163
Gentile, Giovanni, 68 f., 160, 164, 214, 307, 457 ff., 461, 476, 760 f., 777
Gentile reform, 757, 761 ff., 773 f.; and teacher preparation, 587
Geography, teaching of, 382, 413 f., 688, 735; in Germany, 445
George Reed Act, 319
Georgia, 325, 344, 619

German, teaching of, in Germany, 444
Germany, administration in, 228, 281 ff.
Germany, elementary education in, 351, 356, 425 ff.; compulsory attendance, 436 f.; curriculum, 439 ff.; elementary schools, 434 ff.; intermediate education, 446 ff.; organization of, 437 f.; pre-schools, 434; provision of schools, 434 f.; religion and, 436; the Revolution and, 425 ff.
Germany, national character and education in, 32 ff.
Germany, organization of education in, 136 ff.
Germany, parents' associations in, 219
Germany, preparation of elementary school teachers, 565 ff.; admission, 572; curriculum, 574 ff.; examinations and appointment, 577 ff.; faculty, 573; history, 565 ff.; preliminary education, 570; present system, 570 ff.
Germany, preparation of secondary school teachers, 842 ff.
Germany, secondary education in, 635 f., 707 ff.; admission, 719; aims, 726 ff.; curriculum, 733 ff.; examinations, 743 ff.; girls' schools, 750 ff.; history, 707 ff.; organization, 723 ff.; post-War reform, 717 ff.; provision and administration, 712 ff.; school life, 746 f.; school types, 720 ff.; summary, 748 ff.; time-schedules, 738 ff.
Germany, state and church in, 47
Germany, state and education in, 61 ff.
Gesamtkonferenz, 716 f.
Gesamtschulverbände, 292
Gesamtunterricht, 378, 432 f., 441, 482, 515
Gesellschaft zur Förderung haüslicher Erziehung, 294
Gesner, Johann Matthias, 828
Gestalt psychology, 426
Ghisolfa, 472
Gianturco Law, 585
Giardino d'infanzia, 159, 462
Ginnasi, 306, 757 ff.
Ginnasi-licei, 157
Ginnasio, 162
Giovani Italiane, 169, 476
Girard, Père, 400, 464
Girl Scouts, 823
Girls, secondary education of, in France, 698 f.; in Germany, 750 ff.
Giunta per l'istruzione media, 763 f.
Giunta per le scuole medie, 303
Grades, 127
Grado inferiore, 462
Grado preparatorio, 159, 462 f.
Grado superiore, 462 f.
Grammar Schools, England, 645
Gramophone records, 743

Grandes Ecoles, les, 124 f.
Grants for secondary schools, conditions for, England, 649 f.
Gréard, Octave, 396, 407, 676
Greek education, 2 f.
Grundschule, 64, 136, 139 ff., 149, 154, 283 ff., 351, 435, 439 f., 718 f., 727, 751
Grundschulgesetz, 283, 286
Gruppo Balilla, 167
Guidance, vocational, 117 ff., 131, 147, 203 f.
Guidance and selection, 705
Guidance clinics, 115, 204
Guizot, 349, 548, 675
Guizot, Loi, 120, 403, 418
Gymnasium, 145, 707 ff.

Hadow Report, 94, 108 ff.
Hadow, Sir Henry, 670
Haenisch, Karl, 568
Haldane, Lord, 222
Hall, G. Stanley, 801
Hall, Samuel R., 521, 601
Hamburg, 142 ff., 148, 282, 286 f., 293, 433, 582 f.
Hampshire, 363
Handbook of Suggestions for the Consideration of Teachers, 100, 238, 366 f., 373 ff.
Handelshochschulen, 147, 723
Handelsministerium, 286
Harnisch, 520, 566
Harper, President, 822
Harris, William T., 494
Harrow, 105, 638
Hatch Act, 319 f.
Haubinda, 427
Hauptlehrer, 438 f.
Hausarbeitsgesetz, 153
Hausfrauenklasse, 447
Hauslehrerschule, 427
Headmasters' Conference, 639, 642
Health, care of, in Germany, 446
Health, Ministry of, 113
Health and education, 92
Health instruction, 201
Health work in United States, 198 f.
Hecker, J. J., 520
Hegel, 49, 65
Heimatkunde, 426, 431, 433, 441 f., 729, 867
Henning, 520
Herbart, 349 f., 360, 488, 514
Herriot, M., 266, 268, 707
Hesse, 142 ff., 293, 582
Heyne, Christian Gottlieb, 828
Hierarchy in administration, 297, 307
High school, rise of, in United States, 792 ff.
High schools, 194 f.; in England, 645
High schools, *see* United States, secondary education in
Higher Certificate Examination, 664, 666 f.

Higher Council of Education, France, 218; Italy, 218
Higher Council of Public Instruction, France, 126, 268, 416; Italy, 301
Higher education, England, 104; France, 125 f.; Italy, 163; Russia, 179 f.; United States, 195 f.
Higher elementary education, 123, 704; France, 418 ff.
Higher examination, 103
Higher normal schools, 125; Italy, 586
Higher School of Commerce, Paris, 124
Hilfsbüchereien, 743
Hilfsschulen, 152, 436
History, educational, England, 94 ff., 228 ff., 359 f., 520 ff., 637 ff.; France, 119 f., 403 f., 548, 674 ff.; Germany, 137 ff., 565 ff., 707 ff.; Italy, 156 f., 455 f., 585, ff., 757 ff.; Russia, 174; United States, 188 ff., 486 ff., 600 ff., 790 ff.
History, secondary education, France, 674 ff.
History, teaching of, 381, 413 f., 688, 735; Germany, 444 f.; Italy, 470
Höhere Mädchenschulen, 145, 750
Holland, parents' associations in, 219; state and church in, 47
Holy Synod, 174
Home and Colonial School Society, 528
Home Office, England, 237, 259; and juvenile delinquency, 117
Home rooms, 819
Homework, 723, 737
Hoole, Charles, 520
Hoover, President Herbert, 78 f., 198
Hostels, youth, 152, 443, 748
Houston, Texas, 342, 508
Hugo, Victor, 400
Hull University College, 104
Humanism, 636
Humboldt, Wilhelm von, 707 f.
Hungerkandidaten, 710

Idaho, 325, 344, 606, 619
Ideonità examination, 774
Illinois, 344, 619, 621
Illinois State Normal University, 603
Illiteracy in France, 405; in Italy, 156, 165, 456; in Russia, 175, 182 f.
Ilsenburg, 427
Incaricati, 849
Indemnités, 561 f.
Indiana, 192, 325, 344, 605 f., 618 f., 621
Indians, education of, 318 f.
Individual and nationalism, 11 f.
Individual and society, 353 f., 865 f.
Individuality, French concept of, 31, 399
Indoctrination, 184, f., 866 ff.; and education, 357
Infancy, care of, in Italy, 169; in Russia, 176

INDEX 911

Infant schools, 159, 354 f., 366, 373, 376 f., 464 f.; France, 400 ff.; Italy, 464 f.; Russia, 480
Infant welfare, 128
Inglis, A., 798
Inspection, England, 649; France, 415
Inspectors, 304; England, 239 f.; France, 270 ff.; Germany, 289 f.
Institut de France, 271
Institut National Agronomique, 124
Institut National d'Orientation Professionnelle, 131
Instituteur, stagiaire and *titulaire*, 559 f.
Instituteurs, 406
Institutrice, stagiaire and *titulaire*, 559 f.
Institutrices, 406
Insular Bureau, 319
Integrated instruction, 378, 432, 441, 482, 515, 737, 819
Intelligence tests, use of, 201
Interdepartmental Committee on Medical Inspection and Feeding of Children, 113
Interdepartmental Committee on Physical Deterioration, 113
Intermediate education, 138, 144 f.; England, 386 ff.; France, 418 ff.; Germany, 446 ff.
Interna, 227 f., 237 f., 261, 649; and *externa*, 58, 60, 63, 215 f.
Iowa, 325, 330, 344, 619; University of, 493
Iowa State College of Agriculture, 493
Isocrates, 799
Istituti magistrali, 162, 306, 588, 762 ff.
Istituti Superiori di Magistero, 162, 591 f., 762
Istituti tecnici, 306, 757 ff.
Istituto Pedagógico, 831
Italianità, 297
Italy, administration in, 228, 297 ff.; the reform, 297 f.
Italy, educational system of, 83, 155 ff.
Italy, elementary education in, 351, 354, 455 ff.; attendance, 463 f.; curriculum, 467 ff.; elementary schools, 467 ff.; examinations, 473 f.; experiments, 471 f.; history, 455 ff.; *Opera Balilla*, 475 f.; organization, 462 ff.; physical education, 475; pre-schools, 464 ff.; textbooks, 472 f.; time-schedule, 474
Italy, governmental expenditures in, 207
Italy, national character and education in, 32 f., 42 ff.
Italy, preparation of elementary school teachers, 585 ff.; appointment, 590 f.; curriculum, 588 ff.; Gentile reform, 587; history, 585 ff.; present system, 587 ff.; status, salaries and pensions, 594 f.
Italy, preparation of secondary school teachers, 849 ff.
Italy, secondary education in, 636, 757 ff.; admission and fees, 765 f.; aims, 767 f.; curriculum, 766 ff.; examinations, 774 ff.; Gentile reform, 761 ff.; history, 757 ff.; present system, 760 ff.; provision and organization, 763 ff.; school life, 778 ff.; time-schedules, 767 ff.
Italy, state and church in, 47
Italy, state and education in, 64 ff.

Jefferson, Thomas, 78
Jena, University of, 571
Job-analysis, 502, 506 f., 609
Joint Matriculation Board, Northern Universities, 666
Joliet, Ill., Junior College, 822
Journal Officiel, 267
Journey, school, 383
Jugendämter, 152
Jugendbewegung, 426 ff., 584, 730 f., 747
Jugendherbergen, 152, 443, 748
Junior college, 196, 822
Junior high school, 194, 196, 386, 803 ff.
Junior Red Cross, 823
Juvenile Advisory Committees, 254
Juvenile Boards, 152
Juvenile courts, 117, 204
Juvenile delinquency, 117
Juvenile Employment Committees, 254
Juvenile Organizations Committees, 242 f., 255
Juvenile Psychopathic Institute, Chicago, 204

Kalamazoo Case, 79, 86, 190, 793 f.
Kalashnikov, 478
Kansas, 325, 344, 616, 619
Kansas City, school medical inspection in, 199
Kay-Shuttleworth, Sir James, 360, 528 f.
Kent, 253, 378, 384
Kentucky, 325, 344, 619
Kernfächer, 733
Kerschensteiner, Georg, 360, 429 f.
Kindergartens, 140, 191, 355, 434, 481; in United States, 492, 494 f.
Kinderheime, 434
Kinderhorte, 434
Kingsley, James L., 601
Klassengemeinde, 746
Klassenkonferenz, 716 f.
Klassenleiter, 716
Kleinkinderschulen, 434
Kolhozes, 181
Komsomols, 182, 185 f., 311, 481, 485, 788
Konfessionelle Schulen, 142, 436
Konrektor, 143, 438 f.
Koos, L., 811
Kreisärzte, 150
Kreislehrerräte, 293
Kreisschulinspektor, 290

Kriege, Matilde, 494
Krippen, 355, 434
Kropotkin, P. A., 477
Krupskaya, 477
Kultur, 50
Kuratorium, 713
Kursfächer, 733
Kuvenko, S. N., 477

Labor certificate, 474
Labor exchanges, 117
Labor, Ministry of, England, 118
Labor school, unified, 481 ff.
La Chalotois, 48
Laicity in education, 120; France, 399 f.
Laissez faire and administration, 210; in education, 50 ff., 232
Lakanal, 548
Lancashire, 253, 363
Lancaster, Joseph, 521
Landerziehungsheime, 427
Landesmittelschulkasse, 295
Landesschulkasse, 294 f.
Langlois, Ch., 841
Language and nationalism, 5 f.
Language, mother, teaching of, 735
Languages and literature, teaching of, 688
Languages, foreign, 736
Lapie, M., 559, 695
Lateinschulen, 446 f.
Latin-American countries, centralization in, 210
Latin Grammar Schools, 790 f.
Laurea, 850
Laval, M., 683
League of Communist Youth, 185 f., 481
Learning, laws of, 515
Leeds, University of, 104
Lehrerbeiräte, 225
Lehrerkonferenz, 439
Lehrerräte, 290
Lehrerseminare, 520, 524, 567
Lehrervertretungen, 290
Leicester University College, 104
Leicestershire, 363
Leipzig teachers' association, 426
Leipzig, University of, 582
Lenin, 175, 596
Lernschule, 357, 429, 441
Lexington, Mass., normal school, 601
Liard, Louis, 396
Liberal education, 627; definition of, 728 f., in the United States, 798
Libraries, lending, 743
Libro del Stato, 472
Libro e Moschetto, 168
Licei, 757 ff.
Licei classici, 162
Licei femminili, 162, 306, 762

Licei-ginnasi, 306, 762 ff.
Licei scientifici, 162, 306, 762 ff.
Licence, 419, 551, 678; *d'enseignement*, 273, 561, 835 ff.; *ès lettres*, 835 ff.; *ès sciences*, 835 ff.
Licenza, 162; examination, 774
Lietz, Hermann, 427
Life, school, *see* School life.
Ligue de l'Enseignement, 133, 703
Lily, John, 520
Lippe, 144 f., 582
Litt, Theodor, 429
Liverpool, 115; University of, 104
Livret de scolarité, 422
Livret scolaire, 693
Lloyd George, Mr., 243
Loans, 260, 306
Local administration, 208 ff., 221, 224 f., 302, 311, 329 ff.
Local authorities, England, 248 ff.; France, 272 ff.; Prussia, 291; United States, 329 ff.
Local government, English, 249 f.
Local Taxation Act, 1890, 95 f.
Local Taxation (Customs and Excise) Act, 640
Locke, 799
Loi Astier, 124
Lois, 267
Lombardo-Radice, Giuseppe, 299, 308, 460 f.
London, 102, 113, 115, 248 f., 251, 384, 386, 391; University of, 104, 666
London Day Training College, 830
Los Angeles, 493; high school curricula, 816
Loughborough College, 541
Louisiana, 325, 344, 605 f., 619
Lowe, Robert, 230, 361
Lowestoft, 237
Lübeck, 142, 144
Lunacharsky, 477
Lycées, 125, 674 ff.
Lyzeum, 145, 752 ff.

Macerata, University of, 163
Machiavelli, 65
Madariaga, Señor, 27 ff.
Maestri elementari, 591
Maestri ordinari, 591
Maestri straordinari, 591
Magistrat, 291
Maine, 344, 605, 619, 621
Maintenance grants, 101, 146, 706, 720
Maîtres, 682; *d'internat*, 678
Maîtresses, 682
Maladjusted children, 115
Malnutrition, 201
Malthus, 51
Managers, school, 114, 253 f.
Manchester, 102, 251, 255, 257, 387
Manchester Grammar School, 655

INDEX

Manchester, University of, 104
Mann, Horace, 487, 601
Mannheim, 436
Manual training, Germany, 445
Married women teachers, 617
Martini, 758
Maryland, 325, 330, 344, 605, 618 f., 621
Marx, Karl, 478
Massachusetts, 325, 344, 487, 513, 605 f., 617, 619, 621, 791, 793, 804
Maternal schools, 159, 400 ff.
Maternity and Child Welfare Act, 115
Maternity and Child Welfare Act, 1919, 369
Maternity and Infancy Act, 199
Mathematics, teaching of, 688, 736
Matteucci, 758
Maturità examination, 774
Maurois, André, 29
May, Sir George, 545
Mayor, French, and education, 275
McMillan, Margaret, 369, 372, 493
McMillan, Rachel, 369, 493
Mecklenburg-Schwerin, 145, 582
Médecins inspecteurs des écoles, 129
Médecins scolaires, 129
Medical inspection, school, 150, 241; England, 113 ff.; France, 128 f.; Italy, 170; United States, 199 f.
Mental defectives, 201
Mental Deficiency, Committee on, 115
Merchant Taylors', 638
Merrill-Palmer School of Home-Making, 493
Messina, University of, 163
Meteorological Institute, Berlin, 445
Méthode active, 867
Methods, elementary school, French, 411 ff.
Methods of instruction, 357 f., 690 f., 737 f., 867 f.; United States, 514 ff.
Meumann, Ernst, 426
Mexico, state and church in, 47
Michigan, 192, 325, 344, 602, 605, 619, 621; State Normal School, Ypsilanti, 603; University of, 795
Middle schools, 138, 144 f., 446 ff.
Middlesex, 253, 363
Milan, 591; University of, 163
Military service and education, 708
Mill, John Stuart, 52, 56, 220, 232 f., 360
Milwaukee, school medical inspection in, 199
Ministère de l'Hygiène, de l'Assistance Publique, et de la Prévoyance Sociale, 128
Ministerialräte, 287
Ministerium für Landwirtschaft, Forsten, und Domänen, 286
Ministerium für Wissenschaft, Kunst, und Volksbildung, 286 ff.
Ministero dell'Educazione Nazionale, 169, 299
Ministero della Pubblica Istruzione, 299
Ministre de l'Education Nationale, 266
Ministry for Science, Art, and Public Education, 286 ff.
Ministry of Agriculture, 259
Ministry of Agriculture, Forests and Domains, 286
Ministry of Commerce, 286
Ministry of Education in Prussia, 139
Ministry of Health, 241, 260
Ministry of Interior, Federal, and education, 283
Ministry of Labor, 241; Federal, 147
Ministry of Public Instruction and Fine Arts, 266
Ministry of Public Welfare, 286 f.; Prussia, 140, 150 f.
Ministry of Religion, Education, and Public Health, Prussia, 707
Ministry of Social Welfare, 434
Minneapolis, 333
Minnesota, 325, 333, 335, 344, 605, 619, 621
Minority groups, schools for, 149
Mississippi, 192, 325, 344
Missouri, 325, 328, 344, 619
Mittelschulen, 138, 144 f., 386, 446 ff.
Mittlere Schulen, 446 ff.
Modena, University of, 163
Modern Language Enquiry, American, 810
Modern Language Investigation, 858
Monopoly, educational, 126
Montana, 325, 344, 618 f., 621
Monte-pensioni, 594 f.
Montesca, La, 470 f.
Montessori, 140, 176, 280, 355, 377; Maria, 159, 465 f., 471
Monzie, M. Anatole de, 134, 264, 266, 706
Moral instruction, 143; French, 411
Morley, 391
Morrill Acts, 319 f.
Mort, Paul R., 345
Moscow Park of Culture and Rest, 184
Mothers, care of, 128, 169
Mulcaster, Richard, 520
Municipal boroughs, 249
Musée Pédagogique, 271
Muséum d'Histoire Naturelle, 271
Museum für Leibesüngen, 446
Museums, 184
Mussolini, 160, 169, 462, 761
Mutualità scolastica, 166

Nachhilfe-unterricht, 436
Naples, University of, 163
Napoleon, 49, 119, 229, 548, 707; decree of, 209
Narkompros, 309, 600
Nasi, 758
National Adult School Union, 100
National Advisory Committee on Education, 314, 321

INDEX

National Agricultural Institute, 124
National Association of Directors of Educational Research, 317
National Association of Fascist Teachers, 300
National Bureau of Selection and Distribution, 862
National Child Welfare Association, 205
National Children's Home and Welfare Associations, 204
National Committee for Mental Hygiene, 204, 493
National Committee on Child Labor, 202, 205
National Committee on Home Education, 197
National Committee on Mathematical Requirements, 810
National Confederation of Fascist Syndicates, 170
National Conference Committee on Standards of Colleges and Secondary Schools, 806
National Congress of Parents and Teachers, 197, 199, 205, 493
National Consumers' League, 202
National Council of Labor Unions, 100
National Education Association, 317, 488, 505, 602, 623, 796
National Federation of Day Nurseries, 493
National Froebel Union, 541
National Fund for Social Insurance, 166
National Health Insurance, England, 115
National Herbart Society, 488
National Institute for Vocational Guidance, 131
National Organization for Leisure-time Activities, 170 f.
National Playing-Fields Association, 383
National Society for Promoting the Education of the Poor, 94
National Society for the Education of the Poor, 521, 528
National Society for the Study of Education, 505
National Society of College Teachers of Education, 317
National systems of education, characteristics of, 233; distinctiveness of, 14 f.; English, 234 f.
National systems of education, organization, 83 ff.; characteristics of, 83 ff.; England, 94 ff.; France, 119 ff.; Germany, 136 ff.; Italy, 155 ff.; Russia, 175 ff.; United States, 188 ff.
National Union of Teachers, 244, 543 f., 546
Nationalism and education, 1 ff., 864 f.; and culture, 6 f.; and internationalism, 14; and language, 5 f.; and racial origin, 5; and religion, 5 f.; and schools, 12 f.; and the individual, 11 f.; concept of, 9; factors in the development of, 15 ff.; psychology of, 9 f.; significance of, 4 f.
Nationalism in Italian education, 461
Natoli, 758
Natural science, teaching of, Germany, 445
Nozioni varie, 470 f.
Nebraska, 605, 619; denominational schools in, 492
Neohumanism, 707 f., 730
Neugestaltung der Volksschullehrerbildung, 571
Neutrality in education, 120; French, 399 f.
Nevada, 325, 330, 344, 619, 621
New Britain, normal school, 602
New England Association of Colleges and Preparatory Schools, 795, 806
New England Colleges, conference of, 795
New Hampshire, 192, 325, 344, 605, 619
New Jersey, 325, 606, 618 f., 621
New Mexico, 325, 344
New Prospect in Education, The, 109, 111, 367, 385, 671
New Step in Education, A, 109
New York, school medical inspection in, 199
New York Children's Aid Society, 204
New York City, 333
New York State, 325, 328, 333, 344, 601, 603, 606, 618 f., 621, 793; Board of Regents, 796, 805; College, 328; employment certificates in, 203; Normal School, Albany, 602
New York State, provision for blind students, 201
New Zealand, centralization in, 210
Nidi, 159
Non-provided schools, 98 f., 362 f.
Norfolk, Va., 497
Normal schools, 197, 548 ff.; United States, 601 ff.
Normandie Nursery School, Los Angeles, 493
North Carolina, 325, 344, 619
North Central Association, 195 f., 795, 806, 855, 857
North Dakota, 325, 344, 619, 621
Northwest Association of Secondary and Higher Schools, 796, 806, 857
Nottingham University College, 104
Nunn, Sir Percy, 360, 375
Nurseries, 176; day, 355
Nursery school program, 372
Nursery schools, 96 f., 191, 355, 368, f., 493 f.
Nurses, school, 114, 151, 170
Nutrition classes, 201

Oberlin, 400
Oberlyzeum, 752 ff.
Oberrealschule, 145 f., 710 ff.
Oberregierungsräte, 287
Oberschullehrer, 716

INDEX

Oberschulrat, 713
Oberstudiendirektor, 715
Oberstudienrat, 713, 715 f.
Objectives in education, 506 f.
Observatoire de Paris-Meudon, 271
Occupations, courses in, 203
Occupazioni intellettuali recreativi, 470 f.
Octobrists, 185 f., 310, 481
Octroi, 277
Odenwaldschule, 427
Oeuvres complémentaires, 557
Oestreich, Paul, 429
Office National des Pupilles de la Nation, 272
Office National des Recherches Scientifiques et Industrielles et des Inventions, 272
Office National des Universités et Ecoles Françaises, 271 f.
Office of Education, United States, 318
Office of Indian Affairs, 319
Office of Special Inquiries and Reports, 239, 241 f.
Officials, executive, city, 332, 334 ff.; county, 330 f.; state, 326 ff.
Ohio, 344, 619, 621
Oklahoma, 192, 325, 344, 605, 619
"Old Deluder Satan" Law, 487
Oldenburg, 582
Ontario, 76
Opera Balilla, see Opera Nazionale Balilla
Opera contro Analfabetismo, 165
Opera Nazionale Balilla, 166 ff., 461 f., 475 f., 779
Opera nazionale di Assistenza all'Italia Redenta, 164
Opera Nazionale di Assistenza per l'Italia Redenta, 465
Opera Nazionale Dopolavoro, 170 f.
Opera Nazionale per l'Assistenza e la Protezione della Maternità e dell'Infanzia, 169, 465
Ordinance of 1785, 320
Ordinance of 1787, 320
Ordinanze, 300
Ordinarius, 716
Oregon, 325, 344, 606, 619
Oregon Case, 79 f., 198, 492
Organization of national systems of education, 83 ff.
Orlando Law, 156, 455 f.
Ortsschulinspektor, 290
Otto, Berthold, 427
Oundle School, 106
Oxford and Cambridge Joint Board, 639, 665
Oxford and Cambridge Schools Examination Board, 666
Oxford Delegacy for Local Examinations, 666
Oxford Examination Delegacy, 541
Oxford, University of, 104
Oxfordshire, 363

Pädagogische Akademien, 571 ff.
Pädagogische Prüfung, 846
Pädagogisches Zentralblatt, 288
Padua, University of, 163
Palermo, University of, 163
Parental education, 191
Parents' associations, 219
Parents' councils, 293 f., 721
Parents' meetings, 219
Parents, participation of, in administration, 218 f.
Paris, place of, 265
Paritätische Schulen, 142, 436
Parker, Francis, 488
Parkhurst, Helen, 498
Parliament, English, and education, 246
Parliamentary Secretary for Education, 235, 246
Parma, University of, 163
Parochial schools, 492
Part III Authorities, 96, 249, 253, 257
Pasquali, Pietro, 465
Patriotism, 864 f.; teaching of, 413
Patronage, comités de, 129 f., 419, 682
Patronage, committees of, in Italy, 165 f
Patronati scolastici, 165 f., 466, 473
Paulsen, Friedrich, 428
Pavia, University of, 163
Payment by results system, 95, 230
Peabody, Elizabeth, 494
Pécaut, Félix, 396, 399
Pedagogical technicum, 596 ff.
Pennsylvania, 325, 328, 333, 337, 344, 606, 619, 621
Pensions, teachers', England, 546 f.; France, 563; Germany, 581; Italy, 594 f.; United States, 620
People's Commissariat for Education, 309 ff.
Perasso, Giambattista, 167
Percy, Lord Eustace, 214, 246 f.
Pericles, 2
Personality, French concept of, 31, 399
Perugia, University of, 163
Pestalozzi, 360, 464, 488, 520
Philadelphia, 513
Philippines, education in, 319
Philosophy of education, American, 801 f.
Physical defectives, 201
Physical education, administration of, 270; Germany, 446; Italy, 475, 778 f.
Physical training, 383; in Italy, 167 f.
Piccole Italiane, 169, 475
Piedmont, illiteracy in, 456
Pinkevitch, Albert P., 74, 358, 477, 788
Pioneers, 182, 185 f., 311, 481, 485 f., 788
Pirogov, N. I., 477
Pisa, University of, 163
Pius XI, Pope, 47
Pizzigoni, Giuseppina, 472

916 INDEX

Plamann, 520
Plato, 45 f.
Platoon plan, 499
Play afternoons, 446
Playground and Recreation Association, 205
Playgrounds, 205, 383
Podestà, 304
Pokrovski, 477
Political education, 184 f.
Political theory and education, 20 f.
Politics and education, 1 ff., 172 f., 175 f., 180, 182 ff., 281 f., 571, 780 ff.
Polytechnization, 180 f., 782
Popular Party, Italy, 760
Portland, Ore., 497
Porto Rico, education in, 319
Post-elementary education, 101 f.; in Italy, 161
Practice schools, 611
Practice teaching, England, 538; France, 555 f.; Germany, 575 f.; United States, 611
Präparandenanstalten, 567
Pre-asile, 159
Prefect, 274
Preliminary education of teachers, England, 533 f.; France, 553 f.; Germany, 570; United States, 606 f.
Preparation of secondary school teachers, 827 ff.
Preparatory classes, 703
Preparatory schools, England, 642 f.
Pre-schools, 140, 354 f.; England, 96 f., 368 f.; France, 122, 400 ff.; Germany, 140, 434; Italy, 157 f., 462, 464 ff.; Russia, 176 f., 480 f.; United States, 191, 492 ff.
Preside, 764
President, English Board of Education, 235 ff.
Prevention of Cruelty to Children Act, 1904, 252
Priestley, Joseph, 50
Primary School, Report on the, 110, 367 f., 370 ff.
Principal, 682
Principal, elementary school, 438 f.; France, 406
Private education, 148 f., 437; France, 126 f.; Italy, 163 f.
Private schools, 57, 91 f., 229, 365, 764 f.; England, 104 ff., 647 f.; Germany, 427; United States, 197 f., 517 f.
Private teachers, 150
Privileges, 453; and education, 728, 750; Germany, 712, 726 f.; and secondary education, 627, 630 f., 687
Probationary appointment, 591
Probationary year, 828, 842
Probejahr, 828, 842

Professeurs, 682; *de langues vivantes*, 419; *de lettres*, 419; *de sciences*, 419
Professional Preparation of Teachers for American Public Schools, 602, 607
Professionalization of subject matter, 524, 608
Professori ordinari di ruolo, 849, 852
Professori straordinari, 850
Progressive Education Association, 517 f.
Progressive schools, 866
Progymnasium, 145, 708
Project method, 514 f.
Promotion of pupils, United States, 496 ff.
Promotions, 446; secondary school, Germany, 726
Promozione examination, 774
Propaganda and education, 184 f.
Provided schools, 98 f., 362
Provincial School Boards, 151, 288 f., 713
Provinz, in Prussia, 221
Provinzialschulkollegium, 288 f.
Proviseur, 682
Provveditore agli studi, 160 f., 298, 302 f., 307
Prüfstelle für Lehrbücher, 288
Prussia, administration in, 286 ff.; central authority, 286 ff.; educational finance, 294 f.; inspection, 289 f.; local authorities, 291 f.; parents' councils, 293 f.; teachers' councils, 292
Psychology and education, 801 f.
Public, the American, and secondary education, 800
Public Instruction, Ministry of, France, 119
Public school, American, meaning of, 190
"Public Schools," England, 95, 105, 229, 638, 642 ff.
Public Schools Act, 638
Public Works Loan Board, 261
Publicity and education, 338 f.
Pupil teachers, 521, 528 ff.
Pupils, promotion and classification of, 496 ff.
Purnell Act, 319

Quantitative basis for secondary education, 796, 821
Queen's Scholarships, 528
Quintilian, 799

Rabfaks, 180
Race and nationalism, 5, 17 f.
Ratke, 520
Reading, University of, 104
Realgymnasium, 145, 710 ff.
Reali Istituti Superiori di Magistero, 852 ff.
Realprogymnasium, 145, 722
Realschule, 145, 708
Realschule erster Ordnung, 710
Reason in French life, 31 f.
Reason, place of, in French education, 397 f.

INDEX

Recitation method, 383 f.
Recreation and welfare in the United States, 205 f.
Rector, 272
Red Army, 182, 310
Red Corners, 183
Red Cross, 200
Reddie, Cecil, 427
Rédressement Français, le, 424
Reformation and education, 3
Reformgymnasium, 145
Reformrealgymnasium, 145, 721 ff.
Reformschulen, 722
Regierungen, Prussia, 221, 289, 291 ff.
Regierungsräte, 287
Regio ispettore scolastico, 304
Regionalism, 279 f.
Regions in Italy, 221
Registration of teachers, 244 f.
Regolamenti, 300
Regulations for Secondary Schools, 641 ff., 648 ff.
Regulations for the Training of Teachers, 531
Reich and education, 136, 282 ff.
Reichsamt für Arbeitsvermittlung, 147
Reichsarbeitsverwaltung, 147
Reichselternverband, 294
Reichsgesetz betreffs Kinderarbeit, 152
Reichsgesetz für Jugendwohlfahrt, 150, 152
Reichsgewerbeordnung, 152
Reichsschulgesetz, 47, 143, 425
Reichsschulkonferenz, 283, 569, 720, 751
Reichsverband der deutschen Volkshochschule, 147
Reichsverband der Elternbeiräte mittlerer Schulen Deutschlands, 294
Reichsvolksschulgesetz, 283, 286
Reifeprüfung, 138, 743 ff., 757
Reifezeugnis, 745
Rektor, 143, 438 f.
Rektoratschulen, 144, 446 f.
Religion and education, 139, 142 ff.
Religion and nationalism, 5 f.
Religion and schools, in Italy, 160 f.
Religion, educational value of, 459
Religion, French schools and, 399 f.
Religious education, 436; Russia, 479; United States, 491 f.
Religious groups, representation of, on local bodies, 291
Religious instruction, 363 f.; England, 98 f.; Germany, 425; aim of, 444; Italy, 468
Renaissance and education, 3
Rent, indemnity for, 561 f.
Répétiteurs, 682
Répétitrices, 682
Reports, school, 715
Research, bureau of, 340 f.
Research division, N.E.A., 317

Reserve Officers' Training Corps, 319
Rest houses, 184
Retarded children, 115, 130, 436
Revised Code, 95, 361
Rhode Island, 325, 344, 619, 621
Ribot, Alexandre, 676
Ribot Commission, 676
Richert, Hans, 733
Richtlinien, 62, 285, 296, 434, 440 ff., 729, 733 ff., 755
Rinnova, La, 472
Rochester, 333
Roebuck, John Arthur, 521
Roedean, 642
Roman Catholic schools, 198; in United States, 492
Roman education, 3, 46
Rome, 586, 591
Rome, University of, 163
Roscoe, Frank, 233
Rovigliano, 470 f.
Royal College of Art, 236
Royal Commission on Physical Training in Scotland, 113
Royal Commission on Secondary Education, 231
Royal Higher Normal Schools, 304
Royal Higher Teachers Colleges, Italy, 591 f.
Royal Society of Saint George, 246
Royal Society of Teachers, 104, 243, 245, 833
Rugby, 105, 638
Rural Community Councils, 100
Rural school teachers, 541 f.
Rural schools, 192 f.
Rush, Benjamin, 77
Russell, Dr. James E., 315 f.
Russell Sage Foundation, 316
Russell, W. E., 521
Russell, William, 601
Russia, administration of education in, 308 ff.
Russia and religion, 47
Russia, elementary education in, 351, 477 ff.; curriculum, 482 ff.; elementary schools, 481 ff.; pre-schools, 480; theory of, 477 ff.
Russia, national character and education in, 32 f., 42 ff.
Russia, organization of education in, 172 ff.
Russia, preparation of teachers, 596 ff.; curriculum and courses of study, 598 f.; status, salaries, 598 f.
Russia, secondary education in, 636, 780 ff.; aims, 780 f.; curriculum, 781 ff.; school and society, 787 f.
Russia, state and education in, 55, 69 ff.
Russia Socialist Federated Soviet Republic, 308 ff.
Russia Socialist Federated Soviet Republic, 308 ff.

INDEX

Sadler, Sir Michael, 57, 233, 241 f., 360, 371, 669 f.
Saint-Cloud, 123, 549 ff., 560
St. Leonard's, 642
St. Louis, 508
St. Paul, 333
St. Paul's, 638
Salaries, normal school faculty, France, 552 f.
Salaries, secondary school teachers, 835, 841, 849, 859
Salaries, superintendents', 327
Salaries, teachers', England, 544 ff.; France, 561 ff.; Germany, 581; Italy, 593 f.; Russia, 598 f.; United States, 618 ff.
Salle d'asile, 400 f.
Sammelklassen, 143, 436
Sammelschulen, 436
Sanctions, 687
Sanderson of Oundle, 106
Sardinia, Kingdom of, 156
Sassari, University of, 163
Sauzé, M. de, 557
Saxony, 139, 142, 144, 147, 282, 286 f., 293, 571, 582 f.
Schemes, procedure by, 258 f.
Schienmeyer, J. C., 520
Scholarships, 104, 125, 127 f.
Scholarships, France, 679
Scholarships and Free Places, Departmental Committee on, 652 f., 670
School Attendance Bill, 109, 364, 367, 385
School boards, 224
School Certificate Examination, 654
School Journeys Association, 383
Schools Inquiry Commission, 95, 638 f., 828, 831
School life, England 672 ff.; France, 699; German secondary schools, 746 f.; Italy, 778 f.; Russia, 789 f.; United States, 823 ff.
School term, length of, in United States, 192
Schuldeputationen, 291
Schülerausschuss, 746
Schülerheime, 748
Schülerselbstverwaltung, 746
Schülervereine, 746 f.
Schulfürsorgerinnen, 151
Schulgemeinde, 746
Schulheime, 748
Schulkommissionen, 291
Schullandheime, 748
Schulleiter, 438 f.
Schulpflicht, 437
Schulräte, 289 f.
Schulvorstand, 292
Schulwanderungen, 426, 433
Schulze, Johannes, 708 f.
Schurz, Mrs. Carl, 494
Science and Art Department, 95 f., 230 f., 640 f., 665

Science Museum, 236
Sciences, teaching of, 382, 471, 660, 688, 736, 776 f.
Scotland, school elections in, 225
Scuola ausiliaria, 170
Scuola complementare, 161, 306, 467, 762 ff.
Scuola Fascista, 300
Scuola Rinnovata, La, 472
Scuola secondaria di avviamento al lavoro, 160 ff., 463, 367, 762 ff.
Scuola Superiore Fascista, 475
Scuole materne, 159, 462, 466
Scuole medie, 161
Scuole pareggiati, 764 f.
Scuole per i Contadini dell'Agro Romano e delle Paludi Pontine, 164
Second Certificate Examination, 664, 666 f.
Second International Congress on School Hygiene, 113
Secondary education, 625 ff.; European and American, 797 ff.; history of, 625 ff.; meaning of, 392 f.
Secondary education, England, 101 ff., 637 ff.; France, 124 f., 674 ff.; Germany, 138, 145 f., 707 ff.; Italy, 157, 162 f., 756 ff.; Russia, 178, 780 ff.; United States, 194 f., 760 ff.
Secondary education for all, 670 ff.
Secondary Schools Examinations Council, 665, 668
Selby-Bigge, Sir L. Amherst, 240
Selection, 680, 705 f.
Self-government, German secondary schools, 746 f.; Russian secondary schools, 787
Seminaria scolastica, 520
Seminarjahr, 842
Senior high school, 194, 196
Senior school, England, 386 ff.
Senior stage, elementary schools, 380
Service, training in, 580; training of teachers in, 547 f., 560 f., 622 f
Shaftesbury, Lord, 360
Shatsky, S. T., 477
Sheffield, University of, 104
Sheppard-Towner Maternity Aid Act, 319
Shoreditch Technical Institute, 541
Shrewsbury, 105, 638
Sicily, attendance in, 456
Siena, University of, 163
Simon, Jules, 404
Simon, T., 131, 396
Simultanschulen, 139, 142 f., 364, 436
Size of classes, 723
Smith, Adam, 51
Smith College, 493
Smith, Sydney, 39
Smith-Bankhead Act, 319
Smith-Hughes Act, 319
Smith-Lever Act, 197, 319

INDEX

Smithsonian Institution, 319
Social distinctions and education, 85 ff.
Social forces and education, 1 ff.
Social services and education, 92 f., 96, 150; England, 112 f.; France, 128 ff.; Italy, 164 f.; United States, 198 f.
Social status of education, 349, 351 f.
Social studies, 471, 515, 814, 819
Social welfare activities, 254 f.
Societies, German school, 746 ff.
Society and the individual, 353 f., 865 f.
Society for Open Air Schools, 129
Sonnino Law, 156, 456
South Carolina, 325, 344, 619; denominational schools in, 492
South Dakota, 330, 619; denominational schools in, 492
Southampton University College, 104
Southern Association of Secondary Schools and Colleges, 857
Sovhozes, 181
Soviet Republics, *see* Russia
Soviet state, 72
Special classes, 142
Special places, England, 651
Special schools, 130, 152
Spencer, Herbert, 52 f., 350
Spielnachmittage, 446
Spranger, Eduard, 429 f.
Springfield, Mass., 333, 621
Staatliche Auskunftsstelle für Schulwesen, 288, 742
Staatliche Hauptstelle für den naturwissenschaftlichen Unterricht, 288, 743
Staatliche Prüfstelle für die Lehrbücher der höheren Schulen, 742
Staatsexamen pro facultate docendi, 842 ff.
Stadtschulrat, 226, 290 f.
Stadtverordnetenversammlung, 291
Staff, administrative, 339 ff.
Stage pédagogique, 840 f.
Stages in elementary schools, 367
Stagiaire, 559 f.
Standardization of American high schools, 795 f., 805 ff.
Standardization, teachers colleges, 605 f.
Standardizing agencies and teachers, 857
Standardizing associations, 795 f.
Standards, English, 361
Standards, prescription of, 215 ff.
State and church in education, 16
State and education, 45 ff., 187; current tendencies, 53 ff.; history of, 46 ff.; in England, 55 ff., 228 ff., 232 ff., 637 f.; in France, 59 ff.; in Germany, 61 ff.; in Italy, 64 ff.; in Russia, 69 ff.; in United States, 76 ff.
State boards of education, 325 f.
State control in United States, 321 f.
State departments of education, 328 f.
State intervention in England, 210
State Normal School, Cortland, New York, 612 f.
State Teachers College, Fredericksburg Virginia, 612
State Teachers College, Greeley, Col., 613 ff.
State, theory of, and education, 208 ff.
State universities and preparation of teachers, 857 f.
Status, education for, 627, 630 ff.
Stellenbeiträge, 295
Sterling-Towner Act, 199
Stern, Wilhelm, 426
Stowe, Calvin E., 487, 601
Student life, 615
Student-teacher, 530
Studienanstalt, 145, 752 ff.
Studienassessoren, 847
Studiendirektor, 715
Studienrat, 713, 716, 847
Studienreferendare, 715, 845 f.
Studienstiftung des deutschen Volkes, 147
Study, how to, 514
Study, supervised, 692
Sturzo, 760
Suggestions, *see* Handbook of Suggestions; Richtlinien
Suggestions for the Consideration of Teachers and Others Concerned in the Work of Public Elementary Schools, *see* Handbook
Superintendent, school, 316
Superintendent, city. 332, 334 ff.; county, 330 f.; state, 326 ff.
Supervisors, 304; Italy, 591
Supplementary teachers, 542
Supplenti, 849
Surmenage, 424, 687
Surveys, educational, 259, 316 f.
Swift, F. H., 344
Syndicat des Instituteurs, 563

Talleyrand, 48
Taunton Commission, 95, 638
Teachers and curricula, 342
Teachers, certification of, 559 f., 577 ff., 590 f.
Teachers College, Columbia University, 335, 493
Teachers colleges, 197
Teachers' conferences, 716 f.
Teachers' councils, 218, 225, 290, 292 f., 341 406, 439
Teacher's diploma, 832 f.
Teachers, discipline of, 302 f.
Teachers, French elementary school, 406
Teachers, high school, 807, 817 f.
Teachers, higher elementary school, 419

Teachers in *école maternelle*, 402
Teachers' organizations, German, and education, 426
Teachers, participation of, in administration, 211, 217 f., 255, 282, 341 f.; in curriculum-making, 508
Teachers' pensions, 546 f., 563, 581, 594, 620 ff.
Teachers, pre-school, preparation of, 466
Teachers, preparation of elementary school, 520 ff.; history, 520 f.; problems of, 524 ff.; England, 528 ff.; France, 548 ff.; Germany, 138 f., 565 ff.; Italy, 585 ff.; Russia, 596 ff.; United States, 600 ff.
Teachers, private, 150
Teachers' Registration Council, 104, 245, 833
Teachers, registration of, 244 f., 833
Teachers, salaries of, 243 f., 544 ff., 561 ff., 581, 593 f., 598, 618 ff., 835, 841, 849, 859
Teachers, secondary school, preparation of, 827 ff.
Teachers, status of, 520 ff., 543 ff.; 561 f., 580, 593 f., 598 f., 619 ff., 834 f., 841 f., 845 f., 859 f.
Teachers' Superannuation Act, 1925, 546
Teaching, professionalization of, 864
Technical education, 163
Technical Instruction Act, 1889, 95, 230 f., 640 f.
Technicums, 179; pedagogical, 596 ff.
Technische Hochschulen, 147; Dresden, 582
Teeth, care of, 201
Tennessee, 325, 344, 605, 619; state and education in, 80
Tenure, teacher, 617 f.
Testo Unico, 157, 300
Texas, 325, 344, 605, 619
Textbook Commission, 288
Textbooks, England, 383 f.; France, 416; Germany, 437 f., 742 f.; Italy, 472 f.; United States, 513 ff.
Theaters, 184
Theory, educational, and elementary schools, 352 f.
Thomas, Albert, 405
Thorndike, E. L., 197
Thring, Edward, 631, 639
Thuringia, 143 f., 147, 153, 282, 293, 571, 582
Time-schedules, elementary schools, 373 ff., 403, 410, 440, 444; intermediate schools, 388, 392, 421 f., 450 ff.; secondary schools, 658 ff., 686, 733 ff., 753, 755 ff., 767 ff., 782 f.
Titres, 127
Titulaire, 559 f.
Tocqueville, de, 38, 41
Tolstoy, Leo N., 477
Tours, educational, 779
Towns, 329 f.

Townships, 329 f.
Training colleges, England, 528 ff., **534 ff.**
Training of teachers, *see* Teachers, preparation of
Transportation, school, 192
Transfer, theory of, 799 f.
Travaux dirigés, 692
Treasury, England, 259 f.
Trevelyan, Sir Charles, 109, 671
Trotter School, 472
Turin, University of, 163

Umanitaria, 164
Uncertified teachers, 530, 542 f.
Unclassified schools, in Italy, 160, 165
Under-Secretary for Fine Arts and Technical Instruction, France, 123
Under-Secretary of State for Physical Education, 270
Under-Secretary of State for Vocational Education, 269 f.
Unified labor school, 481 ff., 780 ff.
Union of Soviet Socialist Republics, *see* Russia
Union of Teachers, Russia, 218
Union of Workers in Education, 311
Union of Workers in Education and Art, 309
Unione Magistrale Nazionale, 585 f.
United States, administration in, 223
United States, administration of education in, 313 f.; authorities for, 324 f.; characteristics of, 313 f.; city superintendent, 334 ff.; Constitution and, 318; curriculum, 323; educational finance, 342 ff.; experimentation and research in, 315 f.; federal aid, 319 ff.; Federal Government and, 313 ff., 318 ff.; leadership in, 315 f.; local administration, 329 ff.; publicity, 338 f.; state control in, 322; state departments, 328 f.; state superintendent, 326 ff.
United States and religious education, 47
United States Children's Bureau, 188, 199, 202, 205, 318 f.
United States Commissioner of Education, 318
United States Department of Agriculture, 319; 4 H Clubs, 205
United States Department of Commerce and Labor, 319
United States Department of Labor, 202
United States Department of the Interior, 319
United States, elementary education in, 355, 486 ff.; aims, 498 ff.; attendance, 490 f.; curriculum, 504 ff.; educational experiments, 517 f.; elementary schools, 495 ff.; history, 486 ff.; methods of instruction, 514 ff.; pre-schools and kindergartens, 492 ff.; private schools, 517 f.; provision

INDEX

of schools, 489 f.; religious education, 491 f.; textbooks, 513 f.
United States, national character and education in, 38 ff.
United States Office of Education, 188, 199
United States, organization of education in, 188 ff.
United States, parents' associations in, 219
United States, preparation of elementary school teachers, 600 ff.; administration, 604 f.; admission, 606 f.; appointment and tenure, 617 f.; certification, 616 f.; curricula, 607 ff.; history, 600 ff.; pensions, 619 f.; present system, 604 ff.; salaries, 618 ff.; status, 623 f.
United States, preparation of secondary school teachers, 854 ff.
United States, secondary education in, 627 f., 636 f., 790 ff.; accrediting and standardization, 795 f., 805 ff.; aims, 795, 809 ff.; curricula, 812 ff.; enrollments, 802; history, 790 ff.; junior college, 822 f.; organization of, 802 f.; rise of high school, 792 ff.; school life, 823 f.; unique character of, 825 f.
United States, state and education in, 55, 76 ff.
United States War Department, 319
Units, 796, 819 ff.
Universities, American, 195 f.; French, 125 f., Italian, 163
Universities and schools, 749 f.
University Grants Committee, 104, 236
University training departments, 530, 539 f.
Unterrichtspflicht, 437
Urban districts, 249
Uruguay and religious education, 47
Ushinsky, K. D., 477
Utah, 325, 330, 344, 606, 619

Vacation schools, 205
Venetia, attendance in, 456
Verein für das Deutschtum im Ausland, 445
Vermont, 325, 344, 605 f., 619, 621, 804
Versuchsschulen, 149, 433 f., 866
Victoria and Albert Museum, 236
Villari, 758
Vigilatrici, 170
Virginia, 325, 344, 605, 619, 621; religious instruction in, 492; school medical inspection in, 199
Vocational education, 146 f.; France, 123; administration of, in France, 269 f.
Vocational guidance, 117 f., 131, 147, 203 f.
Vocational training, 103
Volkshochschule, 148
Volkshochschulheime, 148
Volksschulen, 138 ff., 434 ff., 442 ff.

Volksschullehrerseminarien, 138
Volkswohlfahrtsministerium, 150, 287, 434
Vollanstalten, 721
Voluntary schools, 98 f.
Voluntary workers, 114, 253 f.
Vom Kinde aus, 433
Vorbereitungsjahre, 842 ff.
Vorschulen, 64, 90, 138 ff., 149, 435, 718 f. 727

Waldeck, 582
Wandern, 433
Wandertage, 443
Wanderungen, 151, 748
Wandervögel, 730
Waples, D., 609
Warwickshire, 251, 255
Washburne, Carleton, 497 f.
Washington, George, 78
Washington, State of, 325, 344, 606, 619, 621
Wealth and education, 802
Welfare, children's, 150
Wells, H. G., 262
Welsh Department, 239
Weltanschauung, 143, 425
Weltliche Schulen, 139 f., 143
Werkschulen, 144
West Riding of Yorkshire, 253, 363 f., 378, 384, 387 f., 668
West Virginia, 325, 344, 619
Westminster, 105, 638
Whiskey money, 231, 260
White House Conference on Child Health and Protection, 198, 206
Wiese, Ludwig, 709
Wilbur, Secretary Ray Lyman, 321
Wilhelm II, Kaiser, 710
Wirtschaftsoberschule, 723
Wilson, H. B., 502
Wilson, Sir Roland K., 233
Winchester, 105, 638
Winnetka, Ill., 497
Wisconsin, 333, 344, 512, 605, 619, 621
Wissenschaftliche Prüfungsämter, 843
Wolf, Friedrich August, 828
Women's Institutes, 100
Work-cards, 153
Workers' Education Association, 100
Workers' faculties, 180
Working Men's Clubs, 100
Wundt, Wilhelm, 426
Württemberg, 142 ff., 282
Wyneken, Gustave, 427
Wyoming, 325, 344, 619

Yale Psycho-Clinic Guidance Nursery, 493
Yorkshire Training Colleges, Board of Administration, 536

Young Men's Christian Association, 100, 205
Young Women's Christian Association, 205
Youth hostels, 383
Youth movement, 426 ff., 730 f.
Ypsilanti, normal school, 602

Zeller, 520

Zemstvos, 174
Zentralblatt für die gesamte Unterrichtsverwaltung in Preussen, 287
Zentralinstitut für Erziehung und Unterricht, 147, 288, 743
Zeungnis der mittleren Reife, 452
Zeugnis der Obersekundareife, 726

TEXAS A&M UNIVERSITY - TEXARKANA